Aġasa Ledford

W9-ATC-930

15

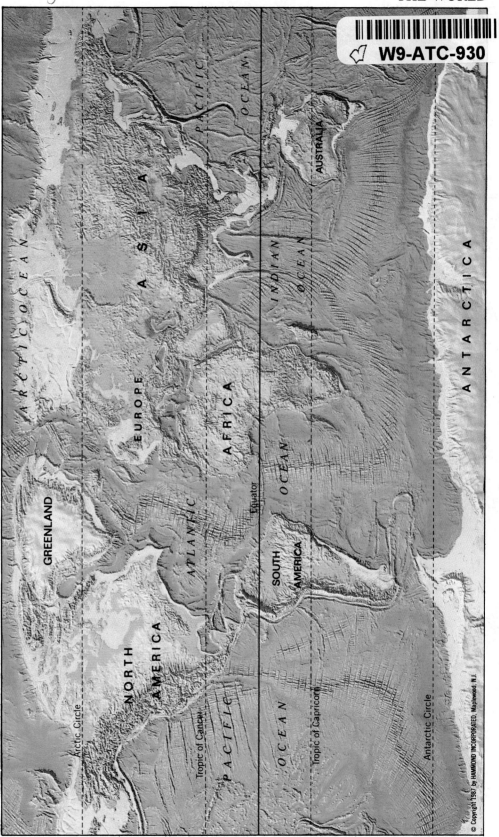

ARCTIC OCEAN

ASIA

EUROPE

AFRICA

PACIFIC OCEAN

AUSTRALIA

INDIAN OCEAN

ANTARCTICA

GREENLAND

ATLANTIC

NORTH AMERICA

SOUTH AMERICA

OCEAN

Equator

Arctic Circle

Tropic of Cancer

PACIFIC

OCEAN

Tropic of Capricorn

Antarctic Circle

EUROPE

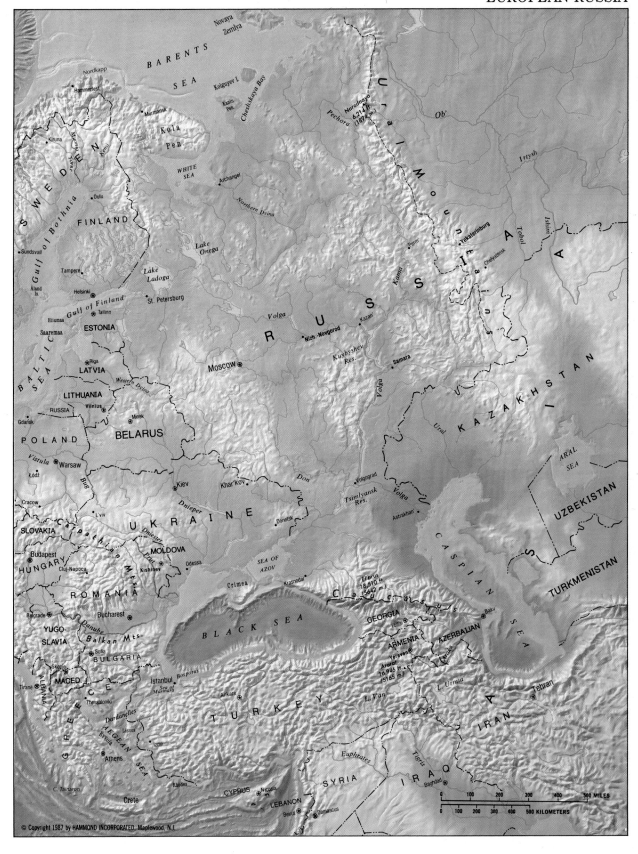

AFRICA

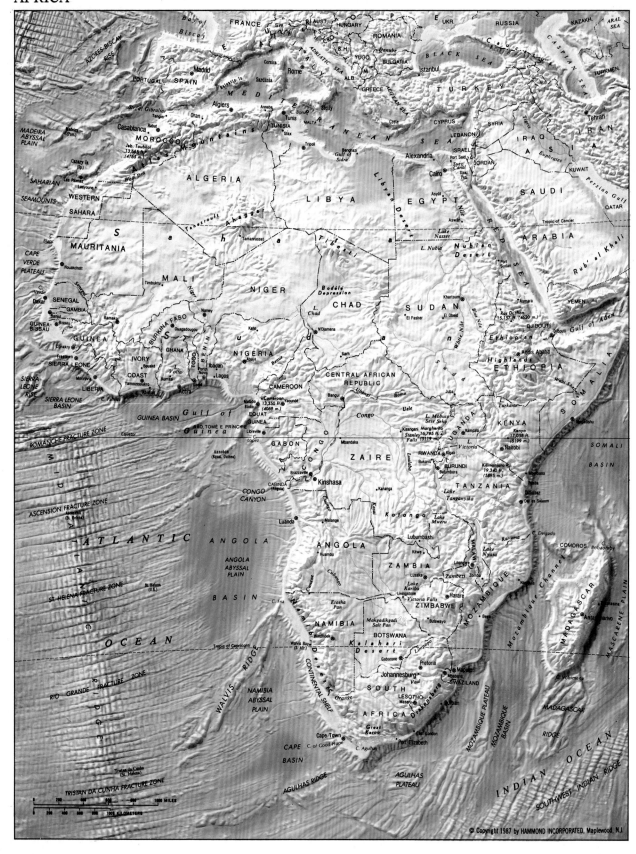

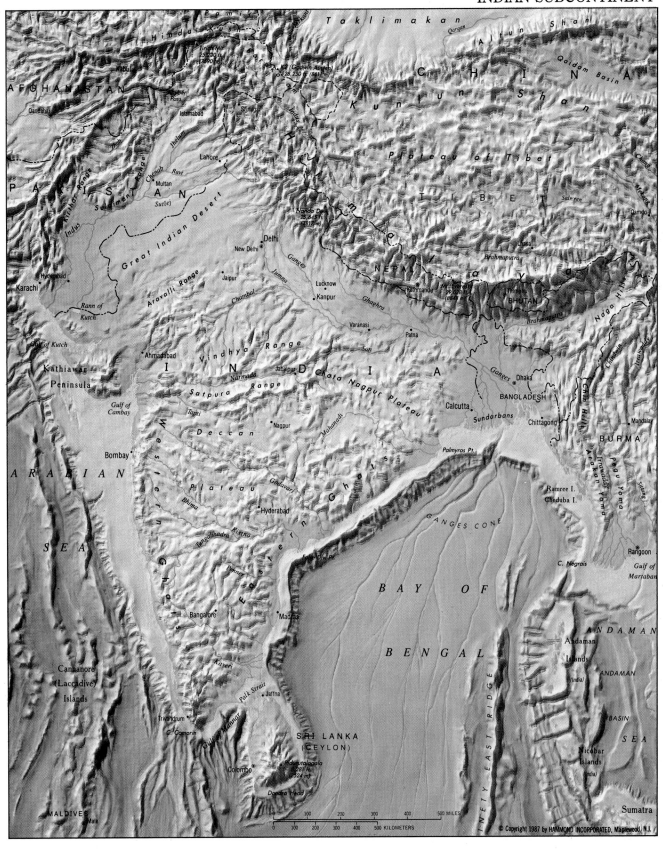

Taklimakan

Qarqan

Altun Shan

Qaidam Basin

CHINA

Tirich Mir
25,230 ft.
7690 m.

Hindu Kush

Pamir

Mustagh

K2 (Godwin Austen)
28,250 ft. (8611 m)

Kunlun Shan

CHINA

Kabul

AFGHANISTAN

Khyber Pass

Islamabad

Srinagar

Plateau of Tibet

TIBET

Salween

Chang

Mekong

Qandahar

Kirthar Range

Suleiman Range

Lahore

Jhelum

Chenab

Ravi

Multan

Sutlej

Indus

Lhasa

Brahmaputra

Kamdo

PAKISTAN

Hyderabad

Karachi

Great Indian Desert

Aravalli Range

Nanda Devi
25,645 ft.
7817 m.

Himalaya

NEPAL

Kathmandu

Mt. Everest
29,028 ft.
(8848 m)

Thimphu

BHUTAN

Brahmaputra

Naga Hills

Rann of Kutch

New Delhi

Delhi

Ganges

Jaipur

Jumna

Chambal

Lucknow

Kanpur

Ghaghra

Varanasi

Patna

Son

Gulf of Kutch

Ahmadabad

Vindhya Range

INDIA

Chota Nagpur Plateau

Ganges

Dhaka

BANGLADESH

Chin Hills

Chindwin

Irrawaddy

Kathiawar Peninsula

Narmada

Satpura Range

Jabalpur

Calcutta

Sundarbans

Chittagong

Gulf of Cambay

Tapti

Deccan

Nagpur

Mahanadi

Palmyras Pt.

BURMA

Mandalay

Bombay

Western Ghats

Plateau

Godavari

Eastern Ghats

Ramree I.
Cheduba I.

Pegu Yoma

Arakan Yoma

Sittang

ARABIAN

Bhima

Hyderabad

Krishna

GANGES CONE

C. Negrais

Rangoon

Gulf of Martaban

SEA

Tungabhadra

Pennar

False Divi Pt.

BAY OF

ANDAMAN

Bangalore

Madras

BENGAL

Andaman Islands

ANDAMAN

(India)

Cannanore (Laccadive) Islands

Kaveri

Palk Strait

Jaffna

NINETY EAST RIDGE

BASIN

SEA

Trivandrum

C. Comorin

Gulf of Mannar

SRI LANKA (CEYLON)

Pidurutalagala
8,281 ft.
2524 m.

Nicobar Islands

(India)

Colombo

Dondra Head

MALDIVES

Male

Sumatra

100   200   300   400   500 MILES

0   100   200   300   400   500 KILOMETERS

© Copyright 1987 by HAMMOND INCORPORATED, Maplewood, N.J.

EAST AND SOUTHEAST ASIA

© Copyright 1987 by HAMMOND INCORPORATED, Maplewood, N.J.

SOUTH AMERICA

NICARAGUA
CARIBBEAN SEA
WEST INDIES
Pts. Gallinas
ARUBA (Neth.)
Curaçao
Bonaire
Willemstad
GRENADA
BARBADOS
TRINIDAD & TOBAGO
Port of Spain
Trinidad
DEMERARA ABYSSAL PLAIN

Barranquilla
Maracaibo
Caracas
L. Maracaibo
Ciudad Guayana
Bolívar (5007 m.)
GUIANA PLATEAU

COSTA RICA
PANAMA
Panama Canal
Malpelo I. (Col.)
PANAMA BASIN

VENEZUELA
Orinoco
Guri Res.
Arauca
Meta

GUYANA
Georgetown
Paramaribo
Cayenne
SURINAME
FRENCH GUIANA

CONTINENTAL SHELF
AMAZON CANYONS
PARA ABYSSAL PLAIN

COLOMBIA
Cali
Putumayo
Vaupés
Mt. Roraima (2094 m.)
Angel Falls
Neblina (3014 m.)
Guiana Highlands
CEARA ABYSSAL PLAIN

Quito
ECUADOR
Chimborazo 20,561 ft. (6267 m.)
Guayaquil
Gulf of Guayaquil

Negro
Amazon
Equator
I. de Marajó
B. de Marajó
Belém
São Luís

Japurá
Içá
Iquitos
Amazon
Javari
Juruá

Manaus
Selvas
Madeira
Purus
Tapajós
Xingu
Teresina
Rep. de Tucuruí

Tocantins
Araguaia
Parnaíba
Caatingas

Ucayali
PERU
Trujillo
Huascarán 22,205 ft. (6768)
Callao
Lima
Cusco

Marmoré
Guaporé
Mamoré
Beni

BRAZIL
Brazilian Highlands
Res. de Sobradinho

PERU-CHILE TRENCH
NAZCA RIDGE
PERU BASIN

BOLIVIA
La Paz
Titicaca
Ancohuma 21,489 ft. (6550 m.)
Cochabamba
Oruro
Sucre

Planalto de Mato Grosso
Grande
Pico da Bandeira 9,482 ft. (2890)
Belo Horizonte
São Francisco
Jequitinhonha
Salvador

Arica
Gran Chaco
Pilcomayo
Paraguay
Campo Grande

Tropic of Capricorn
Antofagasta
CHILE
Vol. Llullaillaco 22,057 ft. (6725 m.)
Pto. del Estado 22,615 ft. (6893 m.)

PARAGUAY
Asunción
Itaipu Res.
Curitiba
Iguaçu
Paraná
São Paulo
Rio de Janeiro
C. de Cabo Frio

Les. San Félix (Chile)
I. San Ambrosio (Chile)
CHILE BASIN

I. Alejandro Selkirk
I. Robinson Crusoe
Juan Fernández Is. (Chile)

Córdoba
Santa Fe
Rosario
Negro

Uruguay
Porto Alegre
Lagoa dos Patos
SANTOS PLATEAU
I. de Santa Catarina
RIO GRANDE PLATEAU

Cerro Aconcagua 22,831 ft. (6959 m.)
Mendoza
Valparaíso
Santiago

Lagoa Mirim
URUGUAY
Buenos Aires
La Plata
Montevideo
Río de la Plata
C. San Antonio

CHALLENGER FRACTURE ZONE
Concepción
Colorado
Negro
Salado
Pampas

ATLANTIC OCEAN

ARGENTINA
Golfo San Matías
Pen. Valdés
Chubut

ARGENTINE BASIN

Puerto Montt
Isla de Chiloé
Archipiélago de los Chonos
Pen. Taitao

Golfo San Jorge
C. Tres Puntas
Deseado

G. de Penas
Archipiélago Reina Adelaida
Bahía Grande
Str. of Magellan
Tierra del Fuego
Falkland Islands (U.K.)
Stanley

MORNINGTON ABYSSAL PLAIN

FALKLAND ESCARPMENT
FALKLAND PLATEAU
FALKLAND RIDGE

Str. of Magellan
Cape Horn
NORTH SCOTIA RIDGE

0 200 400 600 800 MILES
0 200 400 600 800 KILOMETERS

© Copyright 1987 by HAMMOND INCORPORATED, Maplewood, N.J.

CIVILIZATIONS OF THE WORLD

CIVILIZATIONS
OF THE WORLD

The Human Adventure

SECOND EDITION

VOLUME C: FROM 1800

Richard L. Greaves
Florida State University

Robert Zaller
Drexel University

Philip V. Cannistraro
Drexel University

Rhoads Murphey
University of Michigan

■ HarperCollinsCollegePublishers

Executive Editor: Bruce Borland
Director of Development: Betty Slack
Project Editor: Susan Goldfarb
Assistant Art Director: Lucy Krikorian
Text Design: Delgado Design, Inc.
Cover Design: Delgado Design, Inc.
Photo Researcher: Leslie Coopersmith
Production Manager: Willie Lane
Compositor: Waldman Graphics, Inc.
Printer and Binder: R. R. Donnelly & Sons Company
Cover Printer: The Lehigh Press, Inc.

Cover illustration: Beadwork on cloth by Jimoh Buraimoh. In the collection of the artist.

Title page photo: Bahai Temple, New Delhi. Wim Swann.

Part-opening art: Part Five: From contemporary rendering of traditional Japanese Zen Buddhist daily chant (courtesy of Dai Bosatsu Zendo).

Color atlas in front matter copyright © Hammond Incorporated, Maplewood, N.J.

Civilizations of the World: The Human Adventure, Second Edition (Part C: From 1800)

Copyright © 1993 by HarperCollins College Publishers

Library of Congress Cataloging-in-Publication Data

Civilizations of the world : the human adventure / Richard L. Greaves
  . . . [et al.]. — 2nd ed.
      p.   cm.
    Includes indexes.
    Contents: v. A. To 1500 — v. B. From 1300 to 1800 — v. C. From
1800.
    ISBN 0-06-500678-X (v. A). — ISBN 0-06-500679-8 (v. B). — ISBN
0-06-500680-1 (v. C)
    1. Civilization—History.   I. Greaves, Richard L.
CB69.C576   1993c   92-39937
909—dc20   CIP

93 92 91 90 9 8 7 6 5 4 3 2

CONTENTS IN BRIEF

Atlas
Contents in Detail   vii
Chronologies and Genealogies   xxi
Maps and Graphs   xxii
Preface   xxv
Supplements   xxvii
Acknowledgments   xxix
About the Authors   xxxi
A Note on the Spelling of Asian Names and Words   xxxiii

30. The Industrial Revolution   788
31. The Age of Ideology   816

THE VISUAL EXPERIENCE: ROMANTIC AND NEOCLASSICAL ART   *following page 832*

32. The Triumph of Nationalism   843
33. Industrial Society and the Liberal Order   869

GLOBAL ESSAY: WRITING AND COMMUNICATION (II)   895

34. The Age of Western Domination   901

THE VISUAL EXPERIENCE: ART OF MODERN ASIA AND AFRICA   *following page 928*

PART FIVE   THE TWENTIETH CENTURY   932

35. Culture, Society, and the Great War   934

GLOBAL ESSAY: THE HUMAN IMAGE (II)   961

36. Upheaval in Russia and the Middle East   968
37. Totalitarianism and the Crisis of Democracy   995
38. The Second World War and Its Aftermath   1025
39. Revival and Revolution in East Africa   1050
40. Nationalism and Revolution: India, Pakistan, Iran, and the Middle East   1078

GLOBAL ESSAY: MAPS AND THEIR MAKERS (II)   1108

41. Decolonization and Development: Africa and Latin America   1113
42. The Contemporary Age   1142

THE VISUAL EXPERIENCE: ART OF THE MODERN WESTERN WORLD   *following page 1152*

Epilogue: Civilization and the Dilemma of Progress   1171
Index   I-1

CONTENTS

Atlas
Chronologies and Genealogies   xxi
Maps and Graphs   xxii
Preface   xxv
Supplements   xxvii
Acknowledgments   xxix
About the Authors   xxxi
A Note on the Spelling of Asian Names and Words   xxxiii

CHAPTER 30   THE INDUSTRIAL REVOLUTION   788

Background: Population, Energy, and Technology   789
Commerce and the Formation of Capitalist Society   791
The Agricultural Revolution   794
  A New Prosperity?   795
Science, Technology, and the State   795
The Transformation of Britain   796
  The Organization of Labor   797
  Industrial Discipline   798
  Family Life: A Tale of Two Cultures   799
  Capital, Labor, and the Rights of Man   801

  ❦ **Robert Owen, Industrial Reformer   803**

The Population Explosion   805

  ❦ **Manchester, the Factory Town   808**

The Spread of the Industrial Revolution   810
  Exploitation and Resistance   811
  The German Giant   812
  Industrial Development After 1850   812
  The Harnessing of Science   813

  ◎ **Documents**
  Malthus on Population 790 / Child Labor 800 / Luddism 803 /
  Two Views of Manchester 809

CHAPTER 31   THE AGE OF IDEOLOGY   816

The Legacy of Revolution   817
The Congress of Vienna   818
Collective Security   819
The Diplomatic Settlement   819
Reaction and Revolution   820
The Overthrow of Ottoman Rule in Greece   822
The Troubled 1820s   823
Liberalism   825
Romanticism and the Quest for Identity   826
The Dethronement of Tradition   826
The Romantic Hero   826

 Goethe and the Romantic Spirit   827

The Spread of Romanticism   828
Romanticism Beyond the Arts   829
Romanticism and the Image of Women   830
The Liberal Revival and the Revolutions of 1830   831
The July Revolution in France   832
Revolution East and West   832
Britain: Revolution Averted   832
The Socialist Challenge   834
The Demand for Reform   834
From Reform to Revolution   835
Karl Marx   835
The Revolutions of 1848   837
The Causes of the Revolutions   837
The Collapse of the Old Order   838
Counterrevolution in Central Europe   839
France: From Revolution to Empire   840

 Documents
The Mystique of Nationalism 818 / Metternich's Plea for the Old
Order 822 / The Romantic Poet 829 / Mazzini's Call to
Revolution 833 / The June Days 840

THE VISUAL EXPERIENCE: ROMANTIC AND NEOCLASSICAL ART   *following page 832*

CHAPTER 32   THE TRIUMPH OF NATIONALISM   843

The Politics of National Grandeur: Napoleon III in France   844
The Second Empire   845
The Liberalization of the Empire   847
Power Politics and the Unification of Italy   848
The Italian Risorgimento   849
Cavour the Realist   849
The Crisis of Italian Unification   850
Iron and Blood: The Making of the German Empire   852
Nationalism and the German State System   853
Bismarck and the Liberals   853
The Showdown with Austria   854
The Franco-Prussian War and the Forging of German Unification   855
Eastern Europe and the Ottomans   857

❦ Vienna in the Age of Franz Joseph   857

Russia Between Reaction and Reform   858
Alexander II and the Dilemma of Russian Reform   859
The Dissolution of the Ottoman Empire   860
The Jewish Question and the Birth of Zionism   862

❦ Theodor Herzl and the Quest for a Jewish Homeland   862

**The Struggle for National Unity: The United States
and Latin America   864**
The American Civil War   864
National Development in Latin America   865
Brazil: From Empire to Republic   865
Dictatorship and War   866
Argentina and Mexico   866

◉ **Documents**
**The Napoleonic Myth   845   /   Cavour Versus Garibaldi   852   /   Bismarck on
Power Politics   855   /   Tsarist Russia on the Edge of Revolution   860   /
On Anti-Semitism   863**

CHAPTER 33   INDUSTRIAL SOCIETY AND THE LIBERAL ORDER   869

Industrial Development and Monopoly Capitalism   870
The Second Phase of the Industrial Revolution   870
The Rise of Big Business   871
The Social Hierarchy   872
The Aristocracy: Adjustment and Change   872
The Growth of the Middle Classes   872
The Decline of the Working Class   873

☙ **The Urban Landscape   874**

Sexuality, Women, and the Family   875
Bourgeois Respectability   876
Sexual Attitudes   877
Liberalism and the Political Order   877
Britain in the Victorian Age   878
The Third Republic in France   879
Germany Under the Reich   880
The Liberal State in Italy   881
Spain and the Smaller Powers   883
The Rise of Feminism   883
Social Activism and Women's Rights   883
The Suffrage Struggle   885

☙ **Emmeline Pankhurst and the Politics of Confrontation   885**

Science and the Doctrine of Progress   887
The Darwinian Revolution   887
Science and Society   887
Culture and Industrial Society   888
Painting: New Visions of Reality   888
The Literary Response   888
Socialism and the Labor Movement   889
Socialism, Anarchism, and the Paris Commune   889
Trade Unions and the Labor Movement   890
Socialist Parties: Between Reform and Revolution   890
Women of the Left   892

◉ **Documents**
   The Cult of Domesticity 876 / The Principle of Utilitarianism 884 /
   The Suffragette Revolt 886 / Socialist Women 892

〰 **GLOBAL ESSAY: WRITING AND COMMUNICATION (II)   895**

CHAPTER 34   THE AGE OF WESTERN DOMINATION   901

   The New Imperialism   902
      Conflicting Interpretations   902
      Economics and Empire   902
   Africa and the Colonial Powers   904
      Africa on the Eve of Imperialism   904
      Explorers and Missionaries   906
      The Scramble for Africa   906
      Britain, France, and the Perils of Empire   908
      South Africa and the Boer War   909
      Imperialism and Its Consequences   910
   The West in Asia   910
   British Imperial India   912
      Modern Growth   912
      Colonial Government   913

   ❀ **New Delhi: Indian Summer of the Raj   916**

      The Rise of Indian Nationalism   917
   Colonial Regimes in Southeast Asia   918
      The British in Burma and Malaya   918
      French, Dutch, and American Colonialism   918
      Independent Siam   920
      Overseas Chinese   920
   China Besieged   921
      Traders and Missionaries   922
      The Taiping Rebellion   922
      Attempts at Reform   923
      Treaty Ports and Mission Schools   924
      The Boxer Rebellion   924

Japan Among the Powers 925
The Meiji Restoration: Response to the West 925
Economy and Government 926
Japanese Imperialism 926

🏵 **Ito Hirobumi: Meiji Statesman 927**

Australia and the Pacific Islands 927
Australia: Convicts, Wool, and Gold 928
New Zealand: Maori and Missionaries 929
Islands of the Pacific 929

◉ **Documents**
Imperialism and Economics: The Debate 903 / Military Revolution in Africa: The Zulu Warrior 905 / Women and African Society 908 / Opium 922 / Through Each Other's Eyes 923

THE VISUAL EXPERIENCE: ART OF MODERN ASIA AND AFRICA *following page 928*

PART FIVE THE TWENTIETH CENTURY 932

CHAPTER 35 CULTURE, SOCIETY, AND THE GREAT WAR 934

The Crisis of European Culture 935
The Revolt Against Positivism 935
The Dilemmas of Science 936
Realism Abandoned: Literature and Art 937

🏵 **Barcelona and the Modern Temper 937**

Postimpressionists, Cubists, and Futurists 938
Nationalism and Racism 939
The Breakdown of the European Order 939
Bismarck and the Concert of Europe 941
The Triple Entente 941
The Arms Race 942
Europe on the Brink 943
Sarajevo: The Failure of Diplomacy 943

The Ordeal of the West   945
War of Attrition   945
The Eastern Front and Italian Intervention   946
The War Beyond Europe   947
Agony on the Western Front   948
The Social Consequences of Total War   948
American Intervention and the German Collapse   949
The Reordering of Europe   950
The Paris Peace Conference   950
The Treaty of Versailles   950
The Search for Security   952
Society and Culture: The Impact of War   952
Social Change and Economic Crisis   954
The New Morality: Women, Work, and Sex   954

❦ **Josephine Baker: An American in Paris   956**

Science, Literature, and Art   957

◉ **Documents**
**The Futurist Manifesto 940 / The Trauma of Trench Warfare 945 /
The War Guilt Principle 951 / Postwar Sexual Mores 955**

〰**GLOBAL ESSAY: THE HUMAN IMAGE (II)   961**

CHAPTER 36   UPHEAVAL IN EURASIA AND THE MIDDLE EAST   968

The Russian Revolution   969
The Twilight of the Romanovs   969
The March 1917 Revolution   970
Lenin and the Bolshevik Coup   971
Building the Communist State   972
Revolution Under Siege   973

❦ **Alexandra Kollontai and the Women's Question   975**

Stalin Versus Trotsky: The Struggle for Power   976
The Comintern: Russia Between East and West   978
China: Rebels, Warlords, and Patriots   980
Sun Yat-sen and the 1911 Revolution   980

The May Fourth Movement 981
China and the Marxist Model 982
The Nanking Decade 982

❦ **Shanghai: The Model Treaty Port 984**

India: Toward Freedom 986
Gandhi and Mass Action 986
Hindus and Muslims 988

The Nationalist Awakening in the Middle East 989
The Mandate System and the Palestine Question 990
The Modernization of Turkey and Iran 991

◉ **Documents**
**The Bolshevik Strategy 972 / What Price Revolution? 975 /
The Comintern: East Versus West 979 / Gandhi's Message to the
British 987 / The Declaration of Indian Freedom 988**

CHAPTER 37 **TOTALITARIANISM AND THE CRISIS
OF DEMOCRACY 995**

The Nature of Fascism 996
General Characteristics 996
The Origins of Fascism 997

Italy: The Fascist Triumph 997
Benito Mussolini 997
Postwar Crisis in Italy 998
The Fascist Movement 998
The March on Rome 999

Mussolini's Italy 1000
Economic Policy 1000
The Church and Fascism 1001
Regimentation, Propaganda, and Art 1001

❦ **Rome, the Fascist Capital 1003**

The Anti-Fascist Opposition 1003

Germany: From Weimar to Hitler 1003
Revolution and the Weimar Republic 1004
Adolf Hitler and the Rise of Nazism 1004

ᴥ **Bertolt Brecht and Weimar Culture   1007**

   The Nazi Seizure of Power   1008
Nazi Germany   1009
   The Nazi State   1009
   Economic Policy   1010
   Society and Culture   1010
   Hitler and the Jews   1011
Fascism as a World Phenomenon   1012
   Varieties of European Fascism   1012
   Fascism in Asia   1013
   Brazil's Estado Novo   1013
Stalin's Soviet Union   1015
   The Five-Year Plans   1015
   Social Policy   1016
   The Great Purges   1017
The Great Depression and the Crisis of Capitalism   1018
   The Economic Collapse   1018
   Government Response   1019
Britain, France, and the United States: The Trial of Democracy   1019
   Politics and Society   1020
   Toward the Welfare State   1020
Central and Eastern Europe   1021
   The Successor States   1021
   The Decline of Liberalism   1022

◎ **Documents**
   **Theory of the Fascist State 999 / Mussolini's Seizure of
   Power 1001 / Hitler as Demagogue 1005 / Nazism: The Philosophy of
   Domination 1006 / The Brazilian Experience: The Estado Novo 1014**

CHAPTER 38   THE SECOND WORLD WAR AND ITS AFTERMATH   1025

   The Rising Sun: Japanese Expansion in East Asia   1026
   Aggression and Appeasement in the West   1026
      Europe and Africa: The Axis Advance   1027
      The Spanish Civil War   1028
      The Czech Crisis   1030

World War II   1031
The Nazi Onslaught   1031
Allied Resistance and Axis Setbacks   1032
The United States and Japan: The Road to Pearl Harbor   1033
The War in China   1034

☙ **Chungking: Beleaguered Wartime Capital   1035**

India and Southeast Asia   1037
Japan and the Pacific Theater   1037
The Price of Victory   1037
Descent into the Abyss: The Holocaust   1038

☙ **Isabella Katz and the Holocaust: A Living Testimony   1039**

The Grand Alliance: Victory in Europe   1040
The Atomic Bomb and the Defeat of Japan   1042
The World War and the Future   1043
The United Nations   1044
The Cold War   1045
Potsdam and the Origins of the Cold War   1045
From the Truman Doctrine to the Berlin Blockade   1046
The Cold War and American Politics   1048

◉ **Documents**
**Guernica 1029 / Hitler's War Plans 1031 / The End of Emperor
Worship 1044 / The Iron Curtain 1046**

CHAPTER 39   REVIVAL AND REVOLUTION IN EAST ASIA   1050

The Recovery of Japan   1051
The American Occupation   1051
Economic and Social Development   1053
Japan's International Role   1055

☙ **Tokyo and the Modern World   1056**

China in Revolution   1056
Postwar China and the Communist Triumph   1058
Reconstruction and Consolidation   1058
The Great Leap Forward   1059
The Sino-Soviet Split   1059

The Cultural Revolution   1060
China After Mao   1065
The Revolution Reconsidered   1065
Taiwan and Hong Kong   1067
Divided Korea   1068
Southeast Asia Since World War II   1070
The Philippines and Indonesia   1071
Indochina and the Vietnam War   1071
Malaysia, Singapore, Thailand, and Burma   1073
Women in East Asian Society   1074
Rewards and Problems of Modernization   1075

◎ Documents
MacArthur: An Assessment 1052 / Revolution, Chinese
Style 1061 / Attack on the "Revisionists" and "Imperialists" 1062 /
Mao: The Revolutionary Vision 1064

CHAPTER 40   NATIONALISM AND REVOLUTION: INDIA, PAKISTAN, IRAN, AND THE MIDDLE EAST   1078

South Asia: Independence and Political Division   1079
The Kashmir Conflict   1083
India After Independence   1083
India Under Nehru   1083
Indira Gandhi   1085
The Sikhs   1087
India After Indira Gandhi   1087
Bangladesh and Pakistan   1089
Sri Lanka   1090
The Turbulent Middle East   1092
Israel and the Struggle for Palestine   1092

David Ben-Gurion, Israel's Founder   1094

Israeli Society: Challenge and Conflict   1096
The Arab-Israeli Wars   1097

Jerusalem: A City Divided   1098
Arab Nationalism   1098
Nasser and the Egyptian Revolution   1099

The Middle East in the Postwar World   1100
OPEC and the Politics of Oil   1101
Modernization and Revolution in Iran   1101
Women and the Islamic Revolution   1103
The Middle East Today   1104
Legacy of Violence: The Lebanese Civil War and the Gulf War   1105

◉ Documents
Muslim Solidarity: Jinnah's Call 1079 / India and the Sense of
History 1081 / India's World Role 1085 / Israel or
Palestine? 1095 / Militant Islam 1104

🕉GLOBAL ESSAY: MAPS AND THEIR MAKERS (II)   1108

CHAPTER 41   DECOLONIZATION AND DEVELOPMENT:
AFRICA AND LATIN AMERICA   1113

Africa: The Seeds of Revolt   1114
The Achievement of Independence   1115

🕉 Jomo Kenyatta: Kenya's Founding Father   1118

The Quest for Unity   1119
South Africa   1120
North Africa   1122
African Perspectives and Prospects   1124
South America: Reform and Revolution   1124
Brazil: The Unstable Giant   1127

🕉 Brazilia: The Planned City   1128

Argentina: Dictatorship and Democracy   1128
Chile and Peru: Socialism and the Military   1130
Bolivia: Land of Revolutions   1131
Central America and the Caribbean   1132
The Cuban Revolution   1132
Patterns of Violence   1135
The Nicaraguan Revolution   1135
Mexico in the Twentieth Century   1137

Society and Culture in Latin America   1138
Women and the Culture of Machismo   *1139*

◎ **Documents**
**Black Power 1115 / Apartheid and the Oppression of Women 1120 /
Eva Perón on Peronism 1130 / Che Guevara on Guerilla Warfare 1134 /
A Sandinista Woman 1136**

CHAPTER 42   THE CONTEMPORARY AGE   1142

The Soviet Union and Eastern Europe   1143
Postwar Reconstruction in the Soviet Union   1143
From National Fronts to People's Democracies   1143
The Yugoslav Model   1144
De-Stalinization and the Rise of Khrushchev   1144
Dissent and Diversity   1145
Western Europe and North America   1146
The Political Revival of Europe   1146
Women and Social Change in Western Europe and the Communist Bloc   1147
American Society in Transition   1148

ᴥ **Martin Luther King, Jr., and the Struggle for Civil Rights   1149**

The New Activism and American Women   1150
Canada: Economic Expansion and Social Change   1151
From Brinkmanship to Détente   1153
Confrontation and Crisis   1153
Brezhnev and the Return to Repression   1153

ᴥ **Moscow: Russian City, Soviet Capital   1155**

Coexistence and Détente   1156
The Reagan Era   1157
The Superpowers Challenged   1157
The Nonaligned World   1158
The Growth of European Autonomy   1158
The Revolution in Eastern Europe   1160
Toward Unity   1162
The Nuclear Peril   1163
The Quest for Disarmament   1163
The End of the Superpower Age   1163

◎ **Documents**
Letter from Birmingham Jail 1150 / The Cuban Missile Crisis: Two
Views 1154 / *Perestroika:* Reform in Gorbachev's USSR 1165 / Vaclav
Havel on the End of the Modern Era 1166

THE VISUAL EXPERIENCE: ART OF THE MODERN WESTERN
WORLD   *following page 1152*

EPILOGUE   CIVILIZATION AND THE DILEMMA OF PROGRESS   1171

History, Time, and Progress   1172
Global Implications of Progress   1173
Science, Technology, and the Environment   1173
Facing the Future: History as Freedom   1175

Index   I-1

CHRONOLOGIES AND GENEALOGIES

Population Growth, 1750–2000   805
The Industrial Revolution   812
The Revolutions of 1848 and 1849   837
Population of the Major Cities of Continental Europe
  Around 1910   875
Western Colonization, 1800–1900   921
The Road to World War I   944
The Three Russian Revolutions   978

The Road to World War II   1032
East Asia Since 1945   1069
South Asia Since 1945   1090
Conflict in the Middle East Since World War II   1099
Africa Since 1945   1122
The Growth of Selected Latin American Cities   1126
Latin America Since 1945   1139
The Age of the Superpowers   1168

MAPS AND GRAPHS

30.1 European Industrialization, c. 1850   793
30.2 Urbanization in Europe   806
30.3 Railways in Great Britain, 1825–1914   807
31.1 Europe After the Congress of Vienna
      (1815)   821
31.2 Ethnic Composition of the Austro-Hungarian
      Empire   825
31.3 Parliamentary Representation in Britain Before
      1832   834
31.4 Europe's Revolutions of 1848   838
32.1 Europe in 1871   848
32.2 The Unification of Italy, 1859–1870   851
32.3 The Unification of Germany, 1866–1871   856
32.4 The Decline of the Ottoman Empire to
      1914   861
33.1 German and British Industrial Production,
      1882–1912   871
34.1 Africa on the Eve of World War I   907
34.2 Major Ports and Commercially Productive Areas
      in East Asia, 1600–1940   911
34.3 Growth of the British Empire in India   913
34.4 Growth of India's Railway Network   914
34.5 Colonial Empires in Asia   919
34.6 Colonial Empires in the Pacific, c. 1900   928
35.1 The Balkans in 1914   943
35.2 World War I, 1914–1918   946
35.3 Territorial Settlements in Europe,
      1919–1926   953

36.1 Russia in War and Revolution, 1917–1921   974
36.2 China in the 1930s   983
36.3 The Growth of Shanghai   985
36.4 The Middle East After World War I   991
37.1 Unemployment in Germany, 1929–1934   1008
38.1 Central Europe, 1939   1030
38.2 World War II in Europe   1033
38.3 The China-Burma-India Theater in
      World War II   1036
38.4 World War II in Eastern Asia   1043
39.1 Modern Japan   1051
39.2 Modern China   1057
39.3 Modern Korea   1068
39.4 Southeast Asia   1070
40.1 South Asia Today   1082
40.2 Major Languages of the Indian
      Subcontinent   1084
40.3 Sri Lanka   1091
40.4 The Middle East Today   1093
41.1 Africa Today   1117
41.2 Modern South America   1125
41.3 Mexico, Central America, and the
      Caribbean   1133
42.1 Europe, 1945–1989   1159
42.2 The Breakup of Yugoslavia   1162
42.3 The Independent Republics of the Former
      Soviet Union   1169

P R E F A C E

The demise of the Soviet empire and the subsequent restructuring of international relations underscore the premise of this book: Our ability to relate to other cultures and peoples demands some understanding of their history and values, and without this understanding there can be no responsible citizenship, no informed judgment, and no effective commitment to seek peace and dignity for all. Americans do not live in isolation from people in Asia, Africa, Europe, Latin America, and the Middle East. Our ability to understand and respect one another necessitates an awareness of our historical roots.

Civilizations of the World was from its beginning a *world* history—a conscious effort to broaden the Western cultural background of most students by giving substantial coverage to all the major civilizations and by trying to place historical events, customs, and cultures in a global context. The enthusiastic reception of the first edition of *Civilizations of the World: The Human Adventure* has shown the extent to which many of our professional colleagues and their students find this approach meaningful.

BIOGRAPHICAL PORTRAITS

World histories sometimes fail to give students a sense of personal intimacy with the subject. Migratory movements, famines and plagues, trading patterns, and imperial conquests are all important in history, but the individual also matters. Scholars used to write about the past in terms of its "great men" (rarely its women). The great figures still appear in our text, of course, as in any broad historical study. But to give a true sense of the diversity of the human achievement, we have included in most chapters biographical portraits of significant personalities from each epoch and region of the globe, not all famous in their own time but each an important reflection of it. Among them are cultural figures, such as the Greek poet Sappho, the Japanese artist Hokusai, and the German dramatist Bertolt Brecht. Others are religious leaders, such as Guatama Buddha; St. Clare, founder of the Roman Catholic order of Poor Sisters; and the Quaker pamphleteer Margaret Fell. Some were prominent in the political world: the rebel Chinese emperor Hung-wu; the South American liberator Simón Bolívar; India's Indira Gandhi; and David Ben-Gurion, a founding father of Israel. Others, such as England's Mary Wollstonecraft and the Soviet feminist Alexandra Kollontai, were especially concerned with women's rights; some, like Isabella Katz, testified to the endurance of the human spirit. All offer special insights into the times of which they were a part.

URBAN PORTRAITS

Civilization begins with the city, and modern society is increasingly urban. We have therefore provided accounts of how cities around the world have developed. Some of the cities—Italy's Pompeii and Mexico's Teotihuacán, for example—are now in ruins, while others—Shanghai, Baghdad, Moscow—are thriving. Jerusalem, Paris, Tokyo (Edo), and Rome are revisited at different periods to give a sense of how they changed over time. Like the biographical portraits, the urban portraits are fully integrated into the narrative and provide instructors with excellent topics for discussion, essay questions, and unusual lecture themes. Students will find them intriguing subjects for term papers.

WOMEN AND MINORITIES

This text continues to focus particularly on women and minorities. The contributions of women to both Western and non-Western societies—whether as rulers, artists and writers, revolutionaries, workers, or wives and mothers—are systematically considered. The biographical portraits are the most obvious illustrations of the attention given to women, but discussions of their contributions are also interwoven throughout the text's narrative. Special consideration is also given to the role of minorities. Four African or African-American figures are highlighted in the portraits: the dancer and social activist Josephine Baker, the African monarch Mansa Musa, Jomo Kenyatta of modern Kenya, and Dr. Martin Luther King, Jr. As one of the founders of Western civilization and a significant force throughout their history, the Jews are covered more fully in this text than in any comparable work. They are followed from their settlement in ancient Palestine to their persecution and exile under the Romans and from their medieval migrations to their return to Palestine and the founding of modern Israel. By recounting the histories of these groups, we hope to make students aware of their achievements.

SOCIAL AND CULTURAL COVERAGE

Recent scholarship has placed considerable emphasis on social and cultural history. That scholarship is reflected throughout this text, but perhaps most clearly in two chapters that are unique among survey texts. Chapter 7, "The Ancient World Religions," offers a comparative overview of the great religions and philosophies of the ancient world, with a discussion of Islam immediately following, in Chapter 8. Chapter 22, "The Societies of the Early Modern World," provides a broad overview of such key aspects of the world's societies in the sixteenth and seventeenth centuries as marriage, the family, sexual customs, education, poverty, and crime. Moreover, at eight different points throughout the text we pause to consider four significant sociocultural themes: writing and communication, the human image, mapping, and the human experience of death. Here again are special opportunities for distinctive lectures, discussions, essay topics, and research papers.

MAP ATLAS AND FULL-COLOR ART INSERTS

Two types of special color inserts are featured in the book. The first, included in the front matter, is an eight-page full-color atlas showing the physical characteristics of major areas of the globe. This section is intended as a reference that students can use to improve their knowledge of geography. More than 100 maps appear in the text itself.

In addition to the atlas, the combined volume includes eight full-color inserts titled "The Visual Experience," each insert featuring about eight illustrations—of painting, sculpture, architecture, and objets d'art—that are related in a meaningful way to the text's presentation of history. In the split volumes, selected color inserts are included. The text illustrations consist of a separate program of nearly 400 engravings, photographs, and other images chosen for their historical relevance.

PRIMARY SOURCE DOCUMENTS

To enhance the usefulness of this text, we have provided not only a generous complement of maps and illustrations but also a comprehensive selection of primary sources. By studying these documents—usually four or five per chapter—students can sample the kinds of materials with which historians work. More important, they can engage the sources directly and so participate in the process of historical understanding. To emphasize the sense of history as a living discipline, we survey changing historiographic interpretations of the Renaissance, the French Revolution, imperialism, and fascism.

READING LISTS

The discipline of history goes far beyond merely amassing raw data such as names, places, and dates. Historical study demands analysis, synthesis, and a critical sense of the worth of each source. As a guide to students who wish to hone their historical understanding and analytical skills, an up-to-date reading list is provided at the end of each chapter.

MAJOR CHANGES IN THE SECOND EDITION

The most significant change in the second edition involves a substantial increase in the coverage of Africa and the Americas before 1500. Early Africa now has a newly written chapter (Chapter 9) of its own, as do the early Americas (Chapter 10). The latter includes innovative coverage of the Amerindians of North America as well as the Eskimos. The discussion of modern Africa in Chapter 40 has also been substantially rewritten, and recent developments in Asia, Latin America, the Middle East, Europe, and North America are discussed. To take advantage of the latest scholarship, the authors have rewritten the four chapters dealing with western Asia, Egypt, the Greeks, and the Romans (Chapters 1, 4, 5, and 6). A new biographical portrait, featuring Mansa Musa, appears in Chapter 9. The coverage of fascism has been consolidated in Chapter 37, and Chapter 38 now incorporates the origins of the Cold War. Chapter 22, on comparative social history in the early modern period, which students and professors have found highly stimulating, has been likewise revised. Other changes appear throughout the text, reflecting both new scholarship and suggestions from readers.

In revising this book the authors have benefited from the research of many others, all of whom share our belief in the importance of historical study. To the extent that we have succeeded in introducing students to the rich and varied heritage of the past, we owe that success in a very special way to our fellow historians and to the discipline to which we as colleagues have dedicated our careers.

RICHARD L. GREAVES
ROBERT ZALLER
PHILIP V. CANNISTRARO
RHOADS MURPHEY

S U P P L E M E N T S

The following supplements are available for use in conjunction with this book.

For Instructors

- *Instructor's Resource Manual* by Richard L. Greaves and Robert Zaller. Prepared by authors of the text, this instructor's manual includes lecture themes, special lecture topics, topics for class discussion and essays, a film list, identification and map items, and term paper topics. Also included is *Mapping the Human Adventure: A Guide to Historical Geography* by Glee Wilson, Kent State University. This special addition provides over 30 reproducible maps and exercises covering the full scope of world history.

- *Discovering World History Through Maps and Views* by Gerald Danzer, University of Illinois, Chicago. Created by the recipient of the AHA's 1990 James Harvey Robinson Award for his work in the development of map transparencies, this set of 100 four-color acetates is a unique instructional tool. It contains an introduction on teaching history through maps and a detailed commentary on each transparency. The collection includes cartographic and pictorial maps, views and photos, urban plans, building diagrams, and works of art.

- *Test Bank* by Edward D. Wynot, Florida State University. Approximately 50 multiple-choice and 10 essay questions per chapter. Multiple-choice items are referenced by text page number and type (factual or interpretive).

- *TestMaster Computerized Testing System.* This flexible, easy-to-master test bank includes all of the test items in the printed *Test Bank*. The TestMaster software allows you to edit existing questions and add your own items. Tests can be printed in several different formats and can include figures such as graphs and tables. Available for IBM and Macintosh computers.

- *Grades.* A grade-keeping and classroom management software program that maintains data for up to 200 students.

For Students

- *Study Guide* by Richard L. Greaves and Robert Zaller. Prepared by authors of the text, each chapter contains a chapter overview; map exercises; study questions; a chronology; and identification, completion, short answer, and document exercises, along with a list of term paper topics.

- *SuperShell Computerized Tutorial.* This interactive program for IBM computers helps students learn major facts and concepts through drill and practice exercises and diagnostic feedback. SuperShell provides immediate correct answers and the text page number on which the material is discussed. Missed questions appear with greater frequency; a running score of the student's performance is maintained on the screen throughout the session.

- *Mapping World History: Student Activities* by Gerald Danzer, University of Illinois, Chicago. A free map workbook featuring exercises designed to teach students to interpret and analyze cartographic materials as historical documents. The instructor is entitled to a free copy of the workbook for each copy of the text purchased from HarperCollins.

- *TimeLink Computer Atlas of World History* by William Hamblin, Brigham Young University. This HyperCard Macintosh program presents three views of the world—Europe/Africa, Asia, and the Americas—on a simulated globe. Students can spin the globe, select a time period, and see a map of the world at that time, including the names of major political units. Special topics such as the conquests of Alexander the Great are shown through animated sequences that depict the dynamic changes in geopolitical history. A comprehensive index and quizzes are also included.

ACKNOWLEDGMENTS

The authors are grateful to Bruce Borland, history editor; Susan Goldfarb, production editor; and Bruce Emmer, copy editor. This book could not have been completed without the invaluable assistance of Judith Dieker Greaves, editorial assistant to the authors. The authors wish additionally to thank the following persons for their assistance and support: Lili Bita Zaller, Philip Rethis, Kimon Rethis, Robert B. Radin, Julia Southard, Robert S. Browning, Sherry E. Greaves, Stephany L. Greaves, and Professors Eric D. Brose, Roger Hackett, Sean Hawkins, Victor Lieberman, Winston Lo, Donald F. Stevens, Thomas Trautmann, and Edward D. Wynot, Jr.

The following scholars read the manuscript in whole or in part and offered numerous helpful suggestions:

Karl Barbir
Siena College

Robert F. Brinson
Santa Fe Community College

Christopher E. Guthrie
Tarleton State University

Craig Harline
University of Idaho

George J. Lankevich
Bronx Community College

Dennis Reinhartz
University of Texas at Arlington

Irvin D. Solomon
Edison Community College

Gerald Sorin
SUNY—New Paltz

Glee E. Wilson
Kent State University

Edward D. Wynot, Jr.
Florida State University

Donald L. Zelman
Tarleton State University

We are also indebted to the reviewers of the first edition:

Dorothy Abrahamse
California State University, Long Beach

Winthrop Lindsay Adams
University of Utah

George M. Addy
Brigham Young University

Jay Pascal Anglin
University of Southern Mississippi

Charmarie J. Blaisdell
Northeastern University

William A. Bultmann
Western Washington University

Thomas Callahan, Jr.
Rider College

Miriam Usher Chrisman
University of Massachusetts, Amherst

Jill N. Claster
New York University

Cynthia Schwenk Clemons
Georgia State University

Allen T. Cronenberg
Auburn University

John Dahmus
Stephen F. Austin State University

Elton L. Daniel
University of Hawaii at Manoa

Leslie Derfler
Florida Atlantic University

Joseph M. Dixon
Weber State College

John Patrick Donnelly
Marquette University

Mark U. Edwards, Jr.
Harvard University

Charles A. Endress
Angelo State University

Stephen Englehart
California State Polytechnic University,
    Pomona

William Wayne Farvis
University of Tennessee

Jonathan Goldstein
West Georgia College

Edwin N. Gorsuch
Georgia State University

Joseph M. Gowaski
Rider College

Tony Grafton
Princeton University

Coburn V. Graves
Kent State University

Janelle Greenberg
University of Pittsburgh

Udo Heyn
California State University,
   Los Angeles

Clive Holmes
Cornell University

Leonard A. Humphreys
University of the Pacific

Donald G. Jones
University of Central Arkansas

William R. Jones
University of New Hampshire

Thomas Kaiser
University of Arkansas at Little Rock

Thomas L. Kennedy
Washington State University

Frank Kidner
San Francisco State University

Winston L. Kinsey
Appalachian State University

Thomas Kuehn
Clemson University

Richard D. Lewis
Saint Cloud State University

David C. Lukowitz
Hamline University

Thomas J. McPartland
Bellevue Community College

Elizabeth Malloy
Salem State College

John A. Mears
Southern Methodist University

V. Dixon Morris
University of Hawaii at Manoa

Marian Purrier Nelson
University of Nebraska at Omaha

William D. Newell
Laramie County Community College

James Odom
East Tennessee State University

William G. Palmer
Marshall University

William D. Phillips, Jr.
San Diego State University

Paul B. Pixton
Brigham Young University

Ronald R. Rader
University of Georgia

Leland Sather
Weber State College

Kerry E. Spiers
University of Louisville

Paul Stewart
Southern Connecticut State University

Richard G. Stone
Western Kentucky University

Alexander Sydorenko
Arkansas State University

Teddy Uldricks
University of North Carolina at Asheville

Raymond Van Dam
University of Michigan, Ann Arbor

John Weakland
Ball State University

David L. White
Appalachian State University

Richard S. Williams
Washington State University

Glee E. Wilson
Kent State University

John E. Wood
James Madison University

Martin Yanuck
Spelman College

ABOUT THE AUTHORS

Philip V. Cannistraro. A native of New York City, Philip V. Cannistraro, an authority on modern Italian history and culture, received the Ph.D. degree from New York University in 1971. Currently Professor of History at Drexel University, Cannistraro served as head of the Department of History and Politics from 1982 to 1986, and again from 1988 to 1990. He also taught at Florida State University and has been a visiting professor at New York University and St. Mary's College, Rome. He has lectured widely in Italy and in the United States and is American editor of the Italian historical quarterly *Storia Contemporanea.* The recipient of two Fulbright-Hays fellowships, Cannistraro is an active member of the Society for Italian Historical Studies and the American Italian Historical Association. His numerous publications include *La Fabbrica del Consenso: Fascismo e Mass Media* (1975), *Poland and the Coming of the Second World War* (with E. Wynot and T. Kovaleff, 1976), *Italian Fascist Activities in the United States* (1976), *Fascismo, Chiesa e Emigrazione* (with G. Rosoli, 1979), *Historical Dictionary of Fascist Italy* (1981), and *Italian Americans: The Search for a Usable Past* (with R. Juliani, 1989). Cannistraro has coauthored a biography of Margherita Sarfatti due to be published in 1993 and is currently writing a biography of Generoso Pope.

Richard L. Greaves. Born in Glendale, California, Richard L. Greaves, a specialist in Reformation and British social and religious history, earned his Ph.D. degree at the University of London in 1964. After teaching at Michigan State University, he moved in 1972 to Florida State University, where he is now Robert O. Lawton Distinguished Professor of History, Courtesy Professor of Religion, and Co-Director of the Center for British and Irish Studies. A Fellow of the Royal Historical Society, Greaves has received fellowships from the National Endowment for the Humanities, the American Council of Learned Societies, the Andrew Mellon Foundation, the Huntington Library, and the American Philosophical Society. The 22 books he has written or edited include *John Bunyan* (1969), *Theology and Revolution in the Scottish Reformation: Studies in the Thought of John Knox* (1980), *Saints and Rebels: Seven Nonconformists in Stuart England* (1985), *Deliver Us from Evil: The Radical Underground in Britain, 1660–1663* (1986), *Enemies Under His Feet: Radicals and Nonconformists in Britain, 1664–1677* (1989), *Secrets of the Kingdom: British Radicals from the Popish Plot to the Revolution of 1688–1689* (1992), and *John Bunyan and English Nonconformity* (1992). The Conference on British Studies awarded Greaves the Walter D. Love Memorial Prize for *The Puritan Revolution and Educational Thought: Background for Reform* (1969), and his *Society and Religion in Elizabethan England* (1981) was a finalist for the Robert Livingston Schuyler Prize of the American Historical Association. He was president of the American Society of Church History in 1991.

Rhoads Murphey. Born in Philadelphia, Rhoads Murphey, a specialist in Chinese history and in geography, received the Ph.D. degree from Harvard University in 1950. Before joining the faculty of the University of Michigan in 1964, he taught at the University of Washington; he has also been a visiting professor at Taiwan University and Tokyo University. From 1954 to 1956 he was the director of the Conference of Diplomats in Asia. The University of Michigan granted him a Distinguished Service Award in 1974. Currently president of the Association for Asian Studies, Murphey has served as editor of the *Journal of Asian Studies* and *Michigan Papers in Chinese Studies.* The Social Science Research Council, the Ford Foundation, the Guggenheim Foundation, the National Endowment for the Humanities, and the American Council of Learned Societies have awarded him fellowships. A prolific author, Murphey's books include *Shanghai: Key to Modern China* (1953), *An Introduction to Geography* (4th ed., 1978), *A New China Policy* (with others, 1965), *Approaches to Modern Chinese History* (with others, 1967), *The Scope of Geography* (3rd ed., 1982), *The Treaty Ports and China's Modernization* (1970), *China Meets the West: The Treaty Ports* (1975), *The Fading of the Maoist Vision* (1980), and *A History of Asia* (1992). *The Outsiders: Westerners in India and China* (1977) won the Best Book of the Year award from the University of Michigan Press.

Robert Zaller. Robert Zaller was born in New York City and received a Ph.D. degree from Washington University in 1968. An authority on British political history and constitutional thought, he has also written extensively on modern literature, film, and art. He has taught at Queens College, City University of New York; the University of California, Santa Barbara; and the University of Miami. He is currently Professor of History and former head of the Department of History and Politics at Drexel University. He has been a Guggenheim Fellow and is a member of the advisory board of the Yale Center for Parliamentary History and a Fellow of the Royal Historical Society. His book *The Parliament of 1621: A Study in Constitutional Conflict* (1971) received the Phi Alpha Theta prize for the best first book by a member of the society, and he was made a fellow of Tor House in recognition of *The Cliffs of Solitude: A Reading of Robinson Jeffers* (1983), the inaugural volume of the Cambridge Studies in American Literature and Culture series. His other books include *Lives of the Poet* (1974) and *Europe in Transition, 1660–1815* (1984). He has edited *A Casebook on Anaïs Nin* (1974) and *Centennial Essays for Robinson Jeffers* (1991) and has coedited, with Richard L. Greaves, the *Biographical Dictionary of British Radicals in the Seventeenth Century* (3 volumes, 1982–1984). With Richard L. Greaves and Jennifer Tolbert Roberts he is a coauthor of *Civilizations of the West: The Human Adventure* (1992). His recent publications include studies of Samuel Beckett, Philip Guston, Bernardo Bertolucci, and the English civil war.

A Note on the Spelling
of Asian Names and Words

Nearly all Asian languages are written with symbols different from our Western alphabet. Chinese, Japanese, and Korean are written with ideographic characters, plus a phonetic syllabary for Japanese and Korean. Most other Asian languages have their own scripts, symbols, diacritical marks, and alphabets, which differ from ours. There can thus be no single "correct spelling" in Western symbols for Asian words or names, including personal names and place names—only established conventions. Unfortunately, conventions in this respect differ widely and in many cases reflect preferences or forms related to different Western languages. The Western spellings used in this book, including its maps, are to some extent a compromise, in an effort to follow the main English-language conventions but also to make pronunciation for English speakers as easy as possible.

Chinese presents the biggest problem, since there are a great many different conventions in use and since well-known place names, such as Peking or Canton, are commonly spelled as they are here in most Western writings, even though this spelling is inconsistent with all of the romanization systems in current use and does not accurately represent the Chinese sounds. Most American newspapers and some journals now use the romanization system called *pinyin*, approved by the Chinese government, which renders these two city names, with greater phonetic accuracy, as Beijing and Kwangzhou but which presents other problems for most Western readers and which they commonly mispronounce.

The usage in this book follows the most commonly used convention for scholarly publication when romanizing Chinese names, the Wade-Giles system, but gives the pinyin equivalents for modern names (if they differ) in parentheses after the first use of a name. Readers will encounter both spellings, plus others, in other books, papers, and journals, and some familiarity with both conventions is thus necessary.

In general, readers should realize and remember that English spellings of names from other languages (such as Munich for München, Vienna for Wien, and Rome for Roma), especially in Asia, can be only approximations and may differ confusingly from one Western source or map to another.

CIVILIZATIONS OF THE WORLD

The Industrial Revolution

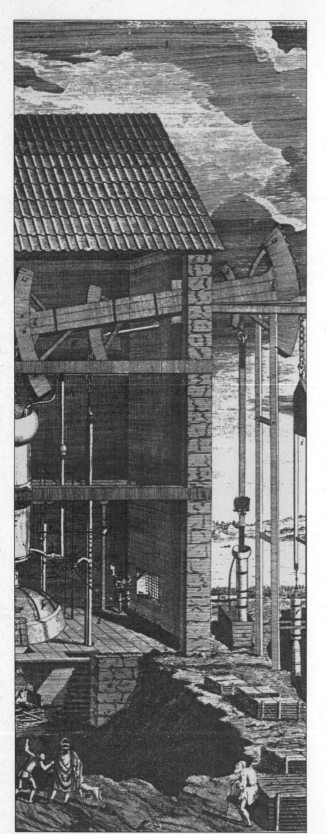

From the beginning of history to the nineteenth century, all physical labor was accomplished by human hands, either directly or with tools held or rigged by human hands or with animals guided by human hands. Power was supplied by muscle reinforced by levers, pulleys, and weights and supplemented by running water, moving air, or fire. Since then, work has been performed increasingly, and in the more developed regions of the world predominantly, by machines powered by steam, electricity, combustible gases, and the exploding atom. The use of new power sources to drive increasingly complex machines is still developing, as may be seen in such contemporary devices as computers and lasers. The enormous consequent increase in productive capacity and technical mastery of the resources of the globe has transformed work, society, and the face of the planet itself more than any single development since the intro-

An early steam-powered engine, based on an English design and built in 1727, pumps water from a Swedish mine. Impressive in scale, it could pump 100 gallons a minute out of flooded shafts. [Trustees of the Science Museum, London]

duction of agriculture. This process is still known by the name given to it by the nineteenth-century British historian Arnold Toynbee: the Industrial Revolution.

Background: Population, Energy, and Technology

The Industrial Revolution began in western Europe, particularly in Great Britain. Europe had achieved an aggregate growth of population, commerce, and energy between the fifteenth and the eighteenth centuries. Such growth, at an even faster relative rate, had been experienced between the eleventh and thirteenth centuries, only to be succeeded by the demographic catastrophe of the fourteenth. Some observers, such as the Englishman Thomas Robert Malthus (1766–1834), feared at the end of the eighteenth century that Europe was on the brink of such a catastrophe again. In his *Essay on Population* (1798), Malthus noted with alarm the surge in Europe's population, apparent since the middle of the century. Asserting that population tended to increase geometrically while production grew only arithmetically, he calculated that Europeans would soon outstrip their resources. The result would be scarcity, famine, and war.

Had the Industrial Revolution not transformed Europe's productive capacity, Malthus' dire prophecy might have come true. By the end of the eighteenth century, the continent's once abundant forests had been seriously depleted by industrial demand and agricultural clearance. The average Parisian, for example, was consuming 2 tons of fuel per year by 1789, almost all of it wood, and French forests had already shrunk to their present-day size. At that rate, the exhaustion of France's major energy source and chief industrial material seemed inevitable.

The solution was the replacement of wood by coal. Coal had become an important fuel source in the sixteenth century in Liège, where it was mined in the surrounding basin, and even more so in Newcastle on the Tyne basin in England, where after 1600 it was used extensively in the production of salt, glass, bricks, and tiles, in metal and sugar refining, and in baking and brewing. But its more general use was restricted by the difficulty and danger of mining it, the lack of overland transportation to distribute it, and the foul-smelling sulfur released in burning it.

One of the chief hazards of coal mining was subsurface water. At the beginning of the eighteenth century, Thomas Savery, a London inventor, and Thomas Newcomen, a Dartmouth blacksmith, developed a steam-powered pump that Savery called "the Miners' Friend."

The efficiency of this pump was increased fourfold when the Scotsman James Watt (1736–1819) developed a condenser that kept the steam from being dissipated into the atmosphere, and demand for the pump skyrocketed. Dissatisfied with the device, Watt continued to experiment until by 1782 he had converted it into a double-action rotary engine capable of turning heavy machinery. By 1800 some 500 such engines were in use in Great Britain.

Just as industrial progress was limited by the use of wood as its primary source of energy, so too was it limited by its dependence on wood and stone as its chief construction materials. Running a poor third to these, though indispensable for such everyday products as nails, needles, wire, spurs, buckles, and rings, as well as heavier implements such as stoves and weapons, was iron. Smelting iron, which involved separating it from its ore, was a complex, labor-intensive process (the Italian city of Brescia, a major iron center, was said to employ 60,000 people to manufacture iron in the late fifteenth century), requiring heavy machinery and great amounts of fuel. The product itself, like coal, was difficult to transport, and most iron for domestic use was produced in small quantities on the village level.

Smelting was accomplished by the use of charcoal, which required that all large ironworks be located near forest areas. The search for an alternative fuel as the forests dwindled led to coke, a waste product obtained from coal essentially as charcoal is from wood. Its high sulfur content resulted in an unacceptably brittle product, however, until the Quaker ironmaster Abraham Darby was able to produce a coke-smelted iron suitable for heavy utensils and military ordnance in 1709. The demand for munitions during the Seven Years' War led to a considerable expansion of coke-fed blast furnaces in Great Britain. But it was not until 1784, when Henry Cort introduced the puddling process for converting crudely cast pig iron into the lighter and more tensile wrought iron necessary for most domestic products, that the iron industry was freed from its dependence on wood.

The result of these technical innovations was that by the 1780s Europe stood on the verge of a great breakthrough in its industrial capacity. The use of steam facilitated the extraction of coal; the use of coal made possible the increased production of iron; and iron (with other metals) was first to supplement and then to replace wood and stone as the prime industrial material. At the same time, transportation was improved by new highways called turnpikes that could bear far heavier loads and by canals that turned Britain's waterways into an integrated transport system. The symbol of the new age was the great iron bridge that Abraham Darby III built across the Severn River in Shropshire in 1779; 50 years later, the first phase of the Industrial Revolution was to culminate in the locomotive, which, made of iron and

◉ Malthus on Population ◉

The English clergyman and economist Thomas Malthus, writing at the beginning of the population explosion, concluded that the permanent pressure of population would frustrate all efforts to achieve a more perfected society, and that only sexual abstinence could prevent widespread misery.

In plants and irrational animals, the view of the subject is simple. They are all impelled by a powerful instinct to the increase of their species; and this instinct is interrupted by no doubts about providing for their offspring. Wherever therefore there is liberty, the power of increase is exerted; and the superabundant effects are repressed afterwards by want of room and nourishment.

The effects of this check on man are more complicated. Impelled to the increase of his species by an equally powerful instinct, reason interrupts his career, and asks him whether he may not bring beings into the world for whom he cannot provide the means of support. If he attend to this natural suggestion, the restriction too frequently produces vice. If he hear it not, the human race will be constantly endeavoring to increase beyond the means of subsistence. But as, by that law of our nature which makes food necessary to the life of man, population can never actually increase beyond the lowest nourishment capable of supporting it, a strong check on population, from the difficulty of acquiring food, must be constantly in operation. This difficulty must fall somewhere, and must necessarily be severely felt in some or other of the various forms of misery, or the fear of misery, by a large portion of mankind.

That population has this constant tendency to increase beyond the means of subsistence, and that it is kept to its necessary level by these causes, will sufficiently appear from a review of the different states of society in which man has existed. But, before we proceed to this review, the subject will, perhaps, be seen in a clearer light if we endeavor to ascertain what would be the natural increase of population if left to exert itself with perfect freedom; and what might be expected to be the rate of increase in the productions of the earth under the most favorable circumstances of human industry.

It will be allowed that no country has hitherto been known where the manners were so pure and simple, and the means of subsistence so abundant, that no check whatever has existed to early marriages from the difficulty of providing for a family, and that no waste of the human species has been occasioned by vicious customs, by towns, by unhealthy occupations, or too severe labor. Consequently in no state that we have yet known has the power of population been left to exert itself with perfect freedom.

Source: T. Malthus, *An Essay on Population* (London: Dutton, 1914), pp. 6–7. First published in 1798.

powered by steam and coal, was to provide industry with an incomparably cheap and efficient method of transportation.

These neatly interlocking developments suggest that the Industrial Revolution was a more or less straightforward consequence of certain technical improvements in mining and metallurgy, prompted by a threatened scarcity of traditional resources. But such an explanation by itself would be misleading. Other societies, including previous European ones, had faced scarcity without finding a key to increased productivity. Other societies had achieved technical levels comparable to those of eigh-

teenth-century Europe without an industrial breakthrough. The Chinese had used coal for domestic heating for several thousand years and for metalworking from about 500 B.C. Their smelting processes were far more sophisticated, and they were able to produce wrought iron and steel of far higher quality. The swords forged with this steel, proceeding westward along the trade routes, had enabled Persian cavalrymen to rout Roman legions in the third century A.D. Western metalworking, despite considerable advances between the eleventh and eighteenth centuries, was still in fact inferior to that of China and India; and when in 1591 the

The first railway track was laid inside this circular enclosure near what is now the site of the great Euston train station in London to demonstrate Richard Trevithick's steam locomotive in 1808. The first commercially usable engine was built in the 1820s, and by the 1840s rail networks had begun to span Europe and the United States. The enormous capital outlays forced business, industry, and the state into partnership on an unprecedented scale. The drawing is by Thomas Rowlandson. [Trustees of the Science Museum, London]

Portuguese captured a cargo of Indian steel, no blacksmith in Lisbon or Spain was able to forge it. Yet at the same time the fine silks and cottons of China and India, so much in demand in eighteenth-century Europe, were woven on looms whose crudeness astonished Western visitors. Clearly, the relation between craft and technology was complex; nor do we fully understand the social processes that inhibited technology in China after the thirteenth century at just the moment it had begun to advance in what had only recently been one of the most backward sectors of the globe, western Europe.

The technical breakthrough of eighteenth-century Europe should therefore be seen not as the beginning but as the end product of a complex process of social change. That process had at least three distinguishable components: commercial, agricultural, and scientific.

Commerce and the Formation of Capitalist Society

Before the term *Industrial Revolution* had been coined, the nineteenth-century social critics Karl Marx (1818–1883) and Friedrich Engels (1820–1895) had identified the banking and commercial classes of Europe—the bourgeoisie—as critical in the development of the new industrial society. "The bourgeoisie," they wrote,

> has subjected the country to the rule of the towns. It has created enormous cities, . . . agglomerated population, centralized means of production, and has concentrated property in a few hands. . . . [It] has created more massive and more colossal productive forces than have all preceding generations together.[1]

Marx and Engels saw the bourgeoisie as a group unique to modern Western society, differing from merchant elites in all previous societies in its ability to grasp, organize, and exploit the basic elements of production: capital, land, and labor. Exaggerated though this view may be, it is certainly true that the development of business and commerce had become critical to the prosperity and expansion of Europe.

Commerce becomes a specialized economic function when consumers no longer obtain their goods directly from producers. In commercial economies, producers and consumers typically consummate their exchange through a person appropriately called a middleman, or merchant. In the simplest case, the commercial exchange involves a seller (the producer) and a buyer (the consumer) linked by a person who both buys (from the producer) and sells (to the consumer). By extending the links in this chain—by adding more intermediaries—goods can be shipped around the world, joining producers and consumers who share no common language or currency or even knowledge of one another's concrete existence. In such a case, the producer produces for a wholly abstract market, the size and nature of which is defined by the number of men in the middle.

What expands this number, and hence the economy itself, is capital. Capital can be defined in stocks of goods or resources, in warehousing and shipping facilities, in command or control of a labor supply. But its simplest form is money, since money is freely interchangeable into all the other elements. The term *capital* in this sense was first used in the West in the twelfth and thirteenth centuries. A *capitalist*, as the term emerged by about the mid-seventeenth century, was someone who possessed a large stock of money, whether or not he chose to invest it. Although the term *capitalism* can be found as early as 1753, it emerged as a description for an economic system characterized by control of the means of production (capital in its modern sense) by a distinct group of private individuals (capitalists) only in the early twentieth century. Marx himself never used the term.

Capitalist society—the distinctive form of the modern West—may then be understood as one in which economic relations are integrated by those who possess, as personal or corporate property, the means of production, through which they command both the labor force and the range of consumer choice. In this sense, capitalism as a fully developed system cannot be said to have existed before the transformation of European society by the Industrial Revolution in the nineteenth century. Yet if the Industrial Revolution made capitalism possible as a distinctive economic system, the capitalist element in the preindustrial economy—the activity of the bourgeois or merchant class—was the most dynamic element in that economy, the activity that enabled it to grow.

Preindustrial capitalism was, in short, commercial capitalism, a capitalism not of producers but of distributors. The two states of eighteenth-century Europe where this capitalism was most advanced were Great Britain and the Netherlands. Dutch prosperity, the envy of Europe in the previous century, was chiefly the result of commercial activity. The Dutch had been merchants and seafarers since the Middle Ages. The Bank of Amsterdam was the greatest commercial institution on the Continent. Through joint-stock companies—limited-liability partnerships of merchants and investors—it financed a worldwide traffic; at its height, Dutch shipping carried half of the world's trade, exclusive of China. Though Dutch industry and agriculture were also advanced, it was the trading of other people's goods that gave the Netherlands the highest standard of living in the seventeenth-century West and enabled it to enjoy great power status with a population barely an eighth the size of France's, and a land area—largely barren of resources—no more than one-twentieth that of France.

The culture of early modern capitalism was nowhere better displayed than in the Netherlands. The Dutch republic was dominated by its town life; as early as 1500, more than half the population of its largest province, Holland, was urban. Dutch towns, with their meandering waterways, humpbacked bridges, and the mellow red brick of their pavements and houses, were connected by a web of canals plied constantly by barges, ferries, and flyboats. Their harbors were crammed with the treasures of the Americas and the Indies—sugar, silks, spices, cocoa, tobacco; their shipyards launched 2,000 new seagoing vessels each year. Cloth manufacturing and finishing remained the staple industry, as it had been since the Middle Ages, but there were hundreds of other industries and specialized trades such as diamond cutting, lens grinding, and bookmaking (Amsterdam alone had between 40 and 50 presses). Business was serviced by a host of bankers, factors, jobbers, and commodity and discount brokers.

The great commercial families, the so-called regent class, ruled with all the aplomb of the traditional European aristocracies. As their city grew, the merchant oligarchs of Amsterdam conceived the bold plan of virtually quadrupling its area by constructing three new concentric canals linked by a system of cross canals and streets. They carried out this extraordinary project in the midst of their war of independence against Spain and with their own profits on it built sumptuous houses for themselves along the new canals. But population pressure on the towns was continuous. A shantytown arose beyond the northern boundary of Haarlem, where, it was reported in 1643, there was "much disorder and mischief not only by night, when the gates of this city are closed, but at all times."[2] The modern problems of overcrowding, poverty, and violence were already in evidence.

The Dutch had had a miniature Industrial Revolution of their own in the sixteenth and seventeenth centuries. The introduction of a movable cap to the windmill, traditionally an important power source in the Netherlands, meant that the central drive shaft no longer had to be turned, only the sails. Windmills and their sails could henceforth be much larger, making them both more powerful and responsive to lighter airs. In the 1590s Cornelis Cornelisz attached a crank to the drive shaft that transformed the rotary motion of the sails into a reciprocating motion driving a series of vertical saw blades. This enabled the Dutch to hew the giant Baltic timbers they used in shipbuilding with far greater precision and efficiency. By adapting the crank to other kinds of implements—hammers, rams, paddles—they were able to convert the windmill to a host of industrial uses: hulling, oilseed crushing, fulling, boring, and paper and dye preparation, among many others. Even more significant was the development of the water-pumping mill, which enabled the Dutch to drain lakes and marshes and thus to add significantly to their land-poor country. Such large-scale reclamation projects were financed by

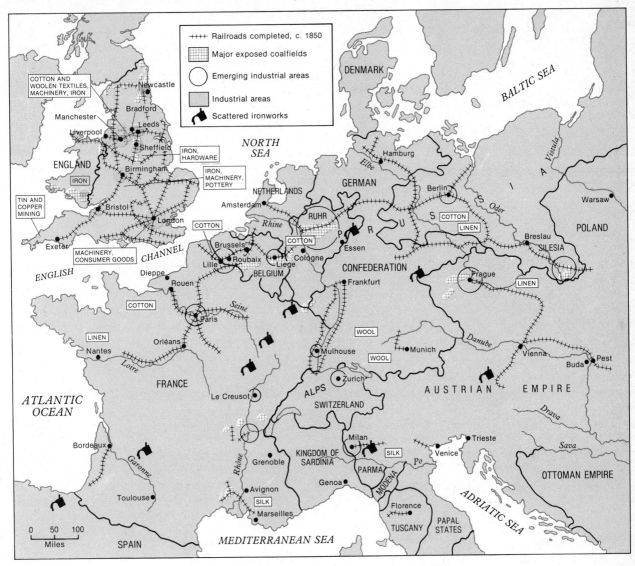

30.1 *European Industrialization, c. 1850*

groups of wealthy merchants, particularly Amsterdammers; thus once again commercial capital, industrial innovation, and economic development went in tandem.

The British were slower to develop as a commercial power, but during the eighteenth century their growing naval and imperial supremacy, their control of the lucrative slave trade, and the systematic creation of capital and credit through the expansion of the national debt enabled them to outstrip the Dutch. In 1688, before the creation of the Bank of England, the public debt was £688,000; by 1713, after the wars against Louis XIV, it had grown to £54 million; in 1815, after the defeat of Napoleon, it stood at £861 million. At first much of this expansion was financed by the Dutch themselves, who

as late as 1776 held 43 percent of the British debt, but this share rapidly declined thereafter. By 1815 it was held almost entirely by the British upper classes themselves: noblemen, gentry, and well-to-do merchants. This oligarchy not only determined the expenditure of the debt through their control of the government but also reaped a direct return through the payment of interest on it, estimated in 1815 at nearly a tenth of the government's revenue. In effect, the British state itself had been converted into a giant corporation paying dividends to its wealthy shareholders. This great capital— the spoil of commercial profit, war, and empire—was a fuel that stoked the engines of the Industrial Revolution no less than coal and steam.

The Agricultural Revolution

The backbone of European society was the traditional peasant village, typically structured around open fields divided into narrow, unfenced strips. These strips were worked by individual peasants, but since they comprised a single large field, the strips were all plowed, sown, and harvested as one. These rhythms enforced the communal cooperation and solidarity that characterized peasant society. The peasants' life was the life of their villages: traditional, conservative, immemorial as the soil and the seasons, and highly resistant to change. But that life was soon not only to change but within a few generations actually to disappear.

The two necessities of the peasant's life were to feed his family and to pay his dues and taxes—to his lord, the church, and the state. These two necessities constituted the task of subsistence—survival—since peasants who could not meet their obligations to the lord would lose the use of the land. Subsistence was difficult in the best of times, and only the wealthiest of peasants could think of producing for the market. The majority dared not experiment with new crops or techniques that promised greater productivity. Their existence held no margin for error.

But changes in both demography and the structure of land ownership undermined these traditional patterns. The general surge in population in the sixteenth century had put great pressure on the food supply, driving up land and food prices. This made life harder for the average peasant, whose increased cost for seed was not compensated by higher food prices, since he did not produce for the market and indeed was often a purchaser of food himself. But it opened great opportunities for those able to speculate in land and sell grain. In England this class of substantial landowners, the gentry, had already been enriched by the purchase of church lands at the time of the Reformation. In the seventeenth and eighteenth centuries they set out to maximize their profits, partly through land acquisition and enclosure and partly through the importation of new techniques developed by the Dutch and the Flemish.

Simply defined, enclosure was the process of appropriating a portion of the village commons, usually by the manorial lord or chief local landowner, by erecting a fence or a hedge. Enclosure removed pastureland and sometimes plowland from the community. The result was hardship and sometimes devastation. Resistance was often violent. A major rebellion in 1549 following a period of heavy enclosure climaxed in an attempt to set up a communistic peasant community in Norfolk under the leadership of Robert Kett.

Most enclosure before the seventeenth century was for the purpose of pasturing sheep, which the gentry raised for market. Thereafter it was increasingly justified as a means of raising agricultural productivity to feed a growing population through the introduction of crops and fertilizers on land that peasants lacked either the means or the desire to "improve." But when the increase in population temporarily leveled off, as it did in the late seventeenth century, the lure of profit did not. Agrarian capitalism—the replacement of small-scale farming for subsistence by large-scale farming for the market—had begun to transform the traditional village; it would end by destroying it.

The improvement of enclosed land involved a variety of new techniques. As in the Low Countries, marshland was extensively drained and filled in. Marl and clay were mixed in sandy soils to make them more productive. Jethro Tull (1674–1741) introduced the planting of seeds in straight, even rows in place of the wasteful old method of sowing them at random (broadcast), while Lord Charles Townshend—"Turnip" Townshend, as he came to be nicknamed—demonstrated that yields could be significantly improved by rotating crops and planting with turnips and clover fields that had previously lain fallow. Both plants replenished the soil and provided winter fodder to sustain animals that would otherwise have been slaughtered for lack of feed. Not only did this substantially increase the size of herds, but thanks to the tireless experiments of the Leicestershire breeder Robert Bakewell, they became larger and heavier as well: between 1710 and Bakewell's death in 1795 the average weight of sheep had trebled and cattle doubled. By the mid-eighteenth century a veritable craze for agricultural improvement had swept the country. More than 1,000 books, pamphlets, and journals on agricultural subjects had been published by the end of the century, 250 of them alone by Arthur Young, at whose urging the governmental Board of Agriculture was established in 1793. King George III himself contributed to Young's journal under the pen name "Farmer George."

Spurred by personal competition and the quest for profits, improving landlords hastened to acquire and enclose more and more land. The unquestioned control of Parliament by the gentry facilitated a policy of legalized confiscations. Between 1760 and 1815 some 3,600 acts of Parliament enclosed 6 million acres of land, or roughly a quarter of the arable land in England. By 1840 the communally farmed open field had ceased to exist.

What emerged in its place was a system of great estates worked by tenant farmers and hired laborers—no longer a peasantry but an agricultural work force. This system, with its vastly greater productivity and efficiency, enabled Britain to feed a population that had begun to grow at an unprecedented rate. In 1700 the population of England was about 5.5 million; by 1801 it had increased to 9 million and by 1851 to 18 million. This growing population provided both the work force and the primary market for the products of the Industrial Revolution, while at the same time the profits of the new agricultural economy, together with those of commerce and empire, constituted yet another major source of capital.

A New Prosperity?

Analysts have vigorously debated whether Britain's new wealth resulted in a higher general standard of living. Certainly the disparity between the immense wealth of the propertied few and the mass of the population had never been greater. Even more significant was the sense of dispossession many English men and women felt from their own country. The small independent proprietor or yeoman sank with the more ordinary village peasant to the status of a mere laborer, no longer owning the land he worked or entitled, even in part, to its fruits. The poet Oliver Goldsmith caught the popular sense of alienation and bitterness in "The Deserted Village," which went through five editions in the year of its publication, 1770:

> *Ill fares the land, to hastening ills a prey*
> *Where wealth accumulates and men decay.*
> *Princes and lords may flourish, or may fade*
> *A breath can make them, as a breath has made*
> *But a bold peasantry, their country's pride*
> *When once destroyed, can never be supplied.*

Even Arthur Young, the foremost propagandist of the new agriculture, came at last to deplore its human cost. "I had rather," he wrote at the end of the eighteenth century, "that all the commons were sunk in the sea than that the poor should in future be treated as they have generally been hitherto."

Apart from Britain, the Low Countries, and Denmark (where Dutch methods were also introduced), the agricultural revolution was slow to spread. Enthusiasm for agricultural improvement ran high in France, particularly among the group of reformers called the Physiocrats, led by François Quesnay (1694–1774); Louis XV wore a potato flower in his lapel in an attempt to popularize the plant. But the French aristocracy was not eager to disturb the system of seigneurial dues that constituted its chief profit from the peasantry, and the peasant insurrection of July 1789 (see Chapter 27) that led to the abolition of the manorial regime left France a nation of small proprietors and delayed the introduction of large-scale capitalist agriculture for a century. Elsewhere, despite some interest in the new methods, change was retarded by the ingrained conservatism of lords and peasants, especially in eastern Europe, where serfdom was still widespread. The agricultural revolution was bound up with the existence of commercial capitalism and the habits of a developed market economy; where these were lacking, little headway was made.

The agricultural revolution was a revolution in soil management and animal husbandry rather than mechanization. The scythe gradually replaced the sickle in the eighteenth century, but it was not until the nineteenth that threshers and reapers were introduced, and their use spread slowly. The abundance of cheap labor—and the necessity to absorb a rapidly growing population—made the introduction of laborsaving machinery in agriculture not only less necessary but also politically dangerous. No similar inhibitions were at work in industry, where machines created more work than they destroyed. But if the agricultural revolution was not in this sense a part of the Industrial Revolution, at least until the introduction of combine harvesters in the 1880s, it was an indispensable precondition of it.

Science, Technology, and the State

The last major element in the Industrial Revolution was the development of machine technology itself. As will now be clear, the new technology was not a cause but rather an effect of conditions that favored and to some degree compelled an attempt to expand productive capacity—the extension of a market economy and the pressure of a growing population.

Technology itself must be viewed not as the mere sum of new methods and inventions but as the outcome of a complex social process in which need precedes opportunity and opportunity precedes design. Time and again in history, seeming technological breakthroughs had failed to yield significant results for lack of sustained economic demand; even in Britain itself, the Newcomen steam pump and Darby's coal-smelting process had little impact for half a century until the need for new energy sources spurred further development.

Nonetheless, cooperative interest in new industrial processes and techniques was growing. The Royal Society (1662), which served as a general clearinghouse for scientific ideas, provided the model for bodies such as the national Society of Arts, which sought improved methods of production. Informal groups of scientists and manufacturers in England and Scotland coordinated efforts to find solutions for specific industrial problems and sponsored prize competitions. Each such solution set a potential agenda for the next.

A case in point was the mechanization of the textile industry. Textiles were the most important element of the European economy after agricultural products. In the early eighteenth century they accounted for three-fourths of all English exports. Traditionally, England had specialized in woolens, but the leading edge of the industry was in cotton, stimulated by the popularity of fine calicoes from India and by the supply of raw cotton provided by slave labor in the colonial plantations. Raw materials were thus available, and a market was waiting, but productive capacity lagged. The first breakthrough occurred in 1733 when a Lancashire clockmaker, John Kay, invented the flying shuttle. This device enabled weavers to drive the shuttle across their looms by pulling strings attached to hammers. At one stroke it doubled the capacity of the loom. Yet the weavers could produce their cloth no faster than spinners could provide them with thread. The Royal Society offered a prize for a spinning machine, but not until James Hargreaves startled his wife at work on her wheel one day in 1764 was a solution found. Jenny Hargreaves' wheel overturned, but it continued to revolve on its side even though the spindle remained upright. Hargreaves envisioned a set of spindles driven by a single wheel, and thus the "spinning jenny" was born. A former barber, Richard Arkwright, attached the jenny to the water frame, a system of rollers that drew the thread taut before it was spun. The supply of thread now exceeded loom capacity until the clergyman Edmund Cartwright invented a power loom that could be operated by water or steam. Arkwright made a fortune and was rewarded with a knighthood in 1786, the first ever given to an industrialist, and Cartwright was voted £10,000 by a grateful House of Commons.

The official recognition given these men of humble status indicated the importance the state attached to commercially viable inventions. Yet the British government was far less directly involved in promoting industrial development than mercantilist France, with its state-sponsored factories, or the Prussia of Frederick the Great. The British concentrated instead on seeking raw materials, opening markets, and securing naval supremacy. From the age of the Navigation Acts (1651–1660), designed to ensure control of the colonial trade, the government pursued a consistent policy of commercial advantage. Britain's wars were fought not for *gloire* but for trading posts and privileges; what it sought above all from the wars against Louis XIV was penetration of the rich market of Spanish America, and when, 70 years later, it obtained logging rights along 300 leagues of wooded Mexican coastline, a British diplomat noted sagely, "If we manage this area wisely, there ought to be enough wood for eternity." If free enterprise and laissez-faire, the gospel so compellingly preached by Adam Smith in *The Wealth of Nations*, were to prove the formula for industrial expansion at home, it was within the framework of unfettered access to world markets and vital resources opened up by a century and a quarter of conscious government policy.

The Transformation of Britain

Between about 1780 and 1830 Great Britain was transformed more profoundly than any nation in recorded history. This transformation affected the size of the population and the distribution and living conditions of the vast majority. It altered the nature and in some respects the very notion of family life, work, and leisure. It profoundly affected the bonds of social organization and even the physical face of the land itself. From Britain the effects of this transformation rippled outward, first to the rest of Europe and then, through the mechanism of imperialism, to the furthest corners of the globe.

During this same period, the eyes of all Europe were fixed not on Britain but on the revolutionary upheavals in France—the great revolution of 1789, the meteoric career of Napoleon, the Bourbon restoration, and finally, in 1830, yet another round of revolution (discussed in Chapter 31) that overthrew the ruling dynasty once more and shook European politics as far away as St. Petersburg. Yet economically and even socially, France in 1830 was still in many respects the France of 1780, a nation of peasant proprietors tilling the soil much as their ancestors had done for hundreds of years.

The events in France were significant, certainly, and indeed they were broadly related to the great transformation in Britain. But if we can in the last analysis see the same fundamental change at work in both countries—the triumph of the capitalist mode of production and its integration with the powers of the state—the method of this change was very different in each. In France, owing to the survival of the seigneurial regime until 1789 and the relative underdevelopment of commercial capitalism, the drama was played out as a contest for control of the state, while in Britain, where the interests of the commercial classes and the state had been completely harmonized, a social transformation of unprecedented magnitude was achieved with relatively little political disturbance, and virtually none at all at the level of national authority. Britain saw only two monarchs between 1780 and 1830, George III and George IV, and even more remarkably, the office of prime minister was occupied for 35 of those 50 years by only two men as well, the brilliant William Pitt the Younger and the colorless Lord Liverpool.

The magnitude of economic change in Britain can best be suggested by statistics. In 1700 Britain produced 2.5 million tons of coal; in 1815 it mined 16 million. Pig iron production rose from 17,000 tons in 1740 to 125,000 in 1796 and then doubled again to 256,000 tons in 1806. Much of this production went to service the booming cotton industry, where output rose from 21 million yards

Coal-mining operations such as the one depicted here in the county of Northumberland, belching their black smoke for miles around, transformed much of the British landscape in the early nineteenth century. [Trustees of the Science Museum, London]

of cloth in 1796 to 347 million by 1830. During this period cotton cloth rose from ninth to first place in the value of British manufactures, accounting for almost half of all exports. Even after 1830 textiles in general and cotton in particular constituted the essential product of the Industrial Revolution.

The Organization of Labor

The enormous increase in production attested by these figures entailed not only new energy sources and new machines but also new methods of commercial and industrial organization. Thus arose the two distinctive institutions of the Industrial Revolution: the bank and the factory. The function of banks was to concentrate capital; of factories, to concentrate labor. There were still only 12 banks in Great Britain outside London in 1750; by 1793 there were nearly 400, and by 1815 about 900. The intimate connection between banking and industrialization was demonstrated by the fact that some of the leading inventor-industrialists of the period—Richard Arkwright and James Watt among them—formed banks of their own as their business expanded.

The modern factory was the result of the machine. Previously, production had been carried on by four more or less distinct means of organization: the small workshop; the "cottage" or "domestic" system of home labor; the urban "manufactory" (to use Marx's term), which concentrated large numbers of workers under the same roof; and the preindustrial factory, or "arsenal," which assembled workers on an open-air site such as a mine, dockyard, or foundry.

Of these four, the first two were by far the most important. The small workshop, consisting typically of a master craftsman, two or three journeymen, and a like number of apprentices, had been characteristic of the medieval city. The workshops were organized on the basis of craft or trade into guild associations, which set general conditions of work and wages and standards of production. The guild system was in decay in the eighteenth century and in Britain had been legally abolished, although the workshop itself, with its distinction among master, journeyman, and apprentice, still remained. The result was that journeymen increasingly tended to organize in defense of their working conditions and wages, a phenomenon noted with deep disapproval by the German Imperial Diet in 1731.

The cottage or domestic system was particularly widespread in the clothing trade, although it was common as well in metalworking and other pursuits. Under this arrangement the clothier provided the yarn and the looms to spinners and weavers who worked at home and whose product the clothier then collected and marketed, thus combining the function of capitalist and merchant in one. On his travels in the English countryside in the 1720s Daniel Defoe noted that the population of whole villages was engaged in cloth production, "so that no hands being unemployed, all can gain their bread." Cloth-producing centers on the Continent were similarly organized. At its most developed, the domestic system converted rural hamlets into integrated productive units in which the workers were separated only by walls.

The urban manufactory was typical of more specialized textile production such as hat, lace, and tapestry making; the Gobelins tapestry works established by Colbert was perhaps the most famous example. The manufactory concentrated as many as 500 workers under a single roof, thus making possible a greater division of labor and a closer supervision of the productive process—both typical of the nineteenth-century factory. The manufactory differed from a factory in the modern sense, as the etymology of its name implies, in that machinery was directly hand-operated and hand-powered; human muscle still supplied the energy.

The eighteenth century reserved the term *factory* itself for industrial or mining operations in which human energy was supplemented by wind, running water, or fire. Iron foundries, arsenals, and shipyards were typical examples. Large-scale water-powered mining was well established in central Europe by the sixteenth century. Yet even though the concentration of labor and the increasing sophistication with which it was organized laid the basis for an industrial breakthrough, it could not of itself bring it about. Far greater concentrations could be found in China, for example, where in Sungkiang, south of Shanghai, over 200,000 workers were employed in the cloth trade. What made the difference was the development of iron machinery powered by coal and steam and the expanding market economy prepared by commercial capitalism. China had neither. Its immense productive base was turned inward on primarily domestic consumption, and its unexcelled craftsmanship had been developed at the expense of its technology.

The factory system of the Industrial Revolution was essentially an adaptation of the urban manufactory to the new machines. These machines doomed the domestic system. The engines that powered them required buildings of unprecedented size and complexity of design. Andrew Ure described one such factory at Stockport:

The building consists of a main body, and two lateral wings, the former being three hundred feet long, and fifty feet wide, the latter projecting fifty-eight feet in front of the body. There are seven stories, including the attics. The moving power consists of two eighty-horse steam-engines, working rectangularly together, which are mounted with their great gearing-wheels on the ground floor . . . and are separated by a strong wall from the rest of the building. This wall is perforated for the passage of the main horizontal shaft, which, by means of great bevel wheels, turns the main upright shaft, supported at its lower end in an immense pier of masonry, of which the largest stone weighs nearly five tons.[3]

Ure described the steam engines as the "two-fold heart" of the factory, whose alternating pulsations caused "an uniformity of impulsive power to pervade every arm of the factory." As this language suggests, the factory was conceived of as a giant organism whose lifeblood was the surging force of its engines and whose vital activity—production—depended on the coordination of all its parts. This was why the factory was, much more than a gigantic enclosure for heavy machinery, an integrated system of production. Ure himself defined the nature of this system: "The term *Factory System* . . . designates the combined operation of many work-people, adult and young, in tending with assiduous skill a series of productive machines continuously impelled by a central power."[4]

Industrial Discipline

Ure's words reflected a profound transformation in attitudes toward work itself. The work patterns of an agrarian society had been dictated by the rhythms of nature. People satisfied with subsistence quit when they had achieved it. But production for the market was open-ended, and long before the advent of the modern factory, entrepreneurs such as the Scotsman John Law had deplored the fact that many agricultural laborers were "idle one half their time." From this equation of leisure time with idleness it was only a short step to regarding the typical worker as lazy and unwilling to work—especially for his employer's profit—except when goaded by necessity. Daniel Defoe was irked when "strolling fellows" refused his offer of day labor, replying that they could earn more money by begging. This did not suggest to prospective employers the desirability of offering better wages; rather, most agreed with Samuel Johnson that "raising the wages of day laborers is wrong for it does not make them live better, but only makes them idler."

In fact, few workers could afford "idleness" in the market-oriented British economy of the eighteenth century, where most of the rural population could make ends meet only by entering the cottage system. But the productivity of workers in their own homes was imperfectly supervised at best; only in factories could a genuine work discipline be enforced. Long before such discipline came to Britain, Colbert had applied it to his state

WOMAN DRACINC COAL | OLD WOMEN AT WORK | CHILDREN PICKINC UP

These horrific images of work in a British coal mine of the 1840s were recorded by a
French visitor. Women and children were preferred for work in the coal galleries because
they were smaller and more docile than men. Notice that the woman in the left frame is
chained to her cart so that she can drag it forward on all fours. The height of the galleries
was approximately that of the hold on a slaving vessel. [Mansell Collection]

factories in France. Overseers pounced on every defect;
at the third mistake, a worker would be put in irons for
two hours next to a sample of the faulty work. No swear-
ing or idleness was permitted; only hymns might be
sung, in a low voice that would not disturb the other
workers.

The mechanized factory carried this process to its
logical conclusion. Instead of assigning one class of
worker, the overseer, the task of imposing discipline on
the rest of the work force, such discipline was now imposed by the rhythm of the machine itself. No longer
did the laborer work a machine; rather, the machine
worked the laborer. The penalties for slackness were
savage. "Idlers"—often women and children, who comprised the majority of the work force in the textile
mills—were flogged, tortured, and hung with weights,
had vises screwed to their ears, or were tied three or
four at a time "on a crossbeam above the machinery,
hanging by our hands," as a witness told an investigating
commission in 1835. Sixteen-hour workdays were not
uncommon, and many workers toppled from weariness
into their machinery: the grisly image of a worker falling
into a vat of lard and becoming a part of the product in
Upton Sinclair's novel *The Jungle* (1906) had its counterpart in fact. Some commentators compared the treatment of factory workers unfavorably to that of West Indian slaves, and conditions were even worse in the
mines.

Family Life:
A Tale of Two Cultures

The early Industrial Revolution had a devastating effect
on traditional patterns of child rearing and family life
among the rural poor. Child labor among the poor had
been common in preindustrial Europe, but parents maintained direct supervision of their children in the field or,

in the cottage system, at the wheel or loom. Once families were brought under the discipline of the factory,
however, it was no longer the father but the overseer
who determined the nature, duration, and rhythm of
work. Adult males were indeed a minority in the typical
textile mill. Employers preferred women and children,
the younger the better; Andrew Ure confessed that it
was "near impossible to convert persons past the age of
puberty . . . into useful factory hands." At the factory of
Samuel Greg, seven workers in ten were under the age
of 18, one in six under the age of 10. Children entered
the factory at the age of 5 or 6, as they enter school
today; in some mills children as young as 3 were employed, and in one recorded case a child of 2. Ure depicted these children as "lively elves" whose work
"seemed to resemble a sport." Unfortunately, the elves
seemed not to live very long: the child mortality rate
among Britain's working poor in the mid-nineteenth century was two to three times that of the suburban middle
class, and the average life expectancy of the poor in the
working-class district of Bethnal Green in London was
two years shorter than that estimated for Cro-Magnon
man. Children who emerged from what the poet William
Blake (1757–1827) called the "dark Satanic mills" of
early industrialism were so puny and stunted that they
seemed to many observers to belong to a separate race.

The relative underemployment of adult males in the
factories left many fathers to serve as "house-husbands"
while their wives and children worked. Many young
women went into domestic service in middle- and upper-
class households; by the middle of the nineteenth century, female servants made up the second largest occupational category in Britain, after farmworkers. Such
women were often sexually exploited by their employers; others went into prostitution in the new factory
towns. Under these circumstances the male-dominated
family unit that had been characteristic of early modern
Europe at all social levels was gravely undermined
among the new working class. Many of what we regard

◉ Child Labor ◉

This testimony was given by Joseph Hebergam, age 17, before a select committee of Parliament in 1832.

Q.: You had fourteen and a half hours of actual labor at 7 years of age?
A.: Yes.
Q.: What means were taken to keep you at your work so long?
A.: There were three overlookers; there was a head overlooker, and then there was one man kept to grease the machines, and then there was one kept on purpose to strap.
Q.: Was the main business of one of the overlookers that of strapping the children up to this excessive labor?
A.: Yes, the same as strapping an old restive horse that has fallen down and will not get up.

• • •

Q.: How far did you live from the mill?
A.: A good mile.
Q.: Was it very painful for you to move?
A.: Yes, in the morning I could scarcely walk, and my brother and sister used out of kindness to take me under each arm, and run with me to the mill, and my legs dragged on the ground. . . .
Q.: Were you sometimes too late?
A.: Yes; and if we were five minutes too late, the overlooker would take a strap, and beat us till we were black and blue.

Source: "Report of the Select Committee on the Factories Bill," in *Industrial Revolution: Children's Employment*, vol. 2 (Shannon: Irish University Press, *British Parliamentary Papers*, 1968–1972), 2: 157–159.

as typical family problems of the modern poor—single-parent, female-headed households, high rates of illegitimacy and child delinquency, participation in the underground economies of prostitution and theft—were already in evidence in early industrial Britain. The Poor Law of 1834 was the culmination of this process. The assumption behind it was that unemployment and destitution were the result not of low wage rates and violent fluctuations in the industrial economy but of personal idleness and unwillingness to work. Paupers were herded into workhouses where husbands were separated from wives, as if in jail, and parents from children. Those who died there were denied church burial. For the first time, poverty itself was made a crime.

In contrast to the working-class family, the bourgeois household was becoming more closely knit. It was also more child-centered than ever before. Children had been viewed traditionally as miniature adults. They were neither the object of family life nor the prime focus of its concern. In peasant families children were put to work as soon as they were able; in aristocratic ones they were boarded out at the age of 7 or 8. But in the wake of such reformers as Rousseau and Pestalozzi childhood

was not only defined negatively as the absence of such adult traits as size, strength, and rationality but also seen as a distinct phase of life with its own experiential value. Rousseau and Pestalozzi were succeeded by a torrent of popular manuals on child rearing with titles such as *The Parents' Handbook*. "The child," declared the poet Wordsworth, "is father to the man," and the bourgeois household was gradually redefined as a kind of factory whose product the child was, an attitude still reflected in our language today when we speak of children as "products" of either good or broken homes.

While thus internalizing the values of industry within the home itself, the bourgeois household was also viewed as a refuge from the competitive pressures of society, "a tent pitch'd in a world not right," in the phrase of the poet Coventry Patmore. The influential Victorian critic John Ruskin called it "the place of peace; the shelter, not only from all injury, but from all terror, doubt, and division." This idealized vision of "home, sweet home" implied a domestic division of labor between a male breadwinner and a woman whose function as wife and mother was to maintain a secure and idyllic refuge. This reinforced the patriarchal dominance of the bourgeois household just when it was being shattered in the working-class one.

The bourgeois wife and mother was expected to subordinate herself totally to her husband and to have no thought or interest beyond his welfare and comfort. Such subordination began in the bedroom. The Victorian woman was taught not merely to put her husband's pleasure before her own but to experience no pleasure at all. As one physician wrote, "A modest woman seldom desires any sexual gratification for herself. She submits to her husband, but only to please him; and, but for the desire of maternity, would far rather be relieved of his attentions."

In every respect then, the working-class and bourgeois family experience was as different as possible. In the bourgeois home the husband was the master and sole provider; in the working-class one it was often the wife who found employment while the husband maintained whatever home life was possible. The bourgeois family exalted the child as the "product" for which it existed, while the children of the working class were expendable units in the dredging of coal or the making of textiles. The result, wrote the novelist and later statesman Benjamin Disraeli, was that Britain had become

two nations between whom there is no intercourse and no sympathy; who are ignorant of each other's habits, thoughts and feelings, as if they were dwellers in different zones, or inhabitants of different planets, who are formed by a different breeding, are fed by a different food, are ordered by different manners, and are not governed by the same laws.[5]

Capital, Labor, and the Rights of Man

Disraeli's two nations might also be given another name: capital and labor. Writing in the 1830s, the French novelist Honoré de Balzac (1799–1850) remarked that the three orders of Old Regime society "have been replaced by what we nowadays call classes. We have lettered [professional] classes, industrial classes, upper classes, middle classes, etc." Balzac's "etc." would include the growing army of industrial laborers, which Marx would call the proletariat and others, more simply, the working class.

The very different thing about the new social division between classes instead of orders was that it no longer assumed a harmony but rather a conflict of interests between the various groupings, particularly between the two broad categories known as capital and labor. The traditional medieval distinction among those who work, those who fight, and those who pray—the peasantry, the aristocracy, and the clergy—was based on the idea that each order had a distinctive function that was essential to the good of the whole and the glory of God; if the role of the fighters and prayers included command over the bodies and souls of the workers, it was on behalf of a common welfare that embraced all. Martin Luther, whose revolution shattered the unity of the priesthood, reinforced the idea of subordination when he preached that each man had a vocation prescribed by God in which it was his duty to labor and to remain content.

The Enlightenment brought with it a fundamental change of attitude. Its prime political documents, the Declaration of Independence and the Declaration of the Rights of Man, asserted the legal equality of all men but said nothing about their economic rights. They thus divorced the political realm, in which citizens might call on the state to enforce their legal rights, from the economic one, in which the state was, optimally, a neutral spectator of the private contractual obligations that individuals had entered into of their own free will. Implicit in this view was John Locke's sharp distinction between society as a voluntary association of equals and the state as the agency designed to provide a secure arena for the interplay of private interests.

This point of view received its most persuasive expression in the Scotsman Adam Smith's (1723–1790) *Inquiry into the Nature and Causes of the Wealth of Nations* (1776). Smith believed that the generation of wealth was the result of each individual pursuing his or her own private interest in an arena of competitive equality. The public interest was the sum of competitive interactions, since the only generalized interest all actors shared in an economic system was to maximize its total wealth, a goal best achieved by ensuring them the liberty to pursue their interests, whether as producers or as consumers, as they saw fit.

From this premise it followed that the obtrusive government regulation characteristic of mercantilism could only dampen initiative and retard the creation of wealth. Such a viewpoint was welcomed not only by late-eighteenth-century entrepreneurs but, at least in Britain and America, by the government as well; as William Pitt the Younger exclaimed to Smith, "We are all your pupils." Thus the political liberalism espoused by John Locke, which contended that government was an instrument created by society for its own well-being, was wedded to an economic liberalism that asserted that in the sphere of trade and industry, such well-being was best secured by being left alone.

To those who predicted that chaos would result from an unregulated market, Smith responded by invoking the idea of an "invisible hand" that guided selfish individual interests toward collective profit and efficiency through the laws of supply and demand. Taking this notion a step further, his successors, notably David Ricardo (1772–1823), argued that the relations between capital and labor were governed by natural laws as fixed and immutable as the laws of physics. Those laws enshrined the clash of interests at the heart of society. Competition, not cooperation, was the law of social life.

For anyone unable to compete, there could be only a struggle to survive. Long before the proletarians began to perceive their employers as class antagonists, however, the spokesmen of the new industrial order had portrayed them as enemies of progress. In effect, the working class was defined negatively as having no interests and hence no social existence. Its only desire, according to writers such as William Temple, was to be as idle as possible. "Great wages and certainty of employment render the inhabitants of cities insolent and debauched," Temple declared. He concluded that "the only way to make [the poor] temperate and industrious is to lay them under a necessity of laboring all the time they can spare from meals and sleep, in order to procure the common necessities of life." Ironically, both Adam Smith and David Ricardo regarded labor as the source of all economic value, an idea that was to be crucial to the thought of Karl Marx. But Smith and Ricardo failed to relate the abstract value of labor to the actual toil of the laborer. In effect, labor was seen as something to be extracted from the recalcitrant body of the worker as coal was hacked out of the side of a hill.

At first workers' resistance to the new industrial order was directed chiefly at the introduction of new machinery or the importation of foreign labor or products. As early as 1675 the silk weavers of East London smashed 35 mechanical looms imported from Holland. In 1719 the weavers rose again to protest the importation of cheap calico fabrics from India and secured an act of Parliament against them. The use of Irish immigrant labor occasioned the riots of 1736, which included a bomb blast in the houses of Parliament. Anti-Irish feeling also sparked the great Gordon riots of 1780, when London burned for six days.

The most sustained violence occurred between 1811 and 1817, a period marked not only by an intensive mechanization of textile production that threw tens of thousands of traditional weavers out of work but also by the general depression that set in with the end of the Napoleonic wars. A destitute rioter in East Anglia summed up the plight of many in 1816: "Here I am between Earth and Sky, so help me God. I would rather lose my life than go home as I am." The rioters were called Luddites after a legendary figure, Ned Ludd, who may have destroyed stocking frames in Yorkshire in the 1780s. *Luddism* has gone into the dictionary as a synonym for mindless opposition to change. In fact, the Luddites were chiefly artisans and skilled workers who put forward a platform of political grievances and demands, including the right to organize. More generally, machine breaking was often used as a bargaining tool in industrial disputes, and workers were surprisingly sophisticated in targeting machines that threatened their livelihood.

Industrialists opposed worker organization for ob-

vious reasons of self-interest but also on the grounds that it interfered with the working of the "objective" laws of economics to the detriment of productive efficiency and hence general prosperity. The doctrine that the free interplay of private market interests produced maximum public benefit in the form of wealth and happiness was known generally as economic liberalism or, in a phrase borrowed from the French, laissez-faire (roughly, "leave it alone").

The philosopher Jeremy Bentham (1748–1832) argued that it was actually possible to calculate social benefits on an arithmetic scale and thereby determine objectively what constituted the public good, which Bentham defined as "the greatest happiness of the greatest number." Bentham agreed with Smith and Ricardo that this happiness could be achieved only by noninterference in economic activity, especially by the state. "Every law is an evil because every law is a violation of liberty," he wrote, "so that the government can only choose between evils."

But if nonintervention was enjoined on the state, it applied equally to organizations, such as guilds or unions, that attempted to raise wages artificially or to reduce working hours. The chief economic role allotted the state in the laissez-faire dispensation was to prevent such organizations from arising to do mischief, and the only good laws the state could enact in the economic sphere were those suppressing them. The government did indeed act, spurred in the 1790s by fear of political clubs organized on the Jacobin model by the London shoemaker Thomas Hardy and by tracts such as Tom Paine's *Rights of Man*, which demanded popular rights, reform of the House of Commons, and abolition of the monarchy and the House of Lords. In 1799 and 1800 it passed the Combination Acts, which forbade workers to organize for any purpose whatever. However, it did nothing about industrial lobbies such as the General Chamber of Manufacturers, organized by Matthew Boulton and Josiah Wedgwood. Nor did most advocates of laissez-faire seem to regard the thousands of enclosure acts passed by Parliament on behalf of private interests as state intervention.

As the catastrophic effects of industrialization on the working class became apparent, however, widespread demand arose for government regulation of at least the conditions of child and female labor. "A feeling very generally exists," the conservative Thomas Carlyle remarked, "that the condition and disposition of the Working Classes is a rather ominous matter at present; that something ought to be said, something ought to be done, in regard to it." That "something," largely the work of reformers such as Francis Place (1771–1854) and the seventh earl of Shaftesbury (1801–1885), was a series of Factory Acts, of which the most significant included the Factory Act of 1833 and the Mines and Collieries Act of 1842, which prohibited the employment of

⊕ Luddism ⊕

This declaration by framework knitters, a formerly prosperous class of artisan workers who possessed a royal charter regulating their production of hosiery, illustrates the grievances of skilled craftsmen, which included complaints about the inferior quality of machine-made goods as well as fears of depressed wages and unemployment. "Ned Ludd" was a symbolic signature, referring to an already mythic figure, and "Sherwood Forest" was meant to evoke not only the legend of Robin Hood but also the freedom and independence traditionally associated with England's woodsmen.

Whereas by the charter granted by our late sovereign Lord Charles II, by the Grace of God King of Great Britain, France, and Ireland, the framework knitters are empowered to break and destroy all frames and engines that fabricate articles in a fraudulent and deceitful manner and to destroy all framework knitters' goods whatsoever that are so made. . . . And we do hereby declare that we will break and destroy all manner of frames whatsoever that make the following spurious articles and all frames whatsoever that do not pay the regular prices heretofore agreed to by the masters and workmen—All print net frames making single press and frames not working by the rack and rent and not paying the price regulated in 1810: warp frames working single yarn or too coarse hole—not working by the rack, not paying the rent and prices regulated in 1809. . . . All frames of whatsoever description the workmen of whom are not paid in the current coin of the realm will invariably be destroyed. . . .

Given under my hand the first day of January 1812. God protect the Trade.

Ned Ludd's Office
Sherwood Forest

Source: A. Aspinall and E. A. Smith, eds., *English Historical Documents*, vol. 11: *1783–1832* (Oxford: Oxford University Press, 1959), p. 531.

children under the age of 9 in textile mills and children under 10 and women underground in mines, and the Factory Act of 1847, which established a ten-hour day for women and children. Slowly, the pulverizing conditions of industrial labor were relaxed, and its devastating impact on the working-class family was mitigated.

ROBERT OWEN, INDUSTRIAL REFORMER

The most sustained opposition to laissez-faire economics came from Robert Owen (1771–1858), industrialist, philanthropist, and founder of British socialism. Owen was born in a small Welsh town, the son of a saddler and ironmonger and a local farmer's daughter. At the age of 15 he migrated to Manchester, where he shared rooms

at one point with Robert Fulton, the inventor of the steamboat, whom he lent £100 out of his first savings. Shy and diffident, Owen was by the age of 19 nonetheless manager of a cotton mill employing 500 people. In 1794 he became a partner in the Chorlton Twist Company, one of Manchester's principal textile firms, and five years later he persuaded his fellow partners to purchase the New Lanark spinning mills near Glasgow from the industrialist David Dale, whose daughter Caroline he married.

Thus far Owen's career resembled that of many of the other self-made industrialists of the era. But he was horrified by child labor and refused to employ anyone under the age of 10. He rebuilt the workers' houses, cleaned and paved their streets, provided cheap coal for heating, and opened a company store that sold goods at cost.

As Owen's views grew more radical (and his profit margins lower), his business partners became restive.

In 1813 he bought them out and formed a new company whose partners, including Jeremy Bentham, agreed to limit themselves to a 5 percent return. This enabled Owen to carry out the educational theories that he had gradually developed, which he first spelled out in *A New View of Society* (1813). Owen argued that people were wholly the products of their environment and education; this alone, he said, made the difference between judges and the persons they sentenced to be hanged or deported. He built a large educational complex at New Lanark, the heart of which was the first nursery school in Great Britain. Owen's theories anticipated much of progressive education. His school was run on the principle of play; no child was forced to do anything against his or her wishes, and no punishment was ever imposed. New Lanark became a mecca for reformers of every stripe and a major tourist attraction as well: between 1816 and 1826 nearly 20,000 visitors streamed through its gates.

Owen himself had meanwhile turned his interests to reform on a national level. His agitation was largely responsible for the passage of the early (though ineffective) Factory Act of 1819. By now he had become convinced of the radical injustice of contemporary society. Always a religious skeptic, he openly denounced the clergy from 1817, thus parting company with mainstream reformers such as William Wilberforce, who sought to mitigate the evils of the Industrial Revolution by an appeal to Christian ethics. Owen shocked a meeting of his fellow magnates by declaring that it would be better for the cotton industry to perish altogether than to be carried on under conditions that destroyed the health of its workers.

Between 1817 and 1820 Owen put forward a sweeping plan to reorganize society on the basis of small, cooperative communities. Each community would contain 500 to 2,000 members and would be both agriculturally and industrially self-sufficient. Owen suggested that such communities might be set up by private philan-thropists, by parishes or counties seeking relief from the burden of their poor, or by associations of tradesmen, workers, and farmers who wished to escape "the evils of the present system." He envisioned such communities as establishing regional and national federations and, ultimately, a worldwide one. It was, he fervently believed, the social, economic, and political form of the future.

Owen traveled widely over the next several years in Ireland and on the Continent to promote his plan, and in 1825, convinced that the New World was a more fertile ground for his ideas than the Old, he set up the model community of New Harmony on a 20,000-acre site in Indiana. Despite initial enthusiasm, it collapsed after three years, having cost Owen the bulk of his fortune.

Owen returned to England in 1829 to find that in his absence he had become a hero to the nascent British labor movement, which, coming into the open after the repeal of the Combination Acts in 1824, had adopted his call for worker self-governance. Owen once more threw himself into reform agitation. He now saw that the potential for organizing a great federation of the producing classes actually existed in the trade union movement, and in October 1833 he launched what was to become the Grand National Consolidated Trades Union, the first nationwide confederation of labor in history. For a few heady months Owen was the acknowledged leader of the worker movement, and as local unions and associations rushed to join, the Grand Union claimed no fewer than 500,000 members by the spring of 1834. Thoroughly alarmed, employers initiated lockouts of workers who joined the Union, and the government cracked down as well, hastily deporting seven Dorset workers who went down in labor history as the Tolpuddle martyrs. What doomed the Grand Union, however, was the very speed at which it had grown, outstripping both its organizational resources and its agreed-on goals. Owen himself was disillusioned as the union, far from evolving peacefully toward communal living, appeared bent on a

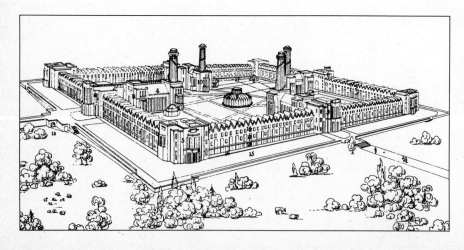

Stedman Whitwell's conception of one of Robert Owen's utopian communities is a cross between a medieval fortress and a planned city, with its fanciful architecture and rigid thoroughfares. The pastoral scene in which it is so incongruously set emphasizes its rejection of commerce. Such communities were designed as self-sufficient living systems for 500 to 2,000 persons. [Granger Collection]

bloody confrontation with capital. By late 1834 it had ceased to exist in all but name, and embittered labor militants turned their backs on socialism in Britain for the next 50 years.

Owen continued to travel and speak widely on behalf of his ideal communities (seven more were founded in Britain between 1825 and 1847). An exchange founded by the flannel weavers of Rochdale in 1844 became the basis of the modern cooperative movement, which still flourishes in the midwestern United States. Owen himself continued to see America as the best hope for the realization of his principles. All four of his sons became U.S. citizens; the eldest, Robert Dale Owen, served in Congress and had a distinguished career as an advocate of educational reform and women's rights. Active to the end, Owen addressed public meetings into his eighty-eighth year. Carried home to die in his native town, he spent the last day of his life planning the reform of education in the parish. The liberation of women was an abiding concern as well, and it is appropriate that the best summation of Owen's character and influence should have come from a pioneer feminist, Harriet Martineau. He was, she said,

> **always a gentle bore in regard to his dogmas and expectations; always palpably right in his descriptions of human misery; always thinking he had proved a thing when he had only asserted it in the force of his conviction; and always really meaning something more rational than he had actually expressed.[6]**

The Population Explosion

An observer visiting our planet about 250 years ago and returning today would probably be struck by two things: first, by how many more human beings were inhabiting it, and second, by how densely concentrated they were in specific areas. The first of these phenomena goes popularly by the name of the population explosion; the second is called urbanization. Both of them are related to the Industrial Revolution, though they are by no means simply its result.

The human population of the earth was probably well under 10 million at the time of the neolithic revolution—the cultivation of plants and the domestication of animals—about 10,000 years ago. Agriculture made historical civilization possible, and civilization, from a very early point, was marked everywhere it developed by city-dwelling. Thus a continuous rise in population and a propensity to urbanization have been characteristic of civilization from the beginning. What has been unprecedented is the steady surge of population since about the mid-eighteenth century. In 1750 the world population was under 800 million. It reached 1 billion by about 1830, 2 billion in 1930, 3 billion in 1960, 4 billion in 1975, and 5 billion in 1986. At the same time, the number of persons engaged in agriculture has been steadily diminishing. In most places, at least 80 percent of the population was engaged in agriculture in 1750; in most industrialized nations today, the figure is less than 5 percent.

These numbers suggest some obvious conclusions. The population explosion began before the advent of the Industrial Revolution, and it was well under way as a worldwide phenomenon long before the effects of industrialization reached beyond Europe. However, its continued rate of increase has unquestionably been sustained by the Industrial Revolution, including the continuous transformation in the productive capacity of agriculture known today as the "green revolution." Despite the fears of Malthus and of many neo-Malthusian commentators today, the food supply has kept pace with population growth; indeed, most of the industrially developed nations suffer at present from excess productive capacity, which has led them to warehouse enormous quantities of food and to subsidize farmers to keep large portions of their acreage fallow—a development that would no doubt have seemed like a world turned upside down to "Turnip" Townshend. It remains true that world

POPULATION GROWTH, 1750–2000 (in millions)

	1750	1800	1850	1900	1950	2000 (projected)
Asia (including territories east of the Urals)	498	630	801	925	1,381	3,458
China	200	323	430	436	560	1,200
India and Pakistan	190	195	233	285	434	1,269
Africa	106	107	111	133	222	768
Europe (including territories west of the Urals)	167	208	284	430	572	880
North America	2	7	26	82	166	354
South and Central America	16	24	38	74	162	638
Australasia and Pacific Islands	2	2	2	6	13	32
World	**791**	**978**	**1,262**	**1,650**	**2,515**	**6,296**

nutritional levels are declining as a whole and that famines have broken out in places like the Sahel region of Africa, but it is quite clear that this is the result of unequal economic development and wealth, often compounded by political breakdown, and not of inadequate productive capacity as a whole.

Although there is much debate about the causes of the population explosion, it has everywhere been associated not with an increase in fertility but with a decrease in mortality. The difference may be summarized by a single statistical comparison. In 1700 only 475 of every 1,000 persons born live would reach the age of 20; by the mid-twentieth century, 960 would do so. The sharp decline in the death rate was essentially the result of a reduction in mortality from infectious diseases and (after the introduction of modern contraceptive devices) infanticide. At the same time, increases in agricultural capacity enabled more developed nations to sustain population growth. The population of England and Wales increased from 5.5 million to 18 million between 1700 and 1850, yet, thanks to the agricultural revolution, food production kept pace. Emigration and the settling of new lands also relieved population pressure; some 60 million Europeans left the continent between 1846 and 1924, mostly for the Western Hemisphere, the Siberian hinterland of Russia, and Australasia. Not all of this resulted in net population gain. White settlers in Australia completely exterminated the native population of the large island of Tasmania, and four-fifths of the Maori population of New Zealand and three-fourths of the Indian population of the United States had been destroyed by the 1870s.

The first great surge in population was to a large ex-

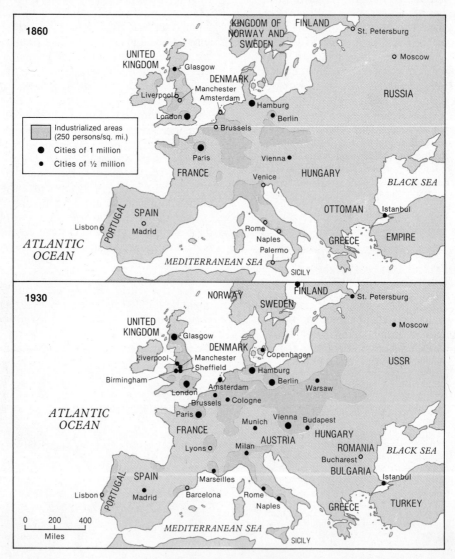

30.2 Urbanization in Europe

tent a European phenomenon. In the absence of reliable data (only Sweden kept mortality statistics before 1800), we can only speculate that a cyclic remission in the incidence of microbial diseases combined with the increase in agricultural productivity in northern Europe generated sufficient thrust to trigger growth. Given the enormously high level of mortality, even a marginal increase in the survival rate could have had a significant impact on population.

Not until after 1850 was control of infectious diseases made possible by the introduction of hygiene and sanitation, particularly in the purification of water supplies and the disposal of waste. These two measures did more to reduce mortality rates than any others, including the development of vaccines and so-called wonder drugs (the sulfa family in 1935 and antibiotics, most notably penicillin, in the 1940s). The concern for sanitation was at first provoked by the appallingly high mortality rates among workers in early industrial towns, but it was extended systematically only after the scientific connection between dirt and disease had been established by the research of Pasteur in France, Lister in Scotland, and Koch in Germany in the 1860s and 1870s. The results were dramatic. Typhoid deaths fell by more than 85 percent in England over a 35-year period, and malaria by nearly as much in Italy over 20 years. It was not the ability to cure infectious disease but the simple reduction of exposure to it that accounted for this progress.

The population of Europe (including Russia) roughly quadrupled between 1650 and 1900, from about 100 to some 430 million, exclusive of emigration. From less than a fifth of the world's population in the mid-seventeenth century, Caucasians had become a third of it by the dawn of the twentieth. This was the high-water mark of European demographic advance. The introduction of Western standards of sanitation to other areas of the globe—essential to preserve the health of European colonizers in the heyday of imperialism—ignited a similar population explosion in Asia and Africa. By the 1980s non-Western peoples again accounted for approximately four-fifths of the world's population.

Perhaps the most significant and far-reaching effect of the Industrial Revolution was the urbanization of Western society. The city had occupied a distinctive place in the West since the Middle Ages. With its walls and towers, it stood off boldly from the surrounding countryside. No less important were the charters and privileges, often won by long struggle, that gave it a unique degree of self-government and political importance. The late-medieval city-states of Italy and the free imperial cities of Germany were the finest flowering of this proudly independent civic culture, and neither the Renaissance nor the Reformation would have been conceivable without them. But the new state-centered global economies that had begun to develop by the late sixteenth century were inimical to them, and their decay

was shortly evident. Machiavelli had written with admiration of the vigor and independence of the German cities of his time; 200 years later Frederick the Great could reply that a word from the emperor sufficed to control them.

The great eighteenth-century cities of London, Paris, and Amsterdam, with their worldwide commercial and financial connections, were prototypes of a new kind of city, the global metropolis. But such cities were still exceptional. With nearly a million inhabitants by 1800, London was ten times larger than the next British city and 100 times or more the size of the majority of Britain's towns, which still served as they had for hundreds of years primarily as markets for the local countryside. Although urbanization had reached 50 percent or more in some highly commercialized regions of the Low Countries, in Britain less than a third and in France less than a quarter of the population lived in towns.

The Industrial Revolution changed all that. Factory towns like Huddersfield sprang up overnight near the

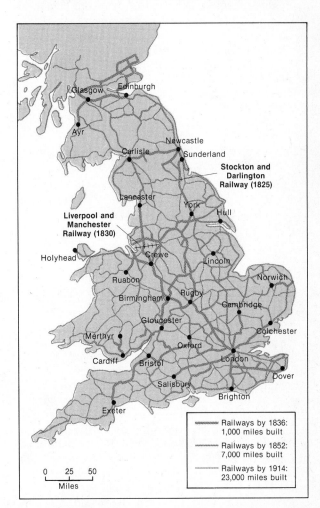

30.3 Railways in Great Britain, 1825–1914

coalfields and iron mines of Britain's industrial heartland. The pulse of manufacturing turned regional marketing centers like Northampton into points on a nationwide distribution grid and old coastal towns like Bristol into international seaports. These in turn were now linked by a new mode of transportation ideally designed for hauling large quantities of goods, the steam locomotive. The British census of 1851 distinguished between manufacturing, mining, and hardware towns, regional centers and seaports, and spas and coastal resorts. Like everything else, the city was now a specialized category, a part of the universal division of labor.

And it was to the city that the rapidly growing British population now came—to London above all. From under a million inhabitants in 1800, London swelled to 2.5 million by midcentury and 4.5 million by the early 1900s. Half again as many people lived in its suburbs. No city of its size had ever been seen before in the world. No other British city approached it, but many others achieved rates of growth that were proportionally no less impressive; Sheffield, for example, grew from 111,000 to 285,000 over a 40-year period, Nottingham from 52,000 to 187,000. By 1851 half the population lived in urban areas, and that number would grow to three-quarters by 1900. The percentage of farm laborers declined correspondingly. In 1851 only two of every nine working Britons were engaged in agriculture; 30 years later that number was 2 of every 16; and on the eve of World War I fewer than 2 out of 25 members of the work force remained on the farm. As the British commentator Robert Vaughan wrote as early as 1843, "If any nation is to be lost or saved by the character of its great cities, our own is that nation."[7]

A river of humanity streams up this impossibly congested street in Gustave Doré's depiction of nineteenth-century London. The vividly gesturing porters and drivers suggest the vigor and tumult of a great commercial metropolis, and the Dickensian fat boy asleep on the pile of cargo in the center adds a touch of humor, but the picture recedes darkly into a sea of anonymous human faces and forms, an ominous comment on the mass society Doré saw taking shape. [Mansell Collection]

MANCHESTER, THE FACTORY TOWN

If any city might have served as a test case for Vaughan's assertion, it was industrial Manchester. Situated in Lancashire west of the Pennine mountains and connected to the port of Liverpool by the river Mersey, Manchester had long been a modestly prosperous regional marketing center whose population on the eve of the Industrial Revolution was about 17,000. The cotton industry transformed it in the 1770s and 1780s, and the grimeblackened factories with their surrounding slums that seemed to mushroom overnight made it the prototype of the new industrial city. By the 1780s its population had grown to 40,000, by 1801 to 70,000, and by 1831 to 142,000: an eightfold increase in 80 years. Visitors commented on the new appearance of what had once been described as the "fairest" town in the region, which as late as 1784 had seemed attractive to a French tourist.

By 1814, however, a Prussian visitor noted the pall that hung over the town. "The cloud of coal vapor may be observed from afar. The houses are blackened by it. The river . . . is so filled with waste dye-stuffs that it resembles a dyer's vat." Another visitor proclaimed it "abominably filthy" and obnoxious to the senses: "the Steam Engine is pestiferous, the Dyehouses noisesome and offensive, and the water of the river as black as ink or the Stygian lake." The Frenchman Alexis de Tocqueville summed up contemporary opinion in 1835 when he wrote of Manchester, "Civilization works its miracles, and civilized man is turned back almost into a savage."

Nowhere else was the confrontation between the classes more starkly posed. A local clergyman noted:

◉ Two Views of Manchester ◉

Two highly contrasting views of Manchester were provided by John Aikin and, some 40 years later, James Kay.

The prodigious extension of the several branches of the Manchester manufactures has likewise greatly increased the business of several trades and manufactures connected with or dependent upon them. The making of paper at mills in the vicinity has been brought to great perfection, and now includes all kinds, from the strongest parcelling paper to the finest writing sorts, and that on which banker's bills are printed. To the ironmongers' shops, which are greatly increased of late, are generally annexed smithies, where many articles are made, even to nails. A considerable iron foundry is established in Salford, in which are cast most of the articles wanted in Manchester and its neighborhood. . . . The tin-plate workers have found additional employment in furnishing many articles for spinning machines; as have also the braziers in casting wheels for the motion-work of the rollers used in them; and the clockmakers in cutting them. . . . To this sketch of the progress of the trade of Manchester, it will be proper to subjoin some information respecting the condition and manners of its tradesmen, the gradual advances to opulence and luxury. . . . Within the last twenty or thirty years the vast increase of foreign trade has caused many of the Manchester manufactures to travel abroad. . . . And the town has now in every respect assumed the style and manners of one of the commercial capitals of Europe.

Manchester, properly so called, is chiefly inhabited by shopkeepers and the laboring classes. . . . The rapid growth of the cotton manufacture has attracted hither operatives from every part of the kingdom, and Ireland has poured forth the most destitute of her hordes to supply the constantly increasing demand for labor. . . . The population . . . is crowded into one dense mass, in cottages separated by narrow, unpaved, and almost pestilential streets, in an atmosphere loaded with the smoke and exhalations of a large manufacturing city. . . . The houses . . . are too generally built back to back, having therefore only one outlet, no yard, no privy, and no receptacle for refuse. Consequently the narrow streets, in which mud and water stagnate, become the common receptacle of offal and ordure. . . .
   [These districts] . . . are inhabited by a turbulent population, which, rendered reckless by dissipation and want, . . . has frequently committed daring assaults on the liberty of the more peaceful portions of the working classes, and the most frightful devastations on the property of their masters. Machines have been broken, and factories gutted and burned at mid-day. . . . The police form . . . so weak a screen against the power of the mob, that popular violence is now, in almost every instance, controlled by the presence of a military force.

Sources: J. Aikin, *A Description of Manchester* (London: John Stockdale, 1795), pp. 176–184 passim; J. Kay, *The Moral and Physical Condition of the Working Classes Employed in the Cotton Manufacture in Manchester*, 2nd ed. (London: Cass, 1970), pp. 20–43 passim.

There is no town in the world where the distance between the rich and the poor is so great. . . . There is far less *personal* communication between the master cotton spinner and his workmen . . . than there is between the Duke of Wellington and the humblest laborer on his estate.

When Friedrich Engels, the colleague of Karl Marx and himself a Manchester industrialist, tried to engage a "middle class gentleman" in conversation about the condition of the city's slums, he received the brusque reply, "And yet there is a great deal of money made here. Good morning, sir."[8] It was no doubt the existence of such attitudes that made an American visitor "thank Heaven that I am not a poor man with a family in England."

Such despair, as the reformer Francis Place noted,

Raw industrial waste was dumped directly into Manchester's river, the Irwell, whose still and blackened water were captured in James Mudd's 1854 photograph. [The Manchester Public Libraries]

growth. Not until 1853, when the population, now in excess of 300,000, had begun to sprawl over into suburbs as chaotic as the center itself, was Manchester formally incorporated as a city.

As the historian Asa Briggs explained:

> **All roads led to Manchester in the 1840s. It was the shock city of the age, and it was just as difficult to be neutral about it as it was to be neutral about Chicago in the 1890s or Los Angeles in the 1930s.**[9]

Reformers focused on the city, and novelists such as Elizabeth Gaskell in *Mary Barton* and Charles Dickens in *Hard Times* depicted it, as Gaskell said, to "give utterance to the agony" of the poor. Manchester's mill owners, protesting the unflattering portraits of themselves in such social novels, complained that their services to the nation in creating new wealth and new opportunity were unfairly disparaged. But whichever side one took in the great class debate, all agreed that Manchester was the crucible of an unprecedented phenomenon, as prodigal of energy and power as it was of misery and despair: the industrial city.

Ironically, Manchester itself had already passed the peak of its industrial importance. Its factories were obsolescent in comparison to newer models elsewhere, and its prosperity rested increasingly on its importance as a trading center. The Manchester Exchange, first opened to the public in 1809 and greatly expanded in 1838, was the largest brokerage facility in Europe. With economic maturity came at least the beginnings of civic responsibility. A local sanitary code, one of the first in the country, was drafted in 1845. The next year Manchester got its first public parks and a bequest to found what became the greatest of the early civic universities. In 1857 it held an exposition that drew more than 1.3 million visitors and led to the founding of an orchestra. By late Victorian times the city that had been described as "the entrance to hell" by the commander sent to quell disturbances there in 1839 had become respectable and almost staid.

had turned large sections of the Manchester working class into potential revolutionaries. In 1817 a band of destitute weavers set out for London to protest their wages, only to be turned back by force. Two years later, in August 1819, troops fired point-blank into a mass rally at St. Peter's Field in the city, killing 11 persons and wounding some 400, including 113 women and children. It was the first battle of modern labor history, and the "Peterloo Massacre," as it was called in mocking comparison to the Battle of Waterloo, symbolized the threat of class war.

In the 1830s and 1840s Manchester often seemed on the verge of anarchy. Popular unrest exploded again with the economic slumps of 1829 and 1836. These were compounded by devastating outbreaks of typhoid and cholera, which were added to the normal toll of respiratory and intestinal diseases taken by air and water pollution and by the appalling lack of sanitation: it was estimated that there was one indoor toilet for every 212 inhabitants of the city. Moreover, despite its phenomenal growth, Manchester was still being governed as if it were a village. There was no regular police force, no provision for social services, and no attempt to regulate

The Spread of the Industrial Revolution

The rest of Europe was not economically idle while Britain was undergoing its great revolution. Population and production, both agricultural and industrial, was rising on the Continent between 1780 and 1830, and cities were growing as well. Arthur Young was impressed with the progressive nature of farming in parts of France on his travels in the 1780s, while German farmers introduced a variety of new crops into their country, including potatoes, beets, hops, and tobacco. Nor were industrial improvements confined to Britain. In France new methods of iron and steel production were developed, and Joseph-Marie Jacquard invented a silk loom. In Germany the world's first sugarbeet refinery began operation. Moreover, interest in the new developments in Britain was intense. British factories drew thousands of foreign visitors, and details about British inventions and techniques spread rapidly. In other respects, too, much of the infrastructure of the Industrial Revolution was in place on the Continent. Swiss and Dutch banking were highly developed, and the eighteenth century saw major improvements in roads, bridges, and harbors and extensive canal-building projects in northern France and Prussia. An observer looking for the likeliest place for the Industrial Revolution to begin would probably have suggested the Netherlands in 1700 or France in 1750.

Exploitation and Resistance

Nonetheless, it was in Britain that the spark caught fire. In France a largely parasitic aristocracy drained off capital investment, a top-heavy governmental bureaucracy often crushed the initiative it was trying to promote, and the absence of a central banking system hampered the flow of credit. Germany suffered from its division into hundreds of tiny principalities and the chaos of internal customs barriers and road and river tolls that this engendered. The Dutch republic, the great commercial success of the seventeenth century, had exhausted itself in struggles with Louis XIV. In eastern Europe, including Prussia, Austria, and Russia, the persistence of serfdom hamstrung the movement of labor so critical to industrial development.

Thus it was not until about 1830 that industrialization per se—the use of power-driven machinery and the organization of labor and production in factories—came to the Continent. It appeared first along a belt that included the Low Countries, northeastern France and western Germany, and northern Italy, where the concentration of a skilled and urbanized work force, plentiful deposits of coal and iron, good road and river communications, and access to seaports were most favorable. Its spread, however, was notably uneven. It advanced most rapidly in Belgium, which profited not only from its commercial connections with the Netherlands, from which it had just achieved independence, but also from its rich deposits of coal.

France, despite its partial development, remained primarily a nation of small farmers throughout the nineteenth century; in 1881 its population was still two-thirds rural. A key variable was social attitude. French capital, long sheltered behind government subsidies and high tariffs, was far more timid and less entrepreneurial than its British counterpart; the Parisian banker Seillière was

all too typical when, returning from a visit to an ironworks in 1836, he was reported "scared out of his wits by the investment going on." Large-scale financing was still a novelty in France, and much of it was introduced by foreign firms, such as the great international banking house of Rothschild. French industry, which specialized in luxury items—silks, carpets, tapestries, porcelain, fashion clothing, vintage wines, and brandies—was craft-oriented and not easily adaptable to mass production. A British visitor at a French industrial exhibit in 1802 remarked that there was not a single item of ordinary consumption on display.

In fact, it was British entrepreneurs who introduced the first power machines into France. William Wilkinson set up the first coke furnace in the country at Le Creusot in 1785; not until 1819 was another built. John Holker, who settled in France in the mid-eighteenth century, was almost single-handedly responsible for setting up a modernized textile industry in Rouen, and as late as 1840 it was observed that the majority of foremen in its plants were from Lancashire. The pace of British investment stepped up considerably in the 1820s. Aaron Manby and Daniel Manton set up a large ironworks plant at Charenton in 1827 that became an industrywide model, and the same partners introduced the first gas lighting in Paris two years later.

As in Britain, industrial expansion in France was at first largely confined to textile manufacturing; cotton production doubled between 1830 and 1846. A railway-building boom in the 1840s brought increased demand for iron and steel as well. At the same time, high tariffs and other barriers to trade began to give way before the increasingly direct control of the levers of government exercised by the commercial bourgeoisie and, especially, banking interests. The ascendancy of such interests was even more open after the revolution of 1848. In the two decades that followed, the French economy entered the industrial era, although many small-scale enterprises continued to flourish. The value of industrial production doubled, foreign trade trebled, internal commerce quadrupled, and railway mileage and total industrial horsepower quintupled.

As in Britain, industrialization was accompanied by ruthless exploitation of the work force, including women and children. Conditions in France had never been idyllic; in 1776 the bookbinders of Paris had struck to win a 14-hour day. But the regime of the factory intensified the worst abuses of the preindustrial workshop. An observer in the department of Nord described working conditions in 1826:

The greed of the manufacturers knows no limits; they sacrifice their workers to enrich themselves. They are not content with reducing these poor creatures to slavery by making them work in unhealthy workshops from which fresh air is excluded, from 5 A.M. to 8 P.M. (and some-

times 10 P.M.) in the summer, and from 6 A.M. to 9 P.M. in the winter; they force them to work a part of Sunday as well. From bed to work and from work to bed—that sums up the life of their victims. . . . They never have a moment for their private affairs; they always breathe a polluted atmosphere; for them the sun never shines.[10]

France, too, had its outbreaks of machine breaking, as at Viennes in 1819, and the industrial riots in Lyons in 1831 and 1834 paralleled those in Manchester. In Charles Fourier (1772–1837) France it had its own utopian reformer as well. Fourier, a mathematician who had been head of the statistical office in Lyons during Napoleon's Hundred Days in 1815, proposed a network of small, self-contained communities called phalansteries similar to Owen's experiments at New Lanark and New Harmony; French attempts to found such communities, like Owen's, were short-lived. More modest goals of reform lagged behind the British example. Despite official concern about the high rate of physical rejection among French army conscripts, the only industrial legislation passed in the first half of the nineteenth century was the Factory Law of 1841, which prohibited the employment of children under the age of 8 in factories.

The German Giant

The Napoleonic wars had been a watershed in German economic development. They had caused serious dislocation, but German industry, sheltering behind the Continental System, had benefited by a respite from competition with British products. They had also radically simplified Germany's political geography, reducing its hundreds of principalities to 39 states, of which an enlarged Prussia, now in control of the coalfields of the Ruhr and the Saar, the main river systems of the north, and the prosperous cities of the Rhineland and West-

phalia, was the most important. The most critical single item on the economic agenda was the removal of internal tolls and tariff barriers. Under Prussian leadership, a free trade zone, the Zollverein, or Customs Union, had been established by 1834, embracing some 34 million people. This formed the basis for a sustained industrial expansion whose rate of growth was unsurpassed on the Continent.

Textiles and metallurgy flourished, and new mining techniques opened up the great coal deposits of the Ruhr. Railways were introduced in 1835, eight years after the French had built their first line; by 1850 there were twice as many miles of track in Germany as in France. Private and public capital were symbiotic in Germany to an extent unparalleled except in tiny Belgium, which was for all practical purposes an extension of Germany's western frontier. By the 1820s and 1830s the great industrial pioneers—Krupp, Stinnes, Mannesmann—had already made their mark. Major capital construction, such as railways, was financed by joint-stock ventures underwritten in part by government funds, and by the late 1840s the first state railways were built. By virtually every measure—population, production, urbanization—Germany was the most economically powerful nation on the Continent by 1850, and within a generation it would be challenging the lead of Britain itself.

Industrial Development After 1850

The wealth and productivity of the West increased exponentially after 1850. In part this increase was stimulated by the same factor that had fueled the economic boom of the sixteenth century: the discovery of gold in the New World. The discovery of gold in 1848 at Sutter's Mill in California (and sizable deposits later in Australia) added as much gold to the world's stocks in the next 20

THE INDUSTRIAL REVOLUTION

Economic developments	Political events
Agricultural revolution (c. 1700–1800)	Enclosure Acts (1760–1840)
Spinning jenny, steam engine (1760s)	Population expansion begins (c. 1750)
First industrial factories (1760–1780)	Adam Smith, *The Wealth of Nations* (1776)
First iron bridge (1779); first wrought iron produced (1784)	Thomas Malthus, *An Essay on Population* (1798); Anticombination Acts (1799–1800)
Canal and turnpike system built (1760–1820)	Luddite revolts (1811–1817)
First locomotive (1825)	Great Reform Bill (1832); Factory Act (1833); Poor Law (1834)
Industrialization spreads to the Continent (c. 1830)	Industrial riots in Lyons (1831)
First telegraph line (1844)	Karl Marx and Friedrich Engels, *The Communist Manifesto* (1847); revolutions of 1848
Bessemer steel furnace (1856)	First public corporations (1859)
Telephone (1876); light bulb (1880); transformer (1881); automobile (1885)	Standard Oil trust (1882)
Wright brothers' airplane (1903)	Sherman Antitrust Act (1890); U.S. Steel (1901)

years as in the preceding 350. As the new supply leveled off, the European economy contracted in the 1870s and 1880s, only to surge forward again with fresh supplies from South Africa and the Klondike. A second source of capital, particularly for Britain and, to a lesser extent, France, was the profits of trade and empire. The traffic of European commerce had constituted 75 percent of the world's trade by 1800. The volume of that trade now skyrocketed, increasing at least 1,200 percent between the 1840s and 1914.

Much of this trade was with the United States, which, already a major economic force by 1860, had become the world's leading industrial power by 1900. The industrialization of the United States marked the triumph of Alexander Hamilton's vision of an America founded on commercial and industrial prosperity over Thomas Jefferson's dream of a pastoral democracy based on independent yeomen. Numerous factors created an ideal climate for expansion: vast deposits of iron, coal, and petroleum, which, with a plenitude of gold and silver, provided an unsurpassed source of both raw materials and specie; a domestic labor and consumer market continually fed by immigration; and a political system firmly controlled by northern banking and industrial interests after the Civil War. By 1890 American iron and steel production had surpassed that of Britain; by 1900 the United States was making more steel than Britain and Germany combined; by 1910 its rail network was carrying a billion tons of freight per year. Huge trusts and monopolies dominated the economy, exploiting the cheap labor drawn primarily from southern and eastern Europe. When the United States Steel Corporation was organized in 1901, it was capitalized at $1.4 billion—a sum greater than the total wealth of the country a century before.

The Harnessing of Science

At the same time, new technological developments greatly extended the scope of the Industrial Revolution. A new age of steel resulted from the refining processes introduced by Sir Henry Bessemer in the 1850s, Werner von Siemen in the 1860s, and the cousins Percy Gilchrist and Sidney Thomas in the 1870s, which permitted both much higher temperatures in blast furnaces and the use of lower grades of ore. In the last three decades of the nineteenth century world steel production increased 50-fold as steel, lighter and more tensile than iron, began to replace it in rail, ship, and building construction.

For the first time as well, applied science and engineering began to feed directly and systematically into technological development, creating new products, processes, and sources of energy. The age of the amateur inventor, the inspired tinkerer working alone, was rapidly drawing to a close; the American Thomas Alva Edison (1847–1931) was the last and greatest of the type. Large firms began to employ their own scientists and engineers, working directly on product development and production improvement. At the same time, the lag time between basic scientific discovery and its technological application was sharply diminished. As crucial to the nineteenth century as steam had been to the eighteenth was electricity, which as a natural phenomenon had attracted the interest of a host of scientists from Benjamin Franklin to Alessandro Volta. Following the conversion of mechanical motion into electric current by Michael Faraday in 1831, the American Samuel F. B. Morse produced the first practical telegraph in the 1840s. The telegraph was the beginning of a communications revolution that paralleled that of the steam locomotive in transportation. The telephone followed in 1879, and in 1896 the Italian Guglielmo Marconi adapted radio waves, discovered by Heinrich Hertz a decade before, to a new mass communications device.

The development of electromagnets, the electrolytic process, and the modern dynamo paved the way for the use of electricity in public places such as railways, docks, theaters, and markets, as well as in some factories. The incandescent light bulb, invented independently by Edison in America and Sir Joseph Swan in Britain, brought electrical illumination into the home and the office in the 1880s. In the same decade the steam turbine began to replace the old reciprocal-action engine. It was soon adapted to coal and then to the fuel source that would power the twentieth century, petroleum. The combustion engine followed in 1886, the airplane in 1903. By the early 1900s, European and American cities were lit electrically by huge generating systems, and their streets were crowded with trams and, increasingly, automobiles. At the same time, organic chemistry (the chemistry of carbon compounds), developed especially in Germany, produced a whole range of synthetic dyes, textiles, paints, and other products. No longer were humans confined to working, blending, crushing, and refining the given raw materials of nature; by manipulating the basic organic components of these materials, new, artificial products could be created.

By every measure—energy produced, goods and services distributed, miles of railway track and telegraph, telephone, and cable line laid—industrialization and the new, unprecedented standards of living it made possible increased by quantum leaps in Europe and the United States during the nineteenth century. But industrial development remained unevenly distributed geographically, and industrial wealth was even more unequally shared socially. Moreover, the disparity between worker and owner in Europe and the United States was greater still between colonizer and colonized as capital penetration and imperial expansion brought the mines, factories, technical processes, and industrial discipline of the West to the far corners of the globe. As this process intensified during the last decades of the century, social

Flags fly proudly over the Crystal Palace, built to house the world's first international industrial exhibition in London in 1851, while a festive bourgeois crowd takes its ease outside the monument. The palace, constructed of cast iron and glass, was itself a triumph of the new technology. [BBC Hulton/Bettmann Archive]

and political dislocation, and in some cases devastation, occurred on a scale that dwarfed the changes that had taken place in Britain and on the Continent. Only a few places outside Europe achieved industrialization on their own before 1900. Chief among them was North America, and particularly the United States, where, with a population nearly equal to that of France or Germany by 1850 and a role as the principal supplier of raw cotton to the European market, integration with the new industrial economy was a foregone conclusion. Beyond the North Atlantic trade circuit, however, only Argentina in the Western Hemisphere and Japan in the Far East had developed a significant industrial base on their own. As the twentieth century dawned, European economic and political hegemony in the world was at its zenith.

The Industrial Revolution and the population explosion that accompanied it both began, independently, in the middle of the eighteenth century, and both have continued unabated the processes of change and upheaval that have transformed the globe. Population pressure spurred agricultural and industrial development, at first in Britain and then elsewhere, and success in sustaining an ever-expanding population generated the market and product demand that fed technological growth. When in 1851 Britain celebrated its role as the "workshop of the world" with a great international industrial exhibition at the Crystal Palace in London, the most important technological advance in hu-

manity's recorded history was already an accomplished fact. The windmill and the waterwheel had given way to the steam engine, the domestic workshop to the factory, the horse and cart to the locomotive and the telegraph. Metals had replaced wood in the construction of harbors, bridges, buildings, and machinery, as coal had replaced it as the source of power. Petroleum in turn was soon to supplement and then largely replace coal, as petroleum itself, having succeeded animal and vegetable oils for lighting, was soon to be replaced by electricity. At the same time, the nature of work and of the social organization that revolved around it was no less radically transformed. The artisan who saw

a job through from start to finish was replaced by the skilled factory worker who was confined to a single part of a process and integrated into a complex market structure that dictated the wages, conditions, and availability of employment. The family circle, the primary preindustrial work unit the world over, began to give way to an impersonal industrial discipline that reshaped and often shattered traditional relationships and modes of living at the most basic level. Inexorably, these changes radiated outward from their European origins to embrace the entire world and to create not merely a new global economy but a new global culture as well.

Notes

1. K. Marx and F. Engels, *The Communist Manifesto* (New York: New York Labor News Co.), pp. 13-14. First published in 1848.
2. A. M. Lambert, *The Making of the Dutch Landscape* (New York: Seminar Press, 1971), p. 195.
3. A. Ure, *Philosophy of Manufactures* (New York: Kelley, 1967), p. 109. Originally printed in 1861.
4. Ibid., p. 13.
5. B. Disraeli, *Sybil, or the Two Nations.* In *The Works of Benjamin Disraeli* (New York: M. W. Dunne, 1904–1905), bk. 2, chap. 5.
6. M. Cole, *Robert Owen of New Lanark* (New York: Oxford University Press, 1953), p. 152. First published in 1857.
7. A. Briggs, *Victorian Cities* (London: Odhams Books, 1965), p. 55.
8. Ibid., p. 102.
9. Ibid., pp. 92–93.
10. W. O. Henderson, *The Industrial Revolution in Europe, 1815–1914* (Chicago: Quadrangle Books, 1961), p. 107.

Suggestions for Further Reading

Ashton, T. S. *The Industrial Revolution, 1760–1830.* London: Oxford University Press, 1961.
Braudel, F. *Civilization and Capitalism.* 3 vols. London: Collins, 1979–1985.
Briggs, A. *Victorian Cities.* London: Odhams Books, 1965.
Chambers, J. D., and Mingay, G. E. *The Agricultural Revolution, 1750–1850.* New York: Schocken Books, 1966.
Cipolla, C. M., ed. *The Industrial Revolution, 1700–1914.* London: Penguin Books, 1973.
Clapham, J. H. *The Economic Development of France and Germany, 1815–1914.* Cambridge: Cambridge University Press, 1928.
Cole, M. *Robert Owen of New Lanark.* New York: Oxford University Press, 1953.
Crafts, N. F. R. *British Economic Growth During the Industrial Revolution.* New York: Oxford University Press, 1986.
Dennis, R. *English Industrial Cities of the Nineteenth Century.* Cambridge: Cambridge University Press, 1984.
Harrison, J. F. C. *The Early Victorians, 1832–1851.* New York: Praeger, 1971.
Henderson, W. O. *The Industrial Revolution in Europe.* Chicago: Quadrangle Books, 1961.
Hobsbawm, E. J. *Industry and Empire.* Harmondsworth, England: Penguin Books, 1970.
Landes, D. *The Unbound Prometheus: Technological Change and Industrial Development in Western Europe from the Seventeenth Century to the Present.* London: Cambridge University Press, 1969.
Mathias, P. *The First Industrial Nation: An Economic History of Britain, 1700–1914.* New York: Scribner, 1969.
McKeown, T. *The Modern Rise of Population.* New York: Academic Press, 1976.
Mokyr, J., ed. *The Economies of the Industrial Revolution.* London: Rowman & Allanheld, 1985.
Perkin, H. *The Origin of Modern English Society, 1780–1860.* London: Routledge & Kegan Paul, 1969.
Thompson, E. P. *The Making of the English Working Class.* Harmondsworth, England: Penguin Books, 1964.
Weber, A. F. *The Growth of Cities in the Nineteenth Century.* Ithaca, N.Y.: Cornell University Press, 1969.
Wilson, C., and Parker, G. *An Introduction to the Sources of European Economic History, 1500–1800.* London: Weidenfeld & Nicolson, 1977.
Zaretsky, E. *Capitalism, the Family, and Personal Life.* London: Pluto Press, 1976.

CHAPTER 31

The Age of Ideology

In the wake of the French Revolution and the Napoleonic conquests, Europe experienced some of its most turbulent and troubled decades. The statesmen of the victorious allies, meeting at Vienna, sought to restore the Old Regime and to find an antidote to revolution. Their attempts foundered on the continuing demands for representative government, free competition, and social justice, often expressed through a fervent desire for national independence or unity. This was in turn linked to the wider cultural movement of Romanticism, which, in its emphasis on the free expressive powers of the individual, questioned traditional values and undermined traditional authority. By 1830 the fragile détente between the old noble elites and the increasingly powerful

Detail from Honoré Daumier's painting *Les Divorceuses*. **At an impassioned meeting of women, one of many held during the Revolution of 1848, a feminist spokeswoman, probably Jeanne Derain, demands reform of the divorce laws. Daumier's portrayal typified the derivsive reaction of the press to the new and disturbing phenomenon of feminist activism. [Bulloz/Musée Carnavalet]**

bourgeoisie had broken down, and a new wave of revolutionary disturbance swept Europe. This was only the precursor of the far more widespread and violent revolutions of 1848, in which the industrial proletariat, fired by the doctrines of socialism, played for the first time a leading role. These revolutions ended largely in apparent failure, but they confirmed the ascendancy of the bourgeoisie as the only barrier to the demand for a new social order.

The Legacy of Revolution

The American Revolution, in declaring all men born "free and equal," and the French Revolution, in asserting liberty, equality, and fraternity to be the goals of a just society, had propounded new political values to the Western world. Freedom or liberty, as the Old Regime understood these terms, meant not general rights applicable to all but privileges enjoyed by particular individuals or corporate groups: the right of a town or locality to charge bridge, river, or road tolls, for example, or the exemption of the clergy from the jurisdiction of secular courts. The foundation of Old Regime society was not equality but hierarchy and subordination; its members were not citizens but subjects.

Even more foreign to the old order was the new revolutionary ideal of fraternity, the voluntary solidarity of all citizens with one another and their patriotic identification with the nation and, beyond borders, with all humanity. In America these principles had inspired the first nation ever created on the basis of citizen equality, though it still excluded women and blacks. The founding of the United States had in turn been a powerful inspiration to the French revolutionaries of 1789. But whereas the United States, an ocean away, had been able to export its revolution only by precept and example, the armies of the French republic, crossing the Alps and the Rhine, had brought theirs by force to much of Europe.

The champions of the old order, led by Britain—whose own revolutions of 1640 and 1688 had been the antecedents of both the French and American ones—had fought and finally defeated the armies of France. Long before Waterloo, however, the ideals of freedom and equality had been tempered in both revolutionary France and democratic America. In the United States the election of senators by state legislatures and of the president and vice-president by an electoral college represented a barrier to direct citizen control of the legislative and executive branches of government. In France a similar retreat was visible as early as 1791 in the distinction between active and passive citizens, and by the time of Napoleon, passive acquiescence in a dictatorial regime was the only function left to citizenship.

Despite this, the ideals of representative government and an egalitarian society remained alive. No longer could the rulers of Europe rely on obedience to authority based on the unquestioned subordination of subject populations to their natural masters, and political agitation everywhere now took the form of demands for basic rights and representation. Of no less importance were the values of freedom and equality in dissolving the traditional barriers to state centralization. The reduction of many particular and individual freedoms was a tedious and sometimes impossible task; the removal of a single set of generalized freedoms required only the suspension of constitutional guarantees by an emergency decree, as first Robespierre and then Napoleon had shown. Liberties extended to all and tyranny exerted over all lay uncomfortably close together as the legacy of the democratic revolutions of the late eighteenth century.

The demand for liberty and equality was often linked to another pervasive political sentiment of the early nineteenth century, nationalism. In its simplest terms, nationalism was a sense of cultural and political identity among a given people. Cultural identity was manifested in shared traditions and the possession of a common language; political identity was expressed in the association with or residency in a particular region or territory. The ultimate expression of a people's identity was the possession of a state.

Nationalism first expressed itself in Germany. The philosopher-critic Johann Gottfried von Herder (1744–1803) argued in the 1770s and 1780s that each people had its own organic development and must pursue its own individual destiny. This contention, like many other early manifestations of Romanticism, went counter to the Enlightenment ideal of a universal reason that would bring an identical justice to all. Herder urged his compatriots to look to their own cultural heritage for meaning and direction, rather than to an imported French model that could only be valid for the French, not the Germans.

Herder's work stimulated a cultural nationalism that was displayed in patriotic literature; research into German philology, folklore, and legend (including the famous collections of the brothers Jacob and Wilhelm Grimm); and attempts to define the German "soul." The Napoleonic conquests galvanized political nationalism in Germany as well. Johann Gottlieb Fichte called on the people of Prussia to regenerate the lost honor of their fatherland, while his fellow Prussian, the philosopher Georg Wilhelm Friedrich Hegel (1770–1831), claimed that the historical dichotomy between the individual and the community was overcome in the unity of the modern nation-state. The highest manifestation of this unity was not, as Fichte expressed it, in the securing of particular benefits such as life, liberty, and personal well-being, as in the Anglo-American tradition, but in a noble patriotism and love of country.

This almost mystical sense of the union, or perhaps submersion of the individual in the nation, suggests that nationalism was not an essentially liberal cause, even though liberals often expressed their aspirations through it and used it as a vehicle of rebellion against the established order. In Russia nationalism would be invoked in the 1840s both by liberal westernizers who wished to see Russia become modern and competitive by adopting western European values and institutions and by conservative Slavophiles who believed that Russia could fulfill its messianic destiny in the world only by remaining true to its traditions. In short, nationalism appealed across the spectrum from economic rationalists, who saw the nation-state as an efficient market mechanism, to religious enthusiasts, who saw it as a communal salvation; from Friedrich List, who dreamed of a tariff-free greater Germany, to Adam Mickiewicz, a Polish poet who identified the history of his nation with the passion of Christ and its longed-for independence with the resurrection.

The result of these conflicting ideologies—civil freedom against local and traditional rights, a society conceived as a body of equal citizens or as a patriotic community versus one conceived as a set of hierarchical orders—was a new and uncertain age in which, for the first time, the very basis of the social order was in dispute. In the aftermath of Napoleon's defeat, the victorious allied powers set about to restore the world they had known before 1789 as far as they could. Their attempts to do so, against not only the countervailing forces unleashed by the French and American revolutions but the as yet unreckoned ones of the Industrial Revolution, determined the course of European politics to the middle of the nineteenth century and beyond.

The Congress of Vienna

The major European powers met in Vienna in September 1814 to try to untangle 20 years of war and revolution. It was the first such general congress of the powers since the one that had settled the Thirty Years' War at Westphalia in 1648. Every state on the Continent sent representatives, including defunct members of the old Holy Roman Empire seeking reinstatement. But only five parties really counted—Austria, Britain, Prussia,

◎ The Mystique of Nationalism ◎

The nationalist fervor that Napoleon stimulated and that ultimately overthrew him was powerfully fed by the antirationalist elements that also produced the Romantic movement. In this passage, the French philosopher Joseph de Maistre (1753–1821), a conservative opponent of the Enlightenment and of the French Revolution, expresses his sense of the "national soul" inherent in all peoples.

Human reason left to its own resources is completely incapable not only of creating *but also of conserving any religious or political association*, because it can only give rise to disputes and because, to conduct himself well, man needs beliefs, not problems. . . . Religion and political dogmas, mingled and merged together, should together form a *general* or *national mind* sufficiently strong to repress the aberrations of the individual reason which is, of its nature, the mortal enemy of any association whatever because it gives birth only to divergent opinions. . . .

What is patriotism? It is this national mind of which I am speaking; it is individual *abnegation*. Faith and patriotism are the two great wonder-workers of the world. Both are divine. All their actions are miracles. Do not talk to them of scrutiny, choice, discussion, for they will say that you blaspheme. They know only two words, *submission* and *belief*; with these two levers, they raise the world. Their very errors are sublime. These two infants of heaven prove their origin to all by creating and conserving; and if they unite, join their forces, and together take possession of a nation, they exalt it, make it divine and increase its power a hundred-fold.

Source: J. Lively, ed., *The Works of Joseph de Maistre* (New York: Macmillan, 1965), pp. 108–109 (modified slightly).

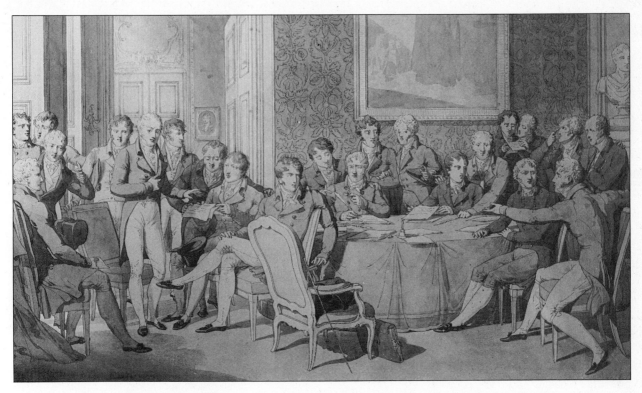

The Congress of Vienna, which redrew the map of Europe in the wake of the Napoleonic era. Metternich stands in the left foreground, Castlereagh is seated in the center with his legs crossed, and Talleyrand is seated to the right with his right arm on the table. [Bulloz]

Russia, and France, represented, respectively, by Prince Metternich, Viscount Castlereagh, Baron Hardenberg, Tsar Alexander I (the only sovereign taking direct part in the proceedings), and the ubiquitous Baron Talleyrand, who after deserting Napoleon had brokered the return of the Bourbon dynasty to France.

Collective Security

What the allies wanted at Vienna, broadly speaking, was to restore the old order of kingship and aristocracy, to prevent the domination of Europe by any single state, and to contain the virus of revolution wherever it might spread. To accomplish this, they created a structure of collective security that was essentially a classical balance-of-power system tinctured by the agreement to suppress all forms of radical activity. This meant that collective security would be brought to bear not only against states that threatened the stability of the system by external action but also against those whose internal stability was threatened by domestic discontent.

The framework for this sytem was already in place in the wartime coalition that had defeated Napoleon; formalized as the Quadruple Alliance in 1815 and extended, after a suitable period of probation, to include France in

1818, it formed the basis of the so-called Concert of Europe, which kept the peace of the Continent, or at any rate took the credit for doing so, down to 1914. The novelty of the system was the recognition that war, because it had the potential to unleash revolution, had become too dangerous a luxury for Europe to afford. Alexander I, for whom it represented not merely a political instrument but a spiritual compact, managed to bully his fellow sovereigns (with the exception of the pope, the Turkish sultan, and the regent of Britain) into signing a "holy alliance" against war and for Christian concord. On a more mundane level, Prince Metternich conceived it as a sanction to intervene in the affairs of any state threatened by revolution. The British were suspicious of the uses to which such an unlimited warrant might be put, however. Reverting to a lone hand after years of marshaling coalitions on the Continent, they refused to commit themselves to any joint command. Prussia, too, was skeptical of any rapprochement between its two powerful eastern neighbors, Austria and Russia.

The Diplomatic Settlement

The strains among the allies at Vienna came into the open over the Polish-Saxon question, which nearly torpedoed the congress. Napoleon had taken away almost all the territory gained by Austria and Prussia in the partitioning of Poland to create a satellite entity, the Grand Duchy of Warsaw. Its collapse with the defeat of his empire again left a power vacuum in eastern Europe. Alexander I insisted on restoring the original prepartition Poland, with himself as king. To win Prussia's support, he offered to cede it Saxony, which had become vulnerable as the last German state to desert Napoleon. Metternich, appalled, sought out Castlereagh and Talleyrand, who agreed to resist the Russian plan, if necessary by force.

The Polish-Saxon question was finally settled by compromise. Alexander received a reduced "congress" Poland that was roughly equivalent to Napoleon's Grand Duchy, and Prussia was compensated with two-fifths of Saxony. But the whole episode pointed up the inherent contradiction of the congress system, which presupposed lasting cooperation between historical rivals whose interests were fundamentally opposed.

The Congress of Vienna did, however, decide a wide range of issues, which set the diplomatic framework of the nineteenth century. Uppermost in the minds of the allies was the creation of buffer zones, primarily against France but more subtly against Russia, whose steady westward encroachment had become a major concern over the preceding 100 years. A new Belgo-Dutch kingdom of the Netherlands was erected as a barrier on France's northern frontier, and Prussia was given a solid bloc of territory along the Rhine to perform a similar function. With the acquisition of the Rhineland—which, with the Saxon strip, made it the largest territorial gainer at the congress—Prussia now overarched all of northern Germany, facing France to the west and Russia to the east. Austria was reinstalled in northern Italy and expanded along the Dalmatian coast, where, from a southern vantage, it could serve as a check against Russian designs on Turkey and French ones on Italy. The British, following the policy they had adopted at the Peace of Utrecht a century before, sought no territory on the Continent but added several key islands and stations in the West Indies and the Far East to their unrivaled sea empire. They now controlled the Mediterranean through Gibraltar, Malta, and the Ionian Islands, the South Atlantic through the West Indies and the Cape of Good Hope, and the Indian Ocean and the South China Sea through Ceylon, Mauritius, and Singapore. Bestriding the major ocean arteries of the world, they were uniquely situated to exploit the productive expansion of the Industrial Revolution and to enjoy a century of extraordinary world dominion.

The thorniest single issue facing the powers was the settlement of Germany. Beset by the rival demands of nationalists who dreamed of a unified German state and the claimants of liquidated states who wanted a return to the benevolent chaos of the Holy Roman Empire, they chose to preserve the states carved from the empire by Napoleon, loosely linked in a body known as the German Confederation, whose main function was to keep the smaller states from gravitating toward France. It was a pragmatic solution that left Prussia in a position of greatly augmented influence and postponed for 50 years the final confrontation between Prussia and Austria for control of Germany.

France itself was treated leniently in an attempt to shore up the restored Bourbon monarchy, whose representative, Talleyrand, was treated nearly as a partner in the peacemaking. The dramatic return of Napoleon from Elba and the ensuing Hundred Days compelled the allies to harsher sanctions. The congress took away some snippets of French territory, imposed an indemnity of 700 million francs, and posted an army of occupation in France for three years. Nevertheless, France's treatment was exceedingly lenient. Events bore out the wisdom of the allies' moderation; the age of French aggression and French preponderance in Europe was over.

By their lights, the diplomats at Vienna accomplished a good deal. They cleared away the debris of a generation of war and converted a wartime coalition into a permanent instrument for maintaining order. The instrument was flawed, and the values it sought to defend—monarchy, aristocracy, and hereditary privilege—were already in eclipse, but the goal of regulating interstate conflict was a first step toward the recognition of the historical obsolescence of war.

What the men at Vienna were unwilling to recognize was the change of their own time. Formed under the Old Regime, their conception of society was still patriarchal; in the words of the Holy Alliance, the sovereigns of Europe were "as fathers of families towards their subjects and armies." In redrawing the map of the Continent, they acted in the high-handed manner of old, parceling out peoples and territories solely according to the abstract scales of power. It would never have occurred to them to ask the Belgians whether they wanted to be under the Dutch, the Venetians under the Austrians, or the Poles under Russia. They rightly calculated that nationalism, the new sentiment that a land belonged to its people and not to its ruler, was incompatible with the preservation of the existing order; they wrongly concluded that they could contain it with treaties, armies, and spies.

Reaction and Revolution

The notion of collective security against revolution—what came to be known as the Congress System—was the brainchild of Prince Klemens von Metternich (1773–1859), who as foreign minister of Austria from

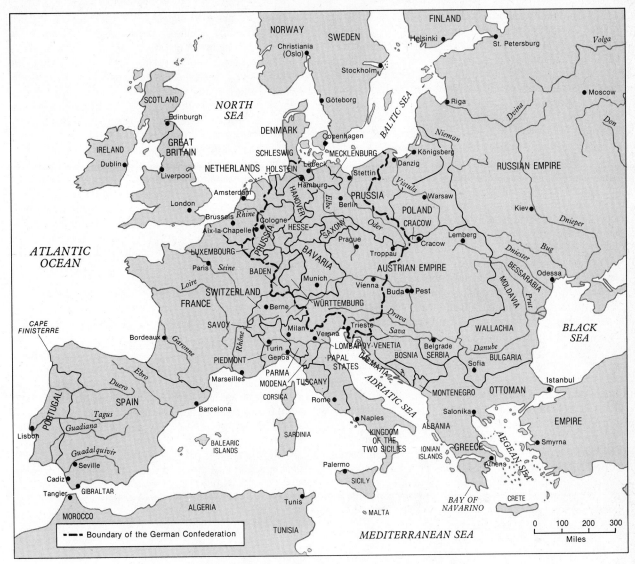

***31.1** Europe After the Congress of Vienna (1815)*

1809 to 1848 put his stamp on the diplomacy of the age. Metternich envisioned the system operating through periodic meetings of the great powers that by monitoring developments in each state could scotch any activity that threatened either internal or external stability. As the Troppau Protocol of 1820 put it:

> **States which have undergone a change of government due to revolution, the results of which threaten other states, *ipso facto* cease to be members of the European alliance. . . . If owing to such alterations immediate danger threatens other states, the powers bind themselves, by peaceful means, or if need be by arms to bring back the guilty state into the bosom of the Great Alliance.**

The opportunity soon arose to test the system. The restored regimes in Spain and the Kingdom of the Two Sicilies were violently unpopular. The Spanish had waged a heroic resistance against Napoleon on behalf of the Bourbon regime to which, after a century, they had transferred their loyalty. When King Ferdinand VII returned to Madrid in 1814 after a six-year exile, he was welcomed rapturously. But enthusiasm for the symbol of Spanish monarchy was not the same as a desire to turn back the clock. The Enlightenment had penetrated Spain, particularly during the reign of Charles III (1759–1788), and the Napoleonic administration, however despised on nationalist grounds, had left its mark in the form of greater tolerance and bureaucratic efficiency. An elected national body, the Cortes, meeting in the free city of Cadiz in 1812, had adopted a liberal constitution on the basis of which Ferdinand had been recalled. But the king swiftly dissolved the Cortes, nullified its acts, scrapped its constitution, and threw its chief leaders and supporters into jail. Restoring the Inquisition and the lands of the church and the aristocracy in full, he proclaimed a return to divine right absolutism. It was a formula for revolution. The economy languished; Seville and Cadiz were full of merchants ruined by the long wars and the revolts of the American colonies, against which the regime seemed helpless to respond. Discontent spread to the military, and secret societies sprang up in defiance of the censorship. Rebellion broke out in early 1820, and Ferdinand, made a virtual prisoner, was compelled to summon the Cortes and to reinstate the constitution of 1812.

Portugal, Spain's Iberian neighbor, was soon touched by an uprising as well when rebels demanded the return of King John VI, who was still in exile in Brazil, but also a constitutional government. At the same time, a series of revolts and disturbances broke out on the Italian peninsula aimed against both Spanish and Austrian rule. They began in Naples, where King Ferdinand I, like his nephew Ferdinand VII in Spain, had abrogated reforms and alienated both the army and the bourgeoisie. Sardinia next attempted to depose its reactionary monarch, Victor Emmanuel I, and there were threats of rebellion in the Papal States as well.

A more complex—and far more broadly based—rebellion broke out in Greece in 1821, which soon became a revolution against 3½ centuries of Ottoman rule.

Within the space of a year, insurrection had sparked across the entire Mediterranean coast from Cape Finisterre to the eastern Aegean.

Metternich called for action but met a divided response. The British dissented from the Troppau Protocol, and the French, unwilling to serve as the agent of Austrian interests in Italy, sat idle. Metternich was more successful with Prussia and Russia, with whose assent an Austrian army descended on Italy and speedily crushed the rebellions in Naples and Sardinia. France was more amenable to action in Spain, where it was anxious to restore its influence, and when the revolutionary government in Madrid rejected an ultimatum to modify its reforms in 1823, it sent troops across the Pyrenees to restore the king it had deposed 15 years before. Despite promises of clemency, Ferdinand VII carried out a bloody purge and plunged Spain back into a civil and clerical autocracy that left a bitter legacy.

The Overthrow of Ottoman Rule in Greece

The case of Greece was more complicated. The Ottoman Empire had revived in the seventeenth century to make a last great assault on Europe, only to be driven back from the walls of Vienna and deep into the Danube basin (see Chapter 20). Battered by the southward expansion of Russia in the eighteenth century, it now faced revolt among the subject peoples within its own borders. The Serbians had risen in 1804 in the beginnings of a strug-

◎ Metternich's Plea for the Old Order ◎

Prince Klemens von Metternich, the preeminent figure in European politics between 1815 and 1848, here forcefully expresses his conservative credo.

Drag through the mud the name of God and the powers instituted by his divine decrees, and the revolution will be prepared! Speak of a social contract, and the revolution is accomplished! The revolution was already completed in the palace of kings, in the drawing-rooms and boudoirs of certain cities, while among the great mass of the people it was still only in a state of preparation. . . .

The first and greatest concern for the immense majority of every nation is the stability of the laws, and their uninterrupted action—never their change. Therefore let the governments govern, let them maintain the groundwork of their institutions, both ancient and modern; for if it is at all times dangerous to touch them, it certainly would not now, in the general confusion, be wise to do so.

Source: K. von Metternich, *Memoirs*, trans. Mrs. A. Napier, vol. 3 (London: Richard Bentley & Son, 1881), pp. 461, 474.

gle for nationhood that was to have profound consequences for all of Europe. Their rebellion aroused little interest, but when the Greeks of the southern Peloponnesus raised the flag of independence in 1821, the Continent took sudden notice. Greek merchants dominated the trade of the eastern Mediterranean, sometimes flying a Russian flag. At the same time, the Greeks were engaged in a great revival of their own culture. The Society of Friends, a secret organization supported by Alexander I (whose horror of rebellions stopped short at those that advanced Russian interests), engineered an uprising after a number of false starts.

Under heavy pressure from his alliance partners, Alexander withdrew his support from the rebels, and the powers waited for the Greek insurrection to burn itself out. But they failed to take into account both the resolve of the Greeks and a new force that the very idea of collective security had helped create—public opinion. A new classical revival spurred chiefly by German scholars and archaeologists in the eighteenth century combined with the nascent Romantic movement to produce a fascination with things Greek. The British government paid £35,000 to acquire the friezes of the Parthenon known as the Elgin marbles, and the French installed the Venus de Milo in the Louvre. "We are all Greeks," the poet Shelley enthused, and his great Romantic contemporary Lord Byron fought and died beside the Greek rebels. Committees to support the Greek cause sprang up spontaneously all over western Europe and the United States. In the face of this, the calculated indifference of the powers could not be kept up. Britain, France, and Russia attempted to impose an armistice on Turkey in 1827 and, failing that, sent out a squadron that first blockaded and then destroyed the Turkish fleet at Navarino in the Peloponnesus. The Turks were compelled to recognize Greek independence by the London Protocol of 1830.

The poet Byron in Greek dress. His struggle on behalf of Greek independence symbolized the Romantic quest for freedom and the recovery of the heroic ideal. [National Portrait Gallery, London]

The Troubled 1820s

The revolt of the Greeks was the political cause célèbre of the 1820s. It gave heart to nationalist movements everywhere, although it showed too that such movements could not hope to succeed merely on the basis of elite elements such as the bureaucracy and the officer corps but required mass support. It left the Congress System in ruins as well. The spectacle of an allied fleet playing midwife to a revolutionary state demonstrated that Metternich's dream of a perpetual status quo could not withstand a united demand for change and that in a crisis each power would consult its own interest first and its treaty obligations second. What emerged was a looser, more informal understanding, the Concert of Europe, by which the great powers would attempt to resolve their major differences and avoid general war.

While only Russia among the major powers underwent an actual rebellion within its borders between 1815 and 1830—the Decembrist revolt of 1825—all experienced significant unrest. We have touched on the Luddite attacks and urban agitation in Britain. In retrospect, it was remarkable that unrest was contained as well as it was in Britain, given the unprecedented social transformation of the Industrial Revolution, whose maximum impact was being felt in these years. It seemed serious enough, however, to the Tory government of Lord Liverpool. In the wake of the Peterloo Massacre, the government passed a series of repressive measures through Parliament, the Six Acts, which suppressed public meetings, curbed the press, and speeded up procedures for prosecuting offenders against the public order. Waterloo's hero, the duke of Wellington, expressed the hope that Britain's example of firmness would be followed by others so that the world might escape "the universal revolution which seems to menace us all." Three months later, in February 1820, a plot to assassinate the entire cabinet and seize control of the government was "discovered," although the conspirators' arms had actually been supplied by the government. It was not until the late 1820s that a less hysterical atmosphere began to prevail.

In France, Louis XVIII (1814–1824) sought a middle ground between the reactionary Ultraroyalist party, which wanted to turn the clock back literally to 1789, and the ex-Bonapartists and republicans, whom Louis knew he would have to conciliate to stabilize his regime. He offered a charter that in essence preserved the structure of the Napoleonic Code and set up a bicameral assembly that could veto royal legislation. The Hundred Days brought a violent Ultra reaction in which hundreds of suspected Jacobin and Bonapartist sympathizers were massacred. No sooner had Louis regained a measure of control than the assassination in 1820 of the duke of Berry, the heir to the throne, set off a new wave of reaction. As Louis' reign ebbed, power passed to his intransigent brother, the count of Artois, who succeeded him as Charles X (1824–1830). A new spate of legislation enacted the program of the Ultras. The Law of Indemnity (1825) compensated nobles who had lost their estates during the revolution by devaluing government bonds held by the bourgeoisie, and the Law of Sacrilege, passed in the same year, imposed the death penalty for the theft of sacred objects and other vaguely defined offenses against the church. When members of the Jesuit order, still officially banned in France, appeared openly in Catholic schools, liberals concluded that they were now directing the government.

Despite its greatly strengthened geopolitical situation, Prussia was content to allow Metternich to play ideological policeman to the rest of Germany, a role he assumed with relish. By the Carlsbad Decrees of 1819, Metternich suppressed the student societies that had taken up the aspirations for national unity thwarted at the Congress of Vienna. These societies were in turn the successors of the quasi-military gymnastic clubs founded by Friedrich Ludwig Jahn (1778–1852) during the Napoleonic wars, whose members, wearing gray-shirted uniforms and imbued with a hatred of "foreign" (including Jewish) influence, strikingly foreshadowed elements of Nazi ideology and practice. Student groups that gathered at Wartburg Castle near Eisenach to commemorate the tricentennial of Luther's Ninety-five Theses in 1817 toasted unity and freedom but also burned conservative and antinationalist books after a torchlight procession, a rather dubious way to protest censorship.

In Austria itself Metternich's chief concern was to suppress nationalist stirrings among the many minority groups that comprised the Habsburg empire. The very name Austria had been adopted no less recently than 1804 to describe the patrimonial lands of the emperor, and whereas the yearning for national identity might encourage a sense of unity in such regions as Germany and Italy and strengthen it in states such as Britain, France, or Spain already established on the basis of a common language and heritage, it could only foster division and separatism in such an amalgam of peoples and tongues as the Habsburg state represented. By skillfully playing rival minorities off against one another, Metternich delayed his day of reckoning for more than 30 years; by failing to provide a genuine accommodation for nationalist aspirations within the framework of the empire, he ensured that that day would come.

Russia was still by far the most autocratic of all European states. Like Catherine the Great, the eccentric Alexander I (1801–1825) began his reign with a flourish of reform. Men of all classes were legally entitled to hold land for the first time, and masters were encouraged to free their serfs. New schools were founded, including six universities, and new ideas entered the country, particularly through the medium of the Freemasons and other secret fraternities, much in vogue at the time. Leo Tolstoy has left a vivid picture of liberal ferment among the early-nineteenth-century urban aristocracy in his novel *War and Peace* (1869). The reforming Count Speransky even drafted plans for a system of representative bodies culminating in a national assembly, though without real legislative power. But the Napoleonic invasions ended these fair hopes, and a chastened Alexander, regarding his country's disaster as a providential judgment, lapsed into a reactionary mysticism that made him Metternich's most zealous if not always most reliable ally in the war against reform.

Frustrated liberal aspirations among the officer corps in conjunction with a succession crisis in December 1825 provoked Russia's first attempt at revolution. Alexander's heir, the Grand Duke Constantine, had secretly resigned his claim to the throne in favor of his brother Nicholas, but when the tsar died suddenly, each brother proclaimed the other. In the resulting chaos, disaffected officers raised the standard of "Constantine and constitution," which some of the soldiers apparently thought referred to the tsar and his wife.

Whatever the comic overtones of the Decembrist uprising, it was ruthlessly suppressed. Hundreds were imprisoned or exiled, and five officers were executed; these officers' courageous bearing made them symbols of resistance under the dreary and despotic reign of Nicholas I (1825–1855). The latent genius of the Russian people flowered in an extraordinary literary generation that included the poets Alexander Pushkin (1799–1837) and Mikhail Lermontov (1814–1841) and the novelists Nikolai Gogol (1809–1852) and Ivan Turgenev (1818–1883). Gogol in particular caught the spirit of Nicholas' Russia in his comic novel *Dead Souls* and his play *The Inspector General*, while the young Feodor Dostoevsky (1821–1881), later one of the century's greatest novelists, began his career by facing a mock firing squad in Siberia for allegedly "socialist" activities. Others, like the

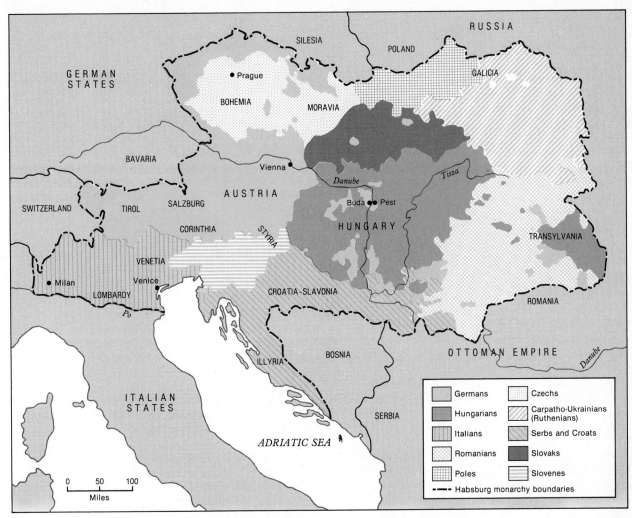

31.2 Ethnic Composition of the Austro-Hungarian Empire

journalist Alexander Herzen (1812–1870), sought haven abroad, thus initiating the long tradition of the Russian exile.

Liberalism

The term most frequently used to describe the varied forms of opposition to the Restoration regimes was *liberalism*, a word that has and continues to bear many different and sometimes contradictory meanings. The origins of liberalism go back to the British philosopher and political theorist John Locke (see Chapter 26), who argued for the supremacy of society over the state or, in practical terms, the control of the Stuart monarchy by the propertied classes. Adam Smith drew out the impli-

cations of Locke's argument for the freedom of commerce from state interference, or what the modern neoliberal philosopher Robert Nozick has called "capitalist acts between consenting adults." Having picked up much of the freight of the Enlightenment as well, liberalism by the early nineteenth century had come to stand broadly for free trade in a laissez-faire marketplace, the limitation of state authority by written constitutions, secular education, and national self-determination. In a general sense, nineteenth-century liberalism may be said to have represented the interests of capitalist enterprise and the aspirations of the commercial bourgeoisie. This was how Karl Marx took it; for him liberalism was simply the ideology of the bourgeoisie. But it was merged as well with a post-Enlightenment skepticism about the role of government and a profound change in cultural sensibility, Romanticism, to form a complex and potent mixture whose appeal extended far beyond narrow economic interests.

Romanticism and the Quest for Identity

Romanticism may be viewed in many ways. The term *Romantic* is often contrasted to the term *classical* to express a mood or movement of art, thought, and cultural sensibility in which feeling and imagination shape form instead of the other way around and in which the expression of individual personality is valued above conformity to established norms of taste and style. As such, it is a tendency that may be observed in many cultures and periods, particularly in the arts.

The Dethronement of Tradition

Historically, the Romantic movement that began in the West in the mid-eighteenth century and continues as its dominant cultural style to the present day represented a final emancipation from the authority of ancient Greece and Rome. That legacy lay heavily over the medieval period in terms of its religion (Christianity, the faith of the late Roman Empire), its law (largely based on the Code of Justinian, itself an adaptation of the Roman civil code), and its thought (influenced first by Aristotle and later by Plato and his followers). So deeply was the culture of the West permeated by the influence of antiquity that even the reaction against scholastic thought and institutions that we call the Renaissance took the form of a renewal of the classical tradition. A similar movement on a smaller scale took place with the classical revival that began in the mid-eighteenth century. This time, however, the reinterpretation of the Greco-Roman tradition took place in the context of a far wider shift in the perspective of Western culture.

Many things contributed to this development. The Renaissance emphasis on the value of the individual and the Reformation idea of personal responsibility for one's own salvation (and one's ethical conduct in the world) laid the first basis for this shift. The scientific revolution, with its revolt against the cosmogony of the ancient and medieval worlds and the traditional Christianity that rested on it, was a second important step. By the end of the seventeenth century, in the debate between the ancients and the moderns (see Chapter 24), it was being confidently asserted for the first time that the modern world was equal if not superior to the ancient one, and by the mid-eighteenth, the doctrine of progress, with its assumption of the inferiority of the past and the indefinite improvement if not ultimate perfectibility of the species, had become widely prevalent. The French Revolution was the political expression of this hope, and it persisted in the utopian schemes of Owen, Fourier, and others.

The result of all this was a new view of human possibility. At the same time, however, the embarkation on an uncertain and uncharted future provoked deep anxiety. The past was no longer the model for the present but merely a record of progress to date; culture was not to be inherited but to be created. For the first time the West took on the burden of originality, of the new and avant-garde, that has characterized its culture ever since. Each generation, each decade, was to be reckoned in terms of its difference from its predecessors. The demand for progress and the measure of progress (whether in art, science, politics, or fashion) by originality speeded up the experience of time no less than the factory whistle, the locomotive, or the newspaper.

The Romantic Hero

The dethronement of tradition and the quest for the new put extraordinary emphasis on the role of the individual. A single person, properly placed, could change the destiny of a nation; a single idea could create a new product or industry or a new artistic form: thus the philosophes exalted the enlightened despot; thus the solitary inventor, like Edison, became a hero; and thus too the lonely artist in his garret or lost amid the wilds of nature became the very symbol of the creative process. Yet these images betrayed pathos too. The great political figure, like Napoleon, might suffer ignominy and exile; the inventor might fail; the starving artist might die in obscurity. Emancipated from tradition, society was now dependent on genius; and genius, wayward and unpredictable, was to be found only in the individual.

What emerged was a confidence in the collective destiny of Western culture—whether in the form of nation building, utopian experiment, missionary zeal, or imperial expansion—that rested paradoxically on the talent and initiative of the isolated individual. The cultural expression of this paradox was Romanticism. The Romantic hero was typically a sensitive, misunderstood young man (much less often a woman) in revolt against his surroundings or a man of destiny boldly seeking knowledge and power no matter what the cost. In the former type, Romanticism portrayed the sense of anxiety and vulnerability that beset the individual in a time of change; in the latter, the vaunting self-confidence of a society that had laid claim to the secrets of nature and would soon take the dominion of the earth.

GOETHE AND THE ROMANTIC SPIRIT

Both kinds of heroes were represented in the work of the great German poet and dramatist Johann Wolfgang von Goethe (1749–1832), whose career spanned the last decades of the Enlightenment and the first ones of Romanticism. Goethe was the son of a town councillor of Frankfurt. He studied and briefly practiced law before turning to a literary career, which by 1775 was prominent enough to secure him an invitation from the young duke of Weimar, Karl August, who had chosen him to be the star of what he hoped to make the most brilliant court in Europe. Arriving with little thought except to gain a temporary sinecure that would free him for writing, Goethe was to remain at Weimar, with the exception of a critical two-year sojourn in Italy in 1786–1788, for the rest of his life.

Goethe was not merely the founding figure of modern German literature but also an artist and natural scientist of distinction. Like Rousseau, he was a keen student of botany, and he put forward an elaborate theory of color in opposition to Newton's. Science in his day had not yet become professionalized, and amateurs continued to dominate it, such as the minister Joseph Priestley, who discovered oxygen, and William Herschel, the organist-astronomer who found Uranus and Neptune, the first planets discovered since antiquity. Goethe's scientific pursuits, however, were closely tied to his conception of nature as a unity composed of innumerable individual elements. "Every living thing," he wrote,

> is not a single unit but a plurality: even if it seems to be an individual, it nevertheless remains an association of living, independent entities, which are similar in idea and plan, but which in appearance may be like and similar or unlike and dissimilar.

From this sprang Goethe's profoundly Romantic idea of the cosmos itself as the ultimate living organism, a notion that nationalist thinkers would find easy to apply to the relationship between the individual citizen and the nation.

But it was as an author that Goethe exerted his greatest influence. His early novel, *The Sorrows of Young Werther* (1774), brilliantly captured the mood of the so-called *Sturm und Drang* ("storm and stress") years of the early Romantic movement in Germany and portrayed its quintessential hero in the student Werther, who commits suicide out of frustrated love. *Werther* was a best-seller all over Europe and sparked a rash of real suicides; its fame was so great that the Chinese painted the young hero and his love, Lotte, on porcelain for the export trade. But Werther's sorrows were as much

This oil painting of the great Goethe with his wife and children, by J. K. Seekatz, is much more than a fancy-dress family portrait. Situated in a pastoral setting typical of eighteenth-century aristocratic portraits, Goethe symbolizes the emergent power of his own bourgeois class and its appropriation of the political and material source of aristocratic power, the land. At the same time, the towering ruin stands for Romantic aspirations and hence Goethe's personal claim to status as an artist. [Freies Deutsches Hochstift—Frankfurt am Main]

metaphysical as amorous, and he thus embodied the Romantic sense of the individual at odds with a world he never made.

Goethe himself was very much the rebellious young man he wrote about in his early years, tempestuous in his love affairs and radical in his politics. It was only much later, as the venerable Sage of Weimar, that he acquired the image of Olympian wisdom and detachment that has been historically associated with his name. Yet a single work that preoccupied him for six decades gave continuity to his entire career as well as matchless definition to the Romantic movement itself, his dramatic poem *Faust*. The Faust legend originated in a sixteenth-century German physician, astrologer, and magician who was probably named Sabellicus but who called himself Faustus and was reputed to have made a pact with the Devil. Contemporary writers used his story as a cautionary tale, though the English dramatist Christopher Marlowe, himself a reputed atheist, made him a semiheroic figure in his *Tragical History of Dr. Faustus* (1592). But Goethe rescued Faust the bogeyman from the carnivals and shows of his day and made him the very symbol of the Romantic quest for forbidden knowledge and experience. Equally important, Goethe's literary Devil, Mephistopheles, is not merely an evil tempter but a tormented being who is a larger symbol of Faust himself. Goethe's difficulty in finishing the poem stemmed from his rejection of the legend of Faust's ultimate damnation; like his fellow Romantics, he believed that the quest for knowledge was the essence of man's being and that good and evil could not be disentangled from it. In the end his Faust finds salvation rather than punishment, though not before coming to understand the limitations of all knowledge and the abiding mystery of existence.

In his later years Goethe was the cultural arbiter of Europe, whose favor and blessing was sought by the great and near-great; Napoleon, who met him at Erfurt in 1808, confessed to having read *Werther* seven times. No other poet since Shakespeare had so profound an influence on his fellow artists; the Romantic composers Beethoven, Schubert, Berlioz, Liszt, Mendelssohn, Schumann, and Wagner were some of the musicians who found inspiration in his work, particularly *Faust*. Goethe himself had a wide and sympathetic interest in younger artists, and he was particularly taken by the English poet Lord Byron (1788–1824), whose death he memorialized in the second part of *Faust*. But his main influence was on his fellow German poets and dramatists.

The Spread of Romanticism

The generation that came to maturity with Goethe in the 1770s and 1780s included the playwrights Gotthold Ephraim Lessing (1729–1781) and Friedrich von Schiller (1759–1805). In these authors particularly the link between Romantic individualism and Romantic nationalism can be seen clearly. In *Laocoön*, Lessing called for the creation of a national, heroic literature and the rejection of classical models, which were likened (as in the ancient statue from which he drew his title) to a giant serpent strangling human creativity. Schiller, who was particularly close to Goethe, answered that call in plays such as *William Tell* and *The Maid of Orleans* that described charismatically led movements of national liberation.

Goethe remained the mentor and example for the most important German writers of the next two generations, including the poets Friedrich von Novalis (1772–1801), Friedrich Hölderlin (1770–1843), and Heinrich Heine (1797–1856), and the playwright Heinrich von Kleist (1777–1811). The last decade of the eighteenth century also saw the advent of Romanticism in Britain, with the poetry of William Wordsworth (1770–1850) and Samuel Taylor Coleridge (1772–1834) and the immensely popular novels of Sir Walter Scott (1771–1832). Coleridge's still widely read *Rime of the Ancient Mariner* (1798) combined Christian symbolism with Romantic quest and atonement; Wordsworth's epic verse autobiography, *The Prelude* (1807), offered the artist himself as hero, a theme that was to preoccupy both the nineteenth and twentieth centuries. These poets' successors, the tragically short-lived John Keats (1795–1821), Percy Bysshe Shelley (1792–1822), and Byron, brought English Romantic poetry to its finest flowering.

It is arguable that France produced the first truly Romantic figure in Jean-Jacques Rousseau, who called for a return to nature as a refuge from the evils of a corrupt civilization and whose candid autobiography, the *Confessions*, was the earliest model of Romantic quest literature. However, the neoclassicism that dominated the arts through most of the eighteenth century retained its hold longer in France than elsewhere. The French Revolution harked back to Rome and Greece for its symbols of republican virtue and patriotism, and Napoleon, giving these a skillful imperial twist, adapted them for his own purposes. Not until after 1815, when defeat had turned France's mood inward, did it produce its first Romantic generation. The crucial transitional figures were the novelist Benjamin Constant (1767–1830), the poet and historian François-Auguste-René de Chateaubriand (1768–1848), and Madame de Staël (1766–1817), whose immensely influential book *On Germany* (1813) popularized German Romantic philosophy in France. Chateaubriand in particular was the herald of a Catholic revival in France that rejected the Deism of the Enlightenment and the revolution and signaled a renewal of interest in medieval piety, soon reflected in a neo-Gothic movement in architecture. Madame de Staël caught this new mood as well: "I do not know exactly what we must believe," she declared, "but I believe that we must believe! The eighteenth century did nothing but deny. The human spirit lives by its beliefs." This new, if rather vague, religiosity blended well with Romantic self-absorption, but it clashed with liberalism. The result was that the Romantics tended to sort out either on the extreme right (Chateaubriand in France, Novalis in Germany) or on the extreme left (Shelley in England), with very few in the political middle.

The post-1815 generation in France included the novelist Stendhal (Marie-Henri Beyle, 1783–1842), whose great novel *The Red and the Black* gave the French their

---

◉ The Romantic Poet ◉

In the preface to his Lyrical Ballads *(1798), William Wordsworth describes the poet as a kind of universal lawgiver, what his younger contemporary Percy Shelley would later call "the unacknowledged legislator of the human race." This proclamation of the sovereign genius of the solitary poet was crucial to the development of Romantic individualism and to the notion of the artist as a uniquely privileged figure in society.*

What is meant by the word Poet? What is a Poet? To whom does he address himself? And what language is to be expected from him? He is a man speaking to men: a man, it is true, with more lively sensibility, more enthusiasm and tenderness, who has a greater knowledge of human nature, and a more comprehensive soul. . . . He is the rock of defense of human nature; an upholder and preserver, carrying everywhere with him relationship and love. In spite of difference of soil and climate, of language and manners, of laws and customs, in spite of things silently gone out of mind and things violently destroyed, the Poet binds together by passion and knowledge the vast empire of human society, as it is spread over the whole earth, and over all time. The objects of the Poet's thoughts are everywhere; though the eyes and senses of men are, it is true, his favorite guides, yet he will follow wheresoever he can find an atmosphere of sensation in which to move his wings. Poetry is first and last of all knowledge—it is as immortal as the heart of man.

Source: The Complete Poetical Works of William Wordsworth (Philadelphia: Porter & Coates, 1851), pp. 664, 666.

---

own Werther in the character of Julien Sorel; the painter Eugène Delacroix (1798–1863), whose depiction of a Turkish atrocity during the war of Greek independence, *The Massacre at Chios*, profoundly influenced European opinion; and the composer Hector Berlioz (1803–1869), whose *Symphonie fantastique* (1830), with its lavish orchestral coloration and rather fevered literary program, was the prototypical Romantic symphony.

Romantic music reached its unquestioned apogee in Germany and Austria, where in the period between 1770 and 1830 four of the greatest geniuses in musical history appeared: Franz Joseph Haydn (1732–1809), Wolfgang Amadeus Mozart (1756–1791), Ludwig van Beethoven (1770–1827), and Franz Schubert (1797–1828). Haydn and Mozart were the supreme masters of the classical style that reigned for most of the latter half of the eighteenth century, with its emphasis on clarity of structure and texture, but their work exhibited elements of the nascent Romantic sensibility as well. Beethoven bridged the classic and Romantic eras, particularly in the nine symphonies that remain to this day the most admired synthesis of personal expression and formal control in music. Beethoven was a critical transitional figure in another respect as well. Whereas Haydn had worn the livery of his aristocratic employers, the Esterhazys, for most of his life, and Mozart too had been at the mercy

of his patrons, Beethoven was the first composer to make an independent living by the sale of his music. The artist, too, no longer sheltered (and subordinated) by clerical or noble patrons, had entered the marketplace.

Romanticism Beyond the Arts

Romanticism touched not only the arts but philosophy, history, religious thought, and the natural sciences as well. Even as the Enlightenment proclaimed the sovereignty of reason, the German philosopher Immanuel Kant fatally undercut its claims by arguing that the human mind was no mere passive receptor of experience, as Locke and other empiricists had believed, but a complex mechanism that gave form and shape to phenomena according to its own internal laws. Accordingly, the world could not be experienced as it was "in itself" but only as filtered through the processes of intellect and emotion and therefore subjectively. There could be no objective and impersonal description of the world, even in science, because no one—except perhaps God—could overcome the limitations of individual perception. Like the blind, we touched a world that was truly real but could never be seen as it really was.

Kant's philosophy went by the name of idealism, after

Ludwig van Beethoven bridged not only the classical and Romantic periods in music but also, as the first musician to support himself primarily from the sale of his own work, the era of aristocratic patronage and of the artist-entrepreneur. [Mansell Collection]

ment of nationally oriented histories, such as those written by Jules Michelet in France and Leopold von Ranke in Germany, as well as such cognate disciplines as ethnology (the study of humankind by racial and cultural divisions) and philology (the study of particular languages). No other thinker of the period made so strenuous and systematic an effort to reconcile the two opposite poles of Romantic thought, the attempt to define oneself in opposition to society, whether as explorer, entrepreneur, or artist, and the desire for patriotic identity within the national group.

Romanticism and the Image of Women

The beginnings of modern feminism coincided with those of Romanticism and may be seen as part of the same process of social transformation. Prior to this time the few women who by sheer force of personality had

Classical philosophy culminated in the work of Georg Wilhelm Friedrich Hegel, whose conception of history as a struggle between dialectically opposed forces embodied Romantic notions of quest and struggle and profoundly influenced Karl Marx. [Mansell Collection]

his distinction between the "ideas" we form of reality through the interaction of world and mind and the world as it exists independently of our perception of it. The implications of Kantian idealism were powerfully but controversially explored by the Prussian philosopher Georg Wilhelm Friedrich Hegel (1770–1831). Hegel argued that all of human history was a great unconscious drama that tended toward the realization of human freedom, which he called the spirit of reason. The agents of this drama were great individuals such as Caesar or Napoleon, through whose personal passions and ambitions this spirit acted; thus Caesar had created the first world empire, and Napoleon had stimulated the sense of national self-identity that Hegel saw as the final phase of the development of freedom.

Hegel's emphasis on the role of great men in history dovetailed neatly with Romantic individualism, while his identification of nationalism with the progress of freedom had immense appeal to liberals in Germany and elsewhere. He also gave great impetus to the develop-

been able to distinguish themselves were regarded as oddities or freaks; Samuel Johnson's cruel jest that a woman preaching was like a dog walking on its hind legs summarized the dominant male attitude toward female intellectual activity in general, even during the Enlightenment. But with the nineteenth century, women began to appear for the first time on a plane of equality with men in a major cultural movement. If Mary Wollstonecraft still had to struggle for recognition because of her sex in the 1790s, Madame de Staël was much more readily accepted only 20 years later, and in the succeeding decades women came to occupy an increasingly prominent place in the arts, particularly literature. We have noted the immense popularity of the British novelist Elizabeth Gaskell in the 1840s and 1850s (see Chapter 30). An analogous position was occupied by the American author and abolitionist Harriet Beecher Stowe, best known for her novel *Uncle Tom's Cabin* (1852), and the French novelist Aurore Dupin (1804–1876), who, taking the pen name George Sand, became as famous for her daring private life—which included a highly publicized liaison with the great Polish composer-pianist Frédéric Chopin—as for her voluminous literary output. At least four Englishwomen stand in the front rank of nineteenth-century literature: Jane Austen (1775–1817), whose social novels reveal a psychological penetration equaled among her contemporaries only by Goethe; the Brontë sisters, Charlotte and Emily; and Mary Anne Evans (1819–1880), known by the pen name George Eliot, whose novel *Middlemarch* is rivaled only by the major works of Charles Dickens. At the same time the reclusive New Englander Emily Dickinson (1830–1886) was writing some of the finest lyric poetry since Sappho.

Nevertheless, the disabilities faced by women attempting to compete in what was still a man's world were obvious. Elizabeth Gaskell was never known by her own forename but simply as "Mrs. Gaskell"; Dupin and Evans both adopted masculine pen names in an effort to gain more serious attention for their work; and Emily Dickinson's poems were never published in her own lifetime. If, moreover, a place in literature and to a lesser extent in the other arts was reluctantly conceded to women, it served only to confirm age-old prejudices against them in the fields of philosophy, politics, and the professions. The German nationalist philosopher Johann Gottlieb Fichte argued that women lacked the "speculative aptitude" for either philosophical inquiry or public office. Hegel made what was to be the fundamental nineteenth-century bourgeois distinction between a public world of work and struggle, in which only men were fit to compete, and the private sphere of "piety and domesticity," for which women were intended by nature. The Frenchman Auguste Comte (1798–1857) doubted that women could be entrusted even with running a household except under male supervision. If women excelled in literature, it only confirmed the prevailing stereotype of them as creatures in whom the imagination prevailed at the expense of the intellect.

The rejection of marriage by women like Mary Wollstonecraft and George Sand and their demand for free sexual companionship reinforced the widespread male belief that women should be confined as tightly within the bounds of "piety and domesticity" as possible. Yet the image of woman had come to stand allegorically for revolution itself. In 1792 the new French republic decreed that it was to be represented officially by a seal that bore the likeness of a woman dressed in ancient style holding a pike. This popular figure of "Marianne," which blended the image of Roman virtue and Joan of Arc with secular allusions to the cult of the Virgin Mary, reached its apotheosis in Delacroix's famous painting of the revolution of 1830, *Liberty on the Barricades*. The painting shows a semiallegorical female figure leading a charge over the bodies of fallen sans-culottes, a top-hatted bourgeois at her side. Her bared breast recalls the classical image of the Amazon warrior, but the realistic touches—the stained petticoats, the hair under the arms—proclaim her as well to be a woman of the people. At the same time, her nudity carries an implicit message of sexual aggressiveness that is only partly offset by her averted, impassive gaze. Far more powerfully than the seal of Marianne, Delacroix's figure conveys the conflicting impulses behind the early Romantic image of woman: the idealized warrior-goddess and the available woman of the street, the symbol of liberation who remains chained in her petticoats, who leads a battle that will be fought by the sans-culottes but won by the bourgeoisie.

The Liberal Revival and the Revolutions of 1830

By the late 1820s dissatisfaction with the reactionary Bourbon dynasty in France and the slow pace of reform in Britain had reached the flashpoint of revolution. A neutral observer, asked to predict where it would actually occur, would probably have chosen Britain. The British political system, unreformed since 1689, had refused even a token accommodation to the new social reality created by the Industrial Revolution. The great new cities, half-anarchic, had virtually no representation in Parliament and no access to central government. Yet Britain alone, of all the major states of Europe, was to avoid revolution in 1830 and the years to come. Not London but Paris was to provide the impetus for the next wave of insurrection.

The July Revolution in France

The new revolutionary crisis began in March 1830 when the French Chamber of Deputies, led by the bankers Jacques Lafitte and Jean-Paul Casimir-Perier, voted no confidence in the government of Charles X and its policies of censorship, suffrage restriction, and clerical control of education. Charles dissolved the assembly, but new elections, even though limited to an electorate of 100,000, produced a decisive opposition majority. The king wavered, but spurred on by his chief minister Polignac, the archbishop of Paris, and Metternich, he responded on July 26 by dissolving the just-elected Chamber before it could meet, imposing new press censorship, reducing the electorate to a hard core of 25,000 aristocrats, and announcing fresh elections on this basis.

The target of these edicts was the regime's bourgeois opposition, but the reaction came from the working-class sections of Paris. The very next day barricades appeared spontaneously in the streets, and the army, called out to clear them, refused to do so. Faced with anarchy, Charles abdicated two days later in favor of his grandson and fled into exile. France was left without a government.

The sudden vacuum of power revealed the clear-cut divisions of the French political spectrum. The bourgeois opposition—bankers, industrialists, and merchants—wanted not the overthrow of the Bourbon monarchy but greater favor within it for themselves. The Parisian workers, students, and radical intellectuals who had taken to the barricades and made the revolution wanted a republic, headed by the venerable marquis de Lafayette as president. A compromise was hastily brokered behind the scenes. The duke of Orléans, a collateral relative of the Bourbons but a republican soldier in the army of 1792, was put forward as a constitutional monarch by a coalition consisting of Talleyrand, the liberal journalist Adolphe Thiers, and Lafitte, the duke's personal banker. When Lafayette publicly endorsed him, the republican opposition melted away. Louis-Philippe, as the new king was called, promised to abide by the charter of 1814, flew the tricolor flag of the 1789 revolution rather than the Bourbon lily, and was the first monarch to wear the contemporary equivalent of a business suit in public. With his paunch and his umbrella, he was indistinguishable from the bourgeoisie that had brought him to power and whose interests he faithfully served.

Revolution East and West

The three-day revolution in France was the signal for major uprisings across the border in Belgium and, for far different reasons, in Poland. The union of Belgium and the Netherlands, arranged at Vienna, had much to recommend it in theory, as the two nations formed a natural economic and geographic unit. The Catholic Belgians, however, long accustomed to relative autonomy under the rule of Spain and Austria, chafed under the domination of a Protestant Dutch king, William I. Heartened by the French example, they rose up in August 1830 and, after fruitless efforts at conciliation, proclaimed independence under a liberal monarchy of their own. When Dutch troops failed to quell them, a hastily arranged big power conference in London recognized the new government to forestall French intervention.

The Polish rebellion was triggered by the news that Tsar Nicholas I, who was also king of Poland, was planning to send Russian troops through that country on its way to help suppress the Belgians. Russian rule was desperately unpopular, however, and almost any pretext might have served. The Polish Diet declared Nicholas deposed, but the tsar's army speedily crushed the revolt. Poland was absorbed directly into the Russian empire and ruled under a state of military emergency that lasted technically from 1833 until the First World War. Thousands of Poles were executed, imprisoned, or banished to Siberia, and many more fled to the West, among them Chopin.

Lesser disturbances also shook Germany, Italy, Switzerland, Spain, and Portugal, though for the most part without significant result. Yet liberals could, with the tragic exception of Poland, count 1830 as a year of victory. The bourgeoisie had reclaimed political primacy in France and, no longer dependent on a dictator such as Napoleon to retain it, had cut a king to their own measure. The powers had been forced to acquiesce in an independent Belgium, nominally a monarchy, whose constitution acknowledged its origin in the sovereignty of the people and provided what was to be for many years the widest electoral franchise in Europe. The autocratic William I was forced to embrace reform in the Netherlands, and liberal gains were made in Switzerland. Above all, 1830 marked the year when history seemed to move again in Europe. The liberal triumph was far from complete, but its outlines at last seemed visible.

Britain: Revolution Averted

Britain accomplished revolutionary change without revolution. The settlement of 1689 had confirmed the supremacy of Parliament over the king. But neither the size of the electorate—less than 4 percent of the population—nor the distribution of seats had changed in nearly a century and a half, and both were now profoundly unrepresentative of the urban, industrialized society that Britain had become. The long and almost un-

THE VISUAL EXPERIENCE
Romantic and Neoclassical Art

Eugène Delacroix, *Massacre at Chios*. This vivid, if stylized, rendering of the massacre of Greek rebels on the island of Chios by the Turks helped mobilize opinion throughout Europe on behalf of the Greek cause. The stereotyped but highly effective images of defenseless womanhood at the mercy of the sword were all calculated to arouse bourgeois outrage. [Giraudon/Art Resource]

Eugène Delacroix, *The Twenty-eighth of July: Liberty Leading the People* [also known as *Liberty on the Barricades*]. This famous painting personifies liberty as a female figure leading a charge over the bodies of fallen sans-culottes, a top-hatted bourgeois at her side. Her bared breast recalls the classical image of the Amazon warrior, but her stained petticoats proclaim her to be a woman of the people. [Louvre/Réunion des Musées Nationaux]

Eugène Delacroix, *George Sand in Masculine Costume*. To make headway in a man's world, the novelist Aurore Dupin adopted a male pen name, George Sand, and male attire as well. Sand's expression, a mix of sensitivity and severity, conveys the ambiguity of her role and the plight of the woman artist in the nineteenth century. [Collection Viollet/Musée Carnavalet, Paris]

Caspar David Friedrich, *Traveler Looking Over a Sea of Fog*. Friedrich's striking vision of a solitary climber staring into the abyss evokes the Romantic confrontation with nature. The artist has posed his hero with his back to the viewer, as if turned away from civilization, but his attire and walking stick proclaim him to be essentially urban and bourgeois. [Hamburg Kunsthalle]

Gustave Courbet, self-portrait, also called "The Man with the Pipe." Courbet painted many self-portraits in a wide variety of moods. Here his averted gaze and musing expression show him lost in private reverie, as indifferent to the viewer as Friedrich's traveler. At the same time, however, the strong brow and the clenched pipe indicate a man preparing to take determined action in the world. [Giraudon/Art Resource]

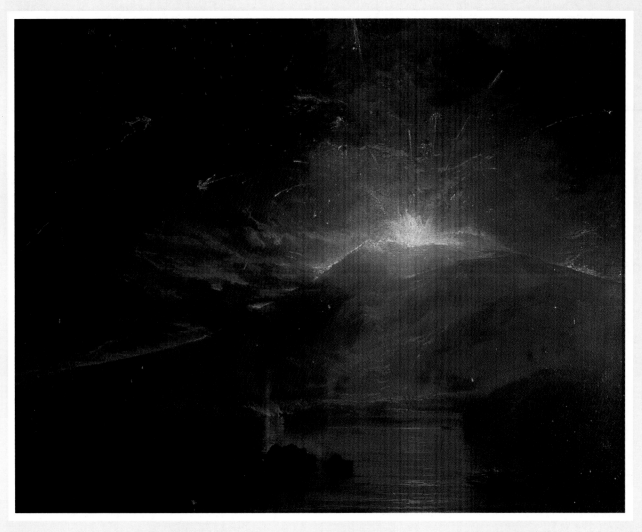

J. M. W. Turner, *Eruption of La Soufrière.* **Turner's image of a volcano suggests the immense force of natural power but also the ambition of industrial civilization to channel that power. [Bridgeman Art Library/Art Resource]**

Édouard Manet, *Déjeuner sur l'Herbe*. Manet's manifesto of sexual and artistic freedom, first exhibited in 1863, caused a scandal. Unlike the nude figures of Delacroix' *Massacre at Chios*, the nude in Manet's painting is not offered up for pity, protection, or erotic fantasy, nor is she the property of the men whose company she shares. In contrast, the modest, stooping figure in the background represents a submissive femininity (as well as the conventions of academic painting) that the new bohemian freedom rejected. [Clíché des Musées Nationaux, Paris]

William Adolphe Bouguereau, *Charity*. Bouguereau's painting deals with a real contemporary problem, urban poverty and abandonment, but in such a way as to blunt perception. The pleading mother is given the guise of a Renaissance Madonna, an effect emphasized by the neoclassical façade she is crouched against and the Italianate building in the distance. Poverty here is removed from all misery and squalor and is presented as feminine dependence, appealing to chivalry and charity. [Birmingham Museums and Art Gallery, England]

Mazzini's Call to Revolution

Despite the failure of the revolutions of 1830, young nationalists took heart at the year that had rocked the kings of Europe on their thrones. Giuseppe Mazzini, the leader of Young Italy, an organization dedicated to the liberation and unification of Italy, here declares both the faith and the method of his revolutionary band. The emphasis on education and guerrilla tactics sounds a particularly modern note.

Young Italy is *Republican*. . . . Republican—because theoretically every nation is destined, by the law of God and humanity, to form a free and equal community of brothers; and the republican is the only form of government that insures this future. . . .

The means by which Young Italy proposes to reach its aims are—education and insurrection, to be adopted simultaneously, and made to harmonize with each other.

Education must ever be directed to teach by example, word, and pen the necessity of insurrection. Insurrection, whenever it can be realized, must be so conducted as to render it a means of national education. . . .

Insurrection—by means of guerrilla bands—is the true method of warfare for all nations desirous of emancipating themselves from a foreign yoke. This method of warfare supplies the want—inevitable at the commencement of the insurrection—of a regular army; it calls the greatest number of elements into the field, and yet may be sustained by the smallest number. It forms the military education of the people, and consecrates every foot of the native soil by the memory of some warlike deed.

Source: N. Gangulee, ed., *Giuseppe Mazzini: Selected Writings* (London: Lindsay Drummond, 1945), pp. 129–134 passim.

broken Conservative domination of British politics from 1760 to 1830 had hardened the nation's rulers in their belief that, as the duke of Wellington put it, the British constitution was already more perfect than any human intelligence could contrive.

In fact, reform had already begun during the ascendancy of George Canning, Castlereagh's successor as foreign minister in Lord Liverpool's government. Tariff duties and colonial trade restrictions, some in effect since the seventeenth century, were relaxed, and the Test Act, which had barred Catholics and Dissenters from public life since 1673, was at last repealed (1829). A gesture was even made toward the lower orders; unions were recognized, and the number of offenses punishable by death was cut by 100—which nevertheless left another 100 on the books. But the one issue that had become symbolic of the liberal cause as a whole—parliamentary reform—remained unaddressed.

The reformers' moment came in 1830, when Wellington's government fell and a Whig ministry under Lord Grey came to power. Despite bitter Tory opposition, Grey at last steered a parliamentary reform bill through both houses in 1832, although the Lords acquiesced only when faced with the king's threat to create enough

Whig peers to override them. It was just in time; riots had broken out all over the country, a tax strike was being organized, and radicals urged a run on the Bank of England as a means of bringing the propertied classes to their knees.

The Reform Act was as important for the revolution it averted as for the rather modest alterations it produced. It changed the image but not the reality of power in Britain. Some 143 seats in the House of Commons, about a quarter of the total, were redistributed. Slightly fewer than half of these went to new industrial towns, such as Manchester, which had previously lacked representation of any kind. Some, but by no means all, of the "rotten boroughs"—decayed constituencies that continued to return members to Parliament with a largely phantom electorate—were eliminated. The franchise was extended from slightly under 500,000 to just over 800,000 voters, still little more than 5 percent of the population. The net effect was a token recognition of the industrial bourgeoisie that kept the balance of electoral power safely in the hands of the gentry and nobility.

But while on some issues the interests of the two groups were genuinely divided, it would be a mistake to see them as fundamentally opposed. The new magnates

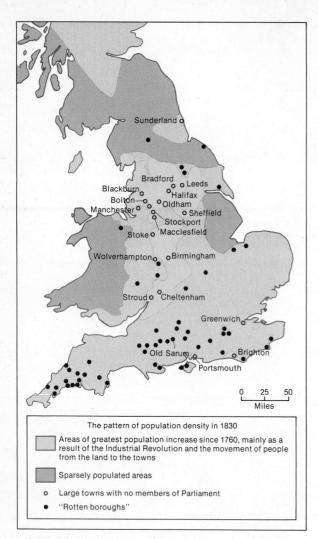

31.3 Parliamentary Representation in Britain Before 1832

The pattern of population density in 1830

Areas of greatest population increase since 1760, mainly as a result of the Industrial Revolution and the movement of people from the land to the towns

Sparsely populated areas

o Large towns with no members of Parliament

● "Rotten boroughs"

The Socialist Challenge

It would be accurate to say that the working classes had fought the revolutions of 1830 and the bourgeoisie had won them. The sans-culottes on the barricades in Paris, the workers who defied the Dutch king in Brussels and Antwerp, and the British laborers who seized Bristol and threatened other towns in their demand for parliamentary representation had all taken an initiative that their betters were quick to convert to their own advantage. Nothing could symbolize the irony of mass politics in the early industrial age more than the spectacle of elderly aristocrats like Lafayette and Lord Grey stage-managing the transference or at any rate the sharing of power between the traditional nobility and the industrial bourgeoisie at the behest of the workers.

The Demand for Reform

The experience of the 1830s and 1840s taught at least the more advanced elements of the working class that their interests could not be encompassed by those of the bourgeoisie. The mass movement that Robert Owen led briefly from 1833 to 1834 (see Chapter 30) was prompted in part by disillusion with the Reform Act, and by the end of the 1830s the first sustained workers' movement had emerged in Britain, the Chartists. It began in 1836 when a small shopkeeper, William Lovett, founded the London Workingmen's Association. The association's relatively modest initial demands were presented in the tradition of social deference to one's superiors. Its tone, however, soon grew more radical. In 1838, with the assistance of the veteran reformer Francis Place, it drew up the first People's Charter. This document rejected the piecemeal reform of Parliament, which was all conventional politics could offer. It demanded a secret ballot, equal electoral districts, annually elected Parliaments on the basis of universal manhood suffrage, the removal of property qualifications for office, and payment for all members of Parliament. The effect of this would have been fully to democratize the political system (at least for men) and to enable workers themselves to stand for and occupy seats in Parliament. Here was a genuine break with the politics of deference, with its assumption that the interest of the working class could be represented satisfactorily by its social betters.

In February 1839 a self-styled workers' convention met in London to press for the People's Charter, now attached to a petition that had gained a million signatures. The delegates called themselves "Members of the Convention," both in evident allusion to the French National Convention of 1792 and to Parliament itself. When the House of Commons rejected the charter, a general strike was proposed. Lacking organization and experi-

of industrial capitalism, like their eighteenth-century predecessors in commerce and finance, had little need of parliamentary representation to make their weight felt. The propertied classes in town and country had adjusted their mutual relations in a manner that more adequately represented the influence of the former. Both agreed that the reins of government would continue to rest with them to the exclusion of the vast majority. The Reform Act of 1832, like the regime of Louis-Philippe in France, reflected that broad consensus. So too did the repeal in 1846 of the Corn Laws, which had kept grain prices high by curtailing foreign imports. Industrialists opposed the Corn Laws because high food prices forced them to pay higher wages; the landowners finally endorsed repeal, not least to preserve the ruling consensus.

enced leadership, it petered out in sporadic agitation from which many existing unions held aloof. Unlike Owen's Grand Union however, the Chartist movement did not collapse with its first defeat but remained a powerful force throughout the 1840s.

A similar rethinking of worker interests was going forward in France, where, having consolidated its position, the government of Louis-Philippe set its face against even token reform. In 1839 the journalist Louis Blanc (1811–1882) argued in a widely read book, *The Organization of Labor*, that the state should socialize all major economic services, including banking, transportation, and insurance, and establish "social workshops," or cooperative factories operated by and for workers. Blanc's reformism derived from the Saint-Simonians, followers of the influential Count de Saint-Simon (1760–1825), who had advocated control of public services and enterprises by a technocratic elite of scientists and engineers. What both Saint-Simon and Blanc ignored, however, like more "utopian" socialists such as Owen and Fourier, was the problem of actual political power. The state, whether controlled by aristocrats, by bourgeoisie, or, as in much of western Europe, by an uneasy combination of both, was highly unlikely to cede authority to either workers or engineers.

From Reform to Revolution

Such was the conclusion drawn by revolutionaries such as Louis-Auguste Blanqui (1805–1881) and Pierre Proudhon (1809–1865), who in turn derived from the martyred Gracchus Babeuf (see Chapter 27) and his Italian disciple, Filippo Maria Buonarotti (1761–1837). Proudhon, unwilling to compromise with any scheme of state ownership, declared roundly that all property was a theft of the value created by labor. He envisioned the abolition of the state in favor of a system of decentralized cooperative enterprises that would produce and exchange goods noncompetitively on the basis of social need. For Blanqui, such an arrangement, however desirable in principle, begged the fundamental question of power: How was such a peaceful system to be established against the resistance of the propertied classes and the state machinery they controlled? Blanqui's answer was armed revolution aimed at establishing a "dictatorship of the proletariat," a phrase he coined. Like his mentor Buonarotti, Europe's first professional revolutionary, Blanqui spent most of his life in jail or on the run; Tocqueville, observing him in 1848 at a rare moment of liberty, said that he had the appearance of a man who had passed his life in the sewers. But with Buonarotti and Blanqui, a new kind of person had appeared on the European scene, convinced of the inevitable struggle between the classes and dedicated to revolution at any cost.

All the thinkers and political activists just considered subscribed to a common critique of the capitalist system. They accepted Adam Smith's definition of labor as the source of all productive value and believed (as Smith did not) that the wealth produced by this labor should be owned socially or collectively: hence the name *socialism* applied to their ideas and demands. The socialists' beliefs were clear-cut: private ownership was the appropriation by force of an excess share of the common social wealth (in the pithy formulation associated with Proudhon, "property is theft"), and unregulated capitalism was the equivalent of unrelieved exploitation. But they disagreed about the remedy. Owen, Fourier, and Proudhon put their faith in small, collectively owned enterprises linked voluntarily into cooperative associations; Saint-Simon and Blanc believed that only state power could break up existing concentrations of private capital and ownership; and Blanqui added that only revolution from below could give the proletariat access to that power. What they all lacked was a theory of social action or, more simply, a credible plan for overthrowing the existing order.

Karl Marx

Karl Marx supplied the theoretical basis for socialism. Until Marx, the socialists had produced no thinker who could conceptually challenge the defense of capitalism put forward by Adam Smith and David Ricardo. For both Smith and Ricardo, private enterprise—economic competition for individual profit—maximized the production of wealth and hence the aggregate social good. Ricardo in particular was sensitive to the high social cost of capitalism: the exploitation of child and female labor, the tendency of worker income to remain at subsistence level, and the "business cycle"—the abrupt spasms of boom and bust to which the industrial system had already shown itself to be vulnerable. These costs were regrettable but, Ricardo felt, for the most part unavoidable. This was particularly true for income stagnation, which Ricardo formulated as the "iron law of wages." In times of industrial expansion when the demand for labor exceeded the supply, Ricardo argued, wages would tend to rise above subsistence level; but the result of relative prosperity was a higher birthrate, which produced excess labor capacity, depressed wages, and caused starvation and misery. For this reason, worker demands for higher wages were self-defeating. Marx was the first socialist thinker to challenge this and similar "laws" of economics on their own ground and in his major work, *Capital*, to advance a comprehensive countertheory to demonstrate that capitalism was not merely unstable but inherently self-destructive as well.

Marx was born in the rapidly industrializing Rhineland city of Trier in 1818. He was descended on both

The founder of modern communism, Karl Marx, in a photograph taken in the mid-1870s. [Globe Photos]

extraordinary and prophetic essays on worker alienation and shed his last attachments to Hegelian idealism. With his friend and lifelong collaborator, Friedrich Engels, he hailed the coming of a new socialist order in *The Communist Manifesto*, but the failed revolutions of 1848 led him into exile instead.

Marx took refuge in London with his large and needy family, living under the watchful eye of the local police and the spies of a dozen nations and on the bounty of Engels, who owned a factory in Manchester. Marx was not embarrassed to live on the profits of capital and himself speculated on the stock market. The task of philosophy, he said, was not to understand the world but to change it, and the man who meant to make that philosophy was not worried about being judged by the rules of the world that would be left behind.

Dismissing his predecessors and rivals, Marx declared his work to be the only "scientific" socialism. It was founded on a grand theory that, arguing humanity's intellectual and social development from its material struggle to wrest the necessities of life from nature, proceeded to describe the stages of history in terms of a social struggle for control of the technical means of production—land, labor, and machinery. Marx described ancient society as founded on slavery, the medieval West on feudalism, and capitalism on wage labor, which he saw as a modern form of slavery. Since, like other socialists, Marx regarded labor as the only source of productive value (capital itself, whether in the form of money, machinery, or tilled lands, being merely labor objectified), all profit extracted from labor by means of the wage system was "surplus" or appropriated value.

Marx praised the bourgeoisie for having greatly expanded the material base of civilization by industrialization and urbanization, even as it simultaneously debased its human content by forcing the great mass of the population to live in conditions of unparalleled exploitation and misery. The contradiction between the prosperity of the few and the poverty of the many would, however, ultimately be too evident to ignore. At the same time, the inherent tendency of capitalist competition to contract and profit margins to shrink would lead to ever-severer contractions of the business cycle and to the growth of monopoly, until the conditions for socialist revolution were ripe.

But revolution could be neither prepared nor accomplished without active class struggle. Marx collaborated (and ultimately quarreled with) all the leading social activists of his day, including the Frenchman Proudhon, the Russian anarchist Mikhail Bakunin (1814–1876), and the German trade unionist Ferdinand Lassalle (1825–1864). Yet he continually stressed the cooperative nature of the proletarian struggle across all borders, rejecting nationalism as a bourgeois phenomenon that reflected the divisive, competitive nature of capitalism itself. In 1864 he was instrumental in founding the Inter-

sides from a long line of rabbis, but his father, like many other Jews of the time, had submitted to Christian baptism to gain entry into the legal profession. Marx studied philosophy at Bonn and Berlin, drank and dueled, and wrote bad poetry, a comic novel, a tragic play, and a doctoral dissertation on the difference between the atomic theories of Democritus and Epicurus. He also became part of a circle of young radicals who were attempting to extend Hegelian philosophy in a leftward direction. As a correspondent for the *Rheinische Zeitung*, he exposed the wretched poverty of the winegrowers of the Trier region in an article that helped lead to the suppression of the newspaper. Quitting Germany in disgust, he settled in Paris, where he produced a series of

national Workingman's Association, later known as the First International, to promote the proletarian cause throughout Europe and America. At his death in 1883, he was clearly the foremost figure of European socialism, as both a thinker and an activist.

Marx never managed to put his mature ideas into finished, comprehensive form. Half his manuscripts lay unpublished at his death, many to remain unknown for decades; even his masterpiece, *Capital*, the first part of which was published in 1867, was only a torso. In part this reflected his own refusal to settle into any mold, even his own; as he once wittily remarked, "I am not a Marxist." Yet, though always controversial and frequently misinterpreted, his thought has been decisive in shaping much of the modern world, and in the universality of his influence he may be regarded as the first nonreligious thinker of world significance. Certainly he takes his place as one of the most important figures in the Western tradition. Before Marx no theory of societal development had advanced much beyond Plato and Aristotle 2,000 years before. There was no theory of historical change that dealt adequately with the concrete problems of subsistence, organization, or technological innovation. There was no theory of the Enlightenment that portrayed humanity as anything more than orphans of reason or suggested the plausibility of a just society.

The Russian émigré Annenkov described Marx as unkempt, domineering, and very nearly offensive in manner; but, he added, "he looked like a man with the right and power to demand respect, no matter how he appeared before you and no matter what he did," a man with "the firm conviction of his mission to dominate men's minds and prescribe them their laws." Much of the twentieth century responded to that force.

The Revolutions of 1848

When late in the year 1847 the young Marx and Engels warned of the imminence of revolution in *The Communist Manifesto*, they may have been the only people in Europe to expect it. Yet within the first four months of 1848 the Continent was rocked by almost 50 separate revolutions in France, Prussia, Austria, and almost all the lesser German and Italian states. Surveying the wreckage of monarchies, Tsar Nicholas I wrote to Queen Victoria that Russia and Britain seemed to be the last two states standing in Europe. The exaggeration in that statement was slight.

The Causes of the Revolutions

Some general causes of the revolutions can be discerned, although they differed with the circumstances of each state or region. The Industrial Revolution, which had begun in earnest on the Continent after 1830, had shaken social and demographic patterns and profoundly altered political ones. Unfulfilled nationalist aspirations were a primary impetus in Germany, Italy, and eastern Europe. These tensions and grievances were also exacerbated, as before 1789 and 1830, by hard times. Harvests were poor in the three years preceding 1848; the Prussian peasantry, lacking bread, survived on potatoes, while in Ireland, the failure in 1845 of the potato crop—the last resort of the poor—led to mass starvation and emigration, which between them reduced the population

THE REVOLUTIONS OF 1848 AND 1849

1848

January	Sicilian uprising against the Kingdom of Naples
February	Naples, Tuscany grant constitutions; revolution in Paris, republic proclaimed
March	Uprisings in Vienna, Venice, Milan, Berlin; serfdom abolished in Austria; Venice proclaims a republic; Frederick William IV promises Prussia a constitution
April	Constituent Assembly elected in France
May	Frankfurt Assembly convenes
June	Troops quell popular uprisings in Prague and Paris
October	Austrian army retakes Vienna from radical students and workers
December	Ferdinand I of Austria abdicates in favor of Franz Joseph; Louis Napoleon elected president of the French Republic

1849

February	Rome proclaims a republic
March	Battle of Novara; Charles Albert abdicates
April	Hungary declares independence from Austria; Frederick William IV refuses the crown of Germany from the Frankfurt Assembly
May–August	Frankfurt Assembly dispersed; absolute monarchy restored in Naples; Russia suppresses the Hungarian revolution; Republic of Venice surrenders

of the country from 8.5 million to 6.5 million in five years. Urban workers were also squeezed by the rising price of food, and the agricultural crisis soon produced industrial depression as well. The integration of agricultural and industrial markets through capitalist development meant that any disturbance in one sector of the system had immediate repercussions in the rest of it, while the new concentration of population in towns and cities provided natural foci of discontent.

The single most pervasive element in the revolutions of 1848, however, was a general questioning of the existing political order. The monarchs of the Old Regime had based their authority on appeals to divine right and a traditional social order, but divinity no longer shielded a ruler who could be forced off his throne by a three-day riot as Charles X had been in 1830 or set up like Louis-Philippe by a backstairs cabal consisting of a diplomat, a journalist, and a banker. Nor could such a ruler appeal to traditional values or deference in a society where the most basic relations of property, production, and authority were being transformed and a new financial, commercial, and industrial elite was busily accumulating power. Still less could rulers legitimate themselves where, as in most of Italy, they served not a native but a foreign interest.

The new bourgeois or quasi-bourgeois regimes established by the events of 1830–1832, though based explicitly or implicitly on popular sovereignty and constitutional guarantees, had proved singularly unwilling to embrace the vast majority of the people in the political process. Except for Belgium, in no European nation with a representative system did the electorate exceed 5 percent of the population. The Chartists pursued their demand for universal manhood suffrage in Britain with petitioning campaigns of 3 million signatures in 1842 and 5 million in 1848, only to meet with continuing rejection in Parliament, while in France, with only 300,000 electors in a population of 30 million, the government of François Guizot set itself resolutely against even a token extension of the franchise. After two revolutions and 60 years, the French Assembly was a less representative body than the Estates General of Louis XVI had been.

The Collapse of the Old Order

The 1848 revolutions began with a stirring in Italy, where on January 12 the people of Sicily rose against Ferdinand II. By the end of the month Milan and Venice had proclaimed their ancient independence as republics

31.4 Europe's Revolutions of 1848

and called on King Charles Albert of Piedmont and Pope Pius IX to help unify the entire peninsula. The French were not far behind. Liberal reformers, blocked from public demonstrations, had adopted the British tactic of holding banquets that were in effect mass political rallies on behalf of a modest extension of the franchise. When the authorities sought to ban one such banquet in Paris in late February, the events of 1830 swiftly repeated themselves. Riots broke out, barricades went up, and the National Guard, called out to quell the disturbances, joined in instead. Louis-Philippe dismissed the unpopular Guizot in a bid to regain middle-class support. But the Parisian workers were not to be duped a second time. Breaking into the Chamber of Deputies, they forced the proclamation of a republic, and Louis-Philippe fled into exile in London.

The news from Paris galvanized dissidents in Germany and Austria. In Berlin the irresolute Frederick William IV (1840–1861) found himself a virtual prisoner of nationalists who demanded that Prussia take the lead in unifying Germany under a liberal constitution. Student rebels and workers joined in Vienna to extract a promise of reform from the emperor, Ferdinand I, and the aged Metternich fled the city in disguise to join Louis-Philippe in exile. More serious were nationalist uprisings by the Bohemians in Prague and the Hungarians in Budapest. The latter, under the leadership of the fiery journalist and orator Louis Kossuth (1802–1894), demanded virtual independence from Austria, with a separate army, government, and system of finance. In addition, the Hungarian Diet, composed exclusively of noblemen and long one of the most reactionary assemblies in Europe, voted for constitutional government, the abolition of serfdom, and the imposition of taxes on the nobility. By the end of March the Austrian Empire was prostrate, while in Germany a group of liberals, meeting spontaneously in Heidelberg, called for the election of an all-German parliament on the basis of universal manhood suffrage and under the supervision of an electoral body, the *Vorparliament*, summoned directly by them. So great was the enthusiasm for unity throughout the country, and so paralyzed were the existing governments, that the election was duly carried out, and on May 18 the 830 delegates of the new parliament convened in Frankfurt to make Germany a nation.

The single most evident fact about this whirlwind of revolutions was the weakness and prostration of the established governments. As Charles X had fallen at what seemed the merest touch in 1830, not only had his successor been toppled, but what seemed the most rock-solid thrones in Europe, Prussia and Austria, had shaken in their foundations before relative handfuls of protesters who made up their demands as they went along. Nothing could have more conclusively demonstrated the ideological bankruptcy of these regimes and their helplessness in the face of even the most disorganized chal-

lenge. At the same time, however, the revolutionaries, united for the moment in the flush of success, were soon as divided from one another as they had been from the kings who served as the common target of their discontent.

Counterrevolution in Central Europe

Among the first revolutions to unravel were in the Austrian Empire. In Italy, Charles Albert had no sooner assumed leadership of the anti-Habsburg coalition than it began to collapse; a counterrevolution restored Ferdinand II in Sicily, while the Venetians made it clear that they had no intention of abandoning their republic to merge with the House of Savoy. In July, Austria badly defeated Charles Albert's forces at the battle of Custozza, and a last attempt to resuscitate the cause ended in disaster at Novara in March 1849. The Italian conflagration was not quite over; in November 1848, Pius IX fled Rome after the assassination of his chief minister, and a republic was proclaimed in February headed by Giuseppe Mazzini (1805–1872), whose impassioned vision of a united, democratic Italy had made him a hero to a generation of young nationalists. Mazzini's government immediately announced the confiscation of church lands and their redistribution to the peasantry, as well as a program of public housing for the urban poor. Although it controlled only the city of Rome and its immediate environs, the republic declared itself the nucleus of a united Italy. But it fell to a French army in July despite stubborn resistance, and with the fall of Venice a month later, the collapse of the revolutionary cause was complete.

In Hungary the Magyar majority under Kossuth rapidly alienated the various minorities under its control by proclaiming what amounted to racial hegemony: it abolished local assemblies in non-Magyar provinces and prescribed that Hungarian be the exclusive language of all higher education as well as of the Diet. This stimulated Slavic nationalism, which culminated in a pan-Slavic congress that convened in Prague in June, only to be suppressed by troops under General Alfred Windischgratz still loyal to the Habsburgs. This victory emboldened the court party to attempt the liberation of Vienna. In October, Windischgratz occupied the city after a bombardment and executed or exiled its radical leaders on the spot. Two months later the feebleminded Ferdinand I was induced to step down in favor of his 18-year-old nephew, Franz Joseph I (1848–1916), who, unhampered by his predecessor's promises to the liberals, completed the process of restoration the following summer by crushing the Hungarian revolt with the aid of 140,000 Russian troops.

In Germany, meanwhile, the Frankfurt Assembly set

to its task of providing the country with a national government and a constitution. The fundamental anomaly of its position, however, was soon apparent. Almost all the delegates were university-educated members of the upper bourgeoisie: lawyers, doctors, scholars, ministers, bankers, merchants, and manufacturers. Their vision was of a world made safe for bourgeois opportunity: free trade, untrammeled growth, an end to the political monopoly of the aristocracy, and a liberal regime presiding benignly over a swelling gross national product. But the masses, whose rebellion had cleared the ground for them, wanted none of these things. They were peasants clamoring for land, artisans demanding protection for their trades, and workers who wanted higher wages and industrial regulation. Free enterprise only meant new chains to them, and free speech was less important than bread they could afford to eat.

While the Frankfurt delegates attempted to thrash out their own manifold differences—whether the new Germany should be a federation or a unitary state, a monarchy, an empire, or a republic, and above all whether it should seek to incorporate German-speaking areas of Austria, Denmark, and Poland within its borders—the existing governments of the German Confederation, supposedly waiting for final extinction but still in control of their armies, slowly recovered their authority. By the time the Assembly had drafted its constitution, which included provisions for freedom of speech,

assembly, and the press, religious toleration, and public education, both Prussia and Austria had become strong enough to reject it out of hand. When Frederick William IV, no doubt with memories of being forced to ride through the streets of Berlin with a revolutionary tricolor in his hat the previous spring, was approached in April 1849 to become "emperor of the Germans," he replied loftily that he would not pick up a crown from the gutter. At that the Frankfurt Assembly began to collapse. The more moderate delegations, unwilling to contemplate a republic, went home, and the radical remnant was dispersed by force in June. The revolution in Germany was over.

France: From Revolution to Empire

In France the course of events was quite different. Here alone (apart from Mazzini's short-lived Roman republic), the monarch of an independent state had actually been deposed and a new provisional government established. A hasty compromise among revolutionary factions, it consisted of seven moderate and three radical (socialist) republicans. Among the latter was Louis Blanc, who urged immediate relief for the unemployed through a Ministry of Progress that would establish his workshop system. Behind Blanc was the specter of Blanqui, white-

◉ The June Days ◉

The French liberal Alexis de Tocqueville describes the June Days of 1848.

I come at last to the insurrection of June, the most extensive and the most singular that has occurred in our history, and perhaps in any other: the most extensive, because, during four days, more than a hundred thousand men were engaged in it; the most singular, because the insurgents fought without a war-cry, without leaders, without flags, and yet with a marvellous harmony and an amount of military experience that astonished the oldest officers.

What distinguished it also, among all the events of this kind which have succeeded one another in France for sixty years, is that it did not aim at changing the form of government, but at altering the order of society. It was not, strictly speaking, a political struggle, in the sense which until then we had given to the word, but a combat of class against class. . . .

It must also be observed that this formidable insurrection was not the enterprise of a certain number of conspirators, but the revolt of one whole section of the population against another. Women took part in it as well as men. While the latter fought, the former prepared and carried ammunition; and when at last the time had come to surrender, the women were the last to yield.

Source: A. T. De Mattos, trans., *The Recollections of Alexis de Tocqueville* (New York: Columbia University Press, 1949), pp. 150–151.

haired and black-clad, "the most complete revolutionary of his time,"[1] who showed his power by mounting a demonstration of 100,000 workers in Paris in March 1848. When Blanc failed to win them the concessions they demanded, one of the marchers denounced him as a traitor. The revolution had already been split.

Most of the wealthier bourgeoisie and nobility had already fled Paris, and the United States was the only foreign power to recognize the French republic. The moderates in the government placed their hopes in speedy elections, which they expected to produce a conservative majority that would isolate the radicals. A Constituent Assembly, elected by universal manhood suffrage in April, convened on May 4 and immediately replaced the provisional government with a five-man executive of its own that contained no socialists. On June 22, following an abortive coup led by Blanqui, the government announced the dissolution of the workshop program, which had been set up as a sop to Blanc but had provided only ill-paid road work for the 200,000 unemployed of Paris. The reaction was immediate. The workers took up arms, the government proclaimed martial law, and the class war heralded only six months before by Marx and Engels in *The Communist Manifesto* became bloody reality in the streets of Paris. Ten thousand people were killed or wounded in a three-day struggle without quarter (June 24–26) until troops under General Louis Cavaignac regained control of the city. Capping victory with vengeance, the Assembly decreed that the 15,000 prisoners taken be deported. An army of 50,000 occupied the French capital until October.

The so-called June Days sent a shudder of terror throughout bourgeois Europe; one woman likened the strife in Paris to the siege of Rome by the barbarians. The feeling was reciprocated, and not by French workers alone. "Every proletarian," wrote the editor of *Red Revolution* in London, "who does not see and feel that he belongs to an enslaved and degraded class is a *fool*." The ideological breach between the classes was complete, and that division remains the formal posture of western European politics to this day.

Looking back on the revolutions of 1848, Karl Marx observed wryly that history repeats itself: the first time as tragedy, the second as farce. There was more than a touch of farce about many of them, but there was much tragedy too, and in the June Days of Paris, an ominous portent of the future. But perhaps the dominant emotion was frustration. For a glorious moment, liberals had dreamed of constitutions, nationalists of unification, and radicals of a classless society in which the workers of every land could embrace as comrades. These dreams were not as yet to be.

The European elite of the mid-nineteenth century—an amalgam of the upper bourgeoisie and the traditional landed aristocracy—was still powerful enough to maintain itself, while its opponents were too diffuse in their aims, too divided among themselves, and too little rooted in the political and social realities of the mass of the population they claimed to represent. Yet the demands they made—political equality, national consolidation, and social justice—reflected deeply felt ideological contradictions within European society. Inherited privilege, the basis of political dominance in Europe for centuries, was no longer self-justifying, while acquired privilege—the accumulation of wealth and capital by the bourgeoisie—was equally suspect as a mandate to rule. If the revolutionaries of 1848 had failed to topple the existing order, they had exposed the essential hollowness and vulnerability of any authority not based on popular consent.

Notes

1. P. Robertson, *Revolutions of 1848* (New York: Harper & Row, 1960), p. 61.

Suggestions for Further Reading

Abrams, M. H. *The Mirror and the Lamp: Romantic Theory and the Critical Tradition.* New York: Oxford University Press, 1953.

Artz, F. B. *Reaction and Revolution, 1814–1832.* New York: Harper & Row, 1963.

Chevalier, L. *Laboring Classes and Dangerous Classes in Paris During the First Half of the Nineteenth Century.* New York: Fertig, 1973.

Clark, K. *The Romantic Rebellion.* New York: Harper & Row, 1973.

Dakin, D. *The Greek Struggle for Independence.* Berkeley: University of California Press, 1973.

De Ruggiero, G. *The History of European Liberalism,* trans. R. G. Collingswood. Boston: Beacon Press, 1959.

Droz, J. *Europe Between Revolutions, 1815–1848*. New York: Harper & Row, 1967.

Friedenthal, R. *Goethe. His Life and Times*. Cleveland: World, 1965.

Hammond, J. L., and Hammond, B. *The Age of Chartism*. Hamden, Conn.: Archon Books, 1962.

Hobsbawm, E. J. *The Age of Revolution: Europe, 1789 to 1848*. New York: New American Library, 1962.

Kohn, H. *The Idea of Nationalism*. New York: Collier Books, 1967.

Krieger, L. *The German Idea of Freedom*. Boston: Beacon Press, 1957.

Lichtheim, G. *A Short History of Socialism*. New York: Praeger, 1970.

Lynch, K. A. *Family, Class, and Ideology in Early Industrial France: Social Policy and the Working-Class Family, 1825–1848*. Madison: University of Wisconsin Press, 1988.

Manuel, F. E. *The Prophets of Paris*. Cambridge, Mass: Harvard University Press, 1962.

McLellan, D. *Karl Marx: His Life and Thought*. New York: Harper & Row, 1973.

Nicolson, H. *The Congress of Vienna*. London: Constable, 1946.

Pinkney, D. H. *The French Revolution of 1830*. Princeton, N.J.: Princeton University Press, 1972.

Pointon, M. "Liberty on the Barricades: Women, Politics and Sexuality in Delacroix," in S. Reynolds, ed., *Women, State and Revolution*. Brighton: Wheatsheaf, 1986.

Robertson, P. *Revolutions of 1848*. New York: Harper & Row, 1960.

Sheehan, J. J. *Germany, 1770–1866*. New York: Oxford University Press, 1990.

Stearns, P. N. *1848: The Revolutionary Tide in Europe*. New York: Norton, 1974.

Taylor, A. J. P. *The Habsburg Monarchy, 1809–1918*. New York: Harper & Row, 1965.

The Triumph of Nationalism

The failure of the 1848 upheavals represented at once a crushing blow to the ideals of Romantic revolution and the last desperate stand of the conservative order established by the Congress of Vienna. In the decades that followed, the forces of order gave way to those of change as a powerful, rapidly spreading nationalism triumphed in Europe.

As the dominant theme of European history over the next half century, nationalism had a powerful appeal to a broad cross section of society, from workers to industrialists and from merchants to aristocrats. Many factors explain the success of nationalism in the post-1848 period. Unlike the abortive nationalist movements of the 1820s and 1830s, it now combined the Romantic celebration of the past and its tortured search for self-identity with a new realism based on the understanding and use of power. Moreover, artists, writers, and musicians explored nationalistic themes in their work, while both higher literacy rates and more skillful propaganda made more and more members of the middle and lower classes sensitive to nationalist symbolism. Most impor-

Princess Victoria of Hohenzollern, the wife of Emperor Frederick William IV of Germany, was at the center of liberal opposition to Bismarck's domestic policies. [Mansell Collection]

tant, in regions where nationalistic aspirations were frustrated by foreign domination, a new generation of practical, tough-minded leaders came into power. Raised during the turbulent days of the Napoleonic empire, these men admired the methods of modern warfare and diplomacy, appreciated the benefits of efficient government, and understood the principles of liberal economics and industrial development. Cavour in Italy and Bismarck in Germany were the two most outstanding examples of this marriage between nationalism and power politics. In an age increasingly under the influence of science and technology, Bismarck and Cavour successfully translated the ideals of an earlier generation into the concrete action of the new.

Although all-pervasive, nationalism reflected local conditions. In Italy and Germany it assumed the form of nation-building. Where centralized states already existed, as in Britain, nationalism merged with liberalism to forge a new ruling elite dedicated to industrial and commercial expansion through overseas conquest or, as in the case of France, to economic development under a restored empire. In the Austrian, Russian, and Ottoman empires, despotic but ineffectual monarchies struggled to control ethnically diverse populations clamoring for independence or self-determination. While the young republic of the United States struggled to restore unity after a destructive civil war, nationalism promoted independence movements and nation-building in Latin America. Finally, the international Zionist movement added a new element to nationalism as it sought to give expression to the centuries-old quest for a Jewish homeland.

The emergence of nationalism in the second half of the nineteenth century is a development of immense importance. As a worldwide phenomenon, its long-range repercussions would be felt in the national antagonisms that twice in the twentieth century erupted into global war, in the twisted ideas that fed the ideologies of fascism between the wars, and in the national rivalries over which the United States and the Soviet Union fought a dangerous ideological war. Ironically, nationalism also inspired the revolt of former colonies against Western rule, which was itself partly a consequence of nationalism.

The Politics of National Grandeur: Napoleon III in France

Nowhere after 1848 was the beguiling appeal of nationalism stronger than in France. In December 1848, partly as a result of the gruesome violence of the June insur-

rection, French males overwhelmingly chose as the president of their new Second Republic Louis-Napoleon Bonaparte, the enigmatic nephew of Napoleon I. Much to everyone's amazement, General Louis-Eugène Cavaignac, the conservative republican hero who had crushed the June riots, received only 1.5 million votes, the socialist Alexandre Ledru-Rollin and the poet Alphonse de Lamartine even less, whereas the virtually unknown Louis-Napoleon won the trust of more than 5.5 million Frenchmen.

Louis-Napoleon (1808–1873) had almost no political experience, but the magic of his name was irresistible. For years he had lived abroad, a dreamy youth caught up in the euphoria of revolutionary Romanticism. Implicated in the 1831 revolt in the Papal States and in two ludicrous plots to overthrow Louis-Philippe, he spent time in exile and then in prison until his escape to England in 1846. French and English reactionaries funded his return to Paris in the midst of the 1848 revolution, whereupon he campaigned for the presidency by invoking the theme of national unity.

Louis-Napoleon's platform, designed to appeal to a strife-torn society, argued that the country needed an authoritarian leader. Like many modern politicians, however, Louis-Napoleon was duplicitous. While appealing to Catholics and other proponents of authority, he also cultivated the support of the working classes.

He proposed to eliminate a corrupt Parliament and political parties to open the way to a direct relationship between the citizens and himself through plebiscites based on universal male suffrage. Unlike the role of the aristocratic Old Regime or the upper-middle-class government of Louis-Philippe, the proper role—indeed, the duty—of government was, in Louis-Napoleon's mind, to wipe out poverty and provide prosperity for all citizens.

These views, first expressed in two pamphlets he wrote while in prison, *On Napoleonic Ideas* and *The Extinction of Poverty*, formed the core of Louis-Napoleon's political thought. But his popularity was derived in large measure from the memory of national greatness attached to Napoleon I. Despite a stocky build and an exaggerated mustache and goatee, Louis-Napoleon had a charismatic appeal that transcended class and social status. He also realized that public opinion could be a powerful instrument of authority. He knew almost by instinct what later, twentieth-century dictators would discover, that an authoritarian state based on nationalist pride and popular consensus and promising both social tranquillity and economic prosperity had a strong appeal in times of stress.

The Second Republic lasted three years. Although its constitution provided for a strong president, the chief executive could serve for only one term. Louis-Napoleon therefore played to the conservatives who dominated the National Assembly by enacting measures in favor of the Catholic church, reducing the suffrage, and restricting

◎ The Napoleonic Myth ◎

In 1839 Louis-Napoleon wrote a pamphlet titled On Napoleonic Ideas. *Praising the reign of his uncle as having been founded on the will of the people, Louis-Napoleon contributed to the popularization of the Napoleonic myth on which he was to base his own rise to power.*

The Emperor Napoleon has contributed more than any other person to hasten the reign of liberty, by preserving the moral influence of the revolution, and diminishing the fears which it inspired. . . .

The government of Napoleon, better than any other, could have sustained liberty, for the simple reason that liberty would have strengthened his throne, though it overthrows such thrones as have not a solid foundation.

Liberty would have fortified his power, because Napoleon had established in France all that ought to precede liberty; because his power reposed upon the whole mass of the nation; because his interests were the same as those of the people; because, finally, the most perfect confidence reigned between the ruler and the governed. . . .

There is no longer any necessity to reconstruct the system of the emperor; it will reconstruct itself. Sovereigns and nations will concur in re-establishing it; because each one will see in it a guaranty of order, of peace, and of prosperity. . . .

In conclusion, let us repeat it, the Napoleonic idea is not one of war, but a social, industrial, commercial idea, and one which concerns all mankind. If to some it appears always surrounded by the thunder of combats, that is because it was in fact for too long a time veiled by the smoke of cannon and the dust of battles. But now the clouds are dispersed, and we can see, beyond the glory of arms, a civil glory greater and more enduring.

Source: Louis-Napoleon Bonaparte, *Napoleonic Ideas*, trans. J. Dorr (New York: Appleton, 1859).

freedom of education and the press. When the legislature refused to amend the constitution to permit him a second term, Louis-Napoleon seized power. On December 2, 1851, he illegally dissolved the Assembly and proclaimed a temporary dictatorship in the name of the people. With the support of the army, he arrested his opponents and crushed an uprising of the workers. In a plebiscite held that same month, 92 percent of the voters gave him the power to draft a new constitution that made him president for ten years. A second plebiscite a year later confirmed by an even greater margin the hold of the Napoleonic legend on the national psyche: Louis-Napoleon was proclaimed Napoleon III, emperor of the French.*

The Second Empire

The structure of imperial government, inspired by the constitution of Napoleon I, was designed to give the

*Napoleon II, son of Napoleon I, died in 1832 without having served as emperor.

impression of a regime responsive to the popular will. An appointed senate was balanced by an assembly chosen every six years by carefully manipulated elections based on universal male suffrage. Parliament could, however, only discuss items submitted by the emperor and had to debate behind closed doors. Napoleon personally controlled the army and the budget and conducted foreign affairs, advised by a handpicked Council of State.

Napoleon's domestic policies, resting on vigorous government intervention in the economy, produced unparalleled prosperity. The emperor deliberately strengthened the middle class by encouraging investment and the modernization of industry. The state-owned railroad increased its mileage fivefold during the first decade of imperial rule, thus stimulating industrial development and commerce. A law passed in 1865 introduced the concept of limited liability to protect corporate stockholders from excessive risk. Investment capital was raised through the *Crédit Mobilier*, a banking institution that sold shares to the public. A free trade agreement with Britain in 1860 resulted in an increase in French exports and eventually a favorable balance of trade. In an effort to advance commerce with the East, French capital financed—and a French engineer, Ferdinand de Lesseps, constructed—the Suez Canal in the decade between 1859 and 1869. These measures bound the middle class to the government, for industrial production had doubled and the vitality of the economy seemed to confirm the wisdom of the French people in putting another Bonaparte on the throne.

Working-class support for Napoleon III was almost as strong as middle-class enthusiasm, for wages kept pace with inflation and the emperor sponsored government health programs, low-cost housing, and numerous public works projects. Despite the fears of many businessmen, in the 1860s he even permitted the formation of trade unions and legalized the right to strike.

The vigorous economic life of the Second Empire was accompanied by a deliberate effort to drape the public image of France in a grand, if at times gaudy, style. The results were most stunning in the imperial capital, where Napoleon appointed Baron Georges Haussmann to direct a massive rebuilding program. Narrow but picturesque medieval streets and unattractive neighborhoods were demolished to make way for 85 miles of broad boulevards and tree-shaded pavements. Along with large squares and stately new buildings, Haussmann also built sewers to provide drainage. Although costly and controversial, these projects not only created jobs but also gave the emperor better security because the wider avenues made it difficult to erect barricades against government troops, as the Parisians had done so often in the past. This experiment in urban renewal transformed Paris into a well-ordered and elegant city. It also created a vast stage on which Napoleon and his consort, Empress Eugénie, performed lavish public ceremonies befitting the renewed splendor of France.

Born Eugénia de Montijo (1826–1920), Eugénie was the beautiful, ambitious daughter of a Spanish father and a Franco-American mother. When she met the French president in 1850, she judged him a man of greatness and offered to finance his coup d'état the next year. They were married in January 1853, after Napoleon became emperor, in a sumptuous ceremony in Notre Dame Cathedral. Together they presided with great elegance over the Second Empire. Just as Napoleon dreamed of the reemergence of his nation as a great power, so Paris was to become once again the arbiter of Europe in matters of taste and culture. After the drab years of Louis-Philippe's bourgeois monarchy, the new imperial court gave at least the appearance of grandeur.

Despite the considerable domestic achievements of the Second Empire, the economic conditions of the working class were depressed, and Napoleon III did nothing to improve the condition of French women. Although his uncle's civil code had declared the equality of all French citizens, women were not included in the definition of citizenship, with the result that the power of men over them was actually strengthened. For example, after marriage, women could not control their own property, engage in a business or profession, or administer children's financial affairs without the consent of their husbands. Divorce laws favored men, and adultery had significantly more serious consequences for wives than for husbands. The law codes thus reinforced women's legal inequality and subordination.

Uniting with the utopian socialists in the 1830s and with the republican socialists in 1848 and 1849, the French feminist movement had been one of the most vigorous and advanced in Europe, pushing hard for women's rights and social reform in general. But the censorship and restrictive domestic policies of the Second Empire repressed the feminists along with other opponents of Napoleon III's rule. Feminist views were therefore restricted largely to the liberal salons of Paris and the underground press, where women writers—no-

Renovation of a Paris neighborhood, as ordered by Baron Haussmann. [Granger Collection]

tably Juliette Lamber and Jenny Héricourt—fought against conservative patriarchy and the equally antifeminist views of former socialist and republican allies such as Pierre-Joseph Proudhon and the historian Jules Michelet. Lamber and Héricourt argued for women's rights in education, the professions, and government and exposed the contradictions implicit in the prevalent attitudes toward marriage, divorce, and the double sexual standard. They and women like them kept social debate alive until the repressive phase of the empire came to an end in the 1860s.

The Liberalization of the Empire

Napoleon III protested that he was a man of peace, but foreign entanglements often threatened to disrupt the stability of the Second Empire. Almost unavoidably, the invocation of the Napoleonic legend raised the specter of war, although Napoleon III had neither the military genius nor the diplomatic astuteness of his uncle. French participation in the Crimean War had been popular, and colonial forays in Africa and Indochina had limited success. But his intervention in Italian affairs backfired when it resulted in the loss of papal territory. More damaging was the disastrous attempt in the 1860s to impose French control over Mexico; even worse was Napoleon's failure to obtain territorial gains from the unification of Germany. The cumulative effect of these mistakes gave rise to domestic criticism, and Napoleon's sensitivity to public opinion led him to make reforms intended to soothe the discontent.

This process of liberalizing the empire, against which Eugénie counseled her husband, began by granting the Assembly increased powers and permitting his political enemies—especially liberals, republicans, and legitimist monarchists—to criticize the government openly. He next lifted the restrictions on parliamentary debate and freedom of the press, a move that encouraged the opposition. The lifting of censorship also led to the emergence of a reinvigorated feminist movement. Women such as Maria Deraismes debated the issue of inequality before large audiences, published feminist newspapers, and established the Association for the Rights of Women. Although Deraismes and her friends were few in number and it would be many decades before their movement scored significant victories, they contributed much to the quality of French political life in the last years of the Second Empire. By 1869, when national elections were held, it became clear that the emperor had lost control of the political situation—almost half of the voters supported opposition candidates and elected 30 republicans to the assembly. Early in 1870 Napoleon institutionalized these changes in a new constitution that for all practical purposes created a parliamentary gov-

Napoleon III and Empress Eugénie with their son. Napoleon III dreamed of imperial grandeur, but this photograph shows the Bonapartes as a proper bourgeois family. [Culver Pictures]

ernment with the emperor serving as head of state. In May the last of Napoleon's plebiscites showed 7.5 million citizens in favor of the new regime and only 1.5 million against.

Whether these sweeping changes reflected Napoleon III's desire to bring France closer to democracy is uncertain, but his days as emperor were numbered. In the summer, drained and in ill health, he went to war against Prussia, and before it was over the Second Empire had collapsed in defeat and the French people had once again turned to a republic.

Material progress made the first decade of Louis-Napoleon's reign some of the best years economically in the history of modern France, at least for the bourgeoisie, yet the price of prosperity was the suppression of political freedom. The second half of his rule saw the

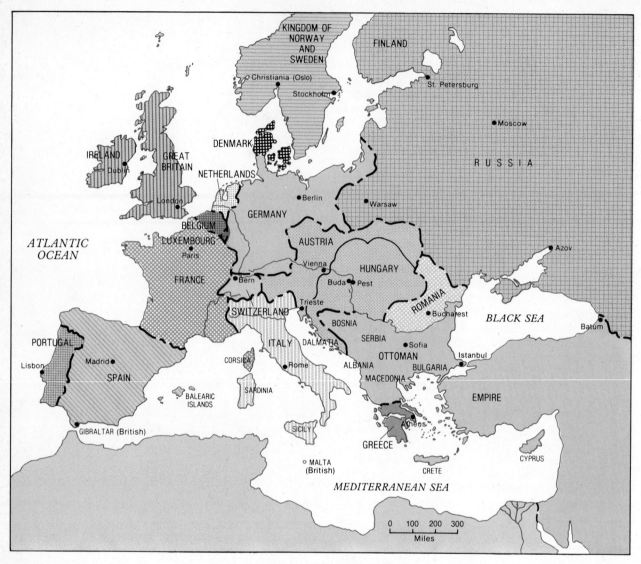

32.1 Europe in 1871

gradual restoration of liberty accompanied by imperialism and war. Once admired as one of the great rulers of the mid-nineteenth century, he died a broken man, scorned by European opinion and repudiated by the French people. He was the victim of the very Napoleonic legend that he represented.

Power Politics and the Unification of Italy

If nationalist pride had made and then destroyed an emperor in France, its impact was even more dramatic in central and southern Europe. There, by 1871, two new nation-states, Italy and Germany, appeared. Italy, in Metternich's famous phrase, had been merely a "geographical expression." The Italian peninsula comprised less than a dozen independent states; Germany was at the same time little more than a name used to describe the region between France and Austria that consisted of some 38 separate kingdoms, principalities, and duchies. Both had had glorious pasts, Italy as the center of the ancient Roman empire and the land of the Renaissance humanists, Germany as the core of the medieval Holy Roman Empire and the site of Luther's Protestant Reformation. But circumstances and history combined to keep each divided and subject to foreign intervention and manipulation.

Nationalism in Italy and Germany was aroused by the French invasions and the wars of Napoleon I. Bonaparte had reduced and rearranged the states in each region and thereby suggested the possibilities of national unification to Italians and Germans, but their nationalism was in part a reaction against foreign occupation. After Waterloo, the Congress of Vienna restored almost all the original rulers of these states to their thrones and replaced French occupation with Austrian influence. In the 1820s and 1830s revolutionary Romanticism failed to bring down the status quo so anxiously guarded by Metternich, although national feeling continued to mature during the next decade. As we have seen, the 1848 revolutions gave rise to the first serious attempts to achieve unification in Italy and Germany, but again Austrian military intervention crushed nationalist hopes.

Out of the defeats of 1849 came one positive result: Piedmont-Sardinia emerged as the only viable Italian state to champion national independence, while Prussian leadership became the focus of the unification effort in Germany. In the 1850s Cavour as prime minister of Piedmont and in the 1860s Bismarck as minister-president of Prussia gave their national movements strong leadership that easily matched Napoleon III in cunning and ambition and, by substituting the principles of power politics for Romantic idealism, achieved unification at last.

Nation building in Italy and Germany demonstrated that midcentury nationalism had secured the consensus of large portions of the middle classes and eventually the nobility. By 1871, when the process was complete, the entrance of Italy and Germany into the European state system profoundly altered the balance of power on the Continent.

The Italian Risorgimento

Strong local traditions and competition characterized the politics of the Italian peninsula since the appearance of city-states in the Middle Ages. Despite some changes wrought at Vienna in 1815, the congress restored the overall structure of the Italian state system. In the south the Kingdom of the Two Sicilies (combining Naples and Sicily) was ruled by a branch of the Bourbon dynasty related through marriage to the Austrian Habsburgs. In central Italy the Papal States remained the temporal possession of the Catholic church and were ruled from Rome by the popes. The north-central region consisted of a patchwork of small states dominated from Florence by the Grand Duchy of Tuscany, where dynastic and political arrangements also gave the Habsburgs considerable influence. In northeastern Italy the Vienna settlement gave the Habsburgs direct control over the provinces of Lombardy and Venetia, which were ruled from Milan by an Austrian viceroy. Finally, in the strategically important northwest corner lay the Kingdom of Sardinia, consisting of the Piedmont and Savoy regions and the island of Sardinia, ruled by the House of Savoy. This ambitious dynasty had pursued a long-standing policy of expansion in Italy, and in the first half of the century Charles Albert had made two dramatic but unsuccessful bids to oust Austria from the peninsula.

Italian nationalists debated a variety of programs that shared the common goal of an Italian "resurgence," or Risorgimento, as the movement for independence and unity was known. Giuseppe Mazzini (1805–1872), one of the great European theorists of nationalism, preached a revolution aimed at creating a united Italian republic based on popular sovereignty and universal suffrage. Mazzini's idealistic propaganda, which educated a generation of Italians to the cause of freedom, posed a radical democratic alternative to the more conservative programs of his contemporaries. The Neo-Guelph* movement, founded by the Piedmontese priest Vincenzo Gioberti, advocated a federation of Italian states led by the papacy and protected by the king of Sardinia. The election of Pope Pius IX in 1846 gave brief impetus to Gioberti's plan, but ultimately his effort to reconcile Italian unification with the temporal interests of the church proved unrealistic. The third alternative, known as the moderate program, was the work of a group of liberal Piedmontese noblemen. Opposed to the revolutionary tactics and democratic principles of Mazzini, the moderates championed a unification imposed from above by Piedmontese armies and a constitutional monarchy under the House of Savoy. The Risorgimento was the climax of Italian nationalism, but from another perspective it was also an ideological civil war fought between radicals and moderates deeply divided over the form and purposes of the unified state that all desired.

Cavour the Realist

Charles Albert's valiant war against Austria in 1848 and 1849 had given credibility to the moderate program. Despite his abdication in 1849, the hapless monarch had left his kingdom a constitution that became the symbol of Italian liberal hopes, one that his son, Victor Emmanuel II (1849–1878), refused to rescind despite Austrian pressure. In 1850 the young king appointed to the cabinet Count Camillo Benso di Cavour (1810–1861), a brilliant statesman into whose hands the leadership of the Risorgimento passed.

Although born into the nobility, Cavour was also the epitome of the nineteenth-century businessman. Portly, nearsighted, and a dull orator who spoke French better than Italian, Cavour was nonetheless crafty and steel-

---

*In the Middle Ages the Guelphs were supporters of the papacy against the ambitions of the Holy Roman emperor.

Count Cavour, whose shrewd policies ultimately unified Italy, is depicted here in a photograph taken at the Congress of Paris in 1856. [Mansell Collection]

willed. Above all, he was a master of power politics, unwilling to allow principle to interfere with objectives and capable of outwitting Europe's shrewdest diplomats. With a successful background in agriculture, industry, and banking, he developed an abiding belief in economic liberalism. First as minister of agriculture and commerce in 1850 and then as prime minister from 1852, he modernized Piedmont's economy and forged an alliance of moderate forces within parliament that was responsible for progressive legislation. He understood fully that Piedmont lacked the strength to rid Italy of the Austrians alone, and his policy hinged on securing the support of powerful foreign allies. Nevertheless, Cavour's view of unification was more limited than Mazzini's, for his goal was originally the creation of a large Piedmontese kingdom covering northern Italy but excluding the Papal States and the Bourbon south.

Cavour's first step in the realization of his plan was a masterstroke of political cynicism. Although Piedmont had no apparent interest in the Near East, in 1854 he intervened in the Crimean War on the side of Britain and France, thus securing a place for himself at the Paris peace talks that followed. Cavour not only succeeded in raising the "Italian question" at the conference but also won the admiration of Napoleon III. The French emperor, who in his youth had developed a strong affection for Italy, believed that his sponsorship of the Italian cause would further his own prestige. In July 1858 he and Cavour negotiated the secret Treaty of Plombières. The agreement pledged French military support for a war against Austria, the goal of which would be Piedmont's annexation of Lombardy and Venetia. Victory was to result in the creation of a kingdom of upper Italy and an Italian federation under the presidency of the pope. For its help, France would receive from Piedmont the provinces of Savoy and Nice. Cavour and Napoleon further agreed to manufacture a suitable pretext for war with Austria, and they promised not to make a separate peace until their goals had been reached.

In the tension-filled months that followed, efforts to settle the Italian problem peacefully threatened to wreck Cavour's plans. In April 1859, however, the Austrians played into his hands by issuing an ultimatum demanding that Piedmont demobilize its armies. The French declared war and, taking advantage of Austrian delays, quickly moved into Italy to join their Piedmontese allies. Lombardy was liberated, but as the allies prepared to press into Venetia the unpredictable Louis-Napoleon suddenly announced the conclusion of an armistice at Villafranca with the Austrian emperor, Franz Joseph. It clearly violated Napoleon's agreement with Cavour, for the Austrians were forced only to surrender Lombardy. Nevertheless, Victor Emmanuel accepted the terms, and the outraged Cavour resigned in protest.

Yet all was not lost. During the fighting in Lombardy, moderate nationalists and liberal businessmen secretly worked in cooperation with Cavour to stage a series of revolts that unseated the rulers of the central Italian duchies. Then, in the wake of the armistice of Villafranca, they engineered popular demonstrations in favor of union with Piedmont. Returning to office in January, Cavour suppressed his anger and struck a bargain with Napoleon that permitted the Piedmontese annexation of these territories. Borrowing one of Napoleon's favorite political tactics, Cavour engineered plebiscites to confirm popular enthusiasm for his territorial aggrandisement. Thus by 1860 Piedmont had been considerably enlarged by the addition of Lombardy and the duchies of central Italy. The first step in the unification of Italy had been taken.

The Crisis of Italian Unification

Until the plebiscites in central Italy, the astute Cavour had managed to shape the course of events, but now the initiative was seized by Giuseppe Garibaldi (1807–1882). A hero in the age of power politics, a determined Romantic in the face of Cavour's cynicism, Garibaldi was nevertheless the greatest guerrilla fighter of the century. Although he believed in Mazzini's republican doctrines, he was above all a patriot determined to see Italy free and united. With a death sentence on his head for having taken part in a Mazzinian plot, Garibaldi fled to South America in 1834 and fought against authoritarian gov-

FRANCE

SWITZERLAND

AUSTRIAN EMPIRE

From Austria

From Austria 1866

To France 1860

SAVOY

PIEDMONT

LOMBARDY

Milan

VENETIA

Trieste

Magenta

Villafranca

Turin

Po

PARMA

Solferino

Venice

MODENA

Bologna

OTTOMAN EMPIRE

To France 1860

Genoa

ROMAGNA

THE MARCHES

NICE

Marseilles

Nice

Pisa

Florence

Tiber

ADRIATIC SEA

TUSCANY

KINGDOM OF SARDINIA

CORSICA (FRANCE)

PAPAL STATES 1870

Rome

SARDINIA

Naples

Bari

Taranto

TYRRHENIAN SEA

KINGDOM OF THE TWO SICILIES

Palermo

Straits of Messina

SICILY

MEDITERRANEAN SEA

- Kingdom of Sardinia before 1859
- To kingdom of Sardinia, 1859
- To kingdom of Sardinia, 1860
- To kingdom of Italy, 1866–1870
- × Major battle
- – · – Boundary of kingdom of Italy after unification

0   50   100
Miles

32.2 The Unification of Italy, 1859–1870

ernment in the jungles of Uruguay. He returned to Italy in 1848 to fight along with Charles Albert and then went to Rome to lead the dramatic defense of Mazzini's republic against the French troops sent there by Louis-Napoleon to restore the pope. By 1859, when Garibaldi again commanded a volunteer army against Austria, he was a popular figure with a rapidly growing following.

Garibaldi's vision of unification encompassed the entire Italian peninsula. In 1860 he decided to complete the process begun by Cavour with a daring military expedition against the Kingdom of the Two Sicilies. Cavour not only mistrusted Garibaldi's republican sentiments but also feared that Napoleon III would intervene if Garibaldi attempted to seize Rome. He therefore played a double game, secretly encouraging Garibaldi's 1,000-man army of "Red Shirts" while simultaneously preparing to stop the guerrilla leader with force should he

threaten Rome. Landing in Sicily in May, Garibaldi outmaneuvered the Bourbon armies, recruited additional volunteers among the disaffected peasants, and captured the island. By September he had crossed to the mainland and taken the Neapolitan capital, declaring a provisional dictatorship over the entire Italian south. In the meantime, a worried Cavour had persuaded Napoleon III to agree to the passage of Piedmontese troops through the Papal States in order to protect the pope. Instead, Victor Emmanuel seized all the papal lands except for the area around Rome. In October, as the Risorgimento reached its climax, Victor Emmanuel and Garibaldi met just north of Naples, thus bringing the moderate and the radical forces face to face. Determined to make Italy a nation rather than plunge it into civil war, Garibaldi relinquished his conquests to the king. In March 1861 the Piedmontese sovereign was proclaimed

⊠ Cavour Versus Garibaldi ⊠

Throughout 1860, while Garibaldi's volunteer army seized the island of Sicily and then the mainland portion of the kingdom of Naples, Count Cavour, the Piedmontese premier, tried to prevent Garibaldi from seizing control of the Italian unification movement. In this letter Cavour describes his political calculations and his efforts to stop Garibaldi.

If Garibaldi proceeds to the mainland of southern Italy and captures Naples just as he has already taken Sicily and Palermo, he will become absolute master of the situation. King Victor Emmanuel would lose almost all his prestige in the eyes of Italians. . . .

We would be forced to go along with his plans and help him fight Austria. I am therefore convinced that the king must not receive the crown of Italy from Garibaldi's hands. . . .

I have no illusions about the grave and dangerous decision I am advocating, but I believe it is essential if we are to save the monarchic principle. Better a king of Piedmont should perish in war against Austria than be swamped by the revolution. The dynasty might recover from a defeat in battle, but if dragged through the revolutionary gutter its fate would be . . . sealed.

Although I have made up my mind how to act if Garibaldi reaches Naples, it is nevertheless my first duty to the king and Italy to do everything possible to prevent his success there. My only hope of foiling him is if I can overthrow the Bourbon regime before Garibaldi crosses to the mainland—or at least before he has had time to reach Naples. If the regime falls, I would then take over the government of Naples in the name of order and humanity, and so snatch out of Garibaldi's hands the supreme direction of the Italian movement.

Source: C. B. di Cavour, letter to Costantino Nigra, August 1, 1860, in D. Mack Smith, ed., *Garibaldi* (Englewood Cliffs, N.J.: Prentice Hall, 1969), pp. 44–45.

Victor Emmanuel II, king of Italy. Two months later Cavour died.

The euphoria of the Risorgimento quickly faded as the Italians encountered the problems of nationhood. Indeed, the kingdom was still incomplete—Venetia was not incorporated until the Austro-Prussian War of 1866, and Rome itself was not seized until the Franco-Prussian War in 1870. When it did occur, the annexation of Rome produced deep hostility between the Catholic church and the new state that plagued Italian affairs for the next half century. Regional differences and local loyalties remained strong, and the gap between the developing industrial interests of the north and the depressed agricultural economy of the south widened. A host of vital public policy issues, including illiteracy, disease, and extreme poverty, placed enormous pressure on a national debt already burdened by the costs of the wars of unification. Added to these difficulties was an often corrupt parliamentary regime that remained unresponsive to the needs of the largely unenfranchised poorer classes and a ruling elite bent on making Italy a great power. The challenge for Cavour's successors, then, would be to resolve these problems of national development and move Italy toward political democracy.

Iron and Blood: The Making of the German Empire

In Germany, as in Italy, the Congress of Vienna mandated a restoration designed to prevent national unification as well as to guarantee Austrian preponderance in German affairs. The creation of the German Confederation, with a diet, or parliament, at Frankfurt representing 38 sovereign states, recognized the irreversibility of Bonaparte's destruction of the Holy Roman Empire and his simplification of the German state system. The confederation included small states with only a few hundred square miles of territory, such as the Thuringian principalities, and much larger units such as the kingdom of Bavaria, which comprised more than 10,000 square miles. Religious differences reinforced political divisions, for while northern Germany was Protestant, the predominantly Catholic south tended to regard Austria as a bulwark against Protestant Prussia. In these circumstances, Austria dominated the divided German states.

Nationalism and the German State System

The kingdom of Prussia, with considerably enlarged territories and a formidable army, was the second most powerful state in the German Confederation. Its autocratic and unstable monarch, Frederick William IV (1840–1861), aspired to expand the Hohenzollern position in Germany. Just as Piedmont vied with Austria for mastery in Italy, so Prussian-Austrian rivalry was the heart of the German power struggle after 1815. The stronghold of German nationalism, however, was not the Prussian monarchy, whose motivation was largely one of dynastic power, but the rapidly growing liberal middle class. The Prussian-sponsored *Zollverein* (customs union) that developed after 1818 not only stimulated trade throughout Germany and underscored the economic advantages of unification but also anticipated the so-called *kleindeutsch* ("small German") solution that sought to exclude Austria from German affairs.

By 1848 these middle-class elements hoped that Prussia would provide the leadership to unify Germany and give it a constitutional monarchy. Twice during the revolutions of 1848, however, these expectations were dashed by the military-aristocratic forces that ruled Prussia. In the fall Frederick William, encouraged by the army and reactionary elements in his court, withdrew his promise to allow an elected constituent assembly to draft a liberal constitution. In March 1849, when the Frankfurt assembly elected him emperor of Germany, he rejected the "crown from the gutter," later issuing a more conservative constitution of his own. This royal document provided for a two-chamber parliament, an appointed upper house and a lower house elected by an unequal and indirect system of universal male suffrage. Although the constitution was ambiguous about the role of the lower house (Landtag) in formulating budget laws, it was clear that the king retained extensive authority. Yet Frederick William's efforts to unify Germany failed. In 1850, when he attempted to solicit an imperial crown from his fellow German monarchs, Austria and Russia coerced him to abandon the plan in a humiliating capitulation at Olmütz.

Bismarck and the Liberals

Despite its commercial and industrial primacy, Prussia's repressive domestic policies, together with Frederick William's timidity in foreign affairs, cast doubt on its ability to bring about German unification. These tendencies were reinforced when William, the monarch's brother, became regent in 1858 and then king in 1861. William I (1861–1888) precipitated a constitutional crisis in Prussia that changed the course of German history.

In February 1860, William presented a bill to the Prussian Landtag that proposed to double the size of the regular army and increase compulsory military service from two to three years. Most controversial, perhaps, was the fact that the king, himself a professional soldier, wished to reduce the role and independence of the civilian militia, whose lack of discipline he regarded with contempt. The liberal middle classes—who, because of the elitist nature of the suffrage law, dominated the Landtag—saw these measures as a constitutional challenge, for they wished both to assert the power of parliament over the king and to reduce the influence of the military in Prussian society. As a result, the military bill was eventually withdrawn. When a later version of the same bill was voted down in 1862, William dissolved the Landtag, but the new elections only increased the liberal majority. Torn between abdicating and forcing a showdown with the liberals, the king appointed Count Otto von Bismarck (1815–1898) as his new minister-president.

Bismarck ranks as one of the dominant figures in modern German history. Although a member of the conservative Junker class of aristocratic landowners, he was neither provincial in his outlook nor ideologically wedded to the past. He cut an imposing figure, stubborn, fiercely combative, and oblivious to the constraints of tradition and constitutional theory. Bismarck was also a master political strategist. His early career had given him wide experience in diplomacy, first as a Prussian delegate to the Frankfurt Diet and then as ambassador in St. Petersburg and in Paris. Though he disdained the parliamentary demands of the liberals, he recognized that they had embraced nationalism and that Prussia needed their industrial skills and wealth. Bismarck's view of unification was at first limited—the imposition of Prussian mastery over largely Protestant northern Germany, a goal he eventually came to believe would require the expulsion of Austria from the German state system.

For Bismarck, the German question and the conflict with the Landtag were linked, for a strong army was needed to deal with Austria. When he found that compromise with the liberals over military reform was impossible, he reorganized the army with funds earmarked for other purposes. The liberals denounced Bismarck's

Bismarck, who forged the modern German state, is shown in 1871, the year the new empire was proclaimed. [Culver Pictures]

German unification would be achieved, for just as Cavour's actions intensified the ideological struggle between Italian moderates and radicals, so Bismarck polarized the German unification movement between liberals and the advocates of power politics.

The Showdown with Austria

Bismarck's determination to extend Prussian authority over northern Germany made a military confrontation with Austria all but inevitable. The showdown evolved between 1863 and 1866 and resulted from a situation involving Schleswig and Holstein, two northern duchies controlled by the king of Denmark although not an actual part of his kingdom. Holstein, inhabited almost entirely by Germans, was part of the confederation, whereas Schleswig's mixed population of Danes and Germans fought bitterly over the issue of membership. When Denmark moved to annex Schleswig in 1863, Bismarck persuaded the Austrians to join Prussia in what proved to be a short and successful war to reclaim the two provinces. The Peace of Vienna that ended the war against Denmark provided that Austria and Prussia would administer the provinces jointly. Discussion as to their future resulted in a deadlock when the Austrians insisted that the provinces become a single state ruled by a German prince, while Bismarck demanded extensive commercial rights that would have made them virtual Prussian provinces. A temporary agreement was established in 1865 according to which Holstein would be run by Austria and Schleswig by Prussia. This awkward arrangement led to continued quarrels between the two allies and eventually gave Bismarck the excuse to provoke a war with Austria.

Like Cavour, Bismarck understood that *Realpolitik* required careful diplomatic preparation among the other European powers. Prussia needed assurance that other nations would not come to Austria's assistance. Because he had offered to help Russia put down a Polish uprising in 1863, Bismarck was fairly certain that Tsar Alexander II would not interfere, but Napoleon III was the unknown element. In the fall of 1865 Bismarck and Napoleon held a secret meeting reminiscent of the Plombières encounter between Napoleon and Cavour. Bismarck secured Napoleon's promise of neutrality in the event of an Austro-Prussian war with vague promises of territorial compensation for France along the Rhine. The following year he negotiated an alliance with Italy that promised Italian military assistance in return for the Austrian-held province of Venetia. After years of preparation, the war came suddenly. On June 1, 1866, the Prussians sent troops into Holstein in protest over what Bismarck claimed was an Austrian violation of their agreement. In response, the Austrians persuaded the German Confederation to vote military action against Prussia. Bis-

high-handed tactics, and the issue was further complicated by public criticism from Frederick, the heir to the throne, who had been influenced by his liberal-thinking wife, Victoria (1840–1901), the oldest daughter of Britain's Queen Victoria and Prince Albert. Victoria envisioned a unified Germany ruled not by the military but by the best traditions of German culture. Her role in the constitutional crisis resulted in her exclusion from public life for many years.

Not only was Bismarck oblivious to the protests of the liberal opposition, but he lectured them on *Realpolitik*. In blunt speeches before the Landtag, he declared that only a policy of "iron and blood" would yield results, that power rather than principle determined the outcome of conflict, and that results justified means. A vigorous program in foreign affairs, he believed, would win over many liberals and critics of his violation of constitutional procedure. Moreover, since the defeats of 1848, the German intellectuals had either emigrated or abandoned politics. Bismarck thus set the terms on which

◉ Bismarck on Power Politics ◉

On September 30, 1862, Bismarck made the following remarks before the Prussian Landtag in order to secure approval of the military reorganization bill proposed by King William I. His words were the quintessential statement on the nature of power politics.

While it is clear that we cannot avoid complications in Germany, we do not seek them. Germany does not look to Prussia's liberalism but to her power. Because the southern states of Germany—Bavaria, Württemberg, and Baden—would like to indulge in liberalism, Prussia's role will not be assigned to them! Prussia must gather her forces and hold them in reserve for the right moment, which we have already missed several times. Since the Treaty of Vienna, our borders have not been designed to ensure a healthy body politic. Not by speeches and majorities will the great questions of the day be decided—that was the mistake of 1848 and 1849—but by iron and blood.

Source: H. Kohl, ed., *Die politischen Reden des Fürsten Bismarck* (Stuttgart: Cotta, 1892–1905). Translated by P. Cannistraro.

marck's answer was to declare the confederation dissolved and order Prussia's armies into action.

The Austro-Prussian War was important for several reasons. Bismarck tried to make the point that the "national development of Germany" was at stake, although in truth Prussian aggression was the real issue. After seven weeks of fighting, Austria was defeated at Königgratz in Bohemia. The Prussian victory was due to the ability to deploy troops rapidly by railroad, the use of a new breech-loading gun, and the brilliant strategist Count Helmuth von Moltke. The king's controversial military reorganization bill had proved itself. Although the war was fought against the other states of the German Confederation as well as Austria, the latter had been poorly prepared and had to fight on both the German and the Italian fronts. By imposing deliberately moderate peace terms on Austria in the Treaty of Prague (August 1866), Bismarck demonstrated once again his mastery of *Realpolitik*. No reparations were extracted from Austria, and a separate agreement forced it only to cede Venetia to the Italians. Bismarck's real goal was achieved by the dissolution of the confederation and Austria's withdrawal from German affairs. The Austrians also had to recognize Prussia's annexation of Schleswig-Holstein and a number of German states in the north. While the southern Catholic states remained independent, they had to pay indemnities and sign military alliances forcing them to fight on Prussia's side in any future war.

After the war, Bismarck presided over the creation of the North German Confederation. Dominated by Prussia, it included all German states north of the river Main.

A constitution made the king of Prussia its president and Bismarck its chancellor. Local affairs remained in the hands of each state, but foreign policy and military authority were controlled by the central government. The parliament of the North German Confederation consisted of the Bundesrat, or upper house, representing each of the states, and a Reichstag, or lower house, elected by universal male suffrage. This system, which later provided the model for the constitution of united Germany, reflected the wide powers of the Prussian king and limited such parliamentary principles as ministerial responsibility. But the liberalized franchise created the sense that wide strata of the people, not just the middle class, now had a stake in Germany's future.

The Franco-Prussian War and the Forging of German Unification

It is difficult to say just how long Bismarck intended the North German Confederation to remain in place. As a Prussian rather than a German nationalist, his vision of unification may well have remained limited despite the events of 1866. But just as Garibaldi had forced Cavour to broaden his view of Italian unification in 1860, so now the diplomatic blunders of Napoleon III pushed Bismarck to complete the process he had begun.

Austria's defeat at the hands of Prussia shocked Napoleon, who had underestimated Prussian power. The suddenness of the Austrian collapse prevented him from intervening, and Prussia's victory had been so complete that Bismarck did not grant the territorial rewards that he had vaguely promised Napoleon. Napoleon's failure to extract concessions from Bismarck, compounded by the fiasco in Mexico, stimulated the emperor's opponents at home, who argued that the war represented a severe blow to French prestige. Napoleon became convinced that the consolidation of German strength on France's borders had to be stopped. For his part, Bismarck came to realize that a war with France would inflame German nationalism and push the southern states, where business circles already favored unification, into a united Germany.

Friction between the two countries mounted steadily, with both Napoleon and Bismarck contributing to the tension. The pretext for war arose from a dispute over whether a German prince related to William I would become king of Spain. The immediate cause for the outbreak of the Franco-Prussian War was the so-called Ems dispatch. When William I agreed to withdraw his support of the Hohenzollern candidate, Napoleon demanded that the Prussian king apologize and promise not to raise the Hohenzollern candidacy again. Meeting with the French ambassador at Ems in July 1870, the Prussian ruler refused to give such a promise and telegraphed the details of the talk to Berlin. Bismarck had the dispatch published in the press after changing the wording to create the impression that William had insulted the French. Newspapers in Paris and Berlin sen-sationalized the telegram and enraged public opinion. On July 19 the French declared war.

As in the case of the struggle with Austria four years earlier, the swiftness of the Franco-Prussian War and the superiority of Prussia's military forces stunned Europe. Thanks to Bismarck's lenient treatment of Austria in 1866, it remained neutral, as did the other great powers; moreover, the military treaties he had forced on the southern German states brought them into the war on the side of Prussia, so that the war became, at least in name, a "national" one. On September 1 the Prussian armies captured Napoleon III along with more than 100,000 French soldiers at Sedan. The news of Napoleon's surrender was followed a few days later in Paris by the proclamation of a republic. The republican forces continued to fight for five additional months despite the siege of the capital and the outbreak of an uprising in March known as the Paris Commune. While Paris held out against starvation and the violence sparked by the Commune, Bismarck consolidated Germany. On January 18, 1871, in the Hall of Mirrors in the palace of Versailles, William I was proclaimed German emperor, and all of Germany was at last unified under a political system virtually identical to the one that had governed the North German Confederation.

At the end of the month the French republic capitulated, and in February a National Assembly was elected and the liberal monarchist Adolphe Thiers chosen as

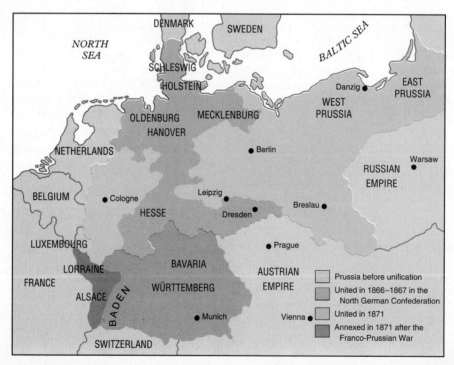

32.3 The Unification of Germany, 1866–1871

chief executive. Thiers, who made peace with the Germans, had little room to negotiate, for Bismarck was in no mood to be generous. The peace of Frankfurt, signed on May 10, was harsh—France had to pay an indemnity of 5 billion francs and accept German occupation until it was paid. Most distressing to the French, however, was the loss of Alsace and most of Lorraine to Germany. These provinces, which contained iron deposits and a prosperous textile industry, were inhabited by German-speaking people who preferred the French to the Prussians, and their annexation remained for the next half century a source of bitterness between Germany and France.

The Franco-Prussian War had profound repercussions. Along with the unification of Germany came the victory of Bismarck's political strategy, which had wedded German nationalism to the conservative-aristocratic forces that ruled Prussia and cowed the liberals into abandoning their opposition in the face of unification. The completion of Italian territorial unity was an unexpected by-product of the Franco-Prussian War, for when Napoleon III brought home the troops stationed in Rome to protect the pope, King Victor Emmanuel III seized the city and made it the capital of Italy. Most immediately the war led to the collapse of Napoleon's Second Empire. Perhaps its most far-reaching result was the shift in the balance of power. By 1871 Italy was demanding recognition as a great power, and the collapse of Austria and France demonstrated that Germany had emerged as the most powerful European state. The Treaty of Frankfurt confirmed the end of the Concert of Europe created by the Vienna peace settlement in 1815, for not only had Austria and France been defeated by the new German colossus, but Britain and Russia had remained aloof from the wars. Napoleon III, Cavour, and Bismarck, each in his own way an embodiment of the nationalist doctrines that dominated the age, had wrought profound changes in the structure of the European state system.

Eastern Europe and the Ottomans

Austria's role in Italian and German affairs after 1815 was symptomatic of its status as a multiethnic empire in an age of rising nationalism. This last dynastic state, ruled by the Habsburgs since the Middle Ages, survived the waves of Romantic nationalism of the 1820s and 1830s, as well as the upheavals of 1848, but its existence was seriously challenged in midcentury as its many nationalities clamored for independence. Twelve million Germans controlled political power and enjoyed special sta-

tus in a state that reached 50 million by 1914 and included 24 million Slavs to the south, 10 million Magyars and 4 million Romanians to the east, as well as Czechs, Slovaks, Poles, Croats, Serbs, Italians, and a variety of other ethnic groups. The Habsburgs made a number of attempts to bring the forces of nationalism under control, but neither reforms, the granting of limited provincial autonomy in 1859, nor the new constitution of 1861 was effective.

The Austro-Prussian War of 1866 demonstrated just how divided and weak the Austrian Empire was, and defeat provoked still one more effort at reform. After difficult negotiations, Emperor Franz Joseph reached a compromise (*Ausgleich*) with Hungarian leaders. The new constitution created the Dual Monarchy, in which Franz Joseph was both king of Hungary and emperor of Austria. Foreign affairs, finance, and military matters were conducted by common ministers, but otherwise the two parts of the monarchy were autonomous, each with its own constitution, official language, and parliament.

The *Ausgleich* did not, of course, eliminate the serious problems facing the empire but merely enabled the Hungarians to share with the Germans in its rule. The other nationality groups continued to demand their freedom. Some industry and a middle class thrived in Bohemia and the area surrounding Vienna, and serfdom had been abolished in 1848. However, in both halves of the Dual Monarchy most inhabitants were landless, backward peasants burdened by conservative landowners and heavy taxes. Despite the ancient lineage of the Habsburgs and the importance of its strategic position in Europe, the Dual Monarchy remained an anachronism in a Europe rapidly dividing along national lines.

VIENNA IN THE AGE OF FRANZ JOSEPH

As the capital of Austria, Vienna was a microcosm of the empire, reflecting its strengths and weaknesses, its brilliance and its contradictions. Since 1278, when the Habsburgs selected the town on the banks of the Danube for their capital, the city had been a center of bureaucracy and aristocratic splendor. Vienna grew rapidly in the modern period, and by the opening of the nineteenth century it contained more than a quarter of a million people. Yet although the Habsburg capital was the government center for a vast multiethnic empire, it remained an essentially German city in language and culture.

Because its economy was built around the court and the government, Vienna had little industry or industrial proletariat until the mid-nineteenth century. It collected and spent tax revenues, and its economic life centered on banking, crafts, and the production of luxury goods, including silk and porcelain. Similarly, the social structure of the city included a wealthy aristocracy, a variety of civil servants, artisans and shopkeepers, a small but prosperous business class, and workers. With the coming of the Industrial Revolution to Vienna in the 1830s and 1840s, tens of thousands of peasants streamed into the city, and by the eve of the revolutions of 1848 its population had increased to 400,000.

As long as Austria remained a great European power, Vienna was a center of European diplomacy, a role it played never more splendidly than as host of the great peace settlement following the Napoleonic wars. In the generation before the revolutions of 1848, the city of Metternich became the capital of the European conservative order, crowded with diplomats, reactionary politicians, and police agents bent on uncovering revolutionaries. Metternich's office, and therefore the nerve center of the bureaucracy, was housed in the Ballhaus chancery, built in the early eighteenth century, but the true grandeur of the Habsburg empire was displayed in the rich array of luxurious royal palaces. Emperor Franz Joseph, who died in 1916 after 68 years on the throne, was installed in the vast Hofburg Palace and moved in the summer months to the ornate Schönbrunn Palace. The important aristocratic families of the realm built lavish residences, of which the most remarkable was the Belvedere, the summer palace of Prince Eugène of Savoy. While the bulk of the population lived in middle-class housing and ugly tenements, much of the European nobility that visited Vienna saw only the splendors of the ruling class. In the 1860s Vienna's beauty was enhanced still further by the demolition of the city's medieval wall and the building of the Ringstrasse, a majestic tree-lined boulevard encircling the city that rivaled Haussmann's work in Paris.

Vienna's importance to Western culture was unequaled in the sphere of music. The city nurtured the greatest concentration of musical brilliance in modern times, for the patronage of the Habsburgs and the nobility attracted the musical giants of Europe—Mozart and Haydn, Beethoven, Schubert and Schumann, Johann and Richard Strauss, Brahms and Mahler. Although the second half of the nineteenth century was a period of crisis and decline for the Habsburg empire, its capital thrived as a refined city basking in sentimentality. The light operatic themes of Franz Lehar's *Merry Widow* (1905), together with the late Romantic lushness of the music of Anton Bruckner and Gustav Mahler, had wide popular appeal. The aging Emperor Franz Joseph, who stood stiffly in uniform braced by his sword while the imperial court danced to the waltzes of Johann Strauss, was the symbol of a fragile and once great empire.

In this time of unabashed nostalgia, Vienna also gave birth to avant-garde movements that challenged the values of the past. Richard Strauss' *Der Rosenkavalier* (1911) represented the swan song of Romantic opera in the classical style—a young composer, Arnold Schönberg, had already broken from the Western tradition of tonality, and two young followers, Alban Berg and Anton Webern, were pushing the revolution in music even further by abandoning the standard Western conception of key. Painters and writers were experimenting with new forms of expression that would later lead to the movement in the arts known as the Vienna Secession. But it was perhaps in the study of a Viennese physician named Sigmund Freud that the most profound transformation was taking place. Freud's investigations suggested that deep-rooted instincts struggled for release and dominance within the human psyche, and the popularization of his work shattered nineteenth-century rationalism.

Vienna also saw the emergence of political movements that challenged the roots of European liberalism, among them the Christian Socialist party of Karl Lüger and the Social Democratic party led by Victor Adler. But whereas the Social Democrats appealed to the city's growing industrial working class, Christian Socialist membership came largely from the petite bourgeoisie. Lüger and his followers identified closely with a growing anti-Semitic sentiment in the city. Lüger was mayor of the city when, in 1907, a teenage German first came to Vienna to study painting. In Vienna the young man discovered anti-Semitism and came to loathe the mixing of nationalities that he saw in the capital. His name was Adolf Hitler.

Russia Between Reaction and Reform

The dilemmas facing a multiethnic empire such as Austria were perhaps more serious still in Russia, where the problems of national minorities were compounded by the vast size of its territory and the complexity of its population. Stretching thousands of miles across two continents, the peoples of the Russian empire included a wide diversity of Europeans and Asians, and for centuries Russia struggled unsuccessfully to define its national identity between the pulls of two civilizations.

Despite its complexity, the social structure of Russia's population was rigidly divided between a small and highly privileged nobility and a huge, impoverished peasant population. Perhaps 95 percent of Russian subjects fell into the peasant category, the great majority of them serfs with no civil rights or property who owed heavy dues and services to the landowning masters. The wealthy nobility owned almost all the land and were exempt from taxes and military service. Because Russia's economy was predominantly agricultural throughout most of the nineteenth century, a small middle class existed only in the larger cities.

In an age when autocracy was disappearing in Europe, the Russian tsar remained an absolute monarch. His will was law, and only the poverty, backwardness, and ineffective bureaucracy of imperial Russia limited his authority. Because no legitimate forms of protest existed, conspiracy and local insurrection were frequent. When faced with such threats, the Romanov dynasty swung between extremes of enlightened reform and brutal repression.

Tsar Alexander I (1801–1825), who recognized that the political and social structure of the empire needed to be modernized, had experimented with constitutionalism and federalism before reverting to autocracy. His brother, Nicholas I (1825–1855), was so obsessed by the fear of revolution that he appointed secret police to hunt down subversives. Nicholas proclaimed the principles of "autocracy, Orthodoxy, and nationalism," by which he meant obedience to the Romanov dynasty, adherence to the Russian Orthodox church, and the advancement of Russian national interests. Censorship and restrictions on intellectual life were combined with the exile of political prisoners to Siberia.

The tsar also ordered a program of Russification of ethnic minorities and supported the Slavophiles, who believed that Russia should live according to its traditional Slavic values in an agrarian society based on Orthodoxy, mysticism, and despotism. Opposed to this position were the Westerners, who argued that Russia should modernize by adopting the European model of industrial society built on rationalism. This debate split the intelligentsia, Russian intellectuals who wanted to achieve political goals.

Alexander II and the Dilemma of Russian Reform

The great issues confronting Russian society in the mid-nineteenth century came to a head after Russia's defeat in the Crimean War. The crisis began when Russia and Turkey went to war in 1853 over the Balkan territories of Moldavia and Wallachia. The next year Britain and France, concerned over Russian attempts to control the Christian holy places in Jerusalem and Palestine and to expand into the eastern Mediterranean, came to the aid of the Turks by invading Russia's Crimean peninsula in the Black Sea. Eventually Piedmont and Austria also sided against Russia, thus involving most of the European powers in a military conflict for the first time since the Congress of Vienna. The Crimean War ended in 1856 with Russia's defeat on the battlefield and diplomatic losses at the Paris peace conference.

Nicholas I died during the war. Like many other Russians, his more liberal son, Alexander II (1855–1881), realized that the Crimean disaster was due in part to the country's military and industrial backwardness, and he at last gave in to demands for reform. In 1861 he issued an imperial edict that emancipated more than 22 million serfs and gave them communal title to a portion of the land on which they worked. A system of local government was begun at the level of the village commune (*mir*), which held the land in common. District councils administered the courts and collected taxes, while indirectly elected provincial councils (*zemstvos*) acted as forums for open discussion of political and social issues and provided elementary education. But the emancipated serfs were forced to compensate their former lords, and their land parcels were generally too small for profitable cultivation. The emancipation edict was thus a step forward in relative terms only, for most of the former serfs quickly fell into debt and wound up as agricultural laborers on the estates of their former masters. Moreover, Alexander began to doubt the wisdom of some of his measures after an assassination attempt in 1866, and in the mid-1870s he reimposed censorship on the press and the universities and curtailed freedom of debate in the *zemstvos*.

The new wave of repression sparked widespread discontent. Socialists such as Alexander Herzen (1812–1870) inspired many of the radical intelligentsia to live in the small villages in an attempt to raise peasant political consciousness. But as these so-called *Narodniki* (from the Russian word *narod*, "people") became disillusioned by the obstacles they faced, many began to proclaim themselves "nihilists," who believed in nothing. In the face of Alexander's return to repression, some of the nihilists came under the influence of the anarchist Mikhail Bakunin (1814–1876), who preached the destruction of the government through "propaganda of the deed," by which he meant individual acts of violence. In 1881 Alexander II was assassinated by such a terrorist act.

Russia descended into deep reaction during the reigns of Alexander III (1881–1894) and his son, Nicholas II (1894–1917). The only positive developments were the economic reforms carried out in the 1890s by Count Sergei Witte (1849–1915), a tough finance minister bent on modernizing the Russian economy along Western lines. Under Witte's leadership, government initiative rather than private capital stimulated industrialization. Until reactionary agrarian interests forced his dismissal in 1903, Witte succeeded in attracting Western investments by putting Russia on the gold standard, launching the trans-Siberian railroad, and stimulating industry. The French, eager for an alliance with Russia, poured capital into the empire. According to one estimate, industrial production doubled in a decade. Yet Witte's programs did not begin to come to grips

◉ Tsarist Russia on the Edge of Revolution ◉

In 1881 Tsar Alexander II was assassinated by an anarchist group known as the "Will of the People." In March that same year the terrorist organization addressed an open letter to the new tsar, Alexander III, of which the following is an excerpt.

A dispassionate glance at the grievous decade through which we have just passed will enable us to forecast accurately the future progress of the revolutionary movement, provided the policy of the government does not change. The movement will continue to grow and extend; deeds of a terroristic nature will increase in frequency and intensity. Meanwhile the number of the discontented in the country will grow larger and larger; confidence in the government, on the part of the people, will decline; and the idea of revolution—of its possibility and inevitability—will establish itself in Russia more and more firmly. A terrible explosion, a bloody chaos, a revolutionary earthquake throughout Russia, will complete the destruction of the order of things. Do not mistake this for a mere phrase. We understand better than anyone else can how lamentable is the waste of so much talent and energy—the loss, in bloody skirmishes and in the work of destruction, of so much strength which, under other conditions, might have been expended in creative labor and in the development of the intelligence, the welfare, and the civil life of the Russian people. . . .

These are the reasons why the Russian government exerts no moral influence and has no support among the people. These are the reasons why Russia brings forth so many revolutionists. These are the reasons why even such a deed as killing a Tsar excites in the minds of a majority of the people only gladness and sympathy. Yes your Majesty! Do not be deceived by the reports of flatterers and sycophants; Tsaricide is popular in Russia.

Source: J. H. Robinson and C. Beard, eds., *Readings in Modern European History*, vol. 2 (Boston: Ginn, 1909), pp. 364–366.

with the monumental social and political problems the country faced.

The Dissolution of the Ottoman Empire

By the start of the nineteenth century, the Ottoman Empire still ruled an estimated 40 million people, but corruption and administrative chaos were rife and, as in the Austrian Empire it bordered, the nationalist aspirations of its subject populations were already threatening to tear it apart. Revolts by Serbs and Greeks were followed later in the century by Bulgarian and Romanian uprisings, while some of the sultan's ambitious regional commanders, such as Muhammad Ali, governor of Egypt, pursued independent policies. The Western view of the Ottoman Empire was summed up by Tsar Nicholas I, who during a state visit to England in 1844 referred to it as a "dying man."

While nationalist movements challenged the unity of the Ottoman Empire, the great powers posed a more serious threat to its existence. By 1830 the Russians had occupied the Danubian principalities of Moldavia and Wallachia, the French had seized Algiers, and with the help of foreign intervention the Greeks had won their independence. As the internal decay of the Turkish system accelerated and the territorial ambitions of the European states grew, the so-called eastern question emerged. Although on one level it involved the interaction between the Ottoman Empire and the great powers, the eastern question may more clearly be understood as the conflict among the great powers over the future of the sultan's domains. One major complication arose from the growing competition between Austria and Russia for predominance in the Balkans; another was due to the centuries-old Russian ambition to gain control over the Turkish Straits in order to have free access from the Black Sea into the Mediterranean. The fate of the Ottoman possessions in the Middle East interested both Britain and France, for the British regarded the area as the gateway to India and the French were concerned over the protection of Christian holy places. Similarly, in North Africa the French were intent on expanding their foothold in Algiers into Morocco and Tunisia at the same time that the British consolidated their interest in Egypt following the completion of the Suez Canal.

The web of competing interests that comprised the eastern question made the Ottoman Empire a sensitive issue in European diplomacy. The Crimean War and the Paris peace conference of 1856 confirmed the neutrality of the Black Sea, ended the Russian occupation of Moldavia and Wallachia—the provinces were merged into the kingdom of Romania a few years later—and left the protection of the Christian populations of the Middle East to the sultan. But if the peace conference basically preserved the Ottoman Empire, succeeding events speeded its disintegration. In 1875 revolts against Turkish rule in Bosnia led to a declaration of war against Istanbul by the semiautonomous states of Serbia and Montenegro, which were eventually assisted by Russia. When the resulting Treaty of San Stefano (1878) threatened to shift the balance of power in the Balkans in favor of Russia, Austria and Britain became alarmed. That summer, therefore, the Russians were forced to the conference table at the Congress of Berlin. Despite Bismarck's claim that he would act as an "honest broker" at the conference, Russian gains from the Treaty of San Stefano were severely reduced. Serbia, Montenegro, and a new state, Bulgaria, were recognized as fully in-

Abdul Hamid II, a cruel despot, ruled the Ottoman Empire until the Young Turks deposed him in 1909. [Bettmann Archive]

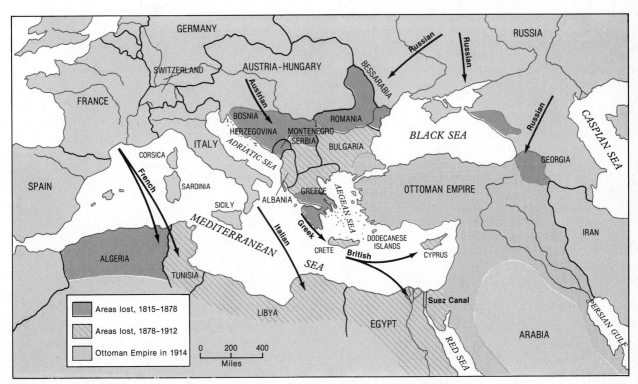

32.4 The Decline of the Ottoman Empire to 1914

dependent from Turkish rule, while the provinces of Bosnia and Herzegovina were placed under Austrian administration. The Ottoman Empire lost half of its European territory. During the next 30 years European powers would strip Turkey of its remaining possessions in North Africa.

The dismemberment of the Ottoman Empire aroused discontent among the sultan's younger, Western-educated subjects and in the army, where opposition to the inefficient rule of the sultans was growing. In 1856 a far-reaching reform edict, the *Hatt-i Humayun*, established a progressive political structure for the empire, but a new sultan, Abdul Hamid II (1876–1909)—known for his brutal tyranny as "Abdul the Damned"—crushed the hopes of the reformers. After issuing a new constitution, Abdul Hamid reimposed tyranny. In the Ottoman Empire, as in Russia, the weight of centuries of repression seemed to move toward revolution.

The Jewish Question and the Birth of Zionism

The Enlightenment had significantly advanced the theoretical equality and the actual emancipation of the Jews, and during the nineteenth century the remaining legal restrictions on them were eliminated in virtually every major country of Europe, although quasi-official sanctions such as educational and professional quotas remained. Despite the fact that religious and social prejudices against them were still deeply rooted in Europe, most Jewish populations were being assimilated into Europe's social, economic, and cultural life.

In an age of self-conscious nationalism, however, the Jewish question grew increasingly complicated. The development of "scientific" theories of race in the late nineteenth century and the resulting merger of nationalism and racism stimulated anti-Semitic discussion. In countries where Catholic and Christian influence blended with political conservatism, anti-Semitism emerged as a political movement with widespread appeal. In Germany, Adolf Stöcker's Christian Socialist Workingman's Union, the Conservative party, and even an Anti-Semitic League advocated an end to Jewish influence in national life, and in 1882 an international anti-Semitic congress was held in Dresden. In France, Edouard Drumont's book *La France juive* (1886) inflamed popular attitudes, and the shocking Dreyfus affair revealed the depth of anti-Semitic sentiment. In the Dual Monarchy, the Christian Socialist party elected Karl Lüger mayor of Vienna on a distinctly anti-Semitic platform.

It was in Russia, where the partitions of Poland in the late eighteenth century had made millions of Jews subjects of the tsar, that systematic repression became state policy. Anti-Semitic measures coincided with the reactionary policies of Alexander I and Nicholas I, and in the wake of the assassination of Alexander II in 1881, violent anti-Semitic campaigns, or pogroms (*pogrom* is Russian for "devastation"), were unleashed, often with official connivance, as Jews were killed and beaten and their homes and shops burned and looted. The infamous May Laws of 1882 provided the basis for the expulsion of Jews from villages and rural centers outside Poland, and even fiercer pogroms broke out in 1902 and 1903. In the period from 1881 to 1910, millions of Russian Jews fled, most of them to the United States.

As a reaction to these persecutions and a defense against the assimilation and secularization of Jewish life, the end of the century saw the development of an organized movement of Jewish nationalism called Zionism. Advocates of Zionism argued that Jews would never find justice and equality until they returned to their biblical homeland and formed their own national state. Rabbi Zevi-Hirsch Kalischer and a number of other Jewish thinkers had already proposed the establishment of a homeland in Palestine, and in 1869 an agricultural colony named Mikveh Yisrael ("Hope of Israel") was founded there. In 1882 Leo Pinsker, a Russian Jewish physician, published an influential pamphlet, *Autoemancipation*, advocating a similar program.

❦
THEODOR HERZL AND THE QUEST FOR A JEWISH HOMELAND

The founder of modern political Zionism was Theodor Herzl (1860–1904). Against overwhelming odds, and at times almost singlehandedly, Herzl set in motion the movement that years after his death resulted in the establishment of the state of Israel.

Herzl was born in Budapest to a merchant family of assimilated Jews. After taking a law degree from the University of Vienna, he turned to writing, immersing himself in the world of sentimental bourgeois culture that characterized the Austrian capital in the 1880s. Although he wrote successful plays, journalism was Herzl's real talent, and he made an international reputation as foreign correspondent for the prestigious *Neue Freie Presse*. A handsome man with a Romantic, narcissistic personality, he moved in literary and aristocratic circles. But in 1891 his Viennese paper sent Herzl to Paris, where his life took a sudden and dramatic turn. In Paris, Herzl discovered his identity as a Jew. France was then in the throes of the Dreyfus scandal, and Herzl witnessed the anti-Semitic frenzy firsthand. Thereafter, Jewish issues began to preoccupy him. The result was his famous pamphlet, drafted in a few intense months in late 1895 and

◉ On Anti-Semitism ◉

The reemergence of anti-Semitism assumed new and more virulent forms in the late nineteenth century and led Jewish leaders such as Theodor Herzl and his friend Max Nordau to found the Zionist movement. Here are two moving statements by them on the nature of anti-Semitism.

Stunned by the hailstorm of anti-Semitic accusations, the Jews forget who they are and often imagine that they are the physical and spiritual horrors which their deadly enemies represent them to be. The Jew is often heard to murmur that he must learn from the enemy and try to remedy the faults ascribed to him. He forgets, however, that the anti-Semitic accusations are meaningless, because they are not a criticism of facts which exist, but are the effects of a psychological law according to which children, wild men, and malevolent fools make the persons and things they hate responsible for their sufferings.

I believe that I understand anti-Semitism, which is really a highly complex movement. I consider it from a Jewish standpoint, yet without fear or hatred. I believe that I can see what elements there are in it of vulgar sport, of common trade jealousy, of inherited prejudice, of religious intolerance, and also of pretended self-defense. I think the Jewish question is no more a social than a religious one, notwithstanding that it sometimes takes these and other forms. It is a national question which can only be solved by making it a political world-question to be discussed and controlled by the civilized nations of the world in council.

    We are a people—One people.

Sources: M. Nordau, speech to the First Zionist Congress, 1897, in A. Hertzberg, ed., *The Zionist Idea* (Garden City, N.Y.: Doubleday, 1959), p. 241; T. Herzl, *The Jewish State: An Attempt at a Modern Solution of the Jewish Question* (New York: Maccabaean Publishing Co., 1904), pp. 4–5.

published the following year as *Der Judenstaat* (*The Jewish State*).

Written in a powerful, crisp style, *The Jewish State* was a radical analysis of the Jewish question. Herzl argued that although many Jews had attempted to assimilate into European society, anti-Semitism had made this impossible. "I consider the Jewish question," he wrote, "neither a social nor a religious one, even though it sometimes takes these and other forms. It is a national question." His solution, therefore, was that Jews all over the world should organize to obtain a land of their own. In his mind, Palestine was the natural site for a Jewish state. But unlike earlier leaders, he insisted that Palestine should be secured not through unofficial immigration and infiltration but rather through an international charter.

Herzl threw himself into the task. Sacrificing his marriage, his wealth, and eventually his health, he spent the rest of his life in a tireless campaign to convince his fellow Jews and to secure the support of world opinion. His efforts resulted in the establishment of the World Zionist Organization. In 1897 he presided over the First Zionist Congress, in Basel, Switzerland, which proclaimed that "Zionism seeks to establish for the Jewish people a publicly recognized, legally secured home in Palestine" and to strengthen "Jewish self-awareness and national consciousness." By 1901 there were local Zionist organizations throughout the world, including 1,034 in Russia and 135 in the United States, and branches as far afield as New Zealand, Chile, and India. Herzl gained the help of influential Jewish leaders and met with heads of state, including Kaiser William II and the Turkish sultan, in efforts to realize the Basel program. In 1903 the British government offered part of its East African possessions as the basis for a Jewish state. Through the work of Herzl's successor, Chaim Weizmann (1874–1952), and the support of the British statesman Arthur Balfour, the British government became increasingly sympathetic to the Zionist cause, but not until World War I did it support a Jewish homeland in Palestine.

Herzl's program provoked great controversy, even within the ranks of the Zionist movement. Some biographers have portrayed him as a man with a messianic complex—he demanded blind obedience from his fol-

The founder of the modern Zionist movement, Theodore Herzl, was driven by the revival of anti-Semitism in the late nineteenth century as well as by the centuries-old aspirations of Jews for a homeland in Palestine. [Granger Collection]

lowers, and everywhere he traveled, especially in eastern Europe and Russia, throngs of poor Jews greeted him with adulation. His argument that assimilation had failed suggested to many that he despaired of liberalism, yet his vision of the new Jewish state was so grounded in tolerance and progressive ideals that it often provoked resentment from cultural Zionists who saw nothing specifically Jewish about it. Similarly, he failed both to understand the importance of socialism within the Zionist ranks and to anticipate the clash between Jews and Arabs that would result from the occupation of Palestine. Yet his methods yielded results, and he galvanized millions of Jews the world over. His despondency over the failure of assimilation, together with his warnings about the dangers of anti-Semitism, gave an urgency to his search for a solution to the Jewish question. Some of his critics charged that he was obsessed by the Zionist program, but his forebodings about the fate of Europe's Jews would prove tragically prophetic.

The Struggle for National Unity: The United States and Latin America

The struggle for national identity in the nineteenth century was by no means limited to Europe, and similar developments were occurring as far away as China and Japan. Perhaps the closest parallels were to be found in newly independent Latin America and the United States, for the governments there had been set up by people who considered themselves European in culture and values and who were inspired by the same Enlightenment principles that nourished the French Revolution.

Even after the American union had adopted its constitution in 1787, the United States continued to wrestle with ideological issues concerning the nature of its democracy. Indeed, the struggle between the Federalists, who represented the conservative northern landowners and the commercial classes, and the southern landowner Democratic-Republicans, who championed the small yeoman farmers of the young republic, was not unlike the European conflict between conservatism and liberalism. The passage of the Bill of Rights in 1791 and the subsequent election of Thomas Jefferson (1801–1809) as president signaled the rejection of a powerful central government dominated by privilege and wealth, a tendency later confirmed in the democratic principles of Andrew Jackson (1829–1837).

The advance of democratic attitudes in the United States went hand and hand with its territorial expansion. In less than half a century huge tracts of land, each larger than most European countries, were added to the United States. The Louisiana Purchase in 1803, the settlement of the old northwestern territories, and the conquest of Texas and California in the Mexican-American War all fulfilled what Americans came to call their "manifest destiny," an attitude first expressed by the Russians in their expansion across Siberia. As more settlers pushed westward into the frontier territories, the pioneer values of hard work, individual worth, and self-reliance were deemed more valuable than birth and status. The seemingly unlimited American continent, with its fertile farmland and natural resources, gave Americans self-assurance and unbridled optimism.

The American Civil War

Yet the American experience was not without serious problems. Sectional disputes, particularly between the agricultural south and the industrializing north, threatened to disrupt the republic. By the 1850s the institution of slavery, on which the southern economy depended, had become a deeply divisive issue. The test of nationhood came in the bitter civil war between 1861 and 1865, in which Abraham Lincoln (1861–1865) sought to preserve national unity just when Cavour had forged an Italian state and Bismarck was striving to create a united Germany. As war leader, Lincoln put the preservation of the nation before the question of abolition. But in response to growing demands, he issued the Emancipation Proclamation on January 1, 1863, abolishing slavery in the secessionist Confederate states. The defeat of the Confederacy achieved both goals of ending slavery in the United States (long after it had been abolished in most other places in the Western world) and preserving the American union.

Following the civil war, the United States entered a period of unrestrained economic development and industrialization. By the end of the century almost 200,000 miles of railroads crisscrossed the continent, and American mills produced a third of the world's steel. The population of the nation, swelled by almost 30 million immigrants from Europe and Asia between 1860 and 1914, settled hundreds of millions of acres of land in the west and swarmed into the burgeoning cities. On the eve of World War I almost half of the nation's 100 million people lived in urban centers. The rapid transformation of the American continent from a frontier society to an industrial giant and the resulting leap in America's status to global power were to have profound consequences for the world.

National Development in Latin America

In Latin America the struggle for national liberation began in 1808, when Napoleon's armies drove the rulers of Spain and Portugal into exile, thereby providing an opportunity for republican nationalists in the colonies to seek self-government. Yet political consolidation did not go as far as in North America, where, apart from Mexico, the entire continent eventually came under the jurisdiction of either Canada or the United States. For one thing, the population of Latin America was more ethnically complex: that of the Spanish colonies was about 45 percent Indian, 30 percent mixed Indian and European (mestizo), 20 percent white, and 5 percent black. In Brazil, where slavery was common, some 50 percent of the population was black, 30 percent mixed (*mamelucos*), and 20 percent white.

By 1821 Mexico and the Central American states—Costa Rica, Salvador, Nicaragua, Guatemala, and Honduras—had secured their independence. Despite an experiment between 1823 and 1839 to unite the five smaller states in a federal republic known as the United Provinces of Central America, regional unity was not permanent. In South America a similar attempt in the 1820s to join Venezuela, Colombia, and Ecuador into Gran Colombia failed, and by 1830 the present grouping of nations—Argentina, Chile, Bolivia, Peru, Ecuador, Colombia, Venezuela, Uruguay, and Paraguay—had been established in what had been Spanish regions of South America.

Brazil: From Empire to Republic

Brazil, the largest nation in Latin America, became independent in 1822 when the Portuguese ruler's son, Dom Pedro (1798–1834), declared its separation from the mother country. As emperor (1822–1831) Pedro proclaimed a constitution that gave him great power and established a parliamentary regime. The emperor's autocratic behavior culminated in an opposition movement that forced him to abdicate in 1831 in favor of his infant son. A regency ruled Brazil until 1841 and enacted a series of constitutional amendments that gave considerable authority to provincial assemblies. Local revolts were widespread in the northern regions, where the sugar and cotton economy experienced difficult times; the coffee-growing areas proved more stable. After the 15-year-old Dom Pedro was proclaimed emperor as Pedro II (1841–1889), order was restored to the country during most of his long reign.

The major issue facing Pedro II was slavery, on which Brazil's social and economic order rested. The agricultural system of large landed estates had been built on slave labor, and when the slave trade ended after 1850, a serious labor shortage resulted. Nevertheless, the abolitionist movement gained in strength, and in 1888 Brazil at last terminated slavery. By then the demand for labor was beginning to be met by European immigrants.

The abolition of slavery brought an end to the only remaining monarchy in Latin America, for the wealthy planters resented the emperor's support for abolition and his failure to indemnify them for the loss of their slaves. In November 1889 a military revolt replaced the imperial government with a republic. Political reforms were followed in 1891 by a new constitution that established a federal system of government that still left numerous powers to provincial assemblies.

While the vast interior remained an agricultural region, Rio de Janeiro, the capital, and other cities became centers of modern economic life. Demands for government subsidies, credits, tariffs, and infrastructures led to the printing of paper currency and inflation, which in turn hurt coffee prices. Domestic manufacturing and the middle classes expanded under the presidency of Marshal Floriano Peixoto (1842–1895), known as the "consolidator of the republic," but the coffee planters combined to drive him out of office in 1894. Over the following decades, overproduction of coffee became a persistent problem, which the government attempted to solve through support programs.

Dictatorship and War

Economic and political development was often hampered in Latin America by two factors: most governments fell at one time or another to dictators, known as caudillos, who subverted the constitutional systems, and the region also experienced violent and costly wars as competing states clashed over territory and position. Among the most important of these struggles was the Paraguayan War (1865–1870). When Paraguay declared independence in 1813, it was the only landlocked state in South America. Despite economic dependence on Argentina, Paraguayan leaders created a prosperous and progressive country. Nevertheless, border disputes, especially over the area known as the Banda Oriental, poisoned relations between Paraguay and Brazil. In 1828 that region secured its independence as the state of Uruguay, but Brazil continued to intervene in its affairs. In May 1865, Brazil, Argentina, and the Brazilian-backed government of Uruguay formed the Triple Alliance against Paraguay. The war ended five years later with the disastrous defeat of Paraguay, whose population of 500,000 was reduced by three-fourths as a result not only of the fighting but also of starvation, disease, and occupation. Paraguay lost large portions of its territory. In the War of the Pacific (1879–1883), Chile defeated Bolivia and Peru, seized the valuable nitrate-rich area of southeastern Peru, and cut Bolivia off from the sea.

Benito Juárez, the son of Indian parents, served as president of Mexico during a difficult period in his country's history. [Organization of American States]

Argentina and Mexico

In Argentina, attempts by the wealthy port city of Buenos Aires, the federal capital, to impose its control over the rest of the country created political tensions. In 1829 Juan Manuel Rosas (1793–1877) became governor of Buenos Aires and arranged a federal pact that allowed the provinces to run their own internal affairs while leaving foreign policy to him. Nevertheless, the vast plains provinces of the pampas, ruled by tough and independent-minded cattlemen known as gauchos, offered continual resistance to centralized government. Rosas, who ruled Argentina as a tyrant and suppressed civil liberties, was overthrown in 1852. The resulting constitution of 1853 resembled that of the United States, creating a federal republic run by an elected president and a two-chamber national legislature. The provinces elected governors and their own legislatures. Over the next 50 years economic development and the creation of an infrastructure—especially the railroad and telegraph networks and a public school system—slowly brought genuine unity to the country. Argentina's population doubled to 4 million between 1870 and 1900, much of the increase owing to migration from Europe.

Unlike most countries in Latin America, Mexico in the nineteenth century had a number of important leaders of mestizo and Indian origin. The Mexican constitution of 1824 was a compromise between middle-class liberals and conservative landowners and military officers. Nineteen states, each with its own legislature, chose the president of the republic. In 1833 Antonio López de Santa Anna (1794–1876), an ambitious and unprincipled general of Creole descent, was elected president on a liberal platform, but his true conservative beliefs soon emerged, and he governed Mexico for 20 years as a dictator. Santa Anna's prestige suffered when the United States annexed Texas in 1845 and acquired California and New Mexico in the Mexican War of 1846–1848.

Benito Juárez (1806–1872), a Zapotec Indian who had been elected governor of Oaxaca, replaced the ousted

Santa Anna. Juárez led a coalition government that reduced the influence of the military and the church and sought to distribute land to the peasants. A new constitution enacted in 1857 sparked a violent civil war—the War of Reform—that ended in victory for Juárez and the liberals.

The war so disrupted economic conditions that the government had to suspend payment on foreign loans. This prompted Napoleon III to send a French army to Mexico in 1862 that toppled the government. Napoleon selected the Austrian Archduke Maximilian (1832–1867) to rule as emperor of Mexico. Although a miserable failure as emperor, Maximilian's downfall resulted from Napoleon's decision to recall French troops to Europe afer Prussia's victory in the 1866 war with Austria. Juárez captured the hapless Maximilian, who was tried and executed in 1867. Juárez then served as president of Mexico until his death, implementing further social and economic reforms.

In 1877 the Mexican government was again overthrown, this time by Porfirio Díaz (1830–1915), a former follower of Juárez of mixed Creole and Indian descent. Díaz ruled Mexico with an iron fist for more than 30 years. He encouraged the investment of foreign capital and sold off the country's natural resources while the condition of the workers and peasants deteriorated. When he was finally forced to resign in 1911, Mexico was on the edge of revolution.

In the second half of the nineteenth century, European history was shaped largely by triumphant nationalism, which underwent a profound transformation. In midcentury a proponent of nationalism such as Giuseppe Mazzini saw no contradictions between his demands for Italian national liberation and the aspirations of other nationalities. Indeed, Mazzini had cast his nationalist ideas in broad international terms, envisioning an interdependent Europe in which free, equal, self-governing peoples cooperated in a spirit of harmony. Mazzini, who died in 1872, lived to see nationalism triumph in Italy and Germany, yet by the end of the century he would hardly have recognized the concept as the same idealistic doctrine he had once preached. Nationalism also encouraged state-building and overcame sectionalism in the United States and Latin America.

Nation-building had been a complex interaction in which patriotism and middle-class liberalism had first joined forces against conservatism. Ironically, however, success subverted nationalist movements, for as military, industrial, and conservative aristocratic elites embraced nationalism, many liberals subsumed or abandoned their political values to the more immediate goal of unification. Once national unity was achieved under the leadership of men such as Bismarck and Cavour, the Mazzinian vision of a new civilization nurtured by a spirit of freedom and equality gave way to an aggressive chauvinism that perceived history as the struggle between nations for power and dominance. Bitter national rivalries resulting from the wars of unification in Europe and Latin America gave concrete form to the larger political and intellectual changes taking place. The nationalists of the postunification period absorbed and twisted the theories spawned by the Darwinian revolution in science, substituting the doctrine of supremacy for belief in equality, rejecting cooperation in favor of competition, and preaching imperialist expansion instead of self-determination. By the end of the century nationalism, which once had promised a new age of peace and security, pointed to an unstable and dangerous future.

Suggestions for Further Reading

Binkley, R. C. *Realism and Nationalism, 1852–1871.* New York: Harper, 1935.

Crankshaw, E. *Bismarck.* New York: Macmillan, 1981.

Emmons, T. *The Russian Landed Gentry and the Peasant Emancipation of 1861.* Cambridge: Cambridge University Press, 1968.

Florinsky, M. T. *Russia: A History and an Interpretation.* New York: Macmillan, 1953.

Griffith, G. O. *Mazzini: Prophet of Modern Europe.* London: Hodder & Stoughton, 1932.

Hamerow, T. S. *The Social Foundation of German Unification, 1858–1871.* 2 vols. Princeton, N.J.: Princeton University Press, 1969.

Hertzberg, A., ed. *The Zionist Idea.* Garden City, N.Y.: Doubleday, 1956.

Keen, B., and Wasserman, M. *A History of Latin America*, 3rd ed. Boston: Houghton Mifflin, 1988.

Kohn, H. *The Idea of Nationalism.* New York: Macmillan, 1944.

Mack Smith, D. *Cavour.* London: Weidenfeld & Nicolson, 1985.

———. *Garibaldi.* London: Hutchinson, 1957.

McPherson, J. M. *Battle Cry of Freedom: The Civil War Era.* New York: Oxford University Press, 1988.

Mosse, W. E. *Alexander II and the Modernization of Russia.* London: English Universities Press, 1958.

Pflanze, O. *Bismarck and the Development of Germany*, vol. 1, rev. ed. Princeton, N.J.: Princeton University Press, 1990.

Schorske, C. E. *Fin-de-Siècle Vienna.* New York: Knopf, 1979.

Seton-Watson, H. *The Decline of Imperial Russia, 1855–1914.* New York: Praeger, 1952.

Shaw, S. J., and Shaw, E. K. *History of the Ottoman Empire and Modern Turkey.* 2 vols. Cambridge: Cambridge University Press, 1977.

Stavrianos, L. S. *The Balkans, 1815–1914.* New York: Holt, Rinehart and Winston, 1963.

Taylor, A. J. P. *Bismarck: The Man and the Statesman.* New York: Knopf, 1955.

———. *The Habsburg Monarchy, 1809–1918.* New York: Harper & Row, 1965.

———. *The Struggle for Mastery in Europe, 1848–1918.* Oxford: Clarendon Press, 1960.

Thompson, J. M. *Louis Napoleon and the Second Empire.* New York: Norton, 1967.

Williams, R. L. *Gaslight and Shadow: The World of Napoleon III.* New York: Macmillan, 1957.

Woolf, S. *A History of Italy, 1700–1860.* London: Methuen, 1979.

Wright, G. *France in Modern Times.* Chicago: Rand McNally, 1960.

Industrial Society and the Liberal Order

In the years from 1871 to 1900 Europe achieved a higher level of material well-being than any previous civilization. Its population was healthier, more nutritiously fed, better educated, and longer-lived, and it enjoyed more physical comforts than any other people in history. Europeans of this generation made remarkable progress in understanding and controlling the physical world. By the end of the century they moved themselves and the products of their industrial culture efficiently not only by steam but also by the internal combustion engine; they turned machines with steam turbines and electrical energy, communicated rapidly around the globe with the telegraph, underwater cable, and telephone, and illuminated the darkness with the light bulb.

These astonishing advancements in science and technology, together with unprecedented prosperity, deter-

The British naturalist Charles Darwin revolutionized science with his theory of evolution. [National Portrait Gallery, London]

mined how the post-1871 generation thought about it-self. Most Europeans looked at the world with faith in the limitless capacity of reason to solve problems. "Progress," inexorable and continuous, was their religion. Believing that they were moving steadily toward an ideal future, Europeans were self-assured about the achievements and superiority of their civilization.

The materialist culture of the era reflected the fact that the middle class had become an influential elite in European life. Liberal doctrines shaped the governments of most Western nations, while entrepreneurs and industrialists extolled unregulated, growth-driven capitalism. As the middle class achieved status and political power, bourgeois notions of order and respectability defined public attitudes toward family, sexuality, the roles of men and women, and social behavior. Middle-class values also set standards of style and comfort as well as artistic taste.

Still, the age was by no means as well ordered as many contemporaries believed. Industrial capitalism spawned unanticipated problems. Beneath the surface of middle-class prosperity lay widespread poverty and dehumanizing drudgery in the workplace, loudly denounced by social critics. Some demanded social and political reforms and a wider suffrage. As the right to vote spread, radical opponents of liberalism, inspired by the Marxist critique of capitalism, joined industrial workers in forming labor unions and socialist parties in an effort to wrench power from the bourgeoisie.

The social implications of the industrial system were enormous. By the end of the century factories had drawn millions of farmers from the countryside and had transformed a once rural and agricultural Europe into a predominantly urban civilization with pressing problems of public welfare. Higher factory wages had also attracted women to the workplace in large numbers, altering the pattern of family life, modifying sexual behavior, and challenging traditional models of male-female relationships.

Industrial Development and Monopoly Capitalism

In the last third of the nineteenth century, Europe's economy was transformed in three important ways: the Industrial Revolution spread more widely to other European nations, new sources of energy and products were developed, and business elites evolved new forms of control over industry and capital. These trends brought the earlier industrialization process to a climax and shaped Western economic life for generations.

The Second Phase of the Industrial Revolution

The first phase of industrialization, led by Great Britain, had been marked by the application of steam power in the manufacturing of two important commodities, iron and textiles. Subsequent changes in science and technology led to a second and equally important phase. Although steam remained the major source of industrial energy until 1914, electric power and internal combustion engines fueled by petroleum products increasingly replaced steam-driven machinery. The new energy sources led to the development of more sophisticated machines that greatly expanded efficiency and output and lowered production costs.

During the second phase of the Industrial Revolution, steel replaced iron as the basic metal, and the chemical industry grew rapidly. Both developments resulted from the application of scientific discoveries to industry. Through the process developed by Henry Bessemer (1830–1898) at midcentury, steel could now be manufactured in large quantities. The strength and flexibility of steel had a profound impact on construction, manufacturing, and transportation. As railroad networks spread across the European and American continents, the production of locomotive engines, cars, and tracks became a major impetus to industry and capital investment and opened significant new markets. In Europe the rail network doubled between 1890 and 1914. In addition, methods for the mass production of chemical substances revolutionized industry by allowing for the creation of such new products as fertilizers, dyes, explosives, plastics, synthetic fabrics, and medicines such as aspirin.

Germany, France, Italy, Russia, the United States, and Japan became industrial nations. Coal and steel provided useful indices of the growth of production during the second phase of the Industrial Revolution. Between 1870 and 1913 world output of coal had risen from 230 million to more than 1.5 billion metric tons, while steel production rose from 550,000 to more than 80 million tons. By 1914 the "inner zone" of Britain, Germany, and France produced 80 percent of Europe's coal, steel, and machinery and 70 percent of its manufactured products. Germany soon emerged as Europe's industrial giant and rapidly outdistanced Britain. By 1900 German steel production had outpaced Britain's, and on the eve of World War I it was more than double that of Britain and second only to the United States, which manufactured almost twice as much as Germany. Germany also led the field in the cast-iron and chemical industries. In the four decades after 1870 Britain's annual growth rate was 2.2 percent, compared to 2.9 percent for Germany and 4.3 percent for the United States.

The sharp increase in productivity that characterized

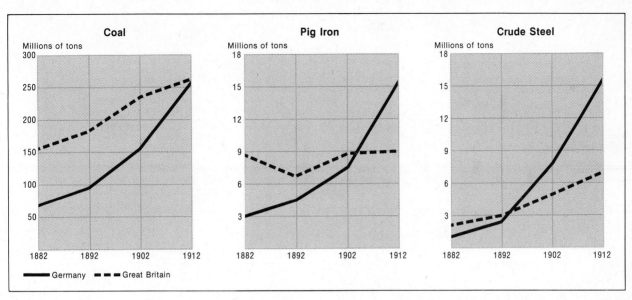

German and British Industrial Production, 1882–1912

the post-1870 period was made possible not only by new energy sources and the spread of industrialism but also by more efficient machines that reoriented production techniques toward standardized parts and specialized tasks. Pioneered by the American automobile manufacturer Henry Ford (1863–1947), the division of labor on assembly lines made cheaper, mass-produced consumer goods available on a wide scale. Although these trends contributed to the material improvement of daily life, they also resulted in overproduction, the further dehumanization of the work process, and a decline in the quality of many products.

The Rise of Big Business

The second phase of the Industrial Revolution bore out Karl Marx's prediction of a trend toward the concentration of wealth in fewer hands. The large numbers of small factories and businesses characteristic of early industrialization gave way to fewer, larger concerns. Business legislation encouraged the trend by extending the concept of "limited liability," which insured the personal assets of investors against business losses. The pattern was not, however, due simply to competition such as took place in retail sales, where department stores forced many independent shopkeepers out of business by buying in large quantities and selling at lower prices. As the cost of such large-scale operations as steel foundries and chemical refineries increased, entrepreneurs required enormous capital, which smaller producers could not afford. Partly for this reason, but largely be-

cause competition drove down the margin of profit, investors created monopolies.

Entrepreneurs often operated through a process known as "horizontal integration," whereby they achieved control over a sector of industry or business such as steel, coal, or oil. Such huge combinations—called amalgamations in Britain, cartels in Germany, and trusts in the United States—dominated industry by the end of the century because they absorbed or drove out competitors and could limit production, fix prices, divide markets, and control labor. By means of "vertical integration," steel manufacturers could buy up coal and iron mines, chemical plants, blast furnaces, and rail companies to ensure control over the entire industrial process.

Unregulated, monopoly capitalism had long-range implications. Investment banking grew in importance, especially with the adoption of the international gold standard for all major currencies. John Pierpont Morgan (1837–1913), the famous American banker, financed governments as well as railroads and steel companies through his firms in New York and London. Industrial monopolies were the work of "captains of industry" such as Andrew Carnegie (1835–1919), who in 1901 merged his Carnegie Steel Company with the United States Steel Corporation, and John D. Rockefeller (1839–1937), owner of the Standard Oil trust, or Alfred Krupp (1812–1887) and August Thyssen (1842–1926) in Germany. Such men were ruthless in their pursuit of profit and accumulated vast fortunes that enabled them to wield unprecedented economic and political power. The social ramifications of the second phase of the Industrial Revolution were far-reaching, especially as the emergence

The giant Krupp manufacturing complex at Essen, Germany (1912), reflected both the new era of early-twentieth-century industrialization and the industrial power of Germany. [Brown Brothers]

of the private-sector bureaucracy enlarged the white-collar class.

The Social Hierarchy

The political and economic changes that transformed Europe in the nineteenth century profoundly affected society. Despite unprecedented material progress, social and economic differences remained sharp, and the quality of life varied greatly between classes.

The Aristocracy: Adjustment and Change

The aristocracy had been the dominant elite before 1789. Most nobles, whose wealth and status had been determined by land ownership, failed to make the transition to modern capitalist agriculture or industrialization. Although land continued to be important, the real wealth of the aristocracy declined along with their income and access to liquid capital. In countries that remained predominantly agricultural, competition from cheaper overseas grain further reduced farm income. Yet in Britain the aristocracy remained stable well into the nineteenth century. The declining influence of the aristocracy appeared sharper than it actually was because of the rapid rise of the middle class. Liberal constitutions gave the bourgeoisie political power, but aristocrats dominated the upper chambers in parliaments. While the spread of civil service examinations and higher education opened administrative positions to the middle classes, there was little competition with the aristocracy for such positions. Ancient lineage and access to royal courts sustained the status of nobles, who remained the point of reference in matters of social prestige and style.

After 1870 the line separating the aristocracy and the upper middle class began to blur, as it had in the sixteenth and seventeenth centuries, as industrial wealth and noble titles sometimes came together through mutually advantageous marriages. Businessmen with surplus capital often bought sumptuous estates as symbols of their rising status. Increasingly, the upper levels of the industrial class copied the living standards of the aristocracy.

The Growth of the Middle Classes

While the aristocracy underwent adjustment in the late nineteenth century, the middle classes enjoyed expansion, though not uniformly. Grouping economic interests and social strata so diverse that they were often mutually antagonistic, the middle classes included wealthy industrialists and bankers as well as shopowners and white-collar workers. In industrialized countries the middle classes represented perhaps one-fifth of the inhabitants, although the powerful industrial and banking families formed a very small percentage of the general population. This elite reaped great benefits from expanded industrial production, earning a third of all national income. Consisting of no more than several hundred families in any given country, this group tended to merge with the old aristocracy, aping their manners and elitist attitudes.

Most middle-class Europeans were members of less wealthy and powerful subgroups: the middle middle

This photograph of an upper-middle-class English family at tea reveals the Victorian ideal of social and domestic property. [Culver Pictures]

class of small entrepreneurs, professional experts, and managers or the lower middle class of shopkeepers and white-collar workers. The ranks of the middle range swelled after 1870 with scientists, engineers, lawyers, and accountants—whose occupations grew more professional—as well as with corporate managers and bureaucrats.

The number of shopkeepers and small business owners grew along with teachers, nurses, and other salaried, nonpropertied members of the lower middle class. The most dramatic increase, however, was among the white-collar employees—clerks, salespeople, secretaries, and low-ranking bureaucrats, most of whom came from the ranks of the working class. White-collar wages were sometimes less than those of skilled workers, but the status of carrying a briefcase, wearing a tie, or having uncallused hands was often seen as compensation for low salaries. The lower middle class expanded rapidly between 1870 and 1900, doubling in Britain to 20 percent of the population.

Although middle- and lower-middle-class groups did not control great wealth, they tended to lead comfortable lives that reflected the values and aspirations of the upper-class bourgeoisie. Yet the status of most of the middle class was precarious in comparison to other groups. Easy social mobility encouraged the lower ranks to strive for greater status and income, but tensions were equally strong. Economic pressure from large industries

and corporations threatened small businessmen and shopkeepers, while people living on fixed incomes from savings and pensions feared that business cycles and recessions could suddenly wipe them out. For white-collar employees, who made every effort to distance themselves from the workers, the greatest fear was that economic adversity would force them back to their working-class origins.

The Decline of the Working Class

Most people—four-fifths of them—lived by physical labor. Industrialization made Europe a predominantly urban civilization, so by the end of the nineteenth century agricultural workers were a distinct minority in most western and central European countries. The agricultural crisis that began in 1873 as a result of huge imports of wheat from the United States reduced the price of European grains. Landowners cut wages and pushed peasants, many of whom already lived close to subsistence, into more extreme poverty. The decline in agricultural earnings, compounded by natural disasters in the 1870s and 1880s, also struck peasant owners, whose land decreased in value. The rural standard of living improved after 1890 with changes in crops and cultivation methods, as well as the introduction of protective tariffs, but agricultural wages remained less than half the average of factory rates.

In industrialized countries the urban working class represented the largest single social stratum and was even more diverse in composition than the middle classes. Among skilled workers, industrialization brought stressful changes as artisans gave way to factory workers who required less skill. Yet there was also a growing need for new kinds of skilled jobs, including metalworkers, machine tool makers, and locomotive engineers. Skilled workers, whose wages were at least twice as high as those of unskilled laborers, saw themselves as an elite with middle-class pretensions. Semiskilled and unskilled workers vastly outnumbered the artisans and the skilled elite. The semiskilled, such as masons, carpenters, plumbers, and some factory workers, earned less money, while the unskilled workers, among whom the largest number were domestic servants, were the lowest paid.

Between the years 1873 and 1896 the West experienced a series of economic crises known collectively as the Long Depression. Primarily an agricultural phenomenon sparked by competition from North American farms, the Long Depression nevertheless affected industry and trade. Rising costs, increased competition, and shrinking markets reduced profits and triggered stock and bank panics. Periods of high unemployment resulted. In Britain, for example, unemployment among unionized workers rose from 1 percent in 1872 to 11 percent in 1879, from 2 percent in 1882 to 10 percent in 1886, and again from 2 percent in 1890 to 7.5 percent in 1893. Such sharp cycles of unemployment not only caused severe hardships among working-class families but also fanned enthusiasm for militant labor unions. Yet even though fluctuations in wages accompanied the crises, during the three decades after 1870 real wages rose by about 37 percent, increasing by a third in France and Germany and by more than half in Britain.

Urban working-class diets improved and became more varied as food prices declined and purchasing power increased, and health conditions in the cities improved with the development of sewage systems, clean water supplies, and the scientific control of disease. Industrial productivity reduced the cost of clothing, so workers were better dressed. The expansion of urban construction made less cramped housing available, and the development of inexpensive railway, subway, and tram services gave workers access to better housing in the suburbs, although they still had to devote large portions of their budgets to rent.

Despite advances in the standard of life for urban workers, production outpaced wages. Although working-class purchasing power expanded and living standards improved for all social groups, the gap between workers and the middle classes widened.

THE URBAN LANDSCAPE

The urbanization of European society—the movement of people from country to city, the growth in the number of urban centers, and the dense concentration of huge populations in them—continued well beyond 1900. Between 1871 and 1911 England's urban population rose from 62 to 78 percent of the whole and France's from 33 to 44 percent. In Germany, which was industrializing rapidly, the increase was spectacular—from 36 to 60 percent. Moreover, 90 percent of Germany's population growth in the same period was in cities. The culture of western Europe had become predominantly urban.

Improved transportation, particularly the railroad, spurred urban growth, and most important cities became hubs of rail lines or port facilities, and frequently both. In large cities the basic infrastructure—drainage systems, water supply, police and fire protection—had already been established by midcentury, and these services were expanded.

Baron Haussmann's redevelopment of Paris during the Second Empire provided the model for a similar project in Vienna, whose Ringstrasse was inspired by Haussmann's grand boulevards. London and Berlin permitted the reconstruction of inner-city zones in the 1870s, when

Behind the exuberant prosperity of Victorian London lay the poverty of much of Britain's working class. This photograph shows an alley in a working-class section of the city.
[Snark/Art Resource]

POPULATION OF THE MAJOR CITIES
OF CONTINENTAL EUROPE AROUND 1910

Paris	2,888,000	Kiev	469,000
Berlin	2,071,000	Turin	428,000
Vienna	2,031,000	Rotterdam	418,000
St. Petersburg	1,908,000	Frankfurt	415,000
Moscow	1,481,000	Lodz	394,000
Hamburg	931,000	Düsseldorf	359,000
Budapest	880,000	Lisbon	356,000
Warsaw	781,000	Stockholm	347,000
Naples	723,000	Palermo	342,000
Brussels	720,000	Nuremberg	333,000
Milan	599,000	Riga	318,000
Madrid	598,000	Charlottenberg	306,000
Munich	596,000	Antwerp	302,000
Leipzig	590,000	Hanover	302,000
Barcelona	587,000	Bucharest	295,000
Amsterdam	568,000	Essen	295,000
Copenhagen	559,000	Chemnitz	288,000
Marseilles	551,000	Stuttgart	286,000
Dresden	548,000	Magdeburg	280,000
Rome	539,000	Genoa	272,000
Lyons	524,000	The Hague	270,000
Cologne	517,000	Bordeaux	262,000
Breslau (Wroclaw)	512,000	Oslo	247,000
Odessa	479,000	Bremen	247,000

town planning revived. By the end of the nineteenth century, advances in engineering, building materials, and construction techniques began to change the face of cities. Reinforced concrete and steel permitted multistory office and apartment buildings, and both the American skyscraper and the metal tower designed by French engineer Gustav Eiffel in the 1890s became symbols of the new, aggressive city. Sewers, sidewalks, and electric lights made urban centers more pleasant places in which to live and work.

France led the way with other distinctive features of the modern city. Using wrought iron and steel, Parisian developers built large, glass-covered galleries in which independent shops and cafés were situated, and by the 1880s Moscow had followed the example. The first major department store was the Bon Marché in Paris. By buying in quantity, department stores could sell a wide range of mass-made goods inexpensively, thus making the products of industrial civilization available to workers and the lower middle class.

Working-class housing, which in the early industrial revolution had consisted of squalid, crammed tenements, improved considerably in this period as a result of health and welfare legislation. The French pioneered middle-class apartment complexes, New York exploited that concept, and British cities added the notion of garden apartments. As urban transportation systems grew, more people escaped urban living for tranquil suburbs, and the city became the metropolis.

Everywhere cities adopted from each other, equipping themselves with London-style parks and suburbs, Paris-style boulevards and cafés, and New York–style office blocks and gridded street plans. All of them acquired grand public buildings and cultural centers such as opera houses, concert halls, museums, and public libraries, and all were afflicted with pollution, noise, and overcrowding. By the end of the century the urban landscape had assumed its modern appearance.

Sexuality, Women, and the Family

The Industrial Revolution and the consequent movement of populations from the country to the cities had significant repercussions on the relationship between men and women, as well as on the family. Urban life tended to erode moral codes and traditional forms of courtship and marriage that were more easily enforced in small villages. At the same time, the employment opportunities and higher wage scales that drew workers to the factories often enabled young men and women to escape family supervision. In the period before 1850 the result had been a dramatic increase in premarital sex (among partners who intended to marry), illegitimate births, and common-law marriages, but this pattern diminished by the last third of the century.

The spread of birth control information contributed to a decline in the birthrate. The French took the lead in contraception, and such traditional methods as the sponge, sheepskin condoms, and the vinegar douche were widely used among the upper classes. In Britain laws prohibited the publication or distribution of contraceptive information until Annie Besant, a socialist, and Charles Bradlaugh, a radical, won a celebrated court case in 1878. Between 1880 and 1900 they distributed more than a million copies of birth control pamphlets that advocated the use of the sponge, syringing with zinc or alum solutions, cervical caps, and rubber condoms. Although Besant aimed her information at the poor, it was the middle class that first made widespread use of these methods, and only by the end of the century did they spread among urban workers. Moreover, middle-class men could more easily afford recourse to brothels, where they found women who were often driven to prostitution by unemployment and poverty.

Industrialization brought mixed results. During the nineteenth century roughly two-thirds of all single women and more than a quarter of married women worked. Life was especially difficult for working women, for most had to function as mothers and wives as well. Married generally in their early and mid-twenties after experiencing the relative independence derived from their jobs, working women subordinated themselves to their husbands. The men ate better food, dressed better, went out without their families in the evenings, and often abused their children and wives. Yet despite the grueling physical and psychological pressures, working mothers managed to keep the basic family structure intact.

The principal female employment categories—domestic service, textile work, and garment making—remained fairly constant into the early twentieth century, but the female work force consisted increasingly of single women; by 1911 only 9.6 percent of married women were employed. The notion that women should "retire" when they married was a product of urban industrial culture. In the cities domestic service employed more women than any other activity in the nineteenth century. Because it promoted such virtues as hard work, clean-liness, and obedience, domestic service was regarded as ideal training for future wives of the working class.

Bourgeois Respectability

The expanding demand for domestic servants reflected both the growing prosperity of the middle class and the new ideal of womanhood that it cultivated. The separation between the male sphere of work and business and the female sphere of home and family reached its most fully developed form among the middle class. Bourgeois respectability required that the home be comfortable, well furnished, and characterized by an atmosphere of warmth and safety from the outside world. Middle-class sensibilities idealized women as gentle and virtuous creatures devoted to bearing and raising children and looking after their husbands. The Victorians evolved a

◉ The Cult of Domesticity ◉

The development of the cult of domesticity, which limited women largely to home maintenance and child rearing, contributed greatly to the social construction of gender roles. In this nineteenth-century handbook for housewives, Mrs. Isabella Beeton explains the principles of household management.

Of all those acquirements, which more particularly belong to the feminine character, there are none which take a higher rank, in our estimation, than such as enter into a knowledge of household duties. . . .

Early rising is one of the most essential qualities which enter into good household management, as it is not only the parent of health, but of innumerable other advantages. Indeed, when a mistress is an early riser, it is almost certain that her house will be orderly and well-managed. . . .

Cleanliness is indispensable to health, and must be studied both in regard to the person and the house, and all that it contains. Cold or tepid baths should be employed every morning, unless, on account of illness or other circumstances, they should be deemed objectionable. . . .

Frugality and economy are home virtues, without which no household can prosper. . . . The necessity of practising economy should be evident to every one. . . .

The treatment of servants is of the highest possible moment, as well to the mistress as to the domestics themselves. On the head of the house the latter will naturally fix their attention; and if they perceive that the mistress' conduct is regulated by high and correct principles, they will not fail to respect her.

After this general superintendence of her servants, the mistress, if the mother of a young family, may devote herself to the instruction of some of its younger members, or to the examination of the state of their wardrobe, leaving the latter portion of the morning for reading, or for some amusing recreation.

Source: I. Beeton, *Book of Household Management* (London: Beeton, 1861), pp. 2–9 passim.

"cult of domesticity" for women that stressed duty, submissiveness, and devotion. A close and emotionally intimate family life was extolled as the social bedrock of the age.

The middle-class family concentrated legal power in the hands of the husband and father. Until midcentury contracts were often used in upper-class families to safeguard the property rights of daughters about to be married, for a husband ordinarily gained control of a wife's property. Most states in America passed married women's property acts, as did Britain in 1882, but these were designed largely to enable fathers who had no sons to pass inheritances to their daughters. Widows almost always had to defer to the relatives of their deceased husbands regarding such matters as their children's education and upbringing. Similarly, divorce was still generally obtainable only by women who could prove that their husbands were impotent or unfit fathers; in most countries husbands could gain a divorce on the grounds of adultery, but women could not. Educational patterns perpetuated the inferior status of women. While middle-class boys usually went to school to receive classical education or professional training in law, medicine, or accounting, girls stayed home to learn painting, needlework, and religion.

Sexual Attitudes

The ideology of bourgeois respectability had a powerful impact on attitudes toward sexuality, though not on its practice. Sexual pleasure was regarded as a male preserve. The assumption that women were not supposed to enjoy sex was a powerful form of male dominance. Public attitudes toward sexuality encouraged a double standard according to which men might, with proper discretion, visit brothels and maintain mistresses to fulfill their "natural" needs. Victorian moral strictures were also imposed on children, whose clothing and physical activities were regulated to repress masturbation and sensations that might lead to sexual arousal. Menstruation—known as "the curse"—was little discussed, and pubescence was regarded as a profoundly disturbing and disagreeable experience.

Diaries and letters, the proliferation of sex manuals and pornography, and the literature of the period demonstrate that despite the strictures fostered by middle-class sexual codes, men and women continued to enjoy sex. The sensational trial and imprisonment in 1895 of the writer Oscar Wilde (1854–1900) because of his love affair with Lord Alfred Douglas made Victorians uncomfortably aware of other sexual orientations. Wilde's account of this experience, *The Ballad of Reading Gaol* (1898), had to be published anonymously, and his "open letter" to Douglas, *De Profundis* (1905), did not appear until after his death. The tension created by the dissonance between moral theory and behavior produced a pyschological anxiety that pervaded the late Victorian age.

Liberalism and the Political Order

The middle class had been a driving force behind the political upheavals that stretched from the American Revolution in 1776 to the revolutions of 1848. They had reacted strongly against the excesses of the French Revolution, but their demands for a share in political power, expressed through the doctrine of liberalism, had made them the foe of absolutism and aristocracy. After 1815 the bourgeoisie stood in sharp opposition to the conservative political principles of the Restoration. In France they brought the "bourgeois king" Louis-Philippe to power in 1830, while in England, where the 1832 Reform Act had enfranchised the industrialists, the propertied classes enjoyed significant political influence. In 1848 and 1849 they came close to establishing constitutional regimes in central and eastern Europe.

The political triumph of the middle classes came after 1850, when they joined forces with elements of the aristocracy in supporting unification movements in Germany and Italy and Napoleon III in France. Thereafter, as the middle classes gained power, they reversed their historical role—whereas once they had acted as a powerful force for change, now they emerged as the champions of order. Liberalism, the doctrine that expressed middle-class aspirations, changed as well.

Over the course of the nineteenth century, liberalism had proved to be a flexible doctrine capable of encompassing a wide range of objectives, from the Enlightenment belief in individual rights to Romanticism and from nationalism to Bismarck's *Realpolitik*. After 1870 the industrial and financial bourgeoisie began to appropriate political liberalism as their special preserve, making it the philosophy of the capitalist establishment.

Though liberalism underwent a transformation after 1870, it continued to stand for the basic premise that government should be based on a written constitution—except in Britain, where an unwritten agreement prevailed—with the middle classes and aristocracy represented in parliamentary institutions elected by limited male suffrage. Liberal parliamentary systems reflected a number of trends: a widening suffrage that eventually encompassed most of the working classes, the appearance of modern political parties representing a range of class and special interests, free elementary education, compulsory military service, the secularization of national culture, and the growing role of the state in social legislation and public policy. Individual countries produced variations in this pattern, but as the century drew to a close, liberalism had permeated the political culture of western Europe almost everywhere. By 1900 all but one of the great European states were part of the "liberal" order; Russia alone stood outside the system.

Britain in the Victorian Age

No nation more completely represented the liberal order than Britain, and no European monarch symbolized that ideal more completely than Queen Victoria (1837–1901). She inherited the throne from her uncle, William IV, at the age of 18. In 1840 she married a German cousin, Prince Albert of Saxe-Coburg-Gotha, who had a formative influence on her character. She learned to express her wishes and opinions forcibly to her ministers and had a strong though discreet influence on politics. After Albert's death in 1861, Victoria lapsed into seclusion as the "widow of Windsor." Her 64-year reign as queen (she was also crowned empress of India in 1876), together with the fact that she was the grandmother of both Kaiser William II of Germany and Tsar Nicholas II of Russia, made Victoria the venerable matriarch of Europe's royalty. But as the symbol of Britain's political stability and industrial power, she was no glittering incarnation of imperial splendor—when she reappeared in public in the 1880s, it was as a matronly icon of bourgeois virtue, dressed in black and wide in girth.

Midway through Victoria's reign, British politics underwent a crucial transformation that resulted in the emergence of new leaders at the head of modernized political parties. Under William Gladstone (1809–1898), the old Whig-radical coalition evolved into the Liberal party. An eloquent orator, Gladstone, the pious son of a merchant, was trained as a classical scholar before entering politics. As chancellor of the Exchequer, he had pushed for a policy of free trade as well as reforms that included a postal savings and insurance system widely used by workers and a reduction in taxes. In 1864, when only one adult male out of six had the right to vote, Gladstone pressed for an extension of the franchise, which had not changed since 1832.

At this time Benjamin Disraeli (1804–1881) was molding the aristocratic, agrarian-based Tories into the new Conservative party. More flamboyant than Gladstone, the brilliant Disraeli was the descendant of Spanish Jews and the author of political novels. He was convinced that the Conservatives needed to broaden their support by appealing to the middle classes. After a successful record of leadership in the House of Commons, he overcame the suspicion of his colleagues, who regarded him as opportunistic, and eventually won the support of Queen Victoria, who preferred the Conservatives to the Liberals.

Queen Victoria and her husband, Prince Albert, were the ideal royal couple, devoted to each other and serious about their duties. [Victoria and Albert Museum]

Gladstone and Disraeli made possible the passage of the Reform Act of 1867. After Gladstone had tried without success to secure passage of a similar bill in 1866, Disraeli—who saw an opportunity for the Conservatives to reap the political credit—maneuvered the measure through the House of Commons. By giving the vote to all middle-class males and the highest-paid urban workers, the second Reform Act doubled the size of the electorate by adding almost a million voters to the rolls.

From 1868 to 1914 the Liberal and Conservative parties alternated in power. First Gladstone and Disraeli, and then their successors, outdid each other in sponsoring political and social legislation. Competitive civil service examinations were introduced in 1870, the secret ballot a year later. After 1884, when Gladstone passed another reform bill that increased the electorate by the addition of 2 million agricultural laborers, Britain continued to evolve toward parliamentary democracy, at least for men.

Before the end of the century the great mass of British workers and farm laborers benefited from a range of reforms—largely modeled on similar legislation introduced in Germany by Bismarck—that included free elementary education; minimum-wage laws; accident, health, and unemployment insurance programs; old-age pensions; and a graduated income tax. Marxist socialism, which was gaining a foothold in less democratic Continental states, had little appeal in Britain. By the eve of World War I, England's upper bourgeoisie believed that their country offered compelling testimony of the wisdom of the alliance between political liberalism and industrial capitalism. Still, as late as 1892 a report found that almost a third of the inhabitants of London—Britain's largest city and the hub of the British Empire—lived in poverty.

The Third Republic in France

For 70 years after 1870 France was governed by a republic born out of military defeat and civil war. The French surrender following the Battle of Sedan had resulted in the overthrow of Napoleon III and the proclamation of a republic (see Chapter 32). The National Assembly chose the liberal royalist Adolphe Thiers (1797–1877) as president. Thiers negotiated the humiliating peace terms with Bismarck that ended the Franco-Prussian War.

In March 1871 the National Assembly moved the government to Versailles, the traditional seat of the French monarchy. There the liberal-monarchist majority further aroused the fury of the Parisians by canceling the debt moratorium and the pay of the civilian National Guard, measures that had kept tens of thousands from starvation during the Prussian siege of the capital. Thiers then tried to confiscate the 200 cannon that had been cast by public subscription during the siege. Angry mobs dragged the cannon to safety and drove off government troops.

Civil war erupted. Extremists in Paris took control of the rebellion and established the Commune, modeled on the revolutionary government of 1792. When the regular army broke through the city's defenses in May, the Communards executed hostages, including the archbishop of Paris, while the Assembly's soldiers summarily shot everyone found with weapons. By the time government troops had secured the city, as many as 20,000 Communards had been executed, and twice that number were deported to penal islands. The repression of the Commune had been bloodier than any civil clash in modern French history. It left a permanent legacy of

class bitterness that polarized French politics and intensified social division.

The Third Republic proved both politically unstable and unpopular. Although the monarchists had a majority in the National Assembly, they could not agree on a suitable candidate for king and continued the republic in effect by default. The constitution of 1875 created a democratic government in which the prime minister and his cabinet were fully responsible to Parliament, whose lower house, the Chamber of Deputies, was elected by universal male suffrage.

Unlike the British, the French failed to develop modern political parties until the end of the century. Poorly organized political groups were held together only by immediate concerns. Royalist sentiment, which remained strong, was the focus of opposition to the Third Republic, but the monarchists remained divided on whether to support the Bourbon, Orléanist, or Bonapartist claimant to the throne. Republican supporters were equally divided. Radical republicans, led by Georges Clemenceau (1841–1929), were anticlerical and anti-German. Moderate republicans were more willing to compromise on major issues. Together, the moderate royalists and the republicans represented the liberal tradition in French politics. The left, which took more than a decade to recover from the disaster of the Commune, was also split into factions. In Parliament, majorities were difficult to form and still more difficult to maintain. More than 50 coalition cabinets governed France during the first 40 years of the republic.

The republic was no friend of social revolution. Reform legislation was slow in coming, and it was 1910 before earlier work and health laws were complemented by accident and social insurance programs. Still, moderates established the supremacy of Parliament and a system of secular state education that slowly engendered republican values in the post-1870 generation.

The strange career of General Georges Boulanger (1837–1891) mirrored the discontent that beset the Third Republic. Originally a radical republican and protégé of Clemenceau, Boulanger became war minister in 1886. He was a popular figure who made a habit of riding a magnificent black horse through the streets of Paris. Chafing under the humiliation of defeat in the Franco-Prussian War, royalists and patriotic admirers saw him as a symbol of French glory. Boulanger lost his cabinet position in 1887 and was sent to the provinces, where he drummed up support for a new constitution and a more authoritarian regime. With the help of right-wing politicians, he planned a coup d'état in 1889 but lost his nerve at the last minute and fled to Brussels.

More serious in its repercussions was the dramatic Dreyfus affair. In 1894 Captain Alfred Dreyfus (1859–1935), a Jewish officer attached to the French General Staff, was court-martialed for treason on charges that he had supplied military secrets to the Germans. A military

After toppling this column bearing a statue of Napoleon I in Paris, the Communard rebels erected the red flag of revolution in its place. [Bulloz/Musée Carnavalet]

court ignored evidence that another officer had been the guilty party. This aroused the radical republicans, who believed that the military had falsely condemned Dreyfus while protecting the real traitor. While Dreyfus languished in prison on Devil's Island, the notorious penal colony, Clemenceau and the novelist Émile Zola (1840–1902) took up his cause and accused the General Staff of harboring clerical, royalist, and anti-Semitic prejudices. In 1899 the army found Dreyfus guilty "with extenuating circumstances" and pardoned him, but his supporters continued to demand a full acquittal, which came only in 1906.

The episode widened the wedge that already separated radicals, socialists, and intellectuals from army leaders, monarchists, and the Catholic church. The crisis unleashed a wave of anti-Semitism that fueled right-wing forces. The Dreyfus case, like the Boulanger affair, revealed that the enemies of the government were strong. Yet the legacy of the French Revolution was equally powerful, and the Third Republic survived for another half century.

Germany Under the Reich

Liberalism in Germany was weaker than in Britain or France because it had been tied so closely to the triumph of Bismarck's unification program. Bismarck had been appointed minister of Prussia to overcome a deadlock between the king and the liberals in the Landtag, which he did by circumventing its control of the budget. In September 1866, however, after his stunning victory over the Austrians, the liberals and others sanctioned his violation of the Prussian constitution.

While Bismarck cowed the liberals, he also forged a powerful alliance between bourgeois industrialists and aristocratic landowners that enabled him to impose political unity on the German states. Prussia ran the federal structure of the German empire through its monarchy, bureaucracy, and army, and, with 236 of 397 seats in the lower house of parliament, the Reichstag, dominated the national assembly. Outwardly, the German parliament conformed to the liberal formula: the Reichstag was elected by universal male suffrage. The Reichstag approved laws and budgets, but it had no real authority over foreign affairs or the imperial ministers. The upper house, the Bundesrat, represented the 26 federated units of the empire and could initiate laws and block measures proposed by the Reichstag. The powers of the emperor were extensive, for he was commander in chief of the army and, in his role as king of Prussia, remained almost an absolute monarch. Moreover, the kaiser appointed the imperial chancellor, who was responsible to him alone.

Bismarck presided over the empire as chancellor for 19 years. Disdainful of his critics, the "Iron Chancellor" rammed his programs through parliament with the support of the conservative landowners and the upper middle class. The interests of the industrialists and bankers were represented by the National Liberals, while the great landowners backed the Conservatives. The Progressives, who spoke for the more radical liberals who had initially opposed Bismarck; the Center party, which spoke for the Catholics; and the Social Democrats, representing the socialist party, were Bismarck's chief sources of opposition.

Bismarck's ruthless methods and high-handed policies were designed to forge a single nation out of the patchwork of states that made up the new empire. He tried to extinguish local loyalties and crush opposition to the central state.

The first target of this policy was the Catholic church, against which he unleashed the so-called *Kulturkampf,* or "battle for civilization"—a campaign to make loyalty to Germany supreme over devotion to the Catholic church. Although the *Kulturkampf* was an extreme example of a growing trend toward secularization all over Europe, Bismarck saw it essentially as a political issue. Germany was predominantly Protestant, but Catholics comprised a third of the population and were strong in Alsace-Lorraine. Bismarck clashed with the church when he sponsored laws that abolished religious orders, imposed state supervision over Catholic education, made civil marriage compulsory, and required government approval of ecclesiastical appointments. When he removed bishops and hundreds of priests, Bismarck succeeded only in making political martyrs of them and found that German Catholics rallied to their church. In the next elections, the Catholic-oriented Center party nearly doubled its representation in the Reichstag. Always the realist, Bismarck eventually reached an accommodation with Pope Leo XIII (1878–1903).

Bismarck also dealt with what he considered the other major national problem, the threat of socialism. The formation of the Social Democratic party in 1875 led him to fear that the socialists would capture the loyalties of workers for the cause of revolution and internationalism. He persuaded the Reichstag to pass legislation restricting socialist activities. Denied an open forum, the socialists organized support underground and elected their candidates to the Reichstag in ever larger numbers. Faced with another political disaster, Bismarck switched his tactics in the 1880s by sponsoring social welfare programs designed to wean the workers away from the socialists while keeping the antisocialist laws intact. Bismarck's social security laws, the most advanced in Europe, provided workers with accident and health insurance and retirement benefits. After 1890 workers were given additional rights, including labor arbitration and better working conditions. These measures failed to reduce working-class support for the socialists, but they did demonstrate that organized political pressure could win substantial material benefits for workers without revolution. As a result, the Social Democratic party grew enormously in electoral strength and by 1912 was the largest party in the Reichstag. At the same time, however, it lost much of its revolutionary impetus.

Bismarck virtually ruled the German empire until 1890, when Kaiser William II (1888–1918) forced him to retire. As erratic as Bismarck was strong-willed, William had come to the throne when he was 29. Strict training had made him deeply attached to military discipline and the spirit of manly virtue that infused the aristocratic Prussian officer corps. Determined to rule Germany himself and unwilling to be dominated by Bismarck as his predecessors had been, William proclaimed, "There is only one master in the Reich [empire], and that is I." Heaping honors on Bismarck, the kaiser retired the man who had created the German empire.

In assuming command of the Second Reich—German nationalists considered the medieval Holy Roman Empire to have been the First—William II now ruled the most powerful state in Europe. Its population was large and growing rapidly, and its modern industrial plant was outpacing other nations in the production of coal, steel, chemicals, and electrical energy. Spectacular economic growth and a system of higher education that stressed technical training produced the most literate and scientifically advanced population in Europe. The German army was the most efficient military force in the world. Stridently nationalistic, the kaiser launched Germany on a new and dangerous course in world affairs.

The Liberal State in Italy

Britain and Germany offered examples of the liberal order at its extremes, one strong and stable, the other weak and shallowly rooted. Italian liberalism evolved between the two extremes. As in the case of Germany, Italian unification owed a great deal to the efforts of one man, Count Cavour. Unlike Bismarck, however, Cavour had been an admirer of British political traditions and was a moderate liberal by conviction.

The headstrong Kaiser William II dismissed
Bismarck in 1890 and assumed personal
direction of German affairs.
[Mansell Collection]

Much as Prussia had done in Germany, Piedmont
had essentially imposed its traditions and institutions on
the Italian states along with unification. The king was
commander in chief of the armed forces and had the
authority to declare war and make treaties. He also appointed the prime minister, who was declared to be "responsible," although whether to the king or to parliament remained unstated. The Chamber of Deputies, or
lower house of the Italian parliament, was elected on the
basis of limited manhood suffrage, with only 2 percent
of the population able to vote. The Chamber controlled
budget appropriations and could initiate legislation. The
Senate, or upper house, could veto measures passed in
the Chamber, and its members, appointed by the king
for life, tended to be conservatives, nobles, and public
officials.

As in France, organized political parties did not
emerge in Italy until after the turn of the century.* Instead, parliamentary deputies considered themselves
members of either the right or the left. These were
largely meaningless labels that had been used during
the unification struggle to describe, respectively, the
supporters of Cavour's program of constitutional monarchy and Mazzini's republican followers. After 1870 the
terms denoted degrees of liberalism, although the differences in outlook were often more a matter of emphasis than substance. In the first years of the kingdom,
when the right was in power, the government pursued
a fiscally conservative program of high taxation and low
expenditure for social reform. When the left came into
power in 1876, it repealed some of the more onerous
taxes, widened the suffrage, and instituted compulsory
elementary education. Significant social and economic
progress came slowly. The lack of clearly defined political parties and programs contributed to the practice of
trasformismo, whereby prime ministers formed coalitions that changed constantly, depending on the specific
issue and the patronage to be distributed.

The euphoria that had accompanied unification
quickly faded as Italians faced the problems of nationhood. The annexation of Rome in 1870 produced deep
hostility between the Catholic church and the new state
that was to plague Italian politics for the next half century. Through the Law of Guarantees, parliament recognized papal sovereignty over Vatican City and offered
financial compensation to the church. But Pius IX, who
declared himself a "prisoner of the Vatican," would not
compromise. He refused to recognize the kingdom and
prohibited Italian Catholics from taking part in political
life. The stalemate, known as the "Roman question,"
weakened the legitimacy of the new state in the eyes of
Italy's overwhelmingly Catholic population.

Regional differences and local loyalties remained
strong in Italy after unification. The gap between the
industrial interests of the north and the depressed agricultural economy of the south widened after 1870, and
illiteracy, disease, and poverty put pressure on a national
debt already burdened by the costs of the wars of unification. Despite the reforms of the left after 1876, the
ruling liberal elite remained unresponsive to the needs
of the unenfranchised poor for many years. Unemployed
migrant workers turned increasingly to brigandage in
the south, while peasant anarchism was widespread in
Sicily and central Italy. In the industrial centers of Milan
and Turin, workers turned to socialism.

The last two decades of the century were a period of
crisis that tested liberalism. From 1887 to 1891 and again
from 1893 to 1896 leadership was in the hands of Francesco Crispi (1819–1901). Like Bismarck, Crispi was de-

---

*The Italian Socialist party, founded in 1892, was the exception.

termined to stem the rise of socialism by suspending constitutional rights and smashing the Socialist party with massive arrests and police harassment. He was also anxious to make Italy a great power through military alliances and colonial conquest, but scandals and military defeat in Africa brought him down. Vigorous action against socialists and anarchists by Crispi's successors climaxed in the bloody suppression of labor demonstrations in 1898. The liberal state in Italy demonstrated its deep hostility to working-class movements.

The accession of Victor Emmanuel III (1900–1946) to the throne in 1900 brought Giovanni Giolitti (1842–1928) to the forefront of national politics. Giolitti served off and on as prime minister for most of the years before World War I. A shrewd politician, he toned down the level of confrontation with labor, coopted moderate socialists into the parliamentary system, and ended strikes through negotiation. Giolitti sought a reconciliation with the church, presided over the development of industry, and sponsored significant factory and social legislation. Finally, in 1911 Giolitti introduced near-universal manhood suffrage. The liberal state had begun its first tentative steps toward democratic reform when the First World War interrupted its progress.

Spain and the Smaller Powers

Instability and unrest, due largely to intrigues surrounding the succession to the throne, marked Spanish political life in the mid-nineteenth century. After a revolution unseated Queen Isabella II (1833–1868), a number of governments—first under the Cortes, then under a king imported from Italy, and finally as a republic—failed to find support and encouraged the church and the army to interfere in politics. Only when Alfonso XII (1874–1885) became king under a liberal constitution did a measure of stability return.

Thereafter, Spain struggled with the problems of social and economic modernization. Small areas of industry existed within an agrarian nation dominated by conservative landed interests. Anarchist and regionalist movements were strong, especially in the Basque region and Catalonia, while industrial growth in Barcelona prompted the rise of socialism. In 1890 universal male suffrage was instituted, but the constant struggle between the Liberal and Conservative parties made social reform difficult.

Events in Spain's colonies added to the nation's problems. When a combination of repressive policies and ineffective administration led to the outbreak of guerrilla resistance in Cuba in 1898, the United States seized the opportunity to wage war with Spain over its possessions. The Spanish-American War resulted in the loss of Cuba and the cession of the Philippines, Puerto Rico, and Guam to the United States. By the end of the century

intellectuals known as the Generation of 1898 were engaged in reassessing Spain's culture and turned increasingly to mystical nationalism in their search for national purpose.

Belgium, the Netherlands, Denmark, Sweden, and Norway followed a more stable pattern. All were constitutional monarchies that by 1914 had introduced universal manhood suffrage. Belgium was the most industrialized nation on the Continent, but the other states underwent rapid economic development that enlarged the middle class.

By 1900 Britain, France, Italy, and Germany represented the range of liberal experience in the European political order. Almost without exception, other nations were variants on the liberal theme. The pace of social and political change differed, depending on the strength of liberalism and the ability of elites to maintain their authority against the emerging political challenge of the working class. As widening suffrage laws involved larger numbers in political life and as governments assumed a greater responsibility for social welfare, the state also claimed more loyalty from its citizens.

The Rise of Feminism

In 1879 the Norwegian dramatist Henrik Ibsen (1828–1906) published a play, titled *A Doll's House*, which exposed the frustration of a wife who felt trapped in what appeared to be a "perfect" marriage. The play ends with Nora, the wife, walking out of her husband's house and slamming the door. Nora became a symbol of female independence for women who sought to escape patriarchy and the middle-class family.

Modern feminism has its roots in the social transformations caused by industrialization as well as in the rebellion against the constraints imposed on women by the ideology of bourgeois respectability. The gulf separating lower-class from middle-class women widened, and not simply because of differences in income and status. Prosperity increased the leisure of middle-class females, who were relieved of household tasks by servants and laborsaving devices. Yet many bourgeois women resented their removal from the workplace, their inferior education, and their confinement in the home.

Social Activism and Women's Rights

To escape their constricted lives, bourgeois women sought outlets in such activities as philanthropy, church work, and temperance drives. British and American women were zealous proponents of abolitionism, although they were forced to take second place to males in abolitionist groups. In the second half of the nineteenth century they did volunteer duty in workhouses, hospitals, and urban tenements, thereby opening up new professions for women in nursing and teaching. After Jane Addams (1860–1935) had established Hull House, Chicago's famous social welfare center, and Beatrice Potter Webb (1858–1943) had disguised herself as an unemployed worker in order to investigate poverty in London's slums, social work also gave women employment opportunities.

Women could not help but be struck by the bitter irony of their efforts to combat racial and industrial slavery while they themselves remained oppressed, and many turned from social activism to feminist militancy in an effort to secure political equality. The beginnings of the modern women's liberation movement can be traced to the world antislavery convention that met in London in 1840, where Elizabeth Cady Stanton (1815–1902) and other women delegates were forced to sit in a curtained galley, separate from the men. In July 1848, Stanton organized a women's rights convention in Seneca Falls, New York, which issued an 18-point "declaration of sentiments" demanding the vote, property and divorce rights, and equal employment opportunities.

In Europe feminists found support in the British reformer John Stuart Mill (1806–1873). Mill was a disciple of the philosopher Jeremy Bentham, who had argued

that the best government was one that gave its citizens access to the greatest pleasure and the least pain. In 1859 Mill published *On Liberty*, which posited that society should permit every individual the fullest degree of liberty consistent with the freedom of others. Government, argued Mill, may restrict freedom only to protect society. Conversely, Mill's democratic sentiments led him to urge government action to eliminate poverty, the exploitation of child labor and economic injustice, and the repression of women.

During the debate over the Reform Act of 1867, Mill, a member of the House of Commons, introduced an amendment to give women the vote. Though defeated 194 to 73, the minority vote was surprisingly large. With contributions from his wife, Harriet Taylor (1807–1859), Mill incorporated the women's rights issue into his theory of liberty in a ground-breaking essay, *The Subjection of Women* (1869). The principle of utility, said Mill, demanded that society eliminate inequality and prejudice, which had prevented women from bringing their talents to bear on public issues. Mill had been arrested in his youth for advocating birth control methods and was convinced that women were the victims of sexual domination. His essay pointed out that men had convinced women of their own inferiority. Later the social scientist Lester Ward (1841–1913) extended Mill's arguments by asserting in *Dynamic Sociology* (1883) a theory of the natural superiority of women.

◉ The Principle of Utilitarianism ◉

The philosophical basis of nineteenth-century liberalism owed much to the work of John Stuart Mill, whose "utilitarian" theories were based on the principle of the greatest good for the greatest number of people. Here Mill explains what he meant by "good."

The creed which accepts as the foundation of morals, Utility, or the Greatest Happiness Principle, holds that actions are right in proportion as they tend to promote happiness, wrong as they tend to produce the reverse of happiness. By happiness is intended pleasure, and the absence of pain; by unhappiness, pain, and the privation of pleasure. To give a clear view of the moral standard set up by the theory, much more requires to be said; in particular, what things it includes in the ideas of pain and pleasure; and to what extent this is left an open question. But these supplementary explanations do not affect the theory of life on which this theory of morality is grounded—namely, that pleasure, and freedom from pain, are the only things desirable as ends; and that all desirable things (which are as numerous in the utilitarian as in any other scheme) are desirable either for the pleasure inherent in themselves, or as means to the promotion of pleasure and the prevention of pain.

Source: J. S. Mill, *Utilitarianism*, 15th ed. (London: Longman, 1907), pp. 9–10.

The Suffrage Struggle

The women's movement spread throughout Europe in the nineteenth century. Often divided over tactics and goals, feminist leaders nevertheless constituted a kind of women's international as they fought against male privilege, government and church policy, and tradition. In 1868 British women founded the National Society for Women's Suffrage. The following year Susan B. Anthony (1820–1906) and Elizabeth Stanton established the National Woman Suffrage Association, which merged with other groups in 1890 to form the National American Woman Suffrage Association. By the 1870s unmarried propertied women had received the municipal franchise in Britain, Sweden, and Finland, and American women had gained the suffrage in a few states.

On the European continent, especially where the Catholic church was strong, the women's movement generally incorporated the suffrage into broader campaigns. In France two generations of feminist activism had been repressed after the 1848 revolutions, but the women's rights struggle revived during the Third Republic under the leadership of Hubertine Auclert, who demanded the vote on the principle of "perfect equality of the sexes before the law and before customs and morality."[1] Anna Maria Mozzoni translated Mill's essay on women into Italian and published a women's journal, while Luise Otto-Peters, who had fought for women's rights during the 1848 revolutions, cofounded the General Association of German Women in 1865. Efforts to forge unity among suffrage forces climaxed in 1902 in the International Alliance of Women, which held congresses in Berlin, Copenhagen, Amsterdam, London, Stockholm, and Budapest.

EMMELINE PANKHURST AND THE POLITICS OF CONFRONTATION

The suffrage movement captured public attention in Britain after the turn of the century under the fiery leadership of Emmeline Pankhurst (1858–1928), a woman of immense determination and eloquence. The daughter of a Manchester textile printer, Pankhurst was educated in Paris and was influenced by French feminists. In 1879 she married Richard Pankhurst, an advocate of women's suffrage with whom she promoted the Women's Property Act.

After working with suffrage groups in Manchester, Pankhurst became convinced that women had to use confrontational, and at times violent, tactics to publicize their cause and win the right to vote. In 1886 she participated in a strike of female workers in a London match factory, an experience that taught her the advantages of direct action. Three years later she helped establish, in

Emmeline Pankhurst, whose radical strategies emboldened British suffragettes, was repeatedly arrested.
[Culver Pictures]

affiliation with the Liberal party, the Women's Franchise League. Because it met with resistance from the Liberals, she subsequently switched her political allegiance to the Independent Labour party. When the death of her husband in 1898 left her alone to raise a son and three daughters, she took a civil service job but was fired because of her suffrage work.

Inspired by her daughter Christabel, also an ardent feminist, in 1903 Pankhurst created the Women's Social and Political Union (WSPU), a London-based suffrage organization without party affiliation. The WSPU opposed candidates for elected office who did not support the women's vote. Together with her daughters Sylvia and Christabel, Pankhurst led an army of women—called "suffragettes" to distinguish them from the "suffragists" of the moderate National Union of Women's Suffrage Societies—in public meetings, marches to Buckingham Palace, and demonstrations before Parliament.

In 1911, after the government's continued refusal to adopt a prosuffrage platform, Pankhurst took control of the WSPU and, with Christabel, directed a window-smashing campaign along fashionable shopping streets, for which Emmeline received a nine-month prison term. Nevertheless, the WSPU's tactics grew more violent. One woman chained herself to the railings at 10 Downing Street, the residence of the prime minister, while shouting "Votes for women!" Some resorted to bombings and arson; one woman smashed the Rokeby Venus, a painting in the National Museum, and another tried to strike the Tory Winston Churchill with a horse whip. Following an attempt to bomb the house of Lloyd George, Pankhurst was sentenced to three years' penal servitude. During repeated jail terms, she and her daughters went on hunger strikes to dramatize their cause and had to be force-fed. In 1913 Emily Davison was killed after flinging herself in front of King George V's horse at the Epsom Derby. As the American suffrage

◉ The Suffragette Revolt ◉

The radical suffragettes of the pre–World War I period declared a feminist war against middle-class society in their efforts to win the vote for women. In this speech, made in London in 1912 after having been released from prison, the British suffragette Emmeline Pankhurst delivered her challenge in no uncertain terms.

Ladies and gentlemen, the only recklessness the militant suffragists have shown about human life has been about their own lives and not about the lives of others, and I say here and now that it never has been and never will be the policy of the Women's Social and Political Union recklessly to endanger human life. We leave that to the enemy. We leave that to the men in their warfare. It is not the method of women. . . . There is something that governments care far more for than human life, and that is the security of property, and so it is through property that we shall strike the enemy. From henceforward the women who agree with me will say, "We disregard your laws, gentlemen, we set the liberty and the dignity and the welfare of women above all such considerations, and we shall continue this war as we have done in the past; and what sacrifice of property, or what injury to property accrues will not be our fault. It will be the fault of that government who admits the justice of our demands, but refuses to concede them. . . ."

Be militant each in your own way. Those of you who can express your militancy by going to the House of Commons and refusing to leave without satisfaction, as we did in the early days—do so. . . . Those of you who can express your militancy by joining us in our anti-government by-election policy—do so. Those of you who can break windows—break them. Those of you who can still further attack the secret idol of property, so as to make the government realize that property is as greatly endangered by women's suffrage as it was by the Chartists of old—do so.

And my last word is to the government: I incite this meeting to rebellion! . . . Take me, if you dare, but if you dare I tell you this, . . . you will not keep me in prison.

Source: E. Pankhurst, *My Own Story* (New York: Hearst's International Library, 1914), pp. 264–266.

leader Carrie Chapman Catt observed, the Pankhursts were "in a state of insurrection" against the British government.[2]

The efforts of Emmeline Pankhurst and other courageous women contributed to the development of feminist consciousness as well as to the vote issue, but the women's movement achieved only limited success before World War I. Pankhurst threw herself into war work after 1914 despite fading health. Her lifelong struggle for women's suffrage bore fruit in 1918 with the passage of the Representation of the People Act.

Science and the Doctrine of Progress

The worship of science and the belief in progress that marked European attitudes in this period weakened the eighteenth-century emphasis on the efficacy of human will. In broad terms, the Enlightenment had taught that people could shape their own destinies and mold society to their needs. Nineteenth-century developments, by contrast, reinforced the view that the scientific method could merely reveal the laws governing the physical and social environment. The process of discovery offered the promise of unending material improvement, but the laws of science could not be changed or suspended. Hence the optimism of the eighteenth century was replaced by a vision of perfectability that portrayed humans as part of a larger process of change.

The Darwinian Revolution

Scientific discoveries and technological advances had made possible Europe's Industrial Revolution and the improvement in its standard of living. The growth of literacy encouraged the popularity of science and the spread of its methods to other disciplines. The French philosopher Auguste Comte (1798–1857) was the first major figure to apply scientific principles to the study of society. In his *System of Positive Philosophy*, worked out in the 1830s, Comte argued that laws of social behavior paralleled the physical laws governing the universe and that both were discoverable through the study of specific data. Observation of individual phenomena, he believed, would demonstrate the similarities between them, which would in turn reveal natural laws. Comte described human thought as having moved from an early "theological" stage in which it was believed that the world operated by divine action to a "metaphysical" phase that sought to understand nature through abstract principles. Comte saw the thought of his own day as the

final, "positive" stage, when observable data rather than metaphysical forces explained human behavior and the physical world.

Although Comte rejected theories of evolution, his work dovetailed with that of a number of natural scientists. Jean-Baptiste Lamarck (1744–1829) had tried to show that plants and animals—including humans—had evolved by adjusting to the environment. Sir Charles Lyell (1797–1875), in his *Principles of Geology* (1830–1833), explained the formation of the earth as the result of a slow process of geologic evolution rather than a sudden cataclysm or act of creation. Lamarck and Lyell relied on the painstaking accumulation of evidence in the development of their theories.

These theories formed the intellectual climate in which the British naturalist Charles Darwin (1809–1882) formulated his theses about evolution. His famous book *On the Origin of Species by Means of Natural Selection* (1859) was not the first work to posit a theory of evolution, but it explained in unprecedented detail how the evolutionary process worked. Darwin's principle of natural selection involved a number of points. Because every species produced more individual life forms than could survive, a struggle for existence took place within and between species. Variations, he asserted, gave some organisms advantages in the competition, so that only the fittest survived. But changing environmental conditions demanded alterations in the definition of fitness. In *The Descent of Man* (1871), Darwin argued that, like other forms of life, humans also evolved—from an ancestral type common to anthropoid apes—by the same principle of natural selection.

Darwin's theory was startling because it challenged both the deistic notion that the universe had been designed by God as well as the biblical account of creation. By claiming that the survival and development of organisms was a mechanistic process, Darwin rejected the notion of divine purpose in nature. His vision of a constantly changing world in which humans were simply another form of animal life seemed to support the spirit of materialism.

Science and Society

Darwin had been influenced by social theorists, including Thomas Malthus, whose *Essay on the Principle of Population* (1798) had predicted that population growth would outstrip food supplies. Social scientists, in turn, used Darwin to support their arguments, but in doing so they took evolution far beyond Darwin's intent. The British political philosopher Walter Bagehot (1826–1877) applied natural selection to politics, asserting the superiority of nations that conquered others. His fellow countryman Herbert Spencer (1820–1903) made the classic case for what, ironically, came to be called Social Darwinism—Darwin himself never endorsed this doctrine. In his *Synthetic Philosophy*, Spencer contended that the economic competition of individuals advanced social progress by eliminating the weak. His arguments reflected an extreme form of laissez-faire liberalism that opposed state assistance to the poor and similar social legislation. By the end of the nineteenth century the Darwinian concept of the survival of the fittest had even been used to justify imperial conquest and racism.

Culture and Industrial Society

European artists and writers were profoundly affected by the new culture of science and industry. The contradictions of industrial civilization gave rise to two opposing trends in the arts during the second half of the nineteenth century. The idealistic fervor of Romantic painting was replaced by an "academic" style descended from the official canons of seventeenth- and eighteenth-century painting that deemphasized the individual's quest for meaning through an encounter with nature. Academic portraits conveyed the values of the middle class, while bucolic landscapes presented orderly treatments of nature.

Other artists responded to industrial society with a powerful "realism" that rejected an idealized version of industrial civilization. The call for a new artistic conscience was sounded by critics such as John Ruskin (1819–1900), who, like many of the realists, was influenced by socialist critiques of industrial capitalism and sought to make painting and literature responsive to the problems of the age.

Painting: New Visions of Reality

Scientific developments affected culture profoundly. Some artists saw the development of the camera in the early decades of the century—the first photograph dates from around 1826—as a threat to painting, especially if they defined art as the reproduction of observable experience. But artists such as the Frenchmen Édouard Manet (1832–1883) and Edgar Degas (1834–1917) and the American Thomas Eakins (1844–1916) used photography to study form and motion. Moreover, the realist painters found inspiration in daily life and approached their subject matter with sensitivity.

The British artist J. M. W. Turner (1775–1851) had taken an important step in this direction with his controversial *Rail, Steam and Speed: The Great Western Railway*

(1845). Although Turner claimed that the scene represented a literal depiction of a train in a snowstorm, the public rejected his energy-charged treatment of a locomotive as subject matter unsuited to true art. The French painters Gustave Courbet (1819–1877) and Honoré Daumier (1808–1879) were the major proponents of realism. Courbet believed that the search for truth required the artist to reveal the ugly as well as the beautiful. Influenced by socialism, Courbet made the working class the focus of his work because modern life relied on its labor. He was a realist not in the sense that he rendered the details of every object but in that he portrayed the harsh reality of workers and peasants without idealizing his subjects. *The Stonebreakers* (1849) depicts two workers whose hidden faces betray the anonymity of grueling labor. Daumier, who had been a cartoonist for a radical newspaper, executed watercolors and drawings of common people that deliberately avoided a romanticized vision of poverty.

In the last third of the nineteenth century some artists moved beyond realism under the impact of scientific theories. From recent discoveries in optics, artists learned that air and light are waves of color joined by the human eye into patterns. Their use of short, broken brushstrokes and specific hues captured the way in which changing sunlight affected objects. In doing so, these artists rejected a frozen rendering of reality in favor of a view that was at once scientific and subjective.

The painting by the Frenchman Claude Monet (1840–1926) titled *Impression: Sunrise* (1873) inspired a hostile critic to dub the new style "Impressionism." Monet's fellow Impressionists, including Camille Pissarro (1830–1903), Auguste Renoir (1841–1919), Henri de Toulouse-Lautrec (1864–1901), and Edgar Degas, were similarly committed to these concerns. The Impressionists depicted subject matter that varied from Monet's early railroad station, *Gare Saint-Lazare, Paris*, to the chorus girls of Toulouse-Lautrec's posters and Manet's *Bar at the Folies-Bergères*. While their vision still concerned how the world appeared to the human eye, it was sharply different from that of realists such as Courbet and Daumier.

The Literary Response

If poetry was the major literary mode of the Romantic era, the novel best suited the industrial age. By midcentury an older generation of writers such as Honoré de Balzac (1799–1850) and Victor Hugo (1802–1885) was already making a transition from Romanticism to realism to express injustice. Whereas Hugo's *Les Misérables* (1862) combined political radicalism with emotionally evocative social criticism, Balzac and Gustave Flaubert (1821–1880) shaped a consciously un-Romantic form. Balzac launched the realist movement with a series of novels collectively titled *The Human Comedy*, and Flaubert's *Madame Bovary* (1857), which was prosecuted for its candid treatment of adultery, revealed the sordid underside of bourgeois life. One of the most powerful works in this genre was Émile Zola's *Germinal* (1885), a portrayal of socialist hopes among French miners. Flaubert and Zola led the way from realism to naturalism by applying the principles of scientific observation to the human condition. Influenced by Darwin, the naturalists demonstrated the effect of social environment on personality.

The works of two Russian writers, Ivan Turgenev (1818–1883) and Leo Tolstoy (1828–1910), and of the Norwegian dramatist Henrik Ibsen revealed the universal character of realism. Flaubert had a pronounced influence on Turgenev. Turgenev's first important work, *A Sportsman's Sketches* (1852), was a strenuous protest against serfdom. His novel *Fathers and Sons* (1862) introduced the term *nihilism* to express his protagonist's rejection of all forms of authority. In the tragic story of *Anna Karenina* (1877), Tolstoy depicted a character similar to Flaubert's Madame Bovary. His masterpiece, the monumental novel *War and Peace* (1869), set against the background of the Napoleonic wars, reflected his sense of Russian nationalism as well as the detailed analysis of characters and events many realists employed.

Ibsen's plays explored the conflict between individual freedom and the bourgeois, materialist culture of the late nineteenth century. Whereas Flaubert and Tolstoy examined the theme of adultery, *A Doll's House* (1879) portrayed a wife who suddenly realizes that she has been living for years with a distant husband who considers her simply a precious possession. Like Mill, Ibsen believed in the obligation of society to further individual freedom, but he was disillusioned by political theories. In *An Enemy of the People* (1882), Ibsen lashed out at the cupidity of the majority who, because their income is endangered, refuse to accept a physician's discovery that the mineral waters of their town are polluted.

The greatest popular success of the realist genre was achieved by the British writer Charles Dickens (1812–1870). His novels were widely read through serialization in newspapers and magazines. His grotesque characters and often improbable plots took Dickens beyond the realm of conventional realism. Yet his novels vividly portrayed the social problems of his times, and his most compelling plots were set in the cities, where social classes played out the contradictions of industrialism. The protagonist of *Oliver Twist* (1838) is an orphan brought up in a workhouse for pauper children, where he is mistreated by a cruel master. Dickens reveals how poverty leads to injustice, crime, and tragedy. In *Hard Times* (1854), Dickens deals with the human consequences of aggressive economic individualism in an industrial city called Coketown, where a selfish businessman obsessed with sales and money destroys the lives of his children.

From industrial Britain to agrarian Russia, nineteenth-century novels and plays came to grips with the harsh realities of industrial capitalism and bourgeois society, adding a powerful voice to the protests of the working class.

Socialism and the Labor Movement

Working-class militancy in Europe struggled against the misery and alienation of industrial capitalism. The sans-culottes of the French Revolution and the Luddites of eighteenth-century Britain, like the utopian idealists Robert Owen and Saint-Simon and the British Chartists and the revolutionaries of 1848, had vented worker rebellion against exploitation. As liberalism triumphed after 1850, some of the harsher aspects of industrialism were blunted by reforms. Nevertheless, laborers devised strategies aimed at improving working conditions, and some advocated the elimination of capitalism itself.

In the second half of the nineteenth century the working-class movement focused around three traditions: trade unionism, anarchism, and the scientific socialism derived from the principles of Karl Marx and Friedrich Engels. Unionism accepted industrial capitalism as a permanent feature of modern life but sought to mitigate its impact by improving wages, benefits, and working conditions. Unionists gradually won a legal basis for organizing and the right to strike. Anarchism and Marxist socialism, by contrast, rejected the permanence of capitalism and saw private property as a source of repression and inequality that could not be reformed. Although Marx himself in later life advocated a political path to socialism, many of his followers continued to believe in violent revolution. Anarchists and Marxists were divided in their attitudes toward the state. Anarchists, rejecting all forms of authority, sought to destroy government, while Marxists wanted to seize control of the state and install the proletariat in power, leaving the destruction of the state for a later stage. These divisions weakened the working-class movement.

Socialism, Anarchism, and the Paris Commune

Initially, socialists, anarchists, and other radicals collaborated in the creation of the International Workingmen's Association, founded in London in 1864. The First International, as it was generally known, tried to coordinate labor activities throughout Europe and provide a vehicle for socialist debate. Marx, who gave its inaugural address and was its dominant figure, clashed with Mikhail Bakunin (1814–1876), the exiled Russian anarchist, and eventually drove nonsocialists from the International.

Marx's triumph came a year after the Paris Commune, a pivotal event in international socialism. Marx contributed to the legend surrounding the Commune with a pamphlet titled *The Civil War in France*, in which he argued that it represented the first clear-cut case of proletarian violence. A few international socialists and anarchists had been involved in the Commune uprising, along with large numbers of radicals and ordinary citizens who had no clear program, but the Commune was by no means a Marxist revolution. Yet socialists everywhere came to regard it as a symbol both of the class struggle and of the bourgeois determination to crush worker agitation. Throughout Europe liberal governments reacted to the Commune by imposing restrictions on the working-class movement.

The First International dissolved in 1872 in the wake of the Commune and the socialist-anarchist split. For two decades thereafter, militant action remained largely in the hands of the anarchists, who increasingly adopted terrorist tactics, which they termed "propaganda of the deed." Anarchists tried twice in the 1870s to assassinate Kaiser William I and succeeded in killing a number of statesmen and heads of state, including Tsar Alexander II of Russia (1881), the French president François Sadi-Carnot (1894), the Spanish prime minister Antonio Cánovas del Castillo (1897), Empress Elizabeth of Austria-Hungary (1898), King Umberto I of Italy (1900), and the American president William McKinley (1901). Despite these acts of terrorism, many anarchist leaders repudiated violence. Prince Peter Kropotkin (1842–1921), a Russian noble exiled in London, argued for peaceful cooperation among workers, and the Italian anarchist Errico Malatesta (1853–1932) stressed the humanitarian nature of anarchism and saw himself as an antiauthoritarian socialist.

Trade Unions and the Labor Movement

Although Marx had predicted the growth and concentration of capitalist wealth, the condition of the working class itself did not worsen. Indeed, the general prosperity that began in the 1850s improved the standard of living of most workers, moderating the attitudes of labor and slowing the growth of unions. By the latter part of the century, however, craft unions, representing skilled trades, were again organizing. In the 1870s the Liberal ministry of Gladstone recognized such unions and legalized the strike. The London dockworkers' strike of 1889 provided the impetus for the organization of unskilled laborers and gave rise to industrial unions representing both skilled and unskilled workers throughout

an entire industry. By the end of the century Britain's 2 million union members represented the largest and most successful union experience in Europe.

Beyond Britain, modern unions developed largely during the two decades of economic depression that stretched into the 1890s, largely under the banner of socialism. Napoleon III had permitted unions in 1864 in France, but they were suppressed after the Commune, and only in 1884 did the Third Republic grant them legal status. In Germany, Bismarck's antisocialist campaign retarded their formation until the Imperial Industrial Code of 1891 permitted the right to strike. By 1900 organized labor counted some 850,000 members in Germany and 250,000 in France; in Italy and Austria-Hungary unions were slower to develop.

In the 1890s unionism on the Continent took a more radical turn under the influence of syndicalist leaders. The Frenchman Georges Sorel (1847–1922) was the major proponent of syndicalism (from the French word *syndicat*, "trade union"). He argued that unions rather than political parties were the logical institutions through which working-class leaders could take power from the middle class and reorganize society. In 1895 syndicalists formed the General Confederation of Labor, a union umbrella organization that undertook strike action and rivaled the socialists for leadership of the labor movement. Syndicalism spread to Italy, where leaders attempted an unsuccessful general strike in 1904. After the 1905 Russian revolution, Rosa Luxemburg (1870–1919), a Polish Jew active in politics, published a pamphlet titled *The Mass Strike, the Party, and the Trade Unions* (1906) in which she defined the strike as a political weapon. In *Reflections on Violence* (1908), Sorel proclaimed the general strike as the only means of achieving socialism. The general strike, he argued, would provoke violent state repression, which would incite the workers to revolt.

Socialist Parties: Between Reform and Revolution

Socialist parties grew rapidly in the years after the Paris Commune. Despite Bismarck's efforts to crush it, German socialism flowered. In 1869 two Marxists, August Bebel (1840–1913) and Wilhelm Liebknecht (1826–1900), founded the Social Democratic Labor party, which elected several deputies to parliament. In 1875 the Social Democrats joined forces with the more moderate followers of Ferdinand Lassalle (1825–1864) to issue the so-called Gotha program, combining Marxist theory with pragmatic Lassallian reforms. Although Marx denounced the mixture of revolutionary doctrine and reformist objectives, the resulting German Social Demo-

Women were active in organizing labor unions and in strike activity. Here is a women's labor parade held in New York City in 1913. [UPI/Bettmann Archive]

cratic party (SPD) became the strongest socialist party in Europe.

The German example inspired socialists elsewhere. In Belgium socialists founded a party in 1879. A non-Marxist Italian Worker party developed in 1882, although the socialists did not develop an organization of their own until ten years later. Meanwhile, Russian exiles in Switzerland formed the Russian Social Democrats in 1883. In both Italy and Russia police repression against socialists and anarchists was particularly severe and forced many radicals to spend years in exile. In France doctrinal disputes led to the creation of separate parties that did not unite until 1905.

British socialism followed the same moderate path as its unions. In 1884 a group of middle-class intellectuals founded the Fabian Society.* Led by the Irish playwright George Bernard Shaw (1856–1950), Sydney Webb (1859–1947), Beatrice Webb, and the novelist H. G. Wells (1866–1946), the Fabians rejected violent revolution. In 1900 socialists formed the Labour party.

As socialist parties gathered strength throughout Europe, their leaders attempted to reawaken international solidarity with the creation in 1889 of the Second International. It served largely to organize congresses, coor-

dinate May Day celebrations in honor of the working class, and provide a forum for consultation. National parties continued to provide the impetus for the socialist movement.

In the two decades before World War I the international working-class movement was dominated by the opposing models offered by German and French socialists. In 1899 Éduard Bernstein (1850–1932) published a theoretical work titled *Evolutionary Socialism*. Bernstein, who had been influenced by the British Fabians, was both a revisionist and a reformist. His revisionism derived from his conviction that Marxist doctrine had to evolve as social, political, and economic conditions changed. In the context of a parliamentary system and an expanding industrial economy such as prevailed in Germany, Bernstein challenged Marx's beliefs in the coming crisis of capitalism, the increasing polarization of classes, and the certainty of working-class revolution. This position led him to abandon revolutionary tactics in favor of achieving concrete gains for workers through parliamentary reform and collaboration with non-Marxist parties. In effect, Bernstein's arguments reflected German socialist policy since the 1870s, although his reformism was bitterly denounced by orthodox Marxists. Indeed, the reformist-revolutionary controversy split socialist parties everywhere.

Bernstein's counterpart in France was Jean Jaurès (1859–1914), a fiery speaker and humanist scholar who urged socialist collaboration with middle-class govern-

---

*Named after the ancient Roman general Quintus Fabius Maximus, who avoided pitched battles with the Carthaginians in favor of harassing operations.

ments to secure reforms. Under pressure from the International, which condemned revisionist "opportunism" and urged French socialists to unite into one party, Jaurès reverted to orthodoxy.

Women of the Left

The development of socialist political parties gave added impetus to the women's movement. Although women experienced resentment even within socialist parties and did not often rise to top positions in labor organizations, they found more acceptance from male comrades than in other parties. Socialists eschewed civil marriage as a bourgeois institution and practiced free love in radical circles. Most socialist parties eventually advocated universal suffrage, divorce laws, and birth control.

Despite German laws that prohibited women from engaging in political activity, the SPD took the lead in organizing women. After the party accepted their right to work, a law forced the creation of separate groups for women. In 1878 Bebel issued his *Women in the Past, Present, and Future*, the first sustained study of the women's question from a socialist perspective. Six years later Engels published *The Origins of the Family, Private Property, and the State*. The core of their arguments remained the idea that the suppression of women evolved as the concept of private property developed.

The party's major theoretician of Marxist feminism was Clara Zetkin (1857–1933), who pioneered female militancy within the SPD as well as in the Second International and edited the magazine *Equality*. Zetkin's theories of female emancipation started out from Marx and Engels' position concerning the nature of the middle-class family. She argued that housework and child rear-

---

◉ Socialist Women ◉

The Russian-born Angelica Balabanoff (1869–1965) was one of the most important figures in the prewar socialist movement. After leaving her wealthy family, she studied and worked in the movement throughout Europe, serving on the executive committee of the Second International for many years. Here she describes her early collaboration with Maria Giudice, an Italian socialist, while both were in St. Gall, Switzerland, in 1904.

One day . . . I received word that a young Italian teacher, an ardent propagandist for Socialism, was coming to St. Gall. She had only recently fled from Italy to escape imprisonment for an article she had written. I wrote the comrades at St. Gall that Maria was to have the use of my room. When I returned I found . . . Maria was experiencing her first pregnancy. She eventually became the mother of seven children and the object of considerable gossip. . . . Several years later, in Italy, the editor of a clerical journal made slurring remarks about Maria's morals. Meeting him in the marketplace one day, Maria, in a loud voice that all round her could hear, inquired of a vegetable woman if this was the man who had gossiped about her. The startled woman . . . nodded her head affirmatively. Maria then stepped in the path of the astonished editor and, before the crowd which had already assembled, gave him a resounding slap in the face. There was little more talk of Maria and her children after that. . . .

At the time Maria lived with me in St. Gall, the Italian Socialists had no special propaganda paper for women. We conceived the notion that one should be started. . . . Both Maria and I were hostile to any form of "feminism." To us the fight for the emancipation of women was only a single aspect of the struggle for the emancipation of humanity. It was because we wanted women, particularly workingwomen, to understand this, to learn that they had to fight not *against* men but *with* them against the common enemy, capitalist society, that we felt the need of this paper. Moving to Lugano, Maria and I founded *Su, Compagne!* (*Arise, Comrades!*). It was an almost instant success. . . .

Source: A. Balabanoff, *My Life as a Rebel* (New York: Harper, 1938), pp. 34–35.

ing represented exploitation in the form of unpaid labor. Bourgeois morality had made women little more than property controlled by men. Hence women's liberation was impossible in isolation but had to take place as part of the broader socialist struggle against capitalism. Because Zetkin believed that female labor was a precondition for the liberation of women from sexual slavery, she urged them to participate in the work force as well as in socialist politics.

The Gotha program of 1875 had advocated universal suffrage but refused to support more radical feminist views. Zetkin and other women eventually forced the SPD to adopt a broader feminist position. In 1894 SPD deputies in the Reichstag first proposed a bill for women's suffrage, although it was defeated.

Together with Rosa Luxemburg, Zetkin opposed Bernstein's revisionist principles. Their denunciations of reform socialism separated them from other women in the SPD as well as from nonsocialists because they argued the incompatibility of the socialist women's movement and bourgeois feminism. Nonsocialist feminists, they argued, sanctioned capitalism, a system of exploitation that repressed men and women alike. Whereas Zetkin made the feminist cause the center of her professional life, Luxemburg subsumed women's issues into the larger question of revolution. The hostility of the revisionist leadership drove Zetkin and Luxemburg further to the left, and on the eve of World War I they were among the extremists who formed the German Communist party.

The rise of feminism and socialism after 1870, like the work of realist painters and novelists, revealed the deep contradictions that beset the liberal order in Europe. The political order moved toward democracy, while advances in education, health, and communications contributed to the modernization of a society in which workers and peasants were more fully integrated into national life. Yet industrial capitalism, which had produced remarkable prosperity, also engendered economic and cultural oppression in the organization of work, gender and family relations, and the accumulation of unprecedented wealth by a new business-financial elite. Nor was the prosperity of the period evenly distributed. Workers' wages rose except during the Long Depression, but poverty was still widespread. Illiter-

acy, infant mortality, and illness remained higher among the workers than in the middle classes.

Constitutional monarchies and parliamentary regimes based on universal male suffrage had replaced absolute monarchy almost everywhere in Europe by the opening of the twentieth century. Nevertheless, in some Western states liberal governments proved no less vigorous than the old autocrats in preserving a stable social order and protecting the interests of industrial capitalism and patriarchy. While Europe remained generally at peace for almost half a century, the international order spawned by liberalism also produced militarism and new forms of nationalism, racism, and imperialism.

Notes

1. C. G. Moses, *French Feminism in the Nineteenth Century* (Albany: State University of New York Press, 1984), p. 213.
2. E. F. Hurwitz, "The International Sisterhood," in *Becoming Visible: Women in European History*, ed. R. Bridenthal and C. Koonz (Boston: Houghton Mifflin, 1977), p. 337.

Suggestions for Further Reading

Bridenthal, R., and Koonz, C., eds. *Becoming Visible: Women in European History*. Boston: Houghton Mifflin, 1977.

Burrow, J. W. *Evolution and Society: A Study in Victorian Social Theory*. Cambridge: Cambridge University Press, 1966.

Cahm, C. *Peter Kropotkin and the Rise of Revolutionary Anarchism*. New York: Cambridge University Press, 1989.

Clark, M. *Modern Italy, 1871–1982*. London: Longman, 1984.

Friedberg, A. L. *The Weary Titan: Britain and the Experience of Relative Decline, 1895–1905*. Princeton, N.J.: Princeton University Press, 1989.

Girouard, M. *Cities and People: A Social and Architectural History*. New Haven, Conn.: Yale University Press, 1985.

Harrison, F. *The Dark Angel: Aspects of Victorian Sexuality*. New York: Sheldon Press, 1977.

Hayes, C. J. H. *The Generation of Materialism, 1871–1900*. New York: Harper, 1941.

Joll, J. *The Second International, 1889–1914*. New York: Harper & Row, 1966.

Joyce, P. *Visions of the People: Industrial England and the Question of Class, c. 1848–1914.* New York: Cambridge University Press, 1991.

Landes, D. *The Unbound Prometheus: Technological Change and Industrial Development in Western Europe from 1750 to the Present.* Cambridge: Cambridge University Press, 1969.

Marsden, G., ed. *Victorian Values: Personalities and Perspectives in 19th-Century Society.* New York: Longman, 1990.

Milward, A. S., and Saul, S. B. *The Development of the Economies of Continental Europe, 1850–1914.* Cambridge, Mass.: Harvard University Press, 1977.

Mosse, G. L. *The Culture of Western Europe.* Chicago: Rand McNally, 1961.

Pflanze, O. *Bismarck and the Development of Germany*, vols. 2–3. Princeton, N.J.: Princeton University Press, 1990.

Pugh, M. *The Making of British Politics, 1867–1939.* Oxford: Blackwell, 1982.

Rewald, J. *The History of Impressionism.* New York: Museum of Modern Art, 1961.

———. *Post-Impressionism.* New York: Museum of Modern Art, 1978.

Sheehan, J. J. *German Liberalism in the Nineteenth Century.* Chicago: University of Chicago Press, 1978.

Stearns, P. N. *European Society in Upheaval: Social History Since 1800.* New York: Macmillan, 1967.

Thoennessen, W. *The Emancipation of Women: The Rise and Decline of the Women's Movement in German Social Democracy, 1863–1933.* London: Pluto Press, 1973.

Thompson, D. *Democracy in France Since 1870.* New York: Oxford University Press, 1969.

Vicinus, M., ed. *Suffer and Be Still: Women in the Victorian Age.* Bloomington: Indiana University Press, 1972.

Vincent, J. *Disraeli.* New York: Oxford University Press, 1990.

Writing and Communication (II)

Throughout the ancient and medieval world, literacy was relatively uncommon, but in time improved printing techniques encouraged its spread. In the Arab world and in Europe the production of books was limited by two factors: each copy of a text had to be written by hand, and the material used for manuscripts was generally either parchment, made from split sheepskins, or vellum (calfskin), both of which were expensive. These limitations were first overcome in China, where paper had been manufactured since the first century A.D. Around the eighth century the Chinese invented a system of printing using blocks of wood. The idea of binding several sheets of paper together followed shortly; the first printed book, consisting of six pages, was published in 868.

The notion of movable type originally had little appeal to the Chinese, whose script is made up of thousands of different characters. But in the eleventh century the Chinese developed movable type in wood, a technique later adopted by the Koreans, who were the first to use it on a large scale. Both the Chinese and the Koreans soon made metal type, which obviously lasted longer and made mass printing possible.

By the eighth century the Arabs had borrowed the Chinese method of manufacturing paper, but they had little interest in block printing, perhaps because the art of writing had become an important skill in itself. Toward the end of the twelfth century the Arabs introduced papermaking into Spain, from where the technique spread slowly into northern Europe; by the beginning of the fifteenth century it had reached Germany and Switzerland.

The introduction in Europe of movable type occurred much later than in China and Korea, in the mid-fifteenth century. The material used for the type was metal, since medieval craftsmen were skilled at engraving medals and coins. The first printed book, the so-called Gutenberg Bible, was published in 1455 at Mainz.

In China the production of books had generally been limited to works for the educated classes. The first major printing project was an edition of the Confucian classics in the tenth century, followed by the Buddhist scriptures, and during the Sung period books on art, literature, science, and philosophy appeared in large numbers. Literacy remained primarily an elite preserve, given the difficulty of the written language, but popular fiction began to grow, and literacy rose among the urban merchants, themselves an expanding group.

The effects of printing in Europe may have been more widespread or more immediate than in Asia, especially as universities and other schools enlarged their enrollments to educate the children of merchants and craftsmen. The demand for texts could now be met. Furthermore, the process was self-reinforcing: the more books there were, the more people learned to read. Thus the impact of printing was not merely to facilitate the circulation of ideas among educated people but also to make available on a popular level a vast range of material to which access had formerly been difficult, such as almanacs, herbals, and prophecies.

It soon became apparent that the new technology could be employed in conducting political, religious, and scholarly debate, and controversial positions were circulated quickly. Among the first masters of the medium was the Protestant Martin Luther, who published a series of printed tracts on church reform in 1520 and a German translation of the Bible (New Testament in 1522, Old Testament in 1534) that became a cornerstone of the Reformation. The Reformation introduced printed pamphlets, hymns, religious texts, and sacred pictures to much of northern Europe, calling for not only religious changes but social ones as well. Subsequently, debate in the Western world has been conducted in large measure in print, now supplemented by radio and television. Print has not been replaced for scholarly, scientific, or religious debate, and access to the media on social issues (except for talk shows) is generally limited to people who have established their positions in print. Only political debate has partly replaced print as the medium of prime communication, but even here print remains indispensable.

Between the Reformation and the French Revolution mass literacy began to develop in Europe and to spread among European colonizers elsewhere in the world. The first battleground for printed texts had been a sacred one, but pamphlets could now be distributed and books published to advocate or even galvanize social and political change, and the spread of popular literature had an enormous impact on the English, American, and French revolutions. Not only did pamphleteers advance specific causes or claim individual wrongs, they also served to make accessible at a popular level ideas that had hitherto been limited to intellectuals.

The pamphleteers of the French wars of religion at the end of the sixteenth century and the English Revolution in the mid-seventeenth argued fundamental religious and political ideas, and their works, often cheaply printed, attracted wide circulation. The Lon-

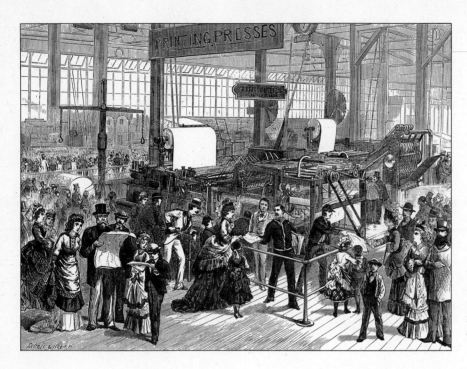

This web press, which was capable of printing on both sides of the paper, was featured at a Philadelphia exhibition in the 1870s. [Granger Collection]

don bookseller George Thomason collected nearly 30,000 books, pamphlets, broadsides, and newssheets published in England between 1640 and 1661, an astonishing output in a country of only 5 million people. The appetite for news persisted, and the seventeenth century saw the first newspapers established in Augsburg, Strasbourg, London, and Paris. The role of print expanded in the eighteenth century, making it possible for growing numbers of westerners in particular to keep abreast of public events and political issues. "Every Englishman, nowadays," said Samuel Johnson, "expects to be promptly and accurately informed upon the condition of public affairs." But not until the advent of the "penny press" in the next century were newspapers fully accessible to the masses. Such exposure required not only literacy and the availability of an extra penny to spend for a paper but also a desire to use the money to acquire the news rather than other goods.

The Enlightenment would have been unthinkable without the printing press, which enabled the philosophes to appeal over the heads of established authority for fundamental reform. Often, however, the most radical thought became available on a popular level only in times of crisis. Tom Paine crystallized revolutionary attitudes in America with a pamphlet appropriately titled *Common Sense*, and the ideas of Jean-Jacques Rousseau became crucial to the thinking of French revolutionaries when they were expressed in popular form by Sieyès in his pamphlet *What Is the Third Estate?* published in January 1789. In China, with

its far greater population, there was from the eleventh century a major increase both in popular fiction and in printed manuals and pamphlets, although, unlike their European counterparts, the latter were rarely critical of the established order.

At the same time, the growth of knowledge and its relatively easy transmission were fundamental to the sudden surge of scientific development in the West. In the eyes of thinkers such as Francis Bacon and René Descartes, it was pointless to continue to depend on ancient writers and their books: new research was needed, and fresh ideas had to be circulated. In medicine and astronomy, chemistry and physics, the basis of modern scientific practice was laid in books published as early as the sixteenth and seventeenth centuries.

Popular literacy was also responsible for something less awesome in scope but equally valuable: instruction and pleasure. From the beginning, many of the most popular books were horoscopes and prophecies, cookbooks, collections of tales, and reports of extraordinary events. New literary forms such as the novel, the short story, and science fiction were created to meet popular demand for fiction and to express new social values and aspirations. All of these forms, including manuals, novels, and even detective stories, appeared in print in China several centuries earlier than in the West, although overall literacy in China probably lagged behind after A.D. 1600. In the nineteenth century, the great age of the novel in the West, New York's dockside was often crowded with readers eagerly awaiting the arrival of the latest installment of a Charles Dickens book from England.

If the invention of writing and printing represent two giant steps in the development of world civilization, the mass communication systems of the twentieth century represent a third. The virtually instantaneous global communication that is possible today was foreshadowed in a series of nineteenth-century inventions that did much to change the role of the written word. A government postal system was introduced in Britain in 1840, much facilitated by the rapid growth of the railway system. Four years earlier, in 1836, the stamp tax on newspapers had been reduced, and by the middle of the century press circulation was three times its former level. The American Samuel Morse invented the telegraph, first used in 1844, and it soon became a valuable means of communication for Julius Reuter's news agency, the first international news service. The Prussian chancellor Otto von Bismarck effectively combined the telegraph and the press in 1870 when he edited a captured French telegram, the Ems dispatch, for publication, knowing that it would probably provoke the French to declare the war he sought; he was right, and the way was prepared for the completion of German unification.

The laying of the first permanent transatlantic cable in 1866 and Alexander Graham Bell's invention of the telephone a decade later made direct, instantaneous communication between Europe and North America possible. During World War II British prime minister

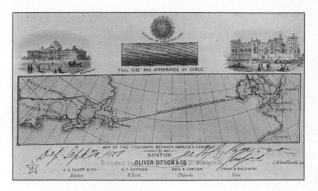

This detail from a sheet music cover commemorated the laying of a transoceanic telegraph cable in 1858. The cable failed after operating for only one month. [Granger Collection]

Winston Churchill and American president Franklin Roosevelt conferred frequently by telephone, using the undersea cable. In the aftermath of the 1961 Cuban missile crisis, Soviet and American leaders approved the creation of a direct communications link, or "hot line," between the Kremlin and the White House to facilitate rapid discussion in the event of future crises.

Another revolutionary development in communications involved the technology of the camera and film. Graphic materials, of course, had been reproduced on printing presses for centuries, but beginning in the 1830s it was possible to transmit, through the new

Alexander Graham Bell demonstrated the telephone he invented by calling Boston from Salem, Massachusetts, on March 15, 1877. [Granger Collection]

Roving photographers such as this one provided valuable documentation for social historians. This photograph was taken at a summer resort in France. [Culver Pictures]

process of photography, the immediate pictorial image of an event. Photographs were vehicles of emotion as well as information, reaching both the illiterate and the educated. The photographs of Mathew Brady (c. 1823–1896) enabled Americans to grasp the horrors that were occurring on the civil war battlefields; his work laid the foundation for modern newsphoto services. Cameras could do more than record battles; they could shape them, particularly after aerial photography became practicable. Although the first aerial shots (from balloons) dated from 1858, the development of the airplane half a century later permitted extensive use of aerial photographs for military purposes, a vital advantage in World War I. Aerial photography has also played an important role in mapping and surveying natural resources, thus facilitating communication about our physical environment.

The initial impact of these changes was limited to Europe and North America, but they were spread elsewhere in part by the Western colonial powers. In India the British founded universities in Calcutta, Bombay, and Madras, and public opinion expressed itself through newspapers. In China the foreign-run Maritime Customs Service began an efficient Western-style postal and telegraph system after 1860, and missionaries published huge numbers of tracts and founded Western-

style schools, colleges, and universities. The Dutch colonial administration of Indonesia, the British in Burma and Malaya, and the Americans in the Philippines did much the same. Japan was first widely exposed to Western influence in 1853 and soon began to employ Western technology.

In Africa the principal beneficiaries of technological progress were the colonial powers themselves. Many parts of Africa had a rich tradition of song and story that went back centuries, but little of it became known beyond the immediate oral range until the twentieth century. In general the African communicative tradition was a spoken one; some of the works of Somali and Swahili poets of the eighteenth and nineteenth centuries were written down, but virtually everything else that is known of earlier times was collected by modern anthropologists. With the arrival of European colonizers and missionaries, a limited number of Africans learned the languages and writing systems of their conquerors, but only the liberation struggles of the twentieth century produced any level of general literacy. Many African writers thus faced the dilemma of having to decide whether to produce works in an alien language for the outside world or use their own tribal language. The same problem still confronts writers in other areas whose native languages and cultures—Basque,

Gaelic, and Welsh for example—struggle to survive in the face of more widely spoken rivals.

The appearance of new inventions—radio, movies, the phonograph—combined with earlier changes to enhance the ability to communicate. In the case of sound transmission, war was again crucial in accelerating the technological development that had begun in the mid-nineteenth century. The transmission of sound using electromagnetic waves rather than wires was discovered by the Italian Guglielmo Marconi in 1895, and within 20 years transmission was possible across both the Atlantic and the Pacific. After World War I, the radio came into common use, bringing with it revolutionary possibilities for political leaders to communicate directly with the masses of their people. Among the early masters of this medium were Franklin Roosevelt, who used the radio for his "fireside chats," and Josef Goebbels, Hitler's propaganda minister. The integration of sight and sound in the cinema was achieved in 1927, when Al Jolson spoke and sang in the first "talkie," *The Jazz Singer*, and by 1930 silent pictures were antiquated. The stage was set for the filming of not only movies for entertainment but also the massive spectacles staged by Hitler at Nuremberg and the patriotic newsreels shown in movie theaters that bolstered morale during World War II.

The phonograph also had roots in the mid-nineteenth century, though only in the 1890s did serious

In the early 1920s the radio became very popular. Early sets required the use of headphones. [Culver Pictures]

manufacturing commence. Improved electrical reproduction came in the 1920s and fine-grooved records in the following decade. Culturally, it was now possible for people in one part of the world to hear and appreciate music from other continents. Perhaps there is no better example of this than the present Japanese fondness for Beethoven's Ninth (Choral) Symphony, performed widely in Japan each year. Moreover, Japanese and Korean conductors and soloists are now some of the best performers of Western music.

Perhaps the most revolutionary development in communications has been television. Although development of electronically transmitted images was under way as early as 1924, only after World War II was intercity network television launched, using coaxial cables. Microwave radio transmission began the same year, 1946, and in 1951 microwave relay made possible the first coast-to-coast television broadcast. The historical ramifications were enormous. In addition to the educational and cultural possibilities television afforded, the medium's ability to provide viewers with virtually immediate coverage of major events created new pressures as well as opportunities for political leaders. Mounting American anger over military involvement in Vietnam in the 1960s resulted at least in part from what people saw on their television screens. The widespread outpouring of sympathy and aid for famine-stricken areas in North Africa in the 1970s and early 1980s was triggered by television pictures of the victims, and television brought home unprecedentedly graphic images of violence and carnage in the Los Angeles riots and the attack on Bosnia in 1992.

Improved communications are changing modern society. Radio and especially television have substantially altered industrial societies by creating mass markets, which have in turn altered labor-management relations and created a greater homogeneity of manufactured goods. Mass communications also facilitate the creation of a consensus for action, while simultaneously providing minorities—in the absence of censorship—with the means to alter majority thinking and behavioral patterns, as Martin Luther King, Jr., demonstrated in the U.S. civil rights movement of the 1960s. Through modern technology, ideas and tastes can be increasingly homogenized, yet it is also possible to use the same means to facilitate the rapid acceptance of new styles and ideas. Television and the movies have even intensified urbanization by popularizing the lure of the cities, which are increasingly attractive both because of their employment possibilities and for their culture and lifestyle.

The pace of the communications revolution still varies considerably from region to region. For every 1,000 people in the United States, for example, there were 408 televisions and 1,417 radios in 1968, compared to 208 and 255, respectively, in Japan and 3 and 74 in

South Korea. Indonesia and India lagged even further behind, with only 14 televisions and 13 radios per 1,000 people, respectively; Nigeria had only one television set for every 1,000 persons in 1968. Such countries are only now experiencing the full brunt of the print revolution. In the period between 1948 and 1968 the number of daily newspapers declined slightly in the Western industrial countries of the United States, Great Britain, France, Italy, and the Netherlands, while they doubled in India, nearly tripled in Pakistan, and jumped nearly sevenfold in Turkey. There are, of course, exceptions to these patterns, often because of political factors such as the rise or fall of authoritarian regimes. The main problem facing developing countries seeking to implement new communications technology is the extraordinary capital outlay required, a problem that will perpetuate the communications gap in the foreseeable future.[1]

Nevertheless, the introduction of communication satellites in the 1970s made possible an operational communications network that is worldwide. Even in areas without electricity, a transistor radio can enable people to hear the news, political messages, and cultural events. But instantaneous communications can complicate international relations. In the nineteenth century, reports of hostile action on another continent could take a week or more to reach a concerned government, but at least that provided time for a considered response. With the advent of the telegraph, and now communication satellites, the pressure for rapid decisions at the expense of deliberate analysis is increased, thereby intensifying the risks of war.

The ability of computers to store and retrieve information is a recent technological advance with major implications for communications. Computers can be programmed with artificial languages to facilitate high-speed transmission of information. Used responsibly, computers are valuable for uses ranging from complex mathematical calculations to scientific experiments. But computers can also be programmed to act in the absence of human reflection, as in the case of the massive computer-generated trading that triggered enormous losses on the New York Stock Exchange in 1987. Ironically, revolutionary advances in communications technology, often generated by wartime research, have simultaneously presented the world with possibilities both deadly and visionary.

Notes

1. Statistics in this paragraph from W. P. Davison, ''The Media Kaleidoscope: General Trends in the Channels,'' in *Propaganda and Communication in World History*, ed. H. D. Lasswell, D. Lerner, and H. Speier, vol. 3 (Honolulu: University Press of Hawaii, 1980), pp. 191–248.

Suggestions for Further Reading

Abel, E., et al. *Many Voices, One World: Communications and Society*. Paris: UNESCO, 1984.

Craig, J. *Thirty Centuries of Graphic Design: An Illustrated History*. New York: Watson-Guptill, 1987.

Frawley, W. *Text and Epistemology*. Norwood, N.J.: Ablex, 1987.

Lasswell, H. D., Lerner, D., and Speier, H., eds. *Propaganda and Communication in World History*, vols. 2 and 3. Honolulu: University Press of Hawaii, 1980.

Logan, R. K. *The Alphabet Effect: The Impact of the Phonetic Alphabet on the Development of Western Civilization*. New York: Morrow, 1986.

Lowenthal, L. *Literature and Mass Culture: Communication in Society*, vol. 1. New Brunswick, N.J.: Transaction Books, 1984.

Schiller, H. I. *Information and the Crisis Economy*. Norwood, N.J.: Ablex, 1984.

Siegel, L., and Markoff, J. *The High Cost of High Tech: The Dark Side of the Chip*. New York: Harper & Row, 1985.

Whalley, J. I. *Writing Implements and Accessories: From the Roman Stylus to the Typewriter*. Detroit: Gale Research, 1975.

CHAPTER 34

The Age of Western Domination

Contemporary world history began during the last three decades of the nineteenth century, when a handful of European countries imposed their domination over major portions of the globe. Britain, France, Germany, and to a lesser extent Italy and Belgium exercised control of a large proportion of the earth's land surface and population. Russia continued to push its borders eastward into Asia, while the United States and Japan extended their presence into the Pacific region. One result of this grab for colonial possessions was the establishment of complex forms of interdependency among world civilizations that still shape our lives. This first major phase in the creation of a "global village" as a product of imperialism is the background of the contemporary age.

Detail of a painting of the Battle of Omdurman (1898), in which the British army under General Horatio Kitchener decisively defeated a Muslim force in the Sudan. [Mansell Collection]

901

The New Imperialism

The process by which this transformation took place is known as the new imperialism, to distinguish it from the previous phase of European colonial expansion that took place between the sixteenth and eighteenth centuries. This newer form of imperialism was characterized not only by its rapid and intense pace but by other unique features as well.

The earlier overseas empires lay chiefly in the Americas and included extensive European-run areas in India and Southeast Asia as well as footholds on the East Asian and African coasts. After 1870 the Western powers moved deep into the interiors of Asia and Africa. Although the older empires traded with local populations, they were generally regarded as sources of direct revenue for the home country—tribute from local rulers, taxation from the indigenous populations, and the expropriation of gold and silver.

Because the new imperialism was the work of advanced industrial-capitalist nations rather than of mercantile economies, it involved the commitment of significant financial investment as well as the deliberate exploitation of the material and human resources of the colonial areas. The economic function of the new imperialism, whether real or perceived, led in turn to the establishment of direct political control over the colonies, administered through elaborate bureaucracies. By the opening of the twentieth century, therefore, a new and direct relationship of unequal exchange had been established among the civilizations of the world, marked by a vast difference between the industrial and technological power of the West and the relative weakness of less technologically developed cultures.

Conflicting Interpretations

Scholars debate the causes and consequences of the new imperialism. One basic fact appears to be generally accepted: by 1870 conditions in Europe were ripe for overseas expansion. The breakdown of the Concert of Europe and the creation of nation-states in Germany and Italy heightened aggressive national rivalry. Moreover, power status was increasingly equated with the possession of overseas colonies, so empire became a matter of national honor. The Long Depression of 1873–1896 convinced some business and government leaders that overseas colonies would solve the problems caused by shrinking European markets and increasingly higher wages. Though policymakers often used economic arguments to explain the necessity for expansion, imperialism had support among all classes, including workers. Even trade union leaders and some socialists were enthusiastic about colonial expansion.

Economics and Empire

Economic rivalry between older industrial states such as Britain and France and newly industrializing states such as Germany and the United States added to the competition for colonies, especially as tariff barriers restricted European markets after 1880. Unprecedented prosperity and military-industrial power produced by the second phase of the Industrial Revolution and advances in science, technology, and industrial organization gave Europeans confidence in the superiority of their civilization. The climax of European development in the last decades of the century thus brought together a growing concern over national pride and security, the desire for continued economic expansion, and an appetite for cultural dominance.

The connection between economics and imperialism is hardly in doubt, although its exact nature is debated. The economic slump that began in the 1870s had increased unemployment, pushed prices for manufactured goods down, and diminished exports, making industrial nations compete fiercely over markets for their manufactured goods at a time when the abandonment of free trade limited the European market. This competition prompted some observers to argue for sheltered colonial markets limited to trade with the home country. An additional stimulus to imperialism arose from the demand for raw materials unavailable in Europe, especially copper, rubber, tin, cotton, jute, and petroleum, as well as foodstuffs such as coconut, coffee, and tea, on which Europeans had come to rely. Not only were raw materials necessary to the new industrial products, but their value was enhanced because cheap colonial labor made mining, extraction, and agriculture especially profitable.

The debate over economic factors centers on accumulated surplus capital. This argument, which later became the major interpretation of Marxist writers, was first proposed in 1902 by the British economic liberal John A. Hobson (1858–1940) in *Imperialism: A Study.* Hobson believed that capitalism suffered from underconsumption—that is, wealth in capitalist societies was poorly distributed as a result of overaccumulation by the rich. The business and financial interests that controlled such surplus capital soon discovered that it could be more profitably invested overseas, where cheap labor and raw materials made a greater return possible. Hobson saw imperialism as the effort of capitalists to find investment outlets for their surplus wealth. He argued that surplus capital could be eliminated if workers were paid higher wages and the rich were taxed more heavily; because these measures would result in greater purchasing power for the working class, the need for new markets—hence imperialism—would disappear.

In 1916 V. I. Lenin (1870–1924), the future Communist leader of the Russian Revolution, wrote the classic

Marxist analysis of the subject, *Imperialism: The Highest Stage of Capitalism*. The scramble for colonies, Lenin noted, coincided with the change in Europe's economy from a phase of free competition to one of intense monopoly through combines, trusts, and the control of finance capital. Imperialism emerges from this "highest" stage of capitalism when business and financial interests in each country seek to extend their monopolies overseas in the search for greater profits. Imperialism was therefore an inevitable response to the "internal contradictions" of monopolistic capitalism. For Lenin, imperialism would result in the breakdown of capitalism.

Hobson and Lenin were partly correct. Between 1860 and 1900 the value of British capital invested abroad grew from $7 billion to $20 billion. By the eve of World War I, one-fifth of the foreign investments of France and Germany was in colonial regions, and about half of Britain's overseas investments was in the colonial world. In many instances, however, foreign rulers needed and requested Western capital, and financial investment hardly explained the imperialist expansion of less developed nations such as Italy and Russia, which had little surplus capital. Nor does colonialism explain the equally large British investments in noncolonial areas, such as Latin America and the United States. Finally, although some colonial possessions were profitable, the military and bureaucratic costs of occupation usually exceeded the financial return.

However important the economic motives behind imperialism, it caught the imagination of the European mind and responded to a popular thirst for the exotic. Scientists, missionaries, hunters, and adventurers poured into Africa and Asia in the late nineteenth century. Yet even the humanitarian instincts of the missionaries, intent on bringing Christianity and modern medicine to "heathens," involved a conviction about the superiority of their own civilization. When the British writer Rudyard Kipling spoke of the "white man's burden," he reflected the view of many Europeans that the civilizing mission was a sacred duty of "more advanced" races—a view supported in more ruthless fashion by believers in Social Darwinism.

◉ Imperialism and Economics: The Debate ◉

Among analysts of the economic causes of the new imperialism, two major authors stand out: Hobson and Lenin.

By far the most important economic factor in imperialism is the influence relating to investments. The growing cosmopolitanization of capital is the greatest economic change of this generation. Every advanced industrial nation is tending to place a larger share of its capital outside the limits of its own political area, in foreign countries, or in colonies, and to draw a growing income from this source.

Imperialism is capitalism in that stage of development in which the dominance of monopolies and finance capital has established itself; in which the export of capital has acquired pronounced importance; in which the division of the world among the international trusts has begun; in which division of all territories of the globe among the great capitalist powers has been completed.

More recent students of imperialism, however, have questioned these earlier views.

In the second half of the twentieth century, it can be seen that imperialism owed its popular appeal not to the sinister influence of the capitalists, but to its inherent attractions for the masses . . . and the adoption of a creed based on such irrational concepts as racial superiority and the prestige of the nation. . . . Imperialism cannot be explained in simple terms of economic theory and the nature of financial capital.

Sources: J. A. Hobson, *Imperialism: A Study* (New York: Pott, 1902), p. 30; V. I. Lenin, *Imperialism: The Highest Stage of Capitalism* (New York: International Publishers, 1939), p. 89; D. K. Fieldhouse, "Imperialism: A Historiographical Revision," *Economic History Review*, 2nd ser., 14 (1961): 209.

German bacteriologists, including the famous Robert Koch (third from left), scrutinize blood samples in East Africa in a search to isolate the microbe that causes sleeping sickness, a major tropical disease. The attitudes of weakness and dependence of the African subjects contrast vividly with the brisk assurance and soldierly dress of the Europeans. [Brown Brothers]

Africa and the Colonial Powers

The most intense phase of the new imperialism unfolded in Africa, a continent four times the size of Europe. For centuries westerners had viewed sub-Saharan Africa as the "Dark Continent," a vast, unexplored expanse where inhospitable climate, diseases, and geography conspired to keep them out. Muslim traders crisscrossed much of West Africa and the Sahara, but as late as the mid-nineteenth century only the coastal settlements and a few interior regions were represented on European maps.

Africa on the Eve of Imperialism

Despite Western ignorance, however, Africa had undergone a major transformation in the centuries before the new imperialism. Iron metallurgy, agricultural techniques, and the introduction of new crops had spread across the continent, and a large increase in population

had caused migrations into central and southern Africa. Diversity of geography and ethnocultural patterns determined development. Sophisticated cultures and effective states marked some regions, especially in the savanna zone of West Africa, where the kingdoms of Ghana, Mali, and Songhai had once flourished, and in Zimbabwe and the Swahili city-states of southeastern Africa. In the rain forests and the southern regions, inhabited mainly by San, Pygmies, and Khoikhoi, political organization revolved around village communities that relied on traditional food-gathering techniques.

Although the British navy tried to suppress the slave trade along the African coast after 1805, slavery continued to flourish inside Africa. Indeed, the decline of the transatlantic slave trade actually drove the price of slaves up, and in many African societies, especially on the west and east coasts and in Ethiopia, slavery became a cornerstone of social and economic life. The Swahili city-states and Dahomey, for example, developed huge plantation systems of slave-based agriculture, similar to those that developed in the United States. In Dahomey and Ashanti slaves were also used to mine gold. In the port cities of West Africa slavery contributed to the rise of a new class of African merchants.

Along with the persistence of slavery, many regions

of Africa witnessed an increase in legitimate trade, especially in ivory, palm oil, cloves, and other agricultural products. In the Niger delta the commercial revival encouraged a unique governing-trading arrangement that extended organized trade into the interior. As a result the inland forest empires of Oyo and Benin, which could not adjust to the new commercial economy, began to decline and were eventually overrun by the Muslim Fulani, who expanded their control as far west as Senegal.

In East Africa the early and mid-nineteenth century saw the development of long-distance caravan routes, first by the Nyamwezi and other African merchants and then by Arab traders. The region experienced serious social upheaval, especially in Malawi, Tanganyika, and northern Mozambique, into which tens of thousands of warriors from southern Africa moved, displacing the lo-

cal populations. Arab slavers and merchants also pushed their way into the interior regions west of lakes Victoria and Tanganyika, where political and social conditions approached chaos. An important exception, however, was the kingdom of Buganda, a powerful centralized state that was in the process of territorial expansion. In South Africa the numerous culturally related Bantu societies had been settled for centuries in the fertile coastal plains. Lacking political cohesion or military defenses, they now found themselves overrun by encroaching white settlers from the Cape Colony and Portuguese slavers from Mozambique, as well as by the fierce Zulu empire. The Zulu were a highly disciplined society of warriors with large, well-organized cities that lived off pillage from the surrounding countryside. These and other struggles resulted in a massive scattering of pop-

◎ Military Revolution in Africa: ◎ The Zulu Warrior

In the 1820s African warfare underwent a major transformation that altered the balance of power among the Bantu-speaking peoples of the southeast. Shaka, the ruler of the Zulu, introduced highly disciplined infantry regiments that were protected by shields and used short, stabbing spears instead of the traditional throwing type. Here is an account of these warriors by Robert Moffat, a British missionary who visited the Zulu a number of years after Shaka's death.

Some thousands of the Matabele [Zulu], composing several regiments, are distinguished by the colour of their shields, as well as the kind and profusion of feathers which generally adorn their heads, having also a long feather of the blue crane rising from their brows, all of which has an imposing effect at their onset. Their arms consist of a shield, short spear, and club. The club, often made of the horn of a rhinoceros or hard wood, they throw with unerring precision, so as even to strike dead the smaller antelope. The spear is not intended for throwing, but for close combat, and such being their mode of warfare, the tribes accustomed to throw their light javelins to a distance, are overtaken by these organized soldiers and mowed down. They must conquer or die, and if one return without his shield or spear, at the frown of his sovereign he is instantly despatched by another. They look best in their war dress, which is only worn on great occasions, and without which they are like the Kafir tribes in a state of nudity. They rarely use a war axe, which distinguishes the Bechuana warrior, and which he only uses when brought into embarrassed circumstances, when his spears are expended, or when butchering the vanquished enemy. Their shields, made of the thickest part of the ox hide, are very different in size and shape. That of the Matabele is sufficiently long to cover the body, while the other is light, and easily manoeuvered so as to throw off the missiles of the enemy. That of the Basuto is smaller still, and seems only capable of defending the left hand, which grasps the spears, and a rod bearing a plume of black ostrich feathers.

Source: R. Moffat, *Missionary Labours and Scenes in Southern Africa* (New York: Carter & Brothers, 1855), p. 351.

ulations out of the region, which in turn displaced other societies and caused considerable social dislocation.

Only two states in Africa were able to maintain their independence in the face of mounting European aggression—Ethiopia and Liberia. After centuries of isolation, the feudal kingdoms of Ethiopia were reunited by a Shoa warrior who dubbed himself Emperor Theodore. He created a modern army and a state administration, although the most fertile lands of the realm continued to be held by nobles and the Coptic Christian church. Liberia, founded in 1821 by Americans as a home for freed blacks returning to Africa from the United States, was politically sovereign but remained dependent on American economic interests.

Changes in military techniques and weaponry also affected conditions in Africa. The earliest of these innovations were the tactics developed by the Zulu. Under their ambitious leader, Shaka (1817–1828), the Zulu steadily conquered new territory. Shaka armed infantry troops with spears designed for fighting at close range. The subsequent introduction of firearms by the British and the Muslims had even more serious consequences. The breech-loading rifle and the Gatling gun, for example, enabled the British to subdue the Zulu in a series of bloody wars in the 1870s. In the hands of westerners and Africans, modern weapons unsettled the political life of numerous African states, which were either consolidated under new rulers or subjugated by foreigners. Thus Sayyid Said, a Muslim contemporary of Shaka, became sultan of Zanzibar in 1806 and for 50 years controlled a vast commercial domain in East Africa. Similarly, the rifle enabled the Boer settlers in South Africa to push into the interior in the face of British and Bantu resistance.

Explorers and Missionaries

Western interest in Africa intensified in the early nineteenth century as a result of the debate over the abolition of the slave trade. Curiosity about the interior of the continent combined with humanitarian concerns to bring a host of explorers and missionaries to Africa. Exploration focused on two unsolved geographic mysteries: the source of the Niger River in West Africa and the source of the Nile in East Africa. As early as 1795 Mungo Park, a Scottish doctor, led an expedition up the Niger, but not until 1830 was the river fully traced. Successive British adventurers made their way from the coast of East Africa in search of the sources of the Nile, including Sir Samuel White Baker and his wife, Lady Florence Baker. In 1864 the Bakers were the first Europeans to see a huge lake, which they called Lake Albert in honor of Queen Victoria's husband. The most famous African explorer of the period was David Livingstone, whose humanitarianism and courage caught the imagination of Europe.

His expeditions in the 1850s sparked public interest. From 1857 to 1863 Livingstone explored the Zambesi River region and in 1866 set out on his last journey, intending to settle the question of the source of the Nile. When no word reached the outside world for five years, an American newspaper sent Henry M. Stanley, a well-known correspondent, to find the lost missionary. The two men met in 1871, but Livingstone, sick and exhausted, refused to return to Britain. When Stanley returned to the Congo in 1878 on behalf of King Leopold of Belgium, he paved the way for a new phase in the history of Western imperialism.

The Scramble for Africa

Portugal had held Angola and Mozambique since the age of exploration, but before 1870, European powers had seized only a few footholds along the coast. France had occupied Algeria and portions of Senegal, and Britain already controlled the Cape of Good Hope, Gambia, and Sierra Leone and had imposed its commercial influence on the Niger River region and Zanzibar. Following the midcentury explorations, the pace of expansion became intense as Western powers scrambled for territory.

The race for colonies was sparked by King Leopold, who planned to exploit the Congo through the privately financed International Congo Association. Establishing a pattern that would be used by other entrepreneurs, hundreds of tribal chieftains were tricked into signing treaties granting the association some 900,000 square miles of land. Karl Peters, founder of the German Colonization Society, followed suit in East Africa, and the Germans seized Southwest Africa; the French army officer Pierre de Brazza secured control over vast tracts north of the Congo River.

In 1885 Bismarck called a conference in Berlin to establish international guidelines for the acquisition of African territory. The conference recognized the Congo Free State as a neutral region. Although the Congo was to be governed by the Belgian king, all nations were to have free access to trade and navigation, and the slave trade was to be suppressed. The diplomats agreed that henceforth a power with coastal possessions had a right to the adjacent hinterland only if it effectively occupied the territory. Future disputes were to be settled by arbitration.

The Congo under Leopold's rule suffered unimaginable exploitation. Private firms used forced labor to squeeze maximum profit out of the rich rubber and ivory resources. Atrocities committed by the labor overseers, together with the toll of disease and climate, claimed more than 10 million lives during the next 20 years. Conditions did not improve until Leopold turned his private ownership of the Free State over to the Belgian govern-

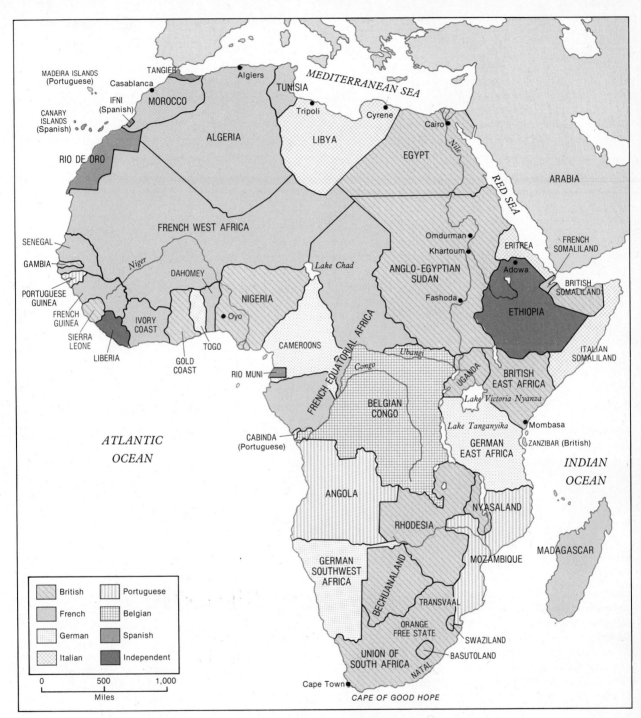

34.1 Africa on the Eve of World War I

ment in 1908, when it was renamed the Belgian Congo.

Following the Berlin conference, nine-tenths of the African continent was rapidly divided among the European powers. Italy and Germany joined the scramble.

When France blocked Italy's ambitions in Tunisia, Italy instead occupied Eritrea and Somaliland, desolate areas along the Red Sea. In 1896 the Italians attempted to conquer the Christian state of Ethiopia, but the forces of its

◉ Women and African Society ◉

Travelers in precolonial Africa encountered long-established social customs that appeared alien to them and that their own cultural arrogance or ethnocentrism made them perceive as primitive. Even David Livingstone, who had a deeper respect for African traditions than most westerners of his day, sometimes misunderstood the import of what he found. This anecdote, which Livingstone's Victorian mind found humorous, revealed the strength of women's roles in one African community.

The person whom Nyakoba appointed to be our guide, having informed us of the decision, came and bargained that his services should be rewarded with a hoe. I showed him the article; he was delighted with it, and went off to show it to his wife. He soon afterward returned, and said that, though he was perfectly willing to go, his wife would not let him. I said, "Then bring back the hoe"; but he replied, "I want it." "Well, go with us, and you shall have it." "But my wife won't let me." I remarked to my men, "Did you ever hear such a fool?" They answered, "Oh, that is the custom of these parts; the wives are the masters." . . . When a young man takes a liking for a girl of another village, and the parents have no objection to the match, he is obliged to come and live at their village. He has to perform certain services for the mother-in-law, such as keeping her well supplied with firewood; and when he comes into her presence he is obliged to sit with his knees in a bent position, as putting out his feet toward the old lady would give her great offense. If he becomes tired of living in this state of vassalage, and wishes to return to his own family, he is obliged to leave all his children behind—they belong to the wife. This is only a more stringent enforcement of the law from which emanates the practice which prevails so very extensively in Africa, known to Europeans as "buying wives." Such virtually it is, but it does not appear quite in that light to the actors. So many head of cattle or goats are given to the parents of the girl "to give her up," as it is termed, i.e., to forego all claim on her offspring, and allow an entire transference of her and her seed into another family. If nothing is given, the family from which she has come can claim the children as part of itself: the payment is made to sever this bond.

Source: D. Livingstone, *Missionary Travels and Researches in South Africa* (New York: Harper, 1858), pp. 667–668.

emperor, Menelik, four times the size of the Italian army, defeated the invaders at Adowa. Although Bismarck was personally opposed to African colonization, he yielded to domestic pressure. Germany proclaimed a protectorate over Southwest Africa and German East Africa (Tanganyika) and eventually added Togo and Cameroon to its empire. When Kaiser William II dismissed Bismarck in 1890, German colonial activities intensified.

Britain, France, and the Perils of Empire

The largest empires in Africa were acquired by France and Britain, whose conflicting ambitions at times brought the two powers to the brink of war. The de Brazza expedition had enabled France to claim a huge portion of equatorial Africa, and by 1896 France had occupied Madagascar as well. The focus of French efforts, however, was in the Sahara. From Algeria, Senegal, and the Ivory Coast the French pushed south, east, and north across the great desert, establishing military outposts while fighting nomads. In 1881 they occupied Tunisia, and by the end of that decade they had gone beyond Lake Chad to the borders of the Sudan. Eventually the French hoped to reach the Nile and perhaps the Red Sea, a plan that brought them into conflict with British aspirations.

By the time the Berlin conference convened, Britain held the Cape Colony in southern Africa and had imposed its control over Egypt. In 1875 Ismail, Egypt's ruler, was unable to repay huge loans from French and British bankers. When, as a result, he was forced to sell his stock in the Suez Canal Company, representing

44 percent of all shares, the British prime minister, Benjamin Disraeli, bought them, giving Britain a vital stake in the strategic waterway. The next year Ismail suspended interest payments on Egypt's foreign debts, and France and Britain assumed joint control of its finances. Foreign intervention sparked nationalist reaction among Egyptian intellectuals and army officers, and in 1882 riots in Alexandria led to a British bombardment of the city and the establishment of a protectorate over the country. For the next 25 years Egypt was ruled by a British governor.

The British next moved to secure the Sudan, an Egyptian dependency to the south. In 1885 a British garrison at Khartoum under General Charles ("Chinese") Gordon was massacred by the armies of the Mahdi, the leader of fierce Muslim tribesmen. Not until 1898 did the British send an expeditionary force, commanded by General Horatio Kitchener, to retake the Sudan. This time the nationalist fervor of the Muslims was no match for the new British machine guns—more than 10,000 tribesmen were wiped out at Omdurman. A few months earlier a French expedition under Captain Jean-Baptiste Marchand had arrived at Fashoda, where it planted the French flag. On September 18, only a few weeks after Omdurman, Kitchener, with a superior force, met Marchand there. An open clash was avoided only when the French government backed down.

British and French imperial plans ran directly counter to each other, for while France sought to create an east-west empire that stretched from the Atlantic to the Red Sea, Britain dreamed of a north-south domain that reached from Egypt to Cape Town. Along with Egypt and the Sudan, Britain already controlled Uganda and British East Africa (Kenya), and a determined British push north from the Cape might connect the parts.

South Africa and the Boer War

The British Cape-to-Cairo scheme was the brainchild of Cecil Rhodes (1853–1902), who had become fabulously wealthy in diamond and gold mining. A fierce nationalist and Social Darwinist, in 1890 Rhodes became prime minister of the Cape Colony and began to formulate a scheme to bring more of Africa under British rule.

The other European powers represented a lesser obstacle to Rhodes than internal conditions in South Africa. The Cape had been settled in the seventeenth century by Dutch immigrants, staunchly independent Calvinist farmers and cattlemen. When Britain annexed the colony after the Napoleonic Wars, these Afrikaners—the British called them Boers, from the Dutch word for farmer—migrated north in the Great Trek, eventually establishing the Orange Free State and the Transvaal

Republic. As they carved out new settlements, the Boers encountered opposition from the Bantu and Zulu populations as well as from the British, and more than 30 years of continuous fighting ensued. Just when a compromise appeared possible, the discovery of gold and diamonds intensified the conflict between the British and the Boers. In the 1880s and 1890s hundreds of thousands of Englishmen poured into the mining towns of the Transvaal, Bechuanaland, and the area later known as Rhodesia, overwhelming the Boers and making open conflict all but inevitable.

The principal Boer spokesman was Paul Kruger (1825–1904). As president of the Transvaal, Kruger pressured the *uitlanders* ("foreigners") by levying discriminatory taxes on them, curbing the use of English, and curtailing the exercise of political rights. In 1895 Rhodes and his agents attempted to overthrow Kruger when a small British force invaded the Transvaal under the command of Dr. Leander Jameson. The Jameson raid failed, but public opinion in Europe condemned the British, and Kaiser William II telegraphed Kruger that the Germans had been ready to help the Boers. In 1899 Britain and the Boer republics went to war; the Boers were defeated and surrendered in 1902. The British eventually granted self-government to the region, and in 1910 the Cape Colony, Natal, the Orange Free State, and the Transvaal were joined as the Union of South Africa.

Paul Kruger, prominent Boer politician and president of the Transvaal.
[Bettmann Archive]

Imperialism and Its Consequences

Imperialism affected both the European conquerors and their colonial subjects. Economic and industrial development in the West responded to the influx of raw materials and the opportunities for overseas investment, and it is probable that the resulting lower prices had a positive effect on the real wages of some European workers. On the diplomatic level, however, competition for colonies increased tensions among the great powers. The impact on Africa was incalculable as the full weight of Western technology descended on the continent, which for centuries had been relatively undisturbed by outside influences. In less than a generation Africans found their social and political structures shattered, their agrarian economy transformed, and their values undermined. Europeans exploited the natural and mineral resources of Africa, extracting huge quantities of gold, diamonds, ivory, rubber, and copper. White settlers seized fertile agricultural land formerly occupied by tribal communities, especially in southern and eastern Africa. The construction of roads, railroads, and telegraph lines stimulated internal trade across long distances and, together with the introduction of a wage-earning structure, transformed the barter economy into a monetary system. Yet enormous manpower was needed to reshape the African economy and build an infrastructure, and the labor supply, poorly paid, was often conscripted by force and treated brutally.

The "modernization" of the continent took a terrible toll on the cultural and political pattern of African life. Broken family and kinship patterns often resulted as workers were required to move over wide distances and tribal communities were stripped of their land. Moreover, imperialism resulted in artificially drawn political boundaries that divided many tribes and merged hostile groups. Even Western humanitarian programs had a mixed impact on local populations. The missionary efforts improved sanitation and agricultural methods and provided Africans with Western education. But these benefits also subverted African identity and undermined traditional values and social mores, for young Africans who were exposed to Western education or converted to Christianity often rejected family and tribal authority.

The speed and relative ease of European conquest obscures the fact that Africans resisted imperialism. The nomads of the Sahara, the Muslims of the Sudan, and the Zulus of southern Africa fought vigorously against Europeans. After the conquest, resistance took more subtle forms. A new class of westernized Africans, many trained at European universities and then appointed to posts in the colonial administrations, eventually emerged. Ironically, these Africans, having absorbed Western political attitudes and values, returned home to provide leadership for their people and sometimes spearheaded the drive for independence.

The West in Asia

Many of the same trends were set in motion by the pressures for westernization in Asia. This was most true in the countries incorporated in Western colonial systems—India, Ceylon, Burma, Malaya, Indochina, Indonesia, and the Philippines—but similar trends were evident in China and even in Japan. Traditional Asian cultures and states were, however, more highly developed than in Africa and could more readily resist or choose from among Western ideas and institutions. For example, a major Christian missionary effort was made, but it produced few converts, although as in Africa it was an important means of introducing Western medicine and education. Much of traditional Asian culture remained vigorous, especially the family system. At the same time, many Asian institutions were remade under Western influence or were augmented by new ones introduced by westerners.

The arrogance as well as the success of Western imperialism was galling to most Asians, especially given their own pride in their ancient traditions of greatness. Western colonialism, and the unequal treaties forced on Siam (Thailand), China, and Japan, stimulated a renewal of the national Asian traditions and an effort to make them relevant to a world dominated by the West and its standards. Thus India saw the Hindu Renaissance and related movements (often under British pressure) to eliminate or restrict institutions now seen as unacceptable, such as *sati* and child marriage. In China similar movements arose against foot-binding, chaste widowhood, and concubinage; in Japan, against premarital promiscuity, class-based restrictions on clothing, and more or less open pornography (known as "spring pictures").

Asians found this forced reexamination of much of their cultural heritage under the eyes of an alien conqueror deeply disturbing. Now more than ever they needed to hold their heads up, convinced that to be Indian or Chinese or Japanese or Southeast Asian was something to be proud of. Many convinced themselves that while the West might have a temporary material advantage, the East was still superior spiritually and in the arts of civilization.

Industrialization was in time pursued vigorously, first in India, then in Japan, and finally in China, although it lagged in Southeast Asia. At least as important as technological change were institutions such as banking and

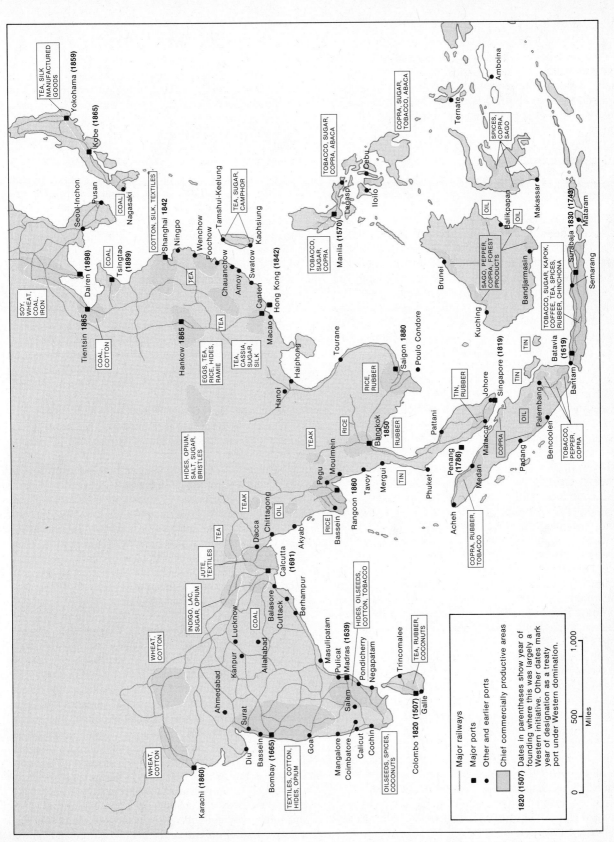

34.2 Major Ports and Commercially Productive Areas in East Asia, 1600–1940

TEA, SILK MANUFACTURED GOODS
Yokohama (1859)
Kobe (1865)
COAL
Nagasaki
Seoul-Inchon
Pusan
COTTON, SILK, TEXTILES
Shanghai 1842
Ningpo
Wenchow
Foochow
Tamshui-Keelung
TEA, SUGAR, CAMPHOR
Chauanchow
Amoy
Swatow
Kaohsiung
Canton
Hong Kong (1842)
Macao
TEA
TEA
EGGS, TEA, RICE, HIDES, RAMIE
TEA, CASSIA, SUGAR, SILK
COAL
Dairen (1898)
Tsingtao (1899)
COAL
Tientsin 1865
Hankow 1865
COAL, COTTON
SOY, WHEAT, COAL, IRON

TOBACCO, SUGAR, COPRA, ABACA
Cebu
COPRA, SUGAR, TOBACCO, ABACA
Ternate
Amboina
SPICES, COPRA, SAGO
Legaspi
Iloilo
Manila (1570)
TOBACCO, SUGAR, COPRA
Makassar
Balikpapan
OIL
OIL
Surabaja 1830 (1743)
Mataram
Semarang
SAGO, PEPPER, COPRA, FOREST PRODUCTS
Brunei
Bandjarmasin
Kuching
TOBACCO, SUGAR, KAPOK, COFFEE, TEA, SPICES, RUBBER, CHINCHONA
Batavia (1619)
Bantam
TIN
TIN
TIN
OIL
TOBACCO, PEPPER, COPRA
Palembang
Bencoolen
Padang
COPRA
Matacca
TIN, RUBBER
Johore
Singapore (1819)
Penang (1786)
Medan
Acheh
COPRA, RUBBER, TOBACCO

Haiphong
Tourane
Hanoi
Saigon 1880
Poulo Condore
RICE, RUBBER
Bangkok 1850
RUBBER
RICE
Pattani
Phuket
Pegu
Moulmein
Mergui
Tavoy
RICE
TEAK
TIN
Rangoon 1860
Bassein
RICE
OIL
Chittagong
Dacca
Akyab
TEAK
HIDES, OPIUM, SALT, SUGAR, BRISTLES

Calcutta (1691)
Berhampur
TEA
JUTE, TEXTILES
Balasore
Cuttack
COAL
Allahabad
Lucknow
Kanpur
INDIGO, LAC, SUGAR, OPIUM
Masulipatam
Pulicat
Madras (1639)
HIDES, OILSEEDS, COTTON, TOBACCO
Pondicherry
Negapatam
Trincomalee
TEA, RUBBER, COCONUTS
Salem
WHEAT, COTTON
Ahmedabad
Surat
Bassein
Bombay (1665)
Diu
Goa
Mangalore
Coimbatore
Calicut
Cochin
OILSEEDS, SPICES, COCONUTS
Colombo 1820 (1507)
Galle
TEXTILES, COTTON, HIDES, OPIUM
WHEAT, COTTON
Karachi (1860)

Major railways
Major ports
Other and earlier ports
Chief commercially productive areas
1820 (1507) Dates in parentheses show year of founding where this was largely a Western initiative. Other dates mark year of designation as a treaty port under Western domination.

0   500   1,000
Miles

joint-stock companies and the particularly Western idea of nationalism. The great Asian empires and states of the past had been cultural and bureaucratic structures different from the nation-states of modern Europe, whose national coherence and drive Asians rightly saw as a source of strength that they lacked but that they must have if they were again to be masters in their own house.

British Imperial India

A divided and weakened India had progressively fallen under the domination of the English East India Company (as described in Chapter 28), and by 1857 most of it was being administered, directly or indirectly, as a single unit. Most Indians exposed to the new British model of Western-style progress admired it, but in the long run being united for the first time yet treated as second-class citizens in their own country led to the emergence of Indian nationalism. The insurrection of 1857 (discussed in Chapter 28) was not yet a war of independence, but it marked the beginning of Indian response to a foreign control increasingly tinged with arrogance. In the wake of the insurrection, the English East Company was dissolved and the so-called Dual System abolished.

The mutiny marked a watershed between the earlier stages of company rule, which saw considerable racial and cultural mixing, and the rise of full-blown imperialism. The British crown assumed direct imperial authority under the Government of India Act (1858), although the façade of Indian principalities was maintained until independence. To complete the transformation, Queen Victoria adopted the title Empress of India in 1877. She took a special interest in her new dominions, which her prime minister, Benjamin Disraeli, called "the brightest jewel in the crown," and is said to have prayed nightly for her Indian subjects. Although she never went there, many Indians revered her as their own empress, part of the long Indian imperial tradition even under alien rulers, and her picture was widely displayed in people's homes.

The British were careful not to displace any more of the native rulers or to take over more territory, a policy kept until Indian independence in 1947. British residents were placed in each of the hundreds of small and a few large Indian-ruled states, but intervention or threats were rarely needed to keep the roughly half of India still formally in native hands in line with British policy. The army remained largely Indian, but the proportion of British officers and troops was increased, and elite regiments of Sikhs, Rajputs, and Gurkhas (from Nepal) were formed. Indians joined the colonial civil service as well and held responsible positions in all fields under overall British supervision.

Modern Growth

The opening of the Suez Canal in 1869, the shift to steam navigation, and the rapid spread of railways brought India much closer to Europe, greatly accelerating the commercialization of the economy. By the end of the century India had by far the largest rail network (25,000 miles) in all of Asia, on a par with many European countries but on a far bigger scale. This too had obvious commercial consequences, but there were social ones as well. British women could now join their husbands more easily in India and raise their families there, thus creating another wedge of separation between the races and cultures. Colonial social life centered in the buildings and grounds of the British Club in each city or town, from which Indians were excluded. This social barrier not only delimited the Indians' inferior status but also kept many of the British in a kind of prison of their own making, cut off both from the subjects they ruled and from fresh ideas and attitudes from home. Thus developed what came to be called the colonial mentality, which preserved a mid-Victorian code of conduct and mores well into the twentieth century.

Indians were the first Asians to experience the impact of Western capitalism and industrialization in their country on a large scale. Many of them were quick to respond as entrepreneurs to the new economic opportunities in commerce and machine manufacturing. As in Britain, industrialization began first with machine-made textiles in Bombay and Calcutta, then in a widening range of other manufacturing. Railways stimulated the growing commercialization of agriculture, especially in industrial crops such as jute (fibers), cotton, indigo, and new plantation production of tea, grown mainly in the hills of Assam, which captured most of the world market. New irrigation projects, especially in the semiarid Punjab and the Indus valley, opened productive farming areas to feed India's booming cities and increased output elsewhere. By 1900 India had the world's largest irrigation system.

Calcutta remained the country's largest city, closely followed by Bombay and then by Madras. Bombay, with its magnificent harbor and its closeness to cotton-growing areas in Gujarat and Maharashtra, became the premier port and the chief center of Indian-owned textile manufacturing. Large new industrial cities also grew inland as the railway linked most of the country in a single market: Ahmedabad in Gujarat, Lucknow, Kanpur, and Allahabad in the central Ganges, Salem and Coimbatore in the south, and many more. Karachi became the port for cotton and wheat from the Indus valley. British industrial and commercial investors, managers, and traders made money and sold goods in this vast new market, but Indians were increasingly prominent as well in the growing modern sector. Indians also entered and in time

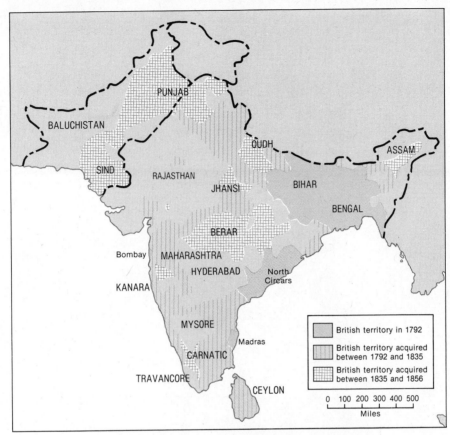

34.3 Growth of the British Empire in India

dominated the new Western-style professions such as law, medicine, engineering, and education. By 1900 India had the world's fourth largest textile industry and by 1920 the biggest steel plant in the British Empire, both, like many other industries, owned and managed largely by Indians.

Colonial Government

The British saw themselves as the bringers of order and "civilization" to their empire, a role that many of them likened to that of the Romans 2,000 years earlier in Europe. Britain was the greatest power in the world from the mid-eighteenth century to the early twentieth. It was also the nursery of industrialization and modern representative government. These things bred a sense of pride and greatness. Britons were fond of describing theirs as an empire on which the sun never set, since it stretched almost around the globe. Indians, they felt, should be grateful to be included, and indeed many were.

British-style education, conducted in English, continued to shape most Indian intellectuals and literate people

to a large degree in the British image. The law of British India, based on English common law, was practiced and administered overwhelmingly by Indians themselves. Nonetheless, the British retained firm control of all senior positions. The prestigious Indian Civil Service (ICS), staffed until the twentieth century almost entirely by Britons trained in Indian affairs, long remained an exclusive supervisory group under the viceroy, the effective head of state in India appointed by London. The ICS was referred to proudly as the "steel framework" whose roughly 900 members ensured the smooth operation of the colonial government.

Despite colonial achievements in agriculture, public health, education, and transportation, however, most Indians remained poor, illiterate, and powerless. Occasional regional famines continued, as in China. Tenancy and landlessness grew with the increasing commercialization of agriculture, and industrial growth was far too slow to absorb or produce adequately for the rising population.

Between 1800 and 1947 the total population of India probably at least doubled, in itself a sign of order and greater economic opportunity, as in eighteenth-century China. The official census begun in 1871 showed a more

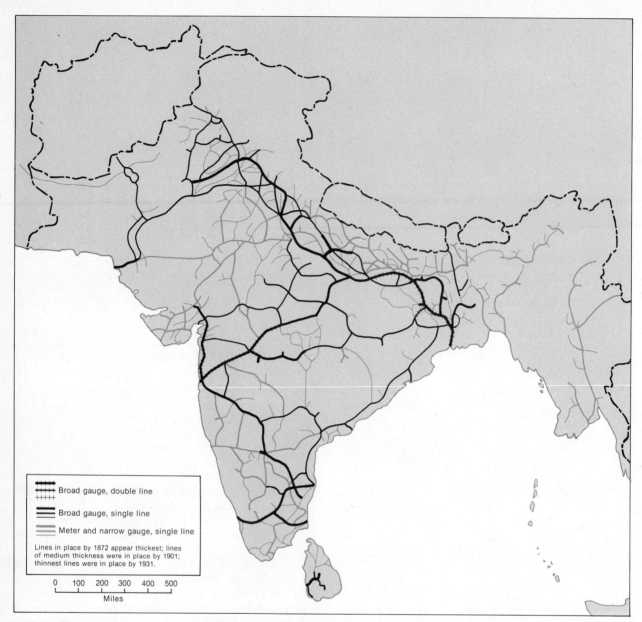

34.4 Growth of India's Railway Network

or less continuous growth of population together with a falling death rate. But this surge in population was barely matched by overall economic growth, which was in any case unbalanced. There was thus little new margin for improved living standards, and while some commercial, professional, and landed groups prospered, much of the peasantry sank deeper into poverty. India remained poor in part because it was poor to begin with after the extravagances, exploitation, and collapse of the Mughals. Industrialization and commercialization directly impoverished some groups and benefited others, as happened in the West too. The hand spinners of cotton, India's single largest manufacturing work force, were devastated by factory production and British imports, although hand weavers benefited from the cheaper machine-spun yarn. The widening market also gave new employment to many farmers, craftsmen, factory or railway workers, and laborers. The pattern in textiles was repeated in other industries and markets and occurred in China as well.

The colonial government was chronically pinched for funds; London insisted that all expenses had to be covered from Indian revenues. The army took much of these, in part for the conquest of Burma, and there was little to spare. Planning was thus difficult, and problems were addressed piecemeal or not at all. Reformers accused the government of playing the role of night watchman while most Indians remained in poverty. Even so, the colonial administration required indirect support, costs that were necessarily borne by ordinary British taxpayers. Thus the imperial system was supported by the middle and lower classes of both countries for the benefit of British and Indian elites.

It would have been impossible for the relative handful of British in India to control the subcontinent and its 350 million people by the 1930s without the support or the active help of most Indians. The British officer contingent in the Indian army reached 40,000 only in the special circumstances of World Wars I and II. The total number of Britons of all levels and in all branches of the civil service, including district officers, judges, and police, was never more than 12,000. In short, colonial India was run mainly by Indians, who until relatively late willingly supported the British raj, or government. By 1910, for example, the police force comprised about 5,000 Britons and over 600,000 Indians. The rest of the civil service employed about 600,000 Indians with only some 5,000 Britons, and the army consisted of about 150,000 native troops and approximately 25,000 British officers.

In contrast, the higher echelons of government remained a British preserve. As if to show their aloofness from the country, they governed in the blazing hot months of summer from hill stations in the Himalayan foothills, first at Darjeeling in northernmost Bengal and later from Simla, north of Delhi. From both they enjoyed spectacular views of the snow-covered mountains, cool, bracing air, Western-style lodges and cottages that reminded them of home, and a round of parties, picnics, and receptions.

As more colonial officers served longer, young British women came or were sent out to India to find a husband, an annual migration at the beginning of the cool weather in autumn irreverently referred to as the "arrival of the fishing fleet." Those who remained unspoken for by the time the hot weather resumed in mid-March often went back to England as "returned empties." As the British community grew, many families by the twentieth century had lived in India for several generations and thought of it as home. They called themselves Anglo-Indians, and they lived in separate residential areas built for them some distance from the Indian towns where they worked. These were known as "civil lines" or "cantonments," since many of them had begun as quarters for troops or garrisons. Their households were staffed by large numbers of Indian servants, whose labor was cheap.

Another group was also known as Anglo-Indians. These were the products of intermarriage, which had been common in the eighteenth and early nineteenth centuries and still occasionally took place in later years. These Anglo-Indians were rejected by both the Indian and British communities, but they usually tried to pass as English and spoke wistfully of "home," meaning an England that most of them had never seen. Many of them became Christians in an effort to raise their status, as did many Untouchables. Missionary efforts made few converts otherwise, although mission schools remained an important means to Western education for many non-Christians as well as for the few Christians.

Social life in the hill stations: a fete at Simla, in a glade nostalgically named Annandale, painted by A. E. Scott around 1845. [British Library]

❀
NEW DELHI:
INDIAN SUMMER OF THE RAJ

Calcutta had long seemed inappropriate as the capital of a British India that had expanded to cover the subcontinent, thousands of miles from Bengal. Although now a thoroughly Indian city, it had been founded by the British themselves and had no indigenous roots or history. Its marginal coastal site further emphasized the foreignness of British rule. For several years after 1900 alternative capital sites were considered, and Delhi, the former Mughal capital, was chosen. At the head of the Ganges valley, Delhi controlled routes both east and south to the heart of India. Successive invaders had to capture Delhi first, mounting their campaigns and ruling their empires from there. The British raj moved too in 1911 to rule from where so many others had before.

It was decided to build a new planned city as an imperial statement, adjacent to the old city and with open space around it but still well within sight of Shah Jahan's Red Fort (see Chapter 20). The remains of other imperial Delhis of the past also showed on the skyline. An artificial hill was built as the setting for the monumental residence and gardens of the viceroy, flanked on each side by two large and stately government buildings known as the Secretariat. From this low rise, broad boulevards and wide vistas led to other buildings and monuments to empire, including the parliament house, by the 1920s filled with mainly Indian members.

Like Paris and Washington, New Delhi was planned before the age of mass transit and the automobile. It was essentially built in a star-shaped pattern with broad tree-lined streets intersecting at angles and punctuated by circles of green area around which traffic had to move. The plan included a large separate commercial and shopping district, with buildings in neoclassical and Anglo-Indian styles, grouped around an immense circle, still called Connaught Circus. Related enterprises lined the streets leading into it at various angles. Pleasant shaded avenues with British names occupied most of the rest of the new planned city, most of them filled with gracious residences and beautiful gardens for civil servants, Indian princes (most of whom maintained extensive establishments in New Delhi), and other members of the upper classes. Lesser officials, workers, and servants commuted the mile or so from Old Delhi, mainly by bicycle, or were housed in the unplanned developments that soon grew around the edges of New Delhi.

The ambitious building plans of 1911 and 1912 were delayed by World War I, but by 1930 the new imperial capital was complete. The architects of New Delhi were of course British, but they made a generally successful effort to combine Western and Indian monumental and

An example of colonial architecture: Victoria Station, Bombay, with a statue of Queen Victoria atop its dome. [Rhoads Murphey]

imperial traditions, consciously using the same red sandstone of which the Red Fort had been built and creating buildings that fit their Indian setting far better than the earlier Victorian extravagances in Calcutta and Bombay. Old Delhi remains a traditional Indian city, centered around the Red Fort. A confusing maze of tiny streets and alleys surrounds the bazaar near Shah Jahan's great mosque, the Jama Masjid. The large unbuilt area in front of the Red Fort remains a vast open-air market and a frequent scene of political rallies. New Delhi became almost automatically the capital of independent India, with no sense of inappropriateness for the world's largest parliamentary democracy, still based on British colonial foundations. Since 1947 Delhi has boomed and become a major industrial center. But Old and New Delhi represent different strands in India's varied past and now also show the two faces of contemporary India, traditional and modern.

The Rise of Indian Nationalism

British-educated Indians, despite their prosperity, were increasingly resentful of the racial discrimination to which they were subject. Many began to demand a larger role in their country's government. Gradually a movement for independence developed. Liberal Englishmen agreed, contending that alien rule was contrary to the British tradition of representative government and political freedom. Gestures toward increasing the participation of Indians in the administration and civil service and elections for some officials and advisers came too slowly to satisfy either Indian or British critics.

The Indian National Congress, which was to become the core of the independence movement, was actually founded by an Englishman in 1885. Indian political leaders made nationalist appeals, among them highly effective and articulate figures such as M. G. Ranade (1842–1901), B. G. Tilak (1856–1920), G. K. Gokhale (1866–1915), and Motilal Nehru (1861–1931), the father of Jawaharlal Nehru (1889–1964), independent India's first prime minister. Their language, culture, and education were as much English as Indian, and they could speak eloquently in terms of British tradition itself against the colonial rule of their country.

Meanwhile, fear of the still expanding Russian empire in central Asia prompted yet another disastrous invasion of Afghanistan in 1878 to install a British puppet on the throne of Kabul. The Afghans murdered the British resident and his entire staff and military escort within a year, and guerrilla fighters stalemated a second invasion until it was withdrawn in 1880 and the Afghans were again "permitted" to choose their own ruler. Opinion in Britain was outraged by both the brutality and the cost of this futile military adventure, and the Disraeli government fell as a result.

The colonial government in India spearheaded other costly ventures as well. In addition to the conquest of Burma, it launched an armed reconnaissance against Tibet in 1903 and 1904 to forestall illusory Russian influence there. The mission showed the flag and obtained an agreement about the frontier. While imperial posturing preoccupied the colonial government and drained the country's resources, poverty in India remained largely unaddressed. Indian nationalists blamed the severe economic distress in many areas on colonial rule. Boycotts of British imports were begun, cutting their value by 25 percent between 1904 and 1908. The government's response was often repressive, and many political leaders were jailed. There were still many British in government with more liberal ideas, and many more outside government, who strove to reduce racial discrimination and urged Indian self-government as Britain's ultimate goal. In 1883, for example, it was agreed that Indian judges could preside over cases involving Europeans. But imperialist attitudes and bureaucratic inertia retarded the giving of Indians a larger and more appropriate role in their own government.

Over a million Indian troops and noncombatants served the British effort in World War I in Europe and the Middle East. Many hoped that this would speed progress toward self-government. When change lagged after the war, civil disobedience movements spread, now led by Mohandas "Mahatma" Gandhi (1869–1948), among others, only to be met by more government repression. In 1919 Indian troops under British command, called in to put down rioting in Amritsar near Lahore, fired on a peaceful and unarmed crowd celebrating a festival, leaving 400 dead. The massacre was a watershed in Anglo-Indian relations. It turned most Indians away from the idea of reform and toward the goal of full independence, creating almost overnight a greatly expanded nationalist movement.

In 1907 the British Parliament had declared that in-

The Amritsar Massacre of April 1919 was followed by further repression in the wake of renewed protests and demonstrations. Here British police officers in Amritsar watch while their Indian assistants search a demonstrator. [BBC Hulton/Bettman Archive]

dependence was Britain's objective in India, a point the British government reaffirmed in 1917 and 1921, but the colonial administration remained slow to move. Although the electoral system was greatly broadened in the 1920s and 1930s and Indian legislatures and officials were given far more power and responsibility, it was too little, too late. Time had run out for British rule in India.

Colonial Regimes in Southeast Asia

The Dutch came to control the largest amount of territory and population in Southeast Asia, incorporating the whole of what is now Indonesia in their colonial empire, from which they largely excluded other Western trade or investment competition. Large numbers of Chinese were already there, however, and their numbers increased to some 3 million as they expanded their control of smaller-scale domestic trade and retailing. The British, along with other westerners, had been trading in Burma since the seventeenth century, but as their Indian empire, and their imperial ambition, grew, they progressively annexed Burma to their colonial holdings. Malaya was thinly settled and unimportant in trade until the tin and rubber boom of the late nineteenth century, but the British hoped to use bases there in an effort to tap the trade with Southeast Asia and with China, a role ultimately performed by Singapore. By the end of the nineteenth century all of Malaya was under British colonial administration, but primarily on an indirect basis through local Malay sultans. French and American colonialists arrived late on the scene. France acquired the Indochinese states of Vietnam, Cambodia, and Laos through conquest by 1885, and the Americans inherited control of the Philippines as a consequence of their defeat of Spain, the former colonial master of the area, in 1898. Each of these Western colonial regimes followed policies with many similarities and some differences. Siam (now Thailand) remained independent as a buffer between rival colonial empires but had to accept the same set of "unequal treaties" as was imposed on China and Japan.

The British in Burma and Malaya

Britain's activity in Southeast Asia had been incidental to its concerns in India and its efforts to break into the China market. It was at first confined to founding bases on the fringes of Dutch power in Malaya. In 1786 a settlement was made at Penang on the northwestern Malay coast, where the British hoped to attract Chinese traders. This was only moderately successful, and they established what soon became their major Southeast Asian trade base at Singapore in 1819.

From the start, Singapore, with its large and excellent harbor commanding the southern entrance to the Molucca Strait, was a commercial center for all of Southeast Asia. Malaya itself remained thinly populated and largely undeveloped until the end of the nineteenth century. Burma was India's immediate geographic neighbor to the east. Its antiquated monarchy periodically made difficulties for British merchants and ignored or insulted British representatives. A brief war from 1824 to 1826 gave the British special rights in the important coastal provinces of Burma. Two more minor wars in 1852 and 1885–1886, for the most part provoked by the British, annexed lower Burma and the rest of the country. Burma was then administered as a province of British India until it was granted separate colonial status in 1937.

Burma and Malaya were rapidly commercialized after 1880 under British rule. Railways were built, and steam navigation was developed. The Irrawaddy delta in lower Burma, including much newly cultivated land, became a major exporter of rice. Upper Burma produced timber, especially teak, for export, and the central valley yielded oil from wells drilled by the British. All this moved out for export through the port of Rangoon, which served as the colonial capital. In Malaya were found rich deposits of tin, a metal in great demand in the industrializing West, and toward the end of the century Malaya also became the world's major producer of plantation rubber. Labor for tin mining and rubber tapping had to be imported, since the local Malays, subsistence farmers, were not interested in such work. The gap was filled mainly from overcrowded South China, and Chinese settlers soon comprised nearly half the population of Malaya. In time many of these Chinese immigrants, who also entered the booming commercial economy of Singapore, became wealthy. The Malays increasingly resented Chinese domination of the commercial economy. Indians also entered, as both laborers and merchants, and with the Chinese and the British controlled the commercial production and foreign trade of both Burma and Malaya. The colonial government of Malaya ruled as much as possible through local sultans and tried to preserve traditional Malay culture, but both countries were economically transformed.

French, Dutch, and American Colonialism

Largely eliminated from India by the end of the eighteenth century, the French sought their own colonial sphere in Asia. They used the persecution of French Catholic missionaries in Vietnam as a pretext for con-

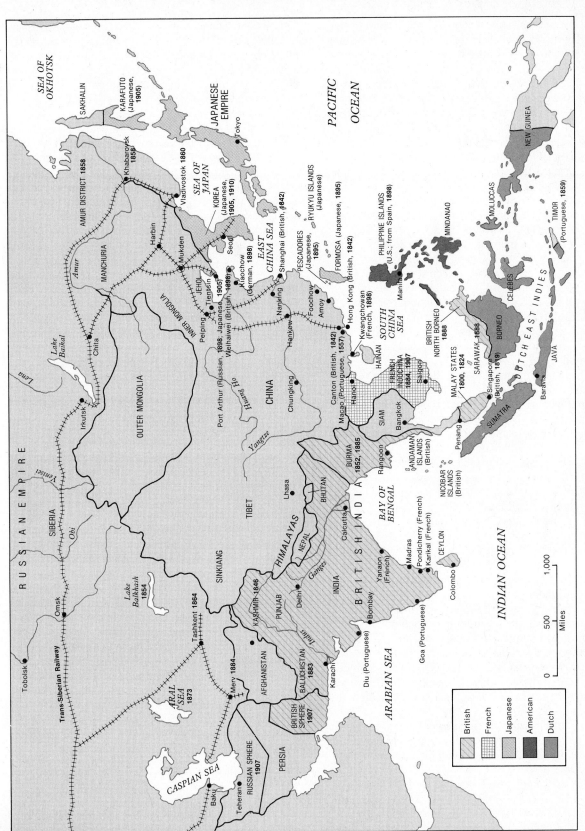

34.5 *Colonial Empires in Asia*

SEA OF
OKHOTSK

SAKHALIN

KARAFUTO
(Japanese,
1905)

JAPANESE
EMPIRE

Tokyo

PACIFIC

OCEAN

AMUR DISTRICT **1858**

Khabarovsk
1858

Vladivostok **1860**

SEA OF
JAPAN

KOREA
(Japanese,
1905, 1910)

NEW GUINEA

Amur

MANCHURIA

Harbin

Mukden

Seoul

EAST
CHINA SEA

Shanghai (British, **1842**)

RYUKYU ISLANDS
(Japanese)

MOLUCCAS

TIMOR
(Portuguese, **1859**)

Lake
Baikal

Chita

JEHOL

Peiping
Tientsin

Port Arthur (Russian, **1898**; Japanese, **1905**)
Weihaiwei (British, **1898**)
Kiaochow
(German, **1898**)

PESCADORES
(Japanese,
1895)

FORMOSA (Japanese, **1895**)

PHILIPPINE
ISLANDS
(U.S.; from Spain, **1898**)

MINDANAO

CELEBES

Irkutsk

RUSSIAN EMPIRE

INNER MONGOLIA

Lena

Huang
Ho

Nanking

Foochow
Amoy

Hankow

HAINAN

DUTCH EAST INDIES

Manila

Yenisei

OUTER MONGOLIA

CHINA

Chungking

Yangtze

Canton (British, **1842**)

Macao (Portuguese, **1557**)

Hong Kong (British, **1842**)

Kwangchowan
(French, **1898**)

SOUTH
CHINA SEA

FRENCH
INDOCHINA
1884–1907

Hanoi

Saigon

BRITISH
NORTH BORNEO
1888

SARAWAK **1888**

BORNEO

JAVA

Batavia

Obi

SIBERIA

Lake
Balkhash
1854

SINKIANG

TIBET

Lhasa

HIMALAYAS

BHUTAN

BURMA
1852, 1885

SIAM

Bangkok

ANDAMAN
ISLANDS
(British)

MALAY STATES
1800, 1824

Singapore
(British, **1819**)

SUMATRA

Penang

Omsk

Tashkent **1864**

NEPAL

Rangoon

BAY OF
BENGAL

Trans-Siberian Railway

Tobolsk

ARAL
SEA
1873

Merv **1884**

KASHMIR **1846**

Indus

PUNJAB

Delhi

INDIA

Calcutta

Ganges

BRITISH INDIA

NICOBAR
ISLANDS
(British)

CEYLON

Colombo

INDIAN OCEAN

AFGHANISTAN

BALUCHISTAN
1883

Karachi

BRITISH
SPHERE
1907

Madras

Pondicherry (French)
Karikal (French)

Yanaon
(French)

Bombay

Diu (Portuguese)

Goa (Portuguese)

ARABIAN SEA

CASPIAN SEA

RUSSIAN SPHERE
1907

PERSIA

Baku

Teheran

British
French
Japanese
American
Dutch

0   500   1,000

Miles

quering the southern provinces in 1862, including the port of Saigon. Later they annexed Cambodia and Laos and in 1885 took over northern Vietnam after defeating Chinese forces sent to protect their tributary state. Under French control, southern Vietnam became a major exporter of rice and rubber grown in the delta of the Mekong River. They were exported through the chief port of Saigon, which was made the colonial capital. Cambodia and Laos remained little developed commercially. Northern Vietnam was already too densely populated to produce surpluses for export, but there was some small industrial growth around the city of Hanoi and in the northern port of Haiphong. The colonial administration tried to impose French culture on these territories, collectively called Indochina.

French rule was oppressive and often ruthless in suppressing all gestures toward political expression. The army was augmented by special security forces and had much of the apparatus of a police state, which executed, jailed, or drove into exile most Vietnamese leaders. These included the young Ho Chi Minh (1890–1969), later the head of the Vietnamese Communist party, who went to Europe in 1911 and later from Paris to Moscow and Canton.

The Dutch left most of Indonesia to native rulers until late in the nineteenth century, content with controlling trade from Batavia (now Djakarta), their colonial capital. Batavia was situated on the tropical island of Java, which produced a variety of plantation crops the Dutch promoted after 1830, including sugar, coffee, tea, and tobacco. By the early 1900s rubber was an important commodity, and Indonesia was second only to Malaya in its production. Oil was also found and exploited. The discovery of more oil and tin and the cultivation of prime land for rubber and tobacco prompted the Dutch to increase their control first of the neighboring island of Sumatra and then of Borneo, Celebes, the Moluccas, Bali, and the hundreds of smaller islands in the archipelago south of the Philippines. New railways and ports were built to expedite trade.

Dutch rule was fiercely contested on some of the islands, especially Sumatra, and it never penetrated effectively into the mountain and jungle interior of Borneo. The northern coast of Borneo was controlled by the British. Dutch rule became increasingly oppressive. Indonesians were excluded from participation in government and the exercise of political rights and were denied access to more than elementary education. Java was systematically exploited by forcing its peasants to grow export crops for Dutch profit. Production and population grew very rapidly, but living standards and the quality of life declined.

In 1898 the United States went to war with Spain over Cuba and acquired the Philippines as its first overseas colony. The 43 years of American control had a greater effect on the culture and economy of the islands than

400 years of Spanish rule. The Americans built roads and hospitals and established an education system up to the university level. Literacy and public health rose to levels second only to Japan in Asia. But America's economic impact was exploitive. In partnership with rich Filipinos, it concentrated on growing commercial crops for export, especially sugar, and often neglected the basic needs of the people as a whole. Manila, the colonial capital, became a rapidly growing commercial center and the chief base of the Filipino middle class and educated elite. The Americans declared as their goal the creation of a democratic society in their own image. To a degree this was achieved, but Philippine politics remained under the control of a landed elite supported by others who profited from the American connection and paid little attention to the dominantly peasant population, who remained exploited. The country had been subjugated only by a brutal war against Filipino nationalist resistance from 1899 to 1902 in which the Americans pursued policies that foreshadowed their later misadventures in Vietnam. Most peasants, still largely illiterate, could not take advantage of free public education or free expression. The United States granted independence to the Philippines in 1946 on terms that ensured its continuing influence and left huge American military bases there.

Independent Siam

While the rest of Southeast Asia was being taken over by imperialist powers, the Thais kept their independence. This was in part the result of geography. Siam lay between the British in Burma and Malaya and the French in Indochina. Neither was willing to let the other dominate the country. British preponderance in Thai foreign trade and investment was balanced by French annexation of territory claimed or occupied by Siam in western Cambodia and Laos. British Malaya detached Siam's southern provinces. Nonetheless, the Thais benefited from a series of able kings who adroitly played the French off against the British and urged the advantages to both of leaving at least part of their country as a buffer state. They had to grant special trade, residence, and legal privileges to the colonial powers, a system like that imposed on China, but there was no foreign effort to take over the government. Nevertheless the Thai economy developed along the same lines as colonial Southeast Asia, with a big new export trade in rice from the delta area, followed later by rubber and tropical hardwoods. Bangkok, the capital, grew rapidly as the chief port for foreign trade and spreading commercialization.

Overseas Chinese

Western development had important demographic consequences for Southeast Asia. Immigrant Chinese began

WESTERN COLONIZATION, 1800–1900

The Americas	Africa	Asia
Dissolution of the Spanish and Portuguese empires (c. 1810–1825)	Britain occupies the Cape Colony (1806)	Britain completes conquest of India (1818), acquires Singapore (1819)
U.S. proclaims Monroe Doctrine (1823)	French occupy Algeria (1830)	Opium War against China (1839–1842); Hong Kong ceded to Britain
	Boers begin Great Trek (1833)	United States forces Japan to end policy of isolation (1853–1854)
French empire in Mexico (1864–1867)	Britain begins systematic exploration of central Africa (1849)	Sepoy Rebellion in India (1857–1858); Second Anglo-Chinese War (1858–1860)
Canada gains Dominion status (1867)		
Spanish-American War; United States acquires Puerto Rico, the Philippines; Cuba becomes U.S. protectorate (1898)	Gold discovered in the Transvaal (1868); scramble for Africa begins (1870)	France colonizes Indochina (1858–1885); Russia annexes Transcaucasus and central Asian steppe (1859–1879), founds port of Vladivostok (1860)
U.S. detaches Panama from Colombia, begins Panama Canal (1903)	Berlin conference (1884–1885); German empire; Congo Free State recognized	Britain annexes Burma to India (1886); U.S. naval base at Pearl Harbor (1887)
	Anglo-Boer War (1899–1902)	Boxer Rebellion (1899–1900)

to flood into all the commercially developed parts of the region in growing numbers after 1870, as plantation and mining labor and as traders. They soon largely monopolized the retail trade in all the cities of Southeast Asia, although they shared it with immigrant Indians in Burma and Malaya. In Bangkok they constituted over half the population and, as in Burma and Vietnam, controlled most of the large export trade in rice. Southeast Asians resented them, especially since they also served as moneylenders and owned most of the shops, but they were often welcomed by the colonialists as useful labor and commercial agents. In Siam, unlike the rest of Southeast Asia, most Chinese were quickly assimilated into Thai society through intermarriage and acculturation. Elsewhere they tended to remain confined to their own quarters and suffered discrimination from the local people. Altogether, Chinese settlers in Southeast Asia totaled about 15 million by the outbreak of World War II.

China Besieged

The Opium War of 1839–1842, in which the British demolished the Chinese forces, was ended by the Treaty of Nanking, which granted Britain most of its demands for trading rights and concessions. The war was provoked by Chinese efforts to end British and American imports of opium, but the larger issues were China's refusal to deal with foreigners as equals or to permit them

to trade where they liked. The port of Hong Kong was ceded outright, and five mainland ports, including Shanghai and Canton, were opened to British trade and residence. Other Western powers, including the United States, negotiated similar treaties the following year. These included the right of extraterritoriality, whereby foreign nationals in China were made immune from Chinese jurisdiction and were dealt with according to their own laws. The war had finally cracked China's proud isolation.

Foreign trade immediately began a rapid increase that continued until the world depression of the 1930s. Tea and silk remained the dominant exports and opium the main import, although it was overtaken after 1870 by cotton yarn, textiles, kerosene, and a variety of other foreign manufactured goods. The treaties further impinged on China's sovereignty by limiting the import tariffs it might impose to 5 percent. This had the effect of giving Western goods virtually unrestricted access to the vast Chinese market. Although China continued to provide most of its own needs, the treaties reduced the country to semicolonial status.

Peking's reluctance to abide by the terms of the treaties led to a second war from 1858 to 1860. British and French troops captured Tientsin (Tianjin) and Peking and burned the imperial summer palace. They saw this as retaliation for Chinese "treachery"—the breaking of successive agreements to observe earlier treaties and to receive the British ambassador in Peking, as well as firing on British forces and imprisoning their representatives.

◉ Opium ◉

The imperial commissioner sent to Canton in 1839 to stop the opium trade wrote a letter in the same year to the young Queen Victoria that read in part as follows.

Magnificently our great emperor soothes and pacifies China and the foreign countries. . . . But there appear among the crowd of barbarians both good and bad persons, unevenly. . . . There are barbarian ships that come here for trade to make a great profit. But by what right do they in return use the poisonous drug [opium] to injure the Chinese people? . . . Of all that China exports to foreign countries, there is not a single thing which is not beneficial. . . . On the other hand, articles coming from outside China can only be used as toys; they are not needed by China. Nevertheless, our Celestial Court lets tea, silk, and other goods be shipped without limit. This is for no other reason than to share the benefit with the people of the whole world.

Source: S. Y. Teng and J. K. Fairbank, *China's Response to the West* (Cambridge, Mass.: Harvard University Press, 1954), pp. 24–26.

Traders and Missionaries

The Treaty of Tientsin, which ended this second war, opened still more ports to residence and trade and allowed foreigners, including missionaries, free movement and enterprise anywhere in the country. Missionaries, the largest number of them American, often served as a forward wave for imperialism, building churches and preaching the Gospel in the interior and then demanding protection from their home governments against Chinese protests or riots. Trouble that missionaries or foreign traders encountered might be answered by sending a warship to the nearest coastal or river port to threaten or shell inhabitants, a practice known as "gunboat diplomacy." When antiforeign mobs assaulted missionaries or their converts, Western governments often used this as a pretext for extracting still more concessions.

Most Chinese were not receptive to the Christian message, especially in the evangelical form of most missionary preaching, and they resented foreigners with special privileges and protection encroaching on their country. Nor did they understand the missionary practice of buying or adopting orphans for charitable and religious purposes and so assumed the worst motives for these practices. Stories circulated that they ate babies or gouged out their eyes for medicine. In 1870 a mob destroyed a French Catholic mission in Tientsin and killed 10 nuns and 11 other foreigners; gunboats and heavy reparations followed.

Unlike the British, the French had no important trade with China and often used protection of their missionaries as a means of increasing their influence. In 1883 they went to war with China over Vietnam when Chinese troops crossed the border to eject them. The French destroyed part of the new Western-style Chinese navy and the dockyards at Foochow on the South China coast, which they had earlier helped to build. China was humbled again.

The Taiping Rebellion

Meanwhile, the greatest of all uprisings against the Ch'ing government erupted in 1850, the Taiping Rebellion. Westerners tend to overemphasize their own role in China as the major influence on events after 1840. China was huge, westerners were few, and their activities were limited to the treaty ports and outlying mission stations. China continued to respond primarily to its own long-standing internal problems, chief among which was a burgeoning population. Having outstripped production, it was falling into poverty and distress in many areas. The Taiping leader, Hung Hsiu-Ch'uan (Hong Xiuquan), was a frustrated scholar who had failed the rigid imperial examinations several times and then espoused an idiosyncratic version of Christianity adapted from missionary teaching. Hung became the leader of a largely peasant group from the impoverished mountain region of southern China, which resented its exclusion from the treaty ports and sought the overthrow of the Manchus. The rebels picked up massive support as they moved north and captured Nanking (Nanjing) in 1853. A northward thrust from there was turned back later that year near Tientsin, but rebel forces won at least a foot-

---

◉ Through Each Other's Eyes ◉

After the Opium War, foreign arrogance increased. Here is a sample from 1858.

It is impossible that our merchants and missionaries can course up and down the inland waters of this great region and traffic in their cities and preach in their villages without wearing away at the crust of the Chinaman's stoical and skeptical conceit. The whole present system in China is a hollow thing, with a hard brittle surface. . . . Some day a happy blow will shiver it [and] it will all go together.

But the Chinese returned the compliment.

It is monstrous in barbarians to attempt to improve the inhabitants of the Celestial Empire when they are so miserably deficient themselves. Thus, introducing a poisonous drug for their own benefit and to the injury of others, they are deficient in benevolence. Sending their fleets and armies to rob other nations, they can make no pretense to rectitude. . . . How can they expect to renovate others? They allow the rich and noble to enter office without passing through any literary examinations, and do not open the road to advancement to the poorest and meanest in the land. From this it appears that foreigners are inferior to the Chinese and therefore must be unfit to instruct them.

Sources: G. W. Cooke, *China: Being the Times Special Correspondence from China in the Years 1857–58* (London: Routledge, 1858), p. v; "A Chinese Tract of the Mid-Nineteenth Century," in E. P. Boardman, *Christian Influence on the Ideology of the Taiping Rebellion* (Madison: University of Wisconsin Press, 1952), p. 129.

---

hold in 16 of China's 18 provinces and dominated the rich Yangtze valley.

The efforts of the Taiping rebels to govern were relatively feeble. Large-scale fighting against the imperial forces continued without significant breaks until its final suppression in 1864. The cost in destruction and loss of life was horrendous. As many as 40 million people died, and much of the productive lower Yangtze region was laid waste. During the same period the Ch'ing also faced three other mass uprisings, in the north, the southwest, and the northwest. The latter two were primarily Muslim rebellions against Ch'ing rule, which lingered until 1873. As one Ch'ing official said, these revolts were like a disease of China's vital organs. In contrast, the activities of the Western powers were a marginal affliction only of the extremities.

Attempts at Reform

One foreign power, however, was still advancing by land: the Russians. Sensing China's weakness, they penetrated the Amur valley in northern Manchuria, from which they had been excluded in 1689. In the treaties following the war of 1858–1860 they detached the mar-

itime provinces of eastern Manchuria and added them to their empire; among their acquisitions was the port of Vladivostok. Muslim rebellion in the northwest after 1862 served as a pretext for Russian intervention in northern Sinkiang (Xinjiang). The Ch'ing government decided that this threat must be met head on, marched an army 2,500 miles from its base in eastern China, and to general surprise defeated both the rebels and the Russians by 1878.

Survival of the Ch'ing regime against the appalling challenges it faced showed that it was still capable of successful action. After 1860 it undertook a policy of "self-strengthening," which included the establishment of new Western-style arsenals, gun foundries, and shipyards. These and other efforts to modernize were handicapped by government red tape, but they achieved some progress. Several outstanding senior officials who realized the need for change rose to power. For a decade or two the Ch'ing seemed to have a new lease on life and to show surprising vigor.

It was not to last. The reformers never won full support from the still archconservative throne or from most of the people. Both remained essentially antiforeign and opposed to adopting Western tactics even to fight westerners. In 1862 a weak boy-emperor came to the throne, dominated by his scheming mother, Tz'u Hsi (Cixi, 1835–1908), a former imperial concubine who had plotted her way to the top. When the emperor died in 1875 at the age of 19, she put her 4-year-old nephew in his place, retaining all real power for herself as the empress dowager until her death in 1908. Tz'u Hsi was clever and politically masterful but narrow-minded and deeply conservative. She had no understanding of what was required to cope with the foreign threat to Chinese sovereignty.

China's first tentative efforts at change were thus for the most part aborted. The Confucian reactionaries, who with few exceptions again dominated the government, grudgingly acknowledged the potency of Western arms but insisted that there could be no abandoning or even altering the traditional Chinese view of the world to deal with them.

Treaty Ports and Mission Schools

Meanwhile the treaty ports, which numbered over 100 by 1910, grew rapidly, attracting Chinese as merchants, partners, and laborers. Manufacturing also began to grow in the treaty ports, especially after 1895 when the Japanese imposed a new treaty that permitted foreign-owned factories to operate in the ports; these produced mainly textiles and other consumer goods. This was the real beginning of modern industrialization in China.

Chinese entrepreneurs and industrialists, many of whom had been blocked or discouraged by the conservative government, welcomed the more enterprising world of the treaty ports. As elsewhere in Asia, imperialist arrogance was growing, and the Chinese found themselves excluded from foreign clubs and parks and treated as second-class citizens in their own cities. Many of them were torn between their ancient cultural pride and their sense of humiliation by westerners on the one hand and their reluctant admiration for the West's power and success on the other. As with their Indian counterparts in colonial Calcutta and Bombay, these conflicts produced the first stirrings of modern nationalism.

The most widespread Western influence on Chinese society came through the efforts of missionaries. The total number of Chinese Christians remained discouragingly small, and many, perhaps most, of them were so-called "rice Christians," who attended church for handouts. Most Chinese looked down on Christian converts as traitors or simply as the dregs of society. Many of the missions came to realize that education and medical help were more attractive than Christian doctrine and might pave a smoother path toward the goal of conversion. Mission-run schools spread rapidly, as did their hospitals. The schools drew many students, in time most of the young Chinese who wanted to study English and

Tz'u Hsi, the empress dowager, was a powerful and unscrupulous ruler. In keeping with the degeneracy of the late Ch'ing period, she favored the overly ornate style in which she decorated many rooms in the Imperial Palace in Peking. [Smithsonian Institution]

Western learning or science. Although most graduates did not become converts, they adopted Western ways of thinking in many respects. Most twentieth-century Chinese nationalists were influenced by mission schools, and nearly all of China's universities were founded by missionaries.

Government schools that included Western curricula were also established, and in 1905 the traditional examination system was abolished. Missionaries and others translated a wide range of Western works, which were read avidly by the new generation of Chinese intellectuals. Many of them began to call for the overthrow of the Ch'ing regime. Ironically, they used the treaty ports, notably Shanghai, as their base, where they were protected from Ch'ing repression by living under foreign law.

The Boxer Rebellion

Missionaries in rural areas continued to provoke anti-foreign riots as their activities spread. In the late 1890s the empress dowager adroitly turned a group of impoverished bandits and rebels in the eastern part of northern China against the missionaries instead of against the dynasty and by extension against all foreigners. By early 1900 this group, which called itself the "Fists of Righteous Harmony" but was known more simply to westerners as the Boxers, went on a rampage, burning mission establishments and killing missionaries and Chinese converts. Converts were resented for their use of foreign intervention in their disputes with other Chinese. By June 1900, with covert imperial support, the Boxers besieged the foreign legations in Peking, which barely held out until relieved by a multinational expedition in mid-August. Having earlier declared war officially against all the foreign powers, the court fled to Sian (Xian). After brutal reprisals, the Western powers (now including a large Japanese contingent) withdrew, and a peace was patched up a year later. A staggering indemnity was forced on China, on top of one already extracted by Japan in 1895. The empress dowager and her reactionary councillors, who had seen the Boxers as the final solution to the "barbarian problem," were left nominally in power.

The Ch'ing dynasty was moribund, but no workable alternative was yet at hand. China had still to learn the lessons of national unity and shared political purpose, which had been unnecessary in the past when the empire controlled "all under heaven" and China had no rivals. The government finally fell in 1911, more of its own weight and incompetence than because of the small, disorganized group of revolutionaries whose uprising joined the defection of disgruntled troops. The fall of the Ch'ing dynasty was hardly a revolution, but it ended the imperial rule by which China had been governed for more than 2,000 years and opened the way for fundamental change.

Japan Among the Powers

As indicated in Chapter 29, the antiquated Tokugawa shogunate was toppled in 1868 and 1869 by a new group of reformers. Their goal was the rapid modernization and westernization of Japan in order to save their country from colonialism and to remove the unequal treaties that had been forced on it. That effort was spectacularly successful. By 1895 new Western-style technology and industry had progressed far and had given Japan new power. With power came new ambition. In a conflict over dominance in Korea, Japan's new navy and army easily defeated China's poorly coordinated forces in 1894–1895 and detached both Korea and Taiwan from Chinese control, adding them to what was now the Japanese colonial empire. In 1904–1905 Japan's new strength enabled it to win early victories against a more formidable opponent, Russia, and then to conclude a treaty that replaced Russian dominance in Manchuria with Japanese. Confidence was high, as Japan was clearly established as a major power in East Asia, and by the early years of the twentieth century Japan was able to get rid of the unequal treaties and to deal with Western powers as an equal. But imperial ambition and military adventuring led the nation into what the Japanese call the "dark valley," beginning with their efforts to take control of much of eastern China in 1915, their formal takeover of Manchuria as part of their empire in 1931, and the morass of their full-scale invasion of China from 1937, a road that led to Pearl Harbor and Hiroshima. Nevertheless, the Meiji period, from 1868 to 1912 (the death of the Meiji emperor), was one of great and constructive progress that laid the foundation of modern Japanese society and economy.

The Meiji Restoration: Response to the West

In contrast to China, the Meiji Restoration in Japan ushered in a period of rapid change and wholesale westernization. Meiji was the reign title of the young emperor, who moved to Tokyo ("eastern capital") in 1869 as the restored head of state, although his role remained symbolic only. He and his successors served as a rallying point for new nationalist sentiment, and most Japanese took inspiration from the fact that their country was once again under imperial rule.

The goal of the new government was to strengthen and modernize Japan and thereby to free it from the unequal treaties (see Chapter 29). Like China, Japan had suffered loss of control over its tariffs and had been forced to concede extraterritoriality and other special privileges to the Western powers. In contrast to the Chinese, however, Japan's leaders realized that regaining their independence depended on mastering Western technology. They also saw that military technology could not be separated from overall industrialization or from the institutional structures that had produced and accompanied it in the West.

Whereas pride rendered these truths unacceptable to the Chinese, Japan showed little hesitation after 1869 in transforming or abolishing traditional institutions. Many Japanese urged wholesale westernization, arguing, "If we use it, that will make it Japanese." Some radical enthusiasts in the early years of Meiji actually tried to destroy traditional temples in their zeal to sweep away the old and make way for the new Japan. Japanese national pride did not rest so much in the culture as in the people's sense of themselves. Although change proved largely bloodless and was accompanied by relatively minor political reorganization, Meiji Japan produced in many ways a real revolution.

Economy and Government

The first priority was rapid industrialization, especially in heavy industries and armaments. Foreign advisers were hired to expedite this growth—from Britain for a modern navy, from Germany for a modern army and armaments industry, and so on. Railways were quickly built to link the major cities, and new ports and facilities were created. The machinery of government and law was wholly remade, modeled on a judicious combination of Western systems. What emerged was a modified constitutional monarchy with a parliament and a largely Western-derived legal system. Such change was important also to demonstrate that Japan was a "civilized" country where foreigners did not need extraterritoriality to protect them.

All Western institutions, and even such details of Western culture as dress and diet, were seen as sources of strength. Samurai discarded their swords and traditional garb, put on Western business suits, learned to waltz, and dominated the new bureaucracy. Some samurai found careers as officers in the new army, and others went into business, government, or manufacturing. The ranks of the army were filled with peasant conscripts; war was no longer a gentlemen's preserve.

The Japanese were rapidly mobilized toward the new goals. They were accustomed to direction, from daimyo, samurai, or other hierarchical superiors, and most came to share the national objectives with genuine enthusiasm. Japan's almost ready-made nationalism, the fruit of an island country with a long history of separateness, was a strong asset. Its people were also linguistically, racially, and culturally homogeneous (as the Chinese and Indians were not), and the country was small and more easily integrated as a unit. In landmass and population, approximately 50 million by 1910, it was about the size of one of China's larger provinces, and some 90 percent of its people were concentrated in the corridor between Tokyo and Osaka. What was decided in Tokyo was quickly carried out everywhere as national policy. Farm output tripled between 1870 and 1940 with the use of new Western technology as well as hard work. In many ways it was the latter that accounted for Meiji Japan's astounding success.

Japanese Imperialism

By the 1890s Japan had a modern navy and army and a fast-growing industrial base. Japanese steamships had won a major place in East Asian trade, and Japanese merchants had acquired a rising share of the China market. In 1894 Britain agreed to relinquish the unequal clauses of the old treaty with Japan by 1899, and other nations soon followed suit.

Having followed the Western lead in modern development, Japan now joined the other imperialist powers in colonial conquests. Korea was the handiest target, and in brief campaigns in 1894 and 1895 the new Japanese fleet and army demolished Chinese forces sent to protect China's tributary dependency. The peace treaty made Japan dominant in a still nominally independent Korea; the Chinese also ceded to them the island of Taiwan (Formosa), a huge indemnity, and the right to operate factories in the China treaty ports.

At the same time, the Russians were extending their influence, railways, and concession areas in Manchuria, whose southern tip they leased from China. The Japanese saw this as a threat to their position in Korea, but in any case they had their own plans for Manchuria. They struck there in 1904 without declaring war, winning a rapid series of land and naval battles against Russia by a combination of dash and willingness to take heavy casualties. The Russians were far from their home base and inadequately prepared; in time their much greater resources would have prevailed, but the Japanese persuaded the American president, Theodore Roosevelt, to arrange a peace at Portsmouth, New Hampshire, in 1905. The Russians were concerned by then with the first stirrings of revolution at home, and the war was expensive and unpopular in Russia. Japan inherited Russia's position in Manchuria and tightened its grip on Korea, which in 1910 became an outright colony in a growing Japanese empire.

Japan's first steps toward empire profited from the tacit support of the Western powers, who saw it as a counterweight against Russia's geographic advantage in the Far East. Japan had been encouraged to attack Russia by the Anglo-Japanese treaty of alliance and friendship signed in 1902, which was welcomed in Japan as a mark of international equality. Theodore Roosevelt saw the Japanese as promising allies, "bully fighters," as he called them. The Russo-Japanese War of 1904–1905 inaugurated a period of new pride, confidence, and continued economic progress.

Japan joined the Allies in World War I, ostensibly as an equal partner, although it took no part in the fighting in Europe apart from sending a few destroyers to join the British Mediterranean fleet. The opportunity was instead used to take over the German concession areas in China, centered in the province of Shantung (Shandong) in the eastern part of northern China. In 1915 Japan presented China with a list of 21 demands that would have made it in effect a Japanese colony. By such bullying tactics, Japan quickly lost the admiration and goodwill built up by its progress since 1869. The Twenty-one Demands also infuriated Chinese patriots and more than any other event spurred the rise of broad-based Chinese nationalism. The demands were rejected, although Japan hung on to the German concessions in Shantung. Meanwhile, the Japanese continued to develop Taiwan, Korea, and Manchuria.

Taiwan offered rice, sugar, and tropical crops to feed Japan's booming population. Korea had rich resources of coal, iron ore, and timber, which Japan appropriated. The Japanese drained the country of every useful commodity, including food crops, to support their growth, leaving the Koreans as an impoverished and exploited labor force. Koreans were forced to adopt Japanese names, and most were denied even elementary education; the public use of their own language was forbidden. Manchuria, still formally part of China but in effect a Japanese sphere, was a storehouse of coal, ores, timber, productive agricultural land, and potential hydroelectric power. Japan exploited all these resources while building an infrastructure of railways, mines, irrigation systems, dams, port facilities, and a colonial administration. In Korea too, railways, mines, factories, and roads were built and basic economic growth was begun, although for Japanese benefit. In Taiwan the infrastructure for economic redevelopment was also laid, primarily in agriculture, leading to new prosperity.

In Manchuria the Japanese built the largest single industrial complex in Asia, including closely integrated mines and factories in the Mukden (Shenyang) area, a dense rail network, and a highly productive commercialized agriculture that generated large surpluses of wheat and soybeans for export to Japan and to world markets through the port of Dairen. Large power dams were built on Manchuria's rivers. The population increased by nearly a million a year from 1900 to the outbreak of the Pacific war in 1941, consisting almost entirely of Chinese who migrated from a disordered and impoverished North China in search of new economic opportunity. Japan's huge investment in Manchuria laid the basis for China's industrialization after Japan's defeat in 1945. But Japan's record as a colonial power, despite the constructive achievements, was marred, as in Korea, by an exploitive approach as well as a disregard for local interests or aspirations.

to learn how to make his country strong and in 1881 became Japan's first prime minister under the new Western-style government. A later visit to Prussia convinced him that a constitutional monarchy was best suited to Japan. Ito was the chief architect of the new constitution proclaimed by the emperor in 1889, which contained many elements of the German imperial constitution. He understood, however, that constitutional government, and the cooperation of the new parliament, could not be made to work without political organization and popular support. In 1898 he left office to form a political party for that purpose, which was dominant in Japan until 1941.

After the Russo-Japanese War in 1905, Ito became the first Japanese resident-general in Korea. The Koreans deeply resented Japanese control, but Ito saw a civilian-based policy as preferable to the complete military occupation urged by powerful voices at home and hoped, against the odds, that he could win the Koreans' goodwill and cooperation in developing their country. In 1909 he was assassinated by a Korean patriot while on a visit to northern Manchuria—an abrupt end to the career of a man who might have played a vital moderating role in subsequent Japanese policies. Ito was an enthusiastic modernizer, especially after his visits to the West, but he also understood the need for compromise in politics and for adapting Western ways to Japanese traditions, circumstances, and values. In some ways he remained at least as traditional as he was modern. His objective was the preservation and development of his country, and westernization was only a means to that end. He believed deeply in the restoration of the emperor's personal rule and aimed to accomplish his goals by working through the throne. But he also understood the rising yearning for a less authoritarian form of government and the need for political parties, a constitution, and a parliament. These aspirations he served well, never letting personal ambition or power cloud his judgment or his dedication to the public welfare.

❧ ITO HIROBUMI: MEIJI STATESMAN

The leading statesman of Meiji Japan, Ito Hirobumi, was born in one of the outer daimyo domains of southwestern Japan in 1841. As a youth, he wanted passionately to save his country from the foreign threat, and at the age of 21 he tried to burn the newly established British embassy in Tokyo. But when he visited Britain the next year, he realized that it was impossible to drive the westerners out by such tactics, and he returned to work for Japan's modernization. After the Meiji Restoration he went with government missions to Europe and America

Australia and the Pacific Islands

Western expansion came late to the Australian continent and most of the Pacific islands. Australia, however, had been inhabited by aborigines for some 50,000 years, and more recently peoples from Southeast Asia had migrated to Australia and the myriad islands of the Pacific. The culture of these peoples varied from that of the aborigines, who lived until Western colonization very much as their Paleolithic ancestors had, to the Maori of New Zealand, skilled seamen whose delicate, filigreed wood-

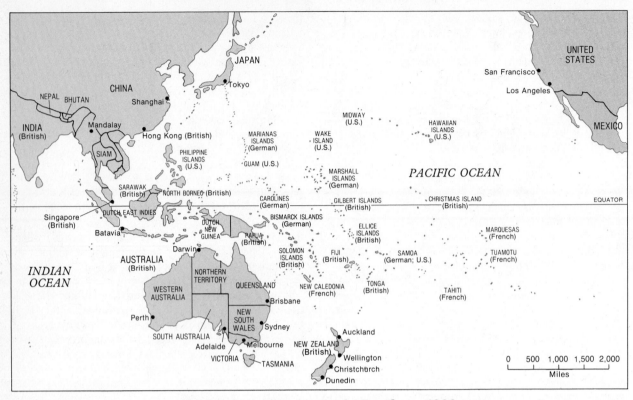

34.6 Colonial Empires in the Pacific, c. 1900

carving had no equal elsewhere in the world. Western explorers called this region Oceania. In addition to Australia and New Zealand, Oceania included Melanesia, extending from New Guinea to Fiji; Micronesia, to the north, embracing the islands from the Marianas to the Gilberts; and Polynesia, the easternmost islands, encompassing Samoa and Hawaii.

Australia:
Convicts, Wool, and Gold

Although Spanish explorers and traders had plied the Pacific throughout much of the sixteenth century, the Dutch were the first westerners to reach Australia, which they called New Holland, in the early 1600s. The English displayed some interest late in the same century, but not until 1770 did a British expedition under James Cook discover land suitable for settlement and claim Australia for Britain. Because the great island continent was not astride the trade routes, it had hitherto been ignored, but the British soon found a use for the latest acquisition to their empire. Having lost the war with the American colonists and having failed to establish penal settlements in West Africa, they could dump unwanted convicts in Australia.

The first British colony was founded at Sydney on the southeast coast in 1788 by Captain Arthur Phillip, who became the first governor. Because the colony was so distant from Britain and so difficult to supply, it was slow to attract free settlers. Many of the earliest free colonists were soldiers who decided to stay in Australia after serving in the British garrison, notwithstanding the fact that the land was described by one officer as "very barren and forbidding." By the mid-nineteenth century it had become the home of some 160,000 transplanted convicts, many of whom were assigned to work a specified number of years for the free colonizers. New South Wales, as the region around Sydney was called, was difficult to farm, especially because of insufficient water, but in the early 1800s the woolen industry developed rapidly, aided by the British government's termination of import duties on colonial wool. Between 1821, when wool was first shipped to Britain, and 1845, wool export increased from 175,000 pounds to 24 million pounds.

By that point exploration was moving rapidly forward, and there were key settlements at Melbourne in the south, Perth in the southwest, and Brisbane to the north. Interest in Australia increased substantially when gold was discovered in New South Wales and its southern neighbor, Victoria, in 1851, two years after the great rush had begun in California. In the ensuing decade the population of New South Wales jumped from 200,000 to

THE VISUAL EXPERIENCE
Art of Modern Asia and Africa

This Congolese carving of a Belgian official and his native driver comments wittily yet perceptively on imperial relationships. [Werner Forman Archive]

Portuguese merchants, greeted by Jesuits, unload goods from India and East Asia at Nagasaki, Japan, in the sixteenth century. Painted by a Japanese artist on gold-leafed paper. [Freer Gallery of Art, Smithsonian Institution]

The "iron horse" in Japan: early Meiji woodblock artists were fascinated by the new railways, as most Japanese were intrigued with the artifacts of the modern West that flooded into their country. [Asian Art Museum, San Francisco]

Western painters, especially the Impressionists, were profoundly influenced by Chinese and especially Japanese styles. Here are two Hiroshige originals from the mid-nineteenth century (left) and two paintings by his Dutch contemporary Vincent van Gogh (right), obvious copies but with some idiosyncratic touches. [Hiroshige: Rijksmuseum, Amsterdam. Van Gogh: Vincent van Gogh Foundation/Van Gogh Museum, Amsterdam.]

Japanese ladies follow the Meiji trend of westernization by learning to play the piano. But they keep their traditional Japanese hairstyles and the cherry tree screen, despite their Western dresses. [Granger Collection]

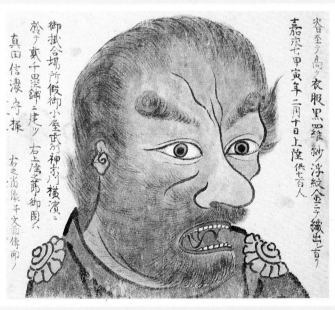

The Japanese were quick to portray the westerners who had forced their way into the country. Here are two representations from 1854, showing Commodore Perry (left) and his second in command, Adams (right). Like the Chinese, the Japanese clearly saw westerners as savages. [Perry: Smithsonian Institution; Adams: Honolulu Academy of Arts, Gift of Mrs. Walter F. Dillingham in memory of Alice Perry Grew, 1960]

IA ORANA MARIA

Paul Gauguin, *Ia Orana Maria* **["We Greet Thee, Mary"]. Gauguin's images of a placid yet sensually inviting South Seas world far removed from the scramble of nineteenth-century Western materialism had great appeal. Gauguin himself had at one time been a stockbroker. [The Metropolitan Museum of Art, Bequest of Sam A. Lewisohn, 1951]**

350,000, and Victoria's rose from 77,000 to 540,000. As the population of the continent as a whole passed 1 million, more attention had to be given to food production, especially when the supply of gold dwindled. As in the American west, bitter conflicts arose between ranchers and farmers, with the latter additionally plagued by water shortages and inadequate transportation facilities. The crisis was gradually resolved only as roads, railways, and irrigation systems were built and as farmers learned to dry-farm and to apply chemical fertilizers.

During the late nineteenth century interest grew in uniting the six Australian colonies, each of which had been given its own legislature by an 1850 British statute. Federation would not only eliminate internal economic barriers but also enhance Australia's ability to withstand potential aggression from one or more of the imperial powers. The resulting commonwealth of Australia, founded in 1901, was a constitutional federation, with the central government, as in the United States, possessing only limited authority.

New Zealand: Maori and Missionaries

The Australian aborigines had been spread too thinly and were too pacific to have posed a serious threat to colonizers. In New Zealand, however, the native Maori were not only relatively more populous, considering New Zealand's smaller size (one-thirtieth the size of Australia), but much better organized and temperamentally more militant. Although Captain Cook had claimed New Zealand for Britain in 1769, interest in settling the islands was slow in developing. Missionary efforts to the Maori, begun in 1814, made striking progress by mid-century. Simultaneously, however, some of the Maori began acquiring European guns, which they turned against rival tribes in an orgy of violence. The island also became a battleground in a different kind of war—one fought ideologically and politically between missionaries, who wanted the land preserved for Christianized Maori, and imperial colonizers, who envisaged a country dominated by white settlers.

Matters came to a head in 1840, thanks largely to the colonizing schemes of Edward Gibbon Wakefield and his New Zealand Land Company. The island, he truthfully told a parliamentary committee, was "the most beautiful country" with a fine climate and productive soil. The British decision to annex New Zealand may have been stimulated as well by a French show of interest in the island nation. The British government formally annexed New Zealand in 1840; the newly appointed governor negotiated a treaty with the Maori, obtaining their recognition of British sovereignty and promising them secure land tenure. But many of the Maori were soon disillusioned as whites from Australia and Britain poured into the islands, and fighting was frequent until 1872, when the Maori finally accepted defeat. By that point the population of the islands was approximately 250,000, of whom less than 40,000 by one estimate were Maori. They were victims not only of the fighting but, like the Australian aborigines and the Amerindians, of the new diseases transmitted by Europeans. Peace provided fresh opportunities for growth, and in the next 30 years the population more than tripled, modern transportation and communications systems were developed, and a democratic political constitution evolved that in 1893 extended suffrage to women.

Islands of the Pacific

Although Spanish and Dutch explorers had discovered some of the islands of Melanesia, Micronesia, and Polynesia, it was not until the late eighteenth century that Europeans began to show serious interest in them. At first their motives were largely economic: whalers and sealers from America, Britain, and France used some of the islands as bases, and merchants traded tools, cloth, and guns for sandalwood, which found a ready market in China. As in New Zealand, much of the early interest in the islands was also religious. Spanish missionaries sought converts in the Marianas, British Protestants in 1797 launched their campaign in Tahiti, and American Protestants began working in Hawaii in 1820. Where the missionaries went, the political interests of their home governments were usually quick to follow. In Tahiti, however, the English Protestants who virtually ran the island were ousted by the French navy in 1843, after which Catholic missionaries taught the natives their version of Christianity.

As imperial rivalry intensified among the great powers in the late nineteenth century, the Pacific islands were increasingly coveted. The interest in converting the native populations continued but was clearly subordinate to economic considerations and imperial advantage. Britain, France, the United States, and Germany competed for the spoils, toppling native states, such as the kingdom of Fiji, in the process. The most notorious example of this occurred in 1893, when American planters, aided by a contingent of 150 marines, overthrew Hawaii's Queen Liliuokalani (1891–1893). Despite the fact that the United States had recognized Hawaii's independence in 1842, the American government waited only until 1900 to annex it, as it had annexed the Philippines and Guam two years earlier. "We need Hawaii just as much and a good deal more than we did California," insisted President William McKinley; "it is manifest destiny."

Thus in 1900 every island in Polynesia, Micronesia, and Melanesia was a colonial possession of Britain, France, Germany, or the United States. Once-mighty

Samoan chieftains and their king listen to the reading of a Western peace treaty in 1881. Note the guard of soldiers in the rear. [Peabody Museum of Salem]

Spain, after losing the Philippines and Guam, had sold its remaining Pacific islands—the Carolines, Marianas, and Marshalls—to Germany the previous year. The Germans, however, would lose those islands to Japan in 1914, the same year they lost northeastern New Guinea to Australia and their part of Samoa to New Zealand. Less than three decades later, conflicting Japanese and American ambitions in the Pacific resulted in the attack on Pearl Harbor that propelled the United States into World War II.

The age of domination saw European powers take control of most of Africa, India, Ceylon, Burma, Malaya, Indochina, Indonesia, and the Philippines, while they and the Americans exercised a strong influence and enjoyed special concessions in Thailand, China, and Japan. The Japanese, taking a lesson from their Western teachers, created their own colonial empire in Korea, Taiwan, and Manchuria.

Imperialism radically challenged the traditional values and structures of the societies it conquered or dominated. The result was dislocation, suffering, and cultural trauma. Much of value was weakened or destroyed. But the West also brought advances in technology, productivity, and medicine that raised the standard of living and increased life expectancy. For better or worse, the colonial impulse united most of the globe in a broad, overarching web of economic and political interdependence for the first time in history. Some of the West's values would be adopted, some contested, some rejected. Many of them would be accepted only after being assimilated to the older cultural patterns that reasserted themselves as the yoke of Western dominance was shaken off. The four great civilizations of Asia each responded differently to the Western challenge. British dominion in India stimulated the development of a nationalist movement that created a modern state on the subcontinent. Similar developments came later in Southeast Asia and were retarded by repressive French and Dutch colonial policies. China, too large to be conquered, would find its own path to modernity after a century of confusion and anarchy. Japan made the most rapid and apparently the easiest transition from a traditional society to a modern, industrial one and in mere decades achieved the status of a world power.

Suggestions for Further Reading

Imperialism and Africa

Curtin, P. D. *Africa and the West: Intellectual Responses to European Culture*. Madison: University of Wisconsin Press, 1972.

Denoon, D., and Nyeko, B. *Southern Africa Since 1800*, rev. ed. New York: Longman, 1984.

Fieldhouse, D. K. *Economics and Empire, 1830–1914*. Ithaca, N.Y.: Cornell University Press, 1973.

Freund, B. *The Making of Africa*. Bloomington: Indiana University Press, 1984.

Hallett, R. *Africa Since 1875*. Ann Arbor: University of Michigan Press, 1974.

Langer, W. L. *The Diplomacy of Imperialism, 1890–1902*, 2nd ed. New York: Knopf, 1965.

Oliver, R. and Atmore, A. *Africa Since 1800*, 3rd ed. Cambridge: Cambridge University Press, 1981.

Perham, M., and Simmons, J., eds. *African Discovery: An Anthology of Exploration*. London: Faber & Faber, 1961.

Robertson, C., and Berger, I., eds. *Women and Class in Africa*. New York: Africana, 1986.

India

Davis, L. E., and Huttenback, R. A. *Mammon and the Pursuit of Empire*. Cambridge: Cambridge University Press, 1988.

Embree, A. T. *1857 in India: Mutiny or War of Independence?* Boston: Heath, 1963.

Forster, E. M. *A Passage to India*. New York: Harcourt, Brace, 1924. (Fiction)

Mason, P. *The Men Who Ruled India*, rev. ed. New York: Norton, 1985.

Seal, A. *The Emergence of Indian Nationalism*. Cambridge: Cambridge University Press, 1968.

Southeast Asia

Bastin, J., and Benda, H. J. *A History of Modern Southeast Asia*. Englewood Cliffs, N.J.: Prentice Hall, 1968.

Hall, D. G. E. *A History of Southeast Asia*, 4th ed. New York: St. Martin's Press, 1984.

Harrison, B. *Southeast Asia: A Short History*. London: Macmillan, 1975.

Orwell, G. *Burmese Days*. New York: Harcourt, Brace, 1934.

Osborne, M. E. *Southeast Asia: An Illustrated Introductory History*. Boston: Allen & Unwin, 1990.

Stanley, P. W. *Reappraising an Empire: The American Impact on the Philippines*. Cambridge, Mass.: Harvard University Press, 1984.

Steinberg, D. J., ed. *In Search of Southeast Asia*. Honolulu: University Press of Hawaii, 1987.

China

Fairbank, J. K. *The Missionary Enterprise in China and America*. Cambridge, Mass.: Harvard University Press, 1974.

Gasster, M. *China's Struggle to Modernize*. New York: Knopf, 1972.

Hsu, I. *The Rise of Modern China*. New York: Oxford University Press, 1975.

Murphey, R. *Shanghai: Key to Modern China*. Cambridge, Mass.: Harvard University Press, 1953.

Pruitt, I. *Daughter of Han*. New Haven, Conn.: Yale University Press, 1945.

Schrecker, J. *Imperialism and Chinese Nationalism*. Cambridge, Mass.: Harvard University Press, 1971.

Japan

Beasley, W. G. *The Meiji Restoration*. Stanford, Calif.: Stanford University Press, 1972.

———. *The Rise of Modern Japan*. New York: St. Martin's Press, 1990.

Borton, H. *Japan's Modern Century*. New York: Ronald Press, 1955.

Myers, R. *The Japanese Colonial Empire*. Stanford, Calif.: Stanford University Press, 1984.

Storry, R. *A History of Modern Japan*, rev. ed. New York: Penguin Books, 1982.

The Twentieth Century

In 1910 King Edward VII of Great Britain died. At his funeral a stately procession of Europe's reigning monarchs—including George V, Edward's successor; Tsar Nicholas II of Russia; Kaiser William II of Germany; Crown Prince Karl of Austria-Hungary; and King Albert of Belgium—paraded on horseback, their helmets and swords glittering in the sun. Looking back on it from the perspective of the present, we are tempted to see great symbolism in the event—the mourning, as it were, for a world that was dying. Within four years the monarchs who had posed so congenially with each other, many of whom were related by marriage or blood, were at war with each other. When that struggle—the "Great War"—was over, some of them had lost their thrones, and those who remained would reign over states with sharply diminished power and prestige.

The world changed rapidly after the Great War of 1914–1918. Revolutionary upheavals in Russia and new ideologies in Italy and Germany proclaimed the entrance of the masses onto the stage of history and the demise of the old liberal order. These Western transformations were accompanied by equally momentous events in India, China, and the Middle East, where anticolonial movements sought both liberation from Western domination and national regeneration. Within 20 years economic crisis and a second world war had completed the decline of Europe as the center of world power. The influence of the traditional European powers was quickly replaced by the emergence of the Soviet Union and the United States as "superpower" states whose military-industrial strength dominated world affairs for almost 50 years. By the early 1990s one of these superpowers—the Soviet Union—had ceased to exist, and the other—the United States—found itself facing increasing economic competition.

By 1945 a fundamental shift had occurred in the relationship between the West and the rest of the world as Asia, Africa, and Latin America completed the transition from colonialism. If the first half of the century began with a few European states controlling huge colonial empires across the globe, the second half draws to a close with a world community consisting of more than 150 independent nations. Indeed, the newer states today play an increasingly more prominent role in shaping a common destiny through a joint international posture of nonalignment, seeking thereby to mitigate the effects of superpower hegemony.

While the twentieth century saw the end of European political supremacy, it also witnessed the extension of Western technology, institutions, and ideas to the newly independent nations. The adoption of Western models of development was both a deliberate weapon in the struggle against colonialism and a legacy of their former subordinate status. But as traditional societies experience the disruptive stresses of modernization, developing nations are searching for alternatives more appropriate to their own cultures.

As we move toward the twenty-first century, a host of vital issues—social and political justice, peace, human rights and equality, and economic well-being—loom ever larger as the joint responsibility of an increasingly interdependent global community. ■

Culture, Society, and the Great War

Until a second global conflict erupted in the 1930s, modern memory recalled only the "Great War" of 1914–1918. World War I was called "great" because its toll on human life, its monetary cost and physical destruction, and the human trauma it caused made all others pale in comparison. It started because rulers and government officials blundered in the summer of 1914, but a half century of diplomatic, social, and cultural history lay behind the immediate events. Many artists and writers had rejected traditional moral and social values, and some glorified violence as a catharsis that would strengthen what they believed was a civilization in decay. Such views anticipated the political breakdown of Europe by creating a climate in which war seemed acceptable, even desirable.

Although the fighting stopped in November 1918, its impact was felt for decades. Four empires disappeared as a result of the conflict—Hohenzollern Germany, Habsburg Austria-Hungary, Ottoman Turkey, and Ro-

Women served at or near the front lines in a number of capacities during World War I. Here a British ambulance driver is shown in France. [Bettmann Archive]

manov Russia. This last was replaced by the world's first state to describe itself as socialist with the goal of transforming itself into a communist society. The shock of the war experience, no less than the conditions of peace imposed on the vanquished, helped shape the twentieth century.

The Great War was not the first worldwide war, for earlier struggles had also been waged on several continents and oceans. In this war military engagements took place in Africa, Asia, and the Middle East, but the fighting was concentrated in Europe. Although imperialism formed part of the background to the war, its causes were almost entirely in the West. Nevertheless, the Great War had worldwide repercussions. In its aftermath, Europe's overseas empires disintegrated as its global supremacy collapsed.

The Crisis of European Culture

In the three decades preceding World War I, European culture underwent a revolution that transformed thought: antirationalists challenged the optimism inherited from the Enlightenment and the materialism of the nineteenth century, while the literary and artistic avant-garde experimented with new ways of experiencing time and space. Philosophers increasingly favored instinct over reason to explain human behavior, while students of the mind proclaimed that beneath the fragile veneer of civilization lurked dark forces. Scientists, who had previously explained the physical world through the observation of recordable data, confronted a universe in which measurement itself was relative to the observer. Literary narrative, which once expressed motives and character, spoke increasingly in the language of ambiguity. The crisis also overturned aesthetic values as artists questioned conventional expressions of reality. Most disturbing, new strains of antidemocratic and racist thought were introduced into politics.

The Revolt Against Positivism

As we have seen (Chapter 33), in the early nineteenth century Auguste Comte had argued that human behavior can be explained by "positive" observable data rather than by metaphysical forces. By the end of the century many intellectuals had turned against materialism and reason in what came to be known as the antipositivist revolt. Its most outspoken proponent was the German Friedrich Nietzsche (1844–1900). A philosopher repelled by the hypocrisy and pettiness of his time, Nietzsche assaulted traditional morality. His scathing

criticism of bourgeois values extended to the roots of Western culture, from Greco-Roman rationalism to the Judeo-Christian belief in compassion, sin, and humility—concepts he said were more suitable to slaves and weaklings than the free and the strong.

To realize freedom and human potential, Nietzsche urged the abandonment of these traditions in favor of instincts and emotions. He called on heroic leaders to guide the masses: "All gods are dead," he proclaimed, "so we now want the superman to live." While he condemned democratic liberalism and equality, he also repudiated militarism and anti-Semitism, although apologists for Nazism later seized on his writings as justification for their doctrines of national and racial superiority. These justifications were part of the philosophical underpinning for European anti-Semitism. Misunderstood during his lifetime, Nietzsche's ideas had a profound influence on European culture. Literary and artistic rebels drew inspiration from his attack on the establishment, and in the 1920s political demagogues were influenced by his concept of the superman.

Nietzsche's stress on the irrational was echoed by the French philosopher Henri Bergson (1859–1941). Distinguishing between the rational intellect and intuitive understanding, Bergson believed the former a useful tool for analyzing knowledge but not for understanding reality. Only intuition could grasp the "life force," which informed all experience and expressed itself in a continuum, or "duration," that instinct alone could describe. Bergson's chief influence lay in underscoring nonrational experience. Although he did not reject science, he undermined the scientists' claim to a monopoly on knowledge.

Sigmund Freud (1856–1939), a Viennese physician, confirmed Bergson's arguments about the limits of reason. Freud's treatment of psychiatric disorders, based on clinical data, convinced him that behavior is the result of powerful and primitive desires such as aggression and sex. These drives usually remain in an irrational unconscious, which he called the id. Freud believed that the id struggles constantly against the ego, which rationalizes and channels these desires according to the constraints of reality and the socially implanted values of the superego.

The superego functions as a kind of conscience, but instead of reflecting absolute moral values or rational truths, it is the product of social conditioning. Because the mind tends to repress the id, the conflict generally remains unconscious. Nevertheless, the resulting tensions can cause crippling experiences of guilt and fear or even mental breakdown. Freud's theories, particularly those concerning infantile and childhood sexuality, shocked bourgeois notions of human nature. Moreover, by positing that some people live emotionally in a frozen past, Freud and other psychoanalysts altered human perception of time as a forward-moving concept.

Like Nietzsche, Freud emphasized the irrational basis of human behavior and social values. For Freud, civilization is built on the repression of powerful individual urges, particularly sexual ones. Socialization, and hence "progress," rests not on reason but on the frustration of instincts that, held continuously in check, threaten to overwhelm it. Nietzsche had questioned whether civilization was worth its cost in terms of human fulfillment. Freud assumed that repression and self-denial are the necessary price of society. World War I seemed to bear out his pessimism about human nature and the stability of civilization, and his influence on postwar thought was enormous.

Freud's leadership within the movement he founded for the study and treatment of the human psyche—psychoanalysis—was challenged by his former disciple, Carl Jung (1875–1961), who elaborated his own theory of a collective unconscious. In recent decades Freud's theories have been sharply challenged. Nonetheless, he has remained one of the most influential thinkers of the century, and his indirect impact on sexual attitudes, artistic expression, and the concept of mental illness has been incalculable. Perhaps no one has done more to change the modern conception of human nature.

The Dilemmas of Science

Ironically, advances in the realm of physical science seemed to reinforce antirationalist arguments. Since the days of Newton, science had sustained the idea that the physical world operated according to immutable laws and predictable mechanical processes. The modern scientific age, which began with investigations into the nature of matter following the discovery of X-rays in 1895 by Wilhelm Röntgen (1845–1923), shattered these illusions. Experiments by Marie Curie (1867–1934) and her husband, Pierre Curie (1859–1906), showed that the atomic weight of elements such as radium changed as they emitted energy in the form of "subatomic" particles. These findings suggested a relationship between matter and energy. By the end of the 1920s a radical revision of the basic assumptions of classical physics had totally recast scientific understanding of the universe.

Early in the twentieth century the German physicist Max Planck (1858–1947) conducted studies of radiation that revealed that contrary to earlier theories, light energy moves not in steady waves but in discontinuous yet calculable spurts, which he called quanta. Working independently, Albert Einstein (1879–1955) also began to revolutionize physics. His "Special Theory of Relativity," published in 1905, rejected the notion that space and time were absolutes, suggesting instead that both were relative to the position of the observer. Einstein showed that light moves through space in particles known as photons and calculated that the energy contained in a

Albert Einstein, whose theories of relativity revolutionized our concepts of the universe, is shown here in his middle years. He received the Nobel Prize for physics in 1921. [Granger Collection]

photon was equal to its mass multiplied by the square of the speed of light—a concept expressed in his famous formula, $E = mc^2$. Hence not only do mass and time vary with velocity, but energy and mass are interchangeable. In 1915 Einstein's "General Theory of Relativity," which explained gravitation, further shook standard views of the physical world: it described the universe as curved, so that when light waves are deflected as they pass through a gravitational field, they eventually return to their point of origin. Einstein's universe was a four-dimensional one in which length, breadth, and height also had to be conceived in terms of time.

In the years between the evolution of Einstein's theories of relativity, Ernest Rutherford (1871–1937) forced contemporaries to abandon still another basic assumption about matter. Rutherford theorized that the atom, which since ancient times had been regarded as a solid, indivisible mass, was actually an arrangement much like a solar system, consisting of a central particle (the nucleus) with a positive electrical charge, surrounded by orbits of negatively charged electrons. He demonstrated that by bombarding substances with subatomic particles, the structure of atoms could be changed.

In the popular mind these theories and findings led to a doubly disturbing conclusion about the physical universe: that it was not unchangeable but shifting and uncertain and that perhaps knowledge of it lay beyond human comprehension. While almost all countries, in an effort to coordinate wireless communications and transportation schedules, were adopting World Standard Time at the beginning of the twentieth century, scientists such as Einstein were shattering the concept of a uniform public time into the infinite variations of private times relative to each individual.

Realism Abandoned: Literature and Art

The revolt against positivism was reflected in literature and painting. Writers and artists not only expressed the social criticism that rejected the values of materialist culture but also probed beyond the conscious mind. Alienation impelled literary figures to take refuge in obscure symbolism, decadence, or aestheticism, while artists provided visual evidence of the breakdown of traditional forms.

The rebellion in literature had begun at midcentury with the publication of *Flowers of Evil* (1857) by the French poet Charles Baudelaire (1821–1867). Like the British poet Algernon Swinburne (1837–1909) and others, Baudelaire was hostile to bourgeois values and deliberately shocked conventional morality. The 1880s saw the birth of the Decadents and Symbolism, two literary movements derived in part from these earlier sources. The Decadents were sophisticated aesthetes such as Oscar Wilde (1854–1900), J. K. Huysmans (1848–1907), and Gabriele D'Annunzio (1863–1938), who extolled the idea of art for art's sake and cultivated exoticism and artificiality.

The Symbolists, represented by Stéphane Mallarmé (1842–1898) and Paul Verlaine (1844–1896), sought to express the inexpressible in experimental verse that relied on symbols to convey images that logic alone could not fathom. They rejected conventional perception in favor of a subjective, inner world. Often proclaiming the values of aestheticism and decadence, the Symbolists portrayed emotions derived from immediate experience, much as Bergson had urged.

In the 1870s Impressionism assaulted both realism and academic art by depicting the disintegrative effects of light. By the 1880s Impressionism was under attack by Postimpressionists, who, like the Symbolists, were moving away from the outer world of visible reality to an inner realm of the individual artist. In his later years, Claude Monet (1840–1926), the leading Impressionist, painted huge canvases depicting waterlilies. These shimmering pools of color, almost devoid of form, represented a transition between the perceived reality of Impressionism and the emotion of Postimpressionism.

One of the most powerful Postimpressionists was Vincent van Gogh (1853–1890), whose works conveyed an imaginative vision of the world. Like Paul Gauguin (1848–1903), who left the materialistic society of France to settle in Tahiti, van Gogh was interested in using the formal, abstract elements of art—line, color, and form—to express an intensely personal view of truth. Paul Cézanne (1839–1906), however, wanted to free art of subjectivity and emotionalism. Following classical principles, he used color to stress the underlying weight and volume of objects. His landscapes define objects only in the most general sense by using contour, color, and mass to convey abstract equivalents for conventional objects.

❧
BARCELONA AND THE MODERN TEMPER

No city better reflected the cultural ferment of turn-of-the-century Europe than Barcelona. Located on Spain's northeastern plain at the edge of the Mediterranean Sea, Barcelona was the center of Catalan regionalism. In many ways the capital of Catalonia province represented the outstanding example of a modern European city, an innovative, rapidly modernizing enclave in a traditional, agrarian nation. By the late nineteenth century Barcelona had become a city marked by bold cultural experimentation.

Founded at the end of the first century B.C. as a Roman administrative center, the town had grown up in the Middle Ages around a military fortress. Its location on the sea made it a natural focus of trade and shipbuilding. The Industrial Revolution reached Spain through Barcelona, where an enterprising middle class emerged in the late eighteenth century. By the 1850s chemical and machinery manufacturers had joined bankers, shipping magnates, and textile producers in forming a powerful liberal oligarchy. Although its members pressed for urban development and economic modernization, they also fought the labor and socialist movements with support from the government.

At midcentury greater Barcelona had a population of several hundred thousand that exhibited the class characteristics of an advanced capitalist society. Demographic growth forced the adoption in 1859 of a new town plan, similar to the plans followed in Paris and elsewhere, that consisted of a square grid pattern of streets and parks cut across by broad diagonal avenues. Less than a generation later, when more than 500,000 people lived there, Barcelona hosted the Universal Exhibition of 1888. The project, which incorporated a huge complex of exhibition halls, hotels, apartment buildings, factories, and urban services into the city plan, gave a strong thrust to construction and the arts.

Despite their reactionary politics, the economic elites that sponsored the Universal Exhibition encouraged an atmosphere of cultural innovation that made Barcelona synonymous with the most avant-garde trends in Europe. Brilliant local architects, working in the so-called *modernista* style, designed new buildings in a wide range of exciting idioms. This eclectic movement found inspiration in Moorish, Romanesque, and Gothic patterns, in the strong craft tradition of Catalonia, and in the international Art Nouveau style of the period.

The most creative architect of the period, Antonio Gaudí (1852–1926), developed a unique style that reconciled form with function and expressed his militant Catholic beliefs. Gaudí's creations, such as the Guell Palace, incorporated organic forms that resembled sculptural modeling. While his designs were derived from both Gothic and Art Nouveau styles, they represented an original architectural vocabulary that was a reaction against what he saw as the falsity of fin-de-siècle design. Many of his ambitious creations remained unrealized or incomplete; a society exists even to this day that seeks to finish his most famous project, the Church of the Holy Family.

While Gaudí and other architects gave the city a bold new face, Barcelona also became a haven for the avant-garde, which included some of Europe's major artists and writers. Four important Spanish-born artists lived and exhibited in Barcelona in the early years of the twentieth century: Pablo Picasso (1881–1973), usually associated with Paris, executed his first mature works in Barcelona, along with Joan Miró (1893–1983), pioneer abstract painter and a native of the city, Julio Gonzalez (1876–1942), a craftsman turned sculptor, and Salvador Dalí (1904–1989), the famed Surrealist painter. The economic boom that Barcelona experienced during World War I drew many foreign artists from war-torn countries to neutral Spain. The French Dadaist and Surrealist painter Francis Picabia (1879–1953) came into contact with Dalí, worked in Barcelona, and was later joined by the Belgian Surrealist René Magritte (1898–1967). In the 1930s the American photographer and painter Man Ray (1890–1976), the Italian sculptor Alberto Giacometti (1901–1966), and the German painter Max Ernst (1891–1976) all exhibited there.

While these and other creative talents pushed art and design toward modernism, the Spanish writer Eugenio d'Ors (1882–1954) founded a more conservative cultural movement known as *Noucentisme* ("Twentieth Century"), which stressed a revival of Mediterranean classicism in the arts. Nevertheless, as Spain headed toward dictatorship and conflict in the 1920s, Barcelona remained a bastion of cultural discourse. The International Exhibition of 1929 was the last symbol of Barcelona's

The highly original talent of the Barcelona architect Antonio Gaudí is seen here in a photograph of the Casa Mila, an apartment house completed in 1910. [Giraudon/Art Resource]

cultural primacy. The brilliant architect Ludwig Mies van der Rohe designed the exhibit's German pavilion in the Bauhaus style, which had come to stand for internationalism and modernity. Ironically, his "Barcelona chair," a pivotal example of modern furniture design, was intended as the official seat for Spain's King Alfonso XIII.

Postimpressionists, Cubists, and Futurists

Postimpressionists such as Cézanne brought painting to the edge of modernism. At the Paris Salon of 1905, the works of a number of Postimpressionist artists—Matisse, Rouault, and others—were hung together because of certain common characteristics. Their distortions, flat patterns, and preoccupation with line and form rather than objective reality, combined with violent, bold colors and stark contrasts, earned these men the title of *fauves* ("wild beasts"). Closely related to Fauvism were two German Expressionist groups, the Bridge and the Blue Rider, formed between 1905 and 1911, whose proponents emphasized bold colors and psychological portraiture.

The most significant step away from the traditional portrayal of reality came with Cubism, launched in Paris by the Spaniard Pablo Picasso and the Frenchman Georges Braque (1882–1963) in 1907. Influenced by Cézanne, Picasso and Braque developed a concept of form and context that enabled them to render the whole structure of an object as well as its position in space. Abandoning the bright colors and striking contrasts of the *fauves*, they focused on the subtleties of intersecting lines and angles and the reduction of objects to abstract forms. The Cubists not only set in motion the revolution in abstract painting, but by fracturing objects into separate elements and fixing them in time-space relationships, they transformed traditional views of reality.

The only major prewar art movement to develop independently of Paris was Futurism, founded by Filippo T. Marinetti (1876–1944) and a group of young Italian writers and artists in 1909. In contrast to most of the avant-garde of the period, the Futurists rejected humanist culture in the name of the machine and industrial civilization. Exalting the speed and energy of modern life, painters such as Umberto Boccioni (1882–1916) and Carlo Carrà (1881–1966) moved toward the elimination of traditional forms. Futurists advocated the destruction of libraries and museums and, influenced by the ideas of Nietzsche, Sorel, and Bergson, preached violence as an act of liberation. Futurism found other disciples in art and literature, notably in the English painter Wyndham Lewis (1882–1957) and the Russian poet Vladimir Mayakovsky (1893–1930).

Nationalism and Racism

The Futurists may have been the most extreme example of the crisis of European culture, but such disturbing concepts also affected public affairs. Some political theorists and social critics rejected the positivist doctrines on which both liberalism and socialism were based. Georges Sorel founded his syndicalist theories on the belief that the working masses could be stimulated to violent action through the general strike. Sorel's ideas were reinforced by the psychologist Gustav Le Bon (1841–1931), whose book *The Crowd* (1895) argued that mobs responded to pathological suggestion, and by others who maintained that instinct determined social conduct.

The characterization of mass behavior as essentially irrational led the Italian sociologist Vilfredo Pareto (1848–1923) to assert the need for government by an elite rather than by the people. The French monarchist Charles Maurras (1868–1952) founded a reactionary political organization known as *Action Française* on the theory that "the mob always follows determined minorities." Such thinking would influence important political leaders of both the right and the left, from Benito Mussolini to V. I. Lenin.

A further manifestation of these trends was the rise of racism and a new form of nationalism. Whereas nationalists of the 1830s and 1840s fought oppression on behalf of subjected peoples, a chauvinistic nationalism now pitted races and nation-states against one another. Influenced by Social Darwinism, the virulent nationalism of the late nineteenth century preached aggression and dominance. In the 1870s the pan-Slavic movement proclaimed Russia's historic mission to unite all Slavic peoples into a great federation for an inevitable struggle against the West, while the Pan-German League, founded in 1893, demanded territorial expansion and a German-dominated central Europe.

The exaggerated nationalism of the period was linked to racist doctrines, which owed much to the Frenchman Arthur de Gobineau (1816–1882), author of "An Essay on the Inequality of the Races." Gobineau argued that the white races—especially the "Aryans" descended from Germanic tribes—had created civilization but had degenerated as a result of intermingling with "inferior" races. His theories impressed the German musical genius Richard Wagner (1813–1883), who condemned "Jewish" influence in music and whose cycle of four powerful operas in *The Ring of the Nibelungen* (1848–1876) glorified Germanic mythology. Wagner's son-in-law, the British expatriate Houston Stewart Chamberlain (1855–1927), espoused the creation of a superior race through genetic breeding. Chamberlain's *Foundations of the Nineteenth Century* (1899) blamed Europe's racial "degeneration" on the Jews.

Although anti-Semitism had existed for centuries, it reappeared in the vicious Russian pogroms of the late nineteenth century and as the basis for political movements spawned by racial doctrines. In Germany political parties inspired by Adolf Stöcker (1835–1909) elected deputies to the Reichstag on anti-Semitic platforms, while the mayor of Vienna, Karl Lüger (1844–1910), used anti-Semitism to generate popular support for his Christian Socialist party. In France, Charles Maurras led a campaign against the Jews during the Dreyfus affair. Nazi anti-Semitism was rooted in the racist atmosphere of the 1890s.

The Breakdown of the European Order

Few topics in modern history are more controversial than the causes of World War I. During and after the conflict, governments on both sides issued volumes of

204 Part Five The Twentieth Century

◉ The Futurist Manifesto ◉

The Futurists were symptomatic of the crisis of prewar European culture. Not only did they rebel against reason, tradition, and conventional standards of beauty, but they also demanded a new civilization based on the aesthetic of the machine. Here is the first Futurist manifesto, drafted by Filippo T. Marinetti and originally published in Paris on February 20, 1909.

We want to praise the love of danger, the attitude of energy and fearlessness.

Courage, audacity, and revolt will be essential elements of our poetry.

Until now literature has exalted pensive immobility, ecstasy, and sleep. We want to exalt aggressive action, a feverish insomnia, the racer's stride, the mortal leap, the punch, and the slap.

We assert that the beauty of the world has been enriched by a new beauty: the beauty of speed. A racing car . . . is more beautiful than the *Victory of Samothrace.*

We want to praise the man at the wheel, who hurls his spiritual lance across the earth, along the circle of its orbit.

The poet must give himself with ardor, splendor, and generosity, to swell the enthusiastic fervor of the primordial elements.

There is no beauty except in struggle. No work without an aggressive character can be a masterpiece. Poetry must be conceived as a violent attack on unknown forces, to reduce and prostrate them before man.

We stand on the last promontory of the centuries! . . . Why must we look back, when what we want is to break down the mysterious doors of the impossible? Time and space died yesterday. We already live in the absolute, because we have already created eternal, omnipresent speed.

We want to glorify war—the world's only hygiene—militarism, patriotism, the destructive gesture of liberators, beautiful ideas worth dying for, and scorn for woman.

We want to destroy museums, libraries, academies of every kind, and want to fight moralism, feminism, every opportunistic or utilitarian cowardice.

We will sing of great crowds excited by work, by pleasure, and by riot; we will sing of the multicolored, polyphonic tides of revolution in modern capitals; we will sing of the vibrant nocturnal fervor of arsenals and shipyards blazing with violent electric moons; of hungry railway stations that devour fire-breathing serpents; factories hung on clouds by the twisted lines of their smoke; bridges that stride the rivers like giant gymnasts, gleaming in the sun with a glitter of knives; adventurous steamers that cut the horizon; deep-chested locomotives whose wheels gallop along the tracks like the hooves of huge steel horses bridled by tubing; and the sleek flight of planes whose propellers flutter in the wind like banners and seem to cheer like an enthusiastic crowd.

Source: L. De Maria, ed., *Per conoscere Marinetti e il futurismo* (Milan: Mondadori, 1973), pp. 5–7. Trans. P. Cannistraro.

documents to justify their positions. In the wake of the Allied victory, a defeated Germany was forced to accept the blame. Since then, historians have taken a more balanced view of the war's origins, separating the long-range developments in which all European nations had participated from the immediate circumstances that led to its outbreak. The controversy erupted again in the 1960s when a German scholar, Fritz Fischer, maintained that his country had deliberately planned a far-reaching program of conquest before 1914. The response to Fischer's thesis has been heated, and today most historians would argue that his explanation focused too narrowly on Germany and underemphasized the broader European causes of the war.

For decades historical antagonisms, colonial rivalries, economic competition, and expansionist aspirations, all fueled by chauvinistic nationalism, had propelled Europe into an arms race and hostile alliances. Diplomatic confrontations increased tensions among the powers, so that most nations came to believe that only military alliances provided safety. When the final crisis came in the summer of 1914, the diplomatic order collapsed through a combination of fear and miscalculation. Science and technology, the twin sources of power and pride that had enabled the West to dominate the globe, made what most statesmen hoped would be an easy war a long and agonizing ordeal from which Europe never fully recovered.

Bismarck and the Concert of Europe

For more than half a century after the defeat of Napoleon in 1815 Europe's international system had been based on the notion that the great powers would act "in concert" to keep the peace established by the Congress of Vienna. The system worked remarkably well until the creation of the German empire in 1871 drastically altered international politics. Bismarck's triumph, won on the ruins of the second French empire, gave birth to a powerful state whose unsurpassed military strength was quickly equaled by its industrial and economic power.

The rapid emergence of Germany upset the European balance of power. Upon achieving unification, Bismarck denied having any further territorial ambitions. For the next 20 years his foreign policy goals remained the preservation of the Concert of Europe and the protection of Germany. Bismarck saw two potentially troublesome situations. On the western frontier the French were obsessed with achieving revenge against Germany after their humiliating defeat in the Franco-Prussian War. For the Iron Chancellor the worst scenario was a military pact between France and Russia that would sandwich Germany between them in a two-front war. To avoid such a "nightmare," as he described it, Bismarck sought to keep France isolated from diplomatic alliances with other powers.

The east presented a more complicated security problem. The rise of nationalism threatened to destabilize east-central Europe and the Balkans by pulling apart both Austria-Hungary, which had been severely weakened by Prussia's lightning victory in 1866, and the deteriorating Ottoman Empire. The Balkans became the focus of this regional instability, for there Austria-Hungary and Russia competed for territory and influence at the expense of the Turks. Conflict between Vienna and St. Petersburg over the Balkans could drag Germany into a major war in the east and allow France to invade from the west. Bismarck responded by creating secret and often mutually contradictory diplomatic and military pacts. His strategy placed Berlin at the center of a complicated web of alliances that exploited competing national interests and fears.

Bismarck took his first step in 1873, when he concluded a mutual consultation treaty, the League of the Three Emperors, with Russia and Austria-Hungary. The league faced a serious crisis in 1877 and 1878. Russia, motivated by a desire for expansion, joined Serbia, Montenegro, and Bulgaria in a war against Turkey. The Treaty of San Stefano freed the Balkan states from Turkish control and gave the tsar a foothold in the region. Assuming the self-professed role of an "honest broker," Bismarck tried to engineer peace at the congress of Berlin and redress the balance of power. Austria secured the right to administer the provinces of Bosnia and Herzegovina, which technically remained Ottoman possessions, and the size of Bulgaria was reduced. Nevertheless, the Berlin congress aroused Slavic hostility against Germany and Austria-Hungary, for the Russians were angered by what they considered Bismarck's perfidy, while Serbia and Montenegro were bitter over Austria's occupation of Bosnia and Herzegovina. Romania and Greece were disappointed at not having gotten territories from the Turks. The Balkans had become a powder keg.

Bismarck moved immediately to protect Germany from reprisal. In 1879 he concluded the Dual Alliance with Austria-Hungary, a defensive military pact. The Russians, sensing their isolation, responded in 1881 by agreeing to a mutual-security pact with Germany. Not only did this ease Russia's fears of encirclement, but it also gave Germany a measure of security by reducing the possibility of a joint attack by France and Russia. Bismarck had successfully played off Austria and Russia.

Two additional treaties closed the circle of Bismarck's diplomatic policy. In 1882 the Triple Alliance drew Italy into a defensive agreement with Germany and Austria. Finally, in 1887 Bismarck secretly negotiated the Reinsurance Treaty with Russia, guaranteeing neutrality by one power if the other were attacked. Thus Russia did not have to worry about Germany in the event of a war with Austria, while Germany no longer feared what Russia would do in case of a war with France. Bismarck could now be confident that German interests were protected—at least as long as he managed German affairs.

The Triple Entente

When Kaiser William II forced Bismarck into retirement in 1890, German foreign policy changed drastically. The new emperor rejected the necessity of an alliance with

Russia and friendship with Britain, two vital premises of Bismarck's diplomacy. Convinced that Austria was Germany's natural ally, William refused Russian requests to renew the Reinsurance Treaty. The inevitable happened: in 1894 France and Russia signed a defensive military agreement that created the "nightmare alliance" Bismarck had dreaded.

Britain had remained aloof from Continental alliances, adhering instead to its traditional "balance of power" policy. But the kaiser, who resented Britain's preeminent world position, was determined to raise German prestige by winning colonial territories and brandishing German power. Britain, whose industrial growth had fallen behind Germany's, grew alarmed at the kaiser's hostility. Abandoning Bismarck's opposition to imperial conquest, William attempted to block the consolidation of British interests in Africa and in 1896 enraged London by expressing pro-Boer sentiments. Between 1898 and 1900 British security interests were again put at risk when Germany began constructing a powerful fleet that challenged Britain's goal of maintaining a two-to-one margin over Germany's naval forces.

German aggressiveness forced Britain to end its diplomatic isolation. An Anglo-Japanese agreement in 1902 was followed two years later by the Entente Cordiale ("friendly understanding") with France, which settled colonial disputes between the two nations. France agreed to a British sphere of influence in Egypt in return for French predominance in Morocco. Outraged by this, Kaiser William visited Tangier to support Moroccan independence. The Algeciras conference of 1906 affirmed the Entente agreements, rebuffing Germany.

In 1906, in the wake of the Moroccan crisis, the British launched the first of a series of battleships known as dreadnaughts, with greater range, speed, and firepower than any previous type of military vessel. The next year the Germans followed suit, unleashing a costly naval race between the two powers. Tensions increased as German plans to construct a Berlin-to-Baghdad railroad made Britain, France, and Russia uneasy over their interests in the Middle East. Encouraged by the French, Russia and Britain negotiated a treaty in 1907 that settled colonial rivalries in Tibet, Afghanistan, and Iran and, like the Entente Cordiale, made possible closer cooperation in Europe.

In the 20 years after Bismarck's retirement, Europe's great powers had aligned themselves into two blocs. Germany, Austria, and Italy were bound by the terms of the Triple Alliance, while Britain, France, and Russia were tied less formally by treaties that together formed a Triple Entente. Separating these military and diplomatic blocs was a pattern of growing hostility. Disputes between members of the rival blocs heightened tensions and made the alliance systems more rigid, for the fear of being left without the protection of friends led nations to support their partners, regardless of the merits of the

issue. The most dangerous consequence of this development was that in times of crisis the alliances limited the options available to each power.

The Arms Race

Even before the division of Europe into opposing blocs, firms such as Krupp in Germany, Schneider in France, and Armstrong-Whitworth in Britain reaped enormous profits from the sale of weapons and exercised great influence on the defense policies of their governments. International rivalries over colonies and markets stimulated armaments industries and were used to justify huge military expenditures. French per capita arms spending more than doubled between 1870 and 1914; Germany's increased more than sixfold. By the eve of World War I both countries were spending almost 5 percent of their national income on weapons.

Improvements in weapons advanced rapidly, yet the nature of technological development made permanent advantage impossible. Reinforced concrete and steel alloys improved defensive systems. Nevertheless, the enormous firepower of heavy artillery—especially long-range howitzers—and more powerful explosives made impregnable fortresses a thing of the past. The British dreadnaughts, designed to revolutionize sea warfare, were mounted with ten 12-inch guns, each capable of hurling an 850-pound shell 10 miles. But the thick armor plating and turbine engines of the dreadnaughts were vulnerable to enemy guns as well as to torpedoes from newly developed submarines and destroyers. Military planners were convinced that the outcome of warfare on land and sea would be determined by artillery.

Despite the technology, infantry soldiers were the basis of war strategy. By 1874 all of the great powers except Britain had introduced compulsory military service. France and Germany doubled their standing armies between 1870 and 1914, each keeping almost half a million men under arms in peacetime. The function of the infantry was modified in the 1880s with the introduction of the magazine rifle and the machine gun, which gave great advantage to defensive positions and guaranteed huge casualties to attacking armies. Despite these changes, European tactics were still based on the Prussian campaigns of 1866 and 1870, with their emphasis on speed, mobility, and surprise. Military plans, based on elaborate transportation networks and exact timetables, contributed to the possibility of war, for generals insisted on rapid mobilization during international crises.

Such was the case with the Schlieffen Plan, worked out in 1905 by the German general staff. Based on the likelihood of a two-front war against France and Russia, the strategy assumed that the Russians would take longer to mobilize than the French. Hence Schlieffen proposed that while Germany remained on the defensive against Russia, two armies—a powerful one sweeping through Luxembourg and Belgium and a weaker force moving from the south to lure the French away from the real attack—would swing rapidly around a central "hinge" and crush the French in a giant pincer. Having defeated France, the Germans could then concentrate their military strength against Russia.

With mass conscription came the introduction of the general staff, also based on the German model, and the growing prestige of a professional officer caste. Although strongest in Germany, the link between the landed nobility and the military command was present in every country. Their aristocratic lineage gave high-ranking officers special access to and influence over their sovereigns, even in representative governments, while their conservative outlook in domestic politics weakened the position of liberal civilians in government circles.

Government propaganda, the sensationalism of the press, and the nationalism imbued in citizens by universal elementary education conditioned the public to conscription and the high cost of armaments. Compulsory military training in turn convinced the public to accept the possibility of war.

35.1 The Balkans in 1914

Europe on the Brink

Relations between the Triple Alliance and the Entente deteriorated as one international crisis succeeded another. The Austro-Russian struggle for hegemony stirred nationalist fervor in the Balkans, where Serbian nationalists sought to create a united Slavic state and looked to Russia—the Slavic "big brother"—for support. Austria-Hungary, which regarded Slavic nationalism as a threat to its multinational empire, opposed Serbia. These forces came to a head in 1908 when Austria attempted to prevent Serbian expansion to the Adriatic Sea by annexing Bosnia and Herzegovina. The angry Serbs, who had hoped to incorporate Bosnia into their greater Slavic state, could do little without Russia, which felt too weak to respond in the face of British and Austrian pressure.

European aggression speeded the disintegration of the Ottoman Empire. In 1911 the kaiser dispatched the gunboat *Panther* to the Moroccan port of Agadir under the guise of protecting German nationals, but his real purpose was to challenge French and British domination in Africa. The crisis dissipated when the French agreed to cede part of Equatorial Africa to Germany, but it had the effect of alarming British opinion and solidifying the Anglo-French Entente. Later that year Italy went to war against the Ottoman Empire and wrested Libya from the Turks.

Encouraged by these events, the Balkan states at-

tacked Turkey in 1912. The Balkan League, consisting of Serbia, Bulgaria, Greece, and Montenegro, easily defeated the Turks. Bulgaria emerged with the lion's share of the spoils. Austria intervened again to prevent the Serbs from gaining access to the Adriatic Sea, and when Russia protested, an international conference resolved the dispute by creating the state of Albania and compensating Serbia with inland territory. No one was satisfied. A month later, in June 1913, a second Balkan war erupted in which Serbia, Romania, Greece, and Turkey stripped Bulgaria of many of its territorial gains.

The Serbs, who had now doubled the size of their country, reoccupied parts of Albania, but their Russian protectors again failed to back them when an Austrian ultimatum forced their withdrawal. In fact, both Vienna and St. Petersburg remained deeply anxious. Throughout 1912 and 1913, the Austrians were bitterly critical of Germany, to whose lack of support they attributed Serbia's expansion. The Russians simultaneously blamed Britain for having prevented Serbia from gaining access to the sea. On both sides an uneasy feeling prevailed that neither the Triple Alliance nor the Entente could survive further internal tensions.

Sarajevo:
The Failure of Diplomacy

On June 28, 1914, three students assassinated Archduke Franz Ferdinand (1863–1914), nephew of the emperor of Austria-Hungary and heir to the throne, while he at-

One of the conspirators responsible for the assassination of Archduke Franz Ferdinand being taken into police custody. [Granger Collection]

tended military maneuvers in Bosnia. The three terrorists—members of Young Bosnia, a Slavic nationalist group—had been trained by Serbian army officers in a secret organization called Unity or Death (also known as the Black Hand). The Austrians did not know that Serbian cabinet members had been aware of the plot for some weeks, although they had not approved of it. Nevertheless, the Austrians expressed outrage and accused Serbian officials of complicity in the assassination. Some officials pushed for quick military action, hoping to crush Serbia permanently. The danger lay in the probability that conflict with Serbia would spark Russian intervention. Austria thus sought the support of Germany before acting.

In response, Kaiser William gave Austria-Hungary a "blank check" on July 5—that is, clear assurance of military support, along with advice to strike while world opinion was still hostile to Serbia. His chancellor, Theobald von Bethmann-Hollweg, acknowledged the risk of a general European war but believed that decisive Austrian action supported by Germany would deter Russia. Britain, he assumed, would not intervene. On July 23, Austria presented Serbia with a stiff ultimatum, including a demand that Austria be permitted to hunt for Franz Ferdinand's assassins on Serbian territory. Although Belgrade's reply was conciliatory, the Serbians refused to accept this provision, which would have undermined their independence. On July 28, Austria declared war on Serbia.

When a reluctant Tsar Nicholas II ordered partial

THE ROAD TO WORLD WAR I

1870	Franco-Prussian War; second French empire collapses
1871	German empire created; France cedes Alsace and Lorraine
1878	Congress of Berlin; partition of Ottoman Empire begins
1879	Dual Alliance between Germany and Austria-Hungary
1882	Italy joins Germany and Austria-Hungry in the Triple Alliance
1890	Bismarck dismissed as chancellor of Germany
1894	Franco-Russian Alliance
1898	Fashoda crisis; Britain and France on the brink of war in the Sudan
1902	Anglo-Japanese alliance
1904	Anglo-French Entente
1905	First Moroccan crisis; Germany challenges French hegemony in North Africa
1908–1909	Bosnian crisis; Austro-Russian tension in the Balkans mounts
1911	Second Moroccan crisis
1911–1913	First and second Balkan wars
1914	Sarajevo crisis; outbreak of war (June 28–August 4)

Russian mobilization on July 30, General Helmuth von Moltke, the kaiser's chief of staff, appealed for an immediate German mobilization in order to put the Schlieffen Plan into operation. Bethmann-Hollweg belatedly tried to persuade the Austrians to negotiate, to no avail. The Austrians announced mobilization against Russia on July 31, and Nicholas responded in kind. The Germans immediately demanded that the tsar pull back, but before he could reply, Germany declared war on Russia on August 1.

The elaborate diplomatic calculations continued to go awry. On August 2 the German ambassador in Brussels delivered an ultimatum demanding free passage through Belgian territory, presaging a preemptive strike against France. The British foreign secretary, Sir Edward Grey (1862–1933), intimated to Berlin that a violation of the international treaty guaranteeing Belgian neutrality would be regarded as a serious matter, but Bethmann-Hollweg ridiculed the idea that Britain would fight over "a scrap of paper." Two days later Germany declared war on Belgium and France and set the Schlieffen Plan in motion. On August 4, Britain declared war on Germany. "The lamps are going out all over Europe," Grey is supposed to have said, and "we shall not see them lit again in our life-time."[1]

The Ordeal of the West

Most countries greeted the coming of war with relief and even enthusiasm, and almost no one thought it would last very long. Within a few weeks, however, these expectations proved illusory. Europe found itself locked in a prolonged ordeal that brought unprecedented death and destruction.

War of Attrition

The rapid war of movement and assault anticipated by military planners turned into a bloody stalemate almost at once. The German armies crossed into Belgium on August 4, but unexpected resistance and last-minute changes in strategy threw off their timetable. By September they had advanced to within 25 miles of Paris, but the French halted them at the Marne River and forced retreat. With the Schlieffen Plan in shambles, the Anglo-French allies and Germany then tried to outflank each other; the line of battle soon reached from the Swiss border to the sea.

Once the Germans failed to strike a death blow

◉ The Trauma of Trench Warfare ◉

As millions of young men poured into the trenches during World War I, the unimagined horrors of modern warfare crushed both the values and the optimism of a generation of Europeans. Here two British soldiers describe their experiences during the Battle of the Somme in the summer of 1916.

There was a terrific smell. It was so awful it nearly poisoned you. A smell of rotten flesh. The old German front line was covered with bodies—they were seven and eight deep and they had all gone black. The smell! These people had been laying since the first of July. Wicked it was! Colonel Pinney got hold of some stretchers and our job was to put the bodies on them and, with a man at each end, we *threw* them into that crater. There must have been over a thousand bodies there. I don't know how many we buried. I'll never forget that sight. Bodies all over the place. I'll never forget it. I was only eighteen, but I thought, "There's something wrong here!"

As far as you could see there were all these bodies lying there—literally thousands of them. . . . Some without legs, some were legs without bodies, arms without bodies. A terrible sight. . . . It didn't seem possible. It didn't get inside me or scare me, but it just made me wonder that these could have been men. It made me wonder what it was all about. And far away in the distance we could see nothing but a line of bursting shells. It was continuous. You wouldn't have thought that anybody could have existed in it, it was so terrific. And yet we knew we were going up into it, with not an earthly chance.

Source: L. Macdonald, *Somme* (London: Michael Joseph, 1983), pp. 113–114.

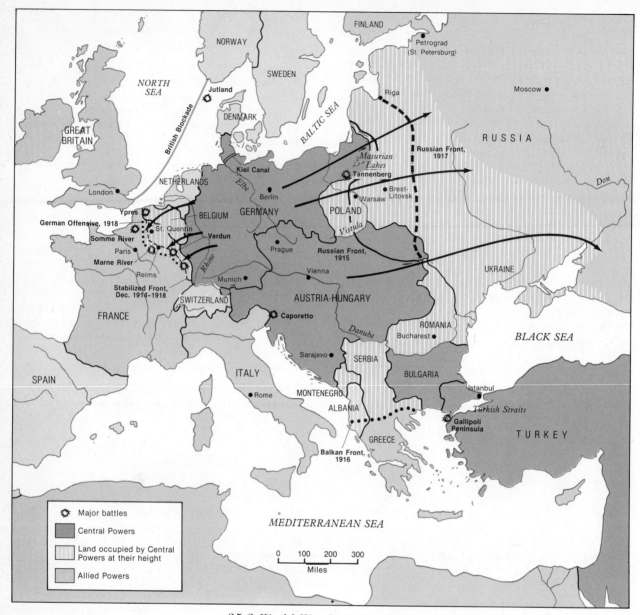

35.2 World War I, 1914–1918

against France, their dream of a rapid victory vanished. Instead, the equally matched combatants now faced each other in a war in which defense proved stronger than attack. On either side of the front, the combatants dug hundreds of miles of trenches, protected by barbed wire, land mines, and machine guns, in which millions of infantry soldiers lived and died. After preparatory artillery barrages, soldiers were ordered to charge the enemy trenches and cross the "no man's land" that separated them, only to be cut down by deadly machine gun fire and artillery. The first four months of fighting alone resulted in 1,640,000 casualties, yet after the first battle of the Marne the front line hardly moved. Generals clung stubbornly to the same tactics for 3½ years, squandering the lives of their men. The conflict had become a war of attrition in which the infliction of casualties rather than the capture of terrain became the measure of success.

The Eastern Front and Italian Intervention

Conditions were far different on the eastern front, where men and supplies had to move over vast distances. In

August the Russians won unexpected victories by moving two separate armies deep into East Prussia. The Germans panicked and withdrew four divisions from Belgium, while the kaiser put the retired general Paul von Hindenburg (1847–1934) in charge of operations and made the major general Erich Ludendorff (1865–1937) his chief of staff. By dealing separately with each of the Russian armies Hindenburg and Ludendorff won major victories at Tannenberg and the Masurian Lakes, and by mid-September the Russians had lost 250,000 men.

Russia fared better against the Austrians, overrunning Galicia and driving into Hungary. The Austrians suffered further setbacks in the Balkans, where the Serbs twice repelled their armies. But Russian fortunes declined with the entrance of Turkey into the war on the side of the Central Powers, for the closing of the Dardanelles straits cut Russia off from critical supplies. Winston Churchill (1874–1965), Britain's First Lord of the Admiralty, conceived a daring plan to force the straits open, but a joint Anglo-French fleet failed to break through in March 1915. This effort was followed by landings on the Gallipoli peninsula, which were commanded by Mustapha Kemal (1881–1938), the future dictator of Turkey. By January the British had withdrawn.

The war widened further in 1915. The Germans struck, advancing some 200 miles against Russia, inflicting more than 2 million casualties and capturing or destroying almost a third of its industries. Allied reverses on the eastern front were mitigated in part by Italy's entrance into the war in May in return for promises of territory on the Italo-Austrian border and on the Dalmatian coast. In September, Bulgaria joined Germany and Austria.

The War Beyond Europe

Although the most crucial military operations took place in Europe, the Great War was a truly global conflict. Some 640,000 Canadians, 329,000 Australians, and 117,000 New Zealanders fought in the Allied forces, as did more than 1 million Indian troops and hundreds of thousands of African soldiers from the French colonies.

Military activity beyond Europe was of little importance to the outcome of the war, but in the Middle East the fighting was to have a direct bearing on postwar events. Arab nationalists meeting in Paris in 1913 had insisted on autonomy within the Ottoman Empire, but during World War I the British deliberately encouraged the Arabs to revolt, thus foiling Turkish efforts to mobilize them against the Allies. When the Ottoman Empire joined the Central Powers in November 1914, the British Indian army sent an expeditionary force to the Persian Gulf and Iraq, nearly reaching Baghdad before being driven back by Turkish forces. Another Indian force guarded the Suez Canal. During the Gallipoli and Dardanelles campaigns, British diplomats pledged to support an Arab revolt and gained the cooperation of Abdul-Aziz ibn-Saud (1880–1953), the sultan who ruled the Nejd region of south-central Arabia.

British promises to the Arabs were designed to help the war effort, not to bring independence to the region. In 1916 Hussein ibn-Ali (1856–1931), a proclaimed descendant of the prophet Muhammad and protector of the holy city of Mecca, instigated a revolt against the Turks, frustrating efforts to launch a holy war against the Allies. With British approval he declared himself king of the Arabs, claiming control over a vast area stretching from the Hejaz along the Red Sea to the Persian Gulf. That same year the British and French concluded the Sykes-Picot Agreement, which divided much of the region into spheres of influence: France would get Syria and Lebanon; Britain, Iraq and Palestine. Throughout 1917 and 1918, T. E. Lawrence (1888–1935), a British archaeologist and soldier—later known as Lawrence of Arabia—assisted Prince Faisal (1885–1933), Hussein's son, who commanded the Arab forces that seized Damascus and Jerusalem.

The dual nature of British policy in the Middle East became clear in November 1917 when Foreign Secretary Arthur James Balfour formally supported Zionist aspirations for a Jewish homeland in Palestine. The Balfour Declaration did not specifically promise Jewish control over all of Palestine, but it contradicted other statements on behalf of Arab nationalist interests.

Elsewhere in the world the war posed a long-range threat rather than an immediate military danger for the West, for Britain and the Dominions feared Japanese expansionism. Allied with Britain since 1902, Japan declared war against the Central Powers in 1914 and swept over the German Pacific islands north of the equator. Australia occupied New Guinea and New Zealand took German Samoa to forestall Japanese expansion in the South Pacific. China declared war against Germany and Austria-Hungary only in 1917, but a 200,000-man Chinese labor battalion served with the Allies in Europe. Yet the Japanese seized the German holdings in China's Shantung province and presented China with the infamous Twenty-one Demands (see Chapters 34 and 36). Unlike China or India, Japan took no part in the war in the West beyond sending several destroyers.

In Africa, British colonial armies, made up of Indian, African, and Afrikaner troops, had little difficulty in taking Togo and Southwest Africa from Germany. But the German commander in East Africa, Paul von Lettow-Vorbeck, matched the daring exploits of T. E. Lawrence in organizing native resistance and conducting guerrilla warfare. He stopped an assault led by the South African general Jan Smuts and invaded Kenya, successfully defending German East Africa until the end of the war.

The British feared German attempts to foment rebellion in Afghanistan and Japanese propaganda in India, but with minor exceptions, the Indian army remained loyal. India was notified that it was automatically at war as part of the empire. Most Indian nationalists, including Gandhi, supported the war, hoping that a British victory would hasten India's freedom. Yet the contributions made by the colonies, together with Allied promises of "liberation" both in the Middle East and in the German possessions, raised questions about the future.

Agony on the Western Front

In 1916 and 1917 the killing on the western front intensified. In February 1916 the Germans massed their forces for an assault against Verdun, hoping that the French would make a costly defense. They were not disappointed. On the first day of the battle the Germans fired about 1 million artillery shells, and when the siege was over months later, 700,000 French and German soldiers were dead. Verdun held, but the bloodletting left deep scars on France. Oblivious to the lessons of Verdun, the British embarked on an offensive at the Somme River in June. Despite a massive preliminary bombardment, 60,000 British soldiers were cut down the first day. The British introduced primitive tanks into the battle with minimal effect, and by November this offensive too was over with little result but slaughter—600,000 British and French and 500,000 German soldiers had been killed or wounded.

In the spring of 1917 the Allies suffered a major blow in the east. On March 12, St. Petersburg erupted in revolution, and three days later Tsar Nicholas abdicated. While awaiting what they now regarded as an inevitable Russian defeat, the Germans retired behind the Hinden-burg Line, a fortified defensive position in the west. The French vainly attacked it in April, suffering 250,000 casualties. From July to November the British fought the Germans at Ypres in the fields of Flanders, despite the new horrors of poison gas. The British suffered another 300,000 casualties.

Europeans could hardly grasp the fearful toll that the fighting had taken—more than 2.5 million dead and wounded alone in the four major western engagements of 1916 and 1917. The enthusiasm of 1914 turned to shock and a sense that civilization had reached the point of collapse. "The higher civilization rises," observed a German general, "the viler man becomes."[2] Churchill, writing about the war a few years later, was equally bleak: "When all was over, Torture and Cannibalism were the only two expedients that the civilized, scientific, Christian States had been able to deny themselves: and these were of doubtful utility."[3]

The Social Consequences of Total War

The futility of the war brought opposition and sometimes revolt. During the spring 1917 offensive in Champagne, some French units had refused to leave the trenches, and the Russian army was rife with mutiny long before the revolution. The shock of the war also spread defeatism among civilians. In Turin, Italian socialists staged an abortive uprising, and in July the German Reichstag passed a peace resolution.

The collapse of morale on both sides raised serious

German dead at the Battle of Verdun. [Bettmann Archive]

concerns about the home front, for in a war of such gigantic proportions, industrial production was as important as front-line fighting. Attrition created huge shortages not only of manpower but also of food, clothing, and munitions. To cope with the economic and political strains, leaders formed cabinets of national unity, representing in some cases even socialist parties. Governments instituted rationing, placed controls on prices and wages, restricted union activity, and set up planning boards to coordinate production of war matériel.

The trend toward the greater militarization of society that had begun in the late nineteenth century accelerated sharply. The military assumed more authority in civilian affairs, and governments imposed censorship on the press and suspended constitutional procedures. Official propaganda called for a "total" war effort that demanded the regimentation of civilian life. Soldiers and civilians were regarded as one in the struggle. To dehumanize the enemy, Allied propaganda spread stories of "Huns" committing barbaric atrocities in Belgium and northeastern France. As civilian morale fell in the face of mounting casualties at the front, propaganda increased the stakes in victory so as to justify the enormous sacrifices. Both sides claimed to be fighting not just for national defense but in the name of civilization and democracy.

The ceaseless demands of war resulted in full employment, an unprecedented situation that provided wages for women and the poor. Hundreds of thousands of women left the home for the factories, and by the end of the war they comprised more than a third of all industrial workers in most countries. Women also filled white-collar jobs ordinarily occupied by men. Their independence grew with their importance to the war effort, and they broke social customs that had previously restrained them in behavior and dress. Women contributed to the war effort by serving as nurses, orderlies, and ambulance drivers. The huge number of casualties created a serious shortage of medical facilities and overwhelmed trained personnel, so that thousands of volunteers staffed field hospitals along with professional nurses. The primitive conditions under which they worked exposed these women not only to infection and disease but also to the dangers of artillery bombardment and the threat of capture, for nursing and Red Cross units were often immediately behind the front.

The most famous nurse of the war was Edith Cavell (1865–1915), a Briton in charge of a Red Cross station in Belgium. She remained at her post to care for the wounded while Germans overran the area. When they learned that she was also helping captured British and French soldiers escape, they shot her for espionage. Although her nonnursing activities had removed her from the protection of international law, Allied propaganda made her death a symbol of enemy "barbarism."

Class distinctions tended to break down under the impact of the common struggle for survival. Aristocratic ladies volunteered for nursing duties along with working women, and union leaders worked side by side with industrialists on government boards. Moreover, although the enlisted ranks of the armies were filled overwhelmingly with workers and peasants, young aristocrats and educated middle-class men made up the lower officer corps. The dynamics of trench warfare, in which the junior officers led the charges over the top, meant that the upper classes actually spilled a larger proportion of their blood on the battlefields.

Total war targeted civilians as part of an overall military strategy that sought to break morale. German zeppelins dropped bombs over British cities, and Austrian artillery shelled Venice. More effective, however, were efforts to starve entire populations into submission through naval blockades. Britain and France continued to receive food and supplies from the United States and the British Empire, while Russia and the Central Powers, virtually cut off from overseas trade, felt the shortages acutely. Germany instituted rationing as early as 1915. During the bitter winter of 1916–1917, the German people suffered from hunger and cold, subsisting on turnips and substituting synthetic products for natural goods.

The British violated international agreements by interfering with neutral shipping to Germany. The Germans responded with a major innovation in naval warfare, the U-boat, or submarine. To be effective, submarines had to fire on ships by surprise from below the surface, without being able to ascertain whether they were enemy or neutral vessels or whether they were carrying war contraband. Submarine warfare antagonized American opinion, especially after the sinking of a commercial liner, the *Lusitania*, in May 1915 with the loss of over 1,000 lives, 128 of them American. That summer U-boat commanders were given restricted orders.

American Intervention and the German Collapse

The submarine was a devastating weapon, sinking 750,000 tons of shipping in 1915 alone. After the stalemate of Verdun and the Somme, the Germans believed it might be decisive as well, despite the risk of bringing the United States into the war. Unrestricted submarine warfare was unleashed on February 1, 1917, and President Woodrow Wilson broke diplomatic relations with Germany two days later. Allied and neutral shipping losses more than doubled in 1917. The U-boats, together with German diplomatic intrigue, Allied propaganda, and the influence of American munitions manufacturers and other trading and banking interests, influenced Congress to declare war against Germany on April 6, 1917. By September 1918 more than 1 million American men had reached Europe; they included 200,000 African-American soldiers who served in labor units, in four infantry regiments attached to the French army, and the entire United States 92nd Division.

American supplies began to tip the balance in favor of the Allies, but before the end of 1917 they suffered two serious setbacks. In October the Battle of Caporetto nearly knocked Italy out of the war. In March 1918 the new Bolshevik government in Russia signed the Treaty of Brest-Litovsk with Germany, taking Russia out of the war. The events of 1917 were partly offset when Wilson seized the political initiative by announcing American commitment to war aims that he hoped would bring "peace without victory." His Fourteen Points, issued in January 1918, proposed an end to secret diplomacy, freedom of the seas, unimpeded international trade, disarmament, self-determination for the peoples of eastern Europe, the adjustment of imperial claims based on the interests of colonial peoples as well as those of the powers, and the creation of an international peacekeeping organization, the League of Nations, among other things.

The last year of the war saw a desperate effort by the Germans to win a military victory. In March, Ludendorff regrouped German troops from the former Russian front and made a massive assault against France, driving once again to the Marne River but failing to break through the Allied lines. On July 18 the Allies, reinforced by some 300,000 American soldiers, began their counteroffensive. By the end of September the German armies, having lost another million men, were in retreat, and civilian morale was on the point of collapse. Convinced that victory was impossible, Ludendorff advised the kaiser to sue for peace.

Germany's request for an armistice on the basis of the Fourteen Points met with a stiff response from Wilson, who demanded that the Germans first implement political reforms. In the meantime, Bulgaria, Turkey, and Austria-Hungary collapsed. On November 3 the German fleet at the port of Kiel mutinied, setting off revolutions in Munich and Berlin. Six days later socialists proclaimed a republic in the capital, and the kaiser abdicated. The armistice, signed on November 11, officially ended the fighting.

The Reordering of Europe

At the close of the Great War, people knew that Europe would never be the same. Thirty-four nations had been engaged in the struggle. Vast tracts of once productive land lay in ruins, and the populations of cities such as Berlin and Vienna were at the edge of starvation. More than 10 million fighting men and at least 1 million civilians had been killed and 20 million wounded. The war had also bled Europe's financial resources of $3.3 billion, turning a continent that had once exported huge amounts of capital into a debtor to the United States. Disillusioned by the experience of total war, Europeans were hopeful that the peace would bring a better world.

The Paris Peace Conference

In January 1919 representatives from 27 victorious nations assembled in Paris to draw up peace treaties with five vanquished states—Germany, Austria, Hungary, Bulgaria, and Turkey. Two reasons accounted for the air of expectancy that surrounded the conference. First, Wilson's presence suggested that the treaties would be equitable, since both sides had accepted his Fourteen Points as the basis for peace. Second, each nation brought a delegation of technical experts who promised to arrange the settlements according to objective, "scientific" principles instead of old-fashioned power politics.

Like the Congress of Vienna 100 years earlier, the Paris peace conference was an impressive gathering of national leaders. Britain was represented by its prime minister, the Welsh Liberal David Lloyd George (1863–1945); France by the Republican premier, Georges Clemenceau (1841–1929); and Italy by its prime minister, Vittorio E. Orlando (1860–1952). Most of the major decisions were the result of negotiations among the "Big Three," Wilson, Lloyd George, and Clemenceau.

Operating in the shadow of the Bolshevik revolution in Russia and the fear that its example would spread, the Big Three excluded Lenin's government from the deliberations. Moreover, public opinion among the victors demanded harsh peace terms for the defeated enemy. Unlike the Congress of Vienna, where France was accorded full diplomatic representation, Germany was permitted to have only observers at the conference and to await terms dictated by the Allied Powers.

The Treaty of Versailles

The most pressing problem was what to do with Germany. Three issues were paramount: French insistence on future security against Germany, the disposition of German colonies, and the reparations the Germans would pay. Because France had twice been invaded within 50 years, Clemenceau demanded the creation of a separate buffer state in the Rhineland between his country and Germany. Wilson objected that such a plan would violate the principle of self-determination, and his debate with Clemenceau became so acrimonious that the American president threatened to leave the conference. In the end, Clemenceau compromised: the Rhineland would be demilitarized and occupied by Allied

The leaders of the principal Allied Powers gather at the Paris peace conference (1919): (from left) David Lloyd George, Vittorio E. Orlando, Georges Clemenceau, and Woodrow Wilson. [Brown Brothers]

troops for 15 years, during which time the coal-rich Saar region was to be administered by the League of Nations for the economic benefit of France and Britain, and the United States promised to conclude a defensive military alliance with France.

France, Britain, and Japan all coveted German colonies. The "mandate principle" offered a solution under which these powers were each given control over some of the territories under League supervision, with the object of preparing them for independence. The principle did not apply, however, to China's Shantung peninsula, which came under full Japanese authority. Reparations were another contentious issue. Britain and France insisted that Germany be responsible for all damage done to civilians, including pensions and family support. As a result, the Allies drafted Article 231, which held German

◎ The War Guilt Principle ◎

The harsh treaty the Allies imposed on Germany at the Paris peace conference contained a unique principle that forced Germany to accept responsibility for having caused World War I. Article 231 of the Treaty of Versailles is known as the "war guilt clause."

The Allied and Associated Governments affirm and Germany accepts the responsibility of Germany and her allies for causing all the loss and damage to which the Allied and Associated Governments and their nationals have been subjected as a consequence of the war imposed upon them by the aggression of Germany and her allies.

Source: U.S. Congress, Senate, *Treaty of Peace with Germany,* 66th Cong., 1st sess., S. doc. 49 (1919).

aggression responsible for the war. The exact amount was fixed two years later at the staggering sum of $33 billion.

John Maynard Keynes (1883–1946), an economist attached to the British delegation, believed the peace treaty put Germany in an untenable position that spelled future disaster. In *The Economic Consequences of the Peace* (1919) he argued that the enormous reparations anticipated were impossible in view of the other economic provisions of the treaty. Large amounts of German coal were allocated to France, many of Germany's ships were given to Britain, and billions of dollars of its foreign assets were confiscated. Territorial losses stripped Germany of half its iron mines and a fifth of its iron and steel industries. The treaty forced Germany to return Alsace and Lorraine to France; on its eastern borders, Germany ceded parts of East Prussia and Upper Silesia to a revived state of Poland, lost the city of Danzig to League control, and gave up territory to newly independent Czechoslovakia. *Anschluss*, or union, was forbidden between Germany and Austria.

Determined that Germany would be in no position to wage another aggressive war, the Allies reduced its army to a 100,000-man volunteer force and limited its navy to a handful of small ships. They also prohibited all offensive weapons, including submarines, airplanes and zeppelins, heavy artillery, tanks, and poison gas. Finally, the treaty provided for the trial of the former kaiser as a war criminal, but the Netherlands, to which he had fled, refused to extradite him. The threat of renewed war forced representatives of the new German government to sign the treaty on June 28, 1919.

The peace terms with Germany's allies were hardly less severe. Austria was reduced to a third of its former size, while Hungary was left with a fourth of its former territory. Bulgaria, too, lost land, and all three states had to reduce their armies. Turkey remained only with Asia Minor and a small strip of territory around Istanbul, and the Turkish straits were demilitarized and opened to international shipping.

The Search for Security

Wilson had insisted that permanent peace rested on the creation of an international body known as the League of Nations. The Covenant, or constitution, of the League was incorporated into each of the peace treaties. It provided for a system of "collective security" by which the League would encourage disarmament and prevent war by arbitrating disputes and applying economic sanctions. The Covenant also established a system of mandates by which the European powers assumed the right to rule a number of non-Western areas that they argued were incapable of self-government. Granting self-determination to some European states, such as Poland and

Yugoslavia, while denying the same right to the colonized peoples of Asia, Africa, and the Pacific reflected racist assumptions. Because it had no armed force to coerce violators, the League lacked the power to enforce its principles. Moreover, when Congress refused to ratify the Treaty of Versailles, the United States itself failed to join the organization; neither Germany nor the Soviet Union was to become a member for years.

France and Germany sought alternatives to the League of Nations to ensure their security. American withdrawal from European diplomatic affairs denied France the defensive treaty that Britain and the United States had promised. Consequently, France created a "little entente" by aligning itself with Czechoslovakia, Romania, and Yugoslavia, hoping thereby to encircle Germany on its eastern borders. Isolated from the community of nations, Germany made common cause with Soviet Russia, another outcast nation. In 1922 they signed the Treaty of Rapallo, opening diplomatic relations and pledging economic cooperation as well as secret military contacts.

France remained uneasy over German intentions, and when the Germans failed to meet their reparations quota in 1923, French and Belgian troops occupied the Ruhr Basin on the eastern bank of the Rhine. Passive resistance among Ruhr factory workers and miners and British and American protests eventually forced a withdrawal, but the fear and hatred between the nations remained deeply rooted.

In 1925 German Foreign Minister Gustav Stresemann (1878–1929) proposed that Germany, France, Britain, Italy, and Belgium guarantee the western European status quo. The result was the Locarno Pact, which relieved some of the international political tension. In 1926 Germany finally joined the League of Nations. In 1927 the French foreign minister, Aristide Briand (1862–1932), and the American secretary of state, Frank Kellogg (1856–1937), sponsored a treaty renouncing war as an instrument of national policy. The Kellogg-Briand Pact of 1928, eventually signed by 65 states, "outlawed" war.

Society and Culture: The Impact of War

A decade after World War I, José Ortega y Gasset (1883–1955), a Spanish philosopher, wrote, "Today, by the very fact that everything seems possible to us, we have a feeling that the worst of all is possible: retrogression, barbarism, decadence."[4] Ortega's irony revealed how deeply disturbed his generation had been by the war. Yet his pessimism makes little sense unless we re-

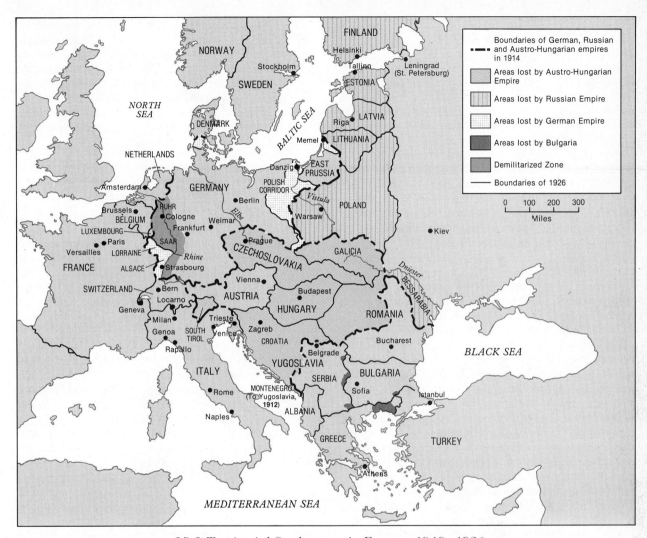

35.3 Territorial Settlements in Europe, 1919–1926

member that even as Europeans rebuilt their cities and mourned their dead, they were haunted by the memory of their former confidence in the superiority of their civilization. This explains why the West experienced a profound crisis of belief after 1919 despite the victory of the democracies and the return of peace.

Ultimately, Ortega's foreboding proved justified. Although European intellectual and cultural life in the postwar period was creative and varied, it was marked by a mood of anxiety. The sense of futility was particularly acute among the veterans who returned to a civilian society beset with political and economic problems and intent on getting back to "normalcy." To these dashed hopes was added the horror of modern warfare. The German author Erich Maria Remarque (1898–1970) captured the shock experienced by soldiers in two best-selling novels, *All Quiet on the Western Front* (1929) and

The Road Back (1931). The mood of despair seemed to confirm the prewar intuitions of Nietzsche and Freud that civilized society was irrational and that humans were unable to control their "primitive" instincts. This atmosphere of skepticism stimulated a transformation of Western culture. A decade after the war's end, the "modern" temper of twentieth-century life had been established.

Distrust of established beliefs, uncertainty about the meaning of life, and anxiety about the future produced what the author Gertrude Stein (1874–1946) termed a "lost generation." The triumph of communism in Russia and the rise of fascism in the 1920s suggested a willingness to abandon democracy. Frustrated material expectations added to the disorientation, for the economic boom after 1919 proved to be only a prelude to the Great Depression.

Social Change and Economic Crisis

The impact of the war was felt differently in each country and class. Everywhere the status and power of the old nobility were seriously weakened, especially in the new states of eastern Europe. The aristocracy had been systematically eliminated in Russia after the Bolshevik revolution, and a large number of young British nobles had been killed in the war. Peasants had been conscripted into military service more heavily than any other class, so the toll in death and disablement among them was also high. After the war many peasants refused to go back to their villages and often formed the rank and file of militant veterans' groups in the cities. When they did go back to the countryside, they frequently led protest movements.

Postwar society in western Europe was predominantly urban. In France, the most agrarian of the industrialized nations, the percentage of the working population engaged in agriculture fell from one-half before 1914 to one-third by 1931. Nevertheless, the number of industrial workers remained fairly stable over the following decades as advances in technology and assembly-line processes made labor more productive. During the first years of the war severe labor shortages had produced higher wages and a modicum of prosperity for the working classes, but government controls and inflation eventually forced wages to lag behind prices, resulting in significant discontent. The support and cooperation that socialist parties and unions gave to the war effort had conditioned many labor leaders to moderate policies. Some working-class leaders, however, reverted to more radical doctrines after the war, and many looked to the Russian Revolution for inspiration. As real wages rose between 1924 and 1929, particularly for the unskilled, worker discontent was once again mitigated, a trend reinforced by new social welfare measures in many countries.

The war affected the middle classes most severely. Greater educational opportunities and the growth of the service sector increased the number of white-collar workers, many of whom came from working-class families. The economic slump of the 1920s, however, slowed middle-class mobility. The pressure was particularly acute on the lower middle class, whose opportunities for advancement into managerial positions in the private sector shrank as the economy slowed. Inflation also limited the earning power of this group and threatened its status. The most extreme distress occurred in Germany, where by 1925 inflation had eaten up more than 50 percent of the capital held by the lower middle class. Retirees, widows, and others living on fixed incomes were hit especially hard, as were property owners whose incomes were frozen by rent regulations. Lower-middle-class earnings fell markedly in the 1920s, and millions of workers were forced back into the factories, where salaries equaled or exceeded those of white-collar employees. Hence the lower middle class felt squeezed between two groups: the wealthy capitalists, whose income was still increasing, and the workers from whose ranks many of them had risen. Lower-middle-class resentment of big business and labor often found political expression in radical right-wing groups.

The New Morality: Women, Work, and Sex

The middle class, which had experienced prewar optimism most fully, now found its values under assault. Wartime conditions disrupted social arrangements and family structures: husbands at the front, women in the factories, strangers crowding into the cities, and the uncertainty of survival had loosened the restrictions of bourgeois society and contributed to the breakdown of traditional morality. Psychological and social stress encouraged a new style of life that celebrated "liberation" from conventional behavior. In the 1920s Europeans were caught up in the spirit of the "jazz age," a name reflecting the popular perception that American life was more modern and less tradition-bound.

Public manifestations of the new morality appeared everywhere. Women's skirts were shorter and dresses more revealing, slinky adaptations of the "flapper" style made famous in Prohibition America. Young people drank and smoked in public, bars and nightclubs proliferated, and dancing took on more expressive—and suggestive—forms. Motion pictures, perhaps the most popular mass entertainment of the period, created the cult of the "vamp," and the private lives of film stars were spread across the front pages of the popular press. The use of chaperons and arranged marriages declined sharply, while illegitimacy and divorce rates rose. Such changes produced a more open attitude toward sexual matters.

Social developments reflected the new morality. Greater tolerance toward sexual minorities evolved. Events once thought sensational, such as Oscar Wilde's trial in the 1890s, seemed quaint to Europeans of the 1920s who openly professed their differing sexual orientation. Paris and Berlin, the two centers of postwar avant-garde culture, were havens for artists, writers, and musicians that included homosexuals as well as American blacks. Gertrude Stein and Alice B. Toklas, the most famous lesbian couple of the period, presided over a brilliant artistic and literary scene in Paris. Sexual minorities still faced formidable obstacles to equality and acceptance, but the more tolerant attitudes of the 1920s brought the issue into the open.

◎ Postwar Sexual Mores ◎

In the decade after World War I, many aspects of nineteenth-century codes of social behavior were abandoned in the West as religious belief, defined gender roles, and public morality were consciously rejected by the "lost generation." Here Walter Lippmann (1889–1974), an American social critic, sees changes in the status of women and advances in birth control as the principal reasons for the freer sexual conduct that marked the 1920s.

Until quite recently the main conventions of sex were enforced first by the parents and then by the husband through their control over the life of the woman. The main conventions were: first, that she must not encourage or display any amorous inclinations except where there was practical certainty that the young man's intentions were serious; second, that when she was married to the young man she submitted to his embraces only because the Lord somehow failed to contrive a less vile method of perpetuating the species. All the minor conventions were subsidiary to these; the whole system was organized on the premise that procreation was the woman's only sanction for sexual intercourse. . . . The virtuous man, by popular standards, was one who before his marriage did not have sexual relations with a virtuous woman. . . . These conventions were not perfectly administered. But they were sufficiently well administered to remain the accepted conventions, honored even in the breach. It was possible, because of the way people lived, to administer them.

The woman lived a sheltered life. That is another way of saying that she lived under the constant inspection of her family. . . . She met young men under the zealous chaperonage of practically the whole community. No doubt, couples slipped away occasionally and more went on than was known or acknowledged. But even then there was a very powerful deterrent against an illicit relationship. This deterrent was the fear of pregnancy. That in the end made it almost certain that if a secret affair were consummated it could not be kept secret and that terrible penalties would be exacted. In the modern world effective chaperonage has become impracticable and the fear of pregnancy has been virtually eliminated by the very general knowledge of contraceptive methods.

The whole revolution in the field of sexual morals turns upon the fact that external control of the chastity of women is becoming impossible. . . .

For when conception could be prevented, there was an end to the theory that woman submits to the embrace of the male only for purposes of procreation. She had to be persuaded to cooperate, and no possible reason could be advanced except that the pleasure was reciprocal.

Source: W. Lippmann, *A Preface to Morals* (New York: Macmillan, 1929), pp. 286–291 passim.

The emancipation of women was another result of the social transformation. An earlier generation of feminist agitation had made important advances in raising the consciousness of women and calling public attention to their demands for equality. Yet despite the work of the middle-class suffragists and the socialist women's movement, Finland and Norway were the only Western nations in which women had won the right to vote before 1914.

Wartime labor shortages created a situation in which women made significant progress toward representation in the workplace. As women crowded into the munitions industries and the service sector, governments made propaganda appeals to them, thus raising expectations for change. Some nations granted women the right to vote: in 1918 the British Parliament extended suffrage to women over 30, and shortly thereafter both the United States and the new German republic gave the vote equally to men and women. Austria, Poland, and Czechoslovakia joined Belgium, the Netherlands, Sweden, and Denmark in following suit.

While these were crucial gains, the suffrage was not

made universal in Spain, France, Switzerland, and Italy until after World War II. Moreover, in many countries marriage and property laws favoring husbands also remained largely intact. After 1919 more women gained access to educational opportunities and a wider range of jobs, although many were forced out of their wartime work by returning soldiers, and in practice some professions remained closed to women. Nor was progress in regard to the status of women and sexual minorities permanent, for serious setbacks occurred in the interwar years when right-wing regimes repressed both with renewed vigor.

✿ JOSEPHINE BAKER: AN AMERICAN IN PARIS

One of the most celebrated figures in Europe between the wars was the black American entertainer Josephine Baker. Born in St. Louis in 1906 to a black mother and a father reputedly of Spanish descent, Baker left school at the age of 8 to help support her family. While living in East St. Louis, she witnessed the race riots that broke out there in 1917, and the sight of white bands burning and killing with impunity left an indelible mark on her.

Baker's talent soon surfaced. She starred in basement musicals as a child and ran away with a vaudeville troupe at the age of 13. Four years later she appeared at Radio City Music Hall in New York in a musical featuring black performers titled, stereotypically, *Shuffle Along*. In 1925 she went to Paris with a show called *La Revue Nègre*, which sought to capitalize on the topical vogue for jazz and for "exotic" black entertainers. The show failed and the company was stranded, but Baker caught on with the Folies Bergère, a club famous for its lavish sets and its scantily dressed performers. She created a sensation in her debut, in which she appeared clad only in a tutu made of rhinestone-studded bananas and three bracelets.

Baker's multiple talents as a singer and dancer, wed to a style of inimitable comic abandon, soon made her an international celebrity. Billed only as Josephine, the former slum child earned and spent enormous sums of money; mimicking her own exotic image, she strolled down the streets of Paris with a pet leopard. After a hugely successful world tour, she appeared in films opposite such French stars as Jean Gabin and ventured into light opera as well.

In 1937 Baker married a wealthy industrialist, Jean Lion, converted to Judaism, and became a French citizen. At the outbreak of World War II she joined the Red Cross and was later recruited into the French Resistance, gathering intelligence and also entertaining Free French forces. At the end of the war she was awarded

The American jazz singer and dancer Josephine Baker was a great celebrity in Paris during the years between the wars. [Granger Collection]

France's highest decorations, the Croix de Guerre and the Légion d'Honneur, as well as the rosette of the Resistance. Baker's wide travel and her experience of poverty and discrimination led her in 1947 to found what she called a World Village at Les Milandes, her estate in southwestern France. Here, she and her second husband, Jo Bouillon, adopted a "rainbow family" of 12 children of all races and religions. She became a center of controversy in 1951 after she protested the refusal to serve her at the Stork Club in New York, but the National Association for the Advancement of Colored People (NAACP) named her its Woman of the Year. Baker began a crusade against segregation in her native country and succeeded in integrating theaters and nightclubs from Las Vegas to Miami. In 1963 she stood with Dr. Martin Luther King, Jr., at the climax of his march on Washington, D.C., and delivered an impassioned speech in front of the Lincoln Memorial.

Bankrupted finally by her debts at Les Milandes, Baker was provided a villa for herself and her children by Princess Grace of Monaco. In 1973 she triumphed at Carnegie Hall in another comeback tour, and despite failing health she repeated her success in Paris in a performance commemorating her fiftieth anniversary in France on April 10, 1975. Two days later, she died of a stroke.

On or off the stage, in or out of controversy, Josephine Baker was for half a century a uniquely vivid symbol of glamour, vitality, compassion, and commitment to the struggle for human equality. At the end of her life a film biography was planned, but, as she told reporters in a 1973 interview, "I would like to meet the woman who has the courage even to play my life story in a film. . . . I do not believe the woman exists who could have had the courage to have *lived* it as I have done." Certainly, few women of the twentieth century have combined careers and interests so daringly, served the human cause so passionately, and triumphed so indomitably.

Science, Literature, and Art

The postwar crisis of belief was especially acute among artists and writers, whose search for meaning led to creative ferment and experimentation. Proclaiming a "crisis of the mind," the French poet and critic Paul Valéry (1871–1945) articulated the state of anxiety and pessimism. His gloomy prognosis of the future was echoed by the German scholar Oswald Spengler (1880–1936). Spengler's immensely popular book *The Decline of the West* (1918) compared the development of Europe with the historical pattern of other civilizations. He argued that the West had entered a period of decay that could be reversed only by an authoritarian "Caesar" capable of imposing peace and order on a chaotic world. In a

similar vein, Ortega y Gasset's *Revolt of the Masses* (1930) warned that democratic society would result in the decline of education and culture.

Science offered no antidote to these laments. Building on the advances in physics at the turn of the century, the Danish physicist Niels Bohr (1885–1962) had formulated a theory of the atom in 1913 that attempted to reconcile Max Planck's quantum theory with Ernest Rutherford's view of atomic structure. By the mid-1920s, however, more complex ideas challenged Bohr's conclusions. The abstract language of differential equations took the place of concepts such as orbits, while Bohr and others revised their earlier hypotheses. In 1927 the German physicist Werner Heisenberg (1901–1976) announced his "uncertainty principle": the behavior of atomic particles did not conform to the laws of cause and effect. The futility of attempting to find a comprehensive explanation of physical phenomena to replace the old Newtonian model became increasingly apparent.

Postwar developments in philosophy both reflected and reinforced the findings of science. Ludwig Wittgenstein (1889–1951), the most forceful advocate of the movement called logical empiricism, maintained that traditional ethical and metaphysical systems were meaningless because philosophy was nothing more than statements of fact clarified by logic. Logical positivists asserted that unless such concepts as "freedom" and "God" could be reduced to the precise language of mathematics and symbolic logic, they were meaningless. Similarly, existentialism, derived from the Danish philosopher Søren Kirkegaard (1813–1855) and later associated with the French philosophers Jean-Paul Sartre (1905–1980) and Albert Camus (1913–1960), presented an image of human helplessness and despair in the face of an existence devoid of meaning and a supreme being. Although the existentialists argued that humans exist without a predetermined purpose, they still asserted the necessity of responsible moral action.

In the world of literature, a no less startling revolution took place. Language and structure gave way to experiments that reflected new theories of the human personality as well as a conscious desire to break away from traditional forms. Authors extended the path opened by Marcel Proust (1871–1922), the French author of *Remembrance of Things Past*, with a new "stream of consciousness" of subjective experience. The year 1922 saw the publication of two influential works in this genre, *Ulysses* by the Irishman James Joyce (1882–1941) and *Jacob's Room* by the Englishwoman Virginia Woolf (1882–1941), followed in 1929 by *The Sound and the Fury* by the American William Faulkner (1897–1962). Each of these works probed the random thoughts and emotions of everyday consciousness and the obscure sources of human motivation that Freud had suggested.

D. H. Lawrence (1885–1930), whose controversial novel *Lady Chatterley's Lover* (1928) was censored for its explicit description of sexual desire, exemplified the postwar liberation from bourgeois mores. The German Thomas Mann (1875–1955), in *The Magic Mountain* (1924), evoked the collapse of meaning. Franz Kafka (1883–1924), a German Jew who lived in Prague, wrote frightening tales of nightmares that haunt the imagination, most notably *The Trial* (1925) and *The Castle* (1929).

While much of the literature of the period between the world wars was so innovative as to confuse and repel readers, the poetry of the Irishman William Butler Yeats (1865–1939) had a more direct appeal, for he combined traditional lyricism with a stoic view of the world. In a similar manner, the German Rainer Maria Rilke (1875–1926) attempted to evoke harmony with nature.

The Italian dramatist Luigi Pirandello (1867–1936) and the poet T. S. Eliot gave the most representative expression to the concerns of the period. In Pirandello's *Six Characters in Search of an Author* (1918), two sets of players, a family and a group of actors, appear on stage at the same time, with the family members asking actors to portray their roles. Both family and actors present versions of the truth peculiar to their own viewpoints. Much as in Einstein's theories, Pirandello's play offered relative truths from which the observer—or the audience—could choose. The absurdity of a world without fixed guideposts was a pervasive theme of interwar European culture. Eliot, in *The Waste Land* (1922), cap-

tured most poignantly the sense of desolation that so many creative thinkers of the postwar world felt. Eliot portrayed the spiritual emptiness of modern London and brought the mood of Symbolism into English poetry. He eventually resolved his personal crisis by joining the Anglican church.

The plastic arts, like literature, caught the spirit of the period. As early as 1915 the horrors of the war had begun to produce the deliberately nonsensical anti-art movement known as Dada (from the French meaning "hobbyhorse"). Other artists embraced a "return to order" that restored representational forms to painting so as to express human alienation and isolation. Surrealism drew from a variety of sources, including the new realism, prewar Cubism, Dadaism, and Freudian psychology. Surrealists such as Salvador Dalí and Giorgio de Chirico (1888–1978) created visions of a dream world and hallucinatory landscapes according to the irrational dictates of the subconscious. Other artists, such as Wassily Kandinsky (1866–1944) and Paul Klee (1879–1940), moved from their earlier Expressionist concerns toward greater abstraction, a trend that Piet Mondrian (1872–1944) brought to its extreme in rigidly nonobjective paintings.

Klee and Kandinsky taught at the Bauhaus, the most famous school of architecture and design in modern times. Founded in Weimar by the architect Walter Gropius (1883–1969), the Bauhaus sought to reconcile art

Walter Gropius founded the Bauhaus, the most important school of modern architectural design, to reconcile art with technology. His functionalist style is apparent in the workshop building, completed in 1926. [Museum of Modern Art, New York]

with science and technology. It advanced an architectural style emphasizing functionalism, the use of glass and prefabricated concrete, and a rejection of ornamentation. The Bauhaus "international style," also championed by the French architect Le Corbusier (1887–1965) and the American Frank Lloyd Wright (1869–1959), testified to the triumph of the modern temper.

The generation that grew to maturity between 1890 and 1919 experienced the stress and excitement of living through the end of one historical era and the birth of another. The second half of the nineteenth century had been generally a period of material growth, optimism, and self-confidence. Science and technology had made life in the West more comfortable and had enabled the Western powers to impose their rule over much of the globe.

Many of the same factors that caused European expansion contributed, however, to a mounting crisis among the Western states. To a litany of old grievances were added new rivalries and competition for increasingly limited resources. While political leaders and capitalist entrepreneurs in one nation worked to outmaneuver their counterparts elsewhere, military officers and ideologues planned strategies of defense and domination. Once the crisis erupted, the West discovered that it had become much better at waging war than it had imagined. But unlike the wars of imperial conquest, the great European powers were more or less evenly matched, and the war consequently became an exercise in self-destruction.

The strain of total war had produced major change. Socialists shared power in wartime governments, and monarchies were overthrown in three major states. In some countries the bloodletting decimated the ruling classes, while in others revolution eradicated or severely wounded traditional elites. Prewar social arrangements were further altered as a result of the massive conscription of peasants, the mobilization of women into the work force, and the disruption of family life.

The postwar age was a new world. Not only had the European map changed with the shifting of frontiers, but new states also appeared on the ruins of old empires. Positive thinkers saw liberal democracy installed in central and eastern Europe for the first time; the more pessimistic questioned the chances for its survival. New forms of political extremism arose everywhere and, in Russia and Italy, soon came to power and threatened to spread. Nor did Europe's world supremacy survive much beyond the war. As the forces of nationalism took hold in the colonies, Western control of the subject peoples of Asia, Africa, and the Middle East weakened.

Science, literature, and art undermined the optimism of an earlier age, expressed the despair of a generation that had experienced shattering trauma, and forged new directions. Some intellectuals turned back to religion as a source of hope and comfort. Even Carl Jung rejected the teachings of Freud, his intellectual mentor, by advocating the therapeutic value of religious faith. In 1934, with the world in the throes of the Great Depression, the British historian Arnold Toynbee published the first of a series of volumes, titled A Study of History, *that likened the development of civilizations to the biological process of life, with cycles of birth, growth, and decline. Unlike Oswald Spengler, however, Toynbee entertained the prospect that Western civilization might revive itself. In the search for meaning, others turned instead to political movements of protest and violence.*

Notes

1. Viscount Grey of Fallodon, *Twenty-five Years, 1892–1916*, vol. 2 (New York: Stokes, 1925), p. 20.
2. K. Robbins, *The First World War* (New York: Oxford University Press, 1984), p. 88.
3. W. S. Churchill, *The World Crisis* (New York: Scribner, 1923), p. 3.
4. J. Ortega y Gasset, *The Revolt of the Masses* (New York: Norton, 1957), p. 45.

Suggestions for Further Reading

Calder, N. *Einstein's Universe.* New York: Penguin Books, 1980.
Cantor, N. F., and Wertman, M. S., eds. *The History of Popular Culture Since 1815.* New York: Macmillan, 1968.

Ellenberger, H. F. *The Discovery of the Unconscious.* New York: Basic Books, 1970.

Evans, R. J. W., and Strandmann, H. P. von, eds., *The Coming of the First World War.* New York: Oxford University Press, 1989.

Fussell, P. *The Great War and Modern Memory.* New York: Oxford University Press, 1975.

Hughes, H. S. *Consciousness and Society: The Reorientation of European Social Thought, 1890–1930.* New York: Knopf, 1958.

Hughes, R. *The Shock of the New: Art and the Century of Change.* New York: Knopf, 1981.

Joll, J. *The Origins of the First World War.* London: Longman, 1984.

Kern, S. *The Culture of Time and Space, 1880–1918.* Cambridge, Mass.: Harvard University Press, 1983.

Lafore, L. *The Long Fuse: An Interpretation of the Origins of World War I.* Philadelphia: Lippincott, 1965.

Martin, M. W. *Futurist Art and Theory, 1909–1915.* Oxford: Clarendon Press, 1978.

Masur, G. *Prophets of Yesterday: Studies in European Culture, 1890–1914.* New York: Macmillan, 1961.

Mayer, A. J. *The Politics and Diplomacy of Peacemaking.* New York: Knopf, 1968.

Mosse, G. *The Culture of Western Europe.* Chicago: Rand McNally, 1969.

Offer, A. *The First World War: An Agrarian Interpretation.* New York: Oxford University Press, 1990.

Pulzer, P. G. *The Rise of Political Anti-Semitism in Germany and Austria.* New York: Wiley, 1964.

Rewald, J. *The History of Impressionism.* New York: New York Graphic Society, 1980.

Robbins, K. *The First World War.* New York: Oxford University Press, 1984.

Sontag, R. V. *A Broken World.* New York: Harper & Row, 1971.

Stearns, P. N. *European Society in Upheaval: Social History Since 1800.* New York: Macmillan, 1967.

Williams, J. *The Other Battleground: The Home Fronts, Britain, France, and Germany, 1914–1918.* Chicago: Regnery, 1972.

Wohl, R. *The Generation of 1914.* Cambridge, Mass.: Harvard University Press, 1979.

The Human Image (II)

Since the primitive carvers of the Old Stone Age some 25,000 years ago, the human figure has been a central theme of artistic representation. Each civilization has accorded it a different emphasis, and artists of every culture have interpreted it from the aesthetic and religious points of view of their times and societies. Throughout much of the ancient period and during the first millennium A.D., the human figure served a number of important purposes, principally as the embodiment of religious themes, as a means of representing notions of beauty, or as a general commentary on the human condition.

While these functions continued to be served by the human image, important changes began to occur in the modern age. The sixteenth century saw a more secularized portrayal of the human figure in cultures as diverse as Europe and India, together with greater stylistic naturalism. At the same time, an exceptionally active artistic patronage began to emerge throughout much of the world. From the court of Ming China to the Mughal Empire in India and the Medici of Florence, rulers turned to painters and sculptors to produce memorials to the greatness of their regimes. Artists had, of course, always served political purposes, but in some cases rulers now developed a new respect for their creative powers. Figures such as Michelangelo achieved the stature of a culture hero in the late European Renaissance, a phenomenon enshrined in Giorgio Vasari's *Lives of the Painters.* Moreover, while patronage elsewhere in the world remained largely in the hands of rulers, in the West private parties began to commission artists to paint their portraits, so in European art the human figure increasingly represented the wider elite.

Mughal culture in India revealed the diversity of Muslim artistic response to figurative art. The court of Akbar and his successors was the center for the production of portrait miniatures, exquisitely delicate works that meticulously recorded their subjects in a narrative style. Unlike Persian miniatures of earlier times, with their fairy-tale decorations, these paintings display an almost unnerving detachment, as in the portrait of a courtier dying of opium addiction. They testify as much to the virtuosity of the artist as to the representation of an individual.

The emperors of Ming China treated artists with less respect than the court of Akbar: Chinese artists worked in palace workshops under tight supervision, a custom that drove many of the more progressive among them to flee the capital for the cities of the south. Free from

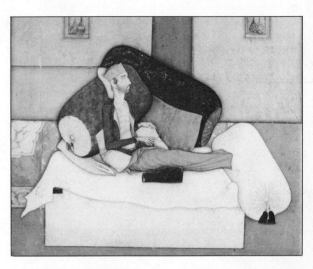

Dying Courtier, c. 1618.
[Bodleian Library, Oxford]

the demands of the emperors, many painters of the period seem to have deliberately avoided the depiction of human beings, thus reinforcing the Chinese preference for landscapes.

During the Ch'ing dynasty (1644–1912) sculptors reverted to smaller-scale works in porcelain, exceeding the technical skill of earlier Chinese ceramists. A small white porcelain statute of Kuan-yin (the Chinese goddess of compassion) from the seventeenth century reveals the softness of form and the deeply humanized rendering of a goddess achieved in this medium. Large quantities of such ceramics were exported to Europe in the eighteenth century, and to this day the term *china* is used to describe fine ceramic wares, especially porcelain.

In contrast to the detached aestheticism of the Mughal image and the refined delicacy of later Chinese porcelains, artists of the early Edo period in Japan depicted the human figure as a means of preserving historic events. Chinese travelers observed that like their own painters, their Japanese neighbors tended to use scroll paintings to narrate events, often without philosophical meaning. A pair of painted Japanese screens from 1610 depict westerners playing music. These are among the interesting works that show Portuguese and Dutch influences on Japanese painting as well as Japanese curiosity at the appearance of the "southern barbarians," as the Jesuit missionaries were known. The figures show little interest in the individuals represented but rather depict their customs, together with their costumes, so drab to Japanese eyes.

Toward the end of the seventeenth century the principal artistic medium in Japan shifted from scroll painting to the woodblock print, which increasingly reflected the lives and tastes of an emerging commercial society. The woodblock allowed for the inexpensive reproduction and wide distribution of popular images and themes, such as the Kabuki actors so admired by the middle class.

When the Portuguese arrived at Benin, West Africa, in the fifteenth century, they found a rich and sophisticated kingdom, whose sculptural tradition may well have been related to that of the earlier civilization of the neighboring city of Ife. Climatic conditions in sub-Saharan Africa have not favored the survival of early wooden carvings, but sculptures made of ivory and

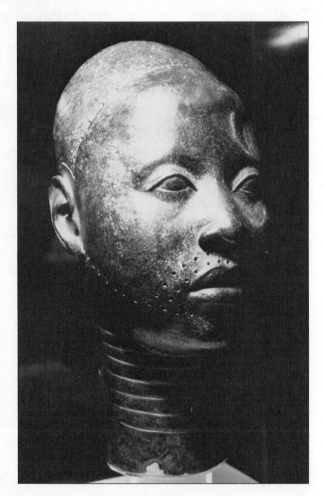

Zinc brass head from Benin, twelfth to fifteenth century. [Ronald Sheridan/Ancient Art and Architecture Collection]

metal reveal skillful renderings of the human form both realistically and in more abstract styles. A fifteenth-century zinc brass head is a delicate and idealized portrait of a king. Like the Japanese, Benin artists recorded the appearance of the newcomers, though in a much more symbolic and stylized form. An ivory portrait mask made for a ruler is topped by a crown composed of a band of long-haired, bearded Portuguese. The carver of this piece is more interested in hairstyles than in dress but shows the same curiosity at strange customs and appearance. The ruler's portrait expresses elegance and power out of all proportion to its size.

No such record survives of the arrival of westerners in the Americas. The art of the last Aztecs retains a strong element of decoration, as in the statues of deities carved to embellish temples. Yet the last period of Aztec art provides at least one outstanding example of an artist's use of the human figure to depict a primal event: the carving of a woman (perhaps a goddess) giving birth. The realism of the straining and the cold, damp look of the skin, produced by a careful working of the stone, are powerfully contrasted with the stylized miniature adult emerging from the womb.

From the sixteenth to the late nineteenth century, European art was molded by the principles of the Italian Renaissance style, which flourished in the fifteenth and early sixteenth centuries. In their efforts to combine the splendors of classical antiquity with Christian values, Renaissance artists turned to the human figure as an image of the highest form of beauty. The face and body reemerged in a way that has been as important for the subsequent development of Western art as its appearance in ancient Greek art in the fifth century B.C. The Renaissance stress on mental and physical prowess and on the ability to control and change environment resulted in the triumph of the human figure as the chief focus of artistic representation in the Western world. Its treatment of the body may best be understood by examining two categories of painting and sculpture: the nude and portraiture.

After centuries of neglect, the female nude was reemphasized in European art in the late fifteenth century. Several of Sandro Botticelli's paintings, including his *Primavera*, were inspired by Hellenistic statuary, especially depictions of Venus, yet they also reflect the early Renaissance philosophical interest in ideal beauty. The classical Venus figure offered the artist an opportunity to depict the female nude, something that could not be done with the Virgin Mary, hitherto the most popular female subject in European art. Titian, the brilliant Venetian painter, displayed the female nude in a reclining form that would remain popular for centuries. His *Venus of Urbino*, vividly and sensuously colored, reflects the Renaissance artist's interest in rendering the human figure in a wholly natural condition, in contrast to the late medieval renditions of naked

Aztec woman, perhaps a goddess, in childbirth. [Dumbarton Oaks, Washington, D.C.]

individualized Renaissance man in his *Portrait of a Young Man*. Here is an elegant, affected youth whose aloof demeanor, handsome face, and elegant hands reveal the haughty arrogance of an educated gentleman of high social position. While Mannerists such as Bronzino emphasized the neck and hands to convey a sense of grace, others, such as El Greco, distorted their figures to highlight the spiritual values of the Counter-Reformation.

The baroque art of the seventeenth century in Europe was characterized by the expression of strong emotions, often religious, and a virtuoso technique. These characteristics can be seen in the works of the Italian sculptor Bernini. In his *St. Theresa in Ecstasy*, the body of the enraptured saint, her robes, and the cloud on which she rests combine to create the illusion of mystical drama. Unlike Michelangelo, Bernini uses the facial expression of his subject, suffused with a passion at once mystical and sensual, to enhance the dramatic effect. Rubens, the Flemish baroque master, concentrated on the human figure as the epitome of the animal body straining against the physical forces

bodies, often shown at the Last Judgment or in hell. Donatello's famous statue of a virtually nude David is a particularly fine example of the combination of Christian and pagan elements in the Renaissance. The subject is a figure from the Old Testament, but the classical stance and the provocative nudity are Greek.

In portraiture Renaissance painters combined an interest in personality and the external world. Leonardo da Vinci's *Last Supper* is both the re-creation of a famous biblical episode and a masterpiece of psychological study in which the viewer is implicitly invited to interpret the emotional responses of Christ's disciples through expressions and physical gestures when they learn one of them is a traitor. No less psychological were the late works of Donatello and Michelangelo, both of whom rejected external beauty in their quest to understand the depths of the penitent soul. A half century later, when the art of the late Renaissance had begun to give way to the sophisticated Mannerist style, the Florentine artist Bronzino brilliantly depicted the

Bronzino's *Portrait of a Young Man*. [Metropolitan Museum of Art, Bequest of Mrs. H. O. Havemeyer, 1929. The H. O. Havemeyer Collection.]

around it, whether in the form of soft, luminous female flesh or muscular, tanned male bodies. Unlike the bodies of El Greco or the late works of Donatello and Michelangelo, those of Rubens vividly represent the zest for physical life that was a dominant element of the baroque spirit.

A more traditional use of the human figure as political icon appears in Hyacinthe Rigaud's portrait of Louis XIV (see page 610), painted at a time when the grandeur of the baroque style was beginning to yield to the more graceful, intimate rococo. Much rococo art was more concerned with shallow aristocratic pastimes than the use of the human form to explore deeper values. However, a strong interest in portraiture, firmly rooted in the Renaissance, continued throughout the period, especially in Britain.

By the late eighteenth century a similar kind of style had developed in Japan, which depicted day-to-day human activities with a directness that marks a distinctly independent school. Much of earlier Japanese art was strongly influenced by Chinese traditions, but no Chinese artist would have produced prints of the kind known as *ukiyo-e* ("pictures of the floating

Love scene by Muhammad Yusuf al-Husaini, c. 1630. [Pierpont Morgan Library, New York]

world") or even recognized them as works of art. One print depicts the scene in a bathhouse, with both naked and dressed figures casually going about their business. In strong contrast to the imposing image of Louis XIV, these figures are given an intentional anonymity, expressing as they do the universality of human experience. This and other prints of the kind made a great impression in Europe when they were first seen there in the nineteenth century. Their influence was strongly felt by the Impressionists.

The later years of the Mughal court saw an increasing informality in the treatment of the human figure, although eighteenth-century Indian art never approached the candor of the *ukiyo-e* prints. The paintings often deal with romantic themes, as in the depiction of a prince embracing his favorite mistress. Lacking the precision of earlier Mughal art, the work remains within

Scene from a Japanese bathhouse, c. 1800. [Museum of Fine Arts, Boston; William Sturgis Bigelow Collection]

the same framework of stylistic refinement, and a common human experience becomes transformed into an episode of elegance and grace: it hardly seems to matter that the faces of the women in the scene are virtually indistinguishable.

Most of the works discussed so far either commemorated an individual or used the human figure to symbolize universal human experience or values. These traditions continued during most of the nineteenth century. The austere Neoclassicism of Jacques-Louis David, as reflected in *The Death of Marat*, glorified the French Revolution. But by the end of the century European artists had begun to employ human images to express anxiety about the state of their world. There are few more disturbing images of tension and neurosis than *The Scream*, by the Norwegian Edvard Munch, in which the distortions of the human body in the painting are reflected in the cosmic upheaval of land and sky.

The years preceding World War I produced traumatic changes throughout the world, in politics and society as well as in cultural life. Munch's attempt to unify figure and landscape to express a transcendent emotion characterized much of the art of the late nineteenth and early twentieth centuries in Europe. In many respects Munch's projection of human emotion onto landscape recalls fourteenth-century Christian art in Italy, but now devoid of religious context.

Years before Munch, the Frenchman Paul Cézanne had begun the effort among modern Western artists to reduce visual experience to simple, abstract forms. This movement was in turn influenced by European contact with the art of Asia, Africa, and Oceania. Western artists found universal messages in the highly stylized art forms of these regions, an impact that may be clearly seen in the paintings of Picasso and Gauguin and the sculptures of Constantin Brancusi. The brutally stylized representations of prostitutes in Picasso's *Demoiselles d'Avignon* (see "The Visual Experience: Art of the Modern Western World") caused a great scandal and presaged his even more radical experiments in abstraction a few years later, in which recognizable images disappeared altogether.

The so-called Expressionist style of Munch, which was taken up by German and Austrian artists shortly before World War I; the flat, abstracted style perfected by Picasso and his colleague Georges Braque, known as Cubism; and the wholly abstract canvases and watercolors of the Russian Wassily Kandinsky all foreshadowed a crisis in the representation of the human image in Western art. The cultural shock of World War I and the impact of Freudian psychology brought further distortions of the image in the form of Surrealism, a movement that dominated European art between the world wars. Seeking to penetrate psychological

states, Surrealist art was, like Expressionism, an attempt to probe beyond the image into inner realms of feeling, and much of it was overtly erotic. But, although it was often accused of being obscure, Surrealism was also capable of powerful political statement, as in Salvador Dalí's *Soft Construction with Boiled Beans—Premonition of Civil War*.

At the same time, Soviet Russia and Nazi Germany were demanding a new official art that would represent their propaganda objectives—the depiction of happy and contented workers in the first case, racially pure Aryans in the second. Hitler banned all abstract or Expressionist art in the Third Reich, and in 1937 he organized a notorious exhibit of "degenerate" art, which showed the work that had been purged from German museums. The exhibition backfired, as audiences streamed in not to mock but to admire some of the finest German painting of the century.

Some artists of the period, such as the British sculptor Henry Moore (1898–1986), continued to represent the human figure in simplified, monumental forms of great power, and Picasso, the most protean and prolific painter of the human image in history, returned to it after World War I. The image was banished again when Abstract Expressionism became the dominant international style after World War II, only to return with the Pop Art of the 1960s. Pop Art, whose images were derived largely from advertising and comic strips, sought to satirize consumerism and both cinematic and political cults of personality, as in the portraits of Marilyn Monroe and Mao Tse-tung by the American Andy Warhol (1928–1987). Pop Art was soon assimilated into a new style of "magic realism," which aimed for photographic illusion, while the former Abstract Expressionist Philip Guston (1913–1980) returned to the image with an effect at once comic and chilling, as in the disembodied head that rolls up an inclined plane in *Untitled*. More recently, the German Anselm Kiefer (born 1945) has turned to the long-disfavored genre of historical portraiture in his remarkable representations of German cultural history.

It is hardly surprising that the history of art has been marked by a continual recourse to the human figure as a source of expression and communication. The range of treatment reflects the diversity of human experience. Works have served religious, political, and aesthetic purposes, have documented events, and sometimes have tried to control them, as in fascist and Soviet art. Differences between cultures seem stylistic rather than reflective of profound divergences: the statue of an Egyptian pharaoh and the portraits of a European, Indian, Chinese, or African sovereign reflect a similar political aim, the exaltation and commemoration of the ruler. If anything seems unexpected, it is that at the end of the twentieth century, a period of unprecedented up-

Salvador Dalí, *Soft Construction with Boiled Beans—Premonition of Civil War*, 1936. [Philadelphia Museum of Art, Louise and Walter Arensberg Collection]

Philip Guston, *Untitled*, 1980. [Bevan Davies/David McKee Inc.]

heaval both in life and in the arts, naturalistic depictions of human beings continue to fascinate us. Such works suggest that the need to "see ourselves as others see us" remains constant.

Suggestions for Further Reading

Clark, K. *The Nude: A Study in Ideal Form.* Princeton, N.J.: Princeton University Press, 1956.

De Dilva, A., and Von Simson, O. *Man Through His Art*, Vol. 6: *The Human Face.* New York: Graphic Society, 1968.

Garland, M. *The Changing Face of Beauty.* New York: Barrows, 1957.

Lee, S. *A History of Far Eastern Art.* New York: Abrams, 1974.

Man: Glory, Jest, and Riddle: A Survey of the Human Form Through the Ages. San Francisco: M. H. de Young Memorial Museum, California Palace of the Legion of Honor, and San Francisco Museum of Art, 1965.

Mayor, A. H. *Artists and Anatomy.* New York: Artist's Limited Edition, 1984.

Mode, H. *The Woman in Indian Art.* New York: McGraw-Hill, 1970.

Neumeyer, A. *The Search for Meaning in Modern Art,* trans. R. Angress. Englewood Cliffs, N.J.: Prentice Hall, 1964.

Relouge, I. E., ed. *Masterpieces of Figure Painting.* New York: Viking, 1959.

Rowland, B. *The Art and Architecture of India.* Baltimore: Penguin Books, 1967.

Segal, M. *Painted Ladies: Models of the Great Artists.* New York: Stein & Day, 1972.

Selz, P. *New Images of Man.* New York: Museum of Modern Art, 1959.

Smart, A. *The Renaissance and Mannerism in Italy.* New York: Harcourt Brace Jovanovich, 1971.

Walker, J. *Portraits: 5,000 Years.* New York: Abrams, 1983.

Wentinck, C. *The Human Figure in Art from Prehistoric Times to the Present Day,* trans. E. Cooper. Wynnewood, Pa.: Livingston Publishing, 1970.

Willett, F. *African Art: An Introduction.* New York: Praeger, 1971.

CHAPTER 36

Upheaval in Eurasia and the Middle East

The twentieth century has been characterized by rapid change, particularly in the transformation of the world's biggest countries, China, Russia, and India, and the similar transformation of the Middle East. Together the four regions hold half the world's population. In China and Russia this change has appropriately been called revolutionary, entailing not only the overthrow of old governments by violence and civil war but also a radical restructuring of social, economic, and political systems in a short period of concentrated effort. The upheavals in each country were engineered and directed by native Communist parties, which made use of mass support by workers and peasants, groups that had previously been excluded from power. Each revolution also created a new set of ideological values.

Leon Trotsky arriving in Paris in 1929, an exile from the Bolshevik USSR he helped found a decade earlier. [*L'Illustration*/Sygma]

Like the French and American revolutions, those in Russia and China inspired others and served as models for change elsewhere in the world. The Chinese Revolution did not prevail until 1949, but its early stages from 1919 to 1934 were strongly influenced and for a time directly guided by Russian communists. When these early revolutionary efforts failed, China left the Soviet path. The ultimate success of the Chinese Revolution in 1949, and its later development, was far more an indigenous phenomenon than a response to the Russian experience.

Although strong differences marked the struggles for independence in India and the Middle East, neither can properly be viewed as a revolution. The Arabs fought Ottoman control with arms during World War I but then came under British and French authority. Indian protests against the British emphasized a nonviolent strategy. In both regions political power was eventually handed over peacefully to nationalist leaders. In the Middle East the League of Nations mandate system and the influx of Jewish settlers into Palestine, negligible until the rise of Nazism but significant thereafter, stimulated resistance from the native Arab population. Yet in the interwar years Arab nationalism failed to become a genuine mass movement as it did in India. There, the independence effort, as in China and Russia, involved peasants and workers under the direction of political organizers. While the nationalist regimes in Turkey and Iran attempted to modernize their countries after World War I, little effort went into radical restructuring of Indian society or its values.

Nevertheless, the changes that took place in India and the Middle East were in some ways revolutionary, for the awakening of nationalism and the end of the colonial system were to have long-range repercussions. India is the outstanding case of a drive for change that used traditional vehicles and symbols to attract support and to accelerate transformation, a pattern that repeated itself in the form of Muslim fundamentalism among Arab states after World War II.

In all of these regions powerful leaders played a key role in planning and directing change, among them Lenin and his successor Stalin in the USSR, Mao Tse-tung in China, Gandhi and his successor Nehru in India, and Faisal, ibn-Saud, Mustapha Kemal, Chaim Weizmann, and Reza Shah Pahlavi in the Middle East. Each of these leaders could claim to have made an enormous impact, not only on his own country but on states far beyond its borders as well. The twentieth century has been called the century of revolution primarily because of the massive upheavals in Russia, China, India, and the Middle East. The ripples that each of these revolutions sent around the world helped to spawn fundamental changes in Asia, Africa, and Latin America. The century of revolution began with dramatic events in Russia in 1917.

The Russian Revolution

In March 1917* the first of two revolutions erupted in war-weary Russia, shattering 300 years of history in the space of a few days: the Romanov dynasty, the last absolute monarchy in Europe, was toppled from the throne it had occupied since 1613. Though laden with drama, the events of March were only a prelude to an even farther-reaching transformation. As if one revolution was insufficient to shift the weight of Russian history, with its virtually unbroken pattern of political and social repression and economic hardship, a second revolution erupted in November. The communist state that arose out of the November revolution became a major force in shaping the twentieth century.

The Twilight of the Romanovs

That the people of Russia were deeply discontented should have come as no surprise to Tsar Nicholas II (1894–1917). The 1905 uprising had been a clear symptom of crisis. Provoked by Russia's defeat in the war with Japan, the "revolution" had climaxed on "Bloody Sunday" (January 22, 1905), when troops fired on protesting workers in St. Petersburg. The growing unrest and strikes finally persuaded Nicholas in October to create an imperial Duma, or assembly, to be elected by broad male suffrage. Within two years, imperial decrees undid most of these reforms. Convinced that his power was divinely ordained, Nicholas was determined to restore his absolute authority. After 1911, following the assassination of Peter Stolypin, a reformist minister who had tried to repress terrorists and reactionaries, he further alienated the educated and professional classes by surrounding himself with conservative advisers. By 1914 some ministers even saw a European war as a positive catalyst for national unity.

Nicholas was an indecisive and not very intelligent leader. After the outbreak of war, he took direct command of the Russian armies—the only European head of state to do so—despite his lack of military training. At first his gesture had a positive symbolic value for the millions of peasants who rallied to the call for arms, but as the imperial armies suffered defeat after defeat, even the least sophisticated Russians began to hold the tsar personally responsible. However, most military officers had been poorly trained in modern strategy. Soldiers sent to the German front were among the worst-fed and worst-equipped in Europe. Tens of thousands lacked

---

*Russia still used the ancient Julian calendar, which had been abandoned in the West centuries earlier. By this time it was 13 days behind the modern Gregorian calendar. Throughout this chapter Gregorian dates will be used.

Tsar Nicholas II and his five children a few years before the revolution that overthrew the Romanov dynasty. [Bettmann Archive]

even a rifle and were told to take one from a fallen comrade or a dead enemy; thus their greatly superior numbers failed to compensate for the country's lack of preparedness. Every setback in the field brought greater disenchantment among the troops. In addition to the incompetence of the generals and the enormous logistical problems stemming from Russia's vastness, Russian society was not sufficiently modernized to organize effectively for or sustain a major war effort. The Romanov dynasty collapsed in part because of the retarded development of the country's industries and infrastructure.

While Russia's war effort deteriorated, Nicholas left the government in the hands of his wife, Tsarina Alexandra (1872–1918), a religious zealot and absolutist. Her harsh, uncompromising attitudes were in part shaped by Grigori Rasputin, an eccentric Russian Orthodox monk whose great influence derived from his ability to convince Alexandra he could relieve her son's hemophilia. Rasputin's power over the tsarina and his manipulation of official policy outraged officials and members of the imperial court who hoped that political reforms would defuse popular discontent. Between September 1915 and November 1916 the Duma was suspended, while severe shortages of food and fuel provoked massive resentment in the cities. In December, hoping to free the

royal family from his influence, conservative aristocrats murdered Rasputin. By then, however, the domestic situation had deteriorated so severely that revolution was imminent. Within the reconvened Duma even conservatives and constitutional monarchists opposed the royal family.

The March 1917 Revolution

On March 8, 1917, disorder erupted in Petrograd.* Food riots led by women spread to the workers, and both a factory lockout and a socialist-inspired Woman's Day celebration filled the streets with protesters. The crisis came when the tsar, still at the front, ordered the revolt suppressed. On March 11 troops fired into a crowd, but the government's inexperienced reinforcements then mingled with the demonstrators. As cries of "Down with the tsar!" rang out, officials found their orders unenforceable. The next day the Duma proclaimed a provisional government under Prince Georgi Lvov and called on Nicholas to step down. With the generals unable to assure him of the army's loyalty—indeed, military leaders supported his stepping down—the last of the Romanov tsars abdicated. He and the imperial family were held under house arrest and were later captured by the Bolsheviks.

After centuries of absolutism and repression, Russia experienced a sudden liberalization. The provisional government planned the election of a constituent assembly on the basis of universal male suffrage and introduced civil liberties. It also implemented the eight-hour workday, ended the persecution of the Jews, and released thousands of political prisoners, although it maintained that only a legally constituted government could resolve the land problem. The new regime enjoyed the support of Western-educated Russians as well as the business and professional classes, while the Duma was dominated by liberals who favored a constitutional monarchy. Even the Entente Powers generally preferred the provisional government to the rule of the tsar, hoping that it would reinvigorate the Russian war effort.

From its inception, however, the provisional government was challenged by the more radical Soviet (council) of Workers' and Soldiers' Deputies, formed in March. Modeled after the organization that had led the 1905 general strike, the Petrograd soviet was in the hands of workers' representatives who had served on the tsar's War Industries Committee. Its executive committee quickly became a barometer of public sentiment. While hundreds of similar groups soon sprang up in army units, industrial centers, and the countryside, the

---

*The tsar had changed the name of the city from St. Petersburg to the Russian form, Petrograd, to emphasize the patriotic nature of the war. Under the Soviets the city was renamed Leningrad, only to revert to the name St. Petersburg in 1991.

Petrograd soviet maintained its preeminence because of its location in the capital, where power had traditionally been concentrated.

In contrast to the Duma, led by liberal elements, the membership of the soviets consisted largely of socialists of various types. The Social Revolutionaries looked to the Russian peasants and their traditional village councils for instituting fundamental change and favored the use of violence. The Mensheviks and the Bolsheviks, factions within the Social Democratic party, were both Marxist in ideology, though sharp differences divided them. The reform-minded Menshevik ("minority") faction sought to build a large party organization along the lines of the Western social democratic movements. They hoped to achieve their goals through peaceful evolution but did not expect to establish socialism in Russia until industrial development was more advanced.

The Bolshevik ("majority") group accepted Marxist goals but followed the teachings of Vladimir Ilyich Lenin (1870–1924), their exiled leader. Lenin rejected Marx's idea that socialist revolution was premature in an underdeveloped country like Russia, where the industrial proletariat was small. He also opposed the evolutionary strategy of the Mensheviks, arguing that peaceful methods were impossible in the tsarist autocracy and that only violent revolution would achieve socialism. Lenin argued for a "vanguard" of professional revolutionaries that would control a disciplined party, educate the workers and peasants, and prepare to seize the initiative.

The soviets, composed of these competing factions and without a clearly articulated ideology, supported the spontaneous actions of the urban crowds and landless peasants. By so doing, they competed with the provisional government for the people's loyalty. As this struggle progressed, the provisional government found itself at a growing disadvantage. The Bolsheviks, the only major group of the left not represented in the government, remained free of responsibility for unpopular policies.

The weaknesses of the provisional government proved to be fatal. The new leaders made no attempt to address the demands of the urban proletariat or to satisfy the land hunger of the peasants. Of more immediate significance, however, was its war policy. Despite the desperate unpopularity of the conflict, the Duma felt duty-bound to honor the alliance with the Entente against Germany. When the government renewed its pledge to support the war effort in May, popular opposition forced many ranking members to resign.

Lenin and the Bolshevik Coup

The Bolsheviks skillfully exploited the shortsightedness of the provisional government as Lenin began to dominate events. A short, stocky man, mostly bald, with a moustache and a goatee, he did not look charismatic.

But John Reed, a young left-wing American writer, understood that although Lenin was a "colorless" man, he had a gift for "explaining profound ideas in simple terms" that any unschooled Russian peasant could understand. He led, said Reed, "purely by virtue of his intellect."[1] Born Vladimir Ilyich Ulyanov, Lenin had been a radical since age 17, when the government had executed his older brother for plotting to assassinate Alexander III. During his twenties he became a Marxist, and his revolutionary activities brought him nearly five years of imprisonment and exile in Siberia. In 1900 he found refuge in western Europe, where he led the Bolshevik break from the Mensheviks.

When the March revolution erupted, Lenin, still in exile in Switzerland, persuaded the German government to grant him passage to Russia. The Germans, hoping that the Bolsheviks would disrupt the Russian war effort, transported him in a sealed train across their lines to the border, and Lenin arrived in Petrograd on April 20. His famous April Theses declared total opposition to the provisional government and instructed his followers to work for a second revolution in Russia, one that would eventually spread to the more industrialized countries of Europe. A communist victory, he said, would contribute to Russia's industrial base and help sustain Marxist socialism permanently.

Early in July soldiers and sailors led a massive uprising in Petrograd. The provisional government put down the revolt and blamed the Bolsheviks. Lenin, disguised as a locomotive fireman, fled to Finland, while a number of his followers—among them Lev Kamenev and Leon Trotsky—were arrested. When the provisional government launched a final military offensive against the Germans in July, soldiers deserted en masse, while in the countryside millions of peasants seized large estates. In an effort to broaden its support, the provisional government replaced Prince Lvov with Alexander Kerensky (1881–1970), a moderate Social Revolutionary. Kerensky's refusal to negotiate a withdrawal from the war served only to discredit him and his Menshevik allies. The final blunder came in September, when Lavr Kornilov, a reactionary military officer, attempted to crush the soviets. Kerensky appeared to welcome the general's action, but he came to believe that Kornilov intended to turn against him as well; he therefore armed the Red Guards, volunteer units from the Petrograd soviet. Pro-soviet railway workers refused to transport Kornilov's equipment, and many of his troops fraternized with the Red Guards.

While Kerensky had prevented a military coup, his power now depended to a great extent on the soviets, which bitterly opposed his determination to continue the war. In the meantime, Bolshevik strength grew rapidly. Lenin's program of "peace, land, and bread" presented a compelling alternative to the provisional government's promises, and his slogan of "all power to the soviets" was a shrewd appeal for popular support. In late Octo-

⊡ The Bolshevik Strategy ⊡

Lenin's revolutionary theories formed the basis for Bolshevik action during the Russian upheaval of 1917. Here Lenin describes the need for a "professional" revolutionary vanguard.

I assert: (1) that no revolutionary movement can endure without a stable organization of leaders maintaining continuity; (2) that the broader the popular mass drawn spontaneously into the struggle, which forms the basis of the movement and participates in it, the more urgent the need for such an organization, and the more solid this organization must be (for it is much easier for all sorts of demagogues to sidetrack the more backward sections of the masses); (3) that such an organization must consist chiefly of people professionally engaged in revolutionary activity; (4) that in an autocratic state, the more we confine the membership of such an organization to people who are professionally engaged in revolutionary activity and who have been professionally trained in the art of combatting the political police, the more difficult will it be to unearth the organization; and (5) the greater will be the number of people from the working class and from the other social classes who will be able to join the movement and perform active work in it.

Source: V. I. Lenin, "What Is to Be Done?" in D. N. Jacobs, ed., *From Marx to Mao and Marchais* (New York: Longman, 1979), p. 45.

ber, as the Bolsheviks gained a majority in the Petrograd soviet as well as in Moscow, Lenin secretly returned to Russia.

With Trotsky, now freed from imprisonment, Lenin planned the seizure of power. Trotsky (1879–1940), born Lev Bronstein, was a brilliant intellectual and strategist who had spent some of his own political exile in the United States. He was the real architect of the Bolshevik coup. He secured control of military power by persuading the Petrograd soviet, which he headed, to appoint him commander of a military revolutionary committee to protect the city. After winning over the soldiers in the Petrograd garrison, his forces captured the telephone exchange, railroad and electric stations, bridges, and government buildings on the night of November 6. Sailors from the Kronstadt naval base brought the cruiser *Aurora* up the Neva River to within firing range of the Winter Palace, seat of the provisional government. The Bolshevik majority in the Congress of Soviets, meeting the next morning in Petrograd, proclaimed that power was now in the hands of the soviets and announced that Lenin was the head of the new government. On November 8, Kerensky fled the city. With almost no bloodshed, the Bolsheviks had won control of Russia. Holding that power, however, would prove a formidable task.

Lenin and Trotsky planned the Bolshevik revolution and won the Russian civil war. They are shown here in a doctored photo. [Bettmann Archive]

Building the Communist State

The seizure of Petrograd and the overthrow of the Kerensky government by no means guaranteed the Bolsheviks a lasting victory. Lenin still had to extend his control to the rest of the country. Setting up an enduring Bolshevik regime would require three more years of bitter struggle amid civil war, political opposition from anti-Bolshevik groups, and invasion by the troops of 14 foreign countries.

Lenin's immediate strategy was to achieve popular

support and a measure of stability by ending war, hunger, and peasant unrest. The Social Revolutionaries had the largest following among Russia's landless rural population, but Lenin stole their thunder by declaring the nationalization of all land and its distribution to the peasants. Although in theory the soviets were to keep the large estates intact as collective farms, in practice the peasants, who were already seizing land on their own initiative, were permitted to keep what they had taken. As revolutionary as these actions were, they failed to solve the hunger crisis. Small property holders jealously withheld their crops from urban consumers. Hoarding increased as a result of the civil war and poor harvests; for years starvation plagued millions.

The promise of peace proved costly to keep. The Germans now sensed victory in the east. German peace terms, however, were so harsh that some Bolshevik leaders, including Trotsky and Nicolai Bukharin, wanted to continue the war as a revolutionary struggle. Lenin's insistence on ending the hostilities ultimately prevailed, and on March 15, 1918, his representatives signed the Treaty of Brest-Litovsk. It ceded to Germany all its wartime conquests as well as eastern Poland, the Ukraine, and the formerly Russian areas of Finland, Estonia, Latvia, and Lithuania. Not until the Nazi-Soviet Pact of 1939 would Russia recover its 1914 frontiers, but the treaty provided Lenin with the much needed opportunity to solidify his authority. Lenin quieted opposition to it within the Communist party—the new official name the Bolsheviks adopted in March 1918—by arguing that the spread of "world revolution" into western Europe would eventually render Russia's losses meaningless.

Despite the euphoria that had greeted the reforms and promises of the provisional government following the March revolution, political liberalism had shallow soil in which to grow. Initially the revolutionaries took democracy far beyond conventional practice, with popular choice entering virtually every area of life. In the soviets a kind of direct democracy prevailed, while in army units soldiers elected officers and in the factories workers organized management councils. Yet there was no tradition of self-government above the village level in Russia. The revolution left a vacuum that inexperienced local councils of semiliterate peasants could hardly fill. Into this void Lenin moved his disciplined organization after the November revolution. Yet his own forces were small and lacked administrative experience.

Lenin's victory destroyed the possibility of democratic government. The Bolsheviks had never pretended to value democracy, and Lenin's program demanded peace and economic well-being, not freedom in the traditional Western sense. He knew, too, that after the distribution of land, universal suffrage would produce a majority representing small landowners. In fact, when the elections for a constituent assembly previously scheduled by the provisional government were held in late

November, the Social Revolutionaries won nearly twice as many delegates as the Bolsheviks. When the assembly met in January 1918, Lenin swiftly demonstrated his intention to create a Marxist-style "dictatorship of the proletariat," disbanding the assembly after only one day of deliberation. For several months Lenin governed in a coalition with left-wing Social Revolutionaries, but when the latter withdrew their support in June, Russia came under one-party rule that retained power until 1991.

During 1918 and 1919 the Bolsheviks began to implement their political and economic policies. Grassroots government yielded to centralized state administration by the Communist party, soldiers' councils were replaced by appointed officers, and factory committees gave way to trade unions controlled by party officials. In the countryside previously independent peasants now had to deliver their "surplus" produce to hungry urban populations. Advances toward self-determination for ethnic minorities and border peoples were eventually replaced by Russian-dominated centralization thinly disguised as a federal state. Lenin believed this system of "war communism" to be necessary under the dual pressure of civil war and foreign invasion. The pressing need for industrial production was not being met by the factory committees, which often lacked necessary technical skills and sometimes resisted state efforts to coordinate labor. Moreover, Lenin saw industrial cartelization as the basis of a socialist economy. Each branch of industry was therefore nationalized and centralized into state trusts. By 1920 about 90 of these trusts existed, all subordinated to the Supreme Council of National Economy, which attempted to direct industrial production throughout the country.

Revolution Under Siege

Early Bolshevik policies and Leninist authoritarianism were shaped in large part by the return of war and strife to Russian soil. The infant Communist regime had to fight for its survival against an array of domestic and foreign enemies: counterrevolutionary legions made up of conservatives, moderates, and even some Social Revolutionaries, known collectively as the White Army; border nationalities seeking independence from Russia; more than 100,000 troops from 14 foreign nations, including the United States, Britain, France, and Japan; and peasants waging a so-called green revolution against the Reds who requisitioned their crops. Between 1918 and November 1920 the Red Army defended Russia's borders in a desperate effort to save the Communist regime.

A combination of military and ideological motives led to the Allied invasion of Russia. The Entente Powers had supported Kerensky's government in order to bolster the war on the eastern front. Lenin's demands for a sepa-

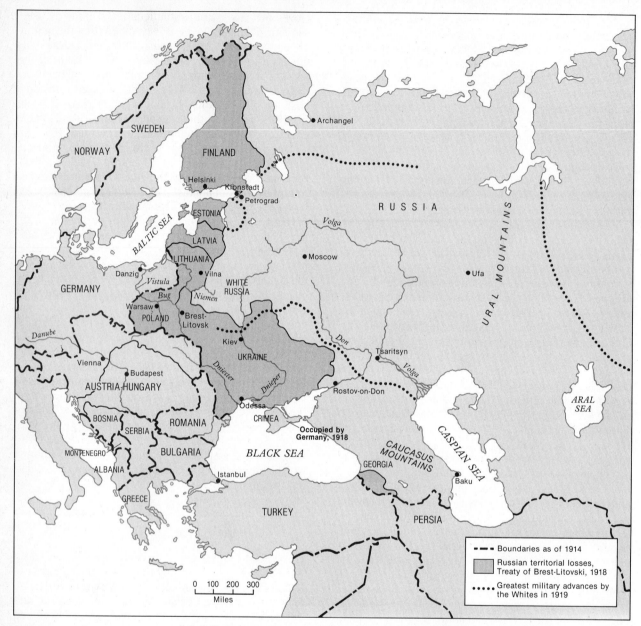

***36.1** Russia in War and Revolution, 1917–1921*

rate peace aroused Allied suspicion that he was a German agent, but they failed to convince the Bolsheviks to reject the German peace terms. With their troops no longer tied down on the Russian front, the Germans broke through Allied lines in the west and marched to a position less than 40 miles from Paris. The German advance was repulsed, but the Allies, fearful that the Bolshevik revolution might spread to their own war-weary population, determined on a preemptive strike.

In June 1918 the Allies decided on military intervention. The French and British sent nearly 24,000 soldiers

to Murmansk and Archangel. On July 16 the Bolsheviks, worried that the Allies might try to liberate the tsar, executed the entire royal family. In Siberia, 40,000 Czech prisoners of war, formerly Austro-Hungarian conscripts, revolted against their Russian guards and commandeered the trans-Siberian railroad in an attempt to reach their homeland, where they hoped to fight for Czech independence. To assist the Czech legion, President Wilson approved a landing at Vladivostok, where 72,000 Japanese and 8,000 American troops eventually arrived. During the winter of 1918–1919 two British divisions seized the rail lines that connected the Black and Caspian seas along the oil-rich Russo-Turkish border. French units, joined by Greek forces, also landed at Odessa on the Ukraine's Black Sea coast.

Allied soldiers remained in Russia after the armistice was signed in November, giving support to the White Army. Against difficult odds, the Bolsheviks possessed a number of advantages. Party discipline and Lenin's leadership kept their forces together while the White Army factions, united only in their opposition to the Communists, were rent with political division. The Bolsheviks also controlled the Russian heartland and could wage war along interior lines, whereas their enemies were scattered along the periphery. Moreover, the Red Army generally had the support of the peasants, who knew the Bolsheviks would never restore the power of the large landowners. Finally, in ethnically Russian areas Bolshevik propagandists shrewdly combined revolutionary rhetoric with a patriotic appeal in the face of foreign invasion.

Bolshevik military operations were commanded by Leon Trotsky, whose abilities as a speaker and Marxist theoretician were matched by brilliant organizational talent. Trotsky raised, equipped, trained, and directed the Red Army, rushing from one front to another in a special train outfitted as a mobile headquarters. He kept troop morale high by means of political propagandists, called commissars, who were attached to Red Army units. His forces repulsed assaults from Siberia, the Ukraine, and the newly independent state of Poland. Late in 1920, Allied ships evacuated more than 100,000 soldiers from Odessa. By the end of the struggle the Bolsheviks had recovered much of the old imperial lands on the western front, except for the Baltic states and the territory lost to Romania and the new states of Czechoslovakia and Poland. With the civil war won, they also regained control over Azerbaijan, Russian Armenia, and Georgia, which separatist forces had threatened to make independent. These and other nominally autonomous states were eventually incorporated into the Union of Soviet Socialist Republics (USSR), established in December 1922. After two years of desperate fighting against invasion, civil war, and famine, the Communist regime was secure but exhausted.

❦

ALEXANDRA KOLLONTAI AND THE WOMEN'S QUESTION

In Russia, as elsewhere in Europe, women had long played an important role in radical movements. Daring women such as Vera Zasulich, who assassinated a cruel provincial governor in 1878, and Olga Liubatovich, who was exiled in Siberia and conspired in St. Petersburg, were but two of the many Russian women active in the revolutionary underground. Others, such as Angelica

---

◈ What Price Revolution? ◈

The great loss of human life during the Russian Revolution and the civil war, criticized by the enemies of bolshevism, was defended by Leon Trotsky as a necessary price for great historical change.

But the misfortunes which have overwhelmed living people? The fire and bloodshed of civil war? Do the consequences of a revolution justify the sacrifices it involves? The question is teleological and therefore fruitless. It would be as well to ask in the face of the difficulties and griefs of personal existence: Is it worth while to be born? Melancholy reflections have not so far, however, prevented people from bearing or being born. Even in the present epoch of intolerable misfortune only a small percentage of the population of our planet resorts to suicide. But the people are seeking the way out of their unbearable difficulties in revolution.

Is it not remarkable that those who talk most indignantly about the victims of social revolutions are usually the very ones who, if not directly responsible for the victims of the world war, prepared and glorified them, or at least accepted them? It is our turn to ask: did the war justify itself? What has it given us? What has it taught?

Source: L. Trotsky, *The Russian Revolution* (Garden City, N.Y.: Anchor/Doubleday, 1959), p. 483. (Originally published in 1930.)

Balabanoff and Anna Kulischiov, achieved prominence as exiled socialist militants, Balabanoff as secretary to the Second International and Kulischiov as a leader of the Italian socialist women's movement. The career of Alexandra Kollontai (1872–1952) illustrates both the role of women in the anti-tsarist movement and the tense relationship between women's liberation and the Bolshevik revolution.

Born into a wealthy landowning family as Alexandra Domontovich, she married a young engineer but after three years left her husband, who viewed her sympathies for the working class as willful defiance of his authority. After studying in Zurich, she returned to St. Petersburg and joined the Menshevik wing of the Social Democratic party. At the time of the 1905 revolution Kollontai recognized "how little our Party concerned itself with the fate of women of the working class and how meager was its interest in women's liberation." She also came to believe that liberation for women "could take place only as the result of the victory of a new social order and a different economic system."[2] Forced into exile because of her radical activities, she lived in western Europe and the United States from 1908 to 1917. In 1915 she broke with the Mensheviks over the war issue and began to correspond with Lenin, returning to Russia at the outbreak of revolution in March 1917.

As a member of the Bolshevik Central Committee, Kollontai supported Lenin's call for an armed uprising. After the November coup she was appointed commissar for social welfare in Lenin's cabinet. Within the party and the government she argued that the revolution would be betrayed unless it destroyed bourgeois moral standards and the authoritarian family. These ideas and her efforts to establish a state-supported system of maternity and infant care drew sharp criticism from her male comrades, who accused her of wanting to "nationalize" Russian women. Her position was undermined when she joined the anti-Leninist faction and pushed to democratize the Communist party through direct worker participation in policymaking. In March 1918 she resigned from the government and later joined the Workers' Opposition movement. Following the civil war, during which she worked as a propagandist with the Red Army in the Ukraine, Kollontai bitterly criticized the new marriage laws established by the Bolshevik regime, which she felt maintained inequality, and demanded full rights for women. Her controversial ideas on women's liberation and sexual freedom were explained in *The New Morality and the Working Class* (1920), the publication of which alienated her still further from the Communist leadership. Although Kollontai's advocacy of sexual relationships based on affection and equality rather than on socially imposed codes offended her more conservative comrades, many others—especially young urban middle-class Russians and intellectuals—agreed.

An early Bolshevik and an ardent feminist, Alexandra Kollontai took part in the first stages of Lenin's government. [Novosti/Sovfoto]

When Joseph Stalin became general secretary of the Communist party in 1922, the Workers' Opposition movement was purged and Kollontai's lover, Alexander Shylapnikov, was killed. Kollontai herself was virtually banished for the next two decades: from 1924 until her retirement in 1945 she served as Russian ambassador to Norway, Mexico, and Sweden and as a representative to the League of Nations. In her last lonely years Kollontai suffered from the knowledge that the revolution she had helped make had fallen short of her hopes.

Stalin Versus Trotsky: The Struggle for Power

Even without the military struggles of the 1918–1920 period, chaotic economic and social conditions would have threatened the Bolshevik regime. Millions of Russians had died as a result of war, epidemics, and famine. Cities and villages lay in ruin, and the transportation system barely functioned. A lack of managers, technicians, and raw materials had brought factories to a virtual standstill, and industrial production had fallen to about 20 percent of its prewar level. Hoarding and drought continued to cause severe food shortages. In the face of these problems, popular support for the Bolsheviks eroded. A wave of peasant uprisings and factory strikes preceded a military revolt, in March 1921, when sailors at the Kronstadt naval base, once a pro-Bolshevik bastion, seized the Winter Palace and proclaimed a "third revolution" against Lenin's regime. The Red Army crushed the movement with much bloodshed, and Lenin knew he had to act swiftly to restore control.

In March 1921, Lenin announced the New Economic Plan (NEP), a retreat from Marxist orthodoxy. The NEP permitted a degree of private enterprise in small industries and the retail trade, ended food requisitioning, and allowed peasants to sell their produce on the open market after paying a small tax. The state, however, continued to own and operate major industries, banking, and transportation and to control wholesale and foreign trade. The NEP slowly achieved success, and by 1928 agricultural and industrial production had returned to prewar levels. The plan, much debated among Communist leaders, resulted in the revival of the rural middle class of kulaks ("large peasants") that ran counter to the Marxist goal of a classless society. The kulaks leased or owned large parcels of land, which they farmed with hired laborers, and raised crops for the market.

As long as Lenin lived, he and the Old Bolsheviks—the group that had made the revolution in 1917—retained control of the Communist party, but he was concerned over the increasing number of bureaucratic careerists entering its ranks. The Soviet constitution of 1923 created the All-Union Congress of Soviets, a representative body in which the highest power theoretically resided. The Congress—its name was changed to the Supreme Soviet in 1936—elected the Council of People's Commissars (changed to the Council of Ministers in 1946), the Executive Committee, and the small Presidium, which acted for the Congress between sessions. In reality, however, the Communist party ran the country through its Central Committee, composed of just under 50 members, which met several times each year. The Central Committee in turn elected the ten-member Politburo, which convened weekly and chose a secretariat of from one to three members to perform executive duties.

In 1922 two strokes removed Lenin from day-to-day leadership. Trotsky appeared to be the logical choice to succeed Lenin, but party members began to unite against him. A temporary troika, or three-member leadership, emerged late in 1922 to carry on Lenin's work, consisting of Grigori Zinoviev, party leader in Petrograd (later named Leningrad); Lev Kamenev, the Communist boss of Moscow; and Joseph Stalin, general secretary of the party and the least known of the three.

Tough, clever, and power-hungry, Stalin (1879–1953) was the only Old Bolshevik of lower-class origin. Born Joseph Djugashvili in the province of Georgia, he was the son of a shoemaker and the grandson of serfs. After being expelled from a theological seminary, he joined the Bolshevik movement at the turn of the century and took the underground name of Stalin, meaning "man of steel." He performed some of the party's most reprehensible tasks, including the robbing of treasury transports to acquire operating funds. Hardened in the tsar's prisons and Siberian exile, Stalin possessed none of the broader culture of his colleagues, most of whom had lived in western Europe during the worst years of tsarist repression. As general secretary he dispensed patronage to build a personal following and came to that office at a time when a new generation of bureaucrats was developing within the party.

Lenin recognized Stalin's power at the very time that the other Old Bolsheviks were growing suspicious of Trotsky. After his second stroke in December 1922, Lenin began to consider the problem of succession. With the help of his wife and closest political assistant, Nadhezhda Krupskaya (1869–1939), he dictated a "testament" in which he reviewed the credentials of possible successors, chiefly Trotsky and Stalin. Although he seemed to favor Stalin, he expressed doubts as to whether Stalin knew how to use his power wisely. Less than two weeks later Lenin added a "codicil," or supplement, to these notes denouncing Stalin as "too rude" and advising the party to appoint someone "more tolerant, more loyal, more polite and more considerate to comrades, less capricious, etc."[3]

Though Lenin had always held reservations about Stalin, his opinion hardened when he learned that Stalin had tried to intimidate Krupskaya. Following Lenin's death early in 1924, the testament and the codicil were read before the party's Central Committee. That summer Krupskaya attempted to have the documents presented before the entire party congress, but Stalin managed to have only minor commissions hear them. Krupskaya survived Stalin's brutal purges and remained on the Central Committee for the rest of her life, but her husband's denunciations of the man who became the dictator of Soviet Russia went unpublished until after Stalin's death.

In 1924 Stalin, who was never known for his mastery of Marxist theory, put forward the novel concept of "socialism in one country." He argued that the Soviet Union could create the industrial economy necessary to sustain socialism without exporting revolution to the rest of Europe. Against this position Trotsky offered the doctrine of "permanent revolution," an unceasing struggle aimed at the elimination of capitalism everywhere. Stalin be-

THE RUSSIAN REVOLUTION AND THE WORLD

Events in Russia	Events abroad
Alexander II emancipates Russia's serfs (1861)	Lincoln's Emancipation Proclamation in the United States (1863)
	Scramble for Africa (1870–1914)
Alexander II assassinated (1881)	Congress of Berlin; Russian gains against Turkey partly annulled (1878)
Accession of Nicholas II (1894)	Franco-Russian Alliance (1894)
Revolution of 1905: tsar promises civil liberties and constitutional government	Russo-Japanese War (1904–1905)
First Duma convenes (1906)	
Reforms of Stolypin (1906–1911)	Instability in the Balkans (1908–1914)
	Revolution in China (1911)
Influence of Rasputin; massive strikes and shortages (1914–1917)	World War I; Russia incurs devastating casualties (1914–1917)
February 1917 revolution; tsar abdicates; Kerensky heads provisional government	United States enters war (April 1917)
October 1917 revolution; Lenin leads Bolshevik coup, leaves war (March 1918)	Allied armies invade Russia (March 1918); war ends in Allied victory (November 1918)
War communism (1918–1920); civil war and famine ravage Russia	Paris Peace Conference (1919)
	Chinese May 4 movement (1919); Gandhi begins nonviolent movement in India (1919)
Kronstadt mutiny; leftist opposition crushed (1921)	Jewish immigrants settle in Palestine (1920–1929)
New Economic Plan (1921–1927)	Fascist seizure of power in Italy (1922)
Lenin dies (1924); Stalin replaces him (1924–1929)	Mustapha Kemal takes power in Turkey (1923)
	Great Depression begins (1929)

lieved that the extension of communist revolution to all capitalist societies required resources that Russia did not have and meant continual armed strife with the West. Stalin eventually won the struggle with Trotsky because he secured control over the party apparatus and won the support of other party leaders. Even leftists such as Zinoviev and Kamenev, whose views corresponded more closely to the permanent revolution theory, feared Trotsky's ambitions, and in 1925 they helped the supposedly safer Stalin strip Trotsky of his position as war commissar. In 1929 Trotsky fled into exile, where, after years of opposition to Stalin's regime that won an often sympathetic hearing from Western socialists, he was murdered in Mexico by a Soviet agent in 1940.

Stalin's skill at maneuvering was consummate. Having used the support of the party's left to weaken Trotsky, he then joined forces with Nicolai Bukharin, leader of the right. Together they removed Stalin's opponents, one by one, from the Central Committee while Stalin increasingly controlled the smaller Politburo. He then turned against his former allies. After the failure of a communist uprising in Bulgaria in 1925, he secured the dismissal of Zinoviev as head of the Communist International and then destroyed Kamenev's authority by having the Moscow party apparatus placed in the hands of the Politburo. In 1928, having crushed the party's left wing, Stalin broke with the right. He did this by favoring the collectivization of agriculture and forced industrialization, positions long associated with the left. When Bukharin opposed these policies, Stalin drove him from office. With Trotsky in exile and the old-guard Bolsheviks outmaneuvered, Stalin emerged as the unchallenged master of the Soviet state.

The Comintern: Russia Between East and West

Stalin's formula for one-country socialism rejected not only Trotsky's insistence on the need for continuing revolution but Lenin's legacy as well. In March 1919, Lenin had invited the world's socialist leaders to Moscow to create a new global organization known as the Communist International, or Comintern. The purpose of this so-called Third International was to convert the Russian Revolution into a world struggle. The instability of the immediate postwar period, marked by the fall of the monarchies in Austria-Hungary and Germany, riots in China, India, and Japan, the seizure of factories by Italian workers, and the establishment of a communist regime in Hungary under Béla Kun, gave Comintern leaders hope, for they saw in such events proof that capitalism and imperialism were about to collapse everywhere. Their optimism was, however, premature, for except in the Soviet puppet state of Mongolia, communism failed to seize permanent power beyond Russia. The Comintern sent agents to every corner of the world to organize and strengthen indigenous communist movements, but in the long run Stalin's policies and the organization's internal limitations hampered its effectiveness.

The Comintern had a divisive impact on the European left. Demanding disciplined followers among the socialists in other countries, Lenin established 21 conditions for foreign parties seeking membership in the Comintern. These included purging themselves of reformists, restructuring their organizations along Bolshevik lines, supporting all communist governments, preparing for the seizure of power in their own countries, and fighting social democrats as well as capitalists. Lenin believed that the moment for world revolution had arrived, but many Western socialist leaders were reluctant to gamble their previous gains on the chance of revolution. Social democrats preferred to achieve socialism without resorting to dictatorship. The result was that socialist parties outside the USSR split into two camps between 1920 and 1921, with most rejecting Lenin's demands in favor of achieving socialism through parliamentary reform. Lenin accused them of wasting a historic opportunity.

Despite these divisions, the Comintern caused panic in Western countries. In the United States a "Red scare" in 1919 led to a government witch-hunt for radicals of every kind. In Europe many frightened members of the middle class abandoned liberalism in favor of fascism and other anti-Communist movements.

The hysteria the Comintern aroused in the West was ironic in view of the fact that revolutionary communism was so unsuccessful elsewhere in the world. The early socialists were essentially Eurocentric in outlook, a characteristic derived in part from Marx's belief that revolution was likely only in advanced capitalist societies. "The founders of Marxism," noted one scholar, "judged non-European civilizations through the prism of Euro-

◉ The Comintern: East Versus West ◉

At the Congress of the Peoples of the East, called by the Communist International in 1920, the representatives of non-Western countries complained bitterly that their concerns were being ignored by Russian leaders. One of the most vocal critics was M. N. Roy, an Indian Communist, who argued that the official report on colonial questions maintained that the fate of the revolutionary movement in Europe depended entirely on the course of the revolution in the East.

Without the victory of the revolution in the Eastern countries, the Communist movement in the West would come to nothing. . . . This being so, it is essential that we divert our energies into developing and elevating the revolutionary movement in the East and accept as our fundamental thesis that the fate of world Communism depends on the victory of Communism in the East.

Here is Lenin's response to Roy's arguments.

Comrade Roy goes too far when he asserts that the fate of the West depends exclusively on the degree of development and the strength of the revolutionary movement in the Eastern countries. In spite of the fact that the proletariat in India numbers five million and there are 37 million landless peasants, the Indian Communists have not yet succeeded in creating a Communist Party in their country. This fact alone shows that Comrade Roy's views are to a large extent unfounded.

Source: F. Claudin, *The Communist Movement: From Comintern to Cominform*, vol. 1, trans. B. Pearce (New York: Monthly Review Press, 1975), pp. 247–248.

pean civilization. The road to progress for the backward peoples they saw as the road of Europeanization, not only from the socio-economic standpoint but also culturally."[4]

Comintern leaders gave little attention to the needs and aspirations of non-Western communists. At the third congress of the Comintern in 1921, the Indian Marxist M. N. Roy attacked the meeting for allowing him only five minutes to report on revolutionary activities in the subcontinent. The next year the Indonesian communist Tan Malaka condemned the Comintern for opposing the pan-Islamic movement, which he said had isolated his party from the Muslim peasants of his country. At the 1924 congress Mexican representatives warned Soviet leaders that they were ignoring potential allies in Latin America, while Sen Katayama of the Japanese Communist party assailed Zinoviev for hardly mentioning the Eastern question. Ho Chi Minh (1890–1969), the Vietnamese activist, complained bitterly that westerners were ignoring revolutionaries in colonial areas and misunderstood the liberation movements.

When the Comintern did support revolutionary activities in the Third World, its approach reflected Soviet concerns. In 1924 the Comintern sent the able but inexperienced Michael Borodin to China to establish a Communist military college at Whampoa, near Canton. The principal of the college was young Chiang Kai-shek (1887–1975), recently returned from a visit to Russia. Despite Chiang's involvement in the Chinese Nationalist party (Kuomintang) and his close ties to bankers, the Comintern ordered the Chinese Communists to integrate themselves into the Kuomintang. On April 12, 1927, Chiang's troops, aided by gangs hired by Shanghai businessmen, launched a surprise attack against Borodin, the Communists, and the trade unions, murdering thousands and imprisoning many more. Nevertheless, for a time the Comintern attempted to mend the ill-fated alliance with the Kuomintang.

Of all the factors that undermined the Comintern, none was more important than Stalin's rise to power. His one-country socialism was essentially a defensive strategy designed to protect the Soviet state. His concern lest revolutionary activities elsewhere endanger the USSR resulted in his using the Comintern only to keep foreign Communist leaders in line. Under Stalin the Communist International became an anachronism, and in a gesture to antifascist unity during World War II, he disbanded it in 1943.

The inability of the Comintern to establish Communist regimes beyond the Soviet Union should not obscure the profound impact of the Russian Revolution. The Bolshevik seizure of power shook the West to its foundations and altered international relations. Stalin was shortsighted only in failing to recognize the Russian Revolution as the first of a series of momentous upheavals that would transform the world.

China: Rebels, Warlords, and Patriots

In contrast to the Russian Revolution, the upheaval in China began almost tentatively, then sputtered and apparently died, and finally broke out in full force only after nearly 40 years of false starts and setbacks. In China too there were perhaps revolutionary implications in the Taiping Rebellion of 1850–1864. All revolutions have their antecedents, but China's was particularly slow in the making. China had first to develop a national political consciousness and a political organization that could pursue revolutionary change, both of which were lacking in its historical experience. The Chinese were accustomed to the overthrow of dynasties grown old and ineffective and their replacement by a new group, which would then administer the traditional system more successfully. The system itself, however, enshrined by the Mandate of Heaven, appeared to be beyond challenge.

But by the twentieth century the traditional model had lost its ability to deal with the now overwhelming problems of mass poverty, technological backwardness, and political weakness. These problems were vividly symbolized by China's helplessness in the face of the imperial powers of the West. It was to take another century to create a new set of solutions and a political structure to pursue them. Meanwhile, China's material welfare and ancient pride continued to suffer.

The Ch'ing dynasty collapsed in 1911, with the gentlest of shoves from a small and poorly organized group of revolutionaries (see Chapter 34). The Ch'ing was widely seen as a failure and was equally resented as an alien dynasty of conquest. Most of the revolutionary support rested on one or both of these grounds rather than on the still only half-formed plans for change. The end of Manchu rule is considered a revolution because the government was overthrown in an armed uprising by people who called themselves revolutionaries and had some new and radical ideas. But they were too few and too politically inexperienced to establish an effective government of their own, and to make matters worse, they were split into factions. The most important revolutionary organization was the Kuomintang, founded around the turn of the century and led by Sun Yat-sen (1866–1925), an idealist with great personal charisma but little sense of practical politics.

Sun Yat-sen and the 1911 Revolution

Sun was born to a peasant family near Canton (Gwangzhou), traditionally a hotbed of separatism and political ferment. At the age of 13, like many Cantonese, he emigrated, joining his older brother in Honolulu, where he went to a church boarding school and became a Christian. At 16 he returned to study in Hong Kong and finished a medical degree there in 1892 at a British mission hospital. After practicing only briefly in Macao, he founded a secret society to overthrow the Manchus, drawing support from overseas Chinese. In 1895 he was forced to flee to Japan, from where he made repeated trips to build Chinese contacts in the United States, Britain, and Hawaii. Other radical leaders and groups in China were also active, and several abortive attempts were made to seize power until an uprising at Wuhan in 1911 was joined by some troops among its garrison. Its successful defiance brought the fall of the imperial government. Sun returned from abroad and became the first president of the newly proclaimed republic. The last Ch'ing emperor, a 6-year-old boy named Pu Yi, abdicated early in 1912, marking the end of an imperial tradition more than 2,000 years old.

China was still hopelessly divided, and even Sun saw that he could not provide unity and strong central government. He agreed to step down in 1912 as president in favor of Yuan Shih-kai (Yuan Shikai, 1859–1916), a leading Ch'ing military man who had thrown his lot in with the republicans. Sun had earlier put together a set of guidelines for a new government called the Three Principles of the People. These were nationalism, democracy, and the people's livelihood, none of which was clearly defined. Nationalism in the modern sense was still a new idea to most Chinese, but they could at least make common cause against the foreign Manchu dynasty in the name of Chinese self-determination. Sun's notion of democracy was heavily indebted to Western models. It implied but did not spell out social and political equality, a notable departure in itself from the hierarchical forms of Confucianism. Democracy was to be assured by a constitution largely on an American pattern, while "livelihood"—a partial redistribution of wealth on behalf of the poorer peasantry—was to be achieved through tax reforms.

China was far from having the requisite basis for democracy, however. There were no true political parties as yet, only a variety of elite or intellectual groups, divided among themselves. When the new Kuomintang won national elections in 1913, Yuan, who had busily concentrated real power in his own hands, arranged the assassination of its leading organizer, Sung Chiao-jen (Song Jiaoren), who had pressed for constitutional government. Sun again fled to Japan, while Yuan tightened his grip as military dictator by force, bribery, and intimidation. In 1915 he had himself declared president for life and took to riding around in an armored car for fear of attack by frustrated revolutionaries. Meanwhile, he dared not confront Western and Japanese imperialism in China because he was dependent on foreigners who

looked to him as a strongman who could ensure order. The revolution had been betrayed.

Several southern and western provinces, where disgruntled military men and revolutionaries were active, broke away from Yuan's control. In 1916 he died suddenly after failing to have himself declared emperor. Political and ideological change had gone much too far to permit any return to such traditional forms, although there was still neither a consensus on what should succeed them nor a semblance of national unity. During the next 12 years China dissolved into virtual anarchy, divided among a number of regionally based warlords and other local military leaders. The Kuomintang and the early revolutionaries had a political ideology of sorts but no army; the warlords had armies but little or no program or party organization. Their troops marched around the countryside like a scourge on the peasants, while a bewildering variety of short-lived regimes or political cliques succeeded each other in Peking as the nominal government of China.

In 1917 Sun returned to Canton, formed a rival government, and began building a more effective political organization. He complained that trying to get the Chinese people to work together was like trying to make a rope out of sand. But although he tried to arouse mass support, he appealed mainly to intellectuals and the few Chinese who were as yet politically conscious. What began to spark Chinese nationalism more effectively were new Japanese encroachments on the nation's sovereignty and spontaneous popular protests against them.

The May Fourth Movement

Japan's Twenty-one Demands on China, issued in 1915, provoked immediate protests from patriotic Chinese, especially after Yuan accepted most of them. China joined the Allied side in World War I in 1917, sent labor battalions to the Western front, and hoped thus to get a hearing at the Paris peace conference. But Japan had secretly obtained Allied agreement to keep what it had taken in China's Shantung province, and it soon appeared that the lofty Western talk about self-determination did not apply to Asia.

When news broke that the warlord government in Peking had also signed secret agreements with Japan, mass demonstrations erupted on May 4, 1919. Chinese nationalism boiled over in what came to be called the May Fourth movement. A new and increasingly radical generation of students in government and mission schools and universities emerged, imbued with Western ideas and dedicated to building a new China. Student protesters beat up a pro-Japanese official and burned a cabinet minister's house. They went on to organize a union and to seek support among the large group of westernized businessmen, industrialists, and shopkeepers in the treaty ports. Strikes and boycotts of Japanese goods attracted widespread support. The cabinet resigned, and China refused to sign the Versailles Treaty.

The May Fourth movement stimulated renewed intellectual ferment as well, especially in Peking and Shanghai, where hundreds of new political and literary periodicals attacked traditional culture, deplored China's weakness, and advocated a variety of more or less radical solutions. The model of the Confucian scholar steeped in the classics gave way to that of "progressive" thinkers who wrote in the vernacular and tried to appeal not only to fellow scholars or intellectuals but to the people as a whole. Parental and family controls, arranged marriages, and the subjugation of women and the young became targets of attack. Women, especially students, played a prominent part in the May Fourth movement; they and their male colleagues urged full-scale female emancipation and an end to the rigidity of the traditional system as a whole. Lu Hsun (Lu Xun, 1881–1936), the greatest modern Chinese writer, voiced bitter indictments of the old society, whose supposed ideals of "benevolence" and "virtue," he alleged, were hypocritical masks for oppression and exploitation. Foreign imperialism was deeply resented, but such critics as Lu Hsun saw it as the result of China's weakness rather than as the cause. The May Fourth movement sought to build a new China in which modern Western ideas of democracy, equality, science, and nationalism would have a prominent place. The example of Meiji Japan was much admired, despite Japanese aggression against China. Like the Meiji leaders, China's new voices called for a clean slate and a national renewal that would incorporate Western ideas.

China and the Marxist Model

Among the Western concepts with particular appeal was Marxism, especially after the success of the Russian Revolution in 1917. Russia too had been a relatively undeveloped country that had embraced the Marxist-Leninist doctrine of centralized organization and collective effort. The Soviet formula seemed to fit China's circumstances, and Marx himself had suggested the relevance of his ideas to China many years earlier. In 1921 a small group of intellectuals, including Mao Tse-tung (Mao Zedong, 1893–1976), then a young student, founded the Chinese Communist party. Representatives from the Comintern helped the new party set up its organization. Soviet experience in political mobilization was also attractive to the Kuomintang, which, like the Communist party, remained largely without any mass base. Sun Yat-sen, still head of the Kuomintang, agreed to an alliance with the Communist party under Comintern direction. Sun's military assistant, Chiang Kai-shek,

was sent to Moscow to study Soviet methods. Party dictatorship was seen as necessary in the early stages of national unification, but Sun's Three Principles of the People and some form of representative government were reasserted as the ultimate goal. Sun may have been moving in the direction of socialism during his last years, but he died suddenly in 1925, and party control passed to Chiang Kai-shek. Chiang, despite his Soviet experience, was a far more conservative figure. With his military background, Chiang saw China's first priority as the achievement of national unity, through force if necessary. He began promisingly by mounting a military and political campaign with Communist help. Moving north from the Kuomintang base in Canton with his Communist allies to defeat the warlords, he established a new national capital at Nanking (Nanjing) in 1927.

The Nanking Decade

Chiang never completely eliminated warlord power in several of the outlying provinces, and although he dominated the Kuomintang, he led it far from its radical origins and progressively lost support. He tried to wipe out his Communist allies in a military coup in Shanghai in 1927 and then in a series of campaigns from 1930 to 1934. Some of the Communists, including Mao, were not in Shanghai in 1927 but in rural areas trying, without success, to organize peasant rebellion. Their small remaining forces retreated to a mountain stronghold in the southeast. Chiang's forces finally drove them out in 1934, forcing them into a retreat known as the Long March. An increasingly ragged column of Communists dodged ahead of Chiang's troops in a zigzag route across western China. The precariously few survivors finally reached a new base area in the remote and mountainous northwest in 1935, centered on Yenan (Yanan). Relatively safe from Chiang's army, they pursued land reform policies and slowly extended their support base in this border area, from which they were to emerge after World War II in 1945 to lead a victorious revolution.

The decade of the Nanking government between 1927 and 1937 was, despite its repressive aspects, a period of at least modest recovery and growth. Chiang permitted no genuine democracy, with the excuse that order and unity must come first. But at least the forms of constitutional government existed, and the economy underwent considerable modernization. Western-trained Chinese developed a central banking system, and a national rail network began to take shape. Industrial growth was still confined almost entirely to the treaty ports but increasingly under Chinese management.

These developments, however, were on a small scale compared to the needs of the country and had little or no impact on most of its predominantly peasant popu-

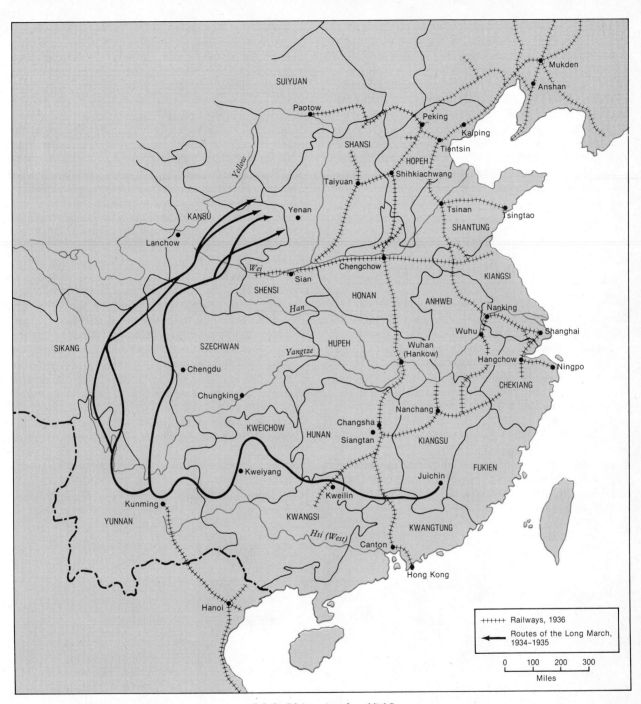

36.2 China in the 1930s

lation. Poverty grew in the countryside. The Kuomintang's political base had become largely a coalition of businessmen from the treaty ports and rural landlords, which sought to suppress agrarian reform and prevent the rise of a politicized peasantry. The Communists,

meanwhile, clung to their small base in the northwest, biding their time.

The situation was transformed by Japan's invasion of China. The Japanese, having reduced Manchuria to an economic colony, invaded it in 1931 and annexed it outright. They watched with concern as Chiang made progress toward national unification and began to build China's military strength. When the militarists who controlled Japan after 1930 saw their hopes for dominance in China and East Asia threatened, they launched a general assault on China in 1937, attacking first at Peking and then at Shanghai; later in the year they moved on to sack Nanking. With its capital in flames, the Kuomintang retreated up the Yangtze, largely to sit out the rest of the war, while the Communists in the north perfected a guerrilla strategy against the invaders and captured the leadership of Chinese nationalism.

✿
SHANGHAI:
THE MODEL TREATY PORT

While the Communists retreated to remote Yenan behind its mountain barriers and began to work out their program for a new China under the leadership of Mao, Shanghai remained a bastion of foreign privilege and Chinese collaborators. But it also harbored the growing group of Chinese dissidents, radicals, and revolutionaries who lived there under the protection of foreign law. Chinese police could not pursue suspects in the foreign settlements, which were ruled by a foreign-dominated municipal council with its own police. The Chinese Communist party had been founded there in 1921 for that reason, by a small group of revolutionaries and writers, part of the much larger number of political refugees living in the city, many of whom were periodically hounded

or captured and executed by the Kuomintang secret police. Chiang Kai-shek's military coup in 1927 killed many of them and drove some of the survivors out, but many remained underground and continued to produce literary and political magazines with titles like *New China, New Youth*, and *New Dawn*, which were avidly read by intellectuals in the rest of China.

After Shanghai passed Peking as China's biggest city about 1910, it became the country's chief center of literature, publishing, and cultural and political ferment. The May Fourth movement spread immediately from Peking to Shanghai; student organizers persuaded many Shanghai merchants to boycott Japanese, and later British, goods. Shanghai joined Peking as a major base for the New Culture movement, sometimes called the Chinese Renaissance, and its efforts to remake Chinese society. Lu Hsun and many other New Culture writers lived in Shanghai.

At the same time, Shanghai remained by far the largest port and commercial center in China, through which over half its foreign trade passed. It also housed over half the country's modern industry. Chinese entrepreneurs, both traditional and westernized, competed and collaborated with foreigners in trade, banking, and manufacturing, and many of them adopted a Western style of living. The foreign settlements at Shanghai were replicas of the modern Western city and looked physically much like Manchester or Chicago. The muddy foreshores of the Huangpu River, a Yangtze tributary that ran along one edge of the city and constituted the harbor, were covered in the nineteenth century by an embankment known as the Bund. It became Shanghai's main thoroughfare, lined with imposing Western banks

Cosmopolitanism in Shanghai, 1933: (from left) the American journalist Agnes Smedley, the playwright George Bernard Shaw, Madame Sun Yat-sen, Ts'ai Yuan-p'ei (a leading intellectual), and Lu Hsun. Shaw was on a visit to China and is here being welcomed by the founders of the China League for Civil Rights. [Eastfoto/Sovfoto]

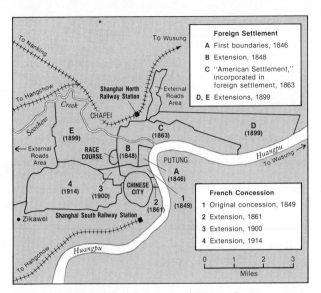

36.3 *The Growth of Shanghai*

and hotels. Nanking Road, the main shopping street, ran at right angles to it, away from the river, and extensive residential areas featured houses in the Western style. The foreign population peaked at about 60,000 in the 1930s, in a city which by then totaled about 4 million, many of whom lived outside the foreign concession areas in sprawling slums or in the walled Chinese city next to the concessions. But the commercial and industrial heart of Shanghai was largely run by foreigners (the Japanese had edged out the British as the majority in-

terest by the 1930s), and they built it in the Western image. They spoke of it as a beacon of "progress" in a vast Chinese sea of "backwardness."

Shanghai was described as "in China but not of it." The city brought silk, tea, and other agricultural goods from the Chinese hinterland for export in return for metals, machinery, and manufactured goods. Overall, however, Shanghai's economic example made relatively little impact, except in the other treaty ports. Elsewhere, it was largely rejected as alien and unsuited to China. The Communists labeled Chinese collaborators in Shanghai and the other treaty ports "running dogs" of the imperialists and were contemptuous of their departure from Chinese ways in favor of westernization.

Shanghai and the other treaty ports cut a deep wound of humiliation in the Chinese psyche, but they also offered an example of the kind of industrial and organizational strength without which China could not hope to chart its own destiny. Shanghai played a major role in stimulating the rise of modern Chinese nationalism and with it a determination to rid the country of its foreign oppressors. The foreign way was rejected, but its technological and industrial achievements were to be adapted to serve Chinese needs. The residents of Shanghai were, of course, the most affected by its example, and it was primarily there that China's modern revolution began. In the end, all foreign privileges were swept away by the revolution, but Shanghai remains China's biggest city and its most advanced industrial and technological center. Shanghai's modernity thus survived the expulsion of the foreigners and shaped basic aspects of the new China.

The Bund, Shanghai, 1986. Except for the vehicles, little has changed since Shanghai's heyday as a treaty port. Most of the buildings shown here date from the 1920s and 1930s. The Huangpu River and floating docks are on the right. [Rhoads Murphey]

India: Toward Freedom

In India the pressures for change were narrowly concentrated on winning freedom from colonial rule. Like China, India suffered from mass poverty, technological backwardness, and foreign domination. Indian nationalists tended to blame colonial oppression for their problems and to see the solution as getting rid of their British overlords. But as in China, a new national consciousness had first to be developed and a national political organization built. India had functioned throughout most of its past not as a national political unit but rather, like China, as a cultural tradition. It took time to get Indians or Chinese to work together for a common political goal. The Indian independence movement did respond to the need for attacking poverty and injustice and for pursuing modern development, but the immediate objective was political freedom. While its final achievement was in some ways a revolutionary change, most Indians saw no need to reject either their own tradition or aspects of the British colonial experience that could help the new nation adapt to the modern world.

India's progress toward freedom is in large part the story of the careers of two men, Mohandas K. Gandhi (1869–1948), often called the Mahatma, or "Great Soul," and Jawaharlal Nehru (1889–1964). Gandhi gave the independence movement what it had not yet had, mass appeal and a mass following. Nehru, in close cooperation with Gandhi, gave practical leadership but acknowledged the charismatic power of Gandhi's example. In the years after World War I the Congress party was transformed under Gandhi's direction from a small group of intellectuals into a truly national party representing a wide range of regional interest groups and mobilizing millions of Indians. Gandhi proved adept at using aspects of the Indian tradition as vehicles of protest against British imperialism and as rallying points for nationalist sentiment and organization.

Gandhi and Mass Action

The son of a minor official in commercial Gujarat, Gandhi followed the path of many upwardly mobile Indians in a rapidly changing society. At 19 he went to London to study law and there became thoroughly westernized. Soon after his return to India, he took a job with an Indian law firm in South Africa, where he spent the next 20 years defending Indian merchants and other immigrants against racist oppression and developing tactics of nonviolent protest and noncooperation.

Back home in 1914, he supported Indian participation in World War I on the Allied side, hoping, as many Indians did, that loyalty to Britain in its hour of need would be rewarded by self-government. The British secretary of state for India announced in 1917 that the government's policy was "the gradual development of self-

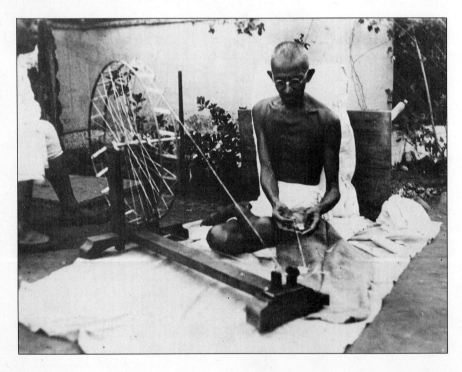

Gandhi the ascetic, spinning cotton yarn. He made it a point to spin 200 yards of yarn every day as a symbolic act, no matter how busy he was. [*L'Illustration*/Sygma]

◎ Gandhi's Message to the British ◎

Gandhi knew England and British culture well, in part from his time there as a student, and he had many British friends. In his Hind Swaraj *(Independent India), he addressed them.*

I admit you are my rulers. . . . I have no objection to your remaining in my country, but . . . you will have to remain as servants of the people. . . . We do not need any European cloth. We shall manage with articles produced and manufactured at home. . . . This is not said to you in arrogance. You have great military resources. . . . If we wanted to fight with you on your own ground, we should be unable to do so but [we must] cease to play the part of the ruled. . . . If you act contrary to our will, we will not help you; and without our help, we know that you cannot move one step forward. . . . You English who have come to India are not good specimens of the English nation, nor can we, almost half-anglicized Indians, be considered good specimens of the real Indian nation. If the English nation were to know all you have done, it would oppose many of your actions. . . . If you will search into your own scriptures, you will find that our demands are just. Only on condition of our demands being fully satisfied may you remain in India; and if you remain under those conditions, we shall learn several things from you and you will learn many from us. So doing we shall benefit each other and the world. But that will happen only when the root of our relationship is sunk in a religious soil.

Gandhi's ideas and personal qualities are well brought out in that passage. Nehru said the following of him in 1935.

I have never met any man more utterly honest, more transparently sincere, less given to egotism, self-conscious pride, opportunism, and ambition. . . . It has been the greatest privilege of our lives to work with him and under him for a great cause. To us he has represented the spirit and honor of India.

Sources: W. T. de Bary, ed., *Sources of Indian Tradition*, vol. 2 (New York: Columbia University Press, 1964), pp. 265–266; J. Nehru, "Mahatma Gandhi," *L'Europe* (February 1936), p. 21.

governing institutions" and an increase of Indians in responsible positions, but with the end of the war it became clear that such change would be painfully slow. Meanwhile, peasant economic suffering and distress among exploited industrial workers were growing. Gandhi traveled through India dressed as a poor peasant, reaching out to the masses and gaining a reputation for personal sanctity. But he also organized and led successful strikes and protest movements, using nonviolent methods with great effect. These and other signs of ferment appeared to members of the government as "seditious conspiracy." Repression followed, culminating in the Amritsar Massacre of 1919 when Indian troops under British command fired on an unarmed and peaceful crowd, leaving 400 dead.

From then on, more and more Indians came to see colonialism as unacceptable. The Congress party began to press for independence, and Gandhi's weapon of non-violent protest and noncooperation attracted more and more followers. Gandhi based his tactics on the ancient Hindu idea of *ahimsa*, or reverence for life, and drew on the redemptive power of love to convert even brutal opponents by its "soul force," or *satyagraha*. Traditional Indian values stressed the avoidance of conflict and the importance of self-control, seeking resolution through compromise and consensus. Nonviolent action was also a practical means for unarmed and powerless people to confront an oppressive state. As the American civil rights leader Martin Luther King, Jr., was later to demonstrate, it worked, both to build a dedicated following and to make its protest against injustice effective.

Gandhi organized boycotts of British imports, an action that caught the popular imagination, as it had in China, and helped build a larger following. He urged Indians to wear only their own cottons and wherever possible to spin and weave for themselves. The spinning wheel became a powerful nationalist symbol, linked also to 5,000 years of the country's history. Some of the Congress party's intellectual elite were scornful of Gandhi's methods, the style of a traditional sadhu (holy man) he adopted, his embrace of the poor, and his personal asceticism. But as both an astute politician and a saintly figure he attracted more support and got more results than the party's politicians had ever done. Gandhi gave the Indian people a sense of their own national identity and inspired them to action through traditional methods and symbols. He succeeded where others had failed in attracting Muslims, Sikhs, Christians, and agnostics to his cause, thus creating India's first truly national movement. He urged his fellow Indians to "get rid of our helplessness" and stand together. As Nehru said of him, "He has given us back our courage, and our pride."

Strikes, boycotts, and demonstrations spread in the early 1920s, but with millions of people now involved, Gandhi could not always guarantee nonviolence. Thousands were jailed, violence occurred on both sides, and in 1922 Gandhi was sentenced to prison for six years. He was released for medical reasons after two but did not resume political agitation until 1930, distressed that his nonviolent campaign had gone astray.

Hindus and Muslims

Meanwhile, the government, affected by Gandhi's popular movement, began to implement many of the reforms previously demanded by the Congress party. It greatly increased the number of Indian officers in the civil service and the army and moved toward the abolition of the tax on cotton. By 1937 all of the British Indian provinces had become self-governing, with legislatures elected by Indian voters. Nehru became mayor of his home city of Allahabad. During this time, rioting between Muslims and Hindus broke out in many areas, a symptom of the general atmosphere of turmoil but also of the efforts of special groups to ensure a better place for themselves in the independent India that was now clearly coming. Hindus and Muslims had worked together for many years in the Congress party. Now Muslims were warned that they had to safeguard their interests against the Hindu majority and that their own party, the Muslim League, led by Mohammed Ali Jinnah (1876–1948), was their only sure protector.

Jinnah pressed for a separate Muslim electorate to vote for candidates for the new posts being opened to Indian officeholders and Indian voters. Meanwhile, Nehru increased his organizational control of the Congress party, although he maintained his loyalty to Gandhi as India's spiritual and symbolic leader. Nehru insisted that the Congress party was the party of all Indians, including Muslims, and that the independence movement would be weakened by factionalism. He was proved tragically right.

The worldwide depression that began in 1929 bore heavily on India and greatly increased its economic distress. When Gandhi resumed political action in 1930, he chose as his targets the tax the government imposed on salt and the official ban on private saltmaking from the sea, arguing that the tax and the monopoly especially hurt the poor. He led a protest march on foot across India to the coast, where he purposely courted arrest by picking up a lump of natural salt and urging Indians to

◎ The Declaration of Indian Freedom ◎

Nehru, as president of the Congress party, declared January 26, 1930, a special day for the assertion of India's right to independence and issued this pledge, which was recited throughout India by millions of nationalists. Note the close similarity, quite conscious on Nehru's part, to the American Declaration of Independence.

We believe that it is the inalienable right of the Indian people, as of any other people, to have freedom and to enjoy the fruits of their toil and have the necessities of life, so that they may have full opportunities of growth. We believe also that if any government deprives a people of these rights and oppresses them, the people have a further right to alter it or abolish it. The British government in India has not only deprived the Indian people of their freedom, but has based itself on the exploitation of the masses, and has ruined India economically, politically, culturally, and spiritually.

Source: S. Wolpert, *A New History of India* (New York: Oxford University Press, 1982), pp. 314–315.

do likewise, as many thousands did. Gandhi, Nehru, and many others were jailed, and there was a wave of strikes. Gandhi had again stirred the conscience of the nation. After eight months in prison, he was released to meet with the viceroy in New Delhi. Gandhi agreed to discontinue civil disobedience; in return, the government sanctioned a movement to promote the use of Indian-made goods and invited Gandhi to a London conference on India later in 1931, together with Jinnah as a representative of the Muslims.

The conference ended in stalemate, and Gandhi was taken back to jail a week after his return. Boycotts, strikes, and violent demonstrations erupted again without Gandhi to restrain them. Meanwhile, economic distress deepened as world markets for India's exports shrank, and a new, more conservative viceroy was appointed. In England, however, popular and parliamentary opinion was turning more and more toward self-government for India. In 1935 a new constitution for India was announced, followed by nationwide elections in 1937 in which nearly 40 million Indians voted. Congress candidates swept the election, and the Muslim League did not even win most of the seats reserved for Muslims. The new constitution granted "safeguard" powers to the colonial government, but Congress ministries took over the provinces. Jinnah was outraged, and until his death he devoted his energies to building first an effective party for Muslims and finally a separate state. Nehru pointed out in reply that the Congress party was a national, not a special-interest, party, and that over 100,000 Muslims belonged to it.

By the outbreak of war in 1939, India was well along the road to self-government, but the war brought the proimperial Winston Churchill to power in Britain and postponed all talk of independence until fascism could be defeated in Europe and Asia. Indians were informed that they were automatically at war with Germany, and later with Italy and Japan. Neither the Congress party's representatives nor other Indian leaders were consulted. Nationalists once again felt betrayed. The Congress party's provincial ministries resigned in protest, leaving the political field to Jinnah and his Muslim League. A belated British offer, reduced at Churchill's insistence from independence to dominion status once the war was over, was rejected. Gandhi called it "a postdated check on a failing bank." He began a series of nonviolent campaigns, culminating in the "Quit India" movement of 1942, a slogan that was scrawled on walls all over the country and shouted at Britons. Nehru spent most of the war in jail, and Gandhi was confined periodically. Jinnah exploited their absence to press for a separate state for Muslims, to be called Pakistan. Independence would come too late to avoid the bloody tragedy of partition.

The British had begun in India as a small group of merchants competing with Arabs, Portuguese, Dutch, French, and Indians for a share of the trade and a few ports. Trading and maintaining the security of routes and warehouses led imperceptibly to more and more political influence and control in an India that lapsed into chaos after 1707. In time the lure of imperial glory captured the British imagination, but there was a kernel of truth in the observation some made that the Indian empire was acquired in "a fit of absence of mind." After 1874 Parliament began to supervise the governance of India, and by 1858 virtually the whole of the subcontinent had been brought under direct or indirect British control.

As early as the 1830s, most Britons agreed that India would one day be independent and that long-term British policy should prepare for this. Indians were quick to learn Western ideas and techniques wherever they saw them as useful, including business and industrial methods and British-style education, law, and parliamentary government. India is still governed today by institutions derived from Britain. The assimilation of British ways also greatly enhanced and accelerated the growth of the independence movement, which Indians saw as itself within the British tradition of political freedom.

If independence had come in 1907, when Parliament first declared it to be Britain's objective, or in the 1920s, when the policy was reaffirmed, it would have been possible to look back on the British era in India in relatively positive terms, though marred in the late eighteenth century by plunder and by the arrogance that led to the 1857 mutiny and its bitter aftermath. But however one assesses the balance or weighs it with other aspects of British rule, especially the failure to combat the fundamental modern Indian problem of poverty, Britain's clearest political error was its delay in giving India independence. Nevertheless, there is little bitterness over the colonial legacy in India, in contrast to much of the rest of Asia, which underwent a harsher rule under the Japanese, French, or Dutch. Many originally British institutions are now firmly a part of South Asian civilization. India has much in common today with other former British colonies, including the United States and Canada, as joint inheritors of many aspects of a common culture.

The Nationalist Awakening in the Middle East

The same nationalist forces that challenged European imperialism in India and China had an equally pronounced impact on the Middle East. Despite ethnic disunity and traditional theological differences within Islam, Arab consciousness had been stimulated by the common experience of Turkish and European exploitation. By the eve of World War I, independence movements, often used as an entering wedge for Western interests, had already dismembered large portions of the weakened Ottoman Empire. The Greeks and most of the Slavic peoples of the Balkans had either freed themselves from Turkish rule or had fallen under Austro-Hungarian control. In North Africa, France had taken Algeria and established protectorates in Morocco and Tunisia, Britain had imposed a sphere of influence over Egypt and the Sudan, and Italy had occupied Libya and Somalia. Besides Turkey proper, only Iraq, Syria, Palestine, and Arabia still remained within the Ottoman sphere.

The Mandate System and the Palestine Question

British success in arousing Arab hostility against the Turks during the war, together with the success of the British adventurer T. E. Lawrence in coordinating Arab resistance, had helped free most of the Middle East from Ottoman control by 1918. When the war was over, Faisal of Iraq and Lawrence lobbied the Paris peace conference for Arab rights, while Chaim Weizmann, who had succeeded Theodor Herzl as the leader of the Zionist movement, continued to push for the creation of a Jewish state. Neither party succeeded. After Faisal's appeals were rejected, an Arab congress declared him ruler of Syria, Palestine, and Lebanon.

While Faisal and Lawrence were in Paris, Abdul-Aziz ibn-Saud took to the deserts with his troops, extending his control over central Arabia. In 1925 he finally forced Hussein to abdicate as ruler of the Hejaz, which he united with his own Nejd sultanate. The British quickly recognized these conquests, and in 1932 ibn-Saud formally changed the name of his realm to the kingdom of Saudi Arabia. Vast oil deposits were soon discovered, and ibn-Saud's hereditary absolute monarchy eventually grew wealthy through the concessions granted to Western oil companies.

Although the Saudi dynasty was successful in Arabia, Arab nationalism continued to be frustrated elsewhere. Faisal's rule over Syria was short-lived, for in 1920 the Allies tacitly recognized the terms of the Sykes-Picot Agreement by approving the League of Nations mandate system, and Turkish control formally gave way to Western domination. The French ejected Faisal from Syria, engendering bitter resistance from the Arab population, and created Lebanon as a separate mandate. In 1926 Lebanon was made a republic, with borders similar to those of the now independent state. The roads, buildings, and irrigation systems constructed under French occupation did not make up for the suppression of civil liberties and the divisive efforts to gain the allegiance of the Christian Arabs of Lebanon. The Lebanon mandate had a rich religious diversity, for in ancient times it had been a place of refuge for religious sects of all kinds.

The Maronite Christians, a Roman Catholic group that followed Eastern Orthodox rites, with roots that went back to the seventh century, comprised about 40 percent of the population; Muslims of various sects made up the bulk of the remaining inhabitants. When the French eventually evacuated the area after World War II, they left behind a legacy of deep hostility.

The British were more successful in their mandate areas. Following an Iraqi rebellion in 1920, which they put down with much bloodshed, they made the popular Faisal king of Iraq, although they continued to run his financial and military affairs for another decade and supervised the creation of a constitutional monarchy. In 1922 Britain granted nominal independence to Egypt but refused to withdraw its troops from the country, and it followed a similar path in Iraq, where independence was recognized in 1930 in exchange for a military alliance that maintained British influence there. Nor did the discovery of rich oil fields in Iraq benefit the population of the region, for foreign companies secured lucrative concessions, further enflaming Arab resentment against the West.

The Palestine problem remained another source of anti-Western hostility as well as a cause of regional unrest. Britain's contradictory policies in the Middle East satisfied neither Arab nor Jewish demands, and throughout the interwar period British governments continued to shift between the two. Arab riots erupted in Palestine immediately after the creation of the British mandate over the area, prompting London to issue assurances that the Balfour Declaration would not be implemented in a way that would damage Arab interests. Yet British statesmen agreed with the Zionist position that the anguished history of the Jews made the creation of an independent Jewish homeland in Palestine a moral necessity. The Jewish community there—the Yishuv—had had a nearly uninterrupted residence since biblical times. It increased as a result of Zionist efforts in the late nineteenth century. By 1919 Jews in the mandate numbered around 60,000, or less than 10 percent of the population. In the early 1920s Britain permitted many Jews to join the Yishuv; by 1939 it had grown to 450,000, almost a third of the total.

Serious violence against Jews, provoked in part by aggressive settlement and the exclusion of Palestinians from newly established factories, broke out in 1929. When Nazi racial policies in Germany and anti-Semitism elsewhere caused another large wave of illegal Jewish immigration in the 1930s, the violence escalated to a virtual state of civil war. The British responded with proposals to create two separate states in the area, but both sides rejected the plan. The bitter struggle between Arab and Jew would reemerge after World War II with far-reaching results.

Despite overwhelming obstacles, Jewish immigrants achieved remarkable success. Although most came

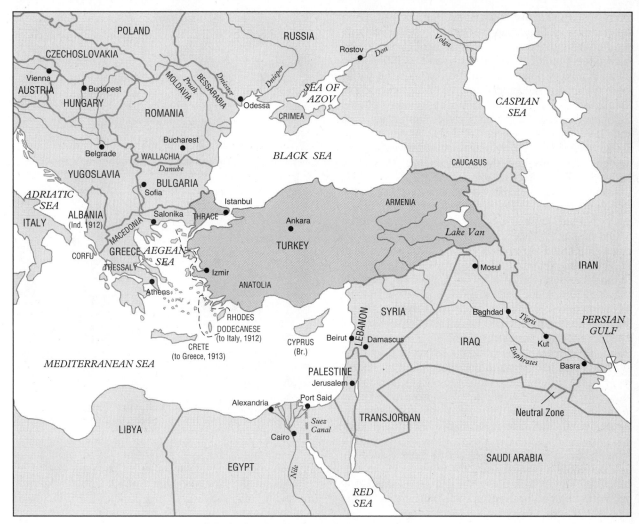

36.4 The Middle East After World War I

from European cities, they adjusted quickly to the rural conditions in Palestine, buying up Arab farmland as well as turning formerly arid terrain into fertile farms and citrus orchards through irrigation, much as the Arabs themselves were doing. The socialist beliefs of many of the early settlers encouraged collective agricultural labor through a farm unit known as the kibbutz, where men and women worked on an equal basis and shared nurseries, dining facilities, and schools as well as the defense of the community. Another form of enterprise was the moshav, a mixture of capitalist and socialist economic features. By 1939 the Jews had created, on socialist principles, an economic infrastructure that encompassed transportation networks, irrigation schemes, and other forms of industrial and agricultural productivity unique in the Middle East at that time. They also built new and prosperous cities, such as Tel Aviv, where a rich intellectual life thrived, based on the Hebrew lan-

guage. This intellectual revival was facilitated by a Hebrew-language publishing industry and theater. Other institutions that elaborated biblical and medieval Jewish cultural themes in a twentieth-century context included art and music academies, a philharmonic orchestra, and the Hebrew University of Jerusalem and its Jewish National Library. By the late 1930s Jewish claims to Palestine, both biblical and historical, were reinforced by their achievements in constructing the foundations of a modern society.

The Modernization of Turkey and Iran

In the second half of the nineteenth century internal problems had made it difficult for the Ottoman Empire to deal effectively with external challenges. The reactionary excesses of the Sultan Abdul Hamid (1876–1909) stimulated opposition among Western-educated reformers and army officers (see Chapter 32). These groups formed the Young Turk movement, which in 1908 forced Abdul Hamid to restore the constitution and the parliament. When the sultan attempted a counterrevolution, the Young Turks unseated him. They soon imposed rigid centralization based on Turkish supremacy on a state that included substantial Arab, Armenian, and Slavic minorities. Wooed by German agents, who trained their army, the Young Turks brought Turkey into World War I on Germany's side.

Military defeat precipitated the final demise of the Ottoman Empire. While the subject Arabs were breaking away from Istanbul, the Allies imposed a harsh peace treaty on Turkey that provided for the partition of its empire. In these circumstances, patriotic Turks turned to Mustapha Kemal (1881–1938), who had defended Gallipoli against the British in 1915. The Western-educated Kemal, charismatic and strong-willed, became the focus of a nationalist movement that revolutionized Turkish life. Setting up a new capital at Ankara, in central Anatolia—a site chosen as deliberately remote from European influence—he won popular acclaim by defying the Allies, abolishing the privileges that foreigners once had in Turkey, and repelling the Greek armies that attempted to wrest further territory from the Turks. While recognizing the inevitability of Arab independence, he was unwilling to surrender Asia Minor, eastern Thrace, or the Dardanelles. In 1923, after creating a republic and defeating a Greek thrust against Asia Minor, he forced a revised peace treaty on the Allies that permitted Turkey to keep Asia Minor and a small strip of territory around Istanbul on the European side of the Turkish Straits.

Kemal—who was given the name Atatürk, or "Father of the Turks"—embarked on a program of massive change designed to bring Turkey into the modern era. Although technically president of the republic, he governed as a dictator under a one-party system with a national assembly elected by indirect vote of a limited electorate, made universal only in 1934. His ability to introduce far-reaching change stemmed in part from an appeal to Turkish nationalism. As the Japanese had done so successfully in their own drive for westernization, Kemal now played on the fear and resentment that Western imperialism had provoked while simultaneously stressing Turkey's historic role as the dominant force in a region of lesser states. With ruthless determination, he abolished ancient customs and swept away cultural patterns that he felt impeded Turkish modernization. Outwardly, the most visible signs of Kemal's revolution were the changes in dress that he decreed. Government officials were required to substitute Western business suits and hats for robes and fezzes. Western-style family names were introduced, and place names were altered

Mustafa Kemal Atatürk, the architect of modern Turkey and its first president. [Culver Pictures]

to symbolize the break from an archaic past. But other changes had a more profound impact. Kemal, who professed no religious beliefs, struck deeply at Islamic tradition by separating church from state and secularizing the nation's educational and legal systems. A simpler, more phonetic alphabet replaced the intricate Arabic script as the written language, and the government launched a far-reaching educational campaign among millions of previously illiterate Turkish citizens.

Kemal's vigorous social reforms inspired a similar modernization experiment in Iran. In a move much like the revolt of the Young Turks, nationalistic Iranian reformers forced the despotic and backward shah to grant a constitution in 1906. The reform momentum was shattered the next year when the British and the Russians divided Iran into spheres of influence and assumed substantive control of the country. When the British tried to impose their authority over the entire country after the war, Reza Khan Pahlavi (1877–1944), a colonel in the Persian Cossack Brigade, took power and assumed the title of shah in 1925.

Reza Shah Pahlavi greatly admired Kemal Atatürk and imitated his modernization program, though with less success. The shah's secularization efforts met with fierce opposition from the powerful Islamic religious leaders, who resented all Western influence and were as strong as the small group of European-trained reformers. Like Kemal, Reza Shah Pahlavi changed place names and westernized dress. He built an efficient army and encouraged trade and industry, but he was personally corrupt, and his government proved tyrannical.

In Turkey, Kemal's reforms radically altered the status of women. Polygamy, still practiced by a minority, was abolished in 1926, and marriage laws were modeled after Western examples. Wealthy women began to attend universities and abandoned their veiled costumes in favor of modern European dress. In 1934 women were enfranchised and made eligible for election to the National Assembly. Reza Shah Pahlavi introduced similar policies in Iran, although there Islamic influence kept a stronger hold on women. These and other changes marked a sharp departure from tradition, whose tribal and Islamic practices had kept women in bondage to men, secluded from public life, and confined by strict codes of behavior. The older customs continued to prevail in Saudi Arabia and elsewhere. Nevertheless, the new social norms fostered by Kemal Atatürk and Reza Shah Pahlavi, together with the emergence of a cohesive Jewish community in Palestine where women labored on an equal basis with men, broke the centuries-old pattern of female subservience in the Middle East.

Early in the twentieth century the largest and oldest societies in the world broke sharply with the patterns of the past. In Russia, China, India, and the Middle East, half of the world's people rejected the political systems that had governed them and strove to remake their societies.

In Russia a corrupt, ineffective, and repressive regime was toppled by an alliance of workers and intellectuals under the charismatic leadership of Lenin. In November 1917 his Bolsheviks swept away the provisional government that had replaced the Romanov dynasty and began a radical experiment in economic and social mobilization. They instituted a program of forced modernization that would enable the Soviet Union, as Russia was now called, to catch up with western Europe and improve the economic condition of its people. On Lenin's death in 1924, leadership passed to the more ruthless, power-conscious Stalin. Lenin's dream of a workers' democracy quickly faded, but Russia's industrial and military power grew rapidly, and the Soviet example of successful revolution and modernization exerted worldwide influence.

In China the revolutionary Kuomintang party succeeded the antiquated Ch'ing dynasty, which collapsed in 1911, but the revolutionaries were too few and too divided to form an effective government. The revolution was betrayed by a military strong man, Yuan Shih-kai, and upon his death in 1916 China disintegrated into a civil war among rival warlords. Under the leadership of Chiang Kai-shek, the Kuomintang managed to form a national government in 1927 but failed to unite the country or to eliminate the rival Chinese Communist party. The Japanese invasion of 1937 mortally weakened the Kuomintang, and civil war after 1945 soon brought the Communists to power with their radical solutions to China's urgent problems of poverty and weakness.

In India the long struggle for independence from British rule made real progress only after 1919, when Mahatma Gandhi greatly widened the movement's support by appealing to mass sentiment. Gandhi restored Indians' pride in their own tradition and identity. With the help of Jawaharlal Nehru, he forged a political instrument, the Congress party, into a successful vehicle for freeing India from colonialism and addressing its inherited problems of economic backwardness and inequality.

In the Middle East both Turkish and European colonial domination was also rejected, and new regimes were created in each country. In 1919 the League of Nations replaced the centuries-long rule of the Ottoman Empire in the Middle East with British and French mandates, designed to provide a transition to independence. The seeds of Arab nationalism grew slowly in the interwar period, for rulers such as Faisal in Iraq and ibn-Saud in Saudi Arabia remained heavily dependent on the European powers, while leaders such as Kemal Atatürk in Turkey and Reza Shah Pahlavi in Iran attempted to modernize their countries according to Western models. The colonization of Palestine by Jewish settlers under British patronage further exacerbated Arab nationalism. Only in the post–World War II era did true independence develop, when several factors combined to bring the new Arab states together against the lingering dominance of the West: the enormous financial strength achieved through the regional coordination of oil resources, a new-found cultural identity inspired by a return to Islamic fundamentalism, and common opposition to the Jewish state of Israel.

Each of these regions linked approaches based on its individual historical experience to the goal of creating new national strength and development. Each swept away unacceptable political systems and built in their place new governments designed to be more effective in responding to urgent national needs. Taken together, the revolutionary changes in these four major regions did indeed shake the world, by fundamentally transforming the half of it that they governed and by inspiring millions in the other half to do the same.

Notes

1. J. Reed, *Ten Days That Shook the World* (New York: Random House, 1960), pp. 170–171.
2. A. Kollontai, *The Autobiography of a Sexually Emancipated Communist Woman*, trans. S. Attanasio (New York: Herder & Herder, 1971), p. 13.
3. D. N. Jacobs, ed., *From Marx to Mao and Marchais: Documents on the Development of Communist Variations* (New York: Longman, 1979), pp. 104–105.
4. F. Claudin, *The Communist Movement: From Comintern to Cominform*, vol. 1, trans. B. Pearce (New York: Monthly Review Press, 1975), pp. 72–73.

Suggestions for Further Reading

Balfour, Baron J. P. *Atatürk: The Rebirth of a Nation*. London: Weidenfeld & Nicolson, 1964.

Bondurant, J. *The Conquest of Violence: The Gandhian Philosophy of Conflict*. Berkeley: University of California Press, 1969.

Brown, J. *Gandhi and Civil Disobedience*. Cambridge: Cambridge University Press, 1977.

Carr, E. H. *The Russian Revolution: From Lenin to Stalin*. New York: Free Press, 1979.

Chamberlin, W. H. *The Russian Revolution, 1917–1921*. New York: Macmillan, 1952.

Chen, J. T. *The May Fourth Movement in Shanghai*. Leiden, Netherlands: Brill, 1971.

Daniels, R. V. *Red October: The Bolshevik Revolution of 1917*. New York: Scribner, 1967.

Deutscher, I. *The Prophet Armed: Trotsky, 1879–1921*. New York: Viking, 1965.

Dirlik, A. *The Origins of Chinese Communism*. New York: Oxford University Press, 1989.

Eastman, L. E. *The Nationalist Era in China, 1927–1949*. Cambridge: Cambridge University Press, 1990.

Edwardes, M. *The Last Years of British India*. London: Cassell, 1963.

Fischer, L. *The Life of Lenin*. New York: Harper & Row, 1965.

Gasster, M. *Chinese Intellectuals and the Revolution of 1911*. Seattle: University of Washington Press, 1969.

Irving, R. G. *Indian Summer: Luytens, Baker, and Imperial New Delhi*. New Haven, Conn.: Yale University Press, 1982.

Iyer, R. *The Moral and Political Thought of Mahatma Gandhi*. New York: Oxford University Press, 1986.

Low, D. A., ed. *Congress and the Raj: Facets of the Indian Struggle, 1917–47*. Columbia: University of Missouri Press, 1977.

Majumdar, R. C. *History of the Freedom Movement in India*. Calcutta: K. L. Mukhopadhyay, 1962.

Pandey, B. N. *Nehru*. London: Macmillan, 1976.

Reed, J. *Ten Days That Shook the World*. New York: Random House, 1960.

Sachar, H. M. *The Emergence of the Middle East, 1914–1924*. New York: Knopf, 1969.

Sheridan, J. E. *China in Disintegration: The Republican Era*. Glencoe, Ill.: Free Press, 1975.

Trotsky, L. *The Russian Revolution*. Garden City, N.Y.: Anchor/Doubleday, 1959.

Ulam, A. B. *The Bolsheviks*. New York: Macmillan, 1965.

———. *Lenin and the Bolsheviks*. London: Collins, 1969.

Upton, J. M. *The History of Modern Iran*. Cambridge, Mass.: Harvard University Press, 1960.

Von Laue, T. H. *Why Lenin? Why Stalin?* London: Weidenfeld & Nicolson, 1966.

Wilbur, C. M. *Sun Yat-sen: Frustrated Patriot*. New York: Columbia University Press, 1976.

Wolfe, B. D. *Three Who Made a Revolution*, rev. ed. New York: Dial Press, 1964.

Wright, M. C. *China in Revolution: The First Phase, 1900–1903*. New Haven, Conn.: Yale University Press, 1968.

Young, E. P. *The Presidency of Yuan Shih-kai*. Ann Arbor: University of Michigan Press, 1977.

Totalitarianism and the Crisis of Democracy

As 1919 opened, Europeans shared a general optimism about the prospects for democracy. Widespread confidence prevailed that the leaders of the victorious Allied Powers who assembled at Paris in January would not only arrange a lasting peace but would also fulfill President Wilson's dream of making the world "safe for democracy." Indeed, the collapse of the imperial autocracies in Russia, Germany, and Austria-Hungary was followed by the creation of parliamentary governments throughout central and eastern Europe. Within two decades, however, liberal ideals and democratic governments were in crisis as fascist movements or authoritarian regimes developed in almost every country. By 1933 fascists had seized power only in Italy and Germany, but their appeal was so pervasive that one historian has characterized the entire interwar period as the "epoch of fascism."* Equally pervasive was the allure of totalitarian-

---

*In this chapter *Fascism* refers to Italian Fascism, *fascism* to the generic variety.

Adolf Hitler salutes upon emerging from a meeting with his diplomatic corps. [FPG]

ism, a political system that was favored by both the fascist dictators and the rulers of the Soviet Union.

Fascism, in contrast to communism, proclaimed itself a spiritual rather than a materialist philosophy, but its appeal nevertheless increased dramatically during periods of economic hardship. The financial crisis that began in 1929 plunged the world into an economic collapse of unprecedented dimensions, causing extreme social distress and challenging capitalism itself. The political consequences of the Great Depression were equally disastrous. The political systems of Britain, France, and the United States, where democracy was deeply rooted, were threatened, though without succumbing to fascism. In the newer states of central and eastern Europe, however, where democracy had been largely the product of the 1919 settlements, liberal governments often fell victim to dictatorship and spawned native fascist movements. Together, fascism and the Great Depression posed a deadly challenge to democracy.

Experiences as diverse as those of Nazi Germany and the Soviet Union demonstrate no causal link between fascism and totalitarianism. Totalitarianism as a form of government imposes complete control over its citizens in order to implement an ideology that seeks to transform society according to supposedly immutable historical laws. Both fascism and communism are totalitarian.

Totalitarian governments are single-party dictatorships in which constitutional rights are severely restricted or eliminated. All political organizations but the official party are outlawed, and in totalitarian states the bureaucracy and the party are closely intertwined. Such regimes are characterized by state terrorism, coercion, police surveillance, government monopoly of the communications media, and strong state economic control. Educational systems indoctrinate citizens from an early age, and social and leisure organizations are designed to mobilize the masses.

Totalitarian rulers are ideological dictators. Men such as Lenin and Mussolini, Stalin and Hitler were driven by a determination to put their doctrines into practice. Though they often compromised for expediency, ideological goals took precedence over traditional moral values. These dictators relied on modern technology—loudspeakers, radio, motion pictures—to achieve social control as well as to reinforce their leadership. In the hands of Mussolini and Hitler the totalitarian state became the instrument for the mobilization of huge industrial, economic, and military resources to unleash wars intended to reshape human life.

The Nature of Fascism

Many Europeans, dissatisfied with liberal governments but unwilling to adopt communism, regarded fascism as an alternative, a "third way" capable of solving the problems of industrial society. Fascists claimed that their system would supersede class struggle and transform society.

Scholars still debate the nature of fascism. Some regard it as a universal phenomenon that possessed a core of similar characteristics in all countries. Despite these similarities, however, Italian Fascism and German Nazism had deep ideological differences, and each in turn differed from fascist movements elsewhere. Although the term *fascist* continues to be applied to noncommunist authoritarian regimes, some observers doubt that we can speak of fascism outside the European setting and beyond the chronological period 1919–1945.

Was fascism a movement of the right or of the left? Was it a revolutionary, a conservative, or a reactionary force? These questions may be resolved in part by recognizing the distinction between fascism as a movement before it came to power and fascism as a regime after it seized control of a government. Once in office, fascist leaders often compromised with traditional power elites to consolidate their authority, and these compromises changed the original aims of their movements.

General Characteristics

Certain characteristics are found in virtually all such movements. The fascists rejected the concept of liberty inherited from the French Revolution and nineteenth-century liberalism. They argued that democracy corrupts the human spirit with greed, sacrifices national interests for the sake of party and class concerns, and fosters alienation and a loss of community. Fascists claimed that they would eliminate the class conflict implicit in Marxism, which divided the national community. In the place of Enlightenment rationalism, fascism proclaimed the superiority of instinct, feeling, and blood, and it glorified violence and action. The fascists promised to restore idealism and youthful activism and to integrate every class and citizen into the all-embracing totalitarian state.

Fascist regimes were sustained by the cult of the charismatic leader, whose authority was unquestioned and to whom all loyalty and obedience were directed. Dictators such as Benito Mussolini (1883–1945) and Adolf Hitler (1889–1945) played crucial roles in the success of fascism. Propaganda and public rituals instilled in the population a fanatical faith in the leader, who, with an elite party, ruled in the name of a single national will. Future leaders would be trained through the party, which acted as a link between the people and the state.

The mass base of fascism came chiefly from the lower middle class. White-collar workers, civil servants, artisans, and shopkeepers resented wealthy capitalists just as they feared the working classes. This lower-middle-class group, from which the early movements filled their ranks, hoped that fascism would solve the postwar economic crisis and restore traditional values—respect for authority, family, and nation. It shared the fascists' alienation from the existing social and political order, whose elites monopolized power and restricted advancement. Fascist programs were, however, tailored to attract diverse interests so that segments of the aristocracy, big business, urban labor, and the peasantry found them appealing.

Fascism's major appeal was to nationalism or racism. Such appeals cut across class lines and economic interests, and fascist propaganda played successfully on the popular desire for national greatness and ethnic dominance. Mussolini's dream of re-creating a Roman empire and Hitler's prophecy of a "thousand-year Reich" reflected the fascist thirst for expansion, and the foreign policies of both dictators were aggressive. For some fascist movements—particularly the German National Socialists—racism was the core of their ideologies, but for others—such as the Italian Fascists—racism represented a later addition. Nevertheless, many fascists emphasized the biological or spiritual distinctiveness of their national "races" and exalted the unity of "blood and soil" in their national histories. Fascism systematically eliminated entire populations as the extreme logic of its racism unfolded: hundreds of thousands of North Africans were slaughtered by Italian Fascist armies, and millions of Jews were murdered by the Nazis in central Europe.

The Origins of Fascism

Some historians regard fascism as a reaction against ruling elites, while others consider it a strategy adopted by those elites to forestall revolution from below. Many scholars agree that we must look for the sources of fascism in the nineteenth century. In Italy and Germany the manner and circumstances in which national unification was achieved may have had an important bearing on the origins of fascism. Unification was the work of political and economic elites who excluded the masses from the process of nation-building and used the instruments of power politics—war and diplomacy—to achieve their purposes. These elites shaped the new national states according to their own interests to secure power. Large segments of the populations of these countries were therefore not integrated into national life and looked to fascism to give them a share in the benefits of nationhood.

The Marxist interpretation asserts that fascism is the product of class struggle common to all capitalist societies. It argues that as the counterrevolutionary form adopted by capitalists to suppress the workers, fascism is an attempt by the industrial and financial interests to save dying capitalism. Most Marxists now consider fascism an independent force distinct from capitalism itself.

In this view, capitalists supported and used fascism as a weapon in their struggle against the working classes. The "Red scare" that spread throughout Europe following the Russian Revolution provided the atmosphere in which fascism rose to power.

Other scholars argue that the origins of fascism are to be found in the moral and cultural crisis that Europe experienced at the turn of the century. The late-nineteenth-century revolt against positivism undermined many of the ideals inherited from the Enlightenment and the French Revolution and challenged the underlying Judeo-Christian ethical principles on which Western civilization was based. The decline of these values affected political behavior and produced social disintegration, and World War I was seen as an irrational triumph over reason. Accordingly, fascism emerged out of the dislocation of the postwar period as an extreme revolt against positivist values.

Marxist and non-Marxist scholars agree that fascism was an immediate result of World War I. In the postwar crisis, a number of elements—the presence of numerous unemployed and alienated veterans, thwarted lower-middle-class aspirations, capitalist fears of revolution, the outrage of nations humiliated in the war or in the peace settlements—were skillfully manipulated by fascist leaders.

Italy: The Fascist Triumph

The life of Benito Mussolini and the history of Italian Fascism were inextricably linked. Italian Fascism and its regime bore the indelible stamp of his personality and ideas, but he never dominated his movement as Hitler did Nazism.

Benito Mussolini

The founder of Fascism was born in 1883 in a small village in northeastern Italy. Mussolini's father, a blacksmith, was a socialist from whom he inherited a radical, anticlerical bias. He displayed a violent personality but a keen intelligence. His mother, a devout schoolteacher, sent him to a Catholic seminary, from which he was expelled for stabbing another pupil. By 1901 Mussolini was teaching elementary school and active in local socialist politics. The next year he fled to Switzerland to avoid the draft, remaining there until 1904. As a center for revolutionary exiles from many countries, Switzerland afforded Mussolini the opportunity to develop his socialist ideas. He read widely and worked as a propagandist for the Italian Socialist party (PSI). After his return to Italy, he distinguished himself as a revolutionary socialist, a public speaker, and a journalist. During the Italo-Turkish

War (1911–1912) he was a staunch pacifist and anti-imperialist, earning a prison term for inciting antiwar riots. In 1912 he helped the revolutionary socialist faction seize control of the PSI and was made editor of the official party daily, *Avanti!*

By the outbreak of World War I, Mussolini had become a prominent socialist leader. During the "interventionist crisis" (1914–1915), in which Italy remained neutral while arranging to enter the war on the Allied side, he rejected some of his socialist principles, particularly his antiwar stance. Concluding that the war could act as a catalyst for revolution, he advocated Italian intervention and as a result was expelled from the PSI in 1915. That year, with money from industrialists and foreign sources, he founded his own newspaper, *Il Popolo d'Italia*, which became the official Fascist organ.

Following a brief stint as a soldier, during which he was wounded and made a sergeant, Mussolini returned to political agitation. He had meanwhile absorbed nationalist ideas and abandoned his belief in the class struggle. By the end of the war Mussolini was a revolutionary without an ideology, a leader in search of a movement.

Postwar Crisis in Italy

Peace was accompanied by a crisis in Italy. To bolster wartime morale the government had promised land for peasants, jobs for workers, and political and social equality. These promises created expectations among Italians of all classes, but postwar realities brought swift disillusionment. Italy's national debt had risen dramatically, the value of its currency had fallen sharply, and foreign trade had been seriously curtailed. The spiraling cost of living hit the working and middle classes hard. Demobilized soldiers demanded jobs, many of which had been filled by women during the war, and the difficulties of converting the economy to peacetime production resulted in more than 2 million unemployed by the end of 1919.

Economic hardships were compounded by a crisis of national prestige. The Treaty of London (1915) that brought Italy into the war had committed the Allies to extensive territorial concessions for Italy, including the Trentino and southern Tirol, the port of Trieste, the Istrian peninsula, the Dalmatian coast, and the Dodecanese islands, which the Italians had occupied since 1912. But at the Paris peace conference Wilson and Lloyd George not only gave Dalmatia to the new Yugoslav state but also refused to compensate Italy with the port city of Fiume, which Prime Minister Orlando demanded. The Italians felt betrayed, and a patriotic frenzy swept the country. Nationalists blamed Orlando's liberal government for what they termed the "mutilated victory," and Fiume became the symbol of Italy's frustrated hopes.

In September 1919 the nationalist writer and adventurer Gabriele D'Annunzio (1863–1938) invaded Fiume with a group of veterans and set up an independent state. Although the Italian government drove him out after a year, the Fiume adventure set a dangerous precedent for military coups and demonstrated the extent of nationalist sentiment. While he ruled Fiume, D'Annunzio adopted symbols and techniques that Mussolini later copied, including the Roman salute, fiery rhetoric, mass torch-lit rallies, and the title of *Duce* ("leader").

Italian frustrations were directed against the liberal regime. In the postwar elections of November 1919, the liberals, who had enjoyed a large majority of seats in the Chamber of Deputies since national unification, suddenly found themselves reduced to the third-ranking party, behind the Socialists and the Italian Popular party, which combined progressive Catholic principles with demands for social and economic reform. The Socialists and Catholics together held enough seats to control the Chamber of Deputies but failed to form a coalition, and King Victor Emmanuel III (1900–1946) continued to select his prime ministers from among the discredited liberals.

Against this background, industrial and agrarian unrest intensified, with more than 1,600 strikes in 1919 alone. In the impoverished south, landless peasants led by veterans and socialists seized uncultivated land, and in September 1920 a major factory sit-in in the northern industrial centers threatened to develop into a revolution. This "occupation of the factories" helped push the industrialists into the arms of the Fascists.

The Fascist Movement

In this context Mussolini founded the Fascist movement. At a meeting of about 100 followers in Milan in March 1919, he established the first *fascio di combattimento* ("combat group"), a mixture of nationalist intellectuals, former socialists and syndicalists, and war veterans. The name of the movement was derived from the Latin word *fasces*, a bundle of rods tied around the shaft of an ax, which had been used by the ancient Romans to symbolize unity and authority. Fascist groups spread throughout northern and central Italy, and membership grew from less than 1,000 in the summer of 1919 to 20,000 by late 1920 and to more than 250,000 by 1922. Most were veterans who sought a sense of community based on the "spirit of the trenches"—comradeship, loyalty, bravery, and action. These alienated young men formed Mussolini's paramilitary squads, whose members came to be known as Squadristi. Their parades and rallies, black-shirted uniforms, and nihilistic slogans vividly symbolized Italy's postwar crisis.

The Squadristi unleashed a reign of terror across the nation under the command of local Fascist chieftains. They launched "punitive expeditions" against socialist

◉ Theory of the Fascist State ◉

Fascist political theory rejected nineteenth-century liberalism, which held that government's function was to guarantee the rights and freedoms of individuals. Instead, fascists argued that service to an all-powerful state was the highest moral goal. In these passages, written in collaboration with the philosopher Giovanni Gentile, Mussolini explained the essence of what he called the totalitarian state.

Against individualism, the Fascist conception is for the State; and it is for the individual in so far as he coincides with the State, which is the conscience and universal will of man in his historical existence. It is opposed to classical Liberalism, which arose from the necessity of reacting against absolutism, and which brought its historical purpose to an end when the State was transformed into the conscience and will of the people. Liberalism denied the State in the interests of the particular individual; Fascism reaffirms the State as the true reality of the individual. And if Liberty is to be the attribute of the real man, and not of that abstract puppet envisaged by individualistic Liberalism, Fascism is for liberty. And for the only liberty which can be a real thing, the liberty of the State, and of the individual within the state, and nothing human or spiritual exists, much less has value, outside the State. In this sense Fascism is totalitarian. . . .

The Fascist State, the highest and most powerful form of personality, is a force, but a spiritual force, which takes over all the forms of the moral and intellectual life of man. It cannot therefore confine itself simply to the functions of order and supervision as Liberalism desired. It is not simply a mechanism which limits the sphere of the supposed liberties of the individual. It is the form, the inner standard and the discipline of the whole person; it saturates the will as well as the intelligence. . . .

Fascism, in short, is not only the giver of laws and the founder of institutions, but the educator and promoter of spiritual life. It wants to remake, not the forms of human life, but its content, man, character, faith. And to this end it requires discipline and authority that can enter into the spirits of men and there govern unopposed. . . .

Source: B. Mussolini, "The Doctrine of Fascism" (1932), in M. Oakeshott, ed., *The Social and Political Doctrines of Contemporary Europe* (Cambridge: Cambridge University Press, 1939), pp. 166, 168.

and trade union offices, urban strikers, and peasant protesters. By 1921 the antisocialist campaign was bringing Fascism financial backing from industrialists and landowners, and the liberal government took no steps to halt Fascist violence. Fascist assaults against city halls and provincial officials were followed by open threats to take over the state.

The March on Rome

While the Blackshirts' violent tactics weakened the Socialists and created the impression that Fascism possessed a strength beyond its numbers, Mussolini maintained the profile of a respectable politician. In 1921 he signed and then violated a peace pact with the PSI and converted the Fascist movement into the National Fascist party (PNF), which won 35 seats in Parliament. Mussolini now had the prestige of being a deputy. The Liberal premier, Giovanni Giolitti, hoped to co-opt the Fascists into the established order by luring Mussolini into a coalition of moderate and conservative parties. Like other liberals, Giolitti failed to understand that Fascism was not a conventional political force.

In 1922 Mussolini marched on Rome to frighten the government into conceding power to Fascism. Between October 26 and 28, tens of thousands of Blackshirts moved toward the capital while Mussolini waited in Milan. King Victor Emmanuel III, uncertain of the army's loyalty and fearful of civil war, refused to impose martial law. On October 29 he asked Mussolini to become prime minister. Mussolini arrived in Rome the following day, dressed in top hat and tails. Only then did the Blackshirts enter Rome, but now to cheer Mussolini before the royal palace. The liberal state had collapsed in the face of a bluff.

Mussolini took office by legal means, but with only 35 Fascist deputies in a chamber of more than 500, he

Mussolini (left) leading the Fascist march on Rome in the fall of 1922. [Brown Brothers]

sition. Over the next four years Mussolini created the first fascist regime in history.

Mussolini's Italy

In the aftermath of the Matteotti crisis, Mussolini laid the foundations of his totalitarian state. He abolished all political organizations except the Fascist party, censored the press, set up a political police force, instituted loyalty oaths for civil servants, created a military court to prosecute anti-Fascists, and secured power to rule by decree. Once Fascists were installed in key government posts, he sought a broad popular consensus.

On the surface Italy was still a parliamentary state with a monarch. The 1861 constitution remained in force, and Mussolini supposedly held office as prime minister at the pleasure of the king. Imposed above this system was the Fascist Grand Council, which in theory combined party and state functions. The council, appointed by Mussolini, selected candidates for election to the Chamber of Deputies and approved policy decisions. In 1939 this body was replaced by the Chamber of Fasci and Corporations, which represented trades and professions rather than parties. Traditional institutions therefore coexisted with new Fascist bodies, and the totalitarian state never fully superseded them.

Economic Policy

The Fascists established strong state control over the economy while preserving capitalism. Mussolini abolished the non-Fascist unions, prohibited strikes, and recognized the rights of industrial associations. In return, the industrialists supported his regime and dealt only with Fascist unions. Having abolished the economic rights of workers, Mussolini established the "corporate state" in the late 1920s by combining unions and employer associations into "corporations" for each major economic sector and industry. The corporate system was touted as an original form of economic organization in which state-supervised cooperation between capital and labor would replace class conflict. In reality, private business continued largely unhindered, and the corporate structure had little impact on economic life, except to control workers.

Mussolini failed to solve Italy's economic problems or temper the long-range effects of the Great Depression. Efforts to impose autarchy, or economic self-sufficiency, made matters worse. Marshlands were drained and cultivated, and farmers were coerced into growing more wheat and less of other crops. Nevertheless, overall agricultural production declined. Higher tar-

moved cautiously. Over the next year and a half he assumed extensive authority, muzzled the press, and passed a new election law designed to ensure a Fascist majority in Parliament. According to this measure, the party that received the largest popular vote, with a minimum of 25 percent, would have two-thirds of the seats in the Chamber of Deputies. In 1924 the Fascists swept the elections by rigging the polls and intimidating opponents with violence, thus securing control of Parliament. Mussolini grew more confident when the army agreed to support the regime in return for the creation of a Fascist militia that would absorb the Blackshirts.

That summer the courageous Socialist leader Giacomo Matteotti (1885–1924), who had exposed the illegality of the Fascist electoral victory, was murdered by Fascist thugs. Popular reaction against Mussolini was so strong that he feared dismissal by the king. Opposition deputies withdrew in protest from the Chamber, and Blackshirt leaders pressured Mussolini to complete the seizure of power. In January 1925, in a forceful speech to Parliament, he assumed total responsibility and proclaimed the Fascist dictatorship. This speech was followed by a "second wave" of violence against the oppo-

◉ Mussolini's Seizure of Power ◉

In late 1924 Mussolini was accused by the opposition of having ordered a secret Fascist police force to assassinate socialist deputy Giacomo Matteotti. After weeks of hesitation, during which pressure from both his enemies and radical Fascist leaders mounted, he assumed full authority and declared a dictatorship in a speech on January 3, 1925.

It is I who in this chamber make accusations against myself. . . . If I had founded a secret police, I would have done so through the kind of violence that is an integral part of history. I have always said . . . that violence, to be effective, must be surgical, intelligent, and high-minded. . . .

I declare here, before the entire Chamber and before the Italian people, that I and I alone assume political, moral, and historical responsibility for everything that has happened.

If this surprising statement is sufficient to indict me, then bring forth the scaffolds! If Fascism has been only castor oil and clubs instead of the superb passion of Italy's best youth, the fault is mine. If Fascism has been a gang of criminals, then I am their leader.

If all the violence in this country has been the result of a special historical, moral, and political climate, I am responsible for that climate because I created it. . . .

When two elements are in inevitable conflict, the solution is force. History has never known another solution.

I tell you now that the problem will be solved. Fascism, the government, the party are all in working order.

You are all under an illusion. You believed that Fascism was finished because I compromised it, but this is not at all the case. Italy wants peace, tranquillity, and calm labor. We will give it these things, with love if possible, but with force if necessary.

Rest assured that within the next twenty-four hours the situation will be clarified in every way.

Source: E. Susmel and D. Susmel, eds., *Opera omnia di Benito Mussolini*, vol. 21 (Florence: La Fenice, 1953), pp. 235–241 passim. Translated by P. V. Cannistraro.

iffs to stimulate industry increased consumer prices and shortages. Despite welfare programs and subsidies to large families, the standard of living of industrial and farm workers declined throughout the 1930s.

The Church and Fascism

Mussolini was more successful in relations with the Catholic church. Though an atheist, he understood the importance of Catholicism in Italian life and saw the church as a bulwark against communism. He thus ended the hostility that had existed between church and state since 1870, when the kingdom of Italy seized Rome from the papacy. The Lateran Pacts of 1929 recognized the independence of Vatican City, which became a separate state within the city of Rome; anticlerical laws were repealed; Catholic youth groups were to be free from interference; the Vatican was to have its own newspaper and radio station; religious instruction in state schools became compulsory; and the government paid the Vatican an indemnity. The Lateran Pacts represented a triumph for Mussolini, for they secured the church's cooperation and gave the regime a respectable image. Most important, Mussolini won the support of many devout Italians. Pope Pius XI (1922–1939) proclaimed him "the man sent to us by Providence."

Regimentation, Propaganda, and Art

The regimentation of life under Fascism affected both thought and behavior. Mussolini created a secret police agency (called OVRA), spied on anti-Fascists, and introduced a new penal code. Nevertheless, a variety of circumstances—Mussolini's penchant for compromise, a long tradition of Italian resistance to bureaucratic authority, and the more limited ideological goals of Fascism—combined to make his system of terror less severe than that in Nazi Germany or the Soviet Union.

Control of the media and cultural life was placed under the Ministry of Popular Culture. Young people were trained in the party's youth organization, which included separate groups for males and females aged 6 through 17. They provided military training, sports, and political indoctrination; by the mid-1930s they had over 3 million members. Leisure activities for workers and peasants were controlled through the party's Dopolavoro ("after-work") organization. By 1940 the party, once an elite vanguard, had been opened to practically all Italians, many of whom viewed membership as a career necessity.

Although Mussolini's early movement had included several female Blackshirts, Fascism held a rigidly chauvinist attitude toward women, who were viewed exclusively as housewives and "mothers of the race." The Duce's highly publicized mistresses enhanced his reputation as a virile lover, and Fascists in general regarded women as objects to be "conquered" by men. The regime fostered conservative social values that reinforced traditional mores. The party trained young females to be wives and mothers, while state agencies provided maternity assistance, hygiene instruction, and child care information. Mussolini had supported giving the vote to women, but once in power he buried political equality. During the Fascist period the percentage of women making up the working population dropped as the depression affected both agriculture and industry.

The party glorified the leader. Mussolini was virtually deified as the farsighted "man of destiny." His skills as an orator, combined with his studied poses and facial expressions, captivated huge throngs. Slogans glorified the Duce and Fascist achievements: "Mussolini is always right," "A minute on the battlefield is worth a lifetime of peace," "Believe! Obey! Fight!"

In the mid-1930s the party introduced programs designed to alter Italian customs. Males were to be molded into the Fascist "new man"—obedient, virile, ruthless, efficient, and selfless. The military salute supplanted the handshake, black shirts were to be worn instead of business suits, and bourgeois pastimes such as golf and tennis were replaced with team sports. Many Italians privately scoffed at such measures, which were observed only superficially. The Fascists idealized imperial Rome as their inspiration, and Mussolini promised to create a new empire in which his people would recapture the Roman traditions of sacrifice and discipline. Mussolini was to be Italy's new Caesar.

With Mussolini in power, Margherita Sarfatti (1880–1961), his constant companion and adviser, emerged as the most influential woman in Italy. She wrote a regular

Margherita Sarfatti, Italian art critic and the author of a popular biography of Mussolini, was the Fascist dictator's lover and cultural mentor for 20 years. This photo was taken in 1931. [Ghitta Carell]

art column and edited Mussolini's official monthly. An international array of prominent writers paid court at her salon in Rome, and she patronized intellectuals and painters, for whom she secured commissions and arranged exhibits.

Sarfatti advocated the "return to order"—the abandonment of abstractionism that had marked prewar artistic modernism—and supported painters who remained committed to a modern style while appreciating older Italian traditions, especially perspective, portraiture, and classical landscape painting. Sarfatti believed that this artistic transformation suited the Fascist emphasis on nationalist values and social order. In 1922 she organized the artists whose work combined modernism and classical ideals into a movement called the Twentieth Century (Novecento) and persuaded Mussolini to inaugurate its first group exhibit. Until the early 1930s the movement came close to representing Fascism's official artistic style, and thus Mussolini's regime encouraged the kind of avant-garde culture that Hitler condemned as "decadent." In promoting the Twentieth Century, Sarfatti struggled against anti-intellectual Fascists who viewed modernism as a product of a corrupt civilization and wanted a "social realist" art that was little more than posterlike propaganda.

🏵 ROME, THE FASCIST CAPITAL

With its ancient grandeur and rich archaeological remains, Rome was ideally suited for Mussolini's imperial dreams. Its history spanned 2,000 years. A city with a complex physical appearance, its ancient ruins and monuments stood against medieval buildings, Renaissance palaces, and baroque churches. Fountains and squares provided relief from the winding, dark streets and bustling shopping districts.

Besides its role as a cultural center, Rome was a seat of government. After the collapse of the ancient empire, the city became the site of the papacy and the Catholic church, dominated by the Vatican and St. Peter's Basilica. When Rome became the capital of Italy in 1870, it began to assume its modern appearance. The influx of white-collar workers to staff the bureaucracy increased the size of the urban community significantly. Rome's population of 200,000 in 1870 doubled by the turn of the century, and by 1936 it had reached almost 1.2 million. During the reign of King Umberto I (1878–1900) the city underwent a construction boom to accommodate its growing population, and elaborately ornate Umbertine architecture took its place alongside older styles.

Like emperors and popes before him, Mussolini determined to redo Rome in order to accent its imperial past, thus making the city the capital of the new Fascist empire. He ordered archaeological excavations and the renovation of ancient sites. He demolished entire residential districts of the inner city to build a grand concourse, the Via dell'Impero ("Imperial Way"), running from the Colosseum along the Forum to the Piazza Venezia, where his office was located. On the walls of the Basilica of Maxentius he placed massive marble maps of the ancient Roman conquests, followed by one showing the Fascist domain. The Piazza Venezia, dominated by a huge monument to Victor Emmanuel II, was the core of Fascist Rome. From the balcony of the Palazzo Venezia, Mussolini harangued enormous crowds. Mussolini also gave the city a modern appearance by constructing monuments and buildings in a modernized classical style characteristic of the regime's taste in architecture. In the 1930s a new complex for the University of Rome was built, as was the Italic Forum, a stadium surrounded by statues of nude athletes to symbolize Fascism's emphasis on physical strength. After the Lateran Pacts of 1929, Mussolini again destroyed residential districts to build a wide boulevard from the Tiber River to St. Peter's.

By the end of the decade plans had been laid for a new minicity in the suburbs between Rome and the ancient port of Ostia. Here modern public buildings were designed in the Fascist style for a world's fair in 1942, but the coming of World War II ended the project.

The Anti-Fascist Opposition

In spite of the enthusiasm Mussolini engendered, many Italians opposed Fascism. Mussolini's enemies came from all political parties and all walks of life. By 1926 most of the well-known anti-Fascists who escaped Blackshirt brutality had been forced into exile, where they established groups with such names as Justice and Liberty. In the early 1930s an underground Communist network had been set up in Italy and, together with Justice and Liberty, kept the hope of freedom alive while refuting Fascist propaganda. Mussolini's irresponsible foreign adventures gave anti-Fascism an added impetus, and his anti-Semitic laws alienated many Italians, who regarded the small Jewish population of 50,000 as loyal and productive. The degree to which Italians were repulsed by Mussolini's anti-Semitic policies reflected their humanist traditions.

Germany: From Weimar to Hitler

Nazism, the German variety of fascism, developed after Mussolini founded his Fascist group, but it took more than a decade longer to come to power. Outwardly, the two movements appeared to be almost identical—radical parties with ideologies inspired by elements of socialism, syndicalism, and nationalism; the cult of the charismatic leader; a rank-and-file membership consisting largely of the lower middle class and veterans disaffected by the postwar crisis; a paramilitary organization with uniforms, slogans, and a philosophy of violence; resentment toward capitalists and hatred for the communists; and a revolutionary determination to destroy parliamentary government.

Despite these similarities, the Nazi regime was generally acknowledged to have been more totalitarian than Mussolini's system. The more overtly racial component in Nazi ideology represented a major difference between the two movements and in part explains the greater brutality of the Third Reich. In its early stages, Mussolini's cabinet included several Jewish ministers, a situation inconceivable in Nazi Germany, and his mistress for almost 20 years, Margherita Sarfatti, was a Jew. During the 1920s Hitler had regarded Mussolini as a mentor, the elder statesman of international fascism; after the Nazi takeover in Germany, however, Hitler emerged as the senior partner in what became known as the Rome-Berlin Axis. This change reflected the disparity between the industrial and military capacities of Italy and Germany.

Revolution and the Weimar Republic

The military collapse of 1918 had a profound impact on Germany's political and social fabric. Revolutionary unrest erupted, and worker and soldiers' councils similar to those in Russia were formed. On November 8, Kurt Eisner, a communist leader in Munich, set up a separate Republic of Bavaria that was put down only after his assassination and a civil war between rightists and leftists. When Kaiser William II abdicated on November 9 and his chancellor resigned, the government was placed provisionally in the hands of Friedrich Ebert and Philipp Scheidemann, both moderate Social Democrats. That same afternoon Scheidemann proclaimed a republic with Ebert as its first chancellor. Extremists on both the left and the right, however, attempted to seize power. To maintain order, Ebert offered the German high command guarantees of protection if the army remained loyal. Revolutionary Marxists, known as Spartacists (after the Thracian gladiator Spartacus, who led a slave uprising against Rome in 73 B.C.), revolted in 1919 under the leadership of Rosa Luxemburg and Karl Liebknecht. During "Spartacist Week" (January 6–15) they battled the government in the streets of Berlin. Luxemburg and Liebknecht were killed by soldiers sent to arrest them. The government also turned for support to private military groups known as the Free Corps, headed by embittered former officers and armed veterans. The Free Corps, from which would come many of the early adherents to the Nazi movement, would eventually turn against the government itself.

After the Spartacist revolt, an array of moderate political parties—the largest of which were the Social Democrats, the Catholic Center party, and the Democrats—met in the National Assembly at Weimar to draft a new constitution. This document (adopted in July 1919), which created the German Republic, reflected progressive social ideas and democratic principles. It provided for universal suffrage, a cabinet system of government with an elected president and an appointed chancellor, and a bill of rights that guaranteed civil liberties, education, and employment.

Although the so-called Weimar Republic was one of the most liberal governments in central Europe, it was burdened from the start with serious problems. In March 1920, militarists led by Wolfgang Kapp attempted a putsch, or coup, by marching on Berlin. Kapp's putsch was suppressed by a socialist-led general strike. In the first election under the new constitution, held three months later, the three-party centrist coalition that had dominated the National Assembly fell from 76 to 47 percent of the popular vote, while the parties on the extreme right and left almost doubled their support. Moderate forces never again regained a majority, and the 13 years

of the Weimar government produced 20 different cabinets. The German people looked on the republic with suspicion, especially since the Allies had forced the kaiser to abdicate. Rightist and leftist extremists regarded the regime as an enemy and plotted against it. Although the army had agreed to protect the government, its high command was uncomfortable with the democratic system and blamed the republic for the humiliating Treaty of Versailles.

Germans found it difficult to understand how their country, once an industrial giant with the best army in the world, could have lost the war. Moreover, they resented the fact that the Allies had forced them to accept total responsibility for the war. Right-wing extremists, monarchists, and army officers manufactured the legend that Germany had been "stabbed in the back" by traitors, whom they identified as Marxists and Jews. Reactionaries pointed to the helpless new republic, shorn of its army, as a symptom of decadence. Extremists assassinated two progressive ministers—Matthias Erzberger in August 1921 and Walther Rathenau a year later.

The economic problems that beset postwar Germany fueled the feeling that the Weimar Republic was too weak to rule. The government responded to the severe unemployment that struck the country by printing huge quantities of paper currency to finance assistance programs and prevent massive starvation. The result was spiraling inflation that devastated much of the middle class, a condition exacerbated by the French occupation of the Ruhr valley in 1923. The German mark, worth about 12 U.S. cents at the end of the war, was now virtually worthless—German shoppers paid for a loaf of bread or a newspaper with sacks of currency. The almost daily rise in the cost of living left salaries far behind, and people on fixed incomes—pensioners, widows, disabled veterans—were virtually wiped out. By 1925 inflation had destroyed 50 percent of the capital of the lower middle class, more than half a million of whom were forced into factory work. The devastating economic collapse caused widespread despair and further undermined public confidence in the republic.

Adolf Hitler and the Rise of Nazism

Adolf Hitler, the founder of the Nazi movement, was born in 1889 in Braunau, Austria, near the Bavarian border. His father, a minor customs official, was unsympathetic to his son's aesthetic leanings, and the young Hitler was always much closer to his mother. Frustrated by his desire to be an artist, he did poorly in his studies and never graduated from high school. In Vienna, where Hitler lived between 1908 and 1913, he evolved his theories of history, politics, and racism. He lived a harsh, bohemian existence, working odd jobs and earning money by

◉ Hitler as Demagogue ◉

Hitler was unequaled as a public speaker. His ability to hold huge numbers of people in his spell, to arouse their passions and whip them into a frenzy of adulation, made him a master of political demagoguery. Although he was a skillful actor on the political platform, his charisma also derived from his conviction of his own destiny. Konrad Heiden, who witnessed many of Hitler's public speeches, provides a vivid description of his ability to sway audiences.

Hitler's special trait is his concentration on greatness. This is the source of his power. When suddenly this man, who has been awkwardly standing around, now and then muttering a remark that by no means dominates the conversation, is seized with determination and begins to speak, filling the room with his voice, suppressing interruptions or contradictions by his domineering manner, spreading cold shivers among those present by the savagery of his declarations, lifting every subject of conversation into the light of history, and interpreting it so that even trifles have their origin in greatness; then the listener is filled with awe and feels that a new phenomenon has entered the room. This thundering demon was not there before; this is not the same timid man with the contracted shoulders. He is capable of this transformation in a personal interview and facing an audience of half a million. The magic power of this image of greatness emanating from human nullity greatly appealed to the German people after the World War, when this people, oppressed by their own nullity, longed for greatness; but a far deeper and more decisive explanation of Hitler's effect is the soul state of modern man, who, in his pettiness, loneliness, and lack of faith, longs for community, conviction, and greatness. Here he sees greatness emerging from a creature who as a man is smaller than you or I—that is what made Hitler an experience for millions.

Source: K. Heiden, *Der Führer: Hitler's Rise to Power* (Boston: Houghton Mifflin, 1944), pp. 377–378.

painting watercolors and postcards. Although he developed some skill as an architectural draftsman, his ambitions were frustrated when he was refused admission to the Vienna School of Architecture.

Hitler absorbed a muddle of ideas and attitudes that ultimately formed the basis of Nazi ideology. Racism, in particular anti-Semitism, had the most powerful impact on him. Vienna's population reflected the mixed ethnic composition of the Austro-Hungarian Empire, and in the late nineteenth century Karl Lüger and Georg von Schönerer channeled Austria's anti-Semitic traditions into political movements. Lüger was the dominant figure in the Christian Socialist party, a Catholic organization supported by reactionary conservatives who elected him mayor of Vienna on an anti-Semitic platform. Schönerer, leader of the lower-middle-class Liberal party and a member of the Austrian parliament, organized student clubs in Vienna on the basis of anti-Semitism and generated widespread worker support for a campaign against the alleged influence of Jewish bankers in the imperial government. Moreover, he believed that the "superior" German race should rule over the "inferior" Slavs of central and eastern Europe—Czechs, Serbs, Poles, and others.

As unemployment and inflation mounted in postwar Berlin, scenes of poverty became painfully familiar. Here Berliners sell tin cans for scrap during the severe inflation of 1923. [Granger Collection]

Under the influence of these sources, Hitler became obsessed with the idea of race. He came to see Judaism and Marxism as twin forms of degeneracy and to identify the Jews as the principal source of moral and cultural decline and corruption in Europe. From Schönerer's pan-German ideology he concluded that Germany and Austria must be united into a "greater Germany," while Lüger's political success suggested that the key to a radical movement was the ability to generate and channel the enthusiasm of the masses.

When World War I broke out, Hitler volunteered in a Bavarian infantry regiment, for he considered himself a German. He fought at the front, was promoted to corporal, and was twice awarded the Iron Cross. The end of the war found him recuperating in a hospital from the effects of poison gas.

At the end of World War I, Hitler worked in Munich as a political informant for the army. In this capacity he joined a small group known as the German Workers' party, one of many such organizations that sought to stimulate German patriotism and infuse the working class with the spirit of nationalism. Hitler spent the next five years developing his political talents and leadership within the party. Like Mussolini, he had a natural oratorical ability and spoke frequently in public, expounding the views he had evolved in Vienna. He was unimpressive in appearance, yet he projected a personal magnetism that gripped a nation. To a far greater degree than Mussolini, Hitler had an uncanny ability to sway the masses and evoke worship. These qualities enabled the Nazi Führer ("leader") to convert his small group into a mass party.

In 1920 the German Workers' party was renamed the National Socialist German Workers' party (NSDAP), shortened in popular usage to "Nazi." It acquired its own newspaper, and its 25-point program called for a Greater Germany incorporating all German-speaking peoples, annulment of the Treaty of Versailles, denial of citizenship to Jews, and socioeconomic reforms to benefit the workers and the middle class. Although Hitler himself

◎ Nazism: The Philosophy of Domination ◎

The Nazis viewed life—and therefore history—as a Darwinian struggle for existence in which the fittest triumphed over the weak. Hitler's call for German rearmament was therefore only the first step in a plan for world domination. Hitler preached his brutal message in a speech in Munich on March 15, 1929.

If men wish to live, then they are forced to kill others. The entire struggle for survival is a conquest of the means of existence which in turn results in the elimination of others from these same sources of subsistence. As long as there are peoples on this earth, there will be nations against nations. . . .

There is in reality no distinction between peace and war. Life, no matter in what form, is a process which always leads to the same result. Self-preservation will always be the goal of every individual. Struggle is ever-present and will remain. This signifies a consistent willingness on the part of man to sacrifice to the utmost. Weapons, methods, instruments, formations, these may change, but in the end the struggle for survival remains. . . .

One is either the hammer or the anvil. We confess that it is our purpose to prepare the German people again for the role of the hammer. For ten years we have preached, and our deepest concern is: How can we again achieve power? We admit freely and openly that, if our Movement is victorious, we will be concerned day and night with the question of how to produce the armed forces which are forbidden us by the peace treaty. We solemnly confess that we consider everyone a scoundrel who does not try day and night to figure out a way to violate this treaty, for we have never recognized this treaty. . . .

We confess further that we will dash anyone to pieces who should dare to hinder us in this undertaking. . . . Our rights will never be represented by others. Our rights will be protected only when the German Reich is again supported by the point of the German dagger.

Source: G. W. Prange, ed., *Hitler's Words* (Washington, D.C.: American Council on Public Affairs, 1944), pp. 10–11.

regarded the socialist provisions as propaganda, some Nazi leaders, such as Gregor and Otto Strasser, took them seriously.

The party also developed a paramilitary wing of storm troopers called the *Sturmabteilung* (SA), with its brown shirts, outstretched-arm salute, "Heil Hitler!" and swastika symbol. Rallies, marches, songs, and banners were incorporated in techniques that Hitler's propaganda machine later developed on a massive scale. The SA membership, like that of Mussolini's Blackshirt squads, consisted of disaffected veterans and Free Corps volunteers, rootless young men, and thugs and criminals. Ernst Röhm, the SA leader, believed that violence and terror would bring about the Nazi revolution.

In 1923 Hitler determined to seize power by force. Inspired by Mussolini's march on Rome, he planned a putsch in Munich with the connivance of local officials and the backing of a popular World War I general, Erich Ludendorff. On the evening of November 8 the Brownshirts surrounded a beer hall in which a political meeting was scheduled. Hitler rushed into the room, jumped onto a table, and fired a pistol in the air, shouting, "The National Socialist revolution has begun!" The putsch ended in fiasco the next day as the police scattered the participants and arrested Hitler. The abortive revolt brought Hitler a five-year prison term, of which he served less than nine months. In jail he wrote his famous testament *Mein Kampf* ("My Struggle"), outlining his racial theories, domestic policies, and plans for world conquest. He also concluded that violence alone would not assure the Nazi conquest of Germany and that the party must combine legal electoral methods with violence.

After the failure of the Munich uprising, Röhm attempted to wrest control of the Nazi movement from Hitler. Röhm saw the SA as the instrument for the conquest of the state and the party. But in Hitler, who wanted to subordinate the SA to the party, Röhm met his match in duplicity. Using murder, blackmail, and slander to reassert his position, Hitler defeated Röhm, who went into exile in Bolivia in 1925. Hitler had become the undisputed leader of the movement.

The inner core of the Nazi leadership, attached to Hitler by loyalty and fear, began to take shape. The hierarchy included the gluttonous Hermann Göring, future air marshal; the tireless party organizer Rudolf Hess; the brilliant propagandist Joseph Goebbels; the rabid ideologue Alfred Rosenberg; and the chilling technocrat of police terror, Heinrich Himmler. The party also developed its organizational apparatus, creating youth groups and the infamous *Schutzstaffel* (SS), an elite defense corps later used in the mass exterminations of World War II. In 1929 Himmler took control of the SS and turned it into one of the principal instruments of Hitler's power. The black uniforms and death's-head insignia of the SS became synonymous with the Nazi terror state.

BERTOLT BRECHT AND WEIMAR CULTURE

In contrast to the political and economic turmoil that beset the Weimar Republic, German cultural life between 1919 and 1933 was marked by a feverish brilliance. In theater, cinema, art, architecture, and literature, Germany exploded with a creative energy that was at once modern, experimental, and tormented. Berlin, with a population of more than 2 million, emerged as the center of Weimar's cultural ferment. War, defeat, and revolution had combined to transform the grim solemnity that had once marked Germany's capital into an irreverent spirit that made the city a mecca for young, talented Germans in search of a faster-paced, modern life. By the early 1920s restaurants, bathhouses, dance halls, and nightclubs—including the dozens of gay and lesbian bars described by British writer Christopher Isherwood in his *Berlin Stories*—gave the city a rowdy allure that rivaled even the attractions of Paris. American jazz became the rage, and the iconoclastic atmosphere also gave rise to a peculiar Berlin institution, cabarets in which political and social satire took the form of musical comedy. The air of unreality became starker in the aftermath of the terrible inflation that struck in 1923 and put a quarter of a million Berliners out of work.

No artist better symbolized Germany's postwar culture than George Grosz (1893–1959). After being courtmartialed from the army for insubordination, Grosz went to Berlin, where he joined in succession the Dada move-

A detail from one of George Grosz' satirical drawings contrasts sober working men with partying "fat cats." [Bildarchiv Preussischer Kulturbesitz]

ment, the Expressionists, and the Spartacists. Inspired by the bitter irony he saw in the cabarets, Grosz' political drawings satirized fat industrialists, militarists, and corrupt politicians and assaulted bourgeois standards of morality. Grosz detested the Nazis and in 1923 executed a startlingly prescient drawing of a monocled officer with a swastika, the first of many anti-Nazi works depicting storm troopers and other symbols of the political reaction stalking Germany.

Grosz' counterpart in theater was Bertolt Brecht (1898–1956), whose plays and poems explored the agony of human isolation and the dilemma of moral and political commitment. A pacifist repelled by the horrors of World War I, Brecht's first critical success came in 1922 with a play titled *Spartacus* (later renamed *Drums in the Night*), about a veteran who chose a comfortable life instead of joining the Spartacist uprising.

In 1924 Brecht moved to Berlin, where the theatrical producer Max Reinhardt and the composer Kurt Weill recognized his genius. In his plays as in his personal life, he struggled to detach himself from the irrationality of violence, sex, and aggression and strove to understand how modern society transformed individuals into groups. In *Man Is Man* (1927) he recognized the powerful forces at work in Germany as he described how a worker had been changed into a bloodthirsty soldier.

After 1929 Brecht's work revealed a growing commitment to Marxism, which he believed to be the only solution to the nihilism of his age. *The Three-Penny Opera* (1928) expressed his cynical distaste for bourgeois materialism by taunting his audiences for their gluttonous appetites and lack of ethical values. Under the growing influence of the Communist party, Brecht shifted to an austere didactic style. His controlled language and aesthetic precision urged self-discipline and self-denial in the interests of humanity—he was, he said, interested in the ideas his characters represented rather than in the characters themselves. These influences led him to the development of the Epic Theater, in which plays were conceived on a grand scale and the audience kept at a distance through the use of signs, posters, and light.

In 1932 his full-length play *St. Joan of the Stockyards*—based in part on Upton Sinclair's novel *The Jungle*—depicted the Great Depression as the story of greedy speculation in the Chicago stock market. Despite his Marxism, Brecht never made himself a blind servant of party discipline. *The Measures Adopted* (1930) brought criticism from German Communist officials because it depicted the murder of a young comrade by party militants. Brecht refused to dramatize revolutionary events, believing that to use the theater for political purposes was to undermine its revolutionary fervor.

Darker forces began to encircle Brecht in the early 1930s. The air of creative genius that had given Berlin's cultural life its brilliance seemed unreal in the midst of the Great Depression, which by 1932 had raised unemployment in the city to 636,000. The ironic contrast between Berlin's cabaret culture and Germany's political realities grew sharper as Hitler's storm troopers spread violence and bloodshed. Brecht left Berlin in 1933, eventually emigrating to the United States.

The Nazi Seizure of Power

At first the Nazi party's electoral prospects were not promising. When the economy began to recover in 1924, political instability seemed to abate. The next year the country elected a new president, the revered Field Marshal Paul von Hindenburg (1847–1934), who provided middle-class Germans with a sense of security. Although Nazi membership increased from 27,000 in 1925 to 178,000 in 1929, the number of Nazi deputies in the Reichstag fell from 32 to 12. By the end of the decade the future of National Socialism was by no means clear. It required the economic shock of the Great Depression to create the mass base Hitler needed to seize power.

No other country suffered greater hardship as a result of the Great Depression than Germany: by 1932, production had fallen by 39 percent and unemployment hit almost 6 million. The economic collapse encouraged the rapid rise of extremist movements. Although other factors enhanced the appeal of Nazism to many Germans, the severe hardship and pervasive fear generated by the crisis produced the ideal environment for Nazi success. The depression polarized German politics. In parliamentary elections held between 1929 and 1932,

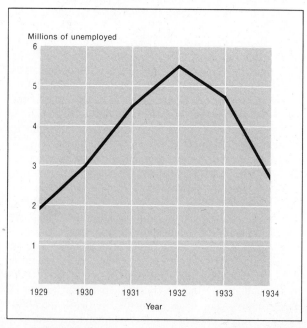

Unemployment in Germany, 1929–1934

Nazi representation rose to 230 seats, while the Communist delegation increased from 54 to 89. Moderate elements were pushed aside as these two sworn enemies battled physically in the streets and meeting halls and verbally in speeches, posters, and handbills. When the 85-year-old Hindenburg decided to run for a second term as president in 1932, Hitler and Communist leader Ernst Thälmann opposed him. Hindenburg and Hitler faced each other in a runoff, but although the now senile field marshal won, Hitler had received more than 13 million votes. The Nazis slipped to 196 seats in the November 1932 elections as the Communists raised their total to 100, encouraging some people to believe that the radical left would assume control of a government that was helpless in the midst of economic, political, and social chaos.

Hitler's followers urged him to seize control of the government forcibly in a coup d'état, while conservative antidemocratic forces—aristocratic landowners, army officers, industrialists, wealthy merchants, and financiers—were both terrified at the prospect of a Communist victory and attracted to Hitler's nationalist slogans. Hoping to manipulate him to stem mass discontent and advance their own interests, some began supplying funds to the Nazis.

On January 30, 1933, Hindenburg, fearful of civil war and pressured by his advisers, appointed Hitler chancellor of the German Republic. Hitler promptly dissolved the Reichstag and called for new elections. When the parliament building was destroyed in a fire of unknown origin, the Nazis blamed the Communists and conducted the balloting in an atmosphere of anti-Communist hysteria and intimidation. Although the Nazis won only 44 percent of the vote, support from extreme nationalists added another 8 percent to give the coalition a legislative majority. Declaring a national emergency, Hitler expelled the Communist deputies from the Reichstag, which then voted him dictatorial powers for four years. After using this authority to outlaw all other political parties, he completed the transition from democracy to dictatorship when he combined the office of president with that of chancellor following the death of Hindenburg in August 1934. Hitler destroyed the short-lived Weimar Republic and became the unchallenged ruler of a Germany that was anxious to restore its economy and regain its place in international affairs.

Nazi Germany

With great self-assurance and clear policies already formulated, Hitler embarked on a total reshaping of German life, thereby establishing the second—and even more brutal—fascist totalitarian state in Europe.

The Nazi State

Hitler created new political and administrative systems. The former states of the German Republic, such as Prussia and Bavaria, were abolished, and a highly centralized government replaced the federal structure established in 1871. Hitler christened his new regime the Third Reich and proclaimed that it would last 1,000 years. He was the Führer, the supreme commander who embodied the sovereignty of his nation. Nazi party members replaced high-ranking officials in the central and local bureaucracies. The party itself was reorganized so that local leaders occupied positions equivalent to their bureaucratic counterparts in government. Although the Reichstag remained intact, it served only to provide Hitler with a forum for public declarations and the legitimation of Nazi programs.

The new German legal system also conformed to Nazi philosophy. Law was defined as the will of the German people acting in the interests of the state and its Führer. "People's courts" replaced the regular judicial system to dispense Nazi justice arbitrarily. To enforce compliance, Hitler established a secret political police— the dreaded Gestapo—and, six months after the Nazi seizure of power, concentration camps—the first one was at Dachau, outside Munich—to hold political prisoners. Under the command of SS leader Heinrich Himmler (1900–1945), ten or more such centers were built in Germany. Prisoners were used as slave labor, while others were beaten, tortured, or starved to death. Medical personnel performed fiendish experiments on living inmates. The Nazi state deliberately abandoned all traditional moral values.

Hitler was cautious in dealing with the armed forces. The officer corps, drawn largely from the elite of Prussian society, had been a powerful and independent force in German life. The generals regarded Hitler and his followers as rabble-rousers who could be cast aside once they had generated a renewed sense of patriotism and crushed the Communist threat. Hitler brought the generals under his control by compromising his own movement and agreeing to preserve the army's independence.

In 1930 Hitler had persuaded Ernst Röhm, the exiled leader of the SA, to return to Germany and resume command of the Brownshirts. After Hitler became chancellor, Röhm pressed him to eliminate the regular army and turn the SA into a revolutionary people's force. But Hitler needed the army both to consolidate his power and to realize his larger plans for world power. In April 1934 he cut a deal with the officer corps: it would support his policies in exchange for the elimination of the SA. The result was a violent end to a major chapter in the history of National Socialism and a dramatic demonstration of Hitler's ruthlessness. On June 30—the "Night of the Long Knives"—Hitler unleashed a bloody purge of the

SA in which Röhm, scores of his associates, and most of Hitler's political enemies were murdered.

Economic Policy

To pull Germany out of the depression and make it economically self-sufficient, Hitler launched extensive public works programs that changed the appearance of Germany through reforestation, swamp drainage, and the construction of superhighways and housing. Farmers received subsidies and protection against debt foreclosure. To avoid dependence on imported raw materials, German scientists developed artificial rubber, plastics, synthetic textiles, and other substitute products.

While unemployment virtually disappeared and living standards began to rise, both employers and workers lost much of their economic freedom. Strength Through Joy, an organization similar to Mussolini's Dopolavoro, offered low-income citizens entertainment, vacations, and travel. Industry and commerce remained privately owned but were placed under strict government control. In 1936 Hitler proclaimed the first of two four-year plans that regimented economic life, including wages, profits, and production decisions. Business and professional associations became arms of the Nazi economic system, and independent labor unions were replaced with the National Labor Front, in which membership was compulsory. Strikes were prohibited, and all labor relations were regulated by the state. Hitler's economic policies and rearmament program did pull Germany out of the worst aspects of the depression, restoring relatively full employment. Yet workers paid a heavy price—the loss of their liberty and a devastating war.

Society and Culture

State coordination also affected social and cultural affairs. Conscious of the need for future soldiers and workers, Hitler promoted the enlargement of German families through a rising birthrate and improved health care. Some 20 percent of Nazi party members were women in the early 1920s, but once in power, Nazi ideologists, like the Fascists in Italy, limited the role of women in national life. In *Mein Kampf*, Hitler had written that for women "the chief emphasis must be on physical training, and only subsequently on the promotion of spiritual and intellectual values. The goal of female education must invariably be the future mother." Official propaganda projected women as symbols of Germanic female virtue in contrast to the warrior image of men.

Nazi women were generally enthusiastic about restoring traditional social values, and Hitler established a large corps of female officials to organize women in local communities. After 1937, when he began to prepare for war, women were encouraged to work in industry, agriculture, and the service sector.

For males Hitler removed many of the social barriers that had previously limited economic or political opportunities. Most middle-class citizens perceived the Nazi regime as a promoter and guardian of this social transformation.

Seamstresses sew Nazi flags in 1933. [Government Photo Archives, Berlin]

A group of young Nazis
confiscating books to be taken
to the Operplatz in Berlin for
burning in May 1933.
[UPI/Bettmann Newsphotos]

Organized religion posed a challenge to the new order and hence came under growing pressure to accept government control. Catholic and Protestant clergy were prohibited from criticizing official policies and found it difficult to maintain ties with churches outside Germany. The state discouraged children from attending religious schools while supporting the revival of anti-Christian movements that worshiped ancient Teutonic gods.

The cultural sphere drew special attention both as a means to promote the cult of the Führer and to construct the Nazi world view. Under the vigilance of the minister of propaganda, Joseph Goebbels (1897–1945), every facet of intellectual and artistic life was harnessed to generate enthusiasm for Nazi doctrine and its leader. Publishing houses came under the control of the government, which eliminated all literature not conforming to officially endorsed ideas; "offensive" books were publicly burned. The government assigned themes to writers, artists, architects, and musicians. As in Fascist Italy, sports were seen as physical demonstration of Nazi virtues. Radio and film, whose potential for shaping mass opinion was immense, were perhaps Goebbels' most powerful propaganda weapons. Leni Riefenstahl, a talented film director, won international acclaim for the seductive power of her visual imagery in such documentary films as *Triumph of the Will* (1935).

Hitler took a keen interest in art and architecture. Viewing modern styles as alien to the "Germanic spirit," he dismissed modern-minded artists and museum curators and in 1935 regimented artists under Nazi party orders. In his inaugural address at the opening of the House of German Art in Munich in 1937, Hitler denounced Impressionism, Futurism, and Cubism as Jewish-inspired "cultural bolshevism." He demanded an art that reflected German values. To illustrate the "depravity" of modernism, the government set up a permanent Exhibition of Degenerate Art. Nazi painting and sculpture reflected a Romantic hero worship inspired by the themes of Nordic mythology made famous by Wagner's operas. This official art lacked originality or creative expression, let alone aesthetic value. Instead, it glorified the Führer as a Germanic warrior, extolled the concept of "blood and soil," idealized the image of mothers and children, and depicted muscle-bound nudes as the embodiment of German strength. The Nazis also attacked modern architecture, closing down the Bauhaus and driving its architects out of Germany. Hitler and his architectural consultant Albert Speer planned to erect in Berlin monumental buildings designed in a pseudo-Greek classicism.

Underpinning all these efforts was the educational system. Schools and universities underwent a thorough reconstruction of their curricula and faculties to ensure that all students received indoctrination and only carefully screened information. The Nazi party formed a comprehensive youth movement—the Hitlerjugend, or Hitler Youth—that reinforced intellectual, psychological, and political conformity.

Hitler and the Jews

The ultimate horror of the Nazi regime began to reveal itself soon after Hitler came to power. More than any other authoritarian or totalitarian movement, National

A stylized realism characterized much
official art in the Third Reich, as in this
depiction of an example of the brave,
dedicated young people of Germany by Anton
Hackenbroich titled *New Youth*.
[Ulstein Bilderdienst, Berlin]

Socialism was based on racial and ethnic hatred. Nazi
ideologues considered the Germans a superior race who
deserved to be masters over such "undesirables" as
Slavs, gypsies, and Latins. But Hitler, whose anti-
Semitism had been formed during his Vienna days, reserved his special animosity for the Jews, whose persecution and ultimate annihilation became his obsession.

Hitler swiftly launched a campaign of official persecution against the Jews. In April 1933 the government
barred Jews from the civil service, while racial laws forbade them to study or teach in the universities or to
practice medicine, law, and other professions. In 1935
the notorious Nuremberg Laws deprived Jews of all civil
rights, including the freedom to marry non-Jews. A campaign of terror against German Jewry followed. "Jewish"
became the characteristic term of official disapproval for
everything considered negative in Nazi eyes—democracy, communism, liberalism, or individual rights.

As the anti-Semitic drive intensified, thousands of
Jews fled Germany. The assassination of a German diplomat in Paris by a young Polish Jew in 1938 was the
pretext for the infamous *Kristallnacht* ("Night of Broken
Glass"), a coordinated wave of violence that destroyed
Jewish homes, businesses, and synagogues and took
many lives; later the Jews were heavily assessed to pay
for the damage. The Western democracies, unwilling to
assume the burden of caring for millions of refugees,
refused to accept mass Jewish immigration. Although
some international protests were lodged against these
outrages, most Germans accepted them.

The Jews still in Germany now found it virtually impossible to leave, having become hostages for whom the
worst horrors still lay ahead. Nazi anti-Semitism drew
on a long tradition of persecution, prejudice, and superstition, but the Nazis went far beyond that tradition in
their effort to impose the domination of the German
"master race" on the "inferior" peoples of Europe. During World War II the fate of Germany's Jews would be
tied to that of Jews throughout the Continent as Hitler
drove anti-Semitism to its ultimate conclusion: the me-
thodical extermination of European Jewry.

Fascism as a World Phenomenon

To many Europeans the postwar world seemed to be
rapidly dividing into two antagonistic systems, communism and fascism. In Europe a struggle unfolded between left and right, between "revolution" and "reaction," that polarized around these extreme ideologies.
No European nation escaped the trauma of ideological
divisiveness or the specter of fascist radicalism. Societies as advanced as Britain's and as underdeveloped as
Romania's experienced their own peculiar brands of fascism: in each state segments of the population looked
to extreme solutions for seemingly unmanageable
problems.

Varieties of European Fascism

In France and Britain fascism was not a genuine threat
to the established order, for right-wing movements
failed to establish a mass base. But France produced
fascistlike political groups, some of which modeled
themselves after Mussolini's or Hitler's example, that
challenged the country's democratic traditions. During
the depression the Parti Populaire Français (French
People's party) had perhaps as many as a half million
members, but it was unable to unify the right. France

also produced more traditional conservative movements that capitalized on nationalism and adopted antidemocratic, anti-Semitic principles. Such groups included Charles Maurras' Action Française (French Action) and the Croix de Feu (Cross of Fire).

In Britain, where Mussolini was a popular figure in the 1920s, fascist organizations were also established. In the early 1930s the wealthy aristocrat Sir Oswald Mosley founded the British Union of Fascists. An admirer of Mussolini, Mosley modeled his union on the Blackshirts. Like Hitler, to whom he gravitated after 1933, Mosley dreamed of a Greater Britain in which all citizens were integrated into a regimented society to revive national glory. Mosley's advocacy of political violence resulted in the outlawing of the movement, and during World War II he was imprisoned.

In Spain, where the struggle between right and left was largely the result of a government unable to solve national problems, a military dictatorship under Miguel Primo de Rivera (1870–1930) emerged after 1923. His son, José António Primo de Rivera, founded a fascist movement called the Falange. In the mid-1930s Spain became the bloody battleground in the conflict between communism and fascism. The Spanish civil war was marked by the military intervention of Hitler and Mussolini on the fascist side as well as that of the Soviet Union on the side of the republican government and ended with the installation of the dictatorship of General Francisco Franco.

In Belgium, a nation bitterly divided between Dutch- and French-speaking ethnic groups, the Rexist movement of Léon Degrelle aimed at national unification in a spiritual and racial sense. A different form of fascism developed in Romania, an agrarian society with a strong Orthodox tradition rooted in peasant society. There Corneliu Codreanu's Iron Guard movement appealed to the traditional associations of soil and religion. In Austria two armed organizations, the urban Social Democratic Schutzbund (Alliance for Defense) and the rural Christian Socialist Heimwehr (Home Guard), vied with each other and with the Austrian Nazi party. Led by Prince von Starhemberg, the reactionary Heimwehr opposed democracy as bitterly as it did Hitler's attempts to Nazify the country. Under the Austrian chancellor, Engelbert Dollfuss, the Heimwehr was given representation in the government, which forged the Fatherland Front to block the union (*Anschluss*) of Austria and Germany. These movements, together with the Nazis, gained ground with the assassination of Dollfuss in 1934.

Fascism in Asia

Mussolini had predicted that fascism would be the dominant political philosophy of the twentieth century, and admirers of fascism were to be found the world over. Demagogues who modeled themselves after Mussolini

and Hitler were so popular in the United States that Anne Morrow Lindbergh, wife of the famous aviator Charles Lindbergh, spoke of fascism as "the wave of the future." In India and the Arab countries of the Middle East some nationalist leaders gravitated to fascism in the hope that it would lead to independence from colonial rule. Fascist influence may even have inspired a group of radical army officers in China to establish the so-called Blue Shirts (more properly, the "Cotton Cloth People"), although their militaristic, authoritarian program was little more than a variant of the nation-building doctrine of the Kuomintang regime of Chiang Kai-shek.

In Japan, as early as 1934 Marxist writers identified the authoritarian, militaristic, expansionist tendencies of the country as a form of fascism. The code of the samurai and emperor worship suggest that the roots of a native fascism were to be found in Japanese history. Young army officers and small ultranationalist groups pressed for radical changes in politics and the economy, and the leading nationalist ideologue of the period, Kita Ikki (1883–1937), seemed to be a Japanese counterpart of Mussolini. Kita was a former Marxist socialist who called for nationalization of some industries, state regulation of the economy, authoritarian government under the emperor, and the creation of a greater East Asian empire. None of the Japanese groups became a significant movement capable of seizing power, and Japan's constitution and political system remained largely unchanged. After Kita Ikki and some of his followers staged a revolt in Tokyo in 1936, they were executed. The continuity of Japan's political and cultural traditions proved stronger and more entrenched than the new fascistlike ferment. Moreover, the military aggression of the 1930s was not due to an indigenous Japanese fascism but was rather the result of a broad nationalist consensus in favor of expansion among Japan's traditional political and military leaders.

Brazil's Estado Novo

In Latin America fascistlike military dictatorships were widespread in the years between the wars. The rule of Getulio Vargas (1883–1954) in Brazil offers the best example of a regime strongly influenced by European fascism but shaped largely by local conditions.

The Brazilian republic, founded by the military in 1889 after the overthrow of Emperor Dom Pedro II, had proved itself unable to deal with problems of national development. The central government, representing a federation of autonomous states, was undermined by regionalism and the power of local bosses. Because the agrarian economy rested largely on coffee production, the conservative plantation owners dominated Brazil's society and its politics. Poverty and illiteracy afflicted the rural population, and the government repressed the labor movement. Only the small Brazilian middle class, represented chiefly by intellectuals and a group of young military officers known as the *tenentes*, wanted industrialization and agrarian reform.

The Great Depression, which ruined the coffee market and made it impossible for the government to repay its staggering foreign debts, brought down the republic. In October 1930 a military coup put Vargas in power as provisional president. He was to rule Brazil, with one interruption, for almost 20 years. Vargas came from a wealthy ranching family and had run unsuccessfully for president. He had few interests in life other than acquiring and exercising power. A shrewd leader, his enemies denounced him as an unprincipled dictator while his followers revered him as the "father of the poor."

Vargas tried to create worker consensus through labor legislation and government-controlled unions while simultaneously encouraging the development of a strong middle class. He diversified agriculture, limited coffee production, and extended tax incentives and government loans to business. Like Mussolini, Vargas expanded his personal power by balancing the conflicting economic and political interests that dominated the country. The left-wing *tenentes* pushed for basic reforms, while the conservatives, resenting his centralization efforts and alarmed by his economic reforms, made an unsuccessful attempt to seize power. On the surface his reforms seemed to support greater democracy and social justice—the electorate was expanded and given the secret ballot, women received the vote, social security laws and educational reforms were enacted, and labor unions were formed. In 1934 Vargas pushed through a new constitution that reduced state autonomy and established government authority over the economy. The new Chamber of Deputies reflected Mussolini's corporatist doctrine by providing for the election of representatives not only by population and area but also by class and profession. The Chamber appointed Vargas president for four years.

Vargas soon shifted to the right. He stripped the *tenentes* of their influence and suppressed the Communists. At the same time, he encouraged the growth of Integralismo, a fascist movement secretly financed by Mussolini. The Integralists, who adopted green-shirted uniforms and a paramilitary organization, railed against democracy, communism, and Jews while preaching rabid nationalism and "Christian virtues."

Vargas could not succeed himself as president, and in 1937 he assumed dictatorial power. From 1937 to 1945 Vargas ruled Brazil under the Estado Novo (New State), a totalitarian government that strongly resembled European fascist regimes. The Estado Novo abolished political parties, imposed rigid censorship, established a special police force, and filled the prisons with political dissidents. Although Vargas did not attempt the kind of mass mobilization that Mussolini and Hitler had undertaken, he denounced democracy as "decadent" and courted the workers with populist rhetoric. Vargas permitted no alternate sources of power to exist—in 1938 he banned all paramilitary groups, and when the Integralists tried to seize power, he crushed them.

◉ The Brazilian Experience: ◉
The Estado Novo

In June 1940, Getulio Vargas outlined his vision of the authoritative state to a group of his officers.

We and all humanity are passing through a historical moment of great repercussions, resulting from a violent shifting of values. We are marching to a future different from the one we knew in the realm of economic, social, and political organization, and we feel that old systems and antiquated formulae have entered into decline. It is not, however, as die-hard pessimists and conservatives maintain, the end of civilization, but the tumultuous and fruitful beginning of a new era. Vigorous peoples, fit for life, need to follow the direction of their aspirations, instead of pausing to contemplate what has crumbled and fallen into ruins. . . . Balanced economy no longer allows privileged classes to enjoy a monopoly of comfort and benefits. . . . The State, therefore, should assume the obligation of organizing the productive forces, to provide the people with all that is necessary for the collective welfare. . . . The era of improvident liberalism, sterile demagoguery, useless individualism, and disorder has passed.

Source: J. W. F. Dulles, *Vargas of Brazil: A Political Biography* (Austin: University of Texas Press, 1967), p. 210.

The economic policies of the Estado Novo were similar to Mussolini's Fascist programs. Vargas banned strikes and lockouts and stripped workers of the right to organize independently of the government. The regime set wages and hours, but although industrial workers benefited from some legislation, Vargas appeased the landowners by excluding agricultural workers from the new laws. He industrialized Brazil through a policy of economic planning and government investment in development ventures that combined public and private ownership. State technocrats expanded and rationalized Brazilian business, while Vargas preached an economic nationalism designed to free Brazil from its dependence on foreign capital. In the end he succeeded too well—he forced Brazil through a period of rapid social change and economic modernization, and his efforts eventually antagonized the traditional elites as well as his supporters.

During World War II, Vargas attempted to liberalize his regime, but in 1945 the army deposed him in a bloodless coup. Vargas, who retained his popularity among Brazilians, was again elected president in 1950. Four years later, when the army tried to force him out of office again, he committed suicide.

Brazil's Estado Novo suggests that fascism can be regarded not only as a political movement in individual countries but also as a model for resolving social and economic problems. Fascism was seen as either a means for speeding up modernization in underdeveloped countries or a method whereby old power elites could retain their authority and status. On still another level, fascism provided an example of how expanded government authority could alter the nature of society. Fascism offered new and brutally direct methods for social organization and control.

Why did fascism succeed in some cases in destroying its liberal enemy? In Italy and Germany the answer seems clear. Liberalism was in crisis at the end of World War I in Italy and poorly rooted in Germany, and traditional leaders were incapable of understanding both the new social forces unleashed by the war and the fascist response. On a more general level, the success of fascism was due to the fear and despair among people whose lives and values were threatened by economic collapse and loss of social status. This sense of desperation that led ordinary people to join fascist movements is aptly expressed in the title of the 1932 novel by German author Hans Fallada, *Little Man, What Now?*

Stalin's Soviet Union

Unlike Hitler or Mussolini, Stalin inherited an established, if not completely shaped, revolutionary system. He had several goals, the first of which was the consol-

Stalin as the genial leader—a photo of a painted portrait. [Mansell Collection]

idation of his hold over the country and its Communist party. He also wished to make Russia economically independent of the hostile capitalist powers, particularly by modernizing industry. In part he was motivated by ideological considerations. Committed to socialism as they perceived it, Stalin and his supporters were uneasy about the NEP policies introduced by Lenin, which had created a kind of market socialism based on nationalized industry, mixed private retail trade and state distribution, and capitalistic agriculture strongly influenced by state prices and quotas. Eliminating the vestiges of capitalism and introducing a new model of development became a priority, now that the economy had recovered from its wartime prostration and Stalin's political power was secure.

The Five-Year Plans

Stalin's device to attain these objectives was the five-year plan. This strategy sought to replace private property and economic activity with a system of production quotas formulated and administered by a central authority under the party's direction. The plan established production goals for every citizen. Heavy industry and transportation received most of the resources at the expense of consumer-oriented manufacturing and agriculture. The quotas were unrealistic—projected increases of 250 percent for heavy industry, 300 percent for steel production, and 150 percent for agriculture. Workers and managers who met or exceeded their targets received bonuses; stiff penalties awaited those who fell short. A new government agency, GOSPLAN, became the vehicle for translating party directives into performance. In sum, the plans attempted to impose centralized state control on resources and labor that capitalism regulated through such market forces as supply and demand or changes in wages, prices, and interest rates.

The initial plan (1928–1932) had mixed success. Frequent breakdowns in planning and implementation caused waste, surpluses, or shortages, and quotas were rarely met. Moreover, the emphasis on quantity resulted in shoddy products. Nonetheless, owing in part to the substantial importation of machinery, skilled workers, and technicians from the advanced industrial countries, production doubled in five years.

Agriculture was another story. Stalin was determined to gain control over the countryside and punish the landowning peasants who had resisted state authority. Moreover, he wanted to collect grain efficiently and pay for his industrialization programs by controlling grain prices. The method adopted was to consolidate the thousands of small family farms into a few hundred large agricultural enterprises that could use the latest mechanization and management techniques. Each huge farm would focus on a specific crop, which could be grown more efficiently. This would result in agricultural surpluses for sale abroad to finance industrialization.

In 1929 Soviet peasants were ordered to surrender their land and farm animals to the state and to become members of cooperative farms known as collectives. Under state control, each collective would receive quotas, much like factory workers or coal miners. Except for their houses and personal belongings, members were to turn over their property to the collective and to share the work and whatever profit or loss the farm recorded. Much of the peasantry—especially the well-to-do kulaks—rebelled against this system, burning crops and seed reserves or slaughtering livestock rather than surrendering them to the collectives. Across rural Russia detachments of police and, occasionally, Red Army troops attacked villages that resisted collectivization. The most capable farmers were either killed or dispatched to labor camps. The scheme was disastrous for Soviet agriculture. Livestock declined by over one-half, and the output of grain barely increased between 1928 and 1938, when it finally reached the prewar level. A famine swept the country in 1932 and 1933, the direct result of forced collectivization. Together Stalin's agrarian policy and the famine killed between 5 and 8 million persons in the Ukraine alone.

In addition to its social and economic impact, collectivization had important political implications. The systematic and brutal intrusion into the countryside saw a significant extension of the Communist party's power, for until then its direct control over the vast majority of Soviet citizens had been limited. Stalin's radical measures represented a vital step toward totalitarian control.

Declaring the five-year plan a success, Stalin announced a second in 1932 and a third six years later. In the later versions, steps were taken to improve quality and eliminate shortcomings in production and distribution. The results in industry were impressive. During the first two plans, the output of iron and steel expanded fourfold, that of coal three times; by 1938 the Soviet Union had become the world's largest producer of tractors and locomotives. Many of the new plants featured the latest equipment from America or western Europe. Agriculture, however, continued to present major problems. Grain production crept upward very slowly, and the country faced constant shortages of meat, fruits, vegetables, and dairy products. By the end of 1932 some 60 percent of all surviving peasant families had joined collective farms; by 1938 the proportion reached 93 percent. The government could count on a reasonably steady supply of basic goods for the cities. Collectivization provided Stalin with at least a political triumph.

Industrial expansion coincided with urbanization, as modern cities rose up in previously isolated areas of Siberia and central Asia. To populate them and meet the demand for labor, millions migrated from rural regions to the new manufacturing centers. Workers lost most of their independence as their unions became instruments of the state and their employment was decided by the central authorities.

Life in Stalin's Russia was harsh. Adequate housing was scarce, and wages failed to keep pace with prices—in 1937 a nonagricultural worker could afford only 60 percent of what he could have purchased in 1928. To material hardships was added the psychological strain of political indoctrination. Everyone was required to attend lectures by party activists, who extolled the virtues of Soviet socialism while warning of capitalist plots. Artists, writers, film producers, playwrights, musicians, and other communicators took seriously Stalin's command that they become "engineers of human minds" and competed as composers of Communist propaganda.

By the mid-1930s another major propaganda theme was added: virtual deification of Stalin. Unlike other dictators, Stalin shunned public appearances at mass rallies and similar functions. Yet his presence, in the form of portraits, statues, and books, was inescapable. Indeed, he became the focal point of a cult of personality comparable to those in Nazi Germany and Fascist Italy.

Social Policy

Stalin's regime offered positive incentives to labor. Unemployment virtually disappeared, and the foundation was laid for free state medical services, pensions for the elderly, subsidized housing, and day-care facilities for children. Perhaps the most meaningful benefit to many was the extension of free education to all, a policy begun in the 1920s. The government declared war on illiteracy, bringing basic schooling to even the most isolated portions of the Soviet Union. Advanced education was provided free to students demonstrating superior aptitude, and a reward system of high salaries, bonuses, and privileges awaited successful graduates. Indeed, a managerial and technocratic class soon emerged that, together with the political and artistic elites, formed a new aristocracy in this supposedly classless society. The welfare system, combined with fear of the consequences of any criticism, effectively muted discontent among the masses.

The status of women underwent significant change during the Stalinist period. The hopes of early Bolshevik feminists such as Alexandra Kollontai that the revolution would achieve equality for women were never fully realized. In 1918 the Zhenotdel, or Party Women's Bureau, was established to educate and recruit women for the Communist party. The Zhenotdel also acted as an advocate for women's interests in the workplace and sponsored women candidates for local elections. Even though it had no powers of enforcement, the Zhenotdel had an uneasy relationship with party officials, and Stalin abolished it in the 1920s.

In that decade, however, Russian women were given legal access to abortion and divorce, and although Stalin minimized the rhetoric of sexual equality, industrial policy and economic necessity resulted in wider opportunities for women. The collectivization of agriculture brought women into the fields in greater numbers, while subsistence salaries for male workers pushed millions of wives and daughters into factory jobs, public works projects, and heavy construction. The most significant change, however, came in educational opportunities, which were now open to women, especially in science, technology, and medicine. Despite the advances in education and employment, the Soviet mobilization of women increased their physical and psychological burdens, for most women were expected to care for children and do housework while working or going to school. Nevertheless, unlike the fascist regimes in Italy and Germany, which relegated women to the roles of wives and mothers, Soviet totalitarianism proclaimed the goal of female equality and made important strides in breaking the pattern of traditional roles for women.

The Great Purges

Stalin's development programs had employed totalitarian mechanisms of state control that made wide use of police terror against the peasants. But as uneasiness over his brutal methods mounted, the internal security forces, known as the NKVD, were soon turned against the Communist elite. Between 1936 and 1938 Stalin unleashed a reign of terror that engulfed eminent party members, high-ranking administrators, and military leaders. Eventually it expanded to include ordinary citizens, many of whom fell victim to sudden arrest and summary execution or exile to a remote labor camp without apparent cause. The reasons behind these "great purges" remain obscure. There is evidence of at least one serious plot against Stalin; paranoia may have so consumed him that he struck out blindly against presumed enemies.

The terror began with the assassination in December 1934 of Sergei Kirov, a close associate of Stalin's and, according to some, his chosen successor. Claiming that Kirov's murder was part of a vast conspiracy led by supporters of the exiled Trotsky, Stalin, who had in reality arranged for the murder himself, ordered mass arrests. In 1936 there began a series of public trials that captured world attention. Sixteen "Old Bolsheviks"—activists who had joined the party prior to 1917—were charged with conspiring to topple Stalin and restore Trotsky to power. Led by Grigori Zinoviev and Lev Kamenev, all confessed and were executed. Similar trials claimed

In the Soviet Union, women were mobilized into virtually all sectors of the labor force. Here a female tractor driver leads a procession to the fields. [Sovfoto]

other Old Bolsheviks, including the theoretician Nikolai Bukharin; all offered identical confessions followed by summary execution. Next the purge reached the army. A secret court-martial in 1937 found Marshal Mikhail Tukhachevsky and other officers guilty of conspiring with the Germans and the Japanese as well as with Trotsky, and all were executed. In addition, thousands of prominent party members, union officials, business executives, and intellectuals lost their liberty or their lives. Stalin culminated the purges by executing the leaders of the very police force that had implemented his program of terror. When the purges were over, millions had fallen victim to his obsession.

The great purges served to remove upper and middle-level officials in the party, state, military, and economic institutions, and Stalin replaced them with younger functionaries who would dutifully obey him. Yet the purges also had the effect of halting the revolutionary changes that had been going on in the Soviet Union since the early 1920s. Thenceforth the regime would follow the path set by Stalin's totalitarian dictatorship.

The Great Depression and the Crisis of Capitalism

By the eve of World War I the capitalist system had grown complex and global in scope. In theory, a free international market set the prices of most basic commodities, although imperialism had long since made the law of supply and demand obsolete in many sectors of the world economy. Moreover, some regions enjoyed special status as the sole producers of specific items sold to the rest of the world. Traditionally, industry and commerce were financed through a system of credit resting on the assumption that lenders or investors could collect the money owed them and that borrowers could earn enough income to repay their loans while continuing to purchase agricultural or industrial products. It was a resilient system, having weathered numerous financial crises—what today might be termed recessions—prior to 1914. But the crisis that erupted in 1929 and lasted in some respects until the outbreak of World War II was more than simply an adjustment in the world economy. Along with major changes in economic theory and practice, it brought untold suffering to millions and raised serious doubts about the viability of capitalism and the liberal political systems on which it rested.

The Economic Collapse

After an initial postwar slump, the 1920s exhibited a surge of economic vitality that brought prosperity to more people than ever before. Much of this growth derived from international trade, construction, and the development of new industries such as the automobile, radio, and motion pictures. While many people believed that the prosperity would last forever, the economic expansion had been financed largely by personal, corporate, and international credit—a shaky foundation whose flaws were exposed in the October 1929 stock market crash. Securities purchases relied heavily on margin trading, whereby investors bought stocks and bonds by putting up only a fraction of the purchase price; the remainder was borrowed from brokers, who in turn obtained credit from banks. Such unregulated practices led to widespread speculation in stocks, whose market value was often many times their actual worth. With installment credit readily available, consumers were encouraged to buy houses, automobiles, and other major items without having the cash to pay for them. Here, too, retailers and wholesalers borrowed funds from banks to pay their suppliers. Manufacturers easily obtained credit for plant expansion, and small nations received foreign loans far beyond their ability to repay. If one link in this credit chain suddenly demanded immediate repayment, the others would be forced to come up with large amounts of cash to meet their debt obligations.

The availability of easy credit concealed other serious flaws in the post–World War I economy. The new prosperity was not evenly distributed, for profits far surpassed wages for nearly all working people, and farm prices continued to lag far behind the prices charged for manufactured goods and basic services. Consequently, despite the abundance of credit, mass purchasing power was never based on solid financial ground. Furthermore, the economic optimism of the day resulted in high levels of production and huge inventories, with the possibility that unsold goods could force cutbacks and eventual job layoffs. At the international level the appearance of new states in central and eastern Europe introduced further volatility into the world economy. Since the economies of these states were immature and their finances precarious, their vulnerability to credit difficulties weakened the global economy in time of trouble.

Strictly speaking, the Great Depression began with the financial collapse touched off by the sudden deflation of the New York Stock Exchange in October 1929. In reality the world agrarian sector had already been experiencing severe hardship as the prices of basic agricultural goods followed an unchecked downward spiral. The stock market crash produced a sudden rush by creditors to call in loans at all levels, and the consequent failure of a major European lender (Austria's *Creditanstalt*) in 1931 gave the crisis an international dimension. The panic soon passed to industry, and even large corporations were forced to halt production as the markets for their goods dried up. By 1933 world production had

Anxious crowds gather outside the New York Stock Exchange in October 1929, following the crash. [UPI/Bettmann Newsphotos]

declined 38 percent and world trade had dropped to one-third its pre-1929 level. When farmers who had escaped previous difficulties were hit by the evaporation of credit and customers, the collapse of the modern capitalist economy appeared complete.

The resulting Great Depression caused mass suffering, desperation, and fear to an extent hitherto unknown in the modern West. Unemployment reached epidemic proportions—Great Britain reported 3 million unemployed in 1933, Germany 6 million, and the United States 13 million. Worldwide, some 30 million people were without jobs when the depression reached its depth in 1932. People living on fixed incomes or running marginal businesses saw their savings disappear, often literally overnight. Skilled and productive employees were reduced to supporting families on what meager welfare was available. As the depression dragged on, demoralization turned to frustration and resentment. Families disintegrated, suicides rose dramatically, and the very fabric of society seemed torn apart.

Government Response

Nations dealt with the crisis in various ways. The reactions of Britain, France, Germany, Italy, the United States, and the Soviet Union are considered individually in this and later chapters, but some general observations will prove useful here.

At first governments pursued deflationary policies that made the problem worse but then switched to pump-priming strategies, including deficit spending, to stimulate economic revival. All states, whether demo-cratic or totalitarian, undertook measures to generate work for their citizens and to limit the economic hardship as much as possible: public works programs, spending cuts, currency controls, and tariffs were among the most widespread efforts. Governments assumed a greater degree of control over economic and social life than ever before as they attempted to come to grips with the immediate consequences of the economic collapse and its long-range implications.

The Great Depression affected the future in ways that were not immediately apparent but had a lasting impact. What had once been an integrated world economy disintegrated into highly competitive national economic systems. Economic competition bred distrust between countries and fostered a spirit of nationalism that shattered post–World War I dreams of international cooperation. Extremist political movements that promised quick solutions to the crisis spread rapidly. While representative government survived in long-established Western democracies, even France, Britain, and the United States experienced profound trauma that altered their political and social traditions.

Britain, France, and the United States: The Trial of Democracy

The Great Depression challenged liberal democratic systems, yet the problems facing each of the three major democracies were unique. Common to Britain, France, and the United States, however, were an extension of state welfare measures, stronger government control over the economy, and the basic survival of democratic institutions.

Politics and Society

After 1919 Britain had to cope with a serious economic slump brought about by the end of the war and the reorientation of the global economy. In the 1920s British governments, led in succession by the Liberals, the Conservatives, and finally the Labour party, grappled with two closely related issues: chronic unemployment—which rose to 18.5 percent in the next decade—and a growing deficit produced in part by social welfare programs. Despite serious labor unrest, most notably a 1926 coal miners' general strike, in periods of severe crisis the Labourites and the Conservatives tended toward ideological convergence. Moreover, the currency policies of successive governments sheltered the British population, particularly its middle class, from the devastating inflationary cycles that ruined other countries.

The postwar period in the United States saw the economic boom of the so-called Roaring Twenties, especially in the construction and automobile industries, and America became obsessed with material wealth. Under Republican presidents Warren G. Harding (1921–1923) and Calvin Coolidge (1923–1929), the country pursued a "return to normalcy" that aimed at a nostalgic recreation of the atmosphere of the prewar era. Although Americans were suspicious of foreign political entanglements, government policies spread American economic influence into Latin America and the Pacific. The labor movement found organized action increasingly difficult in the face of government hostility, and the rapid economic growth that produced nearly full employment and better wages undercut the appeal of unions. Only farmers seemed excluded from the prosperity. Facing declining prices and rising costs well before the depression, farmers received little support from the government, and hard times had begun to grip rural America in the early 1920s.

The difficulties experienced by the farmer were often obscured by the glare of Jazz Age life in the big cities. Despite the Eighteenth Amendment to the U.S. constitution, which banned the production and sale of alcoholic beverages, popular culture was indulgent and iconoclastic. Flashy automobiles, speakeasies, gangster heroes such as Al Capone, and "flappers"—women considered bold and unconventional in behavior and dress—became symbols of America's frenzied modernism, while the election of Republican president Herbert Hoover (1929–1933) epitomized the belief in uninterrupted prosperity.

Aside from the contrasting tone of life in Britain and the United States, both represented relatively stable political states. In France, by contrast, chronic instability had long appeared to be the rule. This was due in part to the tremendous financial investment needed to rebuild the economy after the wartime destruction the country had suffered. Successive cabinets advanced—and then under fierce opposition retreated from—plans for tax increases and other measures designed to finance reconstruction. The result was a large deficit and a serious inflationary spiral. In addition, the electoral system, based on proportional representation, stimulated political factionalism with a multiparty system that necessitated coalition government.

One of the few islands of stability in the period came with the "government of national union" formed in 1926 by Raymond Poincaré (1860–1934). A careful and temperate man, Poincaré governed France for three years, during which time he restored a measure of equilibrium to the country. He stabilized the franc, halted the deficit spending programs of previous administrations, and introduced social legislation that rejuvenated the economy and eased social tensions. As living standards improved by the end of the decade, France reestablished its reputation for cultural leadership. Although Paris again became a thriving center of avant-garde artists and writers, its fame in the 1920s rested largely on its colony of brilliant expatriates, which included the writers James Joyce, Ernest Hemingway, and Gertrude Stein.

Toward the Welfare State

The Great Depression shattered the complacency that had permeated life in the three major democracies. Britain, with the apparatus of the modern welfare state well in place by 1930, endured the economic crisis with the least shock to its political system. British Labour prime minister Ramsey MacDonald (1929–1935) converted his cabinet into a national coalition government in 1931 to eliminate partisan policy disputes. He reduced unemployment compensation in 1931 and sought to stimulate economic recovery by raising taxes, reducing the budget, lowering interest rates, and changing currency and tariff policies. The Conservative governments that followed under Stanley Baldwin (1935–1937) and Neville Chamberlain (1937–1940) continued this approach. Britain weathered the crisis and experienced an economic revival in the late 1930s, based largely on the continued low prices of raw materials from abroad. However, conditions in northern England, Scotland, and Wales remained far more depressed than in the south, encouraging a flight of capital and population from what had once been Britain's industrial heartland that has continued ever since.

Although unemployment in France was not as severe as in other countries, the depression had a critical impact on the country's political system. The government failed to deal effectively with the economic collapse, so as prosperity disappeared after 1932, political tensions resurfaced. The radical right in particular posed such a serious threat that the socialists, Communists, and other leftist elements formed a coalition government under socialist Léon Blum (1936–1937), the so-called Popular Front. Social reforms aimed chiefly at the working and lower classes appeared to reduce social stress, but concerted resistance from the financial and business communities halted the recovery program. By the end of the decade France was economically worse off, more bitterly divided, and more politically unstable than any other leading European power.

The United States underwent the greatest transformation as a result of the depression. Firmly committed to the principles of a free enterprise market economy, the Hoover administration did little to halt the financial collapse of the stock market. By 1932 unemployment had reached 25 percent. Yet the mounting despair of the American people, who increasingly demanded action, did not turn against the fundamental principles of the economic and political system. Hence when Democrat Franklin D. Roosevelt (1933–1945) was elected president by a large majority, he assumed that he had received a mandate for fundamental change that would reform capitalism in order to save it.

Roosevelt represented an alternative to socialism and fascism, favoring forceful intervention by the federal government in economic life. Along with regulating the economy and stimulating business recovery through deficit spending, Roosevelt's New Deal introduced several basic social welfare programs. The result was a resurgence of industrial, commercial, and agricultural activity that, though never attaining predepression levels, stimulated significant recovery and partly cushioned the impact of the economic crisis. By 1938, when deficit spending was reduced, a new recession had set in, and it required the massive production needs of World War II to pull the nation completely out of this economic slump. Despite criticism of Roosevelt's programs, the economic turnabout his policies induced was so successful that most Americans were willing to accept them.

The United States, Britain, and France thus retained both the form and the essence of their democratic systems in the face of severe trials. Although fascistlike demagogues developed followings in all three countries, their citizens did not succumb to dictatorship, in part because these governments adopted public works projects, unemployment and health insurance, and old-age pensions to help blunt the impact of economic adversity. The real welfare state was created after World War II, but its origins were found in the social programs of the 1930s.

President Franklin D. Roosevelt inaugurated major changes in the United States' economic and social life. [UPI/Bettmann Newsphotos]

Central and Eastern Europe

The strength of liberal institutions in the United States and western Europe was not duplicated in most of eastern Europe. New states had arisen after 1919 out of the remnants of the shattered German, Austro-Hungarian, Russian, and Ottoman empires. These "successor states" were Poland, Czechoslovakia, Yugoslavia, Hungary, Austria, Turkey, and the Baltic republics of Estonia, Latvia, and Lithuania. In these nations democracy proved less resistant to the political and economic stress of the postwar period.

The Successor States

Together with the already independent countries of Bulgaria, Greece, Romania, and Albania, the successor states formed a bastion of small nations in the strategic heartland of Europe. They were governed either by constitutional monarchies with representative institutions or by republican systems modeled after Western democracies. The new democracies were considered important in London and Paris as barriers against the spread of communism and the revival of German power. Most of these states eventually abandoned democracy for authoritarian dictatorship. Although a genuinely fascist regime never ruled in any of these nations prior to World War II, the reactionary right came to dominate the political and economic systems throughout the region. The special circumstances of the successor states demanded unique approaches to governing and to socioeconomic organization that the liberal system often could not manage.

In retrospect, it is surprising that there was such confidence in eastern Europe as a proving ground for democracy. Without exception, these nations faced problems that would have staggered wealthier, well-established states. A variety of factors retarded economic development. Before 1918 the region had functioned, directly or indirectly, as colonial territory for larger powers, which had supplied it with investments and manufactured goods in return for agricultural products and raw materials. When the war ended, the area faced the sudden loss of secure markets and the inexpensive resources necessary for industrial modernization. To these problems were added a lack of native investment capital, outmoded commercial and agricultural structures, and inadequate communication and transportation systems. Indeed, except for portions of Czechoslovakia, Poland, and Austria, the economies of eastern Europe resembled those of colonial areas in Asia, Africa, or the Middle East.

Social weaknesses contributed to the economic difficulties in eastern Europe. These societies had been dominated by landowning or entrepreneurial nobility and a religious hierarchy that ruled peasants who lived as virtual serfs, despite the formal abolition of serfdom in the nineteenth century. Again with the exception of Austria, Poland, and Czechoslovakia, there was no substantial middle class of merchants, financiers, or managers to provide the expertise and resources needed for modern industrial and commercial development. The small but influential intelligentsia provided the real leadership on a local level. Much of the middle class that did exist was German or Jewish. Finally, these nations were beset with problems common to underdeveloped societies. Illiteracy, high birth and death rates, primitive health conditions, and poor nutrition combined to retard modernization and undermine the democratic systems.

In addition to the clash of interests between landowners and peasants or between the emergent urban dwellers and the much larger rural population, these states were characterized by enormous ethnoreligious diversity. For historical reasons, nearly all of them had a heterogeneous population composed of groups whose ethnic and religious affiliations were different from those of the ruling majority. In some cases, notably Poland, Czechoslovakia, Yugoslavia, Hungary, and Romania, these minorities formed a substantial proportion of the inhabitants. Except for Greece and Turkey, which solved this problem by exchanging minority groups, governments faced ongoing challenges from the minorities. The minorities' reluctance to accept the supremacy of national states, coupled with the failure of most governments to treat their minorities fairly, was a major barrier to the formation of integrated societies.

The Decline of Liberalism

Liberal democracy in eastern Europe also suffered from political liabilities. The lack of experience in representative government meant that the normal give-and-take and compromise of parliamentary systems were absent from local and national politics, with the result that policymaking was often paralyzed. Many states had a multiplicity of political parties, which made legislative activity difficult. Perhaps the most serious political liability was the intense nationalism that pervaded the region and colored the perceptions of leaders and common people alike. Some areas, such as Poland, Hungary, and Bohemia, had long-established nationalist traditions, but national animosities were deepened by the wartime experience. Those on the losing side—Austria, Hungary, Turkey, Bulgaria—were determined to regenerate patriotic pride and regain lost territory; the victors who were already independent—Romania, Greece, Albania—viewed nationalism as a device to keep the hard-won spoils of war. In the states formed from territory of the defeated empires—Poland, Czechoslovakia, Estonia, Latvia, and Lithuania—uncompromising nationalism was seen as the basis for protecting their newly won sovereignty. Nationalism in eastern Europe produced aggressive international behavior that impeded cooperation among the countries and rendered impossible the formation of regional organizations that might have resolved economic problems.

It is hardly surprising that parliamentary democracies often failed to cope with these difficulties and gave way to authoritarian dictatorships. The first nation to adopt a dictatorial government was Hungary, which turned to Admiral Miklós Horthy after a short-lived Communist regime under Béla Kun in 1919. Authoritarian leaders soon came to power elsewhere: Marshal Józef Pilsudski in Poland (1926), Antanas Smetona in Lithuania (1926), King Zog in Albania (1928), and King Alexander in Yugoslavia (1929). The Great Depression intensified the problems these nations faced and accelerated the trend toward dictatorship. King Carol began to assume dictatorial power in Romania in 1931, and within three years Engelbert Dollfuss in Austria, Konstantin Päts in Estonia, and Karlis Ulmanis in Latvia had followed suit. In 1935 and 1936 King Boris of Bulgaria and General John Metaxas of Greece completed the transformation to authoritarianism in the region. Only Czechoslovakia, under the leadership of Tomáš Masaryk and Edvard Beneš, managed to retain its democratic government, despite authoritarian tendencies and serious internal problems.

Whether they were royal, civilian, or military dictatorships, these regimes shared certain characteristics.

All retained the façade of democratic institutions, but all developed secret police systems, curtailed civil liberties, suppressed political opposition, and relied on centralized bureaucracies to enforce dictatorial decisions. Fascist movements appeared throughout the region, although none came to power before World War II. Instead, the dictators claimed that their regimes represented protection against exploitation, revolutionary unrest, or the persecution of minorities and posed as the embodiment of the national will. The appeals to nationalism and stability in an area beset with competition, mistrust, and insecurity ultimately proved too strong for the democratic experiment in eastern Europe.

As an ideology, fascism drew on the elitist, antidemocratic radicalism and nationalist-racist doctrines that emerged out of Europe's cultural ferment at the turn of the century. At the same time, modern concepts of political communication and social mobilization provided skillful leaders with the techniques for developing a power base and a new style of authoritarian leadership. The impact of World War I and the subsequent economic crisis helped discredit democratic systems and enabled these leaders to channel popular discontent into mass movements. Once in power, Mussolini and Hitler among the fascist dictators and Stalin in the Soviet Union established totalitarian states that aimed to control all aspects of life and indoctrinate their populations with new ideological values.

For contemporaries in the 1930s the world appeared to be engaged in a series of ideological struggles: a battle between democracy and totalitarianism or between capitalism and communism. Fascist victories in Italy and Ger-

many made the prospects for democracy seem dark, while in the USSR Stalin created an equally brutal police state. The Western democracies came through the economic crisis with their political institutions changed but fundamentally intact. Yet little of the democratic experiment in eastern Europe survived the decade. More dangerous still, in Italy, Germany, and the Soviet Union the totalitarian restructuring of political, social, and economic life offered compelling alternatives to the liberal order.

Finally, the spread of totalitarianism had important international repercussions. Both in Europe and in Asia militarism and the thirst for expansion began to undermine peace. With Mussolini and Hitler in power, one of the compelling forces behind the rise of fascism—nationalist frustration over the 1919 settlements—drove the dictators relentlessly toward the destruction of the postwar international order.

Suggestions for Further Reading

Arendt, H. *The Origins of Totalitarianism*, 2nd ed. Cleveland: World Publishing, 1958.

Bracher, K. D. *The German Dictatorship*. New York: Praeger, 1970.

Bullock, A. *Hitler: A Study in Tyranny*. New York: Harper & Row, 1964.

Cassels, A. *Fascism*. New York: Crowell, 1975.

Conquest, R. *The Great Terror: A Reassessment*. New York: Oxford University Press, 1989.

De Felice, R. *Interpretations of Fascism*. Cambridge, Mass.: Harvard University Press, 1977.

Deutscher, I. *Stalin: A Political Biography*, 2nd ed. New York: Oxford University Press, 1967.

Dulles, J. W. F. *Vargas of Brazil: A Political Biography*. Austin: University of Texas Press, 1967.

Friedrich, C. J., and Brzezinski, Z. *Totalitarian Dictatorship and Autocracy*. New York: Praeger, 1956.

Gay, P. *Weimar Culture*. New York: Harper & Row, 1968.

Greene, N. *From Versailles to Vichy*. New York: Crowell, 1970.

Hinz, B. *Art in the Third Reich*. New York: Pantheon Books, 1979.

Kershaw, I. *The Hitler Myth: Image and Reality in the Third Reich*. New York: Oxford University Press, 1987.

Kindleberger, C. P. *The World in Depression, 1929–1939*. Berkeley: University of California Press, 1973.

Laqueur, W., ed. *Fascism: A Reader's Guide*. Berkeley: University of California Press, 1976.

Larsen, S. U., et al., eds. *Who Were the Fascists?* Oslo: Universitetsfϕrlaget, 1982.

Lyttelton, A. *The Seizure of Power: Fascism in Italy, 1919–1929*. London: Weidenfeld & Nicolson, 1973.

Mack Smith, D. *Mussolini*. London: Weidenfeld & Nicolson, 1981.

Maruyama, M. *Thought and Behaviour in Modern Japanese Politics*. London: Oxford University Press, 1963.

Morris, I., ed. *Japan, 1931–1945: Militarism, Fascism, Japanism?* Boston: Heath, 1963.

Payne, S. G. *Fascism: Comparison and Definition*. Madison: University of Wisconsin Press, 1980.

Peukert, D. J. K. *Inside Nazi Germany*. New Haven, Conn.: Yale University Press, 1987.

Schoenbaum, D. *Hitler's Social Revolution: Class and Status in Nazi Germany*. New York: Anchor Books, 1967.

Seton-Watson, H. *Eastern Europe Between the Wars, 1918–1941*. Cambridge: Cambridge University Press, 1962.

Shannon, D. A. *Between the Wars: America, 1919–1941*, 2nd ed. Boston: Houghton Mifflin, 1979.

Tannenbaum, E. R. *The Fascist Experience: Italian Society and Culture, 1922–1945*. New York: Basic Books, 1972.

Taylor, A. J. P. *English History, 1914–1945*. New York: Oxford University Press, 1965.

Toland, J. *Adolf Hitler*. Garden City, N.Y.: Doubleday, 1976.

Ulam, A. *Stalin: The Man and His Era*. New York: Viking, 1973.

The Second World War and Its Aftermath

Some historians see the 20 years separating the two world wars as little more than a pause in an ongoing conflict that began in 1914. Clearly, the origins of World War II are to be found in part in the Great War and in the peace settlements that followed it. Nor is there any doubt that the European war that erupted in 1939 was due chiefly to the aggression of the fascist powers, especially the expansionist ambitions of Hitler.

Even more than the Great War, World War II was a truly global conflict that unfolded in two distinct theaters, Europe and Asia. The Asian war had actually begun much earlier, as Japan began its own expansionist thrust into China in the early 1930s. Japanese ambitions in Asia and the Pacific inevitably drew the United States into the war, and thenceforth America exercised a determining influence in world affairs.

The impact of World War II on the lives of nations and millions of their inhabitants was enormous. The

British Prime Minister Winston Churchill inspects the damage from a German air raid. [Brown Brothers]

waging of "total" war—war in which entire populations, civilian as well as military, were engaged in a life-and-death struggle—proved more extensive and more devastating than in 1914–1918. When it was over, the world had changed drastically and permanently, not least in that the old international system had given way to a new era dominated by two superpowers, the United States and the Soviet Union.

The Rising Sun: Japanese Expansion in East Asia

In the 1920s the Japanese came to view China, with its large territory but internally weak government, as their sphere of interest and had taken advantage of World War I and the Russian civil war to extend their influence on the mainland. In addition to providing an opportunity for territorial expansion, the Great War had also quickened the pace of Japanese industrial growth and enabled Tokyo to capture many regional markets from the Western powers. In the post–World War I period Japan became the main source of textiles and other consumer products for the rest of Asia.

But this thriving economy rested on a precarious base. Lacking essential raw materials, Japan's chief asset was its highly motivated, well-disciplined work force. Indeed, Japanese leaders were able to mobilize workers even more effectively than Europe's totalitarian dictators, producing a modern industrial machine along with a series of related commercial and financial institutions, largely controlled by a few great family trusts known as the *zaibatsu*. Political and economic leaders realized that their nation would continue to prosper only if it had a guaranteed flow of raw materials from abroad, together with secure foreign markets for its finished products. A disruption of this balance would halt the growth of Japanese power and expose its vulnerability to forces beyond its control.

The Japanese political system vigorously pursued the interests of the nation's economic elite. On paper Japan possessed a government strikingly similar to that of many European powers—a written constitution adopted in 1889, universal male suffrage since 1925, and modern parliamentary and judicial systems. But this institutional structure was largely misleading. The Diet (parliament) had sharply limited powers, and ministers governed in the name of the supreme and holy emperor, to whom they were completely responsible. A spirit of militarism pervaded Japanese life and gave the professional officer corps a political influence comparable to that enjoyed by the German military caste prior to World War I. In the 1930s Japan was the only modern nation that required its war and naval ministers to be generals and admirals

on active-duty status. Many of its younger officers, influenced by the national revival that had begun in the mid-nineteenth century, were drawn from a segment of the small landowning nobility that followed the warrior code of the old samurai. The powerful combination of nationalism, militarism, and authoritarianism that dominated Japanese politics determined that in time of crisis, ultimate authority passed to the military leaders.

After World War I, Chinese tariff barriers and the Great Depression threatened Japan's access to raw materials and markets. Younger army officers proposed the conquest of nearby territory from which materials could be obtained and to which manufactured goods—as well as surplus population—could be sent. Military spokesmen added a messianic tone to these arguments by insisting that the prosperity and progress of all Asia depended on the Japanese, who would liberate Asia from Western exploitation. Japan's imperial program thus assumed the guise of a broader campaign in defense of Asian interests.

Manchuria was the first target of Japanese expansionism. Russia, whose territory bordered Manchuria on the north and east, had dominated the area until its defeat in the 1905 war. Thereafter, although it remained nominally part of China, Manchuria became a Japanese sphere. In September 1931, Japanese colonels took advantage of a minor incident involving the South Manchuria Railway at Mukden to invade Manchuria. The civilian government reluctantly approved the army's initiative, and by early 1932 the Japanese conquest of Manchuria was complete.

When the Chinese responded with a boycott of Japanese goods, Tokyo landed 70,000 troops at Shanghai, then withdrew them under pressure from the Western powers. Japan nonetheless renamed its conquered Manchurian territory Manchukuo ("Country of the Manchus") and proclaimed it an independent state under Henry Pu Yi, the last Manchu emperor, who remained a Japanese puppet. Condemned by the League of Nations, the Japanese withdrew their membership, presenting the League with the first real test of its ability to stop aggression. The League failed to meet the challenge, imposing neither economic nor military sanctions. Japan's ambitions were emboldened by the signing of the Anti-Comintern Pact with Germany in 1936, which bound both partners to withhold aid from the Soviet Union should either party go to war with the Soviets.

Aggression and Appeasement in the West

Japan's success in defying the League of Nations encouraged Hitler's and Mussolini's quest for territorial expansion. Mussolini's emphasis on the virtues of war, combined with his dream of creating a new Roman Empire, impelled him toward conquest. Hitler was even more outspoken about his plans for a Greater German Reich in Europe, the corollary of a racial policy that aimed at bringing the "inferior" peoples of the Continent under the domination of the "master" Germanic race.

Europe and Africa: The Axis Advance

Hitler laid the groundwork for expansion while rebuilding German military strength. In October 1933, Germany withdrew from the League of Nations and the following July instigated a coup in Austria aimed at bringing about the union (*Anschluss*) of Austria and Germany. Nazi conspirators murdered Austrian chancellor Engelbert Dollfuss but were halted by Mussolini, who intervened to protect Austrian independence, which he considered vital to Italy's security.

In January 1935, Hitler won a huge majority in the Versailles-mandated plebiscite that returned the Saar region to Germany. In March he openly defied the postwar settlement, declaring that Germany had formed an air force and had reinstituted the military draft. Despite protests, Britain tacitly endorsed Hitler's actions in June 1935 by signing a naval agreement with Germany.

In the summer of 1934 Mussolini had begun preparations for the conquest of Ethiopia, one of the two remaining independent nations in Africa (the other was Liberia). Arousing enthusiasm with a propaganda campaign at home, the Duce launched his invasion in October 1935. The League of Nations promptly imposed economic sanctions, but it omitted oil from the list of products that member nations could not sell to Italy. This important exception, together with the abstention of the United States, Japan, and Germany from the boycott, virtually assured Italy of victory. In May 1936, when Mussolini proclaimed the incorporation of Ethiopia with Italian Somaliland and Eritrea into a new empire called Italian East Africa, the collective security system created at Versailles crumbled.

Hitler took full advantage of these developments. In March 1936, while the conquest of Ethiopia was under way, he ordered German troops into the Rhineland, which the Versailles treaty had established as a demilitarized zone. At the same time, he repudiated the 1925 Locarno treaties that guaranteed Germany's frontiers with Belgium and France and recognized the demilita-

The Italian campaign against Ethiopia pitted modern weapons and technology against traditional warriors and civilians. Here Ethiopian chieftains display their rifles.
[**Archive Photos**]

Hitler and Mussolini review
military plans.
[Culver Pictures]

rized status of the Rhineland. Although the French mobilized their troops, Britain refused to act. Hitler and
Mussolini had shown that the democracies were unwilling to preserve the postwar settlement. In October 1936
the Führer and the Duce agreed to coordinate an anti-
communist campaign in what Mussolini later called the
Rome-Berlin Axis.

The Spanish Civil War

The Axis partnership demonstrated its military capacity
during the Spanish civil war. When Spain became a
democratic republic after the collapse of the Bourbon
monarchy in 1931, the new government launched a cam-

Franco's victory in the
Spanish civil war forced
thousands of civilians to seek
refuge across the border in
France. [UPI/Bettmann]

Pablo Picasso produced *Guernica* to express the agony of the German bombing of the village of Guernica during the Spanish civil war. [A&R/Arxiu MAS]

◉ Guernica ◉

The aerial bombardment of the town of Guernica in April of 1937, during the Spanish civil war, became a symbol of the horror of modern warfare and inspired Pablo Picasso to paint his wrenching painting by that name. Here a British correspondent for the London Times *describes the event:*

Guernica, the most ancient town of the Basques and the center of their cultural tradition, was completely destroyed yesterday afternoon by insurgent air raiders. The bombardment of this open town far behind the lines occupied precisely three hours and a quarter, during which a powerful fleet of airplanes . . . did not cease unloading on the town bombs weighing from 1,000 lb. downwards and, it is calculated, more than 3,000 two-pounder aluminum incendiary projectiles. The fighters, meanwhile, plunged low from above the centre of the town to machine-gun those of the civilian population who had taken refuge in the fields. . . .

At 2 A.M. today when I visited the town the whole of it was a horrible sight, flaming from end to end. The reflection of the flames could be seen in the clouds of smoke above the mountains from 10 miles away. Throughout the night houses were falling until the streets became long heaps of red impenetrable debris. . . .

In the form of its execution and the scale of the destruction it wrought, no less than in the selection of its objective, the raid on Guernica is unparalleled in military history. Guernica was not a military objective. . . .

The rhythm of this bombing of an open town was, therefore, a logical one: first, hand grenades and heavy bombs to stampede the population, then machine-gunning to drive them below, next heavy and incendiary bombs to wreck the houses and burn them on top of their victims.

Source: D. A. Puzzo, ed., *The Spanish Civil War* (New York: Van Nostrand Reinhold, 1969), pp. 155–157.

paign of social and economic reform. Conservative elements, especially the military, the Catholic church, and the aristocracy, opposed the reforms and gained control of the government in 1933. In response, leftist and democratic groups formed the Popular Front, which regained power in the 1936 elections. Unwilling to accept this, army officers under the leadership of General Francisco Franco (1892–1975) revolted in July. Franco was soon joined by extreme nationalists and Spanish fascists, known as the Falange, and the nation was plunged into civil war.

The Spanish civil war was a major barometer of the willingness of democratic and totalitarian forces to act. Hitler and Mussolini poured tanks, planes, and military personnel into Spain on behalf of the Nationalists. Stalin countered by shipping equipment and military advisers to the republican Loyalists. Fearful of escalation, the British and the French adopted a policy of nonintervention. Thousands of liberals, socialists, communists, and anarchists from Europe and America who viewed Spain as an ideological battleground fought as volunteers in international brigades against the Franco forces. The agony of the Spanish people was exemplified by the German bombing of the town of Guernica on April 26, 1937. By the beginning of 1939, the Nationalists had won, and Franco became dictator of Spain.

38.1 *Central Europe, 1939*

The Czech Crisis

Emboldened by the timidity of the Western powers, Hitler annexed Austria, occupying it with German troops in March 1938. He then turned to Czechoslovakia. The 3 million ethnic Germans who lived in the Sudeten border region had never been reconciled to Czech rule. In the aftermath of the Austrian *Anschluss,* the Czech Nazi leader, Konrad Henlein (1898–1945), demanded autonomy for the Sudetenland, a move that Hitler promptly endorsed. The democratic Czech government, headed by President Edvard Beneš (1884–1948), appealed to France and the Soviet Union, with which it had defensive alliances, and mobilized its own forces. Hitler responded by threatening an invasion. War appeared imminent.

The French, unprepared to fight, yielded the diplomatic initiative to Britain's prime minister, Neville Chamberlain (1869–1940). Determined to avoid war, Chamberlain held a series of meetings with Hitler. A final conference, held in Munich with Mussolini and French premier Edouard Daladier (1884–1970) on September 29 and 30, settled the fate of Czechoslovakia. Chamberlain and Daladier accepted the demand for German annexation of the Sudetenland and forced the Czechs to acquiesce. Chamberlain then returned to London to proclaim "peace in our time." Six months later Hitler violated the agreement, moving German troops into Prague

and dismembering what was left of Czechoslovakia. It, like Austria, had ceased to exist as a sovereign state.

The Munich settlement represented the culmination of the Western policy of appeasement. The strategy of appeasement had been calculated to eliminate the dangers of war by satisfying the demands of aggressor states through peaceful negotiation. At the time the policy did not seem as shortsighted as it does in retrospect. Many agreed with Hitler and Mussolini that some aspects of the postwar peace settlements had been unfair, while others saw the instability of the new states in eastern Europe as proof of the failure of Wilsonian self-determination. Appeasement was the policy of people who had survived the horrors of World War I and were determined to avoid another at almost any cost.

Appeasement was all the more compelling because some European statesmen, still haunted by the specter of the Russian Revolution, believed that the upheavals of war would unleash communism in the West. The Great Depression had seriously weakened the economic and social order of capitalism and had shaken Western faith in democratic political systems. The lack of military preparedness in Britain and France reflected these post-1919 developments, whereas for some Western leaders the armed strength of the aggressors made appeasement seem necessary. The policy, however, only whetted the territorial appetites of Mussolini and Hitler.

⊕ Hitler's War Plans ⊕

On November 5, 1937, Hitler held a secret meeting with his military leaders in which he sketched his plans for aggression and war. Hitler's comments were recorded by his aide, Colonel Hossbach.

The aim of German policy is to make secure and to preserve the racial community and to enlarge it. . . .

Germany's future was therefore wholly conditional upon the solving of the need for space. . . .

Germany's problem could only be solved by means of force. . . .

If the *Führer* was still living, it was his unalterable resolve to solve Germany's problem of space at the latest by 1943–45.

Our first objective, in the event of our being embroiled in war, must be to overthrow Czechoslovakia and Austria simultaneously. . . . Our agreements with Poland only retained their force as long as Germany's strength remained unshaken. . . .

Actually, the *Führer* believed that almost certainly Britain, and probably France as well, had already tacitly written off the Czechs. . . .

Military intervention by Russia must be countered by the swiftness of our operations. . . .

Source: Documents on German Foreign Policy, 1918–1945, Series D, I (Washington, D.C.: U.S. Government Printing Office, 1949), Document No. 19.

World War II

At the end of March 1939—when it was clear that Poland would be Hitler's next victim—Chamberlain publicly assured Warsaw that Britain and France would defend Polish independence. By then the dictators had no reason to believe the Western powers meant what they said. On April 3, Hitler secretly ordered the invasion of Poland in September, and five days later Mussolini invaded Albania. In May, after Britain and France extended guarantees to Greece and Romania, Hitler and Mussolini signed the Pact of Steel, a formal military alliance.

In preparation for his assault against Poland, Hitler sought to guard against two possible contingencies: the intervention of Russia and, in the event that the Western powers did fight, a two-front war between Russia in the east and an Anglo-French campaign in the west. The Soviet Union had been negotiating with both sides since early spring, but mutual mistrust in Moscow, London, and Paris ultimately prevented an agreement. From Stalin's perspective, whereas an alliance with Britain and France might mean a war against Germany with no prospect of gain, Hitler offered him tangible benefits—neutrality in the event of war between Germany and the West and a division of eastern European territory. For

Stalin the choice was clear. On August 23, Germany and Russia announced a nonaggression treaty, which contained a secret protocol that divided Poland into German and Russian spheres, gave Lithuania to Germany, and ceded Finland, Latvia, and Estonia to the Soviet Union, thereby almost restoring Russia's 1914 frontiers. The Nazi-Soviet Pact was a consummate act of *Realpolitik* concluded by two bitter ideological enemies. It shattered the loyalty of many communists and supporters of the Soviets around the world. On September 1, German planes and armored columns attacked Poland. Two days later Britain and France declared war on Germany. World War II had begun in Europe.

The Nazi Onslaught

Poland fell in less than four weeks, in what the Germans called a *Blitzkrieg* ("lightning war"), which coordinated air and ground forces in a sudden furious attack. Before the collapse of Warsaw, Stalin rushed troops into eastern Poland to secure the territory promised him in the Nazi-Soviet Pact. Poland, too, was obliterated.

Unable to launch an offensive before the onset of winter, Hitler held back from an all-out assault to the west. Between late September 1939 and April 1940, this "phony war" was interrupted only by German-British

THE ROAD TO WORLD WAR II

1931	Japan invades Manchuria and leaves the League of Nations (September)
1933	Hitler becomes chancellor of Germany (January)
	Reichstag grants Hitler dictatorial powers (March)
	Germany withdraws from League of Nations (October)
1935	Hitler announces German rearmament (March)
	Mussolini invades Ethiopia (October)
1936	Hitler reoccupies the Rhineland (March)
	Outbreak of Spanish civil war (July)
	Rome-Berlin Axis; Anti-Comintern Pact between Germany and Japan (November)
1937	Japan invades China (July)
	Italy withdraws from the League of Nations (December)
1938	Germany annexes Austria (March)
	Munich Pact dismembers Czechoslovakia (September)
1939	German troops occupy Prague (March)
	Italy invades Albania (April)
	Pact of Steel: military alliance between Germany and Italy (May)
	Nazi-Soviet Nonaggression Pact (August)
	Hitler invades Poland (September 1)
	Britain and France declare war on Germany (September 3)

naval engagements. In the meantime, the Soviet Union moved troops into Estonia, Latvia, and (as a result of a new agreement with Germany) Lithuania and on November 30 invaded Finland, conquering it by March 1940 after unexpected resistance. In April, Hitler suddenly struck at Norway and Denmark. The latter fell in less than a day, Norway by the end of the month. Then, on May 10, the full weight of the German war machine was flung against Belgium and the Netherlands. The same day, Chamberlain resigned and was replaced as prime minister by Winston Churchill (1874–1965).

Although the combined British, French, Belgian, and Dutch forces matched Germany's 134 divisions, the Allies were deficient in planes and antiaircraft power and overwhelmed by German *Blitzkrieg* tactics. By the end of May the Germans had pushed the Allied armies to the English Channel, where more than 330,000 French and British troops were evacuated from Dunkirk to England. Bypassing the Maginot Line, a chain of static fortifications that ran north from Switzerland, the Germans pushed rapidly through Belgium into France, outflanking French forces. On June 10, Mussolini, who had kept Italy neutral but now feared that the war might be over before he could act, declared war. French premier Paul Reynaud turned over the government to 84-year-old Marshal Henri Pétain (1856–1951), the hero of Verdun. Determined to salvage what he could, Pétain sued for terms. The armistice, signed on June 22, 1940, granted the Germans occupation of more than three-quarters of France, leaving the southern portion of the country to Pétain, who established a puppet regime in the city of Vichy. A small resistance group led by General Charles de Gaulle (1890–1970) escaped to London and formed the Free French organization. In less than

two months, France, the mainstay of democracy in continental Europe, had fallen.

Allied Resistance and Axis Setbacks

With France defeated, Hitler was certain that Britain would finally seek an accommodation. To hasten this, he unleashed his air force against Britain in July to wreck civilian morale by terror bombing. Churchill, Britain's new leader, was a veteran of its imperialist wars and had served as First Lord of the Admiralty during World War I. In the face of adversity, he also proved to be a stirring orator. A convinced anticommunist, he had once expressed admiration for Mussolini but since 1936 had strongly opposed appeasement. Now he personified the British will to resist. Outnumbered by more than 2 to 1, the Royal Air Force (RAF) fought in the skies over London and other cities, inflicting unexpected casualties on the German *Luftwaffe*. In London, St. Paul's Cathedral remained almost alone in the midst of devastated streets as a symbol of survival, while Churchill rallied the nation in eloquent speeches. Unable to launch an amphibious invasion against a superior navy and facing mounting air losses, Hitler broke off what came to be called the Battle of Britain.

Stymied in Britain, the Axis turned to eastern Europe and North Africa. The Italians assaulted the British stronghold in Egypt in September and were repulsed into Libya, but Hitler salvaged the operation and pushed to within 100 miles of the Suez Canal. The pattern was repeated in October, when Mussolini invaded Greece.

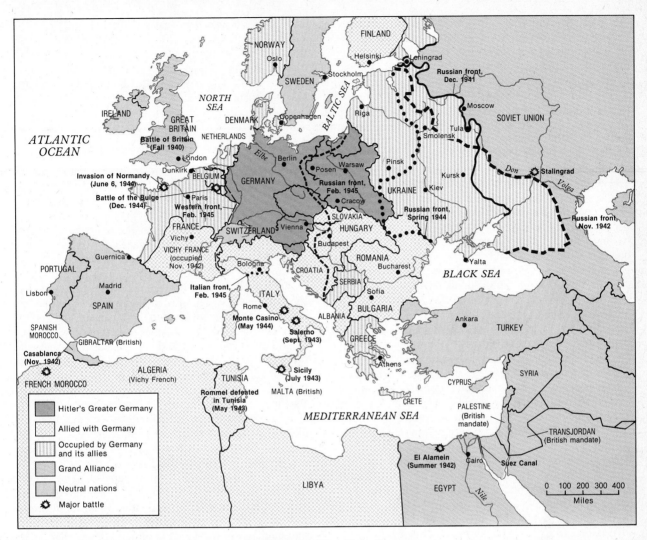

38.2 World War II in Europe

Valiant Greek resistance, British aid, and poor Italian equipment required Hitler to intervene again. Together with Hungarian and Bulgarian troops, the Germans overran Yugoslavia and defeated Greece.

As early as July 1940, Hitler ordered preparations for an invasion of Russia. Despite the Nazi-Soviet Pact, Hitler remained obsessed by the desire to destroy Bolshevism and to gain control of the grain-rich fields of the Ukraine. Once Russia was defeated, he believed, Britain would be forced to capitulate. The Russian invasion began on July 22, 1941. "Operation Barbarossa" moved the mightiest army in history—some 175 German divisions—against a vast, unfortified front. The Germans took the Soviets by surprise and, shattering their weak defenses, killed or captured 2 million soldiers in the first months of the campaign. By late October, Russia appeared about to collapse. But instead of allowing his generals to make a concentrated push against Moscow, Hit-

ler insisted on dispersing his forces along the front. An early winter brought the German offensive to a halt, just as it had Napoleon's Grand Army in 1812. When Stalin's troops counterattacked, first in November and again in December, the Nazi war machine suffered its first setbacks. With Britain holding out in the west and Russia having survived in the east, Hitler now faced the prospect of a two-front war.

The United States and Japan: The Road to Pearl Harbor

Among the great powers of the world, only the United States remained at peace. Disillusionment over the outcome of World War I had nurtured isolationist sentiment among many Americans, and when President Franklin Roosevelt came into office, he moved cautiously to make the nation aware of the precarious state of world affairs. Roosevelt wanted the United States to exert its influence against fascist and Japanese expansionism. But as the threat of war mounted, isolationists in Congress passed neutrality laws that prohibited the export of arms. Nevertheless, the Japanese drive into northern China in the summer of 1937 moved the American government into an openly anti-Japanese position. That October, Roosevelt, in a public statement known as the Quarantine Speech, declared that war was a contagion that had to be contained.

The outbreak of war in Europe found the American public sympathetic to Britain and France but unwilling to become directly involved. Roosevelt, determined to supply France and Britain with weapons, secured a revision of the neutrality laws that enabled the Allies to buy arms on a cash-and-carry basis. As the Nazis stormed across western Europe, he obtained a $1 billion defense appropriation. Public opinion began to rally behind the president during the Battle of Britain, and in September 1940, Congress implemented the first peacetime draft in American history. Two months later, as British resources neared exhaustion, Roosevelt devised the lend-lease program, which extended unlimited goods, instead of credit, to Britain. In the wake of the Nazi invasion of Russia, munitions were also sent to the Soviet Union under the same plan. America had become, in Roosevelt's words, "the arsenal of democracy."

In August, Roosevelt and Churchill met on a cruiser off the Newfoundland coast to sign a statement of principles tantamount to war aims. This Atlantic Charter, signed on August 14, not only called for national self-determination, disarmament, and "freedom from fear and want" but also looked forward to "the final destruction of the Nazi tyranny" and unconditional German surrender.

Asian events finally brought America into the war. United States policy toward Japan had already hardened over China. Now, with the Western powers fighting in Europe, Japanese expansionists saw their opportunity. In September 1940, Japan signed a defensive Tripartite Pact with Germany and Italy, extending the Axis alliance to Asia. America responded by banning the sale of essential raw materials, including iron, steel, and aviation fuel, to Japan. Negotiations initiated with the United States in the spring of 1941 by Prince Konoye, the Japanese premier, resulted in deadlock. Hitler's invasion of Russia freed Japan to move without fear of Soviet interference, and in July it occupied Indochina. Roosevelt immediately froze Japanese assets and joined with Britain in imposing economic sanctions. The failure of negotiations, together with the stiff American response to Japan's conquest of Indochina, played into the hands of the extremists in Tokyo. In October, General Tojo Hideki (1885–1948), a militarist, became premier. On the morning of December 7—without a declaration of war

and while Japanese envoys were meeting with American officials in Washington—two waves of Japanese planes attacked the United States naval base at Pearl Harbor, Hawaii, striking a devastating blow at American power in the Pacific. The next day the United States declared war on Japan.

The War in China

The Second World War was far more a global conflict than the first, and the major theater outside Europe was Asia. More territory and people in Asia were involved in the fighting than in any other part of the world. Asia experienced the first and so far the only use of nuclear weapons, by the Americans against the Japanese, and China suffered the greatest number of war casualties of any nation.

For China the war had actually begun in 1931 with the Japanese invasion of Manchuria and escalated to an all-out battle for survival when the Japanese attacked Peking and Shanghai in 1937 and fought their way to the Kuomintang capital of Nanking. Japanese troops, with the full knowledge of their commanders, went on an orgy of killing when Nanking fell, vowing to punish the Chinese for holding up the imperial army by their resistance in Shanghai and on the route to Nanking. Chiang Kai-shek had committed most of his best soldiers and modern weapons to slowing the Japanese drive for Nanking, but it was innocent civilians—probably as many as 300,000 dead—who suffered in the so-called Rape of Nanking once the Japanese entered the city. Survivors described horrifying sights of raped women impaled on stakes and children sliced in two.

Chiang's government and the remnants of his army retreated westward to Chungking (Chongqing). The Kuomintang war effort was largely spent, its best troops and equipment gone. New conscription drives in the western provinces brought the army to some 5 million men, but they were poorly clothed and fed, often virtually starved, and tyrannized by their officers; they had few or no weapons and very poor morale. The Japanese invasion was stalled by the mountains of western China, by overextended supply lines, and by the effective guerrilla resistance of the Communists in the north, who pinned down 1 million enemy troops but were never themselves eliminated. Japanese planes bombed the cities left under Chinese control almost at will after 1937 but had little military effect except to kill many thousands of civilians.

A few small battles took place, largely ineffective retreating actions by demoralized and poorly led Chinese forces easily brushed aside by Japanese columns probing westward. Near the Burma border in the far southwest, periodic artillery duels across the gorge of the Salween River broke out, but no real battles. In the north a

Aftermath of the Japanese bombing of Shanghai in 1937. [UPI/Bettmann Newsphotos]

different kind of war hurt the Japanese far more. Chinese Communist guerrillas controlled most of the countryside at night, especially west of the coastal plain, bombing bridges, roads, and railways and ambushing Japanese patrols but avoiding pitched battles, given the vast Japanese superiority in equipment. The guerrillas confined the invaders to the cities and towns, and as the war progressed, they won control of much of the rural north while they too depended on mountains and distance to limit enemy occupation to urban areas in the east. When Japan surrendered in August 1945, its armies still held most of the eastern half of China, from which the Chinese never had the strength to drive them.

But although there were only skirmishes rather than major battles after 1937, more than 21 million Chinese died at the hands of the Japanese between 1937 and 1945, most of them civilians. The occupying army was at least as ruthless as the Nazis in Europe, exterminating whole villages as part of a policy of terror and slaughtering noncombatants indiscriminately. Their officially sanctioned slogan was "Kill all, burn all, loot all!" In the occupied territories the Japanese forced Chinese to bow or even kneel to their officers and beat or shot them if they were not sufficiently deferential. The record of the

Japanese was equally bad elsewhere in Asia, but in China they began much earlier and made no real effort to win local support. Like Nazi terror, Japanese brutality stemmed also from a conviction of their own cultural and even racial superiority and from their contempt for the people they conquered. It was a grim period in the history of East Asia. At the end of the war, the Kuomintang had been fatally weakened, and the Communists had grown from a tiny and hunted band to a major military presence in the north. Their effectiveness against the Japanese had won them a broad base of popular support even among many in the Kuomintang-controlled areas, and by mid-1945 they were the real government of much of the north.

❦
CHUNGKING: BELEAGUERED WARTIME CAPITAL

Just before the fall of Hankow (one of the three cities now part of Wuhan) on the central Yangtze in October 1938, China's capital moved farther upriver to Chungking, where it remained for the rest of the war. Chungking sprawled over steep hills at the junction of the Chialing (Jialing) River and the Yangtze near the center of the generally hilly Red Basin of Szechuan (Sichuan), which was in turn surrounded on all sides by mountains. The steep and narrow gorges of the Yangtze about halfway between Hankow and Chungking along the provincial border were easily blocked by a boom. These natural defenses kept Chungking secure from the Japanese army, but it had few defenses against air attack, and Japanese bombing caused great destruction and loss of life. By 1941, before Pearl Harbor, an unofficial American group, the Flying Tigers, paid by the Chinese but with their own fighter planes, had greatly reduced the bombing raids. Chinese morale was high for the first two or three Chungking years, and the wartime capital was a symbol of patriotic resistance. Whole arsenals and factories had been disassembled and carried on the backs of workers to Chungking and elsewhere in Szechuan to escape the Japanese; university faculties and students made the same journey, carrying what they could of their libraries and laboratories. America's entry into the war against Japan in late 1941 gave morale another boost.

But disillusionment spread as the Kuomintang army largely sat the war out while the increasingly corrupt government of Chiang Kai-shek and his cronies stockpiled arms for use against the Communists. Chungking was also notorious for its gray, cloudy weather; its drizzle; its suffocatingly hot summers and cold, damp winters; and its painful overcrowding. More than a million people from all parts of China, including officials and army personnel, were added to the original small population, with too few additions to housing, water supply, and other basics. Fires set by Japanese bombs often burned out of control, and air raid shelters were grossly inadequate. Chungking's main link with the outside world was the extension of the Burma Road through mountainous southwest China and, after the Japanese took Burma, the American airlift from India over the "hump" of the Himalayas. The main airport was a sandbank in the Yangtze hemmed in by steep hills on both sides, flooded every spring and summer by rising river levels and obscured most of the time by heavy low clouds. The summer airport was on the edge of a cliff above the river, which was equally dangerous. There were no railways anywhere in Szechuan. People understandably felt isolated. Prices for everything skyrocketed through a combination of wartime shortages, government ineptitude, and a swollen population. The Szechuanese blamed it on "downriver people," who in turn were contemptuous of "ignorant provincials."

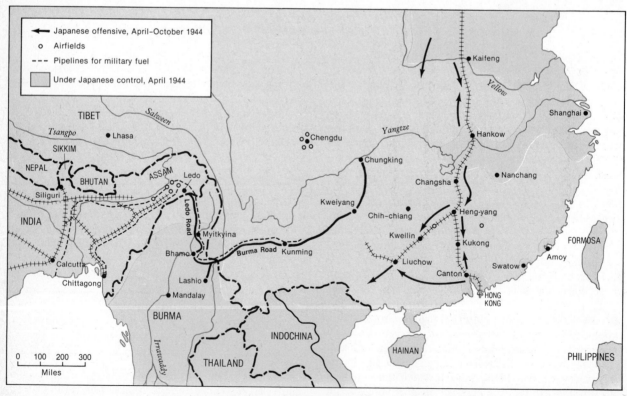

38.3 The China-Burma-India Theater in World War II

Tight "thought control" and the secret police suppressed all free political expression, and people with "dangerous thoughts" or caught with "improper" books in their dwellings were jailed or executed. Those with money and connections lived luxuriously in guarded villas with American-made limousines, but most people in Chungking lived in poverty, mud, and squalor. By 1940 inflation began to rise at about 10 percent per month, accelerating wildly after 1943. Currency might lose half or more of its value between morning and afternoon. The government printed more notes of larger denominations, while its finance minister, H. H. Kung, brother-in-law of Chiang Kai-shek, obtained gold from the United States for his own accounts in overseas banks, as did other Kuomintang officials. Salaries and wages fell hopelessly behind inflation, and malnutrition, tuberculosis, and other diseases of poverty were widespread. Furniture, clothing, books, and heirlooms were sold in a vain attempt to stay afloat. Nearly all officials succumbed to bribery and other forms of corruption, whatever their original principles, if only to save their families. By the end of the war the Chinese were universally demoralized and had lost faith in the Kuomintang. The Chungking years saw the death of Kuomintang hopes to remain the government of a China now sick of its ineffectiveness, corruption, and reaction.

India and Southeast Asia

India was only marginally involved in the war, although 2 million Indian troops fought under British command in several theaters, and India itself became a major military base and supply center for the Allied war effort in Asia. A few Japanese bombs fell on Calcutta, but the big invasion push through northwestern Burma was stopped by British and Indian troops at Imphal, just inside the Indian border, in the spring of 1944, followed by the accelerating collapse of the Japanese position in Burma as British and Indian forces advanced. Ceylon served as a major Allied base and became the headquarters of the Allied Southeast Asia Command under Lord Louis Mountbatten (1900–1979), who directed the reconquest of Burma and Malaya.

A frustrated Bengali and Indian nationalist, Subhas Chandra Bose (1897–1945), who had been passed over for leadership in the Congress party, saw his chance for power in alliance with the Japanese. Bose had visited Mussolini and Hitler in Europe. He escaped from British arrest in 1941, made his way to Berlin, and in 1943 went by German submarine around Africa to Singapore, where the Japanese gave him command of 60,000 Indian prisoners of war. He called them the Indian National Army for the "liberation" of their homeland, but they were used as cannon fodder in the advance wave for the bloody and fruitless assault on Imphal. Bose escaped and was later killed in an air crash, but he remained a national hero to some Indians.

Japan and the Pacific Theater

The chief military action in Asia took place in the Pacific. Following the attack on Pearl Harbor, the Japanese conquered Malaya, Burma, Indonesia, and the Philippines in rapid succession. This onslaught was aided by Japanese use of French bases in Indochina, granted by the Vichy government in mid-1940 and vital to the assault on Southeast Asia.

The speed of the Japanese advance paralleled that of the Nazis in Europe. Japanese dive bombers destroyed the major ships of the British Asian fleet off Singapore as they had sunk most of the American fleet at Pearl Harbor. The Americans now lacked the naval capacity to defend or supply the Philippines, where much of their air force had been destroyed on the ground a few hours after the Pearl Harbor raid. The Japanese had developed a light, fast, maneuverable fighter plane, the Zero, which gave them air supremacy. The Dutch East Indies (Indonesia) were weakly defended, and no help was available for the greatly outnumbered Dutch. Thailand remained neutral, but at the price of granting Japanese use of bases there. By early 1942 Japan had occupied all the smaller islands in the western Pacific and installed garrisons even in the western Aleutians off Alaska.

Japan's thrust southward had long been planned as part of the "Greater East Asia Coprosperity Sphere." Japan claimed that it would liberate Asia from Western colonialism, but the real aim was to combine its technological, industrial, and organizational skills with the labor and resources of the rest of East Asia, thereby creating a single economic entity dominated by Tokyo. Poor in natural resources, Japan sought access to the oil, rubber, tin, and rice of Southeast Asia and the iron ore and coal of the Philippines and China. But Japan ignored the rising force of nationalism, first in China and then in its Southeast Asian conquests. Almost from the beginning, Japanese racist arrogance and brutality made a mockery of "coprosperity" and earned the Japanese bitter hatred everywhere. Western prisoners, including the defeated American forces in the Philippines, were treated with special cruelty. Japan was now master of Asia, and its warrior tradition had only contempt for soldiers who surrendered even when their position was hopeless.

The Price of Victory

The brutality of Japanese rule in Asia was on a massive scale, but it lacked the carefully organized, systematic scope of Nazi atrocities in Europe. As the year 1942 opened, Hitler controlled, directly or indirectly, a huge empire that stretched from the English Channel to the gates of Moscow and from Norway to North Africa. His goal, after victory, was to create out of this area a "New Order" with Germany as its center and around which Europe and the world would revolve. Hitler never developed detailed plans for his empire. Yet the war provided ample evidence of what the New Order would have entailed.

Descent into the Abyss: The Holocaust

Hitler's plans derived from his notions of race, which he believed held the key to world history. Nazi racial ideologues divided Europe's population into three broad categories: the master "Aryan" race of German-speaking or related peoples, below which stood the Latins, and at the bottom the Slavs, Jews, and gypsies. Hitler dealt with the conquered territories according to this scale of values. The inferior populations of the eastern regions would provide Germany with *Lebensraum* ("living space") and a huge supply of cheap or slave labor. Immediately after the conquest of Poland, pockets of German colonists were established there, and more than 1 million Poles were brought to Germany as forced workers. Later even greater numbers of Russian prisoners suffered the same fate.

Nazi policy in eastern Europe was a vital part of Hitler's geopolitical scheme, but the Jews were at the core of his obsession about race. He spoke repeatedly of making Germany *Judenrein*, or free of Jews, and in *Mein Kampf* he described how the Nazi state would breed a population of Aryans free of the sick, the weak, and, most important, the Jewish "contagion." As early as 1919, Hitler had written that "the final objective" of anti-Semitism must "unswervingly be the removal of the Jews altogether."[1]

After the seizure of power, Nazi policies had forced the vast majority of German Jews to emigrate, so that by 1939 few were left in the Reich. Once the war began, large-scale emigration from areas under German control became impossible, and Nazi officials evolved barbaric plans to deal with the millions of Jews in the conquered territories of Poland and eastern Europe. They first schemed to concentrate Europe's Jews in "reservations" in the Lublin district of Poland or on the island of Madagascar. As plans for the invasion of Russia progressed, the removal policy gave way to the Final Solution—the extermination of European Jewry.

Hitler gave SS leader Himmler orders for the Final Solution in the spring or early summer of 1941. As the German army pushed eastward, special SS units—*Einsatzgruppen* ("special-duty groups") commanded by police chief Reinhard Heydrich—herded Jews into ditches behind the front lines and shot them. Mobile gassing vans were also used. By fall the extermination process had been organized on a massive scale as Jews and other victims were transported by rail from all over the Continent to death camps in Poland.

The SS murdered millions in extermination camps such as Auschwitz, Treblinka, and Bergen-Belsen, where tens of thousands of men, women, and children were gassed to death each day. A precedent for the killing had been set earlier by the gassing of 70,000 mentally ill Germans. The bodies of the victims were stripped of clothing, hair, and gold teeth. Corpses were either processed for soap and fertilizer or burnt. Outside the

A group of Polish Jews are marched to the death camps flanked by German Gestapo agents. [UPI/Bettmann Newsphotos]

camps, in Poland and Russia, SS squads continued to slaughter many thousands more, shooting and burying their victims in mass graves.

The Nazis murdered a startling range of victims in their effort to purge Europe of "undesirable" elements, including gypsies, the infirm and mentally ill, Jehovah's Witnesses, and some 60,000 known German homosexuals. But their primary focus remained the Jews. Some estimates suggest that more than 6 million Jews perished in the Holocaust, more than three-fourths of Europe's Jewish population. Beyond the statistics lies the memory of the planned elimination of entire categories of human beings by a modern, technologically advanced society. Modern history has known no more heinous example of human barbarism.

<hr>

❧
ISABELLA KATZ AND THE HOLOCAUST: A LIVING TESTIMONY

<hr>

No statistics can adequately render the enormity of the Holocaust, and its human meaning can perhaps only be understood through the experience of a single human being who was cast into the nightmare of the Final Solution. Isabella Katz was the eldest of six children—Isabella, brother Philip, and sisters Rachel, Chicha, Cipi, and baby Potyo—from a family of Hungarian Jews. She lived in the ghetto of Kisvarda, a provincial town of 20,000 people, where hers was a typical Jewish family of the region—middle-class, attached to Orthodox traditions, and imbued with a love of learning.

In 1938 and 1939 Hitler pressured Hungary's regent, Miklós Horthy, into adopting anti-Jewish laws. By 1941 Hungary had become a German ally, and deportations and massacres were added to the restrictions. Isabella's father left for the United States, where he hoped to obtain entry papers for his family, but after Pearl Harbor, Hungary was at war with America and the family was trapped. In the spring of 1944, when Hitler occupied Hungary, the horror of the Final Solution struck Isabella. On March 19, Adolf Eichmann, an SS officer in charge of deportation, ordered the roundup of Jews in Hungary, who numbered some 650,000. On May 28, Isabella's nineteenth birthday, the Jews in Kisvarda were told to prepare for transportation to Auschwitz on the following morning. Isabella recalled:

And now an SS man is here, spick-and-span, with a dog, a silver pistol, and a whip. And he is all of sixteen years

After the liberation of an extermination camp, German civilians are forced to witness the unspeakable horrors of the Final Solution. [AP/Wide World Photos]

old. On his list appears the name of every Jew in the ghetto. . . . "Teresa Katz," he calls—my mother. She steps forward. . . . Now the SS man moves toward my mother. He raises his whip and, for no apparent reason at all, lashes out at her.[2]

En route to Auschwitz, crammed into hot, airless boxcars, Isabella's mother told her children to "stay alive":

Out there, when it's all over, a world's waiting for you to give it all I gave you. Despite what you see here . . . believe me, there is humanity out there, there is dignity. . . . And when this is all over, you must add to it, because sometimes it is a little short, a little skimpy.[3]

Isabella and her family were among more than 437,000 Jews sent to Auschwitz from Hungary.

When they arrived at Auschwitz, the SS and camp guards divided the prisoners into groups, often separating family members. Amid the screams and confusion, Isabella remembered:

We had just spotted the back of my mother's head when Mengele, the notorious Dr. Josef Mengele, points to my sister and me and says, "Die Zwei" [those two]. This trim, very good-looking German, with a flick of his thumb and a whistle, is selecting who is to live and who is to die.[4]

Isabella's mother and her baby sister perished within a few days.

The day we arrived in Auschwitz, there were so many people to be burned that the four crematoriums couldn't handle the task. So the Germans built big open fires to throw the children in. Alive? I do not know. I saw the flames. I heard the shrieks.[5]

Isabella was to endure the hell of Auschwitz for nine months.

The inmates were stripped, the hair on their heads and bodies was shaved, and they were herded into crude, overcrowded barracks. As if starvation, forced labor, and disease were not enough, they were subjected to unspeakable torture, humiliation, and terror, a mass of living skeletons for whom the difference between life and death could be measured only in an occasional flicker of spirit that determined to resist against impossible odds. Isabella put it this way:

Have you ever weighed 120 pounds and gone down to 40? Something like that—not quite alive, yet not quite dead. Can anyone, can even I, picture it? . . . Our eyes sank deeper. Our skin rotted. Our bones screamed out of our bodies. Indeed, there was barely a body to house the mind, yet the mind was still working, sending out the messages "Live! Live!"[6]

In November, just as Isabella and her family were lined up outside a crematorium, they were suddenly moved to Birnbäumel, in eastern Germany—the Russians were getting nearer and the Nazis were closing down their death camps and moving the human evidence of their barbarism out of reach of the enemy. In January, as the Russians and the frigid weather closed in, the prisoners were forced to march through the snows deeper into Germany, heading toward the camp at Bergen-Belsen. Those who could not endure the trial fell by the side, shot or frozen to death. On January 23, while stumbling through a blizzard with the sound of Russian guns in the distance, Isabella, Rachel, and Chicha made a successful dash from the death march and hid in an abandoned house. Two days later Russian soldiers found them. Philip had been sent to a labor camp, and Cipi made it to Bergen-Belsen, where she died.

Isabella later married and had two children of her own, making a new life in America. Yet the images of the Holocaust remain forever in her memory. "Now I am older," she says, "and I don't remember all the pain. . . . That is not happiness, only relief, and relief is blessed. . . . And children someday will plant flowers in Auschwitz, where the sun couldn't crack through the smoke of burning flesh."[7]

The Grand Alliance: Victory in Europe

By 1942 the Grand Alliance of Russia, Britain, and the United States had been formed against Hitler's New Order. From the first the Allies were plagued by mutual distrust: Churchill feared Soviet territorial designs in Europe and what he believed was America's ignorance of European affairs; Roosevelt suspected Churchill's imperialist ambitions in the Mediterranean and Stalin's political motives; and Stalin suspected both Western statesmen, who hated communism, of wanting to deny the Soviet Union the fruits of victory. Nevertheless, they agreed to make military objectives—defeating first Germany and Italy, then Japan—their immediate goal, postponing political issues until the war was won. In January 1942 the three powers joined with 23 other nations in a declaration that reaffirmed these goals as well as the principles of the Atlantic Charter.

The tide of battle began to turn in favor of the Allies in 1942. In May and June, American forces stopped the Japanese advance in the Pacific in crucial battles in the Coral Sea and at Midway Island. In November the United States and Britain launched Operation Torch, the invasion of North Africa.

Under the pressure of the gigantic battles that were consuming Russian forces on the eastern front, Stalin had repeatedly insisted on the opening of a major second front in the west. No nation sustained a greater burden of physical destruction and death than the Soviet Union, which lost some 20 million men, and no nation contributed more to the defeat of Germany. Since the winter of

1941 the German armies had continued to batter the Russians along an 1,800-mile front, but in August 1942 the German war machine was flung at the southern zone in a protracted battle for Stalingrad. The situation appeared hopeless when the Germans stormed the city in September. But Stalin's armies, circling around from the south and north, caught Hitler's forces in a gigantic pincer movement. Although winter fast approached, Hitler refused to withdraw his soldiers. On February 2, 1943, the last of the 500,000-man Sixth German Army surrendered. That July, German and Russian forces fought bitterly along the Kursk salient, southwest of Moscow, in the biggest tank battle of the war. A clear victory for the Russians, the engagement cost another half million German casualties and spelled ultimate defeat for Hitler.

Churchill and Roosevelt had met in January 1943 in Casablanca, where they made plans for opening the second front. To forestall the Soviets in central Europe, they chose Italy as the target, and in July, Allied troops landed in Sicily from their base in North Africa. The Sicilian invasion precipitated a coup d'état against Mussolini by dissident Fascists and involved King Victor Emmanuel III and Marshal Pietro Badoglio. The king arrested Mussolini and appointed Badoglio prime minister, but Hitler quickly moved German troops into northern Italy and rescued the Duce. By early September, when the Italians signed an armistice and joined the Allies as a co-belligerent against Germany, the Allies had crossed to the mainland. In the north Mussolini established a puppet regime, the Italian Social Republic, under German auspices. Thereafter, for 18 months Italy became the scene of bitter fighting, not only between the Allies and the Axis but also between Fascist loyalists and a massive partisan resistance movement.

In October 1943, Allied foreign ministers meeting in Moscow reiterated their demand for unconditional surrender. They also agreed to the joint occupation of Germany, the purge of Nazism, and the creation of a United Nations organization to replace the discredited League of Nations. A month later Churchill and Roosevelt met with Stalin in Tehran for their first face-to-face conference. The talks focused on plans for the final attack against Hitler's "Fortress Europe." The three agreed to an invasion of western Europe in the spring of 1944.

Operation Overlord began on June 6, 1944—"D day." Under the supreme command of General Dwight D. Eisenhower (1890–1969), the Allies carried out the greatest amphibious landing in history on the coast of Normandy. More than 2 million men and millions of tons of equipment poured into northwestern France over the

The female labor force in the United States more than doubled during World War II. Here women riveters work on an airplane. "Rosie the Riveter," became a popular icon. [UPI/Bettmann Newsphotos]

next few months. By the end of August, Allied armies had driven the *Wehrmacht* to the frontiers of Germany, but the drive stalled. In a desperate effort to stave off defeat, Hitler launched a counteroffensive in December, driving deep into the Allied sector in Belgium and Luxembourg, but the bloody Battle of the Bulge proved to be Germany's last major effort. From the east, Soviet armies poured into Germany in January, coming within 100 miles of Berlin, while British and American troops pushed toward Germany from the west, crossing the Rhine in March.

While the Allies were closing the ring around Germany, Churchill, Roosevelt, and Stalin met in February 1945 at Yalta, on the Black Sea. The Yalta conference revealed the growing tensions that would divide the Allies after the war. Roosevelt, eager to secure Soviet entry into the war against Japan, conceded some of Stalin's demands regarding the future governments of Europe. Soviet armies were already in Poland, Germany, the Balkans, and eastern Europe. Churchill, who had made a secret arrangement with Stalin regarding Soviet and British influence in the Balkans, joined Roosevelt in agreeing to a larger Russian role in eastern Asia and the transfer of Poland's eastern territory to Russia while compensating the Poles with German land. In return, Stalin promised to permit democratic elements in the postwar governments of Poland and the eastern European states.

Three days after American and Russian soldiers met on the Elbe River on April 25, Mussolini was executed by Italian partisans. On April 30, Hitler committed suicide in a secret bunker beneath the ruined streets of Berlin. German representatives signed the surrender in Eisenhower's headquarters on May 7, 1945.

The Atomic Bomb and the Defeat of Japan

With the European conflict at an end, American strategists turned their attention to the Pacific theater, where Japanese defeat was imminent. The naval battle of Midway in June 1942 had been won mainly by American aircraft carriers, which had been on patrol when Pearl Harbor was bombed, and by use of British-developed radar. A long island-hopping campaign began in which American and Australian troops retook the fiercely defended islands of the western Pacific one by one. Bloody battles in the jungles of New Guinea, the Solomon Islands, and the Bismarck Archipelago were followed by a slow northward advance, with hand-to-hand fighting and heavy losses on both sides. The Allies captured Saipan, within bombing range of Japan's big cities, in June 1944, and in October the Japanese suffered a major defeat in the Philippine Sea. By early 1945 the Philippines themselves were retaken, and in June the Allies seized Okinawa, part of Japan's home territory. Fanatical Japanese defenders often fought to the last soldier. Japanese pilots began to make suicidal *kamikaze* ("divine wind") attacks in planes loaded with bombs that purposely crashed into enemy ships. American losses, though serious, were soon replaced. Japan's fleet was by now almost entirely sunk, and American submarines had destroyed the majority of its supply and merchant ships. Meanwhile, American and Chinese forces had joined British and Indian troops in the liberation of Burma, while Allied naval dominance had cut the Dutch East Indies off from Japanese supply lines.

Japan was ready to surrender by the spring of 1945 and had begun peace feelers through the still neutral Russians. American bombers had destroyed nearly all of Japan's cities, using incendiary bombs to start giant firestorms. In one horrible night in Tokyo, fire bombing killed an estimated 100,000 people, the same number slain throughout the war in air raids over Britain. Many of the survivors in the gutted cities starved.

Events in the United States cut short plans for the final assault against the Japanese mainland. Working in secret laboratories on the so-called Manhattan Project, American, British, and European refugee scientists developed a primitive atomic bomb. The weapon was successfully tested on July 16 at Alamogordo in the isolated desert of New Mexico. Harry S Truman (1884–1972), who became president in April on Roosevelt's death, decided to use the awesome new weapon against Japan, a decision that subsequently aroused great controversy. On the one hand, some strategists argued that an invasion of Japan would cost heavy American casualties, although Eisenhower did not believe that the atomic bomb was needed to force Japan's surrender. On the other hand, at Yalta, Stalin had agreed to attack Japan within three months after the defeat of Germany, and Truman, with a decisive weapon at hand, may have been anxious to forestall the Russians. On August 6 an American plane dropped an atomic bomb on the medium-sized town and army base of Hiroshima, obliterating the city and killing over 100,000 civilians. Radiation fallout and other injuries eventually claimed thousands of additional victims. Truman called it "the greatest thing in history." Russia declared war on August 8 and swept into Japanese-occupied Manchuria. The next day the Americans leveled the city of Nagasaki with a second atomic device; more than 65,000 died. On August 15, Emperor Hirohito announced the Japanese surrender.

The war had cost the lives of 2.5 million Japanese soldiers and sailors, and an additional million civilians had died in air raids. The country was in ruins. But the Japanese defeat of colonial regimes in the early years of the war had destroyed the myth of Western invincibility, and Japanese brutality had further stimulated Asian nationalism. Despite the Western victory in Asia, the old Western empires were irretrievably gone.

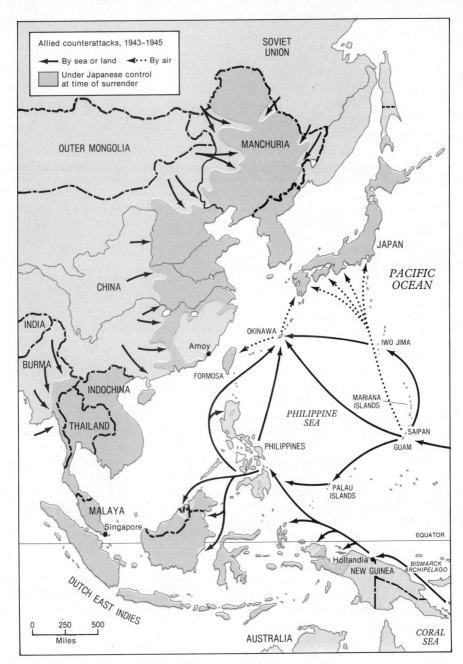

38.4 World War II in Eastern Asia

The World War and the Future

The meeting of Soviet and American troops on the Elbe River in April 1945, amid the rubble of a continent, symbolized the eclipse of Europe as the dominant force in international politics. Germany had been decisively de-feated and occupied. An exhausted Britain found itself the world's greatest debtor nation. France, overrun and occupied by Hitler's armies, had only de Gaulle's Free French and the internal resistance known as the Maquis to remember with any pride. Few could deny that the Soviet Union and the United States had been the prin-cipal architects of victory or that their military strength would determine the future of the globe. Henceforth, the

◎ **The End of Emperor Worship** ◎

On August 15, 1945, after the atomic bombing of Japan by American planes, Emperor Hirohito spoke to his people for the first time over the radio and declared the war lost. Here is how one listener, 10 years old at the time, recalled the impact of the news.

The adults sat around their radios and cried. The children gathered outside in the dusty road and whispered their bewilderment. We were most confused and disappointed by the fact that the Emperor had spoken in a *human* voice, no different from any adult's. None of us understood what he was saying, but we had all heard his voice. One of my friends could even imitate it cleverly. Laughing, we surrounded him—a twelve year old in grimy shorts who spoke with the Emperor's voice. A minute later we felt afraid. We looked at one another; no one spoke. How could we believe that an august presence of such awful power had become an ordinary human voice on a designated summer day?

Source: O. Kenzaburo, *A Personal Matter,* trans. J. Nathan (New York: Grove Press, 1968), pp. vii–viii.

hegemony once exercised by western Europe would be shared by the two superpowers for the next half-century.

The Second World War transformed both nations, and each saw its role in a different light. Stalin, though a brutal dictator, represented the views of most Soviet peoples when he adopted a defensive posture toward postwar geopolitics. Since coming to power in 1924, his foremost concern in foreign affairs had been Soviet national interests. From that viewpoint, he saw the spread of communism primarily as an extension of Soviet influence and only secondarily as the success of an ideology. Three times in as many decades Western powers had invaded his country, and the savage war fought on Soviet soil against the Nazis had taken an enormous toll on his nation's people and resources. Now he was determined to strengthen the USSR against a rearmed Germany and a hostile United States.

The American people emerged from World War II with a vastly different outlook. Attacked directly only at Pearl Harbor, the United States had lost some 390,000 soldiers in the war as compared to 27 million Soviet deaths. Wartime spending had brought full employment after more than a decade of economic depression. In 1945 a wealthy America towered above its devastated allies. In the face of shattered European economies, the United States could look eagerly toward the opening of vast new markets for the products of its businesses and farms. Secure behind the world's only nuclear capability, most Americans wanted rapid demobilization, lower taxes, more consumer goods, and an end to foreign political commitments.

The United Nations

Allied plans for establishing a secure peace were based on the conviction that the fascist regimes had been responsible for the war and should be destroyed. The Allies imposed democratic and educational reforms on Germany, Italy, and Japan and removed compromised officials from positions of influence. They also supervised the drafting of new constitutions establishing parliamentary governments and civil liberties. Furthermore, the discovery of the Nazi death camps led to the establishment of the Nuremberg military tribunal to punish prominent Nazis for "crimes against humanity." Similar trials, on different grounds and sometimes under local jurisdiction, were held in Japan and Italy.

As in 1919, the victors in World War II placed great significance on the creation of an international organization to maintain the peace. Roosevelt, a Wilsonian idealist, was an ardent advocate of a new world body empowered to prevent aggression. The Allies dissolved the League of Nations, which had proven inept in dealing with fascist aggression and in its place created the United Nations, with headquarters in New York City. The formal charter, drafted at a meeting in San Francisco in April, was signed by 50 nations in June 1945.

The UN charter gave one vote to each member state in the General Assembly, which has since grown to more than triple its original size. But real power lay in the Security Council, whose permanent members were the United States, the Soviet Union, Britain, France, and

China. Because each could veto council decisions, the organization was mired in controversy from the start. Subsidiary agencies, such as the World Health Organization and the Food and Agricultural Organization, however, have made important contributions in noncontroversial areas such as combating disease and starvation.

The Cold War

The conflict between Soviet and American national interests that dominated the international scene in the post–World War II period came to be known as the Cold War. As it grew in intensity after 1945, the Cold War assumed the public guise of a clash of ideologies. Many Americans saw themselves as defending capitalist democracy against communist totalitarianism, while the Soviets portrayed themselves as opponents of Western imperialism. In both instances the rhetoric obscured the reality of the Cold War as a struggle for dominance between the world's strongest nations.

Potsdam and the Origins of the Cold War

Historians disagree as to when the Cold War began and who was responsible for breaking Soviet-American wartime collaboration. Some scholars place the beginning as early as 1918, when American troops invaded north-

ern Russia at Archangel to try to topple the Bolshevik regime. Others argue that the growing antagonism between the United States and the Soviet Union, already revealed in wartime discussions among the Allies, did not become irreversible until 1947 or 1948, when anticommunism became the guidepost of American policy. The consensus, however, is that the Cold War emerged out of the conflict between Stalin and Truman over the future of eastern Europe during the Potsdam conference in the summer of 1945.

Stalin had made it clear at Yalta that he wanted a readjustment of borders and an extension of the Soviet frontier into Polish territory. In return, he promised to allow free elections in eastern Europe after the war. Between February and July, however, the situation had changed drastically, for the Red Army had overrun Poland, Romania, Hungary, Bulgaria, and most of Czechoslovakia and Yugoslavia, and pro-Soviet governments dominated by Communists were installed. At Potsdam, with Truman now representing the United States and Clement Attlee, Churchill's successor, representing Great Britain, the issue resurfaced.

An aggressive Truman charged that Stalin had betrayed the Yalta agreement. Stalin's goal was to establish a line of buffer states between Germany and the Soviet Union. With eastern Europe under Red Army occupation, the Soviet leader remained adamant in the face of what some historians believe was Truman's attempt to use America's atomic monopoly to blackmail the Soviets into making concessions.

The division of Europe into Western and Soviet blocs was an accomplished fact when, in March 1946, the former prime minister Winston Churchill set the tone

The Big Three at Potsdam, 1945: Churchill (soon to be replaced by Atlee), Truman, and Stalin confer on post–World War II settlements. [Imperial War Museum, London]

for Cold War rhetoric by declaring that the Soviets had lowered an "iron curtain" across the continent, an expression quickly adopted by Western cold warriors as a symbol of the division between East and West in Europe.

The Soviet-American clash soon took on a more global character. The United States blocked Soviet efforts to secure a foothold in Iran, and in August, when Stalin demanded a voice in controlling the Dardenelles straits, Truman sent an aircraft carrier to the eastern Mediterranean. The future promised a pattern of repeated and dangerous confrontations.

From the Truman Doctrine to the Berlin Blockade

While relying on the nuclear deterrent to safeguard American security, Truman insisted that the United States had to counter a growing communist challenge, especially in Greece, China, and Indonesia, where communist movements were attempting to overthrow local governments. Truman used the Greek situation to arouse American public opinion. Since the liberation of

Greece in 1944, Britain had stationed troops there in support of a corrupt monarch in order to keep Soviet influence out of the Mediterranean. A civil war, led by procommunist wartime resistance fighters, now threatened the political stability of the country. Although Stalin kept his wartime promise to recognize Greece as an Anglo-American sphere of influence, the Communist government of Yugoslavia was aiding the rebels, and the British could no longer sustain the rightist regime.

On March 12, 1947, Truman announced that America must assist nations that were "resisting attempted subjugation by armed minorities or by outside pressures. . . . The free peoples of the world look to us for support in maintaining their freedoms."[8] Urging Congress to appropriate $400 million in military aid to bolster the Greek and Turkish governments, the president inaugurated the Truman Doctrine, the cornerstone of American foreign policy for the next two decades. Soon the word *containment* was being used to describe the basic principle of the Truman Doctrine, according to which the United States should restrict communism to areas already under Soviet control. That July, Congress also passed a measure establishing the National Security Council, which was to coordinate military and diplomatic

◙ The Iron Curtain ◙

As Cold War tensions with the Soviet Union grew, Western leaders adopted the powerful image of the iron curtain to describe the Soviet-controlled areas of Europe. The phrase originated in a speech given by British Prime Minister Winston Churchill while on a visit to the United States in 1946.

From Stettin in the Baltic to Trieste in the Adriatic, an iron curtain has descended across the continent. Behind that line lie all the capitals of the ancient states of Central and Eastern Europe. Warsaw, Berlin, Prague, Vienna, Budapest, Belgrade, Bucharest, and Sophia, all these famous cities and the populations around them lie in the Soviet sphere, and all are subject, in one form or another, not only to Soviet influence but to a very high and, in many cases, increasing measure of control from Moscow. . . .

The Communist parties, which were very small in all these Eastern states of Europe, have been raised to preeminence and power far beyond their numbers and are seeking everywhere to obtain totalitarian control. Police governments are prevailing in nearly every case, and so far, except in Czechoslovakia, there is no true democracy. . . .

Whatever conclusions may be drawn from these facts—and facts they are—this is certainly not the Liberated Europe we fought to build up. Nor is it one which contains the essentials of permanent peace. . . .

Last time I saw it all coming, and cried aloud to my fellow countrymen and to the world, but no one paid any attention. . . .

We surely must not let that happen again.

Source: R. R. James, ed., *Winston S. Churchill: His Complete Speeches, 1897–1963*, vol. 7 (New York and London: Chelsea House, in association with R. R. Bowker), pp. 7290–7293.

policy for the president with the assistance of the newly formed Central Intelligence Agency (CIA). Truman was especially concerned about Third World areas, where professed Marxists often led national anticolonial movements. Soviet propagandists answered the Truman Doctrine by accusing the United States of seeking to preserve colonialism and asserting that the Soviet Union spoke for national liberation.

Containment had its economic as well as its military side. The United States attempted to draw all European states into the American orbit through a massive program of economic development. In June 1947, Secretary of State George C. Marshall offered economic assistance to any European nation that promised to consult with the American government to determine its needs. Although Czechoslovakia, Poland, and Hungary were interested, the Soviet Union vetoed their participation in the Marshall Plan, fearing that Western economic penetration would weaken its hold on the eastern European states. In western Europe, however, the United States pumped $13 billion into Britain, France, Italy, Germany, and other countries. The Marshall Plan proved a huge success, inaugurating a sustained era of European prosperity that helped combat the growth of socialist and communist parties.

In response, the Soviet Union strengthened its hold on eastern Europe. In 1946 Stalin already controlled Poland, Romania, Bulgaria, and Albania, and over the next two years he consolidated Russian influence over Hungary and Czechoslovakia. The Soviet counterpart to the Marshall Plan was COMECON, an economic organization that claimed to integrate the economies of the eastern European states and the Soviet Union. Under the program, some nations, such as Czechoslovakia, were assigned industrial goals, while others, such as Bulgaria, were given agricultural quotas. In place of the old Communist International (Comintern), abolished during the war in the name of Allied cooperation, Stalin created the Communist Information Bureau (Cominform), designed to reassert Moscow's control over the world communist movement.

As the United States and the Soviet Union consolidated their respective positions in Europe, Germany assumed major importance. The future of Germany had been debated since Potsdam, when Stalin had insisted on moving Russia's borders westward at the expense of Poland, which in turn would receive portions of East Prussia as well as the city of Danzig, renamed Gdansk. Germany's eastern border was set at the Oder and Neisse rivers, and the country was broken into four occupation zones to be governed separately by Britain, France, the United States, and the Soviet Union. Berlin, inside the Soviet zone, was similarly divided among the four powers. Yet no formal peace treaty or final resolution of Germany's status ever came, for disputes between the Soviet Union and the West left Germany broken into two separate states. The Soviet Union,

which had suffered such massive casualties and destruction at the hands of Germany, preferred to see it permanently divided.

After 1946 the Western powers agreed to combine the three Western occupation zones into a single economic unit as a prelude to political sovereignty for a "West German" government. In 1948 self-government was instituted on a local level, and the Germans were permitted to write a new constitution. No postwar American action antagonized the Soviet Union as much as these efforts to reestablish a German nation, for Stalin feared both the industrial revival and the remilitarization of a new German state. That June, Stalin restricted access to West Berlin. The Americans promptly closed their sector to Soviet traffic. When Stalin blockaded all road, rail, and water access to Berlin, Britain and the United States followed suit with a counterblockade against goods moving from East to West Germany. Amid fear of war, the United States began to supply West Berlin by air, moving huge quantities of food, fuel, medicines, and other vital goods to the beleaguered city for almost a year until Stalin conceded defeat.

The Berlin blockade hastened the creation of a separate West German government, formally proclaimed on May 21, 1949, as the Federal Republic of Germany, with its capital at Bonn. Parliamentary elections brought to power as chancellor the Christian Democrat Konrad Adenauer (1876–1967), a former mayor of Cologne who had been imprisoned by Hitler. In contrast to Kurt Schumacher, the Social Democratic candidate who advocated nationalization of industry and banks, Adenauer represented America's Cold War position: cooperation with the West, rapprochement with France, and vigorous anticommunism. Five months after the creation of the Bonn government, the Soviet Union formed a Communist regime in the eastern sector, known as the German Democratic Republic, with its capital in East Berlin.

As the decade drew to a close, Cold War tensions heightened. In April 1949 the United States sponsored the North Atlantic Treaty Organization (NATO), a mutual-defense pact in which most Western nations, including Greece and Turkey, pledged to treat an armed attack against one nation as an assault against all. Although Soviet ground strength at the time outnumbered Western troops by about 10 to 1, in 1955 the Soviet Union established a similar defense system, dubbed the Warsaw Pact.

The relationship between the superpowers changed dramatically in September 1949 with news that the Soviet Union had detonated an atomic bomb. Several months later Communist forces under Mao Tse-tung defeated the Nationalist armies of Chiang Kai-shek and seized power in China (see Chapter 39). The end of nuclear monopoly and the Communist takeover in China replaced confidence with uncertainty in American foreign policy.

The Cold War at home:
Senator Joseph R. McCarthy
of Wisconsin (seated) and his
two chief aides, G. David
Shine and Roy Cohn.
[Eve Arnold/Magnum]

The Cold War and American Politics

For Americans, the Cold War had powerful repercussions at home. In February 1950, Senator Joseph R. McCarthy (1908–1957) of Wisconsin claimed to have a list of Communists who held important positions in the State Department and accused Secretary of State Marshall of protecting them by inaction. McCarthy never produced the name of a single Communist and repeatedly changed the number of alleged "traitors" he had discovered in the government. But his message was clear: the Truman administration had bred and coddled the communist enemy within the government.

That a senator could make such accusations against Truman appears incongruous in retrospect, for the president had shown himself to be an enthusiastic cold war-

rior, had imposed a loyalty program on federal employees, and had jailed most leaders of the small and nearly impotent Communist party of the United States. Yet a wave of anticommunist hysteria swept the country.

McCarthy's "Red scare" campaign made him a national figure. Despite the election of a Republican president, Dwight D. Eisenhower (1953–1961), he continued to claim conspiracy in high places. The witch-hunt spread from Communists to other groups, including homosexuals. In televised hearings that ended in mid-1954, McCarthy finally overextended himself when he charged that the army itself was riddled with Communist spies. In December the Senate censured McCarthy, ending his influence. Yet imitators perpetuated his methods, especially in monitoring schoolteachers and blacklisting actors. The anticommunist scare had lasted four years, and in some areas of American life, pools of suspicion lingered far longer.

　　　▨　　　▨　　　▨

As the world began to recover from the ashes of destroyed cities and the loss of some 50 million lives, it could look back on a generation of economic depression, brutal dictatorship, ideological strife, and the bloodiest war in his-

tory. Yet international strife did not end in 1945, for growing tensions had already begun to divide the former Allies—as the postwar recovery got under way, the Cold War struggle between the United States and the Soviet

Union loomed. In this context, the birth of the atomic age, mirrored in the ruins of Hiroshima and Nagasaki, suggested the possibility that humans could one day destroy civilization.

As people everywhere celebrated the triumph over European fascism and Japanese militarism, the task of political and economic reconstruction presented the world with a more pressing challenge than the emerging Cold War. Moreover, out of the tragic and sobering legacy of the war, the prospect of an end to the vast colonial empires that had once held in their grip the peoples of Asia, Africa, and Latin America, augured well for the future.

Notes

1. L. S. Dawidowicz, *The War Against the Jews, 1933–1945* (New York: Holt, Rinehart and Winston, 1975), p. 153.
2. I. K. Leitner and I. A. Leitner, *Fragments of Isabella* (New York: Dell, 1988), pp. 18–19.
3. Ibid., p. 28.
4. Ibid., p. 31.
5. Ibid., p. 32.
6. Ibid., pp. 46–47.
7. Ibid., pp. 102–103.
8. F. Friedel, *America in the Twentiety Century* (New York: Knopf, 1960), pp. 475–476.

Suggestions for Further Reading

Boyle, J. H. *China and Japan at War, 1937–1945*. Stanford, Calif.: Stanford University Press, 1972.

Butow, R. *Japan's Decision to Surrender*. Stanford, Calif.: Stanford University Press, 1954.

Calvocoressi, P., and Wint, G. *Total War*. Harmondsworth, England: Penguin Books, 1972.

Campbell, H., ed. *The Experience of World War II*. New York: Oxford University Press, 1989.

Campbell-Johnson, A. *Mission with Mountbatten*. New York: Dutton, 1953.

Conroy, H., and Wray, H., eds. *Pearl Harbor Reexamined*. Honolulu: University Press of Hawaii, 1990.

Divine, R. A. *The Reluctant Belligerent: American Entry into World War II*. New York: Wiley, 1979.

Eubank, K. *The Origins of World War II*. New York: Crowell, 1969.

Fussell, P. *Wartime: Understanding and Behavior in the Second World War*. New York: Oxford University Press, 1989.

Gaddis, J. L. *The United States and the Origins of the Cold War, 1941–1947*. New York: Columbia University Press, 1972.

Gellately, R. *The Gestapo and German Society: Enforcing Racial Policy, 1933–1945*. New York: Oxford University Press, 1990.

Gilbert, M., and Gott, R. *The Appeasers*. Boston: Houghton Mifflin, 1963.

Havens, T. *The Valley of Darkness*. New York: Norton, 1978.

Herken, G. *The Winning Weapon: The Atomic Bomb in the Cold War, 1945–1950*. Princeton, N.J.: Princeton University Press, 1988.

Hildebrand, K. *The Foreign Policy of the Third Reich*. Berkeley: University of California Press, 1973.

Hsi-sheng, C. *Nationalist China at War*. Ann Arbor: University of Michigan Press, 1982.

Ienaga, S. *The Pacific War*. New York: Pantheon Books, 1978.

Kitchen, M. *A World in Flames: A Short History of the Second World War in Europe and Asia, 1939–1945*. New York: Longman, 1990.

Kolko, G. *The Politics of War*. New York: Random House, 1969.

Langer, W. L., and Gleason, S. E. *The Undeclared War, 1940–41*. New York: Harper & Row, 1953.

Lebra, J., ed. *Japan's Greater East Asia Coprosperity Sphere in World War II*. Kuala Lumpur, Malaysia: Oxford University Press, 1975.

Mastny, V. *Russia's Road to the Cold War*. New York: Columbia University Press, 1979.

Myers, R. H., and Peattie, M. R., eds. *The Japanese Colonial Empire, 1895–1945*. Princeton, N.J.: Princeton University Press, 1984.

Parker, R. A. C. *Struggle for Survival: The History of the Second World War*. New York: Oxford University Press, 1991.

Robertson, E. M. *Mussolini as Empire Builder*. London: Macmillan, 1977.

Spector, D. H. *Eagle Against the Sun*. New York: Free Press, 1989.

Taylor, A. J. P. *The Origins of the Second World War*. New York: Wiley, 1972.

Thomas, H. *The Spanish Civil War*, rev. ed. New York: Harper & Row, 1977.

Ulam, A. *Expansion and Coexistence: The History of Soviet Foreign Policy, 1917–1967*. New York: Praeger, 1974.

White, T., and Jacoby, A. *Thunder out of China*. New York: William Sloane Associates, 1946.

Wright, G. *The Ordeal of Total War, 1939–1945*. New York: Harper & Row, 1968.

Revival and Revolution in East Asia

Much of Asia was devastated by World War II, and no part of it was unaffected. There were more war casualties in Asia than in all of the rest of the world. The heavy human and economic losses were, however, accompanied by the end of colonial rule and Western dominance in Asia. The Japanese conquest of Southeast Asia destroyed the image of Western superiority, while the war in Europe weakened both the power and the desire of the European powers to resume their former positions in Asia. Japan's economy was destroyed by the war, and almost all of its cities were bombed to rubble. Japan lived under American military occupation from 1945 to 1952, but by 1950 the damage to the economy had been largely repaired and rapid new growth that would continue for decades had begun. By 1965 Japan had become the world's third industrial power, after the United States and the Soviet Union, and in the 1970s and 1980s it won a commanding position in world markets for its manufactured exports.

In China long-pent-up pressures for change resulted

"Women hold up half the sky," Mao said, and in China since 1950 they have entered many occupations previously reserved for men. [China Reconstructs]

in civil war, from which the Communists emerged victorious over the Kuomintang (Guomindang) government in 1949. The new revolutionary government quickly repaired war damages, but in 1957 Mao Tsetung, the Communist leader, launched the Great Leap Forward, a radical economic program that ended by plunging the country into mass starvation. It was followed in 1966 by the Cultural Revolution, a destructive effort to revive flagging revolutionary ardor, which ended only with Mao's death in 1976. China began to reopen its contacts with the West in the 1970s and to pursue economic growth rather than ideology. Korea was split by the Cold War into rival states; Vietnam, similarly divided, was unified by a successful war against the United States; and in Southeast Asia a number of new nations emerged, each following a different path.

The Recovery of Japan

Japan had been more completely destroyed by the war than any of the other belligerents. In addition to Hiroshima and Nagasaki, which had been leveled by the atomic bombs, virtually all of Japan's cities, especially Tokyo and Yokohama, had been flattened and burned by massive conventional and incendiary bombing. A notable exception was Kyoto, the old imperial capital, which had been preserved by the intervention of American art historians. The government and what remained of the army in the home islands were still, however, in good order, and there was a smooth transfer of power to the American military government of occupation under General Douglas MacArthur. Japan had surrendered to the Allied forces, including Britain, China, Australia, Canada, New Zealand, and the Soviet Union, although the Soviets had intervened only in the last week of the war. But MacArthur permitted only token representation from each of the other allies in his SCAP (Supreme Commander Allied Powers) regime of occupation, over which he presided like a virtual emperor.

With very few exceptions, the Japanese people, including officials, officers, and troops as well as other civilians, accepted Emperor Hirohito's pronouncement of surrender and his call to "endure the unendurable." Most felt relief that the disastrous war was over. They soon found that the occupying Americans were not the devils some had feared and vented their bitterness on the now discredited military leaders who had so nearly destroyed the nation they were sworn to serve. In general, the occupation, which lasted from late August 1945 to late April 1952, was a period of peaceful reconstruction, with the Japanese doing most of the work of government under American supervision, except at the highest level.

39.1 Modern Japan

The American Occupation

Relief on finding the occupying forces bent on reconstruction rather than revenge was soon joined by gratitude for American aid. Most Japanese had lived at best on an austerity diet during the last years of the war, and many were half starved, living in makeshift shelters in the bombed-out cities. The winter of 1945–1946 would have been far harder if the Americans had not flown in emergency supplies of food and got the main rail lines working again to transport fuel and essential building supplies. Having expected far worse from their new rulers, the Japanese were pleasantly surprised. Many were even enthusiastic about the institutional changes that SCAP began to decree to root out the remnants of militarism and implant American-style democracy.

The big prewar industrial combines were broken up, though they subsequently re-formed. Thousands of political prisoners who had been accused of "dangerous thoughts" and jailed by the military-controlled govern-

✦ MacArthur: An Assessment ✦

Most observers described General Douglas MacArthur as a vain man, ever conscious of his public image. Here is a leading Western historian's assessment of MacArthur in his role as the head of SCAP from 1945 to 1951.

A tendency toward complacent self-dramatization was encouraged by the adulation of a devoted wartime staff that he took with him to Japan. . . . They took almost ludicrous care that only the rosiest reports of the occupation should reach the outside world. In their debased opinion the slightest criticism of S.C.A.P. amounted to something approaching sacrilege. MacArthur took up residence in the United States Embassy in Tokyo. Each day at the same hour he was driven to his office in a large building facing the palace moat; at the same hour each day he was driven home again. . . . He never toured Japan to see things for himself. . . . The irreverent were heard to say that if a man rose early in the morning he might catch a glimpse of the Supreme Commander walking on the waters of the palace moat. There is no doubt that this aloofness impressed Japanese of the conservative type. . . . But it may well be doubted whether this kind of awed respect was compatible with the healthy growth of democratic sentiment. . . . The Japanese perhaps learned more about democracy from MacArthur's dismissal than from anything he himself ever did or said.

Source: R. Storry, *A History of Modern Japan,* rev. ed. (New York: Penguin Books, 1982), pp. 240–241.

ment of the 1930s and 1940s were released. Other Japanese who were identified—sometimes wrongly—as having been too closely associated with Japanese fascism or militant imperialism were removed from their posts, including a number of senior officials. Several hundred Japanese were identified as suspected war criminals, and most were tried by a special tribunal in Tokyo that included Allied representatives. Seven were executed, including the wartime prime minister, Tojo Hideki, and 18 others were sentenced to prison terms. Nearly 1,000 minor war criminals in Japan and Southeast Asia, largely military men, were executed for gross cruelty to prisoners or to the inhabitants of conquered countries. This contrasted with the far more lenient treatment and in some cases even protection of all but the most major Nazi leaders by the United States and its allies in Europe and prompted charges of racism.

A victor's justice in the aftermath of a bitter war is easily criticized, especially when racially tinged, but most Japanese accepted the tribunal's verdict as inevitable and perhaps even appropriate punishment. Most blamed their failed leaders rather than their new masters. The flexibility and adaptability of the Japanese in turn impressed the Americans, who had expected resentfulness and found instead to a surprising degree both liking and admiration. Having fought ruthlessly and with immense dedication, the Japanese proved quite ready to accommodate to a relatively benign new order. Americans were admired because they had won and also because most Japanese truly appreciated their relief and reconstruction program and also their efforts to democratize Japan. After all, the Japanese had suffered horribly under a militaristic police state; they were ready to follow new paths. American ways were imitated uncritically by many, but the basic political reforms of the occupation sent down firm roots.

Most of the changes were reaffirmed after the occupation or, perhaps more accurately, were grafted onto earlier Japanese efforts to adopt Western institutions prior to the years of military government (1931–1945). In addition to a revitalization of electoral and party democracy, government was decentralized by giving more power to local organs. Public education, formerly supervised closely by the central government, was also decentralized and freed as much as possible from bureaucratic control. One of the most successful and permanent changes was the program of land reform, which compensated the large owners whose property was expropriated and sold the land to former tenants, thus ending the last surviving traces of the Tokugawa order. Japanese society began to evolve rapidly toward its present social system, in which status results from achievement rather than birth.

The new constitution drafted by SCAP officials re-

Emperor Hirohito of Japan with General MacArthur at the U.S. Embassy in Tokyo in 1945. [Bettmann Archive]

hardened the American line. Although President Harry Truman fired MacArthur in 1951 for his irresponsible management of the Korean War, Cold War considerations continued to dominate American policy. When the occupation ended in 1952, Japan was bound to the United States by a security treaty that permitted the buildup of a Japanese "self-defense force," the stationing of American troops, and American use of several major bases in Japan. U.S. pressures for Japanese rearmament have continued, and the bases remain, but Article 9 of the constitution still has the support of most Japanese.

Economic and Social Development

Whatever the political shifts as the occupation wore on, economic reconstruction was almost miraculously rapid. By 1950 the shattered cities, factories, and rail lines had been largely rebuilt, and by the end of 1951 industrial production was about equal to what it had been in 1931, now from new and more efficient plants. The Korean War provided an additional economic boost as Japan became the chief base and supplier for American forces in Korea. By 1953, with reconstruction complete, personal incomes had recovered to their prewar levels, and Japan was entering a new period of rapid development. Some credit is due to American aid in the hard years immediately after the war, but the "Japanese miracle" was overwhelmingly the result of the nation's own hard work, organization, and the pursuit of economic success through group effort. The growth of production and income in Japan from 1950 to 1975 was faster than has been measured in any country at any time; in those 25 years, output and incomes roughly tripled. Yet the Japanese continued to maintain a very high rate of personal savings, which as elsewhere helped fuel economic growth through investment.

At the same time, production quality also rose impressively, and in many respects Japanese goods, notably automobiles, cameras, sound reproduction equipment, optics, and many electronic items, became the best in the world market. This was a tribute to advanced Japanese technology and design, as well as to the efficiency of an industrial plant rebuilt with the latest design and equipment. Similar factors were active in the postwar recovery of Germany, while the victorious Allies, including the United States, were saddled with their older and less efficient plants. After 1953 Japan dominated world shipbuilding, although it gave ground increasingly to South Korea in the 1980s. By 1964 Japan had become the world's third largest producer of steel, and by 1980 it had overtaken both the USSR and the United States in steel output while also becoming a major producer and exporter of automotive vehicles. Japan

tained the emperor as a figurehead but vested all real power in a legislature and prime minister elected by universal suffrage. There was a detailed bill of rights for the protection of individuals against arbitrary state power. Article 9 of the constitution forbade Japan to have any armed forces except for police and denied it the right to go to war. To most Japanese this was not only reasonable but welcome, given the ruin that arms had brought them and the aftermath of atomic warfare, of which they were the living witnesses. Japan, many felt, should set an example of the folly of war for the rest of the world. What disillusioned the Japanese about the occupation was the shift in American policy beginning in 1948 toward rebuilding Japan's military capacity and using it as a base of American strategic operation.

The goal of making Japan a Cold War ally of the United States soon took precedence over reform and reconstruction. The Berlin blockade, the Communist victory in China in 1949, and the Korean War all further

also invaded European and American markets on a large scale with its "high-tech" and industrial goods.

Japanese democracy has retained healthy growth, although politics continue to be dominated by a conservative coalition with no effective rival parties. High school education is virtually universal, and literacy among the Japanese is the highest in the world. The press is of high quality and is avidly supported by a public that also buys and reads more books than in any other country, about ten times the figure for Americans. Over half of young Japanese continue with postsecondary education in a great variety of colleges, universities, and other institutions. Overall, the Japanese are now probably the best-educated population in the world.

Education was a major reason for Japan's spectacular economic success. Economic growth largely eliminated the nation's poverty and unemployment. With the postwar disappearance of aristocratic values, Japan became largely a nation of prosperous middle-class people in an orderly society. Despite crowded conditions—population density in its central urban corridor is the highest in the world—there are few slums, little violent crime, and few signs of social malaise. By 1980 Japan achieved the world's highest life expectancy and its lowest murder rate, less than one two-hundredth that of the United States.

Japanese disarmament, a condition at first imposed by the American occupation but now for many an ingrained social value, has also paid handsome dividends. Japan has thus been largely free of the crushing economic burden of maintaining the huge military establishment undertaken by most other large countries in the postwar world. Money was invested instead in economic growth, new technology, full employment, education, and a wide range of social services. Japan is virtually alone in the world in having escaped from most of the cankerous problems that breed in poverty, such as violence, hopelessness, and drugs. The national ethic of work, achievement, and high standards, now in the service of personal and group goals of economic advancement rather than imperial ambition, has produced a new and more constructive society.

Nevertheless, Japanese society has significant problems. The drive for achievement exacts a toll on school-children as well as on adults. Pressures begin for admission to the "right" kindergarten and continue through elementary school, middle (high) school, and college or university. Each stage of schooling is accompanied by fiercely competitive examinations. Childhood, after the age of 5, is a stressful time for most Japanese. Extreme urban crowding and cramped living space add further burdens. Commuting time for people who work in downtown Tokyo *averages* nearly two hours each way and is only slightly less in other big Japanese cities. Parks and recreation facilities are extremely limited. Housing is fearfully expensive, and most urban Japa-

nese, who constitute over 80 percent of the population, live in tiny apartments with minimal amenities. Yet as one of the best-informed and most widely traveled peoples in the world, most Japanese know they are generally very well off despite their cramped quarters.

Notwithstanding the newer values of social equality and status based on achievement, traditional patterns remain, especially the subordinate status of women. Deference to superiors or elders, and of all women to men, is still expected by older Japanese. New generations may well reshape their society on somewhat freer lines, but most would agree that it will be a long time before women achieve anything close to equality. In the workplace women are in subordinate or service roles, with very few exceptions. At the same time, women are often the real powers within the family and household. They usually have control of the family finances and have the preponderant role in the upbringing of children; most fathers work long hours, and their long commute usually gets them home only after the children are in bed.

Tradition meets modernity: a woman in traditional Japanese dress waits at a bus stop. [Ira Kuschenbaum/Stock]

Modern Japanese women still learn traditional arts, and playing the koto is one. Koto players must wear the kimono and usually practice in a thoroughly authentic setting, kneeling on a *tatami* mat. [Shashinka Photo]

Nevertheless, about half of adult Japanese women work outside the house, close to the current American figure, often managing a small family business or neighborhood store. Equality in the professions remains a distant goal.

Nearly half of Japanese women get some form of post–high school education or training. Much of it is vocational, and relatively few attend the prestigious universities, which are minutely ranked; most Japanese can recite the rank order. Many women attend college or university for reasons of social status or to find a husband.

Japan's International Role

Despite their global economic stature, the Japanese have been reluctant to assume the role of a world power in political terms, a role that has brought them tragedy in the past. They have often been uncomfortably aware of this disparity between their economic power and their more hesitant political stance abroad. On a number of occasions they felt their interests ignored in the maneuverings of Cold War diplomacy. As an American client and a bulwark against neighboring communist states, Japan was dumbfounded when in 1971 Washington, re-

versing a 22-year policy, suddenly renewed contact with China without informing Tokyo in advance. The Japanese still refer to this event as the "Nixon shock," and on many other occasions as well, U.S. actions have caused the Japanese to feel slighted or ignored.

It seems likely that in time Japan will come to play an international diplomatic role more in keeping with its economic power, but most Japanese continue to hope that this can be done without adding new military power. Some Japanese have openly favored rearmament to compete in a world dominated by nations with the greatest military power, a policy that deeply concerns Japan's neighbors and former victims of its imperialism. Although the Americans have pressed for it, a rearmed Japan would no longer be their client, which is indeed why some Japanese support rearmament. More positively, by 1988 Japan had become the world's largest donor nation of foreign aid, all of it economic rather than military.

Modern Japan has been a leader in other nonmilitary directions, notably in the control of industrial pollution. Japan is small, and most of its population, cities, and industry are crowded into a narrow coastal corridor only about 400 miles long. Industrial concentration is higher there than anywhere in the world, and hence Japan was the first to notice the lethal effects of air and water pollution as one consequence of its postwar industrial growth. Many deaths and many more health casualties derived from heavy metal toxins and air pollution were traced to specific plants and their poisonous discharges into the water or the atmosphere. Once this became clear and public opinion had been mobilized, national and municipal governments quickly passed stringent legislation, beginning in 1969 with the city of Tokyo, to limit emissions and effluents from industry and vehicles. As industrial growth continues, concentration and crowding will go on generating the same problems, and pollution levels are building up again, while controls have remained incomplete. But Japanese organization, efficiency, and technology have demonstrated that the problems can be managed, given the willingness to confront them. The technology needed to control or even eliminate pollution was developed quickly, and the added expense was extremely modest, estimated at between 1 and 2 percent of total production costs.

Japan has also led the way in reducing energy use through more efficient plants and better engine design. Nearly all Japanese trains are electrified, including the heavily used high-speed line that connects Tokyo with the major cities to the south and southwest and Hokkaido to the north. Trains leave Tokyo every 15 minutes for Osaka, making the 310-mile trip in three hours, including stops at Nagoya and Kyoto, running at speeds up to 140 miles per hour.

Urbanization is higher in Japan than anywhere else in the world, and the coastal area from Tokyo to Osaka and on to northern Kyushu is rapidly becoming a single vast urban-industrial zone. Although the rural Japanese landscape, especially the mountains that cover much of the country, is very beautiful, a good deal of the remaining countryside is increasingly empty as people have flocked to the cities in search of wider economic and cultural opportunity. On weekends and holidays urbanites rush to natural beauty spots, temples or shrines, and resorts, which are often excessively crowded. Crammed onto overloaded trains or buses, most passengers must stand for hours, while many others are locked into gigantic traffic jams on the highways. Much of traditional Japanese culture has been lost or discarded in this avalanche of change. Although many Japanese regret the price they have paid for development, their sense of national identity has remained strong, bound together with many symbolic survivals of traditional culture: customary food and rituals, aesthetic sensitivity, and the commitment to order, self-discipline, and group effort in the pursuit of excellence.

❦
TOKYO AND THE
MODERN WORLD

By about 1965 Tokyo had become the world's largest city and a symbol of Japan's new economic leadership. The urban area had grown outward to merge with that of previously separate cities in the same lowland basin, including Kawasaki and Yokohama. By the 1980s this vast, unbroken conglomeration of dense settlement, commerce, industry, and government measured 50 miles across and included over 30 million people linked by the world's largest and most efficient subway system. Almost nothing is left of the Edo described in Chapter 29, most of which had been in any case periodically destroyed by fires. Modern Tokyo was also largely ruined by a catastrophic earthquake in 1923 and then again by American bombs and firestorms in 1944 and 1945.

The only part of the city that has survived all of these cataclysms unscathed is Tokugawa Ieyasu's massive shogunal castle, surrounded by its moats and stone walls, originally built in the early seventeenth century and since 1869 used as the imperial palace. In the middle of a huge and strikingly modern city of glass, steel, skyscrapers, and expressways, with traffic flowing around it, the palace still stands as a symbol of Japan's traditional past, both as a Tokugawa monument and as the home of a still enthroned emperor whose lineage goes back to before the dawn of Japanese history. Among Japan's many big cities, Tokyo still plays the role of the brash modernist, the focus of change, the center of everything new; but even in Tokyo the Japanese do not forget their past. The palace, though an anachronism, is neverthe-

less an appropriate focal point for the capital of Japan. For all its apparent emphasis on the streamlined or frantic present and future, Tokyo is also a city of the Japanese tradition.

That aspect of the city's character becomes clear beyond the immediate downtown and government areas. Except for the industrial clusters around the fringes of each originally separate municipality, Tokyo is primarily a vast collection of neighborhoods. Many are grouped around a surviving or rebuilt temple, shrine, former daimyo estate, or parklike garden. Wandering through the back streets and alleys of these neighborhoods, it is easy to imagine oneself in Tokugawa Edo. Clouds of steam escape from public bathhouses, enveloping the patrons, who include many dressed in traditional kimonos and walking in wooden clogs, especially in the evening after work. Inside countless tiny restaurants and teahouses with their *tatami* (straw mats), low tables, and wall scrolls, little seems to have changed since Ieyasu's time, including much of the food. Many inhabitants of the tiny houses or apartments maintain miniature Japanese-style gardens the size of a small tabletop or lovingly tend potted plants set out by the doorway or on small balconies to catch the sun. Street vendors, singing traditional chants, peddle roasted sweet potatoes, chestnuts, or *yakitori* (Japanese shish kebab).

Crowds of kimono-clad worshipers, or people simply on an outing, throng the courtyards of rebuilt temples and shrines, especially on festival days. Similar crowds fill the narrow streets and patronize street vendors or shops selling traditional as well as modern goods: fans both manual and electric, silks and nylons, horoscope fortunes and stock market guides, tea and beer, lacquer and plastic, scrolls and comic books. Like Japan itself, Tokyo is both very modern and very traditional, very Japanese and very Western.

China in Revolution

The cataclysmic changes that transformed twentieth-century China constitute the largest revolution in human history, measured by the numbers of people involved and the radicalness and speed of the changes. Although the events of 1911 leading to the overthrow of the Manchu dynasty are called a revolution, the pace of change was slow for many years, and the dominant political party, the Kuomintang, became in time largely a supporter of the status quo rather than a force for radical reform. The Chinese Communist party barely survived Kuomintang efforts to eliminate it, but during the anti-Japanese war from 1937 to 1945 it rapidly gained strength and support in the course of its guerrilla resistance to the invaders. The final contest between the

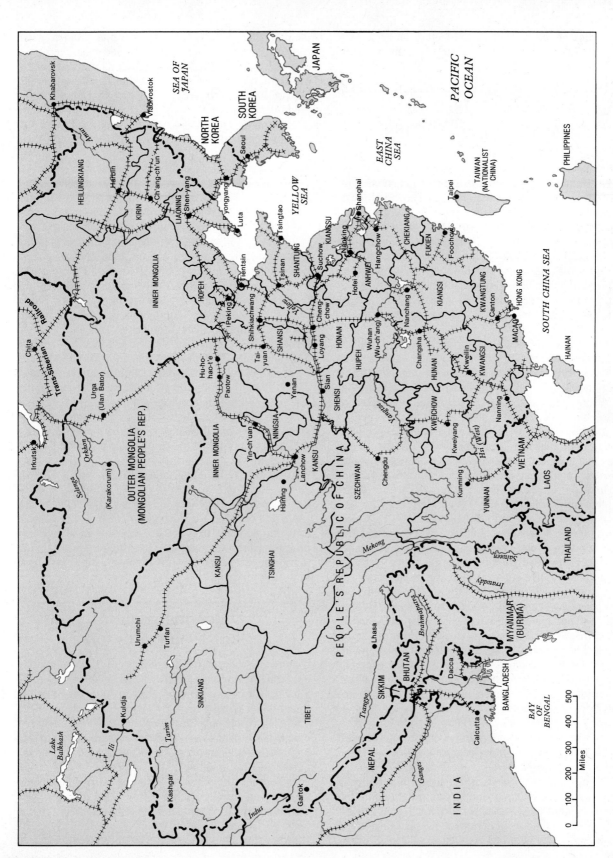

39.2 Modern China

two parties ended in Communist victory in 1949, and fundamental revolution began under a radically new set of ideals.

Postwar China and the Communist Triumph

The Japanese invasion and occupation of China from 1931 to 1945 fatally eroded the power and legitimacy of the Kuomintang government of Chiang Kai-shek. Buttressed by massive American military and economic support, it clung to a nominal authority while American representatives under General George C. Marshall tried to arrange a coalition with the Communists. When this effort predictably failed in 1947, China was torn by full-scale civil war. The Communist forces, meanwhile, had perfected a guerrilla strategy in their long struggle against the Japanese and had attracted millions of Chinese by their defense of the nation and their program of peasant-oriented reform.

Their leader, Mao Tse-tung (Mao Zedong, 1893–1976), offered a return to the simple virtues of hard work and self-sacrifice in order to build a new China, free from foreign influence and humiliation and free also from the now discredited and reactionary elitism of Confucianism and the old order it represented. The Confucian society had deteriorated sadly as China had sunk deeper into poverty, demoralization, and unwillingness to face drastically changed circumstances. People necessarily concentrated on ensuring their own survival rather than on responsibility for others or on group welfare. In their remote frontier base at Yenan (Yanan) in the northwest, where they were centered from 1934 to 1947, the Communists under Mao's direction had worked out a number of ideas for China's regeneration, while at the same time appealing broadly to the masses.

Mao himself, like several other Communist leaders, came from peasant stock, and their program emphasized peasant welfare and peasant values, as the Kuomintang had not. Landlordism and oppression of the peasantry were popular issues in the face of widespread rural poverty and mass suffering. Chinese who collaborated with foreign businessmen in the treaty ports prospered in league with a government that was prone to favor foreign influences. The cities, nearly all of which were foreign-dominated treaty ports as well as centers of Kuomintang strength and the home of "running dogs" (collaborators with the foreigners), were obvious targets for a peasant-oriented revolutionary movement.

Success depended, however, on building a mass support base in the countryside, where most Chinese lived. The Communists initiated land reform programs in the areas they controlled—most of the north—as well as campaigns to politicize and organize the peasants. Intellectuals were also involved in an effort to create a new ideology that could appeal to peasants. Mao himself, though the son of a rich peasant turned grain merchant, was primarily an intellectual as well as a gifted poet in the tradition of the Confucian scholars and emperors. His prescriptions for art and literature that would "serve politics" and "serve the masses" attracted growing numbers of fellow intellectuals disillusioned with the corruption and spiritual bankruptcy of the Kuomintang. As an intellectual organizing peasant rebellion, Mao consciously followed an old Chinese tradition.

The civil war that broke out in 1947 soon became a rout, despite heavy American support for the Kuomintang. The Communists had few weapons except what they could capture from their opponents or make themselves, but their strength quickly multiplied as growing numbers of Kuomintang troops and officers surrendered to them, often voluntarily, with all their equipment. The close American connection, with its connotation of foreign dominance, probably weakened rather than strengthened the Kuomintang in its fight against the Communists and left a legacy of anti-American bitterness when the civil war ended. On October 1, 1949, Mao announced the inauguration of the People's Republic of China from a rostrum in front of the Forbidden City in Peking (Beijing), conscious, as always, of the tradition of China's imperial greatness, to which he was now the heir. "China has stood up," he said, and the great majority of Chinese responded with enthusiasm.

The revolution was the culmination of a long process that began with the overthrow of the old Ch'ing (Qing) dynasty in 1911. After the failure of Sun Yat-sen and the corruption of the Kuomintang, the Communists, originally appealing largely to intellectuals, had finally succeeded in creating a mass political base, with a peasant army forged in the fires of the Japanese war. They called their program "the mass line," claiming to represent the more than 80 percent of the Chinese people who lived in the countryside.

Reconstruction and Consolidation

Chiang Kai-shek and the remnants of the Kuomintang government and army fled to the offshore island of Taiwan (Formosa), where American aid helped them in time build a prosperous economy and gain firm control of the island's population. From this tiny base, sheltered only by American power, Chiang continued to claim sole legitimate authority over China. The United States supported the Kuomintang until the desire to exploit the split between the Chinese Communists and their erstwhile Soviet allies led belatedly to official American recognition of the government in Peking in 1979. Unofficial ties with Taipei (the Taiwan capital) remained, however. On the mainland the new government moved quickly to repair the physical damage of the long years of war and to extend its land reform and political education programs into the newly conquered south and southwest. All over the country what was still called land reform became more violent as party organizers, in an effort to create "class consciousness," encouraged peasants to "speak bitterness" and to identify their landlord-oppressors. Many thousands of the latter were killed by angry mobs, and their land was distributed among the poorer peasants.

Firm central government control was reestablished in all of the former empire, including Manchuria (now called simply "the northeast"), southern or "Inner" Mongolia, Sinkiang (Xinjiang), and Tibet, and a major program of industrialization was begun. War with the United States in Korea from late 1950 to mid-1953 and an American-sponsored embargo on trade with China slowed these efforts but also helped radicalize the country and strengthen dedication to the goals of self-reliance and reconstruction. By 1956 Mao judged that support for the new government was wide and deep enough to invite criticism. In a famous speech, he declared: "Let a hundred flowers bloom; let a hundred schools of thought contend." Many intellectuals and others, including many of China's ethnic minorities such as Tibetans and Muslims, responded with a torrent of criticism aimed at rigid party or government controls. Most of it was pronounced counterrevolutionary, and many of the critics were punished, jailed, or even executed.

The Great Leap Forward

Despite the evidence of dissent, Mao still felt secure enough in the support of the majority of his people that he moved swiftly to collectivize the land. By 1958 he moved beyond the Soviet model of collectivization as China's farms and fields were organized into new communes; private ownership was abolished, and all enterprises were managed collectively. The communes varied widely in area and population but averaged about 25,000 people, frequently incorporating large numbers of previously separate villages. Several villages made up a "production team," several teams a "production brigade," and several brigades a commune. Communes were supposed to include manufacturing enterprises as well, to bring industrialization to the rural areas. Communes were also set up in the cities but added little to existing factories, departments, or offices, and the experiment was short-lived.

Mao announced that 1958 would be the year of the "Great Leap Forward" in which China would overtake Britain in industrial output by united efforts within the commune structure. Communal dining halls were set up so that families need not lose work time by preparing meals. Backyard steel furnaces sprang up all over the rural landscape, using local iron ore and coal or other fuel. Communes were given quotas for production of specific agricultural and industrial goods, but too little attention was paid to the nature of local resources or to rational organization more generally.

The Great Leap was a dismal failure, and the country collapsed into economic chaos in 1959. Peasants had been driven to exhaustion in pursuit of unrealistic goals and by inefficient combinations of tasks and resources. Nearly all of the iron and steel from the backyard furnaces was of unusable quality, and the same was true of much of the other commune industrial output. Crops failed as labor was shifted arbitrarily between different tasks, and for at least three years food was scarce and famine widespread. Probably about 30 million people died of starvation or malnutrition in one of the worst famines in world history. Mao's radical policies had brought disaster, and for several years more moderate leaders such as Chou En-lai (Zhou Enlai, 1898–1976) and Liu Hsiao-chi (Liu Xiaoqi, 1894–1971) eclipsed him, although he remained the party chairman.

The Sino-Soviet Split

The Russians were alarmed by what they saw as the radical excesses of the Great Leap and its departure from the Soviet pattern. They were annoyed also by Mao's assertion that his version of socialism was superior to theirs, his continued support of Stalinist policies after they had been discredited in the USSR, and his accusations that the Soviet Union had now become ideologically impure, or "revisionist." The Russians saw Mao's bellicose stand on the reconquest of Taiwan, for which he requested Soviet nuclear aid, as a threat to world peace, and inevitable tensions arose out of the large-scale Soviet aid program and Soviet advisers in China. In 1959 the Russians withdrew their aid and advisers and moved toward a more antagonistic relationship with China. The next 15 years saw revived territorial disputes and armed border clashes between the two former allies on the long frontier between them, especially in the Amur region of northern Manchuria and along the northern border of Sinkiang.

Each claimed to be the true heir of Marx and Lenin and hence of the correct path to socialism, and in this ideological context long-standing historical conflicts between them surfaced. These dated back to the period of early tsarist expansion into northeastern Asia and to Russia's exploitation of Manchuria and its role as one of the Western imperialist powers during China's years of political weakness. On the other side, China's billion people, bordering thinly settled Siberia and Russia's maritime provinces, were seen as an alarming threat to Soviet Asia. The rhetoric of accusation mounted on both sides; troops were stationed along the frontiers, and

The leaders of Communist China in 1965: (from left) Chou En-lai, Chu Teh, Mao Tse-tung, and Liu Hsiao-chi. [Eastfoto/Sovfoto]

small clashes occurred. But China could not stand alone against the entire world, and its leaders began indirect overtures to the United States. More than a decade later, with the end of their misadventure in Vietnam in sight, the Americans finally responded. A cautious restoration of contact began when President Richard Nixon visited Peking late in 1971. This led to the establishment of diplomatic relations, with full U.S. recognition and an exchange of ambassadors with the People's Republic in 1979.

The Cultural Revolution

During the decade from 1966 to 1976, however, China passed through an unprecedented social cataclysm, the so-called Cultural Revolution, in which hundreds of millions of people suffered. The failure of the Great Leap Forward had necessitated more moderate policies and a period of recovery from economic disaster. By 1966 Mao judged the recovery to be complete, and he launched a new campaign designed to renew a revolution that he saw as having slipped into bureaucratic complacency and opportunism.

Mao remarked that he felt like "an ancestor at his own funeral and at the burial of his hopes." His cure was a purge, though his message was the old one of "serve the people," with its clear echoes of Confucian responsibility. The chief targets of his purge were the members of the elite: party managers and officials, teachers, writers, and intellectuals, as well as others who were allegedly tainted by foreign influence or bourgeois life-

styles or whose class origins were not appropriately peasant or proletarian.

The results were devastating. Millions were hounded out of their jobs. Artists and musicians who showed any interest in Western styles were attacked. Many intellectuals and other "counterrevolutionaries" were beaten or killed, and others were jailed, sent to corrective labor camps, or assigned to the lowest menial tasks as a means of "reeducation." Opera stars, writers, and concert violinists were set to cleaning latrines. All foreign music, art, and literature and the expression of all ideas not approved by the state were banned. Most books disappeared or were burned, to be replaced by the ever-present works of Mao himself and the *Little Red Book* of his sayings. Chinese who had studied abroad were particular targets. People were encouraged to inform on friends, colleagues, and even family members, causing deep trauma and division in a society based on traditional family ties. The accused were often jailed or condemned to corrective labor without evidence. Few people had the courage to try to help them, for fear that they too would meet the same fate. The ensuing turmoil affected the lives of hundreds of millions of people and paralyzed the country. Nor were the rural communes exempt, for there, too, people were obliged to confess ideological sins and subjected to punishment and corrective labor. Many were driven to suicide.

During the height of the Cultural Revolution all universities and colleges were closed, feared as breeding grounds for a new elite. When they slowly began to reopen, it was only to the children of peasants, workers, and party loyalists still in power. The new curriculum

◉ Revolution, Chinese Style ◉

*From the beginning of their revolutionary victory, the Chinese asserted
that their principles and experience should be the guide for the rest of
the world, not the Russian way. Here is Liu Hsiao-chi in 1949.*

The road taken by the Chinese people in defeating imperialism and in founding the
Chinese People's Republic is the road that should be taken by the peoples of many colonial and semi-colonial countries in their fight for national independence and people's
democracy. . . . This is the road of Mao Tse-tung. . . . This is the inevitable road of many
colonial and semi-colonial peoples in the struggle for their independence and liberation.

*Lu Ting-i, director of propaganda of the Central Committee, added in
July 1951:*

Mao Tse-tung's theory of the Chinese revolution is a new development of Marxism-
Leninism in the revolutions of the colonial and semi-colonial countries. . . . It is of universal significance for the world Communist movement. . . . The classic type of revolution in
colonial and semi-colonial countries is the Chinese revolution.

*The Russians replied, in the words of Y. Kovalev, a leading propagan-
dist:*

The decisive prerequisites for the victory of the Chinese revolution were the October Socialist Revolution and the victory of socialism in the U.S.S.R., and the defeat of Japanese
and German imperialism by the Soviet Union in World War II. . . . Stalin's analysis of the
peculiarities of China as a semi-colonial country was taken as the basis for the working out
of the strategy and tactics of the struggle for an independent and democratic China by the
Chinese Communist Party.

*Stalin's successor, Nikita Khrushchev, lectured Mao in 1958 after Mao
suggested that the combined numbers of China and Russia could overcome the capitalist West.*

Comrade Mao Tse-tung, nowadays that sort of thinking is out of date. You can no longer
calculate the alignment of forces on the basis of who has the most men. Back in the days
when a dispute was settled with fists and bayonets it made a difference who had the most
men. . . . Now with the atomic bomb, the number of troops on each side makes practically no difference.

*But the Chinese stuck to their insistence that theirs was the only true
way. This editorial, in characteristic Cultural Revolution style, appeared in* Liberation Army Daily *in May 1966.*

The thought of Mao Tse-tung is the sun in our heart, the root of our life, and the source of
all our strength. Through it one becomes unselfish, daring, intelligent, and able to do anything; no difficulty can conquer him, while he can conquer any enemy. The thought of
Mao Tse-tung transforms man's ideology, transforms the fatherland. . . . Through it the oppressed people of the world will rise.

Source: I. Hsu, *The Rise of Modern China* (New York: Oxford University Press, 1975), pp. 810–813, 859.

◉ Attack on the "Revisionists" ◉ and "Imperialists"

At the Tenth Party Congress in 1973, Vice-Chairman Chou En-lai gave a long address in which he castigated the Russian "revisionists" and lumped them together with the American "imperialists."

There were many instances in the past where one tendency covered another and when a tide came, the majority went along with it, while only a few withstood it. . . . We must not fear isolation and must dare to go against the tide and brave it through. Chairman Mao states: "Going against the tide is a Marxist-Leninist principle. . . . The West always wants to urge the Soviet revisionists eastward to divert the peril toward China, and it would be fine so long as all is quiet in the West. China is an attractive piece of meat coveted by all. But this piece of meat is very tough, and for years no one has been able to bite into it. . . . The U.S.-Soviet contention for hegemony is the cause of world intranquillity. . . . They want to devour China but find it too tough even to bite. . . . U.S. imperialism started to go downhill after its defeat in the war of aggression against Korea. . . . [Khrushchev and Brezhnev in Russia] made a socialist country degenerate into a social imperialist country. Internally it has restored capitalism, enforced a fascist dictatorship and . . . exposed its ugly features as the new tsar and its reactionary nature, namely 'socialism in words, imperialism in deeds.' . . ."

If you are so anxious to relax world tension, why don't you show your good faith by doing a thing or two—for instance, withdraw your armed forces from Czechoslovakia or the People's Republic of Mongolia and return the four northern islands [the Kurile archipelago north of Hokkaido] to Japan? China has not occupied any foreign countries' territory. Must China give away all the territory north of the Great Wall to the Soviet revisionists in order to show that we favor relaxation of world tensions? . . . The Sino-Soviet boundary question should be settled peacefully through negotiations free from any threat. We will not attack unless we are attacked; if we are attacked, we will certainly counterattack.

Source: I. C. Y. Hsu, *The Rise of Modern China* (New York: Oxford University Press, 1975), pp. 878–879.

---

concentrated on "political study." Most high school graduates in the decade after 1966, particularly those in the cities, were assigned to productive labor in the countryside, where, Mao felt, they would learn the value of simple toil and peasant virtues. This was partly a leveling alternative to the universities, partly a means to ease unemployment and housing shortages in the cities, and partly a way to reeducate Chinese too young to have shared the early years of hardship and sacrifice.

Some 17 million young people were sent down in this program by the time it was discontinued in the late 1970s. Most of them saw it as ruinous to their own ambitions and career plans, for which their urban origins and education had prepared them. Nor were most of them very helpful in agricultural or other development work. Their training had not in most cases been relevant, and indeed it had tended, as in China's past, to make them think of themselves as an educated elite who

looked down on peasants and manual labor. The program was understandably unpopular with peasants too, since they had to feed and house disgruntled city youth who, with their higher level of education, were unprepared for farmwork. All white-collar workers were required to spend at least two months each year doing manual labor, mainly in the countryside, which not surprisingly met with resistance from professionals and others.

Mao called on teenagers and students to serve as shock troops for the Cultural Revolution. Like young people everywhere, they had little stake in the status quo, were filled with idealism, and were easily diverted from their studies. They welcomed their exciting new role and the opportunity to exercise authority over their elders. Mao called them Red Guards and permitted them to roam the country freely, ferreting out "rightists" and harassing everyone in responsible positions. Mil-

Building a new irrigation dam and reservoir near Peking in 1982: mass labor and the "mass line." Note the red flags and the absence of mechanical equipment.
[Rhoads Murphey]

lions rode free or commandeered trains and buses to the cities, including Peking, where Mao addressed cheering crowds of Red Guards at mass rallies. Mao and his supporters promoted a personality cult; huge pictures and statues of the "Great Helmsman" and copies of his *Little Red Book* appeared everywhere. Rival factions quickly emerged among the Red Guards, each claiming to be followers of the true line. Many welcomed the opportunity to pay off old grudges and to denounce others, often anonymously. Uncontrolled violence broke out in many cities.

To halt the mounting chaos, Chou En-lai prevailed on Mao to call in the army in 1968. The Red Guards were suppressed, thus creating yet another embittered and dislocated group; the Guards felt they had been betrayed, a "lost generation." But the nightmare went on even after the Red Guards had been sent to the countryside. Politicians at the top, except for Mao himself, were attacked for alleged deviations from the party line, which changed unpredictably. Liu Hsiao-chi (Liu Xiaoqi), a revolutionary comrade Mao had originally picked as his successor, was purged and accused of "rightist revisionism" because of his efforts to rebuild the economy after the disaster of the Great Leap Forward. He died under arrest after public humiliation and beatings. Other high officials suffered similar fates. Professionals in all fields

were scrutinized for their political views and activism. Absence from the endless daily political meetings or silence during them was evidence of "counterrevolutionary tendencies." One of the many slogans of the Cultural Revolution was "Better Red than Expert." No one at any level felt safe.

The Chinese Revolution remained primarily a peasant movement, a Chinese rather than a foreign-style answer to China's problems. This was appealing also on nationalist grounds, especially since nearly all the cities had been tainted by semicolonial foreign dominance. There was thus both a pronounced antiurban bias to the revolution and a determination to exalt the countryside, to put the peasants in charge, and to concentrate efforts on development in the rural areas, the supposed source of all revolutionary values.

This was the theme of both the Great Leap Forward and the Cultural Revolution. All movement of people was controlled, especially to the cities, where housing and ration books for food and household supplies were allocated only to those with assigned employment. Individuals could not choose jobs; they worked wherever the state sent them. In the 1970s a growing number of illegal migrants to the cities lived underground or on forged papers. Most of them are still there, their numbers apparently greatly increased; urban unemployment has be-

◉ Mao: The Revolutionary Vision ◉

The Communist revolution in China was in large part a peasant-based movement against the vested power of the cities. Mao Tse-tung put it dramatically.

Since China's key cities have long been occupied by the powerful imperialists and their reactionary Chinese allies, it is imperative for the revolutionary ranks to turn the backward villages into advanced consolidated base areas, . . . bastions of the revolution from which to fight their vicious enemies.

This equally famous statement of Mao's was published in the periodical Red Flag.

China's 600 million people have two remarkable peculiarities; they are first of all poor, and secondly blank. That may seem like a bad thing, but it is really a good thing. Poor people want change, want to do things, want revolution. A clean sheet of paper has no blotches, and so the newest and most beautiful words can be written on it, the newest and most beautiful pictures painted on it.

Still driven by his revolutionary vision, Mao the poet wrote in 1963, in traditional classic verse:

> So many deeds cry out to be done,
> And always urgently.
> The world rolls on,
> Time passes.
> Ten thousand years are too long;
> Seize the day, seize the hour,
> Our force is irresistible.

Sources: Mao Tse-tung, *The Chinese Revolution and the Chinese Communist Party* (Peking: Foreign Language Press, 1954), p. 17 (written in 1939); *Red Flag*, June 1, 1958, pp. 3–4; "Reply to Kuo Mo-jo" (dated February 5, 1963), in *China Reconstructs* 16 (March 1967): 2.

come a major problem. Despite the official denigration of cities, they remained the places where most people wanted to be.

In the countryside each commune was designed to be self-sufficient as far as possible. The Cultural Revolution promoted a particularly extensive growth of small-scale rural industry, especially in what were labeled the "five smalls": iron and steel, cement, fertilizer, agricultural goods (including tools, machinery, and irrigation equipment), and electric power. There was also considerable production of light consumer goods for local use. Local manufacture did reduce the load on an already overburdened road and rail system and saved transport costs while providing employment and experience to the masses of rural people. But in most cases such production was considerably more expensive than that in larger-scale and better-equipped urban-based plants and

of much lower quality. Decentralized industry has been considered as an alternative to the crowding, pollution, and dehumanization of industrial cities since the eighteenth century, but it has seldom proved economically practicable. Mao's utopian vision of rural development was appealing as an attempt to alleviate the real poverty of the countryside, but it was pursued at dreadful cost. China, meanwhile, lagged farther and farther behind the rest of the world, technologically and educationally.

Mao had said that the major goals of the revolution should be the elimination of the distinctions between city and countryside, between intellectuals and manual workers, and between elites and common people. In pursuit of these aims, workers or janitors became plant managers and university officials; peasants were elevated to power in the communes' "revolutionary committees"; professors, technicians, and skilled managers were humiliated or reduced to the most menial jobs. Even "rich peasants" became targets. All those with any claim to expertise were suspect and were often hounded out of their positions in angry "struggle meetings"; those who refused to join in the denunciations risked being denounced themselves. The moral virtue and practical wisdom of the peasants and the countryside were extolled.

Mao drew heavily on traditional ideas in emphasizing the duty of those in positions of power and responsibility to serve the masses, and he, like the Confucians, used moral examples and slogans to inspire and mold group behavior. He also relied on the new technique of mass campaigns to galvanize people into action. Some were constructive, like the campaigns to eliminate flies or to build new dams and irrigation canals. But most were politically inspired and were aimed at "rightists" and "counterrevolutionaries." The Chinese revolution's radical phase lasted longer and went to greater extremes than similar phases of earlier revolutions, but in time it too faded, if only because the Chinese people were exhausted by constant political campaigns and by the terror itself. Mao's death removed the chief obstacle to a return to more normal conditions, and China turned with relief from its long ordeal.

China After Mao

As Mao lay dying in 1976, a few months after his old comrade-in-arms Chou En-lai had died of overwork and exhaustion while trying to hold the country together, a radical faction led by Mao's widow, Chiang Ch'ing (Jiang Qing), tried to continue his extreme policies. But in 1978 a more moderate leadership emerged under Hua Kuofeng (Hua Guofeng), whom Mao had designated as his successor. Chiang Ch'ing and three of her associates, the so-called Gang of Four, were tried and convicted of "crimes against the people" and sentenced to jail. China began to emerge from its nightmare and to resume cautious interchange with the rest of the world after 30 years of isolation. The universities and their curricula were slowly restored, and students now had to pass entrance examinations rather than merely to demonstrate proper "class origins." Efforts were made to provide somewhat greater freedom for intellectuals, writers, teachers, and managers.

Hua was peacefully replaced by an old party pragmatist, Teng Hsiao-p'ing (Deng Xiaoping, born 1904), who returned to power in 1981 as the real head of state and chief policymaker. Most of Mao's policies were progressively dismantled. The new government acknowledged that China was still poor and technically backward, that it needed foreign technology and investment, and that to encourage production its people needed material incentives rather than political harangues and "rectification campaigns."

The communes were quietly dissolved in all but name. Agriculture, still by far the largest sector of the economy, was organized into a "responsibility system" whereby individual families grew the crops that they judged most profitable in an economy that was now market-oriented. The commune still nominally owned the land and the state still appropriated a share of farm output, but peasants were free to sell the rest in a free market. Those who did well under this system, and urban entrepreneurs who prospered in the small private businesses now permitted, felt free once again to display their new wealth. Expensive houses with television aerials sprouted here and there in the countryside, and in the cities motor scooters, tape recorders, and refrigerators became more common. The new rich and even party officials began to indulge personal tastes in clothing, including Western-style and fashionable outfits, which replaced the drab uniforms decreed in earlier years.

Rural industry remained where it had proved practical, but renewed emphasis was placed on large-scale and urban-based industrial production and on catching up with world advances in technology to make up for the lost years. Many factory and office managers and workers were now rewarded on the basis of their productivity. Technological, managerial, and educational elites also reappeared, and with them the bourgeois lifestyles denounced by Mao as the antithesis of revolutionary socialism. The new pragmatism was illustrated by Teng's pithy remark: "I don't care if a cat is red [socialist] or white [capitalist] as long as it catches mice." At the same time, he affirmed that China was still a socialist country under a Communist government that planned and managed the economy and aimed to provide social justice.

The Revolution Reconsidered

The decade after Mao's death saw a reappraisal of his legacy. The new leadership permitted controlled public criticism of the excesses of the Cultural Revolution and acknowledged the failures of Mao's economic policy. But much had also been accomplished. China remained poor, but there was some growth in agriculture (except for the period 1958–1964), thanks in part to irrigation, better seeds, and fertilization. Industry grew rapidly, if unevenly, from what had been a very small and limited base. In 1964 China tested a nuclear bomb and thereby joined the ranks of the major powers. Thousands of miles of new railways and roads were built. China became a major industrial power. One of China's greatest successes was in delivering basic health care to most of its people, including for several years the system of "barefoot doctors" who traveled even to remote villages to provide basic care and the clinics established in every commune.

As in India, this greatly reduced the death rate, while the birthrate remained high. The result was a rapid growth in population, which nearly doubled between 1949 and 1982, when the first real census was taken. This growth placed great pressure on agriculture, where gains in production barely exceeded population increase. As long as such growth continued, China could expect little progress in terms of per capita well-being, by which real economic growth must be measured. In the 1970s the government began an attempt to control population growth. Beginning in 1983 families were penalized for having more than a single child, a policy seen as necessary for perhaps a generation if China was to escape from poverty.

Chinese socialism has also reduced gross inequities in wealth. Poverty at the bottom has not yet been eliminated, but increased production, better distribution, and the collective welfare system of communes and factories have benefited nearly everyone; recent inflation, however, has hurt many. Health levels, thanks in part to better nutrition as well as improved medical care, are in general high. Literacy has more than doubled since the revolution, and about half the population now gets as far as the early high school grades, although there are places for only about 3 percent in the universities.

The liberation of women, one of the goals of the revolution, is still relatively far from attainment, although there has been much progress. Women are less oppressed than under the old society, but they are still far from equal. The marriage law of 1950 gave them legal equality with men in marital rights, divorce, and the ownership of property, a major step forward. The traditional extended family—three generations living under one roof—has largely disappeared, especially in the cities, and with it the authority of the oldest surviving grandparent. A grandmother, and sometimes a grandfather, may live with a son's family but now serves commonly as baby-sitter, shopper, and general household help, representing the family on neighborhood committees while the mother goes out to work. Nearly all adult women have full-time jobs outside the home, but they are usually not paid equally with men, and at the end of the workday it is usually they who cook the meals, clean the house, and care for the children. However, the state or employers provide extensive child-care facilities for working mothers, far more than in the United States.

The top positions in government, business, industry, and education are held almost exclusively by men, with occasional token female representation on committees. At the same time, nearly all occupations and professions are open to women. There is probably a higher proportion of professionals than in the United States, but most Chinese women work in lower-level or even menial jobs. Despite government efforts to persuade people that daughters are as good as sons, most families still give sons priority since only they can continue the family name and provide some security for aged parents; daughters join their husband's family at marriage. This persistence of traditional custom has unfortunately led, under the pressures of the "one-child policy" since 1983, to widespread female infanticide and abortion of female fetuses. Rural areas cling more to traditional values and often evade the one-child policy or accept the penalties in order to produce one or more sons. Nearly all urban and now rural women do at least keep their own names after marriage, and there is a major change from the old society in the status of and attitudes toward women. But China, like Japan and India, still has a long way to go before women are truly equal members of society.

Despite Mao's efforts, living standards in the cities have risen far more rapidly and substantially than in most rural areas. The growing division between urban and rural lifestyles and levels of affluence is a particular problem for the heirs of a peasant revolution, although it is shared by the rest of the developing world. China's cities are not yet disfigured by masses of visibly homeless and unemployed persons, as are many elsewhere in the developing and even the industrial world, but only because rigid controls on all movement and employment still prevent most rural people from migrating to the cities. Progress in other respects too has been won at the cost of state and collective social controls and the suppression of personal choice. This is not as disturbing to most Chinese as it might be to many westerners, since the subordination of individualism to group effort and welfare has long been central to Chinese tradition.

China's past achievements and its revolutionary progress were due in large part to the primacy of responsibility and the pursuit of common goals over privilege and self-interest. Nevertheless, there have been protests and even student demonstrations against the continuing controls on free expression and choice of employment. As China opened its doors to more normal interchange with the rest of the world, more Chinese have come to see their political system as repressive. The political grievances resulting from this, along with the effects of Western cultural influence, led to remarkable demonstrations in Peking, Shanghai, and other major cities in the spring of 1989 that shook the party hierarchy.

In 1987, 1988, and 1989 the government under Teng Hsiao-p'ing became increasingly repressive in its response to growing disaffection and protests. Meanwhile, inflation mounted, badly hurting most people, and there was bitter resentment of the corruption of party officials and of businessmen and others who had connections to them. Student demonstrations led to a massacre in Peking by army troops and tanks. The demonstrations began in May 1989 in Tienanmen Square, Communist China's chief parade ground, where Mao had once addressed a million cheering followers waving the *Little Red Book*. The students' vague demands for democracy were clearly inspired by the recent increase in contact with the wider world, especially the United States, as well as by unhappiness with censorship, controlled job assignment by the state, inflation, corruption, and political dictatorship. Communist China's 25 million or more officials had become a terrible burden, hated and resented by most people, and China had become the most closely controlled society in history. The demonstrations were never violent, but the government saw them as a threat, and on the night of June 3–4 and the following day the army and its tanks moved in to crush the demonstrators, killing perhaps as many as 1,000 unarmed students. They had challenged an all-powerful state, and it responded as it had so often before. China has never had parliamentary democracy, free expression, or the rule of Western-style law, but the brutality of the massacre in Peking, enacted in front of the world's television cameras, sent shock waves around the globe even as the Soviet Union and eastern Europe were entering an exciting new phase of liberation. China stood out as isolated and condemned, though United States support continued.

In the wake of June 4, the government imprisoned many of the surviving demonstrators as well as thousands of "liberals," executed many, and denounced Western influence and lifestyles. It also continued its brutal suppression of protests in Tibet against Chinese efforts to stamp out expressions of Tibetan identity and Tibetans' requests for a more genuine role in the administration of their supposedly autonomous area.

As of 1992, the future of the regime in Peking remained cloudy. Teng, still the real power, was 88 and in failing health. His passing from the scene was anticipated by many as leading to a power struggle, openly or behind the scenes, between factions urging different approaches to the country's problems. The Chinese people have suffered terribly under successive regimes: the last decades of the deteriorating Ch'ing dynasty, the warlord years after its collapse in 1911, the reactionary and ineffective Kuomintang, and the long nightmare of Maoism, some of which was revived after 1986 when "foreign influences" were again reviled, "bourgeois" and "rightist" tendencies criticized, and, from 1989, "political study" again required of all students. But the government, though still politically repressive, vigorously pursued economic growth, especially in the private sector. In time, China may grow more open to the outside world, and more tolerant of free expression.

Taiwan and Hong Kong

Taiwan had been taken over by the Japanese in 1895 as part of their colonial empire, but with Japan's defeat in 1945 the island was returned to Chinese sovereignty. In 1949 it became the sole remaining base for the defeated Kuomintang. Some 2 million mainland Chinese, including units of the Kuomintang army and government, fled to Taiwan, where they largely excluded the Taiwanese from political power.

The island had originally been settled by Chinese from Fukien (Fujian) province, just across the narrow strait that separates it from the mainland, beginning on a significant scale in the seventeenth century. They had retained their Chinese culture while developing some regional feeling, especially when the island was under Japanese control. They welcomed the mainlanders in 1945, but after violent repressive actions in 1947, and especially after the mass influx of 1949, they tended to regard them as oppressors.

Nevertheless, Taiwan in the 1950s began a period of rapid economic growth, at first with heavy American aid and then, by the early 1960s, on its own. A land reform program gave farmers new incentives as well as increased supplies of fertilizer, new crop strains, and new irrigation. Growing rural prosperity was matched and, by the 1970s, exceeded by industrial growth as Taiwan experienced a small-scale version of the Japanese "economic miracle." Taiwanese developments followed much the same path in technological achievements and both light and heavy manufacturing. Taiwan's trade with the rest of the world quickly exceeded that of mainland China. Taipei, the capital, became a large city and was joined by other rapidly growing industrial centers and ports.

Prosperity, wider relations with the rest of the world, and an unspoken acceptance of political realities in China and East Asia began by the 1980s to soften the harsher aspects of Kuomintang control. Taiwan remained a police state, but more representation and positions were offered to the Taiwanese along with a little more freedom of expression. These trends were still increasing in 1992.

The tiny and rocky island of Hong Kong, just off the mouth of the West River, which leads to Canton, had been ceded to Britain by the Treaty of Nanking, which ended the Opium War in 1842. Additional territory was later leased on the adjacent mainland peninsula to supply Hong Kong with food and water as well as to provide room for expansion. Hong Kong grew rapidly in the nineteenth and twentieth centuries. Although under British control as a crown colony, it remained an overwhelmingly Chinese city, peopled by immigrants from overcrowded southern China who brought with them their interest and skill in commerce and their capacity for hard work. With the Communist victory in China, Hong Kong was isolated from its major market, for which it had served as a leading port for foreign trade. At the same time, it was flooded by waves of refugees from the mainland. The city and its resourceful people survived the crisis by developing a highly successful array of light industries, including textiles and electronics. Although dependent on imported raw materials, they were made profitable by inexpensive labor and efficient factories.

Hong Kong became even more prosperous than it had been before World War II. As China began to resume some trade outside the Communist bloc, Hong Kong regained its former role as a major distribution, commercial, and financial center, a function it also came to perform for much of Southeast Asia. By 1992 the city and its adjacent territories had a population of nearly 6 million. But the Chinese government announced that when the lease on those territories expired in 1997, they and all of Hong Kong would be reclaimed. To this the British agreed. It remains to be seen how this citadel of capitalism will be integrated with the socialist system of the People's Republic.

Divided Korea

Korea had suffered perhaps more than any colonial country in the world under the exceptionally harsh Japanese rule that lasted from 1910 to 1945. Living standards fell sharply during this period as Japan milked Korea of much of its raw materials and food (see Chapter 34). Virtually all nonmenial jobs were filled by Japanese. All efforts at political expression were ruthlessly suppressed, and activists were jailed, killed, or exiled. When the Pacific war ended in 1945, almost no Koreans had the educational or administrative experience to form a viable government.

In the confused weeks after the Japanese surrender, an ad hoc arrangement left Russian troops to occupy the northern half of the country above the 38th parallel while American troops occupied the southern half. The Cold War resulted in both a hardening of this division into a political boundary and the emergence of rival political regimes. A Russian-dominated government emerged in the north with its capital at P'yongyang, and an American client-state was formed in the south, headquartered at Seoul. The conservative, American-educated politician Syngman Rhee (1875–1965) became the first president of the Republic of South Korea, while the Communist leader Kim Il Sung (born 1912) headed the Democratic People's Republic of North Korea. When American and Russian troops withdrew from their respective areas, they left a United Nations commission to keep the peace but also left their two client regimes heavily armed with modern weapons.

On June 25, 1950, the North Koreans, with their new Soviet equipment, launched an invasion across the 38th parallel, although the South was clearly preparing its own strike. Because the Russians were then boycotting

39.3 Modern Korea

the United Nations Security Council, the United States was able to push through a motion condemning North Korea, which the government of the North ignored. A special United Nations emergency force was raised to combat North Korea, but the United States had already committed its soldiers to action, and the United Nations force was largely American, though outnumbered by South Koreans in opposing the North. By September the North Korean forces had overrun the entire peninsula except for a small section in the southeast. General Douglas MacArthur counterattacked behind enemy lines at Inchon. Ignoring his instructions from Washington, he pushed deeply into North Korea, bombed the bridges linking it with China, and massed troops near its frontier. At this critical point, MacArthur openly advocated attacking military bases in Manchuria and using atomic weapons against the Chinese. Chinese forces entered the war in October, driving back MacArthur's

EAST ASIA SINCE 1945

Japan	China	Korea
	Civil war (1947–1949)	
Industrial production equals 1931 level (1951)		Korean war (1950–1953)
	"Great Leap Forward" (1958)	
	Sino-Soviet split (1959)	
		Military rule (1960–1963)
Third largest producer of steel in the world (1964)		
Tokyo becomes largest city in the world (1965)	Cultural Revolution (1966–1976)	
Largest producer of steel in the world (1980)	U.S. recognizes People's Republic (1979)	Assassination of Chung Hee Park (1979)
	Tienanmen Square demonstrations (1989)	

troops and retaking much of the peninsula. Enraged by MacArthur's insubordination, President Truman relieved him of duty, touching off a bitter domestic debate. Dwight Eisenhower, Truman's successor, ended the hostilities. Campaigning for the presidency in 1952 on a pledge that he would bring peace, he approved an armistice signed at Panmunjom in July 1953.

Most of Korea was devastated by the fighting, as the armies of both sides surged back and forth over the country. A million Koreans and an almost equal number of Chinese (compared with 53,000 Americans) died, and 4 million Koreans were made refugees from their shattered homes and villages. Coming on top of the ruthless exploitation of Japanese rule after 1910, the war further reduced Korea to poverty. A pawn in the Cold War rivalries between the superpowers, the nation was left divided, its economy disrupted by the rift. The superpowers continued to supply the police-state regimes in both North and South with arms and economic aid, as their puppets, and the risk of another war between them remains, despite the fervent desire of most Koreans to see their country reunited.

The actions of the United States and the United Nations left most Koreans worse off. The alternative to war would have been a takeover of the entire country by the Communist government of the North, which is, of course, what prompted the American action. But the United States belatedly came to accept Communist governments in China and elsewhere, and it is not easy to argue that a Communist unified Korea would be substantially worse, especially for Koreans, than the present situation, fraught with built-in tensions. American intervention in Korea formed the background for a similar policy in Vietnam, now generally acknowledged as a tragic mistake.

Although the war devastated both halves of the country, Korean culture, language, and national consciousness nevertheless remained one. Both states continued

to pour scarce resources into their military establishments. This was a greater sacrifice in the less developed North than in the South, which included most of the best agricultural land and much of the industry, which the North had earlier supplied with most of its raw materials. By the 1960s South Korea had begun to recover from the war and by the 1970s to leap ahead economically, following the same path of rapid industrial development earlier pursued by Japan.

Syngman Rhee was forced to resign as president in 1960 after his dictatorial style had alienated many of his rivals, to be succeeded by a military junta and from 1963 by equally dictatorial rulers. President Chung Hee Park took office in 1963 but was assassinated in 1979 by his own Korean Central Intelligence Agency. His policies continued under Chun Doo Hwan, while the North remained under the tight control of Kim Il Sung. In both halves of Korea free expression was savagely repressed. In 1987 a wave of student protests erupted in Seoul, and the government of Chun Doo Hwan was obliged to make a few concessions, among them the direct election of the president and somewhat more scope for political parties, including those in opposition. In the first direct presidential election in 16 years, the government's hand-picked candidate, Roh Tae-woo, was chosen president in December 1987 amid charges of massive voting fraud, although he benefited from a split opposition.

Meanwhile, Korean economic growth continued to produce growing prosperity for most people in the South. Rising incomes were spread widely among the population, and the gap between rich and poor was smaller than in most societies. South Korea began to invade world markets in a number of advanced manufacturing sectors, including automobiles. North Korea was largely closed to non-Communist outsiders, but economic development there was substantial, including industrial growth, although less impressive than in the South. As long as Korea remains divided between two implacably hostile governments supported by the United States and Russia, respectively, the peace of this chronically troubled part of the world will continue at risk, and the welfare of its people will suffer. As of 1992 there were some signs that the thaw in American-Russian relations might reduce tensions in Korea and also that South Korea would continue its slow liberalization.

Southeast Asia Since World War II

China's revolutionary resurgence sent shock waves through Southeast Asia, where some 15 million Chinese resided. The Japanese had helped destroy European colonialism in Asia before World War II, but the Chinese revolution now offered a new set of ideas. In neighboring Vietnam the Chinese government aided the Communist party under Ho Chi Minh (1890–1969) in its struggle first against French colonialism and then against American intervention in support of a puppet government in the South (see Chapter 42). In the Philippines the Chinese example helped inspire a peasant Communist

uprising, the Hukbalahaps, whose successors still challenge the government. In Indonesia reports of an alleged coup by Indonesian Communists and Chinese led to an American-supported counterstrike in 1965. Mass killings of innocent Chinese and suspected Communists resulted, and the toll of victims was probably over half a million. Malaya faced an insurrection between 1943 and 1957 by a small group of native Chinese guerrillas, but most Malayan Chinese refused to join it. The rebellion was suppressed by the outgoing British colonial administration when help from China did not materialize.

Neighboring Thailand was wary, but Thai Chinese, who had been assimilated into Thai society much more completely than in any other Southeast Asian country, remained peaceful. In Burma chronic tension existed between the majority Burmans and the numerous minority groups in the mountains around the Irrawaddy plain, and the small Chinese minority in Rangoon was expelled. The military government, which came to power in 1962 under General Ne Win (born 1911), however, modeled its policy in part on the Chinese example by cutting nearly all of Burma's ties with the rest of the world and attempting to promote domestic development through state-directed socialism. Ne Win formally retired in 1989 but continued to control, changing the country's name to Myanmar. In the elections of May

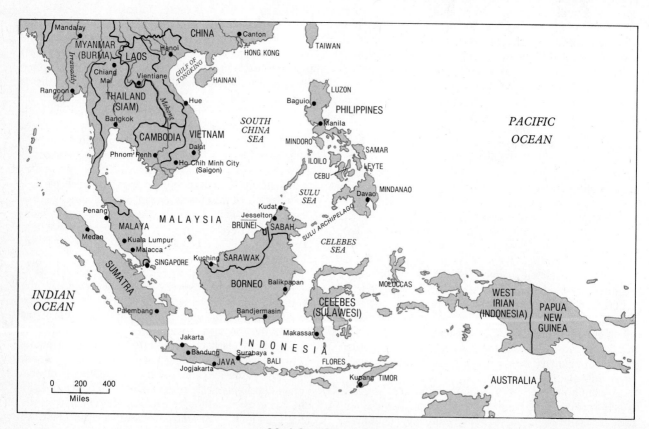

39.4 Southeast Asia

1990 the opposition Socialist party won a sweeping victory, but the military government kept the winning candidate, Aung San Sun Kyi, under arrest, and savage repression continued.

The Philippines and Indonesia

The major event of the years after 1945 in Southeast Asia was the coming of independence to former colonial states. The Philippines in 1946 were the first to achieve it, as the Americans handed over the reins of government, although their continued presence was such that the country remained a virtual protectorate. The first two decades saw some token efforts at land reform. But in 1965 Ferdinand Marcos (1917–1989) became president and soon assumed dictatorial powers, which he used to favor the rich and to suppress free expression. He was finally voted out of office in 1986, and a reformist government under Corazon Aquino (born 1933) began to attempt to repair the damage he had done.

But Aquino had her own ties with rich and powerful families and came from one of them herself. Her connections with the army, the other major Philippine power broker, were uneasy, and she barely survived repeated army rebellions. Given her political base, she was unable, and perhaps unwilling, to push for the kinds of basic change that the Philippines needed if the country was to escape from poverty for most of its citizens, corrupt privilege and wealth for a few, and a political system notorious for cronyism and inefficiency. Aquino chose not to run for reelection in 1992, and a confused contest in May brought in a new government headed by a former general.

In 1949 neighboring Indonesia won its armed struggle for freedom against the Dutch, who left the country unprepared for independence. Like the Koreans, few Indonesians had any administrative or technical experience, and the new government was unable to control inflation or corruption or to spur economic development. The outlying islands resented the dominance of Java, where the capital, Djakarta was located, and regional rebellion became chronic. President Achmed Sukarno (1901–1970), the leader of the independence movement, suspended the ineffective parliamentary government in 1956 and gradually took personal control, together with the army, in the name of what he called "guided democracy." This too failed to deal with Indonesia's mounting problems, and in 1966 General T. N. J. Suharto (born 1921), fresh from his purge of suspected Communists and Chinese, took over, confirming his rule by stage-managed elections in 1971 and 1982. The Suharto regime has made slow progress toward more orderly development despite its repressive nature, but this vast island country of some 180 million people stretched over a 3,000-mile-long archipelago has yet to evolve into full nationhood or to emerge from widespread poverty.

Indochina and the Vietnam War

When Japan surrendered in 1945, Ho Chi Minh, the head of Vietnam's Communist party, declared the independence of all Indochina. From the northern city of Hanoi, he began a war of liberation against French occupation. Under the leadership of General Vo Nguyen Giap, the Communists perfected guerrilla fighting techniques and conducted a war of attrition. Although the

Rice fields in Sumatra, Indonesia. Rice remains the major crop of lowland Southeast Asia, and much of Indonesia resembles this scene, as do the lowland rice-growing areas of Burma, Thailand, Vietnam, Malaysia, and the Philippines. [Henri Cartier-Bresson/Magnum]

French retook southern Vietnam, Ho's forces controlled much of the north. In 1954, after the French-occupied fortress of Dien Bien Phu fell to Giap's forces, a hastily arranged summit conference in Geneva brought together French, Vietnamese, British, American, Soviet, and Chinese representatives. They agreed to break up Indochina temporarily into separate states and to hold national elections to reunify Vietnam within a year. The government under Ho Chi Minh in the north of Vietnam was balanced by an American-backed dictatorship set up in the south under Ngo Dinh Diem based in Saigon, the old French colonial capital. Laos and Cambodia became independent nations.

Diem and the Americans, fearing a Communist victory, refused to permit the national elections agreed to at Geneva. Guerrilla warfare broke out in South Vietnam in 1957, but President Eisenhower limited American involvement to matériel and military advisers. The Kennedy administration escalated the local civil struggle into a major international conflict on the basis of the "domino theory" that a Communist victory in Vietnam would threaten all governments in Southeast Asia. Some 17,000 American military personnel were assigned to Vietnam, but the Communist-led National Liberation Front (NLF) succeeded in capturing most of the countryside. In 1963 Vietnamese generals abetted by the United States killed Diem and ushered in a succession of military regimes.

Under President Lyndon Johnson the conflict be-

came a full-scale war. He ordered air strikes against the Communist North and in August 1964, following a staged naval incident in the Gulf of Tongking (Tonkin), secured passage of a resolution from Congress that gave the president carte blanche to enlarge America's role in the war. By the spring of 1965 the United States was carrying out massive bombardment of North Vietnam and had committed its soldiers to offensive operations. The number of American troops grew steadily, from 184,000 in 1965 to more than 500,000 by the end of 1968.

Despite this buildup, victory eluded the United States and its allies. The attempt to secure territory in the South by so-called search-and-destroy operations against the enemy proved futile, and the administration, fearing Chinese intervention as in Korea, declined to invade the North. Unable to gain victory on the ground, the United States dropped more explosives on tiny Vietnam than the Allies had dropped on all fronts during World War II, and American troops killed thousands of civilians in fruitless efforts to prevent villagers from hiding Communist guerrillas.

The turning point in the war came in February 1968, when the NLF launched a wave of attacks, known as the Tet Offensive, against towns and cities in South Vietnam. In April peace talks between the United States and North Vietnam opened in Paris, and in November, American voters elected the Republican Richard M. Nixon (born 1913) to the presidency. Nixon began the secret bomb-

American soldiers stop to watch as a target in a South Vietnamese village burns. [Philip Jones-Griffiths/ Magnum]

ing of Communist supply routes in Cambodia and Laos in early 1969, concealing the operation through false reports. When Congress learned of the Cambodian bombings, it repealed the Tongking Gulf Resolution. In 1971 the publication of classified war documents heightened antiwar sentiments by revealing earlier deceptions by both Johnson and Nixon. Protests mounted as the 1972 presidential elections approached, but Nixon neutralized them by removing the last American ground troops. The Paris Accords, signed in January 1973, officially ended American involvement in the war. In April 1975 the North Vietnamese captured Saigon, ousted the government of President Nguyen Van Thieu, and unified the country.

The Americans claimed that the struggle was an example of "Communist aggression." Most Vietnamese saw it as a patriotic war of "national liberation" against French colonialism and U.S. imperialism. Peasants came to fear and hate the repressive policies of the puppet government of the South and of their American supporters, as they and most Vietnamese intellectuals had hated French oppression. There were some Vietnamese anti-Communists, including Catholic converts who fled the North, and some who supported the United States–backed government, but they were mainly relatively well-to-do elites and others who benefited from the widespread corruption of the Saigon government or who profited in various ways from the American presence. The war's outcome was ultimately decided by the support of most Vietnamese, including the peasants in this predominantly rural country, for the forces of the National Liberation Front, which they saw as a national rather than a partisan effort.

In many ways the Vietnam War was a repeat of the long struggle of the Chinese Communists against the Kuomintang. In Vietnam, too, the Communist party under Ho had captured the leadership of Vietnamese nationalism by the end of World War II. Like the Chinese, Vietnamese nationalists strove to free their country from foreign domination, and like them, they drew support against a corrupt and repressive regime domestically, which was further weakened politically by its subservience to foreign interests. Between 1.5 and 2 million Vietnamese gave their lives in the struggle; perhaps as many as 4 million were wounded, and over a million were refugees. The Americans suffered 58,000 dead and some 300,000 wounded.

As in Korea but to a far greater extent, American intervention produced in the end nothing but destruction and death. Official policy was based on almost total ignorance of Vietnam, its history of repeated success in repelling vastly superior Chinese armies, and the strength of Vietnamese nationalism. The small nation's guerrilla fighters humbled the military might of the world's greatest superpower, as the Chinese Communists had earlier defeated another United States client,

the Kuomintang. But Vietnam suffered terribly. Its people and its economy have not recovered from what has been called the "endless war" from 1945 to 1975, although for many Vietnamese the struggle against the French had begun in the second half of the nineteenth century. The United States merely prolonged that struggle and, far from preventing a Communist victory, had the effect of hardening the determination and the political rigidity of the government of the North. Since 1975 Vietnam has continued to suffer not only from the effects of unprecedented devastation but also from ideological tension and repression augmented by the long ordeal of conflict. If Ho had been allowed to prevail against the French in 1945 or 1946, as he clearly would have done without massive United States support for the French, most of these tragic problems would have been avoided.

Recovery from the war damage to the economy was slow. As after any civil war, bitterness remained between the victors of the north and the southerners who had opposed them. Large numbers of Vietnamese fled the country, many to the United States. But continued political and ideological tensions further slowed the recovery of Vietnam, which lagged behind much of the rest of Southeast Asia.

Vietnam's war of independence spilled over into neighboring Laos and Cambodia, with appalling human consequences. The overthrow of the neutralist ruler of Cambodia (now Kampuchea), Prince Norodom Sihanouk (born 1919), led to a civil war and subsequently to the genocidal Communist regime of Pol Pot, who was responsible for the deaths of perhaps a third of the country's people from 1976 to 1979 by forced labor, execution, or starvation. Vietnamese military intervention helped a more moderate rival government win control of most of the country in 1979, but Pol Pot's Khmer Rouge forces remain active in their northern bases, supplied by China and the United States. Vietnam was still seen as the enemy of America and now again of China, and its move to eliminate Pol Pot was therefore resisted by both countries for political reasons. Those reasons included Soviet support for Vietnam, which helped sustain it in its war with the United States and which the Chinese also saw as a threat to themselves. Continuing Cold War rivalries in Indochina have thus prolonged its agony, but as of 1990 the United States was edging away from support for Pol Pot, and by 1992 there was agreement among Russia, the United States, and China to hold elections in Cambodia supervised by the United Nations.

Malaysia, Singapore, Thailand, and Burma

Malaya's independence was delayed by the Communist insurgency, but once order was restored, the British quickly handed over power to the new state in 1957. Its major problem has been the diversity of its people. The Malays constituted a bare majority in their own homeland, thanks to massive Chinese immigration since the late nineteenth century. Most Malays were not interested in wage labor, and the booming growth of tin mining and rubber plantations brought in a wave of Chinese workers and entrepreneurs from overcrowded southern China. Many of them went on to become the dominant figures in the commercial life of Malaya and were joined by wives and families from China, as well as by immigrant laborers and merchants from India. By the time of independence Malays made up only about half of the population.

This problem was eased in 1965 by the separation of the island of Singapore, overwhelmingly Chinese, as an independent city-state, and by the addition of former British colonies in northern Borneo, where Chinese were a minority. Since then the state has been called Malaysia, but there have been chronic conflicts between Malays and Chinese. The Chinese are effectively without a political voice, but Malays resent their economic power. A generally stable parliamentary system on the British model was marred in the 1980s by tendencies, like those in Singapore, toward authoritarianism and repression. The economy has remained relatively vigorous and has expanded from its colonial foundations in tin and rubber to include important palm oil production and a rapidly growing light industrial sector.

The tiny Sultanate of Brunei on the north coast of Borneo, formerly a British protectorate, was given its independence following the creation of Malaysia and then rocketed to wealth when rich oil deposits were found there. Independent Singapore continues as a high-income and high-growth center of trade for much of Southeast Asia and has become the world's fourth largest port in volume of traffic.

Thailand, just north of Malaya, was the only nation of Southeast Asia to retain independence throughout the colonial period. Since 1945 it has also enjoyed precarious political stability under democratic forms and has shared in the prosperous commercial growth of Malaya and Singapore through its port and capital of Bangkok, now a rapidly growing Western-style city. Successful military coups, including one in 1991, confirmed the army as the real power, but there was growing dissent among the rising middle class.

Burma won its freedom from Britain in 1948 in the wake of India's independence, but it has been troubled by violence between the dominant Burmans and the diverse minorities who occupy the mountain fringes of the country. Chronic guerrilla-style civil war existed between government forces and rebel groups. General Ne Win's military government was not able to resolve this problem fully, and his policy of isolation from the rest of the world had the effect of further slowing Burma's already sluggish economic growth. Burma has begun to move cautiously toward resuming some external contacts and trade. A new and more responsive government may be able to build a more equitable and consensual national partnership among Burmese and non-Burmese, but the country still has far to go to attain viable nationhood. The military government, moreover, continues to block change and in 1991 outlawed the Socialist party, which had won the May 1990 election.

For Southeast Asia as a whole, the transition from colonialism has been a hard one. Only Singapore and Thailand can be called fully successful states, and both may be regarded as special cases: Thailand never underwent colonial occupation and contains few non-Thai minorities. Singapore is in essence a creation of Western colonialism and capitalism. From the 1980s government policies in Singapore were often repressively applied and free expression was curtailed or silenced. The countries of Southeast Asia are too scattered and too different from each other to work together as a unit, even for common economic purposes. The region is a major sector of the world, but its diversity and the legacy of its colonial domination continue to retard its development.

Women in East Asian Society

The prominence of women political figures such as Chiang Ch'ing, Imelda Marcos, and Corazon Aquino is not representative of the lot of most women in postwar East Asia. In China life for women remained essentially unchanged from the time of Confucius to the beginning of the twentieth century. The Chinese woman was considered a temporary member of her parents' household, to be transferred to her husband's control at marriage. She adopted her husband's surname, only then followed by her own. Upon her death, only her husband's family surname was recorded in her husband's genealogy, so that her personal identity was permanently effaced. Despite the achievement of some women of rank in scholarship and the arts, the average woman was, at least until she bore a son, near the bottom of the status hierarchy.

The impact of Western imperialism in the late nineteenth century brought the first challenge to the traditional system. Mission schools and colleges began to educate women and added support to the movements against foot-binding, chaste widowhood, and the general subjugation of women. After the revolution of 1911, the first women's magazines began to appear, and the demand of the younger generation for greater freedom from parental control opened up new secondary and university education to girls. Pioneer feminists became doctors, lawyers, teachers, and active revolutionaries; there were even banks staffed entirely by women and serving a female clientele. Missionary boarding schools provided an important avenue of mobility for aspiring village girls, while in the cities they offered daughters of the merchant class a Western-oriented education and social contact with foreigners. World War II, with its increased demand for labor power and its dislocation of families, also increased social and economic opportunities for women.

After the revolution of 1949, women in the People's Republic were given basic legal rights for the first time. The Marriage Law of 1950 not only gave women the right freely to choose their husbands and equal responsibility for the raising of children but also established the right of women to own property and to choose an occupation. The effect of this legislation was galvanic. A newspaper estimated in 1953 that 2 million persons had been affected by divorce in Shanghai, Peking, Tientsin, and Wuhan alone. In the same year the Ministry of Justice reported that 70,000 to 80,000 women were being murdered or forced into suicide each year as a result of family conflict or oppression. This backlash presaged a long struggle for genuine equality. By 1958 women comprised 50 percent of the agricultural labor force but were far from equally compensated with men; nor had they advanced far in penetrating the manufacturing sector, where they were still largely confined to the textile and tobacco industries. The commune movement of the late 1950s also had the effect of regimenting women. The top political and professional echelons were still almost entirely reserved for men. Twenty years after the revolution, only 10 percent of the members of the Communist party itself were women.

Official policy toward women in the early decades of the revolution reflected the drive to mobilize labor in general. The traditional extended family was drastically affected by land reform, forced resettlement, and the commune system. Not until 1974, as part of a campaign against the Confucian ethos, was the position of women systematically addressed, particularly the residual dominance of the patrilocal family. Even then, however, the primary impetus was economic rationalization and increased productivity.

The status of women in the newly industrialized nations of Taiwan and Korea, the city-state of Singapore, and the British colony of Hong Kong displays the tension between traditional Chinese or Chinese-influenced family culture and the needs of market capitalism, which tends to treat workers in isolation from the family or other social unit. On the one hand, wage remuneration has given women in these labor-intensive, export-oriented societies some potential economic independence; on the other, they are still expected to remain firmly under family control.

In Southeast Asia, where women have long had independent property rights and have been as active as men in the economy, the primary change in the past several decades has been the increasing differentiation between town and country life. The postwar constitutions of Burma, Thailand, and Indonesia gave legal equality to women, and in South Vietnam the Family Law Bill of 1958 spelled out such equality in detail. In the Islamic states of Malaysia and Indonesia, the special problem of women, apart from the general Islamic subordination of them, is the persistence of polygamy and the ease of divorce, which has mounted in some areas as high as 60 percent.

The situation of Japan is unique in that it is the only East Asian nation in the front rank of the world's industrial powers. Before the twentieth century, women had been subservient to men, as in Confucian China, and unable to inherit property even when male descendants were lacking. As elsewhere in East Asia, a feminist movement had arisen early in the century, led particularly by Hiratsuka Raicho (1886–1971), who founded the first Japanese women's magazine, *Blue Stockings*, in 1911, and Ichikawa Fusae (1893–1981), who was later to serve in the House of Councillors almost continuously from 1953 until her death. A feminist organization, the New Women's Association, was founded after World War I, although it was not until the American occupation that women were able to win formal legal equality and the right to vote. Traditional patterns of deference continued to prevail, however. In 1980 fully 75 percent of the eligible women voted in the nationwide elections, as opposed to 53 percent of the male electorate; yet only 3 percent of the members returned to the Japanese Diet were women.

Social and economic inequality between the sexes continues to characterize Japan. The introduction of co-education in 1950 led to a doubling of girls in secondary schools during the next decade and more than tripled the number of female university students. Yet university women are still regarded as exceptional in Japan. Women now comprise 35 percent of the work force but still lag far behind their male counterparts in earnings and benefits. They are exploited in every sector, including agriculture, where they constitute the majority of the labor force but are almost entirely unpaid workers on family farms. Most working women leave their employment upon marriage, only to reenter 10 to 15 years later at the bottom of the pay scale. Laws have recently been passed, however, providing child care and other benefits for working women. Japanese feminists are particularly active in such causes as consumer and environmental protection, peace and nuclear disarmament movements, and the fight against job discrimination.

Rewards and Problems of Modernization

East Asia as a whole had the highest economic growth rate of any part of the world in the decades following World War II, a pattern that still continues. Hong Kong,

Taiwan, and South Korea rapidly developed in the wake of Japanese economic success after the mid-1950s. Much of this development was on the Japanese model, beginning in light industry and consumer goods and continuing into heavy manufacturing and precision goods. Singapore's growth paralleled that of Hong Kong; both were tiny Chinese city-states that had originally prospered as trade centers and then moved into "high-tech" industrialization and processing. In China, despite the drag exerted by antiurbanism and revolutionary ideology, industrial growth was impressive, and after 1980 overall economic development was rapid. In Southeast Asia several of the major cities besides Singapore, notably Bangkok, Thailand, and Manila, the Philippine capital, grew enormously as booming commercial and light industrial centers.

Much of this growth rested on the East Asian tradition of disciplined hard work and organized group effort, but it was striking enough to attract world attention and speculation about its causes. East Asia does share, to varying degrees, an originally Chinese culture, which has for centuries stressed education, hard work, and group effort, perhaps enough to override other differences in the pursuit of advancement.

But modernization has brought new problems. These include the rapid erosion of traditional cultures (to the distress of many East Asians), the rise of huge cities inadequately supplied with basic services or housing, and fearsome pollution of urban and rural environments. Japan was only the first to suffer dramatically from industrial pollution as a result of the unprecedented concentration of cities and manufacturing in its lowlands. As a high-income and technologically developed society, Japan was also the first to deal successfully with at least some of those problems.

For the rest of East Asia, as in the developing world as a whole, largely unchecked pollution is still increasing, with deeply worrisome long-term consequences for human welfare. Other East Asian countries have passed environmental legislation too, but in most cases it is not effectively enforced. Chinese, Korean, Taiwanese, and Southeast Asian cities are dangerously polluted, their air heavy with soot and fumes, and their water supplies, often inadequate to supply their mushrooming populations and factories, are loaded with poisonous industrial residues. In rural areas heavy applications of chemical fertilizers, the use of largely unregulated chemical pesticides, and the development of factories cause additional environmental damage. Massive cutting of trees to feed the demand for new construction has exposed slopes to erosion, and silt chokes rivers and irrigation systems. In large parts of Southeast Asia the tropical rain forest that covers much of the area is rapidly being depleted to provide lumber for both domestic and world markets, with potentially serious effects on local and world climate.

Most of these countries are bent on rapid industrial and economic growth; they are reluctant to slow that growth or add to its costs, even by limiting the worst of the environmental damage. Such controls, many of them argue, are for rich countries. It may take more human disasters such as Japan experienced to persuade them that their own welfare is at stake. Japan, lacking most industrial raw materials and having to import nearly all of its oil, has invested proportionately more heavily in nuclear power than any country in the world, ignoring its location in one of the world's major earthquake zones. China has huge domestic supplies of coal, most of it with a high sulfur content, which supplies about three-quarters of the nation's energy. These problems may become future disasters as East Asia continues to industrialize.

Urban growth in East Asia has taken place very rapidly and with minimal planning, especially outside China. Even in China industrial and residential areas have not been adequately separated; housing, water supply, and other urban services lag seriously behind demand; Peking has grown uncontrollably. These problems are equally pronounced in urban centers such as Seoul, Taipei, Bangkok, Manila, and Djakarta, where unchecked migration from rural areas has swollen city populations without a substantial increase in basic services.

While the problems of modernization seem especially serious in the cities, it is there also that the chief forces for economic growth are centered. The cities are the major industrial bases, educational centers, commercial and financial hubs, and centers of intellectual and cultural ferment, as they were in the history of the West. So far Asia has tended to repeat the Western experience of economic and industrial development, which in its early and middle stages was unpleasant and unhealthy for most people. As the process has gathered momentum in Asia after World War II, one may hope that the rest of the Western experience will be repeated too, as the cities become, like those in Japan, centers of improved welfare. Their advances can then spread more widely over each country.

The years after 1945 were momentous for East Asia. New nations were born out of the former colonial regimes in Southeast Asia. Korea regained its independence, only to be torn by war and split by superpower tensions. China underwent the largest revolution in history, measured by the numbers of people involved, the scope of its change, and the length of both its gestation and its active course, including the convulsive struggles of the Cultural Revolution. A shattered Japan rebuilt its economy and rose to world industrial leadership. But although each of these major areas had its own internal problems, the dominant trend in all of them was economic growth and industrialization. East Asia as a whole, led by Japan, became the world's largest and most rapidly expanding commercial and industrial network, as it had long been its most populous geographic region. It remains to be seen whether the area's new economic power will be reflected proportionately in new political power on the world scene.

Suggestions for Further Reading

Japan

Cohen, T. *Remaking Japan: The American Occupation as New Deal.* New York: Free Press, 1987.

Dore, R. *City Life in Japan: A Study of a Tokyo Ward.* Berkeley: University of California Press, 1967.

Hane, M. *Modern Japan: A Historical Survey.* Boulder, Colo.: Westview Press, 1986.

Hendry, J. *Understanding Japanese Society.* London: Routledge & Kegan Paul, 1988.

Immamura, H. E. *Urban Japanese Housewives.* Honolulu: University Press of Hawaii, 1986.

Lebra, T. S. *Japanese Women: Constraint and Fulfillment.* Honolulu: University Press of Hawaii, 1984.

Minear, R. *Victor's Justice.* Princeton, N.J.: Princeton University Press, 1971.

Okata, S. *Japan in the World Economy.* Tokyo: Tokyo University Press, 1990.

Reischauer, E. O. *The Japanese.* Cambridge, Mass.: Harvard University Press, 1988.

Saso, M. *Women in the Japanese Workplace.* London: Shipman, 1990.

Stockwin, J. A. *Japan: Divided Politics in a Growth Economy.* London: Weidenfeld & Nicolson, 1975.

Storry, R. *A History of Modern Japan,* rev. ed. New York: Penguin Books, 1982.

Vogel, E. *Japan as Number One: Lessons for America.* Cambridge, Mass.: Harvard University Press, 1979.

China

Bonavia, D. *The Chinese.* New York: Harper & Row, 1984.

Cheng, C. Y. *Behind the Tienanmen Massacre.* Boulder, Colo.: Westview Press, 1990.

Dietrich, C. *People's China: A Brief History.* New York: Oxford University Press, 1986.

Fairbank, J. K. *The Great Chinese Revolution.* Cambridge, Mass.: Harvard University Press, 1986.

Hsu, I. C. Y. *China Since Mao.* New York: Oxford University Press, 1990.

Lee, H. Y. *The Politics of the Chinese Cultural Revolution.* Berkeley: University of California Press, 1978.

Liang, H., and Shapiro, J. *Son of the Revolution.* New York: Knopf, 1984.

Murphey, R. *The Fading of the Maoist Vision.* New York: Methuen, 1980.

Nathan, A. *Chinese Democracy.* Berkeley: University of California Press, 1986.

Riskin, C. *China's Political Economy: The Quest for Development Since 1949.* New York: Oxford University Press, 1987.

Schram, S. *Mao Tse-tung: A Preliminary Reassessment.* New York: Simon & Schuster, 1984.

Schrecker, J. E. *The Chinese Revolution in Historical Perspective.* New York: Praeger, 1991.

Selden, M. *The Yenan Way in Revolutionary China.* Cambridge, Mass.: Harvard University Press, 1971.

Simon, D. F., and Kau, Y. M. *Taiwan: Beyond the Economic Miracle.* New York: Sharpe, 1992.

Sutter, R. G. *Taiwan: Entering the Twenty-first Century.* Washington, D.C.: University Press of America, 1989.

White, M. K., and Parrish, W. *Urban Life in Contemporary China.* Stanford, Calif.: Stanford University Press, 1985.

———. *Village and Family in Contemporary China.* Chicago: University of Chicago Press, 1978.

Wolf, M. *Revolution Postponed: Women in Contemporary China.* Stanford, Calif.: Stanford University Press, 1985.

Woronoff, J. *Asia's "Miracle" Economies.* New York: Sharpe, 1992.

Korea

Clough, R. N. *Embattled Korea.* Boulder, Colo.: Westview Press, 1987.

Lee, K. B. *A New History of Korea,* trans. E. W. Wagner. Cambridge, Mass.: Harvard University Press, 1985.

Southeast Asia

Greene, G. *The Quiet American.* New York: Viking, 1957. (A novel about the Vietnam War.)

Martin, L. K., ed. *The Asian Success Story.* Honolulu: University Press of Hawaii, 1987.

Steinberg, D., ed. *In Search of Southeast Asia: A Modern History,* rev. ed. Honolulu: University Press of Hawaii, 1987.

Nationalism and Revolution: India, Pakistan, Iran, and the Middle East

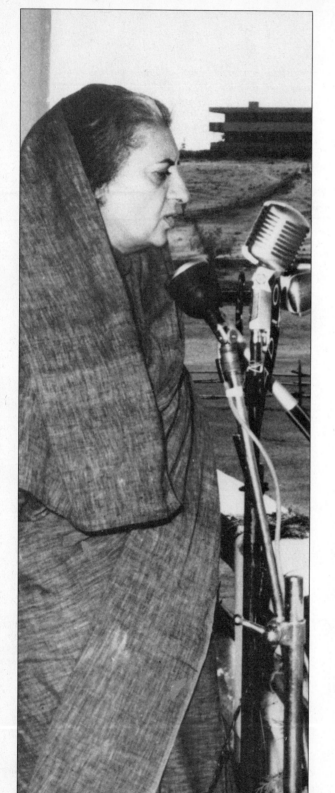

Indira Gandhi in 1972, addressing a crowd at Kolhapur, India. [UPI/Bettmann Newsphotos]

The postwar period was a time of rapid and radical change throughout the Middle East and central Asia. Britain and France withdrew or were forced from their colonial dominions, and a host of new nations emerged, some with ancient roots, others the product of modern nationalism. Among the former, India and Egypt regained their old independence, one as a constitutional democracy, the other as a revolutionary socialist state. Among the latter, Pakistan, the world's third largest Islamic state (after Indonesia and India), emerged from the Muslim-majority regions of pre-1949 India. Some states, such as Jordan, were created primarily as buffer zones or in acts of political compromise, while in other cases nationalist movements, such as those of the Palestinians and the Kurds, remained frustrated. The most controversial new nation to emerge was the state of Israel, where a powerful modern nationalism sought to revive the heritage of a kingdom that had flourished nearly 3,000 years before. Throughout the postwar decades, however, the region as a whole has been characterized by turmoil and instability, culminating in the 1980s in a war between Iran and Iraq that now ranks as the fourth bloodiest conflict of the twentieth century.

South Asia: Independence and Political Division

The Indian subcontinent, known since 1947 as South Asia, is composed of the separate states of Pakistan, India, Bangladesh, Nepal, and Sri Lanka and contains well over a billion people, one-fifth of the world. British colonialism died in the ashes of World War II, and the British were in any case unwilling to continue their rule of an India determined to regain its freedom. Gandhi, Nehru, and other Indian political leaders had spent most of the war years in jail after they had refused to support the war without a promise of independence. Their example inspired many new followers, and by 1945 the independence movement was clearly too strong to be denied by a Britain now both weakened and weary of

colonialism. The conservative wartime leader Winston Churchill was voted out of office. Churchill had been rigidly opposed to Indian independence. During the war he had declared, "I was not made His Majesty's first minister in order to preside over the liquidation of the British Empire," and he was contemptuous of Gandhi. Lord Wavell, military commander in India and the first postwar viceroy, wrote in his diary: "Churchill hates India and everything to do with it. He knows as much of the Indian problem as George III did of the American colonies. . . . He sent me a peevish telegram to ask why Gandhi hadn't died yet."

The new Labour government under Clement Attlee moved quickly toward giving India its freedom. Elections were held in India early in 1946, but by then it had become clear that support for a separate state for Muslims had gained strength. The Muslim League, the chief vehicle for this movement, had been founded as early as 1906, but until 1945 it was supported by only a few Muslims, most of whom remained willing to work with the Congress party as the main agent of politically conscious Indians. The Muslim League's president, Mohammed Ali Jinnah (1876–1948), had earlier been a member of the Congress party and was even for a time its president. He and a few other Muslim leaders became dissatisfied with the Congress party's plans for a secular independent state that deemphasized religious identity and with the party's leaders' unwillingness to reserve what Jinnah regarded as adequate positions and representation for Muslims. Hindus and Muslims had lived to-

◉ Muslim Solidarity: Jinnah's Call ◉

Jinnah made a number of speeches during World War II in his effort to promote Muslim solidarity and political action. Here are excerpts from a 1943 speech.

The progress that Muslims, as a nation, have made during these [past] three years is a remarkable fact. . . . Never before has a nation, miscalled a minority, asserted itself so quickly and so effectively. . . . We have created a solidarity of opinion, a union of mind and thought. . . . Let us cooperate with and give all help to our leaders to work for our collective good. Let us make our organization stronger. . . . We, the Muslims, must rely mainly upon our own inherent qualities, our own natural potentialities, our own internal solidarity, and our own united will to face the future. . . . Train yourselves, equip yourselves for the task that lies before us. The final victory depends upon you and is within our grasp. You have performed wonders in the past. You are still capable of repeating history. You are not lacking in the great qualities and virtues in comparison with other nations. Only you have to be fully conscious of that fact and act with courage, faith, and unity.

Source: W. T. de Bary, ed., *Sources of Indian Tradition,* 4th ed., vol. 2 (New York: Columbia University Press, 1964), pp. 286–287.

Mohammed Ali Jinnah in 1946. Note his totally Western dress. [British Library]

lier career as a British-trained lawyer, he had paid little attention to Islam, and he knew no Urdu, the language of Islam in India. But as he saw his political ambitions threatened by the success of Gandhi and Nehru, he shifted his allegiance to the Muslim League and began to use it to persuade Muslims that a Hindu-dominated India would never, as he put it, give them "justice." He found support among some of the communal-minded (those who put separate group loyalty above national feeling) and also from Muslim businessmen, especially in the port city of Karachi, who saw a possible way of ridding themselves of Hindu competition. Nehru and others insisted that communalism had nothing to do with religion and that the exploitation of religious differences by a few politicians for their own ends fueled communal tensions. Hindus were often more active and more successful in business than Muslims, they were generally more educated, and as the great majority in India they also dominated politics and the professions. But they did not generally discriminate against Muslim intellectuals or professionals. Some other Muslim political figures, like Jinnah, saw greater opportunity for themselves if they could have their own state and supported the League in its campaign to convince Muslims that "Islam was in danger." When such relatively peaceful tactics did not produce enough result, Jinnah and the League began to promote terror and violence, urging Muslims to demonstrate and to attack Hindus in order to call attention to their cause.

gether peacefully for most of nine centuries, even at the village level. Persian Muslim culture had blended in with indigenous elements to form modern Indian civilization. Both groups were long-standing parts of the Indian fabric. It was hard to see them as irreconcilable.

Jinnah, like Nehru, was British-educated. In his ear-

The Congress party was slow to respond or to offer

Nehru and Mountbatten in New Delhi, 1947. The two men took an immediate liking to each other, which greatly eased the transition to independence. [UPI/Bettmann Newsphoto]

Muslims or the League a larger share in an Indian future. Gandhi and Nehru in particular were reluctant even to consider partitioning India just as it was about to win freedom. This tended to increase the League's fear of a Hindu threat to Muslims, and the League resorted to more violent tactics. In the later stages of the long negotiations during 1946 and 1947 Jinnah offered to give up the demand for Pakistan (as the separate Muslim state was to be called) if he could be guaranteed the position of first prime minister of independent India. That demand was rejected, and Jinnah remained adamant in insisting on a separate state that he could head. Successive British representatives tried to work out a solution in sessions with the Congress party and the League, ending with the special mission in 1947 of Lord Louis Mountbatten (1900–1979), the wartime supreme commander in Southeast Asia. Mountbatten was appointed viceroy of India, with the sole charge of working out the terms for independence as quickly as this could be done.

If independence had been granted at any time before 1939, as most Indians and most British had wanted, the issue of partition would not have arisen. Jinnah was able to use the war years, while the Congress party leaders were in jail, to build his political base and then to spread the fear of cultural engulfment and oppression among his followers. Muslim-Hindu violence, once stirred up by the Muslim League, acquired its own dreadful momentum on both sides, especially in regions that were nearly evenly divided between the two religious communities, such as Punjab and East Bengal. Mob riots and mass killing spread widely. Although Mountbatten, like Nehru and Gandhi, hoped to avoid handing over power to a divided India, by July he as well as the party leaders

◉ India and the Sense of History ◉

On the eve of independence, Nehru addressed the Constituent Assembly in 1946 with his characteristic eloquence, stressing the sense of history that many Indians share.

As I stand here, . . . I feel the weight of all manner of things crowding upon me. We are at the end of an era and possibly very soon we shall embark upon a new age. My mind goes back to the great past of India, to the 5000 years of India's history, from the very dawn of that history which might be considered almost the dawn of human history, until today. All that past crowds upon me and exhilarates me, and at the same time somewhat oppresses me. Am I worthy of that past? When I think also of the future, the greater future I hope, standing on this sword's edge of the present between the mighty past and the mightier future, I tremble a little and feel overwhelmed by this mighty task. We have come here at a strange moment in India's history. I do not know, but I do feel, that there is some magic in this moment of transition from the old to the new, something of that magic which one sees when the night turns into day and even though the day may be a cloudy one, it is day after all, for when the clouds move away, we can see the sun again. Because of all this I find a little difficulty in addressing this House and putting all my ideas before it, and I feel also that in this long succession of thousands of years, I see the mighty figures that have come and gone and I see also the long succession of our comrades who have labored for the freedom of India. And we stand now on the verge of this passing age, trying, laboring, to usher in the new. . . .

I think also of the various constituent assemblies that have gone before and of what took place at the making of the great American nation when the fathers of that nation met and fashioned a constitution which has stood the test for so many years. . . . [He then mentions the French and Russian revolutions also.] We seek to learn from their success and to avoid their failures. Perhaps we may not be able to avoid failures, because some measure of failure is inherent in human effort. Nevertheless we shall advance, I am certain . . . and realize the dream that we have dreamed so long.

Source: W. T. de Bary, ed., *Sources of Indian Tradition,* 4th ed., vol. 1 (New York: Columbia University Press, 1964), pp. 350–352.

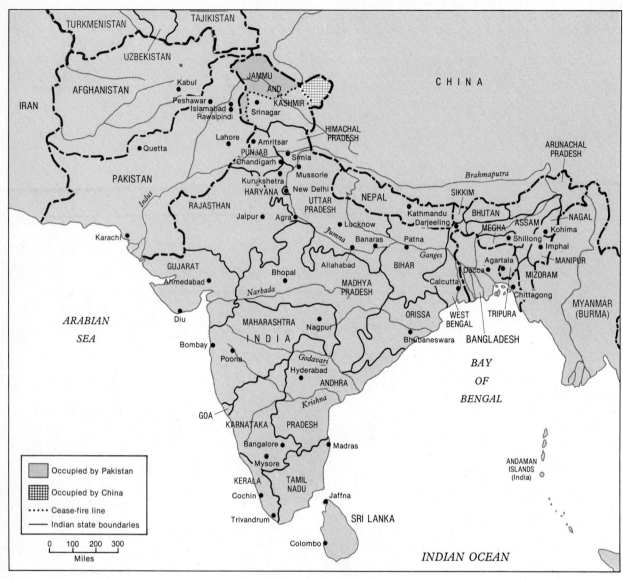

40.1 *South Asia Today*

recognized that partition and the creation of Pakistan were inevitable. Nehru remarked bitterly that "by cutting off the head we will get rid of the headache," while Gandhi continued to regard partition as "vivisection."

Lines were drawn to mark off the predominantly Muslim northwest and western Punjab and the eastern half of Bengal as the two unequal halves of Pakistan, separated from each other by nearly 1,000 miles. At midnight on August 14, 1947, the Republic of India and the Islamic state of Pakistan officially won their independence. Gandhi boycotted the independence day celebrations in New Delhi, going instead to Calcutta to try to quell fresh outbreaks of mass violence there as refugees streamed in from eastern Bengal.

The first months of independence were tragically overshadowed by perhaps the greatest mass refugee movement in history as over 10 million people fled from both sides in 1947 alone, about a million of whom were victims of mob massacre along the route. When it was all over, 50 million Muslims continued to live in India much as before, and India still has more Muslims than Pakistan. For those who chose to migrate to Pakistan, including further millions after 1947, life in the new state (with an initial population of 70 million), was hard in the first chaotic years as Pakistan struggled to cope with the flood of refugees. Hindus remaining in Pakistan soon found that they had little place in an Islamic state that explicitly discriminated against all non-Muslims, and within a few years most of them had migrated to India, depriving Pakistan of many of its more highly educated and experienced people. For the educated elite of both countries, including the army officers who soon faced each other across the new boundaries, partition divided former classmates, friends, and professional colleagues who had shared a common experience, training, and values.

The partition lines also split the previously integrated cultural and economic regions of densely populated Punjab and Bengal and caused immense disruption. Since the division was by agreement based solely on religion, nothing was considered except to separate areas with a Muslim majority, often by a thin margin. Many districts, villages, and towns were nearly evenly balanced between the two religions, which were deeply intertwined over many centuries of coexistence. The partition cut through major road and rail links, divided rural areas from their urban centers, and bisected otherwise uniform regions of culture and language.

The Kashmir Conflict

The still nominally independent native states, under their own Indian rulers, were technically given the choice to join India or Pakistan, but there was really no choice for the few Muslim-ruled states or smaller Muslim-majority areas surrounded by Indian territory, which were absorbed or taken over, including the large state of Hyderabad in the Deccan, Muslim-ruled but with a Hindu majority.

Kashmir, which lay geographically between the two rivals, had a Muslim majority but a Hindu ruler and its own hopes for independence. The ruler, Hari Singh, delayed his decision until his state was invaded by "volunteer" forces from Pakistan, and he agreed to join India in return for military help. Indian paratroops arrived just in time to hold Srinagar, the capital, and the central valley, the only economically important and densely settled part of the state. The cease-fire line, which still stands, gave roughly the western quarter of Kashmir to Pakistan, but the larger issue of which state Kashmir should belong to has never been resolved.

The Kashmir dispute has continued to poison relations between the two states and has sparked three inconclusive wars. Thus to the tragedy of partition and the violence following it has been added chronic Indo-Pakistani tension instead of the cooperation that would be more appropriate between two developing nations born out of the same context and sharing a common cultural tradition. Mahatma Gandhi, who had prayed and labored so hard to stop Hindu-Muslim violence, ironically became one of its victims when he was murdered on January 30, 1948, by a Hindu extremist who considered him too tolerant of Muslims. Nehru saw his death as "the loss of India's soul" and commented, "The light has gone out of our lives and there is darkness everywhere."

India After Independence

In the Republic of India, parliamentary democracy and British-style law have survived repeated tests and remain vigorous. Jawaharlal Nehru, who became prime minister at independence and served until his death in 1964, was a strong and revered leader who effectively dominated the new nation. He presided over the creation of 16 new language-based states within a federal structure. Federalism was necessary in any case given India's size and diversity, and language was the single most obvious basis of regional differences. Although Nehru and others were reluctant to acknowledge the importance of language-based regionalism, it became clear after several years of debate and negotiation that such a concession would have to be made. The states created by 1956 were the size of France, Germany, or Italy in population, and each coincided approximately with the distribution of what were officially declared to be "major" languages out of the many hundreds spoken. Each of these major languages had its own proud history and literary tradition, older, more extensive, and with more speakers than most European languages.

Hindi, the language of the Delhi area and the upper Ganges valley, was declared the official national language, to be used in national government and taught to all Indians in every region, while leaving each state its own regional language in its schools and legislatures. English, familiar to educated people in all the states, was retained as an "associate language" at the national level and continued to be taught in nearly all schools. Indian English has more speakers than American English, and it too has diverged from its British origins. Hindi is the mother tongue of only about 30 percent of the population, and even so consists of several mutually unintelligible dialects. No other native Indian language comes close. Hindi was therefore the obvious choice for a nationwide language, but for most Indians it remains a foreign tongue. It is resented especially by Dravidian-speaking southerners as yet another example of "northern domination" and the "oppression of Delhi."

India Under Nehru

Nehru saw India well launched on the path of economic development, both agricultural and industrial, but he acknowledged the Gandhian legacy by providing special government support for handicraft production and for

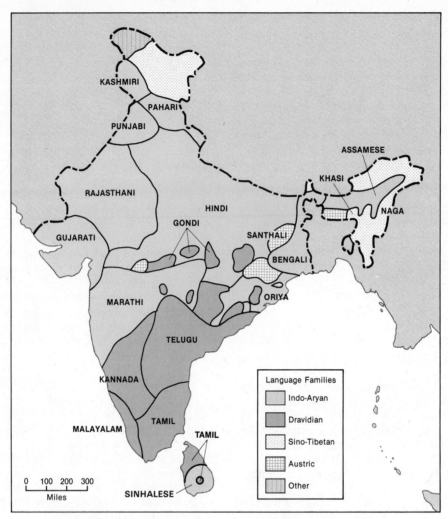

40.2 *Major Languages of the Indian Subcontinent*

small-scale rural industries, especially the hand weaving of cotton cloth. As in China, these were often not economically practical, but symbolically they were important because of their long association with the nationalist movement, and they also offered employment in rural areas, where most Indians still lived. Traditional village councils were revitalized and used as channels for new rural development in agriculture as well as other village enterprises.

But the most rapid growth was in the expanding cities, where industry and new economic opportunity were concentrated for the fortunate and to which streams of rural immigrants were drawn. Housing and other basic human services such as water, sewers, power, education, health care, and urban transport could not keep up with a mushrooming population, including many still unemployed, a familiar problem throughout the developing world. New immigrants took time to make a place for themselves and lived, or squatted, in slums or in the open air, but the wider opportunity that the cities poten-

tially offered continued to attract them despite the squalor and hardships with which most of them had to contend. Calcutta, Bombay, and Delhi–New Delhi, the three largest cities, are among the largest in the world, but like most, including big American cities, they combine luxurious lifestyles for a few and ragged poverty for many.

Despite government efforts to slow it down, India's population continued to grow, owing primarily to improved nutrition from agricultural gains and advances in public health that largely eliminated epidemic disease; life expectancy rose and death rates fell. But rising production, including new industrial output, more than kept pace, and per capita incomes began a slow and steady rise, which still continues. A third or more of the population, however, remained in severe poverty as the top third won new wealth.

The Nehru years were marred by a border dispute with China, in the remote Himalayas, which erupted in brief hostilities in 1962. Fresh from their armed reoc-

◉ India's World Role ◉

Nehru saw India as an emerging power in the modern world and as a major Asian leader. He wrote about this and about East-West relations.

One of the major questions of the day is the readjustment of the relations between Asia and Europe. . . . India, not because of any ambition but because of geography and history . . . inevitably has to play a very important part in Asia . . . [and is] a meeting ground between the East and the West. . . . The Middle East and Southeast Asia both are connected with India. . . . You cannot consider any question concerning the Far East without India. . . . In the past the West ignored Asia, or did not give her the weight that was due her. Asia was really given a back seat . . . and even the statesmen did not recognize the changes that were taking place. There is considerable recognition of these changes now, but it is not enough. . . . I do not mean to say that we in Asia are in any way superior, ethically or morally, to the people of Europe. In some ways, I imagine that we are worse. There is however a legacy of conflict in Europe. . . . We might note that the world progressively tends to become one. . . . [We should] direct [our] policy towards avoiding conflict. . . . The emergence of India in world affairs is something of major consequence in world history. We who happen to be in the government of India . . . are men of relatively small stature. But it has been given to us to work at a time when India is growing into a great giant again.

Source: W. T. de Bary, ed., *Sources of Indian Tradition*, 4th ed., vol. 1 (New York: Columbia University Press, 1964), pp. 352–353.

cupation of Tibet, the Chinese won a quick victory. The Chinese retained control of the small border area they had claimed, which they needed for access into western Tibet, where they were concerned to put down rebellion against their rule. India had refused to discuss the Chinese claim and foolishly tried to eject the Chinese troops, an effort for which the Indian army was poorly prepared. Nehru had attempted, with much success until then, to build pan-Asian friendship and cooperation in partnership with China as the other major Asian power and to promote India as the leader of the nonaligned nations. His death was hastened by the failure of relations with China, which he took as a personal failure, calling it "a Himalayan blunder" (*Himalayan* is understandably used in India to mean "enormous").

With his passing, India felt it had been left leaderless and was fearful about finding an adequate successor. Nehru had been the symbol and architect of the new India and its dominant political figure for more than a generation. But the gap was filled through normal democratic processes by the old Congress party moderate Lal Bahadur Shastri as prime minister. His promising start, including an agreement with Pakistan to reduce tensions, was cut short by his death after only a year and a half. The party then chose Nehru's daughter, Indira Gandhi (no relation to the Mahatma), who quickly established her firm leadership and vowed to continue Nehru's and Shastri's policies.

India had maintained its political stability and democratic system through successive crises, despite a still largely illiterate electorate and the multiple problems of new nationhood, wars, internal and external tensions, and poverty, a record matched by few other new nations. Illiterate voters demonstrated a surprising grasp of political issues, and a far higher proportion of those over 18 voted than in the United States. The Indian press remained freely critical of government shortcomings and offered an open forum for all opinions. India's faithfulness to the system it inherited and has continued to cultivate stands in contrast to the failure of parliamentary democracy and the rise of totalitarianism, dictatorship, censorship, and the police state in so much of the rest of Asia and the world.

♛ INDIRA GANDHI

Like her famous father, Indira Gandhi (1917–1984) was British-educated and widely traveled and came to office with long experience as her father's confidant after her mother's death in 1936, acting as hostess to streams of Indian and foreign visitors who sought Nehru's counsel or favors. She had separated from her husband, Firoze Gandhi, a journalist, a few years after their marriage, and she reared her two sons in her father's house. She impressed all who knew her with her razor-sharp mental powers and her keen grasp of political affairs, but during her father's lifetime she modestly eschewed any public role. After his death in 1964, she accepted the cabinet post of information minister in Shastri's government, but only as one of many able women who had already held cabinet rank and who had been prominent earlier in the long struggle for independence.

The Ministry of Information gave her new public visibility, and when Shastri suddenly died, she entered the contest for Congress party leadership, which ended in her overwhelming victory and subsequent endorsement by the national electorate. She was a consummate politician within the Congress party, and many observers accused her of becoming merely a power broker, but without her father's charisma or deft diplomacy. Indira Gandhi shared her father's commitment to Western values but drew her political strength mainly from left of center. During her years as prime minister, from 1966 to 1977 and from 1980 to her death in 1984, she was a commanding figure.

Drought in 1965 and 1966, which caused much suffering but relatively few deaths, led India to become one of the first countries to launch a major campaign in the so-called green revolution, an agricultural policy that achieved higher yields with improved seeds and expanded irrigation and fertilizer production. By the end of the 1960s there had been a real breakthrough in production, and by 1975 India was again self-sufficient in grains and had a surplus for export, a situation it has since maintained. Industrial growth also continued, but the gap between rich and poor widened. The green revolution benefited farmers with enough land and capital

to use and pay for the new seeds, irrigation, and fertilizers. Small farmers and people in nonagricultural areas sank further into relative poverty, and tenancy and landlessness rose. Upwardly mobile urban workers, managers, professionals, and technicians were more than matched by rising numbers of urban and rural poor. These growing pains were typical of economic development everywhere, including the nineteenth-century West.

In part to quash charges of corruption and to weaken her political opposition, Gandhi in June 1975 proclaimed a state of national emergency in the name of "unity" and "reform." Civil rights were suspended, the press was controlled, opposition leaders and "troublemakers" were jailed, the constitution was amended to keep the courts from challenging the government, and a series of measures was announced to control inflation, inefficiency, hoarding, and tax evasion. It seemed the end of India as the world's largest parliamentary democracy, but Gandhi miscalculated her people's judgment. When she finally permitted a national election in January 1977, she and her party were defeated. The Indian democratic system and its tradition of free expression were soundly vindicated, but the coalition government of non-Congress parties that emerged under the aged Morarji Desai floundered and finally dissolved into bickering, paving the way for Gandhi's return to power in the elections of January 1980.

Although she made no effort to reestablish the "emergency," Gandhi's response to tensions and protests by disaffected regions and groups became increasingly rigid and authoritarian. Meanwhile, economic growth continued in agriculture and industry. By 1983 over a third of India's exports were manufactured goods, many

Grain being fed into a storage silo in New Delhi: one of the results of the green revolution. [UPI/Bettmann Newsphotos]

of them from high-tech industries that competed successfully on the world market. India had become a major industrial power, and its pool of trained scientists and technicians, products of the British-inherited education system, was exceeded only by those of the United States and the Soviet Union. In 1974 its own scientists completed the first Indian nuclear test, though the government continued to insist it would not make nuclear weapons but would instead concentrate on the production of nuclear energy for peaceful purposes. Indian satellites joined American and Russian ones in space, and Indian-made microchips began to revolutionize industry. At the same time, many rural sectors remained in the bullock cart age, and the urban poor slept under bridges near the new luxury apartments of those who had done well in the rapidly growing economy.

The Sikhs

Of the many groups that felt disadvantaged, the most continuously and effectively organized were the Sikhs of Punjab. Ironically, Punjab had led the nation in agricultural progress under the green revolution, and although not all Sikhs were well off, as a group they had prospered more than most others. Part of their discontent was no doubt related to the rising expectations common to periods of development. Having put the green revolution to work with their traditional entrepreneurial talents and hard work, the Sikhs grew increasingly angry at government controls on agricultural prices imposed by Gandhi's fight against inflation, which severely restricted farmers' profits. A religious community founded in the fifteenth century as a reformist offshoot from Hinduism, the Sikhs also wanted greater recognition, increased political status, more control of Punjab state (where they were in fact a minority), and greater provincial autonomy.

Sikhs comprised only about 2 percent of India's population, and Gandhi was reluctant to favor them or to make concessions on provincial autonomy when she had to confront so many similar demands from other discontented groups and protest movements. But her stance on the Sikhs was rigid to a fault; she met violence with more violence, capped by the storming of the Golden Temple in Amritsar, sacred to Sikhism, which a group of extremists had fortified. Four months later, in October 1984, she was gunned down by two of her Sikh guards in the name of Indian freedom. Many others had come to see her as corrupted by power.

India After Indira Gandhi

The Congress party chose Gandhi's son Rajiv (1944–1991) to succeed her, and in January 1985 this choice was overwhelmingly confirmed in a nationwide election.

Rajiv Gandhi offered peace to the Sikhs, granted many of their more reasonable demands (including new borders for Punjab that created a state with a Sikh majority), and in other ways as well showed himself to be a sensitive and responsible leader. As the grandson of Jawaharlal Nehru, Rajiv Gandhi had many of the same qualities of personal charm, ability, and diplomacy. He had never sought power and was accordingly trusted, but the reservoir of popular support for him began to decline as critics claimed that the Congress party under his leadership remained more interested in power-brokering than in serving all the needs of the people. India, in fact, has been a largely one-party democracy since independence, although the Congress party was defeated in 1977 and after Nehru's death became increasingly split into rival factions. Many Indian voters have felt that they were not offered adequate alternatives and that government was often insensitive to their needs. Rajiv Gandhi also sent Indian troops to Sri Lanka in 1987 to try to put down communal violence there. The troops were withdrawn in 1989, but many Sri Lankan Tamils remained bitter, and in May 1991 one of them assassinated Gandhi at an election rally near Madras, the main Tamil base in India. The elections were briefly postponed, and in June a new government emerged, under a former foreign minister, V. N. Rao, but India continued to be torn by communal rioting and by countermeasures that tarnished its democratic tradition.

Three basic problems stubbornly resisted solution: miserable poverty for the bottom third or more of India's people, a population still growing too rapidly (one root of poverty), and continued outbreaks of violence among many of the groups in its highly diverse population. Caste continued to weaken slowly, especially in the cities, but most Indians remained in traditional village worlds, where caste connections still served an important function. Higher or "dominant" castes, as they were often called, resented and tried to suppress the rise of Untouchables. Hindus and Muslims fought one another in some areas. Sikh terrorism and Hindu reprisals threatened to plunge Punjab and Delhi into civil war.

Nationalism grew among Indian intellectuals late in the nineteenth century, but it did not stimulate a mass movement until the 1920s. Even Mahatma Gandhi did not reach all Indians, and the country since independence in 1947 has been moving toward creating a single overriding sense of Indian identity that can take precedence over regional, religious, caste, and other group loyalties. India well illustrates the dictum of the British historian Lord Acton (1834–1902): "The nation is not the cause but the result of the state. It is the state which creates the nation, not the nation the state." To many—perhaps most—Indians it remains more important that they are Bengalis or Marathas or Tamils, Hindus, Sikhs, or Muslims, Brahmins or Untouchables, than that they

Much marketing in India
takes place outdoors. This
scene is in Delhi but might be
almost anywhere in urban
South Asia.
[Rhoads Murphey]

are fellow Indians. It will take more time before such group loyalties can be merged into a common "Indianness" through common experience in a single national state. This problem is shared with most new nations, many of which have difficulties comparable to India's. The difference is partly the scale of India's problem—over 800 million people with a diversity greater than all of Europe—and partly in the recency of its modern experience as a nation-state after 5,000 years of regional and group separatism. Since 1947 the traditional world of the village and its ties has expanded to include considerable integration with the modern world of the cities and with the larger world of regional states sharing a common language and culture.

Within India's federal political structure, central economic planning and an expanding national civil service

Women botany students at
Ludhiana Agricultural
University of Punjab. [© 1981,
Marc and Evelyne Bernheim/
Woodfin Camp]

also help join people in mutual self-interest. Regular bus service on all-weather roads links every village with these wider worlds and with a national network. The sense of nationhood needs time to grow.

The war against poverty, as the government called it, is of course related to communal and intercaste tensions and is the greatest challenge of all developing countries. India has done better economically than most of the so-called Third World, perhaps overall better than China, whose record has been praised by many economists in the West. But India's new wealth has not been well distributed. The hope is that as development proceeds and as efforts to limit population growth succeed, the fight against poverty may make significant headway. This is the same path followed by the West a century earlier as the fruits of the Industrial Revolution eventually raised the economic level of most people. Life expectancy rates and living conditions for most inhabitants are in fact better for modern Calcutta and Bombay than for nineteenth-century Manchester and New York. In India, as in most of Asia, the economic trends are strongly positive, and literacy is growing fast as universal free education spreads. This oldest of world civilizations still keeps much of its ancient tradition alive and draws strength from it as it also pursues the path of modernization.

Bangladesh and Pakistan

East Bengal, which became East Pakistan in 1947, was one of the subcontinent's poorest areas and had virtually no industry of any kind. It had been heavily dependent on Calcutta as its educational, cultural, commercial, industrial, and shipping center, through which its exports and imports moved and where nearly all transport lines were focused. East Bengal contained over half of Pakistan's population and produced three-quarters of its exports, mainly jute, but much of the profit went to Karachi, the national capital in West Pakistan. Moreover, East Bengal was strikingly underrepresented in and underfunded by the national government. Even its language, Bengali, was not officially recognized.

Pakistan continued to be run by and for the small clique of Karachi and Punjabi businessmen and politicians who had pushed for its creation, although the faltering effort at parliamentary government was swept aside by a military dictatorship in 1958. When elections, finally held in late 1970, produced a victory for the East Pakistan party on a platform of greater autonomy, the military government in West Pakistan responded by arresting the party's leader, Sheikh Mujibur Rahman, and then turning its army and tanks against demonstrators in East Pakistan in a mass slaughter. About 10 million

refugees poured across the nearby Indian border by the end of 1971, mainly to already overcrowded Calcutta. Guerrilla actions by Bengalis against the terrorism of the West Pakistani forces finally brought in the Indian army, which in ten days ended the slaughter.

With the Pakistani army defeated, East Pakistan became the new People's Republic of Bangladesh in December 1971. Sheikh Mujib, as he was called, became prime minister, and the refugees returned home, but Bangladesh proved unable to achieve political stability or even effective government. Mujib was murdered by his own army in 1974, following charges of corruption. His military successor was assassinated in 1981, and no clear or successful political order has since emerged. Bangladesh remains one of the world's poorest nations, despite the agricultural productivity of its rice lands, burdened by a still too rapidly growing population and hampered by the lack of forceful planning and leadership. Periodic flooding caused in part by deforestation has compounded Bangladesh's problems.

What remained of Pakistan, in the west, continued to be governed by a military dictatorship, although there was some respectable economic growth in both agriculture and manufacturing. Jinnah died within a year of independence, and in 1958, after a series of corrupt and ineffective prime ministers, the country came under martial law, as it has been much of the time since. The army commander in chief, General Zia-ul-Huq, seized power in a 1977 coup d'état, dissolved the politically corrupt parliamentary system, and in 1979 executed the former prime minister, Zulfikar Ali Bhutto, after he was found guilty of conspiring in the murder of a political opponent. In an effort to break the connection with the "Karachi clique," the capital had been moved in stages between 1961 and 1965 to a new planned site called Islamabad ("City of Islam"), about 10 miles from the city of Rawalpindi in the northwest; the two cities operate as an urban unit, linked by commuting workers and civil servants, and now rival Karachi in size. Lahore, an older and larger city and the chief center of Muslim culture, was more central, but it was thought to be too close to the border with India to be safe. Pakistan lacks most industrial resources, except for some recently discovered oil, and it began in 1947 well below the all-Indian average economic level. Nevertheless, it has avoided major famine, greatly increased irrigation in Punjab and the Indus valley, and built a basic industrial structure. As in India and China, however, economic gains continue to be held back in per capita terms by a growing population. As an Islamic state, Pakistan has been reluctant to promote family planning or to limit the growth of its population. Islamic fundamentalism similar to that in Iran has also won some support in Pakistan.

The government became deeply involved in aiding and providing refuge for the Afghan guerrilla resistance to the Soviet-supported government in Kabul, the Afghan capital, only about 100 miles from the Pakistani frontier. Such activity further strengthened Pakistan's role as a Cold War client of the United States and produced a new flow of American military supplies. But such aid had little relevance to Pakistan's domestic problems and again prompted Indian complaints that the arms were being stockpiled for use against India. The two states have fought two small wars since the partition, in 1965 and 1971, in both of which Pakistan's military power came virtually exclusively from U.S. equipment. Pakistan seemed useful to the United States as a regional anticommunist bulwark against the Soviet Union and as a friend and intermediary with China, particularly during America's resumption of relations with the People's Republic in the early 1970s.

When China became a Soviet rival instead of an ally and soon thereafter came into conflict with India over a border dispute, Pakistan took the Chinese side. In 1971 Washington used the Pakistan-China connection to respond to Chinese overtures, leading to President Richard Nixon's visit to Peking. But these international power ploys had little or nothing to do with Pakistan's people or their needs. Indeed, they put the Pakistanis at serious risk by exposing them to the threat of war, the suffering resulting from further conflict with India, and the massive diversion of resources from urgently needed development into military expenditures. India and Pakistan, with so much history and so many problems in common, have more recently begun to move cautiously toward a less antagonistic relationship, but only after 40 years of tragic tension and conflict. This process was helped by Soviet withdrawal from Afghanistan and by the death of General Zia in a plane crash in 1988. Bhutto's daughter, Benazir, was elected prime minister as Zia's successor in an open contest, thus becoming the first woman to govern an Islamic state, and

Pakistan returned to a more democratic path. But in August 1990 she was removed from office by the president of Pakistan, with army support, and new elections in October brought in Nawaz Sharif as prime minister; he was more acceptable to Islamic fundamentalists than a woman ruler.

Pakistan is a diverse state, resembling India on a smaller scale. It includes a majority whose mother tongue is not the official national language, Urdu, and many groups who feel unrepresented, neglected, or oppressed by the government. Outside the Indus valley and western Punjab, where most of the population is concentrated, Pakistan encompasses arid mountains along its western and northern borders, inhabited by people like the Baluchis and Pathans whose cultures and histories have little in common with those of the lowlands. A truly national state that can include them as partners has not yet emerged. The partition of India has become a permanent fact of life, but Pakistan has still to develop into a nation.

Sri Lanka

The island nation of Ceylon (which changed its name officially to Sri Lanka, an old precolonial name for the country, in 1975) lies across the Palk Strait from India. It made a relatively easy transition to independence in 1948, primarily as a consequence of Indian independence rather than of any strong nationalist movement on the island itself.

Sri Lanka had been under Western domination since the first Portuguese bases there early in the sixteenth century, and its small size and population were easily

SOUTH ASIA SINCE 1945

India	Pakistan	Sri Lanka
Independence (1947)	Independence (1947)	
		Independence (1948)
Assassination of Mahatma Gandhi (1948)	Death of Jinnah (1948)	
		Assassination of S. W. R. D. Bandaranaike (1959)
War with China (1962)		First administration of Sirimavo Bandaranaike (1960–1965)
Death of Nehru (1964)		
	War with India (1965)	
First administration of Indira Gandhi (1966–1977)	War with India (1971)	Second administration of Sirimavo Bandaranaike (1970–1977)
Second administration of Indira Gandhi (1980–1984)		
	Administration of Benazir Bhutto (1988–1990)	India sends troops to quell unrest (1987–1989)
Assassination of Rajiv Gandhi (1991)		

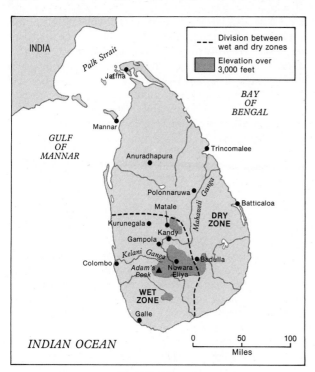

40.3 Sri Lanka

overwhelmed by foreign influences. Many of the elite were more British than Sinhalese (the majority inhabitants) in language and culture, and many regretted the end of their membership in the British Empire. But in the mid-1950s Ceylon was swept by what has been called "second-wave nationalism," a belated but emotional determination to rediscover and assert its own identity. In the elections of 1956 self-serving politicians stirred up communal feelings among the dominant Sinhalese against the minority Tamils, originally immigrants from nearby South India, who form about a fifth of the population. Approximately half of them had lived there, at the northern tip of the island, for over 2,000 years, but the other half were more recently arrived laborers recruited to work the tea plantations in the central highlands. The Tamils are Hindu and speak primarily their own language, which has heightened their distinction from the Buddhist (or for the elite, nominally Buddhist) Sinhalese. They became a convenient scapegoat to stimulate the sense of Sinhalese nationalism, like the Chinese in many Southeast Asian countries.

The tragic pattern of communal violence between Sinhalese and Tamils began with the 1956 election of S. W. R. D. Bandaranaike, on a platform of Sinhalese-only nationalism. Like Jinnah, he had been educated in Britain and was thoroughly westernized; his personal ambition and his keen mind turned to communalism, until then of little interest to him, as a means of creating a new political base for himself. Once called into existence by

his campaign of discrimination, it could not be laid to rest, and he was assassinated in 1959 by a Sinhalese Buddhist who felt that he had not gone far enough.

His place was taken by his widow, Sirimavo Bandaranaike (born 1916), the world's first woman prime minister. She continued most of his policies and ruled with a firm hand for two terms, 1960–1965 and 1970–1977. Like her husband, she was British-educated, sophisticated, and extremely able, showing a talent for both international and domestic diplomacy. Her authoritative rule restored order and relative stability at a time of domestic crisis. Tamils felt more and more excluded and oppressed and took to terrorism as a weapon, finally demanding a separate state.

The Sri Lankan economy was disrupted by chronic fighting, which retarded its generally healthy growth after 1948. Nevertheless, Sri Lanka became self-sufficient in rice by the late 1970s, thanks to major investments in new irrigation and agricultural technology, and at the same time maintained the profitable plantation sector in tea, rubber, and coconuts, although by 1991 the products of light manufacturing—clothing and computers and their components, mainly produced by foreign-owned companies—had become Sri Lanka's main exports. Education, literacy, and public health were improved still further from the relatively high levels established under British colonial control, and per capita incomes remained higher than in any of the other South Asian states, thanks in part to the government's success in limiting population growth. But violence and terrorism on both sides, in an atmosphere close to civil war, eroded the British-inherited system of parliamentary government and the rule of law. In 1987 Rajiv Gandhi agreed to prevent clandestine support from South India from reaching Tamil terrorists in Sri Lanka. Later that year Indian troops were invited in to help restore peace, but they were predictably resented, and were withdrawn at the end of 1989. Much bitterness and tension remained, and violence and terrorism continued unabated.

Sirimavo Bandaranaike is an example of the improving status of women in South Asia. Like China and Japan, South Asia traditionally accorded women a relatively low status, especially during the centuries of Muslim dominance in the north. There were exceptions, including even women military figures and heads of state among the Marathas and other groups and dominant figures at court such as Nur Jahan (see Chapter 20). The westernization that accompanied British control led to increasing education for women; many educated women were prominent in the independence movement and in government and the professions after 1947. In general this was a relatively small group, an intellectual and westernized elite, while most South Asian women, especially in the villages, remained uneducated and subservient to their husbands to a degree that seemed extreme to westerners. There were exceptions, particularly in South India and in the southern state of Kerala, where ancient matriarchal and matrilocal* social forms persisted to some degree. Husbands in this region commonly walk behind wives and defer to them, and property and family names often descend through the female line. Elsewhere in South Asia, women such as Sirimavo Bandaranaike and Indira Gandhi have achieved great prominence on the national scene since independence.

The Turbulent Middle East

When World War II ended, Britain was still the paramount power in the Middle East, directly controlling Egypt, Palestine, Transjordan, Iraq, southern Arabia, and the Persian Gulf. In the next decade, however, it withdrew almost completely from the region, leaving a vacuum of power that was filled by Arab nationalism, superpower rivalry, and the emergence of the state of Israel.

Israel and the Struggle for Palestine

Britain's first withdrawal was from Palestine, where the conflict between Palestinian Arabs and Jewish settlers, compounded by an influx of refugees and Holocaust survivors, had reached a flashpoint. That conflict, in turn, represented a clash between the traditions of two great religions and the aspirations of two nascent nationalisms.

A small number of Jews had always lived in Palestine, to which the faithful believed their people would someday return to reestablish the ancient nation of Israel and await the coming of the messiah. In the mid-seventeenth century a messianic pretender, Sabbatai Zevi, had led an ill-fated expedition of thousands of Jews to Palestine. The serious immigration to the region that commenced two centuries later was spurred, however, not by millennial fervor but by a secular nationalist movement, Zionism.

Zionism was a historic response to Jewish circumstances in nineteenth-century Europe. Emancipation had eliminated most of the civil restrictions that had confined Jews to the ghetto for centuries past without offering them a clear role or place in European society. Many Jews simply attempted to assimilate themselves into the larger nationalities among whom they lived, preserving their religious and cultural traditions while identifying themselves as Frenchmen, Germans, or Russians. To

*In a matrilocal society, a husband joins the wife's family.

Zionist writers, however, as for other nineteenth-century nationalists, political identity as a nation was the final and necessary goal of every people's development. The Zionist position was supported negatively by anti-Semitic writers such as Count Gobineau (1816–1882), who argued that the Jews were an alien, unassimilable element that threatened the racial and cultural integrity of any nation that harbored them. The increasing tempo of anti-Semitic incidents in the late nineteenth century, culminating in the pogroms of Russia and, in the West, in the long, drawn-out agony of the Dreyfus affair (see Chapter 33), suggested to many that assimilation was a mirage. The result was a mass exodus of European Jews, particularly from Russia, from which 3 million emigrated between 1882 and 1914.

The great majority of Jewish emigrants went to the United States, Canada, South America, and Australia; scarcely 1 percent joined the trickle of earlier settlers in Palestine. The real impetus for creating a Jewish state in the Holy Land came from Theodor Herzl, the founder of modern Zionism. Herzl realized that the large-scale settlement necessary to provide a critical mass of population in Palestine would require both organization and capital. His solution was the Jewish National Fund, which undertook the purchase of all land to be occupied by the settlers. He envisioned a society whose growth would be rationally planned rather than subject to the vagaries of speculators and profiteers. New towns would be erected, carefully spaced and separated by belts of collective farmland and linked by express trains and superhighways. In short, the Zionist state was to be a utopian society in which mutualistic socialism was combined with technological progress and centralized planning.

Herzl's vision and Hitler's persecution combined to increase the Jewish population of Palestine tenfold between the end of World War I and the end of World War II. From less than a tenth of the total population of the territory in 1917, it had increased to a third by 1947. The Arab majority greeted the Jewish influx first with suspicion and then with alarm. The entry of Western powers into the formerly Ottoman-controlled lands of the Middle East after World War I stimulated Arab nationalists. For such nationalists, the Jews were a spearhead unit of Western colonization. Their fears were underscored by the report of an American commission Woodrow Wilson sent to the area, which concluded that the Jewish National Fund intended the eventual purchase of the entire territory of Palestine, thereby dispossessing its Arab population. From an Arab perspective, Jewish socialism was simply the handmaiden of British imperialism.

Confronted by bitter and sometimes violent Arab resistance, the British government decided in 1939 to cap Jewish population in Palestine at one-third of the whole and to limit future land purchases severely. These new controls had broader implications, as Britain, the United

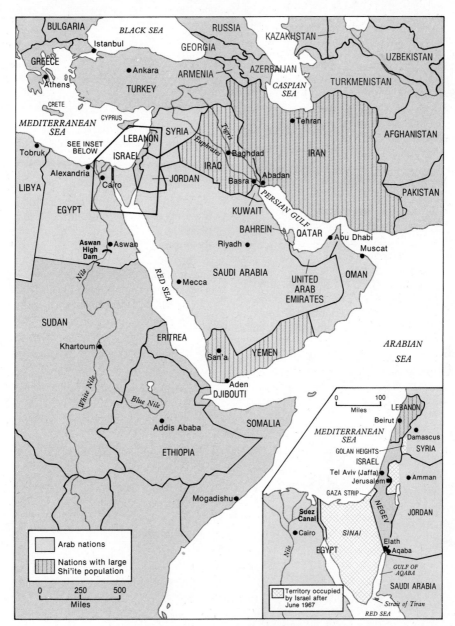

40.4 The Middle East Today

States, and other powers sought to restrict Jewish emigration from Nazi-held Europe in general. When the dimensions of the Holocaust were discovered at the end of World War II, there was general humanitarian pressure to establish Palestine as a refuge for the remnants of European Jewry. The British Labour party, soon to be in power, endorsed Zionist demands for the immediate creation of a Jewish commonwealth and in December 1944 called for the transfer of Palestinian Arabs to neighboring countries. Nothing came of these or more moderate postwar proposals for a federated Jewish-Arab state, which were rejected by both sides. The British, unwilling to maintain their trusteeship in the face of mounting Jewish terrorist attacks and unable to contain the flood of illegal immigrants who ran their blockade, laid the problem before the United Nations in April 1947. After months of lobbying and debate, the General Assembly adopted in November a proposal to divide Palestine into three Jewish and three Arab sectors forming a Jewish and an Arab state, with Jerusalem as an international zone. All seven areas were to be linked in an economic union.

The General Assembly resolution was greeted with rejoicing by the Jews but unanimous rejection throughout the Arab world. The British refused to implement it on the grounds that it had not been accepted by both sides and withdrew their troops without making provision to transfer authority to either one. When the last units departed on May 14, 1948, the Jewish communal government proclaimed the state of Israel. A general struggle immediately ensued for control of Palestine. Armies from Egypt, Syria, Lebanon, Jordan, and Iraq poured across the frontiers to assist the Palestinian Arabs, but the better-organized Jewish forces more than held their own. When a United Nations armistice halted the fighting in 1949, Israel controlled a third more territory than had been granted the Jews under the partition plan, and nearly 750,000 Palestinian Arabs had taken refuge in Lebanon, Syria, Jordan, and the Egyptian-occupied Gaza Strip in southern Palestine.

While still fighting, Israel held its first elections in January. The fiery socialist David Ben-Gurion (1886–1973), founder of the first Jewish agricultural cooperative, or kibbutz, became Israel's first prime minister and its dominant political figure until his retirement in 1966, and the veteran Zionist leader Chaim Weizmann (1874–1952) was installed in the ceremonial office of president.

❦
DAVID BEN-GURION, ISRAEL'S FOUNDER

The single most important figure in the establishment of modern Israel was David Ben-Gurion. Born David Gruen in Plonsk, Poland (then a part of the Russian empire), he was the son of a local Zionist leader. At 17 he startled the local Jewish community by calling for armed resistance against the state-backed pogroms. Three years later, in 1906, he emigrated to Palestine, where he worked as a farmer in Jewish settlements and adopted the Hebrew name Ben-Gurion ("son of the lion"). Expelled by the Ottoman Turks for his political activity at the outbreak of World War I, he eventually reached New York, where he met and married Pauline Munweis, his wife until her death in 1968.

Ben-Gurion responded to the Balfour Declaration by joining the British-sponsored Jewish Legion. Returning to Palestine after its capture from the Turks, he threw himself ardently into political organization and over the next two decades forged the institutions that were to become the nucleus of the Jewish state. In 1920 he founded the Histadrut labor confederation and ten years later its political arm, the Mapai, or Israeli Workers

Israel's leaders in 1955: (from left) General Moshe Dayan, Premier Moshe Sharett, President Itzhak Ben-Zvi, and Prime Minister David Ben-Gurion. [UPI/Bettmann Newsphotos]

◉ Israel or Palestine? ◉

*Two rival nationalisms with ancient roots in the same land put forward
their claims to modern sovereignty over it.*

Declaration of the Establishment of the State of Israel (1948)

The land of Israel was the birthplace of the Jewish people. Here their spiritual, religious, and political identity was shaped. Here they first attained statehood, created cultural values of national and universal significance, and gave to the world the eternal Book of Books. . . .

On the 29th November, 1947, the United Nations General Assembly passed a resolution calling for the establishment of a Jewish state in the land of Israel; the General Assembly required the inhabitants of the land of Israel to take such steps as were necessary on their part for the implementation of that resolution. This recognition by the United Nations of the right of the Jewish people to establish their state is irrevocable. This right is the natural right of the Jewish people to be masters of their own fate, like all other nations, in their own sovereign state.

Palestinian National Charter (1968)

Article 1. Palestine is the homeland of the Arab Palestinian people; it is an indivisible part of the Arab homeland, and the Palestinian people are an integral part of the Arab nation.

Article 2. Palestine, with the boundaries it had during the British mandate, is an indivisible territorial unit.

Article 3. The Palestinian Arab people possess the legal right to their homeland and have the right to determine their destiny after achieving the liberation of their country in accordance with their wishes and entirely of their own accord and will.

Article 4. The Palestinian identity is a genuine, essential, and inherent characteristic; it is transmitted from parents to children. The Zionist occupation and the dispersal of the Palestinian Arab people . . . do not make them lose their Palestinian identity and their membership of the Palestine community, nor do they negate them.

Source: J. N. Moore, ed., *The Arab-Israeli Conflict: Readings and Documents* (Princeton, N.J.: Princeton University Press, 1977), pp. 935–936, 1086.

party, which later merged into the Labour party. Besides leading both organizations, he was elected chairman of the Zionist Executive, the supreme directive body of the Zionist movement, and head of the Jewish Agency, its executive branch.

When Britain, responding to Arab pressure, abruptly pulled back on its commitment to a Jewish homeland in 1939, Ben-Gurion urged and later led armed resistance to it. In May 1942 he assembled an emergency meeting of Zionists in New York that decided on the establishment of a Jewish state as soon as the war in Europe was ended. With the proclamation of Israel six years later, Ben-Gurion became simultaneously its first prime minister and minister of defense, welding its disparate and often conflicting resistance forces into a national army.

With a single brief interval, Ben-Gurion remained Israel's prime minister from 1948 to 1963, firmly shaping Israel's identity as a modern industrial state and a bulwark of Western influence in the Middle East. To critics of his frank espousal of Western interests, including the acceptance of $800 million in reparations from West Germany for Nazi war crimes, he replied characteristically, "What matters is not what Gentiles will say but what the Jews will do." Never wavering in his belief that modern Israel was the direct and legitimate heir of the ancient Jewish state, he was determined at all costs to establish it and to give no quarter to anyone who opposed it. This led him into an assault against Egypt's President Nasser in 1956 that brought about the fall of the Eden government in Britain and contributed to the demise of the

Fourth Republic in France but left Ben-Gurion himself stronger than ever at home. In his last years in office he attempted, unsuccessfully, to institute peace talks with Arab leaders.

Ben-Gurion resigned abruptly in June 1963, in part because of dissension within the Labour party. He founded a new opposition party as a vehicle for his views, but it won only ten seats in the Knesset (parliament). Spent as a political force, he nonetheless remained a charismatic and controversial elder statesman, and to a world public the short, rotund man with the familiar pugnacious features and the halo of white hair remained the image of Israel itself. In failing health, he retired from all political activity in 1970 to spend his last years at a kibbutz in the Negev Desert, writing his memoirs. He lived just long enough to see the twenty-fifth anniversary of the founding of Israel in 1973 and to experience the Yom Kippur War, which revealed how vulnerable, and how far from peace, the new nation still was.

Israeli Society: Challenge and Conflict

The new state chose a system of proportional representation rather than electoral districting for the Knesset, so each member represented the nation as a whole. This meant full representation for minority views but entailed coalition government as well; no single party has won a majority to date. Nevertheless, two basic coalitions have controlled the state since independence: the Labour bloc—strongly Zionist, social-democratic, and secular—and the Likud bloc, which has enjoyed the backing of Orthodox religious parties.

Despite its unity in times of crisis, Israel has been beset by contradictions from the beginning. The ideologically active left wing of the Labour bloc remained attached to the early Zionist ideal of social regeneration through physical labor and communal living exemplified in the kibbutz. The new Jewish man and woman, purged of the effects of centuries of ghettoization and bonded to the soil, would constitute the basis of a genuinely egalitarian society. What emerged instead, however, was an urbanized, consumer-oriented society that bore considerable resemblance to the social-democratic regimes of the West. Class divisions within the Jewish population intensified, particularly between the well-to-do eastern European settlers who dominated the Labour bloc and the so-called oriental Jews who flocked to Israel from the Arab states and Iran in the first two decades of independence and now comprise 65 percent of its Jewish population. This poorer and less literate group, wooed by the Likud coalition of Menachem Begin (1913–1992), turned the Labour coalition out of office after nearly three decades.

The tension between old socialist ideals and the reality of a consumer society is paralleled by that between religious fundamentalists and secular liberals. The fundamentalists, a hard core constituting 15 percent of the Jewish population, retain Orthodox diet, dress, and observance and have successfully insisted on religious controls over marriage, divorce, inheritance, and other social arrangements. Often confrontational, their influence derives not merely from their unity as a single-issue pressure group but from the unresolved debate over the nature of a "Jewish" state.

From its inception, Israel has advertised itself as the homeland of Jews the world over, and under the Law of Return, any Jew emigrating to it is automatically entitled to citizenship. Nonetheless, there is no generally accepted criterion of what defines a Jew, and a prolonged debate in the Knesset in 1960 and 1961 failed to produce one. Originally Semitic, the Jews have become racially heterogeneous through the long centuries of the Diaspora, and fair-haired Scandinavians mix today on the streets of Tel Aviv and Jerusalem with brown-skinned Indians, black Ethiopians, and even Chinese. Still more problematic is the attempt to define them as a "people," since they share few common customs, and fewer than half the population speaks the official language, Hebrew, as a native tongue. Least of all can they be distinguished on the basis of a common faith, since many secularized Jews in Israel and elsewhere no longer keep up religious observances. The fundamentalists alone have developed a clear standard, excluding anyone whose mother was not Jewish or who had not undergone Orthodox conversion. In practice, however, the authorities have simply accepted as a Jew anyone professing to be one. Even Israelis converting to Christianity have continued to be accorded the rights of citizenship.

The unresolved question of what defines a Jew goes to the heart of the central contradiction of present-day Israeli society: the situation of its Arab minority. Although enjoying formal equality, including the right to vote and to sit in the Knesset, the Arabs are clearly second-class citizens in the Jewish state, and their movements and activities are subject to regular military scrutiny and interference. Moreover, while Israelis can justifiably point to levels of health, literacy, and material prosperity among Arabs within their borders considerably higher than those of neighboring countries, they remain far below the national norm as a whole. The problem was compounded by Israeli occupation of the West Bank of the Jordan River as a result of the 1967 war; this doubled the number of Arabs under Israeli jurisdiction. For 20 years the occupation was relatively benign, but in 1987 popular rebellion erupted.

Whether or not the Arabs under Israeli rule would be prepared to accept integration into a multiethnic state remains part of the larger question of Palestinian self-determination and the future of Arab-Israeli relations in general. In either case, their presence poses a challenge to an Israel defined, by whatever standard, as a purely Jewish state.

The Arab-Israeli Wars

The more immediate questions in the Middle East involve the general nonrecognition of the Israeli state by the other powers in the region apart from Egypt, and the insistence of Palestinian Arab nationalists that Palestine be restored to them. Four wars have been fought to date over this question. All have resulted in military victories by the Israelis, none in settlement. The Palestine War of 1948–1949 established Israel as an independent state while creating a major refugee problem. The Israelis refused to allow the 750,000 Palestinians who had fled their homes to return without guarantees of security from the surrounding nations, a point that became moot as the abandoned homes and lands were occupied by the almost equal number of Jewish immigrants, mostly from the other countries of the Middle East, who flocked to the new state in the first two years of its existence. In effect, the massive population transfer envisioned by Zionists had taken place. But neighboring Arab states were both unable and politically unwilling to accept the tide of Palestinian refugees who crowded at their borders. Instead, the refugees were interned in squalid camps along the narrow Gaza Strip and on the West Bank of the Jordan River, previously part of Palestine but now annexed by Jordan. The Palestinian Arabs thus became a people without a country.

Arab nationalists regarded Israel not only as a usurper in the region but also as an agent of Western interests. These suspicions were dramatically confirmed in October 1956 when Israel joined an amphibious Franco-British force in an invasion of Egypt, whose new president, Gamal Abdel Nasser (1918–1970), had nationalized the French- and British-owned Suez Canal Company in response to a cutoff of Western aid. For the British in particular, Egypt's control of the canal threatened important interests in the Far East, while Israel, alarmed at an Egyptian arms buildup, felt that a preemptive strike was essential to its security. With British air support, the Israelis swept across the Sinai peninsula to join assault troops at Port Said. But the war ended in fiasco. The United States, furious at the independent action of its allies, joined the Soviet Union in calling for an immediate cease-fire and withdrawal. Faced with the threat of ruinous economic sanctions, the British and French capitulated. Israel too withdrew, the damaging identification with colonial interests only partly compensated by the opening of the Gulf of Aqaba to Israeli shipping.

The long-term effects of the episode were profound. Nasser emerged as a hero and became the recognized leader of the Arab world until his death. The government of Sir Anthony Eden was forced from office in Britain, and with the assassination of the Iraqi king, Faisal II, and his prime minister, Nuri-es Said, in 1958 the British were forced from their last bases in the Middle East. The United States entered the breach to forestall Soviet influence, and in 1958 its own forces invaded Lebanon in support of pro-Western leadership. With Nasser and other Arab radicals looking to the Soviet Union for aid and the crucial oil resources of the region at stake, the Middle East became an important new area of superpower rivalry.

In the meantime, a new war was brewing between the Arabs and the Israelis. In 1964 Israel began to divert water from the Jordan River to irrigate its southern Negev desert. Jordan protested, and an Arab summit conference in Cairo set up a command force that would coordinate guerrilla activities against Israel and serve as a provisional government for the refugees, the Palestine Liberation Organization (PLO). Terrorist attacks and retaliatory raids increased, while Egypt, Syria, and Jordan announced plans to attack Israel. When Nasser ordered United Nations peacekeeping forces to leave the Sinai in May 1967 and closed the Gulf of Aqaba, the Israelis struck first. In a campaign lasting only six days, Israel swept again across the Sinai; seized the West Bank, including the Arab portion of the city of Jerusalem; and drove Syria off the strategic Golan Heights on the borders of eastern Galilee. Israel had occupied some 28,000 square miles, three times the size of its own territory. It was one of the swiftest and most decisive military victories in history. In November the United Nations Security Council adopted a resolution demanding Israel's withdrawal from the areas it had conquered but also calling for a settlement that would recognize its right to exist as a nation.

Humiliated by the Six Day War, Egypt rearmed with Soviet assistance and planned a new attack with Syria. This time preparations were secret. Israel was caught napping by the Yom Kippur War of 1973, so called because it began with a surprise attack on the annual Jewish day of atonement. Initially repulsed, Israeli forces quickly recovered and with American tactical assistance had regained the offensive when fighting was halted after 18 days on October 24. But they had suffered heavy losses on the ground and in the air, and the conflict brought the superpowers closer to confrontation in the Middle East than ever before.

The Yom Kippur War underlined the dangers posed by continued instability in the Middle East. It brought in its wake a threatened cutoff of oil exports that struck at the very heart of the Western economy. Accordingly, the American secretary of state, Henry Kissinger, conducted arduous "shuttle diplomacy" between the major Arab capitals and Jerusalem in an attempt to find a basis of accommodation. These efforts bore fruit in the Camp David Accords of September 1978 between Egypt and

Israel. The two parties agreed to a phased withdrawal of Israeli troops from the Sinai and a vaguely defined autonomy for the West Bank and the Gaza Strip. President Sadat had ended the humiliating occupation of Egyptian territory and gained a major American subsidy for his ailing economy. Prime Minister Begin had won diplomatic recognition for the first time from an Arab state, secured Israel's western frontier, and divided its two principal antagonists, Egypt and Syria. Both men shared a Nobel Peace Prize. But Sadat was denounced in the Arab world for having made a separate peace with Israel and for failing to secure Palestinian rights. Egypt lost the position of leadership it had enjoyed for the previous quarter century, and Sadat himself was assassinated by Muslim fundamentalists in October 1981.

❀ JERUSALEM: A CITY DIVIDED

The divisions of the contemporary Middle East are nowhere more vividly symbolized than in the historic city of Jerusalem. Today, with its population of around 300,000, it reflects both a rich past and a divided present. The New City, to the west, is a modern capital, with fashionable shops, a convention center, and a Kennedy memorial. It also houses the Knesset, Israel's parliament, and the Israel Museum. The Old City, once shared by Arabs and Jews, is in the Arab quarter, a labyrinth of bazaars, market alleys, and narrow, winding streets. Administratively, the New and Old City are now one; politically, they are as far apart as ever.

After a long history as a religious center first of Judaism and then of Christianity, Jerusalem was conquered by the Muslims in 629. Unlike previous conquerors, they treated the city with great respect. It was sacred to Islam because the Jewish temple was the place to which Muhammad had been carried in his famous vision prior to ascending the seven heavens into the presence of the Almighty. Accordingly, the caliph Omar built a wooden mosque in the temple compound, above which rises today the gold-domed, octagonal structure known as the Haram el-Sharif (Dome of the Rock), still much as it was when completed in 691. For several centuries Christian and Jewish worship was permitted side by side with Islamic. As unrest increased in the Arab world, however, particularly after the ninth century, access to the holy sites became hazardous.

Crusader Europe recaptured Jerusalem and established Christian control of the city again for most of a century (1099–1187) and briefly from 1229 to 1244, expelling Jews and Muslims. Thereafter for nearly 700 years the city again reverted to Islam, first under the Mameluke Turks (1250–1517) and then under their Ottoman successors (1517–1917). It reached a low point in the seventeenth and eighteenth centuries as Ottoman rule decayed, but European influence began to revive it in the nineteenth century, and with the advent of Zionism it became a focus of Jewish immigration.

The British capture of Jerusalem in 1917 inaugurated its modern period. Extensive rebuilding took place, and access to the holy places was given to the three faiths, although at Muslim insistence the ban on Jews entering the Dome of the Rock on the site of the temple mount was maintained. Communal violence between Arabs and Jews erupted as early as 1929, and when the British withdrew from Palestine in 1947, the city (whose population was by now more than 60 percent Jewish) was besieged by the Arab Legion. The armistice of 1949 divided it into an Israeli and an Arab (Jordanian) sector, separated by barbed wire, sandbags, and sniper fire. The Six Day War gave Israel full control of the city, which was itself a major battlefront.

Jerusalem continues to house its three faiths. Its Christian community is particularly variegated, with Protestant, Catholic, Greek Orthodox, Armenian, Abyssinian, and Coptic churches represented. The city's shrines are once again open to all, but its future remains clouded by the Arab-Israeli controversy. As in the days of the prophet Ezekiel, it can be said of the city: "This is Jerusalem; I have set her in the midst of nations."

Arab Nationalism

Until the late nineteenth century, communal identity among the various Arab peoples of the Middle East had little to do with political self-determination or territorial units. Under the Ottoman system members of each religious faith—Muslim, Christian, and Jewish—lived in an independent community governed according to its own law by its clerical hierarchy. Communal consciousness was therefore awareness of religious values and customs rather than ethnic differentiation. Although religious rivalries often had a territorial dimension, not until the final breakup of the Ottoman Empire and the arrival of Western imperialism did such rivalries become identified with control of political entities with discrete boundaries. The idea of nationhood in its modern meaning was, as in so many other parts of the world, a Western import that cut across religious, cultural, and tribal affiliations.

Despite a major Arab cultural revival in the nineteenth century centered in Cairo, Beirut, and Damascus, there was no serious call for Arab separation from the Ottoman Empire until Neguib Azouri, a Palestinian Arab living in Paris, published *The Awakening of the Arab Nation* in 1905, in which he envisioned a united Arab state stretching from the Persian Gulf to the Suez Canal. The

CONFLICT IN THE MIDDLE EAST SINCE WORLD WAR II

1947	United Nations partitions Palestine; Arab League rejects plan
1948	State of Israel proclaimed; defeats Arab League
1952	Revolution brings Nasser to power in Egypt
1953	Mossadegh regime overthrown in Iran
1954–1962	Algerian war of independence
1956	Nasser nationalizes Suez Canal; Anglo-French-Israeli force seizes canal; United States compels it to withdraw
1964	Palestine Liberation Organization (PLO) founded
1967	Six Day War; Israel occupies West Bank and Gaza Strip, annexes East Jerusalem
1973	Yom Kippur War
1975	Civil war in Lebanon; Syria intervenes
1979	Islamic revolution in Iran; Camp David Accords between Israel and Egypt
1980–1988	Iran-Iraq War
1982	Israel invades Lebanon
1983	241 U.S. marines killed in Beirut
1987	*Intifada* begins against Israeli rule in occupied territories
1990	Iraq occupies Kuwait; United Nations demands withdrawal
1991	Gulf War

revival of Turkish nationalism after the Young Turk revolution of 1908 galvanized its Arab counterpart. Moderate Arabs who had been content with the idea of greater political autonomy within the Ottoman framework rather than independence now faced a regime in Istanbul bent on more rigorous controls. When Turkey allied itself with the Central Powers in World War I, Britain, already in quest of oil for its modernized navy in the region, promised support for a united Arab state to the sharif of Mecca, Hussein ibn-Ali, in return for military assistance.

This promise was not kept. In 1920 Britain and France divided the Arab provinces of the former Ottoman Empire between them as mandates under the League of Nations, with Britain adding Palestine, Transjordan, and Mesopotamia (Iraq) to its former protectorate in Egypt and France gaining Syria and Lebanon. Although ibn-Saud united the vast interior of the Arabian peninsula as Saudi Arabia in the 1920s and proclaimed a kingdom in 1932, Britain remained in firm control of most of its coastline. At the same time, American companies began a vigorous exploitation of oil resources in Saudi Arabia and Iraq. World War II saw the Middle East turned into a major theater of operations, with Germany's failure to gain access to the oil fields a crucial factor in its defeat.

The status of some of the Arab trust territories evolved during the interwar period. Iraq had achieved at least enough of the appearance of a state to be admitted to the League of Nations in 1932, although British influence remained strong. In Transjordan a strongman who ruled with British backing, the amir Abdullah, was recognized as a king in 1946, but British control was still so transparent that not until 1955 was the renamed kingdom of Jordan, including the West Bank area seized in the Palestine War, admitted to the United Nations. The pace of change was even slower in Syria and Lebanon,

where the French showed little inclination to prepare their territories for statehood. French control lapsed during the Nazi occupation, however, and in 1946 both states became independent. Although far more advanced economically than Britain's mandates, both countries faced special challenges. Lebanon had no sectarian majority; a variety of Muslim and Christian groups vied for dominance. Syria, despite its proud heritage, was fragmented by religious and tribal divisions among both its majority Muslim and minority Christian populations. In Syria these tensions remain barely under control; in Lebanon they erupted in 1975 in a civil war that precipitated anarchy, invasion, and foreign occupation.

The end of World War II brought rapid changes. In 1945 the League of Arab States was formed under British auspices, consisting originally of Egypt, Syria, Lebanon, Iraq, Transjordan, Saudi Arabia, and Yemen. Although many of these states were as yet in no credible sense independent, they rapidly became so as British influence waned, and it was the league that coordinated the 1948 invasion of Palestine. Defeat at the hands of the tiny Jewish army provoked a military coup in Syria, an upsurge in anti-Western sentiment, and an agonizing reassessment of the wider problems of Arab development and unity.

Nasser and the Egyptian Revolution

The most significant result of this ferment came in Egypt, where in 1952 the military revolution led by Gamal Abdel Nasser drove out the corrupt, British-supported King Farouk, spelling the end of Britain's role in the Middle East and hence of the last direct Western presence in the region.

Nasser was born in 1918, the son of a postal clerk in upper Egypt. Like many young Egyptians of modest origin, he joined the army as a means of gaining educational opportunities and career advancement. His fellow graduates in the 1938 class of the military academy were mostly of similar background, the sons of minor officials, petty merchants, commercial agents, and small landowners. They shared a common sense of frustration at Egypt's continued dominance by Britain and a sense of alienation from the older and wealthier officer corps. Under Nasser's leadership they began to meet on a regular basis to discuss the nation's problems and to plan for its future. By 1942 this group had evolved into a central committee with smaller cells throughout the army. Contacts were also established with religious organizations and foreign Arab leaders. The army's humiliation in the Palestine War strengthened the resolve of the young officers to reform the nation. Now banded together as the Free Officers' Society, they staged a virtually bloodless coup on July 23, 1952, that brought a revolutionary council to power. At first the council attempted to govern the country through its civilian institutions and bureaucracy. When the latter refused to implement the council's directives on land reform, a military dictatorship was proclaimed.

The council's nominal head was a senior general, Muhammad Naguib, but Nasser remained its true leader. It was he who decided on the policy of "guided democracy." Political parties and parliamentary institutions remained the goal of the regime, he declared, but until the masses had been prepared for active political life by reform and education, these could only serve the interests of the few. The press was brought under government regulation, and political activity was exercised through a single mass party, the Arab Socialist Union. In 1954 Nasser assumed direct control of the revolution as prime minister, and two years later he unveiled a constitution guaranteeing basic rights, including racial, religious, and sexual equality.

Nasser's revolution was as much social as political. While most of Egypt's 25 million people lived on an annual per capita income of $60, an elite of 12,000 owned 37 percent of its arable land. Nasser broke up the great estates and distributed them among the peasantry, with the smaller lots subsumed into cooperative farms. The Permanent Council for National Production was established in 1953 to draft first a five- and then a ten-year plan for integrated industrial and agricultural development. Crucial to the success of these plans was the Aswan Dam, which aimed to increase cultivated land by a third by harnessing the Nile River. When the United States, alarmed at Nasser's rising popularity in the Arab world and irked by his lack of enthusiasm for an American-sponsored regional alliance, the Baghdad Pact, announced that it would not help fund the dam, Nasser responded dramatically. He nationalized the Suez Canal,

with the stated purpose of using its income to build the dam, which had now become symbolic not only of his revolution but of Third World hopes in general for independent development. Launched in 1959 with a $300 million loan from the Soviet Union, the dam was completed in 1974 at a cost of more than $2 billion. Although its projected goals for irrigation and hydroelectric power were not fully met and ecological problems such as silting and stagnation continue to plague it, the dam enabled Egypt nearly to double its agricultural output.

Equally significant strides were made in the industrial sector, although much of it remained in handicraft and small-scale production. Nasser's record of accomplishment in one of the world's poorest nations, though politically and economically blemished by the disaster of the Six Day War, was impressive. Nonetheless, these gains were all but negated by unchecked population growth, running at some 3 percent a year. By the late 1970s Anwar el-Sadat had accepted a new client relationship with the United States as the price of economic survival, a policy continued since 1981 by his successor, Hosni Mubarak (born 1929). The heroic age of Nasser had ended.

The Middle East in the Postwar World

Nasser's revolution was a model for many emerging nations in the postwar period, but its influence was most direct on Egypt's North African neighbors. By 1956 the French protectorates of Morocco and Tunisia and the British-occupied Sudan had achieved full self-government, largely under the impetus of Egypt's example, and the former Italian colony of Libya was also granted independence under a feudal monarch, King Idris. However, the French refused to consider withdrawal from Algeria, where a strong settler interest prevailed. A war of national liberation ensued between 1954 and 1962, marked by savagery on both sides and resolved only when Charles de Gaulle, whom the war had brought back to power, arranged a plebiscite.

The rapid formation of new states in the immediate postwar period failed to give definitive shape or stability to Arab nationalism. Tribal groups dispersed over various borders, such as the Kurds of Turkey, Syria, Iran, and Iraq, demanded a homeland of their own. Radical nationalist parties, such as the Ba'ath movement in Syria and Iraq, remained dissatisfied with the conservative, pro-Western regimes left behind in the wake of the imperial powers. Pan-Arabic pressures for political unification between separate states also remained strong. In 1958 Syria and Egypt combined to form the United Arab

Republic, with Nasser as president. Ardent Arab nationalists, particularly Syrian Ba'athists, saw this union as the precursor of a grand Islamic federation but were soon disillusioned when the Egyptians moved to take complete control of Syria's government and economy. Following a Syrian army rebellion in September 1961, the union was dissolved by mutual consent. Similar experiments with other partners have proved equally short-lived, but the dream of a single, unitary state remains deeply embedded in Arab nationalism.

OPEC and the Politics of Oil

The history of the modern Middle East has been to a large extent determined by oil. Otherwise sparing in its gifts, nature has endowed the region with 60 percent of the proven world oil reserves. Britain was already dependent on Iranian oil to power its fleet by the first decade of the twentieth century, and as the West converted rapidly from coal to oil-based energy, the strategic importance of the Middle East grew apace. The discovery of vast new reserves in the desert wastes of Arabia in the 1930s was immediately exploited by the California Arabian Standard Oil Company (later called Aramco) on concessions granted by King ibn-Saud. Almost overnight Saudi Arabia was transformed from a poverty-ridden principality of nomadic tribes to a nation with one of the highest per capita incomes in the world.

In 1960 the Saudis took the initiative in forming the Organization of Petroleum Exporting Countries (OPEC). Originally composed of Saudi Arabia, Iran, Iraq, the tiny and newly independent emirate of Kuwait, and Venezuela, it subsequently expanded to include Algeria, Ecuador, Gabon, Indonesia, Libya, Nigeria, Qatar, and the confederation of small Persian Gulf sheikhdoms known as the United Arab Emirates. At first OPEC confined its activities chiefly to gaining a larger share of the revenues produced by Western oil companies and greater control over levels of production. The persistence of the Arab-Israeli conflict, however, turned it from a simple cartel into a formidable political force. After the Six Day War the Arab members of OPEC formed a separate, overlapping group (OAPEC) for the purpose of concerting policy and exerting pressure on the West over Israel. Egypt and Syria, negligible oil producers but populous and militarily powerful, joined the latter group to underline its intentions.

The Yom Kippur War of 1973 galvanized Arab opinion. Furious at the emergency resupply effort that had enabled Israel to withstand the Egyptian and Syrian assault, the Arabs imposed an oil embargo against the United States, western Europe, and Japan. This was followed by a more than fourfold price increase in the price of oil, causing sudden inflation and economic recession in the noncommunist industrial world and even greater

hardship among the underdeveloped nations. At the same time, the Saudis acquired operating control of Aramco, fully nationalizing it in 1980. As other OPEC nations followed suit, the cartel's income soared. Saudi Arabia, awash in profits, undertook a series of five-year development plans, of which the most ambitious, begun in 1980, called for the expenditure of $250 billion. Other cartel members also undertook major economic programs. For the first time, Third World nations whose resources and labor had long been exploited by the industrial giants had acquired control of a vital commodity, reversing the flow of capital. Some of this income was dispensed in the form of aid to other underdeveloped nations whose economies had been caught between higher prices for oil and the lower prices for their own commodities and raw materials caused by shrinking Western demand. Much of it, however, was reinvested in the West or absorbed in massive arms purchases that exacerbated political tensions, particularly in the Middle East. When reduced demand and overproduction produced a glut on the world market in the mid-1980s, oil prices plummeted and the cartel lost its unity. Producers such as Mexico, Nigeria, and Venezuela, whose economies had expanded recklessly, were plunged into near-bankruptcy, and even Saudi Arabia felt the pinch. The enormous reserves and relative underpopulation of the leading Middle East producers guaranteed the region its continuing strategic importance, but the politics of oil had proved dangerous for all concerned.

Modernization and Revolution in Iran

Iran, though ethnologically and linguistically distinct from its Arab neighbors in the Middle East, has shared its geographic destiny. As elsewhere in the region, social and political controls on the local level were traditionally exercised by the clergy on behalf of tribal landowning elites, with civil law and custom derived directly from religious precepts, although the merchant class of the larger towns had some independent influence. Patriarchal and hierarchical in structure, Iranian society was based on the absolute control of fathers over their families, khans or leaders over their tribes, and the shah as ruler over all, subject only to the ultimate authority of Shi'ite religious principles.

Iran's modernization began with its penetration by two conflicting imperial powers, Russia and Great Britain. In the 1860s and 1870s the first telegraph lines were set up with British assistance, thus ending the country's virtual isolation from the world. Concessions were given to build railroads and develop the country's resources. By 1907 the Russians and the British had formally divided Iran into spheres of influence, but a nationalist uprising in 1921 led by Reza Shah Pahlavi produced a modernizing dictatorship that, like Kemal Atatürk's in Turkey, attempted to introduce Western cultural and industrial models and to reduce the power of the clergy by stressing the nation's pre-Islamic past. New schools and industries were begun, and a conscript army was raised. A trans-Iranian railroad from the Caspian Sea to the Persian Gulf was built from the profits of state monopolies. Wide new avenues were cut through the major towns and named for national folk heroes. Sumptuary laws mandated the wearing of Western dress, and the traditional women's veil, the *chadar*, was made obsolete. In 1935 Reza Shah Pahlavi changed the country's Hellenistic name of Persia to Iran, meaning "land of the Aryans."

This last change was meant to reflect Iran's Indo-European roots but had contemporary significance as well. Reza Shah Pahlavi, dictatorial and often terroristic in his methods, was an ardent admirer of Hitler, and when an Allied force occupied Iran in August 1941, he was forced to abdicate in favor of his son, Muhammad Reza Pahlavi. For the next decade the country was once again a battleground of foreign interests, with the United States replacing Britain soon after World War II and the Soviet Union trying to regain its traditional foothold in the north. A new nationalist insurrection brought Muhammad Mossadegh, a prewar opponent of Reza Shah Pahlavi, to power as prime minister in 1951. Mossadegh nationalized the British-owned Anglo-Iranian Oil Company, thereby reasserting the country's independence. The West retaliated with a boycott of Iranian oil, and a CIA-led army coup deposed him in August 1953.

The shah, who had been briefly forced to flee the country by pro-Mossadegh crowds, returned with American blessing and remained a Western client thereafter. Like his father, however, he harbored grandiose ambitions. A "white revolution" was launched in the early 1960s to complete the process of modernization begun under Reza Shah Pahlavi, although the traditional landed elite remained firmly in control of the countryside. Using the massive oil profits of the 1970s, the shah attempted to turn Iran into the major military power of the Middle East, purchasing $15 billion worth of American arms between 1972 and 1978. But by the latter part of the decade his regime was under general assault. The land hunger of the peasantry remained unsatisfied despite promised reform, while the middle classes cultivated by the shah were frustrated by their exclusion from real power. Showy industrial projects and exotic weapons could not be operated without foreign advisers and technicians, reinforcing a painful sense of dependence on the West. Even the aristocracy, which had never accepted the Pahlavi dynasty, offered little support. The shah's most serious opposition, however, came from the Shi'ite clergy, which bitterly opposed what it took to be his promotion of corrupt Western values and mores. By raising a culturally sensitive issue

that cut across class lines and evoked powerful religious and nationalist sentiment, the clergy brought to focus a general sense of grievance. Their exiled leader, the Ayatollah Ruhollah Khomeini (1900–1989), became the symbol of popular resistance.

The shah responded at first with repression and then, when crippling strikes brought the economy to the verge of bankruptcy, by desperate concessions. In January 1979 he fled into exile, and on February 1, Khomeini returned to Tehran as head of a revolutionary council, which proclaimed an Islamic republic. Real authority, however, emanated from Khomeini himself, who eliminated all political competitors and, armed with nearly absolute powers, embarked on a program of fundamentalist religious reform.

Khomeini's appeal reached far beyond the Shi'ites of Iran. His call to all Muslims to overthrow corrupt and tyrannical rulers and to return to the purity of Islamic law and ritual was particularly attractive to the migrant workers who maintained the economies of Saudi Arabia, Kuwait, and Bahrain. His order to seize 52 American embassy officials and workers in November 1979 was the most dramatically popular act in the Middle East

The Ayatollah Khomeini in 1979, addressing an adoring crowd from his home.
[Alain Dejlan/Sygma]

Iranian demonstrators burn the American flag. [Jean Gaumy/Magnum]

since the nationalization of the Suez Canal. Depicting the United States as a "great Satan" (while at the same time firmly repressing Iran's Communist party and doing pragmatic business with Israel, America's principal surrogate in the area), Khomeini skillfully combined Islamic revivalism with appeals to regional nationalism. In September 1980 Iraq's Saddam Hussein launched an ill-judged invasion of Iran that bitterly divided the Arab world, with Syria, Libya, and South Yemen backing Khomeini and Saudi Arabia and Jordan supporting Iraq. The war enabled Khomeini to keep revolutionary fervor high in Iran while consolidating a theocratic regime that outlasted him and to burnish his image as the leader of Islam's *jihad*, or holy war, against the corrupting influence of the West. It was militarily inconclusive, however, and hostilities were halted by a truce in the summer of 1988.

Women and the Islamic Revolution

The resurgence of Islam has not been confined to Iran. From the Atlantic coast of North Africa to the islands of the Indonesian archipelago, across the great east-west belt where most of the world's 1 billion Muslims live, a major reawakening of Islamic culture has occurred since 1945. In part this has been associated with the emergence of new nation-states along this belt and the consequent testing of one of the world's most important religious traditions with the essentially secular ideology of modern nationalism. In part as well it reflects a struggle for identity in a region whose people are skeptical of

both Western materialism and Communist atheism and are reluctant to align themselves with either of the superpower blocs. But it also has great significance for the social position of one-fifth of the world's women.

Koranic law continues to assign women a subordinate position in society. In the more conservative Middle Eastern states the law has continued to deny them equality in the public sphere and even access to it; in Saudi Arabia women were still not permitted to drive automobiles as late as 1980. In contrast, women had made significant strides in the postwar period in countries either heavily subject to Western influence or unified by socialist revolution. Tunisia, under the presidency of the strongly pro-Western Habib Bourguiba (born 1903), became in 1956 the first Islamic nation to replace the Koranic law on marriage, divorce, and childbearing by a civil code and the first Arab state to ban polygamy. Egypt under Nasser promulgated a constitution giving women full civil equality for the first time, and the socialist governments of Algeria and Yemen have included women's groups within their ruling party organizations. Such developments, however, have tended to affect only the urban middle class, with rural, tribal, and nomadic life continuing along traditional lines. The Iranian revolution of 1979 had a dramatic effect on women; Western attire vanished almost immediately, replaced by the traditional black or gray veil and a shapeless garment covering the entire body. Elsewhere too in the Middle East the *chadar* has again become the norm, sometimes as a symbol of resistance to Western mores, but often a matter of compulsion. Thus while Arab radicalism in the 1950s was at least rhetorically receptive to women's liberation, the fundamentalist revival of the 1980s has tended to

◉ Militant Islam ◉

The view of Islam as historically beleaguered by alien and hostile forces from the West is put forward by the Ayatollah Khomeini in his book Islamic Government.

At its inception, the Islamic movement was afflicted by the Jews, who initiated a counter-activity by distorting the reputation of Islam, by assaulting it, and by slandering it. This has continued to our present day. Then came the role of groups which can be considered more evil than the devil and his troops. This role emerged in the colonialist activity which dates back more than three centuries ago. The colonialists found in the Muslim world their long-sought object. To achieve their colonialist ambitions, the colonists sought to create the right conditions leading to the annihilation of Islam. They did not seek to turn the Muslims into Christians after driving them away from Islam, because they do not believe in either. They wanted control and domination because during the Crusades they were constantly aware that the greatest obstacle preventing them from attaining their goals . . . was Islam with its laws and beliefs and with the influence it exerted on people through their faith. . . . Islam is the religion of the warriors who fight for right and justice, the religion of those seeking for freedom and independence, and those who do not want to allow the infidels to oppress the believers.

The role of women under revolutionary Islam is stated in the constitution adopted by the Islamic Republic of Iran on December 3, 1979.

In creating Islamic social foundations, all the human forces that had up to now been in the service of foreign exploitation will be accorded their basic identity and human rights. And in this regard it is natural that women, due to the greater oppression that they have borne under the idolatrous order, will enjoy more rights.

   The family unit is the foundation of society and the main institution for the growth and advancement of mankind. . . . It is the principal duty of the Islamic government to regard women as the unifying factor of the family unit and its position. They are a factor in bringing the family out of the service of propagating consumerism and exploitation and renewing the vital and valuable duty of motherhood in raising educated human beings. . . . As a result motherhood is accepted as a most profound responsibility in the Muslim viewpoint and will, therefore, be accorded the highest value and generosity.

Source: T. Y. Ismael, *Iraq and Iran: Roots of Conflict* (Syracuse, N.Y.: Syracuse University Press, 1982), pp. 101, 147.

consign women to their former roles, encouraging domesticity, public anonymity, and male dominance.

The Middle East Today

The hope of Camp David, that the Israeli-Egyptian accord would pave the way to a general settlement in the Middle East, has not been realized. No other Arab nation has moved toward recognition of Israel, and the Palestinian issue remains unresolved. During the 1970s the PLO was recognized as the legitimate government of the

Palestinian people by many Arab, Soviet bloc, and Third World nations, and its leader, Yasir Arafat (born 1929), addressed the United Nations as a head of state. His influence declined precipitously in the early 1980s as the PLO's more militant factions fell under Syrian influence. In 1987, however, a popular uprising, the *intifada*, broke out on the West Bank against the Israeli occupation. Seizing this opportunity to reassert his leadership, Arafat began an intensive diplomatic campaign that climaxed in an address before the United Nations in 1988 and the initiation of direct bilateral talks with the United States. In the aftermath of the 1991 Gulf War, Arafat's prestige was again eclipsed by his support for Saddam Hussein, as well as by the loss of Saudi aid and Soviet support. Nonetheless, he remained the chief spokesman for Palestinian nationalism and, directly or indirectly, a key figure in the attempt to reengage the peace process.

The tragic clash between the Israelis and the Palestinians has become, for much of the international public, emblematic of the continuing appeal of nationalism in a globally interconnected world. The Palestinian poet Mahmoud Darwish spoke perhaps best for the common feeling on both sides of the conflict when he wrote:

> *Where shall we go, after the last frontier?*
> *Where will birds be flying, after the last*
> *   sky? . . .*
> *We will cut off the hand of song, so that our*
> *   flesh can complete the song.*
> *Here we will die. Here in the last narrow*
> *   passage. Or here our blood will plant—its*
> *   olive trees.*[1]

Legacy of Violence: The Lebanese Civil War and the Gulf War

A tragic by-product of the Arab-Israeli conflict has been the civil war in Lebanon. On the surface, Lebanon had been one of the most successful of the states to win independence following World War II. Its thriving commercial economy had given it one of the Middle East's highest standards of living, and the political coexistence of a varied community of Christian, Jewish, and Muslim groups had made it a model of religious pluralism. Lebanon's equilibrium was, however, precarious. Urban prosperity masked rural poverty in the central valleys, a rising Muslim birthrate threatened the traditional Christian hegemony, and the country's semiofficial neutrality in the Arab-Israeli conflict brought it under increasing pressure from Arab nationalists. The sudden influx of some 300,000 Palestinian refugees after the Six Day War, followed by others expelled from Jordan in 1971, greatly exacerbated these tensions. The PLO made Lebanon its main base of operations, drawing retaliatory fire from Israel. The Lebanese divided sharply over the Palestinian presence, with Christian groups tending to regard them as unwelcome intruders and Muslims seeing them not only as victims seeking to regain their homeland but as patriots fighting in the common Arab cause against Israel. By 1975 the country had slid into full-scale civil war. When Syrian troops finally enforced a cease-fire 19 months later, 60,000 lives had been lost and nearly a third of the population displaced.

Syria's presence diminished the bloodshed but did nothing to restore stability. The PLO intensified its raids and attacks against Israel, while the Israelis sought to cultivate Christian allies in Lebanon. By 1980 there were approximately 40 separate armed groups in the country. Two years later the Israelis invaded Lebanon, driving the PLO from Beirut and occupying the southern third of the country. This defeat marked the temporary eclipse of Arafat, but the Israelis, now a target for all forces, soon withdrew after heavy losses. An American intervention in 1983 ended even more disastrously, with the death of 241 marines in a commando attack. By the late 1980s Lebanon had vanished as a nation in all but name, the epitome of sectarian anarchy and of the collapse of multiethnic community in the Middle East.

Instability in the region further increased when Iraq invaded oil-rich Kuwait in August 1990. The annexation of Kuwait gave Iraq, with its own substantial oil fields, control of 20 percent of the Persian Gulf reserves. Concerned that Saddam Hussein would order his army—the largest in the Middle East—into neighboring Saudi Arabia, the United States, with support from its allies and many of the Arab states, responded with massive troop deployments along the Saudis' border with Kuwait and Iraq. Cooperation between the United States and the Soviet Union made possible the passage of resolutions in the United Nations Security Council condemning Iraqi aggression and approving naval and air embargoes of Iraq.

When Hussein refused to withdraw from Kuwait, an American-led coalition attacked Iraq in January 1991. The myth of Arab unity was exploded as numerous Arab states, including Egypt, Syria, and Saudi Arabia, joined in the assault. Although Hussein had threatened the allies with "the mother of all battles," the Gulf War lasted only six weeks, with the climactic land campaign taking a mere 100 hours. Much of Iraq's military, the fourth largest in the world, was destroyed by a coalition air assault that featured laser-guided missiles and bombs. By war's end, most of Iraq's economic infrastructure was in ruins, and the damage to the Kuwaiti oil fields, much of it deliberately inflicted by Iraqi troops, had created the worst ecological disaster in history. Some 500 of Kuwait's oil wells were aflame, huge oil slicks polluted the Persian Gulf, and many Iraqi and Kuwaiti refineries were extensively damaged. In the aftermath of the fighting, social and ethnic unrest among Shi'ite Muslims, Kurds, and dissident military units threatened the stability of Hussein's authoritarian regime.

The Gulf crisis was noteworthy in several respects. It marked the first time in the post–Cold War era that the United States and the Soviet Union (which did not participate in the fighting) cooperated diplomatically to condemn aggression. No less important was the fact that Israel, though subjected to attack by Iraqi missiles, refrained from retaliating in order not to provoke Arab states into leaving the coalition. But Hussein had focused renewed attention on the Palestinian problem by promising to withdraw his forces from Kuwait if Israel would relinquish the occupied Arab territories in the West Bank, the Golan Heights, and Gaza. Hussein's proposal further split the Arab world, pitting the moderate Arab states against the PLO and Jordan, with its large Palestinian population.

The increasing polarization of the Middle East was reflected in the prominence of revolutionary Iran; Syria, a state widely linked to support of terrorism; and Libya, whose ruler since 1969, Muammar al-Qaddafi (born 1942), has pursued a policy of military adventurism in North Africa while proclaiming the virtues of Arab unity. At the same time, the influence of militant Shi'ism has grown apace, particularly in countries with large Shi'ite populations, including (besides Iran) Iraq, Yemen, Bahrain, and Lebanon. In addition, economic pressures have intensified on many Middle Eastern countries that overextended themselves financially during the boom years of the 1970s and now face serious problems of unemployment and social unrest. The Iran-Iraq war and the 1991 Gulf War demonstrated the fratricidal tendencies within Islam. Above all, the Arab-Israeli conflict continues to jeopardize hopes for the peaceful development of the region and, on a wider scale, international stability as well.

The forces of religion and nationalism created powerful tides in the postwar period along the great arc stretching from the Middle East to south-central Asia. The new states of India and Pakistan were born in an agony of civil war between their Hindu and Muslim populations, and the state of Israel was created in an equally bitter confrontation between Arabs and Jews. Within Islam itself, divisions between Sunni and Shi'ite Muslims produced bloody conflict as well, most visibly in the Iran-Iraq war. At the same time, the unfulfilled national aspirations of the Palestinians and of the Kurds, the vulnerable oil economy, the problems of poverty and rapid social change, and the continuing unrest in Afghanistan and elsewhere all combine to make this region perhaps the most volatile in the world.

Notes

1. M. Darwish, "Earth Scrapes Us," in *Modern Arabic Poetry: An Anthology*, ed. S. K. Jayyusi (New York: Columbia University Press, 1987), p. 208.

Suggestions for Further Reading

India, Pakistan, and Sri Lanka

Azad, M. *India Wins Freedom*. London: Longman, 1961.

Brown, J. *Modern India: The Origins of an Asian Democracy*. New York: Oxford University Press, 1985.

De Silva, K. M. *A History of Sri Lanka*. Berkeley: University of California Press, 1981.

Franda, M. *India's Rural Development*. Bloomington: Indiana University Press, 1980.

Gold, G. *Gandhi: A Pictorial Biography*. New York: Harper & Row, 1986.

Joshi, R., and Rindle, J. *Daughters of Independence: Gender, Caste, and Class in India*. London: Zed Books, 1986.

Kohli, A. *The State and Poverty in India*. Cambridge: Cambridge University Press, 1987.

Lamb, B. P. *India: A World in Transition*, 4th ed. New York: Praeger, 1975.

Mellor, J. *The New Economics of Growth: A Strategy for India and the Developing World*. Ithaca, N.Y.: Cornell University Press, 1976.

Moon, P. *Divide and Quit*. Berkeley: University of California Press, 1962.

Rosen, G. *Democracy and Economic Change in India*. Berkeley: University of California Press, 1966.

Swamy, S. *Economic Growth in China and India, 1952–1970*. Chicago: University of Chicago Press, 1974.

Tirtha, R. *Society and Development in Contemporary India*. Detroit: Harlo Press, 1980.

Wolpert, S. *Jinnah of Pakistan*. New York: Oxford University Press, 1984.

Ziegler, P. *Mountbatten*. London: Collins, 1985.

The Middle East

Abdulghani, J. *Iran and Iraq*. London: Croom Helm, 1984.

Ajami, F. *The Arab Predicament: Arab Political Thought and Practice Since 1967*. Cambridge: Cambridge University Press, 1981.

Anderson, J. N. D. *Islamic Law in the Modern World*. Westport, Conn.: Greenwood Press, 1975.

Avineri, S. *The Making of Modern Zionism: Intellectual Origins of the Jewish State*. New York: Basic Books, 1981.

Bakhash, S. *The Reign of the Ayatollahs*. New York: Basic Books, 1984.

Devlin, J. *Syria: Modern State in an Ancient Land*. Boulder, Colo.: Westview Press, 1983.

al-Fassi, A. *The Independence Movements in Arab North Africa*, trans. H. Z. Nuseibeh. New York: Octagon, 1970.

Hiro, D. *Holy Wars: The Rise of Islamic Fundamentalism*. London: Routledge & Kegan Paul, 1989.

Kamrava, M. *Revolution in Iran: The Roots of Turmoil*. London: Routledge & Kegan Paul, 1990.

Kurzman, D. *Ben-Gurion: Prophet of Fire*. New York: Simon & Schuster, 1983.

Lacouture, J. *Nasser: A Biography*. New York: Knopf, 1973.

Mortimer, E. *Faith and Power: The Politics of Islam*. New York: Faber & Faber, 1982.

Peretz, D. *Intifada: The Palestinian Uprising*. Boulder, Colo.: Westview Press, 1990.

Rabinovitch, I. *The War for Lebanon, 1970–1983*. Ithaca, N.Y.: Cornell University Press, 1984.

Reich, B. *Israel: Land of Tradition and Conflict*. Boulder, Colo.: Westview Press, 1985.

Said, E. W. *The Question of Palestine*. New York: Times Books, 1979.

Salibi, K. *A History of Arabia*. Delmar, N.Y.: Caravan Books, 1980.

Sampson, A. *The Seven Sisters*. New York: Bantam Books, 1979.

Sifry, M. L., and Cerf, C., eds. *The Gulf War Reader: History, Documents, Opinions*. New York: Random House, 1991.

Taryam, A. O. *The Establishment of the United Arab Emirates, 1950–85*. London: Croom Helm, 1987.

Waterbury, J. *The Egypt of Nasser and Sadat*. Princeton, N.J.: Princeton University Press, 1983.

Maps and Their Makers (II)

The attempt to map the environment began with the earliest human societies. By the middle of the first millennium B.C., the first world map had been produced in Babylonia. Maps of considerable sophistication were drawn in the ancient West and China, but not until the discovery of the Americas and of the Pacific by Columbus and his successors in the late fifteenth and sixteenth centuries were the true dimensions of the earth known with any accuracy.

The discovery of the New World coincided with the development of movable type in the West. Printed maps circulated rapidly, facilitating trade and exploration. In 1570 Abraham Ortelius, a Flemish contemporary of Gerardus Mercator, published his *Theater of the World*, a collection of 70 maps covering the entire globe and incorporating the latest discoveries. It became a traveler's bible, going through 40 editions; a French reader enthused that it was the greatest work in the world after the Holy Scriptures.

Globes came into fashion too, and as Aristophanes had unfolded a map of the world on the ancient Greek stage, so William Shakespeare referred to the first English globe in *The Comedy of Errors*. Shakespeare remarked that "all the world's a stage," and it was no accident that the most important theater of his time was called the Globe. The European imagination of the late sixteenth century was as fascinated with the idea of a knowable world as it was soon to be with its conquest.

The discovery of a new earth stimulated speculation about a new heaven as well. In 1595 the great Mercator's final work was published, called *Atlas*—the first collection of maps to bear this title—and subtitled *Cosmographical Meditations upon the Creation of the Universe, and the Universe as Created*. As this subtitle made clear, Mercator envisioned the mapping of the earth as only a first step toward a new understanding of the cosmos. Fourteen years later, in 1609, Galileo Galilei trained his telescope on the heavens and saw the four largest moons of Jupiter, the first new objects, apart from comets, to be observed in the heavens in thousands of years.

The discovery of these new celestial objects had a very different import from Columbus' discovery of the New World. Although pre-Columbian maps, based on Ptolemy, had underestimated the size of the globe, it was known and accepted that there were places on it where no humans lived and perhaps none had ever gone. The Ptolemaic heavens, however, for all their greater size, were believed to be fully mapped; nor had

the Copernican system, in transposing the earth and the sun, enlarged them. Galileo's four moons changed all that. The cosmos had begun to be explored; as much might be hidden as was known.

If the real exploration of the heavens had to await the development of radio astronomy in the twentieth century, the telescopes of the seventeenth were able to bring at least one celestial body within reach of the cartographers: the moon. Although only one side of it was visible from earth, some 48 craters had been located and named (mostly after ancient philosophers and modern scientists), as well as eight so-called seas. Celestial globes, depicting the sun, the earth, the planets, and the stars, became almost as popular as terrestrial ones. Such representations suggested an attempt to domesticate the cosmos. Europeans began to speculate whether beings like themselves might not inhabit other celestial bodies, and in 1639 the Italian friar Thomas Campanella published one of the earliest works of science fiction, *The City of the Sun*. With the publication of Sir Isaac Newton's *Mathematical Principles of Natural Philosophy* in 1687 (see Chapter 24), the distinction between celestial and terrestrial mechanics that had been maintained since the time of Aristotle collapsed, and it was soon generally accepted that the same physical laws governed both the earth and the heavens.

At the same time, cartography became a weapon in the struggle for commercial advantage and empire. As the imperial initiative passed in the seventeenth and eighteenth centuries from Iberia to England and France, both nations realized the crucial importance of reliable maps. Under Louis XIV mapmaking became a state enterprise. Astronomers were sent to Egypt, South America, and the West Indies to make the celestial observations essential for accurate mapping. The explorer La Salle was commissioned to survey the newly established colony of New France in North America, and a team under Jean-Dominique Cassini, director of the Royal Observatory, set out to produce a true map of France itself. Using the moons of Jupiter as a point of reference for sighting latitude, they discovered that previous maps had placed the port of Brest too far west, in what was actually open sea, and Marseilles too far south. When Louis XIV was shown these results, he exclaimed, "Your work has cost me a good part of my state!"

What France itself lost, however, its colonies regained in Guillaume Delisle's maps of Canada (1703) and Louisiana (1718), which extended French claims in

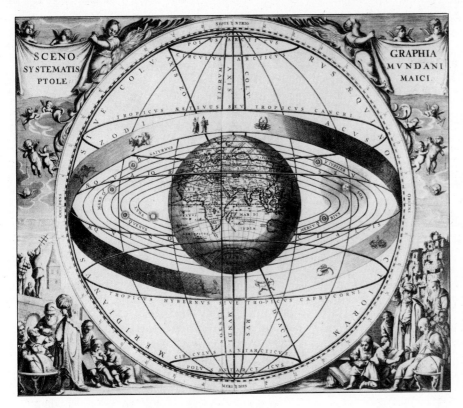

This elegant illustration of the Ptolemaic theory by Pieter Schenk and Gerard Valk dates from 1706, indicating that Ptolemy's model still had advocates into the eighteenth century. The earth is at the center, surrounded by a fiery atmosphere, while the sun, the moon, the five planets then known, and the heavens are represented by mythological figures and cherubs riding on a bed of clouds. At the edge of the system are the divisions of the zodiac. [American Philosophical Society]

the New World at the expense of England's. The British were not slow to respond, and a veritable war of maps ensued in fixing the boundaries of Nova Scotia, ceded by the French at the end of the War of the Austrian Succession (1748), with Britain ironically citing French maps to substantiate its claims to more of the coastline with its rich fisheries and the French citing British maps to limit them.

Despite these conflicts, however, the two nations were able to cooperate occasionally in a common scientific interest. In the 1730s French expeditions to Lapland and Peru confirmed Newton's hypothesis that the earth was not a perfect sphere but, because of its variable motion, a prolate one, bulging at the equator and flattened at the poles. This was important to navigation, because it meant that degrees of latitude and longitude were not uniform but lengthened as they approached the equator and shortened as they receded. Fifty years later a joint team of British and French geographers measured the precise distance between Greenwich, England, and Paris, using French techniques of triangulation and a new British instrument, the theodolite, a 200-pound device consisting of telescopes, reflectors, and angle registers. One hundred years later, in 1884, an international conference established Greenwich as the prime meridian, the point of 0 degrees of longitude from which all divisions of east and west would thenceforth be measured. Among other things, this

made it possible to divide the earth into its present 24 time zones, each 15 degrees of longitude apart. Greenwich thus became, as Babylon, Jerusalem, and Ch'ang An had once been, the center of the earth.

Magellan had crossed the Pacific, but for the next 250 years little was reliably known about its western expanses. It found its geographer at last, however, in James Cook (1728–1779), the son of a Yorkshire laborer who worked himself up to a naval commission, driven by a passion for discovery that, as he confessed, "leads me not only farther than any man has been before me, but as far as I think it possible for man to go." Cook's three voyages set out in search of those will-o'-the-wisps of cartographers, a navigable shortcut to Asia through the Americas called the Northwest Passage and a great southern continent called Terra Australis, hypothesized by the ancient Greeks, popularized by Marco Polo, and still a standard feature of eighteenth-century maps. Cook found neither, but he did map thousands of miles of northwestern American coastline and virtually every island in the Pacific, and he did go farther than any man had been, sailing to within a few hundred miles of both the north pole and Antarctica.

Cook's voyages put a third of the world on the map, although it remained for others to complete his work. The Norwegian Roald Amundsen (1872–1928) finally traversed the chain of bays, straits, and sounds across northern Canada to the Beaufort Sea in 1903–1906.

Antarctica, the true southern continent, was first sighted in 1820; the name Australia was given to the great landmass that the British explorer Matthew Flinders was the first to realize in 1801 was not an archipelago but a continent in its own right. Cook himself was tragically murdered in Hawaii, another of his discoveries, while preparing to make a fourth voyage.

The efforts of Cook, Flinders, and two other Englishmen, George Vancouver and Francis Beaufort, had given a tolerably good idea of the coastal contours of the six habitable continents by the mid-nineteenth century. It remained to map the equally challenging interiors of the Americas, Africa, and central Asia.

One of the first native surveyors of North America was George Washington, who as a young man charted the region between the Potomac River and Lake Erie and, failing to persuade Congress of the urgency of a full geographic survey of the young American republic, left his countrymen at his death a full set of surveying instruments, including parallel rules, compasses, and a theodolite. The acquisition of the Louisiana Territory from France in 1803, however, provided the needed incentive. No one knew exactly what the country had bought. Some people speculated that the Missouri and Columbia rivers might provide a passage to the Pacific. Others imagined the West, as the Greeks had once imagined Terra Australis, as a land of milk and honey. The actual barrier of the Rocky Mountains was barely guessed at.

In 1804 the government dispatched a party of 45 men under Meriwether Lewis and William Clark that two years later, guided by Indian maps, reached the Pacific, laying claim to the western territories beyond Louisiana. They were followed by settlers, adventurers, and, after 1838, the systematic surveys of the Army Corps of Topographical Engineers. In the 1870s John Wesley Powell rafted down the Colorado River, mapping much of the plateau and desert west, and in 1879 the United States Geological Survey was instituted. Its work continues today.

The British mapped India rapidly after its final conquest in 1818, proceeding northward to the Himalayas, where a Bengali clerk surmised that the mountain known as Peak XV and called in Tibetan Chomolungma, or "Goddess Mother of the World," was the tallest in the world. The British renamed it after an Englishman, George Everest. Similarly, the mapping of Africa awaited its intensive colonization after 1870. In contrast, the Jesuits who reached China and Japan in the sixteenth century found an ancient and sophisticated cartographic tradition in both countries. When Matteo Ricci presented a world map to the Chinese emperor in 1602, he tactfully placed China in the center. The Italian Jesuit Martino Martini published the first European atlas of China in 1655, based on Chinese sources. But the Chinese, with their proud isolation, were slow to adopt Western mapping techniques or to accept the results of Western discoveries. The consequence was to place them at a considerable disadvantage in dealing with European imperialism in the nineteenth century.

While the true dimensions and contours of the earth were slowly yielding to exploration and measurement, a similar process was taking place with regard to the heavens. One of the stumbling blocks to the acceptance of the Copernican theory in the seventeenth century was that it suggested a far greater distance to the fixed stars than that of Ptolemy. By the latter part of the century, however, Copernicus had won the day, and French astronomers had calculated the distance between the earth and the sun with better than 90 percent accuracy.

A better appreciation of the scale of the cosmos, however, awaited one of the most important conceptual breakthroughs in history: the realization that the sun itself was a star. Only by means of this could even a rudimentary notion of the immensity of interstellar space be achieved. If any single individual may be credited with it, it was perhaps the martyred Giordano Bruno, who had argued—at the cost of his life—for the idea of an infinity of worlds and hence of an infinite space. A century later the great Dutch astronomer and mathematician Christiaan Huygens (1629–1695), hypothesizing that the star Sirius was a body as bright as the sun, calculated its distance as 27,664 times that of the earth from the sun. Sirius was in reality nearly 20 times farther away, but Huygens' estimate was at least a beginning. William Herschel (1738–1822) took a quantum leap by suggesting that the universe was a sea composed of great galactic islands, of which the sun's island, the Milky Way, was but one. Since Herschel had calculated the equatorial plane of the Milky Way at 7,000 light-years and since the distance between galaxies must necessarily be far larger than their internal dimensions, he was faced with a universe that was, if not infinite, then perhaps ultimately incalculable.

Herschel was the first to realize that the light from the stars he gazed at had traveled so far—millions of years, he thought—that the bodies that had emitted them might no longer exist. At the same time, his slightly older contemporary James Hutton (c. 1726–1797) was suggesting, on the basis of his observation of geologic strata, that the earth itself was not (as had been thought only a century before) only a few thousand years old but many millions. The universe was receding in time as it was expanding in space.

These twin conceptions may have led to a fresh attempt to humanize space by populating it with intelligent life. In 1877 the Italian astronomer Giovanni Schiaparelli observed a network of fine symmetrical lines on the surface of Mars. An American, Percival Lowell, argued that these were elaborate canals built

A sketch of Herschel's 20-inch telescope. Later the astronomer built a giant reflecting telescope with funds provided by Britain's King George III.
[Yerkes Observatory]

by a race of technologically advanced beings. This theory had wide credence in scientific circles and entered popular culture as well; in 1938 millions of Americans were panicked by a radio hoax that announced that Martians had landed in New Jersey. Not until the *Mariner 9* space probe orbited Mars in 1971 and the unmanned *Viking* spacecraft landed on the planet in 1976 were these fantasies laid to rest.

If the period from Columbus' discoveries and Copernican astronomy to Newtonian physics had seen an enormous advance in human knowledge of the earth and the heavens, and that from Newtonian to Einsteinian physics a similar one, the twentieth century marked the beginning of an era of unprecedented exploration and discovery. In 1909 Robert Peary reached the north pole, and in 1911 Roald Amundsen arrived at the south pole. Aerial photography of the Antarctic began in 1928, but not until the postwar period, particularly the International Geophysical Year of 1957–1958 and the U.S. Geologic Survey of 1961–1962, did the continent's true outlines begin to emerge.

At the same time, the oceans and their depths were at last surveyed. Magellan, having probed the depth of the Pacific to about 2,300 feet in 1521, pronounced it immeasurable, and many sailors indeed believed the seas to be bottomless. Not until 1856 was the Pacific's depth roughly ascertained (using tidal wave measurements), and only in the 1950s was the first map of the ocean floors produced. It revealed a planet beneath the planet, with mountain ranges greater than the Himala-

yas, chasms deeper than the Grand Canyon, and plains broader than the Russian steppe.

The discovery of the ocean's great topographic diversity, particularly of the earth's largest single feature, the Midocean Ridge in the Atlantic, led to the realization that the earth was dynamic and the continents themselves in motion. A theory of "continental drift" had been proposed 50 years earlier, to wide ridicule, by the German meteorologist Alfred Wegener. As the discovery of deep space had opened up the geographic dimension of time—as Herschel and his successors had realized that the image of the heavens was a record of past events—so the present generation of cartographers has begun to work backward to reconfigure the continents of past geologic ages. As Wegener had hypothesized, there may have been a single landmass or supercontinent, Pangaea, from which the present seven continents have emerged over the past 200 million years. Such projections may ultimately read forward too, enabling us literally to ascertain the shape of things to come.

At the beginning of the twentieth century the size of the universe was still estimated at no more than 10,000 light-years, and the existence of other galaxies was still an unproven hypothesis. The picture was rapidly transformed by the development of powerful new telescopes, the analysis of light spectra, and the discovery of stars whose variable luminosity enabled astronomers to use them as cosmic yardsticks, like beacons at sea. By 1930 Edwin Hubble (1889–1953) had demonstrated

Kingdoms of space: the great spiral galaxy Andromeda, known as M 31, is similar to our own Milky Way in shape but larger in size, with a diameter of some 180,000 light-years. About 4 billion galaxies, each consisting of billions of stars, lie within reach of modern telescopes. [Observatories of the Carnegie Institution, Washington]

away, but by midcentury that estimate had doubled, and with the introduction of radio telescopes after World War II and the consequent discovery of quasars (quasi-stellar discrete radio sources), it was soon revised tenfold upward again. In the farthest reaches of space, stars may be beaming their light toward us while simultaneously receding from us at a speed nearly equal to that of light itself, and it appears certain that light has reached the earth that was propagated before our planet existed.

It has only been some thousands of years since humans first attempted to mark the distance between here and there on stone, skin, and sand, but our maps have now led us billions of years back in time and billions of light-years outward in space. As astronomers and geologists pursue their visions, the variety, utility, complexity, and sophistication of the mapmakers' art continues to increase. Maps are now indispensable for such diverse projects as weather prediction, flood control, agricultural and urban planning, mining, and—a sad commentary on the human adventure—arms control. At the same time, satellite photography, electronic data processing, and computer simulation have greatly increased the range and precision of mapping. The hand-drawn map, in use for scientific purposes until only a few years ago, may soon go the way of the hand-lettered book. Yet the caution of a nineteenth-century British surveyor remains valid: "All observations are liable to error; no telescope is perfect; no leveling instrument is entirely trustworthy; no instrumental gradations are exact; no observer is infallible."

Suggestions for Further Reading

Bagrow, L. *A History of Cartography.* London: Watts, 1964.

Bricker, C., and Tooley, R. V. *A History of Cartography: 2500 Years of Maps and Mapmakers.* London: Thames & Hudson, 1969.

Brown, L. A. *The Story of Maps.* Boston: Little, Brown, 1980.

Harley, J. B., and Woodward, D., eds. *The History of Cartography.* Chicago: University of Chicago Press, 1987–.

Kopal, Z. *Widening Horizons: Man's Quest to Understand the Structure of the Universe.* New York: Taplinger, 1970.

Schlee, S. *The Edge of an Unfamiliar World: A History of Oceanography.* New York: Dutton, 1973.

Sullivan, W. *Continents in Motion.* New York: McGraw-Hill, 1974.

Thrower, N. J. W. *Maps and Man.* Englewood Cliffs, N.J.: Prentice Hall, 1972.

Wilford, J. N. *The Mapmakers.* New York: Knopf, 1981.

not only that other galaxies existed but also that they were receding at a velocity proportional to their distance from our own. Hubble's law, as this discovery was called, suggested both that cosmic magnitudes were far greater than had been hitherto supposed and that those magnitudes were indefinitely expanding. Estimates of the present size of the universe have been extended continuously since then. Hubble calculated the edge of the universe as 500 million light-years

Decolonization and Development: Africa and Latin America

Africa and Latin America, the two largest landmasses of the Southern Hemisphere, encompass some 800 million inhabitants on 20 million square miles of territory. Each is richly varied in indigenous populations and languages, in climate and geography, and in cultures and natural resources. Each has been profoundly shaped by its contact with European imperialism. In both cases, imperialism has left a legacy of exploitation and underdevelopment, of shattered native traditions and shallowly rooted foreign ones, of resentment, resistance, and continuing dependence. The decline of colonialism after World War II compelled both regions to face similar yet distinct crises of cultural identity, political development, and economic modernization. The result in many cases was chronic instability, civil unrest, and a repeated pattern of military and authoritarian governments. Most daunting of all remain the conditions of poverty and so-

Nigerian students in traditional dress.
[Marilyn Silverstone/Magnum]

cial inequality in which the vast majority of Africans and Latin Americans continue to live.

Europeans maintained through World War II the control they had achieved over most of Africa in the nineteenth century. Few Africans held positions of influence or responsibility in their own lands, and there was little effort to educate native elites for eventual self-government as envisioned by the mandate system of the League of Nations. The Italian conquest of Ethiopia in 1935–1936 extinguished one of the last nominally independent states in Africa. Yet the colonial system disintegrated rapidly after 1945, leading to the unplanned emergence of several dozen new states, most profoundly ill-equipped for independence.

Central and South America had cast aside most direct imperial control in the early nineteenth century but remained divided by the colonial legacy and subject to Great Power influence. Latin American economies were severely affected by the Great Depression and the interruption of trade during World War II. Thus whereas the years following World War II saw the difficult birth of political independence in Africa, Latin America experienced continuing economic decline and external political pressures, particularly from the United States.

Africa: The Seeds of Revolt

African nationalism can be traced back to the career of Edward Wilmot Blyden (1832–1912), a native of the Danish (now American) island of St. Thomas who migrated to Liberia and served it as ambassador, minister plenipotentiary, and secretary of state over a period of four decades. Blyden, a classical scholar who had mastered Latin, Greek, Hebrew, and Arabic, among other tongues, was imbued with the thought of such European figures as Herder, Fichte, Hegel, and Mazzini. Nonetheless, he proudly affirmed his own African heritage. Each race, he asserted, was equal but distinct, with its own powers and endowments. He viewed the Western conquest of Africa as merely a stage in the continent's development and declared that "Africa may yet prove to be the spiritual conservatory of the world." Blyden was thus a forefather of the twentieth-century movement of black consciousness known as "Negritude," which asserted the distinctiveness of the African personality and the uniqueness of the African cultural heritage for black people wherever they might live. He called on Black Africa to absorb the technology of the West while rejecting its cultural imperialism and remaining true to its own traditions.

Other black intellectuals sounded a similar note. The Pan-African Conference held in London in 1900 issued a call "To the Nations of the World," written largely by the American W. E. B. Du Bois (1868–1963), which warned:

> If now the world of culture bends itself towards giving Negroes and other dark men the largest and broadest opportunity for education and self-development, then [imperial] contact is bound to have a beneficial effect upon the world and hasten human progress. But if, by reason of carelessness, prejudice, greed and injustice, the black world is to be exploited and ravished and degraded, the results must be deplorable if not fatal—not simply to them, but to the high ideals of justice, freedom and culture which a thousand years of Christian civilization have held before Europe.[1]

Colonial officials paid lip service to the idea of maintaining native systems of authority, but, as in India, the goal was to minimize costs rather than to preserve indigenous culture; in 1925, for example, Britain governed 20 million Nigerians with a mere 200 administrators. Here as elsewhere throughout Africa, disparate tribes were yoked together under an alien rule that ignored traditional distinctions of language, culture, and governance and erased tribal boundaries that were the result of centuries of political accommodation no less fragile and complex than those of Europe. The result was to sow the seeds of later conflict and civil war when the arbitrarily created nations of imperial convenience were suddenly thrust into independence.

The infrastructure of imperial control had been largely laid by World War I. The Gold Coast railway system was finished by 1903 and those of German East and Southwest Africa before 1914, though the French did not complete their link between Pointe-Noire and Brazzaville in the Middle Congo for another decade, at a cost of 20,000 African lives. The war curtailed virtually all investment in Africa, and little was forthcoming in the 1920s or the depression-ridden 1930s. With the slump in work projects came a rapid decline in European emigration, as most of Europe's labor surplus turned again to North America in search of opportunity. Africa found itself supporting a colonial system that had abandoned any pretext of development in favor of skimming off its natural resources and exploiting its work force.

Resistance to colonial authority took a variety of forms. Some Africans defied it openly, like the Somba of northern Dahomey, who cried, "No more taxation, no more work on the roads, no more soldiering" as they attacked the French in 1917. Others simply migrated across colonial boundaries or disappeared into the bush. Rail strikes erupted in Sierra Leone in 1919 and 1926, in Nigeria in 1921, and in Senegal in 1926, threatening the vulnerable communication links on which imperial control depended. Apart from South Africa, however, where the African National Congress was founded in 1912 and the black Industrial and Commercial Workers Union claimed 100,000 members, there was little significant or-

⊚ Black Power ⊚

The aspirations of African blacks to direct their own destiny was eloquently stated in 1960 by Rashidi Mfaume Kawawa, who would later succeed Julius Nyerere as prime minister of Tanganyika.

The demand for Africanization is made by the black people and means a replacement by them of those of different origin. Despite the wider meaning that the term African has acquired today, the blacks are still at the bottom of every ladder and identify themselves completely and practically with the struggle for change. To ask the indigenous Africans to forget the agony of their past is to ask them to ignore the lesson that their experience has taught them. Asians and Europeans are crying in Tanganyika today for non-racial parties, but just how practical is this? Those non-racial political parties which have been formed in Tanganyika have never succeeded, for they never aimed at emancipating the African, but only at deluding him into satisfaction with the lowest rung. It is the experience of the present that will constitute African reaction in the future; and the place that the Asian and the European will build for themselves in Africa will be governed by the degree of sacrifice they are prepared to make in the cause of a life in joint advancement and dedication with and amongst the Africans.

Source: R. Segal, *African Profiles* (Baltimore: Penguin Books, 1962), pp. 113–114.

ganization until the 1930s. Reflecting the effect of the Great Depression on the African proletariat, a new generation of black intellectuals, including the Jamaican-American Marcus Garvey (1887–1940), the Kenyan Jomo Kenyatta (1891–1978), and the Senegalese Léopold Senghor (born 1906), combined Marxist ideology with appeals to ethnic consciousness. Although Germany's African empire had been seized after World War I, the rise of Hitler reinforced the militants' identification of imperialism with racism, and the brutal conquest of Ethiopia provided fascism with a foothold in Africa.

World War II brought the colonial dilemma in Africa to a head. The French mobilized 100,000 troops for combat in West Africa alone, and Africans comprised almost 9 percent of the fighting force in France itself. Both the Vichy regime in French West Africa and the Gaullist one in Equatorial Africa made heavy demands on their populations, including increased taxes, forced labor, and compulsory deliveries of crops. Similar pressures were exerted in the British colonies, where tens of thousands of natives were conscripted to work in mines and on plantations, and many hundreds died under conditions indistinguishable from slave labor. At the same time the white supremacist regime in South Africa, which had enjoyed dominion status within the British Empire since 1910, profited considerably from its strategic location and emerged from the war as a major regional power.

Neither the bitter divisions among the European powers nor their wartime reversion to the brutal practices of

the colonial past were lost on African leaders, who called for postwar independence. Their position was bolstered by the American military campaign in North Africa and the determination of President Franklin Roosevelt to challenge the Anglo-French colonial monopoly in much of Africa. Thus prodded, the British reaffirmed independence to be the ultimate goal of their African policy, although the French continued to envision their colonies as permanently affiliated with the mother country. There was less pressure on the smaller colonial powers, Belgium and Portugal, both of which resisted change; Portugal, indeed, declared its possessions of Angola, Mozambique, and Portuguese Guinea to be overseas provinces in 1951.

The Achievement of Independence

Between 1957 and 1975 the holdings of the four major colonial powers that survived World War II—Britain, France, Belgium, and Portugal—acquired independence. As a result, 51 new nations emerged, most of them containing a variety of peoples, cultures, languages, and traditions and almost none of them adequately prepared for statehood.

The first postwar decade gave little indication of the rapid decolonization to come. Portugal, as we have seen, moved to integrate its colonies even more closely with itself; Belgium encouraged settler migration; and France, after its expulsion from Syria and Lebanon, tightened its grip on its remaining colonies around the globe. Only Britain moved to prepare its colonies for self-government within the British Commonwealth, promoting education and training African elites. British policy was complicated by the wide developmental variations among its colonies, as well as the resistance of settler populations in Kenya, Uganda, and Tanganyika. At last it settled on the Gold Coast, a prosperous colony with a cocoa-based economy on the bulge of West Africa, where a skillful nationalist leader, Kwame Nkrumah (1909–1972), playing on Western fears of communist influence, secured a commitment to independence. On March 6, 1957, the Gold Coast, renamed Ghana, was proclaimed a sovereign state within the Commonwealth.

Ghana's independence triggered an immediate upsurge of nationalism throughout the continent. This coincided with a radical change of direction in Britain and France. Britain's Suez fiasco in 1956 and 1957 produced a sharp turn in favor of colonial divestiture, while Charles de Gaulle, seeking to bring matters to a head, offered France's black African colonies a choice between membership in a federal community dominated by France or independence with an immediate cessation of aid. Taking up the challenge, the nationalist leader in French Guinea, Sékou Touré (1922–1984), called on his compatriots to opt for "freedom in poverty" rather than continuing dependence. They did so overwhelmingly, and the remaining seven French West African territories, the four of French Equatorial Africa, and the island colony of Madagascar shortly followed suit. By the end of 1960 the sub-Saharan French empire was no more, although de Gaulle, making a virtue of necessity, reversed policy and provided support for the former colonies.

Britain's empire was less easily disassembled. In colonies such as Nigeria, home to more than 200 ethnic and linguistic groups, the problem was finding a viable coalition to hand power to; in others, such as Kenya, there was fierce settler resistance and sometimes savage bloodletting. In general, in territories where either a single tribe predominated or, as in Tanganyika, where a charismatic leader was able to weld a governing consensus among many small tribes, stability could be achieved; elsewhere, most disastrously in Nigeria and Uganda, independence was followed by civil war and by regimes of sometimes appalling brutality.

Britain's most serious difficulties occurred in southern Africa, where two large settler states, Southern Rhodesia and the Union of South Africa, resolutely opposed any challenge to white minority rule. In South Africa

pressures for reform were met by defiance: in March 1960, police opened fire on peaceful black demonstrators in Sharpeville township, killing 67; in October the white electorate voted for a republic, thus renouncing South Africa's dominion status; and in March 1961, South Africa withdrew from the Commonwealth. Southern Rhodesia was nominally part of a central African federation with Northern Rhodesia and Nyasaland; when in 1964 the latter two became independent as Zambia and Malawi, the white settler regime in the south, which had exercised de facto control since 1923, insisted on sovereignty without reform. Negotiations proved fruitless, and in 1965 a renegade Rhodesia declared its independence. Isolated by sanctions and faced with a determined guerrilla movement, the white regime yielded in 1980 to a popularly elected black government led by Robert Mugabe (born c. 1928), and Rhodesia became the Republic of Zimbabwe.

As might be expected, the achievement of independence was most difficult in the colonies of Belgium and Portugal. The world had paid little heed to the Congo since international opinion had forced the Belgians to take it over in 1908 from their royal entrepreneur, King Leopold II. The Belgians now fled at the first approach of insurrectionary violence, and the proclamation of an independent Congo in June 1960 under Patrice Lumumba (1925–1961) was almost immediately followed by the secession of its richest province, Katanga, backed by Western mining interests. After Lumumba's murder by CIA-supported assassins, the Congo became a hotbed of Cold War intrigue, with American, Soviet, Chinese, and residual Belgian interests competing amid virtual civil anarchy. An American-backed strongman, General Joseph Mobutu (born 1930), finally reunited the country, henceforth known as Zaïre, in 1965. The adjoining colony of Ruanda-Urundi split into two states, Rwanda and Burundi, whose rival tribes, the Hutu and the Tutsi, clashed bloodily.

Unlike Belgium, Portugal dug its heels in against the liberation movements in its major colonies, Angola, Mozambique, and Portuguese Guinea, where more than 500,000 whites had settled. After more than a decade of bloodshed the Portuguese military itself rebelled, establishing a new regime in Lisbon that recognized independence in the colonies. The long struggle had produced two black factions in Angola, each with its Great Power sponsor, and civil war raged until 1991. In Mozambique the United States backed rebels against the self-styled Marxist regime of Samora Machel.

In May 1963, representatives of 32 new African states met in Addis Ababa to establish the Organization of African Unity (OAU), which has remained an important (though not always successful) promoter of regional peace and continental interests. The OAU's charter recognized the sovereign equality of all member states and

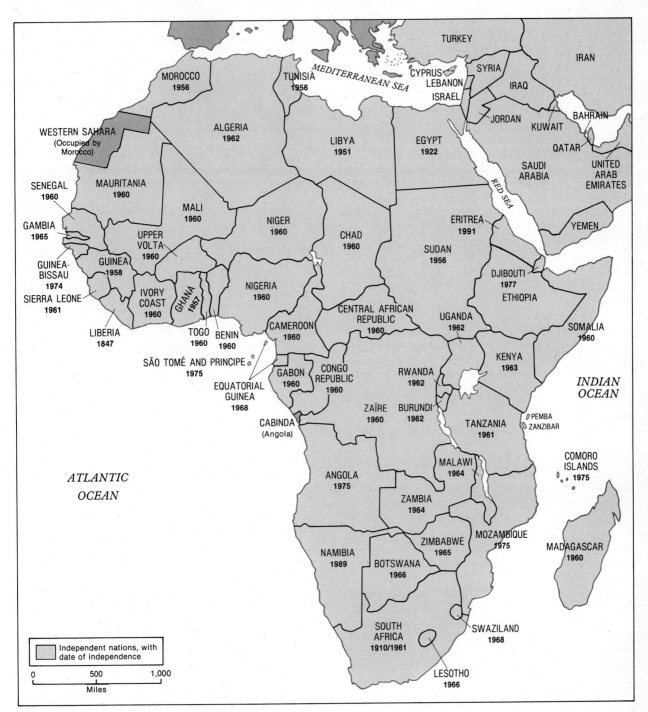

41.4 *Africa Today*

the principle of noninterference in the internal affairs of each and pledged itself to the eradication of all remnants of colonialism in Africa. A historian noted that it thereby "Africanized the European partition,"[2] legitimating the often arbitrary boundaries drawn by the colonial powers, but it is difficult to see what alternative was available. For better or worse, modern Africa, like modern Asia, had been cast in the mold of imperialism and would have to work out its destiny in the forms bequeathed by its departed conquerors.

JOMO KENYATTA: KENYA'S FOUNDING FATHER

Kenyan independence involved some of the most characteristic elements of the African liberation movements: tribal division, settler resistance, a wavering colonial policy, and a charismatic black leader, Jomo Kenyatta. The grandson of a medicine man of the Kikuyu, Kenya's dominant tribe, Kenyatta was unsure of the date and year of his birth, probably 1891. Like other modern revolutionaries, his name was an adopted one; *Jomo* means "burning spear," and *Kenyatta* refers to the beaded belt, or *kinyata*, that he habitually wore.

Kenyatta spent much of his youth traveling in Europe. He returned home in the 1920s, became secretary of the Kikuyu Central Association, and began to involve himself in his country's future. In 1929 and again in 1931 he went to London to argue his tribe's rights to the land on which it had settled. The British government refused to grant his request but allowed the Kikuyu to establish their own schools. Over the following years he attended the London School of Economics and wrote anthropological studies of his people, as well as an autobiography, *Facing Mount Kenya* (1938), that became a bible of the independence movement.

In October 1945, Kenyatta was one of the organizers of the landmark Pan-African Congress that met in Manchester, England. Seizing the postwar moment, young radicals such as Kwame Nkrumah demanded full independence for Africa. When Kenyatta returned to Kenya in September 1946 he became president of the Kenya African Union (KAU), a political party that sought to unify Kenya's tribes. While urging his followers to act with discipline and restraint, he fought for African voting rights, the elimination of racial discrimination, and the return of tribal lands.

When the British rejected these demands, Kikuyu militants organized a terrorist underground, the Mau Mau, which prompted the declaration of a state of emergency. Kenyatta was accused of masterminding the Mau Mau, a charge almost certainly false; unquestionably, however, the KAU had links to the Mau Mau, and in 1952 Kenyatta was imprisoned. British ascendancy was clearly on the wane, however, and with Ghana's independence in 1957, Kenya's drive toward nationhood accelerated. The Kenya African Nationalist Union, now the dominant black party, refused any participation in a transitional government until Kenyatta was freed. In 1961 he returned home in triumph, his captivity having made him the moral leader of his people's struggle. In December 1963 he became the first president of the Republic of Kenya.

Jomo Kenyatta, first president of independent Kenya. [© 1977, Jason Laure/Woodfin Camp]

Kenyatta's firmest base of support was among the Kikuyu, who comprised but 20 percent of the black population of Kenya. As president, he reached out not only to other tribes but also to white and Asian settlers, assuring them of their place in a multiracial society. Europeans continued to serve in his government, and despite his rhetorical commitment to the slogans of "African socialism," he rejected Soviet assistance and built up a wealthy black proprietor class under settlement schemes financed by the British treasury and the World Bank. This elite continued as the backbone of support for his successor, Daniel arap Moi (born 1924).

A man of enormous vitality, Kenyatta, more than any other figure, came to represent the new Africa on the world stage. Never losing touch with his origins—he lived on a farm outside his capital, Nairobi, and regularly worked the land—he became a familiar figure at international conferences and assemblies. Wearing alternately impeccably tailored suits and resplendent tribal robes, he symbolized both the revolutionary charisma that had built modern Africa and the political pragmatism by which he hoped to forge its future. He died, still in office, in 1978.

The Quest for Unity

With independence, Africa contained more nations than any other continent in the world. They varied enormously in size, population, geography, resources, and development. The large, thinly populated states of the southern Sahara—Mauritania, Mali, Upper Volta, Niger, Chad, and the Sudan—were uniformly impoverished, with average per capita income of less than $100 per year, few roads, and virtually no railways. West Africa was chiefly dependent on tropical agriculture and continuing French aid. Nigeria's oil and Zaïre's copper were subject to fluctuating commodity prices. East Africa's economy was based on sisal, coffee, and cotton. Only South Africa had a significant industrial capacity.

Virtually all of the new nations suffered from what political scientists call *underdevelopment*, a term that implies distorted development rather than just a lack of development. In colonial Kenya, for example, the demand for cheap labor to work the coffee plantations led the British to discourage the production of other crops. Such patterns of dependence on a single crop, known as monoculture, left Africans poorly prepared to face the problems of feeding a burgeoning population.

While population increased at a rate of 3 percent a year in the 1960s and 1970s, food production increased at only 2 percent; by 1980, per capita production had thus declined to four-fifths of its 1960 level. This experience contrasted markedly with that of Latin America and Asia, developing areas that achieved per capita increases during the same period. Africa entered the 1980s at the point of a subsistence crisis, which, compounded by drought and civil war, brought serious and recurring episodes of famine to the Sahel region between Mauritania and Chad and to Ethiopia, the Sudan, Somalia, and Mozambique.

Declining agricultural productivity exacerbated the social and political problems that racked sub-Saharan Africa in its first generation of independence. Civil wars that reached genocidal proportions erupted in Nigeria (1967), where a short-lived secessionist state, Biafra, was crushed, and in Burundi, where an estimated 100,000 people were massacred in 1972. Both conflicts had their origins in endemic tribal rivalries that spilled over, with statehood, into a struggle for national power sharing.

Nigeria's civil war was particularly discouraging, as its constitution, worked out over a decade of intense discussion and negotiation between the leading political parties and the dominant Yoruba and Ibo tribes, was thought to be a model of enlightened colonial devolution and native compromise. Equally disillusioning was the fall of Africa's most prominent statesman, Kwame Nkru-mah. During Ghana's first decade, Nkrumah enjoyed unparalleled international stature as leader of Africa's first newly independent nation and the chief spokesman of pan-African unity. At home, however, he indulged in grandiose building projects while suppressing political opposition and moving toward one-party rule. His overthrow in 1966 by a military coup was greeted with general relief, and he died in exile in 1972.

Although several first-generation leaders, notably Kenyatta, Julius Nyerere (born 1922) in Tanzania, and Kenneth Kaunda (born 1924) in Zambia, were able to provide stability and achieve consensual if not democratic government, the typical pattern that emerged in the initial decades of African independence was of autocratic rule. The most notorious examples of this occurred in the Central African Republic, whose ruler, Jean-Bedel Bokassa (born 1921), crowned himself emperor and allegedly participated in the massacre of opponents until his removal in 1979 by a French-sponsored coup, and Idi Amin (born 1925), whose eight-year reign of terror in Uganda (1971–1979) was summed up in the chilling phrase he applied to his opponents: "I ate them before they ate me."

Such excesses, widely condemned both by the African and world community, were the exception. Politics in most African states has often been characterized by personal and factional struggles to control or influence the national government. These struggles have been moderated by private agreements and concessions, prudential concerns, and informal alliances rather than by public laws and institutions. If they bear little resemblance to Western-style parliamentary systems, they reflect traditional power-brokering arrangements that have served African societies in the past and have for the most part provided relatively stable government.

Africa also remained subject to external pressures in the form of Cold War rivalries, economic and sometimes political dependence on former colonial masters, volatile commodity prices, and the politics of aid. The desire of many of the new states to distance themselves from their colonial governors and to redress the consequences of underdevelopment was expressed in the concept of African socialism, which, as practiced in Mali, Benin, the Congo Republic, Mozambique, Somalia, and, after the deposition of Emperor Haile Selassie in 1974, Ethiopia, aimed to promote economic growth and social equality through state control. In the absence of capital resources and technical expertise, these efforts bore little fruit; they did, however, provide an ideological focus for new regimes, as well as a pretext for superpower intervention. The Soviet Union engaged in a long and largely futile effort to extend its influence in Africa through aid to avowedly socialist states, while the United States countered with support for opposition and rebel groups, sometimes of its own invention. The result was the

---

◉ Apartheid and the Oppression of Women ◉

The brutality of apartheid is particularly apparent in its effects on black family life.

Widowhood—a life of void and loneliness; a period of tension, unbalance, and strenuous adjustment. And what can it be to those thousands of African women—those adolescent girls married before they reach womanhood, thrown into a life of responsibility before they have completely passed from childhood to adulthood; those young women in the prime of early womanhood left to face life alone, burdened with the task of building a home and rearing a family; those young women doomed to nurse alone their sick babies, weep alone over their dead babies, dress and bury alone their corpses? What can it mean to those young brides whose purpose has been snatched away, overnight, leaving them bewildered and lost, leaving them with a thirst and hunger that cannot be stilled?

And yet this is the daily lot of tens of thousands of African women whose husbands are torn away from them to go and work in the cities, mines, and farms—husbands who because of the migratory labor system cannot take their wives with them and, because of the starvation wages they receive, are forced to remain in the work centers for long periods—strangers in a strange land—but equally strangers at home to their wives and children.

These women remain alone in the Reserves to build the homes, till the land, rear the stock, bring up the children. They watch alone the ravages of drought, when the scraggy cows cease to provide the milk, when the few stock drop one by one because there is no grass on the veld, and all the streams have been lapped dry by the scorching sun. They watch alone the crops in the fields wither in the scorching sun, their labor of months blighted in a few days. They witness alone the hailstorm sweep clean their mealie lands, alone they witness the wind lift bodily their huts as if they were pieces of paper, rendering them and their children homeless. Alone they bury their babies one by one and lastly their unknown lovers—their husbands, whose corpses alone are sent back to the Reserves. For the world of grinding machines has no use for men whose lungs are riddled with . . . miner's phthisis [tuberculosis of the lungs].

Source: P. Ntantala, in *The Africa Reader: Independent Africa*, ed. W. Cartey and M. Kilson (New York: Vintage Books, 1970), pp. 306–307.

---

lengthy civil wars inflicted on Angola, Mozambique, and Ethiopia, though this last case was complicated by the rebellion of the province of Eritrea. With the waning of the Cold War, settlement was reached in these wars in the early 1990s, including Eritrean independence, and the long-withheld independence of Namibia was finally achieved. However, the bloody collapses of Samuel K. Doe's regime in Liberia and Siad Barre's in Somalia in 1991 were reminders of the inherent instability of many African states and of the limited ability of the OAU to ensure civil peace.

South Africa

In no other region of Africa have the hopes and passions of a new continent been more intently focused than on South Africa. The withdrawal of its Afrikaner-dominated government from the British Commonwealth in 1961 signaled its determination to pursue its policy of apartheid ("separateness," a euphemism for racial segregation) in all walks of life and to deny the black majority any participation in political life. White supremacist rule was inaugurated with the constitution of 1910, which reserved virtually all political power for whites. Subsequently, blacks were driven into sparsely populated and drought-ridden reserves (which the government later called "homelands") and were prohibited from living in towns except when whites required their services. In all, the black population was barred from living in nine-tenths of South Africa.

By the end of World War II, white South Africans comprised nearly a fifth of the population. Most of them were Afrikaners, but there was a large British minority along with numbers of eastern Europeans, particularly Jews, who founded a substantial community in Johan-

Casualties of South Africa's
brutal attempts to maintain
apartheid: Sharpeville, 1960.
[UPI/Bettmann Newsphotos]

nesburg. More than a million Indians had also immi-grated, settling chiefly in the towns. The largest black groups were the Bantu and Khoikhoi tribes.

The Afrikaners remained politically dominant. Their conviction of racial superiority, reinforced by contact with Nazi ideology in the 1930s, was unshaken. Despite the winds of change sweeping the continent, the Afri-kaners held fast to the belief, rooted in their insular Cal-vinist faith, that God had ordained them to rule over black South Africa in perpetuity. As the Dutch Reformed church, representing a majority of Afrikaners, stated in 1950: "God divided humanity into races, languages, and nations. Differences are not only willed by God, but per-petuated by him. . . . Those who are culturally and spir-itually advanced have a mission to leadership and pro-tection of the less advanced."[3] With the triumph of the right-wing National Party in 1948, apartheid was pro-claimed the official ideology of the government. The Population Registration Act of 1950 set up systematic race classifications among whites, blacks, Asians, and "coloreds," persons of mixed European and African par-entage. Marriages across these lines were prohibited, and separate facilities and inferior living areas were al-located for blacks.

In response to this, the African National Congress (ANC) and the South African Indian Congress launched

Nelson Mandela and his wife,
Winnie, bask in popular
adulation at an ANC rally in
the black township of Soweto
shortly after his release
from prison in 1990.
[Peter Turnley/Black Star]

a civil disobedience campaign in alliance with liberal whites. The ANC was outlawed in 1961 following the Sharpeville massacre, and seven of its most prominent leaders, including Nelson Mandela (born 1918), were arrested and sentenced to life in prison. The government ruled by emergency decrees, renewed at frequent intervals, which gave virtually unchecked powers to the police and subverted the constitutional system of justice. Renewed violence broke out after an insurrection in the black township of Soweto in 1976 and was fueled again when the black activist Steve Biko died in detention in 1977. The government of P. W. Botha, seeking to divide the resistance movement, set up separate legislatures for Indians and coloreds in 1978 and cultivated collaborationist leaders in the "homelands," notably the Zulu chieftain Gatsha Buthelezi (born 1929).

By the mid-1980s apartheid was in deep crisis. As violence and repression escalated, the Botha government found itself faced with a new right-wing opposition, the Afrikaner Resistance Movement, as well as economic sanctions from the international community. In August 1989, F. W. de Klerk succeeded the ailing Botha and opened direct negotiations with the ANC. Six months later the ANC was unbanned, together with 35 other political organizations; Nelson Mandela was freed to a hero's welcome around the world; and de Klerk announced his intention to dismantle apartheid and enfranchise all South Africans. By June 1991 most apartheid laws had been repealed, but the prospects for peaceful integration were darkened by the outbreak of black factional and tribal warfare, fanned by elements within the de Klerk government. The future of South Africa—by far Africa's richest and most developed country as well as the world's principal supplier of gold and diamonds—hung in the balance.

North Africa

North Africa has traditionally been a world apart, its culture more closely linked to the Mediterranean basin and the Middle East than to sub-Saharan Africa. The coastal plain, known as the Maghreb, was colonized successively by the Phoenicians, the Romans, and the Arabs, whose influence continues to define the region. The dominant colonial presence was that of the French, whose rule replaced the loose Ottoman suzerainty in Algeria and Tunisia in the nineteenth century and who established a protectorate over Morocco in 1912.

Algeria was the pivot of France's North African empire. First occupied in 1830, it contained a settler population of 1 million, the largest anywhere on the continent except for South Africa. The French considered Algeria a metropolitan territory, and during the Third Republic the settlers, or *colons*, sent six representatives to the lower house of the National Assembly in Paris and three to the upper. The native population was regarded, in the words of one historian of French colonial policy, as "partly a menace and wholly a nuisance." The settlers seized the best land and almost entirely excluded the Muslim majority from industry and commerce. Their attitude was summed up by one of their number after the suppression of a large-scale revolt in 1871: "The Arab must accept the fate of the conquered. He must either become assimilated to our civilization or disappear. European civilization can have no sympathy for the life of savages."[4]

The Nazi defeat of France in 1940 had profound repercussions in North Africa. Germany occupied Tunisia, repatriating the exiled nationalist leader, Habib Bour-

---

AFRICA SINCE 1945

Sub-Saharan Africa	North Africa
South Africa adopts apartheid (1948)	
	Independence of Libya (1951)
	Algerian war of independence (1954–1962)
	Independence of Morocco and the Sudan (1956)
Independence of Ghana (1957)	Independence of Tunisia (1957)
Independence of Guinea (1958)	
Independence of Zaïre and Nigeria (1960)	
South Africa leaves British Commonwealth (1961)	
Organization of African Unity (1963)	
Independence of Zambia (1964)	
	Haile Selassie deposed in Ethiopia (1974)
End of white rule in Zimbabwe (1980)	
	U.S. bombs Libya (1986)
End of civil war in Angola (1991)	
South African government renounces apartheid (1991)	

guiba (born 1903), while in both Morocco and Algeria the overthrow of the Vichy regime by Anglo-American forces gave impetus to nationalist movements. De Gaulle offered concessions to the Muslim elite in Algeria, but these were rejected, and a rebellion broke out in May 1945 that, brutally repressed, left thousands dead. Belatedly, the Fourth Republic offered internal autonomy and majority rule, but this only stiffened the resistance of the *colons*. With a series of coordinated attacks, a full-scale war of independence was launched in November 1954 by a hitherto shadowy organization, the National Liberation Front (FLN). Thus began a seven-year struggle waged with the utmost ferocity on both sides. It ended in 1962 with the rebels victorious but much of the country in ruins and 2 million Algerians homeless.

The French decision to contest the rebellion despite widespread condemnation, particularly in the Arab world, was a complex one. France was smarting from its defeat in another long colonial war in Vietnam, and the very weakness of the Fourth Republic made it difficult to resist the pressure of the *colons*, strongly backed by right-wing forces in the army. Not until Charles de Gaulle was returned to power in what amounted to a coup directed from Algiers did someone wield sufficient authority to break the impasse. De Gaulle, convinced that Algeria was untenable, adroitly sidestepped his sponsors and moved to liquidate the war. He narrowly escaped assassination; France narrowly averted a civil war.

In Morocco and Tunisia the transition to independence was less traumatic, though not without violence. Tunisia gained internal autonomy in 1954 and full independence in 1957, when Bourguiba was installed as president. The Islamic monarchy of Morocco was fully restored in 1956. Both states have enjoyed relative stability since, although Morocco has experienced serious border disputes and guerrilla incursions. Algeria's first years were marked by the problems of reconstruction and by dissension within the revolutionary council. Following a period of internal consolidation and relative isolation, it reemerged as an active neutralist state under the pragmatic leadership of Houari Boumediene. After Islamic fundamentalists heavily defeated the FLN at the polls in 1991, the military staged a preemptive coup. These events presaged an era of instability in North Africa's second most populous country.

The French withdrawal from North Africa, coupled with the antagonism provoked by the creation of the state of Israel, led to the virtual disappearance of the region's flourishing Jewish community. Most of the Jews of Tunis and almost the entire Jewish population of Algeria migrated to France and Israel. The Jewish settlement in Morocco, which at 250,000 had been the largest in Africa, was reduced to a fifth of its former size. A massive Israeli airlift evacuated the Jewish population of Ethiopia, whose residence dated to biblical times, in the spring of 1991.

Much of the external support for the rebellions against French rule in the Maghreb came from Egypt, which under Gamal Abdel Nasser threw off a British protectorate and withstood an Anglo-French effort to seize the Suez Canal. Nasser also played an important role in radicalizing Libya, a former Italian colony that was administered by Britain until it was granted nominal independence in 1951. Under the feudal monarchy of King Idris, Libya remained a postcolonial Western outpost in North Africa and a reliable source of oil. In September 1969 a group of young army officers, inspired by Nasser's pan-Arabism, seized power under the leadership of Colonel Muammar al-Qaddafi (born 1942). After closing Western bases and banning the teaching of English in primary schools, Qaddafi entered a short-lived political union with Egypt and then, going his own way, used the vast oil revenues generated by the OPEC monopoly in the 1970s to fund both development schemes in Africa and terrorist movements around the world. After 1980 he became embroiled in a civil war in neighboring Chad, challenging French influence in its former colony. Friction with the West climaxed in 1986 when American planes bombed Libya in retaliation for alleged Libyan involvement in terrorist incidents; Qaddafi himself was targeted but narrowly escaped.

Egyptian pressure hastened the granting of independence to the Sudan in 1956, which opted neither to join the British Commonwealth nor, as Nasser had hoped, to unite with Egypt. The Sudan was sharply divided between the Muslim north and the Christian south. The threat of an Egyptian-backed coup, together with the increasing ineffectiveness of party government, provoked a military coup in 1958. The nation veered between democratic and military rule in the years thereafter, and a secession attempt by the south in 1974 was bloodily suppressed. The deposition of the Sudan's military strongman, Gaafar Nimeiri, in 1985 failed to produce stable government, and its difficulties were compounded by a spillover of refugees from Ethiopia's civil war as well as famines in the late 1980s.

Few other modern nations have suffered more terribly than Ethiopia. With the expulsion of the Italians by British forces in 1941, Haile Selassie was returned to power. Imperial rule did little to modernize the country; 20 years later, there was only one medical doctor for every 96,000 inhabitants, although the court and the Christian Amharic elite of the northern highlands lived in splendor and the emperor maintained a high international profile. After a period of growing chaos, characterized by student demonstrations, army mutinies, and revelations of corruption, a serious famine brought the regime to crisis. In 1974 a mixed group of moderate and radical army officers deposed Haile Selassie.

Within a short time the radicals had gained control, and under Lieutenant Colonel Mengistu Haile Mariam, Ethiopia's traditional feudal system was replaced with a repressive one-party state. The resulting disruption of food production was only partly offset by Soviet aid. Simultaneously, a rebellion broke out in Eritrea, which had been forcibly assimilated into Ethiopia after World War II, while neighboring Somalia sought to annex the province of Ogaden, largely inhabited by Somali nomads. Cuban troops shortly joined in the fighting, as in Angola. The government in Addis Ababa interdicted food relief to rebel-held areas when famine broke out in the mid-1980s, exacerbating the heavy loss of life. Mengistu was toppled in 1991 following the capture of the Eritrean capital of Asmara by the rebel Popular Liberation Front, whose arms had been scavenged largely from the Ethiopian army itself. In neighboring Somalia, meanwhile, factional fighting broke out, with heavy casualties among the civilian population and starvation among the survivors as rival chieftains fought for control.

African Perspectives and Prospects

In no other continent has change been as rapid or as traumatic as in modern Africa. Within a single generation, from 1870 to 1900, virtually the entire continent was brought under European imperial control, with shattering consequences for centuries-old native polities and traditions; with equal rapidity, the Europeans withdrew between 1945 and 1975, leaving behind a multiplicity of new states, few rooted in African history and most plagued by poverty and tribal division. It is hardly to be wondered that the first generation of African independence has been troubled and sometimes tragic; it is greatly to be admired that in the face of such a daunting challenge, so much has been achieved.

African art and music have enormously enriched the world heritage, and their influence on Western art and American jazz has been profound. In literature, too, Africans are rapidly making their mark. The novels of Chinua Achebe (born 1930) and the plays of Wole Soyinka (born 1934), both Nigerians, have reached a world audience, while the traumas of South African life have been chronicled in the novels and stories of Nadine Gordimer (born 1924) and André Brink (born 1935) and in the plays of Athol Fugard (born 1932). Three African writers have been honored as Nobel laureates in literature in recent years, including Soyinka and Gordimer.

Many problems, however, remain. The revitalization of African agriculture is a high priority as population continues its explosive growth throughout the continent. The problems of urban development must also be addressed in Africa's rapidly expanding cities, as oversimplified models of African socialism give way to a more sophisticated understanding of the importance of diversified growth, appropriate technology, and the complex interaction of town and country. Important public health problems confront most African states, most notably the AIDS epidemic, which has spread more rapidly and more devastatingly in Africa than anywhere else.

High on the agenda of social problems is the role of African women. Despite modernization, most women remain confined to traditional roles. Many of the women of sub-Saharan Africa are still subject to arranged marriages, polygamy, and, in places, sexual mutilation associated with puberty rites. Drought, starvation, forced migration, civil war, and AIDS have compounded these problems in recent years, as has the haphazard urbanization that has broken up the old communal relationships of the countryside in which men and women worked side by side. In sub-Saharan Africa a large proportion of women are involved in subsistence farming. In the cities female underemployment is particularly acute and paid jobs are the exception. Legal equality has gradually emerged, and Ghana took the unprecedented step of reserving ten seats in the national assembly for women. Women have long been active in handicraft production and trading, and when organized they have long been formidable; thousands of Ibo women organized a tax strike against colonial rule in Nigeria in 1923.

The dismantling of apartheid in South Africa, the approaches to regional cooperation in eastern and southern Africa, the end of Cold War rivalries, and the withdrawal of foreign armies from the continent are all hopeful signs for Africa's future. As the 1990s began, there were significant indications that single-party dictatorships were on the wane, particularly in Kenya and Zaïre. In November 1991 a peaceful transfer of power took place in Tanzania when the nation's founding father, Kenneth Kaunda, was defeated at the polls by a trade union leader, Frederick Chiluba (born 1943), an event that set a hopeful precedent for the entire continent.

On the debit side, the threat of civil war in South Africa, the fear of renewed famine in the Sahel, and the problems of forging genuine economic independence still remain. The obstacles to Africa's peaceful development remain high; with ingenuity, statesmanship, and goodwill, they are not insurmountable.

South America: Reform and Revolution

Throughout most of Latin America the mood at the beginning of the twentieth century was one of confidence and optimism. But as the century nears its end, the economic and political progress of the early decades of in-

41.2 Modern South America

dependence has been checked and, in some places, even reversed. Few Latin American governments, democratic or not, have found lasting solutions to the basic social and economic problems that beset the region.

Poverty and overpopulation remain endemic. Wealth and land continue to be concentrated in the hands of a privileged elite that sometimes represents as little as 2 percent of the population and has often protected its own landed and commercial interests by supporting undemocratic regimes. The deep-rooted social ills that afflict

Latin American society are revealed in huge cities such as Buenos Aires and Mexico City, where millions live in overcrowded squalor. The Catholic church has maintained its influence throughout the region. Although at a local level pastoral workers have sought to improve living conditions for the poor, the official image of the church has been compromised in places by its lack of public opposition to repressive regimes.

The main force behind the maintenance of political repression has been the military. Since the mid-

THE GROWTH OF SELECTED LATIN AMERICAN CITIES

	Population (in thousands)					
	1940	1950	1960	1970	1980	Mid-1980s
Buenos Aires (Argentina)	2,410	5,213	7,000	9,400	9,927	10,728
Mexico City (Mexico)	1,560	2,872	4,910	8,567	12,000+	17,000
Rio de Janeiro (Brazil)	1,159	3,025	4,692	5,155	5,542	5,615
Lima-Callao (Peru)	—	947	1,519	2,500	4,601	6,000
Santiago (Chile)	952	1,275	1,907	2,600	4,309	4,750
Havana (Cuba)	936	1,081	1,549	1,700	1,935	1,970
Guayaquil (Ecuador)	—	259	450	800	1,279	1,387
Guatemala City (Guatemala)	186	294	474	770	754	1,800
La Paz (Bolivia)	—	300	400	500	635	950
San Salvador (Salvador)	103	162	239	375	400	1,000
Tegucigalpa (Honduras)	86	72	159	281	485	550
Managua (Nicaragua)	63	109	197	350	608	730

nineteenth century, Latin American political life has been dominated by an endless series of crises and coups provoked by the intervention of the army in civil affairs. Once in power, military leaders have retained control by co-opting the support of the landed and business classes. With the notable exception of Juan Perón in Argentina, these so-called caudillo figures have lacked both charisma and broad-based popular support.

In economic terms, most Latin American countries are dependent on the export of raw materials and are therefore at the mercy of world prices and demand. Continuing political instability has impeded the consistent development of natural resources and industrial production for the benefit of the population at large. The problems of financial instability have been further com-pounded by the inability of countries such as Mexico and Brazil to repay the vast loans made to them by international organizations and foreign banks.

Each nation in Latin America faces its own special problems, in some cases created by its history and in others by its natural environment. Yet for the most part political life has been determined by a single basic principle: revolution, or sudden changes of authority, that merely redistribute power within the old elite. Only in a few instances has the new leadership produced significant change. In Chile a military coup overthrew a left-wing government in 1973 and installed a repressive right-wing dictatorship. In Bolivia the 192 changes of government that had taken place by 1985 only worsened its problems.

The *favelas* of Rio de Janeiro, slums where a quarter of the city's people live in squalid shanties without running water or sewers. [Bruno Barbey/ Magnum]

Since the days of the Monroe Doctrine, the United States has assumed an important and often decisive role in Latin American affairs. In its quest for territorial expansion in the 1840s, the United States seized huge tracts of Mexican territory that later became Texas and California, and in the 1890s it stripped Cuba and Puerto Rico from Spain. Thereafter, a combination of economic and security interests led Washington not only to limit the influence of European powers in Latin America but also to intervene unilaterally in the region. Yet the role played by the United States has varied greatly from one country to another. American involvement in Central American politics increased in the 1980s, and in more repressive regimes such as Chile, the United States has sometimes encouraged their leaders to mitigate the harsher effects of military rule. Direct U.S. intervention established and supported dictatorial regimes in Nicaragua, Haiti, Guatemala, and the Dominican Republic. Successive American administrations have never accepted a left-of-center regime except in Mexico or done more than tolerate centrist governments. When Argentina became embroiled with Britain in 1982 over the Falkland Islands (Islas Malvinas), Washington secretly supported its European ally while professing neutrality. In all cases, American authorities carefully monitor, influence, and often determine events throughout Latin America.

Brazil: The Unstable Giant

Brazil, which occupies almost half of the South American continent—some 3 million square miles—and has a population of more than 140 million, is a far more varied nation than its neighbors. Whereas the other countries in Central and South America speak the Spanish of their conquerors, Brazil's cultural inheritance is mixed. The official language and culture derive chiefly from Brazil's Catholic Portuguese colonizers. That heritage is supplemented by the cultures of the indigenous Indian population and the Africans whose ancestors were imported as slaves in the seventeenth and eighteenth centuries.

The waves of European immigrants who came to Brazil in the nineteenth century included a sizable number of Jews. Continuing Jewish immigration was brought to a halt in 1930 by restrictive legislation, and in 1937 a secret order was circulated to all Brazilian consulates to reject visa applications submitted by Jews. In spite of official discrimination, however, small numbers of skilled workers and professionals escaped to Brazil from Nazi Germany. After World War II the Jewish population rose gradually to about 150,000, concentrating in the larger cities.

In Brazil during the 1930s and 1940s the rule of Getúlio Vargas introduced a period of relative economic and political stability. When Vargas died in 1954, the alliance between nationalism and capitalism that he had forged and maintained for a quarter of a century collapsed. The same forces that produced conflict elsewhere in South America now pitted themselves against each other in Brazil: the working class and the peasants on the one hand, the landowning elite and the military on the other. This conflict unfolded against uncontrolled economic expansion based on foreign loans, used mostly for grandiose public works projects that resulted in profiteering and disastrous inflation.

Expensive public projects took an enormous toll in foreign exchange and political stability. The consequence was growing inflation and an increase in social tension. In 1964 a military government seized power, holding it for a generation. Successive military governments held occasional elections but refused to relinquish control. Although the country has made progress toward economic stability, the gap between the prosperous business class and the poor continues to widen. Uncontrolled development and speculation have led to the spoliation of much of Brazil's land, especially in the Amazon basin. Political repression produced the familiar pattern of rigid censorship, police brutality, and human rights abuse.

By 1975 serious strains had developed in relations between Brazil and the United States. In addition to concern over Brazil's public image as a police state, Washington was alarmed at its growing involvement with nuclear technology. When the Carter administration reduced military aid, the Brazilians retaliated by canceling their military pact with the United States.

From 1979 to 1985 Brazil's military rulers slowly moved toward the reestablishment of civilian government. After parliamentary elections in 1982, a coalition of opposition groups, the Democratic Alliance, chose as its candidate for the presidency Tancredo Neves, a trusted and popular figure. His successor, José Sarney, lacked the ability to command a consensus, and the rest of 1985 was marked by a series of paralyzing strikes. Coming on top of a disastrous drought that devastated Brazil's coffee crop, a major source of exchange, the industrial unrest forced Sarney's government into action. Prices and wages were frozen, and negotiations with the International Monetary Fund and private banks rescheduled Brazil's debts. The nation's problems continued under the corrupt administration of Fernando Collor de Mello.

Economically, Brazil's future seems unclear. A major steel industry has emerged; exports of goods such as chemicals, shoes, and automobiles are increasing; and minerals such as iron and bauxite are bringing in foreign currency. Nonetheless, the repayment of its foreign debts—the largest in the world—reached the breaking point in 1987, when Brazil suspended payments as inflation reached 365 percent per annum. The democratic government has yet to deal with the country's social inequities and has failed to implement land reform. Yet the spirit of optimism that led to the creation of Brasilia is characteristic of Brazilian popular culture and may help the country weather its current crisis.

❀

BRASILIA: THE PLANNED CITY

While Brazil faced financial collapse in the 1950s, its president, Juscelino Kubitschek, inaugurated the country's most ambitious public undertaking, a new capital city, Brasilia. The scheme, commissioned in 1957, was designed to give visible form to the government's faith in Brazil's future. The new capital was situated in the plains of the state of Goias, 600 miles inland. Within three years the master plan of Lucio Costa and the buildings of the architect Oscar Niemeyer had taken sufficient shape for the government to move there. As in Chandigarh, the Indian planned city designed by Le Corbusier, a major city was laid out from the beginning with an eye to its total physical and architectural design, as well as a concern for the day-to-day needs of its inhabitants.

The central part of the city, set on two main axes, north-south and east-west, is surrounded by an artificial lake that divides it from the suburbs. Most of the public buildings are set on the east-west—or "monumental"—axis. At its east end, in the Square of Three Powers, are the legislative, judicial, and executive buildings of government. Given the region's relative inaccessibility, it was necessary to construct a new highway system to connect Brasilia with Rio de Janeiro, the former capital and Brazil's largest city. Brasilia boasts huge water and waste disposal systems and is entirely electrified.

Additional building projects were undertaken in the following decades. The University of Brazil is the center of the city's cultural life, with its auditorium and public library. Public services such as hospitals and clinics and fire and police departments are extensive and modern. By the late 1980s the population had reached about 1.4 million. Many of the original inhabitants came from economically depressed areas of the country to work on the construction of the city, but they have now been supplemented by those employed in local industries, which include printing, furniture, and services.

Brasilia has proved both daring and controversial. The notion of moving Brazil's capital to the interior goes back to the days of Portuguese rule and had been discussed again in the 1820s. Rio de Janeiro certainly exercised a cultural and social monopoly that many Brazilians found stifling. Moreover, the new city is a prosperous one. However, the architectural plans have been criticized as an example of utopian design derived from a Bauhaus aesthetic with totalitarian overtones.

The artificial nature of the project has produced a city that is an exception to most great urban centers throughout the world, which have been almost always the result of a long period of human habitation, the products of accumulated human experience. Diplomats "exiled" to Brasilia complain of its arid climate and the shantytowns that have sprung up around it. Other countries that have followed Brazil's example, such as Nigeria with the construction of a new capital at Abuja, have met with mixed success. Yet the daring speed with which the scheme has been executed, together with the breadth of the concept, compels admiration. Certainly the creation of Brasilia has marked a commitment to urban living as the future basis of a nation that is still predominantly agrarian.

Argentina:
Dictatorship and Democracy

Ever since Argentina's first struggles to win freedom from Spain in the early nineteenth century, political stability has proved elusive. The second largest country in Latin America, after Brazil, Argentina covers an area of just over 1 million square miles and is home to 30 million inhabitants.

Unlike Ecuador, which has a large Indian population, or Colombia and Paraguay, which have mestizo (mixed Spanish and Indian) majorities, Argentinians are overwhelmingly of European origin. The waves of immigrants, mainly Spanish and Italian, who flocked to Argentina in the nineteenth century produced conflicting interest groups that have proved difficult to reconcile. The industrialists of the capital city of Buenos Aires, the ranchers who control the great coastal estates, the farmers of the interior, and radical populists all vie for political recognition and power.

Among the European immigrants were large numbers of Jews attracted to Argentina by its relatively early industrialization. The Jewish community there, almost half a million in number, remains the largest in Latin America. The country's once liberal immigration policies changed, however, in the 1930s, when anti-Semitism made itself felt in Argentina. After World War II Argentina became a haven for escaped Nazi war criminals.

From the time of its rebellion against Spain in 1810, Argentina's history has been dominated by a series of caudillo rulers, most of whom were wealthy landowners or generals devoted to power and money. Only in 1916 were democratic radicals able to defeat the landowners and industrialists in Argentina's first open election and govern the country until 1930. But the Great Depression wrought havoc with the economy and induced the army to replace the government with a conservative coalition of bankers, landowners, and generals. This combination

Juan and Eva Perón established a political system in Argentina that combined dictatorship with populist rhetoric and achieved wide appeal. [Bettmann Archive]

of interests has constituted the single most powerful force in Argentine politics ever since.

By the end of World War II the charismatic Colonel Juan Domingo Perón (1895–1974) had come to dominate the ruling clique. The archetypal caudillo, Perón's ability to mesmerize his fellow citizens owed much to the charm and brilliance of his wife Eva (1919–1952), once a popular radio announcer. By the time of her death, "Evita," who sponsored much of the regime's social reform programs despite her own opulent lifestyle, had become a popular folk heroine to her people. Her memory still remains a powerful force in Argentine politics.

With Eva's encouragement, Perón realized that his personal rule could not continue without the backing of the middle classes and the poor. Gaining control of the trade unions, he was elected president in 1946 with a large majority. Through skillful propaganda and careful attention to interest groups such as the church and the army, the Peróns retained the reluctant support of the right. At the same time, they introduced health and welfare benefits for the poor and stimulated jobs for the unemployed. These measures resulted in increased taxation, which brought a drop in agricultural production and export revenues. Financial chaos and corruption, to-

gether with the death of Eva, undermined support for Perón, who was deposed by the army in 1955.

A series of military regimes followed, alternating with brief periods of civilian rule. By 1973 Perón decided to end his exile in Spain and run for the presidency again. When the army refused to allow his candidacy, he put forward Hector Campora, a Peronist party worker, as his representative. Although Campora won, the Peronist victory led to a bloody civil struggle. In less than two months Campora was compelled to resign, Perón's opponents were forced into retirement, and new elections were called. With his new wife, Isabel, as his running mate, Perón won by a large majority.

Perón's solutions to Argentina's massive problems were contradictory and self-defeating. While courting Communist countries such as the Soviet Union and Cuba, he instituted a repressive domestic policy. Liberal government officials and teachers were dismissed, and the left-wing opposition was crushed. Perón's failures may have been the result of ill health, which prevented him from controlling the conflicting forces within his coalition.

Isabel attempted to take her husband's place after his death in 1974, but the task proved impossible. Many Argentinians resented her efforts to portray herself as Evita's successor. Occupying the highest position ever held by a woman in the Western Hemisphere, the reclusive Isabel found herself unable to control her conspiring ministers. In the 21 months that she held office, she reorganized the cabinet ten times. Nor was she able to rectify Argentina's trade deficit or maintain a policy of economic austerity. Finally, the social life of the country was paralyzed by a rash of kidnappings and assassinations carried out by terrorists of both the left and the right. In 1976 yet another military coup—the sixth in 21 years—installed an army junta.

The army restored some order to the economy, increasing agricultural and industrial production and reducing inflation. The junta raised taxes and froze wages. In the face of mounting foreign debt, however, the value of the Argentine peso fell, and the government devalued it by 70 percent. Thousands of political opponents were rounded up, tortured, and murdered. In protest, the United States suspended military aid to Argentina.

By 1982, with inflation and unemployment again increasing rapidly, the trade unions began a series of strikes, and the banned political parties called for a return to constitutional government. The regime, led by General Leopoldo Galtieri, sought to generate nationalist sentiment by challenging Britain for control of the Falkland Islands, a British crown colony. The Malvinas, as they are called in Latin America, are a group of barren, windswept islands off the southeast tip of Argentina inhabited mainly by sheepherders. In April 1982, Galtieri became an instant national hero when he ordered an invasion of the islands, but the government of British

⊛ Eva Perón on Peronism ⊛

Juan Perón's dictatorship combined populism and nationalism into a political regime that in many ways resembled European fascism. Here Eva Perón, his wife and adviser and herself an important political figure, extolls Peronism with the kind of rhetoric that made the phenomenon so popular among Argentinians.

This is why we, the *peronistas*, may never forget the people; our heart must always be with the humble, the comrades, the poor, the dispossessed, for this is how to carry out best the doctrine of General Perón; and so that the poor, the humble, the working forces, and we ourselves, do not forget, we have pledged to be missionaries of Perón; to do this is to expand his doctrine, not only within our own country, but to offer it to the world as well, as a hope of the rewards always wished for by the working classes. . . .

General Perón has defeated internal capitalism, through social economy, putting capital at the service of the economy, and not vice versa, which only gave the workers the right to die of hunger: the law of the funnel, as it is called, the wide part for the capitalists and the narrow part for the people.

Perón has suppressed imperialist action. Now we have economic independence. He knows well all the insults he will receive for committing the "crime" of defending the country. Some Argentines allied themselves with foreigners in order to slander him, because General Perón was the first to make foreign powers respect Argentina, and treat it as an equal.

Source: E. Perón, *Historia del Peronismo* (Buenos Aires: Presidencia de la Nacion, 1951), trans. in R. Cameron, *Civilization Since Waterloo* (Itasca, Ill.: Peacock, 1971), pp. 529–531.

Prime Minister Margaret Thatcher, assisted by the United States, defeated Argentina.

The military government's popularity plummeted in the wake of its military defeat. The 1983 presidential campaign was won by a political moderate, Raúl Alfonsín. Despite his efforts to prosecute Galtieri and his associates for human rights violations, pressure from the army frustrated the process. Nevertheless, Alfonsín's election helped restore international confidence in his country, and in 1986 he succeeded in negotiating loans from private banks in the United States and from the International Monetary Fund. But lasting democratic solutions to the problems facing Argentina still remain an unrealized goal.

Chile and Peru: Socialism and the Military

Peru and Chile comprise most of South America's west coast. Both contain wide variations in climate and geography and have a population that is overwhelmingly mestizo. In Peru a left-wing military regime has given way to an unstable democracy, while in Chile a demo-

cratically elected socialist leader was replaced by a right-wing military dictatorship.

Throughout the nineteenth and early twentieth centuries Chilean politics was marked by continual struggles between the Liberal party, which first came to power in 1861, and the Conservatives, who represented the army and wealthy landowners. In 1920 the middle classes joined with the workers to bring the populist Arturo Alessandri Palma to power. While his government was ousted and reestablished, left-wing political parties continued to develop. In the 1930s the Radical party replaced the Liberals, and the Socialists and Communists grew in importance. Indeed, by the end of World War II the Communists were the focus of parliamentary opposition.

From 1946 to 1964, as coalitions formed by smaller parties replaced one another, public support for the left increased as a result of a well-organized labor movement. In 1970 Salvador Allende (1908–1973), a Marxist, came to power with a left-wing coalition government. Continuing support for Allende was demonstrated by large victories for his supporters in local elections the next year.

In his three years of power, Allende sought to redress

many of Chile's social and economic inequities. Farms were distributed to peasants, who were provided with a wide range of social benefits. But Allende lacked the resources to pay for his programs, and deficit spending finally produced uncontrolled inflation.

Allende's government was isolated from abroad. His nationalization of American copper mines, together with other industries, led to the suspension of U.S. aid and trade. The United States even refused to sell food to Chile. The Soviets and the Chinese provided some help but not enough to offset a general boycott by noncommunist countries. Finally the army, with assistance from the American CIA, seized control in September 1973 and has remained in power ever since. Allende was slain during the coup. A prolonged period of military rule followed under General Augusto Pinochet. Political parties and unions were banned, and, as in Argentina, thousands of suspected opponents "disappeared." Civilian administration returned in 1989, but Pinochet remained as commander of the army.

Since the overthrow of Allende, Chile, one of South America's pioneers in democracy, has been governed by a repressive military dictatorship. Its leader, General Augusto Pinochet, proclaimed himself president. His well-documented policies of arbitrary arrests, torture, and executions led to a temporary suspension of American aid in 1979, although President Reagan restored it in 1981. Pinochet's constitution provided for his continued rule until 1997. Demonstrations of public opposition in 1985 and 1986 provoked brutal reprisals. Pinochet's presidential rule was repudiated in the elections of 1988, but he remains head of the armed forces and the effective head of the country. It is difficult to imagine a country more different from the revolutionary republic envisioned by its founders.

Like Chile, Peru was the scene of an experimental socialism, but under the unlikely direction of the army. A liberal reformist movement developed among the Peruvian educated classes in the early twentieth century. In 1924 this progressive coalition crystallized in the creation of the American Popular Revolutionary Alliance (APRA). Although anticommunist, the APRA borrowed socialist ideas from the Soviet Union and western Europe and became the focus of an Indian rights movement. Most of Peru's history from the appearance of the APRA to 1968 consisted of periods of liberal government interrupted by army coups and military regimes.

The 1968 coup was unusual. The military leaders proclaimed a policy of "social democracy," intending to follow a middle way between capitalism and communism on the basis of a mixed economy. Banks, mines—some of them U.S.-owned—and other key industries were nationalized, and many large estates were distributed to peasants. Educational programs were expanded and social benefits introduced. The regime suppressed political opposition movements and censored the press.

The international effects of these policies were pre- dictable. The Soviets sent money, weapons, and advisers, while in 1974 the Peruvian government expelled U.S. officials on charges of spying for the CIA. Peru became one of the leading advocates of Third World causes and an outspoken critic of American policies. As a result, foreign investment declined and Peru's economy began to collapse. Some industries were returned to their owners after 1975, but the damage had been done. By 1978 the regime had returned the country to civilian rule.

Both of Peru's subsequently elected presidents have been drawn from the APRA. Their problems—a declining economy, massive debt, drug trafficking, and industrial unrest—have been compounded since 1983 by bands of guerrilla fighters in the countryside of southern Peru. Calling themselves Sendero Luminoso ("shining path," a quotation from Lenin), they are a splinter group of the Peruvian Communist party. In 1984 they were joined by another revolutionary movement, the Tupac Amaru, named after an eighteenth-century Indian who revolted against the Spaniards. The former group is active in rural areas; the latter operates primarily in the cities, including Lima, the capital. Together with the terrorist activities of cocaine traders, the guerrilla groups present serious problems. In 1987 President Alan García survived mutinies and public outrage against police and army brutality, but his successor, Alberto Fujimori, suddenly suspended the constitution after his election in 1991, a move widely condemned both in Peru and abroad. Propped up only by the military, both he and his country faced an uncertain future.

Bolivia: Land of Revolutions

Although the history of Bolivia, with its succession of military coups, superficially resembles that of Argentina, fundamental social differences prevail. The overwhelming majority of Bolivia's population is either of pure Indian or of mixed European and Indian descent. In the early days of independence after 1825 no educated middle class existed to run the state bureaucracy. Wealthy landowners were interested only in protecting their own interests. The military filled the vacuum with 50 years of misrule.

By the end of the nineteenth century, political parties led by Bolivia's landed aristocracy had developed. The Liberal party exploited Bolivia's major resource, tin, and constructed road and rail networks throughout the country. The proceeds from these modernization programs further enriched the wealthy, who became known as the "tin barons," instead of improving living conditions for the poor.

By the 1930s most of Bolivia's mineral wealth had been sold to American investors, and the Great Depression devastated the economy. In 1932 conflict broke out between Bolivia and its southern neighbor, Paraguay, complicating an already difficult situation. The so-called Gran Chaco War ended in 1935 with Bolivia losing a sizable chunk of its territory.

Military governments continued into the postwar period. A brief attempt was made between 1937 and 1939 to introduce social reform for the workers, but its sponsor was murdered, and protests were brutally suppressed. Nevertheless, with great difficulty, Victor Paz Estenssoro managed to unify various urban protest groups into the National Revolutionary Movement (MNR) in 1941. A decade later the MNR won the national elections, but the army refused to allow Estenssoro to take power. Their action finally prompted a revolution that put Estenssoro in office as president.

In 1952 the new government took over the tin mines and raised workers' wages and benefits. Unfortunately, these moves coincided with a fall in tin prices on the world market, pointing up the danger of dependence on a single export. Not until 1966 did the mines return to their former profitability. Estenssoro also tried to redress the grievances of the Indians, most of whom lived in a condition of servitude that had changed little since the sixteenth century. The urban rebellion of the MNR had been accompanied by widespread uprisings and Indian land seizures in the countryside. The government recognized the claims of the Indians in 1953 and distributed land to the farmers.

The democratic government brought genuine social and economic improvement to Bolivia, but it failed to reduce the domination of the military, which seized power once more in 1964. Estenssoro returned to office in 1985 after 20 years marked by a succession of military coups. Most of the regimes were repressive and reactionary, although the pattern was briefly broken by General Juan José Torres, who seized power in 1970. Known for his left-wing sentiments, Torres relied on peasant, worker, and student support and convened a "people's parliament" to represent their views.

In 1972 he was deposed by Colonel Hugo Banzer, who remained in office for six years, a record in Bolivia's political history. Banzer attempted to introduce a coherent economic policy but also sold off the country's natural resources, including oil and natural gas, to foreign business interests. Although these measures stimulated economic growth, the rich gained most of the benefits. Another bewildering succession of coups marked the post-Banzer period. As unfavorable international reaction to drug trafficking and human rights violations grew, the United States broke diplomatic relations with Bolivia, forcing elections in 1982.

The new moderate government of Hernan Siles Zuazo appealed to foreign banks and the International Monetary Fund for help. The aid did little, however, to reduce inflation or satisfy worker demands. In the ensuing chaos, Estenssoro emerged once again, at the age of 77, as president. He promised economic and social reform, but lacking coherent political forces, or even a single charismatic figure such as Perón, Bolivia's history, already witness to nearly 200 changes of government, persistently fulfills gloomy expectations.

Central America and the Caribbean

Private American businesses, especially the United Fruit Company and sugar, coffee, and tobacco firms, had entered Central America and the Caribbean in the late nineteenth century. The United States has maintained a more direct presence in the region since the Spanish-American War. In the wake of its victory over Spain in 1898, the United States declared a protectorate over Cuba and annexed Puerto Rico.

Five years later, when Panamanian rebels revolted against Colombia, which claimed the territory of Panama, Washington supported the rebels and quickly imposed its control over the newly formed republic. Americans then built the Panama Canal on land leased from its new dependency. The strategic importance of the canal for the United States, together with extensive economic interests, have maintained the U.S. presence in the area ever since.

In September 1977, President Jimmy Carter concluded a treaty with Panama whereby the United States would withdraw its military forces from the Canal Zone and transfer control to the Panamanians by the end of the century. The subsequent administration of Ronald Reagan, however, turned against Panama's dictator, General Manuel Noriega, when he ceased to support efforts to overthrow the Sandinista government in Nicaragua. In December 1989, President George Bush ordered an invasion of Panama that resulted in the seizure of Noriega and the installation of a new government. Anti-U.S. feelings remained high in the wake of the widespread devastation caused by the attack.

The Cuban Revolution

Cuba has been one of the most prominent nations in Latin America since 1959, when the country experienced a dramatic political upheaval that has challenged America's sway over the Central American region.

Fidel Castro (born 1927), a charismatic leader and brilliant propagandist, united forces opposed to the corrupt dictator Fulgencio Batista, who had ruled the island since 1936. Yet when Castro's guerrilla campaign overthrew Batista in 1959, his goals were unclear. Although

Ernesto "Che" Guevara and Fidel Castro greet Soviet leader Anastas Mikoyan in 1961. [Sovfoto]

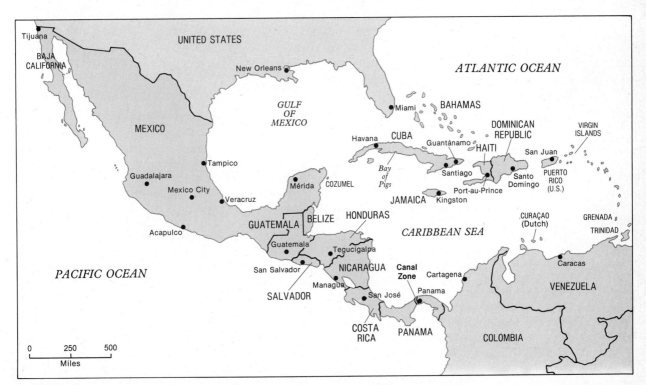

41.3 Mexico, Central America, and the Caribbean

◉ Che Guevara on Guerrilla Warfare ◉

In the course of the revolution against the Batista dictatorship in Cuba, Che Guevara found it necessary to transform Marxist doctrine and Leninist strategy to meet the conditions prevailing in the agrarian societies of Latin America. Here he explains the fundamental principles of guerrilla warfare.

The armed victory of the Cuban people over the Batista dictatorship . . . forced a change in the old dogmas concerning the conduct of the popular masses of Latin America. . . .

We consider that the Cuban Revolution contributed three fundamental lessons to the conduct of revolutionary movements in America. They are:

(1) Popular forces can win a war against the army.

(2) It is not necessary to wait until all conditions for making revolution exist; the insurrection can create them.

(3) In underdeveloped America the countryside is the basic area for armed fighting.

Of these three propositions the first two contradict the defeatist attitude of revolutionaries or pseudorevolutionaries who remain inactive and take refuge in the pretext that against a professional army nothing can be done. . . .

Naturally, it is not to be thought that all conditions for revolution are going to be created through the impulse given to them by guerrilla activity. . . . People must see clearly the futility of maintaining the fight for social goals within the framework of civil debate. . . .

The third proposition is a fundamental of strategy. It ought to be noted by those who maintain dogmatically that the struggle of the masses is centered in city movements, entirely forgetting the immense participation of the country people in the life of all the underdeveloped parts of America.

Source: C. Guevara, *Guerrilla Warfare*, trans. J. P. Moray (Lincoln: University of Nebraska Press, 1985), pp. 47–48.

he had plans to hold elections, he quickly suspended them. By 1961 he had begun introducing state economic and social controls and declared himself a Marxist-Leninist.

Castro's revolution aimed at a radical transformation of Cuba's social and economic structure. His socialist programs drove much of the middle class—some 750,000 people—from the island, and many opponents who stayed were silenced by means of firing squads or imprisonment. Collective farms replaced the estates once owned by large landowners, and the government nationalized the sugar and tobacco industries. Moreover, significant social and educational reforms have improved the lives of Cuba's citizens, and today Cuba's infant mortality and illiteracy rates are the lowest in Latin America. Castro's reforms also gave women equality before the law and open access to education and the professions.

In many ways Cuba's history embodies the dilemma created by America's dealings with its southern neighbors. Batista's rule collapsed only after the withdrawal of informal American support in 1958. Yet Castro anticipated that his radical economic and social policies might bring American intervention. He therefore turned to the Soviet Union, which he hoped would serve as a counterweight to the United States. The Soviets proved powerful and willing patrons in return for a base of operations only 90 miles from the coast of Florida.

In April 1961 the United States sponsored a badly organized invasion by Cuban exiles at the Bay of Pigs on the southern coast of Cuba. The United States, reluctant to engage Cuban forces directly, refused air cover at the last moment, and the invaders were routed. The fiasco confirmed Castro's belief that American imperialism was poised to undermine him and encouraged the Russians to exploit their foothold in Cuba. Weapons, including intercontinental missiles, were deployed on the island, only to be withdrawn in 1962 when an alarmed American government confronted the Soviet Union.

In the 1960s Castro's Cuba served as a center for revolutionary aspirations throughout Latin America. Castro's chief aide in seizing power and organizing the new state had been Ernesto ("Che") Guevara (1928–1967). Guevara now became the principal theorist of guerrilla insurgency as a technique for bringing revolution to the rest of the Americas, personally encouraging rebel forces there and elsewhere. He was killed in Bolivia in October 1967 by U.S.-trained counterinsurgency forces, setting back Castro's policy of exporting revolution.

The Cuban regime has continued to defy American trade boycotts despite the loss of the lucrative U.S. market. The stability of the Cuban economy was maintained largely by Soviet aid. In the 1980s Cuba began to involve itself in revolutions beyond Latin America, including those in Angola and Ethiopia. An apparent easing in relations with the United States in 1984 was reversed the following year, when a private American-based radio station, Radio Martí, began to transmit anti-Castro propaganda to Cuba. Castro himself has been elected president three times, and in 1986 he proclaimed a new emphasis on women, blacks, and young people and appointed his sister-in-law as the first female member of the party council.

The collapse of the Soviet Union in 1991 removed Castro's patron from the scene, and with a continuing U.S. trade boycott Cuba faced increased shortages and hardship. Nonetheless, Castro continued to affirm his brand of socialism and to resist calls for political and economic reform.

Patterns of Violence

Military dictatorships have dominated Central American politics since the turn of the century. In the 1970s elections in Guatemala, Salvador, and Nicaragua were subverted by military intervention. In Guatemala, where half the arable land is owned by 2 percent of the population, each military regime tried to outdo its predecessor in violently repressing popular discontent. The result was some of the bitterest guerrilla warfare in Latin America.

Haiti, which achieved independence from France in 1804 following a slave revolt, has been racked by violence ever since. In 1957 François Duvalier established a police state, which his family maintained for two generations by a combination of brutality and superstition. After Jean-Claude Duvalier succeeded his father, his wife exhausted the country's treasury with extravagant shopping trips to Paris while the people suffered the worst social conditions in the Caribbean. When rioting broke out in 1986, the Duvaliers fled the country, taking

millions of dollars with them. Family rule proved equally unstable in the Dominican Republic, where with American support General Rafael Trujillo maintained a harsh but efficient dictatorship from 1930 until his assassination in 1961. His son failed to retain power and, together with his family, fled the island. United States troops occupied the country between April 1965 and September 1966, thwarting the reformist candidacy of Juan Bosch and installing a rightist regime.

Salvador, a coffee-producing country in which a tiny oligarchy controls three-fifths of the land, remains torn by a civil war that has claimed thousands of civilian casualties. In 1984 a moderate president was elected and negotiations were opened between the regime and the guerrillas, but no satisfactory end to the strife appears in sight. As in Guatemala, American aid, rationalized by a fear of communism, helps finance the government's battle against the guerrillas.

The Nicaraguan Revolution

If fear of Castro's Cuba had earlier dominated American policy in Central America, the Nicaraguan revolution of 1979 set the tone for the 1980s. Like prerevolutionary Cuba, Nicaragua was ruled harshly for more than 30 years by a corrupt and stubborn dictator under Ameri-

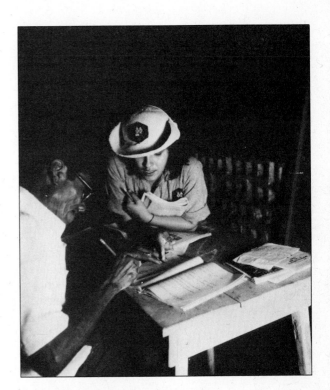

A literacy campaign in Nicaragua.
[Owen Franken/Stock, Boston]

◉ A Sandinista Woman ◉

The revolutionary movement that toppled the repressive government in Nicaragua in 1979 drew dedicated militants from all walks of life, men and women who worked in the underground against difficult odds for years. Here a Sandinista woman leader, Dora Maria, explains the nature of her revolutionary commitment.

Sometimes I wonder, I ask myself why, given the brutal repression in 1973, when the people didn't yet support us, when they informed on comrades who carried out various actions, when they pointed them out on the streets, when the repression shattered us, when thousands of people fell—why did we keep on believing? And why in 1960, in 1961, in 1963, and in 1967 did the militants keep believing that one day the people would rise up?

What makes a man believe in his own potential as a man? What makes a woman believe that she is capable of anything? No one taught us. That is one of the great mysteries about the Revolution. They don't teach it to you at school. You don't learn to believe in humanity on the streets. Religion doesn't teach it. It teaches us to believe in God, not in men and women. So it's difficult to awaken that belief in yourself and in others. But in spite of all that, many women and men did develop that commitment.

It becomes an obsession—the people must rise up, they must. It begins with a vision, an imaginary idea. . . . We had to understand that people are historically capable of making revolutions. . . . But I never understood it as historical law. I think many people didn't. . . . All we knew was that we were going to make the Revolution, however long it took.

Source: M. Randall, *Sandino's Daughters: Testimonies of Nicaraguan Women in Struggle* (Vancouver, Canada: New Star Books, 1981), pp. 53–54.

can protection. When Anastasio Somoza García was finally ousted, the new revolutionary government and the United States confronted each other with mutual suspicion.

The ruling revolutionary party, the Sandinistas (named for César Augusto Sandino, a guerrilla leader of the late 1920s and early 1930s), created a "national reconstruction government" under the presidency of Daniel Ortega. It improved public health, education, and food production through land reform. Sandinista economic policy contained a mix of capitalist and socialist elements. Nevertheless, much government spending was devoted to fighting the U.S.-sponsored *contra* rebels in a war that claimed over 30,000 lives. Much to the displeasure of Washington, the Ortega regime did not implement Western-style democracy or guarantee a free press. While America provided aid to the *contras*, Nicaragua accepted Cuban, Soviet, and Swedish assistance. Fears of intervention in the region were heightened by the American invasion of the Caribbean island of Grenada in 1983 and the installation of a pro-American government there.

At the beginning of that year, representatives of four Latin American countries—Venezuela, Colombia, Panama, and Mexico—met on the island of Contadora off the coast of Panama to develop a peace plan for Central America. The revelation late in 1986 that arms sales to Iran had secretly been used to fund *contra* forces caused a major scandal in the Reagan administration and undermined America's credibility as an opponent of international terrorism.

The war in Nicaragua ended as a result of peace initiatives from other Central American states and Mexico. In 1987 Oscar Arias Sanchez, president of Costa Rica, proposed a plan for the withdrawal of foreign troops, the disarming of the *contras*, and the restoration of democracy in Nicaragua. The Arias plan, monitored by international observers, resulted in a Sandinista agreement to hold free elections in 1990. The victors were a coalition party led by Violeta Barrios de Chamorro, widow of a newspaper editor whose murder in 1978 had sparked the Sandinista revolution. Whether Chamorro will be able to forge genuine national consensus will determine the future of Nicaragua.

Daniel Ortega, the outgoing president of Nicaragua, assists Violetta Barrios de Chamorro at her inauguration in April 1990. [AP/Wide World Photos]

Mexico in the Twentieth Century

Although 300 years of Spanish control over Mexico ended in 1821, the modern republic was not inaugurated until a century later. When Porfirio Díaz resigned the presidency and left Mexico in 1911 (see Chapter 32), the liberal opposition united peasants, workers, and intellectuals behind Francisco Madero (1873–1913), supported by bandit revolutionaries such as Pancho Villa and Emiliano Zapata. Madero assumed the presidency but was murdered in a military uprising openly encouraged by the United States' ambassador to Mexico. After a period of misrule, Madero's last successor, who had held power with American backing, was overthrown in 1920. Mexico was now a republic, with a democratic constitution based on universal male suffrage.

Although since 1920 Mexico has had a parliamentary government, in practice the chief political force, the Institutional Revolutionary Party (PRI), has dominated the country, winning every election since 1929 and providing all of Mexico's presidents. Virtually every aspect of Mexican life is under PRI control, including political patronage, education, the economy, and cultural activities. Lázaro Cárdenas, who served as president from 1934 to 1940, introduced ambitious plans for the redistribution of land, causing confrontation with the Catholic church, and expropriated foreign-owned oil properties in 1938.

Mexico's population, currently more than 75 million, has doubled since 1960. Initial attempts to improve the lives of its vast and underprivileged peasant population gave way after World War II to a drive to industrialize. The result was the creation of large modern cities and an incipient middle class. Yet there has been little change in the lot of the urban or rural poor, whose numbers continue to swell. By the late 1960s the postwar economic boom had begun to decline, and inflation mounted. Following the killing of some 300 university students during a demonstration in 1968, unrest beset the country. In the 1970s the political leadership did little to arrest the erosion of public confidence, borrowing heavily from foreign investors attracted to Mexico's huge oil reserves, the fourth largest in the world.

With the fall of oil prices in 1981, Mexico's economy collapsed. The currency was drastically devalued, and the prices of electricity and gasoline were increased. In the 1982 elections—which featured the candidacy of Rosaria Ibarra de Piedra, the first woman to run for president in the nation's history—the PRI presidential candidate, Miguel de la Madrid, won 74 percent of the votes, a small victory by Mexican standards. The challenge to PRI control was confirmed by a bitterly contested election in 1988.

Mexican society is beset by a wide range of natural and human problems. In 1985 a massive earthquake rocked the capital, Mexico City, leaving thousands dead or homeless. Even with international aid, the damage left irreparable wounds in a city already on the verge of collapse. The plight of Mexico City was, in fact, already one of the country's most serious problems. With more than 17 million people, many living in hovels, and plagued by pollution, it embodies the worst aspects of urbanization, with day-to-day difficulties in energy and public services. Like other Third World urban centers such as Calcutta, Mexico City symbolizes the crisis of city life in the late twentieth century.

Mexico's relations with the United States, always strained, deteriorated in the 1970s. Illegal immigration into America, formerly tolerated by both nations, was more tightly checked. Mexican drug trafficking, a national industry in which even the PRI was implicated, added to these tensions along with a rash of kidnappings and murders of Americans by Mexican bandits posing as policemen.

Mexico's immediate hope must be that oil prices will rise again. Moreover, in 1992 Mexico negotiated a free trade agreement with the United States that, if ratified, promises to improve its economy. The elimination of the harsher inequities that pervade Mexican society represents the major challenge Mexico faces as one of Latin America's most populous countries.

Society and Culture in Latin America

It is difficult to generalize about so vast and varied a region as Latin America, but certain broad principles have applied during the twentieth century. The first is that democratic participation in the political process has been the exception rather than the rule. Paradoxically, because most citizens have been excluded from an active role in government, they have turned to direct political action far more than North Americans or Europeans. The abuses of the secret police in Chile or Guatemala and the massive protests of the "mothers of the disappeared" (missing political prisoners) in Argentina have demonstrated how political realities affect the daily lives of Latin Americans in a direct and often violent manner.

The Catholic church has played an important, if inconsistent, role in Latin American society. Catholicism is deeply rooted in virtually every country of the region, although its external manifestations are often affected by indigenous Indian traditions and its influence varies from country to country. Hence whereas the church occupies an important position as a force for national unity in Argentina, Bolivian Catholicism represents only a thin veneer of European culture on an Indian civilization that goes back to pre-Columbian times. In Mexico the church has almost no influence in public affairs. In the 1970s Latin America saw the growth of so-called liberation theology, a philosophy of social activism that condones the use of violence to promote change in extreme circumstances. Generally developed by worker-priests closely involved in social reform in local communities, this philosophy met with a mixed reception from Catholic religious leaders, both in Latin America and in the church hierarchy. It was condemned by Pope John Paul II, most notably in his 1987 visit to Chile and Argentina.

The reactions of individual national clergy have been determined in part by local conditions. Whereas the archbishop of Salvador played an important part in negotiations there before his assassination in 1979, the confiscation of church property by Nicaragua's Sandinista regime generated official Catholic protests. Yet even though Catholic influence varies throughout Latin America, the phenomenon of secularization that has swept Europe and North America has yet to make serious inroads there.

A third characteristic common to many Latin American countries has been the vitality and persistence of their popular cultures. With the possible exception of Mexico, more directly influenced by its powerful northern neighbor, Latin America shows less cultural conformity than Europe, where American influence has produced a degree of uniformity in popular music, television entertainment, and fast food. The folk songs and dances of Brazil's Carnival, the "reggae" music of Jamaica, the traditional pottery and weaving of Peru, all are manifestations of living and thriving cultural traditions.

Latin American achievements in the arts have also maintained a sense of national character. The Argentinian novelist Jorge Luis Borges (1899–1986) captured the blend of Spanish and Indian mysticism that pervades the life of his country while constructing parables of universal significance. Pablo Neruda (1904–1973), the Chilean writer and diplomat, is probably Latin America's best-known poet and one of four of the region's writers to win the Nobel Prize for literature—the others being his compatriot Gabriela Mistral, the Guatemalan novelist Miguel Angel Asturias, and the Colombian novelist Gabriel Garcia Marquez (born 1928). If there is a feature common to the work of these writers, it is the use of fantasy and magic that provides an escape from reality: Marquez' novel *One Hundred Years of Solitude* describes life in an imaginary town in a remote region of Colombia, where extraordinary events are the order of the day.

LATIN AMERICA SINCE 1945

South America	Mexico and Central America
Perón administration in Argentina (1946–1955)	
	Beginning of police state in Haiti (1957)
	Castro overthrows Batista in Cuba (1959)
	Bay of Pigs invasion (1961)
Military rule in Brazil (1964–1979)	
Allende administration in Chile (1970–1973)	
Military rule in Argentina (1976–1983)	Panama Canal Treaty (1977)
	Sandinista rule in Nicaragua (1979–1990)
Falklands War (1982)	
	Mexico City earthquake (1985)
	Haitian revolution (1986)
	U.S. invasion of Panama (1989)
	Violeta Chamorro elected president of Nicaragua (1990)

Mexico has produced a number of major painters, including Diego Rivera (1886–1957), whose communist sympathies influenced much of his work. Rivera's murals in Rockefeller Center, New York City, were removed after fierce controversy. Among his associates was José Clemente Orozco (1883–1949), famous for the bold realism of his frescoes. By contrast, Rufino Tamayo (1899–1991) created a more cosmopolitan style that invokes a magical world comparable in painting to that of Borges' and Marquez' novels. On the whole, realistic depictions of the lives of workers and peasants have dominated Latin American painting, as in the moving frescoes of Rivera and the Brazilian Cândido Portinari (1903–1962), whose work can be seen at the United Nations building in New York.

Latin American composers have frequently been inspired by the folk music of their homelands. The Brazilian musician Heitor Villa-Lobos (1887–1959) wrote a series of works titled *Bachianas Brasileiras*, in which he treated Brazilian folk motifs in a style reminiscent of Johann Sebastian Bach. Among the works of the Mexican Carlos Chávez (1899–1978), who founded the Mexican Symphony Orchestra, is the *Sinfonia India*, which uses folk motifs to evoke the country's Amerindian past. The generally underdeveloped state of musical conservatories in Latin America has forced most performing artists, including the famous Chilean pianist Claudio Arrau (1904–1991), to study abroad. Yet many capital cities in the region have a thriving operatic tradition that goes back to the nineteenth century. The most famous and most beautiful opera house in South America is the Teatro Colón in Buenos Aires, where performances meet international standards.

The best film production unit in Latin America is the Cuban Film Institute, where young directors and performers are encouraged to develop their skills at government expense. Elsewhere, filmmakers have used their works to document their country's history. The Argentinian film *The Official Story*, which describes events in Argentina after the fall of the military dictatorship in 1983, won an Academy Award as the best foreign film of 1985.

The thriving arts and popular culture of Latin America represent both a reminder of and an escape from the grim realities of everyday life. Unlike much of the rest of the world, the twentieth century has seen little change in age-old social patterns in the region anywhere but in Cuba and Nicaragua. Apart from Mexico, and to a lesser extent Argentina and Brazil, the population remains split into the wealthy few and the many poor, with little sign of a developing middle class. For example, in Brazil, Colombia, and Peru half or more of the households live in absolute poverty, defined as the inability to purchase the barest necessities for subsistence. Yet Latin America has the fastest-growing population in the world, increasing about 3 percent each year. In these same countries approximately one out of five adults is illiterate, and infant mortality remains high. Despite huge potential resources, most of the region is still predominantly agricultural. Industrial production is unequally distributed: as late as 1970 three nations—Argentina, Brazil, and Mexico—accounted for 80 percent of all industrial production in Latin America, and a third of that was confined to the cities of Buenos Aires, São Paulo, and Mexico City.

Women and the Culture of *Machismo*

Women in Central and South American society have only recently begun to regain the position they held in most communities before the Spanish conquest. Among the Aztecs, for example, women came close to legal equality with men. They could possess property, enter into contracts, testify before tribunals, seek divorce, and remarry freely. At the age of 50 they were accorded full equality and enjoyed equal status with men as elders.

Under the colonial regime, women lost most of their rights. The law presumed them to be mentally inferior, and the style of male bravado and presumption known as *machismo* that produced such laws became deeply ingrained in the culture. Yet in colonial times women were allowed to own property and to sign for mortgages in their own names. Independence brought little but lip service to the idea of greater equality for Latin American women. Not until the Mexican revolution in the early twentieth century was legal equality recognized. Argentina, Uruguay, and Chile followed suit in the 1920s and 1930s. Yet women in Argentina did not get the vote until 1947 and in Mexico only in 1953; with the passage of a female suffrage law in Paraguay in 1961, all women in the Americas had won the right to vote.

Despite progress, the goal of full equality remains elusive. Men are still recognized as head of the household in many Latin-American countries, with the legal right to choose the place of domicile, direct the education of children, administer their property, and retain custody in case of divorce. *Machismo* enforces a double standard of sexual morality, with men permitted and even encouraged to form extramarital liaisons as proof of their virility. The result is a very high incidence of rape and illegitimacy, particularly marked in Brazil.

As elsewhere, the position of women is greatly affected by the variables of class, status, and income, by residence in town or country, and by skin color. The women of the elite are in many respects indistinguishable from their counterparts in the industrial West; for those trapped in rural poverty or urban squalor, the still-halting steps toward equality have had little effect. Eva and Isabel Perón notwithstanding, until recent years few women have played a visible part in public life. Beginning in the 1970s, however, more and more women have held appointed or elected positions in government. In Venezuela and Mexico women have served in presidential cabinets, and one woman became governor of the Mexican state of Colima.

Differences in education and training have generally relegated women to lower-paying jobs in the work force, and men usually displace women as a result of technological and unemployment cycles. Thus although women have been part of agricultural labor in Latin America for centuries, mechanization has made it difficult for them to obtain work in that sector. Similarly, ever-larger numbers of Latin American women have moved into factory work, but they are generally paid less than men and hold less skilled jobs. Nevertheless, some exceptions hold out the promise of future change. In Brazil, for example, where the proportion of economically active women is lower than that of men, more women actually hold professional positions. Moreover, the number of working women doubled in the decade after 1970.

Experience has shown that when organized, women can exert a powerful force for change, as in the case of the Argentinian mothers of the disappeared. More revealing still, it has been estimated that women comprised as much as a third of the Sandinista People's Army in Nicaragua. In Cuba legislation passed in 1976 actually provided a legal basis for the sharing of housework and child care. Despite such transformation, however, the pattern of custom and prejudice dies slowly, and *machismo* continues to exert a powerful influence on male attitudes toward women.

ᛥ   ᛥ   ᛥ

Chief among the myriad of problems facing the global community as the second half of the twentieth century draws to a close is the need to secure economic, social, and political well-being for the bulk of the world's inhabitants—an issue symbolized by the status of Africa and Latin America.

Both regions have undergone significant political change since the end of World War II as their peoples struggled against colonialism and continue to work to free themselves from dependence on the more advanced industrialized states. Yet the political systems under which many African and Latin American nations operate have been fraught with instability and a marked tendency toward authoritarianism. In part this political experience has been the result of the massive problems of development that each faces. The economic potential of the regions is vast, but immediate financial resources are limited. In most cases the small, privileged elites that control much of the wealth of these countries have neither directed resources toward the people nor been willing to extend democracy to them. In many areas racial and ethnic tensions contribute to political and social instability. Inefficiency, corruption, and the lack of appropriate technological capacity have combined to retard development, and despite productive agricultural soils, many states cannot feed their rapidly growing populations. Africa and Latin America are burdened with the fastest-growing populations in the world, high illiteracy, daunting health problems, and widespread poverty. Only far-reaching changes in the social and political structures of these regions can, in the long run, resolve such dilemmas.

Though these and other challenges appear at times insurmountable, the future holds substantial promise. Africa and Latin America possess not only extensive natural resources and rich cultural heritages but also populations that have repeatedly proved their creativity and resilience.

Notes

1. G. M. Carter and P. O'Meara, eds., *African Independence: The First Twenty-five Years* (Bloomington: Indiana University Press, 1985), p. 4.
2. J. D. Hargreaves, *Decolonization in Africa* (New York: Longman, 1988), p. 203.
3. J. Hayward, *South Africa Since 1948* (New York: Bookwright Press, 1989), p. 14.
4. Robin Hallett, *Africa Since 1875: A Modern History* (Ann Arbor: University of Michigan Press, 1974), p. 197.

Suggestions for Further Reading

Africa

Amin, S. *Neo-colonialism in West Africa.* New York: Monthly Review Press, 1973.

Benson, M. *Nelson Mandela.* Harmondsworth, England: Penguin Books, 1986.

Bretton, H. *The Rise and Fall of Kwame Nkrumah: A Study of Personal Rule in Africa.* New York: Praeger, 1966.

Carter, G. M., and O'Meara, P., eds. *African Independence: The First Twenty-five Years.* Bloomington: Indiana University Press, 1985.

Davenport, T. *South Africa: A Modern History.* Johannesburg: Macmillan, 1987.

Decalo, S. *Coups and Army Rule in Africa.* New Haven, Conn.: Yale University Press, 1976.

Gifford, P., and Louis, W. R., eds. *The Transfer of Power in Africa: Decolonization, 1940–1960.* New Haven, Conn.: Yale University Press, 1982.

Gordon, D. F. *Decolonization and the State in Kenya.* Boulder, Colo.: Westview Press, 1986.

Hargreaves, J. D. *Decolonization in Africa.* New York: Longman, 1988.

Horne, A. *A Savage War of Peace: Algeria, 1954–1962.* Harmondsworth, England: Penguin Books, 1985.

Jackson, R. H., and Rosberg, C. G. *Personal Rule in Black Africa.* Berkeley: University of California Press, 1982.

Leys, C. *Underdevelopment in Kenya: The Political Economy of Neo-colonialism.* Berkeley: University of California Press, 1974.

Meredith, M. *The First Dance of Freedom: Black Africa in the Postwar Era.* London: Abacus, 1984.

Murray-Brown, J. *Kenyatta.* New York: Dutton, 1973.

Ottaway, M., and Ottaway, D. *Ethiopia: Empire in Revolution.* New York: Africana Publications, 1978.

Price, R. M. *The Apartheid State in Crisis: Political Transformation in South Africa, 1975–1990.* New York: Oxford University Press, 1991.

Verrier, A. *The Road to Zimbabwe.* London: Cape, 1986.

Welch, C. E. *Dream of Unity: Pan-Africanism and Political Unification in West Africa.* Ithaca, N.Y.: Cornell University Press, 1966.

Young, C. *Ideology and Development in Africa.* New Haven, Conn.: Yale University Press, 1982.

———. *Politics in the Congo: Decolonization and Independence.* Princeton, N.J.: Princeton University Press, 1965.

Latin America

Bergmann, E., et al. *Women, Culture, and Politics in Latin America.* Berkeley: University of California Press, 1990.

Blasier, C. *The Hovering Giant: U.S. Responses to Revolutionary Change in Latin America.* Pittsburgh: University of Pittsburgh Press, 1985.

Booth, J. A. *The End of the Beginning: The Nicaraguan Revolution,* 2nd ed. Boulder, Colo.: Westview Press, 1985.

Burns, E. B. *A History of Brazil.* New York: Columbia University Press, 1971.

———. *Latin America: A Concise Interpretive History,* 4th ed. Englewood Cliffs, N.J.: Prentice Hall, 1986.

Calvert, P., and Calvert, S. *Latin America in the Twentieth Century.* New York: St. Martin's Press, 1990.

Keen, B., and Wasserman, M. *A Short History of Latin America,* 2nd ed. Boston: Houghton Mifflin, 1984.

Meyer, M. C., and Sherman, W. L. *The Course of Mexican History.* New York: Oxford University Press, 1979.

Randall, M. *Sandino's Daughters: Testimonies of Nicaraguan Women in Struggle.* Vancouver, Canada: New Star Books, 1981.

Stepan, A., ed. *Authoritarian Brazil: Origins, Politics, and Future.* New Haven, Conn.: Yale University Press, 1976.

Thomas, H. *The Cuban Revolution.* New York: Harper & Row, 1977.

The Contemporary Age

World War II shifted the balance of power from western European states such as Britain, France, and Germany to the United States and the Soviet Union. For the first 20 years of the postwar era, the two superpowers were locked in a Cold War struggle for global hegemony that threatened to end only in nuclear catastrophe. Yet far-reaching changes in both societies, along with the recognition of the larger common danger, brought the superpowers into a new, more optimistic age of understanding and cooperation.

The economic reconstruction of Europe restored political stability in the West and created a mass consumer society characterized by unprecedented prosperity and social justice. In the East, almost half a century of repression ended in the late 1980s as the Soviet Union underwent a profound domestic transformation under the leadership of Mikhail Gorbachev and the peoples of east-

Leading Polish workers in Solidarity, a union movement of great political importance, Lech Walesa speaks to a crowd of strikers outside the Lenin shipyard in Gdansk in 1988. [Reuters/UPI/Bettmann Newsphotos]

ern Europe overthrew their own Communist regimes. In 1991 Communist control there collapsed, followed by the dissolution of the Soviet Union itself.

The Soviet Union and Eastern Europe

In the postwar period Stalin's immediate concerns were to establish a Soviet presence in eastern Europe and to undertake the domestic reconstruction of the Soviet Union. These goals were linked, for he regarded eastern Europe as a region whose economic resources could be used to rebuild Soviet strength.

Postwar Reconstruction in the Soviet Union

The Soviet Union faced an enormous task of reconstruction in the wake of a war that had destroyed much of its industry, many of its cities, and 30 percent of its national wealth. Not satisfied to restore conditions to the 1941 level, Stalin was determined to build an industrial base worthy of the USSR's new role as a world power. The Cold War increased the burden by adding massive expenditures for arms.

Stalin forced the USSR to return to the policies of the 1930s—extracting surplus capital for the development of heavy industry from the work of Soviet men and women. Although the exploitation of eastern Europe aided the work of reconstruction, most Soviets had to sacrifice their living standards again. Between 1946 and 1950 another five-year plan poured more resources into capital investment than had been spent during the 13 years after 1928, yet the economy produced only a minimum of consumer goods and began to stagnate by 1950. Housing remained so scarce that couples had to postpone marriage for years or live with in-laws in a single room.

Stalin's policies had a grimmer side. To meet the demand for workers, he deported huge numbers of people to labor camps, or gulags, across Siberia and central Asia, where thousands died from inadequate food, primitive conditions, and exhaustion. The inhuman conditions of life in the labor camps were brought to the attention of the Western world through the writings of Alexander Solzhenitsyn (born 1918), especially in his monumental work *Gulag Archipelago*. Harsh censorship policies and the repression of intellectuals remained a hallmark of Stalinist rule.

But Stalin's policies produced dramatic economic results. Tremendous increases were achieved in the pro-

duction of iron, coal, steel, oil, chemicals, and electrical power, and science and technology moved ahead at an impressive rate. The USSR exploded an atomic bomb in 1949, tested a hydrogen bomb in 1953, and built high-quality fighter planes that proved themselves against American models during the Korean War (1950–1953). Most impressive, in 1957 the Soviet Union shocked the West by launching *Sputnik*, the world's first artificial satellite.

World War II had relaxed social controls, but during Stalin's final years he reimposed ideological conformity. Secret police chief Lavrenti Beria began massive roundups of "enemies of the state" and transported them to the labor camps. There is also evidence that Stalin was planning another major purge, this time of Jews. He had already accused Soviet Jews of harboring pro-Western and antisocialist views, and in January 1953 he ordered the arrest of nine Jewish physicians on charges that they had attempted to shorten the lives of Soviet officials. Before the alleged "doctors' plot" could unfold, however, a stroke took Stalin's life on March 5. His successors released the physicians and buried Stalin beside Lenin in the Kremlin's mausoleum.

From National Fronts to People's Democracies

The full extent of Stalin's plans for eastern Europe became apparent soon after the war. Unlike the Allies at the end of World War I, Stalin did not attempt to adjust frontiers along ethnic or national lines. Instead, he forcibly relocated entire populations to fit his notions of Soviet security. This entailed the removal of 13 million ethnic Germans, including families that had resided in the Czech Sudetenland, Silesia, and areas east of the Oder and Neisse rivers for centuries. He also moved about 4.5 million Poles westward, replacing them with Russians and Ukrainians, and about 600,000 Balts from their homelands in Estonia, Latvia, and Lithuania, sending half to East Germany and half deep into Russia.

Because most eastern European states had provided troops for Hitler's legions, Stalin forced those countries to pay reparations. The Soviet Union aligned the entire region with its economic system, chiefly as a source of raw materials that satellite states were compelled to sell to the USSR at low prices.

The Soviet Union constructed new governments in states occupied by the Red Army, setting up "national front" coalitions of Communist, Social Democratic, and peasant parties. Each coalition enjoyed a degree of autonomy that varied from country to country. Where Stalin feared a serious threat to Soviet security, as in Poland and Romania, the national fronts were a sham. Bulgaria fared better, since after the arrival of Russian troops in 1944, the Bulgarian army had joined in the war against

Germany. Thus Stalin demanded no reparations from Bulgaria. However, when non-Communist members of the Bulgarian government sought assistance from the Western allies after the war, Stalin manipulated the regime to suit his aims. By contrast, between 1945 and 1947 the national front governments of Hungary and Czechoslovakia were true coalitions in which parties possessed a wide degree of freedom.

The national front regimes lasted less than three years, but they brought about fundamental changes. The Communists joined their coalition partners in breaking up the large, quasi-feudal estates that had characterized eastern European agriculture for centuries, distributing land to millions of peasant families. In addition, between 1945 and 1947 these governments nationalized the coal, steel, banking, and insurance industries.

In the late summer of 1947, Communist parties throughout the region began a concerted attack on their main rivals for popular support, the agrarian parties. Within six months all the national front regimes vanished. In their places appeared one-party Communist governments called "people's democracies." Two pressures probably led to the Soviet crackdown: the desire to use the area's wealth to support reconstruction at home and the decision to impose more direct control on the eastern European states in the face of the Marshall Plan.

The people's democracies geared their economic programs to meet Russia's needs. Governments forced the collectivization of small farms, thus releasing significant numbers of peasants for work in factories under a series of five-year plans. The Soviets intensified their policy of sending high-priced exports to the region while paying low prices for imports. In essence, eastern Europe, an area containing some 90 million people, became an adjunct to the Soviet system. This policy postponed eastern European recovery, leaving the region bleak for many years.

The Yugoslav Model

Direct Soviet hegemony stopped at Yugoslavia, which proved to be an important exception to Russian dominance in eastern Europe. Under the leadership of the Communist leader Marshal Tito (Josip Broz, 1892–1980), the Yugoslav resistance had liberated the country from the Nazis without significant aid from the Red Army. In the postwar period Tito rejected Stalin's claim to preeminence in the Communist world, engaging in a bitter confrontation with Stalin over national sovereignty and Communist strategy.

Tito had aided leftist rebels in Greece against Stalin's orders. When Tito urged Communist leaders in the region to follow his example and ignore Russia's strategic needs, Stalin vowed to discredit him and bring Yugo-

slavia into the Soviet orbit. In September 1947, Stalin located the headquarters of the newly created Cominform in Belgrade, the Yugoslav capital, hoping to use it to spy on Tito and undermine his support. When this tactic failed, Stalin responded in 1948 and 1949 by expelling Yugoslavia from the Cominform, placing an embargo on its economy, and isolating the country from its neighbors.

Within months the resourceful Tito applied for and received American economic assistance, simultaneously abandoning his support for world revolution while proclaiming the need for separate paths to socialism. In 1950 he initiated a policy of political decentralization by transferring authority from Belgrade to workers' councils and communes. These reforms gave workers a larger voice in the management of factories than anywhere else in the world. Tito had not only maneuvered Yugoslavia into a position of nonalignment between the Soviet Union and the West but had also made his country the major world model of independent Marxism.

De-Stalinization and the Rise of Khrushchev

Stalin groomed no successor. In the power struggle that erupted after his death, his closest followers lost out. Beria, dismissed from his posts and expelled from the party, was executed. A collective leadership soon emerged that abolished the office of general secretary of the Communist party, Stalin's base of power for 30 years, and established party secretaries in its place. At the top of this group was Nikita Khrushchev (1894–1971), a miner's son who as party boss had governed the Ukraine from 1939 to 1950. By 1955 he was joined by Nikolai Bulganin and Vyacheslav Molotov, Stalin's longtime foreign minister, to form a three-man troika.

Khrushchev came to personify post-Stalinist Russia. Though he would never wield the arbitrary power that Stalin had, he stood out from his rivals. Illiterate until his twenties, his bald, rotund appearance and outgoing personality belied a keen intelligence. Khrushchev solidified his position in a speech before the Twentieth Congress of the Communist party in 1956 that ranks among the most influential in Soviet history. This speech detailed Stalin's atrocities and attacked him for promoting a cult of personality. Later Khrushchev changed the name of Stalingrad to Volgograd and removed Stalin's body from the Red Square mausoleum. Official statues and portraits of Stalin also vanished.

As details of Khrushchev's speech became public, he began to take controversial action, dissolving the Cominform and meeting personally with Marshal Tito in a bid to improve relations with Yugoslavia. Stalinists on the Politburo attempted to depose Khrushchev, but the Red Army prevented the coup. In 1958 he assumed the

Nikita Khrushchev, who emerged as the leader of the Soviet Union after Stalin's death, initiated a new stage in domestic development and confrontation with the West. [Sergio Larrain/Magnum]

office of premier, thus combining, as Stalin had done, the top party and state offices in his hands. The miner's son had become the leader of the Soviet Union.

Khrushchev introduced a wide range of reforms. Downplaying Stalin's emphasis on the development of heavy industry, he increased the supply of consumer goods and housing and stimulated agricultural production with modern technology. The new policies improved the Soviet standard of living, although shortages of appliances, clothing, and food continued. The judicial system replaced police terror for all but political crimes, and intellectuals had more freedom than ever before. The party bureaucracy, however, still represented a privileged elite.

Dissent and Diversity

Ten days after Khrushchev's meeting with Tito in June 1956, anti-Soviet riots broke out in Poznan, Poland. Sta-

linists were quick to blame them on the liberalized policy toward eastern Europe. Actually, the first serious disorders with the people's democracies had erupted in Czechoslovakia and East Berlin shortly after Stalin's death in 1953. Khrushchev's de-Stalinization program stimulated the discontent that already existed. His speech to the Twentieth Party Congress had undermined the legitimacy of the Stalinists in Poland by reporting that Russian agents had replaced Polish Communist leaders in 1948 with Soviet puppets. Thus in July 1956, when workers in Poznan began publicly demanding "bread and liberty," Polish police and military authorities refused to fire on them. Left with the option of calling in Russian troops or yielding to popular demands, the Polish government promised reforms. Wladyslaw Gomulka (1905–1982), a leader who had lost favor in 1947 for seeking a Polish way to socialism, convinced the Soviet Union to permit his return to power. Gomulka accepted spontaneously formed workers' councils in the factories and began making overtures to the peasants and to the Catholic church while remaining closely linked to Soviet foreign policy.

The October 1956 Hungarian revolution challenged the USSR more directly. When Hungarian police fired on protesters in Budapest, sparking anti-Soviet demonstrations, the government called in Soviet soldiers. Throughout the country, workers' councils formed, demanding free elections, the end of the security police, and the withdrawal of Soviet troops. On October 28, when Imre Nagy (1896–1958) became premier and the Soviets began to withdraw, it appeared that the Hungarians had won. Nagy announced the reestablishment of a multiparty system and a return to the national front coalition of Communists, Social Democrats, and peasant leaders and proclaimed Hungarian neutrality between East and West. Convinced that a failure to respond would provoke further revolts throughout the Soviet bloc, Khrushchev ordered an invasion. Some 2,500 Russian tanks moved into Hungary, shelling Budapest and other cities. When the repression was over, thousands of Hungarians were dead and more than 200,000 refugees had fled. Though some westerners had urged or expected American intervention, none came.

The new Soviet-installed Hungarian premier, János Kádár (1912–1989), cautiously led the nation to a more liberal form of communism over the next three decades. Imprisoned for nationalist activity earlier in his life, Kádár understood his country's desire for reform and independence. By the early 1960s he had removed Stalinists from the Hungarian Communist party and introduced programs that improved the standard of living. Although Kádár's role in the 1956 uprising undermined his leadership in the eyes of many, he remained in power until 1988.

By the early 1960s the countries of the eastern bloc had developed three different socialist systems: on the right stood the Yugoslavs, usually labeled "revisionists" because of their economic and political innovations; a number of "national Communists," such as Gomulka, straddled the middle ground, stressing solidarity with the Soviet Union in foreign policy but demanding domestic freedom to achieve communism; and the "dogmatists," including the followers of Mao Tse-tung in China and the Albanian Stalinists, vehemently opposed revisionism and resisted liberalizing tendencies. Beyond Europe the most significant example of diversity was the split between China and the Soviet Union (see Chapter 39). By the 1970s the Soviet Union remained the acknowledged leader of the Communist world, but its role was limited. The ideological unity of international communism was being eroded by diversity, internecine rivalry, and accommodation with the West.

Western Europe and North America

America's most immediate concern was Europe, to which it exported vast amounts of capital to stimulate economic reconstruction. The Marshall Plan also made possible an economic boom in the United States, for massive military outlays, together with the billions of dollars of aid sent abroad, stimulated the domestic economy. Although partly motivated by humanitarian concerns, that policy also reflected Cold War strategy: American policymakers believed that prosperity would diminish the appeal of communism and provide a basis for stable democratic governments.

The Political Revival of Europe

Much of western Europe's prewar leadership had been discredited by the policy of appeasement or collaboration with Hitler. In the former Axis countries the purges of fascist sympathizers opened bureaucratic positions to former resistance fighters. In Allied nations the disastrous economic conditions that followed the war forced some conservatives, even wartime leaders, out of office. No less a hero than Winston Churchill was defeated at the polls, by the Labourite Clement Attlee (1883–1967), in the 1945 British elections because of his opposition to the extension of public assistance measures.

In France and Italy resistance leaders filled the power vacuum. General Charles de Gaulle, head of the exiled Free French movement, symbolized French efforts to erase the memory of Vichy collaboration with the Nazis, and in 1951 his followers emerged as the nation's largest

President Charles de Gaulle of France and Chancellor Konrad Adenauer of West Germany symbolized the emergence of a western European community based on cooperation and autonomy. [Gamma-Liaison]

political party. In Italy the liberal Ferruccio Parri (1890–1981) and the Christian Democrat Alcide De Gasperi (1881–1954), both former anti-Fascists, succeeded each other as prime minister. Because the Communists had been so prominent in the resistance movements, their support expanded enormously after the war. The Italian Communist party grew to some 2 million members by 1947, the largest in western Europe. In France the Communists were the strongest French party in 1945, and their vote rarely fell below the 25 percent level until 1958.

Despite the Marxist resurgence, western Europe did not face the prospect of social revolution, as it had in 1918 and 1919. The British Labourites and the West German Social Democrats were reformist rather than revolutionary parties. Probably at Stalin's orders, Communist resistance units stacked their arms and until 1947 participated in reformist governments. Moreover, American economic assistance encouraged the development of new center and moderate right parties, of which the progressive Catholic parties, most often called Christian Democrats, were the most significant.

Like the Communists, many of the new Christian Democratic leaders had been in the resistance, but they supported both democratic principles and capitalism. As parties based on Catholic religious loyalties rather than social class, the Christian Democrats appealed to a wide range of voters. The partition of Germany, which placed many Protestant areas under Soviet control, gave the Christian Democrats an unexpected advantage in West Germany, where Catholics predominated.

The potential for rebuilding lay in the destruction of the war, for it cleared away antiquated factories and out-dated technologies. Moreover, refugees willingly offered inexpensive labor, and a rise in the birthrate provided larger internal markets. The Marshall Plan contributed significantly to the reconstruction. The major condition for participation in the program was a willingness to join the Organization for European Economic Cooperation, which encouraged planning and free trade. The Marshall Plan stimulated Europe's economy to such a degree that by the mid-1960s production was almost triple the prewar level, and some western European nations surpassed the United States in per capita standard of living.

Politically, the Marshall Plan weakened the extreme left and strengthened the Christian Democratic parties. When the USSR refused to allow eastern European participation in the plan, Communists in western Europe resigned from governing coalitions or were voted out of office. In the Federal Republic of Germany the Christian Democrats governed from 1949 to 1969, when the Social Democrats under Willy Brandt (born 1913) came to power in coalition with a minority party, the Free Democrats. The Social Democrats, who pumped considerable resources into social programs and education, ran the Bonn government until the early 1980s, when the Christian Democrats under Helmut Kohl (born 1930) returned to office. In Italy, despite frequent changes of government, the Christian Democrats maintained de facto control from 1948 to 1982. The following year the Socialist Bettino Craxi (born 1934) became prime minister, but his policies proved little different from those of his predecessors. Similarly, centrist coalitions dominated France's Fourth Republic until its collapse in 1958 and de Gaulle's return to power. Thereafter, de Gaulle established a more centralized but equally anti-Communist Fifth Republic.

Between 1945 and 1951 Britain's Labourite prime minister, Clement Attlee, introduced the most far-reaching reforms of the period. Attlee nationalized utilities, railroads, airlines, coal mines, the Bank of England, and the iron and steel industries. His Social Welfare Acts covered public housing, free medical care, and national insurance benefits. The Conservatives came back into power in 1951 and since then have alternated with the Labourites in heading the government. Although Conservative governments have not dismantled the British welfare state, from 1979 to 1991 Margaret Thatcher (born 1925)—the United Kingdom's first woman prime minister and the twentieth century's longest-serving one—favored private enterprise and imposed austere fiscal policies on the country. The result was a reduction

Margaret Thatcher, longtime Conservative prime minister of Great Britain, presided over the retrenchment of domestic welfare policies and a tough foreign policy.
[Derek Hudson/Sygma]

of inflation, but at the price of the highest unemployment since the Great Depression and the increasing polarization of society.

Women and Social Change in Western Europe and the Communist Bloc

Though most western European governments avoided full-scale nationalization of industry, they did provide expanded welfare services. Low-cost medical care, family allowances, and unemployment compensation programs all became the rule.

Rapid modernization has marked European society since the end of World War II. Traditional class barriers relaxed, and a salaried managerial elite developed with the growth of public corporations and new technological industries. Social distinctions have also been blurred by a higher standard of living for many and the availability of mass-produced consumer goods. National television networks joined radio and film—which were already widely developed in the 1920s and 1930s—in reaching rural villages. Free higher education virtually eliminated illiteracy. The new prosperity, along with less expensive automobiles and vigorous highway construction, has made for a highly mobile society.

All European states except Liechtenstein and Switzerland gave women the vote after the war, but in other ways the status of women varied greatly from one country to another. The Scandinavian and northern European nations generally adopted legal equality for women more readily than those in the south, but everywhere traditional values have given way to greater opportunity. In 1949 the prominent French intellectual Simone de Beauvoir (1908–1986) published her highly influential book *The Second Sex*, which demonstrated how women had been subordinated by tradition, social custom, and ideology. De Beauvoir's work provided an early theoretical basis for the women's liberation movements that developed in Britain, France, Germany, Italy, and Scandinavia in the 1960s. The revival of Socialist and Communist parties after the war gave practical reinforcement to the new feminist theory, for they combined a long tradition of female militancy with progressive social policies. Hence the representation of women is higher in Socialist and Communist parties than in bourgeois ones. Feminist coalitions and left-wing parties successfully fought for legalized abortion and more liberal divorce laws, even in some Catholic societies.

Women have made up a large percentage of the European work force since the Industrial Revolution. After 1945 they have had access to better jobs along with the growing availability of free higher education. About one out of every three workers is now female, and women have also established a strong presence in labor unions. Nevertheless, most women are still excluded from high-level managerial positions and senior government posts and, like their American counterparts, continue to struggle for full equality.

In the Soviet Union, where women made important gains after Stalin's death, more than half of the workers were female. Abortion was legalized, the divorce law was liberalized, and many more child-care centers were built. In the professions, women represented 67 percent of doctors, 35 percent of lawyers, and more than 58 percent of engineers by the 1980s. (In the United States, by contrast, women make up a much lower percentage of lawyers and physicians.) Khrushchev appointed the first woman member of the Presidium of Ministers, but whereas some 29 percent of party members were women, they held only 4 percent of the high party offices. In general, women's participation in party politics in socialist and communist nations was higher at local levels than in the central governments. For example, in East Germany about 25 percent of district committee members were women in 1981, whereas only 13 percent of the posts in the Central Committee were held by women. Differences in pay and political power between males and females, as well as social inequalities among women, continued to exist, but most women in these nations enjoyed greater access to professions than women in the West.

Nevertheless, life was hard for most Soviet women, despite legal equality. They had few modern conveniences, and married women got almost no support from their husbands for the household duties they were expected to perform in addition to their paid jobs. Mikhail Gorbachev, the last Soviet leader, declared in 1987 that women had "inherent functions: those of mother, wife, the person who brings up children." Yet he took a greater interest in women's issues than any Soviet ruler since Lenin, supporting day-care expansion, flexible work schedules, and increases in the minimum wage for professions held mostly by women. Moreover, his campaign against alcoholism received strong support from Soviet wives.

American Society in Transition

In the 1950s the United States entered an era of economic prosperity and apparent social tranquillity. President Eisenhower attempted to moderate the trend that Roosevelt's New Deal had set in motion toward increasing government involvement in economic and social life. Yet as large numbers of Americans were driven to leave the farms and the cities for life in the suburbs, a federal highway program improved the country's transportation system and spurred the automobile industry. The Eisenhower government, which proved more sympathetic to business than any since 1932, reduced the federal role in the marketplace wherever possible.

Despite the withdrawal of government from social policy, the movement for racial equality made important strides in this period. In 1954 a landmark ruling by the U.S. Supreme Court, *Brown* v. *Board of Education of Topeka*, held that segregated schools violated the constitution's Fourteenth Amendment, which guaranteed all citizens equal protection under the law. Correctly anticipating that the southern states would resist immediate integration, the Court ordered implementation of its ruling "with all deliberate speed." In 1957 Orville Faubus, the governor of Arkansas, summoned the National Guard to block entry of nine black children into Little Rock's Central High School. Eisenhower, who had not been enthusiastic about the *Brown* decision, nevertheless refused to allow such open flaunting of government authority. He ordered federal troops to Little Rock, forcing Faubus to back down.

✤
MARTIN LUTHER KING, JR., AND THE STRUGGLE FOR CIVIL RIGHTS

Black political activism, organized for the first time on a national level, was the driving force in the civil rights struggle. Dr. Martin Luther King, Jr. (1929–1968), a young black Baptist minister, led a mass civil rights movement. Born in Atlanta, Georgia, King was the son of a Baptist preacher. He studied sociology at Morehouse College and then entered the ministry, eventually taking a Ph.D. in theology at Boston University.

In 1954 King became pastor of the Dexter Avenue Baptist Church in Montgomery, Alabama, where he spearheaded the civil rights struggle as leader of the fight against racial segregation on public buses. His eloquent rhetoric and inspiring personality introduced a dynamic new doctrine of nonviolent protest to the nation. A year later the blacks of Montgomery had achieved their goal.

To extend the successful Montgomery action throughout the nation, King organized the Southern Christian Leadership Conference (SCLC), which gave him a national platform. He was convinced that Mahatma Gandhi's tactic of nonviolent disobedience was the answer to the civil rights struggle. In 1960 King became copastor with his father at the Ebenezer Baptist Church in Atlanta but devoted his energies to the SCLC and to a concerted drive against racial injustice. While protesting segregation at a lunch counter, he was arrested and sentenced to state prison on a pretext. The case aroused the interest of then–Democratic presidential candidate John Kennedy (1917–1963).

King's influence reached its peak in the years between 1960 and 1965. The nonviolent strategy of "sit-ins" and protest marches drew a huge interracial following and put pressure on President Kennedy, who proposed a comprehensive civil rights bill in 1963 intended to end legal segregation. King's success also made him the subject of covert FBI surveillance. In the spring of 1963 his efforts to end segregation in Birmingham, Alabama, resulted in national attention as police turned dogs and fire hoses on the demonstrators and arrested King along with hundreds of schoolchildren. From jail King wrote a letter of great eloquence explaining his nonviolent philosophy. In August 1963, King and other civil rights advocates marched on Washington. Before the Lincoln Memorial, his moral passion captivated some 250,000

Martin Luther King, Jr., who popularized the passive resistance strategy that led to victories in the U.S. civil rights movement, leads a march from Selma to Montgomery, Alabama, in 1965. To his left is his wife, Coretta Scott King. [Bob Adelman/Magnum]

peaceful demonstrators as he recounted his "dream" that one day both blacks and whites would be measured by the content of their character rather than by the color of their skin.

Kennedy's legislative proposal was blocked in Congress by a coalition of Republicans and conservative southern Democrats and remained stalled in committee at the time of his assassination in 1963. Kennedy's more politically astute successor, Lyndon B. Johnson (1908–1973), obtained passage of the 1964 Civil Rights Act, which prohibited discrimination in public places and in the use of federal funds. For his contributions to civil rights, King was awarded the Nobel Prize for peace in 1964.

In his final years King's leadership came under in-

◉ Letter from Birmingham Jail ◉

*After the arrest of Martin Luther King, Jr., in 1963, eight fellow clergy-
men published a statement calling his actions "unwise and untimely."
In April, King wrote a lengthy response—scribbled in the margins of a
newspaper and on scraps of paper—explaining "why we can't wait."*

Perhaps it is easy for those who have never felt the stinging darts of segregation to say,
"Wait." But when you have seen vicious mobs lynch your mothers and fathers at will and
drown your sisters and brothers at whim; when you have seen hate-filled policemen curse,
kick, and even kill your black brothers and sisters; when you see the vast majority of your
twenty million Negro brothers smothering in an airtight cage of poverty in the midst of an
affluent society; when you suddenly find your tongue twisted and your speech stammering
as you seek to explain to your six-year-old daughter why she can't go to the public amuse-
ment park . . . and see ominous clouds of inferiority beginning to form in her little mental
sky, and see her beginning to distort her personality by developing an unconscious bitterness toward white people; when you have to concoct an answer for a five-year-old son
who is asking: "Daddy, why do white people treat colored people so mean?" . . . when
you are humiliated day in and day out by nagging signs reading "white" and "colored";
when your first name becomes "nigger," your middle name becomes "boy" (however old
you are) and your last name becomes "John," and your wife and mother are never given
the respected title "Mrs."; when you are harried by day and haunted by night by the fact
that you are a Negro, living constantly at tiptoe stance, never quite knowing what to expect next, and are plagued with inner fears and outer resentments; when you are forever
fighting a degenerating sense of "nobodiness"—then you will understand why we find it
difficult to wait. There comes a time when the cup of endurance runs over, and men are
no longer willing to be plunged into the abyss of despair. I hope, sirs, you can understand
our legitimate and unavoidable impatience.

Source: M. L. King, Jr., *Why We Can't Wait* (New York: Harper & Row, 1963), pp. 83–84.

creasing pressure from more militant blacks, who faulted him for being too cautious. Riots in the Watts district of Los Angeles in 1965 brought attention to the enormous problems of blacks in northern and western cities, where his nonviolent tactics were questioned. King began to broaden his work to include housing discrimination in Chicago, and in 1967 he strongly opposed the war in Vietnam. In April 1968, while in Memphis, Tennessee, to support a strike of sanitation workers, he was assassinated by a white racist.

King's great contribution to civil rights had been his ability to turn regional protests into a national crusade. He had galvanized the black masses into action, and although complex racial problems continued to plague the nation, America would never quite be the same again.

The New Activism and American Women

The same year as the passage of the Civil Rights Act, Johnson ran for election on a platform calling for a "Great Society" made possible by a "war on poverty." The voters returned him to office along with 40 additional Democratic members of Congress, giving the House of Representatives a progressive majority for the first time since 1938. The dramatic triumph of liberalism reflected a new social activism that had been stimulated by the struggle for racial equality.

Since the early 1960s university students in America had been in the forefront of social and political militancy, as they were in Europe. In June 1962 about 60 young people, members of a group known as Students for a Democratic Society (SDS), met at Port Huron, Michigan, to discuss civil rights, foreign policy, education, and welfare. The declaration of principles they issued—the Port Huron Statement—focused on the concept of "participatory democracy," the notion that people should take part in the decisions that affect their lives. SDS organized an interracial movement of the poor in northern cities, took part in sit-ins and demonstrations in the south, and became increasingly militant over the Vietnam War. By the late 1960s SDS had begun to split apart, one faction forming the Weathermen, an extremist group devoted to violent action. Yet the Port Huron Statement left its mark on an entire generation of Americans.

The civil rights movement and student activism transformed American society in other ways. The gay rights movement, born in 1969 when a police raid in New York's Greenwich Village sparked violent protests from men in the Stonewall Bar, raised important issues about sexual oppression and coincided with the emergence of a powerful new impetus toward women's liberation.

Many women who had left the home for the factory during World War II sought job opportunities traditionally closed to them. Feminists were encouraged by the controversial arguments of Betty Friedan (born 1921), whose book *The Feminine Mystique* (1963) argued that women should seek fulfillment beyond their ties to husbands and children. After the war the number of women who worked for pay outside the home rose dramatically, so that by 1960 twice as many women worked as in 1940. Equally significant was the fact that whereas only 15 percent of all wives worked in 1940, the figure exceeded 50 percent by 1980.

Two separate movements took up the challenge of feminism in the 1960s. The National Organization for Women (NOW), at first composed of older professionals, worked for women's rights through the political and legal systems and styled themselves a "militant" organization. Friedan was elected its first president in 1966. The women's liberation movement, which attracted many younger women who had been involved in antiwar and civil rights efforts, was more confrontational. Begin-

ning in 1968 it identified the patriarchal family and socially formed gender patterns as sources of oppression. Not only did radical feminists demand legal equality with men, but they also encouraged women to seek power through female solidarity and "gender consciousness."

Affirmative action regulations designed to enforce equal opportunity brought about improvement in employment patterns and wage scales for minorities and women. Yet in the 1970s a woman earned only 59 cents for every dollar earned by a man. In 1972 Congress passed an equal rights amendment to the constitution, but the measure failed when a number of state legislatures did not ratify it. Racial, ethnic, and sexual prejudice remains deeply entrenched in some segments of American society.

Canada: Economic Expansion and Social Change

Canada and the United States together make up most of the North American continent.* The two nations share a common 3,000-mile border that stretches from the Pacific to the Atlantic and along the eastern frontier of Alaska. Nevertheless, Canada possesses unique historical and cultural traditions and has undergone its

_____

*Mexico, though geographically part of North America, is usually grouped, for linguistic and historical reasons, with the other nations of Latin America.

The new feminism began in the 1960s. Here, at a 1970s fundraiser for the equal rights amendment, are former first lady Betty Ford (speaking), with Bella Abzug on the far right and Betty Friedan second from the left.
[Alex Webb/Magnum]

own social and economic transformation since World War II.

Despite an expanse of nearly 4 million square miles—making it geographically the world's second largest nation (Russia is the largest)–60 percent of Canada's 25 million people live in the Quebec-Windsor corridor, an industrialized region that hugs the U.S.-Canadian border from Detroit to the Atlantic. The rest of the country is a vast, sparsely populated territory of thick forests, productive agricultural prairies, and rich mineral deposits.

Canada's modern history has shown a gradual distancing from Great Britain, its traditional "mother country." The British North America Act of 1867 had defined its political and constitutional structure as a dominion within the British Empire. In 1931, however, the Statute of Westminster conceded full sovereignty to Canada, Australia, New Zealand, and the other dominions, which then became members of the voluntary Commonwealth of Nations. Today Elizabeth II serves as Canada's queen, but an elected prime minister and parliament actually govern. In 1947, after Canadian participation in World War II heightened national self-identity, Parliament passed the Canadian Citizenship Act, which ended the granting of automatic citizenship to British subjects. Only in the mid-1980s did growing national sentiment result in the "patriation" of the constitution to Canada, that is, the replacement of the constitutional provisions of the British North America Act with a new constitution. The new Charter of Rights and Freedoms reinforced basic civil liberties.

Throughout the twentieth century three major parties have dominated the political system. The Liberals, the largest party, have been in power for most of the modern period. The Progressive Conservatives, or "Tories," have a large following that is less inclined to support an extension of the welfare state. The left-of-center New Democratic party follows a social democratic program.

Persistent and at times violent tension has marked relations between Canada's chief linguistic groups, the English- and French-speaking populations. The abiding nationalism of Quebec province, where most French Canadians live, has grown into stiff political resistance against the nation's dominant English element. As a result of pressure from the Parti Québecois and other groups, in 1963 the Royal Commission on Bilingualism and Biculturalism was given a mandate to redress French grievances. The Official Language Act, passed in 1969, established both French and English as the official languages of the nation. Nonetheless, in 1970 the so-called October Crisis erupted in Quebec when a British trade commissioner was abducted and a provincial minister was murdered by the extremist Quebec Liberation Front. Martial law was imposed on the country, but French nationalism did not abate. Several years later the Parti Québecois won control of the provincial government on a separatist platform.

Despite such tensions, the Canadian economy expanded greatly. In the 1960s the diversified manufacturing sector spurred unparalleled prosperity, with the production growth rate reaching 7 percent in 1973 and the GDP (gross domestic product) jumping by 15 percent. Trade expanded, and agricultural exports soared with massive grain sales to China and the USSR. The discovery of large oil reserves in the western province of Alberta increased the nation's economic promise further. Real income rose as much as 6.5 percent a year. Indeed, Canada's growth was so rapid that it had negative consequences by the next decade. The problem, still to be resolved, centers on the fact that the greatly increased manufacturing sector is too large for the small size of the domestic market, which means that continuing prosperity relies too heavily on the vagaries of foreign exchange and economic conditions elsewhere.

Canada's growth in recent decades has been driven in large part by ever-increasing economic ties with the United States. American investments began pouring into Canada in the 1920s. Today about 70 percent of its manufacturing industries are owned and controlled by U.S. companies—the automobile industry, for example, is almost completely American-owned, and the oil and gas concerns are 80 percent foreign-owned. This pattern has meant that major decisions regarding Canadian subsidiaries, especially ones affecting labor and employment conditions, are made abroad. The integration of the two economies has recently been advanced by the signing and ratification of a free trade treaty that aims at creating a single market for the movement of goods across the U.S.-Canadian border. A tripartite free trade treaty between Canada, the United States, and Mexico was tentatively approved in 1992.

To the unequal economic relationship has been added the Americanization of the country's culture, increasingly resented by Canadian intellectuals, who are striving to create a unique cultural life of their own. From Canada's point of view, one of the most pressing issues of the future will be coming to grips with the pervasive feeling that the United States, with far greater wealth and population, is an overshadowing influence.

Canada's widening prosperity has had social consequences, especially in the growth of an affluent middle class, most of which lives in burgeoning urban centers. Toronto and Montreal, each with some 3 million persons, symbolize the Canadian experience. While most of the nation's wealth is still controlled by the English-speaking population and centers on the modern financial network of Toronto, the French-speaking middle class has risen rapidly in recent years. Montreal, a sophisticated and cosmopolitan city, is the hub of a province, Quebec, that is now 70 percent urban and home to an ambitious entrepreneurial class. Although unemployment has been high in recent years, Canada's citizens have since the 1960s enjoyed one of the most advanced

THE VISUAL EXPERIENCE
Art of the Modern Western World

Claude Monet's painting *Impression: Sunrise* (1872), which gave the Impressionist movement its name, reveals the techniques of Impressionism in its early phase. The Impressionists concentrated on the visual effects of light and color rather than on realistic forms. [Giraudon/Art Resource]

Among the Postimpressionist painters, Vincent van Gogh gave powerful expression to his tormented emotional vision through the swirling movement of form and color, as in his painting *The Starry Night*. [1899, oil on canvas, 29 × 36¼″ (73.7 × 92.1 cm). Collection, The Museum of Modern Art, New York. Acquired through the Lillie P. Bliss Bequest.]

In *Mont Sainte-Victoire* and other works, Paul Cézanne reduced landscape elements to flat planes of pure color to emphasize the three essential shapes that he believed comprised all of nature—the cylinder, the sphere, and the cone. [Giraudon/Art Resource]

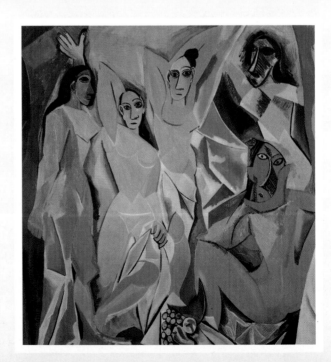

The prostitutes of Avignon Street in Barcelona provided the subject of Pablo Picasso's *Demoiselles d'Avignon*, which reveals the influence of African culture on artists of the period and presages the development of Cubism. Picasso moves from poses reminiscent of classical sculpture on the left to distorted, broken shapes on the right. [1907, oil on canvas, 8′ × 7′8″ (243.9 × 233.7 cm). Collection, The Museum of Modern Art, New York. Acquired through the Lillie P. Bliss Bequest.]

The leading member of the Fauvist movement, Henri Matisse, used flat surfaces of strong color and undulating lines to give his work a primitive flavor. In *Harmony in Red* (also known as *Red Room*), by carrying the blue-on-red pattern of the tablecloth over to the wall and the red of the room over to the pink of the house seen through the window, Matisse reduces the number of tints to a minimum, making color an important structural element in the painting. [George Roos/Art Resource]

The most talented of the Futurists, Umberto Boccioni combined innovative formal artistic elements with a social and political conscience. In *Riot in the Gallery*, the surging demonstrators reveal his concern for the dynamic interaction of motion and space in time. "Everything is in movement," the manifesto of *Futurist Painting* proclaimed; "everything rushes forward, everything is in constant swift change." [Bridgeman/Art Resource]

The most daring step beyond Fauvism and Futurism was taken by a group of painters in Germany known as Der Blaue Reiter ("The Blue Rider"). The leading advocate was the Russian artist Wassily Kandinsky, who abandoned representation and created a nonobjective style using strong colors and dynamic brushwork. In paintings such as *Sketch I for "Composition VII,"* he sought to give spiritual meaning to form and color by eliminating all references to the physical world. [Felix Klee Collection, Kunstmuseum, Bern]

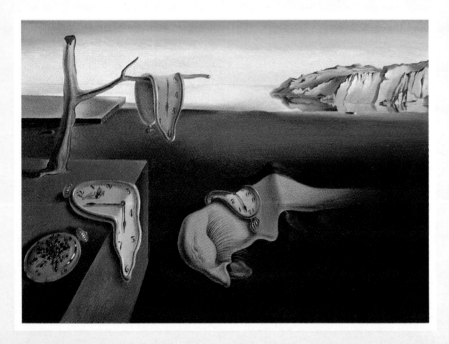

Surrealism was based on Freud's theory of the dream world of the unconscious. In *The Persistence of Memory*, one of the key works of the movement, Salvador Dalí used an almost photographic realism to create an infinite, silent space in which objects cease to comply with the laws of physics. As the watches melt, they suggest the theories of Einstein about the relativity of time and raise questions about what is real and what is not real. [1931, oil on canvas, 9½ × 13″ (24.1 × 33 cm). Collection, The Museum of Modern Art, New York. Given anonymously.]

welfare states in the world, providing cradle-to-grave health care, social security insurance, and an array of other benefits. Canada's future, despite serious challenges, remains bright.

From Brinkmanship to Détente

By the early 1950s the superpowers were enmeshed in a struggle for hegemony. For 25 years the pattern of conflict set in 1947 remained fairly consistent: with American influence predominant in Latin America and western Europe and the Soviet Union supreme in eastern Europe, each superpower challenged the other in peripheral regions of the globe. The danger lay in the possibility that diplomatic confrontations would lead to local military conflict, which could in turn escalate into nuclear war. The Korean War proved to be the first of several such situations.

Confrontation and Crisis

Eisenhower delegated exceptional authority to his secretary of state, John Foster Dulles (1888–1959). A man who combined a brilliant legal mind with righteous moralism, Dulles had been part of Wilson's delegation at the Paris peace conference in 1919. During his long tenure as secretary of state, he was one of the most strident voices of the Cold War, denouncing Truman's containment policy and advocating an offensive program to "liberate" areas under communist control. Dulles emphasized America's nuclear strength, basing foreign policy on repeated warnings that local communist aggression would lead to "massive retaliation" by the United States. The Dulles policy of rattling nuclear missiles whenever international crises erupted was dubbed "brinkmanship," but the eastern European revolts of the 1950s revealed the hollowness of these threats. America stood by in 1956 while anti-Soviet fighters in Hungary battled Soviet tanks with cobblestones and rifles.

The Eisenhower administration never abandoned containment. Using marines or covert operations directed by the CIA, the United States played a key role in overthrowing supposedly procommunist governments around the world, including those in Iran (1953), Guatemala (1954), and Chile (1973). The CIA also plotted the assassination of Congolese leader Patrice Lumumba in 1961 and, with the aid of American gangsters, made several attempts against the Cuban leader Fidel Castro.

Under Kennedy, American Cold War strategy shifted again, but only in emphasis. Kennedy undertook a huge buildup of conventional and nuclear weapons. In his effort to close the "missile gap" with the Soviet Union, he accelerated the nuclear arms race, to which Russia responded in 1961 by detonating a hydrogen bomb in the atmosphere. Kennedy was fascinated with "counterinsurgency" operations, by which he meant the use of limited warfare against communist infiltration of Third World countries. One result of this was the Bay of Pigs fiasco in Cuba (see Chapter 41).

Encounters between Kennedy and Khrushchev brought the world to the edge of nuclear disaster. In the summer of 1961 Khrushchev tried to stem the flow of refugees from East Berlin to the West and threatened to sign a treaty with East Germany that would terminate Western rights in the city. Kennedy ordered reservists on military alert and urged Americans to build fallout shelters. This sharp response may have persuaded Khrushchev to back down, for on August 13 the East Germans sealed off their portion of the city by erecting a wall between the two sections of Berlin.

A year later Khrushchev intruded into the American sphere of influence in Latin America by constructing nuclear missile bases in Cuba. Khrushchev argued the need to prevent another American attempt to overthrow the Castro government, but Kennedy considered the action a direct military threat. In October 1962, when American air reconnaisance revealed Soviet missiles in Cuba, the president imposed a naval quarantine around the island and demanded the missiles' removal. For six tense days Soviet ships sailed toward Cuba and American forces went on war alert. Khrushchev finally drew back by sending Kennedy a letter deploring the horrors of nuclear war and offering a face-saving compromise. The Soviets agreed to withdraw their missiles in return for a public pledge from America not to invade Cuba; unofficially, the United States agreed to dismantle its own offensive missiles in Turkey.

Brezhnev and the Return to Repression

The turbulent Kennedy-Khrushchev era soon came to an end. Kennedy was assassinated in Dallas, Texas, on November 22, 1963. The following summer, while Khrushchev was vacationing in the Crimea, the Communist party's Central Committee stripped him of his power, charging him with a host of errors that included the Cuban crisis, the rift with China, and setbacks in Russia's agricultural and industrial growth. After a brief period of collective leadership, a veteran bureaucrat, Leonid Brezhnev (1906–1982), took Khrushchev's place. Brezhnev served as both Soviet president and Communist party secretary.

During the almost two decades that Brezhnev ruled, the Soviet Union underwent a return to government repression, although not to the extremes of the Stalin

◎ The Cuban Missile Crisis: Two Views ◎

The discovery by the United States in the fall of 1962 that the Soviet Union was installing missile bases in Cuba brought the world to the edge of nuclear war. The first of the following accounts of the crisis is by special White House assistant Arthur M. Schlesinger, Jr., who described President Kennedy's speech of October 19.

Then at seven o'clock the speech: his expression grave, his voice firm and calm, the evidence set forth without emotion, the conclusion unequivocal—"The purpose of these bases can be none other than to provide a nuclear strike capability against the Western Hemisphere." He recited the Soviet assurances, now revealed as "deliberate deception," and called the Soviet action "a deliberately provocative and unjustified change in the status quo which cannot be accepted by this country. . . ." He then laid out what he called with emphasis his *initial* steps: a quarantine on all offensive military equipment under shipment to Cuba; an intensified surveillance of Cuba itself; a declaration that any missile launched from Cuba would be regarded as an attack by the Soviet Union on the United States, requiring full retaliatory response upon the Soviet Union . . . and an appeal to Chairman Khrushchev "to abandon this course of world domination, and to join in a historic effort to end the perilous arms race and to transform the history of man."

Here is Soviet Premier Khrushchev's account.

I want to make one thing absolutely clear: when we put our ballistic missiles in Cuba, we had no desire to start a war. . . . In October, President Kennedy came out with a statement warning that the United States would take whatever measures were necessary to remove what he called the "threat" of Russian missiles in Cuba. . . . In our estimation the Americans were trying to frighten us, but they were no less scared than we were of atomic war. . . .

President Kennedy issued an ultimatum, demanding that we remove our missiles and bombers from Cuba. I remember those days vividly. I remember the exchange with President Kennedy especially well because I initiated it and was at the center of the action on our end of the correspondence. I take complete responsibility for the fact that the President and I entered into direct correspondence at the most crucial and dangerous stage of the crisis. . . .

The climax came after five or six days, when our ambassador to Washington, Anatoly Dobrynin, reported that the President's brother, Robert Kennedy, had come to see him on an unofficial visit. Dobrynin's report went something like this:

"Robert Kennedy looked exhausted. One could see from his eyes that he had not slept for days. He himself said that he had not been home for six days and nights. 'The President is in a grave situation,' Robert Kennedy said, 'and he does not know how to get out of it. We are under very severe stress. In fact we are under pressure from our military to use force against Cuba.'" . . .

We could see that we had to reorient our position swiftly. . . . We sent the Americans a note saying that we agreed to remove our missiles and bombers on the condition that the President give us his assurance that there would be no invasion of Cuba by the forces of the United States or anybody else. Finally Kennedy gave in and agreed to make a statement giving us such an assurance.

Sources: A. M. Schlesinger, Jr., *A Thousand Days: John F. Kennedy in the White House* (Boston: Houghton Mifflin, 1965), pp. 812–813; N. Khrushchev, *Khrushchev Remembers*, trans. S. Talbott (Boston: Little, Brown, 1970), pp. 496–498.

era. Party officials agreed on the need for stability and retrenchment after the changes wrought by Khrushchev. Restraints were reimposed on Russian intellectuals, symbolized by the expulsion of Alexander Solzhenitsyn in 1974. Despite Moscow's acceptance of the human rights provisions of the Helsinki Accords, criticism of government policy by prominent dissidents such as Andrei Sakharov (1921–1989), an internationally acclaimed physicist, brought persecution and long periods of Siberian exile. Recalling Russia's wartime sacrifices, Soviet leaders stressed nationalist traditions and the unity of the Soviet Union, crushing regionalism in the Ukraine and elsewhere.

The new wave of repression also affected the Soviet Union's 1.8 million Jews, who suffered from a long tradition of repression. In the Soviet system, state atheism discouraged Judaism along with all other religions, but the government also claimed that Jewish cultural identity and Zionism undermined the unity of the nation. Khrushchev's liberalization program had hardly affected the Soviet Union's Jews. In the 1960s they formed underground networks to keep Jewish tradition alive, circulating typewritten translations of books such as Leon Uris' novel *Exodus* (1958), which traced the emigration of the Jewish people to Palestine and the founding of the state of Israel. The Brezhnev regime, preoccupied with nationality problems within the Soviet Union and political dissidence, stepped up persecution of the Jews. Emigration to Israel, which had been virtually impossible before, was loosened as a result of international pressure in the 1970s. The exit rate reached a peak in 1979, when over 51,000 Jews left the Soviet Union, but declined steadily thereafter. Only in 1987, under Mikhail Gorbachev's more liberal policies, did the number begin to increase again. Since then, an estimated 600,000 Jews from the former Soviet Union have emigrated to Israel, with others settling elsewhere.

MOSCOW: RUSSIAN CITY, SOVIET CAPITAL

One of the world's great cities, Moscow was not only the political capital of the Soviet Union but also the center of its industrial and cultural life. It embodied the sense of continuity that linked the country's history from its early development to its status as a superpower.

Moscow stands on the Moscow River, in the center of the vast plain of European Russia. Its origins stretch back to the twelfth century, when an early Russian prince built fortifications around an area known as the Kremlin ("citadel"). The town gradually became a thriving trading site, and in 1326 the head of the Russian Orthodox church transferred his seat there. Moscow's

rulers incorporated more of the surrounding countryside and provided defense against repeated Mongol invasions. By the fifteenth century it had become the undisputed core of a unified Russian state under Ivan the Great, who enlarged and strengthened the Kremlin with the crenelated red brick walls and towers that still give it its characteristic appearance.

The establishment of the Romanov dynasty in 1613 added employment in state administration to craft manufacturing. Commercial activity in Moscow centered in a large open market area called Red Square (in Russian, the word meaning "red" also means "beautiful"). In the second half of the eighteenth century Moscow University was founded, and architects from France and Italy were imported to design public buildings. Even after Peter the Great moved the capital to his new city of St. Petersburg, Moscow's industries continued to grow. By 1812, when Napoleon invaded Russia and occupied Moscow, its population had surpassed 275,000.

Following a disastrous fire during the occupation and Napoleon's withdrawal, a great program of rebuilding was undertaken that reconstructed the interior structures of the Kremlin and the Bolshoi Theater. The emancipation of the serfs in 1861 brought many of them to Moscow, whose population had increased to more than 600,000 by 1870. As new rail lines linked the city to the rest of the country during the 1890s, heavy engineering and metal industries developed. The number of inhabitants expanded rapidly, reaching almost 2 million before the outbreak of World War I.

The Soviets gave Moscow much of its modern appearance. Lenin moved the capital back to the city in 1918, and despite the ravages of the civil war its population had doubled by 1939 to more than 4 million, creating serious overcrowding and housing shortages. During World War II, Moscow withstood the onslaught of the German armies, which reached to within 25 miles of the city in late 1941. With Stalin remaining as a symbol of Russian resistance, the citizens of Moscow built antitank defenses, and the Red Army repulsed the Wehrmacht.

Recovery was rapid. In the late 1940s and early 1950s Stalin added ornate "wedding cake" skyscrapers to the Moscow skyline, and in the 1960s Khrushchev began the construction of extensive suburban apartment complexes to relieve the chronic housing shortage. Much of the country's modern industry is concentrated around the periphery.

The eclectic mix of Moscow's architecture reflects the richly diverse history of Russia. The Kremlin still dominates the city. Within its walls is one of the most striking and beautiful architectural ensembles in the world, over which rise the five golden onion-shaped domes of the fifteenth-century Cathedral of the Assumption and the white bell tower built by Ivan the Great. The nineteenth-century Kremlin Great Palace was the seat of

Soviet political power, and the Palace of Congresses, completed in 1961, was used for Communist party meetings. Along the east wall of the Kremlin lies Red Square, the ceremonial center of the capital. Marchers in the annual May Day and the October Revolution parades passed the squat bulk of the Lenin Mausoleum, as well as the domed sixteenth-century Cathedral of St. Basil the Blessed and GUM, the state department store. It was into these same streets that thousands of Soviet citizens poured in August 1991, bringing an end to the Communist government and to the Soviet Union itself.

Coexistence and Détente

In the 25 years following the clash over Cuba, American-Soviet disagreements remained sharp. Yet from the mid-1960s on, superpower relations became clearer as both sides came to realize that nuclear confrontation would be a mutual disaster. Summit meetings and disarmament talks formed the backdrop to a mitigation of tension and a turning away from ideological rhetoric. If, in the 1960s, Cold War propaganda gave way to a public discussion of peaceful coexistence, so in the 1970s the United States and the Soviet Union began to define their relationship in terms of détente, literally a "relaxation of tensions."

American involvement in Vietnamese affairs (see Chapter 39) sparked a political and social crisis at home. The escalation of the war under President Johnson resulted in the sending of more than 500,000 American troops to Vietnam by the end of 1968. A vigorous antiwar movement emerged in America. The protests started on college campuses, but outspoken opponents soon

emerged in Congress and in the press. In 1967 demonstrations spread throughout the country while thousands of young Americans declared themselves conscientious objectors or fled the United States to avoid the draft. Senator Eugene McCarthy (born 1916), campaigning on an antiwar platform, challenged President Johnson for the Democratic nomination. In March 1968, following McCarthy's strong showing in an early primary, the president announced that he would not seek another term.

After the Tet Offensive in February 1968, peace talks with North Vietnam opened in Paris, and in November voters elected the Republican Richard M. Nixon (born 1913) to the presidency. Nixon began the secret bombing of Communist supply routes in Cambodia in early 1969, concealing the operation through false reports. In 1971 the publication of classified war documents heightened antiwar sentiments by revealing earlier deceptions by both Johnson and Nixon. Protests mounted as the 1972 presidential elections approached, but Nixon neutralized them by removing the last American ground troops. The Paris Accords, signed in January 1973, officially ended American involvement in the war.

The 1962 Cuban crisis and the Vietnam War provided the superpowers with an unstated but important lesson in international relations. In withdrawing Soviet missiles from Cuba, Khrushchev had tacitly recognized America's predominance in Latin America. Vietnam had forced the United States to accept the limitations of its military strength. The leaders who followed Johnson and Khrushchev spoke increasingly of tempering Soviet-American relations with détente. Détente actually defined the process by which the superpowers agreed to formalize the dominance that the postwar settlements had given them.

South Vietnam's national police chief executes a Viet Cong officer on a Saigon street. Such scenes aroused opposition to the war in the United States and broad. [Wide World Photos]

This rapprochement was the work of an unlikely pair: Richard Nixon, a lifelong anticommunist, and Leonid Brezhnev, who had opposed Khrushchev's revisionist policies. Nixon repudiated the Dulles doctrine, which had demanded a rollback of Soviet communism, while Brezhnev fell back on Lenin's notion that direct confrontation with the West was unnecessary in light of the inevitable decay of capitalism and the overthrow of colonialism by wars of national liberation.

The scandal known as Watergate ended Nixon's presidency but not the era of détente. It was revealed that Nixon and his aides had illegally manipulated the 1972 presidential election campaign and had authorized surveillance and espionage against his political opponents. The crisis, which climaxed in 1974, exposed Nixon's efforts to cover up illegal White House operations. In August, faced with the possibility of impeachment, the president resigned in disgrace. Nixon's successor, Gerald R. Ford (born 1913), continued the policy of détente.

Détente contributed to the Helsinki Accords. In 1973 the United States and the Soviet Union joined Canada and almost all the European nations at the Conference on Security and Cooperation in Europe, held in Helsinki, Finland. In the final treaty, signed two years later, the Soviets endorsed political and human rights statements and agreed to encourage closer relations with the West. In return, the signatories guaranteed Europe's political boundaries, including the division of Germany into two states. The Soviet Union thus obtained formal recognition of the territorial adjustments in eastern Europe that had been arranged at Yalta and Potsdam. In effect, détente had served to achieve permanent agreement on the postwar settlements that had established the Soviet—and, by implication, the American—sphere of influence in Europe.

American foreign policy remained basically unaltered under Ford's successor, Jimmy Carter (born 1924). Carter denounced repressive governments that violated basic human rights and decried the plight of political dissidents in the Soviet Union, but he continued to support dictatorships in Chile and Iran. He also cited the Soviet military buildup to justify an increase in American arms spending.

The Reagan Era

Despite a stagnant economy, the United States continued to fund and in some cases to expand welfare programs in the 1970s. Dissatisfaction with the costs of government, combined with record levels of peacetime inflation, high interest rates, and the perception that America had lost power and prestige (as exemplified in part by the Carter administration's failure to secure the release of American hostages seized in Iran), resulted in the election of Ronald Reagan (born 1911), the first ideological conservative to win the presidency since the 1920s. Reagan moved swiftly to provide large tax cuts, ostensibly to stimulate investment, while instituting a major military buildup. After a severe economic contraction in 1982–1983 that curbed inflation but left the highest levels of unemployment since the Great Depression, a boom period set in for much of the decade, fueled by real estate speculation and corporate mergers. The end of this period was signaled by a stock market crash in October 1987, and by 1990 the economy was in recession. Reagan's government left a $150 billion annual budget deficit, which by 1992, under Reagan's successor, George Bush (born 1924), had ballooned to nearly $400 billion, partly because of massive bank failures. At the same time, mounting poverty was evidenced by the largest homeless population in the United States since the 1930s.

For all its bellicose rhetoric, the Reagan administration was generally cautious in foreign affairs. The chief exception to this was in Latin America, where the United States invaded Grenada; fought proxy wars in Nicaragua and Salvador; and invaded Panana in December 1989, overthrowing its military strongman, Manuel Noriega. Aside from an ill-fated attempt to garrison war-torn Beirut in 1983 that left 241 marines dead, the major Middle East initiative of the Reagan years was an attempt at a regional peace conference between Arabs and Israelis. Reagan and Bush also provided assistance to the Iraqi dictator Saddam Hussein (born 1937) in his war with Iran, but with Iraq's seizure of the oil-rich emirate of Kuwait in August of 1990 the United States led a United Nations coalition that drove Saddam from Kuwait in February 1991.

The Superpowers Challenged

The Iran hostage crisis demonstrated that the postwar world hegemony jointly exercised by the United States and the Soviet Union had not gone unchallenged. Smaller states have continually sought to mitigate superpower dominance and exert autonomy. In Europe and the non-Western world, national leaders employed a variety of techniques to maneuver between America and the Soviet Union. Within the Communist world, ideological nonconformity proved a powerful means of asserting independence, while in both western and eastern Europe, nationalism was used as a lever against Washington and Moscow.

Outside the immediate areas of superpower hegemony, states often exploited Cold War rivalries to extract economic and political concessions from each side. Neutralism and ideological nonalignment, especially among former colonies, achieved the same results. The balance of nuclear terror actually enhanced such possibilities, for to avoid mutual self-destruction over issues that did not threaten their vital interests, the superpowers were forced to act with restraint. Regional and economic organizations exercised a moderating influence through the control of vital natural resources and markets. The revival of religious fundamentalism among Islamic states, so dramatically demonstrated in the United States–Iran crisis, suggested the availability of still other alternatives.

The Nonaligned World

The colonial territories that gained nationhood after World War II found themselves economically dependent on the industrialized, wealthier Western states. Much-needed developmental resources came through assistance programs sponsored by the United States and the Soviet Union, which vied with each other to capture the political support of the newly independent countries. Yet, rather than becoming pawns in the East-West competition, underdeveloped states devised a strategy that turned the Cold War into what they called "creative confrontation"—playing off the superpowers to their own advantage while maintaining nonaligned status. India's Jawaharlal Nehru saw neutralism as a means of forging a "third force" among nonaligned nations, much as de Gaulle would attempt to do in Europe in the 1960s. The Egyptian leader Gamal Abdel Nasser maneuvered skillfully between the superpowers in pursuit of his goals.

In 1955 a large number of neutralist states convened the Afro-Asian Conference in Bandung, Indonesia, to discuss mutual interests and strategy. The United Nations soon became a focus of Third World nonalignment. The ranks of the General Assembly swelled rapidly as former colonies won independence, thus forming a substantial voting bloc with members from Latin America. Anticolonial sentiment, reinforced by the Soviets, often translated into anti-Western positions, but the primary agenda among nonaligned countries was to secure passage of social and economic assistance measures. Superpower refusal to fund such programs has often undermined the effectiveness of the neutralist coalition, however.

The Bandung conference symbolized continuing efforts to establish regional organizations designed to forge unity of policy and economic cooperation among Third World nations. The Organization of African Unity (OAU) was established because African leaders believed that disunity played into the hands of the superpowers. Founded in 1963, the OAU required a policy of nonalignment from each of its 30 member states and

spawned a number of subregional economic groups similar in concept to the European Common Market. The OAU has also pursued a policy of political cooperation with other Third World regional coalitions, especially with Arab countries.

Much of the frustration expressed by nonaligned nations stemmed from the vastly unequal relationship separating rich and poor states. The resentment, strongest where key resources and local economies have been exploited by multinational Western corporations, has had a major impact on world events. The formation of the Organization of Petroleum Exporting Countries (OPEC) in 1960 reflects these concerns. OPEC devised the strategy of counterpenetration, whereby it hoped to make industrial economies that relied heavily on oil imports vulnerable to Third World pressures. Initially, the strategy had resounding success. Dwindling foreign aid from the United States and its allies, coupled with the West's pro-Israeli policy in the Middle East, angered the Arab nations in OPEC. In 1973 the group quadrupled the price of crude oil. The sudden rise in fuel costs intensified inflation and recession in the West and underscored the interdependence of world societies. The next year the nonaligned bloc in the United Nations passed a resolution demanding the creation of a "new international economic order" in which resources, trade, and markets would be distributed equally.

Nonaligned states forged still other forms of economic cooperation as leverage against the superpowers. OPEC, the OAU, and the Arab League had overlapping members, and in the 1970s the Arabs began extending huge financial assistance to African nations in an effort to reduce African economic dependence on the United States and the Soviet Union. At a 1977 Afro-Arab summit conference in Cairo, oil producers pledged $1.5 billion in aid to Africa. Recent divisions within OPEC have made concerted action more difficult. Nevertheless, the 1973 oil crisis provided dramatic evidence of the potential power of resource suppliers in dealing with the developed world.

The Growth of European Autonomy

European efforts toward economic unity led to a subtle undermining of American influence. In 1950, against the background of the Marshall Plan, French foreign minister Robert Schuman (1886–1963) proposed a plan for cooperating in the production of steel and coal. Belgium, Luxembourg, and the Netherlands joined France, West Germany, and Italy in forming the European Coal and Steel Community (ECSC), which quickly tripled iron and steel output and increased coal production almost 25 percent. By 1957 the ECSC concluded that further

42.1 Europe, 1945–1989

cooperation could strengthen Europe's economies and enable its members jointly to influence the superpowers. As a result, ECSC members created the European Eco-

nomic Community (EEC), better known as the Common Market. Through the elimination of tariff barriers and the free exchange of labor and capital, the Common

Market achieved remarkable success in economic integration. After years of French objection, Britain, Ireland, and Denmark became members in 1973. Although the United States still exercises a major influence in European economic life, Europe has escaped the direct dependence it once had on America. Indeed, while the Common Market brought an increase in American business in Europe, in the 1980s the flow of capital began to move in both directions as European products and investments entered the United States.

Charles de Gaulle, president of France from 1958 to 1969, led a more direct challenge to American hegemony. Proud and intensely nationalistic, he wanted to put France at the center of a Europe that would reassert its autonomy between the United States and the Soviet Union. For that reason, de Gaulle pulled French forces out of NATO, twice vetoed the entry of America's closest ally, Great Britain, into the Common Market, and condemned America's escalating role in Vietnam. More grating still to Washington, the French leader tried to weaken the American economy by demanding gold for the large quantity of U.S. dollars held in Paris.

West Germany also demonstrated more autonomy. When the socialist Willy Brandt became federal chancellor in 1969, he embarked on a policy of reconciliation with the Communist bloc countries of eastern Europe. In exchange for guarantees of West Berlin's freedom and a mutual renunciation of force, Brandt concluded treaties with the Soviet Union, Czechoslovakia, and Poland that formally recognized existing frontiers. Of equal importance, he also began the normalization of relations with East Germany.

The desire for ideological autonomy was linked to the growing identification of Communist parties with the idea of an independent Europe free from the influence of both superpowers. This trend gave rise to the phenomenon known as Eurocommunism, which found its first example in Italy, whose Communist party was inspired by the theoretical writings of Antonio Gramsci (1891–1937). Italian Communists adopted considerable tactical flexibility based on Gramsci's notion that the history of a nation should guide the development of its Communist movement. Not unlike the European Popular Front policies of the 1930s, Italian Communist leaders have accepted both democratic principles and the possibility of sharing power in a coalition with bourgeois parties. The Communists of France, Spain, and most other Western countries moved in the same direction, at times breaking with Moscow over international issues. In 1968 the Italian Communist party, together with its French counterpart, criticized the Soviet Union's invasion of Czechoslovakia. In 1990, as a symbol of the new emphasis on democracy, the Italian party changed its name to the Democratic Party of the Left.

The success of the Common Market, together with the experiences of de Gaulle and Brandt, led to Europe's increasing political independence from Washington. Although some Europeans expressed anxiety at the prospect of an American missile withdrawal, powerful grass-roots peace movements challenged American nuclear policy. Moreover, most European states refused to follow the American lead in applying sanctions against the Soviet Union in 1979 after that nation's invasion of Afghanistan. A similar request was rejected in 1981 following the suppression of the Polish trade union movement, and in 1986 many European states refused an American request for overflight permission during the bombing raid against Libya. With the end of the Cold War and the pledge by the United States and Russia of drastic arms reduction, European dependence on American military power was greatly reduced, although the civil war among the former republics of Yugoslavia demonstrated that regional security in Europe was by no means assured.

The Revolution in Eastern Europe

The trend toward autonomy in eastern Europe had been slower until the late 1980s, when domestic reforms in the Soviet Union released the iron grip that Stalin had imposed on the region. Although the open revolts against Soviet authority in East Germany (1953) and Hungary (1956) were swiftly crushed, cautious ideological divergence from orthodox Communist policy drew many eastern European regimes away from Moscow. Combining Yugoslav nationalism with doctrinal innovation, Marshal Tito steered his country into a quasi-neutral position even during the Stalinist period. Tito's example no doubt contributed to the harsh Soviet reaction against similar efforts in Czechoslovakia. In January 1968, reformists within the Czech Communist party installed Alexander Dubček (born 1921) in office. Dubček lifted censorship and permitted local decision making in factories, unions, and the Communist party itself. The Czech example aroused demands for similar reforms elsewhere in eastern Europe. In August 500,000 Soviet and Warsaw Pact troops poured into Czechoslovakia and arrested Dubček and his reformist supporters. Brezhnev subsequently asserted the Soviet Union's right to intervene in the affairs of any socialist nation whenever necessary—the so-called Brezhnev Doctrine. By the 1970s a subtle shift in Soviet policy was introduced as Moscow sought to reduce the need for military intervention by stimulating economic integration with the eastern European region.

Efforts to achieve autonomy within the Communist world accelerated in Poland. In 1980 a rash of illegal strikes led to a massive work stoppage at the Gdansk shipyards and inspired the formation of the noncommunist Solidarity movement, headed by Lech Walesa (born 1944), a tough union organizer. With support from almost 10 million workers and the Catholic church, Solidarity won major concessions from the government before party leader General Wojciech Jaruzelski (born 1923) imposed martial law and arrested union leaders. Walesa was eventually freed and Solidarity recognized. In the midst of a deepening economic crisis, partially free elections were held in 1989, leading to the formation of a coalition government headed by Tadeusz Mazowiecki, a Solidarity member whose cabinet included both Solidarity representatives and communists. In the spring of 1990 Walesa was elected president of Poland.

In the last months of 1989, decades of Soviet and communist domination in eastern Europe finally ended as the long-suffering peoples of the region, inspired by developments in Poland, drove their governments from power. In late summer East Germans, frustrated by the refusal of Communist party leader Erich Honecker (born 1912) to institute reforms, began leaving their country for the West. As East Germany celebrated its fortieth anniversary in October, mass demonstrations were organized and the number of refugees reached tens of thousands. By the end of the month, Honecker had resigned as party chief.

In an attempt to deter its people from abandoning the country, the East German authorities opened the borders to the West and began to tear down the Berlin Wall, which became the site of huge celebrations. As information about party corruption and government repression became public, the Communists were discredited and new political parties emerged. In March 1990 the first free elections in East German history were held. The Christian Democrats, campaigning on a platform of German unification, won almost half the vote. That July, the economies of the two Germanies were united, and on October 3 political unification was implemented. Serious economic issues, stemming largely from the disparity between the two former societies, remained to be resolved, but a reunited Germany promised to become the most powerful economic unit in Europe.

Inspired by success in Poland and Germany, the people of Hungary and Czechoslovakia moved cautiously toward liberation. In Hungary, despite reforms that permitted small private enterprises, economic setbacks resulted in the fall of János Kádár in 1988. Deep-seated dissatisfaction led to the emergence of new political parties, a change of name in the Hungarian Communist party, and free elections, in which the Communists were repudiated. In Czechoslovakia the government responded harshly to dissident demonstrations, but by late 1989 Prague was awash with rallies of more than 500,000, and the Communist government finally collapsed. The playwright Vaclav Havel (born 1936), one of the leaders of the opposition, became president and began to preside over the democratization of his country. In 1992 long-standing ethnic differences led to discussions concerning the possible division of Czechoslovakia into two separate states.

In Romania, which had remained unaffected by the upheaval in eastern Europe, Nicolae Ceauşescu (1918–

Children at play in the rubble from the dismantled Berlin Wall. [Reuters/Bettmann Newsphotos]

1989) and his wife Elena had created their own form of Communist dictatorship that had strained relations with the Soviet Union. Although Romania experienced food shortages and economic collapse, Ceaușescu had wasted limited resources on sumptuous palaces. In the countryside he destroyed villages and forced their inhabitants into collectives. A vicious secret police kept the population in a state of constant fear.

In December 1989, when demonstrators protested the repressive regime, the police shot and killed some 200 persons. The bloodshed sparked a sharp reaction from the people, who raged through the streets of Bucharest, and resulted in battles between anti-Ceaușescu army units and the secret police. Ceaușescu and his wife attempted to flee but were captured by army rebels and, after a military trial, executed. Despite the end of the dictatorship, however, the prospects for Romanian democracy remained uncertain. Even Bulgaria, a country with virtually no democratic experience, deposed its aging Stalinist dictator, Todor Zhivkov (born 1911), and changed the name of its Communist party to the Bulgarian Socialist party.

In Yugoslavia, where Marshal Tito's death in 1980 had been followed by a collective presidency, the collapse of Soviet hegemony led to radical destabilization. In January 1990 the Communist leadership called for an end to authoritarian government and held multiparty elections. Yet the pace of domestic liberalization was threatened in the summer of 1991 by serious ethnic disorders, as the Croats and Slovenes demanded independence from the federal government. In the summer of 1991, civil war erupted between these districts and the Serbs, who championed unity, and in March of 1992 the war spread to Bosnia-Herzegovina, which had also asserted its independence but failed to stem intercommunal violence that led to the heaviest fighting on European soil since World War II. The European Community recognized Croatian and Slovenian independence. In 1992 Serbia and Croatia seized large portions of Bosnia-Herzegovina, and by the end of the year a much smaller Yugoslav state appeared to be an accomplished fact.

Toward Unity

In 1986 Europe moved closer to economic union when members of the EEC adopted the Single European Act, which called for a unified European internal market and the end of trade barriers by the end of 1992. Moreover, all border formalities would disappear for citizens of the EEC, now known simply as the European Community (EC), and labor and capital would circulate freely. Member states also committed to cooperate in improving the environment and adopting a general plan of social legislation. Some states, especially Britain, opposed the en-

42.2 *The Breakup of Yugoslavia*

vironmental and social aspects of the Single European Act as interference in domestic affairs.

In the late 1980s member nations began to prepare for 1992. Under the plan, the end of all restrictions would place each private corporation in direct competition with others throughout Europe, including service industries such as banking and insurance, which in many cases had been protected by government regulations. Financiers from one country would be free to invest their money in another, and drivers in nations with high insurance rates would be able to insure their automobiles with foreign companies. As a result, insurance firms and other service companies began to diversify their operations throughout the continent, and American and Japanese investors, once discouraged by European protectionism, began to make plans to participate in the vast new market.

European economic unity promised to create a bloc powerful enough to compete successfully with Japan and the United States. By 1987 western Europe had already become the world's largest commercial unit, dealing with 37 percent of the world's trade and holding a third of the world's monetary reserves, despite the fact that the region possesses only 6 percent of the world's population. In the spring of 1992 Danish voters dealt hopes for Europe's political unity an unexpected blow by refusing to ratify the enabling treaty signed by European Community members the previous year at Maastricht. In part this reflected Danish fears of being swallowed up by an entity 340 million strong, but in part as well the resurgence of ethnic divisions in eastern Europe and the flight of foreign refugees from that region to western Europe.

The Nuclear Peril

Despite a history of ideological conflict and Cold War confrontations since the end of World War II, the United States and the Soviet Union remained at peace. Indeed, relations between the superpowers grew less tense in the 1980s, and efforts at political cooperation and disarmament held out the promise of a more peaceful world.

The Quest for Disarmament

Nuclear arms limitations talks have been a feature of diplomatic relations for more than 40 years. Some progress was made; the superpowers were forced to be sensitive to the demands of the international community, and their monopoly over nuclear arms had in any case ended.

In 1946, when it still had the world's only atomic weapons, the United States suggested the creation of an international atomic development authority with the power to inspect all countries to prevent the manufacture of nuclear weapons. America proposed turning its research data and facilities over to the agency. The Soviet Union, in the midst of developing its own atomic capability, vetoed the proposal and in 1949 detonated an atomic device. Thereafter, the United States and the Soviet Union engaged in a costly and dangerous nuclear arms race. Each ultimately possessed enough nuclear weapons to exterminate most of the life on the planet.

During the height of the Cold War the superpowers developed their nuclear arsenals and delivery systems and conducted unrestrained testing of atomic weapons that threatened to destroy the environment. In 1952 the United States exploded a hydrogen bomb, an even more destructive weapon. The following year the Soviets announced their own hydrogen device, and in 1961 they tested a 50-megaton bomb, the equivalent of 50 million tons of TNT.

The first important step in nuclear disarmament came in 1963 with the signing of a test ban treaty that permitted only underground explosions. Although more than 100 nations signed the treaty, some states, hoping to achieve their own nuclear capability, refused. In 1968 the United States and the Soviet Union jointly sponsored a nonproliferation treaty that sought to restrict nuclear weapons to the five nations already in possession of them—the United States, the Soviet Union, Britain, France, and China. The pact called for international inspections to ensure that nuclear energy facilities would be used only for peaceful purposes. Eight countries (Argentina, Brazil, Egypt, India, Israel, Pakistan, South Africa, and Spain) did not sign the agreement. A similar pact in 1977 secured the agreement of 90 nations, but again those approaching nuclear capacity refused. The limited success of the nonproliferation effort not only made disarmament more difficult but also reflected the sobering failure of the superpowers to reach their own accord.

Little progress was made in American-Soviet disarmament until the 1972 SALT I treaty, which froze the number of offensive "strategic" intercontinental missile launchers for five years. The antiballistic missile (ABM) provisions of SALT I limited the number of ABM sites. In theory, ABMs could provide a nuclear defense by intercepting attacking missiles, although the cost would be prohibitive and decoys could make the system ineffective; in a nuclear exchange, even a small margin of error could result in tens of millions of fatalities. The ABM accord was based on the notion of deterrence, which argues that each side would not attack the other because it feared counterattack. By contrast, an unrestricted ABM race might tempt the nation that acquired an effective defense to consider a first strike against the other if nuclear war seemed "winnable."

The SALT I pact was imperfect. The United States possessed a manned nuclear bomber fleet that the Soviets could not match. Moreover, nothing prevented either side from equipping its missiles with multiple warheads (MIRVs), and no restrictions were placed on technical improvements in either missiles or warheads. The 1979 SALT II treaty limited each superpower to 2,400 nuclear launchers, of which only 1,320 could have MIRVs. But the U.S. Senate refused to ratify SALT II because of conservative opposition and the difficulty of maintaining true parity in the face of continued weapon research. The treaty was observed informally until President Reagan exceeded SALT II limits in 1986. Both the United States and the Soviet Union continued to test nuclear weapons, as did France and China.

Soviet president Mikhail Gorbachev continued to press for arms reductions in the later 1980s, but only with the collapse of the Soviet Union did a real breakthrough take place. In June of 1992 Russian president Boris Yeltsin and U.S. president George Bush agreed to cut their missile arsenals by two-thirds by the year 2003, restricting each nation to 3500 missiles apiece. The problem of nuclear proliferation remained, however, as four new nuclear powers emerged from the former Soviet Union, one of which, Ukraine, possessed a significant nuclear capability.

The End of the Superpower Age

Leonid Brezhnev died in November 1982, bequeathing a legacy of political and economic stagnation that was compounded under the brief regimes of his successors, the former secret police chief Yuri Andropov (1904–1984) and the Politburo veteran Konstantin Chernenko (1912–1985), both of whom were preoccupied by the Afghan war and the bellicose tone of the Reagan administration. Using Afghanistan as a pretext, Reagan had begun a massive arms buildup early in his administration. He increased the level of military spending from one-quarter to one-third of the federal budget, aiming at both the achievement of a first-strike nuclear capability and the development of a defensive shield against missile attack, the so-called Strategic Defense Initiative (SDI). Dubbed "Star Wars" by the media, the SDI plan called for the development of satellite-mounted lasers capable of destroying enemy missiles in flight. The Kremlin claimed that such satellites were actually intended for purposes of attack, a charge made credible by attempts to develop space-based offensive systems under the cloak of SDI. The Soviet Union took expensive countermeasures, further burdening its strained economy.

In March 1985, Mikhail Gorbachev (born 1931) succeeded Chernenko as First Secretary of the Communist party. The son of a peasant, Gorbachev had risen through the party's ranks. He had become convinced, however, that only radical reform could arrest the Soviet Union's decline. Moving boldly on both the domestic and foreign fronts, he announced a general program of economic "restructuring," or *perestroika*, while pressing the United States to negotiate major cuts in nuclear weapons.

Gorbachev's initiatives were interrelated. Faced with a declining GDP barely half the size of that of the United States, he knew that he could not match the Reagan military buildup without straining the Soviet economy to the breaking point. Beginning at Geneva in 1985, he pressed negotiations that culminated in 1988 with an agreement to eliminate Soviet and American medium- and short-range land-based missiles. At the same time he withdrew Soviet troops from Afghanistan and ended three decades of frozen relations with China by visiting Peking.

Gorbachev's urbanity and charm disarmed many, as did those of his attractive wife, Raisa. His evocation of Europe as a "common home" spoke tellingly to those who yearned for an end to the division that had beset the continent since 1945. At home he instituted a policy of "openness" (*glasnost*) that included the release of prominent dissidents, most notably the physicist Andrei Sakharov (1921–1989), and the publication of such long-banned works as the novel *Dr. Zhivago*, by Boris Pasternak (1890–1960), and *Requiem*, a memorial to the victims of Stalinism by Anna Akhmatova (1889–1966).

But Gorbachev's essential goals, though broad, were limited. In a speech at Prague in 1987 he spoke of *perestroika* as reconstructing rather than dismantling socialism. At home he remained committed to the Communist party's monopoly of power and to state control of the economy. *Glasnost*, too, revealed its limits.

Gorbachev's initial economic reforms were embodied in the Law on Socialist Enterprise (1987). Individual managers, freed from the control of the all-powerful State Planning Commission, could now buy supplies directly from one another and sell a portion of their output on the market. Prices, however, remained controlled, preventing the formation of wholesale markets and leaving managers dependent on the ministries in Moscow, themselves in disarray. The result was erratic supply, uncertain production, and inefficient distribution. Shortages cropped up everywhere, putting further pressure on official prices and shunting even basic commodities onto the black market.

While party conservatives stubbornly resisted the erosion of their power, free market advocates demanded the complete abandonment of centralized planning. *Glasnost* also produced unexpected results. A loose coalition of youth groups, intellectuals, and academics condemned the abuses of the Soviet system and appealed directly to the public with such tactics as impromptu street polls. Their ranks were swollen by returning veterans from Afghanistan. By 1987 more than 1,000 independent political clubs and study groups had sprung up in Moscow alone.

These new groups were embraced by Boris Yeltsin (born 1931), a maverick politician who broke with Gorbachev and, after being expelled from the Central Committee, dramatically resigned from the Communist party. Gorbachev, assailed from the left and the right, sought to consolidate power on an ever-narrowing base. He created the new executive post of president for himself but clung to his position as General Secretary.

While refusing to submit his presidency to a popular election, Gorbachev replaced the Supreme Soviet in 1989 with a new body, the Congress of People's Deputies. Although a portion of its seats were reserved for party nominees alone, non-Communists were permitted to contest the remainder in the first free elections held in the Soviet Union since 1917. At the same time, reformers swept to power in civic elections in Moscow and Leningrad, and Boris Yeltsin, elected president of the Russian Republic, promptly challenged Gorbachev's right to issue decrees binding on this government.

Sensing weakness at the center, Lithuania, forcibly incorporated into the USSR in 1940, declared its independence, and secession movements arose in the other Baltic republics of Latvia and Estonia as well as in the Ukraine and the Transcaucasus. Communist rule meanwhile collapsed throughout eastern Europe in 1989. The secession of Lithuania posed a threat to the Soviet Union itself. Aligning himself with conservative forces, he imposed an economic blockade on the region and in January 1991 seized public buildings in Vilnius as 14 died. Ethnic strife broke out between Armenia and Azerbaijan and

◉ *Perestroika:* Reform in Gorbachev's USSR ◉

In April 1985, Mikhail Gorbachev announced a policy of far-reaching reform that he called perestroika *("restructuring"). Gorbachev claimed that this policy of delegating more responsibility to the people, of encouraging initiative and openness, was a natural next stage in the development of the Soviet system. Here he describes his goals as a phase in the continuing revolution.*

We have come to the conclusion that unless we activate the human factor, that is, unless we take into consideration the diverse interests of people, work collectives, public bodies, and various social groups, unless we rely on them, and draw them into active, constructive endeavor, it will be impossible for us to accomplish any of the tasks set, or to change the situation in the country. . . .

It is wrong, and even harmful, to see socialist society as something rigid and unchangeable, to perceive its improvement as an effort to adapt complicated reality to concepts and formulas that have been established once and for all. The concepts of socialism keep on developing. . . .

Perestroika is a word with many meanings. But if we are to choose from its many possible synonyms the key one which expresses its essence most accurately, then we can say thus: *perestroika* is a revolution. A decisive acceleration of the socioeconomic and cultural development of Soviet society which involves radical changes on the way to a qualitatively new state is undoubtedly a revolutionary task. . . .

In accordance with our theory, revolution means construction, but it also always implies demolition. Revolution requires the demolition of all that is obsolete, stagnant and hinders fast progress. . . . *Perestroika* also means a resolute and radical elimination of obstacles hindering social and economic development, of outdated methods of managing the economy and of dogmatic stereotype mentality. . . .

And like a revolution, our day-to-day activities must be unparalleled, revolutionary. *Perestroika* requires Party leaders who are very close to Lenin's ideal of a revolutionary Bolshevik. Officialdom, red tape, patronizing attitudes, and careerism are incompatible with this ideal. On the other hand, courage, initiative, high ideological standards and moral purity, a constant urge to discuss things with people, and an ability to firmly uphold the humane values of socialism are greatly honored. . . . We still have a long way to go to achieve this ideal. Too many people are still "in the state of evolution," or, to put it plainly, have adopted a wait-and-see attitude.

Source: M. Gorbachev, *Perestroika: New Thinking for Our Country and the World* (New York: Harper & Row, 1987), pp. 29–55 passim.

elsewhere as Moscow's power waned and other republics defied the center. Embracing the left again, Gorbachev staked the remainder of his prestige on a new Union Treaty, which devolved extensive powers on the republics, leaving Moscow with control over foreign policy, the military, the currency, and other vaguely defined powers of coordination. At the same time, he renounced Marxism-Leninism as the official ideology of the Soviet Union.

On the eve of the treaty's signing in August, hard-line ministers and military chiefs sequestered Gorbachev in his vacation home in the Crimea and announced the seizure of power. The coup collapsed overnight as thousands of citizens poured into the streets of Moscow in protest. A defiant Boris Yeltsin barricaded himself in the Russian parliament building, and most military units withheld their support from the disorganized plotters. Despite its brevity, the coup's effect was decisive. When the shaken Gorbachev returned to Moscow, he found that many were suspicious of his own role, and most held him responsible for the treason of his cabinet.

Although Gorbachev dramatically dissolved the Communist party and offered other new concessions, the re-

◉ Vaclav Havel on the End of the Modern Era ◉

Vaclav Havel, playwright, former dissident, and former president of Czechoslovakia, comments on the significance of the collapse of communism in the Soviet Union and eastern Europe.

The end of Communism is, first and foremost, a message to the human race. It is a message we have not yet fully deciphered and comprehended. In its deepest sense, the end of Communism has brought a major era in human history to an end. It has brought an end not just to the 19th and 20th centuries, but to the modern age as a whole.

The modern era has been dominated by the culminating belief, expressed in different forms, that the world—and Being as such—is a wholly knowable system governed by a finite number of universal laws that man can grasp and rationally direct for his own benefit. This era, beginning in the Renaissance and developing from the Enlightenment to socialism, from positivism to scientism, from the Industrial Revolution to the information revolution, was characterized by rapid advances in rational, cognitive thinking.

This, in turn, gave rise to the proud belief that man, as the pinnacle of everything that exists, was capable of objectively describing, explaining and controlling everything that exists, and of possessing the one and only truth about the world. It was an era in which there was a cult of depersonalized objectivity, an era in which objective knowledge was amassed and technologically exploited, an era of belief in automatic progress brokered by the scientific method. It was an era of systems, institutions, mechanisms and statistical averages. It was an era of ideologies, doctrines, interpretations of reality, an era in which the goal was to find a universal theory of the world, and thus a universal key to unlock its prosperity.

Communism was the perverse extreme of this trend. It was an attempt, on the basis of a few propositions masquerading as the only scientific truth, to organize all of life according to a single model, and to subject it to central planning and control regardless of whether or not that was what life wanted.

The fall of Communism can be regarded as a sign that modern thought—based on the premise that the world is objectively knowable, and that the knowledge so obtained can be absolutely generalized—has come to a final crisis. This era has created the first global, or planetary, technical civilization, but it has reached the limit of its potential, the point beyond which the abyss begins. . . .

What is needed is something different, something larger. Man's attitude to the world must be radically changed. We have to abandon the arrogant belief that the world is merely a puzzle to be solved, a machine with instructions for use waiting to be discovered, a body of information to be fed into a computer in the hope that, sooner or later, it will spit out a universal solution. . . .

We must try harder to understand than to explain. The way forward is not in the mere construction of universal systemic solutions, to be applied to reality from the outside; it is also in seeking to get to the heart of reality through personal experience. Such an approach promotes an atmosphere of tolerant solidarity and unity in diversity based on mutual respect, genuine pluralism and parallelism. In a word, human uniqueness, human action and the human spirit must be rehabilitated.

Demonstrators in Moscow swarm over a tank as they protest the attempted coup against Gorbachev in August 1991. [AP/Wide World Photos]

publics now balked at the treaty, and as the sovereignty of the Baltic republics was recognized and the Ukraine voted overwhelmingly for independence as well, the Soviet Union collapsed. Effective power passed to Yeltsin as leader of the largest of the republics, and in late December Gorbachev resigned as president of a country that had already ceased to exist. Of the 12 non-Baltic republics, 11 adhered to a loose federation brokered by Yeltsin and the presidents of Ukraine and Belarus (Byelorussia), the Commonwealth of Independent States (CIS).

The CIS was little more than a fig leaf over the dissolution of the Soviet empire. From the beginning it was hamstrung by the rivalry between the two most popu-

Mikhail Gorbachev and Boris Yeltsin at the Russian parliament following the abortive coup of August 1991. [De Keerle/Grochowiak/SYGMA]

**Following the coup, angry
Russians topple a statue of
the founder of the KGB
(secret police).
[AP/Wide World Photos]**

lous republics, Russia and Ukraine, which vied for control of the Red Army and the Black Sea fleet. Ethnic violence broke out in Georgia and Moldova and continued between Armenia and Azerbaijan. Unable to secure the cooperation of the other republics, Yeltsin freed prices in Russia on January 2, 1992, effectively severing it economically from the rest of the CIS. The immediate result for Russia itself was unchecked inflation and crippling shortages of food, fuel, medicine, and other commodities. A $24 billion aid package was offered by the Western powers, but staggering problems remained.

History offers no parallel to the breakup of the Soviet empire. Itself the heir of a tsarist state that had gained control of the major part of the Eurasian landmass over

half a millennium, it extended in an unbroken territorial arc from Germany to the Pacific Ocean, and its allies and dependencies had stretched around the globe. For 40 years its rivalry with the United States had structured world politics. With a monolithic bureaucracy, a centrally administered economy, and the world's largest military, it seemed profoundly resistant to change. Yet in only six years, without natural calamity or external conquest, it had ceased to exist. Its demise left a score of new states, most ill-prepared for independence and with no tradition of self-rule, in its wake.

Scholars will long debate the reasons for this stunning denouement, as the world will long live with its consequences. Two observations may perhaps be haz-

THE AGE OF THE SUPERPOWERS

Détente: 1963–1979

1963	Partial Nuclear Test Ban Treaty
1965–1975	Vietnam War
1968	Soviets crush "Prague Spring" reform movement
1972	SALT I treaty
1975	Helsinki Accords

Containment and collapse: 1979–1991

1979–1989	Afghan War
1980	Solidarity movement in Poland
1988	Gorbachev announces unilateral withdrawal of 500,000 Soviet troops from eastern Europe by 1991
1989	Communist ruling parties fall in Poland, East Germany, Czechoslovakia, Romania; Berlin Wall dismantled
1990	Rebellions in the Soviet republics; Germany reunited
1991	Dissolution of the Soviet Union

42.3 The Independent Republics of the Former Soviet Union

arded at this juncture. The Soviet system was, in retrospect, the last of the great empires that had characterized the world of the nineteenth and early twentieth centuries. As the Turkish, Austrian, British, and French empires, weakened by war, collapsed in turn under the pressure of nationalist revolts, so ultimately did that of the Soviets. Yet the Soviet Union was also unique as a political entity, being predicated on the idea of a state whose function, as the dictatorship of the proletariat, was the supersession of all states, including itself. The power and privilege of the Communist party was based on this notion of a temporary stewardship and on its historic role as the solvent of class society. When Mikhail Gorbachev admitted that it had failed in this task and permitted the party to be openly criticized as an entrenched elite, he undermined whatever pretense of legitimacy it retained, and when in his last days of rule he

formally jettisoned Marxism-Leninism and dissolved the party itself, he left no ideology around which his state could cohere.

The moribund state of the Soviet economy, with its outmoded plants, absence of incentive, and lack of price discipline, contributed to the collapse. It was obvious to Gorbachev and his advisers that chaotic breakdown must be avoided as they moved toward a market economy, but production broke down and living standards plummeted. This was compounded by the public's reluctance to accept the consequences of the market. It is unlikely, however, that even a more committed application of market principles could have staved off collapse. In the words of Anatoly Sobchak, the mayor of Leningrad (now again called St. Petersburg), Gorbachev had "tried to reform the unreformable."

The collapse of the Soviet empire had severe secondary consequences. The transition to market economies wreaked havoc in eastern Europe, where fledgling democracies struggled, as after World War I, to overcome a legacy of dependence and autocracy. In Romania, the more or less open sale of children from state orphanages provided a source of hard currency, while in Albania, the last European state to renounce communism, prisoners refused their freedom for fear of going unfed. Yugoslavia disintegrated as its constituent republics renounced their union and savage wars among them claimed tens of thousands of lives.

As the twentieth century approached its end, two distinct political trends were apparent. On the one hand, ethnic particularism seemed triumphant in the former Soviet empire, where a score of new states had emerged and the potential for still further secession remained. On the other, the European Community furnished a model for supranational associations around the globe, suggesting a future of blocs grouped around dominant regional powers. Thus economic integration and political separatism, both growing apace but pulling in different directions, contested the future of the late-twentieth-century world.

Notes

1. F. Freidel, *America in the Twentieth Century* (New York: Knopf, 1960), pp. 475–476.

Suggestions for Further Reading

Ash, T. G. *The Uses of Adversity: Essays on the Fate of Central Europe.* New York: Random House, 1990.

Brzezinski, Z. K. *The Soviet Bloc: Unity and Compromise.* Cambridge, Mass.: Harvard University Press, 1967.

Crankshaw, E. *Khrushchev.* New York: Viking Press, 1966.

Daltrop, A. *Politics and the European Community,* 2nd ed. New York: Longman, 1986.

Dawisha, K. *Eastern Europe, Gorbachev and Reform: The Great Challenge.* Cambridge: Cambridge University Press, 1988.

De Porte, A. W. *Europe Between the Superpowers.* New Haven, Conn.: Yale University Press, 1979.

Epstein, W. *The Last Chance: Nuclear Proliferation and Arms Control.* New York: Free Press, 1976.

Fejto, F. *A History of the People's Democracies: Eastern Europe Since Stalin.* New York: Praeger, 1971.

Freedman, L. *The Evolution of Nuclear Strategy.* New York: St. Martin's Press, 1982.

Kriegel, A. *Eurocommunism.* Stanford, Calif.: Stanford University Press, 1978.

Laqueur, W. *Europe Since Hitler.* London: Weidenfeld & Nicolson, 1972.

Lovenduski, J. *Women and European Politics.* Amherst: University of Massachusetts Press, 1986.

Mazrui, A. A. *Africa's International Relations: The Diplomacy of Dependency and Change.* Boulder, Colo.: Westview Press, 1977.

Milward, A. S. *The Reconstruction of Western Europe, 1945–51.* Berkeley: University of California Press, 1984.

Pinkus, B. *The Jews of the Soviet Union: A History of a National Minority.* Cambridge: Cambridge University Press, 1988.

Rothschild, J. *Return to Diversity: A Political History of East Central Europe.* New York: Oxford University Press, 1989.

Sheehy, G. *Gorbachev: The Man Who Changed the World.* New York: Harper & Row, 1990.

Ulam, A. *Expansion and Coexistence: The History of Soviet Foreign Policy, 1917–1967,* 2nd ed. New York: Praeger, 1974.

Van der Wee, H. *Prosperity and Upheaval: The World Economy, 1945–1980.* Berkeley: University of California Press, 1988.

Von Laue, T. *The World Revolution of Westernization: The Twentieth Century in Global Perspective.* New York: Oxford University Press, 1987.

EPILOGUE

Civilization and the Dilemma of Progress

In the modern era the prevailing view of the historical process has been defined by the concept of progress, which sees history as a steady advance toward a better world. A century ago one proponent of progress, the American writer Edward Bellamy (1850–1898), wrote a popular novel that embodied this belief. In *Looking Backward*, Bellamy imagined a man who fell into a hypnotic sleep in 1887 and awoke in the year 2000. The man discovered a perfect world of universal peace and happiness in which all people shared equally in the wealth and benefits of a society freed from conflict, greed, and even the need for laws. Repelled by the social evils of his own day, Bellamy believed that the future had to be better than the past and that it would inevitably lead to an ideal civilization.

A powerful symbol of twentieth-century technology, the United States space shuttle *Discovery* roars off the launching pad in September 1988. [UPI/Bettmann Newsphotos]

History, Time, and Progress

Looking Backward belongs to a long utopian tradition that stretches back to Plato's fourth-century B.C. *Republic*. Bellamy's optimism for the future stemmed from a prejudice against the past, for his vision of progress did not permit him to see the mixture of good and bad that is present in every period of history. Like many others then and now, he assumed that the passage of time automatically brought with it improvement over what had been before. Those who embrace this view generally assume that the closer in time to our own day, the better human life has been, that the present is superior to the past because it is now rather than then. Yet in his letter from Birmingham Jail, written in 1963, the American civil rights leader Martin Luther King, Jr., pointedly rejected the "strangely irrational notion that there is something in the very flow of time that will inevitably cure all ills."[1] The notion of progress has often obscured the fact that even at moments of relative peace and prosperity, certain groups without power or status—such as workers, racial minorities, and women—have not shared in the broad advances made by society at large.

Bellamy's understanding of progress reflects a relatively modern, peculiarly Western world view that broke with older Western and non-Western traditions alike. Earlier civilizations had viewed progress chiefly in spiritual or theological terms and tended to see history as cyclical rather than progressive. The ancient Greeks of the Classical Age believed that their ancestors had been more "heroic" and thus better. Confucius, whose ethical philosophy dominated Chinese thought, accepted the notion of social improvement through education and good example, but he also inculcated a respect for the knowledge and wisdom of the past and a measured view of the present and future. The Judeo-Christian and Islamic religions prophesied salvation and the attainment of a heavenly paradise through spiritual rectitude but had no place for a secular conception of progress. The Hindu and Buddhist concept of reincarnation, which stressed "progress" from lower to higher states of being, aspired to the ultimate spiritual state of nirvana that would transcend the material world. Indian conceptions of history were decidedly cyclical; the period since about 900 B.C., in which we still live, the *kali-yuga*, was conceived as one of decline and chaos.

Nineteenth-century Western thinkers were thus a minority in viewing progress in secular terms, based on belief in the material perfectibility of society. In this sense the human adventure is measured in terms of our ability to master the physical environment through scientific and technological advances and to improve the level of material well-being and comfort through the ever-increasing accumulation of wealth. Advocates of this conception of progress claimed that improvement would come through the application of knowledge to political, social, and economic problems. History, according to this view, would unfold as the natural laws that governed the universe were discovered and manipulated in the interest of human improvement. The ethos of liberal capitalism sought to unfetter the laws of economics in order to achieve the greatest material good for the greatest number of people.

Even while this conception gained ascendancy in the West, a variety of reform-minded thinkers recoiled against the effects of industrialism by experimenting with socialist utopias in which private ownership of capital was replaced by communal property in rural egalitarian societies. Some utopian socialists even conceived of a technocratic society in which scientists and industrialists governed on behalf of the general populace. Then, in the mid-nineteenth century, "scientific" socialists explained history as the product of class conflict: categories of human beings—classes—competed for ascendancy by seeking control over the means of production and distribution. The Marxist utopia looked forward to the inevitable triumph of the working class over the capitalists and the ultimate creation of a classless society.

Bellamy's utopia was a combination of these visions. It imagined a highly organized industrial society in which a secular state exercised complete authority and evoked voluntary compliance from its citizens because it provided them with material comfort and well-being. Though repelled by the poverty and exploitation that characterized the expanding industrialization of his time, Bellamy remained a believer in the ability of technology to resolve the ills of modern society.

More than a century after the publication of *Looking Backward*, modern writers have become less sanguine about the benefits of a technological society. In 1932, in the midst of the Great Depression, the British author Aldous Huxley published *Brave New World*, a novel that depicted a totalitarian society in which people lacked no bodily comfort but were without freedom or creativity. In 1949, following World War II, George Orwell portrayed a dehumanized totalitarian society of the future in his book *Nineteen Eighty-four*. The appalling nature of such totalitarian regimes as those of Hitler and Stalin and the specter of the atomic bomb provided the impetus for Orwell's novel and its bleak vision of the future. Orwell's message, in the words of the psychologist Erich Fromm, was intended to awaken us to the common "danger of a society of automatons who will have lost every trace of individuality, of love, of critical thought, and yet who will not be aware of it."[2]

Global Implications of Progress

The materialist theory of progress provided a powerful rationale for the imperialism that conquered much of the non-Western world in the late nineteenth century. Many Europeans believed that they were bringing the benefits of their technologically superior civilization to unfortunate primitive peoples. Western science and industry, on which the theory of progress was based, in turn made possible imperialist domination over much of the rest of the world.

As we have seen, the reaction of the non-Western world to the Western intrusion has been mixed. The Chinese effort to keep all Western influences out of their country was by no means the norm, for the Japanese aggressively adopted Western-style industrialization and technology, both to resist Western domination and to extend their own hegemony over East Asia. Similarly, some southern African tribes conquered their neighbors with European firearms, and Arab traders used Western weapons to capture Africans for the slave market. In the early twentieth century Turkish and Iranian admirers of Western technology attempted to "modernize" their countries along the Western model, but more recently Islamic fundamentalists, particularly in Iran, have strenuously repudiated Western influences.

The Western idea of progress continues to influence both Western policies toward the nonindustrialized nations and Third World thinking about how to solve the immense social, economic, and cultural problems endemic to their own countries. Since World War II, industrialized nations have systematically exported their notion of progress to underdeveloped states as they emerged from colonial status to independence. In 1961 President John F. Kennedy announced a massive program of economic assistance for Latin America that he called the Alliance for Progress.

As Western developmental strategies for "modernization" replaced imperialism as the basis of the global dynamic, new forms of dependence have been substituted for older forms of subjugation. During the struggle for India's independence from the British, Mahatma Gandhi—who recognized the relationship between imperialism and the materialist notion of progress—rejected the Western model of development by urging his fellow Indians to adopt the traditional spinning wheel as the symbol of freedom and national regeneration.

Despite Gandhi's rejection of modern technology, his successors embraced Western-style industrialization, making India one of the first Third World countries to develop not only conventional electrical energy sources but a nuclear capability as well. Most other underdevel-

oped nations followed suit, generally adopting an enthusiastic attitude toward technology, with its capacity to enhance health as well as material comforts. Thus agricultural societies often seek to build huge dams, hydroelectric plants, and nuclear energy stations in order to electrify and industrialize their economies, but sometimes at the expense of destroying millions of acres of irreplaceable forests in the process of extracting raw materials and constructing factories. The problem is clearly one of balance; industrialization and conservation need not be mutually antagonistic.

Reliance on Western technology has at times been seriously disruptive to the Third World. The technology of advanced industrial nations and the accompanying infrastructures of such technology are not necessarily ideal or suited for developing countries. Historically, modern technology has been marked by its complex and large-scale character, and its success has depended on extensive national markets, skilled labor, and substantial investment capital. Because developing countries generally lack these resources, simple and inexpensive machinery that does not require extensive education and training may be more appropriate to agrarian societies. Moreover, since 1945 most technological development in the Third World has been undertaken with extensive loans borrowed from Western nations; the resultant economic dependence has crippled the debtor nations, most of which are unable to repay their huge obligations.

In recent years a rethinking of the Western notion of material progress has been unfolding. Not only has the idea of "appropriate technology" gained currency, but it is now increasingly recognized that Third World nations need not necessarily undergo the same stressful stages of development experienced by earlier industrial societies. It is probable, nonetheless, that the rapid transformation of the globe and of its human societies will continue, driven by technological change and its political ramifications.

Science, Technology, and the Environment

As the twentieth century draws to a close, civilization appears to be beset with a host of unparalleled problems. There is irony in the fact that science and technology have made the lives of millions of people more comfortable, yet they have also been the source of unanticipated dilemmas, not the least of which is the ultimate challenge of avoiding nuclear war.

Advances in health care have been startling, especially in the prevention and cure of human d

Foremost among them has been the discovery in 1930 of penicillin, which led to the development of numerous other antibiotics to combat bacteria. Equally important was the discovery of microscopic organisms called viruses, which can reproduce inside living cells and cause such diseases as poliomyelitis and measles. These achievements eventually enabled scientists to explain the cause of a host of dangerous diseases and to develop vaccines against them.

Yet such medical breakthroughs have resulted in lower mortality rates and longer lives, so that a global population explosion threatens to engulf the poorer societies of the Third World in a relentless cycle of poverty and social despair. Although new agricultural methods have increased food productivity, natural disasters and political upheavals periodically create crises of starvation and malnutrition for millions. Nor has medical science shown itself to hold all the answers to health problems. The human race, for example, is now faced with a medical challenge of immense scope that offers no immediate hope of resolution: AIDS (acquired immune deficiency syndrome). First recognized in 1981, AIDS is a viral disorder, spread through blood or body fluids, that affects the body's disease-fighting mechanisms. Although perhaps as many as 20 million people are currently infected by the AIDS virus throughout the world, especially in Africa, there is as yet no known cure.

Despite the Western reliance on the vision of unrestricted progress, one of the most serious problems facing the global community is the challenge of improving and protecting the environment. The earth's ecological balance is maintained by a complex series of biological and chemical subsystems, all of which are kept in balance by delicate interaction with one another. The danger lies in the fact that the demands of industrialization and other forms of economic development, which have despoiled much of the globe's forests, rivers, seas, and air, may push environmental destruction beyond the point of salvation.

Factories and automobiles have already polluted the air over large American and European cities with dangerous levels of carbon monoxide, nitrogen oxides, and sulfur dioxide. One result has been that as chemicals fill the air above the planet, the normal composition of the atmosphere has begun to change. Some scientists believe that these chemicals trap infrared rays within the atmosphere, producing the so-called greenhouse effect, whereby the earth's temperatures are increasing. No less critical is the fact that the coastal waters of the Mediterranean are so damaged by chemical pollutants that much of the seafood caught there is now inedible. Industrial plants pour millions of gallons of chemical waste into rivers and oceans, while synthetic products that are not biodegradable—that is, that cannot be broken down by biological process—accumulate in ever-greater

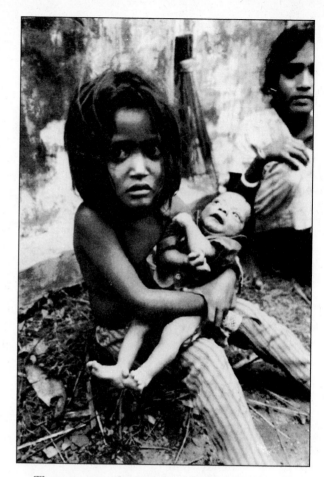

The poverty and social despair that plague the Third World are vividly reflected in this photograph of two children rendered homeless by a hurricane that struck Bangladesh in the spring of 1991. [AP/Wide World Photos]

amounts. In this connection, the disposal of nuclear waste from energy production has become an especially critical issue, for such waste products become nonradioactive only after thousands of years. Government and private attempts to bury nuclear waste deep in the deserts of the United States have met with stiff resistance from local inhabitants and environmentalists.

However serious its impact, the pollution of the environment is only one side of the ecological damage wrought by humans. The other is represented by the wasteful destruction of limited natural resources. Serious efforts to conserve fossil fuels, for example, have been resisted by both private industry and government policy. Now that the depletion of finite energy resources looms as a distinct possibility, the harnessing of atomic power as an energy alternative is fraught with other dangers, as dramatized by the 1979 meltdown at the Three

Mile Island nuclear power plant in Pennsylvania and the 1986 disaster at the plant in Chernobyl, Ukraine.

In the United States and elsewhere, lumber interests and developers have pressed for ever-greater access to forest lands, and in the state of Washington ancient forests have fallen to the timber saw. More startling, however, has been the deliberate destruction of the rain forests in the Amazon region of South America as well as in Costa Rica, Indonesia, and Malaysia. Every day, millions of acres of these dense tropical forests are destroyed, mainly by burning, as enormous population pressures prompt governments to clear land for agricultural purposes. Yet the tragic irony of this process is that rain forest soil is unsuited to crop production and much of the land is quickly abandoned, although it cannot easily return to its original state. If the destruction continues at the present rate, most of the immense rain forests of the globe will be gone in 20 years.

These and similar problems are international in scope. Industrial fumes from factories in the United States, for example, have caused environmental problems in Canada through acid rain, in which atmospheric pollution is brought back down to earth in rainfall. Similarly, the fallout from Chernobyl has reached western European nations. The need to combat all forms of ecological damage grows more pressing every day. Concerted efforts in this direction may yet reverse the harm already done, but the urgency is critical. Today, material "progress" is more than ever a two-edged sword as the human race faces the prospect of self-destruction.

Facing the Future: History as Freedom

Despite advances achieved in the struggle for human rights by racial minorities, women, and other oppressed groups, vast inequities in economic justice and political freedom continue to exist—in Third World countries, in ex-Communist nations, and in the Western world. These and other issues are compelling and dangerous, but the problems of our age are unique only in the particular forms they now assume. If nothing else, history provides us with perspective: war and conflict, disease and hunger, prejudice and exploitation, torture and state repression are some of the less pleasant features of history that our age has in common with all civilizations of the past. Over the course of 5,000 years, all societies have at times perceived the challenges facing them as insurmountable. Yet history also suggests that even though the problems recur relentlessly, determined people continue to seek durable solutions to them.

Change, often rapid and unpredictable, has been the hallmark of history. Even the most conservative of cultures, as in ancient Egypt or medieval China, underwent sudden and dramatic shifts in social and religious beliefs and political structure. Later generations do, of course, inherit traditions and values from the past, but they sometimes choose to discard them in the light of new circumstances. Those moments when people have overcome adversity represent recurrent evidence of the open-endedness of history. Perhaps the only constraint under which our own age operates is the fact that as the world develops into a truly global community, we increasingly share the same human experience and thus equal responsibility for the world we make.

Notes

1. M. L. King, Jr., *Why We Can't Wait* (New York: Harper & Row, 1963), p. 89.
2. E. Fromm, "Afterword," in G. Orwell, *Nineteen Eighty-four* (New York: New American Library, 1961), p. 267.

Aachen [*ah*-kun] (Aix-la-Chapelle),
332–333
Abbas, Shah, 560–561
Abbasids [*ab*-uh-sidz, uh-*bah*-sidz],
217–218, 221, 332, 559
Abdul Hamid II, 862, 992
Abdullah, Amir, 1099
Abelard [*ab*-uh-lahrd], Peter, 379
Abolitionist movement, 701–702
Aborigines, 507
Abortion, 163, 598, 1148
Abraham, 33, 184–185
Abstract Expressionism, 965
Abu Bakr [ah-boo *bahk*-uhr], 215
Abyssinia. *See* Ethiopia
Academy (Athens), 125
Academy (Florence), 423, 432
Achaean [uh-*kee*-uhn] League, 130–131
Achebe, Chinua, 1124
Acid rain, 1125
Acre [*ah*-ker], 352
Acropolis (Athens), 116–119
Act in Restraint of Appeals (1533), 467
Acts and Monuments (Foxe), 473
Action Française [ek-syon frahn-*sez*], 939,
1013
Actium [*ak*-tee-uhm], battle of, 153
Act of Supremacy (1534), 468
Adams, Abigail, 702
Adams, John, 674, 702
Addams, Jane, 884
*Address to the Christian Nobility of the
German Nation* (Luther), 457
Adelard of Bath, 372
Adena culture, 276–277
Adenauer [*ah*-d'n-ow-er], Konrad, 1047
Adler, Victor, 858
Adoptive emperors, 158–159
Adowa [*ah*-doh-wah], battle of, 908
Adrianople [ay-dree-uhn-*noh*-puhl], battle
of, 169, 201
Adulis, 239
Adultery, 208
Aeneid [ih-*nee*-ihd] (Virgil), 156–157
Aequi [*ee*-kwye], 146
Aeschylus [*es*-kih-luhs], 120

Aetolian [ee-*tohl*-yuhn] League, 130–131
Affirmative action, 1151
Afghanistan, 215, 285, 548, 550, 745, 758,
761, 917, 942, 1089–1090, 1160, 1164
Africa: geography, 232–233; agriculture
and ironworking, 233–235; early society and culture, 235–236; kingdom of
Kush, 236–238; kingdom of Axum,
238–239; introduction of Christianity,
238–239; early trading patterns,
239–243; the slave trade, 241–243;
kingdom of Ghana, 243; empire of
Mali, 244–247; empire of Songhai,
247–248; Kanem-Bornu and the Hausa
states, 248–250; states of the Guinea
coast, 250; states of East Africa,
250–253; southern Africa, 253–254;
Nok culture, 447; Ife sculpture,
447–448; women in the early modern
period, 595; sexual customs in, 597; African views of death, 737; and the New
Imperialism, 904–910; on the eve of
World War I, 943; in World War I, 947;
seeds of independence, 1114–1115;
granting of independence, 1115–1120;
modern South Africa, 1120–1122; African National Congress, 1114,
1121–1122
Afrikaners. *See* Boers
Afro-Asian Conference (1955), 1158
Agadir [ah-gah-*deer*] crisis, 943
Agamemnon, 92
Agincourt [ah-zhan-*koor*], battle of, 395
Agra [*ah*-gra], 548, 553–554, 557, 743,
744, 746
Agricola, 162
Agricola, Rudolf, 425
Agriculture: origins of, 8–9; Neolithic,
8–9, 10–11, 47; Mesopotamian, 18–19,
21; Hittite, 37; origins in India, 47; in
ancient China, 70, 71, 73, 77; in classi-
cal Athens, 106; Hellenistic, 132; early
Roman, 145; classical Roman, 150, 155;
Byzantine, 204–205; in early Africa,
233–235; in ancient Ethiopia, 238; in
Ghana, 243; prehistoric American, 257;

Maya, 263; Aztec, 268; in medieval
Southeast Asia, 300, 301; in ancient
China, 306, 318; in medieval Europe,
336–338; in early modern Europe,
481–482, 502; in Spanish America,
498–499; in Ming China, 569; in the
Americas, 660; in early modern Britain,
668; in Ch'ing China, 768–770, 774;
and the first phase of the Industrial
Revolution, 794–795; in the Soviet
Union, 1016; in modern China, 1059; in
modern India, 1086, 1087
Agrippina [ag-rih-*pee*-nuh], 157
Ahimsa [ah-*hihm*-suh], 173
Ahmed Chelebi, Ahi, 547
Ahmedi, 547
Ahmose, 28
Ahura-Mazda [ah-*hoo*-rah *mahz*-duh],
183, 184
AIDS, 1124, 1174
Ainu [*eye*-noo], 323
Airplane, invention of, 813
Aix-la-Chapelle [*eks*-lah-shah-*pell*], Treaty
of, 670, 749
Akbar [*ak*-bahr], 548–552, 559
Akhmatova, Anna, 1164
Akkadians [uh-*kay*-dee-uhnz], 20–21, 226
al-Abbas, Abu, 217
Alalia, battle of, 143
Alamogordo, nuclear testing at, 1042
Alaric [*al*-uh-rik], 170
Alaska, 256, 280–281, 675
al-Bakri [al-bah-*kree*], 243
Albania, 943; between the world wars,
1021–1022; Italian invasion of, 1031;
after World War II, 1047, 1146
Albert (Belgium), 932
Alberta, Canada, 1152
Albertus Magnus [al-*bur*-tuhs *mag*-nuhs],
370, 372
Albigensian [al-bih-*jehn*-see-uhn] Cru-
sade, 364
Albigensians, 364
Albizzi [ahl-*beet*-tsee] family, 410
Albuquerque, Affonso de [uh-*fahn*-zoh
dih uhl-boo-*ker*-kuh], 491

Alcala [ahl-kah-*lah*], University of, 469
Alchemy [*al*-kuh-mee], 181, 221, 372
Alcibiades [al-sih-*bye*-uh-deez], 112
Alcuin [*al*-kwin], 332
Alemanni [*ahl*-eh-mahn-ee], 166, 170
Alembert, Jean d' [dal-ehm-*behr*], 691
Aleutian islands, 280, 1037
Aleuts [uh-*lootz*], 280
Alexander (Yugoslavia), 1022
Alexander I (Russia), 730, 732, 733, 819, 820, 823, 824, 859, 862
Alexander II (Russia), 854, 859, 860, 862, 890
Alexander III (Russia), 859, 860
Alexander VI, Pope, 407, 408, 410, 428, 454, 486
Alexander of Hales, 369–370
Alexander the Great, 54–55, 58, 127–129, 136
Alexandra, 970
Alexandria, 59; and the Hellenistic Kingdoms, 128, 129; and the Ptolemies, 134; women in, 138; in the Roman Empire, 152, 166; and the Byzantine Empire, 201; and the Black Death, 391; and the Ottomans, 545; modern, 909
Alexius I Comnenus [uh-*lek*-see-uhs kuhm-*nee*-nuhs], 208, 330, 350–351
Alfonsín, Raúl, 1130
Alfonso V, "the Magnanimous" (Aragon), 408
Alfonso VI (Castile), 354
Alfonso VII (Castile), 354
Alfonso X, "the Wise" (Castile), 366, 380
Alfonso XII (Spain), 883
Alfred the Great (England), 376
Algeciras [ahl-jeh-*seer*-uhs] Conference, 942
Algeria, 906, 908, 1100, 1103, 1122–1123
al-Ghazali [al-ga-*zah*-lee], Muhammad ibn, 222
Algiers, 860, 861
Algoa [al-*goh*-uh], 488
Alhambra (palace), 355
al-Haytham (Alhazen), 222
Ali [ah-*lee*], 215
Ali, Hussein [hoo-*sayn*] ibn-, 947, 1099
Ali, Muhammad, 860
Ali, Sunni [*soh*-nee], 247–248
al-Khwarizmi [al-*khwah*-rahz-mee], Muhammad ibn-Musa, 222
al-Kindi [al-*kihn*-dee], Yaqub, 222
Allende, Salvador [sahl-vah-*dohr* ah-*yane*-day], 1130–1131
Alliance for Progress, 1173
All Quiet on the Western Front (Remarque), 953
Almagest (Ptolemy), 135
al-Mansur, Abu Ja'far, 217
Almohades [*al*-moh-haydz], 355
Almoravids [al-*moh*-rah-vyedz], 243, 245, 354, 355
al-Muntazar, Muhammad, 215
Alphabet, 33, 93, 226–230, 321, 322
al-Rahman, Abd, 217
al-Rashid, Harun, 221
al-Razi [ahl *rah*-zee] (Rhazes), 221–222
Alsace [ahl-*zahs*], 407, 617, 857, 952

Alva, Duke of, 518
Amarna, 28–30
Amasis [a-*mah*-sis], 100
Amenhotep IV (Akhenaton) [ah-kuhn-*ah*-tahn], 28–30
American Civil War, 675
American Popular Revolutionary Alliance (APRA), 1131
Americas, European conquest of, 495–500
Amerindians. *See* Mesoamerica, Amerindians of; North America, Amerindians of; South America, Amerindians of
Amherst, Lord, 773, 774
Amiens [ah-*myahn*], 375; Peace of, 729
Amin, Idi [ee-dee ah-*meen*], 1119
Ammianus, Marcellinus, 170
Amon-Re [*ah*-men-ray], 25
Amorites [*am*-uh-rites], 22
Amos, 186
Amoy, 577
Amritsar [um-*riht*-ser], 556; massacre at, 917, 987, 1087
Amsterdam, 527–528, 611, 792, 807
Amundsen, Roald, 1109, 1111
Amur [ah-*moor*] River, 494
Amur valley, 923
Anabaptists, 465–466
Analects, 75
Anarchists, 859, 889, 890
Anasazi (Pueblo) culture, 278–279
Anatolia [an-uh-*toh*-lee-uh], 36, 42, 350
Anatomy, in the scientific revolution, 639
Anaxagoras of Clazomenae [an-aks-*ag*-oh-rahs of klah-*zom*-eh-nee], 123
Anaximander [uh-*nahk*-suh-man-dur], 122–123, 508, 634
Anaximenes [an-aks-*ihm*-eh-neez], 123
Ancestor worship, 71, 180, 386
Andes [*an*-deez] Mountains, 257, 273–274
Andronicus I [an-druh-*nee*-kuhs], 207
Andropov, Yuri [*yoo*-ree uhn-*droh*-poff], 1164
Angad, 555–556
Angelico, Fra [frah an-*jel*-ih-koh], 420
Anger, Jane, 702
Angevin [*an*-juh-vihn] Empire, 340
Angkor [*ahng* kohr], 298, 299–300
Angles, 170, 331
Anglo-Saxon Chronicle, 376
Anglo-Indians, 915
Anglo-Saxons, 194
Angola, 488, 489, 906, 1115, 1116, 1119
Anguissola [ahn-*gwee*-soh-lah], Sofonisba, 436
Animals, domestication of, 70
Anjou [*ahn*-zhoo], 340, 407, 612
Ankara [*ang*-kuh-ruh], 992
Annam [ah-*nam*], 301
Anne (England), 619–620, 630
Anne of Austria, 525
Anne of Bohemia, 398
Anne of Cleves, 477
Anschluss [*ahn*-schloos], 952, 1013, 1027, 1030
Anselm [*an*-selm], 369
Antarctica, 1110

Anthony, 193
Anthony, Susan B., 704, 886
Anti-Comintern Pact, 1026
Antigone [an-*tig*-uh-nee] (Sophocles), 121–122
Antigonus [an-*tig*-uh-nuhs], 130
Antioch [*an*-tee-ahk], 129–130, 132, 166, 201, 204, 351, 352
Antiochus I [an-*tee*-oh-kuhs], 56, 129, 138
Antiochus III, 133, 139
Anti-Semitism: medieval, 393; early modern, 474, 476, 699–700; modern, 858, 862, 863, 864, 880, 935, 939, 1005–1006, 1012, 1014, 1038–1040, 1092, 1128
Antoninus (Caracalla) [an-toh-*nye*-nuhs], 159
Antwerp [*an*-twurp], 481, 503–504, 519
Anuradhapura [ah-*noo*-rah-dah-*poo*-rah], 61
Anyang [*ahn*-yahng] (Yin), 70–71, 84, 228
Apache, 279, 281
Apartheid [uh-*pahrt*-ayt], 1120–1122, 1124
Appeasement, policy of, 1030
Aqaba [*ah*-kah-bah], Gulf of, 1097
Aqueducts (Roman), 161
Aquinas [uh-*kwye*-nuhs], Thomas, 369–370
Aquino [ah-*keen*-oh], Corazon, 1071, 1072
Aquitaine [*ak*-wih-tayn], 340, 344, 394–395
Arabia, 212–213, 216, 218, 947
Arab-Israeli Wars: 1948–1949, 1094; 1967 (Six Day War), 1097; 1973 (Yom Kippur War), 1096, 1097
Arab League, 1158
Arabs: early history, 212–213; rise of Islam, 213–215; Umayyads, 215–217; Abbasids, 217–218; medieval economy, 218–219; medieval society, 219–220; scripts of, 229–230; invasion of Europe, 333; and the struggle for Palestine, 1092–1095; Arab-Israeli wars, 1097–1098; and nationalism, 1098–1099; Egyptian revolution, 1099–1100
Arafat, Yasir, 1104–1105
Aragon [*air*-uh-gahn], 354, 355, 404–405, 513, 526
Archaeology, 753
Archaic period (Greece), 95–96
Archaic period (the Americas), 256–257
Archangel, 500, 623, 1045
Archilochus [ahr-*kihl*-oh-kuhs], 96
Archimedes [ahr-kih-*mee*-deez] of Syracuse, 135, 638
Architecture: in ancient Egypt, 32; in Ceylon, 61; in ancient China, 71; classical Greek, 116–119; classical Roman, 158, 159–160, 164–165; Buddhist, 177–178; Byzantine, 209–210; Kushite, 236; in Mali, 247; Olmec, 257–258; Maya, 260, 262, 264; medieval Indian, 293; Indonesian, 301; Japanese, 326; Islamic Spanish, 355; Romanesque, 373; Gothic, 374–375; Italian Renaissance,

436–437; in the Reformation, 476; Taj Mahal, 554; Baroque, 650; in Ch'ing China, 771; modern Western, 938, 958–959; in Nazi Germany, 1011

Archons, 100, 104

Arezzo [ah-*rayt*-tsoh], 155

Areopagus, 100, 102

Argentina: colonial, 678; in the first phase of the Industrial Revolution, 814; modern, 865, 866, 1127, 1128–1130, 1138, 1139, 1140

Argos [*ahr*-gahs], 126

Arianism [*air*-ee-an-ism], 193

Arias Sanchez [*ahr*-ee-uhs *san*-chez], Oscar, 1136

Ariosto [ah-ree-*os*-toh], Ludovico, 648

Aristagoras, 508

Aristarchus [ar-ihs-*tahr*-kuhs] of Samos, 135, 509, 634

Aristocracy: ancient Chinese, 71, 82–83; Etruscan, 144; early Roman, 145; Byzantine, 207; in the early Islam world, 219; Aztec, 268–269; Inca, 274–275; Japanese, 325–326; in medieval Europe, 335, 339; in early modern Europe, 481–482, 588–590, 591–592; in early modern Britain, 666–668; nineteenth-century European, 872; in Russia, 954. *See also* Daimyo

Aristodama [ar-ihs-toh-*dah*-mah] of Smyrna, 138, 139

Aristophanes [ar-ihs-*toff*-uh-neez], 122, 124, 508

Aristotle, 106, 125–126, 127, 634

Ark of the Covenant, 187, 238

Arkwright, Richard, 797

Arles [ahrl], Council of, 193

Armenia [ahr-*mee*-nee-uh], 201, 215, 216, 350, 975, 1164, 1168

Arminians, 527, 529

Arms races: pre-1914, 942–943; post-1945, 1163

Arno River, 418

Arrau, Claudio [*klow*-dyoh ahr-*rah*-oo], 1139

Arsinoë [ahr-*sihn*-oh-ee] II, *138*

Arthashastra, 55, 64

Arthurian legends, 378

Articles of Confederation, 674

Article 231, 951–952

Art of Love, The (Ovid), 157

Aryans [*ar*-yenz], 173, 227; migrations of, 47, 52; domination of India, 52-53; culture of, 53

Asceticism, 173, 174, 193–194

Ashanti [ah-*shahn*-tee], 484, 904

Ashikaga [ah-shee-*kah*-gah] shogunate, 326–328

Ashkenazim, 698

Ashoka [ah-*shoh*-kah], 56–58, 65, 176, 227, 230

Ashurnasirpal [ah-shoor-*nas*-ihr-pahl], 39

Asia Minor: and the Hittites, 36–38; ancient, 40, 102; in the fourth century B.C., 126, 128; in the Hellenistic period, 126, 128, 131; medieval, 201, 216, 218, 250, 352, 353; and the Ottomans, 539; modern, 992

Asiatic Society of Bengal, 753, 758

Assam, 915

Assembly (Athens), 102, 103, 104

Assembly of Notables, 710

Assyrians, 36, 38, 39–40, 235; defeat of the Kushites, 236

Astell, Mary, 531

Astrology, 133, 137, 372

Astronomy: Hellenistic, 135; in Ming China, 579–580; in the Middle Ages, 634–635; in the Scientific Revolution, 636–639; and mapping, 1108–1112

Asturias [as-*tew*-rih-ahs], Miguel Angel, 1138

Aswan Dam, 1100

Atahualpa [ah-tah-*wahl*-pah], 276, 496

Atatürk [at-ah-*turk*]. *See* Mustapha Kemal

Athabaskans, 281

Athens, 201; emergence of democracy, 99–102; and the Persian Wars, 102–103; in the Age of Pericles, 103–108; and the Peloponnesian War, 109–112; and Philip of Macedon, 126–127, 130; role of women, 138; Stoics in, 139, 140; in Roman Empire, 161; slaves and metics in, 106; architecture in, 116–119; drama in, 120–122; and the Ottomans, 545

Athletics: early Greek, 99; in classical Rome, 160; Maya, 260; Hohokam, 278; Chinese, 308

Atlantic Charter, 1034, 1040

Atomic bomb, 1042

Atomic theory, 66, 123, 140

Aton, 28, 30

Attalus III [*at*-uh-luhs], 148

Attila [uh-*till*-uh], 201

Attlee, Clement, 1079, 1146, 1147

Auclert, Hubertine, 886

Audiencias [ou-*thyen*-syahz], 497–498

Auerstadt [*ow*-er-shtaht], battle of, 730

Augsburg [*owks*-boork], 339, 482, 603; Diet of, 461; Peace of, 461, 522

August, Karl, 731

Augustine [*ah*-guh-steen], 194–195

Augustinians, 362

Augustus [ah-*guss*-tuhs], 154–157, 161, 231, 445. *See also* Octavius (Octavian)

Augustus the Strong (Saxony), 650

Aung San Sun Kyi, 1071

Aurangzeb [*ah*-rung-zehb], 554–557, 558–559, 743, 749

Aurelian [ah-*ree*-lee-uhn], 167

Auschwitz, 1038, 1039–1040

Ausgleich [*ows*-glyek], 857

Austen, Jane, 831

Austerlitz [*os*-ter-lits], battle of, 730

Australia, 674, 675, 806, 812, 947; in World War II, 1042; recent, 1152

Austria: conquered by Matthias Corvinus, 415; after the Thirty Years' War, 532; wars with Louis XIV, 617–620; from Ferdinand II to Charles VI, 625–626; in the War of the Austrian Succession, 669–670; in the Seven Years' War, 670–671; under Joseph II, 695–696; and the Napoleonic wars,

729–730, 732–733; and the Congress of Vienna, 818–820; in the early nineteenth century, 824; Revolution of 1848, 839, 840; war with France (1859), 850; Austro-Prussian War, 854–855; Dual Monarchy, 857; in the Crimean War, 859; Vienna in the age of Franz Joseph, 857–858; and the Pacific Islands, 927–929; and the origins of World War I, 941–945; in World War I, 947; and the Peace of Paris (1919), 952; between the world wars, 1021–1023; union with Germany, 1027, 1030. *See also* Holy Roman Empire

Austria-Hungary: and the origins of World War I, 941–945; Austrian Netherlands, 724, 733; Austrian Succession, War of the, 669–670

Austro-Prussian War, 857

Autos-de-fé [ow-tohs duh *fay*], 516

Avars [*ah*-vahrs], 332

Averroës [uh-*vehr*-oh-eez] (Ibn-Rushd), 222–223, 370

Avesta, 183

Avicenna (Sina, Ibn) [ibn-*see*-nah], 221–222, 372, 634

Avignon [ah-vee-*nyohn*], papacy at, 396–397

Axum, kingdom of, 232, 238–239

Ayuthia (Ayutia) [ah-*yoo*-tee-ah], 299

Azerbaijan [*ah*-zer-bye-jahn], 975, 1164, 1168

Azores [uh-*zohrz*, ay-*zohrz*], 498

Azouri, Neguib, 1098

Azov [*ay*-zof], 621

Aztecs [*az*-teks], 231, 259, 260, 267–272, 495, 657, 962, 1139–1140

Ba'ath movement, 1100–1101

Babeuf, François "Gracchus" [grah-*koos* bah-*behf*], 726

Babur [*bah*-ber] "the Tiger," 290, 548, 549

Babylon [*bab*-uh-lahn], 36, 40, 42, 43

Babylonian Captivity (1309–1377), 396–397

Babylonians, 36

Bacchae, The [bak-ee] (Euripides), 122

Bach, Carl Philipp Emanuel, 705

Bach, Johann Sebastian, 650, 705

Bacon, Roger, 372

Bacon, Sir Francis, 640, 643, 896

Bactria, 54, 131, 132

Badoglio, Pietro [*pye*-troh bah-*doh*-lyoh], 1041

Bagehot [*bahj*-ot], Walter, 887

Baghdad [bagh-*dahd*, *bag*-dad], 217, 221, 540, 545, 560

Baghdad Pact, 1100

Bahadur [bah-*hah*-dour], Teg, 556

Bahadur Shah, 761

Bahamas, 485

Bahrain [bah-*rayn*], 1106

Baker, Josephine, 956–957

Baker, Sir Samuel White, 906

Bakewell, Robert, 794

Baki, Muhammad Abd ul-, 547

Bakunin, Mikhail [myih-kuh-*eel* buh-*koo*-nyin], 836, 859, 890
Balabanoff, Angelica, 892, 975–976
Balboa, Vasco Núñez de [*vahs*-koh *nuh*-nyays day bahl-*boh*-uh], 488, 509
Baldwin, King of Jerusalem, 351
Baldwin, Stanley, 1020
Balfour [*bal*-fur], Arthur, 863, 947, 1094
Balfour Declaration, 947, 990
Bali [*bahl*-ee], 297, 920
Balkan League, 943
Balkans: early history, 201, 350; and the Ottomans, 539; in the late nineteenth century, 861–862; and World War I, 941, 943, 947; in World War II, 1042
Balkan Wars, 943
Ball, John, 394, 395
Baltic, 623
Baluchistan [bah-loo-chih-*stahn*], 216
Balzac, Honoré de [oh-noh-*ray* duh bahl-*zak*], 801
Banda Bairagi, 556
Bandaranaike [buhn-druh-*nye*-uhk], Sirimavo, 1091–1092
Bandaranaike, S. W. R. D., 1091
Bandung Conference. *See* Afro-Asian Conference
Bangkok, 299, 920, 1074, 1076
Bangladesh, 1089
Banking: medieval European, 338, 402; early modern European, 482, 572, 629, 664–665, 669, 729, 792, 793, 797; modern Western, 811, 1147
Bank of Amsterdam, 629, 792
Bank of England, 629, 669, 793, 1147
Bank of France, 729
Bantu, 235, 250–252, 253, 254, 387, 906, 909, 1121
Banzer, Hugo, 1132
Baptism, 184, 191, 192
Baptists, 530
Barbados, 662, 663
Barbauld [*bahr*-bold], Anna, 703
Barcelona, 339, 394, 526, 937–938
Bar-Kochba, Simon, 159
Bar mitzvah, 188
Barnabites, 469
Baroque [buh-*roke*], 649–650, 739
Basedow [*bah*-zee-doh], Johann, 697
Basel [*bah*-zuhl], 462, 477, 603; Council of, 461
Basil, 194
Basil II (Byzantium), 350
Basque [bask] region, 883
Bastardy, 599
Bastille [bah-*steel*], 714
Batavia (Djakarta), 535
Batista, Fulgencio [fool-*hen*-see-oh bah-*tees*-tah], 1132–1135
Battle of Britain, 1032
Battle of the Bulge, 1042
Battle of the Nations, 733
Battle of the Saints, 674
Battuta, Ibn, 240, 245–246, 252, 315
Batu [*bah*-too], 357
Baudelaire [bohd-ler], Charles, 937
Bauhaus [*bow*-hous] school, 958–959
Bavaria, 332, 475, 523, 670, 853, 1004, 1009

Bayezid I [bah-yeh-*zeed*], 539
Bayle [bel], Pierre, 645, 647
Bay of Pigs invasion, 1134, 1153
Beard, Charles A., 675
Beaufort [*boo*-fort], Francis, 1110
Beauharnais [bow-ahr-*neh*], Josephine de, 732
Beaumer [*boh*-mer], Madame de, 690
Beauvais [boh-*vay*], 374
Beauvoir [deh boh-*vwar*], Simone de, 1148
Bebel [*bay*-behl], August, 890, 892
Beccaria [bake-ah-*ree*-ah], Cesare [*chay*-zah-ray] Bonesana, Marquis de, 691
Bechuanaland, 909
Becket, Thomas à, 342–343
Bede "the Venerable," 376
Beethoven [*bay*-toh-vehn], Ludwig van, 706, 732, 828, 829, 858, 899
Begin, Menachem [may-*nah*-kehm *bay*-ghin], 1096, 1098
Behn [bayn], Aphra, 430, 596, 702
Beirut [bay-*root*], 1157
Belarus (Byelorussia), 1167
Belgian Congo. *See* Congo
Belgium: and Napoleon, 733; in the first phase of the Industrial Revolution, 811, 812; and the Congress of Vienna, 820; Revolution of 1830, 832; universal manhood suffrage, 883; in World War I, 943, 944; between the world wars, 952, 1027; in World War II, 1032, 1042; end of imperialism in Africa, 1115, 1116; after World War II, 1158–1159
Belgrade, 540, 1144
Belisarius [bel-ih-*sar*-ee-uhs], 201, 203
Bell, Alexander Graham, 897
Bellamy, Edward, 1171–1172
Bellarmine, Robert, 635
Bellini, Gentile [jen-*tee*-lay bel-*lee*-nee], 540
Bellini, Giovanni, 420
Benedictines, 361, 763
Benedict of Nursia [*ner*-shuh], 194, 361
"Benefit of clergy," 342
Beneš [*beh*-nesh], Edvard, 1023, 1030
Bengal: medieval, 285, 289, 291; early modern, 535, 550, 557, 671, 737, 743, 744, 745, 749; and the English, 746, 750, 751, 752, 753, 755; modern, 1081–1083, 1089
Bengal Renaissance, 754
Ben-Gurion, David, 1094–1096
Benin, 250, 488, 905, 962, 1119
Bentham [*ben*-tham], Jeremy, 802, 804, 884
Bentinck [*bent*-ink], William, 757, 758–759
Beowulf [*bay*-oh-wulf], 375
Berbers, 216, 240, 247, 355
Berenice, 138
Berg, Alban, 858
Bergen-Belsen, 1038, 1040
Bergson, Henri [ahn-*ree* berg-*sohn*], 935
Beria, Lavrenti, 1143
Berkeley, George, 698
Berlin, 874, 950, 953, 1004, 1007–1008, 1047, 1145, 1153, 1160, 1161
Berlin, Congress of, 861–862, 941

Berlin blockade, 1047
Berlin Conference (1885), 906–907
Berlin-to-Baghdad railroad, 942
Berlioz, Hector [*ek*-tor ber-*lyohz*], 828, 829
Bernard of Clairvaux [klare-*voh*], 362, 373
Bernini [bur-*nee*-nee], Gianlorenzo, 649, 651, 739, 963
Bernstein, Éduard, 891
Berry [beh-*ree*], Duke of, 824
Besant, Annie, 875
Bessemer, Henry, 813, 870
Bethmann-Hollweg, Theobald von [*tay*-oh-bahlt fohn bate-mahn *hole*-vake], 944
Bhagavadgita [bahg-ah-*vahd gee*-tah], 173
Bhakti movement, 291, 555, 737
Bhutto [*bou*-toh], Benazir, 1090
Bhutto, Zulfkar Ali, 1089
Biafra [bee-*ahf*-ruh], 1119
Bible, 453, 455, 459, 462, 466; New Testament, 189, 192; Old Testament [Hebrew Scripture], 33, 188–189, 192; English versions, 397; Tyndale's edition, 466; Coverdale (1535), 468; Vulgate, 472; Geneva (1560), 473; King James' (1611), 528; textual criticism, 647
Biblical scholarship, 455
Biko [*bee*-koh], Steve, 1122
Bill of Rights (1689), 629
Bindusara, 56
Birmingham, Alabama, 1149
Bismarck, Otto von, 853–857, 880–881, 897, 906, 908, 941, 942
Bismarck Archipelago, 1042
Black Death. *See* Plague
Black Sea, 92, 693
Blackshirts (Italy), 998–999, 1002
Blake, William, 799
Blanc [blanh], Louis, 835, 840–841
Blanqui [blanh-*kee*], Louis-Auguste, 835
Blenheim [*blen*-im], battle of, 620
Blitzkrieg [*blits*-kreeg], 1031, 1032
Blois [bleh-*wah*], Stephen, Count of, 350
Blücher, Gerhard von [*ger*-hart fohn *blue*-ker], 733
Blue Rider movement (art), 939
Blue Shirts, 1013
Blum, Léon [*lay*-on bloom], 1021
Blyden, Edward Wilmot, 1114
Boccaccio, Giovanni [joh-*vah*-nee bohk-*kaht*-choh], 422, 473
Boccioni [boht-*choh*-nee], Umberto, 939
Bodhisattvas [boh-dih-*saht*-vahz], 177
Bodin, Jean [zhan boh-*dahn*], 524
Boers [bohrz], 909, 1120–1122
Boer War, 909
Bohemia, Bohemians, 357, 398, 415, 461, 522–523, 532, 625, 626, 695, 839, 857, 1022; Anabaptists in, 465
Böhme [*beh*-muh], Jacob, 697
Bohr [bohr], Niels, 957
Bokassa, Jean-Bedel, 1119
Boleslav [*boh*-leh-slav] the Pious, 380
Boleyn [*buhl*-ihn, buh-*lin*], Anne, 466–468, 477

Bolívar [boh-*lee*-vahr], Simón, 677–678, 680

Bolivia, 865, 866, 1126, 1131–1132, 1138

Bologna [buh-*lun*-yah], University of, 365–366, 371

Bolsheviks, 971–978 *passim*

Bolshoi [*bohl*-shoy] Theater, 1155

Bombay, 184, 747, 749, 751, 752, 756, 757, 912, 1084

Bonaparte, Jerome, 730

Bonaparte, Joseph, 677, 730

Bonaparte, Louis-Napoleon, 844–848. *See also* Napoleon III

Bonaparte, Napoleon, 724–725, 727–734, 828

Bonaventure [boh-nah-vayn-*too*-rah], 370

Boniface VIII [*bahn*-ih-fuhs], Pope, 345, 348–349, 396

Bonn, 1047

Book of Changes, 72

Book of Common Prayer, 468, 473

Book of Lord Shang, 55

Book of Rituals, 72

Book of Songs, 72

Book of the Courtier, The (Castiglione), 424

Book of the Dead, 25

Bora, Katherine von, 458

Bordeaux [bohr-*doh*], 339, 714

Borges [bohr-hays], Jorge Luis, 1138

Borgia, Cesare [*chay*-zah-ray bohr-jah], 408, 410

Boris (Bulgaria), 1023

Borneo, 920, 1074

Borobodur [*boh*-roh-boo-*door*], 301

Borodin [buh-ruh-*deen*], Michael, 980

Borodino [buh-ruh-dee-*noh*], battle of, 733

Borromini, Francesco [frahn-*cheh*-skoh bohr-roh-*mee*-nee], 650, 652

Bosch, Hieronymus [hee-*rahn*-ih-muhs bahsh], 389, 437–438

Bosch, Juan [hwahn bohsh], 1135

Bose, Subhas Chandra, 1037

Bosnia, 861, 862, 941, 943, 944, 1162

Bosporus, 200

Bossuet, Jacques-Bénigne [zhahk boh-*sway*], 614, 647

Boston, Mass., 673

Boswell, James, 705

Bosworth Field, battle of, 406

Botha, P. W., 1122

Botany, 135

Bothwell, Earl of, 519

Botticelli, Sandro [*sahn*-droh baht-tih-*chel*-lee], 432, 962

Boucher, François [frahn-*swah* boo-*shay*], 704

Boulanger, Georges [zhorzh boo-lahn-*zhay*], 879

Boulton [*bohl*-ton], Matthew, 802

Boumediene, Houari [oo-*ah*-ree boo-may-dee-*ehn*], 1123

Bourbon [boor-*buhn*] dynasty, 521, 524–526, 611–621, 709–719 *passim*

Bourgeoisie: French, 716–717; Chinese, 774; Japanese, 782, 784; nineteenth-century European, 791, 872–873; in the first phase of the Industrial Revolution, 800–801; after World War I, 954

Bourguiba, Habib [hah-*beeb* boor-*ghee*-bah], 1103, 1122–1123

Bouvines [boo-*veen*], battle of, 343, 348

Boxer Rebellion, 924–925

Boyars, 403

Boyle, Katherine, 596

Braddock, Edward, 671

Bradlaugh, Charles, 875

Brady, Mathew, 898

Brahe [brah], Tycho, 638, 643

Brahma, 174

Brahmans, 175, 299

Brahmi script, 227, 230

Brahms, Johannes, 858

Bramante [brah-*mahn*-tay], Donato, 437

Brancusi [brahng-koosh], Constantin, 965

Brandenburg, 523, 626

Brandenburg-Prussia, 623

Brandt, Willy [*vill*-ee brahnt], 1147, 1160

Braque, Georges [zhorzh brak], 939, 965

Brasilia, 1128

Brave New World (Huxley), 1172

Brazil, 257; missions in, 471; discovery of, 485, 486; colonial, 499, 535, 662; modern, 677, 678, 865–866, 1127–1128, 1138, 1139, 1140; and the Estado Novo, 1013–1015; University of, 1128

Brecht, Bertolt [*ber*-tohlt brekht], 1008

Brest-Litovsk [brest lih-tofsk], Treaty of, 950, 973

Brezhnev, Leonid [lay-*oh*-need brehzh-neff], 1153–1155, 1157, 1160, 1163

Brezhnev Doctrine, 1160

Briand, Aristide [ah-ree-*steed* bree-*ahn*], 952

Bridge (art movement), 939

Bridget of Sweden, 397

Brill, 519

"Brinkmanship," 1153

Brink, André, 1124

Brisbane, 928

Brissot, Jacques [zhahk bree-*soh*], 723

Bristol, 808, 834

Britain: conquered by the Romans, 157; in the Roman Empire, 162; invaded by Angles and Saxons, 170; and the American colonies, 660–661, 671–673; colonial trade of, 662–665; age of Walpole, 666; triumph of the elite, 666–668; in the War of the Austrian Succession, 669–670; in the Seven Years' War, 669–670; and the Revolutionary War, 673–674; support for Latin American independence movements, 679–680; and the Napoleonic wars, 729–730, 733; in the first phase of the Industrial Revolution, 788–810 *passim*; and the Congress of Vienna, 818–820; in the early nineteenth century, 823–824, 832–835, 838; in the Crimean War, 850, 859; in the second phase of the Industrial Revolution, 870, 871, 874; in the Victorian Age, 878–879; colonies in Africa, 908–909; rule in India, 912–918, 986–989; impe-rialism in the Pacific, 929; and the origins of World War I, 941–945; in World War I, 945–950; and the Peace of Paris (1919), 950; after World War I, 952; fascists in, 1013; in the Great Depression, 1019–1021; events leading to World War II, 1028, 1030–1031; in World War II, 1031–1034, 1037, 1040–1042, 1046; after World War II, 1047, 1147, 1160; end of imperialism in Southeast Asia, 1074; and the independence of India, 1079–1081; and the Palestine dispute, 1092–1095; mandates of, 1099; end of imperialism in Africa, 1115–1116, 1118; war with Argentina, 1129–1130

British East Africa (Kenya), 909

British North America Act (1867), 675, 1152

British Union of Fascists, 1013

Brittany, 406, 407, 615

Brontë [*bron*-tay], Charlotte, 831

Brontë, Emily, 739, 831

Bronze Age, 11, 15, 16, 89–90, 93, 143, 144; writing in, 229

Bronzino [bron-*dzee*-noh], Alessandro, 963

Brown v. *Board of Education*, 1148

Broz [brawz], Josip. *See* Tito

Bruckner [*brook*-ner], Anton, 858

Brueghel [*bruh*-gehl], Pieter, 438, 503

Bruges [broozh], 339, 503

Brunei [broo-*neye*], 1074

Brunelleschi [broo-nel-*les*-kee], Filippo, 436–437

Bruni [*broo*-nee], Leonardo, 422–423

Bruno, Giordano, 473, 637, 1110

Brunswick, 394

Brussels, 719

Brutus, Marcus, 153

Bucer [*bew*-sur], Martin, 460

Bucharest [*boo*-kah-rest], 1162

Budapest, 839, 1145

Buddha, Gautama, 64, 175–177, 195, 445

Buddhism, 193; in India, 56–58, 63, 285; in Ceylon, 61; in Burma, 61; life of Buddha, 175–176; Four Noble Truths, 176; Hinayana and Mahayana schools, 177–178; Theravada, 177–178; role of women, 195; in Southeast Asia, 177, 182, 296, 298, 299, 300, 301; in China, 305, 308–309, 310; in Korea, 320, 321; in Japan, 323, 326, 327; Zen (Ch'an), 178, 326–327; conceptions of death, 386–387, 736–737; Chinese secret societies, 564; and the Mongols, 568; Tantric, 597

Budé, Guillaume [gee-*yohm* bew-*day*], 425

Buenos Aires [*bway*-nohs *ay*-rays], 866, 1125, 1128, 1139

Buganda, 905

Bugenhagen [*boo*-gehn-hah-gehn], Johannes, 459

Bukharin [boo-*kah*-reen], Nicolai, 973, 978, 1018

Bulavin, Kondraty, 623

Bulganin [bool-*gah*-nyin], Nikolai, 1144

Bulgaria, 861; in World War I, 941, 947, 950; between the world wars, 952, 1021–1023; in World War II, 1033; after World War II, 978, 1045, 1047, 1143–1144, 1162
Bulgars (Bulgarians), 333, 350
Bullinger [*bool*-ing-er], Heinrich, 462
Bundesrat, 855, 881
Buonarotti [bwo-nahr-*rot*-tee], Filippo Maria, 835
Burbage, 648
Burckhardt, Jacob [*yah*-kohp *boork*-hahrt], 439, 440
Burgoyne [bur-*goin*], John, 673
Burgundians, 331, 395
Burgundy, 347, 407, 413, 513
Burgundy, Mary of, 413
Burial practices: in ancient Egypt, 25–26, 385; in India, 65; in ancient China, 71; in the Cyclades, 90; Hindu, 150, 737; Confucian, 180, 387; Zoroastrian, 183; in Ghana, 243; Maya, 261; Adena and Hopewell cultures, 277; Mississippian culture, 278; Neanderthal, 385; in Mesopotamia, 385; in ancient Greece, 385–386; early Christian, 388; medieval Christian, 388–389; Buddhist, 736–737; in Islam, 737, 738; in Indonesia, 737–738; Huron practices, 738; in early modern Europe, 739; in the modern West, 739–740. *See also* Death
Burke, Edmund, 673, 704, 717
Burma: ancient, 61; religion in, 177; writing in, 230; medieval, 296, 298–299; attacked by China, 317, 771; colonial rule, 917, 918, 921; and World War II, 1036, 1037, 1042; after World War II, 1070–1071; independence, 1074; women in modern Burma, 1075
Bursa, 545
Burundi, 1116, 1119
Bush, George, 1132, 1157, 1163
Buthelezi, Gatsha, 1122
Butler, Eleanor, 703
Butler, Joseph, 697
Buyids [*boo*-yihdz], 218
Byng, John, 671
Byron, Lord, 823, 828
Byzantine Empire: early history, 200–201; reign of Justinian, 201–204; economy, 204–206; society, 206–208; Constantinople, 208–210; and the Christian church, 210–211; culture, 211–212; relations with Arabs, 215–216; relations with Franks, 332, 333; and the crusades, 349–351; after the crusades, 353–354
Byzantine mosaics, 446
Byzantium, 200–201. *See also* Constantinople

Cabalists, 380
Cabot, John, 486–488, 499
Cabral [kuh-*brahl*], Pedro, 485
Cadiz, 33, 519, 528, 822
Caesar [*see*-zuhr], Julius, 151–153
Caesaropapism, 210

Cairo [*kye*-roh], 218, 219, 339, 391
Calais [kah-*lay*], 395
Calas, Jean [zhahn kah-*lah*], 687
Calcutta: in the eighteenth century, 744, 747, 748, 749–750, 751, 752, 753, 756; Black Hole of, 750; as a colonial capital, 755; modern, 757, 912, 915, 1037, 1082, 1084, 1089
Calderón de la Barca, Pedro, 648
Calendar, 86, 142, 152, 260–261, 276, 508, 624, 719
Calicut, 489, 490, 491
California, 500, 536, 675, 812, 864, 866, 1127. *See also* Los Angeles
Caligula [kah-*lig*-you-lah] (Gaius), 157
Calixtus II, Pope, 346
Callicrates [kah-*lik*-rah-teez], 118
Calligraphy, 230
Callimachus, 138
Calonne [ka-*lon*], Charles de, 709–710
Calvin, John, 425, 453, 461, 462–465, 475, 477
"Calvinist Fury," 518
Cambay, 296
Cambodia: religion in, 177; writing in, 230; early history, 296, 299–300; colonial rule, 918, 920_ the Vietnam War, 1072, 1073, 1156
Cambrai [kahn-*bray*], 482; League of, 411–412
Cambridge, 339; University of, 366, 425
Cambyses [kam-*bye*-seez], 42
Camels, 240–241
Cameroons, 908
Campanella, Thomas, 1108
Campanus of Novara, 634
Camp David Accords, 1097–1098
Campo Formio, Treaty of, 724
Campora, Hector, 1129
Camus [ka-*moo*], Albert, 957
Canaanites, 33, 228–229
Canada, 671, 673, 674, 738; in the nineteenth century, 675; in the twentieth century, 1151–1153
Canary Islands, 498
Candide (Voltaire), 687
Canisius, Peter, 475
Cannae [*kahn*-ee], battle of, 147
Canning, Lord Charles, 760
Canning, George, 760, 833
Canon law, 371
Canossa, 346
Cánovas del Castillo [*kah*-noh-bahs del kahs-*tee*-lyoh], Antonio, 890
Canterbury Tales (Chaucer), 400, 422
Canticle of the Sun (Francis of Assisi), 364, 378
Canton, 316, 535, 577, 579, 767, 770, 773, 776, 921
Canton (Guangzhou) delta, 76
Cape Breton, 486
Cape Colony, 909
Cape Hatteras, 488
Capellanus, Andreas, 377
Cape of Good Hope, 489, 657, 820, 906
Cape Trafalgar, battle of, 730
Cape Verde Islands, 488
Capital (Marx), 835, 837

Capitalism, 338, 500–503, 792–793, 902–903, 912
Capital punishment, 607
Capone, Al, 1020
Caporetto, battle of, 950
Capuchins [*kap*-yoo-chinz], 469
Capucines [kah-pyoo-*seen*], 469
Caracalla, 166
Caracas, 678
Caraffa, Giampietro [jahm-*pyeh*-troh], 473
Caraka, 66
Caravaggio [kah-rah-*vahd*-joh], 649–650
Caravels, 483–484
Carbon-14 dating, 3, 8
Cárdenas [kahr-thay-nahs], Lázaro, 1137
Cardinals, College of, 346
Carlsbad Decrees, 824
Carlyle, Thomas, 802
Carmelites, 516
Carnegie, Andrew, 871
Carol (Romania), 1023
Caroline islands, 930
Carolingian [kar-uh-*lihn*-jee-uhn] dynasty, 331–333
Carrà [kahr-*rah*], Carlo, 939
Carranza [kahr-*rahn*-sah], Bartolomé de, 515
Carter, James Earl ("Jimmy"), 1127, 1132, 1157
Cartesianism, 641
Carthage [*kahr*-thij], 33, 143, 193, 235; in the Punic Wars, 146–148
Carthaginians, 143, 146–149
Carthusians, 362
Cartwright, Edmund, 796
Casablanca Conference, 1041
Casimir-Perier [*ka*-zee-meer *pay*-ryay], Jean-Paul, 832
Cassian, John, 361
Cassini [kah-*see*-nee], Jean-Dominique, 1108
Cassius, Gaius, 153
Caste, 53, 587, 1087
Castellio [kas-*tell*-yoh], Sebastian, 466
Castiglione, Baldassare [bahl-dahs-*sah*-ray kah-steel-*yoh*-nay], 424
Castile [kah-*steel*], 354–355, 404–405, 513, 526
Castlereagh [kassl-*ray*], Viscount, 819, 820
Castro, Fidel, 1132–1135, 1153
Catalan rebellion, 526
Çatal Hüyük [*shah*-tahl *hoo*-yook], 11
Catalonia, 526, 883
Cateau-Cambrésis [kah-*toh*-kahn-bray-*zee*], Treaty of, 513
Cathari [*kath*-uh-ree], 364
Catherine II, "the Great," 692–693
Catherine of Aragon, 406, 466, 467
Catherine of Braganza, 747
Catherine of Siena, 397
Catholicism: struggle with Holy Roman Empire, 346–349; papal authority, 347, 349; early monastic communities, 361; monastic reform, 361–362; mendicant orders, 362–364; medieval heretics, 364; Scholastics, 369–370; late medieval, 396–397; and the challenges of

Wyclif and Hus, 397–398; and the Counter-Enlightenment, 697–698; and the French Revolution of 1789, 716–717; in Napoleonic France, 729; and Italian Fascism, 1001; in Nazi Germany, 1011; in Latin America, 1138; and the Kulturkampf, 881

Catholic League (France), 521

Catholic League (German states), 522

Cato [*kay*-toh], 164

Catullus [kuh-*tull*-us], 164

Caucasus [*kaw*-kah-suhs], 216

Caudillos, 866, 1126

Cavafy [kuh-*vah*-vee], Constantine, 134

Cavaignac [kah-veh-*nyak*], Louis-Eugène, 841, 844

Cavaliers, 530

Cavell, Edith, 949

Cavour, Camillo Benso di [cah-*mee*-loh kah-*voor*], 849–852, 881

Ceaușescu, Nicolae [nee-koh-*lee* chew-*shehs*-koo], 1161–1162

Celebes [sel-eh-*beez*], 920

Cellini, Benvenuto [bayn-vay-*noo*-toh cheh-*lee*-nee], 432

Central America, after World War II, 1132, 1135–1136

Censorate, 81

Center Party (Germany), 1004

Centilivre [sent-*liv*-er], Susan, 596, 702

Central African Republic, 1119

Central Intelligence Agency (CIA), 1047, 1153

Cervantes, Miguel de [mee-*gell* day suhr-*vahn*-tays], 516, 649

Cerveteri [cher-*veh*-tay-ree], 144

Ceuta [*soo*-tah], 484

Ceylon [see-*lahn*], 294; early history, 60–61; religion in, 176, 177; writing in, 230; early modern, 490, 745, 746, 752–753, 820; in World War II, 1037

Cézanne [say-*zahn*], Paul, 937, 965

Chad, 1119, 1123

Chadar, 1102, 1103

Chaeronea [ker-oh-*nee*-ah], battle of, 127

Chakri [*chah*-kree] dynasty, 299

Chaldeans, 40

Chamberlain, Houston Stewart, 939

Chamberlain, Neville, 1020, 1030, 1031, 1032

Chamber of Fasci and Corporations, 1000

Chambord [shahn-*bohr*], 476

Chamorro, Violetta Barrios de, 1136

Champagne, 377; fairs, 367

Champagne, Marie of, 341, 377

Champollion, Jean-François [zhahn shahn-pawl-*yohn*], 32

Chancellor, Richard, 500

Chandigarh, 1128

Chandragupta Maurya [chun-druh-*goop*-tuh *mow*-ree-uh]], 55, 56

Chang (Zhang) [chahng], 583

Ch'ang An (Qangan) [chahng-ahn], 81, 84, 85, 305, 307, 311, 339

Chang Chü-cheng (Zhang Juzheng), 581

Changsha [chahng-shah], 577

Chansons d'amour [shahn-*sohn* dah-*moor*], 377–378

Chansons de geste [shahn-*sohn* duh zhehst], 376–377

Chapelier Law, Le [luh shah-peh-*lyay*], 718

Chardin [shar-*dan*], Pierre, 704

Charlemagne [*shahr*-leh-mayn], 331–333

Charles I (England), 528–530, 683

Charles II (England), 530, 628–629, 747

Charles II (Spain), 526, 617, 619

Charles III (Spain), 696, 821

Charles IV (Holy Roman Empire), 413

Charles V (Holy Roman Empire), 409, 413–414, 434, 457–458, 460, 461, 466, 471, 473, 483, 488, 513

Charles VI (Holy Roman Empire), 626, 669

Charles VII (France), 395, 407

Charles VIII (France), 407, 408

Charles IX (France), 520

Charles X (France), 824, 832

Charles XII (Sweden), 623, 650

Charles Albert, Elector of Bavaria, 669

Charles Albert (Piedmont), 839, 849

Charles Martel, 331

Charles of Anjou, 354

Charles the Bold (Burgundy), 407

Charter Act (1833), 757

Chartist movement, 834–835, 838

Chartres [*shahr*-treh], 365, 375

Chateaubriand [sha-toh-bree-*ahn*], François-Auguste-René de, 828

Chaucer, Geoffrey [*jef*-free *chahs*-uhr], 400, 422

Chávez, Carlos, 1139

Chavín [*chah*-vihn] culture, 272–273

Chavín de Huantár, 272–273

Chengdu, 79, 577

Cheng Ho (Zhenghe), 567–568

Chernenko, Konstantin, 1164

Chernobyl Nuclear Plant, 1175

Chia Ch'ing (Ja Qing), 772

Chiang Ch'ing (Jiang Qing), 1065, 1074

Chiang Kai-shek [jee-*ahng* kye-*shek*], 980, 982, 1013, 1034, 1036, 1047, 1058

Chiaroscuro [kyah-roh-*skoo*-roh], 431

Chichén Itzá [cheh-chen et-*sah*], 265, 267

Ch'ien Lung (Qian Long), 768, 771–772, 773

Chile [*chil*-ee, *chee*-lay], 257, 678, 865, 866, 1126, 1130–1131, 1138, 1140, 1153, 1157

Chiluba, Frederick, 1124

Ch'in (Qin) [chihn, cheen] dynasty, 73, 76–79

China, ancient: geography of, 68; origins of, 69–70; Lung Shan culture, 69; Hsia dynasty, 69–70; early cities, 69–70, 72, 84–86; Shang dynasty, 70–71; Chou (Zhou) dynasty, 71–72; age of warring states, 72–74; teachings of Confucius, 74–76; Ch'in (Quin) conquest, 76–77; Ch'in authoritarianism, 77–79; Han dynasty, 79–84; reign of Wu Ti, 79–81; early trading patterns, 81-82; Han culture, 82–84; Han legacy, 86–87; religion in, 176, 178; religion and philosophy in, 179–182; writing in, 228; art, 445–446

China (sixth to fourteenth centuries): reunification, 305; T'ang dynasty, 305–310; Sung dynasty, 310–314; Southern Sung period, 314–316; Yuan dynasty, 316–317, 357; culture, 317–319; influence on Japan, 323, 324; sculpture, 447; missionaries in, 471

China, Ming: and Russian expansion, 494; origins, 563–564; reign of Hung-wu, 564–566; naval expeditions, 566–568; conservatism, 568–569; economy, 569–572; culture, 572–577; imperial Peking, 577–579; decline, 579–583; Manchu conquest, 583–584; social hierarchy in the early modern period, 588

China, modern: Manchu rule, 766–768; influence on eighteenth-century Europe, 768; economic and demographic growth, 768–770; Kang Hsi and Ch'ien Lung, 770–772; Ch'ing decline, 772–773; westerners in, 773–776, 921–925; Opium wars, 776; Boxer rebellion, 924–925; in World War I, 947–948; 1911 Revolution, 980–981; May Fourth Movement, 981–982; Nanking decade, 982–984; Shanghai, 984–986; Blueshirts in, 1013; between the world wars, 1026; in World War II, 1034-1037, 1042; postwar China, 1046, 1047, 1056–1059; Great Leap Forward, 1059; Sino-Soviet split, 1059–1060; Cultural Revolution, 1060–1065; China after Mao, 1065–1067; women in modern China, 1075; modern industrialization, 1076; border dispute with India, 1084–1085

Chinese Revolution (1911), 980–981

Ch'ing (Qing) dynasty, 583–584

Chinghis (Genghis) [*jehn*-gihs] Khan, 316, 317, 321, 357, 509

Chinoiserie [shin-*wahz*-uh-ree], 705

Chirico, Giorgio de [*jor*-joh *kir*-ih-koh], 958

Chivalry, 377, 399–400

Choiseul [shwah-*zul*], Duke of, 669

Chola, 60, 61, 62, 260, 292, 293–295, 301

Cholula, 267

Chopin, Frédéric [fray-day-*reek* shoh-*pan*], 831, 832

Chou (Zhou) [joh] dynasty, 71–72

Chou En-lai (Zhou Enlai) [joh en-*lye*], 1059, 1062, 1063

Christian Brethren, 466

Christian Democratic Party (Italy), 1146–1147

Christian Democratic Party (West Germany), 1146–1147

Christian Humanists, 454–456

Christianity, early history of: in India, 59; in early Southeast Asia, 182, 184; life and teachings of Jesus, 189–191; Paul's contribution, 191–192; and the Roman Empire, 192–193; early heresies, 193; monasticism, 193–194; origins of the papacy, 194; role of Augustine, 194–195; women in the early church, 195–196

Christianity, medieval: in the Byzantine empire, 202–203, 210–212; in East Africa, 239; missions to Asia, 328; conceptions of death, 388–389; late medieval, 396–398, 453–454

Christianity, early modern: humanist demands for reform, 454–456; Protestant Reformation, 456–469; Catholic Reformation, 469–474; eighteenth-century revival, 697–698. *See also* Missionaries

Chrysoloras [krih-suh-*lawr*-uhs], Manuel, 423

Chrysostom, John, 388

Ch'u (Qu) [choo], 73

Chuang-tze (Zhuangzi) [jwahng-dzuh], 181

Chu Hsi (Zhuxi) [joo she], 181, 315

Chungking (Chongqing), 1034, 1035–1037

Churchill, Winston: early career, 947, 948; in World War II, 897, 989, 1032, 1034, 1040, 1041, 1042; after World War II, 1045, 1079, 1146

Church of England, 468, 473

Chu Yüan-chang (Zhu Yuan-zhang), 564

Cicero [*sis*-uh-roh], Marcus Tullius, 151, 164

Ciompi [*chom*-pee] rebellion, 394, 410

Circumcision, 184–185, 192

Circus Maximus, 160

Cistercians [sis-*tur*-shuhnz], 362, 381

Cities: origins of, 11–12; in ancient Mesopotamia, 17–19; in ancient India, 50–51; in ancient China, 84–86; founded by Alexander the Great, 129; Hellenistic, 132, 134; Etruscan, 144–145; in the Roman Empire, 161; in early Africa, 241–242, 243, 245, 247, 249, 250, 252–254; Teotihuacán, 258–260; Aztec, 267–268; medieval Indian, 292–293; medieval Southeast Asian, 299–300; Chinese, 307–309, 311, 315; medieval European, 336, 338, 339–340; in the Ottoman empire, 545; in Ming China, 566, 577–579; in the first phase of the Industrial Revolution, 807–810; in British India, 912, 916; in modern Japan, 1055–1056; in modern China, 1066; in modern East Asia, 1076; in modern Africa, 1124; in modern Latin America, 1125–1126, 1128, 1138. *See also specific cities.*

City of God, The (Augustine), 194–195

Civic Humanists, 422–423

Civil Code of 1804, 729

Civil Constitution of the Clergy, 716, 717

Civilization: definition of, 1, 2; origins of, 10–13, 14–15, 16–17

Civil Rights Act (1964), 1149

Civil rights movement, 1148–1151

Clapham sect, 702

Clarendon, Earl of, 628

Clare of Assisi, 363–364

Clark, William, 1110

Clarke, Samuel, 697

Clarkson, Thomas, 702

Claudius, 157

Cleisthenes [*klice*-thee-neez], 101–102

Clemenceau, Georges [zhorzh klay-mahn-*soh*], 879, 880, 950

Clement, 192

Clement V, Pope, 349

Clement VII ("anti-pope"), 397

Clement VII, Pope, 414, 466

Cleomenes [klee-*ahm*-ee-neez], 101

Cleon [*klee*-ahn], 112

Cleopatra, 129, 152–154

Clermont [klair-*mahn*], Council of, 350, 351

Cleves [kleevz], 626

Clive, Robert, 749, 750–751

Cloots [klohtz], Anarchasis, 717

Clovis [*kloh*-vihs], 170, 331

Cluniac order, 362

Cluny [*kloo*-nee], 362

Coal, 789, 796, 811, 812, 813, 870

Code Napoleon, 729, 730, 733

Codreanu [koh-dray-*ah*-noo], Corneliu, 1013

Coen [koon], Jan Pieterzoon, 535

Coffee, 746

Cognac [kahn-*yahk*], League of, 413

Coinage: invention of, 38; Persian, 42, 102; early Greek, 98; Hellenistic, 138; ancient Japanese, 323

Cokayne, Sir William, 501

Coke [cook], Sir Edward, 528

Colbert, Jean-Baptiste [zhahn kohl-*bayr*], 612–613, 643, 661, 798

Cold War: origins of, 1045–1047, 1163; and American politics, 1048; and the Korean War, 1068–1069; Pakistan in, 1090; in Africa, 1116, 1119–1120

Coleridge, Samuel Taylor, 828

Colet, John, 425, 455, 466

Coligny [ko-*lee*-nyee], Gaspard de, 520

Cologne [koh-*lohn*], 338, 339

Colombia, 675, 678, 865, 1128, 1132

Colombo, 61, 490, 745, 753

Coloni, 207

Colonies, early Greek, 93–94

Colonna, Egidio, 365

Colonna, Vittoria, 426–427

Colorado River, 1110

Colosseum (Rome), 160

Columbia, 1138, 1139

Columbus, Christopher, 485–486, 494, 509, 510

Combustion engine, 813

COMECON, 1047

Comintern (Third International), 978–980

Committee of Public Safety, 722, 723

Commodus, 166

Common Life, Brethren and Sisters of the, 402, 453

Common Market, 1159–1160

Commonwealth of Independent States (CIS), 1167–1168

Commonwealth of Nations, 1152

Communist Information Bureau (Cominform), 1047, 1144

Communist Manifesto, The (Marx and Engels), 836

Communist Party (France), 1146

Communist Party (Germany), 1009

Communist Party (Italy), 1146, 1160

Comnena [kohm-*nee*-nah], Anna, 208

Comnenian dynasty, 207–208

Computers, 900

Comte [kohnt], Auguste, 831, 887, 935

Concentration camps, 1009, 1038–1040

Concert of Europe, 819, 823, 941

Conciliar Movement, 397

Concordat of 1801, 729

Concordat of Worms, 346–347

Condorcet [kon-dohr-*say*], Marquis de, 727

Condottiere [kohn-doht-*tyay*-ray], 408

Confessions (Augustine), 194

Confucianism, 193; Confucius and Mencius, 178–179; ideals, 179–181; in Japan, 182, 323–324; revival in China, 310, 313–314, 315; in Korea, 321

Confucius [kohn-*fyoo*-shuhs], 74–76, 82, 179–180, 599, 1172

Congo, 906–907, 114, 1116, 1153. *See also* Belgian Congo

Congo River, 489, 657

Congregationalists, 530

Congregation of the Holy Angels, 469

Congress of Vienna, 818–820, 852

Congress Party, 986, 987–988, 989, 1079–1081, 1086, 1087

Connecticut, 660

Conquistadors [kohng-kee-stah-*dohrs*], 495–496

Conrad III (Holy Roman Empire), 352

Conscription, 79, 85, 722

Conservative Movement (Judaism), 701

Conservative Party (Britain), 1020, 1147

Consistory (Geneva), 464

Constance, 460, 462; Council of, 397, 398, 456, 461; Peace of, 347

Constance (Sicily), 347

Constant, Benjamin, 828

Constantine, 168, 169, 187, 193, 200, 208–209

Constantine, Donation of, 425

Constantine, Grand Duke (Russia), 824

Constantine XI (Byzantium), 201, 403

Constantinople: founding of, 168–169; patriarchs of, 194; in the early Byzantine empire, 205, 206, 208–210, 215–216, 218; late medieval, 336, 352; and the Black Death, 391; fall of, 539

Constituent Assembly (France, 1789), 716–717, 718

Constitution of the Year I, 722

Constitutions of Clarendon, 342

Consuls (Roman), 145, 151

Consumption, 149–150

Contarini [kahnt-eh-*ree*-nee], Cardinal Gasparo, 427

Continental Congress, 673–674

Continental System, 730, 733

Contraception, 163, 598

Contra rebels, 1136

Conversos, 406, 516

Conway, Anne, Vicountess, 596

Cook, James, 507, 928, 929, 1109–1110

Coolidge, Calvin, 1020

Copernicus [koh-*puhr*-nih-kuhs], Nicolaus, 636–638, 643

Coral Sea, battle of, 1040
Corbusier, Le [leh kor-bu-zyay], 959, 1128
Córdoba [*kohr*-doh-vah], 217, 218, 221, 354, 355
Corinth, 95, 109–112, 126, 161; battle of, 148
Corneille [kor-*nay*], Pierre, 649
Cornelisz [kor-*nay*-lihs], Cornelis, 792
Corn Laws, 834
Cornwallis, Charles, 752
"Corporate state" (Italy), 1000
Corpus Juris Civilis, 203, 371
Corregidors [koh-*reg*-ih-dohrz], 405
Corsica, 143, 727–728
Cort, Henry, 789
Cortes [kor-*tez*], 354, 405, 513, 526, 822, 883
Cortés, Hernando [ayr-*nahn*-doh kohr-*tehz*], 265, 272, 495, 507, 657, 660
Corvée (conscript labor), 61
Corvinus, Mathias, 414–415
Cossacks [*kahs*-aks], 532–534, 623
Costa, Lucio, 1128
Costa Rica, 678, 865
Council of Five Hundred, 105
Council of Four Hundred (Athens), 100, 102
Council of Troubles, 518
Counter-Enlightenment, 697–698
Courbet [koor-*bay*], Gustave, 888
Courtly love tradition, 341–342, 381
Courtly romance, 378
Coverdale, Miles, 468, 504
Cracow, 474
Cranmer, Thomas, 467, 468
Crassus [*kras*-uhs], 152
Craxi [*krahx*-ee], Bettino, 1147
Creation, accounts of, 19–20, 24–25, 35
Crécy [*kray*-see], battle of, 395
Crédit-Mobilier [*kray*-dee moh-bee-lee-*yay*], 845
Creeks, 279
Cremation, 388
Creoles, 675
Crete [kreet], 90, 540
Crime: and poverty in the early modern period, 605–606; control in the early modern period, 606–608
Crimean [krye-*mee*-uhn] War, 847, 850, 859
Crispi, Francesco [frahn-*cheh*-skoh *kris*-pee], 882–883
Croatia [kroh-*ay*-shah], 625, 626, 1162
Croix de Feu [krwah deh feh], 1013
Cro-Magnon culture, 5–6
Cromwell, Oliver, 530, 535
Cromwell, Thomas, 467
Crop rotation, 502, 505
Crossbow, 74
Croton, 93
Crusades, 350–353, 379
Crystal Palace (London), 814
Cuba, 486, 498, 658; modern, 677, 679, 883, 1127, 1132–1135, 1139, 1140, 1153–1154, 1156
Cuban missile crisis, 1134–1135, 1153–1154

Cubists, 939, 965
Cult of Death, 399
Cultural Revolution (China), 1060–1065
Cumae [*kew*-mee], battle of, 146
Cumans [*koo*-mahnz], 356
Cuneiform [kyoo-*nee*-ih-form], 12, 17, 20, 48, 226, 229
Curie [*kew*-ree], Marie, 936
Curie, Pierre, 936
Cursus honorum, 145
Cusa [*kew*-suh], Nicholas of, 635
Custozza, battle of, 839
Cuzco [*koos*-koh], 273–276, 496
Cybele [*sihb*-uh-lee], 38, 137
Cyclades [*sik*-lah-deez], 90
Cynicism, 139–140
Cynics, 130
Cyprus, 215, 517, 540
Cypselus [*sihp*-see-luhs], 95
Cyrus [*sye*-ruhs] the Great, 42, 102
Czechoslovakia: after World War I, 952, 975; between the world wars, 1021-1023; Nazi takeover, 1030; after World War II, 1045, 1047, 1144, 1145, 1160, 1161

Dachau [*dak*-au], 1009
Dacians [*day*-shee-ahns], 162
Dadaists, 958, 1007–1008
Dahomey, 904
D'Ailly [da-yee], Pierre, 397
Daimyo [*dye*-myoh], 588, 777, 778, 779, 781, 784
Daladier, Edouard [*ay*-dwahr dah-lah-*dyay*], 1030
D'Albret [*dal*-breh], Jeanne, 465
Dalí [*dah*-lee], Salvador, 938, 958, 965, 966
Dalmatia, 548, 820, 998
Damascus [duh-*mass*-kuhs], 34, 215–217, 218, 362, 947
D'Amboise, Georges [zhorzh dahn-*bwaz*], 469
Danby, Earl of, 628
Dance, in ancient India, 65
D'Annunzio [dahn-*noon*-tsyoh], Gabriele, 937, 998
Danse macabre [dahns ma-*kabr*], 399
Dante Alighieri [*dahn*-tay ah-lay-*gyeh*-ree], 400, 422
Danton, Georges [zhorzh dahn-*tohn*], 720, 724
Danzig [*dahn*-tsig], 402, 952, 1047
Darby, Abraham, 789
Dardanelles [dahr-duh-*nelz*], 947, 1046
Darius I [duh-*rye*-uhs] (Persia), 42, 43, 44, 102, 128
Dark Age (Greece), 92–93
Darnley, Henry Lord, 519
Darwin, Charles, 887–888
Darwish, Mahmoud, 1105
Daumier, Honoré [oh-noh-*ray* doh-mee-*yay*], 888
David, Jacques-Louis [zhahk dah-*veed*], 965
David (Israel), 34, 187
"D Day," 1041
Dead Sea Scrolls, 185

Death, conceptions of: in ancient India, 65; in early China, 71; Neanderthal, 385; Mesopotamian, 385; Egyptian, 385; early Greek, 385–386; Hindu, 386; in Buddhism, 386, 736–737; Taoist, 386–387; Chinese, 387; Hebrew, 388; in early Christianity, 388; medieval European, 388–389, 399; cult of, 399; in traditional Japan, 736–737; Muslim views, 736–738; and the Protestant Reformation, 737, 739; African views, 737; in British India, 737; Sumbanese views, 737–738; Huron views, 738; suicide, 738; martyrdom, 738-739; Jewish views, 739; and the baroque, 739; and the Enlightenment, 739; in the modern West, 739–740. *See also* Burial practices
Deborah, 35
De Brazza, Pierre, 906
Decadents, 937
Decameron (Boccaccio), 422, 473
Deccan, 59, 287–288, 289, 292, 293, 550, 555, 558, 745
Decembrist Revolt, 823, 824
Decius [*dee*-shuhs], persecutions of, 192, 193
Declaration of Independence, 674
Declaration of Pillnitz, 718
Declaration of the Rights of Man and the Citizen, 715, 717, 801
Declaratory Act (1719), 672–673
Decline of the West (Spengler), 957
Decretum [duh-*kree*-tum] (Gratian), 366, 369
Deductive method, 640–641
Defender of the Peace (Marsiglio of Padua), 397, 398
Defoe, Daniel, 631, 649, 702, 705, 798
Degas [day-*gah*], Edgar, 888
De Gasperi [day *gahs*-peh-ree], Alcide, 1146
De Gaulle [duh *gohl*], Charles, 1032, 1100, 1116, 1123, 1146, 1147, 1160
D'Eglantine [*deg*-lahn-tyne], Philippe Fabre, 719
Deinocrates [dye-*nak*-rah-teez], 134
Deism, 684–685, 722–723
Dekker, Thomas, 648
De Klerk, F. W., 1122
De la Cosa, Juan, 509
Delacroix, Eugène [ur-*zhahn* duh-lah-*krwah*], 829, 831
Delagoa, 488
De la Madrid, Miguel, 1138
De la Tour, George, 650
Del Cano, Juan Sebastián, 488
Delft, 528
Delhi: ancient, 218; medieval, 285, 288, 289; under the Mughals, 548, 557, 743, 744, 745; under the English, 751, 760, 761
Delhi Sultans, 286–289
Delian [*dee*-lih-uhn] League, 110, 117
Delisle, Guillaume [gee-*yohm* deh-*leel*], 1108
Delos [*dee*-lahs], 132, 137; role of women in, 138

Delphi [*del*-fye], 99, 119, 126, 131
Democratic Party (Germany), 1004
Democritus, 123, 634
Demography: prehistoric, 7–8; Meso-america and Peru, 257; medieval, 336, 391-392; early modern, 481, 499, 770, 794; and the first phase of the Industrial Revolution, 805–808; modern, 837–838, 913–914, 928–929, 1066, 1119, 1139
Demosthenes [dih-*mahs*-thuh-neez], 126–127
Dendrochronology, 3–4
Denmark: Reformation in, 461; early modern, 523, 623; and the Enlightenment, 697; in the first phase of the Industrial Revolution, 795; in the period 1860–1914, 854, 883; in World War II, 1032; after World War II, 1160, 1162
Deraismes, Maria, 847
Derozio, H. L., 754
Dervishes, 540
Desai [deh-*sye*], Morarji, 1086
Descartes, René [ruh-*nay* day-*kart*], 640–642, 643, 896
Desmoulins [day-moo-lan], Camille, 718
D'Étaples, Lefèvre [leh-*fevr* day-*tapl*], 425
Détente, 1156–1157
Devolution, War of, 616
Devotio moderna, 402
Devshirme, 542, 543
De Witt, Jan [yahn deh *viht*], 617
Dharma [*dahr*-mah], 173–174, 175, 182
Dhimmis, 219
Dialectic method, 369
Dialogue Concerning the Two Chief World Systems (Galileo), 638
Dias, Bartholomeu [bahr-tuh-luh-*may*-uh *dee*-ush], 485, 489
Diaspora [dye-*ahs*-poh-rah], 137, 187, 188
Díaz [*dee*-ahz], Porfirio, 867
Dickens, Charles, 810, 889, 897
Dickinson, Emily, 831
Dictator (Roman), 151, 152
Diderot, Denis [deh-*nee* dee-duh-*roh*], 687, 688, 691, 692, 705
Diem, Ngo Dinh [uhng-*oh* dihn zih-*em*], 1072
Dien Bien Phu [dyen byen foo], battle of, 1072
Diet: Chinese, 318; medieval European, 336; in the Americas, 499, 505; early modern European, 603
Diet (Holy Roman Empire), 413
Dilmun, 50
Dimensionality, illusion of, 430–431
Dimini, 90
Dimitri [dee-*mee*-tree], Grand Prince, 403
Diocletian [dye-uh-*klee*-shuhn], 167–168, 193
Diogenes [dye-*ahj*-eh-neez] of Sinope, 140
Dionysius II, 125
Directory, 724–725, 727, 728
Disease, 391–393, 499
Disraeli [diz-*ray*-lee], Benjamin, 801, 878, 909, 912, 917
Divan, 541

Divination, 71
Divine Comedy, The (Dante), 400, 422
Divorce: in classical Athens, 107; in classical Rome, 163; view of Jesus, 190; in early Islamic society, 220; Maya, 263; in the early modern world, 593–594; in modern Europe, 877; in modern Asia, 1075
Djakarta, 1071, 1076
Dodocanese, 998
Doe, Samuel K., 1120
Dollfuss [*dole*-fuss], Engelbert, 1023, 1027
Doll's House, A (Ibsen), 883
Dome of the Rock (Jerusalem), 1098
Domesday [*doomz*-day] Book, 341
Domestic (cottage) system, 797–798
Domesticity, Cult of, 876–877
Dominic, 362
Dominican Republic, 1127, 1135
Dominicans, 362, 369–370, 380, 381
"Domino theory," 1072
Domitian [doh-*mish*-uhn], 158, 160
Domna, Julia, 163, 166, 192
Donatarios, 499
Donatello [dahn-uh-*tell*-oh], 434–435, 963
Donation of Constantine, 425
Donations of Alexandria, 153
Donatists, 193
Donne [dun], John, 640
Don Quixote [kee-*hoh*-tay] (Cervantes), 516, 649
Dopolavoro, 1002
Doric order, 116
D'Ors, Eugenio, 938
Dostoevsky [doss-tuh-*yev*-ski], Feodor, 824
Douglas, Alfred, 877
Dover, Treaty of, 628
Dow, Alexander, 754
Drake, Sir Francis, 500, 519, 528
Drama: classical Greek, 120–122, 137–138; Noh, 327; late-sixteenth-century, 516; early modern European, 648–649; Romantic, 828; Kabuki, 782; modern Western, 889, 958, 1008
Dreyfus, Alfred, 879–880
Dreyfus Affair, 879–880
Drogheda [*draw*-uh-duh], Statutes of, 406
Drumont [droo-*mon*], Edouard, 862
Dual Alliance, 941
Dualism, 182, 183, 184, 364
Dual Monarchy, 857
Dubček [*doob*-chek], Alexander, 1160
Du Bois [doo *bois*], W. E. B., 1114
Dulles, John Foster, 1153
Dulles doctrine, 1157
Duma, 969, 970, 971
Dunkirk, 530, 1032
Dupleix [doo-*pleks*], Joseph, 749
Dürer, Albrecht [*ahl*-brehkt *dur*-uhr], 432, 476–477, 503
Durham Report, 675
Dutch East Indies (Indonesia), 535, 1037, 1042
Dutch War (1665–1667), 536
Dutch War (1672–1678), 616–617
Dutch West Indies Company, 535

Duvalier, François [frahn-*swah* doo-*vah*-yay], 1135
Duvalier, Jean-Claude, 1135

Eakins, Thomas, 888
Earth Mother, 90
East Africa, 250–253
Eastern Orthodoxy, 194
East Germany, 1047, 1153, 1160, 1161
East India Companies: Dutch, 527, 535, 657; English, 535, 561, 657, 673, 742, 746–756 *passim*, 776, 912; French, 749
Ebert, Friedrich [*free*-drik *ay*-bert], 1004
Ebla, 21
Ecbatana, 43
Ecclesiastical History of the English Nation (Bede), 376
Eck [ek], Johann, 457
Eckhart, Meister, 400–401
Ecuador, 678, 865, 1101, 1128
Eddas, 377
Eden, Sir Anthony, 1097
Edessa [ih-*dess*-uh], 351, 352
Edict of Milan, 169
Edinburgh, 339
Edirne [ee-*deer*-neh], 545
Edison, Thomas Alva, 813
Edo [*ay*-doh], 494, 779, 782, 784, 785. *See also* Tokyo
Education: in ancient India, 65; in Confucianism, 75; in Legalism, 77–78; in China, 82; in Sparta, 108; at Plato's Academy, 125; in early Africa, 242–243; in Mali, 247; Aztec, 270; Carolingian, 332–333; in Granada, 355; in medieval Europe, 364–366; humanist views, 423–424; for Renaissance women, 424, 425–426, 427; and Lutheranism, 459; in Calvin's Geneva, 464; and the Jesuits, 470; in the Ottoman Empire, 544–545, 602–603; in Ming China, 577; in early modern Asia, 600–601; in early modern Europe, 601–602; in modern India, 759; in Manchu China, 772; in Nazi Germany, 1011; in the Soviet Union, 1016–1017; in modern Japan, 1054; in modern China, 1060–1062; in modern East Asia, 1074–1075
Edward I (England), 343, 349, 380
Edward III (England), 394, 395, 410, 418
Edward IV (England), 406
Edward V (England), 406
Edward VI (England), 468–469
Edward VII (Britain), 932
Egypt, 333: geography of, 23; development of civilization in, 23; Old Kingdom, 23–24; traditional religion, 24–26; Middle Kingdom, 26–28; New Kingdom, 28–31; society of ancient, 31–32; culture of ancient, 32–33; Hebrews in, 33; and the Hittites, 36–37, 38; conquered by Persians, 42; contacts with Minoans, 91; Greek colonies in, 93; conquered by Alexander the Great, 128; under the Ptolemies, 129; conquered by Romans, 153–154; under Roman rule, 155; under the Byzantines, 201; conquered by the Persians,

209; early Muslim rule, 215, 218; writing in, 226; under Kushite rule, 236; relations with Axum, 238–239; and the crusades, 352; ancient art, 444; and the Ottomans, 540; and Napoleon I, 728; modern, 908–909, 942, 990, 1032, 1094, 1097–1105 passim, 1123, 1158
Eichmann [ike-mahn], Adolf, 1039
Eiffel [eye-fel] Tower, 875
Eightfold path, 176
"Eight-legged essay," 577
Einstein, Albert, 936
Eisenhower, Dwight D.: in World War II, 1041, 1042; presidency of, 1048, 1069, 1072, 1148
Eisenmenger, Johann Andreas, 699
Eisner [eyes-ner], Kurt, 1004
Elagabulus, 166
Elbe [ehl-buh] River, 1042
Eleanor of Aquitaine [ak-wih-tayn], 341–342, 377
Electricity, discovery of, 813
Elements, The (Euclid), 135, 372
Eleven Thousand Virgins, Brotherhood of the, 453
Elgin marbles, 823
Elijah, 388
Eliot, George (Mary Anne Evans), 831
Eliot, T. S., 958
Elizabeth I (England), 468, 473, 500, 513, 519–520, 521, 522, 528, 535, 598
Elizabeth II (Britain), 1152
Elizabeth of Austria-Hungary, 890
Elizabeth of Braunschweig [broun-shvyck], 459
Elizabeth of Valois [vahl-wah], 513
Elizabeth of York, 406
El Mirador, 260
El Salvador. See Salvador
Émile [ay-meel] (Rousseau), 697
Empedocles, 123, 634
Ems dispatch, 897
Enclosure movement, 668, 794
Encomenderos [ayn-koh-men-day-ros], 496
Encomienda [ayn-koh-mee-ayn-dah], 658
Encyclopedia (ed. Diderot), 687, 691, 692, 702–703
Engels, Friedrich [free-drik ehn-guhls], 791, 809, 836, 889, 892
England: Norman Conquest, 331, 333, 334, 341; Norman rule, 341–343; Edward I, 343; Wat Tyler rebellion, 394; Hundred Years' War, 394–396; War of the Roses, 406; Yorkists, 406; Henry VII's reign, 406; Renaissance in, 425, 436; humanists in, 455–456; and the spread of Calvinism, 465; reforms of Henry VIII, 466–468; the Edwardian reformation, 468–469; Counter-Reformation in, 473–474; exploration in North America, 499–500; Anglo-Spanish War, 519–520; reign of Elizabeth I, 521–522; under the early Stuarts, 528–529; English Revolution, 529–530; early interests in Asia, 534–535; colonial rivalry in the Americas, 535–536;

wars with Louis XIV, 618–621; under the later Stuarts, 628–631; early interests in India, 745–749; English Revolution, 529–530. See also Britain
Enlightened despots: nature of, 691, 696–697; Catherine the Great, 692–693; Frederick the Great, 693–695; Joseph II, 695–696
Enlightenment: roots of, 683; Deism, 684; idea of progress, 684–686; influence of Locke, 686; philosophes, 686–690; Voltaire, 687; Rousseau, 688–689; Montesquieu, Morelly, Mandeville, and Adam Smith, 689; censorship, 690-691; Encyclopedia, 691, 692; and the Jews, 698–701; and abolitionism, 701-702; and women, 702–704; views on death, 739
Ennius [en-ee-uhs], 164
Enragés, 722–723
Entente Cordiale [ahn-tahnt kohr-dyahl], 942
Environmental concerns, 1055, 1076, 1174–1175
Ephesus [ehf-uh-suhs], 108, 119
Epic of Gilgamesh [gihl-guh-mesh], 19–20, 385
Epictetus [ehp-ihk-teet-ehs], 139
Epicureanism, 138, 139–140
Epicurus [ehp-ih-kyoor-uhs], 139–140
Equal rights amendment, 1151
Equestrians (Roman), 150
Erasistratus [er-a-sis-trah-tuhs], 136
Erasmus, Desiderius [des-ih-deer-ee-uhs ih-rahz-muhs], 402, 425, 430, 455, 459, 466, 477
Eratosthenes [er-uh-toss-thuh-neez], 135, 508, 634
Erechtheum [ee-rek-thee-um], 117, 119
Eretrea, 102
Eritrea [ehr-ih-tree-ah], 907, 1027, 1120, 1124
Ernst, Max, 938
Erzberger, Matthias, 1004
Escorial [ays-koh-ree-ahl], 515
Eskimos (Inuit), 280–281, 507
Essay Concerning Human Understanding, An (Locke), 645, 686
Estado Novo, 1014, 1015
Estates General (Dutch), 527
Estates General (French), 345, 349, 396, 407, 524, 611, 710–713
Estenssoro, Victor Paz, 1132
Esterhazy [ess-ter-hah-zee] family, 705
Estonia, 623, 973, 1021–1023, 1031, 1032, 1143, 1164
Ethiopia, 238, 906, 907–908, 1027, 1119, 1120, 1123–1124
Etruscans [ih-trus-kenz], 143–145, 146, 160, 229
Euclid [yoo-klid], 135, 372
Eugene of Savoy, Prince, 626
Eugénie [yoo-jay-nee], Empress, 846
Eumenes [yoo-mee-neez] I, 131
Eumenes II, 131, 148
Eunuchs, 84
Euphrates [yoo-fray-teez] River, 17
Euripides [yoo-rip-ih-deez], 120–122, 137

Eurocommunism, 1160
European Coal and Steel Community, 1158–1159
European Community, 1162
Eusebius [you-see-bih-uhs], 168, 193
Evangelical Union, 522
Evans, Arthur, 90
Everest, George, 1110
"Ever-normal granary system," 79, 311
Everyman, 378
Evolution, theory of, 123
Evolutionary Socialism (Bernstein), 891
Exchequer, 342
Excommunication, 361
Exekias, 100
Existentialism, 957
Experimental method, 372
Exploration: technological background, 483–484; Portuguese motives, 484–485; voyages of, 485–488
Expressionists, 965, 1007
Eyck [ike, eck], Jan van, 437
Eylau [eye-lou], battle of, 730
Ezana, 239

Fabian Society, 891
Fabliaux [fah-blee-oh], 378
Factories, in the first phase of the Industrial Revolution, 797–799
Factory Acts, 802–803, 804
Faerie Queene (Spenser), 522
Fa Hsien [fah-shyen], 62
Fairs: Byzantine, 206; medieval European, 338, 367
Faisal [fye-sahl], Prince (later Faisal I), 947, 990
Faisal II (Iraq), 1097
Falange [fay-lanj], 1013, 1030
Falkland Islands (Islas Malvinas), 1127, 1129
Family: Neolithic, 9; in Mesopotamia, 22–23; and Confucianism, 179; in the Byzantine Empire, 207; Bantu, 235; in early modern Asia, 590–591; in early modern Europe, 591–592; in early modern Africa, 594; in Napoleonic France, 729; in the first phase of the Industrial Revolution, 799–801; in the modern West, 875–877
Famine, 391, 499, 525, 558, 583, 618–619, 837–838, 1059, 1119, 1124
Fanti [fahn-tee], 484
Faraday, Michael, 813
Farel, Guillaume [gee-yohm fah-rel], 462
Farouk (Egypt), 1099
Fascism: nature and origins, 996–997; in Italy, 997–1003; in Germany, 1003–1012; varieties of, 1012–1015
Fashoda incident, 909
Fatamids [fat-uh-mihdz], 218
Fatehpur Sikri [fut-eh-poor see-kree], 552, 746
Fathers and Sons (Turgenev), 889
Faubus, Orville, 1148–1149
Faulkner, William, 957
Faust (Goethe), 827–828
Fauves [fohvz], 938–939
Fell, Margaret, 531–532

Feminist movement, 883–887
Fénelon [fayn-el-*oh*], François, 618
Ferdinand, Archduke Franz, 943–944
Ferdinand I (Austria), 839
Ferdinand I (Holy Roman Empire), 513
Ferdinand I (Naples), 822
Ferdinand II (Holy Roman Empire),
Ferdinand II (Naples), 838, 839
Ferdinand III (Holy Roman Empire), 625
Ferdinand VII (Spain), 485, 677, 821–822
Ferdinand of Aragon, 404–405, 408, 410
Ferdinand of Styria (Bohemia), 522–523
Ferguson, Wallace, 439
Festivals, 368–369, 378, 553, 576, 597, 651
Feudal order: parallels in ancient China, 72; parallels in South India, 292; in Japan, 325–326, 335; in Europe, 334–335, 381; bastard feudalism, 406
Fichte [*fik*-teh], Johann Gottlieb, 717, 732, 817, 831
Ficino, Marsilio [mahr-*see*-lyoh fee-*chee*-noh], 423, 432
Fiefs [feefs], 335
Fielding, Henry, 631, 705
Fiji [*fee*-jee], 928, 929
Filioque [fihl-ee-*oh*-kwee] controversy, 211
Filippo Maria (Milan), 408
Filmer, Robert, 524
Films, 899, 1139
Finland, 973; Reformation in, 461 in World War II, 1031, 1032
Firdawsi (Firdausi) [fihr-*dow*-see], 223
First International, 837, 889–890
First Triumvirate, 152
Fischer, Fritz, 940
Fisher, John, 468
Fitch, Ralph, 746
Fiume [*fyoo*-may], 998
Five Hundred, Council of (*Boule*), 102
Five-Year Plans (USSR), 1015–1016
Flagellants, 392
Flanders, 338, 395, 402, 616, 617, 620, 670, 696
Flaubert [floh-*bair*], Gustave, 888–889
Flavian dynasty, 157–158
Fleury [flur-*ree*], Cardinal André-Hercule de, 669
Flinders, Matthew, 1110
Florence, 338, 339, 391, 394, 402, 410–411, 849; in the Renaissance, 418-419, 422, 423, 428, 436–437, 440, 482
Florida, 471, 500, 536, 671, 674, 675
Flying Tigers, 1036
Fontenelle [fon-teh-*nel*], Bernard de, 685
Foochow (Fuzhou), 577
Food and Agricultural Organization (UN), 1045
Forbidden City, 578, 579
Ford, Gerald R., 1157
Ford, Henry, 871
Forli [fohr-*lee*], 409–410
Formosa, 535. *See also* Taiwan
Fort William. *See* Calcutta
Forty-two Articles, 468
Forum (Rome), 154, 159–160
Fouquet [foo-*kaye*], Nicholas, 613

Fourier [*foor*-yay], Charles, 812
Four Noble Truths, 176
Fourteen Points, 950
Fox, George, 531, 532
Foxe, John, 473
Fragonard [fra-goh-*nar*], Jean-Honoré, 704
France, medieval: and the Vikings, 333–334; and the feudal order, 335; and the Angevin Empire, 341; Capetian period, 343–345; reign of Philip IV, 344–345; Jacquerie, 393–394; Languedoc risings, 394; Hundred Years' War, 394–396; early Valois period, 407–408
France, early modern: Renaissance in, 425; and the spread of Calvinism, 465; civil war, 520–521; and the Thirty Years' War, 523–524; early Bourbons, 524-526; colonial rivalry in the Americas, 536; age of Louis XIV, 611–621; under Louis XV, 668–669; colonies of, 660, 661, 662; in the War of the Austrian Succession, 669–670; in the Seven Years' War, 669–670; and the American Revolutionary War, 673–674; Enlightenment in, 686–691; the revolution of 1789, 709–719; the radical revolution (1792–1794), 719–724; the Thermidorian Reaction, 724–725; legacy of the revolution, 725–727; the Napoleonic era, 727–733; the Bourbon restoration, 733–734
France, modern: in the first phase of the Industrial Revolution, 795, 810–812; and the Congress of Vienna, 819–820; in the early nineteenth century, 824; revolution of 1830, 832; under Louis-Philippe, 835; revolution of 1848, 839, 840–841; Second Republic, 844–845; Second Empire, 845–848; Franco-Prussian War, 855–857; in the Crimean War, 847, 850; in the second phase of the Industrial Revolution, 870, 874; and the Third Republic, 879–880; colonies in Africa, 908–909; colonial regimes in Southeast Asia, 918–920; and the origins of World War I, 941–943, 945; in World War I, 945–950; and the Peace of Paris (1919), 950–952; after World War I, 952; fascism in, 1012–1013; in the Great Depression, 1019–1021; events leading to World War II, 1027–1028, 1030–1031; in World War II, 1031–1032, 1034, 1041–1042, 1043; after World War II, 1047, 1146, 1158–1159, 1160; and the Vietnam War, 1071–1072; mandates of, 1099; end of imperialism in Africa, 1115–1116, 1122–1123
Franche Comté [frahnch kohn-*tay*], 616
Francis I (France), 399, 408, 413, 425, 476, 513
Francis II (France), 513
Franciscans, 362–363, 369–370, 381
Francis of Assisi [ah-*see*-zee], 363
Franck, Sebastian, 466
Franco, Francisco, 1013, 1030
Franco-Prussian War, 856–857

Frankfurt, 339, 839, 852
Frankfurt, Treaty of, 857
Frankfurt Assembly, 839–840
Franklin, Benjamin, 690, 813
Franks, 166, 170, 331–333
Franz Joseph I (Austria), 839, 850, 857, 858
Frederick, Elector of Saxony, 457
Frederick I, "Barbarossa" (Holy Roman Empire), 347, 366
Frederick II (Holy Roman Emperor), 338, 348, 352–353, 366, 380
Frederick II, "the Great" (Prussia), 627–628, 650, 669, 670–671, 687, 693–695
Frederick III (Prussia), 627
Frederick V (Palatinate), 523
Frederick William, "the Great Elector," 626–627
Frederick William I (Prussia), 669, 690
Frederick William IV (Prussia), 718, 839, 840, 853
Free Corps, 1007
Free Democrats (West Germany), 1147
Free French, 1004, 1032, 1043
Freemasons, 690, 824
French Academy of Sciences, 643
French Equatorial Africa, 1115, 1116
French Guinea, 1116
French Revolution (1789–1799): roots of the revolution, 709–711; the revolution of 1789, 711–715; the bourgeois order (1789–1791), 716–717; European reactions, 717–718; the fall of the monarchy, 718–719; the radical revolution (1792–1794), 719–724; the Thermidorian reaction, 724–725; the legacy, 725–727
French Revolution (1830), 832
French Revolution (1848), 839, 840–841
French Revolution (1870), 856
French West Africa, 1115
Fresco, 430
Freud [froid], Sigmund, 858, 935–936
Friedan, Betty, 1151
Friedland [*freet*-lahnt], battle of, 730
Fröbel [*fruh*-behl], Friedrich, 697
Fronde [frohnd], 525–526
Frontinus, Sextus, 165
Frumentius, 239
Fuchou (Foochow, Fuzhou), 315
Fugard, Athol, 1124
Fugger [*foog*-uhr], Jakob, 482, 483
Fugger family, 482, 504
Fujimori, Alberto, 1131
Fujiwara [foo-jee-*wahr*-uh] clan, 324, 325
Fukien (Fujian), 1067
Fulton, Robert, 803
Funan, 299
Fur trade, 660
Fusae, Ichikawa, 1075
Futurists, 939, 940
Fuzuli [foo-zoo-*lih*], Mehmet ibn Suleiman, 547

Gabelle [gah-*bell*], 396, 611
Gabon, 1101
Gainsborough, Thomas, 705

Galen [*gay*-luhn], 634
Galicia [geh-*lish*-uh], 947
Galileo [gal-ih-*lay*-oh], 638–639
"Gallican liberties," 407
Gallipoli [gah-*lip*-oh-lee] campaign, 947
Galtieri [gahl-*tyair*-ee], Leopoldo, 1129
Gama, Vasco da, [*vash*-koh dah *gah*-muh], 484, 485, 491, 510
Gambia, 906
Gandhara, 54
Gandhi [*gahn*-dee], Indira, 1085–1087
Gandhi, Mohandas K., 173, 174, 917, 948, 986–989, 1079–1083, 1173
Gandhi, Rajiv, 1087
Ganges [*gan*-jeez] Valley, 52, 54, 56, 548, 744, 746–747, 752, 760. *See also* Hindustan
"Gang of Four," 1065
Gao, 241–242, 246, 247, 248
Garamantes, 240
Garcia, Alan, 1131
García Marquez [*mahr*-kes], Gabriel, 1138
Gargantua (Rabelais), 425
Garibaldi, Giuseppe, 850–852
Garvey, Marcus, 1115
Gascons, 395
Gascony, 344
Gaskell, Elizabeth, 810, 831
Gauchos, 866
Gaudí [gow-dee], Antonio, 938
Gaugamela [goh-ga-*mee*-lah], battle of, 128
Gauguin [goh-*ganh*], Paul, 937, 965
Gaul [gahl], 146, 152, 166–167; invaded by Franks, 170, 331
Gauls [gahlz], 131
Gay Rights movement, 1151
Gaza Strip, 1094, 1097, 1098, 1106
Gdansk (formerly Danzig), 1047
Geisha [*gay*-shuh], 597, 782
General Association of German Women, 885
Generalife, 355
Geneva [juh-*nee*-vuh], 462, 463–465; University of, 464
Geneva Conference, 1072
Genoa [*jehn*-oh-ah], 338, 339, 402, 411, 418, 603
Gentile [jehn-*tee*-lay], Giovanni, 999
Gentileschi [jent-el-*ehs*-kee], Artemisia, 596
Gentry (English), 794
Geoffrey of Monmouth [*jef*-ree of *mon*-muth], 378
Geography, 135
George I (Britain), 648, 666, 669
George II (Britain), 666, 671
George III (Britain), 673, 773, 794
George V (Britain), 932
Georgia, USA, 660
Georgia, USSR, 975, 1168
Georgics (Virgil), 157
German Confederation, 820, 852–853, 854–855
German East Africa, 947
Germania (Tacitus), 165
Germanic tribes, 331

Germany: medieval, 333, 335; Renaissance in, 425; Reformation in, 457–461; Anabaptists in, 465–466; in the Thirty Years' War, 522–524; victim of Louis XIV's aggression, 618–619; and Napoleon, 729, 731; in the first phase of the Industrial Revolution, 810–812; in the early nineteenth century, 832; revolution of 1848, 839–840; unification of, 852–857; in the second phase of the Industrial Revolution in, 870, 871, 874; Second Reich, 880–881; imperialism in the Pacific, 929–930; colonies in Africa, 907–908; and the origins of World War I, 940–945; in World War I, 945–950; and the Peace of Paris (1919), 950–952; Nazism, 1003–1012; events leading to World War II, 1026–1030; in World War II, 1031–1033, 1037–1042; postwar division of, 1047; reunification of, 1161. *See also* Holy Roman Empire
Gerson, Jean [zhahn *zher*-sohn], 397
Gersonides [gur-*sohn*-ih-deez], 223
Gestapo, 1009
Ghana [*gah*-nah], 243, 488, 1116, 1119, 1124
Ghazis [*gahw*-zehs], 539
Ghent [gehnt], 339, 394
Ghibellines [*gib*-uh-leenz], 408
Ghiberti [gee-*ber*-tee], Lorenzo, 434–435
Giacometti [jah-koh-*met*-tee], Alberto, 938
Giap [jyopp], Vo Nguyen, 1071–1072
Gibbon, Edward, 2, 170
Gibraltar, 620, 674, 820
Gilbert, William, 637, 642
Gilbert Islands, 928
Gilchrist, Percy, 813
Gioberti, Vincenzo [veen-*chayn*-tsoh joh-*bair*-tee], 849
Giolitti [joh-*leet*-tee], Giovanni, 999
Giotto [*joht*-toh], 431
Girondins [jih-*rohnd*-inz], 720, 722, 724
Giudice [*joo*-dee-chay], Maria, 892
Gladstone, William, 878, 890
Glasnost, 1164
Glorious Revolution (1688), 629
Glory of the Kings, The, 238
Gluck [glook], Christoph Willibald von, 705
Gnostics [*nahs*-tiks], 192
Goa [*goh*-uh], 488, 490, 745, 746
Gobi [*goh*-bee] Desert, 391
Gobineau [goh-bee-*noh*], Arthur de, 939, 1092
Go-Daigo, 326
Godfrey of Bouillon [boo-*yohn*], 350, 351
Godwin, William, 704
Goebbels [*ger*-buls], Joseph, 899, 1007, 1011
Goes [goos], Benedict de, 471
Goethe, Johann Wolfgang von [*ger*-tah], 575, 731, 827–828
Gogh [goh, gok], Vincent van, 937
Gogol [*goh*-gol], Nikolai, 824
Gokhale [*goh*-kah-lay], G. K., 917
Golan Heights, 1097, 1106

Gold Coast, 1114, 1116
Golden Book, 411
Golden Bull, 413
Golden Horde, 357
Golden Lotus, The, 574
Goldsmith, Oliver, 795
Gomulka, Wladyslaw [vlah-*dihss*-lahff guh-*mool*-kuh], 1145, 1146
Gonzalez [gawn-*sah*-lehs], Julio, 938
Goodman, Christopher, 473
Gorbachev [gor-beh-*chof*], Mikhail, 1142, 1148, 1155, 1163–1169 *passim*
Gordimer, Nadine, 1124
Gordon, Charles ("Chinese"), 909
Gordon riots, 802
Göring [*gur*-ing], Hermann, 1007
GOSPLAN, 1015–1016
Gotha [*goh*-tah] Program, 890, 893
Gothic style, 374–375, 419
Goths, 166, 169–170
Göttingen [*gurt*-ing-ehn], 459
Gouges, Olympe de, 726
Government of India Act, 912
Goya, Francisco, 730
Gracchus [*grak*-uhs], Cornelia, 150–151
Gracchus, Gaius [*gay*-uhs], 150–151, 161
Gracchus, Tiberius [tye-*beer*-ee-uhs], 150–151
Gramsci [*grahm*-shee], Antonio, 1160
Granada, 354, 355, 405
Gran Chaco [grahn *chah*-koh] War, 1132
Grand Alliance (World War II), 1040–1042
Granicus [gruh-*nee*-kuhs] River, battle of, 128
Granth Sahib, 556
Gratian [*gray*-shun], 366, 369
Gravity, theory of, 123
Great Chain of Being, 683
Great Depression, 1008–1009, 1014, 1018–1021, 1022–1023, 1026, 1128, 1131
"Greater East Asia Co-prosperity Sphere," 1037
Great Fear (France), 714
Great Interregnum, 348, 412
"Great Leap Forward," 1059
Great Northern War, 623
Great Purges (USSR), 1017–1018
"Great Silk Way," 219
"Great Society," 1150
Great Trek (South Africa), 909
Great Wall, 77, 80, 305, 568, 577–578, 580
Grebel [*gray*-bel], Conrad, 465
Greco, El [el *grek*-oh] (Domenico Theotokopoulos), 516, 963
Greece, ancient: Neolithic Age, 89–90; Minoans, 90–91; Mycenaeans, 91–92; Dark Age, 92–93; age of expansion, 93–94; geography of, 94; emergence of the *polis*, 94–95; age of Tyranny, 95; Archaic culture, 95–98; growth of the *polis*, 98–99; birth of Athenian democracy, 99–102; Persian Wars, 102–103; Periclean Athens, 103–108; women in classical Athens, 106–107; Sparta,

Greece, ancient (*Continued*)
108–109; Peloponnesian War,
109–112; the classical ideal, 115–117;
classical art, 117–120, 444–445; classical drama, 120–122; pre-Socratic science, 122–123; classical philosophy,
123–126; Macedonian conquest,
126–127; age of Alexander the Great,
127–129; Hellenistic Greeks, 129–132;
Hellenistic trade, 132; Hellenistic economic patterns, 132–134; Hellenistic
science, 134–136; Hellenistic religion,
136–137; Hellenistic women, 137–139;
later Greek philosophy, 139–140; conquered by the Romans, 148
Greece, medieval, 350
Greece, modern: in the early nineteenth
century, 822–823; independence of,
860; in the early twentieth century,
941, 943; between the world wars,
1021–1023; in World War II, 1031,
1032–1033; after World War II, 1046,
1047, 1144
"Greek fire," 215
Greeks: in ancient India, 58–59; defeated
by Romans in southern Italy, 146; al-
phabet of, 229. *See also* Greece
Greenland, 280, 333
Green revolution, 1086, 1087
Greenwich [*grehn*-ich] Mean Time, 1109
Gregory I, Pope, 194
Gregory VII, Pope, 346, 347, 350
Gregory IX, Pope, 364, 366
Gregory XI, Pope, 397
Gregory XIII, Pope, 520, 521
Grenada, 1136, 1157
Grey, Sir Edward, 945
Grey, Lady Jane, 469
Grey, Lord, 833, 834
Grimm, Jacob, 817
Grimm, Wilhelm, 817
Grocyn [*groh*-sin], William, 425
Groote [groht], Gerhard, 402
Gropius [*grow*-pee-uhs], Walter, 958
Grosseteste [*groh*-test], Robert, 372
Grosz [grohs], George, 1007–1008
Grotius [groh-shih-uhs], Hugo, 527
Grumbach, Argula von, 459, 460
Grünewald [grew-neh-vahlt], Matthias,
476
Guadeloupe [gwah-thay-*loo*-pay], 662, 671
Guam [gwom], 883, 929, 930
Guatemala [gwah-tuh-*mah*-luh], 657, 865,
1127, 1135, 1138, 1153
Gudea [goo-*day*-ah], 21
Guelfs [gwelfs], 408, 419
Guernica [gair-*nee*-kah], bombing of,
1029, 1030
Guernica (Picasso), 1029
Guevara, Ernesto "Che" [air-*ness*-toh
"chay" gay-*vah*-rah], 1134, 1135
Guiana [ghee-*ah*-nah], 535
Guicciardini, Francesco [frahn-*cheh*-skoh
gweet-chahr-*dee*-nee], 428–429
Guilds: Byzantine, 206–207; medieval,
338, 339–340, 402, 596; Florentine,
418; Ottoman, 545; Chinese, 571; early
modern, 590, 797

Guinea, 250, 484
Guise [gheez], Mary of, 521
Guise family, 519, 520–521, 589
Guizot, François [frahn-*swah* gee-zoh],
838, 839
Gujarat [goo-jah-*raht*], 290, 296, 550, 743,
745, 746, 752, 912
Gulag Archipelago (Solzhenitsyn), 1143
Gulags, 1143
Gulf War, 1105–1106, 1157
Gunpowder, 305, 306, 316
Guptas, 61–63, 230
Gurkhas, 773, 912
Gustavus Adolphus [guh-*stay*-vuhs uh-
doll-fuhs], 523
Guston, Philip, 965, 966
Gutenberg, Johann [*yoh*-hahn *goo*-tuhn-
berkh], 429
Guti [*goo*-tee], 21
Gypsies, 1012, 1039

Haarlem, 528
Habsburg [*habz*-burg] dynasty, 413–414.
See also individual emperors
Habsburg-Valois Wars, 413–414
Haciendas, 498
Hadith [*heh*-deeth], 214
Hadrian [*hay*-dree-uhn], 158–159, 161
Hafiz [hah-*feez*], Shams ud-din, 216, 223
Hagia Sophia [*hah*-juh soh-*fee*-uh],
209–210, 544
Haiphong [hye-*fong*], 920
Haiti [*hay*-tee], 677, 1127, 1135
Hajj [hahj], 214
Halberstadt [*hahl*-ber-shtaht], 626
Halle [*hahl*-eh], University of, 601, 697
Hamburg, 333, 339, 365, 402, 460
Hamilton, Alexander, 813
Hammurabi [hah-moo-*rah*-bee], 22–23
Hampton Court (palace), 476
Han [hahn] dynasty, 79–87
Han Fei [hahn fay], 78
Hangchow, 314, 315, 316
Hankow (Hankou) [*hang*-kou], 577, 1035
Hannibal, 147–149
Hanoi, 301, 920, 1071
Hanover, 459
Hanoverian dynasty, 666
Hanseatic [han-see-*at*-ik] League, 338,
402
Hanukkah, 137
Harappa [huh-*rahp*-uh], Harappans, 47,
49, 51, 174, 444, 753
Hardenburg, Prince, 732, 819
Harding, Warren G., 1020
Hard Times (Dickens), 810
Hardy, Thomas, 802
Harem system, 221
Hargreaves, James, 796
Hari Singh, 1083
Harold, 341
Harsha, 63
Harvey, William, 639
Hasan, Abi bin, 250
Hasdai ibn-Shaprut, 380
Hasidim [hah-*see*-dim] and Hasidism,
380, 700

Haskalah movement, 700
Haskins, Charles Homer, 439
Hastings, battle of, 341
Hastings, Warren, 751–752
Hatshepsut [hat-*shep*-soot], 28
Hattusas [hat-too-shuhs], 36, 38
Hattusilis III, 37
Hausa [*hou*-sah] city-states, 249–250
Haussmann, Georges [zhorzh ohs-
mann], 846, 874
Havana, 671
Havel, Vaclav, 1161, 1166
Hawaii, 928, 929
Hawkins, John, 500, 519, 535
Hawkins, William, 746
Haydn [*hye*-d'n], Franz Joseph, 705, 829,
858
Haywood, Eliza, 702
Hébert, Jacques, 722
Hebrews: early history of, 33–34; king-
dom of Israel, 34, 35–36; ancient soci-
ety of, 34–35; in the Hellenistic Age,
137; early writing, 229; conceptions of
death, 388. *See also* Jews
Hecataeus, 508
Hegel [*hay*-guhl], Georg Wilhelm Fried-
rich, 732, 817, 830
Heian [hay-ahn] Era, 324–325
Heidelberg, University of, 425
Heimwehr [*hyem*-vair], 1013
Heine [*hye*-neh], Heinrich, 828
Heinsius [*hyen*-see-uhs], Antonius, 618,
620
Heisenberg [*hye*-zehn-berk], Werner, 957
Hejaz [hee-*jaz*], 990
Hejira [hih-*jye*-ruh], 215
Helena (mother of Constantine), 193
Hellenistic kingdoms: Ptolemies, 129; Se-
leucids, 129–130; Macedon, 130–131;
Pergamum, 131–132; Bactria, 131
Hellespont, 112
Helots [*hel*-uhts], 108
Helsinki [hel-*sing*-kee] Accords (1973),
1155, 1157
Hemingway, Ernest, 1020
Henlein [*hen*-line], Konrad, 1030
Henrietta Maria, 529
Henry, Duke of Guise [gheez], 520–521
Henry I (England), 342
Henry I (Germany), 345
Henry II (England), 341, 342–343, 366
Henry II (France), 513
Henry III (France), 521
Henry IV (England), 406
Henry IV (France), 521, 524, 683
Henry IV (Holy Roman Empire), 346
Henry V (Holy Roman Empire), 346
Henry VI (England), 406
Henry VI (Holy Roman Empire), 347
Henry VII (England), 406
Henry VIII (England), 399, 436, 454,
466–468, 476, 477
Henry of Navarre, 521. *See also* Henry IV
(France)
Henry the Navigator, Prince, 485, 510
Heraclides [her-ah-*klye*-deez], 135
Heraclitus [her-ah-*klye*-tuhs] of Ephesus,
123

Herculaneum [her-kew-*lay*-nee-uhm], 162, 705
Herder, Johann Gottfried von, 705, 731, 817
Heresy, 193, 203, 397–398, 464, 466, 473
Héricourt [ay-ree-*koor*], Jenny, 847
"Hermes Trismegistus," 635–636
Hermeticism, 635–636
Herod, 187
Herodotus [hih-*rod*-uh-tuhs], 26, 93, 102–103, 109, 111, 508
Herophilus [hee-*rof*-ih-luhs], 136
Herrera, Juan de, 515
Herschel, William, 827, 1110
Hertz, Heinrich, 813
Herzegovina, 862, 941, 943, 1162
Herzen [*hair*-tsin], Alexander, 825, 859
Herzl [*herts*-l], Theodor, 862–864, 1092
Hesiod [*hee*-see-uhd], 93, 96
Hess, Rudolf, 1007
Hesse [hehs, *hehs*-ee], Philip of, 465
Heydrich [*hye*-drich], Reinhard, 1038
Hiawatha, 279
Hidalgo [ee-*dahl*-goh], Father, 678
Hidalgos [ee-*dahl*-gohs], 405
Hideyoshi [hee-deh-yoh-shee], Toyotomi, 322, 328, 779
Hieroglyphics [*hye*-ruh-*glif*-iks], 25, 32, 226–227, 231
High Commission, Court of, 528, 529, 530
Himalayas, 1084–1085, 1110
Himmler, Heinrich, 1007, 1009
Hinayana (Theravada) Buddhism, 177–178
Hindenburg, Paul von, 947, 1008–1009
Hindi, 1083
Hinduism, 182, 193; in India, 50, 52–53; in Ceylon, 61; writings, 173–174; belief in reincarnation, 174–175; views on evil and suffering, 175; diversity of, 175; role of women, 195–196; Bhakti movement, 291; in Southeast Asia, 301–302; in the Philippines, 302; conceptions of death, 386, 387
Hindustan, 54, 55, 285, 289, 548, 744. *See also* Ganges Valley
Hipparchus [hih-*pahr*-kuhs], 100–101, 135
Hippias [*hip*-ee-uhs], 100–101
Hippocrates [hih-*pahk*-ruh-teez], 135–136
Hippodrome, 203
Hirohito [hee-roh-*hee*-toh], 1042, 1044, 1051
Hiroshige [hee-roh-*shee*-geh], 783, 784
Hiroshima [hee-*rahsh*-mah], 1042, 1051
Hispaniola, 486, 498, 499, 500, 658
Historical study, 2–5
History: sources for, 3–4, 72, 87; fields of, 3
History of Rome (Livy), 157
History of the Peloponnesian War (Thucydides), 111–112
History of the Persian Wars (Herodotus), 103
Hitler, Adolf, 858, 996, 1004–1012, 1026–1033 *passim*, 1038–1042 *passim*
Hitler Youth, 1011

Hittites, 15, 31, 36–38, 52, 53
Hobbes, Thomas, 530, 644–645, 646, 686, 688
Hobson, John A., 902–903
Ho Chi Minh, 920, 980, 1070, 1071–1073
Hogarth, William, 705
Hohenlinden, battle of, 729
Hohenstaufen [*hoh*-uhn-shtow-fuhn] dynasty, 347–348
Hohenzollern [*hoh*-ehn-*tsol*-ern] dynasty, 626
Hohokam culture, 278
Hokusai [hoh-koo-sye], 783, 784–785
Holbach, Baron d', 688
Holbein, Hans [hahns *hohl*-byne], 436, 453, 477
Hölderlin, Friedrich, 828
Holker, John, 811
Holocaust, 1038–1040
Holstein, 854, 855
Holy Alliance, 819, 820
Holy League (1494), 410; (1511–1513), 408, 411; (1571), 517, 540
Holy Roman Empire: early history, 345–346; struggle with Catholic church, 346–349; rise of the Habsburgs, 412–414; and the Thirty Years' War, 522–524; after the Thirty Years' War, 532; in the later seventeenth century, 532, 625–626; in the eighteenth century, 620, 626; in the War of the Austrian Succession, 669–670; in the Seven Years' War, 670–671; reign of Joseph II, 695–696; and the Napoleonic wars, 729–730, 732
Homer, 89, 92–93, 229
Homo erectus [*hoh*-moh ih-*rek*-tuhs], 5
Homo neanderthalis. See Neanderthal culture
Homo sapiens [*hoh*-moh *say*-pee-uhnz], 5
Homosexuality, 476, 598–599, 1039
Honduras, 678, 865
Honecker [*hah*-neh-kehr], Erich, 1161
Hong Kong, 921, 1067–1068, 1075, 1076
Honshu, 779
Hoover, Herbert, 1020
Hopewell culture, 276–277
Hoplites, 95
Horace, 157
Hortensian Law, 145–146
Horthy [*hor*-tee], Miklós, 1022, 1039
Horus, 25
Ho-shen (he shen), 771–772
Hospitals: in ancient India, 62; in medieval England, 372; in Geneva, 464; in the Catholic Revival, 469; Ottoman, 547; foundling, 598
Hsia (Xia) [shyah] dynasty, 69–70
Hsiung-nu (Xiung-nu) [shung-noo], 41, 81, 83, 84
Hsuan Tsang [shwahn-dzahng], 63
Hsuan-tsung (Xuan-zong) [schwahn dzung], 310
Hsun-tzu (Xunzi) [shuhn-tsoo], 76
Hua Kuo-feng (Hua Guofeng), 1065
Huáscar [*wahs*-kahr], 276
Hubble, Edwin, 1111–1112
Hudson River, 500

Hudson Strait, 500
Hue [hway], 301
Hugh Capet [kah-*pay*], 343
Hugo, Victor, 888
Huguenots [*hyoo*-guh-nots], 520–521, 524–525, 621
Human figure, representations of, 442–449, 961–967
Humanists: Renaissance, 420–426; civic, 422–423; Christian, 454–456
Human origins, 5–7
Human sacrifice, 264, 265, 267, 270–271, 276, 278
Humayun [hou-*mah*-yoon], 549
Hume, David, 698
Hundred Days, 820, 824
Hundred Years' War, 394–396
Hungarians, 350
Hungary: medieval, 333, 352, 357, 414–415; early modern, 465, 532, 540, 548, 625, 626, 669, 695, 696; revolution of 1848, 839; Dual Monarchy, 857; and World War I, 947, 952, 979; between the world wars, 979, 1021–1022; in World War II, 1033, 1039–1040; after World War II, 1045, 1047, 1144, 1145, 1160, 1161
Hung Hsiu-Ch'uan (Hong Xiuquan), 922
Hung-wu, 564–566, 580
Huns, 169, 201. *See also* Hsiung-nu
Hunter-gatherers, 5
Hunyadi [*hoo*-nyo-dee], János, 414–415
Huron Indians, 279, 738
Hus [huhs], John, 398, 453, 457
Husayn [Husein, hoo-*sayn*], 215, 738
Hussein, Sadam, 1105–1106, 1157
Hutchinson, Anne, 702
Hutten, Ulrich von, 454–455
Hutton, James, 1110
Huxley, Aldous, 1172
Huygens [*hye*-genz], Christiaan, 1110
Huysmans [*hois*-mahns], J. K., 937
Hwan, Chun Doo, 1069
Hyderabad, 744, 750, 751, 1083
Hydrogen bomb, 1163
Hydrostatics, 135
Hyksos [*hik*-sahs], 27–28, 32, 33, 53

Iberian peninsula, 212, 216, 331, 353
Ibn-Khaldun, 509
Ibo, 1119, 1124
Ibrahim [ib-rah-*heem*], 290
Ibsen, Henrik, 883, 889
Iceland, 333
Iconoclastic controversy, 210–211, 212
Ictinos [ik-*tye*-nahs], 116, 118
Idealism, 698, 829–830
Ideographs, 12
Idris [ih-*drees*] Aloma (Libya), 249
Ife, 250
Igbo, 595
Ignatius Loyola, 470–471, 515
Ikki, Kita, 1013
Île de France [eel duh *frahns*], 343–344
Iliad, 92–93
Illuminated manuscripts, 373–374
Illyria, 147
Illyrian [ih-*lihr*-ee-ahn] Wars, 148

Imarets, 544–545
Imhotep, 24
Imitation of Christ, The (Thomas à Kempis), 402
Impressionism, 037
Inca, 273–276, 495–496, 593, 605, 657
Incest, 208, 599
Index of Prohibited Books, 473, 690
India, ancient: and the Persians, 42; geography of, 46, 47; origins of civilization in, 47; Indus civilization, 47–52; Aryan invasion, 52–53; Mauryan period, 54–58; Kushan and Greek invasions, 58–59; ancient Southern India, 59–60; Gupta period, 61–63; women in ancient India, 63–65; heritage of ancient India, 65–66; diversity of, 65; invasion by Alexander the Great, 128; contact with Greeks, 131; contact with the Seleucids, 132–133; trade with Rome, 155; religions of, 173–178, 191; writing in, 227, 230; art, 444
India, medieval: spread of Islam, 216, 283–286; Delhi sultans, 286–292; southern India, 292–296
India, Mughal: origins, 548; reign of Babur, 548–549; age of Akbar, 549–552; Jahangir and Shah Jahan, 553–554; age of Aurangzeb, 554–557; society and culture, 557–559; decline, 559
India, early modern: missionaries in, 471; early westerners, 535, 745–749; and the caste system, 587; Mughal collapse, 742–745; Anglo-French rivalry, 749–751; early British rule, 751–753; Orientalists and the Bengal renaissance, 753–754; subjugation of India, 755–759; 1857 mutiny, 759–761
India, modern: British rule, 675; in World War I, 947–948; between the world wars, 986–989; in World War II, 1037; independence and political division, 1079–1083; after independence, 1083–1089; 1158
India Act, 751, 752
Indian Ocean, 746
Indochina, 1034, 1037, 1071–1073
Indo-European languages, 52
Indo-Europeans, 36–38
Indonesia: early history, 296, 297–298, 301; colonial rule, 737, 746, 918; in the twentieth century, 1037, 1046, 1070, 1071, 1075, 1101
Inductive method, 640, 642–643
Indulgences, 350, 397, 455, 456, 457, 458, 462, 472
Indus civilization: origins of, 47–48; relations with Sumer, 48–50; cities, 50–51; decline and fall, 51–52
Indus River, 47, 49, 216
Industrial Revolution, first phase: demographic and technological roots, 789–791; capitalist society, 791–793; agricultural developments, 794–795; machine technology and the state, 795–797; the factory system, 797–799; impact on the family, 799–801; industrial workers, 801–803; Robert Owen,

803–805; demographic growth, 805–808; Manchester, 808–810; the spread of industrialization, 810–813; applied science and engineering, 813–814
Industrial Revolution, second phase, 869–872
Industry: in late medieval Europe, 402; in early modern Europe, 502–503; modern Japanese, 1053–1054
Indus Valley, 46, 52, 54, 752
Infanticide, 108, 163, 594, 598, 806
Ingria [*ing*-grih-ah], 623
Inheritance laws, 382. *See also* Primogeniture
Inner Mongolia, 81, 83
Innocent III, Pope, 343, 347–348, 352, 364
Innocent IV, Pope, 366
Innocent XI, Pope, 626
Inquisition, 364, 405, 473
Institutes of the Christian Religion (Calvin), 462, 463
Institutional Revolutionary Party (Mexico), 1137
Instrument of Government, 530
Insurance, 527, 631
Intendants, 525, 611, 709
Interdict, 361
International Alliance of Women, 885
International Monetary Fund, 1127, 1130, 1132
Intifada, 1104
Investiture Controversy, 346–347, 371
Ionia [eye-*oh*-nee-uh], 102
Ionian School, 122–123
Ionic order, 116
Iran: in the Middle Ages, 215, 217, 218; in the Mongol Empire, 357; rise of the Safavids, 559–561; in the eighteenth century, 761–763; in the twentieth century, 942, 992–993, 1046, 1101–1104, 1153, 1157
Iranian Revolution, 1102–1103
Iran-Iraq War, 1103
Iraq [ih-*rak*]: in the Middle Ages, 215, 216, 217, 218; views of death, 738; in the twentieth century, 947, 990, 1094, 1099, 1101, 1157; war with Iran, 1103, 1105–1106
Ireland, 333, 672–673, 837–838, 1160; rebellion in 1641, 530
Irene, 207, 211, 333
Irnerius, 371
Iron Age, 89–90, 143, 145
Iron Curtain, 1046
Iron Guard, 1013
Iroquois [*ir*-oh-kwoi] Confederation, 279–280, 675, 738
Irrawaddy Delta, 918, 1070
Isabella (Castile), 404–406, 513, 522
Isabella II (Spain), 485, 883
Isaiah [eye-*zay*-yuh], 36, 186, 189
Isenheim altarpiece, 476
Isfahan, 560
Isherwood, Christopher, 1007
Isis [*eye*-sis], 25, 137
Islam: Muhammad and the rise of,

213–214; Sunnis, Shi'ites and Sufis, 214–215, 216; role of women, 220–221; in early Africa, 242–243, 245, 247, 249–250, 252; in India, 283–292; in Southeast Asia, 284–285, 296–298, 302; and the crusades, 350–353; view of death, 736–738
Islamabad, 1089
Islamic civilization: economy, 218–219; society, 219–220; medicine and science, 221–222; philosophy, 222–223; literature, 223
Ismail [ees-mah-*eel*] (Egypt), 908
Ismail (Iran), 560
Isocrates [eye-*sok*-rah-teez], 126
Isopolity, 131
Israel: early, 34–36, 186; founding the modern state, 1092–1097; Arab-Israeli wars, 1097–1098; Jerusalem, 1098; and the Lebanese civil war, 1105; and the Gulf War, 1105–1106
Issus [*ihs*-uhs], battle of, 128
Istanbul, 543–545, 546, 861
Istrian Peninsula, 998
Italian East Africa, 1027
Italian League, 408
Italian Social Republic, 1041
Italo-Turkish War, 943
Italy: and Hellenistic trade, 132; unification of, by Romans, 146–148; medieval, 331, 333, 334, 338, 350; late medieval period, 402, 407–412; Renaissance in, 418–425, 426–429, 431–437; in the Napoleonic era, 724, 731; in the first phase of the Industrial Revolution, 811; in the early nineteenth century, 832; and the revolution of 1848, 838–839; unification of, 848–852, 857; in the Austro-Prussian War, 854–855; the Liberal state, 881–883; colonies in Africa, 907–908; and the origins of World War I, 942, 943; in World War I, 947, 948; and the Peace of Paris (1919), 950; after World War I, 952; Fascism, 997–1003; events leading to World War II, 1026–1028, 1030, 1031; in World War II, 1032–1033, 1041; after World War II, 1047, 1146–1147, 1158, 1160. *See also* Romans; Rome
Ito [ee-toh] Hirobumi, 927
Iturbide [ee-toor-*bee*-thay], Agustín, de, 678
Ivan III, "the Great" (Russia), 403–404
Ivan IV, "the Terrible" (Russia), 533
Ivory Coast, 908

Jackson, Andrew, 864
Jacobins, 718, 722, 727
Jacquard [zha-kar], Joseph-Marie, 811
Jacquerie [zhahk-uh-*ree*], 393–394
Ja'fariyah sect, 761
Jahan [juh-*hahn*], Shah, 553–554, 559
Jahangir [jah-*hahn*-geer], 535, 552–553, 559, 746
Jahn [yahn], Friedrich Ludwig, 824
Jainism [*jye*-nizm], 175
Jamaica, 530, 535, 662–663, 674, 677, 1138

James I (England), 528, 535, 746
James II (England), 618, 619, 629
James IV (Scotland), 406
James VI (Scotland), 519, 528. *See also* James I (England)
Jameson Raid, 909
Jamestown, 536, 599, 660
Jami [*jah*-mee], 223
Janissaries [*jan*-ih-sar-eez], 542
Jansen, Cornelius [kor-*nay*-lihs *yahn*-suhn], 646
Jansenists [*jant*-suh-nists], 601, 697–698
Japan, early: religion in, 178, 181, 182 ; Neo-Confucianism in, 181; Confucianism in, 181, 182; Shinto in, 182; geography, 323; early history, 323; Nara period, 323–324; Heian period, 324–325; Kamakura Shogunate, 325-326; Ashikaga Shogunate, 326–328; sculpture, 447
Japan, early modern: early European traders, 489–490; christianity in, 494; and Ming China, 566; reunification under the Tokugawa, 766, 776–781; expulsion of foreigners, 781–782; culture, 782–784; foreign pressures, 785-786
Japan, modern: in the first phase of the Industrial Revolution, 814; in the second phase of the Industrial Revolution, 870; modernization of, 925–926; imperialism, 926–927; Ito Hirobumi, 927; in World War I, 947; in World War II, 1034–1037, 1042; fascists in, 1013; expansion between the world wars, 1026, 1034; in World War II, 1033–1037, 1042; after World War II, 1050–1056; women in modern Japan, 1075; environmental concerns, 1076
Jarmo, 11
Jaruzelski, Wojciech [*voi*-chek *yahr*-oo-zehl-skee], 1161
Jatis, 587
Jaurès, Jean [zhahn zhoh-res], 891–892
Java, 297, 298, 301, 302, 490, 746, 920, 1071
"Jazz Age," 954
Jebb, Ann, 703
Jebusites, 187
Jefferson, Thomas, 673, 813, 864
Jehovah's Witnesses, 1039
Jena [*yay*-nuh], battle of, 730, 732; University of, 459
Jenne, 241–242, 247
Jeremiah, 36, 186
Jericho [*jehr*-ih-koh], 11, 444
Jerome of Prague, 398
Jerusalem: ancient, 34–35, 36, 148, 158, 187; and the crusades, 351, 352; and the Ottomans, 545; modern, 859, 947, 1097, 1098
Jesuits (Society of Jesus), 470–471, 492–494, 551, 579, 601, 649, 697, 763, 824
Jesus of Nazareth, 187, 189–191, 194, 195
Jews: in Alexandria, 134; rebel against the Romans, 148, 158, 159; in Islamic Spain, 216; in early Islamic society,

219, 222; in Africa, 242; in medieval Europe, 345, 378–380; and the crusades, 350, 351; in medieval Spain, 354, 355, 405–406; in Venice, 412; in the Reformation, 474, 476; in seventeenth-century England, 530; and education in early modern Europe, 601; in the Ottoman Empire, 544, 545, 546; in early modern Rome, 652; emancipation of, 698–701; birth of Zionism, 862–864; migration to Palestine before World War II, 990–991; in Fascist Italy, 1003; in Nazi Germany, 1011–1012; and the Holocaust, 1038–1040; and the state of Israel, 1092–1098; in South Africa, 1120–1121; in North Africa, 1123; in Argentina, 1128; in the USSR, 1155
Jihad [djih-*hahd*], 214
Jinnah [*jihn*-ah], Muhammed Ali, 988, 989, 1079–1081, 1089
Joan of Arc, 395
Johannesburg, 1120–1121
John (England), 341, 343
John II (Portugal), 485
John VI (Portugal), 822
John XII, Pope, 346
John Albert (Poland), 415
John of the Cross, 516
John of Damascus, 212
John of Leiden, 465
John of Salisbury, 369, 371–372
John Paul II, Pope, 486, 1138
Johnson, Lyndon B., 1072, 1073, 1149, 1156
Johnson, Samuel, 701, 705, 798, 831
John "the Baptist," 189
Joint-stock companies, 503
Joinville, Jean de [zhahn duh zhwahn-veel], 378
Jolson, Al, 899
Jones, Sir William, 753, 754
Jonson, Ben, 648
Jordan, 1094, 1097, 1099
Joseph, 28, 32, 33
Joseph II (Austria), 695–696, 700
Joshua, 34
Journal des dames, 690
Joyce, James, 957, 1020
Juarez, Benito [bay-*nee*-toh *hwah*-rays], 866–867
Judah [*joo*-dah], kingdom of, 36
Judah ha-Levi, 380
Judaism: Covenant, 184–185; Torah, 185–186; prophets, 186–187; role of Jerusalem, 187; Talmud, 187–189; role of women, 195–196; and the Sabaeans, 238; Haskalah movement, 700; Hasidism, 700; Reform movement, 700–701; Reconstructionist movement, 701; Conservative movement, 701; Orthodox tradition, 700–701
Judas Maccabaeus [mak-ah-*bee*-uhs], 137
Jugurtha [joo-*gur*-thuh], 149
Juliana of Norwich, 649
Julian "the Apostate," 169
Julio-Claudian dynasty, 157
Julius II, Pope, 408, 411–412, 420, 433, 456

Jumna River, 548
June Days (1848), 841
Jung [yoong], Carl, 936
Junkers [*yoong*-kers], 853
Jurchen [*joor*-chehn], 314, 316
Justinian, 201–204, 209
Just price, 500
Jutes [jootz], 331
Juvenal [*joo*-vuh-nuhl], 159, 165

Kabir [kah-*beer*], 223
Kabir of Banaras, 291, 292, 737
Kabuki, 782
Kabul [*kah*-bool], 758, 1089
Kádár, János [*yah*-nohsh *kah*-dahr], 1145, 1161
Kaesong [*kye*-song], 321
Kafka, Franz, 958
Kaifeng [*kye*-fung], 308, 311, 314, 316, 318
Kalahari desert, 233, 235
Kalibangan, 47, 49
Kalidasa [kah-lee-*dah*-suh], 62–63, 601
Kalingas [kah-*lihng*-gahs], 56
Kalischer, Zevi-Hirsch, 862
Kamakura [kah-mah-*koor*-uh] shogunate, 325–326
Kamasutra, 597
Kamenev [*kah*-mihn-yif], Lev, 971, 977, 978, 1017
Kampuchea. *See* Cambodia
Kandinsky, Wassily, 958, 965
Kandy [*kan*-dih], 61, 746, 753
Kanem Bornu, 248–249
K'ang Hsi (Kangxi), 494, 583, 765, 768, 770–771
Kano, 249–250
Kansu (Gansu) [kan-soo], 81, 310
Kant [kahnt], Immanuel, 687, 698, 717, 829–830
Kao-tsung (Gao-zong), 305
Kappel [*kahp*-el], battle of, 462
Kapp putsch, 1004
Karacaoglan, 547
Karachi [kuh-*rah*-chee], 912, 1080, 1089
Karelia (Karelian Peninsula), 623
Karim Khan, 762–763
Karlowitz [*kahr*-loh-vitz], Treaty of, 548, 626
Karma, 173, 175, 176, 177
Karnak [*kahr*-nak], 31
Kashmir, 752, 758, 1083
Kasim, Abul, 372
Kassites, 36, 38–39, 52, 53
Katanga, 1116
Katip Chelebi (Mustafa ibn Abdullah), 547
Katsina, 248
Katz, Isabella, 1039–1040
Kaunda, Kenneth, 1119, 1124
Kaunitz [*kow*-nihts], Prince Wenzel von, 670
Kautilya [*kow*-tihl-yah], 55
Kawasaki, 1056
Kawawa, Rashidi Mfaume, 1115
Kay, John, 796
Keats, John, 828
Kellogg, Frank, 952

Kellogg-Briand Pact, 952
Kemal Atatürk [keh-*mahl* ah-tah-*turk*], Mustapha, 947, 992, 993
Kempis, Thomas à, 402
Kennedy, John F., 1072, 1149, 1153, 1154, 1173
Kenya [*ken*-yah, *keen*-yah], 947, 1116, 1118, 1119, 1124
Kenyatta [ken-*yah*-tuh], Jomo, 1115, 1118
Kepler, Johannes, 638, 639
Kerensky [kuh-*ren*-skee], Alexander, 971, 972
K'e t'ou (kowtow), 566, 773
Keynes [kaynz], John Maynard, 952
Khadija, 213
Khalji, Ala-ud-din, 288–289
Khaldun, Ibn [*ih*-buhn kahl-*doon*], 223
Kharijites, 215, 217
Khartoum [kahr-*toom*], massacre at, 909
Khmelnitsky [hmil-*nyeet*-ski], Bogdan, 533
Khmer Rouge [kmehr rooj], 1073
Khmer Empire, 298, 299–300
Khoikhoi [koi-koi], 235, 253, 904, 1121
Khomeini [koh-*may*-nee], Ayatollah Ruhollah, 1102–1103, 1104
Khrushchev, Nikita [niyh-*kee*-tuh *kroos*-choff], 1061, 1144–1145, 1148, 1153–1154, 1155, 1156
Kibbutz, 991
Kiefer [*kee*-fur], Anselm, 965
Kiel [keel] mutiny, 950
Kierkegaard, Søren [*sur*-en *kyair*-kuh-gahr], 957
Kiev [*kee*-eff], 333, 356, 621
Kikuyu [kee-*koo*-yoo], 597, 1118
Kilwa, 252–253
Kim il Sung, 1068, 1069
King, Martin Luther, Jr., 899, 1149–1150, 1172
King William's War, 618
Kipling, Rudyard, 755, 903
Kirov, Sergei [syir-*gay* kee-*ruff*], 1017
Kissinger, Henry, 1097
Kitchener, Horatio, 909
Klee [klay], Paul, 958
Kleist [klyest], Heinrich von, 828
Knesset, 1096
Knights Hospitalers, 351–352
Knights of the Garter, 589
Knights Templars, 345, 352
Knossos [*nahs*-uhs], 90, 91
Knox, John, 473, 519, 522, 602
Koch, Robert, 807
Koguryo, 320–321
Kohl [kohl], Helmut, 1147
Kolikovo, battle of, 403
Kollontai [ko-lon-*tye*], Alexandra, 976, 1017
Königgratz [*ke*-nich-grahts], battle of, 855
Königsberg [*ke*-nichs-berk], 627
Konoye [koh-*noh*-yee], Prince, 1034
Koran, 214, 215, 220, 223
Korea: and the Han Empire, 80, 83; religion in, 176, 178, 181; Neo-Confucianism in, 181; and the Sung Dynasty, 310; Mongol conquest of, 316, 317; Paekche, Silla, and Koguryo king-

doms, 320–321; Yi dynasty, 321–323; influence on Japan, 323, 324, 925, 927; Japanese invasion of (1592), 328, 580, 583, 779; after World War II, 1068–1070; women in the modern period, 1075; industrialization, 1076
Korean War, 1068–1069
Kornilov, Lavr [*lah*-ver ker-*nyee*-luff], 971
Koryo, 321
Kossuth [koh-*sooth*], Louis, 839
Kremer, Gerhard, 639
Kremlin, 403
Krishna, 173, 174
Krishna Deva Raya, 295
Kristallnacht, 1012
Kronstadt [*krohn*-shtaht] mutiny, 972
Kropotkin [kroh-*pot*-kin], Peter, 890
Kruger [*kroo*-ger], Paul, 909
Krupp, Alfred, 871
Krupskaya, Nadhezhda, 977
Kuan Yin, 195
Kubilai [*koo*-blye] Khan, 316–317, 326, 357
Kufah [*koo*-fah], 219
Kukulcán, 264
Kulaks, 1016
Kulischiov, Anna, 976
Kulturkampf [kool-toor-kahmpf], 881
Kumbi Saleh, 241–242, 243
Kun [koon], Béla, 979, 1022
Kuomintang [*kwoh*-min-tang] (Guomindang), 980, 982, 983, 1013, 1035, 1036, 1037, 1056–1058, 1067
Kuprili [koo-pree-*lee*], Muhammad, 548
Kurds, 1100, 1105
Kushans, 58, 236–238, 239
Kuwait, 1101, 1105, 1157
Kweichou (Guizhou) [*kway*-chow; gway-joh], 80, 769
Kyoto [*kyoh*-toh], 323, 324, 326, 776–778, 779, 786, 1051
Kyushu [*kyoo*-shoo], 779

Laborers, Statute of, 393
Labour Party (Britain), 1020, 1146, 1147
Labour Party (Israel), 1095–1096
Labrador, 486
Laconia [leh-*koh*-nee-eh], 108
Lady Chatterley's Lover (Lawrence), 957
Lafayette [lah-fay-*et*], Marquis de, 712, 832, 834
Lafitte [la-*feet*], Jacques, 832
Lagash [*lay*-gash], 18, 19
Lagos [*lah*-gohs], battle of, 671
Lahore, 290, 745, 761, 1089
Laissez-faire, 802, 825
Lake Chad, 908
Lamarck, Jean-Baptiste, 887
Lamartine [lah-mar-*teen*], Alphonse de, 844
Lamber, Juliette, 847
La Mettrie [la me-tree], Julian, 688
Lancashire, 808
Lancaster, house of, 406
Landtag (Prussia), 853
Langland, William, 400
Langton, Stephen, 343
Languedoc [lahn-geh-*dok*], risings in, 394

Laos [*lah*-ohs]: religion in, 177, 296; early history, 300; colonial rule, 918, 920; and the Vietnam War, 1072, 1073
Lao-tze (Laozi) [laoh-dzuh], 181
Lapis lazuli, 37, 41
Laplace [lah-*plahs*], Pierre Simon de, 652
La Rochelle [lah roh-*shell*], 525
La Salle, Sieur de [syur duh lah *sahl*], 1108
Las Casas, Bartolomé de [bahr-toh-loh-*may* day lahs *kah*-sahs], 496
Lascaux [lahs-*koh*] caves, 6
Las Navas de Tolosa [lahs *nah*-vahs day toh-*loh*-sah], battle of, 354
Lassalle, Ferdinand, 836, 890
Lateran Councils: Third, 380; Fourth, 364, 380; Fifth, 469
Lateran Pacts (1929), 1001
Latifundia (estates) [lad-uh-*fun*-dih-uh], 150, 155
Latimer, Hugh, 473
Latin America: origins of the Old Colonial System, 657–659; emancipation, 677–680; in the nineteenth century, 865–867; Estado Novo in Brazil, 1013–1015; general over-view, 1124–1127; modern Brazil, 1127–1128; modern Argentina, 1128–1130; modern Chile and Peru, 1130–1131; modern Bolivia, 1131–1132; the Cuban revolution, 1132–1135; modern Central America, 1135–1136; modern Mexico, 1137–1138; society and culture, 1138–1140; Latin Kingdom of Constantinople, 352, 354
Latin League, 146
Latins, 143, 145, 146
Latvia, 623, 973, 1021–1023, 1031, 1032, 1143, 1164
Laud [lawd], William, 529
La Venta, 257
Law: code of Hammurabi, 22–23; ancient Hebrew, 35; Hittite, 37–38; in classical Athens, 104–105; reforms of Julius Caesar, 152; classical Roman, 165–166; Byzantine, 203; Bantu, 235; in medieval Europe, 370–371; Russian, 404, 621, 624; Ottoman, 542; and women in early modern Europe, 596–597; Napoleonic Code, 729, 730, 733; in British India, 758–759
Law, John, 669, 798
Lawrence, D. H., 957
Lawrence, T. E., 947, 990
League of Augsburg, 618
League of Nations, 950, 952, 1026, 1027, 1044, 1099
League of the Three Emperors, 941
League of Venice, 407
Lebanon, 947, 990, 1094, 1097, 1099, 1105, 1106
Lebensraum, 1038
Le Bon, Gustav, 939
Lechfeld [*lek*-felt], battle of, 346
Ledru-Rollin [le-*drew* roh-*lahn*], Alexandre, 844
Legalism, 77–78
Lehar [*lay*-hahr], Franz, 858

Leibniz [*lyep*-nitz], Gottfried Wilhelm von, 642, 705, 768
Leiden [*lye*-dehn], 519
Leignitz, battle of, 670
Leipzig [*lype*-zihg], 733
Lend-Lease Program, 1034
Lenin (Vladimir Ilyich Ulyanov), 902–903, 971–973, 977, 979
Leningrad, 1164, 1169
Leo I, Pope, 194
Leo III, Pope, 210–211, 333
Leo IX, Pope, 346
Leo X, Pope, 428, 456, 457
Leo XIII, Pope, 881
Leon [lay-*ohn*], 354
Leonardo da Vinci [*vihn*-chee], 432–433, 435, 963
Leonidas [lee-*on*-eye-duhs], 102
Leopold I (Holy Roman Empire), 619, 625, 650
Leopold II (Austria), 718, 1116
Leopold II (Belgium), 906
Lepanto [lay-*pahn*-tok], battle of, 517, 540
Lepcis Magna, 161
Lermontov [*lyair*-mun-toff], Mikhail, 824
Lesseps [luh-*seps*], Ferdinand de, 846
Lessing, Gotthold Ephraim, 700, 705, 828
Letters of Obscure Men (Hutten and Rubeanus), 454
Lettow-Vorbeck [*let*-oh *fohr*-bek], Paul von, 947
Leucippus [loo-*sip*-uhs], 123, 634
Leuctra [*look*-trah], battle of, 126
Leuthen, battle of, 670
Levellers, 530
Leviathan [luh-*vye*-uh-thuhn] (Hobbes), 644
Lewis, Meriwether, 1110
Lewis, Wyndham, 939
Lewis and Clark expedition, 1110
Leycester, Judith, 596
Liberalism, 825–826, 877–883; decline of, 1022–1023
Liberal Party (Britain), 1020
Liberal Party (Canada), 1152
Liberation theology, 1138
Liberia, 906, 908, 1120
Liberty of the Christian Man, The (Luther), 457
Libon of Elis, 116
Libya, 943, 1032, 1100, 1101, 1106, 1123, 1160
Licinius [lih-*sihn*-ee-uhs], 193
Liebknecht [*leep*-k'nekt], Karl, 1004
Liebknecht, Wilhelm, 890
Liechtenstein, 1148
Liège [lee-*ayzh*], 339, 482, 789
Likud [lih-*kood*] coalition, 1096
Liliuokalani [lee-*lee*-oo-oh-kah-*lah*-nee] (Hawaii), 929
Lima [*lee*-mah], Peru, 496, 497, 678
Linacre, Thomas, 425
Lincoln, Abraham, 865
Lindbergh, Anne Morrow, 1013
Lindisfarne, 333
Linear A (script), 91
Linear B (script), 92
Linguet, Simon-Henri, 689

Li Ping (Bing) [lee bihng], 78–79
Li Po (Li Bo), 309
Lisbon, 354
Li Ssu [lee-*soo*], 55, 77, 78, 79
List, Friedrich, 818
Lister, Joseph, 807
Liszt, Franz, 828
Literacy: general, 231, 895; in Africa, 247; in Asia, 600, 601–602, 1066, 1089, 1091; in the Soviet Union, 1016–1017; in Latin America, 1139; in Europe, 1148
Literature: early Greek, 92–93, 96–98; classical Roman, 156–157, 164–165; Islamic, 223; ancient Chinese, 309–310; Japanese, 324–325, 326–327; medieval European, 375–378, 400–401; European Renaissance, 421–422, 423, 425; in the late sixteenth century, 516; in the Ottoman Empire, 547; in Ming China, 573-575; early modern European, 648–649; in the Enlightenment, 705; early-nineteenth-century Russian, 824; Romantic, 827–829, 831; modern Western, 888-889, 937, 938, 957–958; African, 1124; modern South American, 1138
Lithuania, 357, 403, 415; in the twentieth century, 973, 1021, 1031, 1032, 1143, 1164
"Little Entente," 952
Little Ice Age, 273, 391
Little Red Book (Mao Tse-tung), 1060, 1063
Li Tzu-ch'eng (Li Zicheng), 583
Liubatovich, Olga, 975
Liu Hsiao-chi (Liu Xiaoqi), 1059, 1063
Liu Pang (Liu Bang) [lyoo bahng], 79, 82, 85
Liu Shao-ch'i, 1061
Liverpool, 664–665
Liverpool, Lord, 823
Lives of the Painters, The (Giorgio Vasari), 420
Livingstone, David, 906
Livonia, 623
Livy, 149, 157
Lloyd George, David, 950, 998
Locarno Pact, 952
Locarno Treaties, 1027
Locke, Anne, 426
Locke, John, 645, 684, 686, 702, 801, 825
Lodis, 290, 548
Logical Empiricism, 957
Lollards, 398, 466
Lombard, Peter, 369, 383
Lombard League, 347
Lombards, 194, 332
Lombardy, 347, 849, 850
Londinium (Roman London), 162
London: medieval, 339, 343, 344, 402; late Stuart and Hanoverian, 630–631, 807, 808; in the nineteenth century, 874, 879; Treaty of (1915), 998
London Protocol, 823
London Workingmen's Association, 834
Long Depression (1873–1896), 873–874
Long March, 982

Lope de Vega [*loh*-pay day *bay*-gah], 516, 648
Lord Shang, 78
Lord's Supper, 192
Lorrain [loh-*rehn*], Claude, 704
Lorraine [loh-*rehn*], 345, 407, 857, 952
Lorris [lo-rees], William de, 378
Los Angeles, California, 1150
Lothal, 50, 52
Louis (Carolingian), 333
Louis VII (France), 341, 352
Louis IX (France), 345, 349, 367, 378, 380
Louis XI (France), 407
Louis XII (France), 407–408, 411
Louis XIII (France), 524–525
Louis XIV (France), 525, 611–621, 626, 650, 683
Louis XV (France), 668–669, 709, 795
Louis XVI (France), 709–717 *passim*
Louis XVIII (France), 733, 824
Louise of Savoy, 414
Louisiana, 669, 675
Louisiana Purchase, 1110
Louis-Philippe [loo-*ee* fee-*leep*] (France), 832, 835, 839
Lovett, William, 834
Lowell, Percival, 1110
Loyang [loh-*yahng*], 72, 83, 84, 305, 316
Luanda, 489
Lübeck [*luh*-bek], 365, 394, 402
Lublin, 474
Lucan [*loo*-kuhn], 165
Lucca, 410
Lucknow, 744, 760
Lucretius [loo-*kree*-shuhs], 164
Luddism, 802, 803
Ludendorff, Erich, 947, 950, 1007
Luder, Peter, 425
Ludovico il Moro. *See* Sforza, Ludovico
Lüger, Karl, 858, 862, 939, 1005, 1006
Lu Hsun (Lu Xun), 982, 984
Lumumba, Patrice, 1116, 1153
Lunéville [loo-nay-*veel*], Treaty of, 729
Lung Shan culture, 69–70, 84, 228
Lusitania, sinking of, 949
Luther, Martin, 456–461, 473, 474–475, 477, 801, 895
Lutheranism, 457–461
Lützen [*lurt*-suhn], battle of, 523
Luxembourg, 617, 943, 1042, 1158–1159
Luxemburg, Rosa, 890, 893, 1004
Lvov [lyuh-*voff*], Prince Georgi, 970
Lyceum (Athens), 125
Lycurgus [lye-*kur*-guhs], 108
Lydia, 42, 102, 137
Lydians, 38
Lyell, Sir Charles, 887
Lyons [lee-*ohn*], 603, 714, 722, 812
Lysippus [lye-*sihp*-uhs], 120
Lysistrata (Aristophanes), 122

Maastricht [*mahs*-trikt], Treaty, 1162
Macao [muh-*kow*], 490
MacArthur, Douglas, 1051, 1052, 1053, 1068–1069
Macartney, Viscount, 773, 774, 775
Macaulay, Catherine, 702

Macaulay, Thomas Babington, 757, 758, 759
Maccabean revolt, 148
McCarthy, Eugene, 1156
McCarthy, Joseph R., 1048
MacDonald, Ramsay, 1020
Macedonia [mass-uh-dohn-yah] (Macedon): rise of, 126–127; and Alexander the Great, 127–129; and the Hellenistic Greeks, 130–131
Macehuales, 269
Machel, Samora, 1116
Machiavelli, Niccolò [nee-koh-loh mah-kyah-vell-ee], 2, 410, 428–429, 455, 473
Machismo, 1140
Machu Picchu [ma-choo peek-choo], 496
McKinley, William, 890, 929
Macrinus, 166
Madagascar, 908, 1116
Madeira [muh-deer-uh], 488
Maderna (Maderno), Carlo, 650
Madero, Francisco, 1137
Madison, James, 674, 675
Madras [muh-drahs], 535, 670, 747, 748, 749, 750, 751, 756, 912
Madrid, 514–515
Madurai [mahd-oo-rye], 60, 293, 294
Magadha [mahg-uh-dah], kingdom of, 56
Magdeburg [mahk-duh-boorkh], 460, 626
Magellan [muh-jel-uhn], Ferdinand, 302, 488, 509
Magellan, Straits of, 488
Maghreb [mahg-reb], 1122, 1123
Magic, 137, 181, 247, 392
Maginot [mahzh-ih-noh] Line, 1032
Magna Carta, 343, 344
Magnetic compass, 306, 315
Magritte [ma-greet], René, 938
Magyars [mag-yahrz], 333, 335, 345, 626
Mahabharata [mah-hah-bah-rah-tah], 52, 53, 298
Maharashtra, 288, 743, 751, 755, 912
Mahayana [mah-huh-yah-nuh] Buddhism, 177–178
Mahdali [mah-dah-lee] dynasty, 252
Mahler, Gustav, 858
Mahmud [mah-mood] of Ghazni [gahz-nee], 285, 286
Mahrathas [muh-rah-tehz], 288
Maimonides [mye-mon-ih-deez] (Moses ben Maimon), 370, 372, 380
Maine [mayn], France, 341, 407
Maintenon [man-teh-nohn], Madame de, 616
Mainz [myentz], 339
Maistre, Joseph de [zhoh-zef duh mess-truh], 690, 818
Majapahit [mah-jah-pah-heet], 301–302
Malabar coast, 490
Malacca [mah-lak-ah], 297, 301, 302, 490, 491
Malaka, Tan, 980
Malaria, 755
Malatesta, Errico, 890
Malawi [meh-lah-wee], 905, 1116
Malaya: early history, 296, 297, 298, 299, 301, 490; colonial rule, 918, 921; in World War II, 1037; after World War II, 1070, 1073–1074

Malaysia, 1073–1074, 1075
Mali [mah-lee], Empire of, 244–247, 489, 1119
Malindi, 252
Mallarmé, Stéphane [stay-fahn ma-lahr-may], 937
Manda, 252
Malleus Maleficarum, 474, 475
Malpighi [mahl-pee-gee], Marcello, 639
Malplaquet [mahl-plah-kay], battle of, 620
Malta, 218, 820
Malthus [mahl-thuhs], Thomas, 789, 790, 805, 887
Mameluke [mahm-luk] dynasty, 288
Manchester, 803, 808–810
Manchu conquest, 766–768
Manchus, 583–584
Manchukuo [mahn-choo-kwoh], 1026
Manchuria: early history, 80, 83, 305, 310, 314, 318; and the Ming dynasty, 566; and early Manchu rule, 583, 766, 767, 770; in the nineteenth and early twentieth centuries, 923, 925, 926, 927, 983; in World War II, 1026, 1034, 1042; after World War II, 1059
Mandan, 279
Mandate of Heaven, 79, 81, 180, 564, 583, 773, 980
Mandates (League of Nations), 951, 990
Mandela, Nelson, 1122
Mandeville [man-de-vihl], Bernard de, 689
Manegold of Lautenbach, 371
Manet [ma-nay], Édouard, 888
Manhattan Project, 1042
Manichaeans [man-ih-kee-uhns], 203
"Manifest Destiny," 675
Manila [muh-nihl-uh], 671, 769, 920, 1076
Manila galleon, 488
Manley, Mary de la Riviere, 702
Mann [mahn], Thomas, 958
Mannerists, 963
Manors, 335–336
Manucci, Niccolò [nee-koh-loh mah-noo-chee], 492
Manutius, Aldus [ahl-duhs mah-noo-shee-uhs], 429–430
Manzikert [man-zih-kurt], battle of, 350
Maori [mah-oh-ree], 806, 927, 929
Mao Tse-tung [mou dzuh-doong] (Mao Zedong), 982, 1047, 1051, 1058–1065, 1066, 1146
Mapping, 507–511, 1108–1112
Marat [mah-rah], Jean-Paul, 718
Maratha Confederacy, 752
Marathas, 555, 556–557, 558, 743–745, 747, 749, 751
Marathon, battle of, 102
Marburg, 462, 523; University of, 459
Marchand [mar-shahn], Jean-Baptiste, 909
March on Rome (1922), 999–1000
Marcion [mahr-shuhn], 192
Marconi [mahr-koh-nee], Guglielmo, 813, 899
Marcos, Ferdinand, 1071
Marcos, Imelda, 1074
Marcus Aurelius [mahr-kuhs ah-ree-lee-uhs], 139, 159, 166

Marengo, battle of, 729
Margaret of Anjou, 406
Margaret of Austria, 414
Margaret of Parma, 518, 521
Marguerite d'Angoulême [dahn-goo-lem], 425
Marguerite of Navarre, 649
Marguerite of Valois [vahl-wah], 520
Mari, 21
Mariam, Mengistu Haile, 1123
Marianas, 928, 930
Marian exiles, 473
Maria Theresa (Austria), 669, 694
Marie Antoinette, 719, 720
Marie-Louise (Austria), 732
Marie-Therese [ma-ree tay-rez] (France), 616
Marinetti, Filippo T., 939, 940
Marius [mahr-ee-uhs], 151
Marivaux [ma-ree-voh], Pierre de, 697
Mark Antony, 153
Marlborough, John Churchill, Duke of, 620
Marlowe, Christopher, 828
Marne: first battle of, 945; second battle of, 950
Maronite Christians, 990
Marriage: in Mesopotamia, 22–23; in ancient Egypt, 32; among the ancient Hebrews, 35; Hittite, 37–38; in classical Athens, 107; in classical Rome, 156, 163; Confucian views on, 180–181; view of Apostle Paul, 191; Augustine's view, 195; Muhammad's view, 214; in early Islamic society, 220-221; in East Africa, 252; Maya, 263; Aztec, 269–270, 495; Inca, 274, 275, 593; in medieval Europe, 382; in Anabaptist Münster, 465; in the Ottoman Empire, 542–543; in early modern Europe, 591–592; in early modern Asia, 592-593; in early modern Africa, 594; Enlightenment views, 702, 703, 704; in modern Turkey, 993; in modern Africa, 1124; in modern Europe, 875, 877; in British India, 915
Marseilles [mahr-say], 338, 339
Marshall, George C., 1047, 1058
Marshall Islands, 507, 930
Marshall Plan, 1047, 1144, 1147
Marsiglio [mahr-seel-yoh] of Padua, 397, 398
Martel, Charles, 331
Martial [mahr-shel], 165
Martin V, Pope, 397, 408
Martineau [mahr-tih-noh], Harriet, 704, 805
Martini [mahr-tee-nee], Martino, 1110
Martini, Simone [see-moh-nay mahr-tee-nee], 194
Martinique [mahr-tih-neek], 662
Martyrdom, 739
Marx, Karl, 791–792, 802, 825, 835–837, 889
Mary, Virgin, 195, 446; cult of, 381
Mary I (England), 469, 513, 521
Mary II (England), 618, 629
Maryland, 536
Mary of Hungary, 436

Mary Stuart, 519, 521
Masaccio [mah-*saht*-choh], 431–432
Masai [mah-*sye*], 597
Masaryk [*mah*-sah-rik], Tomáš , 1023
Massachusetts, 660, 674
Massachusetts Bay, 536
Massachusetts Bay Company, 657
Mass communication systems, 897–900
Masurian [mah-*zur*-ih-ahn] Lakes, battle of, 947
Mathematical Principles of Natural Philosophy (Newton), 642
Mathematics: in ancient Asia, 65, 70; Pythagoras, 123; Hellenistic, 134–135; Islamic, 222; Confucian, 322; in the Scientific Revolution, 642
Mathiez, Albert, 726
Matisse [mah-*tees*], Henri, 938
Matteotti, Giacomo [*jaw*-ko-moh mah-tay-oh-tee], 1000, 1001
Matthias I Corvinus, 414–415
Mau Mau, 1118
Maupeou [moh-*poo*], René Charles de, 669, 709
Maurice of Nassau, 527
Mauritania, 1119
Mauritius [mo-*rish*-uhs], 820
Maurras [moh-ra], Charles, 939, 1013
Mauryan [*mow*-ree-uhn] India, 54–58
Mawali, 219
Maximilian, Archduke (Austria), 867
Maximilian [mak-sih-*mill*-yuhn], Emperor, 407, 411, 415, 454
Mayakovsky, Vladimir, 939
Maya, 231, 260–264
Mayeques, 269
May Fourth Movement, 981–982, 984
Mazarin [mah-zah-*ranh*], Giulio, Cardinal, 525–526, 612
Mazowiecki [mah-zoh-vee-*ehts*-kee], Tadeusz, 1161
Mazzini, Giuseppe [joo-*zep*-pay mah-*tsee*-nee], 833, 839, 849, 850, 851
Mecca, 213, 214, 215
Medea (Euripides), 137–138
Medes [meedz], 40, 41–42
Medici [*mehd*-ih-chee, *may*-dee-chee], Catherine de', 520, 521
Medici, Cosimo [*koh*-zee-moh] de', 410–411, 418, 423
Medici, Lorenzo [loh-*rehn*-tsoh], "the Magnificent," 411, 428
Medici, Marie de', 524
Medici, Piero de', 428
Medici family, 418, 428, 432, 482
Medicine: in ancient India, 53, 66; in the Hellenistic Age, 135–136; Chinese, 181, 573; Islamic, 221–222; medieval European, 372; and the Black Death, 393; in the Ottoman Empire, 547; in Ming China, 573; in the Scientific Revolution, 639; in the first phase of the Industrial Revolution, 807; modern, 1173–1174
Medina [mih-*dee*-nah] (Yath'rib), 215
Medina Sidonia, duke of, 519
Meditations (Marcus Aurelius), 139
Medrese, 547, 603

Megasthenes [mee-*gas*-thee-neez], 56, 133
Mehmet II, "the Conqueror," 539–540, 541, 543–544
Meiji [may-jee] Restoration, 786, 925
Mein Kampf (Hitler), 1007, 1038
Mekong [mee-kong] Delta, 301
Melanchthon [muh-*langk*-thuhn], Philip, 459
Melanesia, 928, 929
Melbourne, 928
Memphis, 236
Mencius [*men*-shuhs], 77, 179–180
Mendelssohn, Moses, 700
Mendelssohn-Bartholdy, Felix, 828
Mendicant orders, 362
Menelik, 238, 908
Mengele, Josef, 1040
Mennonites, 466
Mensheviks, 971
Mentuhotep, 27
Mercantilism, 501
Mercator, Gerardus (Gerhard), 511, 639, 1108
Merchant capitalism, 500–503, 659–660
Merchants: Byzantine, 206; in medieval Europe, 339–340; in early modern Europe, 482–483, 590; in the Ottoman Empire, 545–546; in Ming China, 571–572
Merici [meh-*ree*-chee], Angela, 469–470
Meroë [*mehr*-oh-ee], 32, 236, 237
Merovingian [mehr-uh-*vin*-jee-uhn] dynasty, 331
Mersenne [mer-*sen*], Marin, 643
Mesoamerica, Amerindians of: earliest inhabitants, 256–257; Olmecs, 257–258; Teotihuacán, 258–260; Maya, 260–264; the Toltecs, 265–267; Aztecs, 267–272, 495–496, 499; Inca, 495–496, 499
Mesopotamia: birth of civilization in, 12–13; ancient civilization in, 17–23; Sumerian period, 17–19; religion in, 19–20; Akkadian and Babylonian culture, 20–21; Hammurabi, 22–23; Kassites, 38–39; Assyrians, 39–40; Chaldeans, 40; writing in, 226
Mesta [*may*-stah], 405
Mestizos [may-*stee*-sohs], 499
Metals: copper, 11, 15, 16, 34, 41, 70, 235, 240, 241, 245, 250, 253, 254, 482, 666; bronze, 11, 15, 16, 69, 72, 90, 234, 241, 323; iron (in the ancient world), 15, 33, 34, 37, 41, 72, 92, 98, 143, 323, 790; iron (in the medieval world), 235, 236, 237, 240, 250, 253, 254, 311, 402; iron (in early Africa), 904; iron (in the early modern era), 482, 666, 763, 789, 796, 798; iron (in modern industry), 811, 813, 870, 952, 1016, 1059; steel, 53, 219, 241, 311, 763, 789, 791, 870, 913, 952, 1016, 1053, 1059; tin, 15, 16, 70, 254, 918, 928–929, 1131; lead, 70; zinc, 70; gold, 11, 235, 240, 241, 243, 245, 246, 252, 254, 498, 659–660, 812–813, 904, 910; silver, 11, 482, 488, 498, 570–571, 658–659, 769, 813
Metalworking, 11–12
Metaxas [meh-tah-*ksahs*], John, 1023

Methodists, 697
Metics [*meh*-tiks], 106, 107–108
Metternich [*meht*-ur-nik], Prince Klemens von, 733, 819, 820–824, 832, 858
Meun, Jean de [zhahn deh men], 378
Mexican-American War, 864, 866
Mexico: Olmecs, 257–258; Teotihuacán, 258–260; Maya, 260–265; Toltecs, 265–267; Aztecs, 267–272; Jesuit missions to, 471; Spanish conquest of, 495; University of, 495; Spanish rule in, 657–660, 678; in the nineteenth century, 866–867; in the twentieth century, 1101, 1137–1138, 1139, 1140.
Mexico City, 495, 497, 1125, 1138, 1139
Michael VII, 350
Michelangelo [mee-kel-*ahn*-jeh-loh] Buonarroti, 427, 431, 433–434, 435, 963
Michelet [*meesh*-le], Jules, 726, 830, 847
Mickiewicz [meets-*kye*-veech], Adam, 818
Micronesia, 928, 929
Middle East: Black Death in, 393; Ottoman Empire, 539–548; rise of Safavid Iran, 559–561; women in the early modern period, 595; eighteenth-century Iran, 761–763; dissolution of the Ottoman Empire, 860–862; nationalist awakening, 989–993; the struggle for Palestine, 1092–1096; Israeli society, 1096–1097; the Arab-Israeli wars, 1097–1098; Arab nationalism, 1098–1099; the Egyptian revolution, 1099–1100; OPEC, 1101; the Iranian revolution, 1101–1103; women in the Islamic revolution, 1103–1104; recent trends and the Gulf War, 1104–1106
Middleton, Thomas, 648
Midway Island, battle of, 1040, 1042
Mies Van der Rohe [*mee*-uhs vahn der *roh*-uh], 938
Mikveh Yisrael, 862
Milan [mih-*lahn*]: medieval, 339; in the late medieval and early modern periods, 408–409, 411, 414, 482, 513; Renaissance in, 418, 420 in the nineteenth century, 838, 849
Milan, Edict of, 193
Miletus [mye-*lee*-tuhs], 95, 102, 131
Mill, John Stuart, 884
Millets, 542
Miltiades [mihl-*tye*-ah-deez], 102
Milton, John, 649
Milvian Bridge, battle of, 168
Minamoto clan, 325–326
Mindanao, 302
Ming dynasty, 564–583 *passim*
Mining, 338, 482, 498, 658–659, 812
Minnesingers [*mihn*-ih-sing-uhrs], 377–378
Minoans [mih-*noh*-uhnz], 89, 90–91, 229, 444
Minorca [mihn-*ohr*-kuh], 620, 671, 674
Minos [*mye*-nahs], 90
Min river, 79
Mirabeau, Count Honoré [oh-no-*ray* mee-rah-*boh*], 718, 721
Miracle plays, 378
Miró [mee-*roh*], Joan, 938

Miserables, Les [lay mee-zay-*rabl*] (Hugo), 888
Mishneh Torah (Maimonides), 380
Missions: Christian, 470–471; medieval, 363; early modern, 492–494, 499, 579, 756, 763, 781–782; modern, 898, 906, 915, 918, 922, 924, 929
Mississippian culture, 277–278
Mississippi Bubble, 669
Mississippi Company, 669
Mississippi River, 660
Mistral [mees-*trahl*], Gabriela, 1138
Mithraism, 184
Mixtecs, 231, 272
Mnesicles [*nes*-ih-kleez], 119
Mobutu [moh-*boo*-too], Joseph, 1116
Modena, University of, 473
Moderate Realists, 369
Mogadishu, 252
Mogollon culture, 278
Mohammed Shah, 761
Mohács [mah-*hahch*], battle of, 413, 461
Mohenjo Daro [moh-*hen*-joh *dahr*-oh], 47, 49, 50, 753
Moi, Daniel arap, 1118
Moksha [*mok*-shuh], 174, 175, 386
Moldavia, 859, 860, 861
Moldova, 1168
Molière [moh-*lyair*] (Jean-Baptiste Poquelin), 649
Molotov, Vyacheslav [vyih-cheh-*slaff moh*-luh-toff], 1144
Moltke [*molt*-keh], Helmuth von, 855, 945
Moluccas, 488, 490, 920
Mombasa, 252, 489
Monasteries, dissolution of, 458, 468
Monasticism, 181, 193–194, 361–362
Mondino de' Luzzi, 372
Mondrian [*mon*-dree-ahn], Piet, 958
Monet [moh-*nay*], Claude, 888, 937
Mongolia, 83, 305, 310, 494, 566, 767, 770, 979, 1059
Mongols, 81, 218, 288, 289, 298, 301, 326, 568, 583; conquest of China, 316–317; Yuan dynasty, 317–319, 321; conquest of Russia, 355–358
Monophysites, 201, 203, 204, 210, 239
Monotheism, 28, 36, 137, 175, 186, 213
Mons, 298
Montagnards, 720
Montagu, Mary Wortley, 703
Montaigne [mon-*tayn*], Michel de, 645
Monte Cassino [*mohn*-tay kahs-*see*-noh], 361
Montenegro [mon-te *neh*-groh], 861, 941, 943
Montesquieu [mohn-tes-*kyoo*], Baron de, 689, 690, 691, 699, 702
Monteverdi [mohn-tay-*vare*-day], Claudio, 650
Montezuma II [mahn-teh-*soo*-mah], 267, 271–272, 495
Montpellier [mon-peh-*lyay*], University of, 372
Montreal, 671, 1152
Moore, Henry, 965
Moors, 331, 332

Moravia [muh-*ray*-vee-uh], 357, 415, 625; Anabaptists in, 465
Moravian Brethren, 697
More, Hannah, 702
More, Sir Thomas, 425, 454, 455–456, 468, 477
Morelly, Abbé, 689
Morgan, John Pierpont, 871
Moriscos, 406, 516
Morocco, 217–218, 248, 861, 942, 943, 1100, 1122–1123
Morse, Samuel F. B., 813, 897
Mosaics, 200, 204, 211, 446
Moscow, 357, 403, 733, 875, 972, 1033, 1155–1156, 1164; University of, 1155
Moses, 33, 34, 185
Moshav, 991
Mosley, Sir Oswald, 1013
Mossadegh [*moh*-sa-dek], Muhammad, 1102
Mossi, 247
Mo-tzu (Mozi) [moh-dzu], 75
Mountbatten, Louis, 1037, 1081
Mozambique [moh-zuhm-*beek*], 489, 905, 906, 1115, 1116, 1119, 1120
Mozarabs, 354, 355
Mozart, Wolfgang Amadeus, 690, 705, 829, 858
Mozzoni [mots-*soh*-nee], Anna Maria, 886
Muawiya [moo-*ah*-wee-ah], 215
Mubarak [moo-*bahr*-ek], Hosni, 1100
Muftis, 542
Mugabe [moo-*gah*-bay], Robert, 1116
Mughal (Mogul) [*moh*-guhl] dynasty: founding, 290, 548; from Akbar to Aurangzeb, 548–559; decline, 742–745
Muhammad (Mohammed), 213–215, 218, 219, 220–221
Muhammad Reza Pahlavi, 1102
Mujib, Sheikh (Mujibur Rahman), 1089
Mukden (Shenyang) [*mook*-den], 583, 927
Mummification, 25–26
Munch [mungk], Edvard, 965
Munich [*myoo*-nik], 950, 1007
Munich Conference, 1030
Munich putsch, 365
Münster [*muhn*-ster] (Germany), Kingdom of, 465–466
Müntzer [*mewn*-tser], Thomas, 466
Murasaki [moor-uh-*sah*-kee], Lady, 324–325, 600–601
Murat II, 547
Murmansk, 974
Musa [*moo*-sah], Mansa, 246–247
Muscovy, 403–404
Muscovy Company, 500
Museum (Alexandria), 134
Music: in the Reformation, 477; Baroque, 650, 705; Neoclassical, 705–706; Romantic, 828, 829; Classical, 829; in Vienna, 858; Wagner, 939; Latin American, 1139
Muslim League, 988, 1079–1081
Muslims: Muhammad's teachings, 213–214; Sunnis, Shi'ites, and Sufis, 214–215; in the Umayyad period, 215–217; in the Abbasid period,

217–218; civilization of, 218–223; and the Reconquista, 354–355; view of Black Death, 393
Mussolini [moos-soh-*lee*-nee], Benito, 996–1003, 1026–1027, 1030–1031, 1041
Mustafa, Kara, 617
Mutiny of 1857 (India), 759–761
Mycenae [mye-*see*-nee], 89, 91–92
Mycenaeans, 37, 53, 89, 91–92, 229
Mysore, 743, 751, 752
Mystery cults, 137
Mystery plays, 378
Mystics, mysticism: Christian, 173, 401–402, 466, 516, 587; Sufism, 215–216, 288, 290
Myths, 3, 9

Nabateans [nab-ah-*tee*-uhns], 229–230
Nadir Quli, 761–762
Nadir Shah [*nah*-dur shah], 556, 745
Nagasaki [nah-gah-*sah*-kee], 494, 535, 781, 782, 1042, 1051
Naguib [nah-*geeb*], Muhammad, 1100
Nagy, Imre [*im*-reh nazh], 1145
Naima Efendi, Mustafa, 547
Nairobi [nye-*roh*-bee], 1118
Namibia, 1120
Nanak [*nah*-nuk], 555
Nan Chao [nahn chow], 317
Nanking (Nanjing), 305, 564, 566, 776, 922, 982, 984; Treaty of, 776, 921, 1067; in World War II, 1034
Nanna, 18
Nantes [nahnt], Edict of, 521, 525, 618
Naples, 339, 407, 408, 414, 513, 526, 822, 851; University of, 366
Napoleon I. *See* Bonaparte, Napoleon
Napoleon III, 845–848, 850, 851, 854, 855–857, 867, 890
Napoleonic Code, 729, 730, 733
Napoleonic wars, 729–733
Nara Period, 323–324
Naram-Sin [nah-rahm-*sin*], 21
Narbonne, 216
Narva, battle of, 623
Naseby, battle of, 530
Nasrid dynasty, 355
Nasser, Gamal Abdel, 1095, 1097, 1099–1100, 1123, 1158
Natal [nuh-*tahl*], 909
Nathan the Wise (Lessing), 700
National American Woman Suffrage Association, 885
National Assembly (France), 713, 715–717
National Convention (France), 719–720, 724
"National Fronts," 1143–1144
Nationalism: in the eighteenth century, 817–818, 820; in the nineteenth century, 849, 856, 857, 859; in the twentieth century, 917–918, 926, 939, 981, 989–990, 992, 1022, 1087–1088, 1098–1099, 1114–1115
National Labor Front, 1010
National Liberation Front (FLN), 1123
National Organization for Women, 1151

National Revolutionary Movement (MNR), 1132
National Woman Suffrage Association, 885
NATO. See North Atlantic Treaty Organization
Navaho, 278, 279, 281
Navarino [nah-vah-*ree*-noh], battle of, 823
Navarre [nuh-*vahr*], 354, 513
Navigation Acts (1651, 1660), 662, 796
Nazi Party, 1006–1012 passim
Nazi-Soviet Pact, 1031
Neanderthal culture, 5, 172, 385
Nebuchadnezzar [neb-uk-uhd-*nez*-uhr], 40
Necker, Jacques, 709, 711, 713
Nefertiti [nef-uhr-*tee*-tee], 28–31
Negev Desert, 1097
"Negritude," 1114
Nehru, Jawaharlal [jah-*wah*-har-lahl *nay*-roo], 986, 988, 989, 1079–1085, 1158
Nehru, Motilal, 917
Neisse [*nye*-suh] River, 1047
Nelson, Horatio, 730
Nemea [*nee*-mee-ah], 99
Neo-Babylonians, 40
Neoclassicism, 828, 965
Neo-Confucianism, 181, 315, 370
Neo-Guelphs, 849
Neolithic Age, 7–10, 23, 69, 70, 89–90, 226, 442, 444
Neoplatonism, 423, 427, 432, 433
Nepal [nuh-*pol*], 285, 771, 773
Nerchinsk [*nyer*-chinsk], Treaty of, 770
Nero, 157, 160
Neruda [nay-*roo*-thah], Pablo, 1138
Nerva, 158
Netherlands: Renaissance in, 436, 437–438; spread of Calvinism in, 465; Anabaptists in, 465; rebellion against Spain, 517–519; in the seventeenth century, 526–528; early interests in Asia, 534–535; colonial rivalry in the Americas, 536; war with France (1672–1678), 616–617; late wars with Louis XIV, 618–620; Spanish, 619, 626; colonial trade of, 662; in the Napoleonic era, 724, 730; interests in India, 745–747; in the first phase of the Industrial Revolution, 792–793, 811; in the nineteenth century, 820, 832, 883; colonies of, 918–920; in the twentieth century, 952, 1032, 1158–1159
Neves, Tancredo, 1127
Nevsky, Alexander, 357
New Amsterdam, 660
Newcastle upon Tyne, 789
Newcastle, Margaret Cavendish, Duchess of, 596
Newcomen, Thomas, 789
New Deal, 1021
New Delhi, 916, 1084
New Democratic Party (Canada), 1152
New Economic Policy (NEP), 977, 1015
Newfoundland, 499, 500, 620, 671, 672
New Granada, 657, 678
New Guinea, 928, 930, 947
New Harmony, Indiana, 804

New Heloise, The (Rousseau), 697
New Imperialism: historiographical debate, 902–903; in Africa, 904–910; in India, 910–918; in Southeast Asia, 918–921; in East Asia, 921–927; in Australasia and the Pacific, 927–930
Ne Win, 1070, 1074
New Jersey, 536
New Lanark, 803
New Mexico, 675, 866
New South Wales, 928
New Spain, 660
Newspapers, 602, 631, 718, 847, 896, 898, 900
Newton, Sir Isaac, 642, 684, 1108
New York, 536, 660
New York City, 875
New York Stock Exchange, 1018
New Zealand, 675, 806, 929, 930, 947, 1132
Niani, 247
Nibelungenlied [*nee*-buh-lung-en-*leet*], 377, 400
Nicaea [nye-*see*-uh], 353–354; Council of, 169, 193
Nicaragua, 678, 865, 1127, 1132, 1135–1136, 1138, 1139, 1140, 1157
Nice [nees], 724, 850
Nicene Creed, 193
Nicholas I (Russia), 824, 832, 837, 859, 862
Nicholas II (Russia), 859, 878, 932, 944–945, 948, 969–970
Nicholas V, Pope, 420, 425
Nicias [*nish*-uhs], 112
Nicopolis [nih-*kah*-puh-lis], battle of, 539
Niemeyer [*nee*-mye-er], Oscar, 1128
Nietzsche [*nee*-chah], Friedrich, 935, 936
Niger [*nye*-jer], 1119
Niger delta, 905
Nigeria, 595; modern, 1101, 1114, 1116, 1119, 1124, 1128
Niger River, 906
"Night of the Long Knives," 1009–1010
Nihilists, 859
Nijmegen [*nye*-may-guhn], Treaty of, 617
Nikon, 623
Nile River, 23, 906
Nimeiri, Gaafar [*gaf*-ahr nee-*mer*-ee], 1123
Ninety-five Theses (Luther), 457
Nineveh [*nihn*-uh-vuh], 40, 42
Nine Years' War (1688–1697), 618
Nirvana, 176
Nixon, Richard, 1060, 1072, 1073, 1090, 1156–1157
Nkrumah, Kwame [*kwah*-may nkroo-mah], 1116, 1118, 1119
Nobili [*noh*-bee-lee], Roberto de, 471
Nobunaga, Oda, 327–328, 778
Noh [noh] drama, 327, 782
Nok culture, 235–236, 447
Nominalists, 369, 401
Nonaligned nations, 1158
Nonaggression Pact (1939), 1031
Nonviolence, ideal of, 58, 173, 175
Noriega, Manuel, 1132, 1157
Norman Conquest, 341

Normandy, 334, 612
Normandy, Robert, Duke of, 350
Normandy invasion, 1041
Normans, 334, 347, 350
Norsemen. See Vikings
North, Frederick Lord, 673
North Africa: ancient, 146–148, 170; medieval, 201, 212, 215, 216, 218, 331; early modern, 540; and the dissolution of the Ottoman Empire, 860–861; in World War II, 1032, 1040–1041; after World War II, 1100, 1103, 1122–1124
North America, Amerindians of, 675, 806; Adena and Hopewell cultures, 256, 276–277; Mississippian culture, 277–278; Mogollon culture, 278; Hohokam culture, 278; Anasazi (Pueblo) culture, 278–279; later native cultures, 279–280; Eskimos, Aleuts, and Athabaskans, 280–281
North America, settlement of, 660–661
North Atlantic Treaty Organization (NATO), 1047, 1160
Northern Rhodesia, 1116
Northern Wei [way] kingdom, 305
North German Confederation, 855, 856
North Sea, 499
Northumberland, John Dudley, Duke of, 468–469
Northwest Ordinance, 675
Northwest Passage, 1109
Norway, 883; Reformation in, 461; in World War II, 1032
Notables, Assembly of, 710
Nottingham, 808
Noucentisme, 938
Novalis [noh-*vah*-lis], Friedrich von, 828
Novara, battle of, 839
Nova Scotia, 536, 620
Novels: Japanese, 324–325; Chinese, 573–575, 772; picaresque, 606; in the Enlightenment, 705; Romantic, 810, 827–829, 831; early nineteenth-century Russian, 824; modern Western, 888–889, 953, 957–958; African, 1124; modern Latin American, 1138
Novgorod [*nov*-guh-rut], 357–358, 403
Novikov [*noh*-vee-kuf], Nikolai, 693
Nubia, 27, 28, 32, 239
Nuremberg, 460
Nuremberg Laws, 1012
Nuremberg Trials, 1044
Nurhachi, 583
Nur Jahan [noor juh-*hahn*], 553
Nurredin [noo-reh-*deen*], 352
Nyasaland, 1116
Nyerere [nye-eh-*ray*-ray], Julius, 1119
Nystad [*noo*-stahd], Treaty of, 623

Oceania, 928
Ochino [oh-*kee*-noh], Bernardino, 427
Ockham, William of, 401
Octavia, 153
Octavius (Octavian), 153–154. See also Augustus
October Crisis (Canada), 1152
Oder [*oh*-der] River, 1047
Odyssey [*ahd*-ih-see], 92–93

Oedipus the King (Sophocles) [*ed*-ih-puhs], 120
Ogaden [oh-*gah*-dayn], 1124
O'Higgins, Bernardo, 678
Ohio River, 673
Ohio Valley, 276–277, 671
Okinawa, 1042
"Old Bolsheviks," 1017–1018
Old Colonial System, 657–659
Oldenbarneveldt, Jan van [yahn vahn *ol*-den-*bahr*-nuh-velt], 527
Olivares [oh-lee-*vah*-rays], Count of, 526
Oliver Twist (Dickens), 889
Olmecs [*ol*-meks], 257–258, 270
Olmütz, 853
Olympia, 99, 116, 119
Olympias, 127
Olympic pantheon, 136
Omdurman [om-der-*man*], battle of, 909
On Architecture (Vitruvius), 164
On Liberty (Mill), 884
Ontario, 675
On the Nature of Things (Lucretius), 164
On the Origin of Species (Darwin), 887
On the Revolution of the Heavenly Spheres (Copernicus), 636
OPEC, 1101, 1158
Open Door policy, 785
Opera: Chinese, 576; European, 650, 858, 939
Operation Barbarossa, 1033
Operation Overlord, 1041
Operation Torch, 1040
Opium Wars, 776
Oppenheimer, Samuel, 699
Oprichnina, 533
Optics, 372
Oral history, 4
Orange, house of, 527
Orange Free State, 909
Oration on the Dignity of Man (Pico della Mirandola), 423
Oratory of Divine Love, 469
Oratory of Jesus, 601
Order of the Golden Fleece, 589
Oregon, 675
Oresme [o-rehm], Nicholas of, 635
Oresteia [oh-rehs-*tee*-uh] (Aeschylus), 120, 122
Organic chemistry, 813
Organization for European Economic Co-operation, 1147
Organization of African Unity (OAU), 1116–1117, 1120, 1158
Orientalists (India), 753–754, 758
Origen, 192
Orlando, Vittorio E., 950, 998
Orléans [ahr-lay-*ahn*], 462; siege of, 395
Orléans, Philip, Duke of, 668, 832
Orozco [oh-*rohs*-koh], José Clemente, 1139
Ortega [or-*tay*-gah], Daniel, 1136
Ortega y Gasset [or-*tay*-gah ee gah-*set*], José, 952, 957
Ortelius [or-*tee*-lih-uhs], Abraham, 1108
Orthodox Judaism, 700–701
Orwell, George, 1172
Osaka [oh-*sah*-kah], 327, 494, 778, 779, 781, 785

Oscans, 229
Osiris [oh-*sye*-ris], 25
Osman [*oz*-mun, os-*mahn*], 539
Osnabrück [*os*-nah-brook], 460
Ostracism, in classical Athens, 105
Ostrogoths, 201, 331
Otto I, 333, 335, 345–346
Ottoman Empire, 218; origins, 539; Mehmet the Conqueror, 539–540; Suleiman the Magnificent, 540–541; society, 541–543; Istanbul, 543–545; urban life, 545; economy and culture, 545–548; war against the Holy League (1571), 517, 540; decline, 548; education in the early modern period, 602–603; invasion of the Austrian empire, 625–626; in the eighteenth century, 761; dissolution of, 860–862; and the origins of World War I, 941, 943; in World War I, 947; end of, 991–992
Ottoman Turks, 625–626
Otto of Brunswick, 348
Otto-Peters, Luise, 886
Oudenaarde [ou-duh-*nahr*-duh], battle of, 620
Oudh [oud], 744, 760
Ou-yang Hsiu, 313
Ovid, 157
OVRA, 1001
Owen, Robert, 803–805, 834, 835
Oxford, 366; University of, 425
Oyo, 905

Pacification of Ghent, 519
Pacific Ocean, 1111
Pact of Steel, 1031
Padua [*pad*-yo-ah], University of, 366
Paekche [*payk*-cheh], 320
Paestum [*pes*-tuhm] (Poseidonia), 98
Pagan, Burma, 298
Pahlavi [*pah*-luh-vee] dynasty, 992–993
Paine, Thomas, 701, 717, 723, 802, 896
Painting: in ancient Egypt, 30, 32; in Ceylon, 61; ancient Chinese, 87; early Greek, 100; classical Greek, 117; Buddhist, 177–178; Byzantine, 211–212; Maya, 264, 265; ancient Chinese, 304, 308, 309, 315, 319; Japanese, 326; Romanesque, 373–374; Italian Renaissance, 430–434, 436, 962–963; Northern Renaissance, 436, 437–438; Islamic, 446; medieval Indian, 446–447; in the Reformation, 476–477; in the late sixteenth century, 516; in Mughal India, 550, 961, 964–965; in Ming China, 563, 572–573, 961; baroque, 649-650, 963–964; rococo, 704; eighteenth-century English, 705; Goya, 730; in Ch'ing China, 774; in Tokugawa Japan, 782–783; Romantic, 831; realist, 888; Impressionist, 888, 937; modern Western, 937, 938–939, 958, 965, 1007–1008; in early modern Japan, 961–962; Mannerist, 963; Neoclassical, 965; and Italian Fascism, 1002; in Nazi Germany, 1011; modern Latin American, 1139
Pakistan, 675, 989, 1081, 1082–1083, 1089–1090

Palatinate, 522, 618
Palembang [pah-lem-*bahng*], 301
Palenque [peh-*lehn*-kay], 262
Paleolithic Age, 5, 70, 442
Palestine: ancient, 27–28, 31; Hebrew conquest of, 33, 34; in Byzantine Empire, 201; writing in, 228–229; and the crusades, 350, 353; and the Ottomans, 540; and Russia, 859; birth of Zionism, 863–864; modern, 947, 969, 990–991, 1092–1096, 1099, 1104
Palestine Liberation Organization (PLO), 1097, 1104, 1105
Palestinian National Charter, 1095
Palestrina, Giovanni [joh-*vahn*-nee pah-lay-*stree*-nah], 477
Palk Strait, 490
Palladio, Andrea [ahn-*dray*-ah pah-*lah*-dee-oh], 437
Pallava, 60, 62, 292, 293
Palma, Arturo Alessandri, 1130
Palmyra, 166–167
Pan-African Conference, 1114
Panama, 1132, 1157
Panama Canal, 1132
Pan Ch'ao (Ban Qao) [pahn chow], 83
Pandya, 60, 62, 292, 293, 294
Pan-German League, 939
Panipat [*pah*-nih-put], battles of, 290, 548, 557
Pankhurst, Christabel, 886–887
Pankhurst, Emmeline, 885–887
Pankhurst, Sylvia, 886–887
Pan Ku (Bangu) [pahn goo], 87
Panmunjom Armistice, 1069
Pan-Slavic Movement, 939
Pantagruel (Rabelais), 425
Pantheon, 159, 165
Papacy: origins of, 194; and the Iconoclastic Controversy, 211; late medieval, 396–397, 408. *See also individual popes*; Papal States
Papago, 278
Papal bulls: *Clericis laicos* [*klehr*-ih-sis *lay*-ih-kos] (1296), 349; *Unam sanctam* (1302), 349; *Parens scientiarum* (1231), 366; *Exsurge domine* (1520), 457
Papal States, 408, 410, 411, 474, 822, 849
Paper, 86, 219, 306, 318, 320, 338, 402, 429, 601, 634, 895
Paracelsus [par-uh-*sell*-suhs], 639
Paradise Lost (Milton), 649
Paraguay, 865, 866, 1128, 1132, 1140
Paraguayan War, 866
Parakrama Bahu (Ceylon), 61
Pareto [pah-*ray*-toh], Vilfredo, 939
Parallel Lives (Plutarch), 165
Paris: in the Middle Ages, 333, 339, 343, 366–369, 394, 402; early modern, 462, 807; and the revolution of 1789–1799, 713–714, 718–719, 726; modern, 811, 832, 839, 841, 846, 874, 875, 879, 954
Paris, Peace of (1763), 671; (1856), 859, 861; (1919), 950–952
Paris, Treaty of (1783), 674; (1814), 733
Paris, University of, 365, 370, 397
Paris Accords (1973), 1073, 1156
Paris Commune, 879, 890
Park, Chung Hee, 1069

Park, Mungo, 906
Parlement [pahr-luh-*mahn*], 345, 525, 709, 710
Parliament (England): medieval, 343, 396; Reformation, 467–468; under Edward VI, 468; under Mary Tudor, 473; later Stuart, 528; early Stuart, 528–529; Short, 529; Long, 529–530; Rump, 530; Barebones, 530; Convention (1660), 628; Cavalier (1661–1679), 628; under William III and Anne, 629, 630; age of Walpole, 666; Reform bills, 833, 878–879, 884; and the Chartists, 834
Parliament (France), 845, 879
Parliament (Germany). *See* Bundesrat; Reichstag
Parliament (Diet, Japan), 1026, 1053, 1075
Parliament (Italy), 883–884, 998–1000
Parma, Duke of, 519
Parmenides [pahr-*mehn*-ih-deez] of Elea, 123
Parri [*pahr*-ree], Ferruccio, 1146
Parsees, 184
Parthenon, 116, 117–119
Parthians, 81, 155
Parti populaire français [frahn-*say*], 1012
Parti Québécois [kay-bay-*kwah*], 1152
Partnerships, 338
Pascal, Blaise [blays puhs-*kuhl*], 640, 641, 645–646, 684
Passarowitz [pah-sah-*roh*-vitz], Treaty of, 548
Pasternak, Boris, 1164
Pasteur [pahs-ter], Louis, 807
Pataliputra [*pah*-tuh-lih-*poo*-truh], 55, 56, 58, 61
Patricians, Roman, 145–146, 149
Patronage, 419–420, 434
Päts, Konstantin, 1023
Paul the Apostle, 191–192, 195, 388
Paul III, Pope, 470, 471
Paul IV, Pope, 474
Paul V, Pope, 650
Paulette, 524
Pavia [pah-*vee*-ah], battle of, 413, 513
Pax Romana [paks roh-*mahn*-nuh]], 157
Pays d'état [pay day-*tah*], 611, 613
Pearl Harbor, 1034, 1037, 1042
Peary [*pir*-ee], Robert, 1111
Peasantry: in ancient Egypt, 31; in ancient China, 83; Maya, 261–263; Aztec, 269; in Byzantine Empire, 204–205; in medieval Europe, 335–336; in early modern Europe, 481–482; in early modern Russia, 621; on the eve of the first phase of the Industrial Revolution, 794; in the agricultural revolution, 794; in nineteenth-century Russia, 858; impact of World War I, 954; in the Soviet Union, 1016
Peasants' Revolt (1524–1525), 461, 466, 482
Pechenegs [pech-uh-*negz*], 333, 350, 356
Pedro (Brazil), 678, 865
Pedro II (Brazil), 865
Pegu [peh-*goh*], 299
P'ei Hsiu (Bei Xiu), 509
Peixoto, Floriano, 865

Peking (Beijing), 308, 316, 317, 471; in Ming Dynasty, 564, 568, 577–579, 582, 583; under the Manchus, 766, 767; modern, 921, 984, 1034, 1058
Pelagius [puh-*lay*-juhs], 195
Peloponnesian [pehl-uh-puh-*nee*-zhun] War, 109–112
Peloponnesus [pehl-uh-puh-*nee*-suhs], 91, 92, 131
Penance, sacrament of, 192–193, 456
Penang [pee-*nang*], 918
Peninsular War, 730–731
Pennsylvania, 536, 660
Pentateuch [*pehn*-tah-tewk], 33
"People's Democracies," 1144
Peoples of the Sea, 31, 33, 38, 92
Pepin [*pep*-ihn] the Short, 331
Perestroika, 1164, 1165
Pergamum, 131, 148
Periander, 95
Perioikoi, 108
Pericles [*per*-ih-kleez], 103–104, 112
Periplus of the Erythrean Sea, 59
Perón [pay-*rohn*], Eva, 1129, 1130
Perón, Isabel, 1129
Perón, Juan [hwahn] Domingo, 1129
Perry, Matthew C., 785
Persepolis [per-*sep*-uh-lis], 43–44, 128
Persia: rise of ancient, 40–42; imperial government of, 42; capitals of, 43-44; wars with the Greeks, 102–103; renewed conflict with Greeks, 126; conquered by Alexander the Great, 128–129; religion in, 182–184; Islam in, 218, 223
Persian Gulf, 1105
Persians: ancient, 36, 41–44; invade the Roman Empire, 167, 169; relations with Byzantine Empire, 201–202. *See also* Persia
Persian Wars, 102–103
Perth, Australia, 928
Peru: prehistoric settlement, 256, 257; Chavín culture, 272–273; the Inca, 273–276, 657; Jesuit missions, 471; Spanish conquest of, 495–496; colonial rule, 658, 659, 660, 677, 678; in the late nineteenth century, 865, 866; in the twentieth century, 1130, 1131, 1138, 1139
Pestalozzi, Johann Heinrich [*yoh*-hahn pest-ah-*lot*-see], 697, 800
Pétain, Henri [ahn-ree pay-*tenh*], 1032
Peter I, "the Great" (Russia), 621–625, 650, 692, 761
Peter III (Russia), 693
Peterloo Massacre, 810, 823
Peters, Karl, 906
Peter the Apostle, 191, 192, 194
Peter the Hermit, 350
Petition of Right (1628), 528–529
Petrarch, Francesco [frahn-*cheh*-skoh *pee*-trahrk], 417, 421–422, 438
Petrograd (St. Petersburg), 970, 971, 972
Petronius [peh-*troh*-nee-es], 165
Pfefferkorn, Johann, 454
Pharaoh, position of in ancient Egypt, 23–24, 31
Pharisees, 190

Pharos (Alexandria), 134
Pharsalus [fahr-*say*-luhs], battle of, 152
Phidias [*fid*-ee-uhs], 118
Philadelphia, 674
Philaret, 623
Philip, Arthur, 928
Philip II, "Augustus" (France), 343, 344–345, 348, 352, 366, 368, 379
Philip II (Macedon), 126–127
Philip II (Spain), 436, 473, 512–521 *passim*
Philip III (Spain), 526
Philip IV, "the Fair" (France), 345, 349, 380, 396
Philip IV (Spain), 526
Philip V (Macedon), 148
Philip V (Spain), 619, 620
Philip VI (France), 394
Philippi [fih-*lip*-eye], battle of,153
Philippines: early history, 296, 302; medieval culture in, 298; and Magellan, 488; missions in, 494; colonial rule, 883, 918, 920, 929–930; in the twentieth century, 1037, 1042, 1070, 1071
Philip the Good (Burgundy), 407
Philistines, 34, 92
Philosophes [feel-oh-*sohfs*], 686–690
Philosophy: in Vedic India, 53; in ancient China, 74–76, 77–79; early Greek, 123–124; Socrates, 124; Plato, 124–125; Aristotle, 125–126; Stoicism, 137, 138, 139; Epicureanism, 138, 139–140; in the Hellenistic Age, 139–140; Cynicism, 139–140; Islamic, 222–223; Neo-Confucianism, 315; Scholastic (Europe), 369–370; Neoplatonism, 423; in Ming China, 576; Descartes and Pascal, 640–642; Hobbes, 644–645; Locke, 645, 686, 825; Skepticism, 645–647; Pascal, 645–646; Spinoza, 647–648; in the Enlightenment, 683–689; Voltaire, 687; Rousseau, 688–689; Liberalism, 825–826; Kant and Hegel, 829–830; Nietzsche and Bergson, 935; in the modern West, 957
Phnom Penh [peh-*nahm* pehn], 300
Phoenicians [fih-*nee*-shuhnz], 33, 34, 42, 93, 229, 235
Phonograph, 899
"Phony War," 1031
Photography, 898
Phrygia [*frij*-ih-ah], 137
Phrygians, 38
Physics: in the scientific revolution, 642; modern, 936–937, 957
Physiocrats, 795
Picabia [pee-*kah*-bya], Francis, 938
Picasso, Pablo, 938, 939, 965, 1029
Pico della Mirandola, Giovanni [joh-*vahn*-nee *pee*-koh day-lah mee-*rahn*-doh-lah], 423
Piedmont-Sardinia, Kingdom of, 849, 850, 859, 882
Piedra, Rosaria Ibarra de, 1137
Pietists, Pietism, 601, 697
Pilgrimages, 293, 397, 455, 458
Pillars of Islam, 213–214
Pillnitz, Declaration of, 718, 729
Pilsudski [peel-*soot*-skee], Józef, 1022

Pima, 278
Pinochet, Augusto [ow-*goos*-toh pee-noh-*chet*], 1131
Pinsker, Leo, 862
Piracy, in Ming China, 581
Pirandello [pee-rahn-*del*-loh], Luigi, 958
Pisa [*pee*-sah], 339, 419; Council of, 397
Pisan, Christine de [kree-*steen* duh pee-*zahn*], 426, 427, 649
Pisistratus [pye-*sis*-truh-tuhs], 100–101
Pissarro [pee-*sah*-roh], Camille, 888
Pitt, William, the Elder, 671
Pitt, William, the Younger, 729, 730, 801
Pius II, Pope, 453
Pius V, Pope, 683
Pius VI, Pope, 716
Pius VII, Pope, 728, 730
Pius IX, Pope, 839, 849, 882
Pius XI, Pope, 1001
Pizarro [pih-*zah*-roh], Francisco, 273, 276, 495–496, 497
Place, Francis, 802, 809, 834
Plague (Black Death), 391–393, 419
Planck [plahngk], Max, 936
Plassey, battle of, 671, 750, 751
Plataea [plah-*tee*-ah], battle of, 103
Plato, 124–125, 126, 179, 635
Plautus [*plah*-tuhs], 164
Plebian assembly (Roman), 145, 150
Plebeians, Roman, 145–146, 149–150
Pleistocene epoch, 5
Pliny [*plih*-nee] the Elder, 81, 165
Pliny the Younger, 165
Plombières [plon-bee-*yair*], Treaty of, 850
Plow, invention of, 9
Plutarch, 165
Plymouth, Mass., 536
Poem of My Cid, 377
Poetics (Aristotle), 126
Poetry: Tamil, 60; in ancient India, 62–63; early Greek, 92–93, 96–98; Hellenistic, 138; classical Roman, 157, 164–165; Byzantine, 211; Islamic, 216, 223; Hindu, 291, 292; Chinese, 309–310, 312–313; Japanese, 327; medieval European, 400–401; in the Ottoman Empire, 547; early modern European, 648, 649; Romantic, 828; modern Western, 937, 957, 958; modern South American, 1138
Poggio Bracciolini [*pod*-joh braht-choh-*lee*-nee], 422
Pogroms, 862
Poincaré [pwahn-kah-*ray*], Raymond, 1020
Poitiers [pwah-*tyay*], 341, 373, 377
Poitou [pwah-too], 341, 612
Poland: medieval, 357, 415; early modern, 465, 474, 532–533, 626, 694–695; in the Napoleonic era, 730; and the Congress of Vienna, 820; revolution of 1830, 832; between the world wars, 952, 973, 975, 1021–1022; Nazi conquest of, 1031; in World War II, 1039, 1042; after World War II, 1045, 1047, 1143, 1145, 1160–1161. *See also* Grand Duchy of Warsaw
Pole, Reginald, 427

Polignac [poh-lee-*nyak*], Jules de, 832
Polis, 94–95, 98–99, 108–109, 113
Politburo, 977
Political theory: medieval European, 371–372; Bodin and Filmer, 524; Machiavelli, 428–429; Hobbes and Locke, 644–645, 686; Rousseau and Montesquieu, 688–689
Polo, Marco, 287, 315, 317, 318, 483, 509
Polonnaruwa, 61, 294
Pol Pot, 1073
Poltava [pol-*tah*-vuh], battle of, 623
Polybius [poh-*lib*-ee-uhs], 133
Polyclitus [pahl-ih-*klye*-tuhs] of Argos [*ahr*-gahs], 116
Polycrates [peh-*lihk*-reh-teez], 95
Polygamy, 214, 221, 252, 275, 928, 929, 1075, 1124
Polynesia, 929
Pomerania, 626
Pompadour [*pom*-pah-dohr], Madame de, 669
Pompeii [pahm-*pay*], 161–162, 705
Pompey [*pahm*-pee], 151–152
Pondicherry, 749
Ponet, John, 473
Ponsonby, Sarah, 703
Pontiac, 673
Poona, 556
Poor Clares, 363–364
Poor Laws (England), 800
Poor Relief: in Constantinople, 209; in early modern Europe, 464, 603–604; in early modern Asia, 604–605; in early modern Africa, 605; among the Inca, 605
Pop Art, 965
Pope, Alexander, 689
Popular Front (France), 1021
Popular Front (Spain), 1030
Porcelain, 86, 306–307, 320, 321, 488, 490, 571, 573, 577, 782, 784, 961
Port Huron Statement, 1150–1151
Portinari [por-tee-*nah*-ree], Cândido, 1139
Portolani, 484
Port Royal, Acadia, 536
Portugal: and the reconquista, 354; motives for overseas expansion, 484–485; early involvement in Africa, 488–489; colonization in Brazil, 499; annexed by Spain (1580), 517; war of liberation, 526; American colonies of, 660; and the Enlightenment, 697; in the Napoleonic era, 730; interests in India, 745-747; in the early nineteenth century, 822, 832; end of imperialism in Africa, 1115–1116
Portuguese Guinea, 1115, 1116
Porus, 54, 128
Positivism, 935
Postimpressionists, 937, 938–939
Potosí [poh-toh-*see*], 498, 658–659
Potsdam, 694
Potsdam Conference, 1045
Pottery: prehistoric, 9, 11–12, 13, 16; of ancient India, 47; ancient Chinese, 86; Greek, 90, 91; classical Roman, 155; Olmec, 257; Maya, 264; Chavín, 273

Poverty: in ancient India, 65, 66; in Constantinople, 209; in early modern Europe, 598, 603–604; in early modern Asia, 604–605; and crime in the early modern period, 605–606
Powell, John Wesley, 1110
Poznan riots, 1145
Praetorian Guard, 155, 166
Pragmatic Sanction (1713), 626, 669
Pragmatic Sanction of Bourges [boorzh], 407
Prague [prahg], 339, 523
Prague, Treaty of, 839, 855
Praise of Folly (Erasmus), 455
Praxiteles [prak-*siht*-el-eez], 106, 120, 138, 445
Predestination, 195, 462, 463, 466
Presbyterians, 530
Pre-Socratics, 122–123
Prester (Elder) John, 484, 509, 510
Price, Richard, 703
Price Revolution (Europe), 501–502
Priestley, Joseph, 827
Primo de Rivera, José António, 1013
Primo de Rivera, Miguel, 1013
Primogeniture [*prye*-moh-*jen*-ih-chur], 76, 83, 382, 592, 674
Prince, The (Machiavelli), 428, 473
Printing: in Asia, 306, 312, 320, 321, 322, 571, 601, 895; in Europe, 402, 429–430, 453, 459, 463, 504, 690, 895–897
Procopius [proh-*koh*-pee-uhs], 203, 205, 210
Progress, concept of, 684–686, 826
Progressive Conservative Party (Canada), 1152
Prohibition (United States), 1020
Prophets, Hebrew, 186–187
Prostitution, 56, 60, 64–65, 107; early modern, 469, 599
Protagoras, 124
Proudhon [proo-*dohn*], Pierre-Joseph, 835, 836, 847
Proust [proost], Marcel, 957
Provence [pro-vahns], 407
Prussia: rise of, 626–628; in the War of the Austrian Succession, 669–670; in the Seven Years' War, 670–671; under Frederick the Great, 693–695; and the Napoleonic wars, 729–730, 732–733; and the Congress of Vienna, 818–820; in the early nineteenth century, 824, 853–857; and the revolution of 1848, 837, 839, 840; and the Second Reich, 880–881; after World War I, 952; and the Third Reich, 1009; after World War II, 1047
Psychoanalysis: Freud, 935–936; Jung, 936
Ptolemies [*tahl*-uh-meez], 129, 131, 132, 133, 134
Ptolemy [*tahl*-uh-mee], Claudius, 135, 509, 510, 634, 636–637
Ptolemy I, 129, 134, 136, 137
Ptolemy II, 138
Ptolemy III, 138
Ptolemy IV, 133, 134
Ptolemy VII, 151

Puduhepa, 37
Puerto Rico, 498, 658, 679, 883, 1127
Pufendorf [*poo*-fuhn-dorf], Samuel, 644
Pugachev, Emilian [yeh-myil-*yan* poo-gah-*choff*], rebellion of, 693
Puhar, 62
Punic [*pyoo*-nik] Wars, 146–149
Punjab [pun-*job*]: ancient, 47, 54, 56; medieval, 285, 290; early modern, 548, 555, 556, 743, 752, 758, 760; modern, 1081–1083, 1087, 1090
Purdah, 297, 556
Purgatory, 456, 457, 472
Puritans, 528, 529, 530, 536
Pushkin [*poosh*-kyin], Alexander, 824
Putney Debates, 531
"Putting out," system of, 502
Pu Yi, Henry, 1026
Pydna [*pihd*-nuh], battle of, 148
Pygmies, 904
Pylos [*pye*-lahs], 92
Pyongyang [pyahng-yahng], 320, 1068
Pyramids, 24–25, 259, 260, 261, 265, 267, 278
Pyrenees, Treaty of the, 524, 526
Pyrrhic [*pihr*-ik] Wars, 146
Pyrrhus [*pihr*-uhs], 146
Pythagoras [pih-*thag*-uh-ruhs] of Samos, 123, 508, 634, 635, 638
Pytheas, 134

Qaddafi, Muammar al-[moo-uh-*mar* el kah-*dah*-fee], 1106, 1123
Qajar, Agha Muhammad, 763
Qajar dynasty, 763
Qatar [*kaht*-er], 1101
Quadrivium, 333, 366
Quadruple Alliance, 819
Quakers (Society of Friends), 530–532
Quebec [kwuh-*bek*], 536, 671, 675, 1152
Quebec Act, 673
Quesnay, François [frahn-*swah* keh-*nay*], 795
Quetzalcoatl, 259, 260, 265, 268, 272
Quiberon [keeb-*rohn*] Bay, battle of, 671
Quietism, 697
Quintilian, 165

Rabelais, François [frahn-*swah* rah-*blay*], 425, 438, 648
Racine, Jean [zhahn bah-*teest* rah-*seen*], 649
Racism, 939, 1005–1006, 1027, 1038–1040
Radical Reformation: Anabaptists, 465–466; Spiritualists and Rationalists, 466
Radio, 813, 899, 900
Radischev, Alexander, 693
Rahman, Mujibur, 1089
Raicho, Hiratsuka, 1075
Railroads: in Asia, 757, 759, 912, 918, 926, 927; in Europe, 812, 813, 845, 859, 870; in the United States, 865, 870; in Africa, 910, 1114; in Australia, 929; in the Middle East, 1102; in Bolivia, 1131
Rajasthan [*rah*-juh-stahn], 285, 555, 743, 752

Rajput Confederacy, 290
Rajputs [*raj*-pootz], 285, 289, 548, 550, 555, 745, 912
Rakoczi [*rah*-koh-tsee], Ferenc, 626
Raleigh, Sir Walter, 500, 536
Ramadan [rah-mah-*dahn*], 214
Ramananda, 291
Ramayana, 52, 53, 298
Rambouillet [rahn-boo-*yay*], Catherine de, 649
Rameau [ra-*moh*], Jean-Philippe, 705
Ramillies [*ram*-ih-leez], battle of, 620
Ramses II [*ram*-seez], 31
Ramses III, 31
Ranade [*rah*-nah-day], Mahadeo Govind, 917
Randolph, Edmund, 674
Rangoon, 918, 1070
Ranke [*rahng*-kuh], Leopold von, 830
Rao, V. N., 1087
Rapallo, Treaty of, 952
Raphael [*raf*-ay-uhl] Sanzio, 433, 437
Rasputin [rahs-*poo*-tyin, ras-*pew*-tin], Grigori, 970
Rastadt [*rah*-shtaht, *rahs*-taht], Treaty of, 626
Rathenau, Walther [*vahl*-ter *rah*-teh-noo], 1004
Rationalists, 466
Ravenna [rah-*vehn*-nah], 204, 332
Rawalpindi, 1089
Ray, Man, 938
Raya, Krishna Deva, 295
Raymond II, count of Toulouse, 350
Razin, Stenka, 534
Reagan, Ronald, 1131, 1132, 1136, 1157, 1164
Realist movement (art), 888
Realists (medieval), 369
Real patronato, 405
Realpolitik, 854, 855
Reconquista, 354–355
Reconstructionist Movement (Judaism), 701
Red Fort, 745, 916
Red Guards (China), 1062–1063
Red Turbans, 564
Reflections on the Revolution in France (Burke), 717
Reform Acts: (1832), 833, 834; (1867), 878, 884; (1884), 878–879
Reformation, Catholic (Counter): origins and characteristics, 469; Ursulines and Jesuits, 469–471; Council of Trent, 471–473; in England, 473–474
Reformation, impact of: on Jews, 474; witchcraft persecutions, 474–476; on art and music, 476–478
Reformation, Protestant: conditions in the late medieval church, 453–454; humanist demands for reform, 454–456; Lutheran movement, 456–461; Reformed tradition, 461–465; radical reformation, 465–466; English reformation, 466-469
Reformed Protestantism, 461–463
Reform movement (Judaism), 700–701
Regulated companies, 502

Reichstag [*rikes*-tahk], 855, 880–881, 1008, 1009
Reincarnation, 174–175, 176
Reinhardt, Max, 1008
Reinsurance Treaty, 941, 942
Relativity, theory of, 936
Religion: prehistoric, 10; in ancient Mesopotamia, 19–20; in ancient Egypt, 24–26, 29–31; Hittite, 38; in ancient India, 50; in ancient China, 71, 85; in the Cyclades, 90; Minoan, 91; in the Hellenistic Age, 136–137; in classical Rome, 155; foundations of, 172–173; Asian attitudes, 182; Bantu, 235; Kushite, 236; in early Africa, 243; Olmec, 258; Maya, 261, 263, 264; Aztec, 270–271; Chavín, 273; Inca, 276; Southern Cult, 278; Anasazi (Pueblo), 278. *See also major religions by name*
Religious freedom, 466
Remarque [ruh-*mahrk*], Erich Maria, 953
Rembrandt van Rijn [rine], 650
Remus [*ree*-muhs], 145
Renaissance, European: urban background, 418–419; patronage, 419–420; humanists, nature of, 420–421; age of Petrarch, 421–422; civic humanists, 422–423; Neoplatonists, 423; education and scholarship, 423–425; northern humanists, 425; role of women, 425–427, 435–436; Machiavelli and Guicciardini, 427–429; role of printing, 429–430; and the fine arts, 430–438, 962–963; interpretations of, 438–440
Renoir [ruh-*nwar*], Auguste, 888
Repartimiento, 658
Republic, The (Plato), 124–125
Republic of Virtue, 722–723
Residencia, 657
Reuchlin, Johann [*yoh*-hahn *roik*-luhn], 454
Revolutions of 1830, 832
Revolutions of 1848, 837–841
Rexist movement, 1013
Reynaud [ray-*noh*], Paul, 1032
Reynolds, Joshua, 705
Reza Shah Pahlavi, 992–993, 1101–1102
Rhee, Syngman [*sing*-muhn *ree*], 1068, 1069
Rheims [reemz], 365
Rhenish League, 338
Rhine, Confederation of the, 730
Rhineland, 475, 812, 820, 950, 1027–1028
Rhode Island, 660
Rhodes, 130, 132, 215, 540, 909
Rhodes, Cecil, 909
Rhodesia, 909
Rhône [rohn] Valley, 331
Riario, Girolamo, 409
Ribero, Diego, 509
Ricardo, David, 801–802, 835
Ricci [*reet*-chee], Matteo, 471, 492–494, 572, 579, 580, 583, 1110
Richard I (England), 341, 352
Richard II (England), 394, 398, 406
Richard III (England), 406
Richardson, Samuel, 697, 705
Richelieu [*ree*-sheh-lyuh], Cardinal, 525

Riefenstahl, Leni, 1011
Rigaud [ree-*goh*], Hyacinthe, 964
Rights of Man, The (Paine), 802
Rig Veda [rig *vay*-dah], 174
Rilke [*rihl*-kuh], Rainer Maria, 958
Rime of the Ancient Mariner (Coleridge), 828
Rio de Janeiro [*ree*-oh duh juh-*nayr*-oh], 499, 865, 1128
Rio de la Plata, 488
Risorgimento [ree-sor-jee-*men*-toh], 849–852
Rivera [ree-*vay*-rah], Diego, 1139
Roads: in ancient India, 56, 76, 80; Roman, 161; Inca, 276; Chinese, 305, 569; in Iran, 561
Roanoke Island, 500, 536
Robespierre, Maximilien [max-see-*mee*-lyenh roh-bes-*pyair*], 690, 718, 720, 721–724
Robinson Crusoe (Defoe), 631, 649
Rockefeller, John D., 871
Rococo art, 964
Rodin [roh-*danh*], Auguste, 444
Rodney, George, 674
Roe, Sir Thomas, 746
Röhm [ruhm], Ernst, 1007, 1009
Roland [ro-*lahn*], Madame, 723–724
Romance of Reynard the Fox, 378
Romance of the Rose, 378
Romance of the Three Kingdoms, 85
Roman Empire: conquest of the Mediterranean, 146–149; reign of Augustus, 154–157; the Julio-Claudians, 157; the Flavians and the "Good" Emperors, 157-159; the imperial capital, 159–161; provincial life, 161–162; women in Roman society, 162–164; the Roman achievement, 164–165; Roman law, 165–166; the third-century crisis, 166–167; Diocletian's reign, 167–168; the reign of Constantine, 168–169; the decline of the empire in the West, 169–170; contact with Kushites, 237–238
Romanesque style, 373–374
Romania (Rumania): and World War I, 941, 943; between the world wars, 952, 975, 1021–1023; in World War II, 1031; after World War II, 1045, 1143, 1161-1162
Romanov [ruh-*mah*-noff], Mikhail, 533
Romanov dynasty, origins of, 533–534
Romans, Classical: contributions of, 142–143, 170; origins of, 143, 533–534; rule of Etruscans, 143–144; the early republic, 144–146; unification of Italy, 146–148; Punic Wars, 146–148, 149; conquests in Greece and Asia, 148; decline of the republic, 149–154; age of Augustus, 154–157; literature, 156-157, 164–165; art and architecture, 157, 158, 165; the early empire (A.D. 14–138), 157–159; life in the city of Rome, 159–161; provincial life, 161–162; Roman women, 162–164; law and justice, 165–166; the later empire (A.D. 192–476), 166–170; adopt alphabet, 229

Romanticism, 698, 826–831; view of death, 739
Rome: demand for Chinese silk, 80–81; trade with Asia, 81–82; founding of, 143, 144–145; in the classical period, 159–161; early Christianity in, 192-193; medieval, 339; sack of (1527), 414; Renaissance in, 420, 433; early modern, 481; in the age of the Baroque, 650–652; and the revolution of 1848, 839, 851; unification with Italian state, 852, 857; under Mussolini, 1003. *See also* Romans, Classical
Rome, University of, 366
Rome-Berlin Axis, 1003
Romulus [*rahm*-yoo-luhs], 145
Romulus Augustulus [ah-*gus*-tyoo-luhs], 170
Röntgen [*rent*-guhn], Wilhelm, 936
Roosevelt, Franklin D., 897, 1021, 1033–1034, 1040, 1041, 1042, 1044, 1115
Roosevelt, Theodore, 926
Rosas, Juan Manuel, 866
Roscellin [ro-seh-*lan*], 369
Rosenberg, Alfred, 1007
Rosetta Stone, 32
Rossbach, battle of, 670
Rossi [*rohs*-see], Properzia, 436
Rouault [roo-*oh*], Georges, 938
Rouen [roo-*ahn*], 339, 394, 811
Roundheads, 530
Rousseau, Jean-Jacques [zhahn-zhahk roo-*soh*], 686, 688–689, 690, 691, 697, 698, 800, 828, 896
Roux [roo], Jacques, 720
Roy, Manabendra Nath, 979, 980
Roy, Ram Mohun, 754
Royal Society (England), 530, 795, 796
Roye, Madeleine Mailly, Comtesse de, 465
Rubber, 753
Rubeanus, Crotus, 454
Rubens [*rew*-binz], Peter Paul, 503, 963–964
Rubicon River, 152
Rudolf of Habsburg, 413
Ruhr [roor] Valley, 952, 1004
Ruskin, John, 800, 888
Russia: Viking conquest of, 333; Mongol conquest, 355–358; rise of Muscovy, 403–404; expansion in Asia, 494–495; in the sixteenth and seventeenth centuries, 533–534; under Peter the Great, 621–625; in the Seven Years' War, 670, 671; under Catherine the Great, 691–693; and the Napoleonic wars, 729-730, 733; relations with Iran in the eighteenth century, 761; and the Congress of Vienna, 819–820; in the early nineteenth century, 823, 824–825, 858–859; in the late nineteenth century, 859–860; Decembrist revolt (1825), 823, 824; Second Industrial Revolution in, 870; relations with China and Japan, 923, 925, 926; and the origins of World War I, 941–945; in World War I, 947, 948; Russian Revolution, 969–973; civil war in, 973–975;

after the collapse of the USSR, 1168–1169. *See also* Union of Soviet Socialist Republics
Russian Academy of Sciences, 624
Russian Revolution, 969–973
Russo-Japanese War, 926
Russo-Turkish Wars (1768–1774; 1787–1792), 693
Rutherford, Ernest, 936
Rwanda, 1116
Ryswick [*riz*-wik], Treaty of, 619

SA (*Sturmabteilung*), 1007, 1009–1010
Saar [zahr] basin (Saarland), 617, 951, 1027
Sabaeans [sah-*bee*-ahnz], 132–133
Sacraments, 192, 457, 462, 465, 468, 472
Sacred Congregation of the Holy Office, 473
Sadat, Anwar el-, 1098, 1100
Sadducees, 190
Sadi-Carnot, François, 890
Safavid dynasty, rise of, 560–561
Sagres [sah-*greesh*], 485
Sahara desert, 233, 240–241, 248, 908
Said [sah-*eed*], Nuri es-, 1097
Said, Sayyid, 906
Saigon [sye-*gon*], 301, 920, 1072, 1073
St. Augustine, Florida, 536
St. Bartholomew's Day Massacre, 520–521
St. Cyr [sahn seer] school, 616
St. Denis [sahn duh-nee], Abbey church at, 374
Saint-Lambert, 685
St. Lawrence River, 660
St. Peter's Basilica, Rome, 437, 456
St. Petersburg, 623, 969, 1169. *See also* Petrograd
Saint-Simon [sahn-see-*monh*], Count de, 835
Saipan [sye-*pan*], 1042
Sakas. *See* Scythians
Sakharov, Andrei, 1155, 1164
Saladin [*sal*-uh-dihn], 352
Salamis [*sal*-uh-mihs], battle of, 103
Salat, 214
Salerno, University of, 372
Salons, 689–690, 702, 723, 846, 1002
Salt, 241, 253, 254
SALT Treaties, 1163
Salutati [sah-loo-*tah*-tee], Coluccio, 422
Salvador (El Salvador), 678, 865, 1135, 1138, 1157
Samanids, 218
Samaria, 36
Samarkand [*sam*-ur-*kand*], 81
Samnites, 143, 146
Samnite Wars, 146
Samoa, 928, 930, 947
Samos, 95, 128
Samsara, 386
Samurai, 325–326, 588, 777, 778, 781, 926
San, 235, 904
Sancho the Great, 354
Sand [sahnd], George (Aurore Dupin), 831
Sandinistas, 1136, 1140

Sanhedrin [san-*hee*-drin], 158
San Juan de Uluá, 500
San Lorenzo Tenochtitlán [tay-nohch-tee-*tlahn*], 257, 258
San Marcos, University of, 496
San Martín, José de, 678, 680
San Salvador. *See* Salvador
Sans-culottes [sahn-koo-*lohts*], 716, 718, 720, 724, 726, 727
Sanskrit, 52, 230
San Stefano, Treaty of, 861, 941
Santa Anna, Antonio López de, 866–867
Santo Domingo, 657, 662
São Paulo [soun *pou*-loo], 1139
Sappho [*saff*-oh], 96–98
Sarai [sah-*rye*], 357
Sarajevo [sah-rah-*yeh*-voh], 545
Sarapis [sah-*ray*-pihs], 137
Saratoga, New York, 673
Sardinia, 218, 822
Sarfatti, Margherita, 1002, 1003
Sargon I [*sahr*-gon], 20–21
Sargon II, 40
Sarney, José, 1127
Sartre, Jean-Paul [zhan-pol *sahr*-truh], 957
Sassanids [suh-*sah*-nidz], 184
Sati [*sah*-tee] (suttee), 65, 556, 594, 737, 753, 754, 910
Saud [sah-*ood*], Abdul-Aziz ibn-, 947, 990, 1099, 1101
Saudi Arabia, 990, 1099, 1101, 1105
Saul, 34
Savery, Thomas, 789
Savonarola, Girolamo [jee-*roh*-lah-moh sah-voh-nah-*roh*-lah], 410, 411, 428
Savoy, 724, 850
Savoy dynasty, 849
Saxons, 170, 331
Saxony, 523, 820
Scala [*skah*-lah], Alessandra, 426
Scandinavia, 333. *See also* Denmark; Finland; Norway; Sweden
Scapulimancy, 228
Scheidemann [*shye*-duh-mahn], Philip, 1004
Schiaparelli [skyah-pah-*rehl*-lee], Giovanni, 1110
Schiller [*shil*-er], Friedrich von, 732, 828
Schlesinger, Arthur M., 1154
Schleswig [*sles*-vig], 854, 855
Schlieffen [*shleef*-ehn] Plan, 942–943, 945
Schliemann, Heinrich [*hine*-rik *shlee*-mahn], 92
Schmalkaldic League, 461
Scholastics, 369–370
Schönberg [*shen*-berk], Arnold, 858
Schönerer, Georg von, 1005, 1006
Schubert, Franz, 706, 828, 829, 858
Schumacher [*shoo*-mah-kur], Kurt, 1047
Schuman, Robert, 1158
Schumann, Robert, 828, 858
Schütz [shoots], Heinrich, 650
Science: early Greek, 122–123; pre-Socratic, 122–123; Hellenistic, 134–136; Islamic, 221–222; medieval European, 372, 634–635; Scientific Revolution, 633–643; in antiquity, 634; Hermetic challenge, 635–636; in East Asia, 783;

and the First Industrial Revolution, 795–796, 813–814; in the modern West, 887–888, 936–937, 957
Scientific method, 642–643
Scientific Revolution, 633–643
Scipio [*sip*-ee-oh], 148
Scotland: and the spread of Calvinism, 465; Reformation in, 473
Scott, Sir Walter, 828
Scudéry [skoo-*day*-ree], Madeleine de, 649
Sculpture: Paleolithic, 6, 442; Neolithic, 10, 442, 444; in ancient India, 46, 49, 51, 54, 58, 59; in Ceylon, 61; ancient Chinese, 68, 72, 73, 86; in the Cyclades, 90; archaic Greek, 95–96; early Greek, 100; classical Greek, 116–120; Hellenistic, 131, 134–136, 138; Buddhist, 131–132, 172; Etruscan, 144; classical Roman, 157, 165, 188; Bantu, 235–236; of the Yoruba, 250, 251; Olmec, 257–258; Teotihuacán, 260; Maya, 264; medieval Indian, 294–295; medieval Chinese, 308–309, 447; Korean, 320; Romanesque, 373, 374; Gothic, 375, 376, 446; Italian Renaissance, 434–435, 963; early Japanese, 447; early African, 447–448; Baroque, 649, 963; African, 962; Aztec, 962; modern Western, 965
Scythians [*sith*-ee-uhns] (Sakas), 41, 42, 58
Second Hundred Years' War, 666
Second International, 891–892
Sedan, battle of, 856
Seine [sen] River, 366
Sekigahara, battle of, 779
Selassie, Haile [*hye*-lee seh-*lass*-ee], 1119, 1123
Seleucids [sih-*loo*-sihds], 129–130, 131, 132, 133
Seleucus [sih-*loo*-kuhs], 129
Selim I, "the Grim," 540
Seljuk [sel-*jook*] Turks, 218, 350–353, 560
Semitic languages, 228–229
Semites, 212, 238
Senate (Roman), 145–146, 149–155 *passim*, 158, 166
Sendero Luminoso, 1131
Seneca, 165
Seneca Falls Convention, 884
Senegal, 674, 906, 908, 1114
Senghor [sahn-*gohr*], Léopold, 1115
Senufo, 595
Seoul [sohl], 321, 1068
Separation of church and state, 674
Sephardim [seh-*fahr*-dim], 698
Septuagint, 134
Serbia, 548, 822–823, 861, 941, 943, 944, 947, 1162
Serfdom: in China, 72; in Sparta, 108; in Byzantine Empire, 204–205; in medieval Europe, 335–336; in Russia, 693; in Prussia, 694; in Austria, 696; and the Napoleonic Code, 730
Sermon on the Mount, 190
Servetus [ser-*vee*-tuhs], Michael, 464
Sesklo, 90

Sesostris [see-*sos*-tris] III, 27
Seven Years' War, 670–671, 749
Severi, 166
Severus, Alexander, 166
Severus, Septimius, 166, 192
Sévigné [*say*-vee-*nyay*], Marie de, 649, 723
Seville [suh-*vihl*], 221, 333, 355, 394, 499, 822; University of, 366
Sexto-Licinian Laws, 145
Sexual customs: in classical Athens, 107; in classical Rome, 156, 163; Augustine's view, 195; in the Byzantine Empire, 208; in early modern Asia, 597; in early modern Africa, 597; in early modern Europe, 598–599; in the modern West, 877, 954–955
Seymour [*see*-mohr], Jane, 468, 477
Sforza [*sfohr*-tsah], Caterina, 409–410
Sforza, Francesco [frahn-*cheh*-skoh], 408, 411
Sforza, Ludovico, 407–408
Shaftesbury, 3rd Earl of, 684, 802
Shahada, 213, 215
Shah-Nameh [shah-nah-*mah*] (Firdawsi), 223
Shaka [*shah*-kah], 906
Shakespeare, William, 522, 648
Shang [shahng] dynasty, 69, 70–71
Shanghai, 773, 776, 921, 984–986, 1026, 1034
Shantung (Shandong), 73, 926, 947, 951
Sharif, Nawaz, 1090
Sharpeville Massacre, 1116, 1122
Shastri, Lal Bahadur, 1085
Shaw, George Bernard, 891
Shays' Rebellion, 674
Sheffield, 808
Shelley, Percy Bysshe, 823, 828, 829
Shen Kuo (Shen Guo), 509
Shih (Di) [shew], 76–78, 87
Shi'ite [*shee*-ite] Muslims, 215, 217, 218, 761–762, 1101, 1102, 1105, 1106
Shinto, 178, 182, 195, 324, 783
Shiva [*shee*-vah], 173, 174, 195, 299
Shivaji, 556–557
Siam. *See* Thailand
Siberia, 256, 494, 974, 975
Sicilian Vespers, 354
Sicily: ancient, 112, 146; medieval, 201, 218, 222, 334, 338, 347, 353, 354; early modern, 526; modern, 838, 839, 851, 1041
Sidon [*sye*-dun], 132
Siemens [*see*-menz], Werner von, 813
Sienna, 419
Sierra Leone, 906, 1114
Sieyès [*syay*-yahs], Emmanuel, 711, 724, 727, 896
Sigismund (Holy Roman Empire), 397, 398, 414
Sigismund I (Poland), 474
Sigismund II (Poland), 415
Sigismund III (Poland), 532
Sihanouk [sih-hahn-*uk*], Norodom, 1073
Sikandar [sih-*kun*-dahr], 290
Sikhism [*seek*-izm], Sikhs, 175, 555–556, 743, 745, 758, 912, 1087

Silesia [sih-*lee*-zhuh], 357, 625, 669, 671, 694, 952, 1143
Silk Road, 80–81
Silk trade, 205–206, 307, 482, 488, 490, 545
Silla, 320–321
Simon, Richard, 647
Simons, Menno, 466
Sina, Ibn. *See* Avicenna
Sinai [*sye*-nye] Peninsula, 1097, 1098
Sinclair, Upton, 1008
Sind, 285, 289, 752, 758
Singapore, 820, 918, 1037, 1074, 1075, 1076
Sinhalese, 60–61, 746, 1091
Sinkiang (Xinjiang, Chinese Turkestan), 80, 81, 83, 84, 305, 310, 566, 767, 770, 771, 923, 1059
Sino-Soviet split, 1059–1060
Sistine Chapel, 433
Sitva-Torok, Treaty of, 625
Six Articles (1539), 468
Six Dynasties, 84
Sixtus IV, Pope, 409, 411, 420
Sixtus V, Pope, 650
Skepticism, 645–647, 698
Slavery: in ancient Mesopotamia, 19, 23; in ancient Egypt, 31–32; in Assyria, 40; in ancient China, 70–71; in classical Athens, 107; in the Hellenistic Age, 132; in classical Rome, 151, 156, 163; in early Islam, 214, 219–220; in early Africa, 240–241, 248, 249, 250, 251, 252; in the Aztec empire, 269; in the Portuguese colonies, 485, 488–489; in Spanish America, 498–499, 500, 505; in the West Indies, 535; in the Ottoman Empire, 542, 543; in the Americas, 660–664; Abolitionist Movement, 701–702; in Brazil, 865; in nineteenth-century Africa, 904, 905
Slavophils, 859
Slavs, 1012
Slovenia, 1162
Smallpox, 499
Smetona [smeh-to-*nah*], Antanas, 1022
Smith, Adam, 677, 689, 768, 796, 801, 802, 825, 835
Smolensk [smo-*lyensk*], 403
Smollett, Tobias, 705
Smyrna, 131
Smuts, Jan, 947
Sobieski [so-*byes*-kee], Jan, 617, 626
Soboul, Albert, 726
Social Contract, The (Rousseau), 688
Social Darwinism, 887–888
Social Democratic Party (SPD, Germany), 890–891, 1004, 1146, 1147
Social hierarchies, 587–590
Socialism, 835, 889–893
Socialist Party (Italy), 997–998
Social Revolutionary Party (Russia), 971, 972
Social War, 151
Society of Jesus. *See* Jesuits
Socinians, 466
ocrates [*sahk*-ruh-teez], 124
lidarity movement (Poland), 1161

Solinus, 509
Solomon, 34, 35–36, 187, 238
Solomon Islands, 1042
Solon [*soh*-luhn], 100
Solzhenitsyn [sol-zhuh-*neet*-sin], Aleksandr, 1143, 1155
Somalia, 1119, 1124
Somaliland, 907, 1027
Somaschi [soh-*mahs*-kee], 469
Somerset, Edward Seymour, Duke of, 468
Somme [*som*-eh], battle of, 948
Somoza García, Anastasio, 1136
Songhay [song-*hye*], empire of, 246, 247–248
Song of Igor's Campaign, 377
Song of Roland, 377, 400
Sonnenfels, Joseph von, 690
Soochow (Suzhou), 577
Sophists, 123–124
Sophocles [*sahf*-uh-kleez] 120–121
Sorbonne, 366, 369
Sorel, Georges, 890, 939
Sorrows of Young Werther, The (Goethe), 827, 828
South Africa, 253–254, 813, 909, 1115, 1119, 1120–1122, 1124; Union of (1910), 675
South America, Amerindians of: the earliest inhabitants, 256–257; the Chavín culture, 272–273; the Inca, 273–276
Southeast Asia: early farming in, 8; early religion in, 176, 177; spread of Islam to, 296–298, 357; in the medieval period, 298–302, 357; early European traders, 535; colonial regimes in, 918–921; in World War II, 1037; since World War II, 1070–1074, 1076; women in the modern period, 1075
Southern Christian Leadership Conference (SCLC), 1149
Southern Cult, 278
Southern Rhodesia, 1116
South Sea Bubble, 670
South Sea Company, 669
South Vietnam, 1071–1073
Southwest Africa, 489, 906, 908, 947
Soweto, 1122
Soyinka, Wole, 1124
Sozzini, Faustus [*fow*-stuhs soht-*tsee*-nee], 466
Sozzini, Lelio, 466
Space exploration, 1143, 1171
Spain: Second Punic War, 147–148; under the Visigoths, 170, 201; Muslims in, 217–218, 222; medieval, 331, 333, 336; during reconquista, 354–355; Jews in, 380; age of Ferdinand and Isabella, 404–406; colonial rule in the Americas, 496-499, 535–536, 657–660; under Philip II, 512–517; and the rebellion in the Netherlands, 517–519; Anglo-Spanish War, 519–520; in the early seventeenth century, 523–524, 526; colonial rivalry in the Americas, 535–536; colonies of, 657–660; and the American Revolutionary War, 673–674; loss of American empire, 677–680; in

the Napoleonic era, 730; in the nineteenth century, 821–822, 832, 883; loss of Pacific islands, 930; between the world wars, 1013; civil war in, 1028–1030; Spanish-American War, 883
Spanish Armada, 519–520
Spanish Civil War, 1028–1030
"Spanish Fury," 519
Spanish Inquisition, 515
Spanish Succession, War of the, 619–621
Sparta: in the classical period, 101, 108–109; and the Persian Wars, 102; in the Peloponnesian War, 109–112; and the rise of Macedon, 126
Spartacists (Germany), 1004, 1008
Spartacus [*spahr*-tuh-kuhs], revolt of, 151
Speer, Albert, 1011
Spencer, Herbert, 887–888
Spener [*shpay*-ner], Philip Jakob, 697
Spengler, Oswald, 957
Spenser, Edmund, 522
Speyer [*shpye*-er], Diet of, 461
Spice trade: ancient, 82, 133; medieval, 213, 238–239, 353, 402; early modern, 482–483, 485, 489, 490, 504, 546, 657, 745
Spinning jenny, 796
Spinoza, Baruch [*bah*-rook spih-*noh*-zah], 647–648, 699
Spirit of the Laws, The (Montesquieu), 689
Spiritual Exercises (Ignatius Loyola), 471
Spiritualists, 466
Squadristi, 998
Sri Lanka [sree *lahng*-kah], 1087, 1090–1092. *See also* Ceylon
Sri Vijaya [sree wih-*joh*-yah], 293, 301
SS (Schutzstaffel), 1007, 1038
Ssu-ma Ch'ien (Simaqian) [see-mah chyehn], 79, 87
Staël [stahl], Madame Germaine de, 828, 831
Stained glass, 374–375
Stalin, Joseph, 976–978, 1015–1018, 1030, 1033, 1040–1047 *passim*, 1143–1145, 1155
Stalingrad, 1144; battle of, 1041
Stamp Act Congress, 673
Stanley, Henry M., 906
Stanton, Elizabeth Cady, 704, 884
Star Chamber, 406, 529, 530
Starhemberg, Prince von, 1013
Stein [shtyne], Baron Karl vom, 732
Stein, Gertrude, 953, 954, 1020
Stendhal (Marie-Henri Beyle), 828–829
Sterne, Laurence, 705
Stöcker, Adolf, 862, 939
Stoicism, 137, 138, 139
Stolypin [stuh-*lee*-pyin], Peter, 969
Stowe, Harriet Beecher, 831
Strafford, Earl of, 529–530
Strasbourg, 459, 460, 462, 617, 714
Strasser, Gregor, 1007
Strasser, Otto, 1007
Strategic Defense Initiative (SDI), 1164
Stratonice, 138
Strauss, Johann, 858

Strauss, Richard, 858
Stresemann [*shtray*-zuh-mahn], Gustav, 952
Stuart dynasty, 406 528–530, 629
Students for a Democratic Society, 1150
Stupas [*stoop*-uhs], 61, 178
Sturm [shturm], Johannes, 459
Sturm und Drang movement, 827
"Successor States," 1021–1023
Suchou (Soochow, Suzhou), 315
Sudan, 233, 909, 1100, 1119, 1123; western and central, 243–250
Sudeten [soo-*day*-tuhn] crisis, 1030
Sudetenland, 1030, 1143
Suetonius [swee-*toh*-nih-uhs], 157
Suez Canal, 846, 861, 912, 947, 1100
Suez Canal Company, 908, 1097
Suffragettes, 885–887, 955
Sufism, 215, 216, 221, 223, 288, 291
Sugar, 498, 499, 505, 535, 571, 660, 661–663, 763
Suger [sur-*zhehr*], Abbot, 374
Suharto, T. N. J., 1071
Suicide, 594, 738
Sui [swee] dynasty, 305
Sukarno, Achmed, 1071
Suleiman I [soo-lay-*mahn*], 461, 540–541, 544
Sulla [*suhl*-uh], 151
Sully, Duke of, 524
Sumatra, 297, 301, 302, 490, 920
Sumba, Sumbanese, 737–738
Sumer [*soo*-mer], Sumerians, 12–13, 17–20, 47; relations with India, 48–50; writing in, 226
Summa Theologica (Aquinas), 370
Sundiata, 244–245
Sung dynasty, 310–316
Sunni [*soon*-ee] Muslims, 215, 761–762
Sun Yat-sen [soon yaht-sehn], 980–981, 982
Suppiluliumas [soo-pee-loo-lee-*oo*-mas], 36–37
Suppliant Women, The (Euripides), 122
Surat [soo-*raht*], 296, 535, 550, 556, 746, 747, 749, 752
Surrealists, 938, 958, 965
Suryavarman II, 300
Susa, 43
Su Shih (Su Tung-p'o, Su Dongpo), 312–313
Swabia, Philip of, 348
Swahili city-states, 252–253, 904
Swan, Joseph, 813
Swatow, 577
Sweden: and the Vikings, 333; Reformation in, 461; early modern, 523, 626; in the Napoleonic era, 733; modern, 883
Swift, Jonathan, 691
Swinburne, Algernon, 937
Swiss Brethren, 465
Swiss Confederation, 407, 524
Switzerland: Reformation in, 461–465; in the Napoleonic era, 724, 733; in the early nineteenth century, 832, 891; recent, 1148. *See also* Swiss Confederation
Sydney, 928

Sykes-Picot [syeks-pee-*koh*] Agreement, 947, 990
Symbolists, 937
Symonds, John Addington, 439, 440
Sympolity, 131
Symposium, The (Plato), 124–125
Syndicalism, 939
Syracuse, 93, 135
Syria: ancient, 27, 28, 31, 36–37, 38, 128; in the Byzantine Empire, 201; conquered by the Arabs, 215, 218; and the crusades, 351, 352; and the Ottomans, 540; modern, 947, 990, 1094, 1097, 1098, 1099, 1100, 1105, 1106
Szechuan (Sichuan) [seh-chwahn], 73, 583, 769, 1036

Table of Ranks, 623
Tacitus [*tass*-ih-tuhs], Cornelius, 157, 165
Tae-woo, Roh, 1069
Tagore [tah-*gohr*], Dwarkanath, 754
Tagore, Rabindranath, 754
Tahiti, 929
Tahmasp I [tah-*mahsp*], 560
Tahmasp II, 761
Taille [tah-yuh], 396, 407, 611
Taine [ten], Hippolyte, 725
Taipei [tye-pay], 1058, 1067, 1076
Taiping Rebellion, 922–923
T'ai-tsung (Taizong), 305, 306
Taiwan [tye-wahn] (Formosa), 583, 770, 925, 926, 927, 1058, 1059, 1067, 1075, 1076
Taj Mahal, 554
Talas River, battle of, 306
Tale of Genji [*gehn*-jee], *The* (Lady Murasaki), 324–325, 600
Talleyrand, Charles Maurice de, 732, 819, 820, 832
Talmon, J. L., 725
Talmud, 187–189, 474, 700
Tamayo, Rufino, 1139
Tamerlane, 290, 292, 539, 560, 568
Tamils, 61, 294, 1091
Tamralipiti, 56
Tanganyika [tang-guhn-*yee*-kuh], 905, 908, 1116
T'ang [tahng] dynasty, 305–310
Tangier [tan-*jir*], 942
Tanjore [tan-*johr*], 293
Tannenberg, battle of, 947
Tanzania, 1119, 1124
Taoism (Daoism) [*dow*-izm], 181–182, 193; conceptions of death, 386–387
Tapti [*tahp*-tee] River, 59
Tara Bai, 557
Tarascans, 271
Tarquinia, 144
Tarsus, 132
Tartars [*tah*-turz]. *See* Mongols
Tasmania, 806
Tasso [*tahs*-soh], Torquato, 648
Tatar-Pazarjik [tah-*tahr* pah-zahr-*jik*], 545
Taylor, Harriet, 884
Tea, 307, 753, 769, 912, 921
Tea ceremony, 327
Tecumseh [tee-*kum*-suh], 675
Teerling, Levina, 436

Teheran, 762
Teheran [te-*rahn*] Conference, 1041
Tel Aviv, 991
Telegraph, 813, 900
Telephone, 897
Television, 899–900
Tellier [tehl-*yay*], Michel le, 612, 614
Temple, William, 802
Ten Commandments, 185
Teng Hsiao-p'ing (Deng Xiaoping), 1065, 1066, 1067
Tennis Court Oath (1789), 713
Tenochtitlán [tay-nohch-tee-*tlahn*], 258–260, 267–268, 270, 271, 272, 495, 496
Teotihuacán [*tay*-oh-*tee*-wah-kahn], 264, 270
Terence, 164
Teresa of Avila [*ah*-vee-lah], 516
Teresa of Calcutta, Mother, 196
Terror, The (France), 722
Tertullian [tur-*tuhl*-yuhn], 192
Test Act (1673), 629, 833
Tet offensive, 1072
Tetrarchy (Roman Empire), 167–168
Tetzel, Johann, 457
Teutonic [too-*tahn*-ik] Knights, 352
Texas, 675, 864, 866, 1127
Textiles: in ancient India, 56, 63; cotton, 63, 82, 241, 545, 546, 558, 569, 577, 745, 746, 749, 757, 763, 796–797, 808, 912, 914, 921; hemp, 569; linen, 482, 569; silk, 69, 80–81, 82, 219, 241, 307, 482, 545, 546, 557, 561, 569, 570, 763, 769, 802, 811, 921; wool, 402, 557, 928
Thailand [*tye*-land] (Siam): religion in, 177; writing in, 230; Buddhism in, 296, 298–299; early history, 317; modern, 918, 920, 921, 1037, 1070, 1074, 1075, 1076
Thales [*thay*-leez] of Miletus [mye-*lee*-tuhs], 122
Thälmann [*tel*-mahn], Ernst, 1009
Thatcher, Margaret, 1130, 1147
Theaters, 648–649
Thebes [theebz], Egypt, 25
Thebes, Greece, 89, 110, 126, 127–128
Theme system, 207
Themistocles [thuh-*miss*-tuh-kleez], 102, 105
Theocritus [thee-*ok*-rih-tuhs], 138
Theodora, 203–205, 207
Theodoric, 201
Theodosius [thee-oh-*doh*-shuhs], 169
Theogony (Hesiod), 96
Theophrastus, 134–135
Thermidorian Reaction, 724–725
Thermopylae [thur-*mahp*-ih-lee], battle of, 102–103
Thessalonica, 206
Thessaly, 90
Thiers [tyehr], Adolphe, 832, 856–857, 879
Thieu [tyoo], Nguyen Van, 1073
Third International, 978–980
Third Reich, 1009
Thirty-nine Articles, 473
Thirty Years' War, 522–524

Thomas, Sidney, 813
Thomason, George, 896
Thomas the Apostle, 59, 191
Thousand and One Nights, 223
Three Mile Island nuclear accident, 1174–1175
Three Principles of the People, 981
Thucydides [thoo-*sid*-ih-deez], 2, 111
Thutmose III, 28
Thyssen [*tis*-ehn], August, 871
Tiberius [tye-*beer*-ee-uhs], 157
Tibet: Buddhism in, 285; early history, 305, 310, 317, 318; early modern, 566, 767, 770, 771; modern, 917, 942, 1059, 1067, 1085
Tienanmen Square demonstrations, 1066–1067
Tientsin (Tianjin), 577, 773, 921; Treaty of, 922
Tiglath-Pileser III, 39
Tigris [*tye*-grihs] River, 17
Tikal [tih-*kahl*], 260, 262, 263, 264
Tilak, Bal Gangadhar, 917
Tilsit, Treaty of, 733
Timbuktu [tim-buk-*too*], 241–242, 243, 245, 247, 248, 489
Time, nature of, 4–5
Time of Troubles (Russia), 533
Tintoretto, 516
Tirol [teh-*rohl*], 696, 998
Tirso de Molina [*teer*-soh day moh-*lee*-nah], 648
Tiryns [*tye*-rinz], 92
Titian [*tih*-shun], 432, 434, 516, 962
Tito (Josip Broz), 1144, 1160, 1162
Titus [*tye*-tuhs], 158
Tlatelolco, 267
Tlaxcala [tlahs-*kah*-lah], 495
Tlaxcaltecs, 271, 272
Tocqueville [*toke*-veel], Alexis de, 675, 726, 808, 835
Togo, 908, 947
Tojo Hideki, 1034, 1051
Toklas, Alice B., 954
Tokugawa [toh-koo-*gah*-wah] Ieyasu [ee-yeh-*yah*-soo], 328, 779–780, 781
Tokugawa shogunate, 779–783, 925
Tokyo, 786, 925, 1042, 1051, 1055–1056. *See also* Edo
Toledo [toh-*lay*-doh], 354, 515
Tolstoy, Leo, 824, 889
Toltecs [*tohl*-teks], 265–267, 270
Tongking, 300, 301; Gulf of, 1072, 1073
Tongking Gulf Resolution, 1073
Topa Inca Yupanqui [yoo-*pahng*-kee], 272
Topiltzin, 265–266, 268
Torah, 185–186
Tordesillas [tohr-day-*see*-lyahs], Treaty of (1494), 486
Torgau, battle of, 670
Tories, 629
Tornabuoni [tor-nah-*bwoh*-nee], Lucrezia, 426
Toronto, 1152
Torquemada [tor-kwee-*mah*-duh], Tomás de, 405
Torres [tohr-*rays*], Juan José, 1132
Totalitarianism, nature of, 995–996

Toulon [too-*lohn*], 728
Toulouse [too-*looz*], 731; University of, 366
Toulouse-Lautrec, Henri de [*ahn*-ree duh too-*looz* loh-*trek*], 888
Toungoo [taung-goo] dynasty, 298–299
Touraine [too-*rayn*], 341
Touré, Sékou, 1116
Tours [toor], battle of, 331
Toussaint L'Ouverture, François [frahn-swah too-*sanh* loo-ver-*toor*], 677
Townshend, Lord Charles, 794
Toynbee, Arnold, 2
Trade unions, 889, 890
Trading patterns: Paleolithic, 7; Neolithic, 9; in ancient Egypt and Mesopotamia, 27, 28, 32; of the Canaanites and Phoenicians, 33; of the ancient Hebrews, 34; Hittite, 37; ancient Persian, 42; in ancient India, 48-50, 58–59, 62, 63; in ancient China, 80–82; Minoan, 91; Mycenaean, 92; early Greek, 93–95, 98–99; in the Hellenistic Age, 132–134; in the Roman Empire, 155; Byzantine, 205–206; and the early Arabs, 213; in the early Islamic world, 218–219; Kushite, 236–237; role of Axium, 238–239; in trans-Sahara trade, 240–243; role of Mali, 245; in East Africa, 250–253; in southern Africa, 253–254; Adena and Hopewell cultures, 277; in medieval Southeast Asia, 298; ancient Chinese, 314–315; in medieval Europe, 336–338, 402–403; in early modern Europe, 482–483, 504, 659–660, 661–663; and the age of exploration, 488–490; in the Ottoman Empire, 546; in Ming China, 569–571, 577; in early modern India, 745–749; Iranian, 763; in early modern China, 769, 770–771; in early modern Japan, 777; in modern Asia, 984–986, 1026
Trafalgar, battle of, 730
Trajan [*tray*-juhn], 158–159, 162
Transcaucasus, 1164
Transjordan, 1099
Transubstantiation, 397, 472
Transvaal [trans-*vahl*] Republic, 909
Transylvania, 548, 625, 626
Trasformismo, 882
Treaty Ports (China), 924, 984–986
Treblinka [tre-*bleeng*-kah], 1038
Trent, Council of, 471–473, 477
Trentino [tren-*tee*-noh], 998
Tres Zapotes, 257
Tribonian [tri-*boh*-nih-uhn], 203
Tribunes (Roman), 145, 150, 151, 154
Tributary system (China), 566–567
Trieste [tree-*est*-uh], 998
Trinity, doctrine of the, 192, 193, 464, 466
Tripartite Pact, 1034
Tripitaka, 176
Triple Alliance, 941, 943
Triple Entente, 941–942, 943
Tripoli, 352
Trivium, 333, 366
Trojan War, 92, 93

Troppau [*trop*-ou] Protocol, 821, 822
Trotsky, Leon, 971–972, 973, 975, 977–978, 1017–1018
Trotula, 372
Troubadours [*troo*-buh-dohrz], 342, 377, 381, 400
Troy, 92
Troyes, Chrétien de [kray-*tyahn* duh trwah], 378
Trujillo [troo-*hee*-yoh], Rafael, 1135
Truman, Harry S, 1042, 1045–1048, 1053, 1069
Truman Doctrine, 1046–1047
Tudor dynasty, 406, 466–469, 528
Tu Fu (Du Fu) [too foo], 309–310
Tughluq, Firuz, 289–290
Tughluq, Muhammad, 289
Tughluqs, 289
Tukhachevsky [too-hah-*chef*-skee], Mikhail, 1018
Tula, 265–267, 272
Tull, Jethro, 794
Tung Lin (Donglin), 581
Tunisia, 215, 218, 333, 861, 907, 1100, 1103, 1122–1123
Tupac Amaru [too-pahk ah-*mah*-roo], 1131
Turgenev [too-*gyay*-nyeff], Ivan, 824, 889
Turgot, Anne-Robert [ahn roh-*bair* toor-goh], 709
Turhan, 543
Turkestan, 216, 218
Turkey: and the origins of World War I, 941, 943; and the Peace of Paris (1919), 952; the modern state, 992, 993, 1099; between the world wars, 1021-1022; in NATO, 1047
Turks, Seljuk, 216, 218, 285, 290. *See also* Ottoman Turks
Turner, J. M. W., 888
Tuscany, 143, 849
Tutankhamen [toot-ahng-*kah*-muhn], 30, 31
Twelve Tables (Rome), 145
Twenty-one Demands (1915), 926, 947, 981
Two Sicilies, Kingdom of the, 821, 849, 851
Two Treatises of Government (Locke), 686
Tyler, Wat, 394
Tyndale, William, 454, 466, 504
Tyrannicide, theory of, 371–372, 473
Tyrants, early Greek, 95, 100–101
Tyre [tihr], 352
Tzu Hsi (Cixi), 924

Uganda, 909, 1116, 1119
Ugarit, 33
Uighurs (Uigurs) [*wee*-gurz], 81
Ukraine [yew-*krayn*], 357, 532, 623, 973, 975, 1016, 1033, 1155, 1163, 1164, 1167, 1168
Ulema, 542, 547
Uli, 245
Ulm, battle of, 730
Ulmanis [*ool*-mah-nis], Karlis, 1023
Ulozhenie, 620
Ultraroyalists, 733

Ulysses (Joyce), 957
Umar, 215
Umayyad [oo-*mah*-yahd] caliphate, 215–217
Umberto I (Italy), 890, 1003
Umbrians, 143, 229
Union of Arras [*a*-rahs], 519
Union of Brussels, 519
Union of South Africa, 909, 1116
Union of Soviet Socialist Republics (USSR): after World War I, 952; founding of, 975; under Stalin, 977–980. 1015–1018, 1045–1047; events leading to World War II, 1030–1031; in World War II, 1031–1033, 1034, 1040–1042, 1044; and the origins of the Cold War, 1045–1047; Sino-Soviet split, 1059–1060; and the Arab-Israeli wars, 1097; postwar reconstruction, 1143; postwar relations with eastern Europe, 1143–1144, 1145; the Khrushchev era, 1144-1145; role of women, 1148; postwar relations with the United States, 1153–1155, 1156–1157, 1163; Moscow, 1155–1156; and the revolutions in eastern Europe, 1160–1162; disarmament negotiations, 1163; Gorbachev and the collapse of the USSR, 1163-1169
Union Treaty, 1165
United Arab Emirates, 1101
United Arab Republic, 1100–1101
United Nations (UN): founding, 1041, 1044–1045; and Korea, 1065–1069; and the Middle East, 1093–1094, 1097, 1105
United States: colonial origins, 671–673; revolutionary war, 673–674; founding the nation, 674–675; constitution, 674–675; westward expansion, 675-676; during the first phase of the Industrial Revolution, 813; westward expansion, 864; civil war, 864–865; during the second phase of the Industrial Revolution, 870–871; and the Mexican War, 866; imperialism in the Pacific, 929; in World War I, 949–950; and the Peace of Paris (1919), 950–952; after World War I, 952; in the Great Depression, 1018–1021; in World War II, 1033–1034, 1036, 1037, 1040–1042, 1044; and the origins of the Cold War, 1045–1048; postwar occupation of Japan, 1051–1053; and the Vietnam War, 1072–1073; and the Arab-Israeli wars, 1097; and the Gulf War, 1105; invasion of Panama, 1132; Cuban missile crisis, 1134–1135; and the Nicaraguan revolution, 1136; civil rights movement, 1148–1150; role of women, 1150–1151; relations with Canada, 1151–1152; relations with USSR after the Cold War, 1153–1155, 1156–1157, 1163
United States Geological Survey, 1110
Universal Exhibition (1888), 937–938
Universities, 365–366, 459. *See also* specific schools
Upanishads [oo-*pah*-nih-shahdz], 64, 173, 386

Upper Volta, 1119
Ur, 18–19
Urban II, Pope, 351
Urban VI, Pope, 397
Urban VIII, Pope, 650
Urban planning: in ancient China, 85; early Greek, 98; Hellenistic, 134; classical Roman, 162; Aztec, 258–259; Chinese, 307–308; modern European, 874-875
Ure, Andrew, 798
Uris, Leon, 1155
Ursulines, 469–470, 601
Uruguay, 865, 866, 1140
Uruk, 12, 226
Ussher, James, 683
Usury, 218, 463, 500
Uthman, 215
Utilitarianism, 884
Utopia (More), 455–456
Utrecht [*yoo*-trekt], Peace of, 620
Utrecht, Union of, 519

Vaddas, 60
Vakaranga [vah-kah-*rahng*-gah], 489
Valencia, 221
Valens, 201
Valéry [va-lay-ree], Paul, 957
Valla, Lorenzo [loh-*rayn*-tsoh *vah*-lah], 420, 424–425, 427
Valladolid, 515
Valmy [*val*-mee], battle of, 719
Valois [vahl-*wah*] dynasty, 407–408, 520–521
Vancouver, George, 1110
Vandals, 170, 331
Van den Vondel, Joost, 648
Van Dyck [van *dike*], Anthony, 650
Van Hemessen, Catharina, 436
Vargas [*vahr*-guhs], Getúlio, 1013–1015, 1127
Varro, 164
Vasari [vah-*zah*-ree], Giorgio, 420, 435, 438, 961
Vassals, 335
Vassy [*va*-see], massacre at, 520
Vasvar, Truce of, 626
Vatican City, 882, 1001
Vedas [*vay*-dahs], 52, 53, 64, 173, 175
Vedic culture, 53
Veii [*vee*-eye], 144, 146, 151
Velázquez [vay-*lahs*-keth], Diego, 650
Vendée [vahn-*day*], 720, 722
Venetia [vuh-*nee*-shuh], 849, 850, 852, 854
Venezuela, 678, 680, 865, 1101, 1140
Venice: medieval, 338, 339, 340, 402, 411–412; Renaissance in, 418, 420, 429–430, 434; early modern, 517, 724, 820; modern, 838, 839
Veracruz, 495
Verbiest, Ferdinand, 578
Verdun [ver-*duhn*], battle of, 948
Verdun, Treaty of, 333
Vergerio, Pietro Paolo, 423–424
Verlaine [ver-*len*], Paul, 937
Versailles [vehr-*sye*], Palace of, 615–616, 650, 712, 715, 726, 879

Versailles, Treaty of, 950–952
Verus, Lucius, 166
Vesalius [vih-*say*-lee-uhs], Andreas, 639
Vespasian [veh-*spay*-zhuhn], 157–158
Vespucci, Amerigo [ah-may-*ree*-goh vay-*spoot*-chee], 488, 509
Vesuvius [vuh-*soo*-vee-uhs], 161
Vichy [*vee*-shee] France, 1032, 1037
Victor Emmanuel I (Sardinia), 822
Victor Emmanuel II (Italy), 851–852
Victor Emmanuel III (Italy), 857, 883, 998, 999, 1041
Victoria (Great Britain), 878, 912
Victoria (Prussia), 843
Victorian Age, 878–879
Vienna [vee-*ehn*-uh], 339, 532, 540, 541, 617, 626, 705–706, 874, 1004–1005; University of, 459; in the age of Franz Joseph, 857–858
Vienna, Congress of, 818–820, 852
Vienna, Peace of, 854
Vietnam: early history, 79, 83, 299, 300–301, 305, 310, 317; religion in, 181; writing in, 230; and China, 566, 581, 771; Neo-Confucianism in, 181; colonial rule, 918, 920, 921; since World War II, 1070–1073
Vietnam War, 1071–1073, 1156
Vigée-Lebrun [vee-*zhay*-leh-*bren*], Elizabeth, 704
Vijaya [*vij*-ah-ya], 60
Vijayanagar [*vij*-ah-ya-nuhg-er], 295–296, 745
Vikings, 333–334, 345
Villa [*vee*-yah], Pancho, 1137
Villafranca [veel-lah-*frahng*-kah], armistice of, 850
Villa-Lobos [vee-luh-*loh*-boos], Heitor, 1139
Villanovan culture, 143
Villehardouin [veel-ahr-*dwahn*], Geoffrey de, 378
Villon, François [frahn-*swah* vee-yon], 400–401
Vindhyas, 556
Vindication of the Rights of Woman, A (Wollstonecraft), 704
Virgil, 156–157
Virginia, 471
Virginia Bay Company, 657
Visconti [vees-*kahn*-tee] family, 408
Vishnu [*vish*-noo], 173, 174
Visigoths, 169–170, 201
Vision of Piers Plowman, The (Langland), 400
Vitruvius [vih-*troo*-vee-uhs], 164
Vittorino da Feltre [*fel*-tray], 424
Vladimir [*vlad*-uh-meer], 357
Vladivostock [vlad-ih-*vah*-stock], 923, 974
Volgograd, 1144
Volsci [*vol*-sye], 146
Volta, Alessandro, 813
Voltaire (François-Marie Arouet), 439, 687, 690, 691, 693, 702, 705, 768
Von Bell, Adam Schall, 579
Vulgate, 425, 472

Wagner, Richard [*rik*-art *vahg*-nur], 828, 939

Wakefield, Edward Gibbon, 929
Walata, 241–242
Waldensians, 364, 381
Waldo, Peter, 364
Waldseemüller, Martin, 509
Walesa, Lech [lek vah-*wenz*-ah], 1161
Wallachia [wo-*lay*-kih-uh], 859, 860, 861
Wallenstein [*vahl*-ehn-shtyne], Albrecht von, 523
Walpole, Robert, 666
Walther von der Vogelweide [*vahl*-ter fon der *foh*-guhl-vye-duh], 378
Wang Mang, 83
Wang Yang-ming, 576
Wan-li, 493, 581, 583
War and Peace (Tolstoy), 824, 889
"War communism," 973
Ward, Lester, 884
Warfare: ancient Chinese, 73–74; early Greek, 95; classical Greek, 102–103, 111–112; Aztec, 272; Turkish, 285; Mongol, 316–317; late medieval, 394–395; early modern, 666
Warhol, Andy, 965
War of 1812, 675, 733
War of the Pacific, 866
Warsaw, Grand Duchy of, 730, 733, 820
Warsaw Pact, 1160
Wars of the Roses, 406
Washington, George, 671, 674, 675, 1110
Waste Land, The (Eliot), 958
Watergate scandal, 1157
Waterloo, battle of, 733–734
Water Margins, 573–574
Watt, James, 789, 797
Watteau [wah-*toh*], Antoine, 704
Watts riots (Los Angeles), 1150
Wavell, Archibald, Earl of, 1079
Wealth of Nations, The (Adam Smith), 677, 689, 796, 801
Weathermen, 1150
Webb, Beatrice Potter, 884, 891
Webb, Sydney, 891
Webern [*vay*-bern], Anton, 858
Wedgwood, Josiah, 773, 802
Wegener [*vay*-guh-ner], Alfred, 1111
Wei, 581
Wei [way] dynasty, 84
Weill [vyel], Kurt, 1008
Weimar [*vye*-mahr], 827
Weimar Republic, 1004, 1007–1008, 1009
Wei [way] Valley, 71–72, 77, 81, 305
Weizmann [*vyets*-mahn], Chaim, 863, 990, 1094
Wellesley, Richard, 752
Wellington, Sir Arthur Wellesley, Duke of, 730, 733, 823, 833
Wells, H. G., 891
Wenceslas [*wen*-suhs-los], 398
Wesley, Charles, 697
Wesley, John, 697, 698
West Germany, 1047, 1146–1147, 1158, 1160
West Indies, 535, 662, 663, 672, 674, 820
Westminster, Statute of (1931), 1152
Westphalia [west-*fayl*-yah], 730, 812; Peace of, 523–524; Conference of, 626
...t nursing, 595–596

Wheel, invention of, 13
When the Gods Were Men, 20
Whigs, 629–630
White Army, 973
Whitefield, George, 697
White Huns, 63
White Lotus sect, 564, 772, 773
White Mountain, battle of, 523
White Sea, 500
White Terror, 724
Widows, 877
Wilberforce, William, 702, 804
Wilde, Oscar, 877, 937, 954
Wilkinson, William, 811
William, Duke of Normandy, 334, 341
William I (Germany), 853, 855, 890
William I (Netherlands), 832
William II (Germany), 863, 878, 881, 908, 909, 932, 941–942, 944, 950, 1004
William II (Netherlands), 527
William III (England; William of Orange), 617–619, 622, 629–630
William the Good, Duke, 362
William the Silent, 518–519
Willoughby, Sir Hugh, 500
Wilson, Woodrow, 949, 950, 952, 974, 998, 1092
Winckelmann [*ving*-kuhl-mahn], Johann Joachim, 705
Windischgratz [*vin*-dish-*grahts*], Alfred, 839
Winstanley, Gerrard, 530, 646, 686
Witchcraft, 393, 464, 474–476
Witte, Sergei [syir-*gyay*-ee *vit*-uh], 859
Wittenberg [*vit*-uhn-berk], 458; University of, 457, 459
Wittgenstein [*vit*-ghen-shtyne], Ludwig, 957
Wolff [volf], Christian, 690, 705
Wollstonecraft, Mary, 703–704, 831
Women: in prehistory, 9, 10; in ancient Mesopotamia, 19; in ancient Egypt, 28–31, 32; ancient Hebrew, 35; Hittite, 37–38; in ancient India, 63–65; in Madurai, 60; in classical Athens, 106–107; Aristotle's view of, 126; in the Hellenistic Age, 137–139; in classical Rome, 162–164; in early Christianity, 191; in the ancient world religions, 195–196; in Byzantine empire, 207–208; in early Islamic society, 220–221; in Ghana, 243; in Mali, 245–246; in East Africa, 252; Maya, 263; Aztec, 269–270; Inca, 275–276; Chinese, 308; in medieval Europe, 335; in medieval Christianity, 363–364; and Gothic art, 374–375; and medieval literature, 377–378; in medieval Europe, 381–383; in the European Renaissance, 424, 425–427, 430, 435–436; in the early Lutheran movement, 458–459, 460; Calvin's view of, 464–465; and Anabaptists, 465; as witchcraft victims, 475–476; as rulers in the late sixteenth century, 521-522; Quaker, 530–532; in the Ottoman Empire, 542–543; in early modern Europe, 591–592, 595–597; in early modern Asia, 592–593, 594–595; in the

early modern Middle East and Africa, 595; in the Enlightenment, 702–704; in the French Revolution, 723–724, 726; in Napoleonic France, 729; in Tokugawa Japan, 783; in the first phase of the Industrial Revolution, 799–801; and Romanticism, 830–831; in the France of Napoleon III, 846–847; in modern Europe before World War I, 875–877, 883–887, 892–893; in World War I, 949; between the World Wars in the West, 954–957; in the Soviet Union, 1017; in the modern Middle East, 993; and Italian Fascism, 1002; in Nazi Germany, 1010; in modern Japan, 1054–1055; in modern China, 1066; in modern East Asia, 1074-1075; in modern South Asia, 1091–1092; and the Islamic revolution, 1103-1104; in Latin America, 1136, 1139–1140; in modern Africa, 1124; in postwar western Europe, 1147–1148; in the postwar Soviet Union, 1148; in the postwar United States, 1150–1151
Women's liberation movements, 1148, 1151
Women's Social and Political Union (WSPU), 886
Women's suffrage, 885–887, 955, 1148
Woolf [wulf], Virginia, 957
Wordsworth, William, 717, 828, 829
Working class, modern, 873–874, 875, 952–959 *passim*
Works and Days (Hesiod), 96
World Health Organization, 1045
World War I: origins of, 939–945; the fighting, 945–948, 949–950; social consequences, 948–949, 954–956; peace settlement, 950–952
World War II: origins of, 1025–1030; in Europe, 1031–1033, 1037–1038, 1040-1042; America's entry, 1033–1034; in Asia, 1033–1037, 1042; the Holocaust, 1038–1040
World Zionist Organization, 863
Worms [vorms], Diet at, 457–458
Wren, Christopher, 631
Wright, Frank Lloyd, 959
Writing, 12, 47, 58, 60, 69, 70, 72, 76, 91, 92, 226–231, 238, 260, 323, 333
Wu Chao (Wuzhao), 305–306
Württemberg [*vuhrt*-tem-berk], 461
Wu Ti [woo tee], 79–81
Wyatt, Sir Thomas, 473
Wyclif [*wik*-liff], John, 397–398, 466

Xavier [*zay*-vih-er], Francis, 471, 492, 494
Xenophon [*zen*-uh-fuhn], 111
Xerxes [*zurk*-seez], 42, 102
Ximenes [hee-*may*-nes], Francisco, 405–406, 469

Yalta Conference, 1042, 1045
Yamato Plain, 323
Yang Shao [yahng show] culture, 69–70
Yang Ti [yahng tee], 305
Yangtze delta, 315
Yangtze [*yahng*-tsee] River, 86

Yangtze Valley: ancient, 70, 72, 73, 76, 306, 311, 314, 317; in the Ming era, 564, 578; in the modern era, 773, 923
Yaroslav [yahr-uh-*slahv*] the Wise, 356
Yasovarman I, 299
Yathrib (Medina), 215
Yeats [yates], William Butler, 958
Yellow River, 69, 78
Yeltsin, Boris, 1163, 1164–1168
Yemen, 239, 1099, 1103, 1106
Yenan (Yanan), 982, 1058
Yi dynasty, 321–323
Yin and Yang, 181, 196
Yokohama, 1051, 1056
Yom Kippur [yom kih-*poor*], 188
Yom Kippur War, 1096, 1101
York, house of, 406
Yorktown, battle at, 674
Yoruba [*yoh*-roo-bah], 250, 595, 1119
Young, Arthur, 710, 794, 795, 810
Young Bosnia movement, 944
Young Italy movement, 833
Young Turk Movement, 992, 1099
Ypres [*ee*-pruh], 339; battle of, 948
Yü [yoo], 70
Yuan [yoo-ahn] dynasty, 317–319, 564
Yuan Shih-kai (Yuan Shikai), 981
Yucatán [yoo-kuh-*tan*] Peninsula, 258, 265

Yüeh (Yue), kingdom of, 76, 79
Yugoslavia: between the world wars, 952, 1021–1022; in World War II, 1033; after World War II, 1045, 1046, 1144, 1146, 1160, 1162
Yukon, 280
Yung-lo (Yongluo), 566, 573, 576, 577
Yunnan [yewn-*nahn*], 80, 769

Zaibatsu, 1026
Zaïre [zah-*eer*], 1116, 1119, 1124
Zakat [*zuh*-kaht], 214
Zama [*zay*-muh], battle of, 148
Zambesi [zam-*bee*-zee] River, 657, 906
Zambia, 1116, 1119
Zanzibar, 906
Zapata [sah-*pah*-tah], Emiliano, 1137
Zara [*dzah*-rah], 352
Zaria, 249
Zasulich, Vera, 975
Zealots, 190
Zemski sobor [*zem*-skee soh-*bohr*], 533
Zemstvos [*zemst*-vohze], 859
Zen (Ch'an) Buddhism, 178, 326–327
Zenghi, 352
Zeno [*zee*-noh] of Elea, 130, 137, 139
Zenta, battle of, 626
Zetkin, Clara, 892–893
Zevi, Sabbatai, 699, 1092

Zhenotdel, 1017
Zhivkov, Todor, 1162
Zia-ul-Huq, General, 1089
Ziggurat [zih-guh-*rat*], 18
Zimbabwe [zim-*bah*-bway], 253–254, 904
Zinoviev [zyih-*noff*-yeff], Grigori, 977–978, 980, 1017
Zinzendorf [*tsin*-tsen-dorf], Nicholas von, 697
Zionism, 862–864, 990, 1092–1096 *passim*
Zirid dynasty, 355
Zoë [*zoh*-ee], 403
Zog (Albania), 1022
Zola, Émile [*ay*-meel zoh-*lah*], 880, 889
Zollverein [*tsol*-fur-ine], 812, 853
Zorndorf, battle of, 670
Zoroaster [*zohr*-oh-as-ter] (Zarathustra), 182–183
Zoroastrianism [zoh-roh-*as*-tree-uhn-izm], 182–184
Zoser, 24
Zuazo, Hernan Siles, 1132
Zulu, 905, 906, 909, 910, 1122
Zurbarán [thoor-bah-*rahn*], Francisco de, 649
Zurich [*zoo*-rik], 462, 465
Zwickau [*tsvik*-ou], 466
Zwingli, Ulrich [*tsving*-lee], 461–462, 465, 477

BRAND NAME	ANALGESIC	ANTIHISTAMINE	DECONGESTANT	COUGH SUPPRESSANT	EXPECTORANT	DOSAGE
ANTIHISTAMINES + DECONGESTANTS + ANALGESICS *(Continued)*						
Theraflu Warming Relief Nighttime Severe Cold & Cough Syrup	Acetaminophen 325mg/15mL	Diphenhydramine HCl 12.5mg/15mL	Phenylephrine HCl 5mg/15mL			**Adults & Peds ≥12 yrs:** 2 tbl (30mL) q4h. **Max:** 6 doses (12 tbl or 180mL)/24h.
Theraflu Warming Relief Sinus & Cold Syrup	Acetaminophen 325mg/15mL	Diphenhydramine HCl 12.5mg/15mL	Phenylephrine HCl 5mg/15mL			**Adults & Peds ≥12 yrs:** 2 tbl (30mL) q4h. **Max:** 6 doses (12 tbl or 180mL)/24h.
Vicks NyQuil Sinex Nighttime Sinus Relief LiquiCaps	Acetaminophen 325mg	Doxylamine succinate 6.25mg	Phenylephrine HCl 5mg			**Adults & Peds ≥12 yrs:** 2 caps q4h. **Max:** 4 doses/24h.
COUGH SUPPRESSANTS						
Children's Delsym 12 Hour Cough Relief Liquid*				Dextromethorphan HBr 30mg/5mL		**Adults & Peds ≥12 yrs:** 2 tsp (10mL) q12h. **Max:** 4 tsp (20mL)/24h. **Peds 6–12 yrs:** 1 tsp (5mL) q12h. **Max:** 2 tsp (10mL)/24h. **Peds 4–<6 yrs:** ½ tsp (2.5mL) q12h. **Max:** 1 tsp (5mL)/24h.
Children's Robitussin Cough Long-Acting				Dextromethorphan HBr 7.5mg/5mL		**Adults & Peds ≥12 yrs:** 4 tsp (20mL) q6-8h. **Peds 6–<12 yrs:** 2 tsp (10mL) q6-8h. **Max:** 4 doses/24h.
Delsym 12 Hour Cough Relief Liquid*				Dextromethorphan HBr 30mg/5mL		**Adults & Peds ≥12 yrs:** 2 tsp (10mL) q12h. **Max:** 4 tsp (20mL)/24h. **Peds 6–<12 yrs:** 1 tsp (5mL) q12h. **Max:** 2 tsp (10mL)/24h. **Peds 4–<6 yrs:** ½ tsp (2.5mL) q12h. **Max:** 1 tsp (5mL)/24h.
Robitussin Lingering Cold Long-Acting Cough				Dextromethorphan HBr 15mg/5mL		**Adults & Peds ≥12 yrs:** 2 tsp (10mL) q6-8h. **Max:** 4 doses/24h.
Robitussin Lingering Cold Long-Acting CoughGels				Dextromethorphan HBr 15mg		**Adults & Peds ≥12 yrs:** 2 caps q6-8h. **Max:** 8 caps/24h.
Triaminic Long-Acting Cough Syrup				Dextromethorphan HBr 7.5mg/5mL		**Peds 6–<12 yrs:** 2 tsp (10mL) q6-8h. **Peds 4–<6 yrs:** 1 tsp (5mL) q6-8h. **Max:** 4 doses/24h.

(Continued)

BRAND NAME	ANALGESIC	ANTIHISTAMINE	DECONGESTANT	COUGH SUPPRESSANT	EXPECTORANT	DOSAGE
COUGH SUPPRESSANTS *(Continued)*						
Vicks BabyRub Soothing Aroma Ointment				Petrolatum, fragrance, aloe extract, eucalyptus oil, lavender oil, rosemary oil		**Peds ≥3 months:** Gently massage on the chest, neck, and back to help soothe and comfort.
Vicks DayQuil Cough Liquid				Dextromethorphan HBr 15mg/15mL		**Adults & Peds ≥12 yrs:** 2 tbl (30mL) q6-8h. **Peds 6–12 yrs:** 1 tbl (15mL) q6-8h. **Max:** 4 doses/24h.
Vicks VapoDrops*				Menthol 1.7mg (cherry); Menthol 3.3mg (menthol)		**Adults & Peds ≥5 yrs:** 3 drops (cherry). **Adults & Peds ≥5 yrs:** 2 drops (menthol).
Vicks VapoRub Topical Ointment				Camphor 4.8%, Menthol 2.6%, Eucalyptus oil 1.2%		**Adults & Peds ≥2 yrs:** Apply to chest and throat. **Max:** 3 times/24h.
Vicks VapoSteam				Camphor 6.2%		**Adults & Peds ≥2 yrs:** 1 tbl/quart of water or 1½ tsp/pint of water (for use in a hot steam vaporizer). **Max:** 3 times/24h.
COUGH SUPPRESSANTS + ANTIHISTAMINES						
Children's Dimetapp Long Acting Cough Plus Cold Syrup		Chlorpheniramine maleate 1mg/5mL		Dextromethorphan HBr 7.5mg/5mL		**Adults & Peds ≥12 yrs:** 4 tsp (20mL) q6h. **Peds 6–<12 yrs:** 2 tsp (10mL) q6h. **Max:** 4 doses/24h.
Children's Robitussin Cough & Cold Long-Acting		Chlorpheniramine maleate 1mg/5mL		Dextromethorphan HBr 7.5mg/5mL		**Adults & Peds ≥12 yrs:** 4 tsp (20mL) q6h. **Peds 6–<12 yrs:** 2 tsp (10mL) q6h. **Max:** 4 doses/24h.
Coricidin HBP Cough & Cold		Chlorpheniramine maleate 4mg		Dextromethorphan HBr 30mg		**Adults & Peds ≥12 yrs:** 1 tab q6h. **Max:** 4 tabs/24h.
Robitussin Maximum Strength Nighttime Cough DM Liquid		Doxylamine succinate 12.5mg/10mL		Dextromethorphan HBr 30mg/10mL		**Adults & Peds ≥12 yrs:** 2 tsp (10mL) q6h. **Max:** 4 doses/24h.
Vicks Children's NyQuil Cold & Cough Liquid		Chlorpheniramine maleate 2mg/15mL		Dextromethorphan HBr 15mg/15mL		**Adults & Peds ≥12 yrs:** 2 tbl (30mL) q6h. **Peds 6–11 yrs:** 1 tbl (15mL) q6h. **Max:** 4 doses/24h.
Vicks NyQuil Cough Liquid		Doxylamine succinate 12.5mg/30mL		Dextromethorphan HBr 30mg/30mL		**Adults & Peds ≥12 yrs:** 2 tbl (30mL) q6h. **Max:** 4 doses/24h.

BRAND NAME	ANALGESIC	ANTIHISTAMINE	DECONGESTANT	COUGH SUPPRESSANT	EXPECTORANT	DOSAGE
COUGH SUPPRESSANTS + ANALGESICS						
PediaCare Children Cough & Sore Throat Plus Acetaminophen	Acetaminophen 160mg/5mL			Dextromethorphan HBr 5mg/5mL		**Peds 6-11 yrs (48-95 lbs):** 2 tsp (10mL) q4h. **Max:** 5 doses/24h.
Triaminic Cough & Sore Throat Syrup	Acetaminophen 160mg/5mL			Dextromethorphan HBr 5mg/5mL		**Peds 6-<12 yrs:** 2 tsp (10mL) q4h. **Peds 4-<6 yrs:** 1 tsp (5mL) q4h. **Max:** 5 doses/24h.
COUGH SUPPRESSANTS + ANTIHISTAMINES + ANALGESICS						
Contac Cold + Flu Night Instant Cooling Relief Liquid	Acetaminophen 500mg/15mL	Doxylamine succinate 6.25mg/15mL		Dextromethorphan HBr 15mg/15mL		**Adults & Peds ≥12 yrs:** 2 tbl (30mL) q6h. **Max:** 6 tbl (90mL)/24h.
Coricidin HBP Day & Night Multi-Symptom Cold	Acetaminophen 500mg (nighttime dose only)	Chlorpheniramine maleate 2mg (nighttime dose only)		Dextromethorphan HBr 10mg (daytime dose), 15mg (nighttime dose)	Guaifenesin 200mg (daytime dose only)	(Day) **Adults & Peds ≥12 yrs:** 1-2 softgels q4h. **Max:** 6 caps/12h. (Night) **Adults & Peds ≥12 yrs:** 2 tabs hs and q6h. **Max:** 4 tabs/12h.
Coricidin HBP Maximum Strength Flu	Acetaminophen 500mg	Chlorpheniramine maleate 2mg		Dextromethorphan HBr 15mg		**Adults & Peds ≥12 yrs:** 2 tabs q6h. **Max:** 8 tabs/24h.
Coricidin HBP Nighttime Multi-Symptom Cold Liquid	Acetaminophen 500mg/15mL (10 fl oz bottle), Acetaminophen 325mg/15mL (12 fl oz bottle)	Doxylamine succinate 6.25mg/15mL		Dextromethorphan HBr 15mg/15mL		**Adults & Peds ≥12 yrs:** 2 tbl (30mL) q6h. **Max:** 4 doses/24h.
Delsym Night Time Multi-Symptom Liquid	Acetaminophen 325mg/15mL	Doxylamine succinate 6.25mg/15mL		Dextromethorphan HBr 15mg/15mL		**Adults & Peds ≥12 yrs:** 2 tbl (30mL) q6h. **Max:** 4 doses/24h.
PediaCare Children Cough & Runny Nose Plus Acetaminophen	Acetaminophen 160mg/5mL	Chlorpheniramine maleate 1mg/5mL		Dextromethorphan HBr 5mg/5mL		**Peds 6-11 yrs (48-95 lbs):** 2 tsp (10mL) q4h. **Max:** 5 doses/24h.
Robitussin Peak Cold Nighttime Cold + Flu Liquicaps	Acetaminophen 325mg	Doxylamine succinate 6.25mg		Dextromethorphan HBr 15mg		**Adults & Peds ≥12 yrs:** 2 caps q6h. **Max:** 8 caps/24h.
Triaminic Multi-Symptom Fever Syrup	Acetaminophen 160mg/5mL	Chlorpheniramine maleate 1mg/5mL		Dextromethorphan HBr 7.5mg/5mL		**Peds 6-<12 yrs:** 2 tsp (10mL) q6h. **Max:** 4 doses/24h.
Vicks Alcohol Free NyQuil Cold & Flu Relief Liquid	Acetaminophen 650mg/30mL	Chlorpheniramine maleate 4mg/30mL		Dextromethorphan HBr 30mg/30mL		**Adults & Peds ≥12 yrs:** 2 tbl (30mL) q6h. **Max:** 4 doses/24h.
Vicks NyQuil Cold & Flu Relief LiquiCaps	Acetaminophen 325mg	Doxylamine succinate 6.25mg		Dextromethorphan HBr 15mg		**Adults & Peds ≥12 yrs:** 2 caps q6h. **Max:** 4 doses/24h.

(Continued)

BRAND NAME	ANALGESIC	ANTIHISTAMINE	DECONGESTANT	COUGH SUPPRESSANT	EXPECTORANT	DOSAGE
COUGH SUPPRESSANTS + ANTIHISTAMINES + ANALGESICS *(Continued)*						
Vicks NyQuil Cold & Flu Relief Liquid	Acetaminophen 650mg/30mL	Doxylamine succinate 12.5mg/30mL		Dextromethorphan HBr 30mg/30mL		**Adults & Peds ≥12 yrs:** 2 tbl (30mL) q6h. **Max:** 4 doses/24h.
COUGH SUPPRESSANTS + ANTIHISTAMINES + ANALGESICS + DECONGESTANTS						
Alka-Seltzer Plus Cold & Cough Formula Effervescent Tablets	Aspirin 325mg	Chlorpheniramine maleate 2mg	Phenylephrine bitartrate 7.8mg	Dextromethorphan HBr 10mg		**Adults & Peds ≥12 yrs:** 2 tabs q4h. **Max:** 8 tabs/24h.
Alka-Seltzer Plus Cold & Cough Formula Liquid Gels	Acetaminophen 325mg	Chlorpheniramine maleate 2mg	Phenylephrine HCl 5mg	Dextromethorphan HBr 10mg		**Adults & Peds ≥12 yrs:** 2 caps q4h. **Max:** 10 caps/24h.
Alka-Seltzer Plus-D Multi-Symptom Sinus & Cold Liquid Gels	Acetaminophen 325mg	Chlorpheniramine maleate 2mg	Pseudoephedrine HCl 30mg	Dextromethorphan HBr 10mg		**Adults & Peds ≥12 yrs:** 2 caps q4h. **Max:** 8 caps/24h.
Alka-Seltzer Plus Night Cold Formula Effervescent Tablets	Aspirin 500mg	Doxylamine succinate 6.25mg	Phenylephrine bitartrate 7.8mg	Dextromethorphan HBr 10mg		**Adults & Peds ≥12 yrs:** 2 tabs q4-6h. **Max:** 8 tabs/24h.
Alka-Seltzer Plus Night Cold & Flu Formula Liquid Gels	Acetaminophen 325mg	Doxylamine succinate 6.25mg	Phenylephrine HCl 5mg	Dextromethorphan HBr 10mg		**Adults & Peds ≥12 yrs:** 2 caps q4h. **Max:** 10 caps/24h.
Alka-Seltzer Plus Severe Cold & Flu Formula Effervescent Tablets	Acetaminophen 250mg	Chlorpheniramine maleate 2mg	Phenylephrine HCl 5mg	Dextromethorphan HBr 10mg		**Adults & Peds ≥12 yrs:** 2 tabs q4h. **Max:** 8 tabs/24h.
Alka-Seltzer Plus Severe Sinus Congestion Allergy & Cough Liquid Gels	Acetaminophen 325mg	Doxylamine succinate 6.25mg	Phenylephrine HCl 5mg	Dextromethorphan HBr 10mg		**Adults & Peds ≥12 yrs:** 2 caps q4h. **Max:** 10 caps/24h.
Children's Dimetapp Multi-Symptom Cold & Flu Syrup	Acetaminophen 160mg/5mL	Chlorpheniramine maleate 1mg/5mL	Phenylephrine HCl 2.5mg/5mL	Dextromethorphan HBr 5mg/5mL		**Adults & Peds ≥12 yrs:** 4 tsp (20mL) q4h. **Peds 6-12 yrs:** 2 tsp (10mL) q4h. **Max:** 5 doses/24h.
PediaCare Children Flu Plus Acetaminophen	Acetaminophen 160mg/5mL	Chlorpheniramine maleate 1mg/5mL	Phenylephrine HCl 2.5mg/5mL	Dextromethorphan HBr 5mg/5mL		**Peds 6-11 yrs (48-95 lbs):** 2 tsp (10mL) q4h. **Max:** 5 doses/24h.
PediaCare Children Multi-Symptom Cold Plus Acetaminophen	Acetaminophen 160mg/5mL	Chlorpheniramine maleate 1mg/5mL	Phenylephrine HCl 2.5mg/5mL	Dextromethorphan HBr 5mg/5mL		**Peds 6-11 yrs (48-95 lbs):** 2 tsp (10mL) q4h. **Max:** 5 doses/24h.
Theraflu Warming Relief Nighttime Multi-Symptom Cold Caplets	Acetaminophen 325mg	Chlorpheniramine maleate 2mg	Phenylephrine HCl 5mg	Dextromethorphan HBr 10mg		**Adults & Peds ≥12 yrs:** 2 tabs q4h. **Max:** 12 tabs/24h.
Tylenol Cold Multi-Symptom Nighttime Liquid	Acetaminophen 325mg/15mL	Doxylamine succinate 6.25mg/15mL	Phenylephrine HCl 5mg/15mL	Dextromethorphan HBr 10mg/15mL		**Adults & Peds ≥12 yrs:** 2 tbl (30mL) q4h. **Max:** 10 tbl (150mL)/24h.

BRAND NAME	ANALGESIC	ANTIHISTAMINE	DECONGESTANT	COUGH SUPPRESSANT	EXPECTORANT	DOSAGE
COUGH SUPPRESSANTS + ANTIHISTAMINES + ANALGESICS + DECONGESTANTS *(Continued)*						
Vicks Nyquil Severe Cold + Flu Liquid	Acetaminophen 650mg/30mL	Doxylamine succinate 12.5mg/30mL	Phenylephrine HCl 10mg/30mL	Dextromethorphan HBr 20mg/30mL		**Adults & Peds ≥12 yrs:** 2 tbl (30mL) q4h. **Max:** 4 doses/24h.
COUGH SUPPRESSANTS + ANTIHISTAMINES + DECONGESTANTS						
Children's Dimetapp Cold & Cough Syrup		Brompheniramine maleate 1mg/5mL	Phenylephrine HCl 2.5mg/5mL	Dextromethorphan HBr 5mg/5mL		**Adults & Peds ≥12 yrs:** 4 tsp (20mL) q4h. **Peds 6-<12 yrs:** 2 tsp (10mL) q4h. **Max:** 6 doses/24h.
COUGH SUPPRESSANTS + DECONGESTANTS						
Children's Sudafed PE Cold & Cough Liquid			Phenylephrine HCl 2.5mg/5mL	Dextromethorphan HBr 5mg/5mL		**Peds 6-11 yrs:** 2 tsp (10mL) q4h. **Peds 4-5 yrs:** 1 tsp (5mL) q4h. **Max:** 6 doses/24h.
PediaCare Children Daytime Multi-Symptom Cold			Phenylephrine HCl 2.5mg/5mL	Dextromethorphan HBr 5mg/5mL		**Peds 6-11 yrs (48-95 lbs):** 2 tsp (10mL) q4h. **Peds 4-5 yrs (36-47 lbs):** 1 tsp (5mL) q4h. **Max:** 6 doses/24h.
PediaCare Children Nighttime Multi-Symptom Cold			Phenylephrine HCl 2.5mg/5mL	Diphenhydramine HCl 6.25mg/5mL		**Peds 6-11 yrs (48-95 lbs):** 2 tsp (10mL) q4h. **Max:** 6 doses/24h.
Triaminic Day Time Cold & Cough Syrup			Phenylephrine HCl 2.5mg/5mL	Dextromethorphan HBr 5mg/5mL		**Peds 6-<12 yrs:** 2 tsp (10mL) q4h. **Peds 4-<6 yrs:** 1 tsp (5mL) q4h. **Max:** 6 doses/24h.
COUGH SUPPRESSANTS + DECONGESTANTS + ANALGESICS						
Alka-Seltzer Plus Day & Night Cold & Flu Formula Liquid Gels	Acetaminophen 325mg	Doxylamine succinate 6.25mg (nighttime dose only)	Phenylephrine HCl 5mg	Dextromethorphan HBr 10mg		**Adults & Peds ≥12 yrs:** 2 caps q4h. **Max:** 10 caps/24h.
Alka-Seltzer Plus Day & Night Multi-Symptom Cold Formula Effervescent Tablets	Aspirin 325mg (day); Aspirin 500mg (night)	Doxylamine succinate 6.25mg (nighttime dose only)	Phenylephrine bitartrate 7.8mg	Dextromethorphan HBr 10mg		(Day) **Adults & Peds ≥12 yrs:** 2 tabs q4h. **Max:** 8 tabs/24h. (Night) **Adults & Peds ≥12 yrs:** 2 tabs q4-6h. **Max:** 8 tabs/24h.
Alka-Seltzer Plus Day Non-Drowsy Cold & Flu Formula Liquid Gels	Acetaminophen 325mg		Phenylephrine HCl 5mg	Dextromethorphan HBr 10mg		**Adults & Peds ≥12 yrs:** 2 caps q4h. **Max:** 10 caps/24h.

(Continued)

BRAND NAME	ANALGESIC	ANTIHISTAMINE	DECONGESTANT	COUGH SUPPRESSANT	EXPECTORANT	DOSAGE
COUGH SUPPRESSANTS + DECONGESTANTS + ANALGESICS *(Continued)*						
Alka-Seltzer Plus Severe Sinus Congestion & Cough Liquid Gels	Acetaminophen 325mg		Phenylephrine HCl 5mg	Dextromethorphan HBr 10mg		**Adults & Peds ≥12 yrs:** 2 caps q4h. **Max:** 10 caps/24h.
Robitussin Peak Cold Daytime Cold + Flu Liquid-Filled Capsules	Acetaminophen 325mg		Phenylephrine HCl 5mg	Dextromethorphan HBr 10mg		**Adults & Peds ≥12 yrs:** 2 caps q4h. **Max:** 12 caps/24h.
Sudafed PE Pressure + Pain + Cough Caplets	Acetaminophen 325mg		Phenylephrine HCl 5mg	Dextromethorphan HBr 10mg		**Adults & Peds ≥12 yrs:** 2 tabs q4h. **Max:** 10 tabs/24h.
Theraflu Daytime Severe Cold & Cough Powder Packets	Acetaminophen 650mg/packet		Phenylephrine HCl 10mg/packet	Dextromethorphan HBr 20mg/packet		**Adults & Peds ≥12 yrs:** 1 pkt q4h. **Max:** 6 pkts/24h.
Theraflu Multi-Symptom Severe Cold with Lipton Green Tea & Honey Lemon Flavors Powder Packets	Acetaminophen 500mg/packet		Phenylephrine HCl 10mg/packet	Dextromethorphan HBr 20mg/packet		**Adults & Peds ≥12 yrs:** 1 pkt q4h. **Max:** 6 pkts/24h.
Theraflu Warming Relief Daytime Multi-Symptom Cold Caplets	Acetaminophen 325mg		Phenylephrine HCl 5mg	Dextromethorphan HBr 10mg		**Adults & Peds ≥12 yrs:** 2 tabs q4h. **Max:** 12 tabs/24h.
Theraflu Warming Relief Daytime Severe Cold & Cough Syrup	Acetaminophen 325mg/15mL		Phenylephrine HCl 5mg/15mL	Dextromethorphan HBr 10mg/15mL		**Adults & Peds ≥12 yrs:** 2 tbl (30mL) q4h. **Max:** 6 doses/24h.
Tylenol Cold Multi-Symptom Daytime Caplets	Acetaminophen 325mg		Phenylephrine HCl 5mg	Dextromethorphan HBr 10mg		**Adults & Peds ≥12 yrs:** 2 caps q4h. **Max:** 10 caps/24h.
Tylenol Cold Multi-Symptom Daytime Liquid	Acetaminophen 325mg/15mL		Phenylephrine HCl 5mg/15mL	Dextromethorphan HBr 10mg/15mL		**Adults & Peds ≥12 yrs:** 2 tbl (30mL) q4h. **Max:** 10 tbl (150mL)/24h.
Vicks DayQuil Cold & Flu Relief LiquiCaps	Acetaminophen 325mg		Phenylephrine HCl 5mg	Dextromethorphan HBr 10mg		**Adults & Peds ≥12 yrs:** 2 caps q4h. **Max:** 4 doses/24h.
Vicks DayQuil Cold & Flu Relief Liquid	Acetaminophen 325mg/15mL		Phenylephrine HCl 5mg/15mL	Dextromethorphan HBr 10mg/15mL		**Adults & Peds ≥12 yrs:** 2 tbl (30mL) q4h. **Peds 6–<12 yrs:** 1 tbl (15mL) q4h. **Max:** 4 doses/24h.

BRAND NAME	ANALGESIC	ANTIHISTAMINE	DECONGESTANT	COUGH SUPPRESSANT	EXPECTORANT	DOSAGE
COUGH SUPPRESSANTS + DECONGESTANTS + EXPECTORANTS						
Children's Mucinex Congestion & Cough Liquid			Phenylephrine 2.5mg/5mL	Dextromethorphan HBr 5mg/5mL	Guaifenesin 100mg/5mL	**Peds 6-<12 yrs:** 2 tsp (10mL) q4h. **Peds 4-<6 yrs:** 1 tsp (5mL) q4h. **Max:** 6 doses/24h.
Children's Mucinex Multi-Symptom Cold Liquid			Phenylephrine 2.5mg/5mL	Dextromethorphan HBr 5mg/5mL	Guaifenesin 100mg/5mL	**Peds 6-<12 yrs:** 2 tsp (10mL) q4h. **Peds 4-<6 yrs:** 1 tsp (5mL) q4h. **Max:** 6 doses/24h.
Children's Robitussin Cough & Cold CF			Phenylephrine HCl 2.5mg/5mL	Dextromethorphan HBr 5mg/5mL	Guaifenesin 50mg/5mL	**Adults & Peds ≥12 yrs:** 4 tsp (20mL) q4h. **Peds 6-<12 yrs:** 2 tsp (10mL) q4h. **Max:** 6 doses/24h.
Mucinex Maximum Strength Fast-Max Severe Congestion & Cough Caplets			Phenylephrine HCl 5mg	Dextromethorphan HBr 10mg	Guaifenesin 200mg	**Adults & Peds ≥12 yrs:** 2 tabs q4h. **Max:** 12 tabs/24h.
Mucinex Maximum Strength Fast-Max Severe Congestion & Cough Liquid			Phenylephrine HCl 10mg/20mL	Dextromethorphan HBr 20mg/20mL	Guaifenesin 400mg/20mL	**Adults & Peds ≥12 yrs:** 4 tsp (20mL) q4h. **Max:** 6 doses/24h.
Robitussin Peak Cold Maximum Strength Multi-Symptom Cold CF			Phenylephrine HCl 10mg/10mL	Dextromethorphan HBr 20mg/10mL	Guaifenesin 400mg/10mL	**Adults & Peds ≥12 yrs:** 2 tsp (10mL) q4h. **Max:** 6 doses/24h.
Robitussin Peak Cold Multi-Symptom Cold CF			Phenylephrine HCl 5mg/5mL	Dextromethorphan HBr 10mg/5mL	Guaifenesin 100mg/5mL	**Adults & Peds ≥12 yrs:** 2 tsp (10mL) q4h. **Max:** 6 doses/24h.
COUGH SUPPRESSANTS + DECONGESTANTS + EXPECTORANTS + ANALGESICS						
Children's Mucinex Cold, Cough & Sore Throat Liquid	Acetaminophen 325mg/10mL		Phenylephrine HCl 5mg/10mL	Dextromethorphan HBr 10mg/10mL	Guaifenesin 200mg/10mL	**Peds 6-<12 yrs:** 2 tsp (10mL) q4h. **Max:** 5 doses/24h.
Children's Mucinex Multi-Symptom Cold & Fever Liquid	Acetaminophen 325mg/10mL		Phenylephrine HCl 5mg/10mL	Dextromethorphan HBr 10mg/10mL	Guaifenesin 200mg/10mL	**Peds 6-<12 yrs:** 2 tsp (10mL) q4h. **Max:** 5 doses/24h.
Delsym Day Time Cough + Cold Liquid	Acetaminophen 650mg/20mL		Phenylephrine HCl 10mg/20mL	Dextromethorphan HBr 20mg/20mL	Guaifenesin 400mg/20mL	**Adults & Peds ≥12 yrs:** 4 tsp (20mL) q4h. **Max:** 6 doses/24h.
Mucinex Maximum Strength Fast-Max Cold, Flu & Sore Throat Caplets	Acetaminophen 325mg		Phenylephrine HCl 5mg	Dextromethorphan HBr 10mg	Guaifenesin 200mg	**Adults & Peds ≥12 yrs:** 2 tabs q4h. **Max:** 12 tabs/24h.

(Continued)

BRAND NAME	ANALGESIC	ANTIHISTAMINE	DECONGESTANT	COUGH SUPPRESSANT	EXPECTORANT	DOSAGE
COUGH SUPPRESSANTS + DECONGESTANTS + EXPECTORANTS + ANALGESICS *(Continued)*						
Mucinex Maximum Strength Fast-Max Cold, Flu & Sore Throat Liquid	Acetaminophen 650mg/20mL		Phenylephrine HCl 10mg/20mL	Dextromethorphan HBr 20mg/20mL	Guaifenesin 400mg/20mL	**Adults & Peds ≥12 yrs:** 4 tsp (20mL) q4h. **Max:** 6 doses/24h.
Mucinex Maximum Strength Fast-Max Severe Cold Liquid	Acetaminophen 650mg/20mL		Phenylephrine HCl 10mg/20mL	Dextromethorphan HBr 20mg/20mL	Guaifenesin 400mg/20mL	**Adults & Peds ≥12 yrs:** 4 tsp (20mL) q4h. **Max:** 6 doses/24h.
Mucinex Maximum Strength Fast-Max Severe Congestion & Cold Caplets	Acetaminophen 325mg		Phenylephrine HCl 5mg	Dextromethorphan HBr 10mg	Guaifenesin 200mg	**Adults & Peds ≥12 yrs:** 2 tabs q4h. **Max:** 12 tabs/24h.
Sudafed PE Pressure + Pain + Cold Caplets	Acetaminophen 325mg		Phenylephrine HCl 5mg	Dextromethorphan HBr 10mg	Guaifenesin 100mg	**Adults & Peds ≥12 yrs:** 2 tabs q4h. **Max:** 10 tabs/24h.
Theraflu Max-D Severe Cold & Flu Powder Packets	Acetaminophen 1000mg/packet		Pseudoephedrine HCl 60mg/packet	Dextromethorphan HBr 30mg/packet	Guaifenesin 400mg/packet	**Adults & Peds ≥12 yrs:** 1 pkt q6h. **Max:** 4 pkts/24h.
Tylenol Cold & Flu Severe Caplets	Acetaminophen 325mg		Phenylephrine HCl 5mg	Dextromethorphan HBr 10mg	Guaifenesin 200mg	**Adults & Peds ≥12 yrs:** 2 tabs q4h. **Max:** 10 tabs/24h.
Tylenol Cold & Flu Severe Warming Liquid	Acetaminophen 325mg/15mL		Phenylephrine HCl 5mg/15mL	Dextromethorphan HBr 10mg/15mL	Guaifenesin 200mg/15mL	**Adults & Peds ≥12 yrs:** 2 tbl (30mL) q4h. **Max:** 10 tbl (150mL)/24h.
Tylenol Cold Multi-Symptom Severe Liquid	Acetaminophen 325mg/15mL		Phenylephrine HCl 5mg/15mL	Dextromethorphan HBr 10mg/15mL	Guaifenesin 200mg/15mL	**Adults & Peds ≥12 yrs:** 2 tbl (30mL) q4h. **Max:** 10 tbl (150mL)/24h.
Vicks Dayquil Severe Cold & Flu Relief Caplets	Acetaminophen 325mg		Phenylephrine HCl 5mg	Dextromethorphan HBr 10mg	Guaifenesin 200mg	**Adults & Peds ≥12 yrs:** 2 tabs q4h. **Max:** 4 doses/24h.
COUGH SUPPRESSANTS + EXPECTORANTS						
Alka-Seltzer Plus Max Cough, Mucus & Congestion Liquid Gels				Dextromethorphan HBr 10mg	Guaifenesin 200mg	**Adults & Peds ≥12 yrs:** 2 caps q4h. **Max:** 12 caps/24h.
Children's Delsym DM Cough + Chest Congestion Liquid				Dextromethorphan HBr 5mg/5mL	Guaifenesin 100mg/5mL	**Adults & Peds ≥12 yrs:** 2-4 tsp (10-20mL) q4h. **Peds 6-<12 yrs:** 1-2 tsp (5-10mL) q4h. **Peds 4-<6 yrs:** ½-1 tsp (2.5-5mL) q4h. **Max:** 6 doses/24h.
Children's Mucinex Cough Liquid				Dextromethorphan HBr 5mg/5mL	Guaifenesin 100mg/5mL	**Peds 6-<12 yrs:** 1-2 tsp (5-10mL) q4h. **Peds 4-<6 yrs:** ½-1 tsp (2.5-5mL) q4h. **Max:** 6 doses/24h.

BRAND NAME	ANALGESIC	ANTIHISTAMINE	DECONGESTANT	COUGH SUPPRESSANT	EXPECTORANT	DOSAGE
COUGH SUPPRESSANTS + EXPECTORANTS (Continued)						
Coricidin HBP Chest Congestion & Cough				Dextromethorphan HBr 10mg	Guaifenesin 200mg	**Adults & Peds ≥12 yrs:** 1-2 caps q4h. **Max:** 12 caps/24h.
Delsym DM Cough + Chest Congestion Liquid				Dextromethorphan HBr 20mg/20mL	Guaifenesin 400mg/20mL	**Adults & Peds ≥12 yrs:** 4 tsp (20mL) q4h. **Max:** 6 doses/24h.
Mucinex Cough Mini-Melts				Dextromethorphan HBr 5mg/packet	Guaifenesin 100mg/packet	**Adults & Peds ≥12 yrs:** 2-4 pkts q4h. **Peds 6-<12 yrs:** 1-2 pkts q4h. **Peds 4-<6 yrs:** 1 pkt q4h. **Max:** 6 doses/24h.
Mucinex DM				Dextromethorphan HBr 30mg	Guaifenesin 600mg	**Adults & Peds ≥12 yrs:** 1-2 tabs q12h. **Max:** 4 tabs/24h.
Mucinex DM Maximum Strength				Dextromethorphan HBr 60mg	Guaifenesin 1200mg	**Adults & Peds ≥12 yrs:** 1 tab q12h. **Max:** 2 tabs/24h.
Mucinex Maximum Strength Fast-Max DM Max Liquid				Dextromethorphan HBr 20mg/20mL	Guaifenesin 400mg/20mL	**Adults & Peds ≥12 yrs:** 4 tsp (20mL) q4h. **Max:** 6 doses/24h.
PediaCare Children Cough & Congestion				Dextromethorphan HBr 5mg/5mL	Guaifenesin 100mg/5mL	**Peds 6-11 yrs (48-95 lbs):** 1-2 tsp (5-10mL). **Peds 4-6 yrs (36-47 lbs):** ½-1 tsp (2.5-5mL). **Max:** 6 doses/24h.
Robitussin Maximum Strength Cough + Chest Congestion DM Liquid-Filled Capsules				Dextromethorphan HBr 10mg	Guaifenesin 200mg	**Adults & Peds ≥12 yrs:** 2 caps q4h. **Max:** 12 caps/24h.
Robitussin Peak Cold Cough + Chest Congestion DM				Dextromethorphan HBr 10mg/5mL	Guaifenesin 100mg/5mL	**Adults & Peds ≥12 yrs:** 2 tsp (10mL) q4h. **Max:** 6 doses/24h.
Robitussin Peak Cold Maximum Strength Cough + Chest Congestion DM				Dextromethorphan HBr 10mg/5mL	Guaifenesin 200mg/5mL	**Adults & Peds ≥12 yrs:** 2 tsp (10mL) q4h. **Max:** 6 doses/24h.
Robitussin Peak Cold Sugar-Free Cough + Chest Congestion DM				Dextromethorphan HBr 10mg/5mL	Guaifenesin 100mg/5mL	**Adults & Peds ≥12 yrs:** 2 tsp (10mL) q4h. **Max:** 6 doses/24h.
Vicks DayQuil Mucus Control DM Liquid				Dextromethorphan HBr 10mg/15mL	Guaifenesin 200mg/15mL	**Adults & Peds ≥12 yrs:** 2 tbl (30mL) q4h. **Peds 6-<12 yrs:** 1 tbl (15mL) q4h. **Max:** 6 doses/24h.

(Continued)

BRAND NAME	ANALGESIC	ANTIHISTAMINE	DECONGESTANT	COUGH SUPPRESSANT	EXPECTORANT	DOSAGE
DECONGESTANTS						
Children's Sudafed Nasal Decongestant Liquid			Pseudoephedrine HCl 15mg/5mL			**Peds 6-11 yrs:** 2 tsp (10mL) q4-6h. **Peds 4-5 yrs:** 1 tsp (5mL) q4-6h. **Max:** 4 doses/24h.
Children's Sudafed PE Nasal Decongestant Liquid			Phenylephrine HCl 2.5mg/5mL			**Peds 6-11 yrs:** 2 tsp (10mL) q4h. **Peds 4-5 yrs:** 1 tsp (5mL) q4h. **Max:** 6 doses/24h.
Dristan 12-hr Nasal Spray			Oxymetazoline HCl 0.05%			**Adults & Peds ≥12 yrs:** 2-3 sprays in each nostril q10-12h. **Max:** 2 doses/24h.
Mucinex Sinus-Max Full Force Nasal Spray			Oxymetazoline HCl 0.05%			**Adults & Peds ≥6 yrs:** 2-3 sprays in each nostril q10-12h. **Max:** 2 doses/24h.
Mucinex Sinus-Max Moisture Smart Nasal Spray			Oxymetazoline HCl 0.05%			**Adults & Peds ≥6 yrs:** 2-3 sprays in each nostril q10-12h. **Max:** 2 doses/24h.
Nostrilla			Oxymetazoline HCl 0.05%			**Adults & Peds ≥6 yrs:** 2-3 sprays in each nostril q10-12h. **Max:** 2 doses/24h.
Sudafed 12-Hour Tablets			Pseudoephedrine HCl 120mg			**Adults & Peds ≥12 yrs:** 1 tab q12h. **Max:** 2 tabs/24h.
Sudafed 24-Hour Tablets			Pseudoephedrine HCl 240mg			**Adults & Peds ≥12 yrs:** 1 tab/24h. **Max:** 1 tab/24h.
Sudafed Congestion Caplets[†]			Pseudoephedrine HCl 30mg			**Adults & Peds ≥12 yrs:** 2 tabs q4-6h. **Max:** 8 tabs/24h. **Peds 6-11 yrs:** 1 tab q4-6h. **Max:** 4 tabs/24h.
Sudafed PE Congestion Tablets[†]			Phenylephrine HCl 10mg			**Adults & Peds ≥12 yrs:** 1 tab q4h. **Max:** 6 tabs/24h.
Vicks Sinex 12-Hour Decongestant Nasal Spray			Oxymetazoline HCl 0.05%			**Adults & Peds ≥6 yrs:** 2-3 sprays in each nostril q10-12h. **Max:** 2 doses/24h.
Vicks Sinex 12-Hour Decongestant UltraFine Mist Moisturizing Nasal Spray			Oxymetazoline HCl 0.05%			**Adults & Peds ≥6 yrs:** 2-3 sprays in each nostril q10-12h. **Max:** 2 doses/24h.

BRAND NAME	ANALGESIC	ANTIHISTAMINE	DECONGESTANT	COUGH SUPPRESSANT	EXPECTORANT	DOSAGE
DECONGESTANTS *(Continued)*						
Vicks Sinex 12-Hour Decongestant UltraFine Mist Nasal Spray			Oxymetazoline HCl 0.05%			**Adults & Peds ≥6 yrs:** 2-3 sprays in each nostril q10-12h. **Max:** 2 doses/24h.
Vicks VapoInhaler			Levmetamfetamine 50mg			**Adults & Peds ≥12 yrs:** 2 inhalations in each nostril q2h. **Peds 6-<12 yrs:** 1 inhalation in each nostril q2h.
DECONGESTANTS + ANALGESICS						
Advil Cold & Sinus Caplets/ Liqui-Gels	Ibuprofen 200mg		Pseudoephedrine HCl 30mg			**Adults & Peds ≥12 yrs:** 1-2 caps q4-6h. **Max:** 6 caps/24h.
Advil Congestion Relief Tablets	Ibuprofen 200mg		Phenylephrine HCl 10mg			**Adults & Peds ≥12 yrs:** 1 tabs q4h. **Max:** 6 tabs/24h.
Contac Cold + Flu Maximum Strength Non-Drowsy Caplets	Acetaminophen 500mg		Phenylephrine HCl 5mg			**Adults & Peds ≥12 yrs:** 2 tabs q6h. **Max:** 8 tabs/24h.
Robitussin Peak Cold Nasal Relief	Acetaminophen 325mg		Phenylephrine HCl 5mg			**Adults & Peds ≥12 yrs:** 2 tabs q4h. **Max:** 12 tabs/24h.
Sudafed 12-Hour Pressure + Pain Caplets	Naproxen sodium 220mg		Pseudoephedrine HCl 120mg			**Adults & Peds ≥12 yrs:** 1 tab q12h. **Max:** 2 tabs/24h.
Sudafed PE Pressure + Pain Caplets	Acetaminophen 325mg		Phenylephrine HCl 5mg			**Adults & Peds ≥12 yrs:** 2 tabs q4h. **Max:** 10 tabs/24h.
Tylenol Sinus Congestion & Pain Daytime Caplets	Acetaminophen 325mg		Phenylephrine HCl 5mg			**Adults & Peds ≥12 yrs:** 2 caps q4h. **Max:** 10 caps/24h.
Vicks DayQuil Sinex Daytime Sinus Relief LiquiCaps	Acetaminophen 325mg		Phenylephrine HCl 5mg			**Adults & Peds ≥12 yrs:** 2 caps q4h. **Max:** 4 doses/24h.
DECONGESTANTS + EXPECTORANTS						
Children's Mucinex Stuffy Nose & Cold Liquid			Phenylephrine HCl 2.5mg/5mL		Guaifenesin 100mg/5mL	**Peds 6-<12 yrs:** 2 tsp (10mL) q4h. **Peds 4-<6 yrs:** 1 tsp (5mL) q4h. **Max:** 6 doses/24h.
Entex T			Pseudoephedrine HCl 60mg		Guaifenesin 375mg	**Adults & Peds ≥12 yrs:** 1 tab q4h. **Peds 6-<12 yrs:** ½ tab q4h. **Max:** 4 doses/24h.

(Continued)

BRAND NAME	ANALGESIC	ANTIHISTAMINE	DECONGESTANT	COUGH SUPPRESSANT	EXPECTORANT	DOSAGE
DECONGESTANTS + EXPECTORANTS *(Continued)*						
Mucinex D			Pseudoephedrine HCl 60mg		Guaifenesin 600mg	**Adults & Peds ≥12 yrs:** 2 tabs q12h. **Max:** 4 tabs/24h.
Mucinex D Maximum Strength			Pseudoephedrine HCl 120mg		Guaifenesin 1200mg	**Adults & Peds ≥12 yrs:** 1 tab q12h. **Max:** 2 tabs/24h.
Sudafed PE Non-Drying Sinus Caplets†			Phenylephrine HCl 5mg		Guaifenesin 200mg	**Adults & Peds ≥12 yrs:** 2 tabs q4h. **Max:** 12 tabs/24h.
Triaminic Chest & Nasal Congestion Syrup			Phenylephrine HCl 2.5mg/5mL		Guaifenesin 50mg/5mL	**Peds 6–<12 yrs:** 2 tsp (10mL) q4h. **Peds 4–<6 yrs:** 1 tsp (5mL) q4h. **Max:** 6 doses/24h.
DECONGESTANTS + EXPECTORANTS + ANALGESICS						
Mucinex Maximum Strength Fast-Max Cold & Sinus Caplets	Acetaminophen 325mg		Phenylephrine HCl 5mg		Guaifenesin 200mg	**Adults & Peds ≥12 yrs:** 2 tabs q4h. **Max:** 12 tabs/24h.
Mucinex Maximum Strength Fast-Max Cold & Sinus Liquid	Acetaminophen 650mg/20mL		Phenylephrine HCl 10mg/20mL		Guaifenesin 400mg/20mL	**Adults & Peds ≥12 yrs:** 4 tsp (20mL) q4h. **Max:** 6 doses/24h.
Mucinex Maximum Strength Sinus-Max Pressure & Pain Caplets	Acetaminophen 325mg		Phenylephrine HCl 5mg		Guaifenesin 200mg	**Adults & Peds ≥12 yrs:** 2 tabs q4h. **Max:** 12 tabs/24h.
Mucinex Maximum Strength Sinus-Max Severe Congestion Relief Caplets	Acetaminophen 325mg		Phenylephrine HCl 5mg		Guaifenesin 200mg	**Adults & Peds ≥12 yrs:** 2 tabs q4h. **Max:** 12 tabs/24h.
Sudafed PE Pressure + Pain + Mucus Caplets	Acetaminophen 325mg		Phenylephrine HCl 5mg		Guaifenesin 200mg	**Adults & Peds ≥12 yrs:** 2 tabs q4h. **Max:** 10 tabs/24h.
Sudafed Triple Action Caplets†	Acetaminophen 325mg		Pseudoephedrine HCl 30mg		Guaifenesin 200mg	**Adults & Peds ≥12 yrs:** 2 tabs q4-6h. **Max:** 8 tabs/24h.
Theraflu Warming Relief Cold & Chest Congestion Liquid	Acetaminophen 325mg/15mL		Phenylephrine HCl 5mg/15mL		Guaifenesin 200mg/15mL	**Adults & Peds ≥12 yrs:** 2 tbl (30mL) q4h. **Max:** 6 doses/24h.
Tylenol Cold Head Congestion Severe Caplets	Acetaminophen 325mg		Phenylephrine HCl 5mg		Guaifenesin 200mg	**Adults & Peds ≥12 yrs:** 2 tabs q4h. **Max:** 10 tabs/24h.
Tylenol Sinus Congestion & Pain Severe Caplets	Acetaminophen 325mg		Phenylephrine HCl 5mg		Guaifenesin 200mg	**Adults & Peds ≥12 yrs:** 2 tabs q4h. **Max:** 10 tabs/24h.

BRAND NAME	ANALGESIC	ANTIHISTAMINE	DECONGESTANT	COUGH SUPPRESSANT	EXPECTORANT	DOSAGE
EXPECTORANTS						
Children's Mucinex Chest Congestion Liquid					Guaifenesin 100mg/5mL	**Peds 6–<12 yrs:** 1-2 tsp (5-10mL) q4h. **Peds 4–<6 yrs:** ½-1 tsp (2.5-5mL) q4h. **Max:** 6 doses/24h.
Mucinex					Guaifenesin 600mg	**Adults & Peds ≥12 yrs:** 1-2 tabs q12h. **Max:** 4 tabs/24h.
Mucinex Maximum Strength					Guaifenesin 1200mg	**Adults & Peds ≥12 yrs:** 1 tab q12h. **Max:** 2 tabs/24h.
Mucinex Mini-Melts (Bubble Gum Flavor)					Guaifenesin 100mg/packet	**Adults & Peds ≥12 yrs:** 2-4 pkts q4h. **Peds 6–<12 yrs:** 1-2 pkts q4h. **Peds 4–<6 yrs:** 1 pkt q4h. **Max:** 6 doses/24h.
Mucinex Mini-Melts (Grape Flavor)					Guaifenesin 50mg/packet	**Peds 6–<12 yrs:** 2-4 pkts q4h. **Peds 4–<6 yrs:** 1-2 pkts q4h. **Max:** 6 doses/24h.
Robitussin Mucus + Chest Congestion Liquid					Guaifenesin 200mg/10mL	**Adults & Peds ≥12 yrs:** 2-4 tsp (10-20mL) q4h. **Max:** 6 doses/24h.
EXPECTORANTS + ANALGESICS						
Theraflu Flu & Chest Congestion Powder Packets	Acetaminophen 1000mg/packet				Guaifenesin 400mg/packet	**Adults & Peds ≥12 yrs:** 1 pkt q6h. **Max:** 4 pkts/24h.
ANTIHISTAMINES + ANALGESICS						
Advil PM Caplets	Ibuprofen 200mg	Diphenhydramine citrate 38mg				**Adults & Peds ≥12 yrs:** 2 tabs hs. **Max:** 2 tabs/24h.
Advil PM Liqui-Gels	Ibuprofen 200mg	Diphenhydramine HCl 25mg				**Adults & Peds ≥12 yrs:** 2 caps hs. **Max:** 2 caps/24h.
Coricidin HBP Cold & Flu	Acetaminophen 325mg	Chlorpheniramine maleate 2mg				**Adults & Peds ≥12 yrs:** 2 tabs q4-6h. **Max:** 12 tabs/24h. **Peds 6–<12 yrs:** 1 tab q4-6h. **Max:** 5 tabs/24h.

(Continued)

A85

BRAND NAME	ANALGESIC	ANTIHISTAMINE	DECONGESTANT	COUGH SUPPRESSANT	EXPECTORANT	DOSAGE
ANTIHISTAMINES + ANALGESICS *(Continued)*						
Motrin PM Caplets	Ibuprofen 200mg	Diphenhydramine citrate 38mg				**Adults & Peds ≥12 yrs:** 2 tabs hs. **Max:** 2 tabs/24h.
Tylenol PM Caplets[†]	Acetaminophen 500mg	Diphenhydramine HCl 25mg				**Adults & Peds ≥12 yrs:** 2 tabs hs. **Max:** 2 tabs/24h.

*Multiple flavors available.
†Product currently on recall or temporarily unavailable from manufacturer, but generic forms may be available.

ANALGESIC PRODUCTS

BRAND	INGREDIENT(S)/STRENGTH(S)	DOSAGE
ACETAMINOPHENS		
Children's Tylenol Meltaways Chewable Tablets*†	Acetaminophen 80mg	**Peds 11 yrs (72-95 lbs):** 6 tabs q4h. **Peds 9-10 yrs (60-71 lbs):** 5 tabs q4h. **Peds 6-8 yrs (48-59 lbs):** 4 tabs q4h. **Peds 4-5 yrs (36-47 lbs):** 3 tabs q4h. **Peds 2-3 yrs (24-35 lbs):** 2 tabs q4h. **Max:** 5 doses/24h.
Children's Tylenol Oral Suspension*	Acetaminophen 160mg/5mL	**Peds 11 yrs (72-95 lbs):** 3 tsp (15mL) q4h. **Peds 9-10 yrs (60-71 lbs):** 2.5 tsp (12.5mL) q4h. **Peds 6-8 yrs (48-59 lbs):** 2 tsp (10mL) q4h. **Peds 4-5 yrs (36-47 lbs):** 1.5 tsp (7.5mL) q4h. **Peds 2-3 yrs (24-35 lbs):** 1 tsp (5mL) q4h. **Max:** 5 doses/24h.
FeverAll Children's Suppositories	Acetaminophen 120mg	**Peds 3-6 yrs:** 1 supp q4-6h. **Max:** 5 doses/24h.
FeverAll Infants' Suppositories	Acetaminophen 80mg	**Peds 12-36 months:** 1 supp q4-6h. **Max:** 5 doses/24h. **Peds 6-11 months:** 1 supp q6h. **Max:** 4 doses/24h.
FeverAll Jr. Strength Suppositories	Acetaminophen 325mg	**Adults & Peds ≥12 yrs:** 2 supp q4-6h. **Max:** 6 doses/24h. **Peds 6-12 yrs:** 1 supp q4-6h. **Max:** 5 doses/24h.
Infants' Tylenol Oral Suspension*	Acetaminophen 160mg/5mL	**Peds 2-3 yrs (24-35 lbs):** 1 tsp (5mL) q4h. **Max:** 5 doses/24h.
Jr. Tylenol Meltaways Chewable Tablets*†	Acetaminophen 160mg	**Peds 11 yrs (72-95 lbs):** 3 tabs q4h. **Peds 9-10 yrs (60-71 lbs):** 2.5 tabs q4h. **Peds 6-8 yrs (48-59 lbs):** 2 tabs q4h. **Max:** 5 doses/24h.
PediaCare Children Fever Reducer/Pain Reliever Acetaminophen Oral Suspension	Acetaminophen 160mg/5mL	**Peds 11 yrs (72-95 lbs):** 3 tsp (15mL) q4h. **Peds 9-10 yrs (60-71 lbs):** 2.5 tsp (12.5mL) q4h. **Peds 6-8 yrs (48-59 lbs):** 2 tsp (10mL) q4h. **Peds 4-5 yrs (36-47 lbs):** 1.5 tsp (7.5mL) q4h. **Peds 2-3 yrs (24-35 lbs):** 1 tsp (5mL) q4h. **Max:** 5 doses/24h.
PediaCare Infants Fever Reducer/Pain Reliever Acetaminophen Oral Suspension*	Acetaminophen 160mg/5mL	**Peds 2-3 yrs (24-35 lbs):** 1 tsp (5mL) q4h. **Max:** 5 doses/24h.
Triaminic Children's Fever Reducer Pain Reliever Syrup*†	Acetaminophen 160mg/5mL	**Peds 11 yrs (72-95 lbs):** 3 tsp (15mL) q4h. **Peds 9-10 yrs (60-71 lbs):** 2.5 tsp (12.5mL) q4h. **Peds 6-8 yrs (48-59 lbs):** 2 tsp (10mL) q4h. **Peds 4-5 yrs (36-47 lbs):** 1.5 tsp (7.5mL) q4h. **Peds 2-3 yrs (24-35 lbs):** 1 tsp (5mL) q4h. **Max:** 5 doses/24h.
Triaminic Infants' Fever Reducer Pain Reliever Syrup*†	Acetaminophen 160mg/5mL	**Peds 11 yrs (72-95 lbs):** 3 tsp (15mL) q4h. **Peds 9-10 yrs (60-71 lbs):** 2.5 tsp (12.5mL) q4h. **Peds 6-8 yrs (48-59 lbs):** 2 tsp (10mL) q4h. **Peds 4-5 yrs (36-47 lbs):** 1.5 tsp (7.5mL) q4h. **Peds 2-3 yrs (24-35 lbs):** 1 tsp (5mL) q4h. **Max:** 5 doses/24h.
Tylenol 8 HR Caplets†	Acetaminophen 650mg	**Adults & Peds ≥12 yrs:** 2 tabs q8h prn. **Max:** 6 tabs/24h.
Tylenol Arthritis Pain Caplets†	Acetaminophen 650mg	**Adults:** 2 tabs q8h prn. **Max:** 6 tabs/24h.
Tylenol Extra Strength Caplets	Acetaminophen 500mg	**Adults & Peds ≥12 yrs:** 2 tabs q6h prn. **Max:** 6 tabs/24h.

(Continued)

BRAND	INGREDIENT(S)/STRENGTH(S)	DOSAGE
ACETAMINOPHENS *(Continued)*		
Tylenol Regular Strength Tablets	Acetaminophen 325mg	**Adults & Peds ≥12 yrs:** 2 tabs q4-6h prn. **Max:** 10 tabs/24h. **Peds 6-11 yrs:** 1 tab q4-6h prn. **Max:** 5 tabs/24h.
ACETAMINOPHEN COMBINATIONS		
Excedrin Back & Body Caplets	Acetaminophen/Aspirin buffered 250mg-250mg	**Adults & Peds ≥12 yrs:** 2 tabs q6h. **Max:** 8 tabs/24h.
Excedrin Extra Strength Caplets	Acetaminophen/Aspirin/Caffeine 250mg-250mg-65mg	**Adults & Peds ≥12 yrs:** 2 tabs q6h. **Max:** 8 tabs/24h.
Excedrin Menstrual Complete Express Gels	Acetaminophen/Aspirin/Caffeine 250mg-250mg-65mg	**Adults & Peds ≥12 yrs:** 2 caps q4-6h. **Max:** 8 caps/24h.
Excedrin Migraine Caplets	Acetaminophen/Aspirin/Caffeine 250mg-250mg-65mg	**Adults:** 2 tabs. **Max:** 2 tabs/24h.
Excedrin Sinus Headache Caplets	Acetaminophen/Phenylephrine HCl 325mg-5mg	**Adults & Peds ≥12 yrs:** 2 tabs q4h. **Max:** 12 tabs/24h.
Excedrin Sinus Headache Tablets	Acetaminophen/Phenylephrine HCl 325mg-5mg	**Adults & Peds ≥12 yrs:** 2 tabs q4h. **Max:** 12 tabs/24h.
Excedrin Tension Headache Caplets	Acetaminophen/Caffeine 500mg-65mg	**Adults & Peds ≥12 yrs:** 2 tabs q6h. **Max:** 8 tabs/24h.
Excedrin Tension Headache Express Gels	Acetaminophen/Caffeine 500mg-65mg	**Adults & Peds ≥12 yrs:** 2 caps q6h. **Max:** 8 caps/24h.
Excedrin Tension Headache Geltabs	Acetaminophen/Caffeine 500mg-65mg	**Adults & Peds ≥12 yrs:** 2 tabs q6h. **Max:** 8 tabs/24h.
Goody's Back & Body Pain Powder	Acetaminophen/Aspirin 325mg-500mg per powder	**Adults & Peds ≥12 yrs:** Place 1 powder on tongue q6h prn.‡ **Max:** 4 powders/24h.
Goody's Cool Orange Powder	Acetaminophen/Aspirin/Caffeine 325mg-500mg-65mg per powder	**Adults & Peds ≥12 yrs:** Place 1 powder on tongue q6h prn.‡ **Max:** 4 powders/24h.
Goody's Extra Strength Caplets	Acetaminophen/Aspirin/Caffeine 250mg-250mg-65mg	**Adults & Peds ≥12 yrs:** 2 tabs q6h. **Max:** 8 tabs/24h.
Goody's Extra Strength Headache Powder	Acetaminophen/Aspirin/Caffeine 260mg-500mg-32.5mg per powder	**Adults & Peds ≥12 yrs:** Place 1 powder on tongue q6h prn.‡ **Max:** 4 powders/24h.
Goody's Headache Relief Shot	Acetaminophen/Caffeine 1000mg-65mg	**Adults & Peds ≥12 yrs:** 1 shot q6h prn. **Max:** 4 shots/24h.
Midol Complete Caplets	Acetaminophen/Caffeine/ Pyrilamine maleate 500mg-60mg-15mg	**Adults & Peds ≥12 yrs:** 2 tabs q6h prn. **Max:** 6 tabs/24h.
Midol Complete Gelcaps	Acetaminophen/Caffeine/ Pyrilamine maleate 500mg-60mg-15mg	**Adults & Peds ≥12 yrs:** 2 caps q6h prn. **Max:** 6 caps/24h.
Midol Teen Formula Caplets	Acetaminophen/Pamabrom 500mg- 25mg	**Adults & Peds ≥12 yrs:** 2 tabs q6h prn. **Max:** 6 tabs/24h.
Pamprin Cramp Caplets	Acetaminophen/Magnesium salicylate/Pamabrom 250mg-250mg-25mg	**Adults & Peds ≥12 yrs:** 2 tabs q4-6h prn. **Max:** 8 tabs/24h.
Pamprin Max Caplets	Acetaminophen/Aspirin/Caffeine 250mg-250mg-65mg	**Adults & Peds ≥12 yrs:** 2 tabs q4-6h prn. **Max:** 8 tabs/24h.
Pamprin Multi-Symptom Caplets	Acetaminophen/Pamabrom/ Pyrilamine maleate 500mg-25mg-15mg	**Adults & Peds ≥12 yrs:** 2 tabs q4-6h prn. **Max:** 8 tabs/24h.

BRAND	INGREDIENT(S)/STRENGTH(S)	DOSAGE
ACETAMINOPHEN COMBINATIONS *(Continued)*		
Premsyn PMS Caplets	Acetaminophen/Pamabrom/ Pyrilamine maleate 500mg-25mg-15mg	**Adults & Peds ≥12 yrs:** 2 tabs q4-6h prn. **Max:** 8 tabs/24h.
Vanquish Caplets	Acetaminophen/Aspirin/Caffeine 194mg-227mg-33mg	**Adults & Peds ≥12 yrs:** 2 tabs q6h. **Max:** 8 tabs/24h.
ACETAMINOPHENS/SLEEP AIDS		
Excedrin PM Caplets	Acetaminophen/Diphenhydramine citrate 500mg-38mg	**Adults & Peds ≥12 yrs:** 2 tabs hs prn. **Max:** 2 tabs/24h.
Excedrin PM Express Gels	Acetaminophen/Diphenhydramine citrate 500mg-38mg	**Adults & Peds ≥12 yrs:** 2 caps hs prn. **Max:** 2 caps/24h.
Goody's PM Powder	Acetaminophen/Diphenhydramine citrate 500mg-38mg per powder	**Adults & Peds ≥12 yrs:** 2 powders hs prn.‡
Midol PM Caplets	Acetaminophen/Diphenhydramine citrate 500mg-38mg	**Adults & Peds ≥12 yrs:** 2 tabs hs prn.
Tylenol PM Caplets†	Acetaminophen/Diphenhydramine HCl 500mg-25mg	**Adults & Peds ≥12 yrs:** 2 tabs hs. **Max:** 2 tabs/24h.
Tylenol PM Geltabs†	Acetaminophen/Diphenhydramine HCl 500mg-25mg	**Adults & Peds ≥12 yrs:** 2 tabs hs. **Max:** 2 tabs/24h.
Unisom PM Pain SleepCaps	Acetaminophen/Diphenhydramine HCl 325mg-50mg	**Adults & Peds ≥12 yrs:** 1 tab hs. **Max:** 1 tab/24 hrs.
NONSTEROIDAL ANTI-INFLAMMATORY DRUGS		
Advil Caplets	Ibuprofen 200mg	**Adults & Peds ≥12 yrs:** 1-2 tabs q4-6h prn. **Max:** 6 tabs/24h.
Advil Film-Coated Caplets	Ibuprofen 200mg	**Adults & Peds ≥12 yrs:** 1-2 tabs q4-6h. **Max:** 6 tabs/24h.
Advil Film-Coated Tablets	Ibuprofen 200mg	**Adults & Peds ≥12 yrs:** 1-2 tabs q4-6h. **Max:** 6 tabs/24h.
Advil Gel Caplets	Ibuprofen 200mg	**Adults & Peds ≥12 yrs:** 1-2 tabs q4-6h prn. **Max:** 6 tabs/24h.
Advil Liqui-Gels	Ibuprofen 200mg	**Adults & Peds ≥12 yrs:** 1-2 caps q4-6h prn. **Max:** 6 caps/24h.
Advil Migraine Capsules	Ibuprofen 200mg	**Adults:** 2 caps. **Max:** 2 caps/24h.
Advil Tablets	Ibuprofen 200mg	**Adults & Peds ≥12 yrs:** 1-2 tabs q4-6h prn. **Max:** 6 tabs/24h.
Aleve Caplets	Naproxen sodium 220mg	**Adults & Peds ≥12 yrs:** 1 tab q8-12h. May take 1 additional tab within 1h of first dose. **Max:** 2 tabs/8-12h or 3 tabs/24h.
Aleve Gelcaps	Naproxen sodium 220mg	**Adults & Peds ≥12 yrs:** 1 tab q8-12h. May take 1 additional tab within 1h of first dose. **Max:** 2 tabs/8-12h or 3 tabs/24h.
Aleve Liquid Gels	Naproxen sodium 220mg	**Adults & Peds ≥12 yrs:** 1 cap q8-12h. May take 1 additional cap within 1h of first dose. **Max:** 2 caps/8-12h or 3 caps/24h.
Aleve Tablets	Naproxen sodium 220mg	**Adults & Peds ≥12 yrs:** 1 tab q8-12h. May take 1 additional tab within 1h of first dose. **Max:** 2 tabs/8-12h or 3 tabs/24h.
Children's Advil Suspension*	Ibuprofen 100mg/5mL	**Peds 11 yrs (72-95 lbs):** 3 tsp (15mL) q6-8h. **Peds 9-10 yrs (60-71 lbs):** 2.5 tsp (12.5mL) q6-8h. **Peds 6-8 yrs (48-59 lbs):** 2 tsp (10mL) q6-8h. **Peds 4-5 yrs (36-47 lbs):** 1.5 tsp (7.5mL) q6-8h. **Peds 2-3 yrs (24-35 lbs):** 1 tsp (5mL) q6-8h. **Max:** 4 doses/24h.

(Continued)

BRAND	INGREDIENT(S)/STRENGTH(S)	DOSAGE
NONSTEROIDAL ANTI-INFLAMMATORY DRUGS *(Continued)*		
Children's Motrin Suspension	Ibuprofen 100mg/5mL	**Peds 11 yrs (72-95 lbs):** 3 tsp (15mL) q6-8h. **Peds 9-10 yrs (60-71 lbs):** 2.5 tsp (12.5mL) q6-8h. **Peds 6-8 yrs (48-59 lbs):** 2 tsp (10mL) q6-8h. **Peds 4-5 yrs (36-47 lbs):** 1.5 tsp (7.5mL) q6-8h. **Peds 2-3 yrs (24-35 lbs):** 1 tsp (5mL) q6-8h. **Max:** 4 doses/24h.
Infants' Advil Concentrated Drops	Ibuprofen 50mg/1.25mL	**Peds 12-23 months (18-23 lbs):** 1.875mL q6-8h. **Peds 6-11 months (12-17 lbs):** 1.25mL q6-8h. **Max:** 4 doses/24h.
Infants' Motrin Concentrated Drops	Ibuprofen 50mg/1.25mL	**Peds 12-23 months (18-23 lbs):** 1.875mL q6-8h. **Peds 6-11 months (12-17 lbs):** 1.25mL q6-8h. **Max:** 4 doses/24h.
Junior Strength Advil Chewable Tablets	Ibuprofen 100mg	**Peds 11 yrs (72-95 lbs):** 3 tabs q6-8h. **Peds 9-10 yrs (60-71 lbs):** 2.5 tabs q6-8h. **Peds 6-8 yrs (48-59 lbs):** 2 tabs q6-8h. **Max:** 4 doses/24h.
Junior Strength Advil Tablets	Ibuprofen 100mg	**Peds 11 yrs (72-95 lbs):** 3 tabs q6-8h. **Peds 6-10 yrs (48-71 lbs):** 2 tabs q6-8h. **Max:** 4 doses/24h.
Midol Extended Relief Caplets	Naproxen sodium 220mg	**Adults & Peds ≥12 yrs:** 1 tab q8-12h. May take 1 additional tab within 1h of first dose. **Max:** 2 tabs/8-12h or 3 tabs/24h.
Midol Liquid Gels	Ibuprofen 200mg	**Adults & Peds ≥12 yrs:** 1-2 caps q4-6h prn. **Max:** 6 caps/24h.
Motrin IB Caplets	Ibuprofen 200mg	**Adults & Peds ≥12 yrs:** 1-2 tabs q4-6h prn. **Max:** 6 tabs/24h.
Pamprin All Day Caplets	Naproxen sodium 220mg	**Adults & Peds ≥12 yrs:** 1 tab q8-12h prn. May take 1 additional tab within 1h of first dose. **Max:** 2 tabs/8-12h or 3 tabs/24h.
PediaCare Children Pain Reliever/ Fever Reducer IB Ibuprofen Oral Suspension	Ibuprofen 100mg/5mL	**Peds 11 yrs (72-95 lbs):** 3 tsp (15mL) q6-8h. **Peds 9-10 yrs (60-71 lbs):** 2.5 tsp (12.5mL) q6-8h. **Peds 6-8 yrs (48-59 lbs):** 2 tsp (10mL) q6-8h. **Peds 4-5 yrs (36-47 lbs):** 1.5 tsp (7.5mL) q6-8h. **Peds 2-3 yrs (24-35 lbs):** 1 tsp (5mL) q6-8h. **Max:** 4 doses/24h.
PediaCare Infants Pain Reliever/ Fever Reducer IB Ibuprofen Concentrated Oral Suspension	Ibuprofen 50mg/1.25mL	**Peds 12-23 months (18-23 lbs):** 1.865mL q6-8h. **Peds: 6-11 months (12-17 lbs):** 1.25mL q6-8h. **Max:** 4 doses/24h.
NONSTEROIDAL ANTI-INFLAMMATORY DRUG SLEEP AIDS		
Advil PM Caplets	Diphenhydramine citrate/ Ibuprofen 38mg-200mg	**Adults & Peds ≥12 yrs:** 2 tabs hs. **Max:** 2 tabs/24h.
Advil PM Liqui-Gels	Diphenhydramine HCl/Ibuprofen 25mg-200mg	**Adults & Peds ≥12 yrs:** 2 caps hs. **Max:** 2 caps/24h.
Motrin PM Caplets	Diphenhydramine citrate/ Ibuprofen 38mg-200mg	**Adults & Peds ≥12 yrs:** 2 tabs hs. **Max:** 2 tabs/24h.
SALICYLATES		
PLEASE REFER TO ASPIRIN PRODUCTS TABLE		

*Multiple flavors available.
†Product currently on recall or temporarily unavailable from manufacturer, but generic forms may be available.
‡May stir powder into a glass of water or other liquid.

ASPIRIN PRODUCTS

BRAND	INGREDIENT(S)/STRENGTH(S)	DOSAGE
SALICYLATES		
Bayer Advanced Aspirin Extra Strength Tablets	Aspirin 500mg	**Adults & Peds ≥12 yrs:** 1-2 tabs q4-6h. **Max:** 8 tabs/24h.
Bayer Aspirin Extra Strength Caplets	Aspirin 500mg	**Adults & Peds ≥12 yrs:** 1-2 tabs q4-6h. **Max:** 8 tabs/24h.
Bayer Aspirin Safety Coated Caplets	Aspirin 325mg	**Adults & Peds ≥12 yrs:** 1-2 tabs q4h. **Max:** 12 tabs/24h.
Bayer Genuine Aspirin Tablets	Aspirin 325mg	**Adults & Peds ≥12 yrs:** 1-2 tabs q4h or 3 tabs q6h. **Max:** 12 tabs/24h.
Bayer Low Dose Aspirin Chewable Tablets*	Aspirin 81mg	**Adults & Peds ≥12 yrs:** 4-8 tabs q4h. **Max:** 48 tabs/24h.
Bayer Low Dose Aspirin Safety Coated Tablets	Aspirin 81mg	**Adults & Peds ≥12 yrs:** 4-8 tabs q4h. **Max:** 48 tabs/24h.
Ecotrin Low Strength Tablets	Aspirin 81mg	**Adults & Peds ≥12 yrs:** 4-8 tabs q4h prn. **Max:** 48 tabs/24h.
Ecotrin Regular Strength Tablets	Aspirin 325mg	**Adults & Peds ≥12 yrs:** 1-2 tabs q4h prn. **Max:** 12 tabs/24h.
St. Joseph Aspirin Chewable Tablets	Aspirin 81mg	**Adults & Peds ≥12 yrs:** 4-8 tabs q4h prn. **Max:** 48 tabs/24h.
St. Joseph Rapid Dissolving Melts	Aspirin 81mg	**Adults & Peds ≥12 yrs:** 1-2 tabs q4h prn. **Max:** 12 tabs/24h.
St. Joseph Regular Strength Safety Coated Tablets	Aspirin 325mg	**Adults & Peds ≥12 yrs:** 1-2 tabs q4h prn. **Max:** 12 tabs/24h.
St. Joseph Safety Coated Low Dose Tablets	Aspirin 81mg	**Adults & Peds ≥12 yrs:** 4-8 tabs q4h prn. **Max:** 48 tabs/24h.
SALICYLATES, BUFFERED		
Alka-Seltzer Extra Strength Effervescent Tablets	Aspirin/Citric acid/Sodium bicarbonate 500mg-1000mg-1985mg	**Adults ≥60 yrs:** 2 tabs dissolved in 4 oz water q6h. **Max:** 3 tabs/24h. **Adults & Peds ≥12 yrs:** 2 tabs dissolved in 4 oz water q6h. **Max:** 7 tabs/24h.
Alka-Seltzer Lemon Lime Effervescent Tablets	Aspirin/Citric acid/Sodium bicarbonate 325mg-1000mg-1700mg	**Adults ≥60 yrs:** 2 tabs dissolved in 4 oz water q4h. **Max:** 4 tabs/24h. **Adults & Peds ≥12 yrs:** 2 tabs dissolved in 4 oz water q4h. **Max:** 8 tabs/24h.
Alka-Seltzer Original Effervescent Tablets	Aspirin/Citric acid/Sodium bicarbonate 325mg-1000mg-1916mg	**Adults ≥60 yrs:** 2 tabs dissolved in 4 oz water q4h. **Max:** 4 tabs/24h. **Adults & Peds ≥12 yrs:** 2 tabs dissolved in 4 oz water q4h. **Max:** 8 tabs/24h.
Bayer Aspirin Extra Strength Plus Caplets	Aspirin 500mg buffered with Calcium carbonate	**Adults & Peds ≥12 yrs:** 1-2 tabs q4-6h. **Max:** 8 tabs/24h.
Bayer Women's Low Dose Aspirin Caplets	Aspirin 81mg buffered with Calcium carbonate 777mg	**Adults & Peds ≥12 yrs:** 4-8 tabs q4h. **Max:** 10 tabs/24h.
Bufferin Tablets	Aspirin 325mg buffered with Calcium carbonate/Magnesium carbonate/Magnesium oxide	**Adults & Peds ≥12 yrs:** 2 tabs q4h prn. **Max:** 12 tabs/24h.
SALICYLATE COMBINATIONS		
Anacin Caplets	Aspirin/Caffeine 400mg-32mg	**Adults & Peds ≥12 yrs:** 2 tabs q6h. **Max:** 8 tabs/24h.
Anacin Max Strength Tablets	Aspirin/Caffeine 500mg-32mg	**Adults & Peds ≥12 yrs:** 2 tabs q6h. **Max:** 8 tabs/24h.
Anacin Tablets	Aspirin/Caffeine 400mg-32mg	**Adults & Peds ≥12 yrs:** 2 tabs q6h. **Max:** 8 tabs/24h.

(Continued)

BRAND	INGREDIENT(S)/STRENGTH(S)	DOSAGE
SALICYLATE COMBINATIONS *(Continued)*		
Bayer Back & Body Extra Strength Caplets	Aspirin/Caffeine 500mg-32.5mg	**Adults & Peds ≥12 yrs:** 2 tabs q6h. **Max:** 8 tabs/24h.
Bayer Headache Relief Caplets	Aspirin/Caffeine 500mg-32.5mg	**Adults & Peds ≥12 yrs:** 2 tabs q6h. **Max:** 8 tabs/24h.
Bayer Migraine Formula Caplets	Aspirin/Acetaminophen/Caffeine 250mg-250mg-65mg	**Adults:** 2 tabs qd. **Max: 2** tabs/24h.
BC Arthritis Strength Powder	Aspirin/Caffeine 1000mg-65mg per powder	**Adults & Peds ≥12 yrs:** Place 1 powder on tongue q6h prn. May stir powder into glass of water. **Max:** 4 powders/24h.
BC Powder*	Aspirin/Caffeine 845mg-65mg per powder	**Adults & Peds ≥12 yrs:** Place 1 powder on tongue q6h prn. May stir powder into glass of water. **Max:** 4 powders/24h.
SALICYLATES/SLEEP AIDS		
Bayer PM Caplets	Aspirin/Diphenhydramine citrate 500mg-38mg	**Adults & Peds ≥12 yrs:** 2 tabs hs prn.
*Multiple flavors available.		

COMMONLY USED HERBAL PRODUCTS

NAME	ACCEPTED USES	UNPROVEN USES	INTERACTIONS
Aloe vera	**Topical:** Resolution of psoriatic plaques, reduce desquamation, erythema, and infiltration **Oral:** Constipation	**Topical:** Burns, frostbite, herpes simplex, sunburn, wound healing **Oral:** Diabetes, ulcerative colitis, hyperlipidemia	Antidiabetics, digoxin, diuretics, sevoflurane, stimulant laxatives, warfarin
Black cohosh	Menopausal symptoms (eg, hot flashes)	Labor induction, osteoporosis	Atorvastatin, cisplatin, drugs metabolized by the liver (CYP2D6 substrates), hepatotoxic drugs
Black psyllium	Constipation, hypercholesterolemia	Cancer, diarrhea, irritable bowel syndrome	Antidiabetics, carbamazepine, digoxin, lithium
Capsicum	**Topical:** Pain, fibromyalgia, prurigo nodularis **Intranasal:** Cluster headache, perennial rhinitis (nonallergic, noninfectious)	**Oral:** Dyspepsia, peptic ulcers, swallowing dysfunction **Intranasal:** Migraine headaches, sinonasal polyposis, allergic rhinitis	Cocaine, ACE inhibitors, anticoagulants, antiplatelets, theophylline, coca
Chamomile	Colic, dyspepsia, oral mucositis	Restlessness, insomnia, menstrual cramps, diarrhea, fibromyalgia	Benzodiazepines, CNS depressants, contraceptives, drugs metabolized by the liver (CYP1A2, CYP3A4 substrates), estrogens, tamoxifen, warfarin
Cranberry	Urinary tract infections	Benign prostatic hyperplasia, urine deodorant	Drugs metabolized by the liver (CYP2C9 substrates), warfarin
Echinacea	**Oral:** Common cold, vaginal candidiasis	**Oral:** Influenza **Topical:** Superficial wounds, burns	Caffeine, drugs metabolized by the liver (CYP1A2, CYP3A4 substrates), immunosuppressants, midazolam
Eucalyptus		Asthma, upper respiratory tract inflammation, wounds, burns, congestion, ulcers, acne, bleeding gums, bladder disease, diabetes, fever, flu, loss of appetite, arthritis pain, liver/gallbladder problems	Drugs metabolized by the liver (CYP1A2, CYP2C19, CYP2C9, CYP3A4 substrates), antidiabetics, herbs that contain hepatotoxic pyrrolizidine alkaloids
Evening primrose oil	Mastalgia, osteoporosis	Rheumatoid arthritis, Sjogren's syndrome, chronic fatigue syndrome	Anesthesia, anticoagulants, antiplatelets, phenothiazines
Feverfew	Migraine headaches	Fever, menstrual irregularities, arthritis, psoriasis, allergies, asthma, dizziness, nausea, vomiting, earache, cancer, common cold	Drugs metabolized by the liver (CYP1A2, CYP2C19, CYP2C9, CYP3A4 substrates), anticoagulants, antiplatelets
Flaxseed	Diabetes, hypercholesterolemia, systemic lupus erythematosus nephritis	Breast cancer, cardiovascular disease, colorectal cancer, constipation, endometrial cancer, lung cancer, mastalgia, prostate cancer, menopausal symptoms	Acetaminophen, antibiotics, anticoagulants, antiplatelets, antidiabetics, estrogens, furosemide, ketoprofen, metoprolol, decreased absorption of oral medications
Garlic	**Oral:** Atherosclerosis, gastric cancer, hypertension, tick bites **Topical:** Tinea corporis (ringworm), tinea cruris (jock itch), tinea pedis (athlete's foot)	**Oral:** Benign prostatic hyperplasia, common cold, preeclampsia, prostate cancer **Topical:** Corns, warts	Anticoagulants, antiplatelets, contraceptives, cyclosporine, drugs metabolized by the liver (CYP2E1, CYP3A4 substrates), isoniazid, non-nucleoside reverse transcriptase inhibitors, saquinavir, warfarin

(Continued)

NAME	ACCEPTED USES	UNPROVEN USES	INTERACTIONS
Ginger	Dysmenorrhea, morning sickness, osteoarthritis, postoperative nausea and vomiting, vertigo	Chemotherapy-induced nausea and vomiting, migraine headache, myalgia, rheumatoid arthritis	Anticoagulants, antiplatelets, antidiabetics, calcium channel blockers, phenprocoumon, warfarin
Ginkgo	Age-related memory impairment, cognitive function, dementia, diabetic retinopathy, glaucoma, peripheral vascular disease, premenstrual syndrome, Raynaud's syndrome, vertigo	Age-related macular degeneration, anxiety, ADHD, colorectal cancer, fibromyalgia, hearing loss, ovarian cancer, radiation exposure, schizophrenia, stroke, vitiligo	Alprazolam, anticoagulants, antiplatelets, anticonvulsants, antidiabetics, buspirone, drugs metabolized by the liver (CYP1A2, CYP2C19, CYP2C9, CYP2D6, CYP3A4 substrates), efavirenz, fluoxetine, hydrochlorothiazide, ibuprofen, omeprazole, seizure threshold-lowering drugs, trazodone, St John's wort, warfarin
Ginseng	Diabetes, respiratory tract infections	ADHD, breast cancer	Antidiabetics, monoamine oxidase inhibitors, warfarin
Licorice	Dyspepsia	Atopic dermatitis, hepatitis, muscle cramps, peptic ulcers, weight loss	Cardiac glycoside-containing herbs (eg, digitalis), stimulant laxative herbs (eg, aloe), antihypertensives, corticosteroids, drugs metabolized by the liver (CYP2B6, CYP2C9, CYP3A4 substrates), digoxin, diuretics, estrogens, ethacrynic acid, furosemide, warfarin, grapefruit juice, salt
Milk thistle	Diabetes, dyspepsia	Alcohol-related liver disease, *Amanita* mushroom poisoning, hepatitis B or C, toxin-induced liver damage	Drugs metabolized by the liver (CYP2C9, CYP3A4 substrates), estrogens, drugs that undergo glucuronidation (eg, metronidazole), HMG-CoA reductase inhibitors ("statins"), tamoxifen
Peppermint	**Rectal:** Barium enema-related colonic spasm **Oral:** Dyspepsia, irritable bowel syndrome **Topical:** Tension headache	**Topical:** Postherpetic neuralgia	Antacids, cyclosporine, drugs metabolized by the liver (CYP1A2, CYP2C19, CYP2C9, CYP3A4 substrates), H_2-blockers, proton pump inhibitors
Saw palmetto	Benign prostatic hyperplasia	Androgenic alopecia, prostate cancer, prostatitis and chronic pelvic pain syndrome	Anticoagulants, antiplatelets, contraceptives, estrogens
Senna	Constipation, bowel preparation	Hemorrhoids, irritable bowel syndrome, weight loss	Digoxin, diuretics, warfarin, horsetail, licorice, stimulant laxatives
St. John's wort	Depression, menopausal symptoms, somatization disorder, wound healing	Obsessive-compulsive disorder, premenstrual syndrome, seasonal affective disorder	Numerous medications
Valerian	Insomnia	Anxiety, dyssomnia	Alcohol, alprazolam, drugs metabolized by the liver (CYP3A4 substrates), benzodiazepines, CNS depressants, herbs and supplements with sedative properties

Source: Jellin JM, Gregory PJ, et al. Natural Medicines Comprehensive Database. www.naturaldatabase.com. Accessed March 19, 2014.

ANGINA TREATMENT OPTIONS

GENERIC (BRAND)	HOW SUPPLIED	DOSAGE	RENAL/HEPATIC DOSAGE ADJUSTMENT
BETA BLOCKERS			
Atenolol (Tenormin)	**Tab:** 25mg, 50mg, 100mg	**Initial:** 50mg qd. **Titrate:** May increase to 100mg qd after 1 week. **Max:** 200mg qd.	Renal
Metoprolol succinate (Toprol-XL)	**Tab, ER:** 25mg, 50mg, 100mg, 200mg	**Initial:** 100mg qd. **Titrate:** May gradually increase weekly until optimum response is achieved or there is pronounced slowing of HR. **Max:** 400mg/day. Reduce dose gradually over 1-2 weeks if to be d/c.	Hepatic
Metoprolol tartrate (Lopressor)	**Tab:** 50mg, 100mg, (generic) 25mg, 50mg, 100mg	**Initial:** 100mg/day in 2 divided doses. **Titrate:** May gradually increase weekly until optimum response is achieved or there is pronounced slowing of HR. **Effective Range:** 100-400mg/day. **Max:** 400mg/day. Reduce dose gradually over 1-2 weeks if to be d/c.	Hepatic
Nadolol (Corgard)	**Tab:** 20mg, 40mg, 80mg	**Initial:** 40mg qd. **Titrate:** May gradually increase in 40-80mg increments at 3- to 7-day intervals until optimum response is achieved or there is pronounced slowing of HR. **Maint: Usual:** 40 or 80mg qd. Doses up to 160 or 240mg qd may be needed. **Max:** 240mg/day. Reduce dose gradually over 1-2 weeks if to be d/c.	Renal
Propranolol HCl	**Sol:** 20mg/5mL, 40mg/5mL; **Tab:** 10mg, 20mg, 40mg, 60mg, 80mg	80-320mg/day given bid-qid. Reduce dose gradually over several weeks if to be d/c.	
Propranolol HCl (Inderal LA)	**Cap, ER:** 60mg, 80mg, 120mg, 160mg	**Initial:** 80mg qd. **Titrate:** May gradually increase at 3- to 7-day intervals until optimum response is achieved. **Maint:** 160mg qd. **Max:** 320mg/day. Reduce dose gradually over a few weeks if to be d/c.	
CALCIUM CHANNEL BLOCKERS (DIHYDROPYRIDINES)			
Amlodipine besylate (Norvasc)	**Tab:** 2.5mg, 5mg, 10mg	**Initial:** 5mg qd. **Usual:** 5-10mg qd. **Max:** 10mg qd.	Hepatic
Nicardipine	**Cap:** 20mg, 30mg	**Initial:** 20mg tid. **Titrate:** Allow at least 3 days before increasing dose. **Effective Range:** 20-40mg tid.	Renal/Hepatic
Nifedipine (Procardia XL)	**Tab, ER:** 30mg, 60mg, 90mg	**Initial:** 30 or 60mg qd. **Titrate:** Increase over a 1- to 2-week period (usual), but may proceed more rapidly if symptoms warrant. **Max:** 120mg/day.	
CALCIUM CHANNEL BLOCKERS (NON-DIHYDROPYRIDINES)			
Diltiazem HCl (Cardizem CD, Cartia XT)	**Cap, ER:** (Cardizem CD/ Cartia XT) 120mg, 180mg, 240mg, 300mg; (Cardizem CD) 360mg	**Initial:** 120mg or 180mg qd. **Titrate:** Increase over a 1- to 2-week period when necessary. **Max:** 480mg qd.	
Diltiazem HCl (Cardizem LA)	**Tab, ER:** 120mg, 180mg, 240mg, 300mg, 360mg, 420mg	**Initial:** 180mg qd (am or hs). **Titrate:** Increase at 1- to 2-week intervals if adequate response is not achieved. **Max:** 360mg.	
Diltiazem HCl (Cardizem)	**Tab:** 30mg, 60mg, 90mg, 120mg	**Initial:** 30mg qid (before meals and hs). **Titrate:** Increase gradually (given in divided doses tid-qid) at 1- to 2-day intervals until optimum response obtained. **Usual:** 180-360mg/day.	

(Continued)

GENERIC (BRAND)	HOW SUPPLIED	DOSAGE	RENAL/HEPATIC DOSAGE ADJUSTMENT
CALCIUM CHANNEL BLOCKERS (NON-DIHYDROPYRIDINES) *(Continued)*			
Diltiazem HCl (Dilacor XR)	**Cap, ER:** 120mg, 180mg, 240mg	**Initial:** 120mg qd. **Titrate:** Increase to a dose of up to 480mg qd. May be carried out over a 1- to 2-week period when necessary.	
Diltiazem HCl (Taztia XT, Tiazac)	**Cap, ER:** (Taztia XT) 120mg, 180mg, 240mg, 300mg, 360mg; (Tiazac) 120mg, 180mg, 240mg, 300mg, 360mg, 420mg	**Initial:** 120-180mg qd. **Titrate:** Increase over 1-2 weeks when necessary. **Max:** 540mg qd.	
Verapamil HCl (Calan)	**Tab:** 40mg, 80mg, 120mg	**Usual:** 80-120mg tid. Upward titration should be based on therapeutic efficacy and safety evaluated approximately 8 hrs after dosing. **Titrate:** May increase daily (eg, patients with unstable angina) or weekly, until optimum response is obtained.	Hepatic
Verapamil HCl (Covera-HS)	**Tab, ER:** 180mg, 240mg	**Initial:** 180mg qhs. **Titrate:** If inadequate response with 180mg, increase to 240mg qhs, then 360mg (two 180mg tab) qhs, then 480mg (two 240mg tab) qhs.	Hepatic
CALCIUM CHANNEL BLOCKERS/HMG COA REDUCTASE INHIBITORS			
Amlodipine besylate-Atorvastatin calcium (Caduet)	**Tab:** 2.5-10mg, 2.5-20mg, 2.5-40mg, 5-10mg, 5-20mg, 5-40mg, 5-80mg, 10-10mg, 10-20mg, 10-40mg, 10-80mg	**Initial:** 5-10mg or 5-20mg qd. **Max:** 10-80 mg qd.	Hepatic
COAGULATION MODIFIERS			
Abciximab (ReoPro)	**Inj:** 2mg/mL	0.25mcg/kg IV bolus followed by 10mcg/min infusion for 18-24 hrs, concluding 1 hr after PCI.	
Bivalirudin (Angiomax)	**Inj:** 250mg	Give with ASA (300-325mg/day). **Patients Without HIT/HITTS:** 0.75mg/kg IV bolus, then 1.75mg/kg/hr infusion for the duration of the PCI/PTCA procedure. An activated clotting time should be performed 5 min after the bolus dose and an additional 0.3mg/kg bolus should be given if needed. **Patients With HIT/HITTS:** 0.75mg/kg IV bolus, then 1.75mg/kg/hr infusion for the duration of the procedure. **Ongoing Treatment Post-Procedure:** Continuation of infusion following PCI/PTCA for up to 4 hrs post-procedure is optional. After 4 hrs, an additional infusion may be initiated at a rate of 0.2mg/kg/hr (low-rate infusion), for up to 20 hrs, if needed.	Renal
Clopidogrel bisulfate (Plavix)	**Tab:** 75mg, 300mg	**LD:** 300mg. **Maint:** 75mg qd. Initiate ASA (75-325mg qd) and continue in combination with clopidogrel.	
Dalteparin sodium (Fragmin)	**Inj:** (Syringe) 2500 IU/0.2mL, 5000 IU/0.2mL, 7500 IU/0.3mL, 10,000 IU/0.4mL, 10,000 IU/1mL, 12,500 IU/0.5mL, 15,000 IU/0.6mL, 18,000 IU/0.72mL; (MDV) 95,000 IU/3.8mL, 95,000 IU/9.5mL	**Prophylaxis of Ischemic Complications in Unstable Angina:** 120 IU/kg q12h with PO ASA (75-165mg qd) until clinically stabilized. **Usual Duration:** 5-8 days. **Max:** 10,000 IU q12h.	Renal

GENERIC (BRAND)	HOW SUPPLIED	DOSAGE	RENAL/HEPATIC DOSAGE ADJUSTMENT
COAGULATION MODIFIERS *(Continued)*			
Enoxaparin (Lovenox)	**Inj:** [100mg/mL] (Prefilled Syringe) 30mg/0.3mL, 40mg/0.4mL; (Graduated Prefilled Syringe) 60mg/0.6mL, 80mg/0.8mL, 100mg/mL; (MDV) 300mg/3mL; [150mg/mL] (Graduated Prefilled Syringe) 120mg/0.8mL, 150mg/mL	1mg/kg SQ q12h with PO ASA (100-325mg qd) until clinically stabilized. **Usual Duration:** 2-8 days (up to 12.5 days in clinical trials).	Renal
Prasugrel (Effient)	**Tab:** 5mg, 10mg	**LD:** 60mg. **Maint:** 10mg qd with ASA (75-325mg/day). **<60kg:** Consider lowering the maintenance dose to 5mg qd.	
Ticagrelor (Brilinta)	**Tab:** 90mg	**LD:** 180mg with ASA (usually 325mg). **Maint:** 90mg bid with ASA (75-100mg/day).	
VASODILATORS			
Isosorbide dinitrate (Dilatrate-SR)	**Cap, ER:** 40mg	40mg bid; separate doses by 6 hrs. **Max:** 160mg/day. Allow a dose-free interval of >18 hrs.	
Isosorbide mononitrate (Imdur)	**Tab, ER:** 30mg, 60mg, 120mg	**Initial:** 30mg (given as single tab or as ½ of a 60mg tab) or 60mg (given as single tab) qam on arising. **Titrate:** May increase to 120mg (given as single tab or as two 60mg tabs) qam after several days. Rarely, 240mg qam may be required.	
Isosorbide mononitrate (Monoket)	**Tab:** 10mg, 20mg	20mg bid (give doses 7 hrs apart). **Small Stature Patients: Initial:** 5mg (½ of a 10mg tab). **Titrate:** Increase to ≥10mg by 2nd or 3rd day.	
Nitroglycerin (Nitrolingual)	**Spray:** 400mcg/spray	**Acute Relief:** 1 or 2 sprays at the onset of attack onto or under the tongue. **Max:** 3 sprays/15 min. If chest pain persists, prompt medical attention is recommended. **Prophylaxis:** May be used 5-10 min prior to engaging in activities that might precipitate an acute attack.	
Nitroglycerin (Nitromist)	**Spray:** 400mcg/spray	**Acute Relief:** 1 or 2 sprays at the onset of attack onto or under the tongue. May repeat every 5 min PRN. If 2 sprays are used initially, may only administer 1 more spray after 5 min. **Max:** 3 sprays/15 min. If chest pain persists after a total of 3 sprays, prompt medical attention is recommended. **Prophylaxis:** May be used 5-10 min before engaging in activities that might precipitate an acute attack.	
Nitroglycerin (Minitran, Nitro-Dur)	**Patch:** (Minitran) 0.1mg/hr, 0.2mg/hr, 0.4mg/hr, 0.6mg/hr; (Nitro-Dur) 0.1mg/hr, 0.2mg/hr, 0.3mg/hr, 0.4mg/hr, 0.6mg/hr, 0.8mg/hr	**Initial:** 0.2-0.4mg/hr patch for 12-14 hrs/day. Remove patch for 10-12 hrs/day.	

(Continued)

GENERIC (BRAND)	HOW SUPPLIED	DOSAGE	RENAL/HEPATIC DOSAGE ADJUSTMENT
VASODILATORS (*Continued*)			
Nitroglycerin (Nitrostat)	**Tab, SL:** 0.3mg, 0.4mg, 0.6mg	**Acute Relief:** 1 tab SL or in buccal pouch at onset of attack. May repeat every 5 min until relief is obtained. If pain persists after a total of 3 tabs in 15 min, or if pain is different than typically experienced, prompt medical attention is recommended. **Prophylaxis:** May be used 5-10 min prior to engaging in activities that might precipitate an acute attack.	
Nitroglycerin (Nitro-Bid)	**Oint:** 2%	**Initial:** ½-inch (7.5mg) bid (one in the am and one 6 hrs later). **Titrate:** May increase to 1 inch bid, then to 2 inches bid. Allow a dose-free interval of 10-12 hrs.	
Nitroglycerin in 5% Dextrose	**Inj:** 100mcg/mL, 200mcg/mL, 400mcg/mL	**Initial:** 5mcg/min IV. **Titrate:** Increase by 5mcg/min at intervals of 3-5 min. If no response at 20mcg/min, may use increments of 10 and even 20mcg/min. Once some hemodynamic response is observed, dosage increments should be smaller and less frequent.	
MISCELLANEOUS			
Ranolazine (Ranexa)	**Tab, ER:** 500mg, 1000mg	**Initial:** 500mg bid. **Titrate:** May increase to 1000mg bid, PRN, based on clinical symptoms. **Max:** 1000mg bid.	

Refer to full FDA-approved labeling for additional product information.

Abbreviations: ASA = aspirin; HIT/HITTS = heparin induced thrombocytopenia/heparin induced thrombocytopenia and thrombosis syndrome; PCI = percutaneous coronary intervention; PTCA = percutaneous transluminal coronary angioplasty.

CHOLESTEROL-LOWERING AGENTS

GENERIC (BRAND)	HOW SUPPLIED (MG)*	USUAL DOSAGE RANGE†	T-CHOL (% DECREASE)	LDL (% DECREASE)	HDL (% INCREASE)	TG (% DECREASE)
HMG-COA REDUCTASE INHIBITORS (STATINS)						
Atorvastatin (Lipitor)	Tab: 10, 20, 40, 80	10-80mg/day	29 to 45	39 to 60	5 to 9	19 to 37
Fluvastatin (Lescol)	Cap: 20, 40	20-80mg/day	17 to 27	22 to 36	3 to 6	12 to 18
Fluvastatin (Lescol XL)	Tab, ER: 80	80mg/day	25	35	7	19
Lovastatin (Altoprev)	Tab, ER: 20, 40, 60	20-60mg/day	17.9 to 29.2	23.8 to 40.8	9.4 to 13.1	9.9 to 25.1
Lovastatin	Tab: 10, 20, 40	10-80mg/day	17 to 29	24 to 40	6.6 to 9.5	10 to 19
Pitavastatin (Livalo)	Tab: 1, 2, 4	1-4mg/day	23 to 31	32 to 43	5 to 8	15 to 19
Pravastatin (Pravachol)	Tab: 10, 20, 40, 80	40-80mg/day	16 to 27	22 to 37	2 to 12	11 to 24
Rosuvastatin (Crestor)	Tab: 5, 10, 20, 40	5-40mg/day	33 to 46	45 to 63	8 to 14	10 to 35
Simvastatin (Zocor)	Tab: 5, 10, 20, 40, 80	5-40mg/day	19 to 36	26 to 47	8 to 16	12 to 33
FIBRATES‡						
Fenofibrate (Antara)	Cap: 30, 90	30-90mg/day	16.8 to 22.4	20.1 to 31.4	9.8 to 14.6	23.5 to 35.9
Fenofibrate (Fenoglide)	Tab: 40, 120	40-120mg/day	16.8 to 22.4	20.1 to 31.4	9.8 to 14.6	23.5 to 35.9
Fenofibrate (Lipofen)	Cap: 50, 150	50-150mg/day	16.8 to 22.4	20.1 to 31.4	9.8 to 14.6	23.5 to 35.9
Fenofibrate (Lofibra)	Tab: 54, 160; Cap: 67, 134, 200	54-160mg/day, 67-200mg/day	16.8 to 22.4	20.1 to 31.4	9.8 to 14.6	23.5 to 35.9
Fenofibrate (Tricor)	Tab: 48, 145	48-145mg/day	16.8 to 22.4	20.1 to 31.4	9.8 to 14.6	23.5 to 35.9
Fenofibrate (Triglide)	Tab: 50, 160	50-160mg/day	16.8 to 22.4	20.1 to 31.4	9.8 to 14.6	23.5 to 35.9
Fenofibric acid (Fibricor)	Tab: 35, 105	35-105mg/day	16.8 to 22.4	20.1 to 31.4	9.8 to 14.6	23.5 to 35.9
Fenofibric acid (Trilipix)	Cap, DR: 45, 135	45-135mg/day	16.8 to 22.4	20.1 to 31.4	9.8 to 14.6	23.5 to 35.9
Gemfibrozil (Lopid)	Tab: 600	1200mg/day in divided doses	Moderate reduction	4.1	12.6	Significant reduction
BILE-ACID SEQUESTRANTS						
Cholestyramine (Prevalite)	Powder for Oral Suspension: 4g/packet or level scoopful	2-6 packets or level scoopfuls (8-24g)/day	7.2	10.4	N/A	N/A
Colesevelam HCl (Welchol)	Tab: 625; Powder for Oral Suspension: 3.75g packet, 1.875g packet	3750mg/day	7	15	3	10

(Continued)

GENERIC (BRAND)	HOW SUPPLIED (MG)*	USUAL DOSAGE RANGE†	T-CHOL (% DECREASE)	LDL (% DECREASE)	HDL (% INCREASE)	TG (% DECREASE)
BILE-ACID SEQUESTRANTS *(Continued)*						
Colestipol (Colestid)	**Granules for Suspension:** 5g/packet or level scoopful; **Tab:** 1000	**Granules for Suspension:** 1-6 packets or level scoopfuls/ day; **Tab:** 2-16g/day	N/A	N/A	N/A	N/A
CHOLESTEROL ABSORPTION INHIBITORS						
Ezetimibe (Zetia)	**Tab:** 10	10mg/day	13	18	1	8
NICOTINIC ACID DERIVATIVES						
Niacin, ER (Niaspan)	**Tab, ER:** 500, 750, 1000	1000-2000mg/ day	3 to 10	5 to 14	18 to 22	13 to 28
LIPID-REGULATING AGENTS						
Omega-3-Acid Ethyl Esters (Lovaza)	**Cap:** 1000	4g/day	9.7	+44.5	9.1	44.9
COMBINATIONS						
Amlodipine/ Atorvastatin (Caduet)	**Tab:** 2.5/10, 2.5/20, 2.5/40, 5/10, 5/20, 5/40, 5/80, 10/10, 10/20, 10/40, 10/80	5/10mg – 10/80mg/day	N/A	32.3 to 48.0	N/A	N/A
Ezetimibe/ Simvastatin (Vytorin)	**Tab:** 10/10, 10/20, 10/40, 10/80	10/10mg – 10/40mg/day	31 to 43	45 to 60	6 to 10	23 to 31
Niacin, ER/Lovastatin (Advicor)	**Tab, ER:** 500/20, 750/20, 1000/20, 1000/40	1000/20mg – 2000/40mg/day	N/A	30 to 42	20 to 30	32 to 44
Niacin, ER/Simvastatin (Simcor)	**Tab, ER:** 500/20, 500/40, 750/20, 1000/20, 1000/40	1000/20mg – 2000/40mg/day	1.6 to 11.1	5.1 to 14.3	15.4 to 29.0	22.8 to 38.0
Sitagliptin/ Simvastatin (Juvisync)	**Tab:** 50/10, 50/20, 50/40, 100/10, 100/20, 100/40	50/10mg – 100/40mg/day	23 to 31	29 to 41	8 to 13	15 to 28

Abbreviations: DR = delayed-release; ER = extended-release; N/A = not applicable.

*Unless otherwise indicated.

† Usual Dosage Range shown is for adults and may need to be adjusted to individual patient needs. For specific dosing and administration information including pediatric, geriatric, and renal/hepatic impairment dosing, please refer to the individual monograph listing or the FDA-approved labeling. According to NCEP-ATP III guidelines, lipid-altering agents should be used in addition to a diet restricted in saturated fat and cholesterol only when the response to diet and other nonpharmacological measures has been inadequate.

‡ Refer to the FDA-approved labeling for the lipid parameter changes observed for the treatment of hypertriglyceridemia; LDL increases reported.

Major Contraindications (refer to the FDA-approved labeling for a complete list of warnings and precautions):

Statins: Active liver disease or unexplained persistent elevations of hepatic transaminase levels; women who are pregnant or may become pregnant; nursing mothers.

Fibrates: Severe renal dysfunction (including patients receiving dialysis), active liver disease, gallbladder disease, nursing mothers.

Bile-acid sequestrants: History of bowel obstruction; serum triglycerides >500mg/dL; history of hypertriglyceridemia-induced pancreatitis.

Cholesterol absorption inhibitors: Statin contraindications apply when used with a statin: active liver disease or unexplained persistent elevations in hepatic transaminase levels, women who are pregnant or may become pregnant, nursing mothers.

Nicotinic acid derivatives: Active liver disease or unexplained persistent elevations in hepatic transaminases; active peptic ulcer disease; arterial bleeding.

Combinations: Refer to individual therapeutic class contraindications.

COAGULATION MODIFIERS

GENERIC (BRAND)	HOW SUPPLIED	INDICATIONS	MECHANISM OF ACTION	SPECIAL INSTRUCTIONS
THROMBOLYTICS				
Alteplase (Activase)	Inj: 50mg, 100mg	• AMI • Acute ischemic stroke • PE	Tissue plasminogen activator	• Monitor for signs/symptoms of bleeding, cholesterol embolism, and allergic reactions. • Monitor BP. • Monitor bleeding from recent puncture sites. • Monitor during and for several hours after infusion for signs of orolingual angioedema.
Reteplase (Retavase)	Inj: 10.4 U (18.1mg)	• AMI	Tissue plasminogen activator	• Do not administer other medications simultaneously via the same IV line. • Monitor for signs/symptoms of bleeding, internal and superficial bleeding sites, bleeding at recent puncture sites, cholesterol embolism (eg, livedo reticularis, "purple toe" syndrome, MI, cerebral infarction, HTN, gangrenous digits), and arrhythmias. • Monitor renal/hepatic function.
Tenecteplase (TNKase)	Inj: 50mg	• AMI	Tissue plasminogen activator	• Check for signs/symptoms of bleeding; if serious bleeding occurs, concomitant heparin or antiplatelet agents should be discontinued immediately. • Monitor for cholesterol embolization (eg, livedo reticularis, "purple toe" syndrome, acute renal failure), arrhythmia, and hypersensitivity reactions (eg, anaphylaxis).
PLATELET AGGREGATION INHIBITORS				
Abciximab (ReoPro)	Inj: 2mg/mL	• Adjunct to percutaneous coronary intervention	Glycoprotein IIb/IIIa inhibitor	• Monitor for signs/symptoms of bleeding; document and monitor vascular puncture sites. • If hematoma develops, monitor for enlargement. • Monitor for allergic reactions (eg, anaphylaxis) and thrombocytopenia. • Check aPTT or ACT prior to arterial sheath removal; should not be removed unless aPTT ≤50 seconds or ACT ≤175 seconds. • Monitor platelet counts 2-4 hrs following bolus dose and 24 hrs prior to discharge.

(Continued)

GENERIC (BRAND)	HOW SUPPLIED	INDICATIONS	MECHANISM OF ACTION	SPECIAL INSTRUCTIONS
PLATELET AGGREGATION INHIBITORS *(Continued)*				
Anagrelide HCl (Agrylin)	**Cap:** 0.5mg, (generic) 0.5mg, 1mg	• Thrombocytopenia, secondary to myeloproliferative disorders	Not established; suspected to reduce platelet production	• Dose adjustment is required for patients with moderate hepatic impairment. • Contraindicated in severe hepatic impairment. • Monitor for signs/symptoms of cardiovascular effects, interstitial lung diseases, and thrombocytopenia. • Monitor platelet counts every 2 days during 1st week of treatment and at least weekly thereafter until maint dose is reached. • Monitor blood counts, renal function, and LFTs. • Not for use in nursing.
Cilostazol (Pletal)	**Tab:** 50mg, 100mg	• Intermittent claudication	Not established; suspected to inhibit phosphodiesterase activity and suppress cyclic adenosine monophosphate	• Consider dose adjustment with CYP3A4 and CYP2C19 inhibitors. • Monitor for signs/symptoms of thrombocytopenia, leukopenia, and agranulocytosis. • Not for use in nursing.
Clopidogrel bisulfate (Plavix)	**Tab:** 75mg, 300mg	• ACS • Recent MI • Recent stroke • Peripheral artery disease	$P2Y_{12}$ platelet inhibitor	• Assess for CYP2C19 genotype. • Avoid use with omeprazole or esomeprazole. • Monitor for bleeding, TTP, and hypersensitivity. • Not for use in nursing.
Dipyridamole (Persantine)	**Tab:** 25mg, 50mg, 75mg	• Thrombosis prevention	Inhibits uptake of adenosine into platelets, endothelial cells, and erythrocytes	• Monitor for elevations of hepatic enzymes, hepatic failure, and chest pain in patients with coronary artery disease.
Dipyridamole-Aspirin Extended-Release (Aggrenox)	**Cap:** (Dipyridamole-Aspirin Extended-Release) 200mg-25mg	• Stroke	**Dipyridamole:** Inhibits uptake of adenosine into platelets, endothelial cells, and erythrocytes **Aspirin:** Irreversibly inhibits platelet cyclooxygenase and thus inhibits the generation of thromboxane A2	• Monitor for signs/symptoms of allergic reactions, GI effects, elevated hepatic enzymes, hepatic failure, and for bleeding.
Eptifibatide (Integrilin)	**Inj:** 20mg/10mL, 75mg/100mL, 200mg/100mL	• ACS • Percutaneous coronary intervention	Glycoprotein IIb/IIIa inhibitor	• Contraindicated in patients with renal dialysis dependency. • Monitor for signs/symptoms of bleeding, thrombocytopenia, and hypersensitivity reactions. • Monitor platelet count in patients with low platelet counts.
Prasugrel (Effient)	**Tab:** 5mg, 10mg	• Thrombosis prevention	$P2Y_{12}$ platelet inhibitor	• Monitor for signs/symptoms of bleeding, TTP, hypersensitivity, stroke, and transient ischemic attack.

GENERIC (BRAND)	HOW SUPPLIED	INDICATIONS	MECHANISM OF ACTION	SPECIAL INSTRUCTIONS
PLATELET AGGREGATION INHIBITORS *(Continued)*				
Ticlopidine HCI	**Tab:** 250mg	• Stroke • Thrombosis prevention	Interferes with platelet membrane function by inhibiting adenosine diphosphate-induced platelet fibrinogen binding and subsequent platelet-platelet interactions	• Contraindicated with severe hepatic impairment. • Monitor for signs/symptoms of neutropenia, agranulocytosis, TTP, aplastic anemia, and bleeding. • During first 3 months of therapy, monitor CBC including absolute neutrophil count, platelet count, and peripheral smear every 2 weeks. If therapy is discontinued before 3 months, monitor for 2 weeks following discontinuation. • If liver dysfunction suspected, obtain LFTs. • Monitor serum cholesterol and TG levels. • Not for use in nursing.
Tirofiban HCI (Aggrastat)	**Inj:** 50mcg/mL	• Thrombosis prevention	Glycoprotein IIb/IIIa inhibitor	• Dose adjustment required with renal impairment. • Do not administer through the same IV line as diazepam. • Monitor for signs/symptoms of bleeding, hypersensitivity reaction (eg, anaphylaxis), and thrombocytopenia. • Monitor platelet counts beginning about 6 hrs after treatment initiation and daily thereafter. • Not for use in nursing.
COAGULATION FACTOR INHIBITORS				
Dalteparin sodium (Fragmin)	**Inj:** (Syringe) 2500 IU/0.2mL, 5000 IU/0.2mL, 7500 IU/0.3mL, 10,000 IU/0.4mL, 10,000 IU/1mL, 12,500 IU/0.5mL, 15,000 IU/0.6mL, 18,000 IU/0.72mL; (MDV) 95,000 IU/3.8mL, 95,000 IU/9.5mL	• UA • MI • DVT prevention • Symptomatic venous thromboembolism	Low molecular weight heparin	• Dose adjustment required for cancer patients with thrombocytopenia or renal insufficiency. • Do not mix with other inj or infusions unless compatible. • Monitor for signs/symptoms of neurological impairment, bleeding, and thrombocytopenia. • Monitor for signs/symptoms of spinal or epidural hematomas in patients receiving neuraxial anesthesia or undergoing spinal puncture. • Perform periodic CBC with platelet count, blood chemistry, and stool occult blood tests. • Monitor anti-Xa levels in patients with severe renal impairment or if abnormal coagulation parameters or bleeding occurs.

(Continued)

GENERIC (BRAND)	HOW SUPPLIED	INDICATIONS	MECHANISM OF ACTION	SPECIAL INSTRUCTIONS
COAGULATION FACTOR INHIBITORS *(Continued)*				
Enoxaparin sodium (Lovenox)	**Inj:** (MDV) 300mg/3mL; (Syringe) 30mg/0.3mL, 40mg/0.4mL, 60mg/0.6mL, 80mg/0.8mL, 100mg/mL, 120mg/0.8mL, 150mg/mL	• DVT • UA • MI • ST-elevation MI	Low molecular weight heparin	• Refer to PI for dosage regimen with severe renal impairment (CrCl <30mL/min). • Monitor for signs/symptoms of hemorrhage and thrombocytopenia. • Monitor for epidural or spinal hematomas, and for neurological impairment if used concomitantly with spinal/epidural anesthesia or spinal puncture. • Monitor for signs/symptoms of hyperkalemia. • Periodically monitor CBC, including platelet count, and stool occult blood tests. • If bleeding occurs, monitor anti-factor Xa levels. • Not for use in nursing.
Fondaparinux sodium (Arixtra)	**Inj:** 2.5mg/0.5mL, 5mg/0.4mL, 7.5mg/0.6mL, 10mg/0.8mL	• DVT • PE	Specific factor Xa inhibitor	• Monitor for signs/symptoms of bleeding and thrombocytopenia. • In patients undergoing neuraxial anesthesia or spinal puncture, monitor for epidural or spinal hematomas and neurologic impairment. • Perform periodic CBC (including platelet count), stool occult blood tests, and renal function (including SrCr level) tests. • Contraindicated in severe renal insufficiency.
Heparin sodium	**Inj:** (Heparin Inj) (Preservative-Free) 1000 U/mL [2mL], 5000 U/mL [0.5mL]; (With Benzyl Alcohol) 5000 U/mL [10mL], 10,000 U/mL [4mL]; (With Parabens) 1000 U/mL [1mL, 10mL, 30mL], 5000 U/mL [1mL], 10,000 U/mL [1mL, 5mL], 20,000 U/mL [1mL]; (Heparin in Dextrose) 20,000 U [500mL], 25,000 U [250mL, 500mL]; (Heparin IV) 12,500 U [250mL], 25,000 U [250mL, 500mL]	• Thrombosis prevention **Heparin in Dextrose:** • PE • Arterial thrombosis **Heparin Inj:** • PE • DVT **Heparin Inj/IV:** • Anticoagulant in extracorporeal circulation and dialysis procedures	Glycosaminolycan; inhibits reactions that lead to blood clotting and the formation of fibrin clots	• Monitor for signs/symptoms of hemorrhage, thrombocytopenia, heparin resistance, hypersensitivity reactions, and hyperaminotransferasemia. • Perform periodic monitoring of platelet counts, Hct, and tests for occult blood in stool during entire therapy course, and frequent coagulation tests if given therapeutically. • If given by continuous IV infusion, monitor coagulation time every 4 hrs in early stages of treatment. • If given intermittently by IV inj, perform coagulation tests before each inj during the initial phase of treatment and then at appropriate intervals thereafter. • If given IV, monitor for fluid/solute overload and hypokalemia.

GENERIC (BRAND)	HOW SUPPLIED	INDICATIONS	MECHANISM OF ACTION	SPECIAL INSTRUCTIONS
COAGULATION FACTOR INHIBITORS *(Continued)*				
Protein C concentrate (human) (Ceprotin)	**Inj**: 500 IU, 1000 IU	• Venous thrombosis • Purpura fulminans	Vitamin K-dependent anticoagulant glycoprotein	• Maintenance of trough protein C activity levels above 25% is recommended. • Monitor for hypersensitivity/allergic reactions, bleeding episodes, transmitted infections, heparin-induced thrombocytopenia, sodium overload, platelet count and protein C activity levels, and coagulation parameters.
Warfarin sodium (Coumadin, Jantoven)	**Inj**: (Coumadin) 5mg; **Tab**: (Coumadin, Jantoven) 1mg*, 2mg*, 2.5mg*, 3mg*, 4mg*, 5mg*, 6mg*, 7.5mg*, 10mg*	• Venous thrombosis • PE • MI • Thrombosis prevention	Vitamin K-dependent coagulation factor inhibitor	• Refer to PI for recommended dosing durations, conversion from other anticoagulants (heparin), and dosing recommendations with consideration of genotype. • Pregnancy Category D (with mechanical heart valves) or Category X (for other pregnant populations). • Monitor for signs/symptoms of bleeding, necrosis/gangrene of skin and other tissues, systemic atheroemboli, cholesterol microemboli, and "purple toe" syndrome. • Perform periodic INR testing.
THROMBIN INHIBITORS				
Antithrombin (recombinant) (ATryn)	**Inj**: 1750 IU	• Thrombosis prevention	Antithrombin; plays a central role in the regulation of hemostasis	• Contraindicated with known hypersensitivity to goat and goat milk proteins. • Monitor for antithrombin activity levels once or twice/day, coagulation tests suitable for other anticoagulants used (eg, aPTT, anti-factor Xa activity), allergic-type hypersensitivity reactions (eg, hives, chest tightness, hypotension), hemorrhage, thrombosis, and infusion-site reactions.
Antithrombin III (human) (Thrombate III)	**Inj**: 500 IU	• Hereditary antithrombin III (AT-III) deficiency	Inactivation of thrombin by AT-III	• Monitor for any signs/symptoms of infection (eg, viruses) and other adverse reactions. • Monitor AT-III plasma levels.
Argatroban	**Inj**: 100mg/mL; 1mg/mL	• Thrombosis in patients with heparin induced thrombocytopenia • Percutaneous coronary intervention	Inhibits thrombin-catalyzed or thrombin-induced reactions, including fibrin formation	• Refer to PI for tabulated recommended doses and infusion rates, dose adjustments in patients with hepatic impairment, and for instructions for conversion to oral anticoagulant therapy. • Monitor for signs/symptoms of hemorrhagic events (eg, unexplained fall in Hct/Hgb, fall in BP). • Monitor aPTT 2 hrs after initiation of therapy. • Monitor ACT 5-10 min after bolus dosing, after changes in infusion rate, and at the end of percutaneous coronary intervention procedure, and every 20-30 min during prolonged procedure. • Monitor INR when combined with warfarin. • Not for use in nursing.

(Continued)

GENERIC (BRAND)	HOW SUPPLIED	INDICATIONS	MECHANISM OF ACTION	SPECIAL INSTRUCTIONS
THROMBIN INHIBITORS *(Continued)*				
Bivalirudin (Angiomax)	**Inj:** 250mg	• Percutaneous transluminal coronary angioplasty • Percutaneous coronary intervention	Inhibits thrombin by specifically binding both to the catalytic site and to anion-binding exosite of circulating and clot-bound thrombin	• Infusion dose may need to be adjusted in patients with renal impairment. • Monitor for signs/symptoms of hemorrhage (eg, decreases in BP or Hct), and thrombus formation in gamma brachytherapy. • For patients with renal impairment, monitor anticoagulant status.
Dabigatran etexilate mesylate (Pradaxa)	**Cap:** 75mg, 150mg	• Stroke	Direct thrombin inhibitor; prevents the development of a thrombus	• Monitor for bleeding, GI adverse reactions, and hypersensitivity reactions. • Periodically monitor renal function as clinically indicated. • When necessary, monitor anticoagulant activity by using activated PTT or ecarin clotting time, and not INR.

Refer to full FDA-approved labeling for additional information.

Abbreviations: ACS = acute coronary syndrome; ACT = activated clotting time; AMI = acute myocardial infarction; aPTT = activated partial thromboplastin time; CBC = complete blood count; DVT = deep vein thrombosis; PE = pulmonary embolism; TTP = thrombotic thrombocytopenic purpura; UA = unstable angina.

*Scored

HEART FAILURE TREATMENT OPTIONS

GENERIC (BRAND)	HOW SUPPLIED	DOSAGE	RENAL/HEPATIC DOSAGE ADJUSTMENT
ACE INHIBITORS			
Captopril	Tab: 12.5mg, 25mg, 50mg, 100mg	**Initial:** 25mg tid. **Usual:** 50-100mg tid. **Max:** 450mg/day.	Renal
Enalapril maleate (Vasotec)	Tab: 2.5mg, 5mg, 10mg, 20mg	**Initial:** 2.5mg qd. **Usual:** 2.5-20mg bid. **Max:** 40mg/day in divided doses.	Renal
Fosinopril sodium	Tab: 10mg, 20mg, 40mg	**Initial:** 10mg qd. **Usual:** 20-40mg qd. **Max:** 40mg qd.	Renal
Lisinopril (Prinivil)	Tab: 5mg, 10mg, 20mg	**Initial:** 5mg qd. **Usual:** 5-20mg qd.	Renal
Lisinopril (Zestril)	Tab: 2.5mg, 5mg, 10mg, 20mg, 30mg, 40mg	**Initial:** 5mg qd. **Usual:** 5-40mg qd. **Max:** 40mg/day.	Renal
Quinapril (Accupril)	Tab: 5mg, 10mg, 20mg, 40mg	**Initial:** 5mg bid. **Usual:** 20-40mg/day given in 2 equally divided doses.	Renal
Ramipril (Altace)	Cap: 1.25mg, 2.5mg, 5mg, 10mg	**Post-MI: Initial:** 2.5mg bid (switch to 1.25mg bid if hypotensive). **Titrate:** Increase (if tolerated) to target dose of 5mg bid at 3-week intervals after 1 week of initial dose.	Renal
Trandolapril (Mavik)	Tab: 1mg, 2mg, 4mg	**Post-MI: Initial:** 1mg qd. **Titrate:** Increase (as tolerated) to target dose of 4mg qd; if not tolerated, continue with the greatest tolerated dose.	Renal/Hepatic
ALDOSTERONE BLOCKERS			
Eplerenone (Inspra)	Tab: 25mg, 50mg	**Post-MI: Initial:** 25mg qd. **Titrate:** Increase to 50mg qd, preferably within 4 weeks as tolerated.	
ALPHA/BETA BLOCKERS			
Carvedilol (Coreg)	Tab: 3.125mg, 6.25mg, 12.5mg, 25mg	**Initial:** 3.125mg bid for 2 weeks. **Titrate:** May double dose over successive intervals of at least 2 weeks up to 25mg bid as tolerated. Maintain on lower doses if higher doses not tolerated. **Max:** 50mg bid if >85kg with mild-moderate HF. Reduce dose if HR <55 beats/min.	
Carvedilol phosphate (Coreg CR)	Cap, ER: 10mg, 20mg, 40mg, 80mg	**Initial:** 10mg qd for 2 weeks. **Titrate:** May double dose over successive intervals of at least 2 weeks up to 80mg qd as tolerated. Maintain on lower doses if higher doses not tolerated. Reduce dose if HR <55 beats/min.	
ANGIOTENSIN II RECEPTOR ANTAGONISTS			
Candesartan cilexetil (Atacand)	Tab: 4mg, 8mg, 16mg, 32mg	**Initial:** 4mg qd. **Titrate:** Double the dose at 2-week intervals, as tolerated, to the target dose of 32mg qd.	
Valsartan (Diovan)	Tab: 40mg, 80mg, 160mg, 320mg	**Initial:** 40mg bid. **Titrate:** May increase to 80mg or 160mg bid (use highest dose tolerated). Consider dose reduction of concomitant diuretics. **Max:** 320mg/day in divided doses.	
BETA BLOCKERS			
Metoprolol succinate (Toprol-XL)	Tab, ER: 25mg, 50mg, 100mg, 200mg	**Initial:** (NYHA Class II HF) 25mg qd or (Severe HF) 12.5mg qd for 2 weeks. **Titrate:** Double dose every 2 weeks to the highest dose level tolerated. **Max:** 200mg. Reduce dose if experiencing symptomatic bradycardia.	Hepatic

(Continued)

GENERIC (BRAND)	HOW SUPPLIED	DOSAGE	RENAL/HEPATIC DOSAGE ADJUSTMENT
DIURETICS (POTASSIUM SPARING)			
Spironolactone (Aldactone)	**Tab:** 25mg, 50mg, 100mg	**Initial:** 25mg qd. **Titrate:** If tolerated, may increase to 50mg qd as clinically indicated. May reduce to 25mg qod if not tolerated.	
VASODILATORS			
Isosorbide dinitrate- Hydralazine HCl (Bidil)	**Tab:** 20mg-37.5mg	**Initial:** 1 tab tid. **Titrate:** Increase to a maximum of 2 tabs tid, if tolerated. **Intolerable Side Effects:** May decrease to as little as ½ tab tid. Titrate up as soon as side effects subside.	
Nitroglycerin in 5% Dextrose	**Inj:** 100mcg/mL, 200mcg/mL, 400mcg/mL	**Initial:** 5mcg/min IV. **Titrate:** Increase by 5mcg/min at intervals of 3-5 min. If no response at 20mcg/min, may use increments of 10 and even 20mcg/min. Once some hemodynamic response is observed, dosage increments should be smaller and less frequent.	
MISCELLANEOUS			
Digoxin (Lanoxin)	**Inj:** (Lanoxin) 250mcg/mL, (Lanoxin Pediatric) 100mg/mL; **Sol:** (generic) 50mcg/mL; **Tab:** (Lanoxin) 62.5mcg, 125mcg, 187.5mcg, 250mcg	**LD:** (Sol) 10-15mcg/kg PO. (Inj, Tab) Administer ½ the total LD initially, then ¼ the LD q6-8h, twice. (Inj) 8-12 mcg/kg IV, (Tab) 10-15mcg/kg PO. **Maint:** (Sol) 3-4.5mcg/kg qd PO. **Initial:** (Inj) 2.4-3.6mcg/kg qd IV, (Tab) 3.4-5.1mcg/kg qd PO. **Titrate:** (Inj, Tab) May increase every 2 weeks based on response, serum drug levels, and toxicity.	
Milrinone lactate	**Inj:** 1mg/mL	**LD:** 50mcg/kg IV given slowly over 10 min. **Maint: Continuous IV Infusion: Minimum:** 0.59mg/kg/day at 0.375mcg/kg/min. **Standard:** 0.77mg/kg/day at 0.5mcg/kg/min. **Titrate:** Adjust to desired response. **Max:** 1.13mg/kg/day at 0.75mcg/kg/min.	Renal
Nesiritide (Natrecor)	**Inj:** 1.5mg	2mcg/kg IV bolus over 60 sec, then 0.01mcg/kg/min continuous IV infusion.	

Refer to full FDA-approved labeling for additional information.

Abbreviations: ER = extended-release; HF = heart failure; MI = myocardial infarction.

HYPERTENSION TREATMENT OPTIONS

GENERIC (BRAND)	HOW SUPPLIED	ADULT DOSAGE	PEDIATRIC DOSAGE
ACE INHIBITORS			
Benazepril HCl (Lotensin)	**Tab:** 5mg, 10mg, 20mg, 40mg	**Initial:** 10mg qd or 5mg qd if on diuretic. **Maint:** 20-40mg/day given qd or bid. **Max:** 80mg/day.	**≥6 Yrs: Initial:** 0.2mg/kg qd. **Max:** 0.6mg/kg or 40mg/day.
Captopril	**Tab:** 12.5mg*, 25mg*, 50mg*, 100mg*	**Initial:** 25mg bid or tid. **Titrate:** May increase to 50mg bid or tid after 1 or 2 wks. **Usual Range:** 25-150mg bid or tid. **Max:** 450mg/day.	
Enalapril (Epaned)	**Sol:** 1mg/mL [150mL]	**Initial:** 5mg qd or 2.5mg qd if on diuretics. **Titrate:** Increase dose prn. **Max:** 40mg/day.	**>1 Month: Initial:** 0.08mg/kg (up to 5mg) qd. **Max:** 0.58mg/kg or 40mg/day.
Enalapril maleate (Vasotec)	**Tab:** 2.5mg*, 5mg*, 10mg*, 20mg*	**Initial:** 5mg qd or 2.5mg qd if on diuretic. **Usual:** 10-40mg/day given qd or bid.	**1 Month-16 Yrs: HTN: Initial:** 0.08mg/kg (up to 5mg) qd. **Max:** 0.58mg/kg or 40mg/day.
Enalaprilat	**Inj:** 1.25mg/mL [1mL, 2mL]	**Usual:** 1.25mg IV over 5 min q6h for ≤48 hrs. **Max:** 20mg/day. **Concomitant Diuretic: Initial:** 0.625mg over 5 min, may repeat after 1 hr. **Maint:** Additional 1.25mg dose q6h.	
Fosinopril sodium	**Tab:** 10mg*, 20mg, 40mg	**Initial:** 10mg qd. **Usual:** 20-40mg qd. **Max:** 80mg/day.	**>50kg:** 5-10mg qd.
Lisinopril (Prinivil, Zestril)	**Tab:** (Prinivil) 5mg*, 10mg*, 20mg*; (Zestril) 2.5mg, 5mg*, 10mg, 20mg, 30mg, 40mg	**Initial:** 10mg qd or 5mg qd if on diuretic. **Usual:** 20-40mg qd. **Max:** 80mg/day.	**≥6 Yrs: Initial:** 0.07mg/kg qd (up to 5mg). **Max:** 0.61mg/kg or 40mg.
Moexipril HCl (Univasc)	**Tab:** 7.5mg*, 15mg*	**Initial:** 7.5mg qd 1 hr ac or 3.75mg qd 1 hr ac if on diuretic. **Usual:** 7.5-30mg/day given qd or bid. **Max:** 60mg/day.	
Perindopril erbumine (Aceon)	**Tab:** 2mg*, 4mg*, 8mg*	**Initial:** 4mg qd. **Maint:** 4-8mg/day given qd or bid. **Max:** 16mg/day.	
Quinapril HCl (Accupril)	**Tab:** 5mg*, 10mg, 20mg, 40mg	**Initial:** 10-20mg qd or 5mg qd if on diuretic. **Titrate:** According to BP at 2-wk intervals. **Usual:** 20-80mg/day given qd or bid.	
Ramipril (Altace)	**Cap:** 1.25mg, 2.5mg, 5mg, 10mg	**Initial:** 2.5mg qd. **Maint:** 2.5-20mg/day given qd or bid.	
Trandolapril (Mavik)	**Tab:** 1mg*, 2mg, 4mg	**Initial:** 1mg qd in nonblack patients; 2mg qd in black patients or 0.5mg qd if on diuretic. **Titrate:** According to BP at 1-wk intervals. **Usual:** 2-4mg qd. **Max:** 8mg/day.	

(Continued)

GENERIC (BRAND)	HOW SUPPLIED	ADULT DOSAGE	PEDIATRIC DOSAGE
ACE INHIBITORS-CALCIUM CHANNEL BLOCKERS			
Amlodipine besylate-Benazepril HCl (Lotrel)	Cap: (Amlodipine-Benazepril) 2.5mg-10mg, 5mg-10mg, 5mg-20mg, 5mg-40mg, 10mg-20mg, 10mg-40mg	**Initial:** 2.5mg-10mg qd. **Titrate:** May increase up to 10mg-40mg qd if BP remains uncontrolled.	
Trandolapril-Verapamil HCl (Tarka)	Tab, ER: (Trandolapril-Verapamil ER) 2mg-180mg, 1mg-240mg, 2mg-240mg, 4mg-240mg	Combination may be substituted for same component doses.	
ACE INHIBITORS-THIAZIDE DIURETICS			
Captopril-HCTZ	Tab: (Captopril-HCTZ) 25mg-15mg*, 25mg-25mg*, 50mg-15mg*, 50mg-25mg*	**Initial:** 25mg-15mg qd 1 hr ac. **Titrate:** Adjust at 6-wk intervals, unless situation demands more rapid adjustment. **Max:** 150mg captopril and 50mg HCTZ per day.	
Enalapril-HCTZ (Vaseretic)	Tab: (Enalapril-HCTZ) 5mg-12.5mg, 10mg-25mg*; (Vaseretic) 10mg-25mg*	**Not Controlled with Enalapril or HCTZ Monotherapy: Initial:** 5mg-12.5mg or 10mg-25mg qd. **Titrate:** May increase after 2-3 wks. **Max:** 20mg enalapril and 50mg HCTZ per day.	
Fosinopril sodium-HCTZ	Tab: (Fosinopril-HCTZ) 10mg-12.5mg, 20mg-12.5mg*	**Not Controlled with Fosinopril or HCTZ Monotherapy:** 10mg-12.5mg tab or 20mg-12.5mg tab qd.	
Lisinopril-HCTZ (Zestoretic)	Tab: (Lisinopril-HCTZ) 10mg-12.5mg, 20mg-12.5mg, 20mg-25mg	**Not Controlled with Lisinopril or HCTZ Monotherapy: Initial:** 10mg-12.5mg or 20mg-12.5mg qd, depending on current monotherapy dose. **Titrate:** May increase after 2-3 wks.	
Moexipril HCl-HCTZ (Uniretic)	Tab: (Moexipril-HCTZ) 7.5mg-12.5mg*, 15mg-12.5mg*, 15mg-25mg*	**Not Controlled with Moexipril or HCTZ Monotherapy: Initial:** 7.5mg-12.5mg, 15mg-12.5mg, or 15mg-25mg qd 1 hr ac. **Titrate:** May increase after 2-3 wks. **Max:** 30mg moexipril and 50mg HCTZ per day.	
Quinapril HCl-HCTZ (Accuretic)	Tab: (Quinapril-HCTZ) 10mg-12.5mg*, 20mg-12.5mg*, 20mg-25mg	**Not Controlled with Quinapril Monotherapy: Initial:** 10mg-12.5mg or 20mg-12.5mg qd. **Titrate:** May increase after 2-3 wks.	
ALDOSTERONE BLOCKERS			
Eplerenone (Inspra)	Tab: 25mg, 50mg	**Initial:** 50mg qd. **Titrate:** May increase to 50mg bid. **Max:** 100mg/day.	
ALPHA ADRENERGIC AGONISTS			
Clonidine HCl (Catapres, Catapres-TTS)	Patch, ER (TTS): (TTS-1) 0.1mg, (TTS-2) 0.2mg, (TTS-3) 0.3mg; Tab: 0.1mg, 0.2mg, 0.3mg	(Patch) **Initial:** 0.1mg/24 hrs patch wkly. **Titrate:** May increase after 1-2 wks. **Max:** 0.6mg/24 hrs. (Tab) **Initial:** 0.1mg bid. **Titrate:** May increase by 0.1mg/day wkly. **Usual:** 0.2-0.6mg/day in divided doses. **Max:** 2.4mg/day.	

GENERIC (BRAND)	HOW SUPPLIED	ADULT DOSAGE	PEDIATRIC DOSAGE
ALPHA ADRENERGIC AGONISTS-THIAZIDE DIURETICS			
Clonidine HCl-Chlorthalidone (Clorpres)	**Tab:** (Clonidine-Chlorthalidone) 0.1mg-15mg*, 0.2mg-15mg*, 0.3mg-15mg*	0.1mg-15mg tab qd-bid. **Max:** 0.6mg-30mg/day.	
ALPHA/BETA BLOCKERS			
Carvedilol (Coreg, Coreg CR)	**Cap, ER:** 10mg, 20mg, 40mg, 80mg; **Tab:** 3.125mg, 6.25mg, 12.5mg, 25mg	(Cap, ER) **Initial:** 20mg qd. **Titrate:** May double dose every 7-14 days. **Max:** 80mg/day. (Tab) **Initial:** 6.25mg bid. **Titrate:** May double dose every 7-14 days. **Max:** 50mg/day.	
Labetalol HCl	**Inj:** 5mg/mL [20mL, 40mL]; **Tab:** 100mg*, 200mg*, 300mg	(Inj) **Repeated Inj: Initial:** 20mg over 2 min. **Titrate:** May give additional 40mg or 80mg at 10-min intervals. **Max:** 300mg. **Slow Continuous Infusion:** 200mg (1mg/mL) at 2mg/min. **Alternate:** 200mg (2mg/3mL) at 3mL/min. **Effective Dose Range:** 50-200mg. **Max:** 300mg. (Tab) **Initial:** 100mg bid. **Titrate:** After 2-3 days, may increase in increments of 100mg bid every 2-3 days. **Maint:** 200-400mg bid. **Severe:** 1200-2400mg/day given bid.	
ALPHA₁ RECEPTOR BLOCKERS (QUINAZOLINE)			
Doxazosin mesylate (Cardura)	**Tab:** 1mg*, 2mg*, 4mg*, 8mg*	**Initial:** 1mg qd (am or pm). **Titrate:** May increase to 2mg and if necessary to 4mg, 8mg, and 16mg qd.	
Prazosin HCl (Minipress)	**Cap:** 1mg, 2mg, 5mg	**Initial:** 1mg bid-tid. **Titrate:** May slowly increase to 20mg/day in divided doses. **Usual:** 6-15mg/day in divided doses.	
Terazosin HCl	**Cap:** 1mg, 2mg, 5mg, 10mg	**Initial:** 1mg hs. **Usual:** 1-5mg qd. Slowly increase dose or use bid regimen if substantially diminished response at 24 hrs. **Max:** 40mg/day.	
ANGIOTENSIN II RECEPTOR ANTAGONISTS			
Azilsartan medoxomil (Edarbi)	**Tab:** 40mg, 80mg	**Usual:** 80mg qd. **With High Dose Diuretics: Initial:** 40mg qd.	
Candesartan cilexetil (Atacand)	**Tab:** 4mg*, 8mg*, 16mg*, 32mg*	**Monotherapy without Volume Depletion: Initial:** 16mg qd. **Usual:** 8-32mg/day given qd or bid.	Administer qd or divide into 2 equal doses. **6-<17 Yrs: >50kg: Initial:** 8-16mg. **Usual:** 4-32mg/day. **<50kg: Initial:** 4-8mg. **Usual:** 2-16mg/day. **1-<6 Yrs: Initial:** (PO Sus) 0.20mg/kg. **Usual:** 0.05-0.4mg/kg/day.
Eprosartan mesylate (Teveten)	**Tab:** 400mg, 600mg	**Initial (Monotherapy and Not Volume-Depleted):** 600mg qd. **Usual:** 400-800mg/day given qd-bid. May give bid using same total daily dose or consider dose increase if effect is inadequate. **Max:** 800mg/day.	

GENERIC (BRAND)	HOW SUPPLIED	ADULT DOSAGE	PEDIATRIC DOSAGE
ANGIOTENSIN II RECEPTOR ANTAGONISTS *(Continued)*			
Irbesartan (Avapro)	**Tab:** 75mg, 150mg, 300mg	**Initial:** 150mg qd. **Titrate:** May increase to 300mg qd. **Max:** 300mg qd.	
Losartan potassium (Cozaar)	**Tab:** 25mg, 50mg, 100mg	**Initial:** 50mg qd. **Usual:** 25-100mg/day given qd or bid.	**≥6 Yrs: Initial:** 0.7mg/kg qd (up to 50mg total). **Max:** 1.4mg/kg/day or 100mg/day.
Olmesartan medoxomil (Benicar)	**Tab:** 5mg, 20mg, 40mg	**Initial:** 20mg qd. **Titrate:** May increase to 40mg qd after 2 wks.	**6-16 Yrs: ≥35kg: Initial:** 20mg qd. **Titrate:** May increase to 40mg qd after 2 wks. **Max:** 40mg qd. **20-<35kg: Initial:** 10mg qd. **Titrate:** May increase to 20mg qd after 2 wks. **Max:** 20mg qd.
Telmisartan (Micardis)	**Tab:** 20mg, 40mg, 80mg	**Initial:** 40mg qd. **Usual:** 20-80mg/day.	
Valsartan (Diovan)	**Tab:** 40mg*, 80mg, 160mg, 320mg	**Initial:** 80mg or 160mg qd. **Max:** 320mg/day.	**6-16 Yrs: Initial:** 1.3mg/kg qd (up to 40mg total). **Max:** 2.7mg/kg (up to 160mg) qd.
ANGIOTENSIN II RECEPTOR ANTAGONISTS-CALCIUM CHANNEL BLOCKERS-THIAZIDE DIURETICS			
Amlodipine-Valsartan-HCTZ (Exforge HCT)	**Tab:** (Amlodipine-Valsartan-HCTZ) 5mg-160mg-12.5mg, 5mg-160mg-25mg, 10mg-160mg-12.5mg, 10mg-160mg-25mg, 10mg-320mg-25mg	**Usual:** Dose qd. May increase after 2 wks. **Max:** 10mg-320mg-25mg qd.	
Olmesartan medoxomil-Amlodipine besylate-HCTZ (Tribenzor)	**Tab:** (Olmesartan-Amlodipine-HCTZ) 20mg-5mg-12.5mg, 40mg-5mg-12.5mg, 40mg-5mg-25mg, 40mg-10mg-12.5mg, 40mg-10mg-25mg	**Usual:** Dose qd. May increase after 2 wks. **Max:** 40mg-10mg-25mg qd.	
ANGIOTENSIN II RECEPTOR ANTAGONISTS-THIAZIDE DIURETICS			
Azilsartan medoxomil-Chlorthalidone (Edarbyclor)	**Tab:** (Azilsartan-Chlorthalidone) 40mg-12.5mg, 40mg-25mg	**Initial:** 40mg-12.5mg qd. **Titrate:** May increase to 40mg-25mg after 2-4 wks. **Max:** 40mg-25mg.	
Candesartan cilexetil-HCTZ (Atacand HCT)	**Tab:** (Candesartan-HCTZ) 16mg-12.5mg*, 32mg-12.5mg*, 32mg-25mg*	**Not Controlled on 25mg HCTZ qd or Controlled on 25mg HCTZ qd with Hypokalemia:** 16mg-12.5mg qd. **Not Controlled on 32mg Candesartan qd:** 32mg-12.5mg qd, and then 32mg-25mg qd.	
Eprosartan mesylate-HCTZ (Teveten HCT)	**Tab:** (Eprosartan-HCTZ) 600mg-12.5mg, 600mg-25mg	**Usual (Not Volume-Depleted):** 600mg-12.5mg qd. **Titrate:** May increase to 600mg-25mg qd. **Max:** 600mg-25mg qd.	
Irbesartan-HCTZ (Avalide)	**Tab:** (Irbesartan-HCTZ) 150mg-12.5mg, 300mg-12.5mg	**Initial:** 150mg-12.5mg qd. **Titrate:** May increase after 1-2 wks. **Max:** 300mg-25mg qd.	
Losartan potassium-HCTZ (Hyzaar)	**Tab:** (Losartan-HCTZ) 50mg-12.5mg, 100mg-12.5mg, 100mg-25mg	**Usual:** 50mg-12.5mg qd. **Max:** 100mg-25mg qd.	

GENERIC (BRAND)	HOW SUPPLIED	ADULT DOSAGE	PEDIATRIC DOSAGE
ANGIOTENSIN II RECEPTOR ANTAGONISTS-THIAZIDE DIURETICS *(Continued)*			
Olmesartan medoxomil-HCTZ (Benicar HCT)	**Tab:** (Olmesartan-HCTZ) 20mg-12.5mg, 40mg-12.5mg, 40mg-25mg	**Usual:** 1 tab qd. **Titrate:** May adjust at intervals of 2-4 wks. **Max:** 1 tab/day.	
Telmisartan-HCTZ (Micardis HCT)	**Tab:** (Telmisartan-HCTZ) 40mg-12.5mg, 80mg-12.5mg, 80mg-25mg	**Not Controlled on 80mg Telmisartan or Controlled on 25mg/day HCTZ with Hypokalemia: Initial:** 80mg-12.5mg tab qd. **Not Controlled on 25mg/day of HCTZ: Initial:** 80mg-12.5mg qd or 80mg-25mg tab qd. **Titrate/Max:** Increase to 160mg-25mg after 2-4 wks.	
Valsartan-HCTZ (Diovan HCT)	**Tab:** (Valsartan-HCTZ) 80mg-12.5mg, 160mg-12.5mg, 160mg-25mg, 320mg-12.5mg, 320mg-25mg	**Initial:** 160mg-12.5mg qd. **Titrate:** May increase after 1-2 wks. **Max:** 320mg-25mg qd.	
BETA BLOCKERS			
Acebutolol HCl (Sectral)	**Cap:** 200mg, 400mg	**Mild-Moderate: Initial:** 400mg/day, given qd-bid. **Usual:** 200-800mg/day. **Severe/Inadequate Control:** 1200mg/day, given bid.	
Atenolol (Tenormin)	**Tab:** 25mg, 50mg*, 100mg	**Initial:** 50mg qd. **Titrate:** May increase to 100mg qd after 1-2 wks. **Max:** 100mg qd.	
Betaxolol	**Tab:** 10mg*, 20mg*	**Initial:** 10mg qd. **Titrate:** May increase to 20mg qd after 7-14 days. **Max:** 20mg/day.	
Bisoprolol fumarate (Zebeta)	**Tab:** 5mg*, 10mg	**Initial:** 5mg qd. **Titrate:** May increase to 10mg and then, if necessary, to 20mg qd.	
Metoprolol succinate (Toprol-XL)	**Tab, ER:** 25mg*, 50mg*, 100mg*, 200mg*	**Initial:** 25-100mg qd. **Titrate:** May increase at wkly (or longer) intervals. **Max:** 400mg/day.	**≥6 Yrs: Initial:** 1mg/kg qd up to 50mg qd. **Max:** 2mg/kg (up to 200mg) qd.
Metoprolol tartrate (Lopressor)	**Tab:** (Generic) 25mg*, 50mg*, 100mg*; (Lopressor) 50mg*, 100mg*	**Initial:** 100mg/day qd or in divided doses. **Titrate:** May increase at wkly (or longer) intervals. **Effective Range:** 100-450mg/day. **Max:** 450mg/day.	
Nadolol (Corgard)	**Tab:** 20mg*, 40mg*, 80mg*	**Initial:** 40mg qd. **Titrate:** May gradually increase in 40-80mg increments. **Maint: Usual:** 40 or 80mg qd. Doses up to 240 or 320mg qd may be needed.	
Nebivolol (Bystolic)	**Tab:** 2.5mg, 5mg, 10mg, 20mg	**Initial:** 5mg qd. **Titrate:** May increase at 2-wk intervals. **Max:** 40mg.	
Penbutolol sulfate (Levatol)	**Tab:** 20mg*	**Initial/Maint:** 20mg qd.	
Pindolol	**Tab:** 5mg*, 10mg*	**Initial:** 5mg bid. **Titrate:** May adjust dose in increments of 10mg/day at 3- to 4-wk intervals. **Max:** 60mg/day.	

(Continued)

GENERIC (BRAND)	HOW SUPPLIED	ADULT DOSAGE	PEDIATRIC DOSAGE
BETA BLOCKERS *(Continued)*			
Propranolol HCl	**Inj:** 1mg/mL; **Sol:** 20mg/5mL, 40mg/5mL [500mL]; **Tab:** 10mg*, 20mg*, 40mg*, 60mg*, 80mg*	**Initial:** 40mg bid. **Usual Maint:** 120-240mg/day. In some instances, 640mg/day may be required.	
Propranolol HCl (Inderal LA)	**Cap, ER:** 60mg, 80mg, 120mg, 160mg	**Initial:** 80mg qd. **Titrate:** May increase to 120mg qd or higher. **Maint:** 120-160mg qd. 640mg/day may be required.	
Propranolol HCl (Innopran XL)	**Cap, ER:** 80mg, 120mg	**Initial:** 80mg qhs. **Titrate:** May increase to 120mg qhs.	
Timolol maleate	**Tab:** 5mg, 10mg*, 20mg*	**Initial:** 10mg bid. **Maint:** 20-40mg/day. Wait at least 7 days between dose increases. **Max:** 60mg/day given bid.	
BETA BLOCKERS-THIAZIDE DIURETICS			
Atenolol-Chlorthalidone (Tenoretic)	**Tab:** (Atenolol-Chlorthalidone) 50mg-25mg*, 100mg-25mg	**Initial:** 50mg-25mg tab qd. **Titrate:** May increase to 100mg-25mg tab qd.	
Bisoprolol fumarate-HCTZ (Ziac)	**Tab:** (Bisoprolol-HCTZ) 2.5mg-6.25mg, 5mg-6.25mg, 10mg-6.25mg	**Not Controlled on 2.5-20mg/day Bisoprolol or Controlled on 50mg/day HCTZ with Hypokalemia: Initial:** 2.5mg-6.25mg qd. **Titrate:** May increase at 14-day intervals. **Max:** 20mg-12.5mg (two 10mg-6.25mg tabs) qd.	
Metoprolol succinate-HCTZ (Dutoprol)	**Tab:** (Metoprolol ER-HCTZ) 25mg-12.5mg, 50mg-12.5mg, 100mg-12.5mg	25-100mg of metoprolol succinate ER and 12.5-50mg of HCTZ qd. **Titrate:** Every 2 wks. **Max:** 200mg-25mg.	
Metoprolol tartrate-HCTZ (Lopressor HCT)	**Tab:** (Metoprolol-HCTZ) 50mg-25mg*, 100mg-25mg*, 100mg-50mg*; (Lopressor HCT) 50mg-25mg*, 100mg-25mg*	**Combination Therapy: Metoprolol:** 100-200mg/day given qd or in divided doses. **HCTZ:** 25-50mg/day given qd or in divided doses. **Max:** 50mg/day.	
Nadolol-Bendroflumethiazide (Corzide)	**Tab:** (Nadolol-Bendroflumethiazide) 40mg-5mg*, 80mg-5mg*	**Initial:** 40mg-5mg qd. **Titrate:** May increase to 80mg-5mg qd.	
Propranolol HCl-HCTZ	**Tab:** (Propranolol-HCTZ) 40mg-25mg*, 80mg-25mg*	**Usual:** 1 tab bid. **Max:** 160mg-50mg/day.	
CALCIUM CHANNEL BLOCKERS (DIHYDROPYRIDINE)			
Amlodipine besylate (Norvasc)	**Tab:** 2.5mg, 5mg, 10mg	**Initial:** 5mg qd. **Titrate:** 7- to 14-day intervals. If clinically warranted, titrate more rapidly. **Max:** 10mg qd.	**6-17 Yrs:** Usual: 2.5-5mg qd. **Max:** 5mg qd.
Clevidipine (Cleviprex)	**Inj:** 0.5mg/mL [50mL, 100mL]	**Initial:** 1-2mg/hr. **Titrate:** May double dose at 90-sec intervals. As BP approaches goal, interval should be lengthened to every 5-10 min. **Maint:** 4-6mg/hr. **Max:** 16mg/hr.	

GENERIC (BRAND)	HOW SUPPLIED	ADULT DOSAGE	PEDIATRIC DOSAGE
CALCIUM CHANNEL BLOCKERS (DIHYDROPYRIDINE) *(Continued)*			
Felodipine	**Tab, ER:** 2.5mg, 5mg, 10mg	**Initial:** 5mg qd. **Titrate:** May decrease to 2.5mg qd or increase to 10mg qd at intervals of not <2 wks. **Range:** 2.5-10mg qd.	
Isradipine	**Cap:** 2.5mg, 5mg	**Initial:** 2.5mg bid. **Titrate:** May adjust in increments of 5mg/day at 2- to 4-wk intervals after 2-4 wks of initiation. **Max:** 20mg/day.	
Nicardipine HCI	**Cap:** 20mg, 30mg	**Initial:** 20mg tid. **Titrate:** Allow at least 3 days before increasing dose. **Usual:** 20-40mg tid.	
Nicardipine HCI (Cardene IV)	**Inj:** 2.5mg/mL [10mL], 0.1mg/mL [200mL], 0.2mg/mL [200mL]	**Patients Not Receiving PO Nicardipine: Initial:** 5mg/hr IV infusion. **Titrate:** May increase by 2.5mg/hr every 5 min (for rapid titration) to 15 min (for gradual titration). **Max:** 15mg/hr.	
Nicardipine HCI (Cardene SR)	**Cap, SR:** 30mg, 60mg	**Initial:** 30mg bid. **Effective Range:** 30-60mg bid.	
Nifedipine (Nifedical XL, Procardia XL)	**Tab, ER:** (Nifedical XL) 30mg, 60mg; (Procardia XL) 30mg, 60mg, 90mg	**Initial:** 30 or 60mg qd. **Titrate:** Usual: 7- to 14-day period. May proceed more rapidly if needed. **Max:** 120mg/day.	
Nisoldipine (Sular)	**Tab, ER:** 8.5mg, 17mg, 25.5mg, 34mg	**Initial:** 17mg qd. **Titrate:** May increase by 8.5mg/wk or longer intervals. **Maint:** 17-34mg qd. **Max:** 34mg qd.	
CALCIUM CHANNEL BLOCKERS (DIHYDROPYRIDINE)-ANGIOTENSIN II RECEPTOR ANTAGONISTS			
Amlodipine-Olmesartan medoxomil (Azor)	**Tab:** (Amlodipine-Olmesartan) 5mg-20mg, 5mg-40mg, 10mg-20mg, 10mg-40mg	**Initial:** 5mg-20mg qd. **Titrate:** May increase dose after 1-2 wks. **Max:** 10mg-40mg qd.	
Amlodipine-Valsartan (Exforge)	**Tab:** (Amlodipine-Valsartan) 5mg-160mg, 10mg-160mg, 5mg-320mg, 10mg-320mg	**Initial:** 5mg-160mg qd. **Titrate:** May increase after 1-2 wks. **Max:** 10mg-320mg qd.	
Telmisartan-Amlodipine (Twynsta)	**Tab:** (Telmisartan-Amlodipine) 40mg-5mg, 40mg-10mg, 80mg-5mg, 80mg-10mg	**Initial:** 40mg-5mg qd or 80mg-5mg qd. **Titrate:** May be increased after at least 2 wks. **Max:** 80mg-10mg qd.	
CALCIUM CHANNEL BLOCKERS (DIHYDROPYRIDINE)-HMG COA REDUCTASE INHIBITORS			
Amlodipine besylate-Atorvastatin calcium (Caduet)	**Tab:** (Amlodipine-Atorvastatin) 2.5mg-10mg, 2.5mg-20mg, 2.5mg-40mg, 5mg-10mg, 5mg-20mg, 5mg-40mg, 5mg-80mg, 10mg-10mg,	**Amlodipine: Initial:** 5mg qd. **Titrate:** Adjust generally every 7-14 days. **Max:** 10mg qd. **Atorvastatin: Initial:** 10mg or 20mg qd (or 40mg qd for LDL reduction >45%). **Titrate:** Analyze lipids within 2-4 wks and adjust accordingly. **Usual:** 10-80mg qd.	**Amlodipine: 6-17 Yrs: Usual:** 2.5-5mg qd. **Max:** 5mg qd. **Atorvastatin: 10-17 Yrs: Initial:** 10mg/day. **Titrate:** Adjust at intervals of ≥4 wks. **Max:** 20mg/day.

(Continued)

GENERIC (BRAND)	HOW SUPPLIED	ADULT DOSAGE	PEDIATRIC DOSAGE
CALCIUM CHANNEL BLOCKERS (DIHYDROPYRIDINE)-HMG COA REDUCTASE INHIBITORS *(Continued)*			
Amlodipine besylate- Atorvastatin calcium (Caduet) *(Continued)*	10mg-20mg, 10mg-40mg, 10mg-80mg		
CALCIUM CHANNEL BLOCKERS (DIHYDROPYRIDINE)-RENIN INHIBITORS			
Aliskiren-Amlodipine (Tekamlo)	**Tab:** (Aliskiren- Amlodipine) 150mg-5mg, 150mg-10mg, 300mg-5mg, 300mg-10mg	**Initial:** 150mg-5mg qd. **Titrate:** May increase after 2-4 wks. **Max:** 300mg-10mg qd.	
CALCIUM CHANNEL BLOCKERS (DIHYDROPYRIDINE)-RENIN INHIBITORS-THIAZIDE DIURETICS			
Aliskiren-Amlodipine- HCTZ (Amturnide)	**Tab:** (Aliskiren- Amlodipine-HCTZ) 150mg-5mg-12.5mg, 300mg-5mg-12.5mg, 300mg-5mg-25mg, 300mg-10mg-12.5mg, 300mg-10mg-25mg	**Usual:** Dose qd. **Titrate:** May increase after 2 wks. **Max:** 300mg-10mg-25mg.	
CALCIUM CHANNEL BLOCKERS (NON-DIHYDROPYRIDINE)			
Diltiazem HCl (Cardizem CD, Cardizem LA, Cartia XT)	**Cap, ER:** (Cardizem CD, Cartia XT) 120mg, 180mg, 240mg, 300mg, (Cardizem CD) 360mg; **Tab, ER:** (Cardizem LA) 120mg, 180mg, 240mg, 300mg, 360mg, 420mg	(Cardizem CD, Cartia XT) **Initial (Monotherapy):** 180-240mg qd. **Usual:** 240-360mg qd. **Max:** 480mg qd. (Cardizem LA) **Initial (Monotherapy):** 180-240mg qd (am or hs). **Range:** 120-540mg qd. **Max:** 540mg/day.	
Diltiazem HCl (Dilacor XR, Diltia XT)	**Cap, ER:** (Dilacor XR) 240mg; (Diltia XT) 120mg, 180mg, 240mg	**Initial:** 180mg or 240mg qd. **Usual:** 180-480mg qd. **Max:** 540mg qd.	
Diltiazem HCl (Taztia XT, Tiazac)	**Cap, ER:** (Taztia XT) 120mg, 180mg, 240mg, 300mg, 360mg; (Tiazac) 120mg, 180mg, 240mg, 300mg, 360mg, 420mg	**Initial (Monotherapy):** 120-240mg qd. **Usual Range:** 120-540mg qd. **Max:** 540mg qd.	
Verapamil HCl (Calan)	**Tab:** 40mg, 80mg*, 120mg*	**Initial (Monotherapy):** 80mg tid (240mg/day). **Usual:** 360-480mg/day. **Max:** 480mg/day.	
Verapamil HCl (Calan SR)	**Tab, ER:** 120mg, 180mg*, 240mg*	**Initial:** 180mg qam. **Titrate:** May increase to 240mg qam, then 180mg bid (am and pm) or 240mg qam plus 120mg qpm, then 240mg q12h.	
Verapamil HCl (Covera-HS)	**Tab, ER:** 180mg, 240mg	**Initial:** 180mg qhs. **Titrate:** May increase to 240mg qhs, then 360mg (two 180mg tabs) qhs, then 480mg (two 240mg tabs) qhs.	
Verapamil HCl (Verelan)	**Cap, SR:** 120mg, 180mg, 240mg, 360mg	**Usual:** 240mg qam.	
Verapamil HCl (Verelan PM)	**Cap, ER:** 100mg, 200mg, 300mg	**Usual:** 200mg qhs.	

GENERIC (BRAND)	HOW SUPPLIED	ADULT DOSAGE	PEDIATRIC DOSAGE
LOOP DIURETICS			
Furosemide (Lasix)	**Sol:** (Generic) 10mg/mL [60mL, 120mL], 40mg/5mL [500mL]; **Tab:** (Lasix) 20mg, 40mg*, 80mg	**Initial:** 40mg bid.	
Torsemide (Demadex)	**Inj:** (Generic) 10mg/mL [2mL, 5mL]; **Tab:** (Demadex) 5mg*, 10mg*, 20mg*, 100mg*	**Initial:** 5mg qd. **Titrate:** May increase to 10mg qd after 4-6 wks.	
POTASSIUM-SPARING DIURETICS			
Amiloride HCl (Midamor)	**Tab:** 5mg	**Initial:** 5mg qd. **Titrate:** May increase to 10mg/day.	
Spironolactone (Aldactone)	**Tab:** 25mg, 50mg*, 100mg*	**Initial:** 50-100mg/day given qd or in divided doses for at least 2 wks.	
POTASSIUM-SPARING DIURETICS-THIAZIDE DIURETICS			
Amiloride HCl-HCTZ	**Tab:** (Amiloride-HCTZ) 5mg-50mg*	**Initial:** 1 tab/day. **Titrate:** May increase to 2 tabs/day if necessary. **Max:** 2 tabs/day.	
Spironolactone-HCTZ (Aldactazide)	**Tab:** (Spironolactone-HCTZ) 25mg-25mg, 50mg-50mg*	**Usual:** 50-100mg of each component as single dose or in divided doses.	
Triamterene-HCTZ (Dyazide)	**Cap:** (Triamterene-HCTZ) 37.5mg-25mg	1-2 caps qd.	
Triamterene-HCTZ (Maxzide, Maxzide-25)	**Tab:** (Triamterene-HCTZ) (Maxzide) 75mg-50mg*, (Maxzide-25) 37.5mg-25mg*	(Maxzide-25) 1-2 tabs qd, given as a single dose or (Maxzide) 1 tab qd.	
QUINAZOLINE DIURETICS			
Metolazone (Zaroxolyn)	**Tab:** 2.5mg, 5mg, 10mg	2.5-5mg qd.	
RENIN INHIBITORS			
Aliskiren (Tekturna)	**Tab:** 150mg, 300mg	**Initial:** 150mg qd. **Titrate:** May increase to 300mg qd. **Max:** 300mg/day.	
RENIN INHIBITORS-THIAZIDE DIURETICS			
Aliskiren-HCTZ (Tekturna HCT)	**Tab:** (Aliskiren-HCTZ) 150mg-12.5mg, 150mg-25mg, 300mg-12.5mg, 300mg-25mg	**Add-On/Initial Therapy:** Initiate with 150mg-12.5mg qd. **Titrate:** May increase after 2-4 wks. **Max:** 300mg-25mg qd.	
THIAZIDE DIURETICS			
Chlorothiazide (Diuril)	**Sus:** (Diuril) 250mg/5mL [237mL]; **Tab:** (Generic) 250mg*, 500mg*	**Initial:** 0.5-1g/day given qd or in divided doses. **Max:** 2g/day in divided doses.	**Usual:** 10-20mg/kg/day given qd-bid. **Max: 2-12 Yrs:** 1g/day. **≤2 Yrs:** 375mg/day. **<6 Months:** Up to 30mg/kg/day given bid.
Chlorthalidone (Thalitone)	**Tab:** (Generic) 25mg, 50mg*; (Thalitone) 15mg	**Initial:** 25mg qd. **Titrate:** May increase to 50mg qd, then to 100mg qd. **Max:** 100mg qd. **Maint:** May be lower than initial.	

(Continued)

GENERIC (BRAND)	HOW SUPPLIED	ADULT DOSAGE	PEDIATRIC DOSAGE
THIAZIDE DIURETICS *(Continued)*			
Hydrochlorothiazide	**Tab:** 12.5mg, 25mg*, 50mg*	**Initial:** 25mg qd. **Titrate:** May increase to 50mg/day given qd or in 2 divided doses.	1-2mg/kg/day given qd or in 2 divided doses. **Max: 2-12 Yrs:** 100mg/day. **Infants up to 2 Yrs:** 37.5mg/day. **<6 Months:** Up to 3mg/kg/day given in 2 divided doses may be required.
Hydrochlorothiazide (Microzide)	**Cap:** 12.5mg	**Initial:** 12.5mg qd. **Max:** 50mg/day.	
Indapamide	**Tab:** 1.25mg, 2.5mg	**Initial:** 1.25mg qam. **Titrate:** May increase to 2.5mg qd after 4 wks, then to 5mg qd after additional 4 wks.	
Methyclothiazide	**Tab:** 5mg*	**Usual:** 2.5-5mg qd.	
VASODILATORS			
Hydralazine HCl	**Inj:** 20mg/mL; **Tab:** 10mg, 25mg, 50mg, 100mg	(Tab) **Initial:** 10mg qid for the first 2-4 days. **Titrate:** Increase to 25mg qid for the rest of the 1st wk, then increase to 50mg qid for 2nd and subsequent wks. **Resistant Patients:** ≤300mg/day. (Inj) **Usual:** 20-40mg only when drug cannot be given PO.	(Tab) **Initial:** 0.75mg/kg/day given qid. **Titrate:** Increase gradually over 3-4 wks. **Max:** 7.5mg/kg/day or 200mg/day. (Inj) **Usual:** 1.7-3.5mg/kg divided in 4-6 doses only when drug cannot be given PO.

Refer to full FDA-approved labeling for additional information.

*Scored.

Abbreviations: ACE = angiotensin-converting enzyme; ER = extended-release; HCTZ = hydrochlorothiazide; SR = sustained-release.

PULMONARY ARTERIAL HYPERTENSION AGENTS

GENERIC (BRAND)	HOW SUPPLIED	DOSAGE	SPECIAL INSTRUCTIONS
ENDOTHELIN RECEPTOR ANTAGONISTS			
Ambrisentan (Letairis)	Tab: 5mg, 10mg	**Adults: Initial:** 5mg qd. **Titrate:** May increase to 10mg qd if 5mg is tolerated. **Max:** 10mg qd.	• Monitor for fluid retention, pulmonary edema, PVOD, and hepatotoxicity. • Obtain pregnancy test prior to the initiation of treatment and monthly thereafter. • Monitor Hgb levels at initiation, at 1 month, and periodically thereafter. • Not recommended in moderate or severe hepatic insufficiency. • Pregnancy Category X. • Not for use in nursing.
Bosentan (Tracleer)	Tab: 62.5mg, 125mg	**Adults: Initial:** 62.5mg bid for 4 wks. **Maint/Max:** 125mg bid. **Pediatrics: >12 Yrs: <40kg: Initial/ Maint:** 62.5mg bid. **Treatment Discontinuation:** Consider gradual dose reduction (62.5mg bid for 3-7 days).	• Refer to PI for dosage adjustment in patients developing aminotransferase elevations and in patients receiving ritonavir for at least 10 days or having ritonavir added to treatment with Tracleer. • Monitor for clinical symptoms of hepatotoxicity, increases in bilirubin ≥2X ULN, fluid retention, signs of pulmonary edema, and PVOD. • Measure serum aminotransferase levels prior to initiation of treatment, and then monthly. • Obtain monthly pregnancy tests. • Monitor Hgb levels after 1 and 3 months of treatment, then every 3 months thereafter. • Avoid use in moderate or severe hepatic insufficiency. • Not for use in nursing.
Macitentan (Opsumit)	Tab: 10mg	**Adults:** 10mg qd. **Max:** 10mg qd.	• Monitor for signs/symptoms of pulmonary edema, PVOD, and hepatic impairment. • Obtain pregnancy test before initiation of treatment, monthly during treatment, and 1 month after discontinuation. • Monitor liver enzyme tests and Hgb levels as clinically indicated. • Pregnancy Category X. • Not for use in nursing.
PHOSPHODIESTERASE-5 INHIBITORS			
Sildenafil citrate (Revatio)	Inj: 10mg [12.5mL vial]; Susp: 10mg/mL; Tab: 20mg	**Adults: PO:** 20mg tid, 4-6 hrs apart. **Max:** 20mg tid. **IV:** 10mg (12.5mL) IV bolus tid.	• Monitor for signs of pulmonary edema, decreased/sudden loss of vision or hearing, epistaxis, priapism, and vaso-occlusive crises. • Monitor BP.
Tadalafil (Adcirca)	Tab: 20mg	**Adults:** 40mg qd.	• Refer to PI for dosage adjustment in patients receiving ritonavir for at least 1 wk or having ritonavir added to treatment with Adcirca. • Dose adjustment required in mild or moderate hepatic/renal insufficiency. • Avoid use in severe hepatic/renal insufficiency. • Monitor for signs/symptoms of anginal chest pain, vision or hearing loss, pulmonary edema, nonarteritic anterior ischemic optic neuropathy, prolonged erections >4 hrs, and priapism. • Monitor BP.

(Continued)

GENERIC (BRAND)	HOW SUPPLIED	DOSAGE	SPECIAL INSTRUCTIONS
SOLUBLE GUANYLATE CYCLASE STIMULATOR			
Riociguat (Adempas)	**Tab:** 0.5mg, 1mg, 1.5mg, 2mg, 2.5mg	**Adults: Initial:** 1mg tid; consider 0.5mg tid for patients who may not tolerate the hypotensive effect. **Titrate:** Increase by 0.5mg tid if systolic BP remains >95mmHg and patient has no signs/symptoms of hypotension. Dose increases should be no sooner than 2 wks apart. **Max:** 2.5mg tid. If at any time symptoms of hypotension occur, decrease dose by 0.5mg tid. **Dose Interruption:** Retitrate if treatment is interrupted for ≥3 days.	• Dose adjustment required in smokers. • Monitor for signs/symptoms of hypotension, bleeding, pulmonary edema, and PVOD. • Obtain pregnancy test before initiation of treatment, monthly during treatment, and 1 month after discontinuation. • Not recommended in patients with CrCl <15mL/min, on dialysis, or in patients with severe hepatic insufficiency (Child-Pugh C). • Pregnancy Category X. • Not for use in nursing.
VASODILATORS			
Epoprostenol (Veletri)	**Inj:** 0.5mg, 1.5mg [10mL vials]	**Adults: Chronic Infusion: Initial:** 2ng/kg/min IV. **Titrate:** Increase in increments of 1-2ng/kg/min q15 min or longer if symptoms of PAH persist or recur. Identify a lower dose if initial infusion rate is not tolerated. If dose-limiting pharmacologic effects occur, decrease gradually in 2ng/kg/min decrements q15 min or longer until dose-limiting effects resolve.	• Refer to PI for administration, reconstitution, and infusion rate instructions. • Monitor for signs of recurrence or worsening of pulmonary HTN, pulmonary edema, and abrupt withdrawal symptoms. • Monitor standing and supine BP and HR for several hrs following dose adjustments.
Epoprostenol sodium (Flolan)	**Inj:** 0.5mg, 1.5mg [17mL vials]	**Adults: Chronic Infusion: Initial:** 2ng/kg/min IV. **Titrate:** Increase in increments of 1-2ng/kg/min q15 min or longer if symptoms of PAH persist or recur. Identify a lower dose if initial infusion rate is not tolerated. If dose-limiting pharmacologic effects occur, decrease gradually in 2ng/kg/min decrements q15 min or longer until dose-limiting effects resolve.	• Refer to PI for administration, reconstitution, and infusion rate instructions. • Monitor patient for signs of recurrence or worsening of pulmonary HTN, pulmonary edema, and abrupt withdrawal symptoms. • Monitor standing and supine BP and HR for several hrs following dose adjustments.
Iloprost (Ventavis)	**Sol, Inh:** 10mcg/mL, 20mcg/mL [1mL ampule]	**Adult: Initial:** 2.5mcg. **Titrate:** If 2.5mcg is well tolerated, increase to 5mcg and maintain at that dose; otherwise maintain at 2.5mcg. Give 6-9X/day (no more than once q2h) during waking hrs, according to individual need and tolerability. **Max:** 45mcg/day (5mcg 9X/day).	• Dose adjustment required in hepatic insufficiency. • Monitor vital signs while initiating treatment. • Monitor for exertional syncope, pulmonary edema, and bronchospasms. • Not for use in nursing.

GENERIC (BRAND)	HOW SUPPLIED	DOSAGE	SPECIAL INSTRUCTIONS
VASODILATORS *(Continued)*			
Nitric oxide (Inomax)	**Gas, Inh:** 100ppm, 800ppm [353L, 1963L]	**Pediatrics: Term/Near-Term (>34 Wks) Neonates: Usual:** 20ppm. Maintain treatment for up to 14 days or until underlying oxygen desaturation has resolved and the neonate is ready to be weaned from therapy. **Max:** 20ppm.	• Monitor for rebound pulmonary HTN syndrome, airway inflammation, and damage to lung tissues. • Monitor for PaO_2 and inspired NO_2 during administration. • Measure methemoglobin within 4-8 hrs after initiation of therapy and periodically throughout treatment. • Monitor for pulmonary edema, increased pulmonary capillary wedge pressure, worsening of left ventricular dysfunction, systemic hypotension, bradycardia, and cardiac arrest in patients with left ventricular dysfunction.
Treprostinil (Orenitram)	**Tab, ER:** 0.125mg, 0.25mg, 1mg, 2.5mg	**Adults: Initial:** 0.25mg bid. **Titrate:** Increase in increments of 0.25mg or 0.5mg bid every 3-4 days. Consider titrating slower if 0.25mg bid increments are not tolerated. **TDD:** Can be divided and given tid, titrating by increments of 0.125mg tid. **Max:** Determined by tolerability. If intolerable pharmacologic effects occur, decrease in 2ng/kg/min decrements.	• Consider a temporary infusion of SQ or IV treprostinil in a planned treatment interruption for patients unable to take oral medications. • Dose adjustment required in mild hepatic impairment (Child-Pugh Class A) and concomitant administration with CYP2C8 inhibitors. • Contraindicated in severe hepatic impairment (Child-Pugh Class C). • Avoid use in moderate hepatic impairment (Child-Pugh Class B). • Monitor for abrupt withdrawal symptoms. • Monitor for bleeding, particularly in patients receiving anticoagulants. • Monitor for tablets lodged in a diverticulum, in patients with diverticulosis. • Not for use in nursing.
Treprostinil (Remodulin)	**Inj:** 1mg/mL, 2.5mg/mL, 5mg/mL, 10mg/mL [20mL vials]	**Adults: Continuous Infusion: Initial:** 1.25ng/kg/min SQ or IV. Reduce rate to 0.625ng/kg/min if not tolerated. **Titrate:** Increase in increments of 1.25ng/kg/min per wk for the first 4 wks, then 2.5ng/kg/min per wk thereafter, depending on clinical response. If therapy is interrupted for a few hrs, restart at same dose rate; longer periods of interruption may require retitration.	• Can dilute for IV infusion using SWFI, 0.9% NaCl, or sterile diluent for epoprostenol sodium. • Dose adjustment required in mild or moderate hepatic insufficiency. • Monitor for worsening of symptoms or lack of improvement, bloodstream infections, sepsis, and for abrupt withdrawal symptoms.

(Continued)

GENERIC (BRAND)	HOW SUPPLIED	DOSAGE	SPECIAL INSTRUCTIONS
VASODILATORS *(Continued)*			
Treprostinil (Tyvaso)	**Sol, Inh:** 0.6mg/mL [2.9mL ampule]	**Adults:** Dose in 4 separate, equally spaced treatment sessions (approximately 4 hrs apart) per day, during waking hrs. **Initial:** 3 breaths (18mcg) per treatment session qid. If not tolerated, reduce to 1 or 2 breaths and subsequently increase to 3 breaths, as tolerated. **Maint:** Increase by an additional 3 breaths at approximately 1- to 2-wk intervals, if tolerated, until target dose of 9 breaths (54mcg) is reached per treatment session qid as tolerated. If adverse effects preclude titration to target dose, continue at the highest tolerated dose. If a scheduled treatment session is missed or interrupted, resume as soon as possible at the usual dose. **Max:** 9 breaths per treatment session qid.	• Caution in hepatic/renal insufficiency. • Monitor for worsening of lung disease, loss of drug effect, symptomatic hypotension, and bleeding.

Refer to full FDA-approved labeling for more information.

Abbreviations: PAH = pulmonary artery hypertension; PVOD = pulmonary veno-occlusive disease; SWFI = sterile water for injection.

ACNE MANAGEMENT

GENERIC (BRAND)	HOW SUPPLIED	DOSAGE
SYSTEMIC AGENTS		
Isotretinoin (Absorica)	**Cap:** 10mg, 20mg, 30mg, 40mg	**Adults & Peds ≥12 yrs:** 0.5-1mg/kg/day given in 2 divided doses for 15-20 wks. **Max:** 2mg/kg/day.
Isotretinoin (Amnesteem, Claravis)	**Cap:** (Amnesteem) 10mg, 20mg, 40mg; (Claravis) 10mg, 20mg, 30mg, 40mg	**Adults & Peds ≥12 yrs:** 0.5-1mg/kg/day given in 2 divided doses for 15-20 wks. **Max:** 2mg/kg/day.
Minocycline HCl (Solodyn)	**Tab, Extended-Release:** 55mg, 65mg, 80mg, 105mg, 115mg	**Adults & Peds ≥12 yrs:** 1mg/kg qd for 12 wks.
TOPICAL AGENTS		
Adapalene (Differin)	**Cre:** 0.1%	**Adults & Peds ≥12 yrs:** Apply a thin layer to affected area qpm.
	Gel: 0.1%, 0.3%	**Adults & Peds ≥12 yrs:** Apply a thin layer to affected area qpm after washing.
	Lot: 0.1%	**Adults & Peds ≥12 yrs:** Apply a thin layer to cover the entire face and other affected area qd after washing.
Azelaic acid (Azelex)	**Cre:** 20%	**Adults & Peds ≥12 yrs:** Wash and dry skin. Massage gently but thoroughly into affected area bid (am and pm).
Benzoyl peroxide (BenzEFoam, BenzEFoam Ultra)	(BenzEFoam) **Foam:** 5.3%	**Adults & Peds ≥12 yrs:** Rub into affected area qd or ud until completely absorbed. **Facial Acne:** Use a dollop the size of a marble. **Back/Chest Acne:** Use a dollop the size of a whole walnut.
	(BenzEFoam Ultra) **Foam:** 9.8%	**Adults & Peds ≥12 yrs:** Rub into affected area qd, then bid-tid prn or ud until completely absorbed. Rinse off after 2 min.
Benzoyl peroxide (NeoBenz Micro SD, NeoBenz Micro Wash)	(SD) **Cre:** 5.5%	**Adults & Peds ≥12 yrs:** Apply to affected area qd-bid.
	(Wash) **Sol:** 7%	
Benzoyl peroxide	**Gel:** 2.5%, 5%, 10%	**Adults & Peds ≥12 yrs: (2.5%) Initial:** Apply to affected area qd for 1 week, then bid. **(5%, 10%)** May be initiated in patients demonstrating accommodation to 2.5% gel.
Clindamycin phosphate (Evoclin, Cleocin T, Clindagel)	**Foam:** 1%	**Adults & Peds ≥12 yrs:** Apply to affected area qd.
Clindamycin phosphate (Cleocin T)	**Gel:** 1%	**Adults & Peds ≥12 yrs:** Apply thin layer to affected area bid.
	Lot: 1%	
	Sol: 1%	
Clindamycin phosphate (Clindagel)	**Gel:** 1%	**Adults & Peds ≥12 yrs:** Apply thin layer to affected area qd.
Dapsone (Aczone)	**Gel:** 5%	**Adults & Peds ≥12 yrs:** Apply pea-sized amount to affected area bid.
Erythromycin (Akne-Mycin Ointment)	**Oint:** 2%	**Adults:** Apply to affected area bid (am and pm).
Erythromycin	**Gel:** 2%	**Adults:** Wash and dry skin. Apply a thin layer to affected area qd-bid. Do not rub in; spread lightly.
	Pledgets: 2%	**Adults:** Rub pledget or apply sol to affected area bid (am and pm).
	Sol: 2%	
Gentamicin sulfate	**Cre:** 0.1%	**Adults & Peds >1 yr:** Apply small amount to affected area tid-qid.
	Oint: 0.1%	

(Continued)

GENERIC (BRAND)	HOW SUPPLIED	DOSAGE
TOPICAL AGENTS *(Continued)*		
Tazarotene (Fabior)	Foam: 0.1%	**Adults & Peds ≥12 yrs:** Wash and dry skin. Apply thin layer to affected area of face and/or upper trunk qpm. Massage into skin.
Tazarotene (Tazorac)	Cre: 0.1% Gel: 0.1%	**Adults & Peds ≥12 yrs:** Wash and dry skin. Apply thin layer to affected area qpm.
Tretinoin (Atralin)	Gel: 0.05%	**Adults & Peds ≥10 yrs:** Apply thin layer to affected area qhs.
Tretinoin (Avita)	Cre: 0.025% Gel: 0.025%	**Adults:** Apply thin layer to affected area qpm.
Tretinoin (Retin-A)	Cre: 0.025%, 0.05%, 0.1% Gel: 0.01%, 0.025%	**Adults:** Apply thin layer to affected area qhs.
Tretinoin (Retin-A Micro)	Gel: 0.04%, 0.08%, 0.1%	**Adults & Peds ≥ 12 yrs:** Apply thin layer to affected area qhs.
Tretinoin (Tretin-X)	Cre: 0.025%, 0.0375%, 0.05%, 0.075%, 0.1%	**Adults & Peds ≥ 12 yrs:** Apply thin layer to affected area qhs.
COMBINATION PRODUCTS, TOPICAL		
Adapalene-Benzoyl peroxide (Epiduo)	Gel: 0.1%-2.5%	**Adults & Peds ≥9 yrs:** Apply pea-sized amount to affected area of face and/or trunk qd after washing.
Benzoyl peroxide-Clindamycin phosphate (Acanya)	Gel: 2.5%-1.2%	**Adults & Peds ≥12 yrs:** Apply pea-sized amount to face qd.
Benzoyl peroxide-Clindamycin phosphate (BenzaClin)	Gel: 5%-1%	**Adults & Peds ≥12 yrs:** Wash and dry skin. Apply to affected area bid or ud.
Benzoyl peroxide-Clindamycin phosphate (Duac)	Gel: 5%-1.2%	**Adults & Peds ≥12 yrs:** Wash and dry skin. Apply thin layer to face qpm or ud.
Benzoyl peroxide-Erythromycin phosphate (Benzamycin)	Gel: 5%-3%	**Adults & Peds ≥12 yrs:** Wash and dry skin. Apply to affected area bid or ud.
Clindamycin phosphate-Tretinoin (Veltin)	Gel: 1.2%-0.025%	**Adults & Peds ≥12 yrs:** Apply pea-sized amount lightly covering the entire affected area qpm.
Clindamycin phosphate-Tretinoin (Ziana)	Gel: 1.2%-0.025%	**Adults & Peds ≥12 yrs:** Apply pea-sized amount onto 1 fingertip, dot onto chin, cheeks, nose, and forehead, then gently rub over entire face qhs.
Hydrocortisone acetate-Iodoquinol (Alcortin-A)	Gel: 2%-1%	**Adults & Peds ≥12 yrs:** Apply to affected area tid-qid or ud.
Sodium sulfacetamide-Sulfur (Avar Cleanser, Avar Cleansing Pads, Avar LS Cleanser, Avar LS Cleansing Pads, Avar-e Cream, Avar-e Green Cream, Avar-e LS Cream)	Pads: (Avar Cleansing Pads) 9.5%-5%; (Avar LS Cleansing Pads) 10%-2%	**Adults & Peds ≥12 yrs:** Wash affected area qd-bid or ud.
	Cre: (Avar-e Cream, Avar-e Green Cream) 10%-5%; (Avar-e LS Cream) 10%-2%	**Adults & Peds ≥12 yrs:** Cleanse affected area. Apply a thin layer to affected area qd-tid or ud. Massage into skin.
	Sol: (Avar Cleanser) 10%-5%; (Avar LS Cleanser) 10%-2%	**Adults & Peds ≥12 yrs:** Wash affected area qd-bid or ud.
Sodium sulfacetamide-Sulfur (Sumadan)	Wash: 9%-4.5%	**Adults & Peds ≥12 yrs:** Apply to affected area qd-bid or ud.
Sodium sulfacetamide-Sulfur (Klaron)	Lot: 10%	**Adults & Peds ≥12 yrs:** Apply thin layer to affected area bid.

GENERIC (BRAND)	HOW SUPPLIED	DOSAGE
COMBINATION PRODUCTS, TOPICAL *(Continued)*		
Sodium sulfacetamide-Sulfur	**Lot:** 10%-5%	**Adults & Peds ≥12 yrs:** Apply thin layer to affected area with light massaging qd-tid or ud.

Refer to full FDA-approved labeling for additional information.

PSORIASIS MANAGEMENT: SYSTEMIC THERAPIES*

GENERIC (BRAND)	HOW SUPPLIED	ADULT DOSAGE	FREQUENT SIDE EFFECTS
ANTIMETABOLITES			
Methotrexate (Otrexup, Rheumatrex, Trexall)*	**Inj:** (Otrexup) 10mg/0.4mL, 15mg/0.4mL, 20mg/0.4mL, 25mg/0.4mL, (Rheumatrex) 25mg/mL, 1g; **Tab:** (Rheumatrex) 2.5mg, (Trexall) 5mg, 7.5mg, 10mg, 15mg	**Initial:** 10-25mg PO/IM/IV as a single dose qwk, or 2.5mg PO q12h for 3 doses. **Titrate:** May adjust gradually to achieve optimal response. **Max:** 30mg/wk.	Ulcerative stomatitis, leukopenia, N/V, abdominal distress, malaise, undue fatigue, chills, fever, dizziness, and decreased resistance to infections.
IMMUNOSUPPRESSIVES			
Cyclosporine (Gengraf, Neoral)	**Cap:** 25mg, 100mg; **Sol:** 100mg/mL	**Initial:** 1.25mg/kg bid for ≥4 wks. **Titrate:** May increase by 0.5mg/kg/day at 2-wk intervals, as tolerated. **Max:** 4mg/kg/day.	Renal dysfunction, headache, hypertension, hypertriglyceridemia, hirsutism/hypertrichosis, paresthesia or hyperesthesia, influenza-like symptoms, N/V, diarrhea, abdominal discomfort, lethargy, and musculoskeletal or joint pain.
MONOCLONAL ANTIBODIES			
Ustekinumab (Stelara)	**Inj:** 45mg/0.5mL, 90mg/mL	**SQ: >100kg:** 90mg initially and 4 wks later, 90mg q12wks. **≤100kg:** 45mg initially and 4 wks later, 45mg q12wks.	Nasopharyngitis, upper respiratory tract infection, headache, and fatigue.
MONOCLONAL ANTIBODIES/TNF BLOCKERS			
Adalimumab (Humira)	**Inj:** 20mg/0.4mL, 40mg/0.8mL	**SQ:** 80mg initial dose, followed by 40mg every other wk starting 1 wk after the initial dose.	Infections (eg, upper respiratory tract, sinusitis), inj-site reactions, headache, and rash.
Infliximab (Remicade)	**Inj:** 100mg/vial	Infuse over ≥2 hrs. **IV: Induction:** 5mg/kg at 0, 2, and 6 wks. **Maint:** 5mg/kg q8wks.	Infections (eg, upper respiratory tract, sinusitis, pharyngitis), infusion-related reactions, headache, and abdominal pain.
PSORALENS			
Methoxsalen† (8-Mop, Oxsoralen-Ultra)	**Cap:** 10mg	Take 2 hrs before UVA exposure with some food or milk. **<30kg:** 10mg; **30-50kg:** 20mg; **51-65kg:** 30mg; **66-80kg:** 40mg; **81-90kg:** 50mg; **91-115kg:** 60mg; **>115kg:** 70mg. **Titrate:** May increase by 10mg after 15th treatment under certain conditions ud. **Max:** No more than once qod.	Nausea, nervousness, insomnia, depression, pruritus, and erythema.
RETINOIDS			
Acitretin (Soriatane)*	**Cap:** 10mg, 17.5mg, 25mg	**Initial:** 25-50mg/day as a single dose with the main meal. **Maint:** 25-50mg/day.	Cheilitis, rhinitis, dry mouth, epistaxis, alopecia, dry skin, erythematous rash, skin peeling, nail disorder, pruritus, paresthesia, paronychia, skin atrophy, sticky skin, xerophthalmia, arthralgia, rigors, spinal hyperostosis, and hyperesthesia.

(Continued)

GENERIC (BRAND)	HOW SUPPLIED	ADULT DOSAGE	FREQUENT SIDE EFFECTS
TNF-BLOCKING AGENTS			
Etanercept (Enbrel)	**Inj:** 25mg; 50mg	**SQ: Initial:** 50mg twice weekly for 3 months. **Maint:** 50mg once weekly.	Infections and inj-site reactions.

Refer to full FDA-approved labeling for additional information.
*Contraindicated in pregnancy.
†Oxsoralen-Ultra and 8-MOP should not be used interchangeably.

PSORIASIS MANAGEMENT: TOPICAL THERAPIES*

GENERIC (BRAND)	HOW SUPPLIED	USUAL ADULT DOSAGE	COMMON SIDE EFFECTS
RETINOIDS			
Tazarotene (Tazorac)	**Cre:** 0.05%, 0.1% [30g, 60g]; **Gel:** 0.05%, 0.1% [30g, 100g]	Apply a thin film to lesions qpm.	Pruritus, burning/stinging, erythema, irritation, dry skin, rash.
VITAMIN D DERIVATIVES AND COMBINATIONS			
Calcitriol (Vectical)	**Oint:** 3mcg/g [5g, 100g]	Apply to affected areas bid (am and pm). **Max:** 200g/wk.	Skin discomfort, pruritus, hypercalciuria, lab test abnormality, urine abnormality.
Calcipotriene (Dovonex, Dovonex Scalp, Sorilux)	**Cre:** (Dovonex) 0.005% [60g, 120g]; **Sol:** (Dovonex Scalp) 0.005% [60mL]; **Foam:** (Sorilux) 0.005% [60g, 120g]	Apply to affected areas bid; rub in gently and completely.	Skin irritation, rash, pruritus, application-site erythema/pain.
Calcipotriene-Betamethasone dipropionate (Taclonex)	**Oint:** 0.005%-0.064% [60g, 100g]; **Sus:** 0.005%-0.064% [60g, 120g]	**Max:** 100g/wk. **Oint:** Apply to affected areas qd for up to 4 wks. **Sus:** Apply to affected areas qd for up to 8 wks.	Pruritus, burning sensation, folliculitis, scaly rash.
MISCELLANEOUS AGENTS			
Anthralin (Dritho-Crème, Zithranol-RR, Zithranol Shampoo)	**Cre:** (Dritho-Crème) 1% [50g]; **Cre:** (Zithranol-RR) 1.2% [15g, 45g]; **Shampoo:** (Zithranol) 1% [85g]	**Cre:** Apply qd as directed. **Shampoo:** Apply to wet scalp 3-4 times per wk. Lather, leave on scalp for 3-5 min, and then rinse thoroughly.	Transient primary irritation, staining (skin and fabric), temporary discoloration of hair and fingernails.

Refer to full FDA-approved labeling for additional information.

*Please refer to the *Topical Corticosteroids* table for additional details.

(Continued)

TOPICAL CORTICOSTEROIDS

STEROIDS	DOSAGE FORM(S)	STRENGTH (%)	POTENCY	FREQUENCY
Alclometasone dipropionate (Aclovate)	Cre, Oint	0.05	Low-Medium	bid/tid
Amcinonide	Lot	0.1	Medium*	bid/tid
	Cre, Oint	0.1	High*	bid/tid
Augmented betamethasone dipropionate (Diprolene, Diprolene AF)	Lot, Oint	0.05	Super High	qd/bid
	Cre (AF)	0.05	High	qd/bid
Betamethasone dipropionate	Cre, Lot	0.05	Medium*	**Cre:** qd/bid; **Lot:** bid
	Oint	0.05	High*	qd/bid
Betamethasone valerate (Luxiq)	Cre, Oint	0.1	Medium*	qd/tid
	Foam (Luxiq)	0.12	Medium	bid
	Lot	0.1	Low*	bid
Clobetasol propionate (Clobex, Olux, Olux E)	Cre, Foam (Olux, Olux-E), Gel, Lot (Clobex), Oint, Shampoo (Clobex), Sol, Spray (Clobex)	0.05	Super High	**Cre, Foam, Gel, Lot, Oint, Sol, Spray:** bid; **Shampoo:** qd
Clocortolone pivalate (Cloderm)	Cre	0.1	Medium	tid
Desonide (Desonate, DesOwen, Verdeso)	Cre (DesOwen), Lot (DesOwen), Oint (DesOwen), Foam (Verdeso), Gel (Desonate)	0.05	Low-Medium	**Cre, Lot, Oint:** bid-tid; **Foam, Gel:** bid
Desoximetasone (Topicort)	Cre	0.05	Medium*	bid
	Gel	0.05	High*	bid
	Cre, Oint	0.25	High*	bid
	Spray	0.25	High-Super High	bid
Diflorasone diacetate (ApexiCon E)	Cre (ApexiCon E)	0.05	Medium-High	qd-tid
	Oint	0.05	High-Super High	qd-tid
Fluocinolone acetonide (Capex, Derma-Smoothe/FS, Synalar)	Cre (Synalar), Oint (Synalar)	0.025	Medium*	bid-qid
	Cre, Sol (Synalar)	0.01	Low*	bid-qid
	Oil (Derma-Smoothe/FS)	0.01	Low-Medium	**Adults:** tid; **Peds:** bid
	Shampoo (Capex)	0.01	Low-Medium	qd
Fluocinonide (Vanos)	Cre, Gel, Oint, Sol	0.05	High*	bid-qid
	Cre (Vanos)	0.1	Super High	qd/bid
Flurandrenolide (Cordran)	Cre, Lot	0.05	Medium*	bid/tid
	Tape	4mcg/cm^2	Super High†	qd/bid
Fluticasone propionate (Cutivate)	Cre	0.05	Medium	qd/bid
	Lot (Cutivate)	0.05	Medium‡	qd
	Oint	0.005	Medium	bid
Halcinonide (Halog)	Cre, Oint	0.1	High‡	bid/tid

(Continued)

STEROIDS	DOSAGE FORM(S)	STRENGTH (%)	POTENCY	FREQUENCY
Halobetasol propionate (Ultravate)	Cre, Oint	0.05	Super High	qd/bid
Hydrocortisone (Anusol HC, Ala Cort)	Cre (Ala Cort)	1	Low*	bid-qid
	Oint	1	Low*	bid-qid
	Cre (Anusol HC), Lot, Oint	2.5	Low*	bid-qid
Hydrocortisone acetate (Micort-HC)	Cre	2	Low‡	bid-qid
Hydrocortisone butyrate (Locoid, Locoid Lipocream)	Cre, Oint, Sol	0.1	Medium‡	bid/tid
	Lot	0.1	Medium‡	bid
Hydrocortisone probutate (Pandel)	Cre	0.1	Medium	qd/bid
Hydrocortisone valerate	Cre, Oint	0.2	Medium	bid/tid
Mometasone furoate (Elocon)	Cre, Lot, Oint	0.1	Medium	qd
Prednicarbate (Dermatop)	Cre, Oint	0.1	Medium	bid
Triamcinolone acetonide (Kenalog, Triderm)	Cre, Lot, Oint	0.025	Medium*	bid-qid
	Cre, Lot, Oint	0.1	Medium*	bid/tid
	Cre, Oint	0.5	Medium*	bid/tid
	Cre (Triderm)	0.5	Medium*	bid-qid
	Spray	0.147mg/g	Medium	tid/qid

Refer to full FDA-approved labeling for additional information.

*Source: Knowledge Center: Steroid Potency Comparison. Fougera & Co. website. http://www.fougera.com/knowledge_center/steroidpotency.asp. Accessed March 26, 2014.

†Source: Info for Healthcare Professionals, About Cordran Tape. Cordran Tape website. http://www.cordrantape.com/hcp-about.asp. Accessed March 26, 2014.

‡Source: Topical Steroids Potency Chart. National Psoriasis Foundation website. http://www.psoriasis.org/about-psoriasis/treatments/topicals/steroids/potency-chart. Accessed March 26, 2014.

DIABETES SCREENING AND DIAGNOSIS IN ADULTS

Diabetes is a significant healthcare problem in the US and worldwide. It is the leading cause of kidney failure, non-traumatic lower-limb amputations, and new cases of blindness among adults in the US. Diabetes is a major cause of heart disease and stroke and is the seventh leading cause of death. The disease affects 25.8 million people in the US, or 8.3% of the population.

CLASSIFICATION OF DIABETES

CATEGORIES	PATHOLOGY
Type 1	β-cell destruction, usually leading to absolute insulin deficiency
Type 2	Progressive insulin secretory defect on the background of insulin resistance
Others	Genetic defects of the β-cell Genetic defects in insulin action Diseases of the exocrine pancreas Drug- or chemical-induced
Gestational	Diabetes diagnosed during pregnancy that is not clearly overt diabetes

SCREENING/DIAGNOSIS

PREDIABETES (INCREASED RISK FOR DIABETES)

FPG 100mg/dL (5.6mmol/L) to 125mg/dL (609mmol/L) (IFG)

OR

2-h PG in the 75-g OGTT 140mg/dL (7.8mmol/L) to 199mg/dL (11.0mmol/L) (IGT)

OR

A1C 5.7-6.4%

For all three tests, risk is continuous, extending below the lower limit of the range and becoming disproportionately greater at higher ends of the range.

DIABETES

A1C ≥6.5%.

OR

FPG ≥126mg/dL (7.0mmol/L)

OR

2-h PG ≥200mg/dL (11.1mmol/L) during an OGTT

OR

Hyperglycemia symptoms with a random plasma glucose ≥200mg/dL (11.1mmol/L)

GLYCEMIC, BLOOD PRESSURE, AND LIPID GOALS IN PATIENTS WITH DIABETES

Glycemic Control* Hb A1C Preprandial capillary plasma glucose Peak postprandial capillary plasma glucose	<7% 70-130mg/dL <180mg/dL
Blood Pressure†	<140/80mmHg
Lipids‡ LDL Triglycerides HDL	<100mg/dL <150mg/dL >50mg/dL

*Individualize glycemic goals based on duration of diabetes, age/life expectancy, comorbid conditions, known cardiovascular disease or advanced macrovascular complications, hypoglycemia awareness, etc.

†Lower systolic blood pressure targets may be appropriate based on patient characteristics and response to therapy.

‡In individuals with overt cardiovascular disease, a lower LDL cholesterol goal of <70mg/dL (while using a high dose of a statin) is an option.

(Continued)

GESTATIONAL DIABETES MELLITUS SCREENING AND DIAGNOSIS

TIMELINE*	SCREENING	DIAGNOSTIC CRITERIA	DIAGNOSIS
1st prenatal visit	Screen for undiagnosed type 2 diabetes mellitus in those with risk factors	Diagnosis is made when one or more of the following values are met[†]: • A1C ≥6.5% • FPG ≥126mg/dL • 2-h PG ≥200mg/dL during an OGTT • In a patient with classic symptoms of hyperglycemia or hyperglycemic crisis, a random PG ≥200mg/dL	Women with a positive diagnosis of diabetes receive a diagnosis of overt, not gestational, diabetes.
24 to 28 weeks gestation	Screen all women not previously known to have diabetes at 24 to 28 weeks	Diagnosis of GDM is made when any of the following PG values are exceeded[‡]: • Fasting ≥92mg/dL • 1 h ≥180mg/dL • 2 h ≥153mg/dL	Women who test positive for GDM will need to screen for persistent diabetes at 6-12 weeks postpartum using the OGTT and nonpregnancy diagnostic criteria.

HISTORY OF GESTATIONAL DIABETES MELLITUS

6 to 12 weeks postpartum	Any history of GDM warrants lifelong screening for development of diabetes or prediabetes at least every 3 years	Diagnosis is made using 75g OGTT: • 2-h PG ≥200mg/dL Use of A1C for diagnosis of persistent diabetes at postpartum visit is not recommended because of prepartum treatment for hyperglycemia.	Women with a history of GDM and who develop prediabetes should be offered lifestyle interventions or metformin to prevent diabetes.

*According to the American Diabetes Association guidelines, pregnant women are to be screened for type 2 diabetes at their first prenatal visit and screened for GDM 24-28 weeks into pregnancy.

[†]In the absence of unequivocal hyperglycemia, results should be confirmed by repeat testing.

[‡]Perform 75g OGTT, with plasma glucose measurement fasting and at 1 and 2 hours, at 24 to 28 weeks gestation in women not previously diagnosed with overt diabetes. This OGTT should be performed in the morning after an overnight fast of at least 8 hours.

GLYCEMIC GOALS IN PREGNANT WOMEN

These targets are based on recommendations from the Fifth International Workshop-Conference on Gestational Diabetes Mellitus.

Preprandial: ≤95mg/dL (5.3mmol/L)

AND EITHER

1-h postmeal: ≤140mg/dL (7.8mmol/L)

OR

2-h postmeal: ≤120mg/dL (6.7mmol/L)

GLYCEMIC GOALS IN PREGNANT WOMEN WITH TYPE 1 OR TYPE 2 DIABETES WHO BECOME PREGNANT

• Premeal, bedtime, and overnight glucose 60–99mg/dL (3.3–5.4mmol/L)

• Peak postprandial glucose 100–129mg/dL (5.4–7.1mmol/L)

• A1C <6.0%

Please refer to the *Oral Antidiabetic Agents* table and the *Insulin Formulations* table for pharmacological treatment options.

Abbreviations: FPG = fasting plasma glucose; GDM = gestational diabetes mellitus; IFG = Impaired fasting glucose; IGT = impaired glucose tolerance; OGTT = oral glucose tolerance test; PG = plasma glucose.

Sources:

Standards of Medical Care in Diabetes-2014. *Diabetes Care.* 2014;37(Suppl):S14-S26; S36-S39.

2011 National Diabetes Fact Sheet. Centers for Disease Control and Prevention website. http://www.cdc.gov/diabetes/pubs/factsheet11/fastfacts.htm. Updated October 24, 2013. Accessed March 6, 2014.

American Diabetes Association website. http://www.diabetes.org/. Accessed March 6, 2014.

INSULIN FORMULATIONS

TYPE OF INSULIN	BRAND	CLASS (RX/OTC)	ONSET*	PEAK*	DURATION*
Rapid-acting					
Insulin glulisine	Apidra	Rx	15 mins	0.5-1.5 hrs	3-5 hrs
Insulin lispro	Humalog	Rx	15 mins	0.5-1.5 hrs	3-5 hrs
Insulin aspart	NovoLog	Rx	15 mins	0.5-1.5 hrs	3-5 hrs
Short-acting					
Regular insulin	Humulin R†	OTC	30-60 mins	2-4 hrs	5-8 hrs
	Novolin R	OTC	30-60 mins	2-4 hrs	5-8 hrs
Intermediate-acting					
NPH	Humulin N	OTC	1-3 hrs	8 hrs	12-16 hrs
	Novolin N	OTC	1-3 hrs	8 hrs	12-16 hrs
Long-acting					
Insulin glargine	Lantus	Rx	1 hr	Peakless	20-26 hrs
Insulin detemir	Levemir	Rx	1 hr	Peakless	20-26 hrs
Combinations					
NPH (70%)/regular insulin (30%)	Humulin 70/30	OTC	30-60 mins	Varies	10-16 hrs
NPH (70%)/regular insulin (30%)	Novolin 70/30	OTC	30-60 mins	Varies	10-16 hrs
Insulin aspart protamine (70%)/ insulin aspart (30%)	NovoLog Mix 70/30	Rx	5-15 mins	Varies	10-16 hrs
Insulin lispro protamine (50%)/ insulin lispro (50%)	Humalog Mix 50/50	Rx	10-15 mins	Varies	10-16 hrs
Insulin lispro protamine (75%)/ insulin lispro (25%)	Humalog Mix 75/25	Rx	10-15 mins	Varies	10-16 hrs

Refer to full FDA-approved labeling for detailed information.

*Onset, peak, and duration will vary among patients and dosage should be determined by the healthcare professional familiar with the patient's metabolic needs, eating habits, and other lifestyle variables.

†Also available as 500 U/mL (Rx only) for insulin-resistant patients (rapid onset [within 30 mins]; up to 24-hr duration).

Source: Types of Insulin. National Diabetes Information Clearinghouse (NDIC) website. http://diabetes.niddk.nih.gov/dm/pubs/medicines_ez/insert_C.aspx. Updated February 16, 2012. Accessed February 4, 2013.

ORAL ANTIDIABETIC AGENTS

BRAND (GENERIC)	HOW SUPPLIED	INITIAL* & (MAX) DOSAGE	USUAL DOSAGE RANGE*	PROPERTIES
BIGUANIDES				
Fortamet† (Metformin HCl)	**Tab, ER:** 500mg, 1000mg	500-1000mg qd with evening meal (2500mg/day)	500mg-2500mg/day	**Mechanism:** Activates AMP-Kinase **Action(s):** Hepatic glucose production ↓, intestinal glucose absorption ↓, insulin action ↑ **Advantages:** No weight gain, no hypoglycemia, reduction in cardio-vascular events and mortality **Disadvantages:** GI side effects (diarrhea, abdominal cramping), lactic acidosis (rare), vitamin B12 deficiency
Glumetza† (Metformin HCl)	**Tab, ER:** 500mg, 1000mg	**Metformin-Naive:** 500mg qd with evening meal (2000mg/day)	500mg-2000mg/day	
Glucophage†, Riomet† (Metformin HCl)	**Tab:** 500mg, 850mg, 1000mg **Sol:** 500mg/5mL	500mg bid or 850mg qd with meals (2550mg/day)	850mg-2000mg/day	
Glucophage XR† (Metformin HCl)	**Tab, ER:** 500mg, 750mg	500mg qd with evening meal (2000mg/day)	500mg-2000mg qd or divided doses	
BILE-ACID SEQUESTRANTS				
Welchol (Colesevelam HCl)	**Tab:** 625mg; **Sus:** 3.75g, 1.875g [pkt]	**Tab:** 1875mg bid or 3750mg qd with meal and liquid; **Sus:** 1.875g pkt bid or 3.75g pkt qd with meal	3750mg/day	**Mechanism:** Binds bile acids/ cholesterol **Action(s):** Unknown **Advantages:** No hypoglycemia. LDL cholesterol ↓ **Disadvantages:** Constipation, triglycerides ↑, may interfere with absorption of other medications, may decrease absorption of fat-soluble vitamins
DIPEPTIDYL PEPTIDASE-4 INHIBITORS				
Tradjenta (Linagliptin)	**Tab:** 5mg	5mg qd	5mg/day	**Mechanism:** Inhibits DPP-4 activity, prolongs survival of endogenously released incretin hormones **Action(s):** Active GLP-1 concentration ↑, active GIP concentration ↑, insulin secretion ↑, glucagon secretion ↓ **Advantages:** No hypoglycemia, weight "neutrality" **Disadvantages:** Occasional reports of urticaria/angioedema, cases of pancreatitis observed, nasopharyngitis, headache, upper respiratory tract infection, long-term safety unknown
Onglyza (Saxagliptin)	**Tab:** 2.5mg, 5mg	2.5-5mg qd	2.5-5mg/day	
Januvia (Sitagliptin)	**Tab:** 25mg, 50mg, 100mg	100mg qd	100mg/day	
GLUCOSIDASE INHIBITORS				
Precose (Acarbose)	**Tab:** 25mg, 50mg, 100mg	25mg tid at start of each meal, or qd to minimize GI side effects (≤60kg: 50mg tid, >60kg: 100mg tid)	50-100mg tid	**Mechanism:** Inhibits intestinal α-glucosidase **Action(s):** Delayed glucose absorption **Advantages:** Nonsystemic medication, postprandial glucose ↓ **Disadvantages:** GI side effects (gas, flatulence, diarrhea), dosing frequency
Glyset (Miglitol)	**Tab:** 25mg, 50mg, 100mg	25mg tid at start of each meal, or qd to minimize GI effects (300mg/day)	50-100mg tid	

(Continued)

BRAND (GENERIC)	HOW SUPPLIED	INITIAL* & (MAX) DOSAGE	USUAL DOSAGE RANGE*	PROPERTIES
MEGLITINIDES				
Starlix (Nateglinide)	**Tab:** 60mg, 120mg	120mg tid 1-30 min before meals	120mg tid	**Mechanism:** Closes KATP channels on β-cell plasma membranes
Prandin (Repaglinide)	**Tab:** 0.5mg, 1mg, 2mg	0.5-2mg within 30 min before each meal (16mg/day)	0.5-4mg with each meal	**Action(s):** Insulin secretion ↑ **Advantages:** Accentuated effects around meal ingestion **Disadvantages:** Hypoglycemia, weight gain, upper respiratory tract infections, may blunt myocardial ischemic preconditioning, dosing frequency
SODIUM-GLUCOSE COTRANSPORTER 2 INHIBITORS				
Invokana (Canagliflozin)	**Tab:** 100mg, 300mg	100mg qd before the first meal (300mg/day)	100-300mg qd	**Mechanism:** Inhibits sodium-glucose-cotransporter 2 in the proximal renal tubules
Farxiga (Dapagliflozin)	**Tab:** 5mg, 10mg	5mg qd in the am (10mg/day)	5-10mg qd	**Action(s):** Urinary glucose excretion ↑ **Advantages:** No weight gain **Disadvantages:** BP ↓, impairment in renal function, hyperkalemia, genital mycotic infections, LDL ↑
SULFONYLUREAS				
(Chlorpropamide)	**Tab:** 100mg, 250mg	250mg qd with breakfast (750mg/day)	<100-500mg qd; most patients controlled with 250mg qd	**Mechanism:** Stimulates the release of insulin from the pancreas
Amaryl (Glimepiride)	**Tab:** 1mg, 2mg, 4mg	1-2mg qd with breakfast or first main meal (8mg/day)	1-8mg/day	**Action(s):** Insulin secretion ↑ **Advantages:** Generally well tolerated
Glucotrol (Glipizide)	**Tab:** 5mg, 10mg	5mg qd 30 min before breakfast (40mg/day)	5-40mg qd; divided doses if >15mg/day	**Disadvantages:** Relatively glucose-independent stimulation of insulin secretion; GI effects; hypoglycemia; weight gain; ↑ risk of cardiovascular mortality; low "durability"
Glucotrol XL (Glipizide)	**Tab, ER:** 2.5mg, 5mg, 10mg	5mg qd with breakfast (20mg/day)	5-10mg/day	
Diabeta (Glyburide)	**Tab:** 1.25mg, 2.5mg, 5mg	2.5-5mg qd with breakfast or first main meal (20mg/day)	1.25-20mg/day in single or divided doses	
Glynase PresTab (Glyburide, micronized)	**Tab:** 1.5mg, 3mg, 6mg	1.5-3mg qd with breakfast or first main meal (12mg/day)	0.75-12mg/day in single or divided doses	
(Tolazamide)	**Tab:** 250mg, 500mg	100-250mg qd with breakfast or first main meal (1000mg/day)	100-1000mg/day; divided doses if >500mg/day	
(Tolbutamide)	**Tab:** 500mg	1000-2000mg qd in single or divided doses (3000mg/day)	250-3000mg/day in single or divided doses	
THIAZOLIDINEDIONES				
Actos‡ (Pioglitazone HCl)	**Tab:** 15mg, 30mg, 45mg	15-30mg qd (45mg/day)	15-45mg/day	**Mechanism:** Activates the nuclear transcription factor PPAR-γ
Avandia‡ (Rosiglitazone maleate)	**Tab:** 2mg, 4mg, 8mg	2mg bid or 4mg qd (8mg/day)	4-8mg/day	**Action(s):** Peripheral insulin sensitivity ↑ **Advantages:** No hypoglycemia; (Actos) HDL cholesterol ↑, triglycerides ↓ **Disadvantages:** Weight gain, edema, heart failure, bone fractures; (Avandia) LDL cholesterol ↑, CV events ↑, FDA warnings on CV safety

BRAND (GENERIC)	HOW SUPPLIED	INITIAL* & (MAX) DOSAGE	USUAL DOSAGE RANGE*	PROPERTIES
COMBINATIONS				
(Glipizide/ Metformin HCl)†	**Tab:** 2.5mg/250mg, 2.5mg/500mg, 5mg/500mg	2.5mg/250mg qd or 2.5mg/500mg bid with meals (20mg/2000mg/day)	2.5mg/250mg qd-5mg/500mg bid	
Glucovance† (Glyburide/ Metformin HCl)	**Tab:** 1.25mg/250mg, 2.5mg/500mg, 5mg/500mg	1.25mg/250mg qd or bid with meals (20mg/2000mg/day)	1.25mg/250mg qd-5mg/500mg bid	
Jentadueto† (Linagliptin/ Metformin HCl)	**Tab:** 2.5mg/500mg, 2.5mg/850mg, 2.5mg/1000mg	2.5mg/500mg bid with meals (5mg/2000mg/day)	2.5mg/500mg-2.5mg/1000mg bid	
Duetact‡ (Pioglitazone/ Glimepiride)	**Tab:** 30mg/2mg, 30mg/4mg	30mg/2mg or 30mg/4mg qd with first meal (45mg/8mg/day)	30mg/2mg-30mg/4mg/day	
Actoplus Met†‡ (Pioglitazone/ Metformin HCl)	**Tab:** 15mg/500mg, 15mg/850mg	15mg/500mg bid or 15mg/850mg qd with food (45mg/2550mg/day)	15/500mg bid-15/850mg qd	
Actoplus Met XR†‡ (Pioglitazone/ Metformin HCl)	**Tab, ER:** 15mg/1000mg, 30mg/1000mg	15mg/1000mg or 30mg/1000mg qd with meal (45mg/2000mg/day)	15mg/1000mg-30mg/1000mg/day	
PrandiMet† (Repaglinide/ Metformin HCl)	**Tab:** 1mg/500mg, 2mg/500mg	1mg/500mg bid 15-30 min before meals (10mg/2500/day or 4mg/1000mg/meal)	1mg/500mg-2mg/500mg bid or tid	
Avandaryl‡ (Rosiglitazone/ Glimepiride)	**Tab:** 4mg/1mg, 4mg/2mg, 4mg/4mg, 8mg/2mg, 8mg/4mg	4mg/1mg qd or 4mg/2mg qd with first meal (8mg/4mg/day)	4mg/1mg-4mg/2mg qd	
Avandamet†‡ (Rosiglitazone/ Metformin HCl)	**Tab:** 2mg/500mg, 4mg/500mg, 2mg/1000mg, 4mg/1000mg	2mg/500mg bid with meals (8mg/2000mg/day)	2mg/500mg-4mg/1000mg qd	
Kombiglyze XR† (Saxagliptin/ Metformin HCl)	**Tab, ER:** 5mg/500mg, 5mg/1000mg, 2.5/1000mg	5mg/500mg or 2.5mg/1000mg qd with evening meal (5mg/2000mg/day)	5mg/500mg-2.5/1000mg qd	
Janumet† (Sitagliptin/ Metformin HCl)	**Tab:** 50mg/500mg, 50mg/1000mg	50mg/500mg or 50mg/1000mg bid with meals (100mg/2000mg/day)	50mg/500mg-50mg/1000mg bid	
Janumet XR† (Sitagliptin/ Metformin HCl ER)	**Tab:** 100mg/1000mg, 50mg/500mg, 50mg/1000mg	50mg/1000mg or 100mg/1000mg qd with meals (100mg/2000mg/day)	50mg/1000mg-100mg/1000mg qd	

*Usual dosage ranges are derived from FDA-approved labeling. There is no fixed dosage regimen for the management of diabetes mellitus with any hypoglycemic agent. The initial and maintenance dosing should be conservative, depending on the patient's individual needs, especially in elderly, debilitated, or malnourished patients, and with impaired renal or hepatic function. Management of type 2 diabetes should include blood glucose and HbA1c monitoring, nutritional counseling, exercise, and weight reduction as needed. For more detailed information, refer to the individual monograph listings or FDA-approved labeling.

†**BOXED WARNING:** Products containing metformin may cause lactic acidosis due to metformin accumulation. Refer to package insert for more details.

‡**BOXED WARNING:** Products containing thiazolidinediones, including pioglitazone or rosiglitazone, may cause or exacerbate congestive heart failure in some patients. Refer to package insert for more details regarding this warning.

ANTIEMETICS

GENERIC (BRAND)	HOW SUPPLIED	INDICATIONS				
		MOTION SICKNESS/N/V	POSTOPERATIVE N/V	CHEMOTHERAPY N/V	RADIATION N/V	
ANTICHOLINERGIC AGENTS						
Scopolamine (Transderm Scop)	**Patch:** 1mg/72 hrs	**Prevention:** Apply 1 patch behind one ear at least 4 hrs before needed.	**Prevention:** Apply 1 patch the evening before surgery or 1 hr prior to caesarian section. Keep in place for 24 hrs following surgery.			
ANTIHISTAMINES						
Dimenhydrinate	**Inj:** 50mg/mL	**Prevention/Treatment:** (IM) 50mg q4h; may increase to 100mg q4h if drowsiness is desirable. (IV) Must dilute each mL of solution in 10mL of 0.9% sodium chloride inj, USP and inject over 2 min.				
Meclizine HCl (Antivert)	**Tab:** 12.5mg, 25mg, 50mg	**Prevention/Treatment:** 25-50mg 1 hr prior to trip/departure. May repeat dose q24h prn.				
Promethazine HCl (Promethegan)	**Inj:** 25mg/mL, 50mg/mL	**Prevention/Treatment:** 12.5-25mg IV/IM. May repeat q4h prn. Do not give IV administration >25mg/mL and at a rate >25mg/min.	**Prevention:** 12.5-25mg IV/IM. May repeat q4h prn. Reduce dosage of analgesics and barbiturates. Do not give IV administration >25mg/mL and at a rate >25mg/min.			
	Liq: 6.25mg/5mL [118mL, 473mL]	(N/V) **Prevention/Treatment: 25mg.** 12.5-25mg may be repeated prn q4-6h. (Motion Sickness) **Prevention/ Treatment:** 25mg bid, first dose 0.5-1 hr prior to trip/departure; repeat after 8-12 hrs if needed.	**Prevention:** 25mg q4-6h prn.			

(Continued)

GENERIC (BRAND)	HOW SUPPLIED	INDICATIONS				
		MOTION SICKNESS/N/V	POSTOPERATIVE N/V	CHEMOTHERAPY N/V	RADIATION N/V	
ANTIHISTAMINES *(Continued)*						
Promethazine HCl (Phenergan) *(Continued)*	**Sup:** 50mg (Promethegan); 12.5mg, 25mg **Tab:** 12.5mg, 25mg, 50mg	(N/V) **Prevention/Treatment: 25mg**. 12.5-25mg may be repeated prn q4-6h. (Motion Sickness) **Prevention/ Treatment:** 25mg bid, first dose 0.5-1 hr prior to trip/departure; repeat after 8-12 hrs if needed.	**Prevention:** 25mg q4-6h prn.			
CANNABINOIDS						
Dronabinol (Marinol)	**Cap:** 2.5mg, 5mg, 10mg			**Treatment: Initial:** 5mg/m² given 1-3 hrs before chemotherapy, then q2-4h after chemotherapy, up to 4-6 doses/day. **Titrate:** May increase by 2.5mg/m² increments prn. **Max:** 15mg/m²/dose.		
Nabilone (Cesamet)	**Cap:** 1mg			**Treatment: Usual:** 1mg or 2mg bid. Give initial dose 1-3 hrs before chemotherapy. A dose of 1mg or 2mg the night before may be useful. May be given bid-tid during chemotherapy cycle and, if needed, for 48 hrs after the last dose of each cycle. **Max:** 6mg/day given in divided doses tid.		
5-HT₃ ANTAGONISTS						
Dolasetron mesylate (Anzemet)	**Inj:** 20mg/mL		**Prevention:** 12.5mg IV single dose 15 min before cessation of anesthesia or as soon as N/V presents.			
	Tab: 50mg, 100mg			**Prevention:** 100mg PO within 1 hr before chemotherapy.		

GENERIC (BRAND)	HOW SUPPLIED	INDICATIONS				
		MOTION SICKNESS/N/V	POSTOPERATIVE N/V	CHEMOTHERAPY N/V	RADIATION N/V	

5-HT₃ ANTAGONISTS *(Continued)*

GENERIC (BRAND)	HOW SUPPLIED	MOTION SICKNESS/N/V	POSTOPERATIVE N/V	CHEMOTHERAPY N/V	RADIATION N/V
Granisetron HCl (Granisol)	**Inj:** 0.1mg/mL, 1mg/mL			**Prevention:** 10mcg/kg IV within 30 min before chemotherapy.	
	(Granisol) **Sol:** 2mg/10mL [30mL]			**Prevention:** 2mg qd up to 1 hr before chemotherapy or 1mg bid (given up to 1 hr before chemotherapy and 12 hrs later).	**Prevention:** 2mg qd within 1 hr of radiation.
	Tab: 1mg				
Granisetron Transdermal System (Sancuso)	**Patch:** 3.1mg/24 hrs			**Prevention:** Apply 1 patch to upper outer arm 24 hrs prior to chemotherapy. The patch may be applied up to a maximum of 48 hrs before chemotherapy. Remove patch a minimum of 24 hrs after completion of chemotherapy. Patch can be worn for up to 7 days depending on duration of chemotherapy regimen.	
Ondansetron (Zuplenz)	**Film, Oral:** 4mg, 8mg		**Prevention:** 16mg 1 hr before induction of anesthesia.	**Prevention: HEC:** 24mg 30 min before chemotherapy. **MEC:** 8mg bid; give first dose 30 min before chemotherapy, then next dose 8 hrs later, then q12h for 1-2 days after completion of chemotherapy.	**Prevention:** 8mg tid. **Total Body Irradiation:** 8mg 1-2 hrs before each fraction of radiotherapy administered each day. **Single High-Dose Fraction Radiotherapy to Abdomen:** 8mg 1-2 hrs before therapy then q8h after first dose for 1-2 days after completion of therapy. **Daily Fractionated Radiotherapy to Abdomen:** 8mg 1-2 hrs before therapy then q8h after first dose for each day radiotherapy is given.

(Continued)

GENERIC (BRAND)	HOW SUPPLIED	INDICATIONS				
		MOTION SICKNESS/N/V	POSTOPERATIVE N/V	CHEMOTHERAPY N/V	RADIATION N/V
5-HT₃ ANTAGONISTS (Continued)					
Ondansetron HCl* (Zofran)	**Inj:** 2mg/mL		**Prevention:** 4mg undiluted IM/IV immediately before anesthesia or <2 hrs after surgery if nausea or vomiting occurs; as IV, administer over 2-5 min.	**Prevention:** Three 0.15mg/kg doses (Max: 16mg/dose); give first dose (infuse IV over 15 min) 30 min before chemotherapy. Subsequent two doses 4 and 8 hrs after first dose.	
	Sol: 4mg/5mL [50mL]		**Prevention:** 16mg bid 1 hr before anesthesia.	**Prevention: MEC:** 8mg bid, first dose 30 min before chemotherapy, then 8 hrs later, then bid for 1-2 days after chemotherapy.	**Prevention:** 8mg tid. **Total Body Irradiation:** 8mg 1-2 hrs before each fraction of therapy daily. **Single High-Dose Therapy to Abdomen:** 8mg 1-2 hrs before therapy then q8h after first dose for 1-2 days after completion of therapy. **Daily Fractionated Therapy to Abdomen:** 8mg 1-2 hrs before therapy, then q8h after first dose for each day radiotherapy is given.
	Tab: 4mg, 8mg			**Prevention: HEC:** 24mg (three 8mg tabs) 30 min before chemotherapy. **MEC:** 8mg bid, first dose 30 min before chemotherapy, then 8 hrs later, then bid for 1-2 days after chemotherapy.	
	Tab, Disintegrating: 4mg, 8mg			**Prevention: MEC:** 8mg bid, first dose 30 min before chemotherapy, then 8 hrs later, then bid for 1-2 days after chemotherapy.	
Palonosetron HCl (Aloxi)	**Inj:** 0.25mg/5mL, 0.075mg/1.5mL		**Prevention:** 0.075mg IV single dose over 10 sec immediately before induction of anesthesia.	**Prevention:** 0.25mg IV single dose over 30 sec, 30 min before start of chemotherapy.	

GENERIC (BRAND)	HOW SUPPLIED	INDICATIONS			
		MOTION SICKNESS/N/V	POSTOPERATIVE N/V	CHEMOTHERAPY N/V	RADIATION N/V
MISCELLANEOUS					
Droperidol	**Inj:** 2.5mg/mL		**Prevention: Initial/Max:** 2.5mg IM or slow IV. May give additional 1.25mg doses cautiously to achieve desired effect. Doses should be individualized.		
Metoclopramide (Reglan)	**Inj:** 5mg/mL		**Prevention:** 10–20mg IM near end of surgery.	**Prevention:** 1-2mg/kg IV over not less than 15 min, 30 min before chemotherapy then q2h for 2 doses, then q3h for 3 doses. Give 2mg/kg for highly emetogenic drugs for initial 2 doses.	
Trimethobenzamide HCl (Tigan)	**Cap:** 300mg		300mg tid-qid.		
	Inj: 100mg/mL		200mg IM tid-qid.		
PHENOTHIAZINE DERIVATIVES					
Prochlorperazine (Compro)	**Inj:** 5mg/mL	(N/V) **Treatment: IM:** 5-10mg q3-4h. **Max:** 40mg/day. **IV:** 2.5-10mg slow IV injection or infusion (not bolus) at rate ≤5mg/min. **Max:** 10mg single dose or 40mg/day.	**Prevention: IM:** 5-10mg 1-2 hrs before anesthesia (repeat once in 30 min if needed) or to control acute symptoms during or after surgery. **IV:** 5-10mg slow IV injection or infusion (not bolus) at rate ≤5mg/min 15-30 min before anesthesia or to control acute symptoms during or after surgery (repeat once if needed). **Max:** 10mg single dose and 40mg/day.		
	(Compro) **Sup:** 25mg	(N/V) **Treatment:** 25mg bid.			
	Tab: 5mg, 10mg	(N/V) **Treatment:** 5-10mg tid-qid. Doses >40mg/day only in resistant cases.			

(Continued)

GENERIC (BRAND)	HOW SUPPLIED	INDICATIONS			
		MOTION SICKNESS/N/V	POSTOPERATIVE N/V	CHEMOTHERAPY N/V	RADIATION N/V
SUBSTANCE P/NEUROKININ-1 RECEPTOR ANTAGONISTS					
Aprepitant (Emend)	**Cap:** 40mg, 80mg, 125mg		**Prevention:** 40mg within 3 hrs prior to induction of anesthesia.	**Prevention:** Given for 3 days with a corticosteroid and a 5-HT$_3$ antagonist. Day 1: 125mg 1 hr prior to chemotherapy. Days 2 and 3: 80mg qam.	
Fosaprepitant dimeglumine (Emend for Injection)	**Inj:** 115mg, 150mg			Part of a regimen that includes a corticosteroid and a 5-HT$_3$ antagonist. **Prevention: HEC (Single Dose Regimen):** 150mg on Day 1 only as an infusion over 20-30 min initiated approx. 30 min prior to chemotherapy. **HEC and MEC Chemotherapy-Induced N/V (3-Day Dosing Regimen):** 115mg on Day 1 as an infusion over 15 min initiated approx. 30 min prior to chemotherapy. 80mg capsules are given orally on Days 2 and 3.	

Refer to full FDA-approved labeling for additional information and for pediatric dosages.

Abbreviations: HEC = highly emetogenic cancer chemotherapy; MEC = moderately emetogenic cancer chemotherapy; N/V = nausea and vomiting.

CROHN'S DISEASE TREATMENTS

GENERIC	BRAND	HOW SUPPLIED	ADULT DOSAGE	PEDIATRIC DOSAGE
CORTICOSTEROIDS				
Betamethasone sodium phosphate-Betamethasone acetate	Celestone Soluspan	**Inj:** 3mg-3mg/mL [5mL, multidose]	**Initial:** 0.25-9mg/day IM.*	**Initial:** 0.02-0.3mg/kg/day in 3 or 4 divided doses IM.*
Budesonide	Entocort EC	**Cap:** 3mg	**Usual:** 9mg qam for up to 8 wks. **Recurring Episodes:** Repeat therapy for 8 wks. **Maint:** 6mg qd for up to 3 months, then taper to complete cessation.	
Dexamethasone	Generic	**Sol:** 0.5mg/5mL, 1mg/mL; **Tab:** 0.5mg†, 0.75mg†, 1mg†, 1.5mg†, 2mg†, 4mg†, 6mg†	**Initial:** 0.75-9mg/day.*	**Initial:** 0.02-0.3mg/kg/day in 3 or 4 divided doses.*
	Generic	**Inj:** 4mg/mL [1mL, 5mL, 30mL], 10mg/mL [10mL]	**Initial:** 0.5-9mg/day IV/IM.*	
Hydrocortisone	Cortef	**Tab:** 5mg†, 10mg†, 20mg†	**Initial:** 20-240mg/day.*	**Initial:** 20-240mg/day.*
	Solu-Cortef	**Inj:** 100mg, 250mg, 500mg, 1000mg	**Initial:** 100-500mg IV/IM. May repeat dose at 2-, 4-, or 6-hr intervals. High-dose therapy should continue only until patient is stabilized, usually not beyond 48-72 hrs.*	**Initial:** 0.56-8mg/kg/day IV/IM in 3 or 4 divided doses.*
Methylprednisolone	Depo-Medrol	**Inj:** 20mg/mL, 40mg/mL, 80mg/mL	**Initial:** 4-120mg IM.*	**Initial:** 0.11-1.6mg/kg/day.*
	Medrol	**Tab:** 2mg†, 4mg†, 8mg†, 16mg†, 32mg†; (Dose-Pak) 4mg† [21s]	**Initial:** 4-48mg/day.* Refer to PI for detailed information for ADT.	**Initial:** 4-48mg/day.* Refer to PI for detailed information for ADT.
	Solu-Medrol	**Inj:** 40mg, 125mg, 500mg, 1g, 2g	**Initial:** 10-40mg IV/IM inj or IV infusion. **High-Dose Therapy:** 30mg/kg IV over at least 30 min. May repeat dose q4-6h for 48 hrs. High-dose therapy should continue only until patient is stabilized, usually not beyond 48-72 hrs.*	**Initial:** 0.11-1.6mg/kg/day in 3 or 4 divided doses.*
Prednisolone	Flo-Pred	**Sus:** 15mg/5mL [37mL, 52mL, 65mL]	**Initial:** 5-60mg/day.*	**Initial:** 0.14-2mg/kg/day in 3 or 4 divided doses.*
	Orapred	**Sol:** 15mg/5mL [237mL, 20mL]; **Tab, Disintegrating:** 10mg, 15mg, 30mg	**(Sol) Initial:** 5-60mg/day. **(Tab, Disintegrating) Initial:** 10-60mg/day.*	**Initial:** 0.14-2mg/kg/day in 3 or 4 divided doses.*
	Pediapred	**Sol:** 5mg/5mL [120mL]	**Initial:** 5-60mg/day.*	**Initial:** 0.14-2mg/kg/day in 3 or 4 divided doses.*

GENERIC	BRAND	HOW SUPPLIED	ADULT DOSAGE	PEDIATRIC DOSAGE
CORTICOSTEROIDS *(Continued)*				
Prednisolone *(Continued)*	Generic	**Syrup:** 5mg/5mL [120mL], 15mg/5mL [240mL, 480mL]; **Tab:** 5mg†	**Initial:** 5-60mg/day.* Refer to PI for detailed information for ADT.	**Initial:** 5-60mg/day.* **(Tab)** Refer to PI for detailed information for ADT.
Prednisone	Rayos	**Tab, Delayed-Release:** 1mg, 2mg, 5mg	**Initial:** 5-60mg/day.*	**Initial:** 5-60mg/day.*
	Generic	**Sol:** 5mg/mL [30mL], 5mg/5mL [120mL, 500mL]; **Tab:** 1mg†, 2.5mg†, 5mg†, 10mg†, 20mg†, 50mg†	**Initial:** 5-60mg/day.* Refer to PI for detailed information for ADT.	**Initial:** 5-60mg/day.* Refer to PI for detailed information for ADT.
Triamcinolone	Kenalog-40	**Inj:** 40mg/mL [1mL, 5mL, 10mL]	**Initial:** 2.5-100mg/day.*	**Initial:** 0.11-1.6mg/kg/day in 3 or 4 divided doses.*
MONOCLONAL ANTIBODIES				
Adalimumab	Humira	**Inj:** 20mg/0.4mL, 40mg/0.8mL	**Initial:** 160mg SQ on Day 1 (given as four 40mg inj in 1 day or as two 40mg inj/day for 2 consecutive days); then 80mg after 2 wks (Day 15). **Maint:** 40mg every other wk beginning wk 4 (Day 29).	
Certolizumab Pegol	Cimzia	**Inj:** 200mg/mL	**Initial:** 400mg (given as 2 SQ inj of 200mg) initially and at wks 2 and 4. **Maint:** 400mg q4wks.	
Infliximab	Remicade	**Inj:** 100mg/20mL	**Induction:** 5mg/kg IV at 0, 2, and 6 wks. **Maint:** 5mg/kg q8wks. **Patients Who Respond and Lose Their Response:** May increase to 10mg/kg. Refer to PI for administration and preparation instructions.	**≥6 yrs: Induction:** 5mg/kg IV at 0, 2, and 6 wks. **Maint:** 5mg/kg q8wks. Refer to PI for administration and preparation instructions.
Natalizumab	Tysabri	**Inj:** 300mg/15mL	300mg IV infusion over 1 hr q4wks.	

Refer to full FDA-approved labeling for additional information.

Abbreviation: ADT = alternate day therapy.

*Maintenance dose should be determined by decreasing initial dose in small decrements to lowest effective dose. Withdraw gradually after long-term therapy.
†Scored.

H₂ ANTAGONISTS AND PPIs COMPARISON*

	DRUG	HOW SUPPLIED	Heartburn	PUD	GERD	Esophagitis	Zollinger-Ellison	Helicobacter pylori	NSAID Induced†	Upper GI Bleeding‡	Duodenal Ulcer
H₂ ANTAGONISTS	**CIMETIDINE**										
	Generic	**Sol:** 300mg/5mL		X	X	X	X				X
		Tab: 200mg, 300mg, 400mg, 800mg									
	FAMOTIDINE										
	Pepcid	**Inj:** 10mg/mL (Generic)		X	X	X	X				X
		Sus: 40mg/5mL									
		Tab: 20mg, 40mg									
	NIZATIDINE										
	Axid	**Cap:** 150mg, 300mg (Generic)	X	X	X	X					X
		Sol: 15mg/mL									
	RANITIDINE										
	Zantac	**Inj:** 25mg/mL		X	X	X	X				X
		Cap: 150mg, 300mg (Generic)	X	X	X	X	X				X
		Syrup: 15mg/1mL									
		Tab: 150mg, 300mg									
PROTON PUMP INHIBITORS	**DEXLANSOPRAZOLE**										
	Dexilant	**Cap, DR:** 30mg, 60mg	X		X	X					
	ESOMEPRAZOLE										
	Nexium	**Cap, DR:** 20mg, 40mg	X		X	X	X	X	X		
		Sus, DR: 2.5mg, 5mg, 10mg, 20mg, 40mg (granules/pkt)									
	Nexium I.V.	**Inj:** 20mg, 40mg			X	X					
	LANSOPRAZOLE										
	Prevacid	**Cap, DR:** 15mg, 30mg	X	X	X	X	X	X	X		X
		Tab, Disintegrating: 15mg, 30mg									
	Prevpac	**Cap:** (Amoxicillin) 500mg						X			X
		Tab: (Clarithromycin) 500mg									
		Cap, DR: (Lansoprazole) 30mg									

(Continued)

H₂ Antagonists and PPIs Comparison

	DRUG	HOW SUPPLIED	INDICATIONS								
			Heartburn	PUD	GERD	Esophagitis	Zollinger-Ellison	Helicobacter pylori	NSAID Induced†	Upper GI Bleeding‡	Duodenal Ulcer
PROTON PUMP INHIBITORS	**OMEPRAZOLE**										
	Prilosec	**Cap, DR:** 10mg, 20mg, 40mg	X	X	X	X	X	X			X
		Sus, DR: 2.5mg, 10mg (granules/pkt)									
	Zegerid	**Cap:** (Omeprazole-Sodium bicarbonate) 20mg-1100mg, 40mg-1100mg	X	X	X	X				X	X
		Pow: 20mg-1680mg/pkt, 40mg-1680mg/pkt									
	PANTOPRAZOLE										
	Protonix	**Tab, DR:** 20mg, 40mg	X		X	X	X				
		Sus, DR: 40mg (granules/pkt)									
	Protonix I.V.	**Inj:** 40mg			X	X	X				
	RABEPRAZOLE										
	Aciphex	**Tab, DR:** 20mg	X	X	X		X	X			X

Refer to full FDA-approved labeling for additional information.

Abbreviations: DR = delayed-release; GERD = gastroesophageal reflux disease; GI = gastrointestinal; NSAID = nonsteroidal anti-inflammatory drug; PUD = peptic ulcer disease.

*Rx products only. For OTC products, refer to the *Antacid and Heartburn Products* table.

† Prevention of NSAID-induced gastric ulcers.

‡ Prevention of upper GI bleeding in critically ill patients.

ULCERATIVE COLITIS TREATMENTS

GENERIC	BRAND	HOW SUPPLIED	ADULT DOSAGE	PEDIATRIC DOSAGE
AMINOSALICYLATES				
Balsalazide disodium	Colazal	**Cap:** 750mg	3 caps tid for up to 8 wks (or 12 wks if needed). May open cap and sprinkle on applesauce.	**5-17 yrs:** 1 or 3 caps tid for up to 8 wks. May open cap and sprinkle on applesauce.
	Giazo	**Tab:** 1.1g	**Male:** 3 tabs bid for up to 8 wks.	
Mesalamine	Apriso	**Cap, ER:** 0.375g	4 caps qam. Avoid with antacids.	
	Asacol	**Tab, DR:** 400mg	2 tabs tid for 6 wks. **Maint:** 1600mg/day in divided doses.	**5-17 yrs: 54-90kg:** 27-44mg/kg/day up to 2400mg/day. **33-<54kg:** 37-61mg/kg/day up to 2000mg/day. **17-<33kg:** 36-71mg/kg/day up to 1200mg/day.
	Asacol HD	**Tab, DR:** 800mg	2 tabs tid for 6 wks.	
	Delzicol	**Cap, DR:** 400mg	2 caps tid for 6 wks. **Maint:** 1600mg/day in divided doses. Should be taken at least 1 hr before or 2 hrs after a meal.	
	Lialda	**Tab, DR:** 1.2g	**Induction:** 2-4 tabs qd with a meal. **Maint:** 2 tabs qd with a meal.	
	Pentasa	**Cap, CR:** 250mg, 500mg	1000mg qid for up to 8 wks.	
	SF Rowasa	**Rect Sus:** 4g/60mL	1 instillation (4g) qhs for 3-6 weeks. Retain for 8 hrs.	
Olsalazine	Dipentum	**Cap:** 250mg	1000mg/day in 2 divided doses.	
Sulfasalazine	Azulfidine	**Tab:** 500mg*	**Initial:** 3-4g/day in evenly divided doses with dose intervals ≤8 hrs. May initiate at 1-2g/day to reduce GI intolerance. **Maint:** 2g/day.	**≥6 yrs: Initial:** 40-60mg/kg/day divided into 3-6 doses. **Maint:** 30mg/kg/day divided into 4 doses.
	Azulfidine EN-tabs	**Tab, DR:** 500mg		
CORTICOSTEROIDS				
Betamethasone sodium phosphate-Betamethasone acetate	Celestone Soluspan	**Inj:** 3mg-3mg/mL [5mL, multidose]	**Initial:** 0.25-9mg/day IM.†	**Initial:** 0.02-0.3mg/kg/day in 3 or 4 divided doses IM.†
Budesonide	Uceris	**Tab, ER:** 9mg	9mg qam for up to 8 wks.	

(Continued)

GENERIC	BRAND	HOW SUPPLIED	ADULT DOSAGE	PEDIATRIC DOSAGE
CORTICOSTEROIDS *(Continued)*				
Dexamethasone	Generic	**Sol:** 0.5mg/5mL, 1mg/mL; **Tab:** 0.5mg*, 0.75mg*, 1mg*, 1.5mg*, 2mg*, 4mg*, 6mg*	**Initial:** 0.75-9mg/day.†	**Initial:** 0.02-0.3mg/kg/day in 3 or 4 divided doses.†
	Generic	**Inj:** 4mg/mL [1mL, 5mL, 30mL], 10mg/mL [10mL]	**Initial:** 0.5-9mg/day IV/IM.†	
Hydrocortisone	Anusol-HC	**Sup:** 25mg	**Nonspecific Proctitis:** 1 sup rectally bid for 2 wks. **More Severe Cases:** 1 sup rectally tid or 2 sup rectally bid. **Factitial Proctitis:** Use up to 6-8 wks.	
	Colocort	**Rect Sus:** 100mg/60mL	1 instillation (100mg) qhs for 21 days or until remission. Retain for ≥1 hr, preferably all night.	
	Cortef	**Tab:** 5mg*, 10mg*, 20mg*	**Initial:** 20-240mg/day.†	**Initial:** 20-240mg/day.†
	Proctocort	**Sup:** 30mg	**Nonspecific Proctitis:** 1 sup rectally bid for 2 wks. **More Severe Cases:** 1 sup rectally tid or 2 sup rectally bid. **Factitial Proctitis:** Use up to 6-8 wks.	
	Solu-Cortef	**Inj:** 100mg, 250mg, 500mg, 1000mg	**Initial:** 100-500mg IV/IM. May repeat dose at 2-, 4-, or 6-hr intervals. High-dose therapy should continue only until patient is stabilized, usually not beyond 48-72 hrs.†	**Initial:** 0.56-8mg/kg/day IV/IM in 3 or 4 divided doses.†
Methylprednisolone	Depo-Medrol	**Inj:** 20mg/mL, 40mg/mL, 80mg/mL	**Initial:** 4-120mg IM.†	**Initial:** 0.11-1.6mg/kg/day.†
	Medrol	**Tab:** 2mg*, 4mg*, 8mg*, 16mg*, 32mg*; (Dose-Pak) 4mg* [21s]	**Initial:** 4-48mg/day.† Refer to PI for detailed information for ADT.	**Initial:** 4-48mg/day.† Refer to PI for detailed information for ADT.
	Solu-Medrol	**Inj:** 40mg, 125mg, 500mg, 1g, 2g	**Initial:** 10-40mg IV/IM inj or IV infusion. **High-Dose Therapy:** 30mg/kg IV over at least 30 min. May repeat dose q4-6h for 48 hrs. High-dose therapy should continue only until patient is stabilized, usually not beyond 48-72 hrs.†	**Initial:** 0.11-1.6mg/kg/day in 3 or 4 divided doses.†
Prednisolone	Flo-Pred	**Sus:** 15mg/5mL [37mL, 52mL, 65mL]	**Initial:** 5-60mg/day.†	**Initial:** 0.14-2mg/kg/day in 3 or 4 divided doses.†
	Orapred	**Sol:** 15mg/5mL [237mL, 20mL]; **Tab, Disintegrating:** 10mg, 15mg, 30mg	(Sol) **Initial:** 5-60mg/day. (Tab, Disintegrating) **Initial:** 10-60mg/day.†	**Initial:** 0.14-2mg/kg/day in 3 or 4 divided doses.†
	Pediapred	**Sol:** 5mg/5mL [120mL]	**Initial:** 5-60mg/day.†	**Initial:** 0.14-2mg/kg/day in 3 or 4 divided doses.†
	Generic	**Syrup:** 5mg/5mL [120mL], 15mg/5mL [240mL, 480mL]; **Tab:** 5mg*	**Initial:** 5-60mg/day.† (Tab) Refer to PI for detailed information for ADT.	**Initial:** 5-60mg/day.† (Tab) Refer to PI for detailed information for ADT.

GENERIC	BRAND	HOW SUPPLIED	ADULT DOSAGE	PEDIATRIC DOSAGE
CORTICOSTEROIDS (Continued)				
Prednisone	Rayos	**Tab, DR:** 1mg, 2mg, 5mg	**Initial:** 5-60mg/day.†	**Initial:** 5-60mg/day.†
	Generic	**Sol:** 5mg/mL [30mL], 5mg/5mL [120mL, 500mL]; **Tab:** 1mg*, 2.5mg*, 5mg*, 10mg*, 20mg*, 50mg*	**Initial:** 5-60mg/day.† Refer to PI for detailed information for ADT.	**Initial:** 5-60mg/day.† Refer to PI for detailed information for ADT.
Triamcinolone	Kenalog-40	**Inj:** 40mg/mL [1mL, 5mL, 10mL]	**Initial:** 2.5-100mg/day.†	**Initial:** 0.11-1.6mg/kg/day in 3 or 4 divided doses.†
MONOCLONAL ANTIBODIES				
Adalimumab	Humira	**Inj:** 20mg/0.4mL, 40mg/0.8mL	**Initial:** 160mg SQ on Day 1 (given as four 40mg inj in 1 day or as two 40mg inj/day for 2 consecutive days); then 80mg after 2 wks (Day 15). **Maint:** 40mg every other wk beginning Wk 4 (Day 29). Continue only with evidence of clinical remission by 8 wks (Day 57) of therapy.	
Golimumab	Simponi	**Inj:** 50mg/0.5mL, 100mg/mL	**Induction:** 200mg SQ at Week 0, then 100mg at Week 2. **Maint:** 100mg q4wks. Refer to PI for administration and preparation instructions.	
Infliximab	Remicade	**Inj:** 100mg/20mL	**Induction:** 5mg/kg IV at 0, 2, and 6 wks. **Maint:** 5mg/kg q8wks. Refer to PI for administration and preparation instructions.	**≥6 yrs: Induction:** 5mg/kg IV at 0, 2, and 6 wks. **Maint:** 5mg/kg q8wks. Refer to PI for administration and preparation instructions.

Refer to full FDA-approved labeling for additional information.

Abbreviations: ADT = alternate day therapy; CR = controlled-release; DR = delayed-release; ER = extended-release.

*Scored.

†Maintenance dose should be determined by decreasing initial dose in small decrements to lowest effective dose. Withdraw gradually after long-term therapy.

ANTIVIRALS TREATMENT COMPARISON

GENERIC (BRAND)	HOW SUPPLIED	INDICATIONS							
		HIV	HBV	HCV	Genital Herpes	Herpes Zoster	Herpes Labialis	CMV Retinitis	Influenza
ADAMANTANES									
Rimantadine HCl (Flumadine)	**Tab:** 100mg								✓-A
BIOLOGICAL RESPONSE MODIFIERS									
Interferon alfa-2b (Intron A)	**Inj:** (Pen) 18 MIU, 30 MIU, 60 MIU; (Powder) 10 MIU, 18 MIU, 50 MIU; (Vial) 18 MIU, 25 MIU		✓	✓					
Interferon alfacon-1 (Infergen)	**Inj:** 9mcg/0.3mL, 15mcg/0.5mL			✓					
CCR5 ANTAGONISTS									
Maraviroc (Selzentry)	**Tab:** 150mg, 300mg	✓							
DOPAMINE RECEPTOR AGONISTS									
Amantadine HCl	**Cap:** 100mg; **Syr:** 50mg/5mL [473mL]; **Tab:** 100mg								✓-A
FUSION INHIBITORS									
Enfuvirtide (Fuzeon)	**Inj:** 90mg/mL [108mg]	✓							
GUANOSINE NUCLEOSIDE ANALOGUES									
Entecavir (Baraclude)	**Sol:** 0.05mg/mL [210mL]; **Tab:** 0.5mg, 1mg		✓						
HIV-INTEGRASE STRAND TRANSFER INHIBITORS									
Dolutegravir sodium (Tivicay)	**Tab:** 50mg	✓							
Raltegravir (Isentress)	**Sus Powder:** 100mg/pkt; **Tab:** 400mg; **Tab, Chewable:** 25mg, 100mg	✓							
NEURAMINIDASE INHIBITORS									
Oseltamivir phosphate (Tamiflu)	**Cap:** 30mg, 45mg, 75mg; **Sus:** 6mg/mL [60mL]								✓
Zanamivir (Relenza)	**Powder, Inh:** 5mg/inh								✓-A,B
NON-NUCLEOSIDE REVERSE TRANSCRIPTASE INHIBITORS									
Delavirdine (Rescriptor)	**Tab:** 100mg, 200mg	✓							
Efavirenz (Sustiva)	**Cap:** 50mg, 200mg; **Tab:** 600mg	✓							

(Continued)

GENERIC (BRAND)	HOW SUPPLIED	INDICATIONS							
		HIV	HBV	HCV	Genital Herpes	Herpes Zoster	Herpes Labialis	CMV Retinitis	Influenza
NON-NUCLEOSIDE REVERSE TRANSCRIPTASE INHIBITORS *(Continued)*									
Etravirine (Intelence)	**Tab:** 25mg, 100mg, 200mg	✓							
Nevirapine (Viramune, Viramune XR)	**Sus:** 50mg/5mL [240mL]; **Tab:** 200mg; **Tab, ER:** 100mg, 400mg	✓							
Rilpivirine (Edurant)	**Tab:** 25mg	✓							
NUCLEOSIDE ANALOGUES									
Acyclovir (Zovirax Oral)	**Cap:** 200mg; **Sus:** 200mg/5mL [473mL]; **Tab:** 400mg, 800mg				✓	✓			
Acyclovir (Zovirax Cream)	**Cre:** 5% [2g, 5g]						✓		
Acyclovir (Zovirax Ointment)	**Oint:** 5% [30g]				✓				
Acyclovir sodium	**Inj:** 50mg/mL				✓	✓			
Famciclovir (Famvir)	**Tab:** 125mg, 250mg, 500mg				✓	✓	✓		
Ganciclovir sodium (Cytovene)	**Inj:** 500mg/10mL							✓	
Penciclovir (Denavir)	**Cre:** 1% [1.5g, 5g]						✓		
Ribavirin (Copegus)	**Tab:** 200mg			✓					
Ribavirin (Rebetol)	**Cap:** 200mg; **Sol:** 40mg/mL [100mL]			✓					
Ribavirin (Ribasphere Capsules)	**Cap:** 200mg			✓					
Ribavirin (Ribasphere Tablets)	**Tab:** 200mg, 400mg, 600mg			✓					
Valacyclovir HCl (Valtrex)	**Tab:** 500mg, 1000mg				✓	✓	✓		
Valganciclovir (Valcyte)	**Sol:** 50mg/mL [88mL]; **Tab:** 450mg							✓	
NUCLEOSIDE REVERSE TRANSCRIPTASE INHIBITORS									
Abacavir (Ziagen)	**Sol:** 20mg/mL [240mL]; **Tab:** 300mg	✓							

GENERIC (BRAND)	HOW SUPPLIED	INDICATIONS							
		HIV	HBV	HCV	Genital Herpes	Herpes Zoster	Herpes Labialis	CMV Retinitis	Influenza
NUCLEOSIDE REVERSE TRANSCRIPTASE INHIBITORS *(Continued)*									
Didanosine (Videx, Videx EC)	**Cap, DR:** (Videx EC) 125mg, 200mg, 250mg, 400mg; **Sol:** (Videx) 10mg/mL [2g, 4g]	✓							
Emtricitabine (Emtriva)	**Cap:** 200mg; **Sol:** 10mg/mL [170mL]	✓							
Lamivudine (Epivir)	**Sol:** 10mg/mL [240mL]; **Tab:** 150mg, 300mg	✓							
Lamivudine (Epivir-HBV)	**Sol:** 5mg/mL [240mL]; **Tab:** 100mg		✓						
Stavudine (Zerit)	**Cap:** 15mg, 20mg, 30mg, 40mg; **Sol:** 1mg/mL [200mL]	✓							
Telbivudine (Tyzeka)	**Tab:** 600mg; **Sol:** 100mg/5mL [300mL]		✓						
Zidovudine (Retrovir)	**Cap:** 100mg; **Inj:** 10mg/mL; **Syrup:** 10mg/mL [240mL]; **Tab:** 300mg	✓							
NUCLEOTIDE ANALOGUE INHIBITORS									
Sofosbuvir (Sovaldi)	**Tab:** 400mg			✓					
NUCLEOTIDE ANALOGUE REVERSE TRANSCRIPTASE INHIBITORS									
Adefovir dipivoxil (Hepsera)	**Tab:** 10mg		✓						
Tenofovir disoproxil (Viread)	**Powder:** 40mg/g [60g]; **Tab:** 150mg, 200mg, 250mg, 300mg	✓	✓						
PEGYLATED VIRUS PROLIFERATION INHIBITORS									
Peginterferon alfa-2a (Pegasys)	**Inj:** 135mcg/0.5mL, 180mcg/0.5mL, 180mcg/mL		✓	✓					
Peginterferon alfa-2b (PegIntron)	**Inj:** 50mcg/0.5mL, 80mcg/0.5mL, 120mcg/0.5mL, 150mcg/0.5mL			✓					
PROTEASE INHIBITORS									
Atazanavir sulfate (Reyataz)	**Cap:** 150mg, 200mg, 300mg	✓							

GENERIC (BRAND)	HOW SUPPLIED	INDICATIONS							
		HIV	HBV	HCV	Genital Herpes	Herpes Zoster	Herpes Labialis	CMV Retinitis	Influenza
PROTEASE INHIBITORS *(Continued)*									
Boceprevir (Victrelis)	**Cap:** 200mg			✓					
Darunavir (Prezista)	**Sus:** 100mg/mL [200mL]; **Tab:** 75mg, 150mg, 400mg, 600mg, 800mg	✓							
Fosamprenavir calcium (Lexiva)	**Sus:** 50mg/mL [225mL]; **Tab:** 700mg	✓							
Indinavir sulfate (Crixivan)	**Cap:** 100mg, 200mg, 400mg	✓							
Nelfinavir mesylate (Viracept)	**Powder:** 50mg/g [144g]; **Tab:** 250g, 625mg	✓							
Ritonavir (Norvir)	**Cap, Tab:** 100mg; **Sol:** 80mg/mL [240mL]	✓							
Saquinavir mesylate (Invirase)	**Cap:** 200mg; **Tab:** 500mg	✓							
Simeprevir (Olysio)	**Cap:** 150mg			✓					
Telaprevir (Incivek)	**Tab:** 375mg			✓					
Tipranavir (Aptivus)	**Cap:** 250mg; **Sol:** 100mg/mL [95mL]	✓							
PYROPHOSPHATE BINDING INHIBITORS									
Foscarnet sodium	**Inj:** 24mg/mL							✓	
VIRAL DNA SYNTHESIS INHIBITORS									
Cidofovir (Vistide)	**Inj:** 75mg/mL							✓	

Refer to full FDA-approved labeling for additional information.

Abbreviations: CMV = cytomegalovirus; HBV = hepatitis B virus; HCV = hepatitis C virus; HIV = human immunodeficiency virus.

SEXUALLY TRANSMITTED DISEASES GUIDELINE-BASED TREATMENT

DISEASE	DRUG	RECOMMENDED DOSAGE REGIMENS
BACTERIAL VAGINOSIS		
Nonpregnant Women	Metronidazole *OR* Clindamycin *OR* Metronidazole	500mg PO bid x 7d. 2% cre: 1 full applicator (5g) intravaginally qhs x 7d. 0.75% gel: 1 full applicator (5g) intravaginally qd x 5d.
Alternative Regimens Nonpregnant Women	Clindamycin *OR* Clindamycin ovules Tinidazole	300mg PO bid x 7d. 100mg intravaginally qhs x 3d. 2g PO qd x 2d *OR* 1g PO qd x 5d.
Pregnant Women	Metronidazole *OR* Clindamycin	250mg PO tid x 7d *OR* 500mg PO bid x 7d. 300mg PO bid x 7d.
CHANCROID		
	Azithromycin *OR* Ceftriaxone *OR* Ciprofloxacin *OR* Erythromycin base	1g PO single dose. 250mg IM single dose. 500mg PO bid x 3d. 500mg PO tid x 7d.
CHLAMYDIAL INFECTION		
Nonpregnant Women	Azithromycin *OR* Doxycycline	1g PO single dose. 100mg PO bid x 7d.
Pregnant Women	Azithromycin *OR* Amoxicillin	1g PO single dose. 500mg PO tid x 7d.
Alternative Regimens Nonpregnant Women	Erythromycin base *OR* Erythromycin ethylsuccinate *OR* Ofloxacin *OR* Levofloxacin	500mg PO qid x 7d. 800mg PO qid x 7d. 300mg PO bid x 7d. 500mg PO qd x 7d.
Pregnant Women	Erythromycin base *OR* Erythromycin ethylsuccinate	250mg PO qid x 14d *OR* 500mg PO qid x 7d. 400mg PO qid x 14d *OR* 800mg PO qid x 7d.
EPIDIDYMITIS		
Gonococcal *OR* Chlamydial Infection	Ceftriaxone *PLUS* Doxycycline	250mg IM single dose. 100mg PO bid x 10d.
Acute Epididymitis Most Likely Caused by Enteric Organisms	Ofloxacin *OR* Levofloxacin	300mg PO bid x 10d. 500mg PO qd x 10d.
GRANULOMA INGUINALE (DONOVANOSIS)		
	Doxycycline	100mg PO bid for at least 3 wks and until all lesions have completely healed.
Alternative Regimens	Ciprofloxacin *OR*	750mg PO bid for at least 3 wks and until all lesions have completely healed.
	Erythromycin base (during pregnancy) *OR* Azithromycin *OR*	500mg PO qid for at least 3 wks and until all lesions have completely healed. 1g PO once wkly for at least 3 wks and until all lesions have completely healed.
	Trimethoprim/Sulfamethoxazole *PLUS* Aminoglycoside (eg, gentamicin) can be considered if improvement is not evident within the first few days of therapy.	1 double-strength tab (160mg/800mg) PO bid for at least 3 wks and until all lesions have completely healed. 1mg/kg IV q8h.

(Continued)

DISEASE	DRUG	RECOMMENDED DOSAGE REGIMENS
HERPES SIMPLEX VIRUS (HSV)		
First Episode	Acyclovir OR	400mg PO tid x 7-10d OR 200mg PO 5x/d x 7-10d.
	Famciclovir OR	250mg PO tid x 7-10d.
	Valacyclovir	1g PO bid x 7-10d. Treatment can be extended if healing is incomplete after 10 days of therapy.
Episodic Therapy for Recurrent Genital Herpes	Acyclovir OR	400mg PO tid x 5d OR 800mg PO bid x 5d OR 800mg PO tid x 2d.
	Famciclovir OR	1g bid x 1d OR 125mg PO bid x 5d OR 500mg once followed by 250mg bid x 2d.
	Valacyclovir	500mg PO bid x 3d OR 1g PO qd x 5d.
Suppressive Therapy for Recurrent Genital Herpes	Acyclovir OR	400mg PO bid.
	Famciclovir OR	250mg PO bid.
	Valacyclovir	500mg PO qd (<10 episodes/yr) OR 1g PO qd.
HUMAN PAPILLOMAVIRUS (HPV) INFECTION		
External Genital Warts	Podofilox OR	0.5% sol OR gel: (patient-applied) bid x 3d, wait 4d, repeat as necessary x 4 cycles. Limit application to 0.5mL/day and to ≤10cm^2 total wart area treated.
	Imiquimod OR	5% cre: (patient-applied) hs, 3 times a wk for up to 16 wks.
	Sinecatechins	15% oint: (patient-applied) tid (0.5cm strand/wart) x ≤16 wks.
	Cryotherapy OR	Provider-administered w/liquid nitrogen or cryoprobe q1-2 wks.
	Podophyllin resin	10-25% (provider-administered) Treatment may be repeated wkly prn. Limit application to <0.5mL and to <10cm^2 wart area per session. Do not apply to area with open lesions or wounds.
	Trichloroacetic acid OR	80-90% (provider-administered) Treatment may be repeated wkly prn.
	Bichloroacetic acid OR Surgical removal	80-90% (provider-administered) Treatment may be repeated wkly prn.
Alternative Regimens	Intralesional interferon OR Photodynamic therapy OR Topical Cidofovir	
Vaginal Warts	Cryotherapy OR	With liquid nitrogen.
	Trichloroacetic acid OR	80-90% (provider-administered) Treatment may be repeated wkly prn.
	Bichloroacetic acid	80-90% (provider-administered) Treatment may be repeated wkly prn.
Urethral Meatus Warts	Cryotherapy OR	With liquid nitrogen.
	Podophyllin resin	10-25% in compound tincture of benzoin. (provider-administered) Treatment may be repeated wkly prn.
Anal Warts	Cryotherapy OR	With liquid nitrogen.
	Trichloroacetic acid OR	80-90% (provider-administered) Treatment may be repeated wkly prn.
	Bichloroacetic acid OR Surgical removal	80-90% (provider-administered) Treatment may be repeated wkly prn.

DISEASE	DRUG	RECOMMENDED DOSAGE REGIMENS
LYMPHOGRANULOMA VENEREUM		
	Doxycycline	100mg PO bid x 21d.
Alternative Regimens (including pregnancy/lactation)	Erythromycin base	500mg PO qid x 21d.
NONGONOCOCCAL URETHRITIS		
	Azithromycin *OR*	1g PO single dose.
	Doxycycline	100mg PO bid x 7d.
Alternative Regimens	Erythromycin base *OR*	500mg PO qid x 7d.
	Erythromycin ethylsuccinate *OR*	800mg PO qid x 7d.
	Ofloxacin *OR*	300mg PO bid x 7d.
	Levofloxacin	500mg PO qd x 7d.
Recurrent and Persistent Urethritis	Metronidazole *OR*	2g PO single dose.
	Tinidazole *PLUS*	2g PO single dose.
	Azithromycin	1g PO single dose (if not used for initial episode).
PEDICULOSIS PUBIS		
	Permethrin *OR*	1% cre: Apply to affected area and wash off after 10 min.
	Pyrethrins with piperonyl butoxide	Apply to affected area and wash off after 10 min.
Alternative Regimens	Malathion *OR*	0.5% lot: Apply for 8-12 hours and wash off.
	Ivermectin	250mcg/kg PO; repeat in 2 wks.
PELVIC INFLAMMATORY DISEASE		
Parenteral Regimen A	Cefotetan *OR*	2g IV q12h.
	Cefoxitin *PLUS*	2g IV q6h.
	Doxycycline	100mg PO/IV q12h.
Parenteral Regimen B	Clindamycin *PLUS*	900mg IV q8h.
	Gentamicin	LD: 2mg/kg IM/IV. MD: 1.5mg/kg IM/IV q8h. May substitute with 3-5mg/kg IM/IV single daily dose.
Alternative Parenteral Regimens	Ampicillin/Sulbactam *PLUS*	3g IV q6h.
	Doxycycline	100mg PO/IV q12h.
Oral Regimen	Ceftriaxone *PLUS*	250mg IM single dose.
	Doxycycline *W/ or W/O*	100mg PO bid x 14d.
	Metronidazole *OR*	500mg PO bid x 14d.
	Cefoxitin and Probenecid *PLUS*	2g IM single dose and probenecid 1g PO administered concurrently in a single dose.
	Doxycycline *W/ or W/O*	100mg PO bid x 14d.
	Metronidazole *OR*	500mg PO bid x 14d.
	Other parenteral 3rd Gen Cephalosporin (eg, ceftizoxime or cefotaxime) *PLUS*	
	Doxycycline *W/ or W/O*	100mg PO bid x 14d.
	Metronidazole	500mg PO bid x 14d.
Alternative Oral Regimen may be considered if parenteral cephalosporin therapy is not feasible (If the community prevalence and individual risk for gonorrhea are low)	Levofloxacin *OR*	500mg PO qd x 14d.
	Ofloxacin *W/ or W/O*	400mg PO bid x 14d.
	Metronidazole	500mg PO bid x 14d.

(Continued)

DISEASE	DRUG	RECOMMENDED DOSAGE REGIMENS
PROCTITIS		
	Ceftriaxone *PLUS*	250mg IM.
	Doxycycline	100mg PO bid x 7d.
SCABIES		
	Permethrin *OR*	5% cre: Apply to body from the neck down and wash off after 8-14h.
	Ivermectin	200mcg/kg PO; repeat in 2 wks.
Alternative Regimen	Lindane	1% lot *OR* cre: Apply 1 oz of lot *OR* 30g of cre in a thin layer to body from the neck down and wash off after 8h (should not be used on people with extensive dermatitis, pregnancy, lactating women, or children <2 yrs).
SYPHILIS		
Primary and Secondary Disease	Benzathine penicillin G	**Adults:** 2.4 MU IM single dose. **Peds ≥1 mo:** 50,000 U/kg IM single dose. **Max:** 2.4 MU/dose.
Penicillin Allergy (non-pregnant patients)	Doxycycline *OR*	100mg PO bid x 14d.
	Tetracycline	500mg PO qid x 14d.
Early Latent Disease	Benzathine penicillin G	**Adults:** 2.4 MU IM single dose. **Peds ≥ 1 mo:** 50,000 U/kg IM single dose. **Max:** 2.4 MU/dose.
Late Latent or Latent of Unknown Duration	Benzathine penicillin G	**Adults:** 2.4 MU IM qwk x 3 doses. **Peds ≥1 mo:** 50,000 U/kg IM qwk x 3 doses. **Max:** 2.4 MU/single dose and 7.2 MU/total dose.
Tertiary Disease	Benzathine penicillin G	2.4 MU IM qwk x 3 doses.
Neurosyphilis	Aqueous crystalline penicillin G	3-4 MU IV q4h *OR* continuous infusion x 10-14d (total 18-24 MU per day).
Alternative Regimen	Procaine penicillin *PLUS*	2.4 MU IM qd x 10-14d.
	Probenecid	500mg PO qid x 10-14d.
TRICHOMONIASIS		
	Metronidazole *OR*	2g PO single dose.
	Tinidazole	2g PO single dose.
Alternative Regimen	Metronidazole	500mg PO bid x 7d.
Pregnant Women	Metronidazole	2g PO single dose at any stage of pregnancy.
UNCOMPLICATED GONOCOCCAL INFECTIONS		
Cervix, Urethra, and Rectum	Ceftriaxone *PLUS*	250mg IM single dose.
	Azithromycin *OR*	1g PO single dose.
	Doxycycline	100mg PO bid x 7d.
Alternative Regimens	If ceftriaxone is not available:	
	Cefixime *PLUS*	400mg PO single dose.
	Azithromycin *OR*	1g PO single dose.
	Doxycycline	100mg PO bid x 7d.
	(*PLUS* Test-of-cure in 1 wk)	
	OR	
	If the patient has a severe cephalosporin allergy:	
	Azithromycin	2g PO single dose.
	(*PLUS* Test-of-cure in 1 wk)	

DISEASE	DRUG	RECOMMENDED DOSAGE REGIMENS
UNCOMPLICATED GONOCOCCAL INFECTIONS *(Continued)*		
Pharynx	Ceftriaxone *PLUS*	250mg IM single dose.
	Azithromycin *OR*	1g PO single dose.
	Doxycycline	100mg PO bid x 7d.
VULVOVAGINAL CANDIDIASIS		
Intravaginal Agents	Butoconazole *OR*	2% cre: 5g intravaginally x 3d. (OTC)
	Butoconazole *OR*	2% cre: 5g intravaginally single dose. (Rx)
	Clotrimazole *OR*	1% cre: 5g intravaginally x 7-14d.
	Clotrimazole *OR*	2% cre: 5g intravaginally x 3d.
	Miconazole *OR*	2% cre: 5g intravaginally x 7d.
	Miconazole *OR*	4% cre: 5g intravaginally x 3d.
	Miconazole *OR*	200mg vaginal supp x 3d.
	Miconazole *OR*	100mg vaginal supp x 7d.
	Miconazole *OR*	1200mg vaginal supp single dose.
	Nystatin *OR*	100,000 U vaginal tab x 14d.
	Tioconazole *OR*	6.5% oint: 5g intravaginally single dose.
	Terconazole *OR*	0.4% cre: 5g intravaginally x 7d.
	Terconazole *OR*	0.8% cre: 5g intravaginally x 3d.
	Terconazole *OR*	80mg vaginal supp x 3d.
Oral Agent	Fluconazole	150mg tab PO single dose.

Source: Centers for Disease Control and Prevention. Sexually Transmitted Diseases Treatment Guidelines 2010. *MMWR.* 2010;59(No. RR-12):1-109.

HIV/AIDS PHARMACOTHERAPY

GENERIC [BRAND]	HOW SUPPLIED	USUAL ADULT DOSAGE	PEDIATRIC DOSAGE	FOOD EFFECT	BOXED WARNING*
CCR5 ANTAGONISTS					
Maraviroc (MVC) [Selzentry]†	**Tab:** 150mg, 300mg	**≥16 yrs:** Give in combination with other antiretrovirals. **W/ Strong CYP3A4 Inhibitors (w/ or w/o CYP3A inducer):** 150mg bid. **W/ NRTIs, Tipranavir/Ritonavir, Nevirapine, Raltegravir, Enfuvirtide, Other Drugs That Are Not Strong CYP3A Inhibitors/Inducers:** 300mg bid. **W/ Strong CYP3A Inducers (w/o strong CYP3A inhibitor):** 600mg bid.		Take without regard to meals.	Hepatotoxicity
HIV INTEGRASE STRAND TRANSFER INHIBITORS (INSTIs)					
Raltegravir [Isentress]	**Sus (Powder):** 100mg/pkt; **Tab:** 400mg; **Tab, Chewable:** 25mg, 100mg‡	400mg bid. **W/ Rifampin:** 800mg bid.	Check labeling for age/weight-based dosing.	Take without regard to meals.	
NUCLEOSIDE REVERSE TRANSCRIPTASE INHIBITORS (NRTIs)					
Abacavir (ABC) [Ziagen]§	**Sol:** 20mg/mL [240mL]; **Tab:** 300mg‡	300mg bid or 600mg qd.	(Sol) **≥3 mos:** 8mg/kg bid. **Max:** 300mg bid. (Tab) **≥30kg:** 300mg bid (am and pm). **>21–<30kg:** 150mg qam, 300mg qpm. **14–21kg:** 150mg bid (am and pm).	Take without regard to meals.	Hypersensitivity reactions/lactic acidosis/severe hepatomegaly
Didanosine (ddI) [Videx Powder for Oral Sol; Videx EC]†	**Sol:** 10mg/mL [2g, 4g]; **Cap, DR:** (Videx EC) 125mg, 200mg, 250mg, 400mg	**≥60kg:** (Cap) 400mg qd; (Sol) 200mg bid or 400mg qd. **<60kg:** (Sol) 125mg bid or 250mg qd. **W/ ddI:** 250mg qd or 200mg qd if <60kg. **25–60kg:** (Cap) 250mg qd. **20–25kg:** (Cap) 200mg qd.	**2 wks–8 mos:** (Sol) 100mg/m² bid. **>8 mos:** (Sol) 120mg/m² bid.	Take on an empty stomach at least 30 min before or 2 hrs after meals. Swallow caps whole.	Pancreatitis/lactic acidosis/hepatomegaly with steatosis
Emtricitabine (FTC) [Emtriva]†	**Cap:** 200mg; **Sol:** 10mg/mL [170mL]	**≥18 yrs:** (Cap) 200mg qd; (Sol) 240mg (24mL) qd.	**0–3 mos:** (Sol) 3mg/kg qd. **3 mos–17 yrs:** (Cap) **>33kg:** 200mg qd. (Sol) 6mg/kg qd. **Max:** 240mg (24mL) qd.	Take without regard to meals.	Lactic acidosis/severe hepatomegaly with steatosis/posttreatment exacerbation of hepatitis B

(Continued)

GENERIC [BRAND]	HOW SUPPLIED	USUAL ADULT DOSAGE	PEDIATRIC DOSAGE	FOOD EFFECT	BOXED WARNING*
NUCLEOSIDE REVERSE TRANSCRIPTASE INHIBITORS (NRTIs) *(Continued)*					
Lamivudine [Epivir]†	Sol: 10mg/mL [240mL]; Tab: 150mg†, 300mg	>16 yrs: 150mg bid or 300mg qd.	3 mos-16 yrs: (Sol) 4mg/kg bid. Max: 150mg bid. (Tab) ≥30kg: 150mg bid (am and pm). >21-<30kg: 75mg qam and 150mg qpm. 14-21kg: 75mg bid (am and pm).	Take without regard to meals.	Lactic acidosis/posttreatment exacerbations of hepatitis B in coinfected patients/different formulations of Epivir
Stavudine (d4T) [Zerit]†	Cap: 15mg, 20mg, 30mg, 40mg; Sol: 1mg/mL [200mL]	≥60kg: 40mg q12h. <60kg: 30mg q12h.	Birth-13 days: 0.5mg/kg q12h. ≥14 days: <30kg: 1mg/kg q12h. ≥30kg: Adult dosing.	Take without regard to meals.	Lactic acidosis/hepatomegaly with steatosis/pancreatitis
Tenofovir disoproxil fumarate (TDF) [Viread]†	Tab: 150mg, 200mg, 250mg, 300mg; Powder: 4mg/g [60g]	300mg qd or 7.5 scoops of oral powder if unable to swallow tabs.	≥12 yrs: ≥35kg: 300mg qd or 7.5 scoops of oral powder if unable to swallow tabs. 2-12 yrs: 8mg/kg qd. Max: 300mg qd. Refer to PI for age/weight-based dosing recommendation.	Take without regard to meals.	Lactic acidosis/severe hepatomegaly with steatosis/ posttreatment exacerbation of hepatitis B
Zidovudine (AZT, ZDV) [Retrovir]†	Cap: 100mg; Inj: 10mg/mL; Syrup: 10mg/mL [240mL]; Tab: 300mg	(Cap, Syrup, Tab) 600mg/day in divided doses (300mg bid or 200mg tid). (Inj) 1mg/kg IV over 1 hr 5-6 times/day.	4 wks-18 yrs: ≥30kg: 600mg/day given bid or tid. ≥9-<30kg: 18mg/kg/day given bid or tid. 4-<9kg: 24mg/kg/day given bid or tid. Alternative: 480mg/m²/day in divided doses (240mg/m² bid or 160mg/m² tid).	Take without regard to meals.	Risk of hematological toxicity/ myopathy/lactic acidosis
NON-NUCLEOSIDE REVERSE TRANSCRIPTASE INHIBITORS					
Delavirdine (DLV) [Rescriptor]	Tab: 100mg, 200mg	≥16 yrs: 400mg tid.		Take without regard to meals. Separate doses from antacids by 1 hr.	
Efavirenz (EFV) [Sustiva]	Cap: 50mg, 200mg; Tab: 600mg	W/ Protease Inhibitors and/or NRTIs: 600mg qd at bedtime. W/ Voriconazole: 300mg qd using cap formulation; increase voriconazole to 400mg q12h. W/ Rifampin: ≥50kg: 800mg qd.	≥3 mos: 32.5-<40kg: 400mg qd. 25-<32.5kg: 350mg qd. 20-<25kg: 300mg qd. 15-<20kg: 250mg qd. 7.5-<15kg: 200mg qd. 5-7.5kg: 150mg qd. 3.5-<5kg: 100mg qd.	Take on an empty stomach, preferably at bedtime.	

GENERIC [BRAND]	HOW SUPPLIED	USUAL ADULT DOSAGE	PEDIATRIC DOSAGE	FOOD EFFECT	BOXED WARNING*
NON-NUCLEOSIDE REVERSE TRANSCRIPTASE INHIBITORS (Continued)					
Etravirine (ETR) [Intelence]	**Tab:** 25mg‡, 100mg, 200mg	200mg bid.	**6-<18 yrs: ≥30kg:** 200mg bid. **25-<30kg:** 150mg bid. **20-<25kg:** 125mg bid. **16-<20kg:** 100mg bid.	Take following a meal.	
Nevirapine (NVP) [Viramune; Viramune XR]	**Sus:** 50mg/5mL [240mL]; **Tab:** 200mg‡; **Tab, ER:** 100mg, 400mg	(Tab, Sus) 200mg qd for first 14 days (lead-in period), then 200mg bid. (Tab, ER) **Not Currently Taking IR Nevirapine:** One 200mg IR tab qd for first 14 days, then one 400mg ER tab qd. **Switching from IR Nevirapine to ER Tab:** May switch to 400mg qd without 14-day lead-in period if already taking IR nevirapine bid.	(Tab, Sus) **≥15 days:** 150mg/m² qd for 14 days (lead-in period), then 150mg/m² bid. **Max:** 400mg/day. (Tab, ER) **6-<18 yrs: Lead-In Period:** 150mg/m² qd (as IR tab or sus) up to 200mg/day for the first 14 days. **After Lead-In Period: BSA ≥1.17m²:** 400mg qd. **BSA 0.84-1.16m²:** 300mg qd. **BSA 0.58-0.83m²:** 200mg qd. **Max:** 400mg/day.	Take without regard to meals or antacid.	Life-threatening hepatotoxicity/ skin reactions
Rilpivirine [Edurant]	**Tab:** 25mg	25mg qd.		Take with a meal.	
PROTEASE INHIBITORS					
Atazanavir (ATV) [Reyataz][19]	**Cap:** 150mg, 200mg, 300mg	**Therapy-Naïve:** 400mg qd or (ATV 300mg + RTV 100mg) qd. **W/ EFV:** (ATV 400mg + RTV 100mg) qd. **Therapy-Experienced:** (ATV 300mg + RTV 100mg) qd. **W/ TDF, H₂RA, PPIs, or EFV:** Refer to PI for proper administration and dose adjustments.	**6-<18 yrs: ≥40kg:** (ATV 300mg + RTV 100mg) qd. **20-<40kg:** (ATV 200mg + RTV 100mg) qd. **15-<20kg:** (ATV 150mg + RTV 100mg) qd. **Therapy-Naïve: ≥13 yrs: ≥40kg:** If intolerant to RTV, give ATV 400mg qd. **W/ TDF, H₂RA, or PPIs:** Do not administer without RTV.	Take with food. If you are taking antacids, take atazanavir 2 hrs before or 1 hr after.	
Darunavir (DRV) [Prezista]	**Tab:** 75mg, 150mg, 400mg, 600mg, 800mg; **Sus:** 100mg/mL [200mL]	**Therapy-Naïve or Therapy-Experienced W/ No DRV Resistance-Associated Mutations:** (DRV 800mg + RTV 100mg) qd. **Therapy-Experienced Patients W/ at Least 1 DRV Mutation:** (DRV 600mg + RTV 100mg) bid.	Check labeling for age/weight-based dosing.	Take with food. (Sus) 8mL doses should be taken as two 4mL administrations with supplied oral dosing syringe.	

(Continued)

GENERIC [BRAND]	HOW SUPPLIED	USUAL ADULT DOSAGE	PEDIATRIC DOSAGE	FOOD EFFECT	BOXED WARNING*
PROTEASE INHIBITORS *(Continued)*					
Dolutegravir sodium [Tivicay]	**Tab:** 50mg	**Therapy-Naïve or Therapy-Experienced INSTI-Naïve:** 50mg qd. **W/ Strong UGT1A/CYP3A Inducers, INSTI-Experienced W/ Certain INSTI-Associated Resistance Mutations or Suspected INSTI Resistance:** 50mg bid. **Max:** 50mg bid.	**≥12 yrs; ≥40kg: Therapy-Naïve or Therapy-Experienced INSTI-Naïve:** 50mg qd. **W/ EFV, (Fosamprenavir/RTV or Tipranavir/RTV) or Rifampin:** 50mg bid.	Take without regard to meals.	
Fosamprenavir (FPV) [Lexiva]§	**Tab:** 700mg; **Sus:** 50mg/mL [225mL]	**Therapy-Naïve:** 1400mg bid or (FPV 1400mg + RTV 200mg) qd or (FPV 1400mg + RTV 100mg) qd or (FPV 700mg bid + RTV 100mg) bid. **Protease Inhibitor-Experienced:** (FPV 700mg + RTV 100mg) bid.	Check labeling for age/weight-based dosing.	(Tab) Take without regard to meals. (Sus) **Adults:** Take without food. **Peds:** Take with food.	
Indinavir (IDV) [Crixivan]§	**Cap:** 100mg, 200mg, 400mg	800mg q8h. **W/ DLV, Itraconazole, Ketoconazole:** 600mg q8h. **W/ ddI:** Administer ≥1 hr apart on an empty stomach. **W/ Rifabutin:** 1000mg q8h (reduce rifabutin by ½).		Take with water 1 hr before or 2 hrs after meals; may take with skim milk, juice, coffee, tea, or a light meal.	
Nelfinavir (NFV) [Viracept]§	**Powder:** 50mg/g [144g]; **Tab:** 250g, 625mg	**≥13 yrs:** 1250mg bid or 750mg tid. **Max:** 2500mg/day. Refer to PI for concomitant therapies dosing adjustments.	Check labeling for age/weight-based dosing. **2–<13 yrs:** 45–55mg/kg bid or 25–35mg/kg tid. **Max:** 2500mg/day. Refer to PI for weight-based and concomitant therapies dosing recommendations.	Take with meals.	
Ritonavir (RTV) [Norvir]	**Cap, Tab:** 100mg; **Sol:** 80mg/mL [240mL]	**Initial:** 300mg bid. **Titrate:** Increase every 2–3 days by 100mg bid. **Maint/Max:** 600mg bid.	**>1 mo: Initial:** 250mg/m² bid. **Titrate:** Increase by 50mg/m² bid every 2–3 days. **Maint:** 350–400mg/m² bid or highest tolerated dose. **Max:** 600mg bid. Refer to PI for further pediatric dosage guidelines.	Take with meals.	Coadministration with sedative hypnotics, antiarrhythmics, or ergot alkaloid preparations
Saquinavir (SQV) [Invirase]	**Cap:** 200mg; **Tab:** 500mg	**>16 yrs:** (SQV 1000mg + RTV 100mg) bid or (SQV 1000mg + LPV/RTV 400mg/100mg) bid (no additional RTV).		Take within 2 hrs after a meal.	

GENERIC [BRAND]	HOW SUPPLIED	USUAL ADULT DOSAGE	PEDIATRIC DOSAGE	FOOD EFFECT	BOXED WARNING*
PROTEASE INHIBITORS *(Continued)*					
Tipranavir (TPV) [Aptivus]	Cap: 250mg; Sol: 100mg/mL [95mL]	(TPV 500mg + RTV 200mg) bid.	**≥2-18 yrs:** TPV 14mg/kg + RTV 6mg/kg (or TPV 375mg/m² + RTV 150mg/m²) bid. **Max:** (TPV 500mg + RTV 200mg) bid.	(TPV taken with RTV tab) Take with meals. (TPV taken with RTV cap or sol) Take without regard to meals.	Hepatotoxicity/intracranial hemorrhage
FUSION INHIBITORS					
Enfuvirtide (T20) [Fuzeon]	Inj: 90mg/mL [108mg]	90mg SQ bid.	**6-16 yrs: Usual:** 2mg/kg SQ bid. **Max:** 90mg SQ bid. Refer to PI for weight-based dosing.		
COMBINATIONS					
3TC/ZDV [Combivir]	**Tab:** (Lamivudine-Zidovudine) 150mg-300mg‡	**≥30kg:** 1 tab bid. Do not give if CrCl <50mL/min or if <30kg weight.	**≥30kg:** 1 tab bid. Do not give if CrCl <50mL/min or if <30kg weight.	Take without regard to meals.	Risk of hematological toxicity/myopathy/lactic acidosis/exacerbations of hepatitis B
ABC/3TC [Epzicom]	**Tab:** (Abacavir-Lamivudine) 600mg-300mg	**≥18 yrs:** 1 tab qd. Do not give if CrCl <50mL/min.		Take without regard to meals.	Risk of hypersensitivity reactions/lactic acidosis/severe hepatomegaly/exacerbations of hepatitis B
ABC/ZDV/3TC [Trizivir]	**Tab:** (Abacavir-Lamivudine-Zidovudine) 300mg-150mg-300mg	**Adults/Adolescents ≥40kg:** 1 tab bid. Do not give if CrCl <50mL/min.	**Adults/Adolescents ≥40kg:** 1 tab bid. Do not give if CrCl <50mL/min.	Take without regard to meals.	Risk of hypersensitivity reactions/hematologic toxicity/myopathy/lactic acidosis/severe hepatomegaly/exacerbations of hepatitis B
EFV/FTC/TDF [Atripla]	**Tab:** (Efavirenz-Emtricitabine-Tenofovir Disoproxil Fumarate) 600mg-200mg-300mg	1 tab qd, preferably at bedtime. Do not give if CrCl <50mL/min. **W/ Rifampin: ≥50kg:** Additional 200mg/day of EFV.	**≥12 yrs: ≥40 kg:** 1 tab qd, preferably at bedtime. Do not give if CrCl >50mL/min. **W/ Rifampin: ≥50kg:** Additional 200mg/day of EFV.	Take on an empty stomach.	Lactic acidosis/severe hepatomegaly with steatosis/posttreatment exacerbation of hepatitis B
Elvitegravir/Cobicistat/FTC/TDF [Stribild]	**Tab:** (Elvitegravir-Cobicistat-Emtricitabine-Tenofovir Disoproxil Fumarate) 150mg-150mg-200mg-300mg	**≥18 yrs:** 1 tab qd. Do not give if CrCl <70mL/min.		Take with a meal.	Lactic acidosis/severe hepatomegaly with steatosis/posttreatment exacerbation of hepatitis B

(Continued)

GENERIC [BRAND]	HOW SUPPLIED	USUAL ADULT DOSAGE	PEDIATRIC DOSAGE	FOOD EFFECT	BOXED WARNING*
COMBINATIONS (Continued)					
LPV/RTV [Kaletra]	**Tab:** (Lopinavir-Ritonavir) 200mg-50mg; 100mg-25mg; **Sol:** (Lopinavir-Ritonavir) 80mg-20mg/mL [160mL]	400mg/100mg bid. **<3 Lopinavir Resistance-Associated Substitutions:** 800mg/200mg qd. **Concomitant Therapy W/ EFV, NVP, or NFV:** (Tab) 500mg/125mg bid; (Sol) 533mg/133mg bid. Refer to PI for concomitant therapy dosing recommendations.	Check labeling for age/weight-based dosing.	(Tab) Take without regard to meals. (Sol) Take with meals.	
FTC/TDF [Truvada]	**Tab:** (Emtricitabine-Tenofovir Disoproxil Fumarate) 200mg-300mg	**CrCl ≥50mL/min:** 1 tab qd. **CrCl 30-49mL/min:** 1 tab q48h. Do not give if CrCl <30mL/min.	**≥12 yrs: ≥35kg:** 1 tab qd.	Take without regard to meals.	Lactic acidosis/severe hepatomegaly with steatosis/posttreatment acute exacerbation of hepatitis B/risk of drug resistance with use for pre-exposure prophylaxis in undiagnosed early HIV-1 infection
FTC/Rilpivirine/TDF [Complera]	**Tab:** (Emtricitabine-Rilpivirine-Tenofovir Disoproxil Fumarate) 200mg-25mg-300mg	**≥18 yrs:** 1 tab qd. Do not give if CrCl <50mL/min.		Take with a meal.	Lactic acidosis/severe hepatomegaly with steatosis/posttreatment acute exacerbation of hepatitis B

Refer to full FDA-approved labeling for additional information.

Abbreviations: DR = delayed-release; ER = extended-release; H_2RA = H_2-receptor antagonist; IR = immediate-release; PPI = proton pump inhibitor.

*Refer to monograph for full Boxed Warning and for detailed dosing information.

†Refer to monograph for renal dose adjustment.

‡Scored.

§Refer to monograph for hepatic dose adjustment.

HIV/AIDS-RELATED COMPLICATIONS AND TREATMENTS

COMPLICATION	GENERIC (BRAND)	RECOMMENDED DOSAGE
ASPERGILLOSIS, INVASIVE		
Recommended Treatment Regimen	**Voriconazole** (Vfend)*	Refer to *Oral and Systemic Antifungals* table.
Alternative Treatment Regimen	**Amphotericin B cholesteryl sulfate** (Amphotec)	
	Amphotericin B Liposome (AmBisome)	
	Amphotericin B Lipid Complex (Abelcet)	
	Caspofungin (Cancidas)	
	Itraconazole (Sporanox)	
	Posaconazole (Noxafil)	
CANDIDIASIS		
Prevention/Treatment	**Amphotericin B Lipid Complex** (Abelcet)	Refer to *Oral and Systemic Antifungals* table.
	Amphotericin B Liposome (AmBisome)	
	Anidulafungin (Eraxis)	
	Caspofungin (Cancidas)	
	Fluconazole (Diflucan)	
	Itraconazole (Sporanox)	
	Micafungin (Mycamine)	
	Posaconazole (Noxafil)	
	Voriconazole (Vfend)*	
CYTOMEGALOVIRUS RETINITIS		
Treatment	**Cidofovir** (Vistide)	**Adults: Induction:**† 5mg/kg IV infusion once wkly x 2 wks. **Maint:** 5mg/kg IV q2wk. Give at a constant rate over 1 hr.
	Foscarnet	**Adults: Induction:** 90mg/kg over 1.5-2 hrs IV infusion q12h or 60mg/kg over ≥1 hr IV infusion q8h x 2-3 wks. **Maint:** 90-120mg/kg/d IV over 2 hrs.
	Ganciclovir (Cytovene)	**Adults: Induction:** 5mg/kg IV infusion q12h x 14-21 days. **Maint:** 5mg/kg IV qd, 7 days/wk or 6mg/kg IV qd, 5 days/wk. Give at a constant rate over 1 hr.
	Valganciclovir (Valcyte)	**Adults: Induction:** 900mg PO bid x 21 days. **Maint:** 900mg PO qd.
CRYPTOCOCCAL MENINGITIS		
Treatment	**Amphotericin B Liposome** (AmBisome) *PLUS* **Flucytosine** (Ancobon)	Refer to *Oral and Systemic Antifungals* table.
	Fluconazole (Diflucan)	
HERPES SIMPLEX VIRUS		
Recommended Regimen for Daily Suppressive or Episodic Infections Therapy	**Acyclovir**	Refer to *Sexually Transmitted Diseases Guideline-Based Treatment* table.
	Famciclovir (Famvir)	
	Valacyclovir	

(Continued)

COMPLICATION	GENERIC (BRAND)	RECOMMENDED DOSAGE
KAPOSI'S SARCOMA		
Treatment	**Alitretinoin** (Panretin)	**Adults: Initial:** Apply bid to lesions. May increase to tid-qid based on individual lesion tolerance. Temporarily discontinue if severe irritation occurs.
	Daunorubicin (DaunoXome)	**Adults:** 40mg/m^2 IV over 60 min q2wk. Blood counts should be repeated prior to each dose. Hold dose if absolute granulocyte <750 cells/mm^3.
	Doxorubicin (Doxil)	**Adults:** 20mg/m^2 IV q3wk. **Initial Rate:** 1mg/min. May be increased to administer over 1 hr if tolerated.
	Interferon alfa-2b (Intron A)	**Adults:** 30 million IU/m^2/dose SQ/IM tiw until disease progression or max response achieved after 16 wks.
	Paclitaxel	**Adults:** 135mg/m^2 IV over 3 hrs q3wk or 100mg/m^2 IV over 3 hrs q2wk. **Dose Intensity:** 45-50mg/m^2/wk.
***MYCOBACTERIUM AVIUM* COMPLEX**		
Prevention/Treatment	**Azithromycin** (Zithromax)	**Adults: Prevention:** 1200mg once wkly. **Treatment:** 600mg PO qd w/ ethambutol 15mg/kg qd.
Prevention/Treatment	**Clarithromycin** (Biaxin)	**Prevention/Treatment: Adults:** 500mg PO bid. **Peds:** 7.5mg/kg bid up to 500mg bid.
Prevention	**Rifabutin** (Mycobutin)	**Adults:†** 300mg PO qd. **N/V or GI Upset:** 150mg bid w/ food.
***PNEUMOCYSTIS CARINII* PNEUMONIA**		
Prevention/Treatment	**Atovaquone** (Mepron)	**Adults/Peds 13-16 yrs: Prevention:** 1500mg PO qd w/ meals. **Treatment (Mild-Moderate):** 750mg PO bid w/ meals x 21 days. **TDD:** 1500mg.
	TMP/SMX (Bactrim)	**Adults/Peds: Treatment:** 15-20mg/kg/d TMP and 75-100mg/kg/d SMX in equally divided doses q6h x 14-21 days.
	TMP/SMX (Bactrim DS)	**Adults: Prevention:** 1 DS tab (160/800mg) qd. **Peds: Prevention:** 150mg/m^2/d TMP w/ 750mg/m^2/d SMX PO bid in equally divided doses on 3 consecutive days/wk. **Max TDD:** 1600mg SMX/320mg TMP.
VISCERAL LEISHMANIASIS		
Treatment	**Amphotericin B Liposome** (AmBisome)	Refer to *Oral and Systemic Antifungals* table.
WEIGHT LOSS		
Anorexia	**Dronabinol** (Marinol)	**Adults:†** 2.5mg PO bid; before lunch and supper. **Max:** 20mg/d in divided doses.
Anorexia, Cachexia, Unexplained weight loss	**Megestrol** (Megace)	**Adults: Initial:** 800mg/d. **Usual:** 400-800mg/d.
Cachexia/Wasting	**Somatropin** (Serostim)	**Adults: >55kg:** 6mg SQ qhs. **45-55kg:** 5mg SQ qhs. **35-45kg:** 4mg SQ qhs. **<35kg:** 0.1mg/kg SQ qhs. **Max:** 6mg/d.

This table is not all inclusive of opportunistic infections. Please refer to www.CDC.gov or www.aidsinfo.nih.gov for detailed information. Refer to full FDA-approved labeling for additional information.

Abbreviations: TDD = total daily dose; TMP/SMX = trimethoprim-sulfamethoxazole.

*Use cautiously in patients on protease inhibitors and efavirenz.
†Check monograph for detailed dosing guidelines (eg, CrCl, Urine Protein, SrCr).

Source: Panel on Opportunistic Infections in HIV-Infected Adults and Adolescents. Guidelines for the prevention and treatment of opportunistic infections in HIV-infected adults and adolescents: Recommendations from the Centers for Disease Control and Prevention, the National Institutes of Health, and the HIV Medicine Association of the Infectious Diseases Society of America. Available at http://aidsinfo.nih.gov/contentfiles/lvguidelines/adult_oi.pdf. Accessed March 21, 2014.

ORAL ANTIBIOTICS TREATMENT COMPARISON

GENERIC (BRAND)	HOW SUPPLIED	ABECB	AECB	Bone & Joint	CAP	Endocarditis	GI	Intra-Ab	LRTI	URTI	Lyme Disease	MAC	Meningitis	Oph	Otitis Media	PCP	Septicemia	Sinusitis	SSSI	SSTI	TB	UTI	UGI	Gyn
CEPHALOSPORINS																								
1st Generation																								
Cefadroxil	**Cap:** 500mg; **Susp:** 250mg/5mL, 500mg/5mL; **Tab:** 1g									X									X			X		
Cephalexin (Keflex)	**Cap:** 250mg, 500mg, (Keflex) 250mg, 500mg, 750mg; **Susp:** 125mg/5mL, 250mg/5mL; **Tab:** 250mg, 500mg			X					X	X					X				X			X	X	
2nd Generation																								
Cefaclor	**Cap:** 250mg, 500mg; **Susp:** 125mg/5mL, 187mg/5mL, 250mg/5mL, 375mg/5mL								X	X					X				X			X		
Cefaclor ER	**Tab, ER:** 500mg	X							X	X									X					
Cefprozil	**Susp:** 125mg/5mL, 250mg/5mL; **Tab:** 250mg, 500mg	X							X	X					X			X	X					
Cefuroxime axetil (Ceftin)	**Susp:** 125mg/5mL, 250mg/5mL; **Tab:** 250mg, 500mg	X (Tab)							X (Tab)	X	X (Tab)				X			X (Tab)	X (Tab)			X (Tab)		
3rd Generation																								
Cefdinir	**Cap:** 300mg; **Susp:** 125mg/5mL, 250mg/5mL		X		X					X					X			X	X					

(Continued)

A173

GENERIC (BRAND)	HOW SUPPLIED	ABECB	AECB	Bone & Joint	CAP	Endocarditis	GI	Intra-Ab	LRTI	URTI	Lyme Disease	MAC	Meningitis	Oph	Otitis Media	PCP	Septicemia	Sinusitis	SSSI	SSTI	TB	UTI	UGI	Gyn
CEPHALOSPORINS *(Continued)*																								
3rd Generation (Continued)																								
Cefditoren pivoxil (Spectracef)	**Tab:** 200mg, 400mg	X			X														X					
Cefixime (Suprax)	**Cap:** 400mg; **Susp:** 100mg/5mL, 200mg/5mL, 500mg/5mL; **Tab:** 400mg; **Tab, Chew:** 100mg, 150mg, 200mg		X							X					X							X	X	X
Cefpodoxime proxetil	**Susp:** 50mg/5mL, 100mg/5mL; **Tab:** 100mg, 200mg	X			X					X					X			X	X			X	X	X
Ceftibuten (Cedax)	**Cap:** 400mg; **Susp:** 90mg/5mL, 180mg/5mL	X								X					X									
FLUOROQUINOLONES																								
Ciprofloxacin (Cipro)	**Susp:** 250mg/5mL, 500mg/5mL; **Tab:** 250mg, 500mg			X			X		X									X	X			X		
Ciprofloxacin (Cipro XR)	**Tab, ER:** 500mg, 1000mg																					X		
Gemifloxacin mesylate (Factive)	**Tab:** 320mg	X			X																			
Levofloxacin (Levaquin)	**Sol:** 25mg/mL; **Tab:** 250mg, 500mg, 750mg	X			X				X									X	X			X	X	
Moxifloxacin HCl (Avelox)	**Tab:** 400mg	X			X			X										X	X					

GENERIC (BRAND)	HOW SUPPLIED	ABECB	AECB	Bone & Joint	CAP	Endocarditis	GI	Intra-Ab	LRTI	URTI	Lyme Disease	MAC	Meningitis	Oph	Otitis Media	PCP	Septicemia	Sinusitis	SSSI	SSTI	TB	UTI	UGI	Gyn
FLUOROQUINOLONES *(Continued)*																								
Norfloxacin (Noroxin)	**Tab:** 400mg																					X	X	X
Ofloxacin	**Tab:** 200mg, 300mg, 400mg	X			X				X										X			X	X	X
MACROLIDES																								
Azithromycin (Zithromax)	**Susp:** 100mg/5mL, 200mg/5mL; **Tab:** 250mg, 500mg				X					X					X			X	X				X	X
Azithromycin (Zithromax)	**Susp:** 1g/pkt; **Tab:** 600mg				X							X						X					X	X
Azithromycin (Zmax)	**Susp, ER:** 2g (27mg/mL)				X																			
Clarithromycin (Biaxin)	**Susp:** 125mg/5mL, 250mg/5mL; **Tab:** 250mg, 500mg	X			X		X (Tab)			X		X			X			X	X				X	X
Clarithromycin (Biaxin XL)	**Tab, ER:** 500mg	X			X													X						
Erythromycin (ERYC)	**Cap, DR:** 250mg						X		X	X				X					X			X	X	X
Erythromycin (Ery-Tab)	**Tab, DR:** 250mg, 333mg, 500mg						X		X	X				X					X			X	X	X
Erythromycin (PCE)	**Tab:** 333mg, 500mg						X		X	X				X					X			X	X	X
Erythromycin base	**Tab:** 250mg, 500mg						X		X	X				X					X			X	X	X
Erythromycin ethylsuccinate (E.E.S.)	**Susp:** 200mg/5mL; **Tab:** 400mg						X		X	X				X					X			X	X	X

(Continued)

A175

ORAL ANTIBIOTICS TREATMENT COMPARISON

GENERIC (BRAND)	HOW SUPPLIED	ABECB	AECB	Bone & Joint	CAP	Endocarditis	GI	Intra-Ab	LRTI	URTI	Lyme Disease	MAC	Meningitis	Oph	Otitis Media	PCP	Septicemia	Sinusitis	SSSI	SSTI	TB	UTI	UGI	Gyn
MACROLIDES *(Continued)*																								
Erythromycin ethylsuccinate (EryPed)	**Susp:** 200mg/5mL, 400mg/5mL						X		X	X				X					X			X	X	X
Erythromycin ethylsuccinate/ Sulfisoxazole acetyl	**Susp:** 200–600mg/5mL														X									
Erythromycin stearate (Erythrocin)	**Tab:** 250mg, 500mg						X		X	X				X					X			X	X	X
Fidaxomicin (Dificid)	**Tab:** 200mg						X																	
PENICILLINS																								
Amoxicillin	**Cap:** 250mg, 500mg; **Susp:** 125mg/5mL, 200mg/5mL, 250mg/5mL, 400mg/5mL; **Tab:** 500mg, 875mg; **Tab, Chew:** 125mg, 250mg						X		X	X									X				X	
Amoxicillin (Moxatag)	**Tab, ER:** 775mg									X														

GENERIC (BRAND)	HOW SUPPLIED	ABECB	AECB	Bone & Joint	CAP	Endocarditis	GI	Intra-Ab	LRTI	URTI	Lyme Disease	MAC	Meningitis	Oph	Otitis Media	PCP	Septicemia	Sinusitis	SSSI	SSTI	TB	UTI	UGI	Gyn
PENICILLINS *(Continued)*																								
Amoxicillin-Clavulanate potassium (Augmentin)	**Susp:** 125-31.25mg/5mL, 200-28.5mg/5mL, 250-62.5mg/5mL, 400-57mg/5mL; **Tab:** 250-125mg, 500-125mg, 875-125mg; **Tab, Chew:** 125-31.25mg, 200-28.5mg, 250-62.5mg, 400-57mg								X						X			X	X			X		
Amoxicillin-Clavulanate potassium (Augmentin XR)	**Tab, ER:** 1000-62.5mg				X													X						
Amoxicillin-Clavulanate potassium	**Susp:** 600-42.9/5mL												X		X									
Ampicillin	**Cap:** 250mg, 500mg; **Susp:** 125mg/5mL, 250mg/5mL						X		X	X			X										X	
Penicillin V potassium (Penicillin VK)	**Susp:** 125mg/5mL, 250mg/5mL; **Tab:** 250mg, 500mg								X	X										X				
TETRACYCLINES																								
Demeclocycline HCl	**Tab:** 150mg, 300mg						X		X	X				X					X			X	X	X

(Continued)

INDICATIONS

GENERIC (BRAND)	HOW SUPPLIED	ABECB	AECB	Bone & Joint	CAP	Endocarditis	GI	Intra-Ab	LRTI	URTI	Lyme Disease	MAC	Meningitis	Oph	Otitis Media	PCP	Septicemia	Sinusitis	SSSI	SSTI	TB	UTI	UGI	Gyn
TETRACYCLINES *(Continued)*																								
Doxycycline (Vibramycin)	**Cap:** (Hyclate) 100mg; **Susp:** (Monohydrate) 25mg/5mL; **Syrup:** (Calcium) 50mg/5mL; **Tab:** (Vibra-Tabs) 100mg						X		X	X				X					X			X	X	X
Doxycycline hyclate (Doryx)	**Tab, DR:** 75mg, 100mg, 150mg, 200mg						X		X	X				X					X			X	X	X
Doxycycline monohydrate (Monodox)	**Cap:** 50mg, 75mg, 100mg						X		X	X				X					X			X	X	X
Minocycline HCl (Dynacin)	**Tab:** 50mg, 75mg, 100mg						X		X	X				X					X			X	X	X
Minocycline HCl (Minocin)	**Cap:** 75mg, (Minocin) 50mg, 100mg						X		X	X				X					X			X	X	X
Tetracycline HCl	**Cap:** 250mg, 500mg						X		X					X						X		X	X	X
MISCELLANEOUS																								
Clindamycin (Cleocin, Cleocin Pediatric)	**Cap:** (HCl) 75mg, 150mg, 300mg; **Sol:** (Palmitate HCl) 75mg/5mL							X	X								X			X			X	X
Fosfomycin tromethamine (Monurol)	**Powder:** 3g/sachet																					X		
Isoniazid-Pyrazinamide-Rifampin (Rifater)	**Tab:** 50-300-120mg																				X			

GENERIC (BRAND)	HOW SUPPLIED	INDICATIONS																						
		ABECB	AECB	Bone & Joint	CAP	Endocarditis	GI	Intra-Ab	LRTI	URTI	Lyme Disease	MAC	Meningitis	Oph	Otitis Media	PCP	Septicemia	Sinusitis	SSSI	SSTI	TB	UTI	UGI	Gyn
MISCELLANEOUS *(Continued)*																								
Isoniazid-Rifampin (Rifamate)	**Cap:** 150-300mg																				X			
Linezolid (Zyvox)	**Susp:** 100mg/5mL; **Tab:** 600mg			X	X				X										X					
Metronidazole (Flagyl)	**Cap:** 375mg; **Tab:** 250mg, 500mg			X		X	X	X	X				X				X		X					X
Nitrofurantoin (Furadantin)	**Susp:** 25mg/5mL																					X		
Nitrofurantoin macrocrystals (Macrodantin)	**Cap:** 25mg, 50mg, 100mg														X							X		
Nitrofurantoin macrocrystals and Nitrofurantoin monohydrate (Macrobid)	**Cap:** 100mg															X						X		
Rifampin (Rifadin)	**Cap:** 150mg, 300mg																				X			
Sulfamethoxazole-Trimethoprim (Bactrim, Bactrim DS, Sulfatrim)	**Susp:** (Sulfatrim) 200-40mg/5mL; **Tab:** (Bactrim) 400-80mg, (Bactrim DS) 800-160mg		X				X								X							X		
Telithromycin (Ketek)	**Tab:** 300mg, 400mg				X																			
Trimethoprim	**Tab:** 100mg, 200mg																					X		

(Continued)

GENERIC (BRAND)	HOW SUPPLIED	INDICATIONS																						
		ABECB	AECB	Bone & Joint	CAP	Endocarditis	GI	Intra-Ab	LRTI	URTI	Lyme Disease	MAC	Meningitis	Oph	Otitis Media	PCP	Septicemia	Sinusitis	SSSI	SSTI	TB	UTI	UGI	Gyn
MISCELLANEOUS *(Continued)*																								
Trimethoprim HCl (Primsol)	**Sol:** 50mg/5mL														X							X		
Vancomycin HCl (Vancocin)	**Cap:** 125mg, 250mg						X																	

Refer to full FDA-approved labeling for additional information.

Abbreviations:
ABECB = acute bacterial exacerbation of chronic bronchitis
AECB = acute exacerbation of chronic bronchitis
CAP = community-acquired pneumonia
GI = gastrointestinal
LRTI = lower respiratory tract infection
MAC = *Mycobacterium avium* complex
PCP = *Pneumocystis jiroveci* pneumonia
SSSI = skin and skin structure infection
SSTI = skin and soft tissue infection
TB = tuberculosis
UGI = urogenital infection
URTI = upper respiratory tract infection
UTI = urinary tract infection

SYSTEMIC ANTIBIOTICS TREATMENT COMPARISON

GENERIC (BRAND)	HOW SUPPLIED	INDICATIONS																	
		AECB	Bone & Joint Inf	CAP	Endocarditis	GI Inf	Gyn Inf	Intra-Ab Inf	LRTI	URTI	Meningitis	Otitis Media	PCP	Septicemia	Sinusitis	SSSI	SSTI	TB	UTI
AMINOGLYCOSIDES																			
Amikacin sulfate	Inj: 50mg/mL, 250mg/mL		X					X	X	X	X			X		X			X
Gentamicin sulfate	Inj: 10mg/mL, 40mg/mL; Isotonic Inj: 60mg, 80mg, 100mg, 120mg		X			X		X	X	X	X			X		X	X		X
Streptomycin sulfate	Inj: 1g				X				X		X							X	
Tobramycin sulfate	Inj: 10mg/mL, 40mg/mL		X					X	X	X	X					X			X
CARBAPENEMS																			
Cilastatin sodium-Imipenem (Primaxin IV)	Inj: 250-250mg, 500-500mg		X		X		X	X						X		X			X
Doripenem (Doribax)	Inj: 250mg, 500mg							X											X
Ertapenem (Invanz)	Inj: 1g			X			X	X								X			X
Meropenem (Merrem)	Inj: 500mg, 1g							X			X					X			
CEPHALOSPORINS																			
1st Generation																			
Cefazolin	Inj: 500mg, 1g*		X		X					X				X		X			X
2nd Generation																			
Cefotetan	Inj: 1g, 2g*		X				X	X	X					X		X			X
Cefoxitin	Inj: 1g, 2g*		X				X	X	X					X		X			X
Cefuroxime (Zinacef)	Inj: 750mg, 1.5g*		X				X	X	X		X			X		X			X

(Continued)

A181

GENERIC (BRAND)	HOW SUPPLIED	AECB	Bone & Joint Inf	CAP	Endocarditis	GI Inf	Gyn Inf	Intra-Ab Inf	LRTI	URTI	Meningitis	Otitis Media	PCP	Septicemia	Sinusitis	SSSI	SSTI	TB	UTI
CEPHALOSPORINS *(Continued)*																			
3rd Generation																			
Cefotaxime sodium (Claforan)	**Inj:** 500mg, 1g, 2g*		X				X	X	X		X			X		X			X
Ceftazidime (Fortaz)	**Inj:** 500mg, 1g, 2g*		X				X	X	X		X			X		X			X
Ceftazidime (Tazicef)	**Inj:** 1g, 2g*		X				X	X	X		X			X		X			X
Ceftriaxone sodium (Rocephin)	**Inj:** (Rocephin) 500mg, 1g; (Generic) 250mg, 500mg, 1g, 2g*		X				X	X	X		X	X		X		X			X
4th Generation																			
Cefepime HCl (Maxipime)	**Inj:** 500mg, 1g, 2g							X	X							X			X
5th Generation																			
Ceftaroline fosamil (Teflaro)	**Inj:** 400mg, 600mg			X												X			
FLUOROQUINOLONES																			
Ciprofloxacin (Cipro IV)	**Inj:** 200mg/100mL, 400mg/200mL	X	X	X				X	X							X			X
Levofloxacin (Levaquin)	**Inj:** 5mg/mL, 25mg/mL	X		X					X						X	X			X
Moxifloxacin HCl (Avelox)	**Inj:** 400mg/250mL	X		X				X							X	X			
MACROLIDES																			
Azithromycin (Zithromax)	**Inj:** 500mg						X												
MONOBACTAMS																			
Aztreonam (Azactam)	**Inj:** 1g, 2g, 1g/50mL, 2g/50mL						X	X	X					X		X			X

GENERIC (BRAND)	HOW SUPPLIED	INDICATIONS																	
		AECB	Bone & Joint Inf	CAP	Endocarditis	GI Inf	Gyn Inf	Intra-Ab Inf	LRTI	URTI	Meningitis	Otitis Media	PCP	Septicemia	Sinusitis	SSSI	SSTI	TB	UTI
PENICILLINS																			
Ampicillin sodium	Inj: 125mg, 250mg, 500mg, 1g, 2g*				X	X			X	X	X			X					X
Ampicillin sodium-Sulbactam sodium (Unasyn)	Inj: 1-0.5g, 2-1g*						X	X								X			
Penicillin G benzathine-Penicillin G procaine (Bicillin C-R)	Inj: 600,000-600,000 U/2mL								X	X		X					X		
Penicillin G benzathine-Penicillin G procaine (Bicillin C-R 900/300)	Inj: 900,000-300,000 U/2mL								X	X		X					X		
Penicillin G benzathine (Bicillin L-A)	Inj: 600,000 U/mL, 1,200,000 U/2mL, 2,400,000 U/4mL									X									
Penicillin G benzathine (Permapen)	Inj: 600,000 U/mL									X									
Penicillin G potassium (Pfizerpen)	Inj: 5 MU, 20 MU			X	X				X		X								
Piperacillin sodium-Tazobactam (Zosyn)	Inj: 2-0.25g/50mL, 3-0.375g/50mL, 4-0.5g/100mL, 2-0.25g, 3-0.375g, 4-0.5g*						X	X	X							X			
Ticarcillin disodium-Clavulanate potassium (Timentin)	Inj: 3g-100mg, 3g-100mg/100mL*		X				X	X	X					X		X			X

(Continued)

A183

GENERIC (BRAND)	HOW SUPPLIED	AECB	Bone & Joint Inf	CAP	Endocarditis	GI Inf	Gyn Inf	Intra-Ab Inf	LRTI	URTI	Meningitis	Otitis Media	PCP	Septicemia	Sinusitis	SSSI	SSTI	TB	UTI
TETRACYCLINES																			
Doxycycline hyclate (Doxycycline IV)	Inj: 100mg					X			X	X									X
Minocycline HCl (Minocin)	Inj: 100mg		X			X	X		X	X	X					X			X
MISCELLANEOUS																			
Clindamycin (Cleocin Phosphate)	Inj: 150mg/mL, 300mg/50mL, 600mg/50mL, 900mg/50mL						X	X	X					X		X			
Dalfopristin-Quinupristin (Synercid)	Inj: 350-150mg															X			
Daptomycin (Cubicin)	Inj: 500mg				X														
Linezolid (Zyvox)	Inj: 2mg/mL			X					X							X			
Metronidazole	Inj: 500mg/100mL		X		X		X	X	X		X			X		X			
Rifampin (Rifadin)	Inj: 600mg																	X	
Sulfamethoxazole-Trimethoprim	Inj: 80-16mg/mL												X						X
Telavancin (Vibativ)	Inj: 250mg, 750mg								X							X			

GENERIC (BRAND)	HOW SUPPLIED	INDICATIONS																
		AECB	Bone & Joint Inf	CAP	Endocarditis	GI Inf	Gyn Inf	Intra-Ab Inf	LRTI	URTI	Meningitis	Otitis Media	PCP	Septicemia	Sinusitis	SSSI	SSTI	TB	UTI
MISCELLANEOUS *(Continued)*																			
Tigecycline (Tygacil)	**Inj:** 50mg/5mL, 50mg/10mL			X				X								X			
Vancomycin HCl	**Inj:** 500mg, 750mg, 1g*		X		X				X					X		X			

Refer to full FDA-approved labeling for additional information.

*Also available as a Pharmacy Bulk Package.

Abbreviations:
AECB = acute exacerbations of chronic bronchitis
CAP = community-acquired pneumonia
GI = gastrointestinal
LRTI = lower respiratory tract infection
PCP = *Pneumocystis jiroveci* pneumonia
SSSI = skin and skin structure infection
SSTI = skin and soft tissue infection
TB = tuberculosis
URTI = upper respiratory tract infection
UTI = urinary tract infection

ORAL AND SYSTEMIC ANTIFUNGALS

GENERIC (BRAND)	INDICATIONS	DOSAGE FORM	ADDITIONAL COMMENTS
Amphotericin B	• Aspergillosis • Cryptococcosis • North American blastomycosis • Systemic candidiasis • Coccidioidomycosis • Histoplasmosis • Zygomycosis • Sporotrichosis • Infections due to *Conidiobolus* and *Basidiobolus* species • Leishmaniasis	Inj: 50mg	BW: Used primarily to treat progressive and potentially life-threatening fungal infections. • Doses greater than 1.5mg/kg should not be given. • Verify product's name and dosage preadministration and use caution to prevent inadvertent overdosage that may result in cardiopulmonary arrest. • Administer by slow IV infusion.
Amphotericin B lipid complex (Abelcet)	• Fungal infections in patients refractory to or intolerant of conventional amphotericin B therapy	Inj: 5mg/mL	• If the infusion time exceeds 2 hrs, mix the contents by shaking the infusion bag every 2 hrs. • Administer IV.
Amphotericin B lipid complex (Amphotec)	• Aspergillosis in patients with renal impairment, unacceptable toxicity, or previous failure to amphotericin B deoxycholate	Inj: 50mg, 100mg	• Infusion time may be shortened to a minimum of 2 hrs if no evidence of intolerance or infusion-related reactions. • If patient experiences acute reactions or cannot tolerate the infusion volume, the infusion time may be extended. • Administer IV.
Amphotericin B liposome (AmBisome)	• Infections due to *Aspergillus*, *Candida*, and/or *Cryptococcus* species refractory to amphotericin B deoxycholate or where renal impairment or unacceptable toxicity precludes the use of amphotericin B deoxycholate • Visceral leishmaniasis • Empirical therapy for presumed fungal infections in febrile neutropenic patients • Cryptococcal meningitis in HIV-infected patients	Inj: 50mg	• AmBisome should be administered by IV infusion using a controlled infusion device over a period of approximately 120 minutes. • Administer IV.
Anidulafungin (Eraxis)	• Candidemia and other forms of *Candida* infections • Esophageal candidiasis	Inj: 50mg, 100mg	• The rate of infusion should not exceed 1.1mg/min. • Administer IV.
Caspofungin acetate (Cancidas)	• Candidemia • Intra-abdominal abscesses, peritonitis, and pleural space infections due to *Candida* • Esophageal candidiasis • Aspergillosis in patients who are refractory to or intolerant of other therapies • Empirical therapy for presumed fungal infections in febrile neutropenic patients	Inj: 50mg, 70mg	• Maximum LD and daily maintenance dose should not exceed 70mg, regardless of the patient's calculated dose. • Administer by slow IV infusion over approximately 1 hr.
Clotrimazole	• Oropharyngeal candidiasis • Prevention of oropharyngeal candidiasis in immunocompromised conditions	Loz: 10mg	• Not indicated for treatment of systemic mycoses, including systemic candidiasis.

(Continued)

GENERIC (BRAND)	INDICATIONS	DOSAGE FORM	ADDITIONAL COMMENTS
Fluconazole (Diflucan)	• Vaginal, oropharyngeal, and esophageal candidiasis • UTIs and peritonitis caused by *Candida* • Systemic *Candida* infections, including candidemia, disseminated candidiasis, and pneumonia • Cryptococcal meningitis • Prevention of candidiasis in patients undergoing bone marrow transplantation who are receiving chemotherapy and/or radiation therapy	**Inj:** 200mg/100mL, 400mg/200mL; **Sus:** 10mg/mL, 40mg/mL; **Tab:** 50mg, 100mg, 150mg, 200mg	• Diflucan may be administered orally or by IV infusion. • The IV infusion of Diflucan should be administered at a maximum rate of approximately 200mg/hr as a continuous infusion.
Flucytosine (Ancobon)	• Septicemia, endocarditis, and UTIs caused by *Candida* • Meningitis and pulmonary infection caused by *Cryptococcus*	**Cap:** 250mg, 500mg	**BW:** Use with extreme caution in patients with impaired renal function; monitor hematologic, renal, and hepatic status. • Ancobon should be used in combination with amphotericin B for the treatment of systemic candidiasis and cryptococcosis because of the emergence of resistance to Ancobon.
Griseofulvin (Grifulvin V)	• Tinea capitis • Tinea corporis • Tinea pedis • Tinea unguium • Tinea barbae • Tinea cruris	**Sus:** 125mg/5mL; **Tab:** (Grifulvin V) 500mg	• Periodic monitoring of organ system function, including renal, hepatic, and hematopoietic, should be done. • Medication must be continued until the infecting organism is completely eradicated as indicated by appropriate clinical or laboratory examination.
Griseofulvin (Gris-PEG)	• Tinea capitis • Tinea corporis • Tinea pedis • Tinea unguium • Tinea barbae • Tinea cruris	**Tab:** 125mg, 250mg	• Periodic monitoring of organ system function, including renal, hepatic, and hematopoietic, should be done. • Medication must be continued until the infecting organism is completely eradicated as indicated by appropriate clinical or laboratory examination.
Itraconazole (Sporanox)	**Cap:** • Blastomycosis (pulmonary/ extrapulmonary) • Histoplasmosis (eg, chronic cavitary pulmonary disease and disseminated, nonmeningeal) • Aspergillosis (pulmonary/ extrapulmonary) if refractory to or intolerant of amphotericin B therapy • Onychomycosis of the toenail and fingernail in nonimmunocompromised patients **Sol:** • Oropharyngeal and esophageal candidiasis	**Cap:** 100mg; **Sol:** 10mg/mL	**BW:** Sporanox should not be administered for the treatment of onychomycosis in patients with evidence of ventricular dysfunction. Coadministration of cisapride, oral midazolam, nisoldipine, felodipine, pimozide, quinidine, dofetilide, triazolam, levacetylmethadol, lovastatin, simvastatin, ergot alkaloids, or methadone is contraindicated. • Sporanox Capsules is a different preparation than Oral Solution; these should not be used interchangeably. • Take Sporanox Capsules with a full meal.
Ketoconazole	Treatment of the following systemic fungal infections in patients who have failed/are intolerant to other therapies: • Blastomycosis • Coccidioidomycosis • Histoplasmosis • Chromomycosis • Paracoccidioidomycosis	**Tab:** 200mg	**BW:** Oral use of ketoconazole has been associated with hepatic toxicity. Coadministration of terfenadine, cisapride, and astemizole is contraindicated. Tablets should not be used for treatment of fungal meningitis.

GENERIC (BRAND)	INDICATIONS	DOSAGE FORM	ADDITIONAL COMMENTS
Micafungin sodium (Mycamine)	• Candidemia • Acute disseminated candidiasis • *Candida* peritonitis and abscesses • Esophageal candidiasis • Prevention of *Candida* infection in patients undergoing hematopoietic stem cell transplantation	**Inj:** 50mg, 100mg	• LD is not required. • Infuse IV over 1 hour.
Miconazole (Oravig)	• Oropharyngeal candidiasis	**Tab, Buccal:** 50mg	• Oravig should not be crushed, chewed, or swallowed.
Nystatin	**Sus:** • Oral candidiasis **Tab:** • Non-esophageal mucous membrane GI candidiasis	**Sus:** 100,000 U/mL; **Tab:** 500,000 U	• Not indicated for treatment of systemic mycoses.
Posaconazole (Noxafil)	• Prevention of *Aspergillus* and *Candida* infections **Sus:** • Oropharyngeal candidiasis, including oropharyngeal candidiasis refractory to itraconazole and/or fluconazole	**Sus:** 40mg/mL; **Tab, DR:** 100mg	• DR tablet and oral suspension are not interchangeable. • Each dose of Noxafil should be administered during or immediately (ie, within 20 minutes) following a full meal. • DR tablet should be swallowed whole, and not be divided, crushed, or chewed. It should be taken with food. • In patients who cannot eat a full meal, each dose of Noxafil should be administered with a liquid nutritional supplement or an acidic carbonated beverage.
Terbinafine HCl (Lamisil)	**Granules:** • Tinea capitis **Tab:** • Onychomycosis of the toenail or fingernail	**Granules:** 125mg/pkt, 187.5mg/pkt; **Tab:** 250mg	• (Tab) Prior to initiating treatment, appropriate nail specimens for laboratory testing (potassium hydroxide preparation, fungal culture, or nail biopsy) should be obtained to confirm the diagnosis of onychomycosis.
Voriconazole (Vfend)	• Aspergillosis • Esophageal candidiasis • Candidemia in non-neutropenic patients • Disseminated infections in skin and infections in abdomen, kidney, bladder wall, and wounds caused by *Candida* • Fungal infections caused by *Scedosporium apiospermum* and *Fusarium* spp. including *Fusarium solani*	**Inj:** 200mg; **Sus:** 40mg/mL; **Tab:** 50mg, 200mg	• Vfend Tablets or Oral Suspension should be taken at least one hour before or after a meal. • Vfend IV for Injection requires reconstitution to 10mg/mL and subsequent dilution to 5mg/mL or less prior to administration as an infusion, at a maximum rate of 3mg/kg per hour over 1 to 2 hours. • Do not administer as an IV bolus injection.

Refer to full FDA-approved labeling for additional information.

Abbreviations: BW = Boxed Warning; DR = Delayed-Release.

TREATMENT OF TUBERCULOSIS

TREATMENT ALGORITHM FOR TUBERCULOSIS

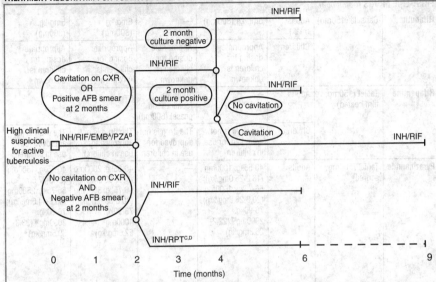

Abbreviations: CXR = chest radiograph; EMB = ethambutol; INH = isoniazid; PZA = pyrazinamide; RIF = rifampin; RPT = rifapentine.

A EMB may be discontinued when results of drug susceptibility testing indicate no drug resistance.

B PZA may be discontinued after it has been taken for 2 months (56 doses).

C RPT should not be used in HIV-infected patients with tuberculosis or in patients with extrapulmonary tuberculosis.

D Therapy should be extended to 9 months if 2-month culture is positive.

Source: Centers for Disease Control and Prevention. Treatment of Tuberculosis, American Thoracic Society, CDC, and Infectious Diseases Society of America. MMWR. 2003;52(No. RR-11):6.

DOSES* OF ANTITUBERCULOSIS DRUGS FOR ADULTS AND CHILDREN†

DRUG	PREPARATION	ADULTS/ CHILDREN	DOSES			
			DAILY	1X/WK	2X/WK	3X/WK
FIRST-LINE DRUGS						
Isoniazid	Tablets (50mg, 100mg, 300mg); elixir (50mg/5mL); aqueous solution (100mg/mL); for intravenous or intramuscular injection	Adults (max)	5mg/kg (300mg)	15mg/kg (900mg)	15mg/kg (900mg)	15mg/kg (900mg)
		Children (max)	10-15mg/kg (300mg)	—	20-30mg/kg (900mg)	—
Rifampin	Capsule (150mg, 300mg); powder may be suspended for oral administration; aqueous solution for intravenous injection	Adults‡ (max)	10mg/kg (600mg)	—	10mg/kg (600mg)	10mg/kg (600mg)
		Children (max)	10-20mg/kg (600mg)	—	10-20mg/kg (600mg)	—

(Continued)

DRUG	PREPARATION	ADULTS/ CHILDREN	DOSES			
			DAILY	1X/WK	2X/WK	3X/WK
FIRST-LINE DRUGS *(Continued)*						
Rifabutin	Capsule (150mg)	Adults[‡] (max)	5mg/kg (300mg)	—	5mg/kg (300mg)	5mg/kg (300mg)
		Children	Appropriate dosing for children is unknown	Appropriate dosing for children is unknown	Appropriate dosing for children is unknown	Appropriate dosing for children is unknown
Rifapentine	Tablet (150mg, film coated)	Adults	—	10mg/kg (continuation phase) (600mg)	—	—
		Children	The drug is not approved for use in children	The drug is not approved for use in children	The drug is not approved for use in children	The drug is not approved for use in children
Pyrazinamide	Tablet (500mg, scored)	Adults	40-55kg: 1000mg (18.2-25.0mg/kg); 56-75kg: 1500mg (20.0-26.8mg/kg); 76-90kg: 2000mg[m] (22.2-26.3mg/kg)	—	40-55kg: 2000mg (36.4-50.0mg/kg); 56-75kg: 3000mg (40.0-53.6mg/kg); 76-90kg: 4000mg[m] (44.4-52.6mg/kg)	40-55kg: 1500mg (27.3-37.5mg/kg); 56-75kg: 2500mg (33.3-44.6mg/kg); 76-90kg: 3000mg[m] (33.3-39.5mg/kg)
		Children (max)	15-30mg/kg (2.0g)	—	50mg/kg (2g)	—
Ethambutol	Tablet (100mg, 400mg)	Adults	40-55kg: 800mg (14.5-20.0mg/kg); 56-75kg: 1200mg (16.0-21.4mg/kg); 76-90kg: 1600mg[m] (17.8-21.1mg/kg)	—	40-55kg: 2000mg (36.4-50.0mg/kg); 56-75kg: 2800mg (37.3-50.0mg/kg); 76-90kg: 4000mg[m] (44.4-52.6mg/kg)	40-55kg: 1200mg (21.8-30.0mg/kg); 56-75kg: 2000mg (26.7-35.7mg/kg); 76-90kg: 2400mg[m] (26.7-31.6mg/kg)
		Children[§] (max)	15-20mg/kg daily (1.0g)	—	50mg/kg (2.5g)	—
SECOND-LINE DRUGS						
Cycloserine	Capsule (250mg)	Adults (max)	10-15mg/kg/d (1.0g in two doses), usually 500-750mg/d in two doses[¶]	There are no data to support intermittent administration	There are no data to support intermittent administration	There are no data to support intermittent administration
		Children (max)	10-15mg/kg/d (1.0g/d)	—	—	—

DRUG	PREPARATION	ADULTS/ CHILDREN	DOSES			
			DAILY	1X/WK	2X/WK	3X/WK
SECOND-LINE DRUGS *(Continued)*						
Ethionamide	Tablet (250mg)	Adults# (max)	15-20mg/kg/d (1.0g/d), usually 500-750mg/d in a single daily dose or two divided doses#	There are no data to support intermittent administration	There are no data to support intermittent administration	There are no data to support intermittent administration
		Children (max)	15-20mg/kg/d (1.0g/d)	There are no data to support intermittent administration	There are no data to support intermittent administration	There are no data to support intermittent administration
Streptomycin	Aqueous solution (1-g vials) for intravenous or intramuscular administration	Adults (max)	**	**	**	**
		Children (max)	20-40mg/kg/d (1g)	—	20mg/kg	—
Amikacin/ Kanamycin	Aqueous solution (500-mg and 1-g vials) for intravenous or intramuscular administration	Adults (max)	**	**	**	**
		Children (max)	15-30mg/kg/d (1g) intravenous or intramuscular as a single daily dose	—	15-30mg/kg	—
Capreomycin	Aqueous solution (1-g vials) for intravenous or intramuscular administration	Adults (max)	**	**	**	**
		Children (max)	15-30mg/kg/d (1g) as a single daily dose	—	15-30mg/kg	—
p-Aminosal- icylic Acid (PAS)	Granules (4-g packets) can be mixed with food; tablets (500mg) are still available in some countries, but not in the United States; a solution for intravenous administration is available in Europe	Adults	8-12g/d in two or three doses	There are no data to support intermittent administration	There are no data to support intermittent administration	There are no data to support intermittent administration
		Children	200-300mg/kg/d in two to four divided doses (10g)	There are no data to support intermittent administration	There are no data to support intermittent administration	There are no data to support intermittent administration
Levofloxacin	Tablets (250mg, 500mg, 750mg); aqueous solution (500-mg vials) for intravenous injection	Adults	500-1000mg daily	There are no data to support intermittent administration	There are no data to support intermittent administration	There are no data to support intermittent administration
		Children	††	††	††	††
Moxifloxacin	Tablets (400mg); aqueous solution (400mg/250mL) for intravenous injection	Adults	400mg daily	There are no data to support intermittent administration	There are no data to support intermittent administration	There are no data to support intermittent administration
		Children	‡‡	‡‡	‡‡	‡‡

(Continued)

DRUG	PREPARATION	ADULTS/ CHILDREN	DOSES			
			DAILY	1X/WK	2X/WK	3X/WK
SECOND-LINE DRUGS *(Continued)*						
Gatifloxacin	Tablets (400mg); aqueous solution (200mg/20mL; 400mg/40mL) for intravenous injection	Adults	400mg daily	There are no data to support intermittent administration	There are no data to support intermittent administration	There are no data to support intermittent administration
		Children	§§	§§	§§	§§

Abbreviations: EMB = ethambutol; INH = isoniazid; RIF = rifampin.

* Dose per weight is based on ideal body weight. Children weighing more than 40kg should be dosed as adults.

† For purposes of this document, adult dosing begins at age 15 years.

‡ Dose may need to be adjusted when there is concomitant use of protease inhibitors or nonnucleoside reverse transcriptase inhibitors.

§ The drug can likely be used safely in older children but should be used with caution in children less than 5 years of age, in whom visual acuity cannot be monitored. In younger children EMB at the dose of 15mg/kg per day can be used if there is suspected or proven resistance to INH or RIF.

¶ It should be noted that, although this is the dose recommended generally, most clinicians with experience using cycloserine indicate that it is unusual for patients to be able to tolerate this amount. Serum concentration measurements are often useful in determining the optimal dose for a given patient.

The single daily dose can be given at bedtime or with the main meal.

** Dose: 15mg/kg per day (1g), and 10mg/kg in persons more than 59 years of age (750mg). Usual dose: 750-1000mg administered intramuscularly or intravenously, given as a single dose 5-7 days/week and reduced to two or three times per week after the first 2-4 months or after culture conversion, depending on the efficacy of the other drugs in the regimen.

†† The long-term (more than several weeks) use of levofloxacin in children and adolescents has not been approved because of concerns about effects on bone and cartilage growth. However, most experts agree that the drug should be considered for children with tuberculosis caused by organisms resistant to both INH and RIF. The optimal dose is not known.

‡‡ The long-term (more than several weeks) use of moxifloxacin in children and adolescents has not been approved because of concerns about effects on bone and cartilage growth. The optimal dose is not known.

§§ The long-term (more than several weeks) use of gatifloxacin in children and adolescents has not been approved because of concerns about effects on bone and cartilage growth. The optimal dose is not known.

¶¶ Maximum dose regardless of weight.

Source: Centers for Disease Control and Prevention. Treatment of Tuberculosis, American Thoracic Society, CDC, and Infectious Diseases Society of America. MMWR 2003;52(No. RR-11):4-5.

ARTHRITIS TREATMENT COMPARISON

GENERIC (BRAND)	HOW SUPPLIED	AS	GA	JIA	JRA	OA	OA of Knee	PsA	RA
CHELATING AGENTS									
Penicillamine (Cuprimine)	**Cap:** 250mg								✓
Penicillamine (Depen)	**Tab:** 250mg								✓
CYCLIC POLYPEPTIDE IMMUNOSUPPRESSANTS									
Cyclosporine (Gengraf, Neoral)	**Cap:** 25mg, 100mg; **Sol:** 100mg/mL								✓
CYCLOOXYGENASE-2 INHIBITORS									
Celecoxib (Celebrex)	**Cap:** 50mg, 100mg, 200mg, 400mg	✓			✓	✓			✓
DIHYDROFOLIC ACID REDUCTASE INHIBITORS									
Methotrexate	**Inj:** 25mg/mL; **Tab:** 2.5mg				✓				✓
Methotrexate (Trexall)	**Tab:** 5mg, 7.5mg, 10mg, 15mg				✓				✓
INTERLEUKIN RECEPTOR ANTAGONISTS									
Anakinra (Kineret)	**Inj:** 100mg/0.67mL								✓
Tocilizumab (Actemra)	**Inj:** 20mg/mL, 162mg/0.9mL			✓					✓
GOLD COMPOUNDS									
Auranofin (Ridaura)	**Cap:** 3mg								✓
Gold sodium thiomalate (Myochrysine)	**Inj:** 50mg/mL				✓				✓
HYALURONAN AND DERIVATIVES									
Hyaluronan (Orthovisc)	**Inj:** 30mg/2mL						✓		
Sodium hyaluronate (Euflexxa)	**Inj:** 1%						✓		
Sodium hyaluronate (Hyalgan)	**Inj:** 10mg/mL						✓		
Sodium hyaluronate (Supartz)	**Inj:** 2.5mL						✓		
HYLAN POLYMERS									
Hylan G-F 20 (Synvisc, Synvisc One)	**Inj:** 8mg/mL						✓		
KINASE INHIBITORS									
Tofacitinib (Xeljanz)	**Tab:** 5mg								✓
MONOCLONAL ANTIBODIES									
Ustekinumab (Stelara)	**Inj:** 45mg/0.5mL, 90mg/mL							✓	
MONOCLONAL ANTIBODIES/CD20-BLOCKERS									
Rituximab (Rituxan)	**Inj:** 100mg/10mL, 500mg/50mL								✓

(Continued)

GENERIC (BRAND)	HOW SUPPLIED	AS	GA	JIA	JRA	OA	OA of Knee	PsA	RA
MONOCLONAL ANTIBODIES/TNF-BLOCKERS									
Adalimumab (Humira)	Inj: 20mg/0.4mL, 40mg/0.8mL	✓		✓				✓	✓
Golimumab (Simponi)	Inj: 50mg/0.5mL, 100mg/mL	✓						✓	✓
Infliximab (Remicade)	Inj: 100mg	✓						✓	✓
NON-STEROIDAL ANTI-INFLAMMATORY DRUGS (NSAIDs)									
Diclofenac potassium (Cataflam)	Tab: 50mg					✓			✓
Diclofenac sodium	Tab, DR: 25mg, 50mg, 75mg	✓				✓			✓
Diclofenac sodium (Pennsaid)	Sol: 1.5%						✓		
Diclofenac sodium (Voltaren Gel)	Gel: 1%					✓	✓		
Diclofenac sodium (Voltaren-XR)	Tab, ER: 100mg					✓			✓
Diflunisal	Tab: 500mg					✓			✓
Etodolac	Cap: 200mg, 300mg; Tab: 400mg, 500mg					✓			✓
Etodolac Extended-Release	Tab, ER: 400mg, 500mg, 600mg				✓	✓			✓
Fenoprofen calcium (Nalfon)	Cap: 200mg, 400mg; (Generic) Tab: 600mg					✓			✓
Ibuprofen	Tab: 400mg, 600mg, 800mg					✓			✓
Indomethacin (Indocin)	Sup: 50mg	✓	✓			✓			✓
Indomethacin Extended-Release	Cap, ER: 75mg	✓				✓			✓
Ketoprofen	Cap: 50mg, 75mg					✓			✓
Ketoprofen Extended-Release	Cap, ER: 100mg, 150mg, 200mg					✓			✓
Meloxicam (Mobic)	Susp: 7.5mg/5mL; Tab: 7.5mg, 15mg				✓	✓			✓
Nabumetone	Tab: 500mg, 750mg					✓			✓
Naproxen (Naprosyn, EC-Naprosyn)	(Naprosyn) Susp: 125mg/mL; Tab: 250mg, 375mg, 500mg; (EC-Naprosyn) Tab, DR: 375mg, 500mg	✓			✓	✓			✓
Naproxen sodium (Anaprox, Anaprox DS)	Tab: (Anaprox) 275mg; (Anaprox DS) 550mg	✓			✓	✓			✓
Naproxen sodium (Naprelan)	Tab, CR: 375mg, 500mg, 750mg	✓				✓			✓
Oxaprozin (Daypro)	Tab: 600mg				✓	✓			✓

GENERIC (BRAND)	HOW SUPPLIED	AS	GA	JIA	JRA	OA	OA of Knee	PsA	RA
NON-STEROIDAL ANTI-INFLAMMATORY DRUGS (NSAIDs) *(Continued)*									
Piroxicam (Feldene)	**Cap:** 10mg, 20mg					✓			✓
Salsalate	**Tab:** 500mg, 750mg					✓			✓
Sulindac	**Tab:** 150mg, 200mg	✓	✓			✓			✓
Tolmetin	**Cap:** 400mg; **Tab:** 200mg, 600mg				✓	✓			✓
PHOSPHODIESTERASE-4 INHIBITORS									
Apremilast (Otezla)	**Tab:** 10mg, 20mg, 30mg							✓	
PURINE ANTAGONIST ANTIMETABOLITES									
Azathioprine (Azasan)	**Tab:** 75mg, 100mg								✓
Azathioprine (Imuran)	**Tab:** 50mg								✓
PYRIMIDINE SYNTHESIS INHIBITORS									
Leflunomide (Arava)	**Tab:** 10mg, 20mg, 100mg								✓
QUININE DERIVATIVES									
Hydroxychloroquine sulfate (Plaquenil)	**Tab:** 200mg								✓
SELECTIVE COSTIMULATION MODULATORS									
Abatacept (Orencia)	**Inj:** 125mg/mL, 250mg			✓					✓
5-AMINOSALICYLIC ACID DERIVATIVES/SULFAPYRIDINES									
Sulfasalazine (Azulfidine EN-tabs)	**Tab, DR:** 500mg				✓				✓
TNF-RECEPTOR BLOCKERS									
Certolizumab pegol (Cimzia)	**Inj:** 200mg/mL	✓						✓	✓
Etanercept (Enbrel)	**Inj:** 25mg, 50mg	✓		✓				✓	✓
COMBINATION PRODUCTS									
NSAIDs/H$_2$-RECEPTOR ANTAGONISTS									
Ibuprofen/Famotidine (Duexis)	**Tab:** 800mg/26.6mg					✓			✓
NSAIDs/PROTON PUMP INHIBITORS									
Naproxen/Esomeprazole magnesium (Vimovo)	**Tab, DR:** 375mg/20mg, 500mg/20mg	✓				✓			✓
NSAIDs/PROSTAGLANDIN ANALOGS									
Diclofenac sodium/ Misoprostol (Arthrotec)	**Tab:** 50mg/200mcg, 75mg/200mcg					✓			✓

Refer to full FDA-approved labeling for additional information.

Abbreviations: AS = ankylosing spondylitis; DR = delayed-release; ER = extended-release; GA = gouty arthritis; JIA = juvenile idiopathic arthritis; JRA = juvenile rheumatoid arthritis; OA = osteoarthritis; PsA = psoriatic arthritis; RA = rheumatoid arthritis.

DIETARY CALCIUM INTAKE

RECOMMENDED CALCIUM INTAKE	
AGE	DAILY INTAKE (MG)
Birth-6 months	200
6 months-1 year	260
1-3 years	700
4-8 years	1000
9-18 years	1300
19-50 years	1000
51-70 years (male)	1000
51-70 years (female)	1200
>70 years	1200

Source: Calcium and Vitamin D: Important at Every Age. National Institute of Arthritis and Musculoskeletal and Skin Diseases website. http://www.niams.nih.gov/Health_Info/Bone/Bone_Health/Nutrition/. Updated January 2012. Accessed February 14, 2014.

ESTIMATING DAILY DIETARY CALCIUM INTAKE		
PRODUCT	CALCIUM/SERVING (MG)	POINTS
Baked beans, 1 cup	142	1
Boiled turnips, ½	99	1
Canned sardines, 3 oz.	324	3
Canned salmon, 3 oz.	181	2
Cereal, fortified, 1 cup	100-1000	1-10
Cooked soybeans	261	3
Cottage cheese with 1% milk fat, 1 cup	138	1
Ice cream, vanilla-flavored, ½ cup	85	1
Lasagna, 1 cup	125	1
Low fat plain yogurt, 1 cup	300	3
Milk, non-fat, 1 cup	302	3
Milkshake, 1 cup	300	3
Oatmeal, fortified, 1 pkt	350	3
Orange juice, fortified, 6 oz.	200-260	2-3
Pudding made with 2% milk, ½ cup	153	2
Pizza, plain cheese, 1 slice	100	1
Raw broccoli, 1 cup	90	1
Shredded cheddar cheese, 1 ½ oz.	306	3
Soft-serve vanilla frozen yogurt, ½ cup	103	1
Soy milk, fortified, 1 cup	80-500	1-5
Tofu, with calcium, ½ cup	204	2
Waffles, fortified, 2	100	1

(Continued)

RECOMMENDED POINTS NEEDED FOR AGE GROUPS

AGE	POINTS
0-3	2-7
4-8	10
9-17	13
18-49	10
50-69	10-12
>70	12

Source: The Surgeon General's Report on Bone Health and Osteoporosis: What It Means to You. National Institute of Arthritis and Musculoskeletal and Skin Diseases website. http://www.niams.nih.gov/Health_Info/Bone/SGR/surgeon_generals_report.asp. Updated March 2012. Accessed March 18, 2014.

FACTORS RELATED TO VITAMIN D THAT MAY AFFECT CALCIUM ABSORPTION

• The National Osteoporosis Foundation recommends an intake of 800 to 1000 IU of vitamin D per day for adults ≥50 years and 400 to 800 IU of vitamin D per day for adults <50 years.

• There are 2 types of vitamin D supplements: vitamin D_2 (ergocalciferol) and vitamin D_3 (cholecalciferol); they are both equally good for bone health.

• The safe upper limit for vitamin D intake for most adults is 4000 IU per day.

• Patients with celiac disease or inflammatory bowel disease, or those who are housebound (eg, living in nursing homes), obese or very overweight, or have limited sun exposure, may need vitamin D supplements.

Source: Calcium and Vitamin D: What You Need to Know. National Osteoporosis Foundation website. http://nof.org/articles/10. Accessed February 14, 2014.

GOUT AGENTS

GENERIC (BRAND)	HOW SUPPLIED	USUAL ADULT DOSAGE
ALKALINIZING AGENTS		
Citric acid monohydrate/Potassium citrate monohydrate (Cytra-K Crystals)	**Crystals:** 1002mg-3300mg/pkt	1 pkt qid after meals and hs, or ud. Reconstitute with ≤6 oz of cool water or juice.
Citric acid monohydrate/Potassium citrate monohydrate (Cytra-K Oral Solution)	**Sol:** 334mg-1100mg/5mL	15-30mL diluted with a glass of water, qid after meals and hs, or ud.
Citric acid monohydrate/Potassium citrate monohydrate/Sodium citrate dihydrate (Cytra-3 Syrup)	**Syr:** 334mg-550mg-500mg/5mL	15-30mL diluted with water, qid after meals and hs, or ud.
CORTICOSTEROIDS		
Hydrocortisone (Cortef)	**Tab:** 5mg, 10mg, 20mg	**Acute Gout:** Individualized dosing.
Hydrocortisone sodium succinate (A-Hydrocort)	**Inj:** 100mg/2mL	**Acute Gout:** Individualized dosing. May repeat dose at intervals of 2, 4, or 6 hrs, based on patient response.
Methylprednisolone (Medrol)	**Tab:** 2mg, 4mg, 8mg, 16mg, 32mg	**Acute Gout:** Individualized dosing.
Prednisone	**Sol:** 5mg/mL, 5mg/5mL; **Tab:** 1mg, 2.5mg, 5mg, 10mg, 20mg, 50mg	**Acute Gout:** Individualized dosing.
Prednisolone	**Syr:** 5mg/5mL, 15mg/5mL; **Tab:** 5mg*	**Acute Gout:** Individualized dosing.
NONSTEROIDAL ANTI-INFLAMMATORY DRUGS		
Indomethacin (Indocin)	**Cap:** (Generic) 25mg, 50mg; **Supp:** 50mg; **Sus:** 25mg/5mL	**Acute Gout:** 50mg tid until pain is tolerable, then d/c.
Naproxen (Naprosyn)	**Sus:** 125mg/5mL; **Tab:** 250mg*, 375mg, 500mg*	**Acute Gout:** 750mg followed by 250mg q8h until attack subsides.
Naproxen Sodium (Anaprox)	(Anaprox) **Tab:** 275mg	**Acute Gout:** 825mg followed by 275mg q8h until attack subsides.
(Anaprox DS)	(Anaprox DS) **Tab:** 550mg*	
(Naprelan)	**Tab, Controlled-Release:** 375mg, 500mg, 750mg	**Acute Gout:** 1-1.5g qd on the 1st day, then 1g qd until attack subsides.
Sulindac	**Tab:** 150mg*, 200mg*	**Acute Gout:** 200mg bid with food, usually for 7 days. **Max:** 400mg/day.
PHENANTHRENE DERIVATIVES		
Colchicine (Colcrys)	**Tab:** 0.6mg*	**Acute Gout:** 1.2mg at 1st sign of flare, then 0.6mg 1 hr later. **Max:** 1.8mg/hour. **Prophylaxis:** 0.6mg qd-bid. **Max:** 1.2mg/day.
RECOMBINANT URICASES		
Pegloticase (Krystexxa)	**Inj:** 8mg/mL	**Chronic Gout:** 8mg IV infusion q2wks.
URICOSURIC AGENTS		
Probenecid	**Tab:** 500mg	250mg bid x 1 wk, then 500mg bid thereafter. May increase by 500mg q4wks if symptoms are not controlled or 24-hr uric acid excretion <700mg. **Max:** 2g/day.

(Continued)

GENERIC (BRAND)	HOW SUPPLIED	USUAL ADULT DOSAGE
XANTHINE OXIDASE INHIBITORS		
Allopurinol (Zyloprim)	**Tab:** 100mg*, 300mg*	**Mild Gout:** 200-300mg/day. **Moderately Severe Gout:** 400-600mg/day. Give in divided doses if >300mg. **Max:** 800mg/day.
Febuxostat (Uloric)	**Tab:** 40mg, 80mg	**Chronic Gout: Initial:** 40mg qd. Increase to 80mg qd if serum uric acid ≥6mg/dL after 2 wks.
COMBINATIONS		
Colchicine/Probenecid	**Tab:** 0.5mg-500mg*	1 tab qd for 1 wk, then 1 tab bid thereafter. May increase by 1 tab q4wks if symptoms are not controlled or 24-hr uric acid excretion is <700mg. **Max:** 4 tabs/day.

Refer to full FDA-approved labeling for additional information.
*Scored.

OSTEOPOROSIS DETECTION, PREVENTION, AND TREATMENT

OSTEOPOROSIS RISK FACTORS

NONMODIFIABLE RISK FACTORS

Gender	Women (postmenopausal) > Men
Age	>50 years old
Body	Low body weight (small and thin), broken bones or height loss during adult years
Ethnicity	Caucasian/Asian > Hispanic/African American
Family history	History of fractures or osteoporosis

MODIFIABLE RISK FACTORS

Lifestyle	Cigarette smoking, weight loss, excessive alcohol (≥3 drinks/day)
Exercise	Inactive
Diet	Low intake of calcium, vitamin D, fruits, and vegetables; high intake of protein, salt, and caffeine

Drugs that may cause bone loss
- Aluminum-containing antacids
- Anticoagulants (heparin)
- Antiseizure drugs
- Aromatase inhibitors
- Barbiturates
- Cancer chemotherapeutic drugs
- Cyclosporine A and tacrolimus
- Glucocorticoids (≥5mg/day of prednisone or equivalent for ≥3 months)
- Gonadotropin-releasing hormone agonists
- Lithium
- Medroxyprogesterone acetate for contraception
- Methotrexate
- Proton pump inhibitors
- Selective serotonin reuptake inhibitors
- Tamoxifen
- Thiazolidinediones
- Thyroid hormones in excess

Diseases/conditions that may cause bone loss
- AIDS/HIV
- Ankylosing spondylitis
- Blood and bone marrow disorders
- Breast cancer
- Celiac disease
- Chronic obstructive pulmonary disease (COPD), including emphysema
- Cushing's syndrome
- Depression
- Diabetes
- Eating disorders, especially anorexia nervosa
- Female athlete triad (includes loss of menstrual periods, an eating disorder, and excessive exercise)
- Gastrectomy
- Gastrointestinal bypass procedures
- Hyperparathyroidism
- Hyperthyroidism
- Inflammatory bowel disease, including Crohn's disease and ulcerative colitis
- Kidney disease that is chronic and long lasting
- Liver disease that is severe, including biliary cirrhosis
- Low levels of testosterone and estrogen in men
- Lupus
- Lymphoma and leukemia
- Missing periods
- Multiple myeloma
- Multiple sclerosis
- Organ transplants

(Continued)

- Parkinson's disease
- Polio and postpolio syndrome
- Poor diet, including malnutrition
- Premature menopause
- Prostate cancer
- Rheumatoid arthritis
- Scoliosis
- Sickle cell disease
- Spinal cord injuries
- Stroke
- Thalassemia
- Thyrotoxicosis
- Weight loss

Note: This list is not inclusive of all drugs, diseases/conditions that may increase the risk factors for osteoporosis.

Sources:

Osteoporosis Handout on Health. National Institute of Arthritis and Musculoskeletal and Skin Diseases website. http://www.niams.nih.gov/Health_Info/Bone/Osteoporosis/osteoporosis_hoh.asp. Updated October 2011. Accessed March 21, 2014.

Clinician's Guide to Prevention and Treatment of Osteoporosis. Washington, DC: National Osteoporosis Foundation; 2013.

BONE MINERAL DENSITY CLASSIFICATION/TESTS

WORLD HEALTH ORGANIZATION (WHO) DEFINITION OF OSTEOPOROSIS

Normal	Bone mineral density within 1 standard deviation (SD) of the young adult mean (T-score ≥-1.0)
Osteopenia (low bone mass)	Bone mineral density between 1.0 and 2.5 SD below the young adult mean (-2.5 < T-score <-1.0)
Osteoporosis	Bone mineral density 2.5 SD or more below the young adult mean (T-score ≤-2.5)

Note: The definitions above should not be applied to premenopausal women, men <50 years of age, and children.

BONE MINERAL DENSITY (BMD) TESTS

- BMD tests provide a measurement for bone density at hip and spine to:

  — Establish and confirm a diagnosis of osteoporosis

  — Predict future fracture risk

  — Measure response to osteoporosis treatment

- BMD is measured in grams of mineral per square centimeter scanned (g/cm^2) and compared to the expected BMD for the patient's age and sex (Z-score) or compared with "young normal" adults of the same sex (T-score).

- The difference between the patient's score and the optimal BMD is expressed in SD above and below the mean. Usually 1 SD equals about 10-15% of the bone density value in g/cm^2.

- Negative values for T-score, such as -1.5, -2, or -2.5, indicate low bone mass.

- The greater the negative score, the greater the risk of fracture.

PREVENTION STRATEGIES

A balanced diet rich in calcium and vitamin D along with exercise helps strengthen bones. This alone may not be enough to stop bone loss caused by lifestyle, medications, or menopause.

- The National Osteoporosis Foundation recommends BMD testing for all women ≥65 years and all men ≥70 years. It also recommends BMD testing for postmenopausal women <65 years and men 50-69 years based on their risk factor profile.

- The U.S. Preventive Services Task Force recommends osteoporosis screening for women ≥65 years and in younger women at increased risk for osteoporotic fractures.

OSTEOPOROSIS AGENTS

GENERIC (BRAND)	HOW SUPPLIED	DOSAGE	SPECIAL INSTRUCTIONS
BISPHOSPHONATES AND COMBINATIONS			
Alendronate sodium (Binosto)	Tab, Effervescent: 70mg	**Osteoporosis: Treatment:** 70mg once weekly. **Increase Bone Mass in Men with Osteoporosis:** 70mg once weekly.	Take at least 30 min before 1st food, drink (other than plain water), or medication of day with plain water only. Dissolve tabs in 4 oz room temperature plain water and wait at least 5 min after the effervescence stops. Stir the solution for about 10 sec and ingest. Do not lie down for at least 30 min and until after 1st food of day.
Alendronate sodium (Fosamax)	Sol: 70mg [75mL]; Tab: (Generic) 5mg, 10mg, 35mg, 40mg, 70mg; (Fosamax) 70mg	**Osteoporosis: Treatment:** 70mg once weekly or 10mg qd. **Prevention:** 35mg once weekly or 5mg qd. **Increase Bone Mass in Men with Osteoporosis:** 70mg once weekly or 10mg qd. **Glucocorticoid-Induced:** 5mg qd; 10mg qd for postmenopausal women not on estrogen.	Take at least 30 min before 1st food, drink (other than plain water), or medication of day with plain water only. Take tabs with 6-8 oz water or 2 oz with oral sol. Do not lie down for at least 30 min and until after 1st food of day.
Alendronate sodium/ Cholecalciferol (Fosamax Plus D)	Tab: (Alendronate-Cholecalciferol) 70mg-2800 IU, 70mg-5600 IU	**Osteoporosis: Treatment:** 1 tab (70mg-2800 IU or 70mg-5600 IU) once weekly. **Usual:** 70mg-5600 IU once weekly. **Increase Bone Mass in Men with Osteoporosis:** 1 tab (70mg-2800 IU or 70mg-5600 IU) once weekly. **Usual:** 70mg-5600 IU once weekly.	Take at least 30 min before 1st food, drink (other than plain water), or medication of day. Take with 6-8 oz water. Do not lie down for at least 30 min and until after 1st food of day.
Ibandronate sodium (Boniva)	Inj: 3mg/3mL; Tab: 150mg	**Osteoporosis: Treatment:** Inj: 3mg IV over 15-30 sec every 3 months. **Prevention/Treatment:** PO: 150mg once monthly.	**PO:** Take at least 60 min before 1st food, drink (other than plain water), medication, or supplement of day. Swallow whole with 6-8 oz plain water while standing or sitting upright. Do not lie down for 60 min after dose.
Risedronate sodium (Actonel)	Tab: 5mg, 30mg, 35mg, 150mg	**Osteoporosis: Prevention/ Treatment:** 5mg qd or 35mg once weekly or 150mg once monthly. **Increase Bone Mass in Men with Osteoporosis:** 35mg once weekly. **Glucocorticoid-Induced: Prevention/Treatment:** 5mg qd.	Take at least 30 min before 1st food or drink (other than plain water) of day. Take with 6-8 oz plain water in an upright position. Do not lie down for 30 min after dose.
Risedronate sodium (Atelvia)	Tab, Delayed-Release: 35mg	**Osteoporosis: Treatment:** 35mg once weekly.	Take in am immediately after breakfast. Swallow whole with 4 oz of plain water. Do not lie down for 30 min after dose. Do not chew, cut, or crush tabs.

(Continued)

GENERIC (BRAND)	HOW SUPPLIED	DOSAGE	SPECIAL INSTRUCTIONS
BISPHOSPHONATES AND COMBINATIONS *(Continued)*			
Zoledronic acid (Reclast)	**Inj:** 5mg/100mL	**Osteoporosis: Treatment:** 5mg IV over ≥15 min once a year. **Prevention:** 5mg IV over ≥15 min once every 2 years. **Increase Bone Mass in Men with Osteoporosis:** 5mg IV over ≥15 min once a year. **Glucocorticoid-Induced: Prevention/Treatment:** 5mg IV over ≥15 min once a year.*	Flush IV line with 10mL normal saline after infusion. Administration of acetaminophen after Reclast may decrease acute-phase reaction symptoms.
HORMONE THERAPY††			
Conjugated estrogens (Premarin Tabs)	**Tab:** 0.3mg, 0.45mg, 0.625mg, 0.9mg, 1.25mg	**Osteoporosis: Prevention: Initial:** 0.3mg qd continuously or cyclically (eg, 25 days on, 5 days off). Reevaluate periodically.	
Conjugated estrogens (CE)/ Medroxyprogesterone acetate (MPA) (Premphase)	**Tab:** (CE) 0.625mg and (CE-MPA) 0.625mg-5mg	**Osteoporosis: Prevention:** 1 CE tab qd on Days 1-14 and 1 CE-MPA tab qd on Days 15-28. Reevaluate periodically.	
Conjugated estrogens/ Medroxyprogesterone acetate (Prempro)	**Tab:** (CE-MPA) 0.3mg-1.5mg, 0.45mg-1.5mg, 0.625mg-2.5mg, 0.625mg-5mg	**Osteoporosis: Prevention:** 1 tab qd. Reevaluate periodically.	
Estradiol (Alora)	**Patch:** 0.025mg/day, 0.05mg/day, 0.075mg/day, 0.1mg/day	**Osteoporosis: Prevention:** 0.025mg/day twice weekly. May increase depending on bone mineral density and adverse events. Reevaluate periodically.	Apply to lower abdomen, upper quadrant of buttock, or outer aspect of hip; avoid breasts and waistline. Rotate application sites. Allow 1 week between applications to same site.
Estradiol (Climara)	**Patch:** 0.025mg/day, 0.0375mg/day, 0.05mg/day, 0.06mg/day, 0.075mg/day, 0.1mg/day	**Osteoporosis: Prevention:** 0.025mg/day once weekly. Reevaluate periodically.	Apply to lower abdomen or upper quadrant of buttock; avoid breasts and waistline. Rotate application sites. Allow 1 week between applications to same site.
Estradiol (Estrace)	**Tab:** 0.5mg§, 1mg§, 2mg§	**Osteoporosis: Prevention:** Lowest effective dose has not been determined. Reevaluate periodically.	
Estradiol (Estraderm)	**Patch:** 0.05mg/day, 0.1mg/day	**Osteoporosis: Prevention: Initial:** 0.05mg/day twice weekly. May give continuously in patients without intact uterus. May give cyclically (eg, 3 weeks on, 1 week off) in patients with intact uterus. Reevaluate periodically.	Apply to trunk of body (including buttocks and abdomen); avoid breasts and waistline. Rotate application sites. Allow 1 week between applications to same site.
Estradiol (Menostar)	**Patch:** 14mcg/day	**Osteoporosis: Prevention:** Apply 1 patch weekly. Reevaluate periodically.	Apply to trunk of body (including buttocks and abdomen); avoid breasts and waistline. Rotate application sites. Allow 1 week between applications to same site.

GENERIC (BRAND)	HOW SUPPLIED	DOSAGE	SPECIAL INSTRUCTIONS
HORMONE THERAPY†‡ *(Continued)*			
Estradiol (Vivelle-Dot)	**Patch:** 0.025mg/day, 0.0375mg/day, 0.05mg/day, 0.075mg/day, 0.1mg/day	**Osteoporosis: Prevention: Initial:** 0.025mg/day twice weekly. May give continuously in patients without intact uterus. May give cyclically (eg, 3 weeks on, 1 week off) in patients with intact uterus. Reevaluate periodically.	Apply to lower abdomen; avoid breasts and waistline. Rotate application sites. Allow 1 week between applications to same site.
Estradiol/ Levonorgestrel (Climara Pro)	**Patch:** (Estradiol-Levonorgestrel) 0.045mg-0.015mg/day	**Osteoporosis: Prevention:** Apply 1 patch weekly. Reevaluate periodically.	Apply to lower abdomen or upper quadrant of the buttock; avoid breasts and waistline. Rotate application sites. Allow 1 week between applications to same site.
Estradiol/ Norethindrone (Activella)	**Tab:** (Estradiol-Norethindrone) 1mg-0.5mg, 0.5mg-0.1mg	**Osteoporosis: Prevention:** 1 tab qd. Reevaluate periodically.	
Estradiol/ Norgestimate (Prefest)	**Tab:** (Estradiol) 1mg and (Estradiol-Norgestimate) 1mg-0.09mg	**Osteoporosis: Prevention:** 1 estradiol (peach color) tab for 3 days followed by 1 estradiol-norgestimate (white color) tab for 3 days. Repeat regimen continuously. Reevaluate periodically.	
Estropipate	**Tab:** 0.75mg§, 1.5mg§, 3mg§, 6mg§	**Osteoporosis: Prevention:** 0.75mg qd for 25 days of a 31-day cycle per month.	
Ethinyl Estradiol/ Norethindrone (Femhrt)	**Tab:** (Ethinyl Estradiol-Norethindrone) 2.5mcg-0.5mg, 5mcg-1mg	**Osteoporosis: Prevention:** 1 tab qd. Reevaluate periodically.	
MISCELLANEOUS			
Calcitonin-Salmon (Fortical)	**Nasal Spray:** 200 IU/actuation	**Osteoporosis (>5 yrs Postmenopause): Treatment:** 200 IU qd intranasally. Alternate nostrils daily.	Patients should take supplemental calcium and vitamin D.
Calcitonin-Salmon (Miacalcin)	**Inj:** 200 IU/mL; **Nasal Spray:** 200 IU/actuation	**Osteoporosis (>5 yrs Postmenopause): Treatment:** (Inj) 100 IU IM/SQ every other day. If >2mL, use IM and multiple inj sites. (Spray) 200 IU qd intranasally. Alternate nostrils daily.	Patients should take supplemental calcium and vitamin D.
Denosumab (Prolia)	**Inj:** 60mg/mL	**Osteoporosis: Treatment:** 60mg as a single SQ inj once every 6 months. **Increase Bone Mass in Men with Osteoporosis:** 60mg as a single SQ inj once every 6 months.	Administer in the upper arm, upper thigh, or abdomen. All patients should receive calcium 1000mg and at least 400 IU vitamin D qd.
Raloxifene HCl† (Evista)	**Tab:** 60mg	**Osteoporosis: Prevention/ Treatment:** 60mg qd.	Calcium and vitamin D supplementation is recommended.

(Continued)

GENERIC (BRAND)	HOW SUPPLIED	DOSAGE	SPECIAL INSTRUCTIONS
MISCELLANEOUS (Continued)			
Teriparatide† (Forteo)	**Inj:** 250mcg/mL	**Osteoporosis: Treatment/ Increase Bone Mass in Men/Glucocorticoid- Induced:** 20mcg SQ qd into thigh or abdominal wall. Use of the drug for >2 years during a patient's lifetime is not recommended.	Administer initially under circumstances where patient can sit or lie down if symptoms of orthostatic hypotension occur. Discard pen after 28 days.

Refer to full FDA-approved labeling for additional information.

*Patients on Reclast must be adequately supplemented with calcium and vitamin D if dietary intake is not sufficient. An average of at least 1200mg calcium and 800-1000 IU vitamin D daily is recommended.

† Check FDA-approved labeling for important Boxed Warnings.

‡ When prescribing solely for the prevention of postmenopausal osteoporosis, therapy should be considered only for women at significant risk for osteoporosis; non-estrogen medications should be carefully considered.

§ Scored.

ADHD AGENTS

BRAND (GENERIC)	HOW SUPPLIED	ADULT DOSAGE	PEDIATRIC DOSAGE
Adderall (Amphetamine salt combo)	**Tab:** 5mg, 7.5mg, 10mg, 12.5mg, 15mg, 20mg, 30mg		Give first dose upon awakening and additional doses q4-6h. **≥6 yrs: Initial:** 5mg qd-bid. **Titrate:** May increase weekly by 5mg/day. **3-5 yrs: Initial:** 2.5mg qd. **Titrate:** May increase weekly by 2.5mg/day.
Adderall XR* (Amphetamine salt combo)	**Cap, ER:** 5mg, 10mg, 15mg, 20mg, 25mg, 30mg	**Amphetamine-Naive/Switching from Another Medication:** 20mg qam. **Currently on Amphetamine IR:** Switch to Adderall XR at the same total daily dose, qd. **Titrate:** May increase at weekly intervals.	**Switching from Amphetamine IR:** Switch to Adderall XR at the same total daily dose, qd. **Titrate:** May increase at weekly intervals. **Amphetamine-Naive/Switching from Another Medication: 13-17 yrs: Initial:** 10mg qam. **Titrate:** May increase to 20mg/day after 1 week. **6-12 yrs: Initial:** 5-10mg qam. **Titrate:** May increase weekly by 5-10mg/day. **Max:** 30mg/day.
Concerta† (Methylphenidate HCl)	**Tab, ER:** 18mg, 27mg, 36mg, 54mg	**18-65 yrs: New to Methylphenidate: Initial:** 18mg or 36mg qam. **Range:** 18-72mg/day. **Currently on Methylphenidate: Initial:** 18mg qam if previous dose 10-15mg/day; 36mg qam if previous dose 20-30mg/day; 54mg qam if previous dose 30-45mg/day; 72mg qam if previous dose 40-60mg/day. Conversion dosage should not exceed 72mg/day. **Titrate:** May increase weekly by 18mg/day. **Max:** 72mg/day.	**New to Methylphenidate: 13-17 yrs: Initial:** 18mg qam. **Range:** 18-72mg/day, not to exceed 2mg/kg/day. **6-12 yrs: Initial:** 18mg qam. **Range:** 18-54mg/day. **Currently on Methylphenidate: ≥6 yrs: Initial:** 18mg qam if previous dose 10-15mg/day; 36mg qam if previous dose 20-30mg/day; 54mg qam if previous dose 30-45mg/day; 72mg qam if previous dose 40-60mg/day. Conversion dosage should not exceed 72mg/day. **Titrate:** May increase weekly by 18mg/day. **Max: 13-17 yrs:** 72mg/day. **6-12 yrs:** 54mg/day.
Daytrana (Methylphenidate)	**Patch:** 10mg/9 hrs, 15mg/9 hrs, 20mg/9 hrs, 30mg/9 hrs	Apply to hip area 2 hrs before effect is needed and remove 9 hrs after application. **Recommended Titration Schedule: Week 1:** 10mg/9 hrs. **Week 2:** 15mg/9 hrs. **Week 3:** 20mg/9 hrs. **Week 4:** 30mg/9 hrs.	**≥6 yrs:** Apply to hip area 2 hrs before effect is needed and remove 9 hrs after application. **Recommended Titration Schedule: Week 1:** 10mg/9 hrs. **Week 2:** 15mg/9 hrs. **Week 3:** 20mg/9 hrs. **Week 4:** 30mg/9 hrs.
Desoxyn (Methamphetamine HCl)	**Tab:** 5mg		**≥6 yrs: Initial:** 5mg qd-bid. **Titrate:** May increase weekly by 5mg/day. **Usual:** 20-25mg/day. Total daily dose may be given in 2 divided doses.
Dexedrine Spansules (Dextroamphetamine sulfate)	**Cap, ER:** 5mg, 10mg, 15mg		**≥6 yrs: Initial:** 5mg qd-bid. **Titrate:** May increase weekly by 5mg/day. **Max (Usual):** 40mg/day.
Focalin (Dexmethylphenidate HCl)	**Tab:** 2.5mg, 5mg, 10mg	Take bid, at least 4 hrs apart. **Methylphenidate-Naive: Initial:** 2.5mg bid. **Titrate:** May adjust weekly in 2.5-5mg increments. **Max:** 20mg/day. **Currently on Methylphenidate: Initial:** ½ of methylphenidate dose. **Max:** 20mg/day.	**≥6 yrs:** Take bid at least 4 hrs apart. **Methylphenidate-Naive: Initial:** 2.5mg bid. **Titrate:** May adjust weekly in 2.5-5mg increments. **Max:** 20mg/day. **Currently on Methylphenidate: Initial:** ½ of methylphenidate dose. **Max:** 20mg/day.

(Continued)

BRAND (GENERIC)	HOW SUPPLIED	ADULT DOSAGE	PEDIATRIC DOSAGE
Focalin XR* (Dexmethylphenidate HCl)	**Cap, ER:** 5mg, 10mg, 15mg, 20mg, 25mg, 30mg, 35mg, 40mg	**Methylphenidate-Naive: Initial:** 10mg qam. **Titrate:** May adjust weekly in 10mg increments. **Max:** 40mg/day. **Currently on Methylphenidate: Initial:** ½ of methylphenidate total daily dose. **Currently on Focalin:** May switch to the same daily dose of Focalin XR.	**≥6 yrs: Methylphenidate-Naive: Initial:** 5mg qam. **Titrate:** May adjust weekly in 5mg increments. **Max:** 30mg/day. **Currently on Methylphenidate: Initial:** ½ of methylphenidate total daily dose. **Currently on Focalin:** May switch to the same daily dose of Focalin XR.
Intuniv† (Guanfacine)	**Tab, ER:** 1mg, 2mg, 3mg, 4mg		**6-17 yrs: Non-Weight-Based: Initial:** 1mg/day. **Titrate:** Adjust in increments of ≤1mg/week. **Maint:** 1-4mg/day. **Weight-Based: Initial:** 0.05-0.08mg/kg/day. **Titrate:** May increase up to 0.12mg/kg/day. **Switching from IR:** D/C IR, and titrate with Intuniv according to recommended schedule. **D/C:** Taper in decrements of ≤1mg q3-7 days.
Kapvay† (Clonidine HCl)	**Tab, ER:** 0.1mg, 0.2mg		**6-17 yrs: Initial:** 0.1mg hs. **Titrate:** Adjust in increments of 0.1mg/day at weekly intervals. Doses should be taken bid with equal or higher split dose given hs. **Max:** 0.4mg/day. **D/C:** Taper in decrements of ≤0.1mg q3-7 days.
Metadate CD* (Methylphenidate HCl)	**Cap, ER:** 10mg, 20mg, 30mg, 40mg, 50mg, 60mg		**≥6 yrs: Initial:** 20mg qam before breakfast. **Titrate:** May adjust weekly by 10-20mg. **Max:** 60mg/day.
Metadate ER† (Methylphenidate HCl)	**Tab, ER:** 20mg	(IR Methylphenidate) 10-60mg/day given bid-tid 30-45 min ac. If insomnia occurs, take last dose before 6 pm. (Tab, ER) May use in place of IR tabs when the 8-hr dose corresponds to the titrated 8-hr IR dose.	**≥6 yrs: Initial:** 5mg bid before breakfast and lunch. **Titrate:** Increase gradually by 5-10mg weekly. **Max:** 60mg/day. (Tab, ER) May use in place of IR tabs when the 8-hr dose corresponds to the titrated 8-hr IR dose.
Methylin (Methylphenidate HCl)	**Sol:** 5mg/5mL [500mL], 10mg/5mL [500mL]; **Tab, Chewable:** 2.5mg, 5mg, 10mg	10-60mg/day given bid-tid 30-45 min ac. If insomnia occurs, take last dose before 6 pm.	**≥6 yrs: Initial:** 5mg bid before breakfast and lunch. **Titrate:** Increase gradually by 5-10mg weekly. **Max:** 60mg/day.
ProCentra (Dextroamphetamine sulfate)	**Sol:** 5mg/5mL [473mL]		**≥6 yrs: Initial:** 5mg qd-bid. **Titrate:** May increase weekly by 5mg/day. **Max (Usual):** 40mg/day. **3-5 yrs: Initial:** 2.5mg qd. **Titrate:** May increase weekly by 2.5mg/day.
Quillivant XR (Methylphenidate HCl)	**Sol, ER:** 5mg/mL [60mL, 120mL, 150mL, 180mL]	**Initial:** 20mg qam. **Titrate:** May increase weekly by 10-20mg/day. **Max:** 60mg/day.	**≥6 yrs: Initial:** 20mg qam. **Titrate:** May increase weekly by 10-20mg/day. **Max:** 60mg/day.
Ritalin (Methylphenidate HCl)	**Tab:** 5mg, 10mg, 20mg	10-60mg/day given bid-tid 30-45 min ac. If insomnia occurs, take last dose before 6 pm.	**≥6 yrs: Initial:** 5mg bid before breakfast and lunch. **Titrate:** Increase gradually by 5-10mg weekly. **Max:** 60mg/day.

BRAND (GENERIC)	HOW SUPPLIED	ADULT DOSAGE	PEDIATRIC DOSAGE
Ritalin LA*, **Ritalin SR**† (Methylphenidate HCl)	**Cap, ER (Ritalin LA):** 10mg, 20mg, 30mg, 40mg; **Tab, ER (Ritalin SR):** 20mg	(Cap, ER) **Initial:** 10-20mg qam. **Titrate:** Adjust weekly by 10mg. **Max:** 60mg qam. (Tab, ER) May use in place of IR tabs when the 8-hr dose corresponds to the titrated 8-hr IR dose.	(Cap, ER) **≥6 yrs: Initial:** 10-20mg qam. **Titrate:** Adjust weekly by 10mg. **Max:** 60mg qam. (Tab, ER) May use in place of IR tabs when the 8-hr dose corresponds to the titrated 8-hr IR dose.
Strattera† (Atomoxetine HCl)	**Cap:** 10mg, 18mg, 25mg, 40mg, 60mg, 80mg, 100mg	**Initial:** 40mg/day. **Titrate:** Increase after minimum of 3 days to target dose of about 80mg/day given qam or as evenly divided doses in the am and late afternoon/early evening. After 2-4 weeks, may increase to max of 100mg/day. **Max:** 100mg/day.	**≥6 yrs: ≤70kg: Initial:** 0.5mg/kg/day. **Titrate:** Increase after minimum of 3 days to target dose of about 1.2mg/kg/day given qam or as evenly divided doses in the am and later afternoon/early evening. **Max:** 1.4mg/kg/day or 100mg, whichever is less. **>70kg:** Refer to adult dosing.
Vyvanse (Lisdexamfetamine dimesylate)	**Cap:** 20mg, 30mg, 40mg, 50mg, 60mg, 70mg	**Initial:** 30mg qam. **Titrate:** May increase weekly by 10mg or 20mg. **Max:** 70mg/day.	**≥6 yrs: Initial:** 30mg qam. **Titrate:** May increase weekly by 10mg or 20mg. **Max:** 70mg/day.
Zenzedi (Dextroamphetamine sulfate)	**Tab:** 2.5mg, 5mg, 7.5mg, 10mg	**≥6 yrs: Initial:** 5mg qd-bid. **Titrate:** May increase weekly by 5mg/day. **Max (Usual):** 40mg/day. **3-5 yrs: Initial:** 2.5mg qd. **Titrate:** May increase weekly by 2.5mg/day.

Refer to full FDA-approved labeling for additional information.

Abbreviations: ADHD = attention-deficit hyperactivity disorder; ER = extended-release; IR = immediate-release.

*Swallow cap whole or open cap and sprinkle contents on applesauce; do not chew beads.
†Swallow whole; do not chew, crush, or divide.

ALZHEIMER'S DISEASE AGENTS

GENERIC (BRAND)	HOW SUPPLIED	ADULT DOSAGE	SPECIAL INSTRUCTIONS
Donepezil HCl (Aricept)	**Tab:** 5mg, 10mg, 23mg; **Tab, Disintegrating:** 5mg, 10mg	**Mild-Moderate: Initial:** 5mg qhs. **Usual:** 5-10mg qhs. **Titrate:** May increase to 10mg after 4-6 weeks. **Moderate-Severe: Initial:** 5mg qhs. **Usual:** 10-23mg qhs. **Titrate:** May increase to 10mg after 4-6 weeks, then to 23mg after ≥3 months.	• Monitor for vagotonic effects on sinoatrial and atrioventricular nodes, syncopal episodes, diarrhea, N/V, active/occult GI bleeding, weight loss, bladder outflow obstruction, and generalized convulsions. • Do not split or crush 23mg tablet.
Ergoloid mesylates	**Tab:** 1mg	1mg tid.	• Monitor for transient nausea and gastric disturbances. • Monitor for relief of signs and symptoms.
Galantamine HBr (Razadyne, Razadyne ER)	(Razadyne) **Sol:** 4mg/mL [100mL]; **Tab:** 4mg, 8mg, 12mg; (Razadyne ER) **Cap, ER:** 8mg, 16mg, 24mg	(Sol, Tab) **Initial:** 4mg bid (8mg/day) with am and pm meals. **Titrate:** Increase to initial maint dose of 8mg bid (16mg/day) after a minimum of 4 weeks, then increase to 12mg bid (24mg/day) after a minimum of 4 weeks. Restart at the lowest dose and increase to current dose if therapy is interrupted for several days or longer. (Cap, ER) **Initial:** 8mg qd with am meal. **Titrate:** Increase to initial maint dose of 16mg qd after a minimum of 4 weeks, then increase to 24mg qd after a minimum of 4 weeks.	• Monitor for GI bleeding, cardiac conduction abnormalities, bladder outflow obstruction, and convulsions. • Not recommended for patients with severe renal/hepatic impairment. • Dose adjustment required for moderate renal/hepatic impairment.
Memantine HCl (Namenda, Namenda XR)	(Namenda) **Sol:** 2mg/mL [360mL]; **Tab:** 5mg, 10mg; (Namenda XR) **Cap, ER:** 7mg, 14mg, 21mg, 28mg	(Sol, Tab) **Initial:** 5mg qd. **Titrate:** Increase in 5mg increments to 10mg/day (5mg bid), 15mg/day (5mg and 10mg as separate doses), and 20mg/day (10mg bid) at ≥1-week intervals. Dosage shown to be effective in controlled clinical trials is 20mg/day. (Cap, ER) **Initial:** 7mg qd. **Titrate:** Increase in 7mg increments to 28mg qd at ≥1-week intervals. **Max/Target Dose:** 28mg qd.	• Monitor renal/hepatic function. • Do not divide or crush Namenda XR; capsules may be opened and sprinkled on applesauce. • Administer oral solution with dosing device and do not mix with any other liquid. • Dose adjustment required in severe renal insufficiency.

(Continued)

GENERIC (BRAND)	HOW SUPPLIED	ADULT DOSAGE	SPECIAL INSTRUCTIONS
Rivastigmine tartrate (Exelon)	**Cap:** 1.5mg, 3mg, 4.5mg, 6mg; **Patch:** 4.6mg/24 hrs, 9.5mg/24 hrs, 13.3mg/24 hrs; **Sol:** 2mg/mL [120mL]	(PO) **Initial:** 1.5mg bid. **Titrate:** May increase to 3mg bid after a minimum of 2 weeks, if 1.5mg bid is well tolerated. Subsequent increases to 4.5mg bid and 6mg bid should be attempted after a minimum of 2 weeks at the previous dose. **Max:** 12mg/day (6mg bid). If not tolerated, d/c therapy for several doses and restart at same or next lower dose. If interrupted longer than several days, reinitiate with lowest daily dose and titrate as above. (Patch) **Initial:** Apply 4.6mg/24 hrs patch qd to skin. **Titrate:** Increase dose only after a minimum of 4 weeks at the previous dose, and only if the previous dose is well tolerated. **Effective Dose: Mild-Moderate:** 9.5mg/24 hrs qd or 13.3mg/24 hrs qd. **Severe:** 13.3mg/24 hrs qd. **Max:** 13.3mg/24 hrs. Replace with a new patch q24h. **Interruption of Treatment: ≤3 Days Interruption:** Restart with same or lower strength patch. **>3 Days Interruption:** Restart with 4.6mg/24 hrs patch and titrate as above.	• Monitor for signs/symptoms of active or occult GI bleeding, extrapyramidal symptoms, urinary obstruction, seizures, and GI adverse events. • (Patch) Monitor for skin reactions. • (PO) Administer with meals in divided doses in am and pm. • Dose adjustment required for moderate to severe renal insufficiency, mild to moderate hepatic insufficiency, or low body weight.

Refer to full FDA-approved labeling for additional information.

Abbreviation: ER = extended-release.

ANTIPARKINSON AGENTS

GENERIC (BRAND)	HOW SUPPLIED	ADULT DOSAGE	SIDE EFFECTS
Amantadine HCl	Cap, Tab: 100mg; Sol: 50mg/5mL	Parkinsonism: Usual: 100mg bid. Serious Associated Illness/Concomitant High-Dose Antiparkinson Agent: Initial: 100mg qd. Titrate: May increase to 100mg bid after 1 to several weeks. Max: 400mg/day. Drug-Induced Extrapyramidal Reactions: Usual: 100mg bid. Max: 300mg/day. Renal Impairment: See PI for dosing adjustments.	Nausea, dizziness, insomnia, depression, anxiety and irritability, hallucinations, confusion, anorexia, dry mouth, constipation, ataxia, livedo reticularis, peripheral edema, orthostatic hypotension, headache, somnolence, nervousness, dream abnormality, agitation, dry nose, diarrhea, fatigue
Apomorphine HCl (Apokyn)	Inj: 10mg/mL	Test Dose: 0.2mL (2mg) SQ; assess efficacy/tolerability. See PI for details. Max: 0.6mL (6mg)/dose. Renal Impairment: Test Dose/Initial: 0.1mL (1mg).	Yawning, dyskinesia, nausea, vomiting, somnolence, dizziness, rhinorrhea, hallucinations, edema, chest pain, increased sweating, flushing, pallor
Benztropine mesylate (Cogentin)	Inj: 1mg/mL; (Generic) Tab: 0.5mg, 1mg, 2mg	Initiate with a low dose. Titrate: May increase every 5-6 days by 0.5mg. Max: 6mg/day. Postencephalitic/Idiopathic Parkinsonism: Usual: 1-2mg/day. Range: 0.5-6mg/day. Idiopathic Parkinsonism: Initial: 0.5-1mg PO or IV/IM qhs. Postencephalitic Parkinsonism: Initial: 2mg/day PO or IV/IM given in 1 or more doses. Highly Sensitive Patients: Initial: 0.5mg PO or IV/IM qhs; increase as necessary. Drug-Induced Extrapyramidal Disorders: Usual: 1-4mg PO or IV/IM qd or bid. Give 1-2mg bid or tid for transient extrapyramidal disorders that develop soon after initiation of neuroleptic drugs; d/c and reevaluate necessity after 1 or 2 weeks. May reinstitute therapy if disorders recur.	Tachycardia, paralytic ileus, constipation, vomiting, nausea, dry mouth, confusion, blurred vision, urinary retention, heat stroke, hyperthermia, fever
Bromocriptine mesylate (Parlodel)	Tab, Snap: 2.5mg*; Cap: 5mg	Initial: ½ SnapTab. Titrate: May increase by 2.5mg/day q2-4 weeks. Max: 100mg/day. Take with food. Assess need for medication at 2-week intervals.	Dizziness, insomnia, hallucinations, dyskinesia, visual disturbance, nausea, confusion, drowsiness, vomiting, abdominal pain, hypotension, constipation
Carbidopa (Lodosyn)	Tab: 25mg*	With Sinemet or Levodopa: Determine dose by careful titration. Most patients respond to a 1:10 proportion of carbidopa and levodopa, provided carbidopa dose is ≥70mg/day. Max: 200mg/day. Consider amount of carbidopa in Sinemet when calculating dose. See PI for detailed dosing information.	Dyskinesia (choreiform, dystonic, and other involuntary movements), nausea; check PI for a more comprehensive list of adverse reactions
Carbidopa/Levodopa (Parcopa)	Tab, Disintegrating: (Carbidopa-Levodopa) 10mg-100mg*, 25mg-100mg*, 25mg-250mg*	25mg-100mg Tab: Initial: 1 tab tid. Titrate: Increase by 1 tab qd or qod up to 8 tabs/day. 10mg-100mg Tab: Initial: 1 tab tid-qid. Titrate: Increase by 1 tab qd or qod up to 8 tabs/day. Maint: 70-100mg/day carbidopa required. Max: 200mg/day carbidopa. Conversion from Levodopa: See PI.	Dyskinesia (choreiform, dystonic, and other involuntary movements), nausea; check PI for a more comprehensive list of adverse reactions

(Continued)

GENERIC (BRAND)	HOW SUPPLIED	ADULT DOSAGE	SIDE EFFECTS
Carbidopa/Levodopa (Sinemet, Sinemet CR)	**Tab:** (Carbidopa-Levodopa) 10mg-100mg, 25mg-100mg, 25mg-250mg; **Tab, ER:** 25mg-100mg, 50mg-200mg	(Tab) **25mg-100mg Tab: Initial:** 1 tab tid. **Titrate:** Increase by 1 tab qd or qod up to 8 tabs/day. **10mg-100mg Tab: Initial:** 1 tab tid-qid. **Titrate:** May increase by 1 tab qd or qod up to 8 tabs/day. **Maint:** 70-100mg/day carbidopa required. **Max:** 200mg/day carbidopa. **Conversion from Levodopa:** See PI. (Tab, ER) **No Prior Levodopa Use: Initial:** One 50mg-200mg tab bid at intervals ≥6 hrs. **Titrate:** Increase or decrease dose or interval accordingly. Adjust dose at interval of ≥3 days. **Usual:** 400-1600mg/day levodopa, given in 4-8 hr intervals while awake. **Conversion to ER Tabs:** See PI.	Dyskinesia (choreiform, dystonic, and other involuntary movements), nausea; check PI for a more comprehensive list of adverse reactions
Carbidopa/Levodopa/ Entacapone (Stalevo)	**Tab:** (Carbidopa/Levodopa/ Entacapone): Stalevo 50: 12.5mg/50mg/200mg; Stalevo 75: 18.75mg/75mg/200mg; Stalevo 100: 25mg/100mg/200mg; Stalevo 125: 31.25mg/125mg/200mg; Stalevo 150: 37.5mg/150mg/200mg; Stalevo 200: 50mg/200mg/200mg	**Currently Taking Carbidopa/Levodopa and Entacapone:** May switch directly to corresponding strength of Stalevo with same amounts of carbidopa/levodopa. **Currently Taking Carbidopa/Levodopa without Entacapone:** First, titrate individually with carbidopa/levodopa product and entacapone product, then transfer to corresponding dose once stabilized. **Max:** 8 tabs/day (Stalevo 50, 75, 100, 125, 150); 6 tabs/day (Stalevo 200).	Dyskinesia (choreiform, dystonic, and other involuntary movements), nausea; check PI for a more comprehensive list of adverse reactions
Diphenhydramine HCl Injection	**Inj:** 50mg/mL	**Usual:** 10-50mg IV at ≤25mg/min or deep IM. May use 100mg IM if needed. **Max:** 400mg/day.	Sedation, sleepiness, dizziness, disturbed coordination, epigastric distress, thickening of bronchial secretions
Entacapone (Comtan)	**Tab:** 200mg	**Usual:** 200mg administered concomitantly with each levodopa/carbidopa dose. **Max:** 1600mg/day. Withdraw slowly for discontinuation.	Dyskinesia, hyperkinesia, hypokinesia, dizziness, nausea, diarrhea, abdominal pain, constipation, urine discoloration, fatigue
Hyoscyamine sulfate (Levbid, Levsin)	(Levbid) **Tab, ER:** 0.375mg. (Levsin) **Tab:** 0.125mg; **Tab, SL:** 0.125mg	**Levbid:** 0.375-0.75mg q12h. **Max:** 1.5mg/24 hrs. Do not crush or chew. **Levsin:** 0.125-0.25mg q4h or prn. **Max:** 1.5mg/24 hrs. May chew or swallow SL tab.	Dry mouth, urinary hesitancy and retention, blurred vision, tachycardia, mydriasis, increased ocular tension, loss of taste, headache, nervousness, drowsiness, weakness, fatigue, dizziness, nausea, vomiting
Pramipexole dihydrochloride (Mirapex)	**Tab:** 0.125mg, 0.25mg*, 0.5mg*, 0.75mg, 1mg*, 1.5mg*	**Initial:** 0.125mg tid. **Titrate:** May increase not more frequently than every 5-7 days (eg, Week 2: 0.25mg tid; Week 3: 0.5mg tid; Week 4: 0.75mg tid; Week 5: 1mg tid; Week 6: 1.25mg tid; Week 7: 1.5mg tid). **Maint:** 0.5-1.5mg tid. **Max:** 1.5mg tid.†	Nausea, dizziness, somnolence, constipation, asthenia, hallucinations, vision abnormalities, general and peripheral edema, insomnia, confusion, amnesia, hypoesthesia
(Mirapex ER)	**Tab, ER:** 0.375mg, 0.75mg, 1.5mg, 2.25mg, 3mg, 3.75mg, 4.5mg	**Initial:** 0.375mg qd. **Titrate:** May increase not more frequently than every 5-7 days, first to 0.75mg/day and then by 0.75mg increments based on efficacy and tolerability. **Max:** 4.5mg/day. **Switching from IR to ER:** May switch overnight from IR to ER tablets at same daily dose.†	Somnolence, nausea, constipation, dizziness, fatigue, hallucinations, dry mouth, muscle spasms, peripheral edema, dyskinesia, headache, anorexia

GENERIC (BRAND)	HOW SUPPLIED	ADULT DOSAGE	SIDE EFFECTS
Rasagiline mesylate (Azilect)	**Tab:** 0.5mg, 1mg	**Monotherapy:** 1mg qd. **Adjunctive Therapy: Initial:** 0.5mg qd. **Titrate:** May increase to 1mg qd. Adjust dose of levodopa with concomitant use. **Concomitant Ciprofloxacin or Other CYP1A2 Inhibitors/Mild Hepatic Impairment:** 0.5mg qd.	Headache, accidental injury, arthralgia, depression, fall, flu syndrome, dyskinesia, nausea, weight loss, constipation, postural hypotension, vomiting, dry mouth, rash, somnolence
Rivastigmine (Exelon)	**Cap:** 1.5mg, 3mg, 4.5mg, 6mg; **Patch:** 4.6mg/24 hrs, 9.5mg/24 hrs, 13.3mg/24 hrs; **Sol:** 2mg/mL	(Cap, Sol) **Usual:** 1.5-6mg bid. **Initial:** 1.5mg bid with meals in am and pm. **Titrate:** May subsequently increase to 3mg bid and further to 4.5mg bid and 6mg bid with a minimum of 4 weeks at each dose, based on tolerability. (Patch) **Usual:** 9.5mg/24 hrs or 13.3mg/24 hrs qd. **Initial:** Apply 4.6mg/24 hrs patch qd to clean, dry, hairless, intact skin. **Titrate:** Increase dose only after a minimum of 4 weeks, if well tolerated. Continue effective dose of 9.5mg/24 hrs for as long as therapeutic benefit persists. **Max:** 13.3mg/24 hrs.	Nausea, vomiting, anorexia, dizziness, diarrhea
Ropinirole HCl (Requip, Requip XL)	**Tab:** 0.25mg, 0.5mg, 1mg, 2mg, 3mg, 4mg, 5mg; **Tab, ER:** 2mg, 4mg, 6mg, 8mg, 12mg	**Initial:** 0.25mg tid. **Titrate:** May increase weekly by 0.25mg tid (0.75mg/day) for 4 weeks. After Week 4, may increase weekly by 1.5mg/day up to 9mg/day, then by 3mg/day weekly to 24mg/day. **Max:** 24mg/day. **Withdrawal:** Decrease dose to bid for 4 days, then qd for 3 days. (Tab, ER) **Initial:** 2mg qd for 1-2 weeks. **Titrate:** May increase at ≥1-week intervals by 2mg/day. **Max:** 24mg/day. **Switching from IR to ER:** Closely match total daily IR dose with initial ER dose. See PI for detailed information.	Dyskinesia, hallucinations, somnolence, vomiting, headache, constipation, dyspepsia, abdominal pain, pharyngitis, UTI, increased sweating, asthenia, edema, fatigue, syncope, orthostatic symptoms, dizziness, nausea, viral infection, confusion, abnormal vision
Rotigotine (Neupro)	**Patch:** 1mg/24 hrs, 2mg/24 hrs, 3mg/24 hrs, 4mg/24 hrs, 6mg/24 hrs, 8mg/24 hrs	**Early-Stage: Initial:** 2mg/24 hrs. **Titrate:** May increase weekly by 2mg/24 hrs based on response and tolerability. **Lowest Effective Dose:** 4mg/24 hrs. **Max:** 6mg/24 hrs. **Advanced-Stage: Initial:** 4mg/24 hrs. **Titrate:** May increase weekly by 2mg/24 hrs based on response and tolerability. **Usual:** 8mg/24 hrs.	Nausea, vomiting, somnolence, application-site reactions, dizziness, anorexia, hyperhidrosis, insomnia
Selegiline (Zelapar)	**Tab, Disintegrating:** 1.25mg	**Initial:** 1.25mg qd before breakfast for ≥6 weeks. **Titrate:** After 6 weeks, may increase to 2.5mg qd if the desired benefit is not achieved and patient can tolerate it. **Max:** 2.5mg/day.	Nausea, dizziness, pain, headache, insomnia, rhinitis, skin disorders, dyskinesia, back pain, dyspepsia, stomatitis, constipation, hallucinations, pharyngitis, rash
Selegiline HCl (Eldepryl)	**Cap:** 5mg; (Generic) **Tab:** 5mg	5mg bid at breakfast and lunch. **Max:** 10mg/day. May attempt to reduce levodopa/carbidopa by 10-30% after 2-3 days of therapy. May reduce further with continued therapy.	Nausea, dizziness, lightheadedness, fainting, abdominal pain, confusion, hallucinations, dry mouth

(Continued)

GENERIC (BRAND)	HOW SUPPLIED	ADULT DOSAGE	SIDE EFFECTS
Tolcapone (Tasmar)	**Tab:** 100mg	**Initial:** 100mg tid. Use 200mg tid only if clinical benefit is justified. May need to decrease levodopa dose.	Dyskinesia, nausea, sleep disorder, dystonia, excessive dreaming, anorexia, muscle cramps, orthostatic complaints, somnolence, diarrhea, confusion, dizziness, headache, hallucination, vomiting, constipation, fatigue, upper respiratory tract infection, falling, increased sweating, UTI, xerostomia, abdominal pain, urine discoloration, hepatotoxicity (including liver failure)
Trihexyphenidyl HCl	**Sol:** 2mg/5mL; **Tab:** 2mg*, 5mg*	**Idiopathic Parkinsonism:** 1mg on Day 1. **Titrate:** May increase by 2mg increments at intervals of 3-5 days, until 6-10mg/day is given. **Postencephalitic Patients:** May require 12-15mg/day. **Drug-Induced Parkinsonism: Initial:** 1mg. **Titrate:** If extrapyramidal manifestations not controlled in a few hrs, increase dose until control is achieved. **Usual:** 5-15mg/day. **Concomitant Levodopa or Other Parasympathetic Inhibitors:** See PI.	Dry mouth, blurred vision, dizziness, nausea, nervousness, constipation, drowsiness, urinary hesitancy/retention, tachycardia, pupil dilation, increased intraocular pressure, vomiting, weakness, headache

Refer to full FDA-approved labeling for additional information.

Abbreviations: ER = extended-release; IR = immediate-release; SL = sublingual.

*Scored.

†Refer to FDA-approved labeling for dosing instructions in renally compromised patients.

OPIOID PRODUCTS

GENERIC	BRAND	DEA SCHEDULE	DOSAGE FORMS	ADDITIONAL COMMENTS
MILD TO MODERATELY SEVERE PAIN				
Codeine sulfate		Schedule II	**Tab:** 15mg, 30mg, 60mg; **Sol:** 30mg/5mL	• **BW:** Death related to ultra-rapid metabolism of codeine to morphine • Pregnancy category C, caution in nursing
Codeine phosphate/Acetaminophen		Schedule V	**Sol:** 12mg-120mg/5mL	• **BW:** Hepatotoxicity • Pregnancy category C, not for use in nursing
		Schedule III	**Tab:** 15mg-300mg	
	Tylenol #3	Schedule III	**Tab:** 30mg-300mg	
	Tylenol #4	Schedule III	**Tab:** 60mg-300mg	
MODERATE TO MODERATELY SEVERE PAIN				
Dihydrocodeine bitartrate/Aspirin/ Caffeine	Synalgos-DC	Schedule III	**Cap:** 16mg-356.4mg-30mg	• **BW:** Death related to ultra-rapid metabolism of codeine to morphine • Safety not known in pregnancy, not for use in nursing
Hydrocodone bitartrate/ Acetaminophen	Norco	Schedule III	**Tab:** 5mg-325mg, 7.5mg-325mg, 10mg-325mg	• **BW:** Hepatotoxicity • Pregnancy category C, not for use in nursing
	Vicodin		**Tab:** 5mg-300mg	
	Vicodin ES		**Tab:** 7.5mg-300mg	
	Vicodin HP		**Tab:** 10mg-300mg	
Hydrocodone bitartrate/Ibuprofen	Reprexain	Schedule III	**Tab:** 2.5mg-200mg, 5mg-200mg, 10mg-200mg	• Pregnancy category C, not for use in nursing
	Vicoprofen		**Tab:** 7.5-200mg	
Oxycodone HCl/Acetaminophen	Percocet	Schedule II	**Tab:** 2.5mg-325mg, 5mg-325mg, 7.5mg-325mg, 10mg-325mg	• **BW:** Hepatotoxicity • Pregnancy category C, not for use in nursing
	Roxicet		**Tab:** 5mg-325mg; **Sol:** 5mg-325mg/5mL	
Oxycodone HCl/Aspirin	Percodan	Schedule II	**Tab:** 4.8355mg-325mg	• Pregnancy category B (oxycodone) and D (aspirin), not for use in nursing

(Continued)

GENERIC	BRAND	DEA SCHEDULE	DOSAGE FORMS	ADDITIONAL COMMENTS
MODERATE TO SEVERE OR CHRONIC PAIN				
Buprenorphine	Butrans	Schedule III	**Patch:** 5mcg/hr, 10mcg/hr, 15mcg/hr, 20mcg/hr	• **BW:** Abuse potential, life-threatening respiratory depression, and accidental exposure • Pregnancy category C, not for use in nursing
Fentanyl	Duragesic	Schedule II	**Patch:** 12mcg/hr, 25mcg/hr, 50mcg/hr, 75mcg/hr, 100mcg/hr	• **BW:** Abuse potential, life-threatening respiratory depression, and accidental exposure • Pregnancy category C, not for use in nursing
Hydromorphone HCl	Dilaudid, Dilaudid-HP	Schedule II	**Tab:** 2mg, 4mg, 8mg; **Sol:** 1mg/mL; **Inj:** 1mg/mL, 2mg/mL, 4mg/mL; **HP: Inj:** 10mg/mL [1mL, 5mL, 50mL], 250mg (sterile, lyophilized powder)	• **BW:** Risk of respiratory depression, abuse, and medication errors. Dilaudid-HP injection is for use in opioid-tolerant patients only • Pregnancy category C, not for use in nursing
	Exalgo		**Tab, ER:** 8mg, 12mg, 16mg, 32mg	
Levorphanol tartrate		Schedule II	**Tab:** 2mg	• Pregnancy category C, not for use in nursing
Meperidine HCl	Demerol	Schedule II	**Sol:** 50mg/5mL	• Pregnancy category C, not for use in nursing
			Tab: 50mg, 100mg; **Inj:** 25mg/mL, 50mg/mL, 75mg/mL, 100mg/mL	
Methadone HCl		Schedule II	**Inj:** 10mg/mL	• **BW:** Life-threatening QT prolongation • Pregnancy category C, not for use in nursing
			Sol: 5mg/5mL, 10mg/5mL	• **BW:** Abuse potential, life-threatening respiratory depression, life-threatening QT prolongation, accidental exposure, and treatment for opioid addiction • Pregnancy category C, caution in nursing
	Dolophine		**Tab:** 5mg, 10mg	
	Methadose		**Sol, Concentrated:** 10mg/mL; **Tab:** 5mg, 10mg; **Tab, Dispersible:** 40mg	
Morphine sulfate/Naltrexone HCl	Embeda	Schedule II	**Cap, ER:** 20mg-0.8mg, 30mg-1.2mg, 50mg-2mg, 60mg-2.4mg, 80mg-3.2mg, 100mg-4mg	• **BW:** Abuse potential, life-threatening respiratory depression, accidental exposure, and interaction with alcohol • Pregnancy category C, not for use in nursing
Morphine sulfate		Schedule II	**Tab:** 15mg, 30mg; **Sol:** 10mg/5mL, 20mg/5mL, 100mg/5mL; **Inj:** 2mg/mL, 4mg/mL, 8mg/mL, 10mg/mL, 15mg/mL	• **BW:** (Sol) Risk of medication errors. The 100mg/5mL is indicated for opioid-tolerant patients only • Pregnancy category C, not for use in nursing
	Astramorph/PF		**Inj:** 0.5mg/mL, 1mg/mL	• Pregnancy category C, safety not known in nursing

GENERIC	BRAND	DEA SCHEDULE	DOSAGE FORMS	ADDITIONAL COMMENTS
MODERATE TO SEVERE OR CHRONIC PAIN *(Continued)*				
Morphine sulfate *(Continued)*	Avinza	Schedule II	**Cap, ER:** 30mg, 45mg, 60mg, 75mg, 90mg, 120mg	• **BW:** Abuse potential, life-threatening respiratory depression, accidental exposure, and interaction with alcohol • Pregnancy category C, not for use in nursing
	Duramorph		**Inj:** 0.5mg/mL, 1mg/mL	• **BW:** Risk of severe adverse reactions with epidural or intrathecal route; observe patients in an equipped and staffed environment for at least 24 hrs after initial dose • Pregnancy category C, safety not known in nursing
	Infumorph		**Inj:** 0.5mg/mL (5mg/10mL), 1mg/mL (10mg/10mL), 10mg/mL (200mg/20mL), 25mg/mL (500mg/20mL)	• **BW:** Not recommended for single-dose IV, IM, or SQ administration. Risk of severe adverse reactions; observe patients in an equipped and staffed environment for at least 24 hrs after an initial (single) test dose, and as appropriate, for the 1st several days after catheter implantation • Pregnancy category C, safety not known in nursing
	Kadian		**Cap, ER:** 10mg, 20mg, 30mg, 40mg, 50mg, 60mg, 70mg, 80mg, 100mg, 130mg, 150mg, 200mg	• **BW:** Abuse potential, life-threatening respiratory depression, and accidental exposure • Pregnancy category C, not for use in nursing
	MS Contin		**Tab, ER:** 15mg, 30mg, 60mg, 100mg, 200mg	• **BW:** Abuse potential, life-threatening respiratory depression, and accidental exposure • Pregnancy category C, not for use in nursing
Oxycodone HCl		Schedule II	**Cap:** 5mg; **Sol:** 1mg/mL, 20mg/mL	• **BW:** (Sol) Risk of medication errors. The 100mg/5mL is indicated for opioid-tolerant patients only • Pregnancy category B, not for use in nursing
	Oxecta		**Tab:** 5mg, 7.5mg	
	Roxicodone		**Tab:** 5mg, 15mg, 30mg	
	OxyContin		**Tab, ER:** 10mg, 15mg, 20mg, 30mg, 40mg, 60mg, 80mg	• **BW:** (OxyContin) Abuse potential, life-threatening respiratory depression, and accidental exposure • Pregnancy category B, not for use in nursing
Oxymorphone HCl	Opana	Schedule II	**Inj:** 1mg/mL; **Tab:** 5mg, 10mg	• Pregnancy category C, caution in nursing
	Opana ER		**Tab, ER:** 5mg, 7.5mg, 10mg, 15mg, 20mg, 30mg, 40mg	• **BW:** Abuse potential, life-threatening respiratory depression, accidental exposure, and interaction with alcohol • Pregnancy category C, caution in nursing
Tapentadol	Nucynta	Schedule II	**Tab:** 50mg, 75mg, 100mg	• **BW:** (Nucynta ER) Abuse potential, life-threatening respiratory depression, accidental exposure, and interaction with alcohol • Pregnancy category C, not for use in nursing
	Nucynta ER		**Tab, ER:** 50mg, 100mg, 150mg, 200mg, 250mg	

(Continued)

GENERIC	BRAND	DEA SCHEDULE	DOSAGE FORMS	ADDITIONAL COMMENTS
BREAKTHROUGH PAIN				
Fentanyl	Abstral	Schedule II	**Tab, SL:** 100mcg, 200mcg, 300mcg, 400mcg, 600mcg, 800mcg	• **BW:** Risk of respiratory depression, medication errors, and abuse potential • Pregnancy category C, not for use in nursing
	Fentora		**Tab, Buccal:** 100mcg, 200mcg, 400mcg, 600mcg, 800mcg	
	Lazanda		**Nasal:** 100mcg/spr, 400mcg/spr	
	Subsys		**Spr, SL:** 100mcg/spr, 200mcg/spr, 400mcg/spr, 600mcg/spr, 800mcg/spr, 1200mcg/spr, 1600mcg/spr	
Fentanyl citrate	Actiq	Schedule II	**Loz:** 200mcg, 400mcg, 600mcg, 800mcg, 1200mcg, 1600mcg	• **BW:** Risk of respiratory depression, medication errors, and abuse potential • Pregnancy category C, not for use in nursing

Refer to full FDA-approved labeling for more detailed dosing.

Abbreviations: BW = boxed warning; ER = extended-release; SL = sublingual.

ORAL ANTICONVULSANTS

GENERIC (BRAND)	USUAL ADULT DOSAGE*	THERAPEUTIC SERUM LEVELS	ABSENCE	AKINETIC	LENNOX-GASTAUT SYNDROME	MYOCLONIC	PARTIAL	TONIC-CLONIC	NEUROPATHIC PAIN
BARBITURATES									
Phenobarbital†	60-300mg/day	N/A					X		
Primidone (Mysoline)	750-2000mg/day	5-12mcg/mL					X	X	
BENZODIAZEPINES									
Clobazam (Onfi)	10-40mg/day	N/A			X				
Clonazepam (Klonopin)	1.5-20mg/day	N/A	X	X	X	X			
Clorazepate dipotassium (Tranxene T-Tab)	22.5-90mg/day	N/A					X		
Diazepam (Valium)‡	4-40mg/day	N/A							
HYDANTOINS									
Ethotoin (Peganone)	2000-3000mg/day	N/A					X	X	
Phenytoin (Dilantin, Dilantin-125, Dilantin Infatabs, Phenytek)	300-600mg/day (Sus.: 375-625mg/day)	10-20mcg/mL					X	X	
SUCCINIMIDES									
Ethosuximide (Zarontin)	500-1500mg/day	40-100mcg/mL	X						
Methsuximide (Celontin)	300-1200mg/day	N/A	X						
MISCELLANEOUS									
Carbamazepine (Carbatrol, Tegretol, Tegretol XR)	Epilepsy: 800-1200mg/day Trigeminal Neuralgia: 400-800mg/day	4-12mcg/mL					X	X	X
Divalproex sodium§ (Depakote, Depakote ER, Depakote Sprinkle Capsules)	10-60mg/kg/day	50-100mcg/mL	X				X		

(Continued)

INDICATIONS

GENERIC (BRAND)	USUAL ADULT DOSAGE*	THERAPEUTIC SERUM LEVELS	ABSENCE	AKINETIC	LENNOX-GASTAUT SYNDROME	MYOCLONIC	PARTIAL	TONIC-CLONIC	NEUROPATHIC PAIN
					SEIZURE DISORDERS				
MISCELLANEOUS *(Continued)*									
Valproic acid[6] (Depakene, Stavzor)	10-60mg/kg/day	50-100mcg/mL	X						
Eslicarbazepine (Aptiom)	800-1200mg/day	N/A					X		
Ezogabine (Potiga)	600-1200mg/day	N/A					X		
Felbamate[1] (Felbatol)	2400-3600mg/day	N/A			X		X		
Gabapentin (Neurontin)	Epilepsy: 900-1800mg/day Postherpetic Neuralgia: 1800-3600mg/day	N/A					X		X
Lacosamide (Vimpat)	200-400mg/day	N/A					X		
Lamotrigine (Lamictal, Lamictal ODT, Lamictal XR)	100-500mg/day (Lamictal XR: 200-600mg/day)	N/A			X (IR, ODT)		X	X	
Levetiracetam (Keppra, Keppra XR)	1000-3000mg/day	N/A				X (IR)	X	X (IR)	
Oxcarbazepine (Oxtellar XR, Trileptal)	1200-2400mg/day	N/A					X		
Pregabalin (Lyrica)	Epilepsy: 150-600mg/day Neuropathic Pain Associated with Diabetic Peripheral Neuropathy/Postherpetic Neuralgia: 150-300mg/day	N/A					X		X
Rufinamide (Banzel)	3200mg/day	N/A			X				
Tiagabine HCl (Gabitril)	32-56mg/day	N/A					X		

GENERIC (BRAND)	USUAL ADULT DOSAGE*	THERAPEUTIC SERUM LEVELS	INDICATIONS							NEUROPATHIC PAIN
			SEIZURE DISORDERS							
			ABSENCE	AKINETIC	LENNOX-GASTAUT SYNDROME	MYOCLONIC	PARTIAL	TONIC-CLONIC		
MISCELLANEOUS *(Continued)*										
Topiramate (Qudexy XR, Topamax, Topamax Sprinkle, Trokendi XR)	200-400mg/day	N/A			X		X	X		
Vigabatrin (Sabril)	3g/day	N/A					X			
Zonisamide (Zonegran)	100-400mg/day	N/A					X			

Abbreviation: N/A = not applicable.

* Refer to complete monograph for full dosing information, including pediatric dosing.
† Phenobarbital is also indicated in generalized seizures.
‡ Oral Valium may be used adjunctively in convulsive disorders, although it has not proved useful as the sole therapy.
§ Divalproex sodium and valproic acid are also indicated as adjuncts in multiple seizure types.
¶ For severe epilepsy refractory to other treatment where the risk of aplastic anemia and/or liver failure is deemed acceptable. Fully advise patient and obtain written, informed consent before treatment. Closely monitor patient.

TREATMENT OF SLEEP DISORDERS

GENERIC (BRAND)	HOW SUPPLIED	ADULT DOSAGE	SPECIAL POPULATIONS
INSOMNIA			
H₁ ANTAGONISTS			
Doxepin (Silenor)	**Tab:** 3mg, 6mg	**Initial:** 6mg qd within 30 min of hs. May decrease to 3mg. **Max:** 6mg/day.	**Elderly ≥65 yrs: Initial:** 3mg qd. May increase to 6mg. **Hepatic Impairment: Initial:** 3mg.
BARBITURATES			
Butabarbital sodium (Butisol)	**Sol:** 30mg/5mL; **Tab:** 30mg*, 50mg*	**Daytime Sedative:** 15-30mg tid or qid. **Bedtime Hypnotic:** 50-100mg.	**Elderly/Debilitated/Hepatic or Renal Impairment:** Reduce dose.
Pentobarbital sodium (Nembutal)	**Inj:** 50mg/mL [20mL, 50mL]	**IM: Usual:** 150-200mg (max 5mL/inj) as a single deep inj. **IV:** Inject slowly (max 50mg/min). **70kg: Initial:** 100mg. May give additional small increments up to 200-500mg total dose for normal adults prn.	**Debilitated/Hepatic or Renal Impairment:** Reduce dose. **Elderly:** Start at lower end of dosing range. **Peds: IM: Usual:** 2-6mg/kg (max 5mL/inj) as a single deep inj. **Max:** 100mg. **IV:** Inject slowly (max 50mg/min).
Secobarbital sodium (Seconal)	**Cap:** 100mg	**Hypnotic:** 100mg hs.	**Elderly/Debilitated/Hepatic or Renal Impairment:** Reduce dose.
BENZODIAZEPINES			
Estazolam†	**Tab:** 1mg*, 2mg*	**Initial:** 1-2mg hs.	**Small/Debilitated Elderly: Initial:** 0.5mg hs.
Flurazepam HCl†	**Cap:** 15mg, 30mg	**Usual:** 15-30mg hs.	**Elderly/Debilitated: Initial:** 15mg hs. **Peds ≥15 yrs:** 15-30mg hs.
Quazepam (Doral)	**Tab:** 15mg*	**Initial:** 7.5mg. May increase to 15mg if necessary.	**Elderly:** Start at lower end of dosing range.
Temazepam† (Restoril)	**Cap:** 7.5mg, 15mg, 22.5mg, 30mg	**Usual:** 15mg hs. **Range:** 7.5-30mg. **Transient Insomnia:** 7.5mg hs.	**Elderly/Debilitated: Initial:** 7.5mg hs.
Triazolam† (Halcion)	**Tab:** 0.25mg*	**Usual:** 0.25mg hs. **Max:** 0.5mg.	**Elderly/Debilitated: Initial:** 0.125mg hs. **Max:** 0.25mg.
IMIDAZOPYRIDINE HYPNOTICS			
Zolpidem tartrate (Ambien, Ambien CR, Edluar, Intermezzo, Zolpimist)	(Ambien) **Tab:** 5mg, 10mg	**Initial:** (Women) 5mg qhs, (Men) 5 or 10mg qhs. May increase to 10mg if the 5mg dose is not effective. **Max:** 10mg/day.	**Elderly/Debilitated/Hepatic Insufficiency:** 5mg qhs.
	(Ambien CR) **Tab, ER:** 6.25mg, 12.5mg	**Initial:** (Women) 6.25mg qhs, (Men) 6.25 or 12.5mg qhs. May increase to 12.5mg if the 6.25mg dose is not effective. **Max:** 12.5mg/day.	**Elderly/Debilitated/Hepatic Insufficiency:** 6.25mg qhs.
	(Edluar) **Tab, SL:** 5mg, 10mg	**Initial:** (Women) 5mg qhs, (Men) 5 or 10mg qhs. May increase to 10mg if the 5mg dose is not effective. **Max:** 10mg/day.	**Elderly/Debilitated/Hepatic Insufficiency:** 5mg qhs.
	(Intermezzo) **Tab, SL:** 1.75mg, 3.5mg	**Usual/Max:** (Women) 1.75mg, (Men) 3.5mg once per night prn if a middle-of-the-night awakening is followed by difficulty returning to sleep.	**Elderly >65 yrs/Hepatic Insufficiency:** 1.75mg qhs.

(Continued)

GENERIC (BRAND)	HOW SUPPLIED	ADULT DOSAGE	SPECIAL POPULATIONS
INSOMNIA *(Continued)*			
IMIDAZOPYRIDINE HYPNOTICS *(Continued)*			
Zolpidem tartrate (Ambien, Ambien CR, Edluar, Intermezzo, Zolpimist) *(Continued)*	(Zolpimist) **Spray:** 5mg/spray [8.2g]	**Initial:** (Women) 5mg qhs, (Men) 5 or 10mg qhs. May increase to 10mg if the 5mg dose is not effective. **Max:** 10mg/day.	**Elderly/Debilitated/Hepatic Insufficiency:** 5mg qhs.
MELATONIN RECEPTOR AGONISTS			
Ramelteon (Rozerem)	**Tab:** 8mg	**Usual:** 8mg within 30 min of hs. **Max:** 8mg/day.	**Hepatic Impairment:** (Severe) not recommended, (Moderate) caution.
NONBENZODIAZEPINE HYPNOTICS			
Eszopiclone (Lunesta)	**Tab:** 1mg, 2mg, 3mg	**Initial:** 2mg hs. May be initiated at or raised to 3mg prn.	**Elderly: Difficulty Falling Asleep: Initial:** 1mg hs. May increase to 2mg prn. **Difficulty Staying Asleep:** 2mg hs. **Severe Hepatic Impairment: Initial:** 1mg hs.
Zaleplon (Sonata)	**Cap:** 5mg, 10mg	10mg hs.	**Low Weight Patients:** 5mg hs. **Max:** 20mg. **Elderly/Debilitated:** 5mg hs. **Max:** 10mg. **Mild to Moderate Hepatic Insufficiency:** 5mg hs.
NARCOLEPSY			
CNS DEPRESSANTS			
Sodium oxybate (Xyrem)	**Sol:** 0.5g/mL [180mL]	**Initial:** 4.5g/night in 2 equally divided doses (2.25g hs at least 2 hrs pc, then 2.25g taken 2.5-4 hrs later). Increase by 1.5g/night (0.75g/dose) at weekly intervals to effective dose range of 6-9g/night. **Max:** 9g/night.	**Hepatic Impairment: Initial:** 2.25g/night in 2 equally divided doses (approx. 1.13g hs at least 2 hrs pc, then 1.13g taken 2.5-4 hrs later). **Elderly:** Start at lower end of dose range.
WAKEFULNESS-PROMOTING AGENTS			
Armodafinil (Nuvigil)	**Tab:** 50mg, 150mg, 200mg, 250mg	150mg or 250mg qam.‡	**Severe Hepatic Impairment w/ or w/o Cirrhosis:** Reduce dose. **Elderly:** Consider lower doses.
Modafinil (Provigil)	**Tab:** 100mg, 200mg*	200-400mg qam as single dose.‡	**Severe Hepatic Impairment:** 100mg qam. **Elderly:** Consider dose reduction.
SYMPATHOMIMETIC AMINES			
Amphetamine salt combo (Adderall)	**Tab:** 5mg*, 7.5mg*, 10mg*, 12.5mg*, 15mg*, 20mg*, 30mg*	**Initial:** 10mg/day. May increase by 10mg weekly. **Usual:** 5-60mg/day in divided doses. Give 1st dose upon awakening, and additional doses (1 or 2) q4-6h.	**Peds: ≥12 yrs: Initial:** 10mg/day. May increase by 10mg weekly. **6-12 yrs: Initial:** 5mg/day. May increase by 5mg weekly. **Usual:** 5-60mg/day in divided doses.
Dextroamphetamine sulfate (Dexedrine Spansule, ProCentra, Zenzedi)	(Dexedrine Spansule) **Cap, SR:** 5mg, 10mg, 15mg	**Initial:** 10mg/day. May increase by 10mg weekly. **Usual:** 5-60mg/day in divided doses. May give once daily.	**Peds: ≥12 yrs: Initial:** 10mg/day. May increase by 10mg weekly. **6-12 yrs: Initial:** 5mg/day. May increase by 5mg weekly. **Usual:** 5-60mg/day in divided doses.
	(ProCentra) **Sol:** 5mg/5mL [473mL]	**Initial:** 10mg/day. May increase by 10mg weekly. **Usual:** 5-60mg/day in divided doses. Give 1st dose upon awakening, and additional doses (1 or 2) q4-6h.	**Peds: ≥12 yrs: Initial:** 10mg/day. May increase by 10mg weekly. **6-12 yrs: Initial:** 5mg/day. May increase by 5mg weekly. **Usual:** 5-60mg/day in divided doses.

GENERIC (BRAND)	HOW SUPPLIED	ADULT DOSAGE	SPECIAL POPULATIONS
NARCOLEPSY *(Continued)*			
SYMPATHOMIMETIC AMINES *(Continued)*			
Dextroamphetamine sulfate (Dexedrine Spansule, ProCentra, Zenzedi) *(Continued)*	(Zenzedi) **Tab:** 2.5mg, 5mg*, 7.5mg, 10mg*	**Initial:** 10mg/day. May increase by 10mg weekly. **Usual:** 5-60mg/day in divided doses. Give 1st dose upon awakening, and additional doses (1 or 2) q4-6h.	**Peds: ≥12 yrs: Initial:** 10mg/day. May increase by 10mg weekly. **6-12 yrs: Initial:** 5mg/day. May increase by 5mg weekly. **Usual:** 5-60mg/day in divided doses.
Methylphenidate HCl (Metadate ER, Methylin, Ritalin)	(Generic) **Tab, SR:** 10mg	(IR Methylphenidate) 10-60mg/day given in divided doses bid or tid 30-45 min ac. Take last dose before 6 pm if insomnia occurs. (Tab, SR) May use in place of IR tabs when 8-hr dose corresponds to titrated 8-hr IR dose.	**Peds ≥6 yrs: Max:** 60mg/day. (IR Methylphenidate) **Initial:** 5mg bid before breakfast and lunch. Increase gradually by 5-10mg weekly. (Tab, SR) May be used in place of the IR tabs when the 8-hr dose corresponds to the titrated 8-hr dose of the IR tabs.
	(Metadate ER) **Tab, ER:** 20mg	(IR Methylphenidate) 10-60mg/day given in divided doses bid-tid 30-45 min ac. (Tab, ER) May use in place of IR tabs when 8-hr dose corresponds to titrated 8-hr IR dose.	**Peds ≥6 yrs: Max:** 60mg/day. (IR Methylphenidate) **Initial:** 5mg bid before breakfast and lunch. Increase gradually by 5-10mg weekly. (Tab, ER) May be used in place of the IR tabs when the 8-hr dose corresponds to the titrated 8-hr dose of the IR tabs.
	(Methylin) **Sol:** 5mg/5mL [500mL], 10mg/5mL [500mL]; **Tab, Chewable:** 2.5mg, 5mg, 10mg*	10-60mg/day given in divided doses bid or tid 30-45 min ac. Take last dose before 6 pm if insomnia occurs.	**Peds ≥6 yrs: Initial:** 5mg bid before breakfast and lunch. Increase gradually by 5-10mg weekly. **Max:** 60mg/day.
	(Ritalin) **Tab:** 5mg, 10mg*, 20mg*; **Tab, SR:** 20mg	(Tab) 10-60mg/day given in divided doses bid or tid 30-45 min ac. Take last dose before 6 pm if insomnia occurs. (Tab, SR) May use in place of IR tabs when 8-hr dose corresponds to titrated 8-hr IR dose.	**Peds ≥6 yrs: Max:** 60mg/day. (Tab) **Initial:** 5mg bid before breakfast and lunch. Increase gradually by 5-10mg weekly. (Tab, SR) May be used in place of the IR tabs when the 8-hr dose corresponds to the titrated 8-hr dose of the IR tabs.
SLEEP APNEA			
CNS STIMULANTS			
Caffeine citrate (Cafcit)	**Inj:** 20mg/mL [3mL]; **Sol:** 20mg/mL [3mL]		**Peds 28-<33 Weeks Gestational Age: LD:** 1mL/kg (20mg/kg) IV over 30 min. **Maint:** 0.25mL/kg (5mg/kg) IV over 10 min or PO q24h beginning 24 hrs after LD.

Refer to full FDA-approved labeling for additional information.

Abbreviations: ER = extended-release; IR = immediate-release; SL = sublingual; SR = sustained-release.

*Scored.
†Contraindicated in pregnancy.
‡Also used at this dose to treat obstructive sleep apnea.

MIGRAINE AND TENSION HEADACHE MANAGEMENT

GENERIC (BRAND)	HOW SUPPLIED	ADULT DOSAGE	HEPATIC/RENAL DOSE CONSIDERATIONS
ACUTE MIGRAINE TREATMENT			
5-HT$_{1B/1D}$ AGONISTS (TRIPTANS)			
Almotriptan malate (Axert)	**Tab:** 6.25mg, 12.5mg	**Initial:** 6.25-12.5mg at onset of headache. May repeat after 2 hrs. **Max:** 25mg/24 hrs.	**Renal/Hepatic Impairment:** 6.25mg. **Max:** 12.5mg/24 hrs.
Eletriptan HBr (Relpax)	**Tab:** 20mg, 40mg	**Initial:** 20 or 40mg at onset of headache. May repeat after 2 hrs. **Max:** 40mg/dose or 80mg/24 hrs.	**Severe Hepatic Impairment:** Not recommended for use.
Frovatriptan succinate (Frova)	**Tab:** 2.5mg	**Usual:** 2.5mg. May repeat after 2 hrs. **Max:** 7.5mg/24 hrs.	No adjustment necessary.
Naratriptan HCl (Amerge)	**Tab:** 1mg, 2.5mg	**Usual:** 1 or 2.5mg. May repeat after 4 hrs. **Max:** 5mg/24 hrs.	**Mild-Moderate Renal/Hepatic Impairment: Initial:** 1mg. **Max:** 2.5mg/24 hrs. **Severe Renal/Hepatic Impairment:** Contraindicated.
Rizatriptan benzoate (Maxalt, Maxalt-MLT)	**Tab:** 5mg, 10mg; **Tab, Disintegrating:** (MLT) 5mg, 10mg	**Initial:** 5mg or 10mg. May repeat after 2 hrs. **Max:** 30mg/24 hrs.	No adjustment necessary.
Sumatriptan (Alsuma, Imitrex, Sumavel DosePro, Zecuity)	(Alsuma) **Inj*:** 6mg/0.5mL	**Max Single Dose:** 6mg SQ. May repeat after 1 hr. **Max Dose/24 hrs:** 12mg.	No adjustment necessary.
	(Imitrex, Sumavel DosePro) **Inj*:** 4mg/0.5mL, 6mg/0.5mL	**Max Single Dose:** 6mg SQ. May repeat after 1 hr. **Max Dose/24 hrs:** 12mg.	**Severe Hepatic Impairment:** (Imitrex) contraindicated, (Sumavel DosePro) not recommended for use.
	(Imitrex) **Nasal Spray:** 5mg, 20mg	**Usual:** 5mg, 10mg, or 20mg single dose into 1 nostril. May repeat after 2 hrs. **Max:** 40mg/24 hrs.	**Severe Hepatic Impairment:** Contraindicated.
	(Imitrex) **Tab:** 25mg, 50mg, 100mg	**Usual:** 25mg, 50mg, or 100mg. May repeat after 2 hrs. **Max:** 200mg/24 hrs.	**Mild to Moderate Hepatic Impairment: Max Single Dose:** 50mg. **Severe Hepatic Impairment:** Contraindicated.
	(Zecuity) **Patch:** 6.5mg/4 hrs	1 patch to skin of upper arm or thigh. The patch should remain in place for 4 hrs or until the red LED light goes off. May apply a 2nd patch to a different site no sooner than 2 hrs after activation of the 1st patch. **Max:** 2 patches/24 hrs.	**Severe Hepatic Impairment:** Contraindicated.
Sumatriptan-Naproxen (Treximet)	**Tab:** (Sumatriptan-Naproxen) 85mg-500mg	**Usual:** 1 tab. May repeat after 2 hrs. **Max:** 2 tabs/24 hrs.	**Hepatic Impairment:** Contraindicated. **Advanced Renal Disease:** Not recommended for use.
Zolmitriptan (Zomig, Zomig-ZMT)	**Nasal Spray:** 2.5mg, 5mg; **Tab, Disintegrating:** (ZMT) 2.5mg, 5mg	**Initial:** 2.5mg. **Max Single Dose:** 5mg. May repeat after 2 hrs. **Max Daily Dose:** 10mg/24 hrs.	**Moderate or Severe Hepatic Impairment:** Not recommended for use.
	Tab: 2.5mg, 5mg	**Initial:** 1.25mg. **Max Single Dose:** 5mg. May repeat after 2 hrs. **Max Daily Dose:** 10mg/24 hrs.	**Moderate to Severe Hepatic Impairment:** 1.25mg. **Severe Hepatic Impairment: Max Daily Dose:** 5mg/day.

(Continued)

GENERIC (BRAND)	HOW SUPPLIED	ADULT DOSAGE	HEPATIC/RENAL DOSE CONSIDERATIONS
ACUTE MIGRAINE TREATMENT (Continued)			
MISCELLANEOUS			
Diclofenac potassium (Cambia)	Sol (Powder): 50mg/pkt	1 pkt in 1-2 oz. (30-60mL) of water.	**Advanced Renal Disease:** Not recommended for use.
Dihydroergotamine mesylate (D.H.E. 45, Migranal)	(D.H.E. 45) Inj*: 1mg/mL	1mL IV/IM/SQ. May repeat prn at 1-hr intervals. **Max Daily Dose:** 3mL/24 hrs IM/SQ or 2mL/24 hrs IV. **Max Weekly Dose:** 6mL/wk.	**Severe Renal/Hepatic Impairment:** Contraindicated.
	(Migranal) Nasal Spray: 4mg/mL	1 spray (0.5mL) in each nostril. May repeat after 15 min. **Max Daily Dose:** 3mg/24 hrs. **Max Weekly Dose:** 4mg/wk.	
Ergotamine tartrate (Ergomar)	Tab, SL: 2mg	1 tab (2mg) under the tongue. May repeat every 30 min. **Max Daily Dose:** 3 tabs (6mg)/24 hrs. **Max Weekly Dose:** 5 tabs (10mg)/wk.	**Renal/Hepatic Impairment:** Contraindicated.
Ergotamine tartrate- Caffeine (Cafergot)	Tab: (Ergotamine-Caffeine) 1mg-100mg	2 tabs. May repeat every 30 min. **Max:** 6 tabs/attack. **Max Weekly Dose:** 10 tabs/wk.	**Renal/Hepatic Impairment:** Contraindicated.
MIGRAINE PROPHYLAXIS			
Divalproex sodium (Depakote, Depakote ER)	(Depakote) Tab, DR: 125mg, 250mg, 500mg	**Initial:** 250mg bid. **Max:** 1000mg/day.	**Hepatic Disease/Significant Hepatic Impairment:** Contraindicated.
	(Depakote ER) Tab, ER: 250mg, 500mg	**Initial:** 500mg qd for 1 week. **Titrate:** Increase to 1000mg qd.	
OnabotulinumtoxinA (Botox)	Inj: 100 U, 200 U	**Usual:** 155 U IM as 0.1mL (5 U)/site. Divide inj across 7 specific head/neck muscle areas.	No adjustment necessary.
Propranolol HCl (Inderal LA)	(Generic) Tab: 10mg, 20mg, 40mg, 60mg, 80mg	**Initial:** 80mg/day in divided doses. **Usual:** 160-240mg/day.	**Renal/Hepatic Impairment:** Use with caution.
	(Inderal LA) Cap, ER: 60mg, 80mg, 120mg, 160mg	**Initial:** 80mg qd. **Usual:** 160-240mg qd.	
Timolol maleate	Tab: 5mg, 10mg, 20mg	**Initial:** 10mg bid. **Maint:** 20mg qd. **Max:** 30mg/day in divided doses.	**Renal/Hepatic Impairment:** Dose reduction may be necessary.
Topiramate (Topamax)	Cap: (Sprinkle) 15mg, 25mg; Tab: 25mg, 50mg, 100mg, 200mg	**Initial: Week 1:** 25mg qpm. **Titrate: Week 2:** 25mg bid. **Week 3:** 25mg qam and 50mg qpm. **Week 4:** 50mg bid. **Usual:** 100mg/day in 2 divided doses.	**CrCl <70mL/min:** 50% of usual dose. **Renal/Hepatic Impairment:** Use with caution.
Valproic acid (Stavzor)	Cap, DR: 125mg, 250mg, 500mg	**Initial:** 250mg bid. Some patients may benefit from doses up to 1000mg/day.	**Hepatic Disease/Significant Hepatic Impairment:** Contraindicated.

GENERIC (BRAND)	HOW SUPPLIED	ADULT DOSAGE	HEPATIC/RENAL DOSE CONSIDERATIONS
TENSION HEADACHE TREATMENT			
Butalbital-APAP (Bupap, Phrenilin, Phrenilin Forte)	(Bupap) **Tab:** (Butalbital-APAP) 50mg-300mg	1 or 2 tabs q4h. **Max:** 6 tabs/day.	**Severe Renal/Hepatic Impairment:** Use with caution.
	(Butalbital-APAP) **Cap:** (Phrenilin Forte) 50mg-650mg; **Tab:** (Phrenilin) 50mg-325mg	(Phrenilin Forte) 1 cap q4h. (Phrenilin) 1-2 tabs q4h. **Max:** 6 caps or tabs/day.	
Butalbital-APAP-Caffeine (Esgic, Fioricet, Zebutal)	(Butalbital-APAP-Caffeine) **Cap:** (Fioricet) 50mg-300mg-40mg; (Zebutal) 50mg-325mg-40mg	1 or 2 caps q4h prn. **Max:** 6 caps/day.	**Severe Renal/Hepatic Impairment:** Use with caution.
	(Esgic) **Cap/Tab:** (Butalbital-APAP-Caffeine) 50mg-325mg-40mg	1 or 2 caps or tabs q4h. **Max:** 6 caps or tabs/day.	
	(Generic) **Sol:** (Butalbital-APAP-Caffeine) 50mg-325mg-40mg/15mL	1 or 2 tbsp (15 or 30mL) q4h. **Max:** 6 tbsp/day.	
Butalbital-APAP-Caffeine-Codeine phosphate (Fioricet w/ Codeine)	**Cap:** (Butalbital-APAP-Caffeine-Codeine) 50mg-300mg-40mg-30mg	1 or 2 caps q4h. **Max:** 6 caps/day.	**Severe Renal/Hepatic Impairment:** Use with caution.
Butalbital-ASA-Caffeine (Fiorinal)	**Cap:** (Butalbital-ASA-Caffeine) 50mg-325mg-40mg	1-2 caps q4h. **Max:** 6 caps/day.	**Severe Renal/Hepatic Impairment:** Use with caution.
Butalbital-ASA-Caffeine-Codeine phosphate (Ascomp w/ Codeine, Fiorinal w/ Codeine)	**Cap:** (Butalbital-ASA-Caffeine-Codeine) 50mg-325mg-40mg-30mg	1 or 2 caps q4h. **Max:** 6 caps/day.	**Severe Renal/Hepatic Impairment:** Use with caution.

Refer to full FDA-approved labeling for additional information.
Abbreviations: APAP = acetaminophen; ASA = aspirin; DR = delayed-release; ER = extended-release.
*Also indicated for acute treatment of cluster headaches.

GYNECOLOGICAL ANTI-INFECTIVES

DRUG	CLASS	FORMULATION	ROUTE	RECOMMENDED DOSAGE
ANTIBACTERIALS				
Clindamycin				
Cleocin Vaginal	Rx	**Cre:** 2%	Vaginal	**Bacterial Vaginosis: Adults:** 1 applicatorful qhs x 3 or 7 days (nonpregnant) or x 7 days (2nd or 3rd trimester).
Cleocin Vaginal Ovules	Rx	**Sup:** 100mg	Vaginal	**Bacterial Vaginosis: Adults:** 1 sup qhs x 3 days (nonpregnant).
Clindesse	Rx	**Cre:** 2%	Vaginal	**Bacterial Vaginosis: Adults:** 1 applicatorful as single dose (nonpregnant).
Metronidazole				
Flagyl*	Rx	**Cap:** 375mg; **Tab:** 250mg, 500mg	Oral	**Trichomoniasis: Adults: (Cap)** 375mg bid x 7 days; **(Tab)** 250mg tid x 7 days. **Alternate Regimen (Tab):** If nonpregnant, 2g as single or divided dose.
Flagyl ER*	Rx	**Tab, ER:** 750mg	Oral	**Bacterial Vaginosis: Adults:** 750mg qd x 7 days.
MetroGel Vaginal	Rx	**Gel:** 0.75%	Vaginal	**Bacterial Vaginosis: Adults:** 1 applicatorful qd-bid x 5 days. For qd dosing, administer qhs.
Vandazole	Rx	**Gel:** 0.75%	Vaginal	**Bacterial Vaginosis: Adults:** 1 applicatorful qhs x 5 days (nonpregnant).
MISCELLANEOUS				
Tinidazole				
Tindamax	Rx	**Tab:** 250mg, 500mg	Oral	**Bacterial Vaginosis:** 2g qd x 2 days or 1g qd x 5 days (nonpregnant). **Trichomoniasis:** 2g single dose. Treat sexual partner with same dose and at same time.
ANTIFUNGALS: CANDIDIASIS TREATMENT				
Butoconazole				
Gynazole-1	Rx	**Cre:** 2%	Vaginal	**Adults:** 1 applicatorful as single dose.
Clotrimazole				
Gyne-Lotrimin 3	OTC	**External Cre:** 2% + **Cre:** 2%	Vaginal	**Adults/Peds ≥12 yrs:** 1 applicatorful qhs x 3 days. **(External Cream)** Apply cream bid externally up to 7 days prn.
Gyne-Lotrimin 7	OTC	**External Cre:** 1% + **Cre:** 1%	Vaginal	**Adults/Peds ≥12 yrs:** 1 applicatorful qhs x 7 days. **(External Cream)** Apply cream bid externally up to 7 days prn.
Fluconazole				
Diflucan	Rx	**Tab:** 150mg	Oral	**Adults:** 150mg single dose.
Miconazole				
Monistat 1 Combination Pack	OTC	**External Cre:** 2% + **Ovule Insert:** 1200mg	Vaginal	**Adults/Peds ≥12 yrs:** 1 sup single dose. **(External Cream)** Apply cream bid externally up to 7 days prn.
Monistat 3	OTC	**Cre:** 4%	Vaginal	**Adults/Peds ≥12 yrs:** 1 applicatorful qhs x 3 days.
Monistat 3 Combination Pack	OTC	**External Cre:** 2% + **Ovule Insert:** 200mg or **Cre:** 4%	Vaginal	**Adults/Peds ≥12 yrs:** 1 sup or applicatorful qhs x 3 days. **(External Cream)** Apply cream bid externally up to 7 days prn.
Monistat 7	OTC	**Cre:** 2%	Vaginal	**Adults/Peds ≥12 yrs:** 1 applicatorful qhs x 7 days. **(External Cream)** Apply cream bid externally up to 7 days prn.

(Continued)

DRUG	CLASS	FORMULATION	ROUTE	RECOMMENDED DOSAGE
ANTIFUNGALS: CANDIDIASIS TREATMENT *(Continued)*				
Miconazole *(Continued)*				
Monistat 7 Combination Pack	OTC	**External Cre:** 2% **Cre:** 2% +	Vaginal	**Adults/Peds ≥12 yrs:** 1 applicatorful qhs x 7 days. **(External Cream)** Apply cream bid externally up to 7 days prn.
Sulfanilamide				
AVC	Rx	**Cre:** 15%	Vaginal	**Adults:** 1 applicatorful qd-bid x 30 days.
Terconazole				
Terazol 3	Rx	**Cre:** 0.8%; **Sup:** 80mg	Vaginal	**Adults:** 1 applicatorful or 1 sup qhs x 3 days.
Terazol 7	Rx	**Cre:** 0.4%	Vaginal	**Adults:** 1 applicatorful qhs x 7 days.
Tioconazole				
Monistat 1, Vagistat 1	OTC	**Oint:** 6.5%	Vaginal	**Adults/Peds ≥12 yrs:** 1 applicatorful single dose hs.
Refer to full FDA-approved labeling for more information.				
*Contraindicated in 1st trimester.				

HORMONE THERAPY

GENERIC	BRAND	STRENGTH (MG)*
INTRAMUSCULAR ESTROGEN PRODUCTS		
Estradiol cypionate	Depo-Estradiol	5mg/mL
Estradiol valerate	Delestrogen	10mg/mL, 20mg/mL, 40mg/mL
ORAL ESTROGEN PRODUCTS		
Conjugated estrogens	Premarin	0.3, 0.45, 0.625, 0.9, 1.25
ORAL SYNTHETIC CONJUGATED ESTROGEN PRODUCTS		
Esterified estrogens	Menest	0.3, 0.625, 1.25, 2.5
Estradiol	Estrace	0.5, 1, 2
Estropipate	Generic	0.75 (0.625), 1.5 (1.25), 3 (2.5), 6 (5)
Synthetic conjugated estrogens	Cenestin	0.3, 0.45, 0.625, 0.9, 1.25
	Enjuvia	0.3, 0.45, 0.625, 0.9, 1.25
TRANSDERMAL ESTROGEN PRODUCTS		
Estradiol	Alora	0.025, 0.05, 0.075, 0.1
	Climara	0.025, 0.0375, 0.05, 0.06, 0.075, 0.1
	Divigel	0.1% gel
	Estraderm	0.05, 0.1
	Elestrin	0.06% gel
	Estrogel	0.06% gel
	Evamist	Spray: 1.53mg/spray
	Vivelle-Dot	0.025, 0.0375, 0.05, 0.075, 0.1
Estradiol hemihydrate	Estrasorb	Emulsion: 4.35mg/1.74g [pouch]
VAGINAL ESTROGEN PRODUCTS		
VAGINAL CREAMS		
Conjugated estrogens	Premarin Vaginal Cream	0.625mg/g
Estradiol	Estrace Vaginal Cream	0.01%
VAGINAL RINGS		
Estradiol	Estring	2
Estradiol acetate	Femring	0.05mg/day or 0.1mg/day
VAGINAL TABLETS		
Estradiol	Vagifem	10mcg
ORAL PROGESTOGEN-ONLY PRODUCTS		
Medroxyprogesterone acetate	Provera	2.5, 5, 10
Norethindrone acetate	Aygestin	5
Progesterone	Prometrium	100, 200
ESTROGEN + PROGESTOGEN COMBINATIONS		
ORAL CONTINUOUS-CYCLIC REGIMENS		
Conjugated estrogens (E) + Medroxyprogesterone acetate (P)	Premphase	0.625 (E); 0.625 (E) + 5 (P)
Estradiol (E) + Norgestimate (P)	Prefest	1 (E); 1 (E) + 0.09 (P)
ORAL CONTINUOUS-COMBINED REGIMENS		
Conjugated estrogens (E) + Medroxyprogesterone acetate (P)	Prempro	0.3 (E) + 1.5 (P); 0.45 (E) + 1.5 (P); 0.625 (E) + 2.5 (P) or 5 (P)
Estradiol (E) + Drospirenone (P)	Angeliq	0.5 (E) + 0.25 (P); 1 (E) + 0.5 (P)

(Continued)

GENERIC	BRAND	STRENGTH (MG)*
ESTROGEN + PROGESTOGEN COMBINATIONS *(Continued)*		
ORAL CONTINUOUS-COMBINED REGIMENS *(Continued)*		
Estradiol (E) + Norethindrone acetate (P)	Activella	1 (E) + 0.5 (P); 0.5 (E) + 0.1 (P)
Ethinyl estradiol (E) + Norethindrone acetate (P)	Femhrt	2.5mcg (E) + 0.5 (P); 5mcg (E) + 1 (P)
TRANSDERMAL CONTINUOUS-CYCLIC OR CONTINUOUS-COMBINED REGIMENS		
Estradiol (E) + Levonorgestrel (P)	Climara Pro	0.045mg/day (E) + 0.015mg/day (P)
Estradiol (E) + Norethindrone acetate (P)	CombiPatch	0.05mg/day (E) + 0.14mg/day or 0.25mg/day (P)

Refer to full FDA-approved labeling for additional information.

NOTE: This list is not inclusive of all estrogen and progestogen products available. Indications vary among the different products. Unopposed estrogen replacement therapy (ERT) is for use in women without an intact uterus. For women with an intact uterus, progestin must be added to the ERT for protection against estrogen-induced endometrial cancer. As with any therapy, the lowest possible effective dosage should be used. Reevaluate periodically.

*Units are in mg unless otherwise stated.

ORAL CONTRACEPTIVES

DRUG	ESTROGEN	PROGESTIN	STRENGTH (ESTROGEN/PROGESTIN)
MONOPHASIC			
Aviane 28, Lessina, Lutera, Orsythia, Sronyx†	Ethinyl estradiol	Levonorgestrel	20mcg/0.1mg
Beyaz*, YAZ [Gianvi, Loryna, Vestura]†	Ethinyl estradiol	Drospirenone	20mcg/3mg
Brevicon, Modicon [Necon 0.5/35, Nortrel 0.5/35]†	Ethinyl estradiol	Norethindrone	35mcg/0.5mg
Desogen [Apri, Emoquette, Reclipsen, Solia]†	Ethinyl estradiol	Desogestrel	30mcg/0.15mg
Femcon Fe, Ovcon 35 [Balziva, Briellyn, Philith, Vyfemla Zenchent, Zenchent Fe]†	Ethinyl estradiol	Norethindrone	35mcg/0.4mg
Loestrin 21 1/20, Loestrin Fe 1/20, Loestrin 24 Fe, Minastrin 24 Fe [Gildess Fe 1/20, Junel 1/20, Junel Fe 1/20, Larin 1/20, Larin Fe 1/20, Microgestin 1/20, Microgestin Fe 1/20]†	Ethinyl estradiol	Norethindrone acetate	20mcg/1mg
Loestrin 21 1.5/30, Loestrin Fe 1.5/30 [Gildess Fe 1.5/30, Junel 1.5/30, Junel Fe 1.5/30, Microgestin 1.5/30, Microgestin Fe 1.5/30]†	Ethinyl estradiol	Norethindrone acetate	30mcg/1.5mg
Lo/Ovral [Cryselle, Low-Ogestrel]†	Ethinyl estradiol	Norgestrel	30mcg/0.3mg
Lybrel [Amethyst]†	Ethinyl estradiol	Levonorgestrel	20mcg/0.09mg
[Altavera, Levora, Marlissa, Portia]†	Ethinyl estradiol	Levonorgestrel	30mcg/0.15mg
Norinyl 1/35, Ortho-Novum 1/35 [Alyacen 1/35, Cyclafem 1/35, Dasetta 1/35, Necon 1/35, Nortrel 1/35]†	Ethinyl estradiol	Norethindrone	35mcg/1mg
Necon 1/50, Norinyl 1/50	Mestranol	Norethindrone	50mcg/1mg
Ogestrel 0.5/50†	Ethinyl estradiol	Norgestrel	50mcg/0.5mg
Ortho-Cyclen [MonoNessa, Previfem, Sprintec]†	Ethinyl estradiol	Norgestimate	35mcg/0.25mg
Ovcon 50	Ethinyl estradiol	Norethindrone	50mcg/1mg
Safyral*, Yasmin [Ocella, Syeda, Zarah]†	Ethinyl estradiol	Drospirenone	30mcg/3mg
[Introvale, Jolessa, Quasense]†	Ethinyl estradiol	Levonorgestrel	30mcg/0.15mg
Zovia 1/35E [Kelnor 1/35]†	Ethinyl estradiol	Ethynodiol diacetate	35mcg/1mg
Zovia 1/50E	Ethinyl estradiol	Ethynodiol diacetate	50mcg/1mg
BIPHASIC			
Mircette [Azurette, Kariva]†	Ethinyl estradiol	Desogestrel	**Phase 1:** 20mcg/0.15mg **Phase 2:** 10mcg/NONE
Lo Loestrin Fe, [Lo Minastrin Fe†]	Ethinyl estradiol	Norethindrone acetate	**Phase 1:** 10mcg/1mg **Phase 2:** 10mcg/NONE
LoSeasonique [Amethia Lo]†	Ethinyl estradiol	Levonorgestrel	**Phase 1:** 20mcg/0.1mg **Phase 2:** 10mcg/NONE
Necon 10/11	Ethinyl estradiol	Norethindrone	**Phase 1:** 35mcg/0.5mg **Phase 2:** 35mcg/1mg
Seasonique [Amethia, Camrese]†	Ethinyl estradiol	Levonorgestrel	**Phase 1:** 30mcg/0.15mg **Phase 2:** 10mcg/NONE

(Continued)

DRUG	ESTROGEN	PROGESTIN	STRENGTH (ESTROGEN/PROGESTIN)
TRIPHASIC			
Cyclessa [Caziant, Cesia, Velivet]†	Ethinyl estradiol	Desogestrel	**Phase 1:** 25mcg/0.1mg **Phase 2:** 25mcg/0.125mg **Phase 3:** 25mcg/0.15mg
Estrostep Fe [Tilia Fe, Tri-Legest Fe]†	Ethinyl estradiol	Norethindrone acetate	**Phase 1:** 20mcg/1mg **Phase 2:** 30mcg/1mg **Phase 3:** 35mcg/1mg
Ortho Novum 7/7/7 [Alyacen 7/7/7, Cyclafem 7/7/7, Dasetta 7/7/7, Nortrel 7/7/7]†	Ethinyl estradiol	Norethindrone	**Phase 1:** 35mcg/0.5mg **Phase 2:** 35mcg/0.75mg **Phase 3:** 35mcg/1mg
Ortho Tri-Cyclen [TriNessa, Tri-Previfem, Tri-Sprintec]†	Ethinyl estradiol	Norgestimate	**Phase 1:** 35mcg/0.18mg **Phase 2:** 35mcg/0.215mg **Phase 3:** 35mcg/0.25mg
Ortho Tri-Cyclen Lo [Tri-Lo-Sprintec]†	Ethinyl estradiol	Norgestimate	**Phase 1:** 25mcg/0.18mg **Phase 2:** 25mcg/0.215mg **Phase 3:** 25mcg/0.25mg
Trivora, Enpresse, Levonest†	Ethinyl estradiol	Levonorgestrel	**Phase 1:** 30mcg/0.05mg **Phase 2:** 40mcg/0.075mg **Phase 3:** 30mcg/0.125mg
Tri-Norinyl [Aranelle, Leena]†	Ethinyl estradiol	Norethindrone	**Phase 1:** 35mcg/0.5mg **Phase 2:** 35mcg/1mg **Phase 3:** 35mcg/0.5mg
FOUR-PHASE			
Natazia	Estradiol valerate	Dienogest	**Phase 1:** 3mg/NONE **Phase 2:** 2mg/2mg **Phase 3:** 2mg/3mg **Phase 4:** 1mg/NONE
PROGESTIN-ONLY			
Nor-QD, Ortho-Micronor [Camila, Errin, Heather, Jencycla, Jolivette, Nora-BE]†		Norethindrone	0.35mg
Plan B [Next Choice]†		Levonorgestrel	0.75mg
Plan B One Step [Next Choice One Dose]†		Levonorgestrel	1.5mg
MISCELLANEOUS			
Ella‡		Ulipristal acetate (progesterone agonist/ antagonist)	30mg

Refer to full FDA-approved labeling for additional information.

*Also contains levomefolate calcium.

†Branded generics.

‡Selective progesterone receptor modulator.

CHEMOTHERAPY REGIMENS*

CANCER TYPE	THERAPIES†‡	REFERENCES
BLADDER CANCER		
	Preferred regimens: First-line therapy for metastatic disease: • Gemcitabine and cisplatin (category 1) • Dose-dense methotrexate/vinblastine/ doxorubicin/cisplatin (DDMVAC) (category 1) **Adjuvant intravesical treatment:** • Bacillus Calmette-Guerin (BCG) **Alternative regimens:** First-line therapy for metastatic disease: • Carboplatin- or taxane-based regimens or single-agent therapy (category 2B) **Adjuvant intravesical treatment:** • Mitomycin	Referenced with permission from the NCCN Clinical Practice Guidelines in Oncology (NCCN Guidelines®) for Bladder Cancer V.1.2014. © National Comprehensive Cancer Network, Inc 2013. All rights reserved. Accessed March 25, 2014. To view the most recent and complete version of the guideline, go online to www.nccn.org. NATIONAL COMPREHENSIVE CANCER NETWORK®, NCCN®, NCCN GUIDELINES®, and all other NCCN Content are trademarks owned by the National Comprehensive Cancer Network, Inc.
BREAST CANCER		
Invasive	**Adjuvant (non-trastuzumab-containing)** **(All category 1):** **Preferred regimens:** • Dose-dense doxorubicin/cyclophosphamide (AC) followed by paclitaxel every 2 weeks • Dose-dense AC followed by weekly paclitaxel • Docetaxel and cyclophosphamide (TC) **Other regimens:** • Dose-dense doxorubicin/cyclophosphamide (AC) • Fluorouracil/doxorubicin/cyclophosphamide (FAC/CAF) • Cyclophosphamide/epirubicin/fluorouracil (FEC/CEF) • Cyclophosphamide/methotrexate/fluorouracil (CMF) • AC followed by docetaxel every 3 weeks • AC followed by weekly paclitaxel • Epirubicin/cyclophosphamide (EC) • Fluorouracil/epirubicin/cyclophosphamide followed by docetaxel or weekly paclitaxel (FEC/CEF followed by T) • Fluorouracil/doxorubicin/cyclophosphamide followed by weekly paclitaxel (FAC followed by T) • Docetaxel/doxorubicin/cyclophosphamide (TAC) **Adjuvant (trastuzumab-containing):** **Preferred regimens:** • Doxorubicin/cyclophosphamide followed by paclitaxel plus trastuzumab ± pertuzumab, various schedules (AC followed by T + trastuzumab ± pertuzumab) • Docetaxel/carboplatin/trastuzumab (TCH) ± pertuzumab **Other regimens:** • AC followed by docetaxel + trastuzumab ± pertuzumab • Fluorouracil/epirubicin/cyclophosphamide (FEC) followed by docetaxel + trastuzumab + pertuzumab • FEC followed by paclitaxel + trastuzumab + pertuzumab • Pertuzumab + trastuzumab + docetaxel followed by FEC • Pertuzumab + trastuzumab + paclitaxel followed by FEC	Referenced with permission from the NCCN Clinical Practice Guidelines in Oncology (NCCN Guidelines®) for Breast Cancer V.3.2014. © National Comprehensive Cancer Network, Inc 2014. All rights reserved. Accessed April 2, 2014. To view the most recent and complete version of the guideline, go online to www.nccn.org. NATIONAL COMPREHENSIVE CANCER NETWORK®, NCCN®, NCCN GUIDELINES®, and all other NCCN Content are trademarks owned by the National Comprehensive Cancer Network, Inc.

(Continued)

CANCER TYPE	THERAPIES†‡	REFERENCES
BREAST CANCER *(Continued)*		
Recurrent or metastatic	**Preferred single agents:** • Anthracyclines: doxorubicin, pegylated liposomal doxorubicin • Taxanes: paclitaxel • Antimetabolites: capecitabine, gemcitabine • Other microtubule inhibitors: vinorelbine, eribulin **Other single agents:** • Cyclophosphamide • Carboplatin • Docetaxel • Albumin-bound paclitaxel • Cisplatin • Epirubicin • Ixabepilone **Chemotherapy combinations:** • Cyclophosphamide/doxorubicin/fluorouracil (CAF/FAC) • Fluorouracil/epirubicin/cyclophosphamide (FEC) • Doxorubicin/cyclophosphamide (AC) • Epirubicin/cyclophosphamide (EC) • Cyclophosphamide/methotrexate/fluorouracil (CMF) • Docetaxel/capecitabine • Gemcitabine/paclitaxel (GT) • Gemcitabine/carboplatin • Paclitaxel/bevacizumab	
HER2-positive metastatic	**Preferred first-line regimens:** **Trastuzumab with:** • Pertuzumab + docetaxel (category 1) • Pertuzumab + paclitaxel **Other first-line regimens:** **Trastuzumab alone or with:** • Paclitaxel ± carboplatin • Docetaxel • Vinorelbine • Capecitabine	
Trastuzumab-exposed HER2-positive metastatic	**Preferred regimen:** • Ado-trastuzumab emtansine (T-DM1) **Other regimens:** • Lapatinib + capecitabine • Trastuzumab + capecitabine • Trastuzumab + lapatinib (without cytotoxic therapy) • Trastuzumab + other agents	
COLORECTAL CANCER		
Advanced or metastatic	**Initial (intensive therapy appropriate):** • FOLFOX ± bevacizumab • CapeOX ± bevacizumab • FOLFOX ± panitumumab (KRAS/NRAS wild-type [WT] gene only) • FOLFIRI ± bevacizumab • FOLFIRI ± cetuximab or panitumumab (KRAS/NRAS WT gene only) • 5-FU/leucovorin or capecitabine ± bevacizumab • FOLFOXIRI ± bevacizumab (category 2B) *Refer to NCCN Clinical Practice Guidelines in Oncology (NCCN Guidelines®) for therapy after first, second, and third progression and for non-intensive therapy appropriate patients.*	Referenced with permission from the NCCN Clinical Practice Guidelines in Oncology (NCCN Guidelines®) for Colon Cancer V.3.2014. © National Comprehensive Cancer Network, Inc 2014. All rights reserved. Accessed March 25, 2014. To view the most recent and complete version of the guideline, go online to www.nccn.org. NATIONAL COMPREHENSIVE CANCER NETWORK®, NCCN®, NCCN GUIDELINES®, and all other NCCN Content are trademarks owned by the National Comprehensive Cancer Network, Inc.

CANCER TYPE	THERAPIES[†‡]	REFERENCES
ESOPHAGEAL AND ESOPHAGOGASTRIC JUNCTION CANCERS		
	Preferred regimens (definitive chemoradiation): • Cisplatin and fluorouracil (category 1) • Oxaliplatin and fluorouracil (category 1) • Cisplatin and capecitabine • Oxaliplatin and capecitabine • Paclitaxel and carboplatin **Other regimens (definitive chemoradiation):** • Paclitaxel or docetaxel and cisplatin • Irinotecan and cisplatin (category 2B) • Docetaxel or paclitaxel and fluoropyrimidine (fluorouracil or capecitabine) (category 2B)	Referenced with permission from the NCCN Clinical Practice Guidelines in Oncology (NCCN Guidelines®) for Esophageal and Esophagogastric Junction Cancers V.2.2013. © National Comprehensive Cancer Network, Inc 2013. All rights reserved. Accessed March 25, 2014. To view the most recent and complete version of the guideline, go online to www.nccn.org. NATIONAL COMPREHENSIVE CANCER NETWORK®, NCCN®, NCCN GUIDELINES®, and all other NCCN Content are trademarks owned by the National Comprehensive Cancer Network, Inc.
Locally advanced or metastatic (where local therapy is not indicated)	Trastuzumab can be added to chemotherapy for HER2-neu overexpressing adenocarcinoma • Trastuzumab with cisplatin and fluoropyrimidine (category 1) • Trastuzumab with other chemotherapy agents (category 2B) • Trastuzumab is not recommended for use with anthracyclines **Preferred first-line regimens:** • Docetaxel, cisplatin, and fluorouracil (DCF) (category 1) • Epirubicin, cisplatin, and fluorouracil (ECF) (category 1) • Fluoropyrimidine (fluorouracil or capecitabine) and cisplatin (category 1) • Fluoropyrimidine (fluorouracil or capecitabine) and oxaliplatin • Fluorouracil and irinotecan *Refer to NCCN Clinical Practice Guidelines in Oncology (NCCN Guidelines®) for DCF and ECF modifications.* **Other first-line regimens:** • Paclitaxel with cisplatin or carboplatin • Docetaxel with cisplatin • Docetaxel and irinotecan • Fluoropyrimidine (fluorouracil or capecitabine) • Docetaxel • Paclitaxel	
LEUKEMIA		
Acute lymphoblastic leukemia (ALL) (Adults ≥40 years)	**Ph-positive:** **Induction regimens:** • TKIs + hyper-CVAD: imatinib or dasatinib; and hyper-fractionated cyclophosphamide, vincristine, doxorubicin, and dexamethasone, alternating with high-dose methotrexate and cytarabine • TKIs + multiagent chemotherapy: imatinib; and daunorubicin, vincristine, prednisone, and cyclophosphamide • TKIs (imatinib or dasatinib) + corticosteroids • TKIs + vincristine + dexamethasone • Dasatinib **Maintenance regimens:** • Add TKIs (imatinib or dasatinib) to maintenance regimen • Monthly vincristine/prednisone pulses (for 2-3 years). May include weekly methotrexate + daily 6-mercaptopurine (6-MP) as tolerated	Referenced with permission from the NCCN Clinical Practice Guidelines in Oncology (NCCN Guidelines®) for Acute Lymphoblastic Leukemia V.3.2013. © National Comprehensive Cancer Network, Inc 2014. All rights reserved. Accessed March 25, 2014. To view the most recent and complete version of the guideline, go online to www.nccn.org. NATIONAL COMPREHENSIVE CANCER NETWORK®, NCCN®, NCCN GUIDELINES®, and all other NCCN Content are trademarks owned by the National Comprehensive Cancer Network, Inc.

CANCER TYPE	THERAPIES†‡	REFERENCES
LEUKEMIA *(Continued)*		
Acute lymphoblastic leukemia (ALL) (Adults ≥40 years) *(Continued)*	**Ph-negative:** **Induction regimens:** • CALGB 8811 Larson regimen: daunorubicin, vincristine, prednisone, pegaspargase, and cyclophosphamide; for patients ≥60 years, reduced doses for cyclophosphamide, daunorubicin, and prednisone • Linker 4-drug regimen: daunorubicin, vincristine, prednisone, and pegaspargase • Hyper-CVAD ± rituximab: hyper-fractionated cyclophosphamide, vincristine, doxorubicin, and dexamethasone, alternating with high-dose methotrexate and cytarabine; with or without rituximab for CD20-positive disease • MRC UKALLXII/ECOG2993 regimen: daunorubicin, vincristine, prednisone, and pegaspargase (phase I); and cyclophosphamide, cytarabine, and 6-MP (phase II) **Maintenance regimen:** • Weekly methotrexate + daily 6-MP + monthly vincristine/prednisone pulses (for 2-3 years) *Refer to NCCN Clinical Practice Guidelines in Oncology (NCCN Guidelines®) for AYA patients. All ALL treatment regimens include CNS prophylaxis with systemic therapy and/or IT therapy.*	
Acute myeloid leukemia (AML)	**Treatment Induction:** **Age <60 years:** • Clinical trial (preferred) • Standard-dose cytarabine with idarubicin or daunorubicin (category 1) • Standard-dose cytarabine with daunorubicin and cladribine (category 1) • High-dose cytarabine (HiDAC) with idarubicin or daunorubicin (category 2B) **Age ≥60 years:** • Clinical trial • Standard-dose cytarabine with idarubicin (preferred) or daunorubicin or mitoxantrone • Low-intensity therapy (5-azacytidine, decitabine +/- cytarabine) **Post-induction after standard-dose cytarabine:** **Age <60 years: Significant residual blasts:** • HiDAC • Standard-dose cytarabine with idarubicin or daunorubicin **Significant cytoreduction with low % residual blasts:** • Standard-dose cytarabine with idarubicin or daunorubicin **Age ≥60 years: Residual blasts:** • Clinical trial • Additional standard-dose cytarabine with anthracycline (idarubicin or daunorubicin) or mitoxantrone • HiDAC *Refer to NCCN Clinical Practice Guidelines in Oncology (NCCN Guidelines®) for post-induction therapy after high-dose cytarabine, post-remission therapy, and therapy-related AML for patients ≥60 years. Treatment decisions for age >60 years are dependent on performance score.*	Referenced with permission from the NCCN Clinical Practice Guidelines in Oncology (NCCN Guidelines®) for Acute Myeloid Leukemia V.2.2014. © National Comprehensive Cancer Network, Inc 2014. All rights reserved. Accessed March 31, 2014. To view the most recent and complete version of the guideline, go online to www.nccn.org. NATIONAL COMPREHENSIVE CANCER NETWORK®, NCCN®, NCCN GUIDELINES®, and all other NCCN Content are trademarks owned by the National Comprehensive Cancer Network, Inc.

CANCER TYPE	THERAPIES†‡	REFERENCES
LEUKEMIA *(Continued)*		

Acute promyelocytic leukemia (APL)	**Induction (low/intermediate risk):**
	• Clinical trial
	• ATRA (all trans retinoic acid) plus:
	  o Arsenic trioxide (category 1) or
	  o Daunorubicin and cytarabine (category 1 or category 2A based on dose and schedule)
	  or
	  o Idarubicin (category 1)
	
	Post-remission/first relapse:
	• Arsenic trioxide ± ATRA until count recovery with marrow confirmation of remission
	• ATRA + idarubicin + arsenic trioxide until recovery with marrow confirmation of remission
	
	Refer to NCCN Clinical Practice Guidelines in Oncology (NCCN Guidelines®) for induction (high risk), consolidation and post-consolidation therapy.
		Referenced with permission from the NCCN Clinical Practice Guidelines in Oncology (NCCN Guidelines®) for Acute Myeloid Leukemia V.1.2014. © National Comprehensive Cancer Network, Inc 2014. All rights reserved. Accessed March 25, 2014. To view the most recent and complete version of the guideline, go online to www.nccn.org. NATIONAL COMPREHENSIVE CANCER NETWORK®, NCCN®, NCCN GUIDELINES®, and all other NCCN Content are trademarks owned by the National Comprehensive Cancer Network, Inc.

Chronic lymphocytic leukemia (CLL)	**First-line therapy for CLL without del (11q) or del (17p):** **Age ≥70 years or younger patients with comorbidities:** • Obinutuzumab + chlorambucil • Rituximab + chlorambucil • Bendamustine ± rituximab • Cyclophosphamide, prednisone ± rituximab • Rituximab • Fludarabine ± rituximab • Cladribine • Chlorambucil **Age <70 years or older patients without significant comorbidities:** • Fludarabine, cyclophosphamide, rituximab (FCR) • Fludarabine, rituximab (FR) • Pentostatin, cyclophosphamide, rituximab (PCR) • Bendamustine ± rituximab • Obinutuzumab + chlorambucil **First-line therapy for CLL with del (17p):** • Alemtuzumab ± rituximab • FCR • FR • High-dose methylprednisolone (HDMP) + rituximab • Obinutuzumab + chlorambucil **First-line therapy for CLL with del (11q):** **Age ≥70 years or younger patients with comorbidities:** • Obinutuzumab + chlorambucil • Rituximab + chlorambucil • Bendamustine ± rituximab • Cyclophosphamide, prednisone ± rituximab • Reduced-dose FCR • Rituximab • Chlorambucil **Age <70 years or older patients without significant comorbidities:** • FCR • Bendamustine ± rituximab • PCR • Obinutuzumab + chlorambucil *Refer to NCCN Clinical Practice Guidelines in Oncology (NCCN Guidelines®) for relapsed/ refractory therapy.*	Referenced with permission from the NCCN Clinical Practice Guidelines in Oncology (NCCN Guidelines®) for Non-Hodgkin's Lymphomas V.1.2014. © National Comprehensive Cancer Network, Inc 2014. All rights reserved. Accessed March 25, 2014. To view the most recent and complete version of the guideline, go online to www.nccn.org. NATIONAL COMPREHENSIVE CANCER NETWORK®, NCCN®, NCCN GUIDELINES®, and all other NCCN Content are trademarks owned by the National Comprehensive Cancer Network, Inc.

CANCER TYPE	THERAPIES†‡	REFERENCES
LEUKEMIA (Continued)		
Chronic myelogenous leukemia (CML)	**Primary Treatment:** • Imatinib • Nilotinib • Dasatinib *Refer to NCCN Clinical Practice Guidelines in Oncology (NCCN Guidelines®) for follow-up therapy.*	Referenced with permission from the NCCN Clinical Practice Guidelines in Oncology (NCCN Guidelines®) for Chronic Myelogenous Leukemia V.3.2014. © National Comprehensive Cancer Network, Inc 2014. All rights reserved. Accessed March 25, 2014. To view the most recent and complete version of the guideline, go online to www.nccn.org. NATIONAL COMPREHENSIVE CANCER NETWORK®, NCCN®, NCCN GUIDELINES®, and all other NCCN Content are trademarks owned by the National Comprehensive Cancer Network, Inc.

Hairy cell leukemia	**Initial:**
	• Purine analog:
	  o Cladribine
	  o Pentostatin
	
	Relapse at ≥1 year:
	• Retreat with initial purine analog ± rituximab
	• Alternative purine analog ± rituximab
	
	Relapse at <1 year:
	• Clinical trial
	• Alternate purine analog ± rituximab
	• Interferon alpha
	• Rituximab
		Referenced with permission from the NCCN Clinical Practice Guidelines in Oncology (NCCN Guidelines®) for Non-Hodgkin's Lymphomas V.1.2014. © National Comprehensive Cancer Network, Inc 2014. All rights reserved. Accessed March 25, 2014. To view the most recent and complete version of the guideline, go online to www.nccn. org. NATIONAL COMPREHENSIVE CANCER NETWORK®, NCCN®, NCCN GUIDELINES®, and all other NCCN Content are trademarks owned by the National Comprehensive Cancer Network, Inc.

HEPATOCELLULAR CARCINOMA		
	Inoperable by performance status or comorbidity, local disease, or local disease with minimal extrahepatic disease only: • Sorafenib (Child-Pugh Class A [category 1] or B) • Clinical trial • Locoregional therapy (ablation, arterially directed therapies, external-beam radiation therapy (conformal or stereotactic)[category 2B]) • Best supportive care **Metastatic disease or extensive liver tumor burden:** • Sorafenib (Child-Pugh Class A [category 1] or B) • Clinical trial • Best supportive care	Referenced with permission from the NCCN Clinical Practice Guidelines in Oncology (NCCN Guidelines®) for Hepatobiliary Cancers V.2.2014. © National Comprehensive Cancer Network, Inc 2014. All rights reserved. Accessed April 2, 2014. To view the most recent and complete version of the guideline, go online to www.nccn.org. NATIONAL COMPREHENSIVE CANCER NETWORK®, NCCN®, NCCN GUIDELINES®, and all other NCCN Content are trademarks owned by the National Comprehensive Cancer Network, Inc.
LUNG CANCER		
Non-small cell	**First-line therapy for advanced disease:** • Chemotherapy ± bevacizumab • Cetuximab + vinorelbine/cisplatin (category 2B) • Afatinib and erlotinib (category 1 for both) for patients with sensitizing EGFR mutation • Crizotinib for patients who are ALK positive • Cisplatin or carboplatin with: paclitaxel, docetaxel, gemcitabine, etoposide, vinblastine, vinorelbine, pemetrexed, or albumin-bound paclitaxel. All these doublet chemotherapy regimens are category 1 for PS 0-1. • Bevacizumab or pemetrexed regimens are not recommended for squamous cell carcinoma. • Gemcitabine/docetaxel • Gemcitabine/vinorelbine *Refer to NCCN Clinical Practice Guidelines in Oncology (NCCN Guidelines®) for second and third line therapies.*	Referenced with permission from the NCCN Clinical Practice Guidelines in Oncology (NCCN Guidelines®) for Non-Small Cell Lung Cancer V.3.2014. © National Comprehensive Cancer Network, Inc 2014. All rights reserved. Accessed March 28, 2014. To view the most recent and complete version of the guideline, go online to www.nccn.org. NATIONAL COMPREHENSIVE CANCER NETWORK®, NCCN®, NCCN GUIDELINES®, and all other NCCN Content are trademarks owned by the National Comprehensive Cancer Network, Inc.

CANCER TYPE	THERAPIES†‡	REFERENCES
LUNG CANCER (Continued)		
Small cell	**Limited stage (maximum of 4-6 cycles):** • Cisplatin (category 1) or carboplatin with etoposide **Extensive stage (maximum of 4-6 cycles):** • Cisplatin or carboplatin with etoposide or irinotecan *Refer to NCCN Clinical Practice Guidelines in Oncology (NCCN Guidelines®) for subsequent chemotherapy for relapses.*	Referenced with permission from the NCCN Clinical Practice Guidelines in Oncology (NCCN Guidelines®) for Small Cell Lung Cancer V.2.2014. © National Comprehensive Cancer Network, Inc 2013. All rights reserved. Accessed March 25, 2014. To view the most recent and complete version of the guideline, go online to www.nccn.org. NATIONAL COMPREHENSIVE CANCER NETWORK®, NCCN®, NCCN GUIDELINES®, and all other NCCN Content are trademarks owned by the National Comprehensive Cancer Network, Inc.
LYMPHOMA		
HODGKIN LYMPHOMA		
Classical	• Doxorubicin/bleomycin/vinblastine/dacarbazine (ABVD) ± RT • Doxorubicin/vinblastine/mechlorethamine/ etoposide/vincristine/bleomycin/prednisone (Stanford V) • Escalated bleomycin/etoposide/doxorubicin/ cyclophosphamide/vincristine/procarbazine/ prednisone (BEACOPP) • Escalated BEACOPP followed by ABVD with RT	Referenced with permission from the NCCN Clinical Practice Guidelines in Oncology (NCCN Guidelines®) for Hodgkin Lymphoma V.2.2014. © National Comprehensive Cancer Network, Inc 2014. All rights reserved. Accessed March 28, 2014. To view the most recent and complete version of the guideline, go online to www.nccn.org. NATIONAL COMPREHENSIVE CANCER NETWORK®, NCCN®, NCCN GUIDELINES®, and all other NCCN Content are trademarks owned by the National Comprehensive Cancer Network, Inc.
Nodular Lymphocyte-predominant	• ABVD ± rituximab • Cyclophosphamide/doxorubicin/vincristine/ prednisone (CHOP) ± rituximab • Cyclophosphamide/vincristine/prednisone (CVP) ± rituximab • Single-agent rituximab	
NON-HODGKIN'S LYMPHOMA		
Follicular lymphoma	**First-line:** • Rituximab + bendamustine (category 1) • Rituximab, cyclophosphamide, doxorubicin, vincristine, prednisone (RCHOP) (category 1) • Rituximab, cyclophosphamide, vincristine, prednisone (RCVP) (category 1) • Rituximab *Refer to NCCN Clinical Practice Guidelines in Oncology (NCCN Guidelines®) for first-line therapy for elderly and second-line/subsequent therapy.*	Referenced with permission from the NCCN Clinical Practice Guidelines in Oncology (NCCN Guidelines®) for Non-Hodgkin's Lymphoma V.2.2014. © National Comprehensive Cancer Network, Inc 2014. All rights reserved. Accessed March 25, 2014. To view the most recent and complete version of the guideline, go online to www.nccn.org. NATIONAL COMPREHENSIVE CANCER NETWORK®, NCCN®, NCCN GUIDELINES®, and all other NCCN Content are trademarks owned by the National Comprehensive Cancer Network, Inc.

Mantle cell lymphoma	**Induction:**
	Aggressive therapy:
	• **CALGB regimen:**
	  ○ Treatment 1, 2, 2.5: rituximab + methotrexate with augmented CHOP (Treatment 2.5 is given if the pre-treatment 3 bone marrow biopsy contains >15% MCL)
	  ○ Treatment 3: etoposide, cytarabine, rituximab
	  ○ Treatment 4: carmustine, etoposide, cyclophosphamide/autologous stem cell rescue
	  ○ Treatment 5: rituximab maintenance
	• Cyclophosphamide/vincristine/doxorubicin/ dexamethasone alternating with high-dose methotrexate and cytarabine (HyperCVAD) + rituximab	

(Continued)

CANCER TYPE	THERAPIES†‡	REFERENCES
LYMPHOMA *(Continued)*		
HODGKIN LYMPHOMA *(Continued)*		
Mantle cell lymphoma *(Continued)*	• NORDIC regimen: rituximab + cyclophosphamide/ vincristine/doxorubicin/prednisone (maxi-CHOP) alternating with rituximab + high-dose cytarabine • Alternating RCHOP/rituximab, dexamethasone, cisplatin, cytarabine (RDHAP) • Sequential RCHOP/rituximab, ifosfamide, carboplatin, etoposide (RICE) **Less aggressive therapy:** • Bendamustine + rituximab • CHOP + rituximab followed by consolidation with rituximab maintenance (category 1 for maintenance) • Cladribine + rituximab • Modified rituximab-HyperCVAD with rituximab maintenance in patients >65 years *Refer to NCCN Clinical Practice Guidelines in Oncology (NCCN Guidelines®) for second-line therapy regimens.*	
Diffuse large B-cell lymphoma	**First-line therapy:** • Rituximab/cyclophosphamide/doxorubicin/ vincristine/prednisone (RCHOP) (category 1) • Dose-dense RCHOP (category 3) • Dose-adjusted cyclophosphamide/doxorubicin/ etoposide/vincristine/prednisone (EPOCH) (category 2B) *Refer to NCCN Clinical Practice Guidelines in Oncology (NCCN Guidelines®) for first-line therapy for consolidation and patients with poor left ventricular function and second-line therapy.*	
Burkitt's lymphoma	**Induction:** **Low/high risk-combination regimens:** • CALGB 10002: cyclophosphamide and prednisone followed by cycles containing either ifosfamide or cyclophosphamide; high-dose methotrexate, leucovorin, vincristine, dexamethasone, and either doxorubicin or etoposide or cytarabine; or intrathecal triple therapy (methotrexate, cytarabine, and hydrocortisone) + rituximab • CODOX-M (original or modified): cyclophosphamide, doxorubicin, vincristine with intrathecal methotrexate and cytarabine followed by high-dose systemic methotrexate ± rituximab (3 cycles) • Dose-adjusted EPOCH (cyclophosphamide/ doxorubicin/etoposide/vincristine/prednisone) + rituximab (minimum 3 cycles with one additional cycle beyond CR) (regimen includes intrathecal methotrexate) • HyperCVAD (cyclophosphamide/vincristine/ doxorubicin/dexamethasone) alternating with high-dose methotrexate and cytarabine + rituximab (regimen includes intrathecal therapy) *Refer to NCCN Clinical Practice Guidelines in Oncology (NCCN Guidelines®) for second-line therapy regimens.*	

CANCER TYPE	THERAPIES†‡	REFERENCES
LYMPHOMA *(Continued)*		
HODGKIN LYMPHOMA *(Continued)*		

Peripheral T-cell lymphoma	**First-line:**
	• Clinical trial
	• ALCL, ALK + histology:
	  o Cyclophosphamide, doxorubicin, vincristine, prednisone (CHOP-21)
	  o CHOP-21 + etoposide (CHOEP-21)
	
	Other histologies (ALCL, ALK-; PTCL, NOS; AITL; EATL):
	• CHOEP
	• CHOP-14
	• CHOP-21
	• CHOP followed by ICE (ifosfamide, carboplatin, etoposide)
	• CHOP followed by IVE (ifosfamide, etoposide, epirubicin) alternating with intermediate-dose methotrexate [Newcastle regimen] [studied only in patients with EATL]
	• Dose-adjusted EPOCH (etoposide, prednisone, vincristine, cyclophosphamide, doxorubicin)
	• HyperCVAD alternating with high-dose methotrexate and cytarabine
	
	Refer to NCCN Clinical Practice Guidelines in Oncology (NCCN Guidelines®) for first-line consolidation therapy and second-line therapies.	

OVARIAN CANCER		
Epithelial/fallopian tube/primary peritoneal	**Primary chemotherapy/adjuvant therapy regimens for stage II-IV:** • Paclitaxel/cisplatin (category 1) • Paclitaxel/carboplatin (category 1) • Docetaxel/carboplatin (category 1) • Dose-dense paclitaxel/carboplatin (category 1) • Paclitaxel/carboplatin/bevacizumab (category 3) *Refer to NCCN Clinical Practice Guidelines in Oncology (NCCN Guidelines®) for recurrence therapies.*	Referenced with permission from the NCCN Clinical Practice Guidelines in Oncology (NCCN Guidelines®) for Ovarian Cancer including Fallopian Tube Cancer and Primary Peritoneal Cancer V.2.2014. © National Comprehensive Cancer Network, Inc 2014. All rights reserved. Accessed March 28, 2014. To view the most recent and complete version of the guideline, go online to www.nccn.org. NATIONAL COMPREHENSIVE CANCER NETWORK®, NCCN®, NCCN GUIDELINES®, and all other NCCN Content are trademarks owned by the National Comprehensive Cancer Network, Inc.
PANCREATIC ADENOCARCINOMA		
Locally advanced unresectable	**Good performance status:** • Clinical trial (preferred) • FOLFIRINOX • Gemcitabine • Gemcitabine + nab-paclitaxel or other gemcitabine-based combination therapy • Capecitabine or continuous infusion fluorouracil (5-FU) (category 2B) • Chemoradiation in selected patients (locally advanced without systemic metastases), preferably following an adequate course of chemotherapy **Poor performance status:** • Gemcitabine (category 1) • Palliative and best supportive care *Refer to NCCN Clinical Practice Guidelines in Oncology (NCCN Guidelines®) for salvage therapy regimens.*	Referenced with permission from the NCCN Clinical Practice Guidelines in Oncology (NCCN Guidelines®) for Pancreatic Adenocarcinoma V.1.2014. © National Comprehensive Cancer Network, Inc 2014. All rights reserved. Accessed March 25, 2014. To view the most recent and complete version of the guideline, go online to www.nccn.org. NATIONAL COMPREHENSIVE CANCER NETWORK®, NCCN®, NCCN GUIDELINES®, and all other NCCN Content are trademarks owned by the National Comprehensive Cancer Network, Inc.

CANCER TYPE	THERAPIES†‡	REFERENCES
PANCREATIC ADENOCARCINOMA *(Continued)*		
Metastatic	**Good performance status:** • Clinical trial (preferred) • FOLFIRINOX (category 1) • Gemcitabine + nab-paclitaxel (category 1) • Gemcitabine + erlotinib (category 1) • Gemcitabine-based combination therapy • Gemcitabine (category 1) • Capecitabine or continuous infusion 5-FU (category 2B) **Poor performance status:** • Gemcitabine (category 1) • Palliative and best supportive care *Refer to NCCN Clinical Practice Guidelines in Oncology (NCCN Guidelines®) for salvage therapy regimens.*	
PROSTATE CANCER		
Small cell	• Cisplatin/etoposide • Carboplatin/etoposide • Docetaxel-based regimen • Clinical trial	Referenced with permission from the NCCN Clinical Practice Guidelines in Oncology (NCCN Guidelines®) for Prostate Cancer V.2.2014. © National Comprehensive Cancer Network, Inc 2014. All rights reserved. Accessed March 25, 2014. To view the most recent and complete version of the guideline, go online to www.nccn.org. NATIONAL COMPREHENSIVE CANCER NETWORK®, NCCN®, NCCN GUIDELINES®, and all other NCCN Content are trademarks owned by the National Comprehensive Cancer Network, Inc.
Symptomatic castration-recurrent	**First-line therapy:** • Docetaxel (category 1) • Radium-223 for symptomatic bone metastases (category 1) • Palliative RT or radionuclide for symptomatic bone metastases • Clinical trial • Best supportive care **For patients who are not candidates for docetaxel-based regimens:** • Mitoxantrone • Abiraterone acetate • Enzalutamide	

Abbreviation: RT = radiation therapy.

*Selected cancers. For more detailed information, refer to the individual monograph listings or FDA-approved labeling. Refer to www.cancer.gov for more information, such as therapies for CNS prophylaxis.

†Refer to NCCN Guidelines for categories of evidence and consensus.

‡All recommendations are category 2A unless otherwise indicated.

Referenced with permission from the NCCN Clinical Practice Guidelines in Oncology (NCCN Guidelines®) National Comprehensive Cancer Network, Inc 2014. All rights reserved. Accessed March 25, 2014. To view the most recent and complete version of the guideline, go online to www.nccn.org. NATIONAL COMPREHENSIVE CANCER NETWORK®, NCCN®, NCCN GUIDELINES®, and all other NCCN Content are trademarks owned by the National Comprehensive Cancer Network, Inc.

COLORECTAL CANCER TREATMENT OPTIONS

GENERIC (BRAND)	INDICATIONS	HOW SUPPLIED	ADULT DOSAGE	SPECIAL INSTRUCTIONS
Bevacizumab (Avastin)	• 1st- or 2nd-line treatment of mCRC in combination with IV 5-FU-based chemotherapy • 2nd-line treatment of mCRC, in combination with fluoropyrimidine-irinotecan- or fluoropyrimidine-oxaliplatin-based chemotherapy, in patients who have progressed on a 1st-line bevacizumab-containing regimen	Inj: 100mg/4mL, 400mg/16mL	**In Combination with Bolus-IFL:** Usual: 5mg/kg every 2 weeks. **In Combination with FOLFOX4:** Usual: 10mg/kg every 2 weeks. **In Combination with Fluoropyrimidine-Irinotecan or Fluoropyrimidine-Oxaliplatin-Based Chemotherapy:** Usual: 5mg/kg every 2 weeks or 7.5mg/kg every 3 weeks.	Administer only as an IV infusion. Administer 1st IV infusion over 90 min. If 1st infusion is tolerated, give 2nd infusion over 60 min and all subsequent infusions over 30 min if 2nd infusion is tolerated.
Capecitabine (Xeloda)	• 1st-line treatment of mCRC • As a single agent for adjuvant treatment in patients with Dukes' C colon cancer who have undergone complete resection of the primary tumor, when treatment with fluoropyrimidine therapy alone is preferred	Tab: 150mg, 500mg	**Monotherapy: Metastatic Colorectal Cancer: Usual:** 1250mg/m^2 bid for 2 weeks followed by a 1-week rest period given as 3-week cycles. **Adjuvant Dukes' C Colon Cancer Treatment:** 1250mg/m^2 bid for 2 weeks followed by 1-week rest period, given as 3-week cycles for total of 8 cycles (24 weeks).	Swallow whole with water and within 30 min after a meal. Toxicity may be managed by symptomatic treatment, dose interruptions, and dose adjustments. Reduce dose to 75% of the starting dose in patients with moderate renal impairment (CrCl: 30-50mL/min).
Cetuximab (Erbitux)	• Treatment of *KRAS*-mutation negative (wild-type), EGFR-expressing, mCRC: - In combination with FOLFIRI (irinotecan, 5-FU, leucovorin) for 1st-line treatment; - In combination with irinotecan in patients who are refractory to irinotecan-based chemotherapy; and - As monotherapy in patients who have failed oxaliplatin- and irinotecan-based chemotherapy or are intolerant to irinotecan	Inj: 2mg/mL [50mL, 100mL, vial]	**Colorectal Cancer (Monotherapy/With Irinotecan or FOLFIRI): Initial:** 400mg/m^2 IV over 120 min. Complete administration 1 hr prior to FOLFIRI. **Maint:** 250mg/m^2 IV over 60 min weekly until disease progression or unacceptable toxicity. Complete administration 1 hr prior to FOLFIRI.	Premedication with H$_1$ antagonist (eg, diphenhydramine 50mg) IV 30-60 min prior to 1st dose is recommended. Refer to PI for dose modifications regarding infusion reactions and dermatologic toxicity.

(Continued)

GENERIC (BRAND)	INDICATIONS	HOW SUPPLIED	ADULT DOSAGE	SPECIAL INSTRUCTIONS
Fluorouracil	• Palliative management of carcinoma of the colon and rectum	**Inj:** 50mg/mL [10mL]	12mg/kg IV qd for Days 1-4. If no toxicity observed, give 6mg/kg IV on Days 6, 8, 10, and 12 unless toxicity occurs. **Max:** 800mg/day. **Poor Risk Patients/Inadequate Nutritional State:** 6mg/kg/day IV for Days 1-3. If no toxicity observed, give 3mg/kg IV on Days 5, 7, and 9 unless toxicity occurs. **Max:** 400mg/day. **Maint:** If toxicity has not been a problem, may repeat 1st course every 30 days after last day of previous course; or give 10-15mg/kg/week IV as a single dose when toxic signs from initial course subside (max: 1g/week).	Administer only IV. Patients should be carefully evaluated prior to treatment to accurately estimate the optimum initial dosage. Patient's reaction to the previous course of therapy should be taken into account in determining the amount of the drug to be used, and the dosage should be adjusted accordingly.
Irinotecan HCl (Camptosar)	• As a component of 1st-line therapy in combination with 5-FU and LV for metastatic carcinoma of the colon or rectum • For patients with metastatic carcinoma of the colon or rectum whose disease has recurred or progressed following initial 5-FU therapy	**Inj:** 20mg/mL [2mL, 5mL, 15mL]	**Combination Therapy:** Administer as 90 min infusion followed by LV and 5-FU. **Regimen 1 (6-Week Cycle with Bolus 5-FU/LV):** 125mg/m^2 IV over 90 min on Days 1, 8, 15, and 22. **Regimen 2 (6-Week Cycle with Infusional 5-FU/LV):** 180mg/m^2 IV over 90 min on Days 1, 15, and 29. **Both Regimens:** Begin next cycle on Day 43. **Single Therapy: Regimen 1 (Weekly):** 125mg/m^2 IV over 90 min on Days 1, 8, 15, and 22 followed by 2-week rest. **Titrate:** Subsequent doses may be adjusted to as high as 150mg/m^2 or to as low as 50mg/m^2 in 25-50mg/m^2 decrements. **Regimen 2 (Every 3 Weeks):** 350mg/m^2 IV over 90 min once every 3 weeks. **Titrate:** Subsequent doses may be adjusted as low as 200mg/m^2 in 50mg/m^2 decrements.	Premedication with antiemetic agents at least 30 min prior to therapy. Consider reducing starting dose by at least 1 level for patients known to be homozygous for the UGT1A1*28 allele.
Leucovorin calcium	• Adjunct to 5-FU to prolong survival for palliative treatment of advanced colorectal cancer	**Inj:** 10mg/mL [50mg, 100mg, 200mg], 20mg/mL [350mg]	200mg/m^2 by slow IV over a minimum of 3 min, followed by 5-FU 370mg/m^2 IV qd for 5 days, or 20mg/m^2 IV qd followed by 5-FU 425mg/m^2 IV qd for 5 days. May repeat at 4-week intervals for 2 courses, then may repeat at 4- to 5-week intervals if the patient has completely recovered from the toxic effects of the prior treatment course.	Refer to PI for detailed dosage adjustment based on toxicity. LV and 5-FU should be administered separately.

GENERIC (BRAND)	INDICATIONS	HOW SUPPLIED	ADULT DOSAGE	SPECIAL INSTRUCTIONS
Levoleucovorin (Fusilev)	• Combination chemotherapy with 5-FU in the palliative treatment of patients with advanced mCRC	**Inj:** 50mg, 10mg/mL [17.5mL, 25mL]	100mg/m² slow IV over a minimum of 3 min, followed by 370mg/m² 5-FU IV, daily for 5 days, or 10mg/m² IV, followed by 425mg/m² 5-FU IV, daily for 5 days. May repeat at 4-week intervals for 2 courses, then at 4- to 5-week intervals if the patient has completely recovered from the toxic effects of the prior treatment course.	Refer to PI for detailed dosage adjustment based on toxicity. 5-FU should be administered separately.
Oxaliplatin (Eloxatin)	• In patients who have undergone complete resection of the primary tumor in combination with infusional 5-FU and LV: - Treatment of advanced colorectal cancer - Adjuvant treatment of stage III colon cancer	**Inj:** 5mg/mL [50mg, 100mg]	**Day 1:** 85mg/m² IV infusion and LV 200mg/m² IV infusion; give both over 120 min at the same time in separate bags using a Y-line, followed by 5-FU 400mg/m² IV bolus over 2-4 min, then 5-FU 600mg/m² IV infusion as a 22-hr continuous infusion. **Day 2:** LV 200mg/m² IV infusion over 120 min; followed by 5-FU 400mg/m² IV bolus over 2-4 min, then 5-FU 600mg/m² IV infusion as a 22-hr continuous infusion. Repeat cycle every 2 weeks. **Advanced Colorectal Cancer:** Continue treatment until disease progression or unacceptable toxicity. **Adjuvant Therapy Stage III Colon Cancer:** Treat for 6 months (12 cycles).	Administer oxaliplatin and LV at the same time in separate bags using a Y-line. Refer to PI for dose modification recommendations. Premedication with antiemetics is recommended.
Panitumumab (Vectibix)	• As a single agent for the treatment of EGFR-expressing, mCRC with disease progression on or following fluoropyrimidine-, oxaliplatin-, and irinotecan-containing chemotherapy regimens	**Inj:** 20mg/mL [5mL, 10mL, 20mL]	**Usual:** 6mg/kg IV infusion over 60 min every 14 days. Infuse doses >1000mg over 90 min.	Do not administer as IV push or bolus. Refer to PI for dose modifications for infusion reactions and dermatologic toxicities.
Regorafenib (Stivarga)	• Treatment of mCRC previously treated with fluoropyrimidine-, oxaliplatin-, and irinotecan-based chemotherapy, an antivascular endothelial growth factor therapy, and, if *KRAS* wild-type, an anti-EGFR therapy	**Tab:** 40mg	**Usual:** 160mg qd for the first 21 days of each 28-day cycle. Continue treatment until disease progression or unacceptable toxicity.	Take dose at the same time each day with a low-fat breakfast that contains <30% fat. Swallow tablet whole. Refer to PI for dose modifications.

(Continued)

GENERIC (BRAND)	INDICATIONS	HOW SUPPLIED	ADULT DOSAGE	SPECIAL INSTRUCTIONS
Ziv-aflibercept (Zaltrap)	• In combination with FOLFIRI for the treatment of mCRC that is resistant to or has progressed following an oxaliplatin-containing regimen	**Inj:** 25mg/mL [4mL, 8mL]	4mg/kg IV infusion over 1 hr every 2 weeks. Administer prior to any component of the FOLFIRI regimen on day of treatment. Continue until disease progression or unacceptable toxicity.	Refer to PI for dose modifications.

Refer to full FDA-approved labeling for additional information.

Abbreviations: 5-FU = 5-fluorouracil; EGFR = epidermal growth factor receptor; FOLFIRI = leucovorin, 5-fluorouracil, irinotecan; FOLFOX = leucovorin, 5-fluorouracil, oxaliplatin; IFL = irinotecan, leucovorin, 5-fluorouracil; LV = leucovorin; mCRC = metastatic colorectal cancer.

LUNG CANCER TREATMENT OPTIONS

GENERIC (BRAND)	INDICATIONS	HOW SUPPLIED	ADULT DOSAGE
ANTIFOLATES			
Pemetrexed (Alimta)	• Initial treatment of locally advanced or metastatic nonsquamous NSCLC in combination with cisplatin • Maintenance treatment of patients with locally advanced or metastatic nonsquamous NSCLC whose disease has not progressed after 4 cycles of platinum-based 1st-line chemotherapy • Single-agent for the treatment of patients with locally advanced or metastatic nonsquamous NSCLC after prior chemotherapy	**Inj:** 100mg, 500mg	**Combination with Cisplatin: Usual:** 500mg/m² IV over 10 min on Day 1 of each 21-day cycle. Give cisplatin 75mg/m² over 2 hrs beginning 30 min after the end of administration. **Single Agent: Usual:** 500mg/m² IV over 10 min on Day 1 of each 21-day cycle.
ANTIMICROTUBULE AGENTS			
Docetaxel (Taxotere)	• Treatment of locally advanced or metastatic NSCLC after failure of prior chemotherapy • In combination with cisplatin for treatment of unresectable, locally advanced or metastatic NSCLC in patients who have not previously received chemotherapy	**Inj:** (Generic) 10mg/mL [2mL, 8mL, 16mL], (Taxotere) 20mg/mL [1mL, 4mL, 8mL]	**After Platinum Therapy Failure:** 75mg/m² IV over 1 hr every 3 weeks. **Chemotherapy-Naive:** 75mg/m² IV over 1 hr followed by cisplatin 75mg/m² over 30-60 min every 3 weeks.
Paclitaxel	• 1st-line treatment of NSCLC in combination with cisplatin in patients who are not candidates for potentially curative surgery and/or radiation therapy	**Inj:** 30mg/5mL, 100mg/16.7mL, 150mg/25mL, 300mg/50mL	**Usual:** 135mg/m² IV over 24 hrs every 3 weeks, followed by cisplatin 75mg/m².
Paclitaxel protein-bound (Abraxane)	• 1st-line treatment of locally advanced or metastatic NSCLC, in combination with carboplatin, in patients who are not candidates for curative surgery or radiation therapy	**Inj:** 100mg	100mg/m² IV over 30 min on Days 1, 8, and 15 of each 21-day cycle. Give carboplatin on Day 1 of each 21-day cycle, immediately after paclitaxel.
ANTHRACYCLINES			
Doxorubicin HCl (Adriamycin)	• To produce regression in bronchogenic carcinoma in which the small cell histologic type is the most responsive, compared to other cell types	**Inj:** 10mg, 20mg, 50mg; 2mg/mL [5mL, 10mL, 25mL, 100mL]	**Monotherapy:** 60-75mg/m² as a single IV inj every 21 days. Use lower dose with inadequate bone marrow reserves due to old age, prior therapy, or neoplastic marrow infiltration. **Concomitant Chemotherapy:** 40-60mg/m² as a single IV inj every 21-28 days.
EPIDERMAL GROWTH FACTOR TYROSINE KINASE INHIBITORS			
Afatinib (Gilotrif)	• 1st-line treatment of patients with metastatic NSCLC whose tumors have epidermal growth factor receptor exon 19 deletions or exon 21 (L858R) substitution mutations	**Tab:** 20mg, 30mg, 40mg	**Usual:** 40mg qd until disease progression or no longer tolerated. Refer to PI for therapy with a P-glycoprotein inhibitor.
Crizotinib (Xalkori)	• Treatment of metastatic NSCLC whose tumors are anaplastic lymphoma kinase-positive	**Cap:** 200mg, 250mg	**Usual:** 250mg bid until disease progression or no longer tolerated by the patient.

(Continued)

GENERIC (BRAND)	INDICATIONS	HOW SUPPLIED	ADULT DOSAGE
EPIDERMAL GROWTH FACTOR TYROSINE KINASE INHIBITORS *(Continued)*			
Erlotinib (Tarceva)	• Treatment of locally advanced or metastatic NSCLC after failure of at least 1 prior chemotherapy regimen • Maintenance of locally advanced or metastatic NSCLC that has not progressed after 4 cycles of platinum-based 1st-line chemotherapy	**Tab:** 25mg, 100mg, 150mg	150mg qd. Continue until disease progression or unacceptable toxicity occurs.
NITROGEN MUSTARD ALKYLATING AGENTS			
Mechlorethamine HCl (Mustargen)	• Palliative treatment of bronchogenic carcinoma	**Inj:** 10mg	**Usual:** 0.4mg/kg/course given either as a single dose or in divided doses of 0.1-0.2mg/kg/day. Base dosage on ideal dry body weight; consider presence of edema or ascites.
NUCLEOSIDE ANALOGUE METABOLITES			
Gemcitabine (Gemzar)	• In combination with cisplatin for 1st-line treatment of inoperable, locally advanced (Stage IIIA or IIIB), or metastatic (Stage IV) NSCLC	**Inj:** (Generic) 2g; (Gemzar) 200mg, 1g	**4-Week Cycle:** 1000mg/m^2 IV over 30 min on Days 1, 8, and 15 of each 28-day cycle. Give cisplatin 100mg/m^2 IV on Day 1 after gemcitabine infusion. **3-Week Cycle:** 1250mg/m^2 IV over 30 min on Days 1 and 8 of each 21-day cycle. Give cisplatin 100mg/m^2 IV on Day 1 after gemcitabine infusion.
PHOTOSENSITIZERS			
Porfimer sodium (Photofrin)	• Treatment of microinvasive endobronchial NSCLC in patients for whom surgery and radiotherapy are not indicated • Reduction of obstruction and palliation of symptoms in patients with completely/partially obstructing endobronchial NSCLC	**Inj:** 75mg	2mg/kg IV over 3-5 min followed by photoactivation 40-50 hrs after inj. A 2nd light application may be given 96-120 hrs following initial inj. Refer to PI for detailed procedure. **Max:** 3 courses of photodynamic therapy.
PODOPHYLLOTOXIN DERIVATIVES			
Etoposide	• 1st-line combination therapy for treatment of SCLC.	**Cap:** 50mg; **Inj:** 20mg/mL [5mL, 12.5mL, 25mL, 50mL]	(Inj) **Range:** 35mg/m^2/day IV for 4 days to 50mg/m^2/day for 5 days. (PO) 2 times the IV dose rounded to nearest 50mg.
Etoposide phosphate (Etopophos)	• 1st-line combination therapy for treatment of SCLC.	**Inj:** 100mg	35mg/m^2/day IV for 4 days to 50mg/m^2/day for 5 days at infusion rates 5-210 min.
TOPOISOMERASE I INHIBITORS			
Topotecan (Hycamtin)	• Treatment of relapsed SCLC in patients with a prior complete or partial response and who are at least 45 days from the end of 1st-line chemotherapy	**Cap:** 0.25mg, 1mg	2.3mg/m^2/day PO qd for 5 consecutive days repeated every 21 days. Round calculated dose to nearest 0.25mg and give minimum number of 1mg and 0.25mg caps.
Topotecan HCl (Hycamtin)	• Treatment of SCLC sensitive disease after failure of 1st-line chemotherapy	**Inj:** 4mg	**Max:** 4mg IV. 1.5mg/m^2 by IV infusion qd over 30 min for 5 consecutive days, starting on Day 1 of 21-day course. Minimum of 4 courses recommended in absence of tumor progression.

GENERIC (BRAND)	INDICATIONS	HOW SUPPLIED	ADULT DOSAGE
VASCULAR ENDOTHELIAL GROWTH FACTOR INHIBITORS			
Bevacizumab (Avastin)	• 1st-line treatment of unresectable, locally advanced, recurrent, or metastatic nonsquamous NSCLC in combination with carboplatin and paclitaxel	**Inj:** 100mg/4mL, 400mg/16mL	**Usual:** 15mg/kg every 3 weeks (with carboplatin and paclitaxel).
VINCA ALKALOIDS			
Vinorelbine tartrate (Navelbine)	• Single agent or in combination with cisplatin for 1st-line treatment of ambulatory patients with unresectable, advanced NSCLC, including Stage IV NSCLC • For use in combination with cisplatin for Stage III NSCLC	**Inj:** 10mg/mL [1mL, 5mL]	**Single-Agent:** 30mg/m^2 IV over 6-10 min weekly. **Concomitant Cisplatin:** 25mg/m^2 weekly with cisplatin 100mg/m^2 every 4 weeks, or 30mg/m^2 weekly with cisplatin 120mg/m^2 on Days 1 and 29, then every 6 weeks.

Refer to full FDA-approved labeling for additional information.
Abbreviations: NSCLC = non-small cell lung cancer; SCLC = small cell lung cancer.

PROSTATE CANCER TREATMENT OPTIONS

GENERIC (BRAND)	HOW SUPPLIED	ADULT DOSAGE	SPECIAL INSTRUCTIONS
CHEMOTHERAPY AGENTS			
Cabazitaxel (Jevtana)	**Inj:** 60mg/1.5mL	**Hormone-Refractory Metastatic Prostate Cancer w/ Prior Docetaxel-Containing Treatment:** 25mg/m^2 administered as a 1-hr IV infusion q3wks in combination with prednisone 10mg PO administered qd throughout treatment.	Premedicate at least 30 min prior to each Jevtana with antihistamine, corticosteroid, and H$_2$ antagonist. Administer using an in-line filter of 0.22µm.
Docetaxel (Taxotere)	**Inj:** (Generic) 10mg/mL [2mL, 8mL, 16mL]; (Taxotere) 20mg/mL [1mL, 4mL, 8mL]	**Hormone-Refractory Metastatic Prostate Cancer:** 75mg/m^2 q3wks administered as a 1-hr IV infusion in combination with prednisone 5mg PO bid continuously.	Premedicate with oral dexamethasone 8mg 12 hrs, 3 hrs, and 1 hr before docetaxel infusion.
Estramustine phosphate sodium (Emcyt)	**Cap:** 140mg	**Palliative Treatment of Metastatic and/or Progressive Prostate Cancer:** 14mg/kg/d given tid-qid. Treat for 30-90 days before determining possible benefits of continued therapy.	Take with water at least 1 hr before or 2 hrs after meals. Do not take with milk, milk products, or calcium-rich foods or drugs.
Mitoxantrone	**Inj:** 2mg/mL [10mL, 12.5mL, 15mL]	**Pain Related to Advanced Hormone-Refractory Prostate Cancer Given w/ Corticosteroids:** 12-14mg/m^2 given as a short IV infusion every 21 days.	For IV infusion only.
Sipuleucel-T (Provenge)	**Sus:** 250mL	**Hormone-Refractory Metastatic Prostate Cancer:** Infuse 250mL over 1 hr q2wks for 3 doses.	Premedicate with oral acetaminophen and antihistamine 30 min prior to Provenge administration.
ESTROGENS			
Conjugated estrogens (Premarin)	**Tab:** 0.3mg, 0.45mg, 0.625mg, 0.9mg, 1.25mg	**Palliative Treatment of Advanced Hormone-Refractory Metastatic Prostate Cancer:** 1.25-2.5mg tid. Effectiveness of therapy judged by phosphatase determinations and symptomatic improvement.	
Esterified estrogens (Menest)	**Tab:** 0.3mg, 0.625mg, 1.25mg, 2.5mg	**Palliative Treatment of Advanced Prostate Cancer:** 1.25-2.5mg tid. Effectiveness of therapy judged by phosphatase determinations and symptomatic improvement.	
Estradiol (Estrace)	**Tab:** 0.5mg*, 1mg*, 2mg* *scored	**Palliative Treatment of Advanced Hormone-Refractory Prostate Cancer:** 1-2mg tid. Effectiveness of therapy judged by phosphatase determinations and symptomatic improvement.	
Estradiol valerate (Delestrogen)	**Inj:** 10mg/mL, 20mg/mL, 40mg/mL	**Palliative Treatment of Advanced Hormone-Refractory Prostate Cancer:** 30mg or more every 1 or 2 wks.	

(Continued)

GENERIC (BRAND)	HOW SUPPLIED	ADULT DOSAGE	SPECIAL INSTRUCTIONS
GNRH ANALOGUES			
Goserelin acetate (Zoladex 1-month)	**Implant:** 3.6mg	**Advanced Prostatic Carcinoma:** 3.6mg every 28 days. **Stage B$_2$-C Prostatic Carcinoma (Given w/ Flutamide):** 3.6mg depot 8 wks before radiotherapy, followed by 10.8mg depot 28 days after 1st injection, or 4 doses of 3.6mg depot at 28-day intervals (2 before and 2 during radiotherapy).	Inject SQ into anterior abdominal wall below navel line.
Goserelin acetate (Zoladex 3-month)	**Implant:** 10.8mg	**Advanced Prostatic Carcinoma:** 10.8mg q12wks. **Stage B$_2$-C Prostatic Carcinoma (Given w/ Flutamide):** 3.6mg depot 8 wks before radiotherapy, followed by 10.8mg depot 28 days after 1st injection.	Inject SQ into anterior abdominal wall below navel line.
GNRH ANTAGONISTS			
Degarelix (Firmagon)	**Inj:** 80mg, 120mg	**Advanced Prostate Cancer: Initial:** 240mg at 40mg/mL concentration. **Maint:** 80mg SQ every 28 days at 20mg/mL concentration.	Inject SQ in the abdominal region and rotate sites periodically.
LHRH AGONISTS			
Histrelin acetate (Vantas)	**Implant:** 50mg	**Palliative Treatment of Advanced Prostate Cancer:** 50mg (1 implant) every 12 months. Insert SQ in the inner aspect of upper arm.	
Leuprolide acetate	**Inj:** 5mg/mL [2.8mL]	**Palliative Treatment of Advanced Prostate Cancer:** 1mg SQ qd. Rotate injection sites.	
Leuprolide acetate (Eligard)	**Inj:** 7.5mg, 22.5mg, 30mg, 45mg	**Palliative Treatment of Advanced Prostate Cancer:** 7.5mg SQ monthly, 22.5mg SQ every 3 months, 30mg SQ every 4 months, or 45mg SQ every 6 months. Rotate injection sites.	Injection sites should be an area with sufficient soft or loose subcutaneous tissue.
Leuprolide acetate (Lupron Depot)	**Inj:** 7.5mg, 22.5mg, 30mg, 45mg	**Palliative Treatment of Advanced Prostate Cancer:** 7.5mg IM monthly, 22.5mg IM q12wks, 30mg IM q16wks, or 45mg IM q24wks. Give as single IM injection; rotate injection sites.	
Triptorelin pamoate (Trelstar)	**Inj:** 3.75mg, 11.25mg, 22.5mg	**Palliative Treatment of Advanced Prostate Cancer:** 3.75mg IM q4wks, 11.25mg IM q12wks, or 22.5mg IM q24wks.	Give IM injection in either buttock. Rotate injection sites.
NONSTEROIDAL ANTIANDROGENS			
Abiraterone acetate (Zytiga)	**Tab:** 250mg	**Metastatic Castration-Resistant Prostate Cancer:** 1000mg qd in combination with prednisone 5mg PO bid.	Swallow whole with water at least 1 hr before or 2 hrs after meals. Do not crush or chew tablets.
Bicalutamide (Casodex)	**Tab:** 50mg	**Stage D$_2$ Metastatic Prostate Cancer:** 50mg qd (AM or PM) at same time each day. Initiate simultaneously with an LHRH analogue.	
Enzalutamide (Xtandi)	**Cap:** 40mg	**Metastatic Castration-Resistant Prostate Cancer w/ Prior Docetaxel Treatment:** 160mg qd.	Swallow whole. Do not chew, dissolve, or open the capsules.

GENERIC (BRAND)	HOW SUPPLIED	ADULT DOSAGE	SPECIAL INSTRUCTIONS
NONSTEROIDAL ANTIANDROGENS *(Continued)*			
Flutamide	**Cap:** 125mg	250mg q8h. **Stage B$_2$-C:** With goserelin acetate implant, start 8 wks prior to initiating radiation therapy and continue during radiation therapy. **Stage D$_2$:** Initiate with LHRH agonist and continue until progression.	
Nilutamide (Nilandron)	**Tab:** 150mg	**Stage D$_2$ Metastatic Prostate Cancer w/ Surgical Castration:** Start on the same day as or on the day after surgical castration. **Initial:** 300mg qd for 30 days. **Maint:** 150mg qd.	

Abbreviations: GnRH = gonadotropin-releasing hormone; LHRH = luteinizing hormone-releasing hormone.

Refer to full FDA-approved labeling for additional information and for dose modifications following adverse effects, toxicities, and renal/hepatic impairment.

RISK FACTORS AND TREATMENT OPTIONS FOR BREAST CANCER

UNMODIFIABLE RISK FACTORS	
Gender	Women > Men
Age	1 out of 8 breast cancer diagnoses are in women <45 yrs, while about 2 out of 3 occur in women ≥55 yrs
Genetic	*BRCA1* and *BRCA2* gene mutations, single *ATM* gene mutation, *CHEK2* gene mutation, *TP53* gene mutation, *PTEN* gene mutations, *CDH1* gene mutation, *STK11* gene mutation
Race	Whites > African Americans. Women <45 yrs: African Americans > Whites
Family history	Having a first-degree relative with breast cancer doubles risk; having 2 first-degree relatives increases risk about 3-fold. <15% of women with breast cancer have a family member with the disease
Personal history of breast cancer	Women with cancer in one breast have a 3- to 4-fold increased risk of developing a new cancer in another area of the same breast or in the opposite breast
Benign breast conditions	Nonproliferative lesions, proliferative lesions with or without atypia. Women with a family history of breast cancer and hyperplasia or atypical hyperplasia have an even greater risk
Early menarche	Women who started menstruating at an early age (<12 yrs)
Age at menopause	Women who went through menopause at a late age (>55 yrs)
Personal history of breast abnormalities	Women with lobular carcinoma in situ (LCIS) have a 7- to 11-fold increased risk of developing cancer in either breast
Earlier breast radiation exposure	Women <40 who had radiation therapy to the chest area as treatment for another cancer
Breast tissue density	Women with a higher proportion of dense breast tissue (more glandular and fibrous tissue and less fatty tissue as seen on a mammogram)

Lifestyle factors associated with increased risk of breast cancer

- Alcohol (2-5 drinks/day)
- High body mass index
- Not having children or having them when >30 yrs
- Lack of physical activity
- Not breastfeeding

Drugs associated with increased risk of breast cancer

- Birth control (oral contraceptives, depot-medroxyprogesterone acetate)
- DES (diethylstilbestrol)
- Postmenopausal hormone therapy or hormone replacement therapy

Uncertain risk factors

- Antiperspirants
- Bras
- Breast implants
- Diet and vitamin intake
- Induced abortion
- Night work
- Pollution (chemicals)
- Smoking (active or passive)

Source: What are the risk factors for breast cancer? American Cancer Society website. http://www.cancer.org/cancer/breastcancer/detailedguide/breast-cancer-risk-factors. Updated January 31, 2014. Accessed March 11, 2014.

(Continued)

GENERIC (BRAND)	HOW SUPPLIED	INDICATIONS	ADULT DOSAGE
ANDROGENS			
Fluoxymesterone (Androxy)	**Tab:** 10mg	• Treatment in premenopausal females who have benefited from oophorectomy and have a hormone-responsive tumor • Used secondarily in females with advancing inoperable metastatic (skeletal) disease who are 1-5 yrs postmenopausal	**Palliation of Inoperable Mammary Cancer in Females:** 10-40mg/day in divided doses. Continue therapy ≥3 months to determine objective response. **Palliation of Advanced Mammary Cancer:** Duration of therapy will depend on response to treatment and appearance of adverse effects.
Methyltestosterone (Testred)	**Cap:** 10mg	• Treatment in premenopausal females who have benefited from oophorectomy and have a hormone-responsive tumor • Used secondarily in females with advancing inoperable metastatic (skeletal) disease who are 1-5 yrs postmenopausal	50-200mg/day.
Testosterone enanthate (Delatestryl)	**Inj:** 200mg/mL [5mL]	• Treatment in premenopausal females who have benefited from oophorectomy and have a hormone-responsive tumor • Used secondarily in females with advancing inoperable metastatic (skeletal) disease who are 1-5 yrs postmenopausal	**Palliation of Inoperable Mammary Cancer in Females:** 200-400mg IM every 2-4 weeks.
ANTHRACYCLINES			
Doxorubicin HCl (Adriamycin)	**Inj:** 10mg, 20mg, 50mg; 2mg/mL [5mL, 10mL, 25mL, 100mL]	• To produce regression in disseminated neoplastic disease • Component of adjuvant therapy in women with evidence of axillary lymph node involvement following resection of primary breast cancer	**Monotherapy:** 60-75mg/m² as a single IV inj every 21 days. **Concomitant Chemotherapy:** 40-60mg/m² as a single IV inj every 21-28 days.
Epirubicin HCl (Ellence)	**Inj:** 2mg/mL [25mL, 100mL]	• Adjuvant therapy in patients with evidence of axillary node tumor involvement following resection of primary breast cancer	**Usual:** 100-120mg/m² IV infusion over 15-20 min, repeat at 3- to 4-week cycles. May give total dose on Day 1 of each cycle or divide equally on Days 1 and 8.
ANTIESTROGENS			
Fulvestrant (Faslodex)	**Inj:** 50mg/mL [5mL]	• Treatment of hormone receptor positive metastatic disease in post-menopausal women with disease progression following antiestrogen therapy	Administer on Days 1, 15, and 29, and once monthly thereafter. **Usual:** 500mg IM into buttocks slowly (1-2 min/inj) as two 5-mL inj, one in each buttock. Refer to PI for hepatic impairment dosing.
ANTIMETABOLITES			
Fluorouracil	**Inj:** 50mg/mL [10mL]	• Palliative management of carcinoma of the breast	12mg/kg IV qd for Days 1-4. If no toxicity observed, give 6mg/kg IV on Day 6, 8, 10, and 12 unless toxicity occurs. **Max:** 800mg/day. **Maint:** If toxicity has not been a problem, may repeat 1st course every 30 days after last day of previous course; or give 10-15mg/kg/week IV as a single dose when toxic signs from initial course subside (max: 1g/week).

GENERIC (BRAND)	HOW SUPPLIED	INDICATIONS	ADULT DOSAGE
ANTIMICROTUBULE AGENTS			
Eribulin mesylate (Halaven)	**Inj:** 0.5mg/mL [2mL]	• Treatment of metastatic disease in patients who have previously received at least 2 chemotherapeutic regimens for the treatment of metastatic disease (prior therapy should have included an anthracycline and a taxane in either the adjuvant or metastatic setting)	Administer IV over 2-5 min on Days 1 and 8 of a 21-day cycle. **Usual:** 1.4mg/m². Refer to PI for hepatic impairment dosing.
Ixabepilone (Ixempra)	**Inj:** 15mg, 45mg	• In combination with capecitabine for the treatment of patients with metastatic or locally advanced disease resistant to treatment with an anthracycline and a taxane, or whose cancer is taxane-resistant and for whom further anthracycline therapy is contraindicated • As monotherapy for the treatment of metastatic or locally advanced disease in patients whose tumors are resistant or refractory to anthracyclines, taxanes, and capecitabine	**Usual:** 40mg/m² IV over 3 hrs every 3 weeks. Refer to PI for hepatic impairment dosing.
ESTROGENS			
Conjugated estrogens (Premarin)	**Tab:** 0.3mg, 0.45mg, 0.625mg, 0.9mg, 1.25mg	• Palliative treatment in patients with metastatic disease	10mg tid for minimum 3 months.
Esterified estrogens (Menest)	**Tab:** 0.3mg, 0.625mg, 1.25mg, 2.5mg	• Palliative therapy for metastatic disease in selected men and women	10mg tid for at least 3 months.
Estradiol (Estrace)	**Tab:** 0.5mg, 1mg, 2mg	• Palliative treatment in appropriately selected women and men with metastatic disease	**Usual:** 10mg tid for at least 3 months.
FLUOROPYRIMIDINE CARBAMATES			
Capecitabine (Xeloda)	**Tab:** 150mg, 500mg	• Treatment of metastatic disease in combination with docetaxel after failure of prior anthracycline-containing chemotherapy • Monotherapy for metastatic disease in patients resistant to both paclitaxel and anthracycline-containing chemotherapy regimen or resistant to paclitaxel and for whom further anthracycline therapy is not indicated	**Monotherapy: Usual:** 1250mg/m² bid for 2 weeks followed by a 1-week rest period given as 3-week cycles. **Combination with Docetaxel: Usual:** 1250mg/m² bid for 2 weeks followed by 1-week rest period, combined with docetaxel 75mg/m² as a 1-hr IV infusion every 3 weeks. Refer to PI for renal impairment dosing.
KINASE INHIBITORS			
Everolimus (Afinitor)	**Tab:** 2.5mg, 5mg, 7.5mg, 10mg	• Treatment of postmenopausal women with advanced hormone receptor-positive, HER2-negative disease in combination with exemestane, after failure of treatment with letrozole or anastrozole	**Usual:** 10mg qd.

(Continued)

GENERIC (BRAND)	HOW SUPPLIED	INDICATIONS	ADULT DOSAGE
KINASE INHIBITORS (Continued)			
Lapatinib (Tykerb)	Tab: 250mg	• In combination with capecitabine for the treatment of patients with advanced/metastatic disease whose tumors overexpress HER2 and who had prior therapy, including an anthracycline, a taxane, and trastuzumab • In combination with letrozole for the treatment of postmenopausal women with hormone receptor-positive metastatic disease that overexpresses the HER2 receptor for whom hormonal therapy is indicated	Give at least 1 hr ac or 1 hr pc. **HER2-Positive Metastatic Breast Cancer: Usual:** 1250mg qd on Days 1-21 continuously with capecitabine 2000mg/m²/day (2 doses 12 hrs apart) on Days 1-14 in a repeating 21-day cycle. **Hormone Receptor-Positive, HER2-Positive Metastatic Breast Cancer: Usual:** 1500mg qd continuously with letrozole 2.5mg qd.
LUTEINIZING HORMONE-RELEASING HORMONE AGONISTS			
Goserelin acetate (Zoladex 1-Month)	Implant: 3.6mg	• Palliative treatment of advanced disease in pre- and perimenopausal women	One 3.6mg implant SQ every 28 days. Administer into anterior abdominal wall below the navel line.
MONOCLONAL ANTIBODIES/HER2 BLOCKERS			
Ado-trastuzumab emtansine (Kadcyla)	Inj: 100mg, 160mg	• Single agent treatment of HER2-positive metastatic disease in patients who previously received trastuzumab and a taxane, separately or in combination (patients should have either received prior therapy for metastatic disease, or developed disease recurrence during/within 6 months of completing adjuvant therapy)	**Usual:** 3.6mg/kg IV infusion every 3 weeks (21-day cycle) until disease progression or unacceptable toxicity. **Max:** 3.6mg/kg. **First Infusion:** Administer over 90 min. **Subsequent Infusions:** Administer over 30 min if prior infusions were well tolerated.
Trastuzumab (Herceptin)	Inj: 440mg	• Adjuvant treatment of HER2-overexpressing node-positive or node-negative disease as part of a treatment regimen consisting of doxorubicin, cyclophosphamide, and either paclitaxel or docetaxel, with docetaxel and carboplatin, or as single agent following multimodality anthracycline-based therapy • In combination with paclitaxel for 1st-line treatment of HER2-overexpressing metastatic breast cancer, or as single agent for treatment of HER2-overexpressing breast cancer in patients who have received ≥1 chemotherapy regimen for metastatic disease	**Breast Cancer Adjuvant Treatment:** Administer for 52 weeks. **During and Following Paclitaxel, Docetaxel, or Docetaxel/Carboplatin: Initial:** 4mg/kg IV infusion over 90 min, then at 2mg/kg IV infusion over 30 min weekly during chemotherapy for the first 12 weeks (paclitaxel or docetaxel) or 18 weeks (docetaxel/carboplatin). One week following the last weekly dose, give 6mg/kg IV infusion over 30-90 min every 3 weeks. **As Single Agent within 3 Weeks Following Completion of Multimodality Anthracycline-Based Chemotherapy Regimens: Initial:** 8mg/kg IV infusion over 90 min. **Maint:** 6mg/kg IV infusion over 30-90 min every 3 weeks. **Breast Cancer Metastatic Treatment: Initial:** 4mg/kg as 90-min IV infusion. **Maint:** 2mg/kg once weekly as 30-min IV infusion until disease progression.
NITROGEN MUSTARD ALKYLATING AGENTS			
Cyclophosphamide	Inj: 500mg, 1g, 2g; Tab: 25mg, 50mg	• Treatment of breast carcinoma	(IV) **Monotherapy: Initial:** 40-50mg/kg in divided doses over 2-5 days, or 10-15mg/kg every 7-10 days, or 3-5mg/kg twice weekly. (PO) **Initial/Maint:** 1-5mg/kg/day. (IV/PO) Adjust dose according to evidence of antitumor activity and/or leukopenia.

GENERIC (BRAND)	HOW SUPPLIED	INDICATIONS	ADULT DOSAGE
NUCLEOSIDE ANALOGUES/ANTIMETABOLITES			
Gemcitabine (Gemzar)	**Inj:** (Generic) 2g; (Gemzar) 200mg, 1g	• In combination with paclitaxel for 1st-line treatment of metastatic disease after failure of prior anthracycline-containing adjuvant chemotherapy, unless anthracyclines were clinically contraindicated	1250mg/m² IV over 30 min on Days 1 and 8 of each 21-day cycle. Give paclitaxel 175mg/m² on Day 1 as a 3-hr IV infusion before gemcitabine.
PROGESTINS			
Megestrol acetate	**Tab:** 20mg, 40mg	• Palliative treatment of advanced disease	40mg qid for a minimum of 2 months.
SELECTIVE ESTROGEN RECEPTOR MODULATORS			
Tamoxifen citrate	**Tab:** 10mg, 20mg	• Treatment of metastatic disease in women and men • Treatment of node-positive or axillary node-negative disease in women following total or segmental mastectomy, axillary dissection, and breast irradiation	**Usual:** 20-40mg/day. Give dosages >20mg/day in divided doses (am and pm).
Toremifene citrate (Fareston)	**Tab:** 60mg	• Treatment of metastatic breast cancer in postmenopausal women with estrogen-receptor positive or unknown tumors	**Usual:** 60mg qd. Treat until disease progression is observed.
SELECTIVE NONSTEROIDAL AROMATASE INHIBITORS			
Anastrozole (Arimidex)	**Tab:** 1mg	• First-line treatment of postmenopausal women with hormone receptor-positive or hormone receptor-unknown locally advanced or metastatic disease • Adjuvant treatment of postmenopausal women with hormone receptor-positive early disease • Treatment of advanced disease in postmenopausal women with disease progression following tamoxifen therapy	1mg qd. Continue until tumor progression with advanced breast cancer.
Letrozole (Femara)	**Tab:** 2.5mg	• First-line treatment of postmenopausal women with hormone receptor positive or unknown, locally advanced or metastatic disease • Adjuvant treatment of postmenopausal women with hormone receptor positive early disease • Extended adjuvant treatment of early disease in postmenopausal women, who have received 5 yrs of adjuvant tamoxifen therapy • Treatment of advanced disease in postmenopausal women with disease progression following antiestrogen therapy	2.5mg qd. **Adjuvant Early Breast Cancer:** D/C at relapse. **Advanced Breast Cancer:** Continue until tumor progression is evident. Refer to PI for hepatic impairment dosing.

(Continued)

GENERIC (BRAND)	HOW SUPPLIED	INDICATIONS	ADULT DOSAGE
TAXANES			
Docetaxel (Taxotere)	**Inj:** (Generic) 10mg/mL [2mL, 8mL, 16mL]; (Taxotere) 20mg/mL [1mL, 4mL, 8mL]	• Treatment of locally advanced or metastatic disease after failure of prior chemotherapy • In combination with doxorubicin and cyclophosphamide for adjuvant treatment of operable node-positive disease	**Locally Advanced or Metastatic Breast Cancer:** 60-100mg/m^2 IV over 1 hr every 3 weeks. **Adjuvant to Operable Node-Positive Breast Cancer:** 75mg/m^2 1 hr after doxorubicin 50mg/m^2 and cyclophosphamide 500mg/m^2 every 3 weeks for 6 courses.
Paclitaxel	**Inj:** 30mg/5mL, 100mg/16.7mL, 150mg/25mL, 300mg/50mL	• Adjuvant treatment of node-positive disease administered sequentially to standard doxorubicin-containing combination chemotherapy • Treatment of breast cancer after failure of combination chemotherapy for metastatic disease or relapse within 6 months of adjuvant chemotherapy	**Adjuvant Therapy: Usual:** 175mg/m^2 IV over 3 hrs every 3 weeks for 4 courses given sequentially to doxorubicin-containing combination chemotherapy. **Failure of Initial Chemotherapy for Metastatic Disease or Relapse within 6 Months of Chemotherapy:** 175mg/m^2 IV over 3 hrs every 3 weeks.
Paclitaxel protein-bound (Abraxane)	**Inj:** 100mg	• Treatment of breast cancer after failure of combination chemotherapy for metastatic disease or relapse within 6 months of adjuvant chemotherapy (prior therapy should have included an anthracycline unless clinically contraindicated)	260mg/m^2 IV over 30 min every 3 weeks. Refer to PI for hepatic impairment dosing.
VINCA ALKALOIDS			
Vinblastine	**Inj:** 1mg/mL [10mL]	• Palliative treatment of unresponsive breast carcinoma	Dose at weekly intervals. **1st Dose:** 3.7mg/m^2. **2nd Dose:** 5.5mg/m^2. **3rd Dose:** 7.4mg/m^2. **4th Dose:** 9.25mg/m^2. **5th Dose:** 11.1mg/m^2. **Max:** 18.5mg/m^2. Do not increase dose after dose that reduces WBC count to 3000 cells/mm^3. **Maint:** Administer a dose of 1 increment smaller than this dose at weekly intervals. Do not give next dose until WBC count has returned to at least 4000 cells/mm^3. Do not increase the size of subsequent doses if oncolytic activity occurred before leukopenic effect. **Usual Weekly Dose:** 5.5-7.4mg/m^2. Refer to PI for hepatic impairment dosing.

Refer to full FDA-approved labeling for additional information.
Abbreviation: HER2 = human epidermal growth factor receptor type 2.

ANTIDEPRESSANTS

GENERIC (BRAND)	HOW SUPPLIED	ADULT DAILY DOSE INITIAL (I), USUAL (U), MAX (M)	TITRATE†
AMINOKETONES			
Bupropion HCl (Forfivo XL)	**Tab, ER:** 450mg	**(U,M)**450mg	N/A
(Wellbutrin)	**Tab:** 75mg, 100mg	**(I)**200mg **(U)**300mg **(M)**450mg	Increase in dose should not exceed 100mg/d q3d.
(Wellbutrin SR)	**Tab, SR:** 100mg, 150mg, 200mg	**(I)**150mg **(U)**300mg **(M)**400mg	May increase to 300mg/d as early as Day 4 of dosing, if tolerated. May increase to 400mg/d after several wks if no clinical improvement. Allow at least 8 hrs between doses.
(Wellbutrin XL)	**Tab, ER:** 150mg, 300mg	**(I)**150mg **(U)**300mg **(M)**450mg	May increase to 300mg/d as early as Day 4 of dosing, if tolerated. May increase to 450mg/d after several wks if no clinical improvement. Allow at least 24 hrs between doses.
Bupropion HBr (Aplenzin)	**Tab, ER:** 174mg, 348mg, 522mg	**(I)**174mg **(U)**348mg **(M)**522mg	May increase to 348mg/d as early as Day 4 of dosing, if tolerated.
MONOAMINE OXIDASE INHIBITORS			
Isocarboxazid (Marplan)	**Tab:** 10mg*	**(I)**20mg **(M)**60mg	May increase by 10mg q2-4d to 40mg/d by end of first wk, if tolerated, then increase by increments of up to 20mg/wk, if needed and tolerated, to 60mg/d.
Phenelzine sulfate (Nardil)	**Tab:** 15mg	**(I)**45mg **(U)**15mg qd or qod **(M)**90mg	Dosage should be increased to at least 60mg/d at a fairly rapid pace if tolerated. May need to be increased up to 90mg/d.
Selegiline (Emsam)	**Patch:** 6mg/24 hr, 9mg/24 hr, 12mg/24 hr	**(I,U)**6mg/24 hr **(M)**12mg/24 hr	May increase by 3mg/24 hr at intervals of no less than 2 wks.
Tranylcypromine sulfate (Parnate)	**Tab:** 10mg	**(I,U)**30mg **(M)**60mg	May increase by 10mg/d at intervals of 1-3 wks.
PHENYLPIPERAZINES			
Nefazodone HCl	**Tab:** 50mg, 100mg*, 150mg*, 200mg, 250mg	**(I)**200mg **(U)**300-600mg	Increases should occur in increments of 100-200mg/d at intervals of no less than 1 wk.
SELECTIVE SEROTONIN NOREPINEPHRINE REUPTAKE INHIBITORS			
Desvenlafaxine (Khedezla)	**Tab, ER:** 50mg, 100mg	**(I,U)**50mg **(M)**400mg	N/A
(Pristiq)	**Tab, ER:** 50mg, 100mg	**(I,U)**50mg **(M)**400mg	N/A
Duloxetine HCl (Cymbalta)	**Cap, DR:** 20mg, 30mg, 60mg	**(I)**40-60mg **(U)**60mg **(M)**120mg	N/A
Levomilnacipran HCl (Fetzima)	**Cap, ER:** 20mg, 40mg, 80mg, 120mg	**(I)**20mg **(U)**40-120mg **(M)**120mg	Initial dose of 20mg/d for 2 days. Increase to 40mg/d. May then increase in increments of 40mg of no less than 2 days as necessary.

(Continued)

GENERIC (BRAND)	HOW SUPPLIED	ADULT DAILY DOSE INITIAL (I), USUAL (U), MAX (M)	TITRATE†
SELECTIVE SEROTONIN NOREPINEPHRINE REUPTAKE INHIBITORS *(Continued)*			
Venlafaxine HCl	**Tab:** 25mg*, 37.5mg*, 50mg*, 75mg*, 100mg*	**(I)**75mg **(U)**75-225mg **(M)**375mg	Doses may be increased in increments up to 75mg/d if needed and should be made at intervals of no less than 4 days.
	Tab, ER: 37.5mg, 75mg, 150mg, 225mg	**(I)**37.5-75mg **(U)**75-225mg **(M)**225mg	Doses may be increased in increments up to 75mg/d if needed and should be made at intervals of no less than 4 days.
(Effexor XR)	**Cap, ER:** 37.5mg, 75mg, 150mg		
SELECTIVE SEROTONIN REUPTAKE INHIBITORS/5-HT1A PARTIAL AGONISTS			
Vilazodone HCl (Viibryd)	**Tab:** 10mg, 20mg, 40mg	**(I)**10mg **(U,M)**40mg	Initial dose of 10mg/d for 7 days. Increase to 20mg/d for an additional 7 days, then increase to 40mg/d.
SELECTIVE SEROTONIN REUPTAKE INHIBITORS			
Citalopram HBr (Celexa)	**Sol:** (generic) 10mg/5mL; **Tab:** 10mg, 20mg*, 40mg*	**(I)**20mg **(U,M)**40mg	Dose increase should occur at intervals of no less than 1 wk.
Escitalopram oxalate (Lexapro)	**Sol:** 1mg/mL; **Tab:** 5mg, 10mg*, 20mg*	**(I,U)**10mg **(M)**20mg	If the dose is increased to 20mg/d, it should occur after a minimum of 1 wk.
Fluoxetine HCl (Prozac)	**Cap:** 10mg, 20mg, 40mg; **Sol:** (generic) 20mg/5mL; **Tab:** (generic) 10mg*, 20mg*, 60mg*	**(I)**20mg **(U)**20-80mg **(M)**80mg	Dose increase may be considered after several weeks if insufficient clinical improvement is observed.
(Prozac Weekly)	**Cap, DR:** 90mg	**(I,U,M)**90mg	Weekly dosing is recommended to be initiated 7 days after the last daily dose of Prozac 20mg.
Paroxetine HCl (Paxil)	**Sus:** 10mg/5mL; **Tab:** 10mg*, 20mg*, 30mg, 40mg	**(I)**20mg **(U)**20-50mg **(M)**50mg	Some patients not responding to 20mg dose may benefit from dose increases in 10mg/d increments, up to a max of 50mg/d. Dose changes should occur at intervals of at least 1 wk.
(Paxil CR)	**Tab, CR:** 12.5mg, 25mg, 37.5mg	**(I)**25mg **(U)**25mg-62.5mg **(M)**62.5mg	Some patients not responding to the 25mg dose may benefit from dose increases in 12.5mg/d increments, up to a max of 62.5mg/d. Dose changes should occur at intervals of at least 1 wk.
Paroxetine mesylate (Pexeva)	**Tab:** 10mg, 20mg*, 30mg, 40mg	**(I)**20mg **(U)**20-50mg **(M)**50mg	Some patients not responding to a 20mg dose may benefit from dose increases in 10mg/d increments, up to a max of 50mg/d. Dose changes should occur at intervals of at least 1 wk.
Sertraline HCl (Zoloft)	**Sol:** 20mg/mL; **Tab:** 25mg*, 50mg*, 100mg*	**(I)**50mg **(U)**50-200mg **(M)**200mg	Patients not responding to a 50mg dose may benefit from dose increases up to a max of 200mg/d. Dose changes should not occur at intervals of less than 1 wk.

GENERIC (BRAND)	HOW SUPPLIED	ADULT DAILY DOSE INITIAL (I), USUAL (U), MAX (M)	TITRATE†
TETRACYCLICS			
Maprotiline HCl	**Tab:** 25mg*, 50mg*, 75mg*	**(I)OP:** 25mg-75mg, **IP:** 100mg-150mg **(U)OP:** 75mg-150mg, **IP:** 150mg-225mg **(M)OP:** 150mg-225mg, **IP:** 225mg	**OP:** Initial dosages should be maintained for 2 wks. Dosages may then be increased gradually in 25mg increments, as required and tolerated. **IP:** Most severely depressed patients may be gradually increased as required and tolerated.
Mirtazapine (Remeron, Remeron SolTab)	**Tab:** 15mg*, 30mg*, 45mg; **Tab, Disintegrating:** 15mg, 30mg, 45mg	**(I)**15mg **(U)**15mg-45mg **(M)**45mg	Dose changes should not be made at intervals of less than 1 to 2 wks.
TRIAZOLOPYRIDINES			
Trazodone HCl	**Tab:** 50mg*, 100mg*, 150mg*, 300mg*	**(I)**150mg **(M)OP:** 400mg, **IP:** 600mg	Dose may be increased by 50mg/d q3-4d.
(Oleptro)	**Tab, ER:** 150mg*, 300mg*	**(I)**150mg **(M)**375mg	Dose may be increased by 75mg/d q3d.
TRICYCLICS			
Amitriptyline HCl	**Tab:** 10mg, 25mg, 50mg, 75mg, 100mg, 150mg	**(I)OP:** 50-100mg, **IP:** 100mg **(U)**50-100mg **(M)OP:** 150mg, **IP:** 300mg	In some patients, 40mg/d is a sufficient maintenance dose. **OP:** Dosage may be increased by 25-50mg/d at bedtime, as needed. **IP:** Dosages should be increased gradually.
Amoxapine	**Tab:** 25mg*, 50mg*, 100mg*, 150mg*	**(I)**100-150mg **(U)**200-300mg **(M)OP:** 400mg, **IP:** 600mg	Initial dose may be increased to 200-300mg/d by the end of the first wk. If no response is seen after treatment of 300mg/d for at least 2 wks, dosages may be increased to 400mg/d (OP) or 600mg/d (IP).
Desipramine HCl (Norpramin)	**Tab:** 10mg, 25mg, 50mg, 75mg, 100mg, 150mg	**(U)**100-200mg **(M)**300mg	Dosage should be initiated at a lower level and increased according to tolerance and clinical response. Treatment of patients requiring as much as 300mg should generally be initiated in hospitals.
Doxepin HCl	**Cap:** 10mg, 25mg, 50mg, 75mg, 100mg, 150mg; **Sol:** 10mg/mL	**(I)**75mg **(U)**75-150mg **(M)**300mg	Severely ill patients may require doses with gradual increases to 300mg/d. Patients with mild symptoms may require doses as low as 25-50mg/d. The 150mg capsule is intended for maintenance therapy only.
Imipramine HCl (Tofranil)	**Tab:** 10mg, 25mg, 50mg	**(I)OP:** 75mg, **IP:** 100mg **(U)OP:** 50-150mg, **IP:** 200mg **(M)OP:** 200mg, **IP:** 250-300mg	**IP:** Gradually increase initial dose to 200mg/d as required. May increase to 250-300mg/d if no response after 2 wks. **OP:** Increase initial dose to 150mg/d ud.
Imipramine pamoate (Tofranil PM)	**Cap:** 75mg, 100mg, 125mg, 150mg	**(I)OP:** 75mg, **IP:** 100-150mg **(U)**75-150mg **(M)OP:** 200mg, **IP:** 250-300mg	**OP:** Initial dose may be increased to 150mg/d and then increased to 200mg/d prn. **IP:** Initial dose may be increased to 200mg/d and, if no response after 2 wks, should be increased to 250-300mg/d.

(Continued)

A271

GENERIC (BRAND)	HOW SUPPLIED	ADULT DAILY DOSE INITIAL (I), USUAL (U), MAX (M)	TITRATE†
TRICYCLICS *(Continued)*			
Nortriptyline HCl (Pamelor)	**Cap:** 10mg, 25mg, 50mg, 75mg; **Sol:** 10mg/5mL	**(U)**75-100mg **(M)**150mg	Dosage should begin at a low level and be increased gradually.
Protriptyline HCl (Vivactil)	**Tab:** 5mg, 10mg	**(U)**15-40mg **(M)**60mg	Dosage should be initiated at a low level and increased gradually, noting clinical response and tolerance. Dosage may be increased to 60mg/d if necessary. Increases should be made in the AM dose.
Trimipramine maleate (Surmontil)	**Cap:** 25mg, 50mg, 100mg	**(I)**OP: 75mg, IP: 100mg **(U)**50-150mg **(M)**OP: 200mg, IP: 250-300mg	Dosage should be initiated at a low level and increased gradually, noting clinical response and tolerance. **OP:** Initial dose increases to 150mg/d. **IP:** Initial dose may be increased gradually in a few days to 200mg/d and, if no response after 2-3 wks, may be increased to 250-300mg/d.
MISCELLANEOUS			
Vortioxetine HBr (Brintellix)	**Tab:** 5mg, 10mg, 15mg, 20mg	**(I)**10mg **(U,M)**20mg	Dose should be increased as tolerated.

Refer to full FDA-approved labeling for additional information.

Abbreviations: DR = delayed-release; ER = extended-release; IP = inpatient; OP = outpatient; SR = sustained-release.

*Scored.

†Titration dosing refers to upward titration only. Refer to full product labeling for discontinuation of treatment, as a gradual reduction in dose may be required. For dosing in hepatic/renal impairment or geriatric or adolescent patients, see individual PI.

MENTAL HEALTH TREATMENT OPTIONS

GENERIC (BRAND)	HOW SUPPLIED	INDICATIONS													
		BIPOLAR DISORDER (MAINTENANCE)	BIPOLAR, MANIC EPISODES	BIPOLAR, MIXED EPISODES	BIPOLAR, DEPRESSIVE EPISODES	DEPRESSION	SCHIZOPHRENIA	ANXIETY	OCD	PANIC DISORDER	PTSD	PMDD	IRRITABILITY ASSOCIATED W/ AUTISTIC DISORDER	PSYCHOSIS	RLS
BENZISOXAZOLE DERIVATIVES															
Iloperidone (Fanapt)	**Tab:** 1mg, 2mg, 4mg, 6mg, 8mg, 10mg, 12mg						✓								
Paliperidone (Invega)	**Tab, ER:** 1.5mg, 3mg, 6mg, 9mg						✓								
Paliperidone palmitate (Invega Sustenna)	**Inj, ER:** 39mg, 78mg, 117mg, 156mg, 234mg						✓								
Risperidone (Risperdal Consta)	**Inj:** 12.5mg, 25mg, 37.5mg, 50mg	✓					✓								
Risperidone (Risperdal, Risperdal M-Tab)	**Sol:** 1mg/mL; **Tab:** 0.25mg, 0.5mg, 1mg, 2mg, 3mg, 4mg, **Tab, Disintegrating:** 0.5mg, 1mg, 2mg, 3mg, 4mg		✓*	✓*			✓						✓		
Ziprasidone (Geodon)	**Cap:** 20mg, 40mg, 60mg, 80mg; **Inj:** 20mg/mL	✓* (PO)	✓ (PO)	✓ (PO)			✓								

(Continued)

GENERIC (BRAND)	HOW SUPPLIED	INDICATIONS: BIPOLAR DISORDER (MAINTENANCE)	BIPOLAR, MANIC EPISODES	BIPOLAR, MIXED EPISODES	BIPOLAR, DEPRESSIVE EPISODES	DEPRESSION	SCHIZOPHRENIA	ANXIETY	OCD	PANIC DISORDER	PTSD	PMDD	IRRITABILITY ASSOCIATED W/ AUTISTIC DISORDER	PSYCHOSIS	RLS
BENZODIAZEPINES															
Alprazolam (Niravam)	**Tab, Disintegrating:** 0.25mg, 0.5mg, 1mg, 2mg							✓		✓					
Alprazolam (Xanax)	**Tab:** 0.25mg, 0.5mg, 1mg, 2mg							✓		✓					
Alprazolam (Xanax XR)	**Tab, ER:** 0.5mg, 1mg, 2mg, 3mg									✓					
Chlordiazepoxide HCl (Librium)	**Cap:** 5mg, 10mg, 25mg							✓							
Clonazepam (Klonopin)	**Tab:** (Klonopin) 0.5mg, 1mg, 2mg; **Tab, Disintegrating:** (ODT) 0.125mg, 0.25mg, 0.5mg, 1mg, 2mg									✓					
Clorazepate dipotassium (Tranxene T-Tabs)	**Tab:** 3.75mg, 7.5mg, 15mg							✓							
Diazepam (Valium)	**Tab:** 2mg, 5mg, 10mg							✓							
Lorazepam (Ativan)	**Sol:** 2mg/mL; **Tab:** (Ativan) 0.5mg, 1mg, 2mg							✓							

GENERIC (BRAND)	HOW SUPPLIED	INDICATIONS													
		BIPOLAR DISORDER (MAINTENANCE)	BIPOLAR, MANIC EPISODES	BIPOLAR, MIXED EPISODES	BIPOLAR, DEPRESSIVE EPISODES	DEPRESSION	SCHIZOPHRENIA	ANXIETY	OCD	PANIC DISORDER	PTSD	PMDD	IRRITABILITY ASSOCIATED W/ AUTISTIC DISORDER	PSYCHOSIS	RLS
BENZODIAZEPINES *(Continued)*															
Midazolam HCI	**Syrup:** 2mg/mL							✓							
BENZISOTHIAZOL DERIVATIVES															
Lurasidone HCI (Latuda)	**Tab:** 20mg, 40mg, 60mg, 80mg, 120mg				✓*		✓								
DIBENZAPINE DERIVATIVES															
Asenapine maleate (Saphris)	**Tab, SL:** 5mg, 10mg		✓*	✓*			✓								
Clozapine (Clozaril, Fazaclo, Versacloz)	**Sus:** (Versacloz) 50mg/mL; **Tab:** (Generic) 25mg, 50mg, 100mg, 200mg; (Clozaril) 25mg, 100mg; **Tab, Disintegrating:** (Fazaclo) 12.5mg, 25mg, 100mg, 150mg, 200mg						✓								
Loxapine (Adasuve)	**Powder, Inhalation:** 10mg						✓								

(Continued)

GENERIC (BRAND)	HOW SUPPLIED	INDICATIONS													
		BIPOLAR DISORDER (MAINTENANCE)	BIPOLAR, MANIC EPISODES	BIPOLAR, MIXED EPISODES	BIPOLAR, DEPRESSIVE EPISODES	DEPRESSION	SCHIZOPHRENIA	ANXIETY	OCD	PANIC DISORDER	PTSD	PMDD	IRRITABILITY ASSOCIATED W/ AUTISTIC DISORDER	PSYCHOSIS	RLS
DIBENZAPINE DERIVATIVES *(Continued)*															
Quetiapine fumarate (Seroquel)	**Tab:** 25mg, 50mg, 100mg, 200mg, 300mg, 400mg	✓*	✓*		✓		✓								
Quetiapine fumarate (Seroquel XR)	**Tab, ER:** 50mg, 150mg, 200mg, 300mg, 400mg	✓*	✓*	✓*	✓	✓*	✓								
Olanzapine (Zyprexa, Zyprexa Zydis, Zyprexa IntraMuscular)	**Inj:** 10mg; **Tab:** 2.5mg, 5mg, 7.5mg, 10mg, 15mg, 20mg; **Tab, Disintegrating:** (Zydis) 5mg, 10mg, 15mg, 20mg	✓ (PO)	✓* (PO)	✓* (PO)	✓* (PO)	✓* (PO)	✓ (PO)								
Olanzapine pamoate (Zyprexa Relprevv)	**Inj, ER:** 210mg, 300mg, 405mg						✓								
DOPAMINE RECEPTOR AGONISTS															
Pramipexole dihydrochloride (Mirapex)	**Tab:** 0.125mg, 0.25mg, 0.5mg, 0.75mg, 1mg, 1.5mg														✓

GENERIC (BRAND)	HOW SUPPLIED	INDICATIONS													
		BIPOLAR DISORDER (MAINTENANCE)	BIPOLAR, MANIC EPISODES	BIPOLAR, MIXED EPISODES	BIPOLAR, DEPRESSIVE EPISODES	DEPRESSION	SCHIZOPHRENIA	ANXIETY	OCD	PANIC DISORDER	PTSD	PMDD	IRRITABILITY ASSOCIATED W/ AUTISTIC DISORDER	PSYCHOSIS	RLS
DOPAMINE RECEPTOR AGONISTS *(Continued)*															
Ropinirole HCl (Requip)	**Tab:** 0.25mg, 0.5mg, 1mg, 2mg, 3mg, 4mg, 5mg														✓
Rotigotine (Neupro)	**Patch, ER:** 1mg/24 hrs, 2mg/24 hrs, 3mg/24 hrs, 4mg/24 hrs, 6mg/24 hrs, 8mg/24 hrs														✓
DOPAMINE/NOREPINEPHRINE REUPTAKE INHIBITORS															
Bupropion HBr (Aplenzin)	**Tab, ER:** 174mg, 348mg, 522mg					✓									
Bupropion HCl (Forfivo XL)	**Tab, ER:** 450mg					✓									
Bupropion HCl (Wellbutrin, Wellbutrin SR, Wellbutrin XL)	**Tab:** 75mg, 100mg; **Tab, SR:** (SR) 100mg, 150mg, 200mg; **Tab, ER:** (XL) 150mg, 300mg					✓									
MONOAMINE OXIDASE INHIBITORS															
Isocarboxazid (Marplan)	**Tab:** 10mg					✓									

(Continued)

A277

GENERIC (BRAND)	HOW SUPPLIED	Bipolar Disorder (Maintenance)	Bipolar, Manic Episodes	Bipolar, Mixed Episodes	Bipolar, Depressive Episodes	Depression	Schizophrenia	Anxiety	OCD	Panic Disorder	PTSD	PMDD	Irritability Associated w/ Autistic Disorder	Psychosis	RLS
MONOAMINE OXIDASE INHIBITORS *(Continued)*															
Phenelzine sulfate (Nardil)	**Tab:** 15mg					✓									
Selegiline (Emsam)	**Patch:** 6mg/24 hrs, 9mg/24 hrs, 12mg/24 hrs					✓									
Tranylcypromine sulfate (Parnate)	**Tab:** 10mg					✓									
PARTIAL D$_2$/5HT$_{1A}$ AGONISTS/5HT$_{2A}$ ANTAGONISTS															
Aripiprazole (Abilify, Abilify Discmelt)	**Inj:** 7.5mg/mL; **Sol:** 1mg/mL; **Tab:** 2mg, 5mg, 10mg, 15mg, 20mg, 30mg; **Tab, Disintegrating:** (Discmelt) 10mg, 15mg	✓*	✓*	✓*		✓*	✓						✓		
Aripiprazole (Abilify Maintena)	**Inj, ER:** 300mg, 400mg						✓								
PHENOTHIAZINES															
Chlorpromazine HCl	**Inj:** 25mg/mL; **Tab:** 10mg, 25mg, 50mg, 100mg, 200mg						✓							✓	
Fluphenazine decanoate	**Inj:** 25mg/mL						✓								

INDICATIONS

GENERIC (BRAND)	HOW SUPPLIED	INDICATIONS													
		BIPOLAR DISORDER (MAINTENANCE)	BIPOLAR, MANIC EPISODES	BIPOLAR, MIXED EPISODES	BIPOLAR, DEPRESSIVE EPISODES	DEPRESSION	SCHIZOPHRENIA	ANXIETY	OCD	PANIC DISORDER	PTSD	PMDD	IRRITABILITY ASSOCIATED W/ AUTISTIC DISORDER	PSYCHOSIS	RLS
PHENOTHIAZINES *(Continued)*															
Fluphenazine HCl	Elixir: 2.5mg/5mL; Inj: 2.5mg/mL; Sol, Concentrated: 5mg/mL; Tab: 1mg, 2.5mg, 5mg, 10mg													✓	
Perphenazine	Tab: 2mg, 4mg, 8mg, 16mg						✓								
Thioridazine HCl	Tab: 10mg, 25mg, 50mg, 100mg						✓								
Trifluoperazine HCl	Tab: 1mg, 2mg, 5mg, 10mg						✓	✓							
SEROTONIN/NOREPINEPHRINE REUPTAKE INHIBITORS															
Desvenlafaxine (Khedezla ER)	Tab, ER: 50mg, 100mg					✓									
Desvenlafaxine succinate (Pristiq)	Tab, ER: 50mg, 100mg					✓									
Duloxetine HCl (Cymbalta)	Cap, DR: 20mg, 30mg, 60mg					✓		✓							
Levomilnacipran HCl (Fetzima)	Cap, ER: 20mg, 40mg, 80mg, 120mg					✓									

(Continued)

A279

MENTAL HEALTH TREATMENT OPTIONS

GENERIC (BRAND)	HOW SUPPLIED	BIPOLAR DISORDER (MAINTENANCE)	BIPOLAR, MANIC EPISODES	BIPOLAR, MIXED EPISODES	BIPOLAR, DEPRESSIVE EPISODES	DEPRESSION	SCHIZOPHRENIA	ANXIETY	OCD	PANIC DISORDER	PTSD	PMDD	IRRITABILITY ASSOCIATED W/ AUTISTIC DISORDER	PSYCHOSIS	RLS
SEROTONIN/NOREPINEPHRINE REUPTAKE INHIBITORS *(Continued)*															
Nefazodone HCl	**Tab:** 50mg, 100mg, 150mg, 200mg, 250mg					✓									
Venlafaxine HCl	**Tab:** 25mg, 37.5mg, 50mg, 75mg, 100mg; **Tab, ER:** 37.5mg, 75mg, 150mg, 225mg					✓		✓ (ER)							
Venlafaxine HCl (Effexor XR)	**Cap, ER:** 37.5mg, 75mg, 150mg					✓		✓		✓					
SELECTIVE SEROTONIN REUPTAKE INHIBITORS/5HT₁ₐ PARTIAL AGONISTS															
Vilazodone HCl (Viibryd)	**Tab:** 10mg, 20mg, 40mg					✓									
SELECTIVE SEROTONIN REUPTAKE INHIBITORS AND COMBINATIONS															
Citalopram HBr (Celexa)	**Sol:** (Generic) 10mg/5mL; **Tab:** 10mg, 20mg, 40mg					✓									
Escitalopram oxalate (Lexapro)	**Sol:** 5mg/5mL; **Tab:** 5mg, 10mg, 20mg					✓		✓							
Fluoxetine HCl	**Sol:** 20mg/5mL; **Tab:** 10mg, 20mg, 60mg				✓* (Tab)	✓			✓	✓					
Fluoxetine HCl (Prozac)	**Cap:** 10mg, 20mg, 40mg				✓*	✓*			✓	✓					

SELECTIVE SEROTONIN REUPTAKE INHIBITORS AND COMBINATIONS (Continued)

GENERIC (BRAND)	HOW SUPPLIED	INDICATIONS													
		BIPOLAR DISORDER (MAINTENANCE)	BIPOLAR, MANIC EPISODES	BIPOLAR, MIXED EPISODES	BIPOLAR, DEPRESSIVE EPISODES	DEPRESSION	SCHIZOPHRENIA	ANXIETY	OCD	PANIC DISORDER	PTSD	PMDD	IRRITABILITY ASSOCIATED W/ AUTISTIC DISORDER	PSYCHOSIS	RLS
Fluoxetine HCl (Prozac Weekly)	Cap, DR: 90mg				✓*	✓*			✓	✓					
Fluoxetine HCl-Olanzapine (Symbyax)	Cap: 25-3mg, 25-6mg, 50-6mg, 25-12mg, 50-12mg				✓	✓									
Fluvoxamine maleate	Tab: 25mg, 50mg, 100mg								✓						
Fluvoxamine maleate (Luvox CR)	Cap, ER: 100mg, 150mg								✓						
Paroxetine HCl (Paxil)	Sus: 10mg/5mL; Tab: 10mg, 20mg, 30mg, 40mg					✓		✓	✓	✓	✓				
Paroxetine HCl (Paxil CR)	Tab, Controlled-Release: 12.5mg, 25mg, 37.5mg					✓		✓	✓	✓		✓			
Paroxetine mesylate (Pexeva)	Tab: 10mg, 20mg, 30mg, 40mg					✓		✓	✓	✓					
Sertraline HCl (Zoloft)	Sol: 20mg/mL; Tab: 25mg, 50mg, 100mg					✓		✓	✓	✓	✓	✓			

(Continued)

GENERIC (BRAND)	HOW SUPPLIED	INDICATIONS													
		BIPOLAR DISORDER (MAINTENANCE)	BIPOLAR, MANIC EPISODES	BIPOLAR, MIXED EPISODES	BIPOLAR, DEPRESSIVE EPISODES	DEPRESSION	SCHIZOPHRENIA	ANXIETY	OCD	PANIC DISORDER	PTSD	PMDD	IRRITABILITY ASSOCIATED W/ AUTISTIC DISORDER	PSYCHOSIS	RLS
TETRACYCLIC ANTIDEPRESSANTS															
Maprotiline HCl	**Tab:** 25mg, 50mg, 75mg					✓		✓							
Mirtazapine (Remeron, Remeron SolTab)	**Tab:** 15mg, 30mg, 45mg; **Tab, Disintegrating:** (SolTab) 15mg, 30mg, 45mg					✓									
THIOXANTHENE DERIVATIVES															
Thiothixene	**Cap:** 1mg, 2mg, 5mg, 10mg						✓								
TRICYCLIC ANTIDEPRESSANTS AND COMBINATIONS															
Amitriptyline HCl	**Tab:** 10mg, 25mg, 50mg, 75mg, 100mg, 150mg					✓									
Amitriptyline HCl-Chlordiazepoxide	**Tab:** 12.5-5mg, 25-10mg					✓		✓							
Amitriptyline HCl-Perphenazine	**Tab:** 10-2mg, 25-2mg, 10-4mg, 25-4mg, 50-4mg					✓	✓	✓							
Amoxapine	**Tab:** 25mg, 50mg, 100mg, 150mg					✓									

GENERIC (BRAND)	HOW SUPPLIED	INDICATIONS													
		BIPOLAR DISORDER (MAINTENANCE)	BIPOLAR, MANIC EPISODES	BIPOLAR, MIXED EPISODES	BIPOLAR, DEPRESSIVE EPISODES	DEPRESSION	SCHIZOPHRENIA	ANXIETY	OCD	PANIC DISORDER	PTSD	PMDD	IRRITABILITY ASSOCIATED W/AUTISTIC DISORDER	PSYCHOSIS	RLS
TRICYCLIC ANTIDEPRESSANTS AND COMBINATIONS *(Continued)*															
Desipramine HCl (Norpramin)	**Tab:** 10mg, 25mg, 50mg, 75mg, 100mg, 150mg					✓									
Doxepin HCl	**Cap:** 10mg, 25mg, 50mg, 75mg, 100mg, 150mg; **Sol:** 10mg/mL					✓		✓							
Imipramine HCl (Tofranil)	**Tab:** 10mg, 25mg, 50mg					✓									
Imipramine pamoate (Tofranil-PM)	**Cap:** 75mg, 100mg, 125mg, 150mg					✓									
Nortriptyline HCl (Pamelor)	**Cap:** 10mg, 25mg, 50mg, 75mg; **Sol:** 10mg/5mL					✓									
Protriptyline HCl (Vivactil)	**Tab:** 5mg, 10mg					✓									
Trimipramine maleate (Surmontil)	**Cap:** 25mg, 50mg, 100mg					✓									
VALPROATE COMPOUNDS															
Divalproex sodium (Depakote)	**Tab, DR:** 125mg, 250mg, 500mg		✓												

(Continued)

A283

GENERIC (BRAND)	HOW SUPPLIED	INDICATIONS													
		BIPOLAR DISORDER (MAINTENANCE)	BIPOLAR, MANIC EPISODES	BIPOLAR, MIXED EPISODES	BIPOLAR, DEPRESSIVE EPISODES	DEPRESSION	SCHIZOPHRENIA	ANXIETY	OCD	PANIC DISORDER	PTSD	PMDD	IRRITABILITY ASSOCIATED W/ AUTISTIC DISORDER	PSYCHOSIS	RLS
VALPROATE COMPOUNDS (Continued)															
Divalproex sodium (Depakote ER)	**Tab, ER:** 250mg, 500mg		✓	✓											
MISCELLANEOUS															
Buspirone HCl	**Tab:** 5mg, 7.5mg, 10mg, 15mg, 30mg							✓							
Carbamazepine (Equetro)	**Cap, ER:** 100mg, 200mg, 300mg		✓	✓											
Gabapentin enacarbil (Horizant)	**Tab, ER:** 300mg, 600mg														✓
Lamotrigine (Lamictal, Lamictal ODT)	**Tab, Chewable:** 2mg, 5mg, 25mg; **Tab:** 25mg, 100mg, 150mg, 200mg; **Tab, Disintegrating:** (ODT) 25mg, 50mg, 100mg, 200mg	✓													
Lithium carbonate	**Cap:** 150mg, 300mg, 600mg; **Sol:** 8mEq/5mL; **Tab:** 300mg	✓	✓												

GENERIC (BRAND)	HOW SUPPLIED	INDICATIONS													
		BIPOLAR DISORDER (MAINTENANCE)	BIPOLAR, MANIC EPISODES	BIPOLAR, MIXED EPISODES	BIPOLAR, DEPRESSIVE EPISODES	DEPRESSION	SCHIZOPHRENIA	ANXIETY	OCD	PANIC DISORDER	PTSD	PMDD	IRRITABILITY ASSOCIATED W/ AUTISTIC DISORDER	PSYCHOSIS	RLS
MISCELLANEOUS *(Continued)*															
Lithium carbonate (Lithobid)	**Tab, ER:** 300mg, 450mg; (Lithobid) 300mg	✓	✓												
Trazodone HCl	**Tab:** 50mg, 100mg, 150mg, 300mg					✓									
Trazodone HCl (Oleptro)	**Tab, ER:** 150mg, 300mg					✓									
Valproic acid (Stavzor)	**Cap, DR:** 125mg, 250mg, 500mg		✓												
Vortioxetine (Brintellix)	**Tab:** 5mg, 10mg, 15mg, 20mg					✓									

Refer to full FDA-approved labeling for additional information.

* Has indication to be used as adjunctive therapy or in combination with other drug.

Abbreviations: ER = extended-release; DR = delayed-release; OCD = obsessive-compulsive disorder; PTSD = post-traumatic stress disorder; PMDD = premenstrual dysphoric disorder; RLS = restless legs syndrome.

ASTHMA AND COPD MANAGEMENT

GENERIC (BRAND)	DOSAGE FORM	ADULT DOSAGE	PEDIATRIC DOSAGE
β₂-AGONISTS, LONG-ACTING			
Arformoterol tartrate (Brovana)*	**Sol, Inh:** 15mcg/2mL	15mcg bid (am/pm) via nebulizer. **Max:** 30mcg/day.	
Formoterol fumarate (Foradil Aerolizer)†	**Cap, Inh:** 12mcg	1 cap (inh) q12h. **Max:** 24mcg/day.	**Asthma: ≥5 yrs:** 1 cap (inh) q12h. **Max:** 24mcg/day.
Formoterol fumarate dihydrate (Perforomist)*	**Sol, Inh:** 20mcg/2mL	2mL q12h via nebulizer. **Max:** 40mcg/day.	
Indacaterol maleate (Arcapta Neohaler)*	**Cap, Inh:** 75mcg	1 cap (inh) daily. **Max:** 1 cap/day.	
Salmeterol xinafoate (Serevent Diskus)†	**DPI:** 50mcg/inh	1 inh bid (am/pm q12h). **Max:** 2 inh/day.	**Asthma: ≥4 yrs:** 1 inh bid (am/pm q12h). **Max:** 2 inh/day.
β₂-AGONISTS, SHORT-ACTING			
Albuterol sulfate	**Sol, Inh:** 0.083%, 0.5%	**Usual/Max:** 2.5mg tid-qid via nebulizer over 5-15 min.	**2-12 yrs: Initial:** 0.1-0.15mg/kg/dose. **Max:** 2.5mg tid-qid by nebulization.
	Syr: 2mg/5mL	2mg or 4mg tid-qid. **Max:** 8mg qid.	**>14 yrs:** 2mg or 4mg tid-qid. **Max:** 8mg qid. **6-14 yrs:** 2mg tid-qid. **Max:** 24mg/day. **2-5 yrs: Initial:** 0.1mg/kg tid (not to exceed 2mg tid). **Titrate:** May increase to 0.2mg/kg tid. **Max:** 4mg tid.
	Tab: 2mg‡, 4mg‡	2mg or 4mg tid-qid. **Max:** 8mg qid.	**>12 yrs:** 2mg or 4mg tid-qid. **Max:** 8mg qid. **6-12 yrs:** 2mg tid-qid. **Max:** 24mg/day.
	Tab, ER: 4mg, 8mg	4-8mg q12h. **Max:** 32mg/day.	**>12 yrs:** 4-8mg q12h. **Max:** 32mg/day. **6-12 yrs:** 4mg q12h. **Max:** 24mg/day.
Albuterol sulfate (AccuNeb)	**Sol, Inh:** 0.63mg/3mL, 1.25mg/3mL		**2-12 yrs:** 0.63mg or 1.25mg tid-qid prn via nebulizer over 5-15 min.
Albuterol sulfate (ProAir HFA, Proventil HFA, Ventolin HFA)	**MDI:** 90mcg/inh	2 inh q4-6h or 1 inh q4h.	**≥4 yrs:** 2 inh q4-6h or 1 inh q4h.
Levalbuterol HCl (Xopenex)	**Sol, Inh:** 1.25mg/0.5mL, 0.31mg/3mL, 0.63mg/3mL, 1.25mg/3mL	0.63mg-1.25mg tid (q6-8h) via nebulizer.	**≥12 yrs:** 0.63-1.25mg tid (q6-8h) via nebulizer. **6-11 yrs:** 0.31mg tid via nebulizer. **Max:** 0.63mg tid.
Levalbuterol tartrate (Xopenex HFA)	**MDI:** 45mcg/inh	1-2 inh q4-6h.	**≥4 yrs:** 1-2 inh q4-6h.
Metaproterenol sulfate	**Syrup:** 10mg/5mL; **Tab:** 10mg‡, 20mg‡	20mg tid-qid.	**>9 yrs or >60 lbs:** 20mg tid-qid. **6-9 yrs or <60 lbs:** 10mg tid-qid. **<6 yrs:** (Syrup) 1.3-2.6mg/kg/day.
Pirbuterol acetate (Maxair)	**MDI:** 200mcg/inh	1-2 inh q4-6h. **Max:** 12 inh/day.	**≥12 yrs:** 1-2 inh q4-6h. **Max:** 12 inh/day.

(Continued)

GENERIC (BRAND)	DOSAGE FORM	ADULT DOSAGE	PEDIATRIC DOSAGE
β₂-AGONISTS, SHORT-ACTING *(Continued)*			
Terbutaline sulfate	**Tab:** 2.5mg‡, 5mg‡	2.5-5mg q6h tid. **Max:** 15mg/day.	**12-15 yrs:** 2.5mg tid. **Max:** 7.5mg/day.
	Inj: 1mg/mL	0.25mg SQ into the lateral deltoid area. May repeat dose in 15-30 min if no improvement. **Max:** 0.5mg/4hrs.	**≥12 yrs:** 0.25mg SQ into the lateral deltoid area. May repeat dose in 15-30 min if no improvement. **Max:** 0.5mg/4hrs.
ANTICHOLINERGICS			
Aclidinium bromide (Tudorza Pressair)*	**MDI:** 400mcg/inh	1 inh bid.	
Ipratropium bromide (Atrovent HFA)*	**MDI:** 17mcg/inh	**Initial:** 2 inh qid. May take additional inh prn. **Max:** 12 inh/day.	
Tiotropium bromide (Spiriva HandiHaler)*	**Cap, Inh:** 18mcg	2 inh of contents of 1 cap qd.	
COMBINATION AGENTS			
Budesonide/Formoterol fumarate dihydrate (Symbicort)†	**MDI:** (Budesonide-Formoterol) 80mcg-4.5mcg/inh, 160mcg-4.5mcg/inh	**Asthma: Initial:** 2 inh bid (am/pm q12h). Starting dose is based on asthma severity. **Max:** 160mcg-4.5mcg bid. **COPD:** 2 inh of 160mcg-4.5mcg bid.	**Asthma: ≥12 yrs:** 2 inh bid (am/pm q12h). Starting dose is based on asthma severity. **Max:** 160mcg-4.5mcg bid.
Fluticasone propionate/ Salmeterol xinafoate (Advair Diskus)†	**DPI:** (Fluticasone-Salmeterol) 100mcg-50mcg/inh, 250mcg-50mcg/inh, 500mcg-50mcg/inh	**Asthma:** 1 inh bid (am/pm q12h). Starting dose is based on asthma severity. **Max:** 500mcg-50mcg bid. **COPD:** 1 inh of 250mcg-50mcg bid (am/pm q12h).	**Asthma: ≥12 yrs:** 1 inh bid (am/pm q12h). Starting dose is based on asthma severity. **Max:** 500mcg-50mcg bid. **4-11 yrs:** 1 inh of 100mcg-50mcg bid (am/pm q12h).
Fluticasone propionate/ Salmeterol xinafoate (Advair HFA)	**MDI:** (Fluticasone-Salmeterol) 45mcg-21mcg/inh, 115mcg-21mcg/inh, 230mcg-21mcg/inh	**Initial:** 2 inh bid (am/pm q12h). Starting dose is based on asthma severity. **Max:** 2 inh of 230mcg-21mcg bid.	**≥12 yrs: Initial:** 2 inh bid (am/pm q12h). Starting dose is based on asthma severity. **Max:** 2 inh of 230mcg-21mcg bid.
Fluticasone furoate- Vilanterol trifenatate (Breo Ellipta)*	**Powder, Inh:** (Fluticasone-Vilanterol) 100mcg-25mcg	1 inh qd. **Max:** 1 inh/day.	
Ipratropium bromide/ Albuterol sulfate (Combivent)*	**MDI:** (Ipratropium-Albuterol) 18mcg-90mcg/inh	2 inh qid. May take additional inh prn. **Max:** 12 inh/day.	
Ipratropium bromide/ Albuterol sulfate (Combivent Respimat)*	**MDI:** (Ipratropium-Albuterol) 20mcg-120mcg/inh	1 inh qid. May take additional inh prn. **Max:** 6 inh/day.	
Ipratropium bromide/ Albuterol sulfate (Duoneb)*	**Sol, Inh:** (Ipratropium-Albuterol) 0.5mg-2.5mg/3mL	3mL qid via nebulizer with up to 2 additional 3mL doses/day prn.	
Mometasone furoate/ Formoterol dihydrate (Dulera)	**MDI:** (Mometasone-Formoterol) 100mcg-5mcg/inh, 200mcg-5mcg/inh	**Previous Inhaled Medium-Dose Corticosteroids: Initial:** 2 inh of 100mcg-5mcg bid. **Max:** 400mcg-20mcg/day. **Previous Inhaled High-Dose Corticosteroids: Initial:** 2 inh of 200mcg-5mcg bid. **Max:** 800mcg-20mcg/day.	**≥12 yrs: Previous Inhaled Medium-Dose Corticosteroids: Initial:** 2 inh of 100mcg-5mcg bid. **Max:** 400mcg-20mcg/day. **Previous Inhaled High-Dose Corticosteroids: Initial:** 2 inh of 200mcg-5mcg bid. **Max:** 800mcg-20mcg/day.
Umeclidinium bromide/ Vilanterol trifenatate (Anoro Ellipta)	**Powder, Inh:** (Umeclidinium-Vilanterol) 62.5mcg-25mcg	1 inh qd. **Max:** 1 inh/day	

GENERIC (BRAND)	DOSAGE FORM	ADULT DOSAGE	PEDIATRIC DOSAGE
CORTICOSTEROIDS			
Beclomethasone dipropionate (QVAR)	**MDI:** 40mcg/inh, 80mcg/inh	**Previous Bronchodilators Alone: Initial:** 40-80mcg bid. **Max:** 320mcg bid. **Previous Inhaled Corticosteroids: Initial:** 40-160mcg bid. **Max:** 320mcg bid.	**≥12 yrs:** Refer to adult dosing. **5-11 yrs: Previous Bronchodilators Alone/ Inhaled Corticosteroids: Initial:** 40mcg bid. **Max:** 80mcg bid.
Budesonide (Pulmicort Flexhaler)	**DPI:** 90mcg/inh, 180mcg/inh	**Initial:** 180-360mcg bid. **Max:** 720mcg bid.	**6-17 yrs: Initial:** 180-360mcg bid. **Max:** 360mcg bid.
Budesonide (Pulmicort Respules)	**Sus, Inh:** 0.25mg/2mL, 0.5mg/2mL, 1mg/2mL		**12 mths-8 yrs: Previous Bronchodilators: Initial:** 0.5mg/day given qd or bid. **Max:** 0.5mg/day. **Previous Inhaled Corticosteroids: Initial:** 0.5mg/day given qd or bid. **Max:** 1mg/day. **Previous Oral Corticosteroids: Initial:** 1mg/day given qd or bid. **Max:** 1mg/day.
Ciclesonide (Alvesco)	**MDI:** 80mcg/inh, 160mcg/inh	**Previous Bronchodilator Alone: Initial:** 80mcg bid. **Max:** 160mcg bid. **Previous Inhaled Corticosteroids: Initial:** 80mcg bid. **Max:** 320mcg bid. **Previous Oral Corticosteroids: Initial/Max:** 320mcg bid.	**≥12 yrs:** Refer to adult dosing.
Flunisolide hemihydrate (Aerospan)	**MDI:** 80mcg/inh	**Initial:** 160mcg bid. **Max:** 320mcg bid.	**≥12 yrs: Initial:** 160mcg bid. **Max:** 320mcg bid. **6-11 yrs: Initial:** 80mcg bid. **Max:** 160mcg bid.
Fluticasone propionate (Flovent Diskus)	**DPI:** 50mcg/inh, 100mcg/inh, 250mcg/inh	**Previous Bronchodilators Alone: Initial:** 100mcg bid. **Max:** 500mcg bid. **Previous Inhaled Corticosteroids: Initial:** 100-250mcg bid. **Max:** 500mcg bid. **Previous Oral Corticosteroids: Initial:** 500-1000mcg bid. **Max:** 1000mcg bid.	**≥12 yrs:** Refer to adult dosing. **4-11 yrs: Initial:** 50mcg bid. **Max:** 100mcg bid.
Fluticasone propionate (Flovent HFA)	**MDI:** 44mcg/inh, 110mcg/inh, 220mcg/inh	**Previous Bronchodilators Alone: Initial:** 88mcg bid. **Max:** 440mcg bid. **Previous Inhaled Corticosteroids: Initial:** 88-220mcg bid. **Max:** 440mcg bid. **Previous Oral Corticosteroids: Initial:** 440mcg bid. **Max:** 880mcg bid.	**≥12 yrs:** Refer to adult dosing. **4-11 yrs: Initial/Max:** 88mcg bid.
Mometasone furoate (Asmanex Twisthaler)	**DPI:** 110mcg/inh, 220mcg/inh	**Previous Bronchodilators Alone/Inhaled Corticosteroids: Initial:** 220mcg qpm. **Max:** 440mcg/day. **Previous Oral Corticosteroids: Initial:** 440mcg bid. **Max:** 880mcg/day.	**≥12 yrs:** Refer to adult dosing. **4-11 yrs: Initial/Max:** 110mcg/day qpm.
LEUKOTRIENE MODIFIERS			
Montelukast sodium (Singulair)	**Granules:** 4mg; **Tab:** 10mg; **Tab, Chewable:** 4mg, 5mg	10mg qpm.	**≥15 yrs:** 10mg qpm. **6-14 yrs:** 5mg chewable tab qpm. **2-5 yrs:** 4mg chewable tab or 4mg oral granules pkt qpm. **12-23 mths:** 4mg oral granules pkt qpm.

(Continued)

GENERIC (BRAND)	DOSAGE FORM	ADULT DOSAGE	PEDIATRIC DOSAGE
LEUKOTRIENE MODIFIERS *(Continued)*			
Zafirlukast (Accolate)	**Tab:** 10mg, 20mg	20mg bid. Take at least 1 hr before or 2 hrs after meals.	Take at least 1 hr before or 2 hrs after meals. **≥12 yrs:** 20mg bid. **5-11 yrs:** 10mg bid.
Zileuton (Zyflo, Zyflo CR)	(Zyflo) **Tab:** 600mg‡	**Tab:** 600mg qid. Take with meals and at hs.	**≥12 yrs: Tab:** 600mg qid. Take with meals and at hs.
	(Zyflo CR) **Tab, ER:** 600mg	1200mg bid. Take within 1 hr after am and pm meals.	**≥12 yrs:** 1200mg bid. Take within 1 hr after am and pm meals.
MAST CELL STABILIZERS			
Cromolyn sodium	**Sol, Inh:** 20mg/2mL	20mg nebulized qid.	**≥2 yrs:** 20mg nebulized qid.
METHYLXANTHINES			
Theophylline anhydrous (Elixophyllin)§	**Elixir:** 80mg/15mL	**>45kg: 1-60 yrs: Initial:** 300mg/day divided q6-8h. **After 3 Days if Tolerated:** 400mg/day divided q6-8h. **After 3 More Days if Tolerated:** 600mg/day divided q6-8h. **<45kg: 1-15 yrs: Initial:** 12-14mg/kg/day. **Max:** 300mg/day divided q4-6h. **After 3 Days if Tolerated:** 16mg/kg/day. **Max:** 400mg/day divided q4-6h. **After 3 More Days if Tolerated:** 20mg/kg/day divided q4-6h. **Max:** 600mg/day divided q4-6h. See PI for infant dose.	
Theophylline anhydrous (Theo-24)§	**Cap, ER:** 100mg, 200mg, 300mg, 400mg	**>45kg: 12-60 yrs: Initial:** 300-400mg/day q24h. **After 3 Days if Tolerated:** 400-600mg/day q24h. **After 3 More Days if Tolerated and Needed:** Doses >600mg should be titrated according to blood levels (see PI). **<45kg: 12-15 yrs: Initial:** 12-14mg/kg/day. **Max:** 300mg/day q24h. **After 3 Days if Tolerated:** 16mg/kg/day. **Max:** 400mg/day q24h. **After 3 More Days if Tolerated and Needed:** 20mg/kg/day. **Max:** 600mg/day q24h.	
Theophylline anhydrous	**Tab, ER:** 400mg‡, 600mg‡		
MONOCLONAL ANTIBODIES/IgE-BLOCKERS			
Omalizumab (Xolair)	**Inj:** 150mg/5mL	150-375mg SQ q2 or 4 wks. Determine dose and dosing frequency by serum total IgE level measured before the start of treatment, and body weight. See PI for dose determination charts.	**≥12 yrs:** 150-375mg SQ q2 or 4 wks. Determine dose and dosing frequency by serum total IgE level measured before the start of treatment, and body weight. See PI for dose determination charts.
PHOSPHODIESTERASE-4 INHIBITORS			
Roflumilast (Daliresp) *	**Tab:** 500mcg	500mcg qd.	

GENERIC (BRAND)	DOSAGE FORM	ADULT DOSAGE	PEDIATRIC DOSAGE
SYSTEMIC CORTICOSTEROIDS			
Methylprednisolone (Medrol)	**Tab:** 2mg‡, 4mg‡, 8mg‡, 16mg‡, 32mg‡	**Initial:** 4-48mg/day. Dosage must be individualized based on the disease state and patient response.	
Prednisolone	**Sol:** 5mg/5mL, 15mg/5mL; **Tab:** 5mg‡	**Initial:** 5-60mg/day. Dosage must be individualized based on the disease state and patient response.	
Prednisone	**Sol:** 5mg/5mL, 5mg/mL; **Tab:** 1mg‡, 2.5mg‡, 5mg‡, 10mg‡, 20mg‡, 50mg‡		

Refer to full FDA-approved labeling for additional information.

Abbreviations: DPI = dry-powder inhaler; ER = extended-released; MDI = metered-dose inhaler.

*Indicated for COPD only.

†Indicated for asthma and COPD.

‡Scored.

§The dose of theophylline must be individualized based on peak serum theophylline concentrations.

Adapted from *Expert Panel Report 3 (EPR-3): Guidelines for the Diagnosis and Management of Asthma – Summary Report 2007*. NIH Publication No 08-5846, October 2007.

ASTHMA TREATMENT PLAN*

CLASSIFICATION	LUNG FUNCTION	STEPWISE APPROACH FOR MANAGING ASTHMA IN PATIENTS ≥12 YEARS OF AGE
Intermittent • Symptoms ≤2 days/wk • Short-acting β_2-agonist use for symptom control ≤2 days/wk • Nighttime awakenings ≤2X/month • Interference with normal activity: none • Risk: exacerbations requiring oral systemic corticosteroids 0-1/yr	• Normal FEV_1 between exacerbations • FEV_1 >80% predicted • FEV_1/FVC—normal	**Step 1†** • **Short-acting inhaled β_2-agonists as needed**
Mild persistent • Symptoms >2 days/wk but not daily • Short-acting β_2-agonist use for symptom control >2 days/wk but not daily, and not more than 1X on any day • Nighttime awakenings 3-4X/month • Interference with normal activity: minor limitation • Risk: exacerbations requiring oral systemic corticosteroids ≥2/yr	• FEV_1 >80% predicted • FEV_1/FVC—normal	**Step 2†** • **Low-dose ICS** ALTERNATIVE TREATMENT: • Cromolyn, LTRA, Nedocromil, or Theophylline
Moderate persistent • Daily symptoms • Short acting β_2-agonist use for symptom control daily • Nighttime awakening >1X/wk but not nightly • Interference with normal activity: some limitation • Risk: exacerbations requiring oral systemic corticosteroids ≥2/yr	• FEV_1 >60% but <80% predicted • FEV_1/FVC reduced 5%	**Step 3†** • **Low-dose ICS + LABA** or **medium-dose ICS** ALTERNATIVE TREATMENT: • Low-dose ICS + either LTRA, Theophylline, or Zileuton
Severe persistent • Symptoms throughout the day • Short-acting β_2-agonist use for symptom control several times per day • Nighttime awakenings often 7X/wk • Interference with normal activity: extremely limited • Risk: exacerbations requiring oral systemic corticosteroids ≥2/yr	• FEV_1 <60% predicted • FEV_1/FVC reduced >5%	Consult with asthma specialist if step 4 care or higher is required **Step 4† or Step 5†** • **Medium-dose ICS + LABA (Step 4)** or **High-dose ICS + LABA (Step 5)** AND consider Omalizumab for patients who have allergies (Step 5) ALTERNATIVE TREATMENT: • Medium-dose ICS + either LTRA, Theophylline, or Zileuton (Step 4)

Note: Preferred treatments are in bold.

Key Points:

The stepwise approach is meant to assist, not replace, the clinical decision-making required to meet individual patient needs.

Review treatment every 1-6 months to maintain control. A gradual reduction in treatment may be possible if well controlled for at least 3 months. If control is not maintained, consider step up and reevaluate in 2-6 weeks.

The presence of one of the features of severity is sufficient to place a patient in that category. An individual should be assigned to the most severe grade in which any feature occurs.

Short-acting β_2-agonists as needed for symptomatic relief for all patients. Intensity of treatment will depend on severity of exacerbation; up to 3 treatments at 20-minute intervals as needed. A short course of oral systemic corticosteroids may be needed.

Use of short-acting β_2-agonists >2 days/wk for symptom relief generally indicates inadequate control and the need to step up treatment.

A short course of oral systemic corticosteroids should be considered when initiating treatment for Moderate and Severe Persistent Asthma.

Abbreviations: FEV_1 = forced expiratory volume in one second; FVC = forced vital capacity; ICS = inhaled corticosteroid; LABA = long-acting inhaled β_2-agonist; LTRA = leukotriene receptor antagonist.

*Adapted from *Expert Panel Report 3: Guidelines for the Diagnosis and Management of Asthma. Full Report 2007.* National Heart, Lung, and Blood Institute, National Asthma Education and Prevention Program, U.S. Department of Health and Human Services.

†In 2-6 wks, evaluate level of asthma control achieved and adjust therapy accordingly.

COUGH-COLD-ALLERGY AGENTS

DRUG	ANTIHISTAMINE	DECONGESTANT	COUGH SUPPRESSANT	OTHER CONTENT	ADULT DOSAGE	PEDIATRIC DOSAGE
ANTIHISTAMINES						
Astelin Nasal Spray	Azelastine HCl, 137mcg/spray				**Vasomotor Rhinitis: Usual:** 2 sprays/nostril bid. **Seasonal Allergic Rhinitis: Usual:** 1-2 sprays/nostril bid.	**Vasomotor Rhinitis: ≥12 yrs: Usual:** 2 sprays/nostril bid. **Seasonal Allergic Rhinitis: Usual: ≥12 yrs:** 1-2 sprays/nostril bid. **5-11 yrs:** 1 spray/nostril bid.
Clarinex Oral Solution	Desloratadine, 0.5mg/mL				**Usual:** 10mL qd.	**≥12 yrs:** 10mL qd. **6-11 yrs:** 5mL qd. **12 mths-5 yrs:** 2.5mL qd. **6-11 mths:** 2mL qd.
Clarinex Tablets	Desloratadine, 5mg				**Usual:** 5mg qd.	**≥12 yrs:** 5mg qd.
Clemastine Fumarate Syrup	Clemastine fumarate, 0.5mg/5mL				**Allergic Rhinitis: Initial:** 2 tsp (1mg) bid, may increase prn. **Max:** 12 tsp/d. **Urticaria/Angioedema: Initial:** 4 tsp (2mg) bid. **Max:** 12 tsp/d.	**≥12 yrs: Allergic Rhinitis: Initial:** 2 tsp (1mg) bid, may increase prn. **Max:** 12 tsp/d. **Urticaria/Angioedema: Initial:** 4 tsp (2mg) bid. **Max:** 12 tsp/d. **6-12 yrs: Allergic Rhinitis: Initial:** 1 tsp (0.5mg) bid; may increase prn. **Max:** 6 tsp/d. **Urticaria/Angioedema: Initial:** 2 tsp (1mg) bid. **Max:** 6 tsp/d.
Clemastine Fumarate Tablets	Clemastine fumarate, 2.68mg				**Allergic Rhinitis: Initial:** ½ tab (1.34mg) bid, may increase prn. **Max:** 3 tabs/d. **Urticaria/Angioedema:** 1 tab. **Max:** 3 tabs/d.	**≥12 yrs: Allergic Rhinitis: Initial:** ½ tab (1.34mg) bid, may increase prn. **Max:** 3 tabs/d. **Urticaria/Angioedema:** 1 tab. **Max:** 3 tabs/d.
Cyproheptadine HCl Syrup	Cyproheptadine HCl, 2mg/5mL				**Initial:** 4mg tid. **Usual:** 12-16mg/d. **Max:** 0.5mg/kg/d.	**Total Daily Dose:** 0.25mg/kg/d or 8mg/m². **7-14 yrs:** 4mg bid-tid. **Max:** 16mg/d. **2-6 yrs:** 2mg bid-tid. **Max:** 12mg/d.
Cyproheptadine HCl Tablets	Cyproheptadine HCl, 4mg				**Initial:** 4mg tid. **Usual:** 12-16mg/d. **Max:** 0.5mg/kg/d.	**Total Daily Dose:** 0.25mg/kg/d or 8mg/m². **7-14 yrs:** 4mg bid-tid. **Max:** 16mg/d. **2-6 yrs:** 2mg bid-tid. **Max:** 12mg/d.

(Continued)

DRUG	ANTIHISTAMINE	DECONGESTANT	COUGH SUPPRESSANT	OTHER CONTENT	ADULT DOSAGE	PEDIATRIC DOSAGE
ANTIHISTAMINES *(Continued)*						
Diphenhydramine HCl Capsules	Diphenhydramine HCl, 50mg				25-50mg tid-qid.	**≥20 lb:** 12.5-25mg tid-qid or 5mg/kg/d or 150mg/m²/d. **Max:** 300mg.
Diphenhydramine HCl Injection	Diphenhydramine HCl, 50mg/mL				(IV/IM) 0-50mg at a rate ≤25mg/min, 100mg if required. **Max:** 400mg.	**Peds (no premature infants or neonates):** 5mg/kg/d or 150mg/m²/d divided in 4 doses at a rate ≤25mg/min. **Max:** 300mg/d.
Hydroxyzine HCl Syrup	Hydroxyzine HCl, 10mg/5mL				25mg tid-qid.	**>6 yrs:** 50-100mg/d in divided doses. **<6 yrs:** 50mg/d in divided doses.
Hydroxyzine HCl Tablets	Hydroxyzine HCl, 10mg, 25mg, 50mg				25mg tid-qid.	**>6 yrs:** 50-100mg/d in divided doses. **<6 yrs:** 50mg/d in divided doses.
Vistaril	Hydroxyzine pamoate, 25mg, 50mg (Cap), 100mg (Cap, generic)				25mg tid-qid.	**>6 yrs:** 50-100mg/d in divided doses. **<6 yrs:** 50mg/d in divided doses.
Pataday	Olopatadine HCl, 0.2%				1 drop in each affected eye qd.	**≥2 yrs:** 1 drop in each affected eye qd.
Patanol	Olopatadine HCl, 0.1%				1 drop in each affected eye bid, separated by 6-8 hrs.	**≥3 yrs:** 1 drop in each affected eye bid, separated by 6-8 hrs.
Promethazine HCl Injection	Promethazine HCl, 25mg/mL, 50mg/mL				25mg. May repeat within 2 hrs prn.	**Peds >2 yrs:** ½ adult dose.
Promethazine HCl Solution	Promethazine HCl, 6.25mg/5mL				25mg hs, 12.5mg ac and hs, or 6.25-12.5mg tid.	**≥2 yrs:** 25mg hs, 12.5mg ac and hs, or 6.25-12.5mg tid.
Promethazine HCl Suppositories	Promethazine HCl, 12.5mg, 25mg, 50mg				25mg hs, 12.5mg ac and hs, or 6.25-12.5mg tid.	**≥2 yrs:** 25mg hs, 12.5mg ac and hs, or 6.25-12.5mg tid.
Promethazine HCl Tablets	Promethazine HCl, 12.5mg, 25mg, 50mg				25mg hs, 12.5mg ac and hs, or 6.25-12.5mg tid.	**≥2 yrs:** 25mg hs, 12.5mg ac and hs, or 6.25-12.5mg tid.
Xyzal Solution	Levocetirizine dihydrochloride, 2.5mg/5mL				**Allergic Rhinitis, Urticaria:** 2.5-5mg qpm.	**Allergic Rhinitis, Urticaria:** **≥12 yrs:** 2.5-5mg qpm. **6-11 yrs:** 2.5mg qpm. **Max:** 2.5mg/d. **6 mths-5 yrs:** 1.25mg qpm. **Max:** 1.25mg/d.

DRUG	ANTIHISTAMINE	DECONGESTANT	COUGH SUPPRESSANT	OTHER CONTENT	ADULT DOSAGE	PEDIATRIC DOSAGE
ANTIHISTAMINES *(Continued)*						
Xyzal Tablets	Levocetirizine dihydrochloride, 5mg				**Allergic Rhinitis, Urticaria:** 2.5-5mg qpm.	**Allergic Rhinitis, Urticaria:** **≥12 yrs:** 2.5-5mg qpm. **6-11 yrs:** 2.5mg qpm. **Max:** 2.5mg/d. **6 mths-5 yrs:** 1.25mg qpm. **Max:** 1.25mg/d.
ANTIHISTAMINES + DECONGESTANTS						
Clarinex-D	Desloratadine, 2.5mg (12 Hr), 5mg (24 Hr)	Pseudoephedrine sulfate, 120mg (12 Hr), 240mg (24 Hr)			(12 Hr) 1 tab q12h. **Max:** 2 tab/d. (24 Hr) 1 tab qd. **Max:** 1 tab/d.	(12 Hr) **≥12 yrs:** 1 tab q12h. **Max:** 2 tab/d. (24 Hr) **≥12 yrs:** 1 tab qd. **Max:** 1 tab/d.
Promethazine VC	Promethazine HCl, 6.25mg/5mL	Phenylephrine HCl, 5mg/5mL			1 tsp q4-6h. **Max:** 6 tsp/d.	**≥12 yrs:** 1 tsp q4-6h. **Max:** 6 tsp/d. **6-<12 yrs:** ½ tsp q4-6h. **Max:** 6 tsp/d. **2-<6 yrs:** ¼-½ tsp q4-6h.
Semprex-D	Acrivastine, 8mg	Pseudoephedrine HCl, 60mg			1 cap q4-6h, qid.	**≥12 yrs:** 1 cap q4-6h, qid.
ANTIHISTAMINES + COUGH SUPPRESSANTS						
Promethazine DM	Promethazine HCl, 6.25mg/5mL		Dextromethorphan HBr, 15mg/5mL		1 tsp q4-6h. **Max:** 6 tsp/d.	**6-<12 yrs:** ½-1 tsp q4-6h. **Max:** 4 tsp/d. **2-<6 yrs:** ¼-½ tsp q4-6h. **Max:** 2 tsp/d.
Promethazine w/ Codeine	Promethazine HCl, 6.25mg/5mL		Codeine phosphate, 10mg/5mL		1 tsp q4-6h. **Max:** 6 tsp/d.	**≥12 yrs:** 1 tsp q4-6h. **Max:** 6 tsp/d. **6-<12 yrs:** ½-1 tsp q4-6h. **Max:** 6 tsp/d.
Tussicaps	Chlorpheniramine polistirex, 8mg (FS), 4mg (HS)		Hydrocodone polistirex, 10mg (FS), 5mg (HS)		1 FS cap q12h. **Max:** 2 FS caps/d.	**≥12 yrs:** 1 FS cap q12h. **Max:** 2 FS caps/d. **6-11 yrs:** 1 HS cap q12h. **Max:** 2 HS caps/d.
Tussionex Pennkinetic	Chlorpheniramine polistirex, 8mg/5mL		Hydrocodone polistirex, 10mg/5mL		1 tsp q12h. **Max:** 2 tsp/d.	**≥12 yrs:** 1 tsp q12h. **Max:** 2 tsp/d. **6-11 yrs:** ½ tsp q12h. **Max:** 1 tsp/d.
Vituz	Chlorpheniramine maleate, 4mg/5mL		Hydrocodone bitartrate, 5mg/5mL		1 tsp q4-6h prn. **Max:** 4 doses/d.	

(Continued)

DRUG	ANTIHISTAMINE	DECONGESTANT	COUGH SUPPRESSANT	OTHER CONTENT	ADULT DOSAGE	PEDIATRIC DOSAGE
ANTIHISTAMINES + COUGH SUPPRESSANTS + DECONGESTANTS						
Atuss DS	Chlorpheniramine maleate, 4mg/5mL	Pseudoephedrine HCl, 30mg/5mL	Dextromethorphan HBr, 30mg/5mL		1-2 tsp q12h.	**>12 yrs:** 1-2 tsp q12h. **6-12 yrs:** ½-1 tsp q12h. **2-6 yrs:** ½ tsp q12h. **<2 yrs:** As directed by a physician.
Bromfed DM	Brompheniramine maleate, 2mg/5mL	Pseudoephedrine HCl, 30mg/5mL	Dextromethorphan HBr, 10mg/5mL		2 tsp q4-6h. **Max:** 6 doses/d.	**≥12 yrs:** 2 tsp q4-6h. **6-<12 yrs:** 1 tsp q4h. **2-<6 yrs:** ½ tsp q4h. **6 mths-<2 yrs:** Dose to be established by a physician. **Max:** 6 doses/d.
Promethazine VC w/ Codeine	Promethazine HCl, 6.25mg/5mL	Phenylephrine HCl, 5mg/5mL	Codeine phosphate, 10mg/5mL		1 tsp q4-6h. **Max:** 6 tsp/d.	**≥12 yrs:** 1 tsp q4-6h. **Max:** 6 tsp/d. **6-<12 yrs:** ½-1 tsp q4-6h. **Max:** 4 tsp/d.
Zutripro	Chlorpheniramine maleate, 4mg/5mL	Pseudoephedrine HCl, 60mg/5mL	Hydrocodone bitartrate, 5mg/5mL		1 tsp q4-6h prn. **Max:** 4 doses/d.	
COUGH SUPPRESSANTS						
Tessalon			Benzonatate, 100mg (Perles)		100mg tid prn. May increase to 200mg tid prn. **Max:** 600mg/d.	**≥10 yrs:** 100mg tid prn. May increase to 200mg tid prn. **Max:** 600mg/d.
Zonatuss			Benzonatate, 150mg (Cap)		150mg tid prn. May increase to 200mg tid prn. **Max:** 600mg/d.	**>10 yrs:** 150mg tid prn. May increase to 200mg tid prn. **Max:** 600mg/d.
COUGH SUPPRESSANTS + DECONGESTANTS						
Rezira		Pseudoephedrine HCl, 60mg/5mL	Hydrocodone bitartrate, 5mg/5mL		1 tsp q4-6h prn. **Max:** 4 doses/d.	
COUGH SUPPRESSANTS + EXPECTORANTS						
Cheratussin AC			Codeine phosphate, 10mg/5mL	Guaifenesin, 100mg/5mL	2 tsp q4h. **Max:** 6 doses/d.	**≥12 yrs:** 2 tsp q4h. **Max:** 6 doses/d. **6-<12 yrs:** 1 tsp q4h. **Max:** 6 doses/d

DRUG	ANTIHISTAMINE	DECONGESTANT	COUGH SUPPRESSANT	OTHER CONTENT	ADULT DOSAGE	PEDIATRIC DOSAGE
COUGH SUPPRESSANTS + OTHER CONTENTS						
Hydromet			Hydrocodone bitartrate, 5mg/5mL	Homatropine methylbromide, 1.5mg/5mL (Syr)	1 tsp q4-6h prn. **Max:** 6 tsp/d.	**6-12 yrs:** ½ tsp q4-6h prn. **Max:** 3 tsp/d.
Tussigon			Hydrocodone bitartrate, 5mg	Homatropine methylbromide, 1.5mg	1 tab q4-6h prn. **Max:** 6 tabs/d.	**6-12 yrs:** ½ tab q4-6h prn. **Max:** 3 tabs/d.

Refer to full FDA-approved labeling for additional information.
Abbreviations: FS = full-strength; HS = half-strength.

ERECTILE DYSFUNCTION TREATMENT

GENERIC (BRAND)	HOW SUPPLIED	DOSAGE
PROSTAGLANDINS		
Alprostadil (Edex, Caverject)	**Inj:** (Edex) 10, 20, 40mcg; (Caverject) 20, 40mcg	Use lowest possible effective dose. Patient must stay in physician's office until complete detumescence occurs. If there is no response, give next higher dose within 1 hr. If there is a response, allow 1-day interval before the next dose. Reduce dose if erection lasts >1 hr. **Vasculogenic, Psychogenic, or Mixed Etiology: Initial:** 2.5mcg. **Titration: Partial Response to 2.5mcg:** Increase to 5mcg and then in increments of 5-10mcg, depending upon response, until erection of 1 hr max duration. **No Response to 2.5mcg:** Increase 2nd dose to 7.5mcg followed by increments of 5-10mcg. **Pure Neurogenic Etiology (Spinal Cord Injury): Initial:** 1.25mcg. **Titration:** Increase to 2.5mcg, then to 5mcg, and then by 5mcg increments until erection of 1 hr max duration. **Maint:** Give no more than 3 doses/week; allow at least 24 hrs between doses. (Edex) **Dose range:** 1-40mcg. Give inj over 5- to 10-sec interval. (Caverject) **Max:** 60mcg/dose.
Alprostadil (Muse)	**Supp, Urethral:** 125mcg, 250mcg, 500mcg, 1000mcg	**Initial:** 125-250mcg. **Titration:** Increase or decrease dose based on individual response. **Max:** 2 administrations/day.
PHOSPHODIESTERASE INHIBITORS		
Avanafil (Stendra)	**Tab:** 50mg, 100mg, 200mg	**Initial:** 100mg prn 30 min prior to sexual activity. **Titration:** Increase to 200mg or decrease to 50mg based on efficacy/tolerability. **Max Frequency:** 1 dose/day. **Max Dose:** 200mg.
Sildenafil (Viagra)	**Tab:** 25mg, 50mg, 100mg	**Usual:** 50mg prn 1 hr prior to sexual activity. May be taken ½-4 hrs prior to sexual activity. **Titration:** Increase to 100mg or decrease to 25mg based on efficacy/tolerability. **Max Frequency:** 1 dose/day. **Max Dose:** 100mg.
Tadalafil (Cialis)	**Tab:** 2.5mg, 5mg, 10mg, 20mg	**PRN Use: Initial:** 10mg prior to sexual activity. **Titration:** Increase to 20mg or decrease to 5mg based on efficacy/tolerability. **Max Frequency:** 1 dose/day. **QD Use: Initial:** 2.5mg qd. **Titration:** Increase to 5mg qd based on efficacy/tolerability.
Vardenafil (Levitra)	**Tab:** 2.5mg, 5mg, 10mg, 20mg	**Initial:** 10mg prn 1 hr prior to sexual activity. **Titration:** Increase to 20mg or decrease to 5mg based on efficacy/tolerability. **Max Frequency:** 1 dose/day. **Max Dose:** 20mg.
Vardenafil (Staxyn)	**Tab, Disintegrating:** 10mg	10mg prn 1 hr prior to sexual activity. **Max:** 1 dose/day. Place on tongue to disintegrate. Take without liquid.

Refer to full FDA-approved labeling for additional information.

BENIGN PROSTATIC HYPERTROPHY AGENTS

GENERIC	BRAND	HOW SUPPLIED	DOSAGE	DOSING CONSIDERATIONS
ALPHA-BLOCKERS				
Alfuzosin	Uroxatral	**Tab, ER:** 10mg	**Usual:** 10mg qd.	• Take dose with the same meal each day. Swallow whole. • **Moderate or Severe Hepatic Impairment/ Concomitant Potent CYP3A4 Inhibitors:** Contraindicated.
Doxazosin	Cardura	**Tab:** 1mg, 2mg, 4mg, 8mg	**Initial:** 1mg qd. **Max:** 8mg qd.	• Stepwise titration in 1- to 2-week intervals, if needed.
	Cardura XL	**Tab, ER:** 4mg, 8mg	**Initial:** 4mg qd. **Max:** 8mg qd.	• Take with breakfast. Swallow whole. • Titrate in 3- to 4-week intervals, if needed.
Silodosin	Rapaflo	**Cap:** 4mg, 8mg	**Usual:** 8mg qd.	• Take with food. • **Moderate Renal Impairment (CrCl 30-50mL/min):** 4mg qd. • **Severe Renal Impairment (CrCl <30mL/min)/Severe Hepatic Impairment:** Contraindicated. • Carefully open and sprinkle the powder inside of capsule on a tablespoon of applesauce if difficult to swallow.
Tamsulosin	Flomax	**Cap:** 0.4mg	**Usual:** 0.4mg qd. **Max:** 0.8mg qd.	• Take dose 30 min after the same meal each day. • Titrate after 2-4 weeks if needed. • Restart at 0.4-mg dose if therapy is interrupted. • **Concomitant Strong CYP3A4 Inhibitors:** Avoid use.
Terazosin	Generic	**Cap:** 1mg, 2mg, 5mg, 10mg	**Initial:** 1mg qhs. **Usual:** 10mg qd. **Max:** 20mg/day.	• Increase stepwise as needed. • Restart at initial dose if therapy is interrupted.
5-ALPHA REDUCTASE INHIBITORS				
Dutasteride	Avodart	**Cap:** 0.5mg	**Usual:** 0.5mg qd.	• Swallow whole. May take with or without food. • May be administered with tamsulosin.
Finasteride	Proscar	**Tab:** 5mg	**Usual:** 5mg qd.	• May take with or without food. • May be administered with doxazosin.
PHOSPHODIESTERASE-5 INHIBITORS				
Tadalafil	Cialis	**Tab:** 2.5mg, 5mg, 10mg, 20mg	**Usual:** 5mg qd.	• Take dose at approximately the same time every day. • **CrCl 30-50mL/min:** 2.5mg is recommended. • **CrCl <30mL/min or on Hemodialysis:** Not recommended for once daily use. • Not recommended for use in combination with alpha-blockers for benign prostatic hypertrophy. • **Severe Hepatic Impairment:** Not recommended.
COMBINATIONS				
Dutasteride/ Tamsulosin	Jalyn	**Cap:** 0.5mg/0.4mg	**Usual:** 1 cap qd.	• Swallow whole. • Take dose 30 min after the same meal each day. • **Concomitant Strong CYP3A4 Inhibitors:** Avoid use.

Refer to full FDA-approved labeling for additional information.

Abbreviation: ER = extended-release.

OVERACTIVE BLADDER AGENTS

GENERIC	BRAND	HOW SUPPLIED	DOSAGE	COMMENTS
MUSCARINIC ANTAGONISTS				
Darifenacin	Enablex	**Tab, ER:** 7.5mg, 15mg	**Initial:** 7.5mg qd. **Max:** 15mg qd.	Swallow whole. **Moderate Hepatic Impairment/ Concomitant Potent CYP3A4 Inhibitors:** Do not exceed 7.5mg/day. **Severe Hepatic Impairment:** Avoid use.
Fesoterodine	Toviaz	**Tab, ER:** 4mg, 8mg	**Initial:** 4mg qd. **Max:** 8mg qd.	Swallow whole. **Severe Renal Impairment (CrCl <30mL/min)/ Concomitant Potent CYP3A4 Inhibitors:** Do not exceed 4mg/day. **Severe Hepatic Impairment:** Avoid use.
Oxybutynin*	Generic	**Syrup:** 5mg/5mL; **Tab:** 5mg	**Usual:** 5mg bid-tid. **Max:** 5mg qid.	**Elderly:** A lower starting dose of 2.5mg bid-tid is recommended. **Pediatrics >5 yrs:** 5mg bid. **Max:** 5mg tid.
	Ditropan XL	**Tab, ER:** 5mg, 10mg, 15mg	**Initial:** 5mg or 10mg qd. **Max:** 30mg/day.	Swallow whole. Increase dose by 5mg weekly if needed. **Pediatrics ≥6 yrs:** 5mg qd. **Max:** 20mg/day.
	Gelnique	**Gel:** 3% (28mg/pump), 10% (1g/pkt)	Apply to dry, intact skin on abdomen, upper arms/ shoulders, or thighs. **3%:** 3 pumps qd. **10%:** 1 pkt qd.	Rotate application sites.
	Oxytrol	**Patch:** 3.9mg/day	Apply 1 patch to dry, intact skin on abdomen, hip, or buttock twice weekly (every 3-4 days).	Rotate application sites (avoid using the same site within 7 days).
Solifenacin	Vesicare	**Tab:** 5mg, 10mg	**Usual:** 5mg qd. **Max:** 10mg qd.	Swallow whole. **Severe Renal Impairment (CrCl <30mL/min)/ Moderate Hepatic Impairment/ Concomitant Potent CYP3A4 Inhibitors:** Do not exceed 5mg/day. **Severe Hepatic Impairment:** Avoid use.
Tolterodine	Detrol	**Tab:** 1mg, 2mg	**Initial:** 2mg bid.	Decrease dose to 1mg bid if needed. **Significant Hepatic or Renal Dysfunction/ Concomitant Potent CYP3A4 Inhibitors:** 1mg bid.
	Detrol LA	**Cap, ER:** 2mg, 4mg	**Usual:** 4mg qd.	Swallow whole. Decrease dose to 2mg qd if needed. **Mild-Moderate Hepatic Impairment/Severe Renal Impairment (CrCl 10-30mL/min)/ Concomitant Potent CYP3A4 Inhibitors:** 2mg qd. **Severe Hepatic Impairment/ CrCl <10mL/min:** Avoid use.

(Continued)

GENERIC	BRAND	HOW SUPPLIED	DOSAGE	COMMENTS
MUSCARINIC ANTAGONISTS (Continued)				
Trospium	Sanctura	**Tab:** 20mg	**Usual:** 20mg bid.	Take 1 hr before meals or on empty stomach. **Severe Renal Impairment (CrCl <30mL/min):** 20mg qhs. **Elderly ≥75 yrs:** May titrate down to 20mg qd based on tolerability.
	Sanctura XR	**Cap, ER:** 60mg	**Usual:** 60mg qam.	Take on empty stomach 1 hr before a meal. **Severe Renal Impairment (CrCl <30mL/min):** Avoid use.
MISCELLANEOUS				
Mirabegron	Myrbetriq	**Tab, ER:** 25mg, 50mg	**Initial:** 25mg qd. **Max:** 50mg qd.	Take with or without food. Swallow whole. **Severe Renal Impairment (CrCl 15-29mL/min)/ Moderate Hepatic Impairment:** Do not exceed 25mg/day. **End-Stage Renal Disease/Severe Hepatic Impairment:** Avoid use.
OnabotulinumtoxinA	Botox	**Inj:** (sterile powder) 100 U, 200 U	**Usual:** 100 U. **Max:** 100 U.	Recommended dilution is 100 U/10mL with 0.9% non-preserved saline solution.

*Oxytrol for women (oxybutynin) patch is available as an OTC product for overactive bladder.

IMMUNIZATION SCHEDULES – UNITED STATES, 2014

Recommended immunization schedule for persons aged 0 through 18 years (Figure 1)

Vaccine	Birth	1 mo	2 mos	4 mos	6 mos	9 mos	12 mos	15 mos	18 mos	19–23 mos	2–3 yrs	4–6 yrs	7–10 yrs	11–12 yrs	13–15 yrs	16–18 yrs
Hepatitis B[1] (HepB)	1st dose	←— 2nd dose —→			←——————————— 3rd dose ———————————→											
Rotavirus[2] (RV) RV1 (2-dose series); RV5 (3-dose series)			1st dose	2nd dose	See footnote 2											
Diphtheria, tetanus, & acellular pertussis[3] (DTaP: <7 yrs)			1st dose	2nd dose	3rd dose			←——— 4th dose ———→				5th dose				
Tetanus, diphtheria, & acellular pertussis[4] (Tdap: ≥7 yrs)														(Tdap)		
Haemophilus influenzae type b[5] (Hib)			1st dose	2nd dose	See footnote 5		3rd or 4th dose, See footnote 5									
Pneumococcal conjugate[6] (PCV13)			1st dose	2nd dose	3rd dose		←——— 4th dose ———→									
Pneumococcal polysaccharide[6] (PPSV23)																
Inactivated poliovirus[7] (IPV) (<18 yrs)			1st dose	2nd dose	←——————————— 3rd dose ———————————→							4th dose				
Influenza[8] (IIV; LAIV) 2 doses for some: See footnote 8					Annual vaccination (IIV only)						Annual vaccination (IIV or LAIV)					
Measles, mumps, rubella[9] (MMR)							←——— 1st dose ———→					2nd dose				
Varicella[10] (VAR)							←——— 1st dose ———→					2nd dose				
Hepatitis A[11] (HepA)							←——— 2-dose series, See footnote 11 ———→									
Human papillomavirus[12] (HPV2: females only; HPV4: males and females)														(3-dose series)		
Meningococcal[13] (Hib-MenCY ≥6 weeks; MenACWY-D ≥9 mos; MenACWY-CRM ≥2 mos)							←————————————— See footnote 13 —————————————→							1st dose		Booster

Legend:
- Range of recommended ages for all children
- Range of recommended ages for catch-up immunization
- Range of recommended ages for certain high-risk groups
- Range of recommended ages during which catch-up is encouraged and for certain high-risk groups
- Not routinely recommended

(Continued)

Catch-up immunization schedule for persons aged 4 months through 18 years who start late or who are more than 1 month behind (Figure 2)

Vaccine	Minimum Age for Dose 1	Minimum Interval Between Doses			
		Dose 1 to dose 2	Dose 2 to dose 3	Dose 3 to dose 4	Dose 4 to dose 5
Persons aged 4 months through 6 years					
Hepatitis B[1]	Birth	4 weeks	8 weeks and at least 16 weeks after first dose; minimum age for the final dose is 24 weeks		
Rotavirus[2]	6 weeks	4 weeks	4 weeks[2]		
Diphtheria, tetanus, & acellular pertussis[3]	6 weeks	4 weeks	4 weeks	6 months	6 months[3]
Haemophilus influenzae type b[5]	6 weeks	4 weeks if first dose administered at younger than age 12 months / 8 weeks (as final dose) if first dose administered at age 12 through 14 months / No further doses needed if first dose administered at age 15 months or older	4 weeks[5] if current age is younger than 12 months and first dose administered at <7 months old / 8 weeks and age 12 months through 59 months (as final dose)[5] if current age is younger than 12 months and first dose administered between 7 through 11 months (regardless of Hib vaccine [PRP-T or PRP-OMP] used for first dose); OR if current age is 12 through 59 months and first dose administered at younger than age 12 months; OR first 2 doses were PRP-OMP and administered at younger than 15 months of age. / No further doses needed if previous dose administered at age 15 months or older	8 weeks (as final dose) This dose only necessary for children aged 12 through 59 months who received 3 (PRP-T) doses before age 12 months and started the primary series before age 7 months	
Pneumococcal[6]	6 weeks	4 weeks if first dose administered at younger than age 12 months / 8 weeks (as final dose for healthy children) if first dose administered at age 12 months or older / No further doses needed for healthy children if first dose administered at age 24 months or older	4 weeks if current age is younger than 12 months / 8 weeks (as final dose for healthy children) if current age is 12 months or older / No further doses needed for healthy children if previous dose administered at age 24 months or older	8 weeks (as final dose) This dose only necessary for children aged 12 through 59 months who received 3 doses before age 12 months or for children at high risk who received 3 doses at any age	
Inactivated poliovirus[7]	6 weeks	4 weeks[7]	4 weeks[7]	6 months[7] minimum age 4 years for final dose	
Meningococcal[13]	6 weeks	8 weeks[13]	See footnote 13	See footnote 13	
Measles, mumps, rubella[9]	12 months	4 weeks			
Varicella[10]	12 months	3 months			
Hepatitis A[11]	12 months	6 months			
Persons aged 7 through 18 years					
Tetanus, diphtheria; tetanus, diphtheria, & acellular pertussis[4]	7 years[4]	4 weeks	4 weeks if first dose of DTaP/DT administered at younger than age 12 months / 6 months if first dose of DTaP/DT administered at age 12 months or older and then no further doses needed for catch-up	6 months if first dose of DTaP/DT administered at younger than age 12 months	
Human papillomavirus[12]	9 years	Routine dosing intervals are recommended[12]			
Hepatitis A[11]	12 months	6 months			
Hepatitis B[1]	Birth	4 weeks	8 weeks (and at least 16 weeks after first dose)		
Inactivated poliovirus[7]	6 weeks	4 weeks	4 weeks[7]	6 months[7]	
Meningococcal[13]	6 weeks	8 weeks[13]			

		Persons aged 7 through 18 years
Measles, mumps, rubella[9]	12 months	4 weeks
Varicella[10]	12 months	3 months if person is younger than age 13 years 4 weeks if person is aged 13 years or older

(Continued)

This schedule includes recommendations in effect as of January 1, 2014. Any dose not administered at the recommended age should be administered at a subsequent visit, when indicated and feasible. The use of a combination vaccine generally is preferred over separate injections of its equivalent component vaccines. Vaccination providers should consult the relevant Advisory Committee on Immunization Practices (ACIP) statement for detailed recommendations, available online at http://www.cdc.gov/vaccines/hcp/acip-recs/index.html. Clinically significant adverse events that follow vaccination should be reported to the Vaccine Adverse Event Reporting System (VAERS) online (http://www.vaers.hhs.gov) or by telephone (800-822-7967). Suspected cases of vaccine-preventable diseases should be reported to the state or local health department. Additional information, including precautions and contraindications for vaccination, is available from CDC online (http://www.cdc.gov/vaccines/recs/vac-admin/contraindications.htm) or by telephone (800-CDC-INFO [800-232-4636]).

NOTE: The above recommendations must be read along with the footnotes on the following pages.

The schedules must be read along with the following footnotes.

1. Hepatitis B (HepB) vaccine. (Minimum age: birth)
Routine vaccination:
At birth:
- Administer monovalent HepB vaccine to all newborns before hospital discharge.

- For infants born to hepatitis B surface antigen (HBsAg)-positive mothers, administer HepB vaccine and 0.5 mL of hepatitis B immune globulin (HBIG) within 12 hours of birth. These infants should be tested for HBsAg and antibody to HBsAg (anti-HBs) 1 to 2 months after completion of the HepB series, at age 9 through 18 months (preferably at the next well-child visit).

- If mother's HBsAg status is unknown, within 12 hours of birth administer HepB vaccine regardless of birth weight. For infants weighing less than 2,000 grams, administer HBIG in addition to HepB vaccine within 12 hours of birth. Determine mother's HBsAg status as soon as possible and, if mother is HBsAg-positive, also administer HBIG for infants weighing 2,000 grams or more as soon as possible, but no later than age 7 days.

Doses following the birth dose:
- The second dose should be administered at age 1 or 2 months. Monovalent HepB vaccine should be used for doses administered before age 6 weeks.

- Infants who did not receive a birth dose should receive 3 doses of a HepB-containing vaccine on a schedule of 0, 1 to 2 months, and 6 months starting as soon as feasible. See Figure 2.

- Administer the second dose 1 to 2 months after the first dose (minimum interval of 4 weeks), administer the third dose at least 8 weeks after the second dose AND at least 16 weeks after the **first** dose. The final (third or fourth) dose in the HepB vaccine series should be administered <u>no earlier than age 24 weeks</u>.

- Administration of a total of 4 doses of HepB vaccine is permitted when a combination vaccine containing HepB is administered after the birth dose.

Catch-up vaccination:
- Unvaccinated persons should complete a 3-dose series.

- A 2-dose series (doses separated by at least 4 months) of adult formulation Recombivax HB is licensed for use in children aged 11 through 15 years.

- For other catch-up guidance, see Figure 2.

2. Rotavirus (RV) vaccines. (Minimum age: 6 weeks for both RV1 [Rotarix] and RV5 [RotaTeq])
Routine vaccination:
- Administer a series of RV vaccine to all infants as follows:

  1. If Rotarix is used, administer a 2-dose series at 2 and 4 months of age.

  2. If RotaTeq is used, administer a 3-dose series at ages 2, 4, and 6 months.

  3. If any dose in the series was RotaTeq or vaccine product is unknown for any dose in the series, a total of 3 doses of RV vaccine should be administered.

Catch-up vaccination:
- The maximum age for the first dose in the series is 14 weeks, 6 days; vaccination should not be initiated for infants aged 15 weeks, 0 days or older.

- The maximum age for the final dose in the series is 8 months, 0 days.

- For other catch-up guidance, see Figure 2.

3. Diphtheria and tetanus toxoids and acellular pertussis (DTaP) vaccine. (Minimum age: 6 weeks.
Exception: DTaP-IPV [Kinrix]: 4 years)
Routine vaccination:
- Administer a 5-dose series of DTaP vaccine at ages 2, 4, 6, 15 through 18 months, and 4 through 6 years. The fourth dose may be administered as early as age 12 months, provided at least 6 months have elapsed since the third dose.

Catch-up vaccination:
- The fifth dose of DTaP vaccine is not necessary if the fourth dose was administered at age 4 years or older.

- For other catch-up guidance, see Figure 2.

4. Tetanus and diphtheria toxoids and acellular pertussis (Tdap) vaccine. (Minimum age: 10 years for Boostrix, 11 years for Adacel)
Routine vaccination:
- Administer 1 dose of Tdap vaccine to all adolescents aged 11 through 12 years.

- Tdap may be administered regardless of the interval since the last tetanus and diphtheria toxoid-containing vaccine.

- Administer 1 dose of Tdap vaccine to pregnant adolescents during each pregnancy (preferred during 27 through 36 weeks gestation) regardless of time since prior Td or Tdap vaccination.

Catch-up vaccination:
- Persons aged 7 years and older who are not fully immunized with DTaP vaccine should receive Tdap vaccine as 1 (preferably the first) dose in the catch-up series; if additional doses are needed, use Td vaccine. For children 7 through 10 years who receive a dose of Tdap as part of the catch-up series, an adolescent Tdap vaccine dose at age 11 through 12 years should NOT be administered. Td should be administered instead 10 years after the Tdap dose.

- Persons aged 11 through 18 years who have not received Tdap vaccine should receive a dose followed by tetanus and diphtheria toxoids (Td) booster doses every 10 years thereafter.

- Inadvertent doses of DTaP vaccine:
  - If administered inadvertently to a child aged 7 through 10 years may count as part of the catch-up series. This dose may count as the adolescent Tdap dose, or the child can later receive a Tdap booster dose at age 11 through 12 years.
  - If administered inadvertently to an adolescent aged 11 through 18 years, the dose should be counted as the adolescent Tdap booster.

- For other catch-up guidance, see Figure 2.

5. *Haemophilus influenzae* type b (Hib) conjugate vaccine. (Minimum age: 6 weeks for PRP-T [ACTHIB, DTaP-IPV/Hib (Pentacel) and Hib-MenCY (MenHibrix)], PRP-OMP [PedvaxHIB or COMVAX], 12 months for PRP-T [Hiberix])

Routine vaccination:

- Administer a 2- or 3-dose Hib vaccine primary series and a booster dose (dose 3 or 4 depending on vaccine used in primary series) at age 12 through 15 months to complete a full Hib vaccine series.

- The primary series with ActHIB, MenHibrix, or Pentacel consists of 3 doses and should be administered at 2, 4, and 6 months of age. The primary series with PedvaxHib or COMVAX consists of 2 doses and should be administered at 2 and 4 months of age; a dose at age 6 months is not indicated.

- One booster dose (dose 3 or 4 depending on vaccine used in primary series) of any Hib vaccine should be administered at age 12 through 15 months. An exception is Hiberix vaccine. Hiberix should only be used for the booster (final) dose in children aged 12 months through 4 years who have received at least 1 prior dose of Hib-containing vaccine.

- For recommendations on the use of MenHibrix in patients at increased risk for meningococcal disease, please refer to the meningococcal vaccine footnotes and also to *MMWR* March 22, 2013; 62(RR02);1-22, available at http://www.cdc.gov/mmwr/pdf/rr/rr6202.pdf.

Catch-up vaccination:

- If dose 1 was administered at ages 12 through 14 months, administer a second (final) dose at least 8 weeks after dose 1, regardless of Hib vaccine used in the primary series.

- If the first 2 doses were PRP-OMP (PedvaxHIB or COMVAX), and were administered at age 11 months or younger, the third (and final) dose should be administered at age 12 through 15 months and at least 8 weeks after the second dose.

- If the first dose was administered at age 7 through 11 months, administer the second dose at least 4 weeks later and a third (and final) dose at age 12 through 15 months or 8 weeks after second dose, whichever is later, regardless of Hib vaccine used for first dose.

- If first dose is administered at younger than 12 months of age and second dose is given between 12 through 14 months of age, a third (and final) dose should be given 8 weeks later.

- For unvaccinated children aged 15 months or older, administer only 1 dose.

- For other catch-up guidance, see Figure 2. For catch-up guidance related to MenHibrix, please see the meningococcal vaccine footnotes and also *MMWR* March 22, 2013; 62(RR02);1-22, available at http://www.cdc.gov/mmwr/pdf/rr/rr6202.pdf.

Vaccination of persons with high-risk conditions:

- Children aged 12 through 59 months who are at increased risk for Hib disease, including chemotherapy recipients and those with anatomic or functional asplenia (including sickle cell disease), human immunodeficiency virus (HIV) infection, immunoglobulin deficiency, or early component complement deficiency, who have received either no doses or only 1 dose of Hib vaccine before 12 months of age, should receive 2 additional doses of Hib vaccine 8 weeks apart; children who received 2 or more doses of Hib vaccine before 12 months of age should receive 1 additional dose.

- For patients younger than 5 years of age undergoing chemotherapy or radiation treatment who received a Hib vaccine dose(s) within 14 days of starting therapy or during therapy, repeat the dose(s) at least 3 months following therapy completion.

- Recipients of hematopoietic stem cell transplant (HSCT) should be revaccinated with a 3-dose regimen of Hib vaccine starting 6 to 12 months after successful transplant, regardless of vaccination history; doses should be administered at least 4 weeks apart.

- A single dose of any Hib-containing vaccine should be administered to unimmunized* children and adolescents 15 months of age and older undergoing an elective splenectomy; if possible, vaccine should be administered at least 14 days before procedure.

- Hib vaccine is not routinely recommended for patients 5 years or older. However, 1 dose of Hib vaccine should be administered to unimmunized* persons aged 5 years or older who have anatomic or functional asplenia (including sickle cell disease) and unvaccinated persons 5 through 18 years of age with human immunodeficiency virus (HIV) infection.

Patients who have not received a primary series and booster dose or at least 1 dose of Hib vaccine after 14 months of age are considered unimmunized.

6. **Pneumococcal vaccines. (Minimum age: 6 weeks for PCV13, 2 years for PPSV23)**

Routine vaccination with PCV13:

- Administer a 4-dose series of PCV13 vaccine at ages 2, 4, and 6 months and at age 12 through 15 months.

- For children aged 14 through 59 months who have received an age-appropriate series of 7-valent PCV (PCV7), administer a single supplemental dose of 13-valent PCV (PCV13).

Catch-up vaccination with PCV13:

- Administer 1 dose of PCV13 to all healthy children aged 24 through 59 months who are not completely vaccinated for their age.

- For other catch-up guidance, see Figure 2.

Vaccination of persons with high-risk conditions with PCV13 and PPSV23:

- All recommended PCV13 doses should be administered prior to PPSV23 vaccination if possible.

- For children 2 through 5 years of age with any of the following conditions: chronic heart disease (particularly cyanotic congenital heart disease and cardiac failure); chronic lung disease (including asthma if treated with high-dose oral corticosteroid therapy); diabetes mellitus; cerebrospinal fluid leak; cochlear implant; sickle cell disease and other hemoglobinopathies; anatomic or functional asplenia; HIV infection; chronic renal failure; nephrotic syndrome; diseases associated with treatment with immunosuppressive drugs or radiation therapy, including malignant neoplasms, leukemias, lymphomas, and Hodgkin disease; solid organ transplantation; or congenital immunodeficiency:

1. Administer 1 dose of PCV13 if 3 doses of PCV (PCV7 and/or PCV13) were received previously.
2. Administer 2 doses of PCV13 at least 8 weeks apart if fewer than 3 doses of PCV (PCV7 and/or PCV13) were received previously.
3. Administer 1 supplemental dose of PCV13 if 4 doses of PCV7 or other age-appropriate complete PCV7 series was received previously.
4. The minimum interval between doses of PCV (PCV7 or PCV13) is 8 weeks.
5. For children with no history of PPSV23 vaccination, administer PPSV23 at least 8 weeks after the most recent dose of PCV13.

- For children aged 6 through 18 years who have cerebrospinal fluid leak; cochlear implant; sickle cell disease and other hemoglobinopathies; anatomic or functional asplenia; congenital or acquired immunodeficiencies; HIV infection; chronic renal failure; nephrotic syndrome; diseases associated with treatment with immunosuppressive drugs or radiation therapy, including malignant neoplasms, leukemias, lymphomas, and Hodgkin disease; generalized malignancy; solid organ transplantation; or multiple myeloma:

    1. If neither PCV13 nor PPSV23 has been received previously, administer 1 dose of PCV13 now and 1 dose of PPSV23 at least 8 weeks later.
    2. If PCV13 has been received previously but PPSV23 has not, administer 1 dose of PPSV23 at least 8 weeks after the most recent dose of PCV13.
    3. If PPSV23 has been received but PCV13 has not, administer 1 dose of PCV13 at least 8 weeks after the most recent dose of PPSV23.

- For children aged 6 through 18 years with chronic heart disease (particularly cyanotic congenital heart disease and cardiac failure), chronic lung disease (including asthma if treated with high-dose oral corticosteroid therapy), diabetes mellitus, alcoholism, or chronic liver disease, who have not received PPSV23, administer 1 dose of PPSV23. If PCV13 has been received previously, then PPSV23 should be administered at least 8 weeks after any prior PCV13 dose.

- A single revaccination with PPSV23 should be administered 5 years after the first dose to children with sickle cell disease or other hemoglobinopathies; anatomic or functional asplenia; congenital or acquired immunodeficiencies; HIV infection; chronic renal failure; nephrotic syndrome; diseases associated with treatment with immunosuppressive drugs or radiation therapy, including malignant neoplasms, leukemias, lymphomas, and Hodgkin disease; generalized malignancy; solid organ transplantation; or multiple myeloma.

7. **Inactivated poliovirus vaccine (IPV). (Minimum age: 6 weeks)**
   Routine vaccination:
   - Administer a 4-dose series of IPV at ages 2, 4, 6 through 18 months, and 4 through 6 years. The final dose in the series should be administered on or after the fourth birthday and at least 6 months after the previous dose.

Catch-up vaccination:
- In the first 6 months of life, minimum age and minimum intervals are only recommended if the person is at risk for imminent exposure to circulating poliovirus (i.e., travel to a polio-endemic region or during an outbreak).
- If 4 or more doses are administered before age 4 years, an additional dose should be administered at age 4 through 6 years and at least 6 months after the previous dose.
- A fourth dose is not necessary if the third dose was administered at age 4 years or older and at least 6 months after the previous dose.
- If both OPV and IPV were administered as part of a series, a total of 4 doses should be administered, regardless of the child's current age. IPV is not routinely recommended for U.S. residents aged 18 years or older.
- For other catch-up guidance, see Figure 2.

8. **Influenza vaccines. (Minimum age: 6 months for inactivated influenza vaccine [IIV], 2 years for live, attenuated influenza vaccine [LAIV])**
   Routine vaccination:
   - Administer influenza vaccine annually to all children beginning at age 6 months. For most healthy, nonpregnant persons aged 2 through 49 years, either LAIV or IIV may be used. However, LAIV should NOT be administered to some persons, including 1) those with asthma, 2) children 2 through 4 years who had wheezing in the past 12 months, or 3) those who have any other underlying medical conditions that predispose them to influenza complications. For all other contraindications to use of LAIV, see *MMWR* 2013; 62 (No. RR-7):1-43, available at http://www.cdc.gov/mmwr/pdf/rr/rr6207.pdf.

   For children aged 6 months through 8 years:
   - For the 2013–14 season, administer 2 doses (separated by at least 4 weeks) to children who are receiving influenza vaccine for the first time. Some children in this age group who have been vaccinated previously will also need 2 doses. For additional guidance, follow dosing guidelines in the 2013-14 ACIP influenza vaccine recommendations, *MMWR* 2013; 62 (No. RR-7):1-43, available at http://www.cdc.gov/mmwr/pdf/rr/rr6207.pdf.
   - For the 2014–15 season, follow dosing guidelines in the 2014 ACIP influenza vaccine recommendations.

   For persons aged 9 years and older:
   - Administer 1 dose.

9. **Measles, mumps, and rubella (MMR) vaccine. (Minimum age: 12 months for routine vaccination)**
   Routine vaccination:
   - Administer a 2-dose series of MMR vaccine at ages 12 through 15 months and 4 through 6 years. The second dose may be administered before age 4 years, provided at least 4 weeks have elapsed since the first dose.
   - Administer 1 dose of MMR vaccine to infants aged 6 through 11 months before departure from the United States for international travel. These children should be revaccinated with 2 doses of MMR vaccine, the first at age 12 through 15 months (12 months if the child remains in an area where disease risk is high), and the second dose at least 4 weeks later.

• Administer 2 doses of MMR vaccine to children aged 12 months and older before departure from the United States for international travel. The first dose should be administered on or after age 12 months and the second dose at least 4 weeks later.

Catch-up vaccination:

• Ensure that all school-aged children and adolescents have had 2 doses of MMR vaccine; the minimum interval between the 2 doses is 4 weeks.

10. **Varicella (VAR) vaccine. (Minimum age: 12 months)**
Routine vaccination:

• Administer a 2-dose series of VAR vaccine at ages 12 through 15 months and 4 through 6 years. The second dose may be administered before age 4 years, provided at least 3 months have elapsed since the first dose. If the second dose was administered at least 4 weeks after the first dose, it can be accepted as valid.

Catch-up vaccination:

• Ensure that all persons aged 7 through 18 years without evidence of immunity (see *MMWR* 2007; 56 [No. RR-4], available at http://www.cdc.gov/mmwr/pdf/rr/rr5604.pdf) have 2 doses of varicella vaccine. For children aged 7 through 12 years, the recommended minimum interval between doses is 3 months (if the second dose was administered at least 4 weeks after the first dose, it can be accepted as valid); for persons aged 13 years and older, the minimum interval between doses is 4 weeks.

11. **Hepatitis A (HepA) vaccine. (Minimum age: 12 months)**
Routine vaccination:

• Initiate the 2-dose HepA vaccine series at 12 through 23 months; separate the 2 doses by 6 to 18 months.

• Children who have received 1 dose of HepA vaccine before age 24 months should receive a second dose 6 to 18 months after the first dose.

• For any person aged 2 years and older who has not already received the HepA vaccine series, 2 doses of HepA vaccine separated by 6 to 18 months may be administered if immunity against hepatitis A virus infection is desired.

Catch-up vaccination:

• The minimum interval between the two doses is 6 months.

Special populations:

• Administer 2 doses of HepA vaccine at least 6 months apart to previously unvaccinated persons who live in areas where vaccination programs target older children, or who are at increased risk for infection. This includes persons traveling to or working in countries that have high or intermediate endemicity of infection; men having sex with men; users of injection and non-injection illicit drugs; persons who work with HAV-infected primates or with HAV in a research laboratory; persons with clotting-factor disorders; persons with chronic liver disease; and persons who anticipate close, personal contact (e.g., household or regular babysitting) with an international adoptee during the first 60 days after arrival in the United States from a country with high or intermediate endemicity. The first dose should be administered as soon as the adoption is planned, ideally 2 or more weeks before the arrival of the adoptee.

12. **Human papillomavirus (HPV) vaccines. (Minimum age: 9 years for HPV2 [Cervarix] and HPV4 [Gardasil])**
Routine vaccination:

• Administer a 3-dose series of HPV vaccine on a schedule of 0, 1-2, and 6 months to all adolescents aged 11 through 12 years. Either HPV2 or HPV4 may be used for females, and only HPV4 may be used for males.

• The vaccine series may be started at age 9 years.

• Administer the second dose 1 to 2 months after the first dose (minimum interval of 4 weeks), administer the third dose 24 weeks after the first dose and 16 weeks after the second dose (minimum interval of 12 weeks).

Catch-up vaccination:

• Administer the vaccine series to females (either HPV2 or HPV4) and males (HPV4) at age 13 through 18 years if not previously vaccinated.

• Use recommended routine dosing intervals (see above) for vaccine series catch-up.

13. **Meningococcal conjugate vaccines. (Minimum age: 6 weeks for Hib-MenCY [MenHibrix], 9 months for MenACWY-D [Menactra], 2 months for MenACWY-CRM [Menveo])**
Routine vaccination:

• Administer a single dose of Menactra or Menveo vaccine at age 11 through 12 years, with a booster dose at age 16 years.

• Adolescents aged 11 through 18 years with human immunodeficiency virus (HIV) infection should receive a 2-dose primary series of Menactra or Menveo with at least 8 weeks between doses.

• For children aged 2 months through 18 years with high-risk conditions, see below.

Catch-up vaccination:

• Administer Menactra or Menveo vaccine at age 13 through 18 years if not previously vaccinated.

• If the first dose is administered at age 13 through 15 years, a booster dose should be administered at age 16 through 18 years with a minimum interval of at least 8 weeks between doses.

• If the first dose is administered at age 16 years or older, a booster dose is not needed.

• For other catch-up guidance, see Figure 2.

Vaccination of persons with high-risk conditions and other persons at increased risk of disease:

• Children with anatomic or functional asplenia (including sickle cell disease):

1. For children younger than 19 months of age, administer a 4-dose infant series of MenHibrix or Menveo at 2, 4, 6, and 12 through 15 months of age.
2. For children aged 19 through 23 months who have not completed a series of MenHibrix or Menveo, administer 2 primary doses of Menveo at least 3 months apart.
3. For children aged 24 months and older who have not received a complete series of MenHibrix or Menveo or Menactra, administer 2 primary doses of either Menactra or Menveo at least 2 months apart. If Menactra is administered to a child with asplenia (including sickle cell disease), do not administer Menactra until 2 years of age and at least 4 weeks after the completion of all PCV13 doses.

(Continued)

- Children with persistent complement component deficiency:

  1. For children younger than 19 months of age, administer a 4-dose infant series of either MenHibrix or Menveo at 2, 4, 6, and 12 through 15 months of age.

  2. For children 7 through 23 months who have not initiated vaccination, two options exist depending on age and vaccine brand:

  a. For children who initiate vaccination with Menveo at 7 months through 23 months of age, a 2-dose series should be administered with the second dose after 12 months of age and at least 3 months after the first dose.

  b. For children who initiate vaccination with Menactra at 9 months through 23 months of age, a 2-dose series of Menactra should be administered at least 3 months apart.

  c. For children aged 24 months and older who have not received a complete series of MenHibrix, Menveo, or Menactra, administer 2 primary doses of either Menactra or Menveo at least 2 months apart.

- For children who travel to or reside in countries in which meningococcal disease is hyperendemic or epidemic, including countries in the African meningitis belt or the Hajj, administer an age-appropriate formulation and series of Menactra or Menveo for protection against serogroups A and W meningococcal disease. Prior receipt of MenHibrix is not sufficient for children traveling to the meningitis belt or the Hajj because it does not contain serogroups A or W.

- For children at risk during a community outbreak attributable to a vaccine serogroup, administer or complete an age- and formulation-appropriate series of MenHibrix, Menactra, or Menveo.

- For booster doses among persons with high-risk conditions, refer to *MMWR* 2013; 62(RR02);1-22, available at http://www.cdc.gov/mmwr/preview/mmwrhtml/rr6202a1.htm.

Catch-up recommendations for persons with high-risk conditions:

1. If MenHibrix is administered to achieve protection against meningococcal disease, a complete age-appropriate series of MenHibrix should be administered.

2. If the first dose of MenHibrix is given at or after 12 months of age, a total of 2 doses should be given at least 8 weeks apart to ensure protection against serogroups C and Y meningococcal disease.

3. For children who initiate vaccination with Menveo at 7 months through 9 months of age, a 2-dose series should be administered with the second dose after 12 months of age and at least 3 months after the first dose.

4. For other catch-up recommendations for these persons, refer to MMWR 2013; 62(RR02);1-22, available at http://www.cdc.gov/mmwr/preview/mmwrhtml/rr6202a1.htm.

Recommended adult immunization schedule, by vaccine and age group[1]

VACCINE ▼ / AGE GROUP ▶	19-21 years	22-26 years	27-49 years	50-59 years	60-64 years	≥65 years
Influenza[2,*]	1 dose annually					
Tetanus, diphtheria, pertussis (Td/Tdap)[3,*]	Substitute 1-time dose of Tdap for Td booster; then boost with Td every 10 yrs					
Varicella[4,*]	2 doses					
Human papillomavirus (HPV) Female[5,*]	3 doses	3 doses				
Human papillomavirus (HPV) Male[5,*]	3 doses	3 doses				
Zoster[6]					1 dose	1 dose
Measles, mumps, rubella (MMR)[7,*]	1 or 2 doses					
Pneumococcal 13-valent conjugate (PCV13)[8,*]	1 dose					
Pneumococcal polysaccharide (PPSV23)[9,10]	1 or 2 doses					1 dose
Meningococcal[11,*]	1 or more doses					
Hepatitis A[12,*]	2 doses					
Hepatitis B[13,*]	3 doses					
Haemophilus influenzae type b (Hib)[14,*]	1 or 3 doses					

*Covered by the Vaccine Injury Compensation Program

For all persons in this category who meet the age requirements and who lack documentation of vaccination or have no evidence of previous infection; zoster vaccine recommended regardless of prior episode of zoster

Recommended if some other risk factor is present (e.g., on the basis of medical, occupational, lifestyle, or other indication)

No recommendation

NOTE: The above recommendations must be read along with the footnotes on the following pages.

(Continued)

Recommended vaccinations indicated for adults based on medical and other indications[1]

VACCINE ▼ / INDICATION ►	Pregnancy	Immunocompromising conditions (excluding human immunodeficiency virus [HIV])[4,6,7,8,15]	HIV infection CD4+ T lymphocyte count[4,6,7,8,15] <200 cells/μL	HIV infection ≥200 cells/μL	Men who have sex with men (MSM)	Kidney failure, end-stage renal disease, receipt of hemodialysis	Heart disease, chronic lung disease, chronic alcoholism	Asplenia (including elective splenectomy and persistent complement component deficiencies)[8,14]	Chronic liver disease	Diabetes	Healthcare personnel
Influenza[2,*]	1 dose IIV annually	1 dose IIV annually			1 dose IIV or LAIV annually	1 dose IIV annually					1 dose IIV or LAIV annually
Tetanus, diphtheria, pertussis (Td/Tdap)[3,*]	1 dose Tdap each pregnancy	Substitute 1-time dose of Tdap for Td booster; then boost with Td every 10 yrs									
Varicella[4,*]	Contraindicated	Contraindicated			2 doses						
Human papillomavirus (HPV) Female[5,*]		3 doses through age 26 yrs			3 doses through age 26 yrs		3 doses through age 26 yrs				
Human papillomavirus (HPV) Male[5,*]		3 doses through age 26 yrs			3 doses through age 26 yrs		3 doses through age 21 yrs				
Zoster[6]	Contraindicated	Contraindicated					1 dose				
Measles, mumps, rubella (MMR)[7,*]	Contraindicated	Contraindicated					1 or 2 doses				
Pneumococcal 13-valent conjugate (PCV13)[8,*]						1 dose					
Pneumococcal polysaccharide (PPSV23)[9,10]						1 or 2 doses					
Meningococcal[11,*]						1 or more doses					
Hepatitis A[12,*]						2 doses					
Hepatitis B[13,*]						3 doses					
Haemophilus influenzae type b (Hib)[14,*]		post-HSCT recipients only				1 or 3 doses					

For all persons in this category who meet the age requirements and who lack documentation of vaccination or have no evidence of previous infection; zoster vaccine recommended regardless of prior episode of zoster

Recommended if some other risk factor is present (e.g., on the basis of medical, occupational, lifestyle, or other indications)

No recommendation

*Covered by the Vaccine Injury Compensation Program

NOTE: The above recommendations must be read along with the footnotes on the following pages.

Additional Information

Report all clinically significant postvaccination reactions to the Vaccine Adverse Event Reporting System (VAERS). Reporting forms and instructions on filing a VAERS report are available at www.vaers.hhs.gov or by telephone, 800-822-7967.

Information on how to file a Vaccine Injury Compensation Program claim is available at www.hrsa.gov/vaccinecompensation or by telephone, 800-338-2382. To file a claim for vaccine injury, contact the U.S. Court of Federal Claims, 717 Madison Place, N.W., Washington, D.C. 20005; telephone, 202-357-6400.

Additional information about the vaccines in this schedule, extent of available data, and contraindications for vaccination is also available at www.cdc.gov/vaccines or from the CDC-INFO Contact Center at 800-CDC-INFO (800-232-4636) in English and Spanish, 8:00 a.m.- 8:00 p.m. Eastern Time, Monday - Friday, excluding holidays.

Use of trade names and commercial sources is for identification only and does not imply endorsement by the U.S. Department of Health and Human Services.

The recommendations in this schedule were approved by the Centers for Disease Control and Prevention's (CDC) Advisory Committee on Immunization Practices (ACIP), the American Academy of Family Physicians (AAFP), the American College of Physicians (ACP), American College of Obstetricians and Gynecologists (ACOG) and American College of Nurse-Midwives (ACNM).

These schedules indicate the recommended age groups and medical indications for which administration of currently licensed vaccines is commonly indicated for adults ages 19 years and older, as of February 1, 2014. For all vaccines being recommended on the Adult Immunization Schedule: a vaccine series does not need to be restarted, regardless of the time that has elapsed between doses. Licensed combination vaccines may be used whenever any components of the combination are indicated and when the vaccine's other components are not contraindicated. For detailed recommendations on all vaccines, including those used primarily for travelers or that are issued during the year, consult the manufacturers' package inserts and the complete statements from the Advisory Committee on Immunization Practices (www.cdc.gov/vaccines/hcp/acip-recs/index.html). Use of trade names and commercial sources is for identification only and does not imply endorsement by the U.S. Department of Health and Human Services.

The previous schedules must be read along with the following footnotes.

1. Additional information
- Additional guidance for the use of the vaccines described in this supplement is available at www.cdc.gov/vaccines/hcp/acip-recs/index.html.
- Information on vaccination recommendations when vaccination status is unknown and other general immunization information can be found in the General Recommendations on Immunization at www.cdc.gov/mmwr/preview/mmwrhtml/rr6002a1.htm.
- Information on travel vaccine requirements and recommendations (e.g., for hepatitis A and B, meningococcal, and other vaccines) is available at http://wwwnc.cdc.gov/travel/destinations/list.
- Additional information and resources regarding vaccination of pregnant women can be found at http://www.cdc.gov/vaccines/adults/rec-vac/pregnant.html.

2. Influenza vaccination
- Annual vaccination against influenza is recommended for all persons aged 6 months or older.
- Persons aged 6 months or older, including pregnant women and persons with hives-only allergy to eggs, can receive the inactivated influenza vaccine (IIV). An age-appropriate IIV formulation should be used.
- Adults aged 18 to 49 years can receive the recombinant influenza vaccine (RIV) (FluBlok). RIV does not contain any egg protein.
- Healthy, nonpregnant persons aged 2 to 49 years without high-risk medical conditions can receive either intranasally administered live, attenuated influenza vaccine (LAIV) (FluMist), or IIV. Health care personnel who care for severely immunocompromised persons (i.e., those who require care in a protected environment) should receive IIV or RIV rather than LAIV.
- The intramuscularly or intradermally administered IIV are options for adults aged 18 to 64 years.
- Adults aged 65 years or older can receive the standard-dose IIV or the high-dose IIV (Fluzone High-Dose).

3. Tetanus, diphtheria, and acellular pertussis (Td/Tdap) vaccination
- Administer 1 dose of Tdap vaccine to pregnant women during each pregnancy (preferred during 27 to 36 weeks' gestation) regardless of interval since prior Td or Tdap vaccination.
- Persons aged 11 years or older who have not received Tdap vaccine or for whom vaccine status is unknown should receive a dose of Tdap followed by tetanus and diphtheria toxoids (Td) booster doses every 10 years thereafter. Tdap can be administered regardless of interval since the most recent tetanus or diphtheria-toxoid containing vaccine.
- Adults with an unknown or incomplete history of completing a 3-dose primary vaccination series with Td-containing vaccines should begin or complete a primary vaccination series including a Tdap dose.
- For unvaccinated adults, administer the first 2 doses at least 4 weeks apart and the third dose 6 to 12 months after the second.
- For incompletely vaccinated (i.e., less than 3 doses) adults, administer remaining doses.
- Refer to the ACIP statement for recommendations for administering Td/Tdap as prophylaxis in wound management (see footnote 1).

4. Varicella vaccination
- All adults without evidence of immunity to varicella (as defined below) should receive 2 doses of single-antigen varicella vaccine or a second dose if they have received only 1 dose.
- Vaccination should be emphasized for those who have close contact with persons at high risk for severe disease (e.g., health care personnel and family contacts of persons with immunocompromising conditions) or are at high risk for exposure or transmission (e.g., teachers; child care employees; residents and staff members of institutional settings, including correctional institutions; college students;

(Continued)

military personnel; adolescents and adults living in households with children; nonpregnant women of childbearing age; and international travelers).

- Pregnant women should be assessed for evidence of varicella immunity. Women who do not have evidence of immunity should receive the first dose of varicella vaccine upon completion or termination of pregnancy and before discharge from the health care facility. The second dose should be administered 4 to 8 weeks after the first dose.

- Evidence of immunity to varicella in adults includes any of the following:

  – documentation of 2 doses of varicella vaccine at least 4 weeks apart;

  – U.S.-born before 1980, except health care personnel and pregnant women;

  – history of varicella based on diagnosis or verification of varicella disease by a health care provider;

  – history of herpes zoster based on diagnosis or verification of herpes zoster disease by a health care provider; or

  – laboratory evidence of immunity or laboratory confirmation of disease.

5. Human papillomavirus (HPV) vaccination

- Two vaccines are licensed for use in females, bivalent HPV vaccine (HPV2) and quadrivalent HPV vaccine (HPV4), and one HPV vaccine for use in males (HPV4).

- For females, either HPV4 or HPV2 is recommended in a 3-dose series for routine vaccination at age 11 or 12 years and for those aged 13 through 26 years, if not previously vaccinated.

- For males, HPV4 is recommended in a 3-dose series for routine vaccination at age 11 or 12 years and for those aged 13 through 21 years, if not previously vaccinated. Males aged 22 through 26 years may be vaccinated.

- HPV4 is recommended for men who have sex with men through age 26 years for those who did not get any or all doses when they were younger.

- Vaccination is recommended for immunocompromised persons (including those with HIV infection) through age 26 years for those who did not get any or all doses when they were younger.

- A complete series for either HPV4 or HPV2 consists of 3 doses. The second dose should be administered 4 to 8 weeks (minimum interval of 4 weeks) after the first dose; the third dose should be administered 24 weeks after the first dose and 16 weeks after the second dose (minimum interval of at least 12 weeks).

- HPV vaccines are not recommended for use in pregnant women. However, pregnancy testing is not needed before vaccination. If a woman is found to be pregnant after initiating the vaccination series, no intervention is needed; the remainder of the 3-dose series should be delayed until completion of pregnancy.

6. Zoster vaccination

- A single dose of zoster vaccine is recommended for adults aged 60 years or older regardless of whether they report a prior episode of herpes zoster. Although the vaccine is licensed by the U.S. Food and Drug Administration for use among and can be administered to persons aged 50 years or older, ACIP recommends that vaccination begin at age 60 years.

- Persons aged 60 years or older with chronic medical conditions may be vaccinated unless their condition constitutes a contraindication, such as pregnancy or severe immunodeficiency.

7. Measles, mumps, rubella (MMR) vaccination

- Adults born before 1957 are generally considered immune to measles and mumps. All adults born in 1957 or later should have documentation of 1 or more doses of MMR vaccine unless they have a medical contraindication to the vaccine or laboratory evidence of immunity to each of the three diseases. Documentation of provider-diagnosed disease is not considered acceptable evidence of immunity for measles, mumps, or rubella.

Measles component:

- A routine second dose of MMR vaccine, administered a minimum of 28 days after the first dose, is recommended for adults who:

  – are students in postsecondary educational institutions;

  – work in a health care facility; or

  – plan to travel internationally.

- Persons who received inactivated (killed) measles vaccine or measles vaccine of unknown type during 1963–1967 should be revaccinated with 2 doses of MMR vaccine.

Mumps component:

- A routine second dose of MMR vaccine, administered a minimum of 28 days after the first dose, is recommended for adults who:

  – are students in a postsecondary educational institution;

  – work in a health care facility; or

  – plan to travel internationally.

- Persons vaccinated before 1979 with either killed mumps vaccine or mumps vaccine of unknown type who are at high risk for mumps infection (e.g., persons who are working in a health care facility) should be considered for revaccination with 2 doses of MMR vaccine.

Rubella component:

- For women of childbearing age, regardless of birth year, rubella immunity should be determined. If there is no evidence of immunity, women who are not pregnant should be vaccinated. Pregnant women who do not have evidence of immunity should receive MMR vaccine upon completion or termination of pregnancy and before discharge from the health care facility.

Health care personnel born before 1957:

- For unvaccinated health care personnel born before 1957 who lack laboratory evidence of measles, mumps, and/or rubella immunity or laboratory confirmation of disease, health care facilities should consider vaccinating personnel with 2 doses of MMR vaccine at the appropriate interval for measles and mumps or 1 dose of MMR vaccine for rubella.

8. Pneumococcal conjugate (PCV13) vaccination

- Adults aged 19 years or older with immunocompromising conditions (including chronic renal failure and nephrotic syndrome), functional or anatomic asplenia, cerebrospinal fluid leaks, or cochlear implants who have not previously received PCV13 or PPSV23 should receive a single dose of PCV13 followed by a dose of PPSV23 at least 8 weeks later.
- Adults aged 19 years or older with the aforementioned conditions who have previously received 1 or more doses of PPSV23 should receive a dose of PCV13 one or more years after the last PPSV23 dose was received. For adults who require additional doses of PPSV23, the first such dose should be given no sooner than 8 weeks after PCV13 and at least 5 years after the most recent dose of PPSV23.
- When indicated, PCV13 should be administered to patients who are uncertain of their vaccination status history and have no record of previous vaccination.
- Although PCV13 is licensed by the U.S. Food and Drug Administration for use among and can be administered to persons aged 50 years or older, ACIP recommends PCV13 for adults aged 19 years or older with the specific medical conditions noted above.

9. Pneumococcal polysaccharide (PPSV23) vaccination

- When PCV13 is also indicated, PCV13 should be given first (see footnote 8).
- Vaccinate all persons with the following indications:
  - all adults aged 65 years or older;
  - adults younger than 65 years with chronic lung disease (including chronic obstructive pulmonary disease, emphysema, and asthma), chronic cardiovascular diseases, diabetes mellitus, chronic renal failure, nephrotic syndrome, chronic liver disease (including cirrhosis), alcoholism, cochlear implants, cerebrospinal fluid leaks, immunocompromising conditions, and functional or anatomic asplenia (e.g., sickle cell disease and other hemoglobinopathies, congenital or acquired asplenia, splenic dysfunction, or splenectomy [if elective splenectomy is planned, vaccinate at least 2 weeks before surgery]);
  - residents of nursing homes or long-term care facilities; and
  - adults who smoke cigarettes.
- Persons with immunocompromising conditions and other selected conditions are recommended to receive PCV13 and PPSV23 vaccines. See footnote 8 for information on timing of PCV13 and PPSV23 vaccinations.
- Persons with asymptomatic or symptomatic HIV infection should be vaccinated as soon as possible after their diagnosis.

- When cancer chemotherapy or other immunosuppressive therapy is being considered, the interval between vaccination and initiation of immunosuppressive therapy should be at least 2 weeks. Vaccination during chemotherapy or radiation therapy should be avoided.
- Routine use of PPSV23 vaccine is not recommended for American Indians/Alaska Natives or other persons younger than 65 years unless they have underlying medical conditions that are PPSV23 indications. However, public health authorities may consider recommending PPSV23 for American Indians/Alaska Natives who are living in areas where the risk for invasive pneumococcal disease is increased.
- When indicated, PPSV23 vaccine should be administered to patients who are uncertain of their vaccination status and have no record of vaccination.

10. Revaccination with PPSV23

- One-time revaccination 5 years after the first dose of PPSV23 is recommended for persons aged 19 through 64 years with chronic renal failure or nephrotic syndrome, functional or anatomic asplenia (e.g., sickle cell disease or splenectomy), or immunocompromising conditions.
- Persons who received 1 or 2 doses of PPSV23 before age 65 years for any indication should receive another dose of the vaccine at age 65 years or later if at least 5 years have passed since their previous dose.
- No further doses of PPSV23 are needed for persons vaccinated with PPSV23 at or after age 65 years.

11. Meningococcal vaccination

- Administer 2 doses of quadrivalent meningococcal conjugate vaccine (MenACWY [Menactra, Menveo]) at least 2 months apart to adults of all ages with functional asplenia or persistent complement component deficiencies. HIV infection is not an indication for routine vaccination with MenACWY. If an HIV-infected person of any age is vaccinated, 2 doses of MenACWY should be administered at least 2 months apart.
- Administer a single dose of meningococcal vaccine to microbiologists routinely exposed to isolates of *Neisseria meningitidis*, military recruits, persons at risk during an outbreak attributable to a vaccine serogroup, and persons who travel to or live in countries in which meningococcal disease is hyperendemic or epidemic.
- First-year college students up through age 21 years who are living in residence halls should be vaccinated if they have not received a dose on or after their 16th birthday.
- MenACWY is preferred for adults with any of the preceding indications who are aged 55 years or younger as well as for adults aged 56 years or older who a) were vaccinated previously with MenACWY and are recom- mended for revaccination, or b) for whom multiple doses are anticipated. Meningococcal polysaccharide vaccine (MPSV4 [Menomune]) is preferred for adults aged 56 years or older who have not received MenACWY previously and who require a single dose only (e.g., travelers).

(Continued)

• Revaccination with MenACWY every 5 years is recommended for adults previously vaccinated with MenACWY or MPSV4 who remain at increased risk for infection (e.g., adults with anatomic or functional asplenia, persistent complement component deficiencies, or microbiologists).

12. Hepatitis A vaccination

• Vaccinate any person seeking protection from hepatitis A virus (HAV) infection and persons with any of the following indications:

  – men who have sex with men and persons who use injection or non-injection illicit drugs;

  – persons working with HAV-infected primates or with HAV in a research laboratory setting;

  – persons with chronic liver disease and persons who receive clotting factor concentrates;

  – persons traveling to or working in countries that have high or intermediate endemicity of hepatitis A; and

  – unvaccinated persons who anticipate close personal contact (e.g., household or regular babysitting) with an international adoptee during the first 60 days after arrival in the United States from a country with high or intermediate endemicity. (See footnote 1 for more information on travel recommendations.) The first dose of the 2-dose hepatitis A vaccine series should be administered as soon as adoption is planned, ideally 2 or more weeks before the arrival of the adoptee.

• Single-antigen vaccine formulations should be administered in a 2-dose schedule at either 0 and 6 to 12 months (Havrix), or 0 and 6 to 18 months (Vaqta). If the combined hepatitis A and hepatitis B vaccine (Twinrix) is used, administer 3 doses at 0, 1, and 6 months; alternatively, a 4-dose schedule may be used, administered on days 0, 7, and 21 to 30 followed by a booster dose at month 12.

13. Hepatitis B vaccination

• Vaccinate persons with any of the following indications and any person seeking protection from hepatitis B virus (HBV) infection:

  – sexually active persons who are not in a long-term, mutually monogamous relationship (e.g., persons with more than 1 sex partner during the previous 6 months); persons seeking evaluation or treatment for a sexually transmitted disease (STD); current or recent injection drug users; and men who have sex with men;

  – health care personnel and public safety workers who are potentially exposed to blood or other infectious body fluids;

  – persons with diabetes who are younger than age 60 years as soon as feasible after diagnosis; persons with diabetes who are age 60 years or older at the discretion of the treating clinician based on the likelihood of acquiring HBV infection, including the risk posed by an increased need for assisted blood glucose monitoring in long-term care facilities, the likelihood of experiencing chronic sequelae if infected with HBV, and the likelihood of immune response to vaccination;

  – persons with end-stage renal disease, including patients receiving hemodialysis, persons with HIV infection, and persons with chronic liver disease;

  – household contacts and sex partners of hepatitis B surface antigen–positive persons, clients and staff members of institutions for persons with developmental disabilities, and international travelers to countries with high or intermediate prevalence of chronic HBV infection; and

  – all adults in the following settings: STD treatment facilities, HIV testing and treatment facilities, facilities providing drug abuse treatment and prevention services, health care settings targeting services to injection drug users or men who have sex with men, correctional facilities, end-stage renal disease programs and facilities for chronic hemodialysis patients, and institutions and nonresidential day care facilities for persons with developmental disabilities.

• Administer missing doses to complete a 3-dose series of hepatitis B vaccine to those persons not vaccinated or not completely vaccinated. The second dose should be administered 1 month after the first dose; the third dose should be given at least 2 months after the second dose (and at least 4 months after the first dose). If the combined hepatitis A and hepatitis B vaccine (Twinrix) is used, give 3 doses at 0, 1, and 6 months; alternatively, a 4-dose Twinrix schedule, administered on days 0, 7, and 21 to 30 followed by a booster dose at month 12 may be used.

• Adult patients receiving hemodialysis or with other immunocompromising conditions should receive 1 dose of 40 mcg/mL (Recombivax HB) administered on a 3-dose schedule at 0, 1, and 6 months or 2 doses of 20 mcg/mL (Engerix-B) administered simultaneously on a 4-dose schedule at 0, 1, 2, and 6 months.

14. *Haemophilus influenzae type b* (Hib) vaccination

• One dose of Hib vaccine should be administered to persons who have functional or anatomic asplenia or sickle cell disease or are undergoing elective splenectomy if they have not previously received Hib vaccine. Hib vaccination 14 or more days before splenectomy is suggested.

• Recipients of a hematopoietic stem cell transplant should be vaccinated with a 3-dose regimen 6 to 12 months after a successful transplant, regardless of vaccination history; at least 4 weeks should separate doses.

• Hib vaccine is not recommended for adults with HIV infection since their risk for Hib infection is low.

15. Immunocompromising conditions

• Inactivated vaccines generally are acceptable (e.g., pneumococcal, meningococcal, and inactivated influenza vaccine) and live vaccines generally are avoided in persons with immune deficiencies or immunocompromising conditions. Information on specific conditions is available at http://www.cdc.gov/vaccines/hcp/acip-recs/index.html.

Sources: Birth-18 Years & "Catch-up" Immunization Schedules. Centers for Disease Control and Prevention website. http://www.cdc.gov/vaccines/schedules/hcp/child-adolescent.html. Updated January 31, 2014. Accessed February 28, 2014.

Adult Immunization Schedules. Centers for Disease Control and Prevention website. http://www.cdc.gov/vaccines/schedules/hcp/adult.html. Updated February 3, 2014. Accessed February 28, 2014.

DRUGS THAT MAY CAUSE PHOTOSENSITIVITY

The drugs in this table are known to cause photosensitivity in some individuals. Effects can range from itching, scaling, rash, and swelling to skin cancer, premature skin aging, skin and eye burns, cataracts, reduced immunity, blood vessel damage, and allergic reactions. The list is not all-inclusive, and shows only representative brands of each generic. When in doubt, always check specific product labeling. Individuals should be advised to wear protective clothing and to apply sunscreen while taking the medications listed below.

GENERIC NAME	BRAND NAME
Acetazolamide	Diamox Sequels
Acitretin	Soriatane
Acyclovir	Zovirax
Alendronate sodium	Fosamax
Alendronate sodium/ Cholecalciferol	Fosamax Plus D
Aliskiren hemifumarate/ Amlodipine besylate/HCTZ	Amturnide
Aliskiren/HCTZ	Tekturna HCT
Almotriptan malate	Axert
Amiloride HCl/HCTZ	
Aminolevulinic acid HCl	Levulan Kerastick
Amiodarone HCl	Cordarone, Pacerone
Amitriptyline HCl	
Amitriptyline HCl/ Chlordiazepoxide	
Amitriptyline HCl/ Perphenazine	
Amlodipine/HCTZ/ Olmesartan medoxomil	Tribenzor·
Amlodipine besylate/HCTZ/ Valsartan	Exforge HCT
Amoxapine	
Amphetamine aspartate/ Amphetamine sulfate/ Dextroamphetamine saccharate/ Dextroamphetamine sulfate	Adderall XR
Anagrelide HCl	Agrylin
Aripiprazole	Abilify
Atenolol/Chlorthalidone	Tenoretic
Atovaquone/Proguanil HCl	Malarone
Azithromycin	Zithromax, Zmax
Benazepril HCl	Lotensin
Benazepril HCl/HCTZ	Lotensin HCT
Bendroflumethiazide/Nadolol	Corzide
Benzoyl peroxide/Erythromycin	Benzamycin Pak
Bexarotene	Targretin
Bismuth subcitrate potassium/ Metronidazole/Tetracycline HCl	Pylera
Bismuth subsalicylate/ Metronidazole/Tetracycline HCl	Helidac Therapy
Bisoprolol fumarate/HCTZ	Ziac

GENERIC NAME	BRAND NAME
Brompheniramine maleate	Bromfed DM
Bupropion HBr	Aplenzin
Bupropion HCl	Budeprion SR, Budeprion XL, Buproban ER, Wellbutrin SR, Wellbutrin XL, Zyban SR
Candesartan cilexetil/HCTZ	Atacand HCT
Capecitabine	Xeloda
Captopril	Capoten
Captopril/HCTZ	Capozide
Carbamazepine	Carbatrol, Epitol, Tegretol, Tegretol-XR
Carbinoxamine maleate	Arbinoxa
Carvedilol	Coreg
Carvedilol phosphate	Coreg CR
Celecoxib	Celebrex
Cevimeline HCl	Evoxac
Chloroquine phosphate	Aralen
Chlorothiazide	Diuril
Chlorothiazide sodium	IV Sodium Diuril
Chlorpheniramine maleate/ Dextromethorphan HBr/ Pseudoephedrine HCl	Atuss DS Tannate Suspension
Chlorpheniramine maleate/ Pseudoephedrine HCl	
Chlorpromazine HCl	
Chlorthalidone	Thalitone
Chlorthalidone/Clonidine HCl	Clorpres
Cidofovir	Vistide
Ciprofloxacin	Cipro XR
Citalopram HBr	Celexa
Clemastine fumarate	
Clindamycin phosphate	Clindagel
Clozapine	Clozaril, FazaClo ODT
Cromolyn sodium	Gastrocrom
Cyclobenzaprine HCl	Flexeril
Cyproheptadine HCl	
Dasatinib	Sprycel
Demeclocycline HCl	Declomycin
Desipramine HCl	Norpramin

(Continued)

DRUGS THAT MAY CAUSE PHOTOSENSITIVITY

GENERIC NAME	BRAND NAME	GENERIC NAME	BRAND NAME
Desvenlafaxine	Pristiq, Khedezla ER	Floxuridine	
Dextromethorphan HBr/ Promethazine HCl	Promethazine DM	Flucytosine	Ancobon
		Fluorouracil	Carac, Efudex, Fluoroplex
Dextromethorphan HBr/ Quinidine sulfate	Nuedexta	Fluoxetine HCl/Olanzapine	Symbyax
Diclofenac potassium	Cambia, Cataflam, Zipsor	Fluphenazine decanoate	
		Fluphenazine HCl	
Diclofenac sodium	Solaraze Gel, Voltaren-XR	Flurbiprofen	Ansaid
Diclofenac sodium/Misoprostol	Arthrotec	Flutamide	
Diflunisal		Fluvastatin sodium	Lescol, Lescol XL
Diltiazem HCl	Cardizem, Cardizem CD, Cardizem LA, Cartia XT, Tiazac ER	Fosaprepitant	Emend
		Fosinopril sodium	
		Fosinopril sodium/HCTZ	
Diphenhydramine HCl	Benadryl Injection	Furosemide	Lasix
Dipivefrin HCl	Propine Ophthalmic Solution	Gemfibrozil	Lopid
		Gemifloxacin mesylate	Factive
Divalproex sodium	Depakote, Depakote ER, Depakote Sprinkle	Glimepiride	Amaryl
		Glimepiride/Pioglitazone HCl	Duetact
Doxepin HCl	Silenor, Zonalon	Glimepiride/ Rosiglitazone maleate	Avandaryl
Doxorubicin HCl	Adriamycin		
Doxycycline	Monodox, Oracea	Glipizide	Glucotrol
Doxycycline calcium	Vibramycin	Glyburide	Glynase PresTab, Diabeta
Doxycycline hyclate	Atridox, Doryx, Vibramycin Hyclate		
		Griseofulvin	Grifulvin V, Gris-PEG
Doxycycline monohydrate	Vibramycin Monohydrate	Haloperidol decanoate	Haldol Decanoate
		Haloperidol lactate	Haldol
Duloxetine HCl	Cymbalta	HCTZ	Microzide
Enalapril maleate	Vasotec, Epaned	HCTZ/Irbesartan	Avalide
Enalapril maleate/HCTZ	Vaseretic	HCTZ/Lisinopril	Prinzide, Zestoretic
Enalaprilat		HCTZ/Losartan potassium	Hyzaar
Epirubicin HCl	Ellence	HCTZ/Methyldopa	
Eprosartan mesylate/HCTZ	Teveten HCT	HCTZ/Metoprolol tartrate	Lopressor HCT
Erythromycin ethylsuccinate/ Sulfisoxazole acetyl		HCTZ/Moexipril HCl	Uniretic
		HCTZ/Olmesartan medoxomil	Benicar HCT
Escitalopram oxalate	Lexapro	HCTZ/Propranolol HCl	
Esomeprazole magnesium	Nexium	HCTZ/Quinapril HCl	Accuretic
Esomeprazole magnesium/ Naproxen	Vimovo	HCTZ/Spironolactone	Aldactazide
		HCTZ/Telmisartan	Micardis HCT
Estazolam		HCTZ/Triamterene	Dyazide, Maxzide
Estradiol cypionate	Depo-Estradiol	HCTZ/Valsartan	Diovan HCT
Eszopiclone	Lunesta	Hexachlorophene	pHisoHex
Ethinyl estradiol/ Norelgestromin	Ortho Evra	Hydroxocobalamin	Cyanokit
		Hydroxychloroquine sulfate	Plaquenil
Ethionamide	Trecator	Ibuprofen	Motrin
Etodolac		Imipramine HCl	Tofranil
Ezetimibe/Simvastatin	Vytorin	Imipramine pamoate	Tofranil-PM
Febuxostat	Uloric		
Fenofibrate	Lofibra		

GENERIC NAME	BRAND NAME	GENERIC NAME	BRAND NAME
Indapamide		Norfloxacin	Noroxin
Interferon alfa-2b	Intron A	Nortriptyline HCl	Pamelor
Interferon alfa-n3	Alferon N	Ofloxacin	Floxin
Isocarboxazid	Marplan	Olanzapine	Zyprexa, Zyprexa Zydis
Isoniazid/Pyrazinamide/ Rifampin	Rifater	Olanzapine pamoate	Zyprexa Relprevv
		Olsalazine sodium	Dipentum
Isotretinoin	Amnesteem, Claravis, Sotret	Omeprazole magnesium	Prilosec
Itraconazole	Sporanox	Omeprazole/ Sodium bicarbonate	Zegerid
Ketoprofen		Oxaprozin	Daypro
Ketorolac tromethamine	Toradol	Oxaprozin potassium	Daypro Alta
Lamotrigine	Lamictal, Lamictal ODT	Oxcarbazepine	Trileptal
Leuprolide acetate	Lupron, Lupron Depot	Oxycodone HCl	Roxicodone
Levofloxacin	Levaquin	Paclitaxel	Abraxane
Lisinopril	Prinivil, Zestril	Panitumumab	Vectibix
Losartan potassium	Cozaar	Pantoprazole	Protonix
Lovastatin	Altoprev	Paroxetine HCl	Paxil, Paxil CR
Lovastatin/Niacin	Advicor	Paroxetine mesylate	Pexeva
Maprotiline HCl		Pentosan polysulfate sodium	Elmiron
Mefenamic acid	Ponstel	Perphenazine	
Meloxicam	Mobic	Pilocarpine HCl	Salagen
Mesalamine	Pentasa	Piroxicam	Feldene
Methotrexate		Polymyxin B sulfate/ Trimethoprim sulfate	Polytrim
Methyl aminolevulinate HCl	Metvixia Cream		
Metolazone	Zaroxolyn	Porfimer sodium	Photofrin
Metoprolol succinate	Toprol-XL	Pravastatin sodium	Pravachol
Metoprolol tartrate	Lopressor	Pregabalin	Lyrica
Minocycline HCl	Arestin, Dynacin, Minocin, Solodyn, Ximino	Prochlorperazine	Compro
		Prochlorperazine edisylate	
		Prochlorperazine maleate	
Mirtazapine	Remeron, RemeronSolTab	Promethazine HCl	Phenadoz, Phenergan, Promethegan
Moexipril HCl	Univasc	Promethazine HCl/ Codeine phosphate	
Moxifloxacin HCl	Avelox		
Nabilone	Cesamet	Promethazine HCl/ Phenylephrine HCl	Phenergan VC
Nabumetone			
Naproxen	EC-Naprosyn, Naprosyn	Promethazine HCl/ Phenylephrine HCl/ Codeine phosphate	Phenergan VC with Codeine
Naproxen sodium	Anaprox, Anaprox DS, Naprelan	Protriptyline HCl	Vivactil
Naratriptan HCl	Amerge	Pyrazinamide	
Niacin/Simvastatin	Simcor	Quetiapine fumarate	Seroquel, Seroquel XR
Nifedipine	Adalat CC, Nifediac CC, Nifedical XL, Procardia, Procardia XL	Quinidine gluconate	
		Quinine sulfate	Qualaquin
		Ramipril	Altace
Nilotinib	Tasigna	Rasagiline mesylate	Azilect
Nisoldipine	Sular	Riluzole	Rilutek

(Continued)

GENERIC NAME	BRAND NAME	GENERIC NAME	BRAND NAME
Ritonavir	Norvir	Tigecycline	Tygacil
Rizatriptan benzoate	Maxalt	Tipranavir	Aptivus
Selegiline HCl	Eldepryl	Tolbutamide	
Sertraline HCl	Zoloft	Topiramate	Topamax
Sildenafil citrate	Viagra	Triamcinolone acetonide	Azmacort
Simeprevir	Olysio	Triamterene	Dyrenium
Simvastatin	Zocor	Trifluoperazine HCl	
Sitagliptin/Simvastatin	Juvisync	Trimipramine maleate	Surmontil
Sotalol HCl	Betapace, Betapace AF	Valacyclovir HCl	Valtrex
Sulfamethoxazole/Trimethoprim	Bactrim, Bactrim DS, Septra, Septra DS, Sulfatrim	Valproate sodium	Depacon
		Valproic acid	Depakene, Stavzor DR
		Vandetanib	Caprelsa
Sulfasalazine	Azulfidine, Azulfidine EN-tabs	Varenicline	Chantix
		Vemurafenib	Zelboraf
Sulindac	Clinoril	Venlafaxine HCl	Effexor XR
Sumatriptan	Sumavel DosePro	Verteporfin	Visudyne
Sumatriptan succinate	Alsuma, Imitrex	Voriconazole	Vfend
Tacrolimus	Prograf	Zaleplon	Sonata
Tazarotene	Avage, Fabior, Tazorac	Zolmitriptan	Zomig
Tetracycline HCl	Sumycin	Zolpidem tartrate	Ambien, Ambien CR, Edluar, Zolpimist
Thalidomide	Thalomid		
Thioridazine HCl			
Thiothixene	Navane		

DRUGS THAT MAY CAUSE QT PROLONGATION

BRAND	GENERIC
Abilify, Abilify Maintena	Aripiprazole
Ablavar	Gadofosveset trisodium
AccuNeb	Albuterol sulfate
Advair Diskus, Advair HFA	Fluticasone propionate/Salmeterol
Albuterol sulfate ER	Albuterol sulfate
Aloxi	Palonosetron HCl
Alsuma	Sumatriptan
Amerge	Naratriptan HCl
Anoro Ellipta	Umeclidinium bromide/Vilanterol trifenatate
Anzemet	Dolasetron mesylate
Apokyn	Apomorphine HCl
Arcapta Neohaler	Indacaterol
Astagraf XL	Tacrolimus
Avelox	Moxifloxacin HCl
Betapace, Betapace AF	Sotalol HCl
Biaxin, Biaxin XL	Clarithromycin
Bosulif	Bosutinib
Breo Ellipta	Fluticasone furoate/Vilanterol trifenatate
Brovana	Arformoterol tartrate
Butrans	Buprenorphine
Caprelsa	Vandetanib
Cardene SR	Nicardipine HCl
Celexa	Citalopram HBr
Cipro, Cipro XR	Ciprofloxacin
Clozaril	Clozapine
Coartem	Artemether/Lumefantrine
Combivent	Ipratropium bromide/Albuterol sulfate
Cordarone	Amiodarone HCl
Corvert	Ibutilide fumarate
Definity	Perflutren, lipid
Detrol, Detrol LA	Tolterodine tartrate
Diflucan	Fluconazole
Ditropan, Ditropan XL	Oxybutynin Cl
Dolophine HCl	
Droperidol	Droperidol
Dulera	Formoterol fumarate dihydrate/Mometasone
DuoNeb	Albuterol sulfate/Ipratropium bromide
E.E.S. Granules, Ery-Ped	Erythromycin ethylsuccinate
Effexor XR	Venlafaxine HCl
Eraxis	Anidulafungin
Eryc, Ery-Tab, PCE Dispertab	Erythromycin
Erythrocin stearate	Erythromycin stearate
Exelon	Rivastigmine tartrate

(Continued)

BRAND	GENERIC
Factive	Gemifloxacin mesylate
Fanapt	Iloperidone
Fareston	Toremifene citrate
FazaClo	Clozapine
Firmagon	Degarelix
Fleet	Dibasic/Monobasic sodium phosphate
Foradil	Formoterol fumarate
Foscarnet sodium	
Fosphenytoin	
Geodon	Ziprasidone HCl
Gilenya	Fingolimod
Granisol	Granisetron HCl
Halaven	Eribulin mesylate
Haldol	Haloperidol decanoate
Haloperidol	
Hecoria	Tacrolimus
Imitrex	Sumatriptan succinate
Intuniv	Guanfacine
Invega	Paliperidone
Invega Sustenna	Paliperidone palmitate
Invirase	Saquinavir mesylate
Isradipine	Isradipine
Istodax	Romidepsin
Jevtana	Cabazitaxel
Kaletra	Lopinavir/Ritonavir
Kapvay	Clonidine HCl
Kayexalate Powder, Kionex	Sodium polystyrene sulfonate
Ketek	Telithromycin
Korlym	Mifepristone
Levaquin	Levofloxacin
Levatol	Penbutolol sulfate
Levitra	Vardenafil HCl
Lexapro	Escitalopram oxalate
Lexiscan	
Lupron Depot	Leuprolide acetate
Maxair Autohaler	Pirbuterol acetate
Mefloquine HCl	
Methadone HCl	
Methadose	Methadone HCl
Multaq	Dronedarone
MultiHance	Gadobenate dimeglumine
Namenda, Namenda XR	Memantine HCl
Nexavar	Sorafenib
Nexterone	Amiodarone HCl
Noroxin	Norfloxacin
Norpace, Norpace CR	Disopyramide phosphate

BRAND	GENERIC
Noxafil Oral Suspension	Posaconazole
Nuedexta	Dextromethorphan HBr/Quinidine sulfate
Ofloxacin	
Oleptro	Trazodone HCl
Orap	Pimozide
OsmoPrep	Dibasic/Monobasic sodium phosphate
PCE	Erythromycin
PCE Dispertab	Erythromycin lactobionate
Pepcid	Famotidine
Perforomist	Formoterol fumarate
Pletal	Cilostazol
Potiga	Ezogabine
PrevPAC	Amoxicillin/Clarithromycin/Lansoprazole
ProAir HFA	Albuterol sulfate
Prograf	Tacrolimus
Proventil HFA	Albuterol sulfate
Prozac	Fluoxetine HCl
Qualaquin USP	Quinine sulfate
Quinidine gluconate	
Quinidine sulfate	
Ranexa	Ranolazine
Razadyne	Galantamine HBr
Reyataz	Atazanavir sulfate
Risperdal, Risperdal Consta	Risperidone
Rythmol SR	Propafenone HCl
Sancuso	Granisetron HCl
Sandostatin, Sandostatin LAR	Octreotide acetate
Saphris	Asenapine
Sarafem	Fluoxetine HCl
Serevent Diskus	Salmeterol xinafoate
Seroquel, Seroquel XR	Quetiapine fumarate
Signifor	Pasireotide
Sirturo	Bedaquiline
Sporanox	Itraconazole
Sprycel	Dasatinib
Staxyn	Vardenafil HCl
Strattera	Atomoxetine HCl
Sumavel DosePro	Sumatriptan
Sutent	Sunitinib malate
Symbicort	Budesonide/Formoterol fumarate dihydrate
Symbyax	Fluoxetine/Olanzapine
Tambocor	Flecainide acetate
Tasigna	Nilotinib
Terbutaline sulfate	
Thioridazine HCl	

(Continued)

BRAND	GENERIC
Tikosyn	Dofetilide
Toviaz	Fesoterodine fumarate
Trisenox	Arsenic trioxide
Tykerb	Lapatinib
Ultane	Sevoflurane
Uniretic	HCTZ/Moexipril
Uroxatral	Alfuzosin HCl
Velcade	Bortezomib
Venlafaxine	
Ventolin HFA	Albuterol sulfate
Versacloz	Clozapine
Vesicare	Solifenacin succinate
Vfend	Voriconazole
Vibativ	Telavancin
Viracept	Nelfinavir mesylate
Visicol	Monobasic/Dibasic sodium phosphate
Votrient	Pazopanib
Xalkori	Crizotinib
Xenazine	Tetrabenazine
Xopenex	Levalbuterol HCl
Xopenex HFA	Levalbuterol tartrate
Zelboraf	Vemurafenib
Zithromax, Zmax	Azithromycin
Zofran	Ondansetron HCl
Zoloft	Sertraline HCl
Zomig	Zolmitriptan
Zuplenz	Ondansetron
Zyprexa Relprevv	Olanzapine
Zytiga	Abiraterone acetate

NOTE: This list does not include all of the drugs that may cause QT disturbance. For more information, please refer to the specific product's full FDA-approved labeling.

DRUGS THAT SHOULD NOT BE CRUSHED

Listed below are various slow-release as well as enteric-coated products that should not be crushed or chewed.
Slow-release (sr) represents products that are controlled-release, extended-release, long-acting, or timed-release.
Enteric-coated (ec) represents products that are delayed release.

In general, capsules containing slow-release or enteric-coated particles may be opened and their contents administered on
a spoonful of soft food. Instruct patients not to chew particles, though. (Patients should, in fact, be discouraged from chewing
any medication unless it is specifically formulated for that purpose.)

This list should not be considered all-inclusive. Generic and alternate brands of some products may exist. Tablets intended
for sublingual or buccal administration (not included in this list) should be administered only as intended, in an intact form.

DRUG	MANUFACTURER	FORM	DRUG	MANUFACTURER	FORM
Aciphex	Eisai	ec	Cardizem CD	Biovail	sr
Actoplus Met XR	Takeda	sr	Cardizem LA	Abbott	sr
Adalat CC	Bayer Healthcare	sr	Cardura XL	Pfizer	sr
Adderall XR	Shire U.S.	sr	Cartia XT	Actavis	sr
Adenovirus Type 4 and Type 7 Vaccine	Teva Women's Health, Inc.	ec	Chlor-Trimeton Allergy	Schering Plough	sr
			Cipro XR	Schering Plough	sr
Advicor	Abbott	sr	Clarinex-D 12 Hour	Schering Plough	sr
Afeditab CR	Watson	sr	Clarinex-D 24 Hour	Schering Plough	sr
Aggrenox	Boehringer Ingelheim	sr	Claritin-D 12 Hour	Schering	sr
Aleve-D Cold & Sinus	Bayer Healthcare	sr	Claritin-D 24 Hour	Schering	sr
Aleve-D Sinus & Headache	Bayer Healthcare	sr	Cometriq	Exelixis, Inc	sr
			Concerta	Ortho-McNeil-Janssen	sr
Allegra-D 12 Hour	sanofi-aventis	sr	Coreg CR	GlaxoSmithKline	sr
Allegra-D 24 Hour	sanofi-aventis	sr	Covera-HS	Pfizer	sr
Alophen	Numark	ec	Creon	Abbott	ec
Altoprev	Watson	sr	Cymbalta	Eli Lilly	ec
Ambien CR	sanofi-aventis	sr	Dairycare	Plainview	ec
Ampyra ER	Acorda Therapeutics	sr	Deconex DM	Poly	sr
Amrix	Cephalon	sr	Delzicol	Warner Chilcott	ec
Aplenzin	sanofi-aventis	sr	Depakote	Abbott	ec
Apriso	Salix	sr	Depakote ER	Abbott	sr
Arthrotec	Pfizer	ec	Depakote Sprinkles	Abbott	ec
Asacol	Procter & Gamble	ec	Detrol LA	Pfizer	sr
Asacol HD	Procter & Gamble	ec	Dexedrine Spansules	GlaxoSmithKline	sr
Astagraf XL	Astellas	sr	Dexilant	Takeda	sr
Augmentin XR	GlaxoSmithKline	sr	Diamox Sequels	Duramed	sr
Avinza	King	sr	Diclegis	Duchesnay USA	sr
Azulfidine EN-tabs	Pfizer	ec	Dilacor XR	Watson	sr
Bayer Aspirin Regimen	Bayer Healthcare	ec	Dilantin	Pfizer	sr
Biaxin XL	Abbott	sr	Dilantin Kapseals	Pfizer	sr
Bontril Slow-Release	Valeant	sr	Dilatrate-SR	UCB	sr
Budeprion SR	Teva	sr	Diltia XT	Watson	sr
Calan SR	Pfizer	sr	Dilt-CD	Apotex	sr
Campral	Forest	ec	Ditropan XL	Ortho-McNeil Janssen	sr
Carbatrol	Shire U.S.	sr	Donnatal Extentabs	PBM	sr
Cardene SR	EKR Therapeutics	sr			

(Continued)

DRUG	MANUFACTURER	FORM	DRUG	MANUFACTURER	FORM
Doryx	Mayne	ec	Klor-Con M15*	Upsher-Smith	sr
Duavee	Wyeth	ec	Klor-Con M20*	Upsher-Smith	sr
Dulcolax	Boehringer Ingelheim	ec	Kombiglyze XR	BMS/AstraZeneca	sr
EC Naprosyn	Genentech	ec	K-Tab	Abbott	sr
Ecotrin 81 mg	GlaxoSmithKline	ec	Lamictal XR	GlaxoSmithKline	sr
Ecotrin 325 mg	GlaxoSmithKline	ec	Lescol XL	Novartis	sr
Effexor-XR	Wyeth	sr	Levbid	Meda	sr
Embeda	King	sr	Lialda	Shire	ec
Enablex	Novartis Consumer	sr	Liptruzet	Merck	ec
Entocort EC	Prometheus	ec	Lithobid	Noven Therapeutics	sr
Equetro	Validus	sr	Luvox CR	Jazz Pharmaceuticals	sr
ERYC	Mayne	sr	Mag64	Rising	ec
Ery-Tab	Abbott	ec	MagDelay	Major	ec
Exalgo	Mallinckrodt	sr	Mag-Tab SR	Niche	sr
Ferro-Sequels	Inverness Medical	sr	Maxifed	MCR American	sr
Fetzima	Forest	sr	Maxifed DM	MCR American	sr
Flagyl ER	Pfizer	sr	Maxifed DMX	MCR American	sr
Fleet Bisacodyl	Fleet, C.B.	ec	Maxifed-G	MCR American	sr
Focalin XR	Novartis	sr	Menopause Relief Trio	Mason Vitamins	sr
Folitab 500	Rising	sr	Mestinon Timespan	Valeant	sr
Forfivo XL	IntelGenx	sr	Metadate CD	UCB	sr
Fortamet	Shionogi Pharma	sr	Metadate ER	UCB	sr
Fulyzaq	Salix	ec	Methylin ER	Mallinckrodt	sr
Fumatinic	Laser	sr	Micro-K	Ther-Rx	sr
Galzin	Gate	ec	Micro-K 10	Ther-Rx	sr
Gilphex TR	Gil	sr	Mild-C	Carlson, J.R.	sr
Glucophage XR	Bristol-Myers-Squibb	sr	Mirapex ER	Boehringer Ingelheim	sr
Glucotrol XL	Pfizer	sr	Moxatag	Victory	sr
Glumetza	Depomed	sr	MS Contin	Purdue	sr
Hemax	Pronova	sr	Mucinex	Reckitt Benckiser	sr
Horizant	GlaxoSmithKline	sr	Mucinex D	Reckitt Benckiser	sr
Imbruvica	Pharmacyclics	ec	Mucinex DM	Reckitt Benckiser	sr
Inderal LA	Akrimax	sr	Myfortic	Novartis	ec
Innopran XL	GlaxoSmithKline	sr	Myrbetriq	Astellas	sr
Intuniv	Shire	sr	Namenda XR	Forest	sr
Invega	Ortho-McNeil-Janssen	sr	Naprelan	Victory	sr
Janumet XR	Merck Sharp & Dohme Corp.	sr	Nexium	AstraZeneca	ec
			Niaspan	Abbott	sr
Kadian	Actavis	sr	Nifediac CC	Teva	sr
Kapvay ER	Shionogi	sr	Nifedical XL	Teva	sr
Keppra XR	UCB	sr	Nitro-Time	Time-Cap	sr
Khedezla ER	Par	sr	Norel SR	U.S. Pharmaceutical	sr
Klor-Con 8	Upsher-Smith	sr	Norpace CR	Pfizer	sr
Klor-Con 10	Upsher-Smith	sr	Nucynta ER	Janssen	sr
Klor-Con M10*	Upsher-Smith	sr	Oleptro	LaboPharm	sr

DRUG	MANUFACTURER	FORM	DRUG	MANUFACTURER	FORM
Olysio	Janssen	ec	Stavzor	Noven	ec
Opana ER	Endo	sr	Sudafed 12 hour	McNeil Consumer	sr
Opsumit	Actelion	ec	Sudafed 24 hour	McNeil Consumer	sr
Oracea	Galderma	ec	Sular	Shionogi Pharma	sr
Orenitram	United Therapeutics Corp.	sr	Sulfazine EC	Qualitest	ec
			Symax Duotab	Capellon	sr
Oxtellar XR	Supernus	sr	Symax-SR	Capellon	sr
Oxycontin	Purdue	sr	Tafinlar	GlaxoSmithKline	ec
Pancreaze	Ortho-McNeil-Janssen	ec	Tarka	Abbott	sr
Paser	Jacobus	ec	Taztia XT	Watson	sr
Paxil CR	GlaxoSmithKline	sr	Tecfidera	biogen	ec
PCE Dispertab	Arbor	sr	Tegretol-XR	Novartis	sr
Pentasa	Shire U.S.	sr	Theo-24	UCB	sr
Pentoxil	Upsher-Smith	sr	Tiazac	Forest	sr
Phenytek	Mylan	sr	Toprol XL†	AstraZeneca	sr
Poly Hist Forte	Poly	sr	Totalday	National Vitamin	sr
Poly-Vent	Poly	sr	Toviaz	Pfizer	sr
Prevacid	Takeda	ec	Trental	sanofi-aventis	sr
Prilosec	AstraZeneca	ec	Treximet	GlaxoSmithKline	ec
Prilosec OTC	Procter & Gamble	sr	Trilipix	Abbott	ec
Pristiq	Wyeth	sr	Trokendi XR	Supernus	sr
Procardia XL	Pfizer	sr	Tussicaps	Mallinckrodt	sr
Protonix	Wyeth	ec	Tylenol Arthritis	McNeil Consumer	sr
Prozac Weekly	Eli Lilly	ec	Uceris	Santarus, Inc.	sr
Qsymia	Vivus	sr	Ultram ER	Valeant	sr
Ranexa	Gilead	sr	Urocit-K	Mission	sr
Rayos	Horizon	ec	Uroxatral	sanofi-aventis	sr
Razadyne ER	Ortho-McNeil-Janssen	sr	Verelan	UCB	sr
Requip XL	GlaxoSmithKline	sr	Verelan PM	UCB	sr
Rescon-Jr	Capellon	sr	Videx EC	Bristol-Myers-Squibb	ec
Ritalin LA	Novartis	sr	Vimovo	AstraZeneca	ec
Ritalin-SR	Novartis	sr	Voltaren-XR	Novartis	sr
Rodex Forte	Legere	sr	Vospire ER	Dava	sr
Rythmol SR	GlaxoSmithKline	sr	Votrient	GlaxoSmithKline	ec
SAM-e	Pharmavite	ec	Wellbutrin SR	GlaxoSmithKline	sr
Sanctura XR	Allergan	sr	Wellbutrin XL	GlaxoSmithKline	sr
Seroquel XR	AstraZeneca	sr	Wobenzym N	Marlyn	ec
Simcor	Abbott	sr	Xanax XR	Pfizer	sr
Sinemet CR	Bristol-Myers Squibb	sr	Zenpep	Eurand	ec
Sitavig	Farmea	ec	Zohydro ER	Zogenix	sr
Slo-Niacin	Upsher-Smith	sr	Zyban	GlaxoSmithKline	sr
Slow Fe	Novartis Consumer	sr	Zyflo CR	Cornerstone	sr
Slow-Mag	Purdue	ec	Zyrtec-D	McNeil Consumer	sr
Solodyn	Medicis	sr	*May split in half or dissolve in water.		
St. Joseph Pain Reliever	McNeil Consumer	ec	† May divide tablet.		

DRUGS THAT SHOULD NOT BE USED IN PREGNANCY

Abiraterone acetate
Acetohydroxamic acid
Acitretin
Ambrisentan
Amlodipine besylate/
  Atorvastatin calcium
Anastrozole
Aspirin
Atorvastatin calcium
Atorvastatin/Ezetimibe
Benzphetamine hydrochloride
Bexarotene
Bicalutamide
Boceprevir
Bosentan
Caffeine
Cetrorelix acetate
Chenodiol
Cholecalciferol
Choriogonadotropin alfa
Chorionic gonadotropin
Clomiphene citrate
Danazol
Degarelix
Denosumab
Desogestrel/Ethinyl estradiol
Diclofenac sodium/Misoprostol
Dihydroergotamine mesylate
Dronedarone
Drospirenone/Ethinyl estradiol
Dutasteride
Dutasteride/Tamsulosin hydrochloride
Enzalutamide
Ergotamine tartrate
Estazolam
Estradiol
Estradiol valerate
Estradiol/Norethindrone acetate
Estrogens, Conjugated, Synthetic B
Estropipate
Ethinyl estradiol
Ethinyl estradiol/Ethynodiol diacetate

Ethinyl estradiol/Etonogestrel
Ethinyl estradiol/Ferrous fumarate/
  Norethindrone acetate
Ethinyl estradiol/Levonorgestrel
Ethinyl estradiol/Norelgestromin
Ethinyl estradiol/Norethindrone
Ethinyl estradiol/Norgestimate
Ethinyl estradiol/Norgestrel
Exemestane
Ezetimibe/Simvastatin
Finasteride
Fluorouracil
Fluoxymesterone
Fluvastatin sodium
Follitropin alfa
Follitropin beta
Ganirelix acetate
Genistein aglycone
Goserelin acetate
Histrelin acetate
Iodine I 131 tositumomab
Isotretinoin
Leflunomide
Lenalidomide
Letrozole
Leuprolide acetate
Leuprolide acetate/
  Norethindrone acetate
Levonorgestrel
Lomitapide
Lorcaserin hydrochloride
Lovastatin
Lovastatin/Niacin
Lutropin alfa
Macitentan
Medroxyprogesterone acetate
Megestrol acetate
Menotropins
Mequinol/Tretinoin
Mestranol/Norethindrone
Methotrexate
Methyltestosterone

Mifepristone
Miglustat
Misoprostol
Mitomycin
Nafarelin acetate
Niacin/Simvastatin
Norethindrone
Orlistat
Ospemifene
Oxandrolone
Phendimetrazine tartrate
Phentermine hydrochloride
Phentermine/Topiramate
Pitavastatin
Pomalidomide
Pravastatin sodium
Radium Ra 223 dichloride
Raloxifene hydrochloride
Ribavirin
Riociguat
Rosuvastatin calcium
Simeprevir
Simvastatin
Simvastatin/Sitagliptin
Sofosbuvir
Tazarotene
Telaprevir
Temazepam
Teriflunomide
Tesamorelin
Testosterone
Testosterone cypionate
Testosterone enanthate
Thalidomide
Triazolam
Triptorelin pamoate
Ulipristal acetate
Urofollitropin
Vitamin A palmitate
Warfarin sodium
Zinc bisglycinate

PREGNANCY CATEGORY X

Studies in animals or humans, or investigational or postmarketing reports, have demonstrated fetal risk, which clearly outweighs any possible benefit to the patient.

FDA-APPROVED NEW DRUG PRODUCTS

BRAND	GENERIC	INDICATION
Adempas	riociguat	To treat adults with two forms of pulmonary hypertension.
Anoro Ellipta	umeclidinium/vilanterol	For the once-daily, long-term maintenance treatment of airflow obstruction in patients with chronic obstructive pulmonary disease.
Aptiom	eslicarbazepine acetate	As an add-on medication to treat seizures associated with epilepsy.
Breo Ellipta	fluticasone furoate/vilanterol	For the long-term, once-daily, maintenance treatment of airflow obstruction in patients with chronic obstructive pulmonary disease, including chronic bronchitis and/or emphysema.
Brintellix	vortioxetine	To treat adults with major depressive disorder.
Dotarem	gadoterate meglumine	For use in magnetic resonance imaging of the brain, spine, and associated tissues of patients ages 2 years and older.
Duavee	conjugated estrogens/ bazedoxifene	To treat moderate-to-severe hot flashes (vasomotor symptoms) associated with menopause and to prevent osteoporosis after menopause.
Farxiga	dapagliflozin	To improve glycemic control, along with diet and exercise, in adults with type 2 diabetes.
Fetzima	levomilnacipran	Treatment of major depressive disorder.
Gazyva	obinutuzumab	Treatment of patients with previously untreated chronic lymphocytic leukemia.
Gilotrif	afatinib	For patients with late-stage (metastatic) non-small cell lung cancer whose tumors express specific types of epidermal growth factor receptor gene mutations, as detected by an FDA-approved test.
Hetlioz	tasimelteon	To treat non-24-hour sleep-wake disorder (non-24) in totally blind individuals. Non-24 is a chronic circadian rhythm (body clock) disorder in the blind that causes problems with the timing of sleep.
Imbruvica	ibrutinib	To treat patients with mantle cell lymphoma, a rare and aggressive type of blood cancer.
Invokana	canagliflozin	Used with diet and exercise to improve glycemic control in adults with type 2 diabetes.
Luzu	luliconazole	For the topical treatment of interdigital tinea pedis, tinea cruris, and tinea corporis caused by the organisms *Trichophyton rubrum* and *Epidermophyton floccosum* in patients 18 years of age and older.
Lymphoseek	technetium Tc 99m tilmanocept	A radioactive diagnostic imaging agent that helps doctors locate lymph nodes in patients with breast cancer or melanoma who are undergoing surgery to remove lymph nodes.
Mekinist	trametinib	To treat patients whose tumors express the BRAF V600E or V600K gene mutations.
Olysio	simeprevir	To treat chronic hepatitis C virus infection.
Opsumit	macitentan	To treat adults with pulmonary arterial hypertension, a chronic, progressive, and debilitating disease that can lead to death or the need for lung transplantation.
Sovaldi	sofosbuvir	To treat chronic hepatitis C virus infection.
Tafinlar	dabrafenib	To treat patients with melanoma whose tumors express the BRAF V600E gene mutation.
Tecfidera	dimethyl fumarate	To treat adults with relapsing forms of multiple sclerosis.
Tivicay	dolutegravir	To treat HIV-1 infection.

(Continued)

BRAND	GENERIC	INDICATION
Vizamyl	flutemetamol F 18 injection	A radioactive diagnostic drug for use with positron emission tomography imaging of the brain in adults being evaluated for Alzheimer's disease and dementia.
Xofigo	radium Ra 223 dichloride	To treat men with symptomatic late-stage (metastatic) castration-resistant prostate cancer that has spread to bones but not to other organs.

Note: This list is not comprehensive and only includes new molecular entities that have not been approved by the FDA previously, either as a single ingredient drug or as part of a combination product. For a complete list, please refer to the FDA website, www.accessdata.fda.gov/scripts/cder/drugsatfda/index.cfm?fuseaction=Reports.ReportsMenu.

ISMP's List of Confused Drug Names

This list has been reproduced with permission from the Institute for Safe Medication Practices (ISMP), and includes ISMP's most current updates, which are completed through June 2011.

DRUG NAME	CONFUSED DRUG NAME
Abelcet	amphotericin B
Accupril	Aciphex
acetaZOLAMIDE	acetoHEXAMIDE
acetic acid for irrigation	glacial acetic acid
acetoHEXAMIDE	acetaZOLAMIDE
Aciphex	Accupril
Aciphex	Aricept
Activase	Cathflo Activase
Activase	TNKase
Actonel	Actos
Actos	Actonel
Adacel (Tdap)	Daptacel (DTaP)
Adderall	Inderal
Adderall	Adderall XR
Adderall XR	Adderall
Advair	Advicor
Advicor	Advair
Advicor	Altocor
Afrin (oxymetazoline)	Afrin (saline)
Afrin (saline)	Afrin (oxymetazoline)
Aggrastat	argatroban
Aldara	Alora
Alkeran	Leukeran
Alkeran	Myleran
Allegra	Viagra
Alora	Aldara
ALPRAZolam	LORazepam
Altocor	Advicor
amantadine	amiodarone
Amaryl	Reminyl
Ambisome	amphotericin B
Amicar	Omacor
Amikin	Kineret
aMILoride	amLODIPine
amiodarone	amantadine
amLODIPine	aMILoride
amphotericin B	Abelcet
amphotericin B	Ambisome
Anacin	Anacin-3
Anacin-3	Anacin
antacid	Atacand
Antivert	Axert
Anzemet	Avandamet
Apresoline	Priscoline
argatroban	Aggrastat
argatroban	Orgaran
Aricept	Aciphex
Aricept	Azilect
ARIPiprazole	proton pump inhibitors
ARIPiprazole	RABEprazole
Asacol	Os-Cal
Atacand	antacid
Atrovent	Natru-Vent
Avandamet	Anzemet
Avandia	Prandin
Avandia	Coumadin

DRUG NAME	CONFUSED DRUG NAME
AVINza	INVanz
AVINza	Evista
Axert	Antivert
azaCITIDine	azaTHIOprine
azaTHIOprine	azaCITIDine
Azilect	Aricept
B & O (belladonna and opium)	Beano
BabyBIG	HBIG (hepatitis B immune globulin)
Bayhep-B	Bayrab
Bayhep-B	Bayrho-D
Bayrab	Bayhep-B
Bayrab	Bayrho-D
Bayrho-D	Bayhep-B
Bayrho-D	Bayrab
Beano	B & O (belladonna and opium)
Benadryl	benazepril
benazepril	Benadryl
Benicar	Mevacor
Betadine (with povidone-iodine)	Betadine (without povidone-iodine)
Betadine (without povidone-iodine)	Betadine (with povidone-iodine)
Bextra	Zetia
Bicillin C-R	Bicillin L-A
Bicillin L-A	Bicillin C-R
Bicitra	Polycitra
Bidex	Videx
Brethine	Methergine
Brevibloc	Brevital
Brevital	Brevibloc
buPROPion	busPIRone
busPIRone	buPROPion
Capadex [non-US product]	Kapidex
Capex	Kapidex
Carac	Kuric
captopril	carvedilol
carBAMazepine	OXcarbazepine
CARBOplatin	CISplatin
Cardura	Coumadin
carvedilol	captopril
Casodex	Kapidex
Cathflo Activase	Activase
Cedax	Cidex
ceFAZolin	cefTRIAXone
cefTRIAXone	ceFAZolin
CeleBREX	CeleXA
CeleBREX	Cerebyx
CeleXA	ZyPREXA
CeleXA	CeleBREX
CeleXA	Cerebyx
Cerebyx	CeleBREX

(Continued)

Brand names always start with an uppercase letter. Some brand names incorporate tall man letters in initial characters and may not be readily recognized as brand names. Brand name products appear in black; generic/other products appear in color.

DRUG NAME	CONFUSED DRUG NAME	DRUG NAME	CONFUSED DRUG NAME
Cerebyx	Cele**XA**	Dilaudid	Dilaudid-5
cetirizine	sertraline	Dilaudid-5	Dilaudid
chlordiaze**POXIDE**	chlorpro**MAZINE**	dimenhy**DRINATE**	diphenhydr**AMINE**
chlorpro**MAZINE**	chlordiaze**POXIDE**	diphenhydr**AMINE**	dimenhy**DRINATE**
chlorpro**MAZINE**	chlorpro**PAMIDE**	Dioval	Diovan
chlorpro**PAMIDE**	chlorpro**MAZINE**	Diovan	Dioval
Cidex	Cedax	Diovan	Zyban
CISplatin	**CARBO**platin	Diovan	Darvon
Claritin (loratadine)	Claritin Eye (ketotifen fumarate)	Diprivan	Diflucan
Claritin-D	Claritin-D 24	Diprivan	Ditropan
Claritin-D 24	Claritin-D	disopyramide	desipramine
Claritin Eye (ketotifen fumarate)	Claritin (loratadine)	Ditropan	Diprivan
		DOBUTamine	**DOP**amine
Clindesse	Clindets	**DOP**amine	**DOBUT**amine
Clindets	Clindesse	Doribax	Zovirax
clomi**PHENE**	clomi**PRAMINE**	Doxil	Paxil
clomi**PRAMINE**	clomi**PHENE**	**DOXO**rubicin	**DAUNO**rubicin
clonaze**PAM**	clo**NID**ine	**DOXO**rubicin	**DOXO**rubicin liposomal
clonaze**PAM**	**LOR**azepam	**DOXO**rubicin	**IDA**rubicin
clo**NID**ine	clonaze**PAM**	**DOXO**rubicin liposomal	**DOXO**rubicin
clo**NID**ine	Klono**PIN**	Dulcolax (bisacodyl)	Dulcolax (docusate sodium)
Clozaril	Colazal	Dulcolax (docusate sodium)	Dulcolax (bisacodyl)
coagulation factor IX (recombinant)	factor IX complex, vapor heated	**DUL**oxetine	**FLU**oxetine
codeine	Lodine	Durasal	Durezol
Colace	Cozaar	Durezol	Durasal
Colazal	Clozaril	Duricef	Ultracet
colchicine	Cortrosyn	Dynacin	Dynacirc
Comvax	Recombivax HB	Dynacirc	Dynacin
Cortrosyn	colchicine	edetate calcium disodium	edetate disodium
Coumadin	Avandia	edetate disodium	edetate calcium disodium
Coumadin	Cardura	Effexor	Effexor XR
Cozaar	Colace	Effexor XR	Effexor
Cozaar	Zocor	Enbrel	Levbid
cyclo**SERINE**	cyclo**SPORINE**	Engerix-B adult	Engerix-B pediatric/adolescent
cyclo**SPORINE**	cyclo**SERINE**	Engerix-B pediatric/adolescent	Engerix-B adult
Cymbalta	Symbyax	Enjuvia	Januvia
DACTINomycin	**DAPTO**mycin	e**PHED**rine	**EPINEPH**rine
Daptacel (DTaP)	Adacel (Tdap)	**EPINEPH**rine	e**PHED**rine
DAPTOmycin	**DACTIN**omycin	Estratest	Estratest HS
Darvocet	Percocet	Estratest HS	Estratest
Darvon	Diovan	ethambutol	Ethmozine
DAUNOrubicin	**DAUNO**rubicin citrate liposomal	Ethmozine	ethambutol
DAUNOrubicin	**DOXO**rubicin	Evista	**AVIN**za
DAUNOrubicin	**IDA**rubicin	factor IX complex, vapor heated	coagulation factor IX (recombinant)
DAUNOrubicin citrate liposomal	**DAUNO**rubicin	Fanapt	Xanax
Denavir	indinavir	Femara	Femhrt
Depakote	Depakote ER	Femhrt	Femara
Depakote ER	Depakote	fenta**NYL**	**SUF**entanil
Depo-Medrol	Solu-**MEDROL**	Fioricet	Fiorinal
Depo-Provera	Depo-subQ provera 104	Fiorinal	Fioricet
Depo-subQ provera 104	Depo-Provera	flavox**ATE**	fluvoxa**MINE**
desipramine	disopyramide	Flonase	Flovent
dexmethylphenidate	methadone	Flovent	Flonase
Diabenese	Diamox	flumazenil	influenza virus vaccine
Diabeta	Zebeta	**FLU**oxetine	**PAR**oxetine
Diamox	Diabenese	**FLU**oxetine	**DUL**oxetine
Diflucan	Diprivan	**FLU**oxetine	Loxitane
Dilacor XR	Pilocar	fluvoxa**MINE**	flavox**ATE**
		Folex	Foltx

Brand names always start with an uppercase letter. Some brand names incorporate tall man letters in initial characters and may not be readily recognized as brand names. Brand name products appear in black; generic/other products appear in color.

DRUG NAME	CONFUSED DRUG NAME
folic acid	folinic acid (leucovorin calcium)
folinic acid (leucovorin calcium)	folic acid
Foltx	Folex
fomepizole	omeprazole
Foradil	Fortical
Foradil	Toradol
Fortical	Foradil
gentamicin	gentian violet
gentian violet	gentamicin
glacial acetic acid	acetic acid for irrigation
glipiZIDE	glyBURIDE
glyBURIDE	glipiZIDE
Granulex	Regranex
guaiFENesin	guanFACINE
guanFACINE	guaiFENesin
HBIG (hepatitis B immune globulin)	BabyBIG
Healon	Hyalgan
heparin	Hespan
Hespan	heparin
HMG-CoA reductase inhibitors ("statins")	nystatin
HumaLOG	HumuLIN
HumaLOG	NovoLOG
HumaLOG Mix 75/25	HumuLIN 70/30
Humapen Memoir (for use with HumaLOG)	Humira Pen
Humira Pen	Humapen Memoir (for use with HumaLOG)
HumuLIN	NovoLIN
HumuLIN	HumaLOG
HumuLIN 70/30	HumaLOG Mix 75/25
Hyalgan	Healon
hydrALAZINE	hydrOXYzine
HYDROcodone	oxyCODONE
Hydrogesic	hydrOXYzine
HYDROmorphone	morphine
hydrOXYzine	Hydrogesic
hydrOXYzine	hydrALAZINE
IDArubicin	DAUNOrubicin
IDArubicin	DOXOrubicin
Inderal	Adderall
indinavir	Denavir
inFLIXimab	riTUXimab
influenza virus vaccine	flumazenil
influenza virus vaccine	tuberculin purified protein derivative (PPD)
Inspra	Spiriva
INVanz	AVINza
iodine	Lodine
Isordil	Plendil
ISOtretinoin	tretinoin
Jantoven	Janumet
Jantoven	Januvia
Janumet	Jantoven
Janumet	Januvia
Janumet	Sinemet
Januvia	Enjuvia
Januvia	Jantoven
Januvia	Janumet
K-Phos Neutral	Neutra-Phos-K

DRUG NAME	CONFUSED DRUG NAME
Kaopectate (bismuth subsalicylate)	Kaopectate (docusate calcium)
Kaopectate (docusate calcium)	Kaopectate (bismuth subsalicylate)
Kadian	Kapidex
Kaletra	Keppra
Kapidex	Capadex [non-US product]
Kapidex	Capex
Kapidex	Casodex
Kapidex	Kadian
Keflex	Keppra
Keppra	Kaletra
Keppra	Keflex
Ketalar	ketorolac
ketorolac	Ketalar
ketorolac	methadone
Kineret	Amikin
KlonoPIN	cloNIDine
Kuric	Carac
Kwell	Qwell
LaMICtal	LamISIL
LamISIL	LaMICtal
lamiVUDine	lamoTRIgine
lamoTRIgine	lamiVUDine
lamoTRIgine	levothyroxine
Lanoxin	levothyroxine
Lanoxin	naloxone
lanthanum carbonate	lithium carbonate
Lantus	Lente
Lariam	Levaquin
Lasix	Luvox
Lente	Lantus
leucovorin calcium	Leukeran
Leukeran	Alkeran
Leukeran	Myleran
Leukeran	leucovorin calcium
Levaquin	Lariam
Levbid	Enbrel
Levemir	Lovenox
levETIRAcetam	levOCARNitine
levETIRAcetam	levofloxacin
levOCARNitine	levETIRAcetam
levofloxacin	levETIRAcetam
levothyroxine	lamoTRIgine
levothyroxine	Lanoxin
Lexapro	Loxitane
Lexiva	Pexeva
Lipitor	Loniten
Lipitor	ZyrTEC
lithium carbonate	lanthanum carbonate
Lodine	codeine
Lodine	iodine
Loniten	Lipitor
Lopressor	Lyrica
LORazepam	ALPRAZolam
LORazepam	clonazePAM
LORazepam	Lovaza
Lotronex	Protonix
Lovaza	LORazepam
Lovenox	Levemir
Loxitane	Lexapro
Loxitane	FLUoxetine

(Continued)

Brand names always start with an uppercase letter. Some brand names incorporate tall man letters in initial characters and may not be readily recognized as brand names. Brand name products appear in black; generic/other products appear in color.

A339

DRUG NAME	CONFUSED DRUG NAME	DRUG NAME	CONFUSED DRUG NAME
Loxitane	Soriatane	Neo-Synephrine (phenylephrine)	Neo-Synephrine (oxymetazoline)
Lunesta	Neulasta	Neulasta	Lunesta
Lupron Depot-3 Month	Lupron Depot-Ped	Neulasta	Neumega
Lupron Depot-Ped	Lupron Depot-3 Month	Neumega	Neupogen
Luvox	Lasix	Neumega	Neulasta
Lyrica	Lopressor	Neupogen	Neumega
Maalox	Maalox Total Stomach Relief	Neurontin	Motrin
Maalox Total Stomach Relief	Maalox	Neurontin	Noroxin
Matulane	Materna	Neutra-Phos-K	K-Phos Neutral
Materna	Matulane	NexAVAR	NexIUM
Maxzide	Microzide	NexIUM	NexAVAR
Menactra	Menomune	niCARdipine	NIFEdipine
Menomune	Menactra	NIFEdipine	niCARdipine
Mephyton	methadone	NIFEdipine	niMODipine
Metadate	methadone	niMODipine	NIFEdipine
Metadate CD	Metadate ER	Norcuron	Narcan
Metadate ER	Metadate CD	Normodyne	Norpramin
Metadate ER	methadone	Noroxin	Neurontin
metFORMIN	metroNIDAZOLE	Norpramin	Normodyne
methadone	dexmethylphenidate	Norvasc	Navane
methadone	ketorolac	NovoLIN	HumuLIN
methadone	Mephyton	NovoLIN	NovoLOG
methadone	Metadate	NovoLIN 70/30	NovoLOG Mix 70/30
methadone	Metadate ER	NovoLOG	HumaLOG
methadone	methylphenidate	NovoLOG	NovoLIN
Methergine	Brethine	NovoLOG FLEXPEN	NovoLOG Mix 70/30 FLEXPEN
methimazole	metolazone	NovoLOG Mix 70/30 FLEXPEN	NovoLOG FLEXPEN
methylphenidate	methadone	NovoLOG Mix 70/30	NovoLIN 70/30
metolazone	methimazole	nystatin	HMG-CoA reductase inhibitors ("statins")
metoprolol succinate	metoprolol tartrate	Occlusal-HP	Ocuflox
metoprolol tartrate	metoprolol succinate	Ocuflox	Occlusal-HP
metroNIDAZOLE	metFORMIN	OLANZapine	QUEtiapine
Mevacor	Benicar	Omacor	Amicar
Micronase	Microzide	omeprazole	fomepizole
Microzide	Maxzide	opium tincture	paregoric (camphorated tincture of opium)
Microzide	Micronase	Oracea	Orencia
midodrine	Midrin	Orencia	Oracea
Midrin	midodrine	Organan	argatroban
mifepristone	misoprostol	Ortho Tri-Cyclen	Ortho Tri-Cyclen LO
Miralax	Mirapex	Ortho Tri-Cyclen LO	Ortho Tri-Cyclen
Mirapex	Miralax	Os-Cal	Asacol
misoprostol	mifepristone	OXcarbazepine	carBAMazepine
morphine	HYDROmorphone	oxyCODONE	HYDROcodone
morphine - non-concentrated oral liquid	morphine - oral liquid concentrate	oxyCODONE	OxyCONTIN
morphine - oral liquid concentrate	morphine - non-concentrated oral liquid	OxyCONTIN	MS Contin
Motrin	Neurontin	OxyCONTIN	oxyCODONE
MS Contin	OxyCONTIN	PACLitaxel	PACLitaxel protein-bound particles
Mucinex	Mucomyst	PACLitaxel protein-bound particles	PACLitaxel
Mucinex D	Mucinex DM	Pamelor	Panlor DC
Mucinex DM	Mucinex D	Pamelor	Tambocor
Mucomyst	Mucinex	Panlor DC	Pamelor
Myleran	Alkeran	paregoric (camphorated tincture of opium)	opium tincture
Myleran	Leukeran	PARoxetine	FLUoxetine
naloxone	Lanoxin	PARoxetine	piroxicam
Narcan	Norcuron	Patanol	Platinol
Natru-Vent	Atrovent	Pavulon	Peptavlon
Navane	Norvasc		
Neo-Synephrine (oxymetazoline)	Neo-Synephrine (phenylephrine)		

Brand names always start with an uppercase letter. Some brand names incorporate tall man letters in initial characters and may not be readily recognized as brand names. Brand name products appear in black; generic/other products appear in color.

DRUG NAME	CONFUSED DRUG NAME
Paxil	Doxil
Paxil	Taxol
Paxil	Plavix
PEMEtrexed	PRALAtrexate
Peptavlon	Pavulon
Percocet	Darvocet
Percocet	Procet
Pexeva	Lexiva
PENTobarbital	PHENobarbital
PHENobarbital	PENTobarbital
Pilocar	Dilacor XR
piroxicam	PARoxetine
Platinol	Patanol
Plavix	Paxil
Plendil	Isordil
pneumococcal 7-valent vaccine	pneumococcal polyvalent vaccine
pneumococcal polyvalent vaccine	pneumococcal 7-valent vaccine
Polycitra	Bicitra
PRALAtrexate	PEMEtrexed
Prandin	Avandia
Precare	Precose
Precose	Precare
prednisoLONE	predniSONE
predniSONE	prednisoLONE
PriLOSEC	Pristiq
PriLOSEC	PROzac
Priscoline	Apresoline
Pristiq	PriLOSEC
probenecid	Procanbid
Procan SR	Procanbid
Procanbid	probenecid
Procanbid	Procan SR
Procardia XL	Protain XL
Procet	Percocet
Prograf	PROzac
propylthiouracil	Purinethol
Proscar	Provera
Protain XL	Procardia XL
protamine	Protonix
proton pump inhibitors	ARIPiprazole
Protonix	Lotronex
Protonix	protamine
Provera	Proscar
Provera	PROzac
PROzac	Prograf
PROzac	PriLOSEC
PROzac	Provera
Purinethol	propylthiouracil
QUEtiapine	OLANZapine
quiNIDine	quiNINE
quiNINE	quiNIDine
Qwell	Kwell
RABEprazole	ARIPiprazole
Razadyne	Rozerem
Recombivax HB	Comvax
Regranex	Granulex
Reminyl	Robinul
Reminyl	Amaryl
Renagel	Renvela
Renvela	Renagel

DRUG NAME	CONFUSED DRUG NAME
Reprexain	ZyPREXA
Restoril	RisperDAL
Retrovir	ritonavir
Rifadin	Rifater
Rifamate	rifampin
rifampin	Rifamate
rifampin	rifaximin
Rifater	Rifadin
rifaximin	rifampin
RisperDAL	Restoril
risperiDONE	rOPINIRole
Ritalin	ritodrine
Ritalin LA	Ritalin SR
Ritalin SR	Ritalin LA
ritodrine	Ritalin
ritonavir	Retrovir
riTUXimab	inFLIXimab
Robinul	Reminyl
rOPINIRole	risperiDONE
Roxanol	Roxicodone Intensol
Roxanol	Roxicet
Roxicet	Roxanol
Roxicodone Intensol	Roxanol
Rozerem	Razadyne
Salagen	selegiline
SandIMMUNE	SandoSTATIN
SandoSTATIN	SandIMMUNE
saquinavir	SINEquan
saquinavir (free base)	saquinavir mesylate
saquinavir mesylate	saquinavir (free base)
Sarafem	Serophene
selegiline	Salagen
Serophene	Sarafem
SEROquel	SEROquel XR
SEROquel	Serzone
SEROquel	SINEquan
SEROquel XR	SEROquel
sertraline	cetirizine
sertraline	Soriatane
Serzone	SEROquel
Sinemet	Janumet
SINEquan	saquinavir
SINEquan	SEROquel
SINEquan	Singulair
SINEquan	Zonegran
Singulair	SINEquan
sitaGLIPtin	SUMAtriptan
Solu-CORTEF	Solu-MEDROL
Solu-MEDROL	Depo-Medrol
Solu-MEDROL	Solu-CORTEF
Sonata	Soriatane
Soriatane	Loxitane
Soriatane	sertraline
Soriatane	Sonata
sotalol	Sudafed
Spiriva	Inspra
Sudafed	sotalol
Sudafed	Sudafed PE
Sudafed PE	Sudafed
SUFentanil	fentaNYL
sulfADIAZINE	sulfaSALAzine

(Continued)

Brand names always start with an uppercase letter. Some brand names incorporate tall man letters in initial characters and may not be readily recognized as brand names. Brand name products appear in black; generic/other products appear in color.

DRUG NAME	CONFUSED DRUG NAME	DRUG NAME	CONFUSED DRUG NAME
sulfADIAZINE	sulfiSOXAZOLE	Vexol	Vosol
sulfaSALAzine	sulfADIAZINE	Viagra	Allegra
sulfiSOXAZOLE	sulfADIAZINE	Videx	Bidex
SUMAtriptan	sitaGLIPtin	vinBLAStine	vinCRIStine
SUMAtriptan	ZOLMitriptan	vinCRIStine	vinBLAStine
Symbyax	Cymbalta	Viokase	Viokase 8
Tambocor	Pamelor	Viokase 8	Viokase
Taxol	Taxotere	Vioxx	Zyvox
Taxol	Paxil	Viracept	Viramune
Taxotere	Taxol	Viramune	Viracept
TEGretol	TEGretol XR	Vosol	Vexol
TEGretol	Tequin	VZIG (varicella-zoster immune globulin)	Varivax
TEGretol	TRENtal	Wellbutrin SR	Wellbutrin XL
TEGretol XR	TEGretol	Wellbutrin XL	Wellbutrin SR
Tequin	TEGretol	Xanax	Fanapt
Tequin	Ticlid	Xanax	Zantac
Testoderm TTS	Testoderm	Xeloda	Xenical
Testoderm TTS	Testoderm with Adhesive	Xenical	Xeloda
Testoderm with Adhesive	Testoderm	Yasmin	Yaz
Testoderm with Adhesive	Testoderm TTS	Yaz	Yasmin
Testoderm	Testoderm TTS	Zantac	Xanax
Testoderm	Testoderm with Adhesive	Zantac	ZyrTEC
tetanus diphtheria toxoid (Td)	tuberculin purified protein derivative (PPD)	Zavesca (escitalopram) [non-US product]	Zavesca (miglustat)
Thalomid	Thiamine	Zavesca (miglustat)	Zavesca (escitalopram) [non-US product]
Thiamine	Thalomid	Zebeta	Diabeta
tiaGABine	tiZANidine	Zebeta	Zetia
Tiazac	Ziac	Zegerid	Zestril
Ticlid	Tequin	Zelapar (Zydis formulation)	ZyPREXA Zydis
tiZANidine	tiaGABine	Zestril	Zegerid
TNKase	Activase	Zestril	Zetia
TNKase	t-PA	Zestril	ZyPREXA
Tobradex	Tobrex	Zetia	Bextra
Tobrex	Tobradex	Zetia	Zebeta
TOLAZamide	TOLBUTamide	Zetia	Zestril
TOLBUTamide	TOLAZamide	Ziac	Tiazac
Topamax	Toprol-XL	Zocor	Cozaar
Toprol-XL	Topamax	Zocor	ZyrTEC
Toradol	Foradil	ZOLMitriptan	SUMAtriptan
t-PA	TNKase	Zonegran	SINEquan
Tracleer	Tricor	Zostrix	Zovirax
traMADol	traZODone	Zovirax	Doribax
traZODone	traMADol	Zovirax	Zyvox
TRENtal	TEGretol	Zovirax	Zostrix
tretinoin	ISOtretinoin	Zyban	Diovan
Tricor	Tracleer	ZyPREXA	CeleXA
tromethamine	Trophamine	ZyPREXA	Reprexain
Trophamine	tromethamine	ZyPREXA	Zestril
tuberculin purified protein derivative (PPD)	influenza virus vaccine	ZyPREXA	ZyrTEC
tuberculin purified protein derivative (PPD)	tetanus diphtheria toxoid (Td)	ZyPREXA Zydis	Zelapar (Zydis formulation)
Tylenol	Tylenol PM	ZyrTEC	Lipitor
Tylenol PM	Tylenol	ZyrTEC	Zantac
Ultracet	Duricef	ZyrTEC	Zocor
valACYclovir	valGANciclovir	ZyrTEC	ZyPREXA
Valcyte	Valtrex	ZyrTEC	ZyrTEC-D
valGANciclovir	valACYclovir	ZyrTEC (cetirizine)	ZyrTEC Itchy Eye Drops (ketotifen fumarate)
Valtrex	Valcyte	ZyrTEC-D	ZyrTEC
Varivax	VZIG (varicella-zoster immune globulin)	ZyrTEC Itchy Eye Drops (ketotifen fumarate)	ZyrTEC (cetirizine)
Vesanoid	Vesicare	Zyvox	Vioxx
Vesicare	Vesanoid	Zyvox	Zovirax

Brand names always start with an uppercase letter. Some brand names incorporate tall man letters in initial characters and may not be readily recognized as brand names. Brand name products appear in black; generic/other products appear in color.

ISMP's List of Error-Prone Abbreviations, Symbols, and Dose Designations

This table has been reproduced with permission from the Institute for Safe Medication Practices (ISMP).

The abbreviations, symbols, and dose designations found in this table have been reported to ISMP through the ISMP National Medication Errors Reporting Program (ISMP MERP) as being frequently misinterpreted and involved in harmful medication errors. They should **NEVER** be used when communicating medical information.

This includes internal communications, telephone/verbal prescriptions, computer-generated labels, labels for drug storage bins, medication administration records, as well as pharmacy and prescriber computer order entry screens.

ABBREVIATIONS	INTENDED MEANING	MISINTERPRETATION	CORRECTION
µg	Microgram	Mistaken as "mg"	Use "mcg"
AD, AS, AU	Right ear, left ear, each ear	Mistaken as OD, OS, OU (right eye, left eye, each eye)	Use "right ear," "left ear," or "each ear"
OD, OS, OU	Right eye, left eye, each eye	Mistaken as AD, AS, AU (right ear, left ear, each ear)	Use "right eye," "left eye," or "each eye"
BT	Bedtime	Mistaken as "BID" (twice daily)	Use "bedtime"
cc	Cubic centimeters	Mistaken as "u" (units)	Use "mL"
D/C	Discharge or discontinue	Premature discontinuation of medications if D/C (intended to mean "discharge") has been misinterpreted as "discontinued" when followed by a list of discharge medications	Use "discharge" and "discontinue"
IJ	Injection	Mistaken as "IV" or "intrajugular"	Use "injection"
IN	Intranasal	Mistaken as "IM" or "IV"	Use "intranasal" or "NAS"
HS	Half-strength	Mistaken as bedtime	Use "half-strength" or "bedtime"
hs	At bedtime, hours of sleep	Mistaken as half-strength	
IU**	International unit	Mistaken as IV (intravenous) or 10 (ten)	Use "units"
o.d. or OD	Once daily	Mistaken as "right eye" (OD-oculus dexter), leading to oral liquid medications administered in the eye	Use "daily"
OJ	Orange juice	Mistaken as OD or OS (right or left eye); drugs meant to be diluted in orange juice may be given in the eye	Use "orange juice"
Per os	By mouth, orally	The "os" can be mistaken as "left eye" (OS-oculus sinister)	Use "PO," "by mouth," or "orally"
q.d. or QD**	Every day	Mistaken as q.i.d., especially if the period after the "q" or the tail of the "q" is misunderstood as an "i"	Use "daily"
qhs	Nightly at bedtime	Mistaken as "qhr" or every hour	Use "nightly"
qn	Nightly or at bedtime	Mistaken as "qh" (every hour)	Use "nightly" or "at bedtime"
q.o.d. or QOD**	Every other day	Mistaken as "q.d." (daily) or "q.i.d." (four times daily) if the "o" is poorly written	Use "every other day"
q1d	Daily	Mistaken as q.i.d. (four times daily)	Use "daily"
q6PM, etc.	Every evening at 6 PM	Mistaken as every 6 hours	Use "daily at 6 PM" or "6 PM daily"
SC, SQ, sub q	Subcutaneous	SC mistaken as SL (sublingual); SQ mistaken as "5 every"; the "q" in "sub q" has been mistaken as "every" (e.g., a heparin dose ordered "sub q 2 hours before surgery" misunderstood as every 2 hours before surgery)	Use "subcut" or "subcutaneously"

(Continued)

ABBREVIATIONS	INTENDED MEANING	MISINTERPRETATION	CORRECTION
ss	Sliding scale (insulin) or ½ (apothecary)	Mistaken as "55"	Spell out "sliding scale"; use "one-half" or "½"
SSRI SSI	Sliding scale regular insulin Sliding scale insulin	Mistaken as selective-serotonin reuptake inhibitor Mistaken as Strong Solution of Iodine (Lugol's)	Spell out "sliding scale (insulin)"
i/d	One daily	Mistaken as "tid"	Use "1 daily"
TIW or tiw	3 times a week	Mistaken as "3 times a day" or "twice in a week"	Use "3 times weekly"
U or u**	Unit	Mistaken as the number 0 or 4, causing a 10-fold overdose or greater (e.g., 4U seen as "40" or 4u seen as "44"); mistaken as "cc" so dose given in volume instead of units (e.g., 4u seen as 4cc)	Use "unit"
UD	As directed ("ut dictum")	Mistaken as unit dose (e.g., diltiazem 125 mg IV infusion "UD" misinterpreted as meaning to give the entire infusion as a unit [bolus] dose)	Use "as directed"

DOSE DESIGNATIONS AND OTHER INFORMATION	INTENDED MEANING	MISINTERPRETATION	CORRECTION
Trailing zero after decimal point (e.g., 1.0 mg)**	1 mg	Mistaken as 10 mg if the decimal point is not seen	Do not use trailing zeros for doses expressed in whole numbers
"Naked" decimal point (e.g., .5 mg)**	0.5 mg	Mistaken as 5 mg if the decimal point is not seen	Use zero before a decimal point when the dose is less than a whole unit
Abbreviations such as mg. or mL. with a period following the abbreviation	mg mL	The period is unnecessary and could be mistaken as the number 1 if written poorly	Use mg, mL, etc. without a terminal period
Drug name and dose run together (especially problematic for drug names that end in "l" such as Inderal40 mg; Tegretol300 mg)	Inderal 40 mg Tegretol 300 mg	Mistaken as Inderal 140 mg Mistaken as Tegretol 1300 mg	Place adequate space between the drug name, dose, and unit of measure
Numerical dose and unit of measure run together (e.g., 10mg, 100mL)	10 mg 100 mL	The "m" is sometimes mistaken as a zero or two zeros, risking a 10- to 100-fold overdose	Place adequate space between the dose and unit of measure
Large doses without properly placed commas (e.g., 100000 units; 1000000 units)	100,000 units 1,000,000 units	100000 has been mistaken as 10,000 or 1,000,000; 1000000 has been mistaken as 100,000	Use commas for dosing units at or above 1,000, or use words such as 100 "thousand" or 1 "million" to improve readability

DRUG NAME ABBREVIATIONS	INTENDED MEANING	MISINTERPRETATION	CORRECTION
To avoid confusion, do not abbreviate drug names when communicating medical information. Examples of drug name abbreviations involved in medication errors include:			
APAP	acetaminophen	Not recognized as acetaminophen	Use complete drug name
ARA A	vidarabine	Mistaken as cytarabine (ARA C)	Use complete drug name
AZT	zidovudine (Retrovir)	Mistaken as azathioprine or aztreonam	Use complete drug name
CPZ	Compazine (prochlorperazine)	Mistaken as chlorpromazine	Use complete drug name
DPT	Demerol-Phenergan-Thorazine	Mistaken as diphtheria-pertussis-tetanus (vaccine)	Use complete drug name
DTO	Diluted tincture of opium, or deodorized tincture of opium (Paregoric)	Mistaken as tincture of opium	Use complete drug name
HCl	hydrochloric acid or hydrochloride	Mistaken as potassium chloride (The "H" is misinterpreted as "K")	Use complete drug name unless expressed as a salt of a drug
HCT	hydrocortisone	Mistaken as hydrochlorothiazide	Use complete drug name
HCTZ	hydrochlorothiazide	Mistaken as hydrocortisone (seen as HCT250 mg)	Use complete drug name
MgSO4**	magnesium sulfate	Mistaken as morphine sulfate	Use complete drug name
MS, MSO4**	morphine sulfate	Mistaken as magnesium sulfate	Use complete drug name
MTX	methotrexate	Mistaken as mitoxantrone	Use complete drug name
PCA	procainamide	Mistaken as patient controlled analgesia	Use complete drug name
PTU	propylthiouracil	Mistaken as mercaptopurine	Use complete drug name
T3	Tylenol with codeine No. 3	Mistaken as liothyronine	Use complete drug name
TAC	triamcinolone	Mistaken as tetracaine, Adrenalin, cocaine	Use complete drug name
TNK	TNKase	Mistaken as "TPA"	Use complete drug name
ZnSO4	zinc sulfate	Mistaken as morphine sulfate	Use complete drug name

STEMMED DRUG NAMES	INTENDED MEANING	MISINTERPRETATION	CORRECTION
"Nitro" drip	nitroglycerin infusion	Mistaken as sodium nitroprusside infusion	Use complete drug name
"Norflox"	norfloxacin	Mistaken as Norflex	Use complete drug name
"IV Vanc"	intravenous vancomycin	Mistaken as Invanz	Use complete drug name

SYMBOLS	INTENDED MEANING	MISINTERPRETATION	CORRECTION
ʒ	Dram	Symbol for dram mistaken as "3"	Use the metric system
♏	Minim	Symbol for minim mistaken as "mL"	
x3d	For three days	Mistaken as "3 doses"	Use "for three days"
> and <	Greater than and less than	Mistaken as opposite of intended; mistakenly use incorrect symbol; "< 10" mistaken as "40"	Use "greater than" or "less than"
/ (slash mark)	Separates two doses or indicates "per"	Mistaken as the number 1 (e.g., "25 units/10 units" misread as "25 units and 110 units")	Use "per" rather than a slash mark to separate doses
@	At	Mistaken as "2"	Use "at"

(Continued)

SYMBOLS	INTENDED MEANING	MISINTERPRETATION	CORRECTION
&	And	Mistaken as "2"	Use "and"
+	Plus or and	Mistaken as "4"	Use "and"
°	Hour	Mistaken as a zero (e.g., q2° seen as q 20)	Use "hr," "h," or "hour"
Φ or ⊘	zero, null sign	Mistaken as numerals 4, 6, 8, and 9	Use 0 or zero, or describe intent using whole words

**These abbreviations are included on The Joint Commission's "minimum list" of dangerous abbreviations, acronyms, and symbols that must be included on an organization's "Do Not Use" list, effective January 1, 2004. Visit www.jointcommission.org for more information about this Joint Commission requirement.

OBESITY TREATMENT GUIDELINES

ADULTS

Overweight or obese patients are at an increased risk for developing coronary heart disease (CHD), type 2 diabetes, dyslipidemia, hypertension, stroke, and conditions like osteoarthritis, sleep apnea, gallstones, and some cancers.

ASSESSMENT:

A. Body mass index
- Body mass index (BMI) is integral in classifying a patient into an overweight or obese category.
- Calculate BMI: weight (kg)/height (m²). Overweight is defined as a BMI of 25-29.9 kg/m². Obesity is defined as an excess of total body fat that is documented by a BMI ≥30 kg/m². [**See table**]

B. Waist circumference
- Excess fat in the abdomen is an independent predictor of risk factors and morbidity.
- Waist circumference measurement can assess a patient's abdominal fat content before and during weight loss treatment. [**See table**]
  - High risk = Men >102 cm (>40 in)
  - High risk = Women >88 cm (>35 in)
- High waist circumference is associated with an increased risk for type 2 diabetes, dyslipidemia, hypertension, and cardiovascular disease (CVD) in patients with a BMI in a range of 25-34.9 kg/m².

C. Risk status
- Identify patients at very high absolute risk.
  - Established CHD (history of myocardial infarction, angina pectoris [stable or unstable], coronary artery surgery, coronary artery procedures [angioplasty]), presence of atherosclerotic diseases (peripheral arterial disease, abdominal aortic aneurysm, symptomatic carotid artery disease), type 2 diabetes, sleep apnea.
- Identify other obesity-associated disease.
  - Gynecological abnormalities, osteoarthritis, gallstones and their complications, stress incontinence.
- Identify cardiovascular risk factors that impart a high absolute risk.
  - Overweight patients require equal emphasis on weight loss therapy and control of cardiovascular risk factors.
  - Patients can be classified as being at high absolute risk for obesity-related disorders if they have three or more of the following risk factors:
    - Cigarette smoking; hypertension; high-risk low-density lipoprotein cholesterol (LDL ≥160 mg/dL); low high-density lipoprotein cholesterol (HDL <35 mg/dL); impaired fasting glucose; family history of premature CHD; age: male ≥45 years, female ≥55 years (or postmenopausal); lack of physical activity; high triglycerides.

CLASSIFICATION OF OVERWEIGHT AND OBESITY BY BMI, WAIST CIRCUMFERENCE, AND ASSOCIATED DISEASE RISK*			DISEASE RISK* RELATIVE TO NORMAL WEIGHT AND WAIST CIRCUMFERENCE
	BMI (kg/m²)	Obesity Class	Men >102 cm (>40 in) Women >88 cm (>35 in)
Underweight	<18.5		
Normal†	18.5 - 24.9		
Overweight	25.0 - 29.9		
Obesity	30.0 - 34.9	I	Increased
	35.0 - 39.9	II	
Extreme Obesity	≥40	III	

*Disease risk for CVD and/or presence of obesity-related comorbidities.
†Increased waist circumference can also be a marker for increased risk even in persons of normal weight.

GOALS: *(Based on NHLBI guidelines unless otherwise indicated)*

A. Weight loss
- Initial goal of weight-loss therapy should be to reduce body weight by approximately 10% from baseline.
- Weight loss should be about 1 to 2 lbs/week (resulting from a calorie deficit of 500 to 1000 kcal/day) for a period of 6 months, with the subsequent strategy based on the amount of weight loss.
- American College of Physicians recommendation: Weight loss should be based on the patient's individual risk factors and may include not only weight loss but other parameters like reducing blood pressure or fasting blood glucose.

(Continued)

B. Maintain a lower body weight over the long term
- Maintenance program should be a priority after initial 6 months.
- Successful weight maintenance is defined as a weight regain of <3 kg (6.6 lb) in 2 years and a sustained reduction in waist circumference of at least 4 cm.
- Maintenance is enhanced with dietary therapy, physical activity, and behavioral therapy (continue this indefinitely). May also initiate drug therapy.

C. Prevent further weight gain

TREATMENT:
Each treatment plan should be tailored to the individual patient based on his or her psychobehavioral characteristics, past attempts at weight loss, financial considerations, age, degree of obesity, gender, and ability to exercise, individual health risks, or motivation.

Nonpharmacological
A. Dietary management
- Low-calorie diets (800 to 1500 kcal/day) are recommended for weight loss in overweight or obese patients.
- Low-calorie diets reduce body weight by an average of 8% and reduce abdominal fat content over a period of approximately 6 months.
- Total fat intake: ≤30% of total calories.

B. Physical activity
- Physical activity independently reduces CVD risk factors and improves cardiorespiratory fitness.
- Initiate with moderate levels of activity (30 to 45 minutes, 3 to 5 days per week).
- Long-term goal: Moderate-intensity physical activity ≥30 minutes most or all days per week.

C. Behavioral therapy
- Self-monitoring (eg, keeping food and activity logs), stress management, stimulus control (ie, controlling cues associated with eating), problem solving, rewarding changes in behavior, cognitive restructuring, and social support.
- Binge Eating Disorder: Self-monitoring, regular eating patterns (3 meals/day plus planned snacks), cognitive restructuring, and relapse prevention strategies.

D. Smoking cessation

Pharmacological
Weight loss drugs may be used only as part of a comprehensive weight loss program that includes diet and physical activity for patients with a BMI of ≥30 with no concomitant obesity-related risk factors or diseases, or for patients with a BMI of ≥27 with concomitant obesity-related risk factors or disease.

MEDICATIONS APPROVED FOR WEIGHT LOSS			
DRUG	TREATMENT PERIOD	DOSAGE	SIDE EFFECTS
Diethylpropion	Approved for short-term use Sympathomimetic amine; acts as a CNS stimulant and elevates BP	**IR:** 25 mg TID, 1 hr before meals and in midevening if desired to overcome hunger **CR:** 75 mg/day in midmorning	Arrhythmias, increased blood pressure, seizures, tremor, headache, GI complaints, bone marrow suppression, urticaria, impotence
Phentermine [Adipex-P]	Approved for short-term use Sympathomimetic amine; typical actions include CNS stimulation and elevation of BP	37.5 mg/day before or 1-2 hours after breakfast or 18.75 mg QD-BID	Withdrawal, increased blood pressure, tremor, headache, GI complaints, urticaria, impotence
Orlistat [Alli (OTC), Xenical]	Approved for long-term use Lipase inhibitor; acts peripherally to reduce absorption of dietary fat in the gut	**Alli:** 60 mg up to TID with each fat-containing meal **Xenical:** 120 mg TID with each fat-containing meal	Gas, oily spotting, fecal incontinence or urgency, oily or fatty stool, oily evacuation, increased defecation

Surgery
Bariatric surgery
- An option for weight reduction for patients with severe and resistant obesity.
- GI surgery or gastric bypass is an available option for motivated patients with a BMI ≥40 kg/m^2 or ≥35 kg/m^2 (who have comorbid conditions) and acceptable operative risks.
- Reserve for severely obese patients, in whom efforts with other therapy have failed, and who are suffering from the complications of obesity.

CHILDREN

Intervention in overweight and obese children and adolescents can decrease the risk of developing obesity-related comorbidities (eg, type 2 diabetes, asthma, sleep apnea, dyslipidemia, and hypertension).

ASSESSMENT:
A. BMI
- Diagnosis of a patient is dependent on BMI as well as CDC growth charts, gender, and age.
- Considered overweight if the BMI is at least in the 85th percentile but less than the 95th percentile for age and sex.
- Considered obese if the BMI is at least in the 95th percentile for age and sex.

B. Risk status
- Cardiovascular risk factors
  - Hypertriglyceridemia, high LDL, low HDL, glucose intolerance, and hypertension.
- Comorbidities
  - Type 2 diabetes, asthma, hepatic steatosis, and sleep apnea.

TREATMENT:

Nonpharmacological
A. Dietary management
- Avoid consumption of calorie-dense, nutrient-poor foods (eg, sweetened beverages, sports drinks, fruit drinks and juices, most fast food, and calorie-dense snacks).
- Portion control.
- Reduce saturated dietary fat intake for children older than 2 years of age.
- Increase intake of dietary fiber, fruits, and vegetables.
- Eat timely, regular meals.

B. Physical activity
- 60 minutes of daily moderate-to-vigorous physical activity.
- Sedentary activity (eg, watching television, playing video games, or using computers for recreation) should be limited to 1 to 2 hours per day.

C. Behavioral therapy
- Educate parents about the need for healthy rearing patterns related to diet and activity (eg, model healthy habits, avoid overly strict dieting and using food as a reward or punishment, and set limits of acceptable behaviors).

Pharmacological
In combination with lifestyle modification, pharmacotherapy can be considered in:
- Obese children only after failure of a formal program of intensive lifestyle modification.
- Overweight children only if severe comorbidities persist despite intensive lifestyle modification (particularly with strong family history of type 2 diabetes, or premature CV disease).

Pharmacotherapy should be provided only by clinicians who are experienced in the use of antiobesity agents and aware of the potential for adverse reactions.

Surgery
Bariatric Surgery
- Indicated for adolescents with a BMI >50 kg/m^2 or a BMI >40 kg/m^2 with severe comorbidities in whom lifestyle modifications and/or pharmacotherapy have failed.
- Must be psychologically stable and capable of adhering to lifestyle modifications.
- Not recommended for preadolescent children, pregnant or breastfeeding adolescents, or those who have not mastered principles of healthy eating and physical activity, are planning to become pregnant within 2 years of surgery, have an unresolved eating disorder, or who have an untreated psychiatric disorder or Prader-Willi syndrome.

SOURCES:
About BMI for Children and Teens. Centers for Disease Control and Prevention website. http://www.cdc.gov/healthyweight/assessing/bmi/childrens_bmi/about_childrens_bmi.html. Updated September 13, 2011. Accessed February 20, 2014.

Tips for Parents – Ideas to Help Children Maintain a Healthy Weight. Centers for Disease Control and Prevention website. http://www.cdc.gov/healthyweight/children/index.html. Updated October 31, 2011. Accessed March 20, 2013.

NHLBI Obesity Education Initiative Expert Panel on the Identification, Evaluation, and Treatment of Overweight and Obesity in Adults. *Clinical Guidelines on the Identification, Evaluation, and Treatment of Overweight and Obesity in Adults: The Evidence Report.* Bethesda, MD: National Heart, Lung, and Blood Institute; 1998.

Alli [package insert]. Moon Township, PA: GlaxoSmithKline Consumer Healthcare LP; 2013.

Diethylpropion [package insert]. Corona, CA: Watson Laboratories, Inc.; 2009.

Adipex-P [package insert]. Sellersville, PA: Teva Pharmaceuticals USA; 2012.

Xenical [package insert]. South San Francisco, CA: Genentech; 2013.

Snow V, Barry P, Fitterman N, et al. Pharmacologic and surgical management of obesity in primary care: A clinical practice guideline from the American College of Physicians. *Ann Intern Med.* 2005;142(7):525-531.

August GP, Caprio S, Fennoy I, et al. Prevention and treatment of pediatric obesity: An Endocrine Society clinical practice guideline based on expert opinion. *J Clin Endocrinol Metab.* 2008;93(12):4576-4599.

POISON ANTIDOTES

This information has been assembled by the Illinois Poison Center, as a resource for the uses and suggested minimum stock quantities for poison antidotes for Illinois hospitals with emergency departments. Requirements and special circumstances in other areas of the U.S. may justify different stocking quantities or products (eg, antivenoms for other varieties of snakes, scorpions, spiders). Contact your nearest regional PCC via the nationwide Poison Help Line at **1-800-222-1222** (available 24 hours a day) for treatment information regarding any exposure, including indications for use of antidote therapy.

ANTIDOTE	POISON/DRUG/TOXIN	SUGGESTED MINIMUM STOCK QUANTITY	RATIONALE/COMMENTS
N-Acetylcysteine (Mucomyst, Acetadote)	Acetaminophen Carbon tetrachloride Other hepatotoxins	IV: 300 mL (60 g) Acetadote PO: 750 mL (150 mg) of 20% NAC	Acetaminophen is the most common drug involved in intentional and unintentional poisonings. 750 mL (150 g) of the oral product provides enough to treat three 100 kg adults for 24 h. Several vials may be stocked in the ED to provide a loading dose, and the remaining vials stocked in the pharmacy. 300 mL (60 g) of IV product will treat two 100 kg adult patients for the entire 21-h IV protocol.
Antivenin, *Crotalidae* Polyvalent Immune Fab – Ovine (CroFab)	Pit viper envenomation (eg, rattlesnakes, cottonmouths, and copperheads)	12-18 vials	Advised in geographic areas in Illinois with endemic populations of copperhead, water moccasin, eastern massasauga, or timber rattlesnake. In low-risk areas, know nearest alternate source of antivenin. This product has a lower risk of hypersensitivity reaction than previously marketed equine product. 12 vials will cover 8 h of treatment, while 18 vials will cover 24 h of treatment. Stock in pharmacy. Store in refrigerator. Equine product was discontinued March 31, 2007 and is no longer available for purchase.
Antivenin, *Latrodectus mactans* (Black widow spider)	Black widow spider envenomation	0 to 1 vial	Serious *Latrodectus* envenomations are rare in Illinois. This product is only used for severe envenomations. Antivenin must be given in a critical care setting since it is an equine-derived product that may cause anaphylaxis. Stock in pharmacy. Product must be refrigerated at all times. Know the nearest source of antidote.
Atropine sulfate	Alpha$_2$ agonists (eg, clonidine, guanabenz and guanfacine) Alzheimer drugs (eg, donepezil, galantamine, rivastigmine, tacrine) Antimyasthenic agents (eg, pyridostigmine) Bradyarrhythmia-producing agents (eg, beta blockers, calcium channel blockers and digitalis glycosides)	175 mg or greater Available in various formulations: 0.4 mg/mL (1 mL, 0.4 mg vial); 0.4 mg/mL (20 mL, 8 mg vial); 0.1 mg/mL (10 mL, 1 mg vial) Atropine Sulfate military-style auto-injectors: (Atropen): 2 mg/0.7 mL, 1 mg/0.7 mL, 0.5 mg/0.7 mL, 0.25 mg/0.3 mL Atropine Sulfate 2.1 mg/0.7 mL with Pralidoxime chloride 600 mg/2 mL (DuoDote)	The product should be immediately available in the ED. Some also may be stored in the pharmacy or other hospital sites, but should be easily mobilized if a severely poisoned patient needs treatment. Note: Product is necessary to be adequately prepared for WMD incidents; the suggested amount may not be sufficient for mass casualty events. Auto-injectors are available from Bound Tree Medical, Inc (800-533-0523). Drug stocked in chempack containers is intended only for use in mass casualty events.

(Continued)

ANTIDOTE	POISON/DRUG/TOXIN	SUGGESTED MINIMUM STOCK QUANTITY	RATIONALE/COMMENTS
Atropine sulfate *(Continued)*	Cholinergic agonists (eg, bethanechol)		
	Muscarine-containing mushrooms (eg, *Clitocybe* and *Inocybe*)		
	Nerve agents (eg, sarin, soman, tabun, and VX)		
	Organophosphate and carbamate insecticides		
Botulinum antitoxin As of March 13, 2010, the only botulinum antitoxin available is HBAT (heptavalent types A-G). This product replaces bivalent antitoxins type AB and antitoxin type E. Baby Botulism Immune Globulin (BIG)	Food-borne botulism Wound botulism Botulism as a biological weapon Note: Heptavalent antitoxin not currently recommended for infant botulism	None. Product is stored at 9 CDC regional centers (including the Chicago Quarantine). To obtain antitoxin, hospitals must call their Local or State Department of Public Health, which will contact the CDC in Atlanta. The CDC emergency operation center can be reached at 770-488-7100.	Antitoxin must be given in a critical care setting since it is an equine-derived product. Note: Product must be refrigerated at all times. Heptavalent antitoxin is stored in the CDC SNS. BabyBIG is available for infant botulism types A and B, through the Infant Botulism Treatment and Prevention Program, sponsored by the California Department of Public Health, telephone: 510-231-7600, www.infantbotulism.org/physician/obtain.php.
Calcium disodium EDTA (Versenate)	Lead Zinc salts (eg, zinc chloride)	2x 5 mL vials (200 mg/mL)	One vial provides 1 day of therapy for a child. 2 to 4 g per 24 h may be necessary in adult patients. Stock in pharmacy. Important note: Edetate disodium (Endrate) is not the same as calcium disodium EDTA, and is used primarily as an IV chelator for emergent treatment of hypercalcemia.
Calcium chloride and Calcium gluconate	Fluoride salts (eg, NaF) Hydrofluoric acid (HF) Hyperkalemia (not digoxin-induced) Hypermagnesemia	10% calcium chloride: 10x 10 mL vials 10% calcium gluconate: 30x 10 mL vials	Many vials of calcium chloride may be necessary in life-threatening HF poisoning. Stock in ED. More may be stocked in pharmacy. The chloride salt provides 3x more calcium than the gluconate salt. Calcium chloride is very irritating and administration through a central line is preferable. Topical calcium gluconate or carbonate gels may be extemporaneously prepared by the pharmacy. Calgonate (calcium gluconate 2.5% gel) is not FDA approved but is manufactured in an FDA-GMP approved facility and is distributed by Calgonate Corp in Port St. Lucie, Florida.
Centruroides Immune F(ab)$_2$ – Equine (Anascorp)	Scorpion envenomation	None	This product is manufactured in Mexico by the Instituto Bioclon. In the U.S., it is marketed by Rare Disease Therapeutics, Inc. in Nashville, Tennessee. It was approved by the FDA in 2011 and can be stored at room temperature. Usual dose: 1 to 3 vials.

ANTIDOTE	POISON/DRUG/TOXIN	SUGGESTED MINIMUM STOCK QUANTITY	RATIONALE/COMMENTS
Cyanide Antidote: Sodium nitrite and sodium thiosulfate (Nithiodote)	Acetonitrile Acrylonitrile Bromates (thiosulfate only) Chlorates (thiosulfate only) Cyanide (eg, HCN, KCN, and NaCN) Cyanogen chloride Cyanogenic glycoside natural sources (eg, apricot pits and peach pits) Hydrogen sulfide (nitrites only) Laetrile Mustard agents (thiosulfate only) Nitroprusside (thiosulfate only) Smoke inhalation (combustion of synthetic materials)	2-4 kits Each kit contains: 1 vial (10 mL) sodium nitrite (300 mg); 1 vial (50 mL) sodium thiosulfate (12.5 g) Stocking this kit may be unnecessary if an adequate supply of hydroxocobalamin HCl is available.	Stock 2 kits in the ED. Consider also stocking 2 kits in the pharmacy. Note: This kit has a short shelf life of 24 months. Significant adverse reactions include methemoglobinemia and hypotension. For smoke inhalation victims, thiosulfate without the use of nitrites may be considered. In 2012, the cyanide kit containing 12 amyl nitrite pearls, two 10 mL sodium nitrite vials, and two 50 mL sodium thiosulfate vials was discontinued by the manufacturer and is no longer available in the U.S. Amyl nitrite ampules may be ordered separately.
Deferoxamine mesylate (Desferal)	Iron Deferoxamine has also been used for chronic aluminum toxicity in chronic kidney disease patients.	12-36 g (Available in 500 mg and 2 g vials)	Quantity recommended supplies 8 to 24 h of therapy for a 100 kg adult. Per package insert, the maximum daily dose is 6 g (12 vials). However, this dose may be exceeded in serious acute iron poisonings. Stock in pharmacy.
Digoxin immune Fab (Digibind, Digifab)	Cardiac glycoside-containing plants (eg, foxglove and oleander) Digitoxin Digoxin	15 vials Each vial (38 mg) neutralizes 0.5 mg of digoxin	An initial dose of 2-3 vials for chronic poisoning or 10 vials for acute poisoning may be given to a digoxin-poisoned patient in whom the digoxin level is unknown. More may be necessary in severe intoxications. 15 vials would effectively neutralize a steady-state digoxin level of 15 ng/mL in a 100 kg patient. Know nearest source of additional supply. Stock in ED or pharmacy.
Dimercaprol (BAL in oil)	Arsenic Copper Gold Lead Lewisite Mercury	4x 3 mL vials (100 mg/mL)	This amount provides 3 doses of 3 to 5 mg/kg/dose given q 4 h to treat 1 seriously poisoned adult (up to 100 kg) or provides enough to treat a 15 kg child for more than 24 h. Stock in pharmacy.

(Continued)

ANTIDOTE	POISON/DRUG/TOXIN	SUGGESTED MINIMUM STOCK QUANTITY	RATIONALE/COMMENTS
Ethanol	Ethylene glycol Methanol	Ethanol is unnecessary if adequate amounts of fomepizole are stocked. Consider stocking 180-360 g in the form of 95% ethanol or equivalents (10% ethanol can be prepared from dehydrated alcohol and D5W for IV use).	180 g provides loading and maintenance doses for a 100 kg adult for 8-24 h. More alcohol or fomepizole will be needed during dialysis or prolonged treatment. 95% or 40% alcohol diluted in juice may be given PO if IV alcohol is unavailable. Stock in pharmacy. Note: See also fomepizole in this chart. Ethanol may cause hypotension or metabolic abnormalities (eg, hypoglycemia) especially in pediatric patients. Since ethanol treatment for toxic alcohol poisoning is not FDA approved and fomepizole offers greater efficacy and safety, fomepizole is the preferred alcohol dehydrogenase inhibitor.
Fat emulsion (Intralipid, Liposyn II, Liposyn III)	Local anesthetics and possibly other cardiac toxins (eg, bupropion, calcium channel blockers, cocaine, beta blockers, tricyclic antidepressants)	Quantity determined by institution. Available in 100 mL of 20% emulsion.	Fat emulsion is an experimental therapy showing promise in the reverse of cardiac toxicity induced by local anesthetics and other cardiac toxins. The evidence for the efficacy of fat emulsion therapy is based on animal studies and human case reports, and its safety has not yet been established. Consultation with a regional PCC toxicologist is advised. Initial dose: 1.5 mL/kg IV over 1 minute. Follow with infusion of 0.25 mL/kg/min over 30 minutes. Loading dose may be repeated once. Rate may be increased to 0.5 mL/kg/min for 60 minutes if blood pressure drops. Maximum total dose is 8 mL/kg. Consider storage in pharmacy, ED, and possibly surgical units.
Flumazenil (Romazicon)	Benzodiazepines	Total 6-12 mg Available in 5 and 10 mL vials (0.1 mg/mL)	Due to risk of seizures, use with extreme caution, if at all, in poisoned patients. More may be stocked in the pharmacy for use in reversal of conscious sedation. Stock in ED, pharmacy, and any unit where procedural sedation is performed.
Folic acid and Folinic acid (Leucovorin)	Formaldehyde/ Formic acid Methanol Methotrexate, Trimetrexate Pyrimethamine Trimethoprim	Folic acid: 3x 50 mg vials Folinic acid: 1x 50 mg vial	For adjunctive treatment of methanol-poisoned patients with an acidosis, give 50 mg folinic acid initially, then 50 mg of folic acid q 4 h for 6 doses. For methotrexate-poisoned patients, administer folinic acid only; consult PCC for dosing information. Stock in pharmacy.
Fomepizole (Antizol) 4-methylpyrazole (4-MP)	Ethylene glycol Methanol	1 to 2x 1.5 g vials Note: Available in a kit of 4x 1.5 g vials	One 1.5 g vial provides an initial dose of 15 mg/kg/12 h to an adult weighing up to 100 kg. Hospitals with critical care and hemodialysis capabilities should consider stocking 1 kit of 4 vials or more. More frequent dosing (ie, every 4 h) is required if the patient is dialyzed. Ethanol is unnecessary if adequate supply of fomepizole is stocked. Fomepizole is preferred to ethanol because of ease of use, fewer adverse effects, simplicity of dosing, and less need for close monitoring. Stock in pharmacy. Know where nearest alternate supply is located.

ANTIDOTE	POISON/DRUG/TOXIN	SUGGESTED MINIMUM STOCK QUANTITY	RATIONALE/COMMENTS
Glucagon HCl	Beta blockers	50 to 90x 1 mg vials	This quantity provides 4 to 8 h of maximum dosing, ie, a 10 mg IV bolus dose followed by 10 mg/h. More may be necessary. Know where nearest alternate supply is located. Stock 30 mg in ED and remainder in pharmacy.
Hydroxocobalamin HCl (Cyanokit)	Acetonitrile Acrylonitrile Cyanide (eg, HCN, KCN, and NaCN) Cyanogen chloride Cyanogenic glycoside natural sources (eg, apricot pits and peach pits) Laetrile Nitroprusside Smoke inhalation (combustion of synthetic materials)	2 to 4 kits Each kit contains one 5 g vial. Note: Diluent is not included in the kit.	Seriously poisoned cyanide patients may require 5 to 10 g (1 to 2 kits). Stock 2 kits in ED. Consider also stocking 2 kits in the pharmacy. The product has a shelf life of 30 months post-manufacture.
Hyperbaric oxygen (HBO)	Carbon monoxide and possibly the following: Carbon tetrachloride Cyanide Hydrogen sulfide Methemoglobinemia	Post the location and phone number of nearest HBO chamber in the ED.	Consult PCC to determine if HBO treatment is indicated.
Insulin and dextrose	Calcium channel blockers (diltiazem, nifedipine, verapamil)	Quantity determined by institution. Humulin R is available as 100 units/mL in a 1.5 mL cartridge and 10 mL bottle. Dextrose 50% in water is available in 50 mL ampules and syringes. Dextrose 25% is available in 10 mL vials and syringes for pediatric use.	High dose insulin and dextrose therapy can reverse cardiovascular toxicity associated with calcium channel blocker overdose. IV Bolus: Recommended starting dose of 1 unit/kg regular insulin (with 1 amp D_{50}); The lowest maintenance dose is 0.5-1 units/kg/h. Higher doses may be considered under consultation with medical toxicologist. Stock in ED and pharmacy.
Methylene blue	Methemoglobin-inducing agents including: Aniline dyes Dapsone Dinitrophenol Local anesthetics (eg, benzocaine) Metoclopramide Monomethylhydrazine-containing mushrooms (eg, *Gyromitra*) Naphthalene Nitrates and nitrites Nitrobenzene Phenazopyridine	6x 10 mL vials (10 mg/mL)	The usual dose is 1 to 2 mg/kg IV (0.1 to 0.2 mL/kg). A second dose may be given in 1 h. More may be necessary. 6 vials provide 3 doses of 2 mg/kg for a 100 kg adult. Stock in pharmacy. *(Continued)*

ANTIDOTE	POISON/DRUG/TOXIN	SUGGESTED MINIMUM STOCK QUANTITY	RATIONALE/COMMENTS
Naloxone (Narcan)	Alpha$_2$ agonists (eg, clonidine, guanabenz, and guanfacine) Unknown poisoning with mental status depression Opioids (eg, codeine, diphenoxylate, fentanyl, heroin, meperidine, morphine, and propoxyphene)	Naloxone: total of 40 mg, any combination of 0.4 mg and 2 mg vials	Stock 20 mg naloxone in the ED and 20 mg elsewhere in the institution.
Octreotide acetate (Sandostatin)	Sulfonylurea hypoglycemic agents (eg, glipizide, glyburide)	225 mcg Available in 1 mL vials (0.05 mg/mL, 0.1 mg/mL, and 0.5 mg/mL) and 5 mL multidose vials (0.2 mg/mL and 1 mg/mL)	Octreotide acetate blocks the release of insulin from pancreatic beta cells that, along with IV dextrose, can reverse sulfonylurea-induced hypoglycemia. The usual adult dose is 50 to 100 mcg IV or SC q 6 to 12 h. The usual pediatric dose is 1 to 1.5 mcg/kg IV or SC q 6 to 12 h. 225 mcg provides 4x 75 mcg adult doses. Stock in pharmacy.
D-Penicillamine (Cuprimine)	Arsenic Copper Lead Mercury	None required as an antidote. Available in bottles of 100 (250 mg capsules)	D-Penicillamine is no longer considered the drug of choice for heavy metal poisonings. It may be stocked in the pharmacy for other indications such as Wilson's disease or rheumatoid arthritis.
Physostigmine salicylate (Antilirium)	Anticholinergic alkaloid-containing plants (eg, deadly nightshade and jimson weed) Antihistamines Atropine and other anticholinergic agents	2x 2 mL vials (1 mg/mL)	Usual adult dose is 1 to 2 mg slow IV push. Note: Duration of effect is 30 to 60 minutes. Stock in ED or pharmacy.
Phytonadione (Vitamin K$_1$) (Aquamephyton, Mephyton)	Indandione derivatives Long-acting anticoagulant rodenticides (eg, brodifacoum and bromadiolone) Warfarin	100 mg injectable; 100 mg oral Available as: 0.5 mL vials (2 mg/mL) and 1 mL vials (10 mg/mL) 5 mg tablets in packages of 10, 12, and 100	Patients who are poisoned by long-acting anticoagulant rodenticides may require 50 to 100 mg/day or more for weeks to months to maintain normal INRs. An oral suspension for pediatric patients may be extemporaneously prepared by the pharmacy. Stock in pharmacy.
Pralidoxime chloride (2-PAM) (Protopam)	OPIs Nerve agents (eg, sarin, soman, tabun, and VX) And possibly: Antimyasthenic agents (eg, pyridostigmine) Tacrine	18x 1 g vials. Also available as: Pralidoxime chloride military-style auto-injectors: 600 mg/2 mL Atropine Sulfate 2.1 mg/0.7 mL with Pralidoxime chloride 600 mg/2 mL (DuoDote)	18 g provides an adult dose of 750 mg/h for 24 h. More may be needed in severe poisoning. Healthcare facilities located in agricultural areas where OPIs are used should maintain adequate supplies. Product is necessary to be adequately prepared for WMD incidents; the suggested amount may not be sufficient for mass casualty events. Auto-injectors are available from Bound Tree Medical, Inc (800-533-0523). The drugs stocked in chempack containers are intended for use in mass casualty events only. Stock in ED or pharmacy.

©Illinois Poison Center March, 2014. PDR has secured written permission to reprint the Antidote Chart for the sole purpose of providing an additional educational reference within this publication. Reproduction or resale of this list without the written authorization from the Illinois Poison Center is strictly prohibited.

ANTIDOTE	POISON/DRUG/TOXIN	SUGGESTED MINIMUM STOCK QUANTITY	RATIONALE/COMMENTS
Protamine sulfate	Heparin Low molecular weight heparins (eg, enoxaparin, dalteparin, tinzaparin)	Variable, consider recommendation of hospital Pharmacy and Therapeutics Committee Available as 5 mL vials (10 mg/mL) and 25 mL vials (250 mg/25 mL)	The usual dose is 1 to 1.5 mg for each 100 units of heparin. Stock in pharmacy in refrigerator. Preservative-free formulation does not require refrigeration.
Pyridoxine HCl (Vitamin B_6)	Acrylamide Ethylene glycol Hydrazine Hydrazine MAOIs (isocarboxazid, phenelzine) Isoniazid (INH) Monomethylhydrazine-containing mushrooms (eg, *Gyromitra*)	10 g (100 vials) Available as 1 mL vials (100 mg/mL)	Usual dose is 1 g pyridoxine HCl for each g of INH ingested. If amount ingested is unknown, give 5 g of pyridoxine. Repeat 5 g dose if seizures are uncontrolled. More may be necessary. Know nearest source of additional supply. For ethylene glycol, a dose of 100 mg/day may enhance the clearance of toxic metabolite. Stock in ED or pharmacy.
Silibinin (Legalon-SIL)	Cyclopeptide-containing mushrooms (eg, Amanita phalloides, Amanita verna, Amanita virosa, Galerina autumnalis, Lepiota josserandi, and others)	None 350 mg/vial	Silibinin is a water-soluble preparation of silymarin; a flavolignone extracted from the milk thistle plant. It inhibits uptake of cyclopeptides in hepatocytes. These hepatotoxins are responsible for high morbidity and mortality following ingestion of these mushrooms. Silibinin is manufactured by Madaus, Inc. in Germany, and has been widely used in Europe since 1984. The initial adult loading dose consists of a 1 h infusion of 5 mg/kg followed by the recommended daily dosage of 20 mg/kg via continuous IV infusion. Product is now available in the U.S. under an open-treatment investigational new drug application. Physicians can obtain the product free-of-charge by contacting the primary investigator at 866-520-4412.

(Continued)

ANTIDOTE	POISON/DRUG/TOXIN	SUGGESTED MINIMUM STOCK QUANTITY	RATIONALE/COMMENTS
Sodium bicarbonate	Chlorine gas Hyperkalemia Serum Alkalinization: Agents producing a quinidine-like effect as noted by widened QRS complex on EKG (eg, amantadine, carbamazepine, chloroquine, cocaine, diphenhydramine, flecainide, propafenone, propoxyphene, tricyclic antidepressants, quinidine, and related agents) Urine Alkalinization: Weakly acidic agents (eg, chlorophenoxy herbicides, chlorpropamide, methotrexate, phenobarbital, and salicylates)	20 to 25x 50 mL vials of either 8.4% (50 mEq/50 mL) or 7.5% (44 mEq/50 mL) Consider stocking 4.2% (5 mEq/10 mL) for pediatric patients.	Stock 20 vials in ED and remainder in pharmacy. Nebulized 2.5-5% sodium bicarbonate has been demonstrated in anecdotal case reports to provide symptomatic relief for chlorine gas inhalation.
Succimer (Chemet) Dimercaptosuccinic acid (DMSA)	Arsenic Lead Lewisite Mercury	0 to 10 capsules Available in bottles of 100 capsules (100 mg/capsule)	Initial treatment of severely symptomatic heavy metal poisoning consists of parenterally administered chelators, eg, BAL or calcium disodium EDTA. Patients who markedly improve may eventually be started on oral DMSA. Asymptomatic or minimally symptomatic patients do not require parenteral therapy and are often treated as outpatients with an oral chelator. FDA approved only for pediatric lead poisoning, however it has shown efficacy for other heavy metal poisonings. 10 capsules represent an initial dose of 10 mg/kg in a 100 kg adult. Stock in pharmacy.

ADJUNCTIVE AGENTS			
ADJUNCTIVE AGENT	POISON/DRUG/TOXIN	SUGGESTED MINIMUM STOCK QUANTITY	RATIONALE/COMMENTS
Benztropine mesylate (Cogentin)	Medications causing a dystonic reaction or other EPS	Quantity determined by institution. Available in tablets of 0.5 mg, 1 mg, 2 mg (bottles of 100 or 1,000) and in 1 mg/mL injectable (2 mL vial) form.	Maximum daily adult dose is 6 mg/d. Stock some in ED and some in pharmacy. See also diphenhydramine.

ADJUNCTIVE AGENTS *(Continued)*

ADJUNCTIVE AGENT	POISON/DRUG/TOXIN	SUGGESTED MINIMUM STOCK QUANTITY	RATIONALE/COMMENTS
L-Carnitine (Carnitor)	Valproic acid	Quantity determined by institution. Available as 330 mg and 500 mg tablets, 250 mg capsules, 200 mg/mL IV solution, and 100 mg/mL PO solution.	L-Carnitine may be considered in valproate intoxication associated with elevated serum ammonia levels and/or hepatotoxicity. Doses of 100 mg/kg/d up to 2 g a day PO divided into 3 doses, or 150-500 mg/kg/d IV (maximum 3 g daily) in 3 or 4 divided doses are recommended for a period of 3 to 4 days or until clinical improvement. Stock in pharmacy.
Cyproheptadine HCl (Periactin)	Medications causing serotonin syndrome	Quantity determined by institution. Available in 4 mg tablets (bottles of 100, 250, 500, and 1,000) and 2 mg/5 mL PO solution.	Cyproheptadine HCl is a nonspecific 5-HT antagonist that has been used in the treatment of serotonin syndrome. Adult dose is 12 mg PO initially, followed by 2 mg every 2 h if symptoms persist. Maintenance dose is 8 mg every 6 h. Maximum of 32 mg/day. Pediatric dose is 0.25 mg/kg/day divided every 6 h, with a max dose of 12 mg/day. Stock in pharmacy.
Dantrolene sodium (Dantrium)	Medications causing NMS Medications causing malignant hyperthermia	Quantity determined by institution. Available in 25, 50, and 100 mg capsules (bottles of 100 or 500) and injectable 20 mg/vial form.	The recommended dose for NMS is 1 mg/kg IV; may repeat as needed every 5 to 10 minutes for a maximum of 10 mg/kg. Dantrolene sodium inhibits calcium release from the sarcoplasmic reticulum of skeletal muscle and thereby reduces rigidity. Stock in pharmacy. Any hospital using inhalational anesthetics should strongly consider stocking dantrolene for treatment of malignant hyperthermia.
Diazepam (Valium)	Chloroquine and related antimalarial drugs NMS Serotonin syndrome Severe agitation from any toxic exposure/overdose (eg, cocaine, PCP, methamphetamine)	Quantity determined by institution. Available as 5 mg/mL injectables in 2 mL ampules, 2 mL disposable syringes, and 10 mL multidose vials. Diazepam military-style auto-injectors for nerve agent-induced seizures: 10 mg/2 mL.	Diazepam and other benzodiazepines are also used in poisoned and nonpoisoned patients as an anticonvulsant, muscle relaxant, and antianxiety agent. They are usually the first-line therapy for drug-induced agitation, tachycardia, and hypertension. Benzodiazepines are a mainstay in the treatment of NMS and serotonin syndrome. Stock in ED and pharmacy. Adequate supply is necessary to be prepared for WMD incidents. Auto-injectors are available from Bound Tree Medical, Inc (800-533-0523). Diazepam is used in conjunction with epinephrine for patients with chloroquine/hydroxychloroquine toxicity (seizures, dysrhythmias, hypotension) or if the amount ingested is more than 5 g. Intravenous loading dose 2 mg/kg over 30 minutes. Maintenance dose of 1 to 2 mg/kg per day for 2 to 4 days.

(Continued)

ADJUNCTIVE AGENTS *(Continued)*

ADJUNCTIVE AGENT	POISON/DRUG/TOXIN	SUGGESTED MINIMUM STOCK QUANTITY	RATIONALE/COMMENTS
Diphenhydramine HCL (Benadryl)	Medications causing a dystonic reaction or other EPS	Quantity determined by institution. Available in 25 and 50 mg capsules (bottles of 30, 100, or 1,000). Also in oral liquid formulation of 12.5 mg/5 mL (4 ounce bottle) and 50 mg/mL injectable syringes.	In addition to its use as an anticholinergic agent, diphenhydramine is a widely used antihistamine in the management of minor or severe allergic reactions. Stock in ED and pharmacy.
Glycopyrrolate bromide (Robinul)	OPIs Nerve agents	Quantity determined by institution. Available as 0.2 mg/mL in vials of 1 mL, 2 mL, 5 mL, and 20 mL.	The dose of glycopyrrolate for OPI poisoning is 0.01 to 0.02 mg/kg IV. Glycopyrrolate is a quaternary ammonium antimuscarinic agent that may assist in the control of hypersecretions caused by acetylcholinesterase inhibition. This agent produces less tachycardia and CNS effects than atropine. Stock in ED and pharmacy.
Phentolamine mesylate (Regitine)	Catecholamine extravasation Intradigital epinephrine injection	Quantity determined by institution. Available as a 5 mg/vial powder with 1 mL diluent.	Phentolamine is an alpha-adrenergic antagonist that will reverse vasoconstriction and peripheral ischemia associated with extravasation of adrenergic agents. When phentolamine is not available, consider using subcutaneous terbutaline sulfate (Brethine). Phentolamine also offers an additional option in the management of drug-induced hypertension. Stock in ED and pharmacy.
Sodium nitrite	Hydrogen sulfide (H_2S)	0 to 1 vial. Available as 3% sodium nitrite in 10 mL vials.	Nitrite therapy for H_2S poisoning is controversial. Seriously poisoned patients should receive nitrites within 1 h of exposure. Sodium thiosulfate is not administered in H_2S poisoning. The product is available from Hope Pharmaceuticals in Scottsdale, Arizona. If the amyl nitrite/sodium nitrite/sodium thiosulfate cyanide antidote kits are stocked, additional sodium nitrite vials may not be necessary. Stock in pharmacy.
Sodium thiosulfate	Bromates Chlorates Mustard agents Nitroprusside Smoke inhalation	Quantity determined by institution. Available in 100 mg/mL, 10 mL vials and 250 mg/mL, 50 mL vials.	Sodium thiosulfate (without nitrites) has been advocated in the treatment of smoke inhalation related to cyanide exposure; however, it is not necessary if hydroxocobalamin is available. Sodium thiosulfate may be used in conjunction with cisplatin to reduce toxicity of this chemotherapy agent. Sodium thiosulfate is found in the amyl nitrite/sodium nitrite/sodium thiosulfate cyanide antidote kits; however, additional vials may be stocked. Stock in pharmacy.
Thiamine	Ethanol Ethylene glycol	Quantity determined by institution. Available as 100 mg/mL in 2 mL vials.	Parenteral thiamine precedes IV dextrose in patients with chronic ethanol abuse. Thiamine 100 mg every 6 h enhances clearance of toxic metabolites of ethylene glycol. Stock in ED and pharmacy.

AGENTS FOR RADIOLOGICAL EXPOSURES

AGENT	POISON/DRUG/TOXIN	SUGGESTED MINIMUM STOCK QUANTITY	RATIONALE/COMMENTS
Calcium-diethylenetriamine pentaacetic acid (Ca-DTPA; Pentetate calcium trisodium injection) Zinc-diethylenetriamine pentaacetic acid (Zn-DTPA; Pentetate zinc trisodium injection)	Internal contamination with transuranium elements: americium, curium, plutonium	Quantity determined by institution. Supplied as 200 mg/mL, 5 mL ampules for IV or inhalation administration. The product is sponsored through Hameln Pharmaceuticals, GmbH, of Hameln, Germany. Distributed in the U.S. by Akorn, Inc.	1 ampule provides the usual adult dose of 1 g q 24 h. More would be necessary in a mass casualty event. Ca-DTPA and Zn-DTPA are available through the SNS and REAC/TS, Oak Ridge, Tennessee at 865-576-3131 (business hours) or 865-576-1005 (after hours).
Potassium iodide, KI tablets (Iosat, Thyrosafe) KI liquid (Thyroshield, SSKI)	Prevents thyroid uptake of radioactive iodine (I-131)	Quantity determined by institution. Available in 130 mg and 65 mg tablets, and PO solutions: 65 mg/mL (30 mL bottle) and 1 g/mL (30 mL and 240 mL bottle).	One 130 mg tablet represents the initial daily adult dose. More would be necessary in a mass casualty event. KI tablets and oral solution are OTC. The Illinois Emergency Management Association makes KI tablets available to healthcare facilities and the general public located near nuclear reactors.
Prussian blue, ferric hexacyanoferrate (Radiogardase)	Radioactive cesium (Cs-137), radioactive thallium (Tl-201), and non-radioactive thallium	None recommended at the present time. Available in bottles of 30 capsules (500 mg/capsule).	The usual oral adult dose is 3 g, 3 times a day. The product is manufactured by Haupt Pharma Berlin GmbH for distribution by HEYL Chemisch-pharmazeutische Fabrik GmbH & Co. KG, Berlin, Germany, and is available in the U.S. from Heyltex Corporation. Prussian Blue is also available through the SNS and REAC/TS, Oak Ridge, Tennessee at 865-576-3131 (business hours) or 865-576-1005 (after hours).

Abbreviations: BAL = British anti-Lewisite; CDC = Centers for Disease Control and Prevention; ED = emergency department; EPS = extrapyramidal symptom; NMS = neuroleptic malignant syndrome; OPI = organophosphate insecticide; PCC = poison control center; REAC/TS = radiation emergency assistance center/training site; SNS = Strategic National Stockpile; WMD = weapons of mass destruction.

APPROVED RISK EVALUATION AND MITIGATION STRATEGIES

The Food and Drug Administration Amendments Act of 2007 gave FDA the authority to require a Risk Evaluation and Mitigation Strategy (REMS) from manufacturers to ensure that the benefits of a drug or biological product outweigh its risks. The table below provides a list of products for which current REMS have been approved by FDA, as of publication.

CURRENTLY APPROVED INDIVIDUAL REMS

DRUG NAME (generic name)

Actemra (tocilizumab) Injection

Adasuve (loxapine) Inhalation Powder

Adempas (riociguat) Tablets

Androgel (testosterone) 1% Gel

Androgel (testosterone) 1.62% Gel

Aranesp (darbepoetin alfa) Injection

Axiron (testosterone) Topical Solution

Bydureon (exenatide) Extended-Release for Injectable Suspension

Caprelsa (vandetanib) Tablets

Chantix (varenicline) Tablets

Eliquis (apixaban) Tablets

Entereg (alvimopan) Capsules

Epogen/Procrit (epoetin alfa) Injection

Extraneal (icodextrin) Intraperitoneal Solution

Forteo (teriparatide [rDNA origin]) Injection

Fortesta (testosterone) Gel

Gattex (teduglutide [rDNA origin]) Injection

Gilenya (fingolimod) Capsules

Iclusig (ponatinib) Tablets

Juxtapid (lomitapide) Capsules

Krystexxa (pegloticase) Injection

Kynamro (mipomersen sodium)

Letairis (ambrisentan) Tablets

Lotronex (alosetron hydrochloride) Tablets

Lumizyme (alglucosidase alfa)

Metoclopramide Oral Solution

Mifeprex (mifepristone) Tablets

Multaq (dronedarone) Tablets

Nplate (romiplostim) for Subcutaneous Injection

Nulojix (belatacept)

Omontys (peginesatide) Injection

Opsumit (macitentan) Tablets

Pomalyst (pomalidomide) Capsules

Potiga (ezogabine) Tablets

Prolia (denosumab) Injection

Promacta (eltrombopag) Tablets

Qsymia (phentermine/topiramate) Extended-Release Capsules

DRUG NAME (generic name)

Revlimid (lenalidomide) Capsules

Sabril (vigabatrin) Oral Solution

Sabril (vigabatrin) Tablets

Soliris (eculizumab) Injection

Stelara (ustekinumab) Injection

Suboxone (buprenorphine/naloxone) Sublingual Film

Suboxone (buprenorphine/naloxone) Sublingual Tablets

Subutex (buprenorphine) Sublingual Tablets

Tapentadol Tablets

Testim (testosterone) Gel

Testosterone Gel

Thalomid (thalidomide) Capsules

Tikosyn (dofetilide) Capsules

Tracleer (bosentan) Tablets

Truvada (emtricitabine/tenofovir disoproxil fumarate) Tablets

Tysabri (natalizumab) Intravenous Injection

Versacloz (clozapine) Oral Suspension

Vibativ (telavancin) Injection

Victoza (liraglutide) Injection

Vivitrol (naltrexone) Extended-Release Injectable Suspension

Xarelto (rivaroxaban) Tablets

Xeljanz (tofacitinib) Tablets

Xenazine (tetrabenazine) Tablets

Xiaflex (collagenase clostridium histolyticum) Injection

Yervoy (ipilimumab) Injection

Zyban (bupropion hydrochloride) Sustained-Release Tablets

Zyprexa Relprevv (olanzapine) Extended-Release Injection

CURRENTLY APPROVED SHARED SYSTEM REMS

NAME OF SHARED SYSTEM REMS

Buprenorphine Transmucosal Products for Opioid Dependence (BTOD)

Extended-Release and Long-Acting Opioid Analgesics

Isotretinoin iPLEDGE

Mycophenolate

Rosiglitazone

Transmucosal Immediate-Release Fentanyl (TIRF) Products

SUGAR-FREE PRODUCTS

The following is a selection of sugar-free products and their corresponding manufacturers (in italics), grouped by therapeutic category. When recommending these products to diabetic patients, keep in mind that many may contain sorbitol, alcohol, or other sources of carbohydrates. This list is not comprehensive. Generic and alternate brands may be available. Check product labeling for a current listing of inactive ingredients.

Analgesics

Addaprin Tablets ‡	*Otis Clapp/Dover*
Aminofen Tablets ‡	*Otis Clapp/Dover*
Back Pain-Off Tablets ‡	*Medique*
Children's Slipup Liquid	*Silarx*
I-Prin Tablets ‡	*Medique*
Medi-Seltzer Effervescent Tablets	*Medique*
Methadose Sugar Free Oral Concentrate	*Mallinckrodt*

Antacids/Antiflatulents

Alcalak Chewable Tablets* † ‡ §	*Medique*
Diotame Chewable Tablets* † ‡ §	*Medique*
Pepto-Bismol Caplets † ‡	*Procter & Gamble*
Tums Extra Sugar Free Tablets* §	*GlaxoSmithKline Consumer*

Antiasthmatics/Respiratory Agents

Jay-Phyl Syrup	*JayMac*

Antidiarrheals

Diamode ‡	*Medique*

Corticosteroids

Pediapred Solution* §	*UCB*

Cough/Cold/Allergy Preparations

Arbinoxa Solution* §	*Pernix*
Broncotron Liquid	*Seyer Pharmatec*
Broncotron-D Suspension	*Seyer Pharmatec*
Cetafen Cold Tablets ‡	*Hart Health and Safety*
Cetafen Cough & Cold Tablets ‡	*Hart Health and Safety*
Cheratussin DAC Liquid	*Qualitest*
Children's Sudafed Nasal	*McNeil Consumer*
Children's Sudafed PE Cold & Cough Liquid* † §	*McNeil Consumer*
Despec Liquid	*International Ethical*
Despec-SF Liquid	*International Ethical*
Diabetic Maximum Strength Siltussin-DM DAS-Na	*Silarx*
Diabetic Siltussin DAS-Na	*Silarx*
Diabetic Siltussin-DM DAS-Na	*Silarx*

Diabetic Tussin	*Health Care Products*
Diabetic Tussin DM Liquid §	*Health Care Products*
Diabetic Tussin DM Maximum Strength §	*Health Care Products*
Diphen Capsules ‡	*Medique*
Gilphex TR Tablets ‡	*Gil*
Neotuss-D Liquid † §	*A.G. Marin*
Neotuss S/F Liquid † §	*A.G. Marin*
Poly Hist PD Solution	*Poly*
Scot-Tussin Diabetes CF Liquid	*Scot-Tussin*
Scot-Tussin Expectorant Solution	*Scot-Tussin*
Scot-Tussin Senior Solution	*Scot-Tussin*
Siltussin DAS Liquid* † §	*Silarx*
Siltussin DM DAS Cough Formula Syrup* † §	*Silarx*
Supress DX Pediatric Drops † §	*Kramer-Novis*
Z-Tuss AC Syrup † §	*Magna*
Z-Tuss E Liquid † §	*Magna*

Fluoride Preparations

Fluor-A-Day Liquid	*Arbor*
Fluor-A-Day Tablets* † §	*Arbor*
Sensodyne Tartar Control with Whitening † ‡ §	*GlaxoSmithKline Consumer*
Sensodyne with Fluoride Cool Gel* † ‡ §	*GlaxoSmithKline Consumer*
Sensodyne with Fluoride Toothpaste Original Flavor* † ‡ §	*GlaxoSmithKline Consumer*

Laxatives

Benefiber (All) Products ‡	*Novartis*
Citrucel (All) Products ‡ §	*GlaxoSmithKline Consumer*
Colace Solution	*Purdue Products*
Fiber Choice Tablets* ‡ §	*GlaxoSmithKline Consumer*
Fibro-XL Capsules	*Key*
Konsyl Balance Powder ‡	*Konsyl*
Konsyl Easy Mix Formula Powder ‡	*Konsyl*
Konsyl Fiber Caplets ‡	*Konsyl*
Konsyl Orange SF Powder ‡ §	*Konsyl*
Konsyl Powder ‡	*Konsyl*
Konsyl Psyllium Capsules	*Konsyl*

* Contains sorbitol.
† May contain other sugar alcohols (eg, glycerol, isomalt, maltitol, mannitol, xylitol).
‡ May contain other sources of carbohydrates (eg, cellulose, lactose, maltodextrin, polydextrose, starch).
§ May contain natural or artificial flavors.

(Continued)

Laxatives (Continued)

Konsyl Senna Prompt Capsules	Konsyl
Metamucil Sugar-Free Smooth Texture Powders ‡ §	Procter & Gamble
Metamucil Capsules	Procter & Gamble
Reguloid Capsules	Rugby
Reguloid Powder Orange Flavor ‡ §	Rugby
Reguloid Sugar-Free Powder Regular Flavor ‡	Rugby

Mouth/Throat Preparations

Cepacol Ultra Sore Throat Spray † §	Reckitt Benckiser
Cepacol Sore Throat + Coating Relief Lozenge † §	Reckitt Benckiser
Cepacol Sore Throat Lozenges † §	Reckitt Benckiser
Cheracol Sore Throat Spray †	Lee
Chloraseptic Spray* † §	Prestige
Diabetic Tussin Cough Drops † §	Health Care Products
Fisherman's Friend Sugar Free Mint Lozenges*	Lofthouse of Fleetwood
Listerine Pocketpaks Film ‡ §	Johnson & Johnson
Luden's Sugar Free Wild Cherry Throat Drops † §	Prestige Brands
Medikoff Sugar Free Drops †	Medique
N'ice Lozenges* §	Heritage/Insight
Oragesic Solution* §	Parnell

Vitamins/Minerals/Supplements

Alcalak Tablets* † ‡	Medique
Apetigen Elixir* †	Kramer-Novis
Apptrim Capsules	Physician Therapeutics
Apptrim-D Capsules	Physician Therapeutics
Bevitamel Tablets	Westlake Labs
Bugs Bunny Complete	Bayer
Calcet Petites Tablets	Mission Pharmacal
Calcimin-300 Tablets	Key
Cerefolin NAC Tablets	Pamlab
Cerefolin Tablets	Pamlab
Chromacaps ‡	Key
Delta D3 Tablets ‡	Freeda Vitamins
DHEA Capsules	ADH Health Products
Diatx ZN Tablets ‡	Centrix
Diucaps Capsules	Legere
DL-Phen-500 Capsules	Key
Enterex Diabetic Liquid ‡	Victus
Evening Primrose Oil Capsules †	Nature's Bounty
Extress (All) Tablets	Key
Eyetamins Tablets ‡	Rexall Naturalist

Fem-Cal Citrate Tablets ‡	Freeda Vitamins
Fem-Cal Plus Tablets	Freeda Vitamins
Fem-Cal Tablets ‡	Freeda Vitamins
Ferrocite Plus Tablets ‡	Breckenridge
Folacin-800 Tablets ‡	Key
Folbee AR Tablets ‡	Breckenridge
Folbee Plus CZ Tablets ‡	Breckenridge
Folbee Plus Tablets ‡	Breckenridge
Folbee Tablets ‡	Breckenridge
Folplex 2.2 Tablets ‡	Breckenridge
Gabadone Capsules	Physician Therapeutics
Gram-O-Leci Tablets* † ‡	Freeda Vitamins
Hypertensa Capsules ‡	Physician Therapeutics
Lynae Calcium/Vitamin C Chewable Tablets	Boscogen
Lynae Chondroitin/ Glucosamine Capsules	Boscogen
Lynae Ginse-Cool Chewable Tablets	Boscogen
Magimin Tablets ‡	Key
Magnacaps Capsules ‡	Key
Medi-Lyte Tablets ‡	Medique
Metanx Tablets ‡	Pamlab
Multi-Delyn (All) Liquids †	Silarx
New Life Hair Tablets ‡	Rexall Naturalist
Nutrisure OTC Tablets	Westlake Labs
Nutrivit Solution* † §	Llorens
O-Cal Fa Tablets ‡	Pharmics
Os-Cal 500 + D Tablets ‡	GlaxoSmithKline Consumer
Powervites Tablets ‡	Green Turtle Bay Vitamin
Protect Cardio AF Capsules	Gil
Protect Plus AF Capsules	Gil
Protect Plus Liquid	Gil
Quintabs-M Tablets ‡	Freeda Vitamins
Quintabs Tablets ‡	Freeda Vitamins
Replace Capsules ‡	Key
Replace without Iron Capsules ‡	Key
Samolinic Softgels †	Key
Soy Care for Menopause Capsules	Inverness Medical
Span C Tablets ‡	Freeda Vitamins
Sunnie Tablets	Green Turtle Bay Vitamin
Sunvite Tablets † ‡	Sundown
Super Dec B100 Tablets ‡	Freeda Vitamins
Super Quints B-50 Tablets ‡	Freeda Vitamins
Supervite Liquid	Seyer Pharmatec
Theramine Capsules	Physician Therapeutics
Triamin Tablets	Key
Triamino Tablets* ‡	Freeda Vitamins
Ultramino Powder	Freeda Vitamins
Vitafol Tablets † ‡	Everett
Xtramins Tablets	Key

* Contains sorbitol.
† May contain other sugar alcohols (eg, glycerol, isomalt, maltitol, mannitol, xylitol).
‡ May contain other sources of carbohydrates (eg, cellulose, lactose, maltodextrin, polydextrose, starch).
§ May contain natural or artificial flavors.

Miscellaneous

Acidoll Capsules	*Key*
Alka-Gest Tablets	*Key*
Cytra-2 Solution* §	*Cypress*
Cytra-K Crystals	*Cypress*
Cytra-K Solution* §	*Cypress*
Namenda Solution* † §	*Forest*

* Contains sorbitol.
† May contain other sugar alcohols (eg, glycerol, isomalt, maltitol, mannitol, xylitol).
‡ May contain other sources of carbohydrates (eg, cellulose, lactose, maltodextrin, polydextrose, starch).
§ May contain natural or artificial flavors.

Brand/Generic Index

BRAND/GENERIC INDEX

Organized alphabetically, this index includes the brand and generic names of each drug in the Concise Drug Monographs section. The main monograph names are fully capitalized (eg, ALBUTEROL) and generic names are in initial caps (eg, Abacavir Sulfate). Any brand name associated with an entry is listed under the product.

A

Abacavir Sulfate
  Epzicom 372
  Trizivir 989
  Ziagen 1105
Abatacept
  Orencia 711
Abciximab
  ReoPro 832
ABELCET 1
ABILIFY 1
ABILIFY DISCMELT
  See Abilify 1
ABILIFY MAINTENA 3
Abiraterone Acetate
  Zytiga...............................1138
ABRAXANE 4
ABSORICA................................. 5
ABSTRAL................................... 7
ACANYA.................................... 8
Acarbose
  Precose 764
ACCOLATE 9
ACCUPRIL.................................10
ACCURETIC...............................11
Acebutolol HCl
  Sectral............................. 872
Acellular Pertussis
  Boostrix............................164
  Pediarix 737
ACEON 12
Acetaminophen
  Norco 677
  Ofirmev...........................700
  Percocet.......................... 745
  Roxicet 859
  Ultracet 1002
  Vicodin............................1037
ACETAMINOPHEN AND
  CODEINE TABLETS..............14
ACIPHEX...................................15
ACIPHEX SPRINKLE
  See Aciphex...........................15
Acitretin
  Soriatane......................... 896
Aclidinium Bromide
  Tudorza Pressair 994
ACTEMRA.................................16
ACTIQ.......................................17
ACTIVASE.................................18
ACTIVELLA................................20
ACTONEL 21
ACTOPLUS MET
  See Actoplus Met XR............ 22
ACTOPLUS MET XR................. 22

ACTOS................................... 24
ACULAR 25
ACULAR LS............................ 26
Acyclovir
  Zovirax Oral.....................1129
ADALAT CC 27
Adalimumab
  Humira 478
Adapalene
  Differin 301
  Epiduo............................. 365
ADCETRIS.............................. 28
ADDERALL 29
ADDERALL XR........................ 30
Adefovir Dipivoxil
  Hepsera 470
ADEMPAS.............................. 32
ADENOCARD.......................... 33
Adenosine
  Adenocard........................ 33
ADRENACLICK......................... 34
ADRENALIN............................ 35
ADVAIR DISKUS...................... 36
ADVAIR HFA 37
ADVICOR............................... 39
Afeditab CR
  See Adalat CC 27
AFINITOR 41
AFINITOR DISPERZ
  See Afinitor......................... 41
Aflibercept
  Eylea 395
AFLURIA............................... 42
AGGRASTAT 43
AGGRENOX 44
AGRYLIN
  See Anagrelide 79
ALACORT 45
ALBUTEROL 46
Albuterol
  Combivent Respimat......... 249
Albuterol Sulfate
  Duoneb 329
  ProAir HFA 779
  Ventolin HFA 1024
Alcaftadine
  Lastacaft 545
ALCORTIN-A........................... 47
ALDACTAZIDE 47
ALDACTONE 49
ALDARA................................. 50
Alemtuzumab
  Campath...........................189

ALENDRONATE 51
  Binosto.............................162
  Fosamax Plus D................ 432
Alfuzosin HCl
  Uroxatral 1010
ALIMTA................................. 52
Aliskiren
  Amturnide 78
  Tekamlo........................... 946
  Tekturna 947
  Tekturna HCT.................... 948
Allopurinol Sodium
  Aloprim 53
Almotriptan Malate
  Axert...............................133
Alogliptin
  Kazano 530
  Nesina 659
  Oseni............................... 718
ALOPRIM 53
Alosetron HCl
  Lotronex 584
ALOXI 54
ALPHAGAN P........................ 55
Alprazolam
  Niravam 672
  Xanax..............................1069
  Xanax XR..........................1070
ALREX 56
ALSUMA 57
ALTABAX 58
ALTACE 58
Alteplase
  Activase 18
ALTOPREV............................ 60
ALVESCO 61
Alvimopan
  Entereg 361
AMANTADINE....................... 62
AMARYL............................... 63
AMBIEN................................ 64
AMBIEN CR........................... 65
AMBISOME 66
Ambrisentan
  Letairis 551
AMERGE............................... 67
AMIKACIN............................. 69
Amikacin Sulfate
  Amikacin 69
Aminobenzoate Potassium
  Potaba............................. 758
AMIODARONE
  See Nexterone 668
Amiodarone HCl
  Cordarone 257
  Nexterone........................ 668

AMITIZA 70

Amlodipine
Amturnide 78
Azor 139
Exforge 391
Exforge HCT 392
Tekamlo 946
Tribenzor 982
Twynsta 996

Amlodipine Besylate
Caduet 182
Lotrel 581
Norvasc 682

AMNESTEEM 71

AMOXICILLIN® 72

Amoxicillin
Augmentin 119
Augmentin XR 120
Moxatag 639
Prevpac 773

AMOXICILLIN/
CLAVULANATE 600/42.9 ... 73

Amphetamine Salt Combo
Adderall 29
Adderall XR 30

AMPHOTEC 74

Amphotericin B Lipid Complex
Abelcet 1
Amphotec 74

Amphotericin B Liposome
AmBisome 66

AMPICILLIN INJECTION 75

AMPICILLIN ORAL 76

Ampicillin Sodium
Unasyn 1004

AMPYRA 77

AMRIX 77

AMTURNIDE 78

ANAGRELIDE 79

Anaprox
See Naprosyn 649

Anaprox DS
See Naprosyn 649

Anastrozole
Arimidex 100

ANCOBON 80

ANDRODERM 81

ANDROGEL 82

ANGELIQ 84

ANGIOMAX 85

Anhydrous Citric Acid
Prepopik 771

Anidulafungin
Eraxis 374

ANTARA 86

ANZEMET 87

APIDRA 88

APIDRA SOLOSTAR
See Apidra 88

Apixaban
Eliquis 345

APLENZIN 89

APOKYN 91

Apomorphine HCl
Apokyn 91

Aprepitant
Emend Capsules 349

APRISO 92

APTIOM 92

APTIVUS 94

ARANESP 95

ARAVA 96

ARCAPTA 98

Arformoterol Tartrate
Brovana 172

ARGATROBAN 99

ARICEPT 100

ARIMIDEX 100

Aripiprazole
Abilify 1
Abilify Maintena 3

ARIXTRA 101

Armodafinil
Nuvigil 698

ARMOUR THYROID 103

AROMASIN 104

Artemether
Coartem 242

ARTHROTEC 104

ARZERRA 106

ASACOL HD 107

Asenapine
Saphris 868

ASMANEX 108

Aspirin
Aggrenox 44
Bayer Aspirin 146
Fiorinal 412
Percodan 746

ASTELIN 109

ASTEPRO 110

ATACAND 110

ATACAND HCT 111

Atazanavir Sulfate
Reyataz 842

ATELVIA 112

Atenolol
Tenoretic 951
Tenormin 952

ATIVAN
See Lorazepam Oral 575

ATIVAN INJECTION 113

Atomoxetine
Strattera 911

Atorvastatin
Liptruzet 566

Atorvastatin Calcium
Caduet 182
Lipitor 564

Atovaquone
Malarone 597

ATRIPLA 114

Atropine Sulfate
Donnatal 319
Lomotil 574

ATROVENT HFA 116

ATROVENT NASAL 117

AUBAGIO 118

AUGMENTIN 119

AUGMENTIN XR 120

AVALIDE 121

Avanafil
Stendra 909

AVANDAMET 122

AVANDARYL 124

AVANDIA 125

AVAPRO 126

AVASTIN 127

AVELOX 128

AVIANE 129

AVINZA 131

AVODART 132

AXERT 133

AXID
See Nizatidine 676

AXIRON 134

Axitinib
Inlyta 496

AZACTAM 135

AZASITE 136

Azelastine HCl
Astelin 109
Astepro 110
Optivar 709

AZILECT 137

Azilsartan Medoxomil
Edarbi 336
Edarbyclor 337

Azithromycin
Azasite 136
Zithromax 1109
Zmax 1111

AZOPT 138

AZOR 139

Aztreonam
Azactam 135
Cayston 204

AZULFIDINE 140

AZULFIDINE EN-TABS 141

B

Bactrim
See Sulfamethoxazole/
Trimethoprim 918

Bactrim DS
See Sulfamethoxazole/
Trimethoprim 918

BACTROBAN NASAL 142

BACTROBAN TOPICAL 143

Balsalazide Disodium
Colazal 244
Giazo 448

BALZIVA
See Ovcon-35 721

BANZEL 144
BARACLUDE 145
BAYER ASPIRIN 146
Bayer Aspirin Children's
  See Bayer Aspirin 146
Bayer Aspirin Regimen
  See Bayer Aspirin 146
Bayer Aspirin Regimen with
  Calcium
  See Bayer Aspirin 146
Beclomethasone Dipropionate
  Qvar 814
Belimumab
  Benlysta 150
BELVIQ 147
Benazepril HCl
  Lotensin 579
  Lotensin HCT 580
  Lotrel 581
Bendamustine HCl
  Treanda 977
BENICAR 148
BENICAR HCT 149
BENLYSTA 150
BENTYL
  See Dicyclomine HCl 300
BENZACLIN 151
Benzonatate
  Tessalon 953
Benzoyl Peroxide
  Acanya 8
  BenzaClin 151
  Epiduo.............................365
Bepotastine Besilate
  Bepreve 152
BEPREVE...........................152
Besifloxacin
  Besivance 152
BESIVANCE 152
BETAGAN 153
Betamethasone Dipropionate
  Lotrisone 583
Betamethasone Valerate
  Luxiq 593
BETAPACE.........................153
BETAPACE AF....................155
Betaxolol HCl
  Betoptic S........................158
BETHKIS 156
BETIMOL 157
BETOPTIC S 158
Bevacizumab
  Avastin 127
BEYAZ...............................159
BIAXIN...............................160
BIAXIN XL
  See Biaxin........................160
Bicalutamide
  Casodex 201
Bimatoprost
  Latisse..............................546
  Lumigan 588

BINOSTO 162
Bisacodyl
  HalfLytely 464
Bismuth Subcitrate Potassium
  Pylera 807
Bisoprolol Fumarate
  Zebeta............................1092
  Ziac 1104
Bivalirudin
  Angiomax.......................... 85
Boceprevir
  Victrelis 1041
BONIVA 163
BOOSTRIX 164
BOSULIF 165
Bosutinib
  Bosulif..............................165
Brentuximab Vedotin
  Adcetris 28
BREO ELLIPTA 166
BREVIBLOC 168
BRILINTA 169
Brimonidine Tartrate
  Alphagan P........................ 55
  Combigan.........................246
  Simbrinza 883
BRINTELLIX 170
Brinzolamide
  Azopt 138
  Simbrinza 883
BROMDAY..........................172
Bromfenac
  Bromday 172
Bromocriptine Mesylate
  Parlodel........................... 732
BROVANA 172
BUDEPRION SR
  See Wellbutrin SR 1065
Budesonide
  Entocort EC 362
  Pulmicort.........................806
  Rhinocort Aqua.................844
  Symbicort.........................926
BUMETANIDE..................... 173
BUPRENEX 174
Buprenorphine
  Butrans 177
  Suboxone Film 915
BUPRENORPHINE AND
  NALOXONE 175
Buprenorphine HCl
  Buprenex 174
Bupropion HCl
  Wellbutrin SR...................1065
  Wellbutrin XL...................1067
  Zyban................................1131
Bupropion Hydrobromide
  Aplenzin 89
BUSPIRONE.......................177
Butalbital
  Fiorinal 412
BUTRANS 177
BYDUREON.........................179

BYETTA 180
BYSTOLIC...........................181

C

Cabazitaxel
  Jevtana 522
CADUET 182
Caffeine
  Fiorinal.............................412
CALAN 184
CALAN SR 185
Calcipotriene
  Dovonex 322
  Sorilux.............................897
Calcitonin-Salmon
  Miacalcin 625
Calcitonin-Salmon (rDNA origin)
  Fortical.............................431
Calcitriol
  Rocaltrol.......................... 857
  Vectical 1023
Calcium Acetate
  Phoslyra 754
CALDOLOR........................ 187
CAMBIA 188
CAMPATH 189
CAMPTOSAR 190
CAMRESE
  See Seasonique.................871
CAMRESELO
  See Loseasonique 577
Canagliflozin
  Invokana...........................510
CANASA 191
CANCIDAS 192
Candesartan Cilexetil
  Atacand............................110
  Atacand HCT 111
Capecitabine
  Xeloda............................1074
CAPRELSA.........................193
Capsaicin
  Qutenza...........................813
CAPTOPRIL........................194
CARBAGLU........................196
Carbamazepine
  Equetro 373
  Tegretol...........................944
Carbidopa
  Parcopa 730
  Sinemet CR 887
  Stalevo 902
CARDENE IV 197
CARDENE SR 197
CARDIZEM 198
CARDIZEM CD....................199
Cardizem LA
  See Cardizem CD 199
CARDURA 200
CARDURA XL.....................201

Carfilzomib
    Kyprolis 539
Carglumic Acid
    Carbaglu 196
Carisoprodol
    Soma 894
Cartia XT
    See Cardizem CD 199
Carvedilol Phosphate
    Coreg CR 260
CASODEX 201
Caspofungin Acetate
    Cancidas 192
CATAFLAM 202
CATAPRES 203
CATAPRES-TTS
    See Catapres 203
CAYSTON 204
CEFACLOR 205
CEFACLOR ER 206
CEFADROXIL 207
CEFAZOLIN 207
CEFDINIR 208
Cefepime HCl
    Maxipime 602
Cefixime
    Suprax 922
CEFOXITIN 209
CEFPODOXIME 210
CEFPROZIL 211
Ceftaroline Fosamil
    Teflaro 944
Ceftazidime
    Fortaz 428
    Tazicef 942
CEFTIN 212
CEFTRIAXONE 213
Cefuroxime
    Ceftin 212
Cefuroxime Sodium
    Zinacef 1107
CELEBREX 215
Celecoxib
    Celebrex 215
CELEXA 216
CELLCEPT 217
CEPHALEXIN 219
Certolizumab Pegol
    Cimzia 225
CERVARIX 220
CESAMET 220
Cetuximab
    Erbitux 375
CHANTIX 221
Chlorambucil
    Leukeran 551
Chlordiazepoxide HCl
    Librax 561
    Librium 562
Chlorpheniramine Polistirex
    TussiCaps 995

Chlorthalidone
    Clorpres 240
    Edarbyclor 337
    Tenoretic 951
Cholecalciferol
    Fosamax Plus D 432
CIALIS 222
Ciclesonide
    Alvesco 61
    Omnaris 705
Ciclopirox
    Penlac 742
Cidofovir
    Vistide 1052
Cilostazol
    Pletal 757
CILOXAN 224
CIMZIA 225
Cinacalcet
    Sensipar 875
CIPRO
    See Ciprofloxacin Oral 231
CIPRO HC 226
CIPRO IV
    See Ciprofloxacin Injection .. 229
CIPRO XR 227
CIPRODEX 228
Ciprofloxacin
    Cipro XR 227
    Ciprodex 228
Ciprofloxacin HCl
    Ciloxan 224
    Cipro HC 226
CIPROFLOXACIN
    INJECTION 229
CIPROFLOXACIN ORAL 231
Citalopram HBr
    Celexa 216
Claravis
    See Amnesteem 71
CLARINEX 232
CLARINEX-D 233
Clarithromycin
    Biaxin 160
    Prevpac 773
Clavulanate Potassium
    Augmentin 119
    Augmentin XR 120
    Timentin 960
CLEOCIN 234
CLEOCIN PEDIATRIC
    See Cleocin 234
Clevidipine
    Cleviprex 235
CLEVIPREX 235
Clidinium Bromide
    Librax 561
CLIMARA 236
CLINDAGEL 237
Clindamycin
    Cleocin 234
Clindamycin Phosphate
    Acanya 8
    BenzaClin 151

Clindagel 237
Clindesse 238
    Evoclin 387
    Veltin 1023
    Ziana 1106
CLINDESSE 238
Clobetasol Propionate
    Olux-E 704
CLONAZEPAM 238
Clonidine HCl
    Catapres 203
    Clorpres 240
    Kapvay 528
Clopidogrel Bisulfate
    Plavix 756
CLORPRES 240
Clotrimazole
    Lotrisone 583
CLOZAPINE 241
Clozapine
    Fazaclo 401
    Versacloz 1030
CLOZARIL
    See Clozapine 241
COARTEM 242
Cobicistat
    Stribild 913
COLAZAL 244
Colchicine
    Colcrys 244
COLCRYS 244
Colesevelam HCl
    WelChol 1064
COLESTID 246
Colestipol HCl
    Colestid 246
COMBIGAN 246
COMBIPATCH 248
COMBIVENT RESPIMAT 249
COMBIVIR 250
COMPLERA 251
COMTAN 253
CONCERTA 254
Conjugated Estrogens
    Enjuvia 360
    Premarin Tablets 767
    Premarin Vaginal 768
    Premphase 770
COPAXONE 255
COPEGUS 256
CORDARONE 257
CORDRAN 259
COREG
    See Coreg CR 260
COREG CR 260
CORGARD 261
CORVERT 262
COSOPT 263
COSOPT PF
    See Cosopt 263
COUMADIN 264

COVERA-HS........................ 266
COZAAR............................ 267
CREON 268
CRESTOR........................... 269
CRIXIVAN 270
Crofelemer
Fulyzaq 438
Cryselle
See Lo/Ovral.................. 570
CUTIVATE
See Fluticasone Topical...... 421
CYCLOBENZAPRINE............. 271
Cyclobenzaprine HCl
Amrix 77
CYCLOPHOSPHAMIDE 272
Cyclosporine
Neoral 657
Restasis........................ 835
CYMBALTA 273
CYTOMEL 275

D

Dabigatran Etexilate Mesylate
Pradaxa........................ 758
DACOGEN........................ 276
Dalfampridine
Ampyra 77
Dalfopristin
Synercid 930
DALIRESP........................ 276
Dalteparin Sodium
Fragmin........................ 436
DANTRIUM........................ 277
Dantrolene Sodium
Dantrium 277
Dapagliflozin
Farxiga........................ 400
Darbepoetin Alfa
Aranesp........................ 95
Darifenacin
Enablex 354
Darunavir
Prezista 774
Dasatinib
Sprycel........................ 901
DAYPRO 278
DAYTRANA........................ 279
Decitabine
Dacogen........................ 276
Delavirdine Mesylate
Rescriptor...................... 834
DEMADEX
See Torsemide 972
DEMEROL
See Meperidine Oral.......... 610
DEMEROL INJECTION 281
DENAVIR 281
Denosumab
Prolia.......................... 788
Xgeva......................... 1076
DEPAKENE 282

DEPAKOTE........................ 284
DEPAKOTE ER.................... 286
DEPAKOTE SPRINKLE
See Depakote 284
DEPO-MEDROL................. 288
DEPO-PROVERA................. 289
DEPO-PROVERA
CONTRACEPTIVE
INJECTION 290
DEPO-TESTOSTERONE 292
Desloratadine
Clarinex 232
Clarinex-D 233
Desogestrel
Mircette....................... 632
Desonide
Verdeso.......................1026
Desvenlafaxine
Pristiq......................... 778
DETROL
See Detrol LA 293
DETROL LA....................... 293
Dexamethasone
Ciprodex...................... 228
Maxitrol......................604
TobraDex..................... 966
DEXAMETHASONE
OPHTHALMIC/OTIC 294
DEXAMETHASONE ORAL ... 295
Dexamethasone Sodium
Phosphate
Dexamethasone Ophthalmic/
Otic........................... 294
DEXILANT 296
Dexlansoprazole
Dexilant....................... 296
Dexmedetomidine HCl
Precedex...................... 763
Dexmethylphenidate HCl
Focalin 422
Focalin XR 424
Dexrazoxane
Zinecard......................1108
Dextroamphetamine Sulfate
ProCentra...................... 782
DIABETA 297
Diazepam
Valium.........................1013
Dibasic Sodium Phosphate
Osmoprep 720
DICLEGIS 298
Diclofenac
Zorvolex......................1126
Diclofenac Epolamine
Flector 416
Diclofenac Potassium
Cambia........................188
Cataflam..................... 202
Zipsor........................ 1109
Diclofenac Sodium
Arthrotec......................104
Pennsaid...................... 743
Voltaren Gel..................1057
Voltaren Ophthalmic......1058
Voltaren-XR..................1059

DICLOXACILLIN 299
DICYCLOMINE HCL 300
Didanosine
Videx EC.......................1042
Dienogest
Natazia 653
DIFFERIN......................... 301
DIFICID........................... 302
DIFLUCAN ORAL 303
Digoxin
Digoxin Oral................... 304
DIGOXIN ORAL 304
DILACOR XR..................... 306
DILANTIN 307
Dilantin Infatabs
See Dilantin 307
Dilantin-125
See Dilantin 307
DILAUDID ORAL 309
DILTIA XT
See Dilacor XR............... 306
Diltiazem HCl
Cardizem 198
Cardizem CD..................199
Dilacor XR.................... 306
Tiazac........................ 957
DILTIAZEM INJECTION........310
Dimethyl Fumarate
Tecfidera 943
DIOVAN 311
DIOVAN HCT 312
DIPHENHYDRAMINE
INJECTION 314
Diphenoxylate HCl
Lomotil 574
Diphtheria Toxoid
Pediarix 737
Diphtheria Toxoid, Reduced
Boostrix......................164
Dipyridamole
Aggrenox 44
Disopyramide Phosphate
Norpace 681
Divalproex Sodium
Depakote...................... 284
Depakote ER.................. 286
DIVIGEL.......................... 314
DOCETAXEL 316
Dofetilide
Tikosyn........................ 959
Dolasetron Mesylate
Anzemet....................... 87
DOLOPHINE 317
Dolutegravir
Tivicay........................ 964
Donepezil HCl
Aricept 100
DONNATAL...................... 319
DORIBAX 320
Doripenem
Doribax 320
DORYX 321

Dorzolamide HCl
Cosopt 263
Trusopt.............................., 992
DOVONEX 322
Doxazosin Mesylate
Cardura............................. 200
Cardura XL 201
Doxepin
Silenor.............................. 881
DOXIL................................... 323
Doxorubicin HCl Liposome
Doxil................................. 323
Doxycycline
Oracea 709
Vibramycin 1036
DOXYCYCLINE HYCLATE
See Doryx 321
DOXYCYCLINE IV 324
Doxycycline Monohydrate
Monodox 637
Doxylamine Succinate
Diclegis 298
Dronabinol
Marinol 598
Dronedarone
Multaq................................ 642
Drospirenone
Angeliq............................... 84
Beyaz 159
Yasmin 1083
YAZ...................................1084
Zarah.................................1089
DUETACT.............................. 325
DUEXIS.................................. 326
DULERA 328
Duloxetine HCl
Cymbalta 273
DUONEB................................ 329
DURAGESIC........................... 330
DURAMORPH.......................... 332
Dutasteride
Avodart 132
Jalyn 515
DYAZIDE................................ 333
DYNACIN 334
DYRENIUM............................. 335

E

EC-Naprosyn
See Naprosyn 649
Eculizumab
Soliris............................... 890
EDARBI.................................. 336
EDARBYCLOR......................... 337
EDLUAR................................. 338
EDURANT............................... 339
Efavirenz
Atripla................................114
Sustiva 923
EFFEXOR XR..........................340
EFFIENT 341
EGRIFTA................................ 342

ELDEPRYL
See Selegiline 873
Eletriptan Hydrobromide
Relpax.............................. 827
ELIDEL................................... 343
ELIGARD................................ 344
ELIQUIS 345
ELLA 346
ELOCON 347
ELOXATIN............................... 348
Eltrombopag
Promacta........................... 789
Elvitegravir
Stribild 913
EMEND CAPSULES.................. 349
EMEND FOR INJECTION...... 350
EMLA..................................... 351
EMSAM 352
Emtricitabine
Atripla................................114
Complera............................ 251
Emtriva.............................. 353
Stribild 913
Truvada 993
EMTRIVA................................ 353
ENABLEX................................ 354
Enalapril
Epaned.............................. 364
Enalapril Maleate
Vasotec 1021
ENALAPRIL/HCTZ 355
ENALAPRILAT 357
ENBREL.................................. 358
ENDOCET
See Percocet 745
ENDODAN
See Percodan..................... 746
Enfuvirtide
Fuzeon 441
ENGERIX-B 359
ENJUVIA................................. 360
Enoxaparin Sodium
Lovenox............................. 586
Entacapone
Comtan 253
Stalevo 902
Entecavir
Baraclude.......................... 145
ENTEREG............................... 361
ENTOCORT EC 362
ENULOSE............................... 363
Enzalutamide
Xtandi 1080
EPANED................................. 364
EPIDUO 365
EPIFOAM................................ 365
Epinephrine
Adrenaclick 34
Adrenalin............................. 35
EpiPen............................... 366
EPIPEN 366

EPIPEN JR.
See EpiPen 366
EPIQUIN MICRO 367
Epitol
See Tegretol 944
EPIVIR 368
EPIVIR-HBV 369
Eplerenone
Inspra............................... 498
Epoetin Alfa
Epogen.............................. 370
Procrit 785
EPOGEN 370
Eprosartan Mesylate
Teveten 954
Teveten HCT 955
Eptifibatide
Integrilin 499
EPZICOM 372
EQUETRO 373
ERAXIS.................................. 374
ERBITUX................................ 375
Eribulin Mesylate
Halaven 462
ERIVEDGE 376
Erlotinib
Tarceva............................. 937
Ertapenem
Invanz 505
ERY-TAB 377
Erythromycin
Ery-Tab.............................. 377
Escitalopram Oxalate
Lexapro 559
Eslicarbazepine Acetate
Aptiom 92
Esmolol HCl
Brevibloc...........................168
Esomeprazole Magnesium
Nexium Oral...................... 666
Vimovo.............................1045
Esomeprazole Sodium
Nexium IV.......................... 665
ESTRACE.............................. 378
ESTRADERM......................... 380
Estradiol
Activella.............................. 20
Angeliq............................... 84
Climara 236
CombiPatch...................... 248
Divigel 314
Estrace 378
Estraderm......................... 380
Evamist 385
Vagifem 1011
Vivelle-Dot 1054
Estradiol Valerate
Natazia............................. 653
ESTROSTEP FE 381
Eszopiclone
Lunesta 589
Etanercept
Enbrel............................... 358

Ethinyl Estradiol
Aviane...................................129
Beyaz....................................159
Estrostep Fe........................381
Femcon Fe...........................405
Lo/Ovral...............................570
Loestrin 21..........................571
Loseasonique.......................577
Mircette..............................632
NuvaRing............................696
Ortho Evra...........................712
Ortho Tri-Cyclen..................714
Ortho Tri-Cyclen Lo.............716
Ortho-Cyclen.......................717
Ovcon-35.............................721
Seasonique..........................871
Yasmin...............................1083
YAZ....................................1084
Zarah.................................1089
Ethionamide
Trecator..............................978
Ethosuximide
Zarontin............................1090
ETODOLAC............................382
Etonogestrel
NuvaRing............................696
ETOPOPHOS..........................384
Etoposide Phosphate
Etopophos...........................384
Etravirine
Intelence............................500
EVAMIST................................385
Everolimus
Afinitor................................41
Zortress............................1124
EVISTA..................................386
EVOCLIN................................387
EXALGO.................................388
EXELON..................................389
Exemestane
Aromasin.............................104
Exenatide
Bydureon.............................179
Byetta................................180
EXFORGE...............................391
EXFORGE HCT........................392
EXTAVIA.................................393
EXTINA...................................394
EYLEA....................................395
Ezetimibe
Liptruzet.............................566
Vytorin..............................1061
Zetia.................................1102

F

FACTIVE.................................395
Famciclovir
Famvir.................................397
FAMOTIDINE..........................396
Famotidine
Duexis................................326
FAMVIR..................................397
FANAPT.................................398
FARXIGA................................400

FASLODEX..............................400
FAZACLO................................401
Febuxostat
Uloric...............................1001
Felbamate
Felbatol..............................403
FELBATOL...............................403
FELODIPINE ER.......................404
FEMARA.................................405
FEMCON FE............................405
Fenofibrate
Antara...................................86
Lipofen...............................565
Lofibra................................573
Tricor.................................983
Triglide..............................984
Fenofibric acid
Fibricor...............................410
Trilipix...............................987
Fentanyl
Abstral....................................7
Duragesic...........................330
Lazanda..............................548
Subsys................................917
Fentanyl Citrate
Actiq....................................17
Fentanyl Injection................407
Fentora...............................408
FENTANYL INJECTION.............407
FENTORA................................408
Ferrous Fumarate
Estrostep Fe........................381
Femcon Fe...........................405
Fesoterodine Fumarate
Toviaz.................................973
FETZIMA.................................409
FIBRICOR................................410
Fibrin Sealant
TachoSil..............................933
Fibrinogen Concentrate
(Human)
Riastap................................845
Fidaxomicin
Dificid.................................302
Filgrastim
Neupogen............................661
Finasteride
Propecia..............................794
Proscar................................797
FIORINAL................................412
FLAGYL...................................412
FLAGYL ER..............................414
FLAGYL IV...............................415
FLECTOR.................................416
FLOMAX.................................417
FLONASE.................................418
FLOVENT HFA..........................419
Fluconazole
Diflucan Oral........................303
Flucytosine
Ancobon................................80
FLUDROCORTISONE.................420

Fluocinonide
Vanos................................1018
Fluoxetine HCl
Prozac................................804
Symbyax..............................928
Flurandrenolide
Cordran...............................259
Fluticasone Furoate
Breo Ellipta.........................166
Veramyst...........................1025
Fluticasone Propionate
Advair Diskus.........................36
Advair HFA.............................37
Flonase................................418
Flovent HFA..........................419
Fluticasone Topical...............421
FLUTICASONE TOPICAL...........421
Fluvastatin Sodium
Lescol.................................549
Fluvoxamine Maleate
Luvox CR..............................592
FOCALIN.................................422
FOCALIN XR.............................424
FOLIC ACID.............................425
Fondaparinux Sodium
Arixtra................................101
FORADIL.................................426
Formoterol Fumarate
Foradil................................426
Perforomist..........................748
Formoterol Fumarate Dihydrate
Dulera................................328
Symbicort...........................926
FORTAMET.............................427
FORTAZ...................................428
FORTEO..................................429
FORTESTA...............................430
FORTICAL................................431
FOSAMAX
See Alendronate.....................51
FOSAMAX PLUS D....................432
Fosaprepitant Dimeglumine
Emend for Injection...............350
FOSINOPRIL............................433
FOSINOPRIL/HCTZ....................434
Fospropofol Disodium
Lusedra...............................591
FRAGMIN................................436
FROVA....................................437
Frovatriptan Succinate
Frova...................................437
Fulvestrant
Faslodex..............................400
FULYZAQ.................................438
FUROSEMIDE...........................439
FUSILEV.................................440
FUZEON..................................441

G

Gabapentin
Gralise................................460
Neurontin............................662

Gabapentin Enacarbil
  Horizant 473
GABITRIL............................ 442
Galantamine HBr
  Razadyne ER 819
Ganciclovir
  Vitrasert 1053
GARDASIL 443
Gatifloxacin
  Zymar................................1134
  Zymaxid 1135
GAZYVA..............................444
GEMCITABINE....................445
Gemfibrozil
  Lopid................................ 575
Gemifloxacin Mesylate
  Factive 395
GEMZAR
  See Gemcitabine...............445
GENERLAC
  See Enulose 363
Genuine Bayer Aspirin
  See Bayer Aspirin............146
GEODON 446
GIAZO 448
Gildess 1.5/30
  See Loestrin 21................. 571
Gildess 1/20
  See Loestrin 21................. 571
Glatiramer Acetate
  Copaxone 255
GLEEVEC............................449
Glimepiride
  Amaryl 63
  Avandaryl........................ 124
  Duetact 325
Glipizide
  Glucotrol 453
  Glucotrol XL 454
GLUCAGON 451
Glucagon, rDNA origin
  Glucagon.......................... 451
GLUCOPHAGE
  See Glucophage XR........... 452
GLUCOPHAGE XR 452
GLUCOTROL....................... 453
GLUCOTROL XL 454
GLUCOVANCE 455
GLUMETZA 457
Glyburide
  DiaBeta 297
  Glucovance....................... 455
  Glynase PresTab............... 458
GLYNASE PRESTAB 458
GLYSET.............................. 459
Golimumab
  Simponi........................... 885
Goserelin Acetate
  Zoladex 1-Month 1115
  Zoladex 3-Month...............1116
GRALISE............................ 460
GRANISETRON 460

Granisetron
  Sancuso............................ 866
Griseofulvin
  Gris-PEG.......................... 461
GRIS-PEG 461
Guanfacine
  Intuniv............................. 504

H

Haemophilus B Conjugate
  Hiberix 472
HALAVEN 462
HALCION 463
HALDOL
  See Haloperidol 465
HALFLYTELY...................... 464
HALOPERIDOL.................... 465
HAVRIX.............................. 466
HECORIA 467
HEPARIN SODIUM.............. 469
Hepatitis A Vaccine
  Havrix.............................. 466
Hepatitis B (Recombinant)
  Engerix-B 359
  Pediarix 737
  Recombivax HB 824
HEPSERA........................... 470
HERCEPTIN........................ 471
HIBERIX............................. 472
Histrelin Acetate
  Vantas..............................1019
HORIZANT......................... 473
HUMALOG 474
HUMALOG MIX 75/25 475
Human Papillomavirus
  Recombinant Vaccine,
  Bivalent
  Cervarix........................... 220
Human Papillomavirus
  Recombinant Vaccine,
  Quadrivalent
  Gardasil........................... 443
HUMATROPE 476
HUMIRA............................. 478
HUMULIN 70/30................. 479
HUMULIN N....................... 480
HUMULIN R....................... 481
HYALGAN 483
Hydrochlorothiazide
  Accuretic...........................11
  Aldactazide 47
  Amturnide 78
  Atacand HCT 111
  Avalide 121
  Benicar HCT 149
  Diovan HCT 312
  Dyazide 333
  Exforge HCT 392
  Hyzaar.............................. 485
  Lotensin HCT 580
  Maxzide 605
  Micardis HCT 627
  Microzide 629

Tekturna HCT..................... 948
Teveten HCT 955
Tribenzor 982
Uniretic 1005
Zestoretic........................1099
Ziac 1104
HYDROCHLOROTHIAZIDE... 483
Hydrocodone Bitartrate
  Norco.............................. 677
  Vicodin............................1037
  Vicoprofen.......................1038
Hydrocodone Polistirex
  TussiCaps 995
Hydrocortisone
  Alacort 45
  Alcortin-A......................... 47
  Cipro HC 226
Hydrocortisone Acetate
  Epifoam 365
Hydrocortisone Sodium
  Succinate
  Solu-Cortef...................... 891
Hydromorphone HCl
  Dilaudid Oral................... 309
  Exalgo 388
Hydroquinone
  Epiquin Micro................... 367
Hydroxychloroquine Sulfate
  Plaquenil 754
HYDROXYZINE HCL............484
Hyoscyamine Sulfate
  Donnatal.......................... 319
  Levbid 554
HYZAAR............................. 485

I

Ibandronate Sodium
  Boniva..............................163
Ibritumomab Tiuxetan
  Zevalin 1103
Ibuprofen
  Caldolor 187
  Duexis 326
  Vicoprofen.......................1038
Ibutilide Fumarate
  Corvert............................ 262
Iloperidone
  Fanapt 398
Imatinib Mesylate
  Gleevec............................449
IMDUR.............................. 487
Imipramine HCl
  Tofranil........................... 967
Imiquimod
  Aldara 50
IMITREX.............................488
Inactivated Poliovirus
  Pediarix 737
INCIVEK.............................489
Indacaterol
  Arcapta 98
INDERAL LA 491
Indinavir Sulfate
  Crixivan........................... 270

INDOCIN
  See Indomethacin 492
INDOMETHACIN................ 492
INFERGEN 493
Infliximab
  Remicade 829
Influenza Virus Vaccine
  Afluria 42
INFUMORPH 495
INLYTA 496
INNOPRAN XL 497
INSPRA............................ 498
Insulin Aspart Protamine,
  rDNA origin
  Novolog Mix 70/30 688
Insulin Aspart, rDNA origin
  Novolog........................... 686
  Novolog Mix 70/30 688
Insulin Detemir, rDNA origin
  Levemir 555
Insulin Glargine, rDNA origin
  Lantus 544
Insulin Glulisine, rDNA origin
  Apidra.............................. 88
Insulin Human NPH, rDNA
  origin
  Humulin 70/30.................. 479
  Humulin N....................... 480
Insulin Human, rDNA origin
  Humulin 70/30.................. 479
  Novolin 70/30 685
Insulin Lispro Protamine,
  rDNA origin
  Humalog Mix 75/25 475
Insulin Lispro, rDNA origin
  Humalog.......................... 474
  Humalog Mix 75/25 475
Insulin, Human
  (Isophane/Regular)
  Novolin 70/30.................. 685
Insulin, Human Regular
  (rDNA Origin)
  Humulin R........................481
  Novolin R........................ 685
INTEGRILIN....................... 499
INTELENCE.......................500
Interferon alfa-2b
  Intron A 502
Interferon alfacon-1
  Infergen........................... 493
Interferon beta-1a
  Rebif 821
Interferon beta-1b
  Extavia 393
INTERMEZZO......................501
INTRON A 502
INTUNIV 504
INVANZ 505
INVEGA 506
INVEGA SUSTENNA 508
INVIRASE 509
INVOKANA......................... 510

Iodoquinol
  Alcortin-A........................ 47
Ipilimumab
  Yervoy...........................1086
Ipratropium Bromide
  Atrovent HFA....................116
  Atrovent Nasal..................117
  Combivent Respimat........ 249
  Duoneb 329
Irbesartan
  Avalide............................121
  Avapro 126
Irinotecan HCl
  Camptosar.......................190
ISENTRESS 511
ISONIAZID 512
Isoniazid
  Rifamate......................... 845
  Rifater 847
ISORDIL TITRADOSE
  See Isosorbide Dinitrate 513
ISOSORBIDE DINITRATE 513
Isosorbide Mononitrate
  Imdur 487
Isotretinoin
  Absorica............................ 5
  Amnesteem 71
Itraconazole
  Sporanox........................900
Ivacaftor
  Kalydeco 528
Ixabepilone
  Ixempra 514
IXEMPRA.......................... 514

J
JALYN 515
JANTOVEN
  See Coumadin.................. 264
JANUMET 516
JANUMET XR..................... 518
JANUVIA 519
JENTADUETO 520
JEVTANA.......................... 522
Junel 1.5/30
  See Loestrin 21................ 571
Junel 1/20
  See Loestrin 21................ 571
JUXTAPID......................... 523

K
KADIAN............................ 524
KALETRA 526
KALYDECO 528
KAPVAY............................ 528
KARIVA
  See Mircette.................... 632
KAZANO 530
KEFLEX
  See Cephalexin 219
KEPPRA XR....................... 531
KETEK 532

Ketoconazole
  Extina............................. 394
  Xolegel 1078
KETOCONAZOLE TABLETS . 533
KETOROLAC...................... 534
Ketorolac Tromethamine
  Acular 25
  Acular LS 26
KLONOPIN
  See Clonazepam 238
KLOR-CON
  See Klor-Con M 536
KLOR-CON M 536
KOMBIGLYZE XR................ 537
KRISTALOSE...................... 538
KRYSTEXXA 539
KYPROLIS......................... 539

L
LABETALOL....................... 540
Lacosamide
  Vimpat 1047
Lactulose
  Kristalose 538
LAMICTAL........................ 541
LAMICTAL ODT
  See Lamictal.................... 541
LAMISIL 543
Lamivudine
  Combivir......................... 250
  Epivir............................. 368
  Epivir-HBV....................... 369
  Epzicom 372
  Trizivir 989
Lamotrigine
  Lamictal 541
LANOXIN
  See Digoxin Oral 304
Lansoprazole
  Prevacid 772
  Prevpac.......................... 773
LANTUS............................544
Lapatinib
  Tykerb 998
LASIX
  See Furosemide 439
LASTACAFT....................... 545
Latanoprost
  Xalatan...........................1068
LATISSE........................... 546
LATUDA........................... 547
LAZANDA......................... 548
Leflunomide
  Arava 96
Lenalidomide
  Revlimid 841
Lepirudin
  Refludan.......................... 824
LESCOL 549
LESCOL XL
  See Lescol 549
LETAIRIS...........................551

Letrozole
Femara.................................405

LEUKERAN............................551

Leuprolide Acetate
Eligard...............................344
Lupron Depot-Ped............590

Levalbuterol Tartrate
Xopenex HFA....................1079

LEVAQUIN............................552

LEVBID.................................554

LEVEMIR...............................555

Levetiracetam
Keppra XR..........................531

LEVITRA...............................556

Levobunolol HCl
Betagan............................153

Levocetirizine Dihydrochloride
Xyzal...............................1082

Levodopa
Parcopa............................730
Sinemet CR........................887
Stalevo.............................902

Levofloxacin
Levaquin...........................552
Quixin..............................812

Levoleucovorin
Fusilev..............................440

Levomefolate Calcium
Beyaz................................159

Levomilnacipran
Fetzima.............................409

Levonorgestrel
Aviane...............................129
Loseasonique.....................577
Mirena..............................633
Seasonique........................871

Levothyroxine Sodium
Levoxyl.............................557
Synthroid..........................931
Unithroid.........................1007

LEVOXYL..............................557

LEXAPRO..............................559

LIALDA................................560

LIBRAX.................................561

LIBRIUM...............................562

Lidocaine
EMLA.................................351
Lidoderm Patch.................563
Synera..............................929

LIDODERM PATCH.................563

Linaclotide
Linzess..............................563

Linagliptin
Jentadueto........................520
Tradjenta...........................974

LINZESS...............................563

Liothyronine Sodium
Cytomel............................275
Triostat.............................988

LIPITOR...............................564

LIPOFEN...............................565

LIPTRUZET............................566

Liraglutide (rDNA Origin)
Victoza...........................1040

Lisdexamfetamine Dimesylate
Vyvanse...........................1063

Lisinopril
Prinivil.............................777
Zestoretic........................1099
Zestril.............................1100

Lithium Carbonate
Lithium ER.........................568

LITHIUM ER..........................568

LITHOBID
See Lithium ER..................568

LIVALO................................569

LO/OVRAL.............................570

LOESTRIN 21.........................571

Loestrin 21 1.5/30
See Loestrin 21..................571

Loestrin 21 1/20
See Loestrin 21..................571

LOFIBRA...............................573

Lomitapide
Juxtapid............................523

LOMOTIL..............................574

LOPID..................................575

Lopinavir
Kaletra..............................526

LOPRESSOR
See Metoprolol...................621

LOPRESSOR HCT
See Metoprolol/HCTZ.........623

Lorazepam
Ativan Injection..................113

LORAZEPAM ORAL.................575

Lorcaserin HCl
Belviq...............................147

LORYNA
See YAZ...........................1084

Losartan Potassium
Cozaar..............................267
Hyzaar..............................485

LOSEASONIQUE.....................577

LOTEMAX SUSPENSION...........578

LOTENSIN.............................579

LOTENSIN HCT......................580

Loteprednol Etabonate
Alrex..................................56
Lotemax Suspension...........578
Zylet...............................1133

LOTREL................................581

LOTRISONE...........................583

LOTRONEX............................584

LOVASTATIN..........................584

Lovastatin
Advicor..............................39
Altoprev.............................60

LOVAZA...............................586

LOVENOX.............................586

Low-Ogestrel
See Lo/Ovral......................570

Lubiprostone
Amitiza...............................70

Lumefantrine
Coartem............................242

LUMIGAN..............................588

LUNESTA..............................589

LUPRON DEPOT-PED..............590

Lurasidone HCl
Latuda..............................547

LUSEDRA..............................591

LUVOX CR.............................592

LUXIQ..................................593

LYRICA.................................594

M

Macitentan
Opsumit.............................708

MACROBID............................595

MACRODANTIN......................596

Magnesium Oxide
Prepopik............................771

Magnesium Sulfate
Suprep..............................923

MALARONE............................597

MALARONE PEDIATRIC
See Malarone......................597

Maraviroc
Selzentry...........................874

MARINOL..............................598

MAVIK.................................599

MAXAIR...............................600

MAXALT...............................601

MAXALT-MLT
See Maxalt.........................601

MAXIPIME.............................602

MAXITROL............................604

MAXZIDE..............................605

MAXZIDE-25
See Maxzide.......................605

Measles Vaccine Live
M-M-R II............................634

Meclizine HCl
Zentrip............................1097

MEDROL...............................606

Medroxyprogesterone Acetate
Depo-Provera......................289
Depo-Provera CI..................290
Premphase.........................770
Provera.............................802

MEFLOQUINE.........................607

Mefloquine HCl
Mefloquine.........................607

MEGACE
See Megace ES....................608

MEGACE ES...........................608

Megestrol Acetate
Megace ES..........................608

Meloxicam
Mobic................................635

Memantine HCl
Namenda............................647

MENACTRA............................609

Meningococcal (groups A, C, Y, and W-135) Oligosaccharide Diphtheria CRM 197 Conjugate
Menveo............................609
Meningococcal Polysaccharide Diphtheria Toxoid Conjugate Vaccine
Menactra........................609
MENVEO.............................609
Meperidine HCl
Demerol Injection.........281
MEPERIDINE ORAL.............610
Meropenem
Merrem............................611
MERREM.............................611
Mesalamine
Apriso.............................92
Asacol HD.......................107
Canasa..........................191
Lialda............................560
Pentasa.........................744
SF Rowasa......................880
Mestranol
Norinyl 1/50...................679
METADATE CD....................612
METADATE ER....................613
Metaxalone
Skelaxin.........................889
Metformin HCl
Actoplus Met XR..............22
Avandamet......................122
Fortamet.........................427
Glucophage XR................452
Glucovance.....................455
Glumetza........................457
Janumet.........................516
Janumet XR.....................518
Jentadueto......................520
Kazano...........................530
Kombiglyze XR.................537
Prandimet......................760
Riomet...........................849
Methadone HCl
Dolophine.......................317
METHADONE ORAL SOLUTION AND SUSPENSION.............615
Methimazole
Tapazole.........................936
Methocarbamol
Robaxin..........................856
METHOTREXATE INJECTION......................617
METHYLIN..........................619
Methylnaltrexone Bromide
Relistor..........................826
Methylphenidate
Daytrana.........................279
See Ritalin.....................853
Methylphenidate HCl
Concerta.........................254
Metadate CD...................612
Metadate ER...................613
Methylin.........................619
Quillivant XR...................810
Ritalin............................853

Methylprednisolone
Medrol............................606
Methylprednisolone Acetate
Depo-Medrol...................288
Methylprednisolone Sodium Succinate
Solu-Medrol....................892
METOCLOPRAMIDE.............620
Metolazone
Zaroxolyn.......................1091
METOPROLOL.....................621
Metoprolol Succinate
Toprol-XL........................970
METOPROLOL/HCTZ...........623
METROGEL-VAGINAL...........624
Metronidazole
Flagyl............................412
Flagyl ER........................414
Flagyl IV.........................415
MetroGel-Vaginal.............624
Pylera...........................807
MEVACOR
See Lovastatin................584
MIACALCIN........................625
Micafungin Sodium
Mycamine.......................643
MICARDIS..........................626
MICARDIS HCT...................627
Miconazole
Oravig...........................710
Microgestin 1.5/30
See Loestrin 21...............571
Microgestin 1/20
See Loestrin 21...............571
MICRO-K...........................628
MICROZIDE........................629
Miglitol
Glyset...........................459
Milnacipran HCl
Savella...........................869
MINIPRESS........................629
MINITRAN
See Nitro-Dur..................673
Minocycline HCl
Dynacin..........................334
MIRALAX...........................630
MIRAPEX...........................631
MIRCETTE.........................632
MIRENA............................633
Mirtazapine
Remeron.........................828
Misoprostol
Arthrotec........................104
M-M-R II...........................634
MOBIC..............................635
Modafinil
Provigil..........................803
Moexipril HCl
Uniretic..........................1005
Univasc.........................1009

Mometasone Furoate
Asmanex.........................108
Dulera............................328
Elocon............................347
Mometasone Furoate Monohydrate
Nasonex.........................651
Monobasic Sodium Phosphate Monohydrate
Osmoprep.......................720
MONODOX........................637
MonoNessa
See Ortho-Cyclen............717
Montelukast Sodium
Singulair.........................888
MORPHINE.........................638
Morphine Sulfate
Avinza...........................131
Duramorph......................332
Infumorph.......................495
Kadian............................524
MS Contin.......................641
MOXATAG.........................639
MOXEZA...........................640
Moxifloxacin HCl
Avelox............................128
Moxeza...........................640
Vigamox.........................1043
MS CONTIN.......................641
MULTAQ...........................642
Mumps Vaccine Live
M-M-R II..........................634
Mupirocin Calcium
Bactroban Nasal..............142
Bactroban Topical............143
MYCAMINE.......................643
Mycophenolate Mofetil
CellCept.........................217
Mycophenolic Acid
Myfortic.........................644
MYFORTIC........................644

N

Nabilone
Cesamet.........................220
NABUMETONE....................646
Nadolol
Corgard..........................261
Naloxone
Suboxone Film.................915
Naltrexone
Vivitrol..........................1056
NAMENDA........................647
NAMENDA XR
See Namenda..................647
NAPRELAN........................648
NAPROSYN........................649
Naproxen
Naprosyn.......................649
Vimovo.........................1045
Naproxen Sodium
Naprelan.........................648
Treximet.........................980

Naratriptan HCl
Amerge 67
NARDIL 650
NASONEX............................ 651
NATACYN 652
Natalizumab
Tysabri 999
Natamycin
Natacyn 652
NATAZIA............................. 653
Nateglinide
Starlix.............................. 904
NATRECOR 654
NATROBA 655
NAVANE 656
Nebivolol
Bystolic............................ 181
NECON 1/50
See Norinyl 1/50.............. 679
Nelfinavir Mesylate
Viracept 1048
Neomycin Sulfate
Maxitrol 604
NEORAL 657
Nepafenac
Nevanac 663
NESINA 659
Nesiritide
Natrecor 654
NEULASTA............................ 660
NEUMEGA............................ 660
NEUPOGEN.......................... 661
NEURONTIN.......................... 662
NEVANAC............................. 663
Nevirapine
Viramune XR....................1049
NEXAVAR 664
NEXIUM IV 665
NEXIUM ORAL 666
NEXTERONE........................ 668
Niacin
Advicor 39
Niaspan 669
Simcor............................. 884
NIASPAN 669
Nicardipine HCl
Cardene IV........................ 197
Cardene SR....................... 197
Nifediac CC
See Adalat CC................... 27
NIFEDICAL XL
See Procardia XL.............. 781
Nifedipine
Adalat CC......................... 27
Procardia XL..................... 781
NIFEDIPINE.......................... 670
NILANDRON 671
Nilotinib
Tasigna............................ 939
Nilutamide
Nilandron.......................... 671

NIRAVAM............................. 672
Nisoldipine
Sular................................ 918
NITRO-DUR 673
Nitrofurantoin Macrocrystals
Macrobid 595
Macrodantin 596
Nitrofurantoin Monohydrate
Macrobid 595
Nitroglycerin
Nitro-Dur.......................... 673
Nitrolingual....................... 674
Nitrostat 675
NITROLINGUAL..................... 674
NITROSTAT 675
NIZATIDINE 676
NORCO................................ 677
NORDITROPIN 678
Norelgestromin
Ortho Evra........................ 712
Norethindrone
Femcon Fe........................ 405
Norinyl 1/50...................... 679
Ovcon-35 721
Norethindrone Acetate
Activella 20
CombiPatch 248
Estrostep Fe 381
Loestrin 21 571
Norfloxacin
Noroxin 680
Norgestimate
Ortho Tri-Cyclen 714
Ortho Tri-Cyclen Lo............ 716
Ortho-Cyclen..................... 717
Norgestrel
Lo/Ovral 570
NORINYL 1/50...................... 679
NOROXIN............................. 680
NORPACE 681
NORPACE CR
See Norpace..................... 681
Nortriptyline HCl
Pamelor........................... 729
NORVASC............................. 682
NORVIR............................... 683
NOVOLIN 70/30.................... 685
NOVOLIN R.......................... 685
NOVOLOG 686
NOVOLOG MIX 70/30.......... 688
NOXAFIL 689
NPLATE 690
NUCYNTA 691
NUCYNTA ER 693
NUTROPIN........................... 694
NUTROPIN AQ
See Nutropin..................... 694
NUVARING........................... 696
NUVIGIL.............................. 698
NYSTATIN ORAL 699

O

Obinutuzumab
Gazyva.............................444
Ocella
See Yasmin......................1083
Octreotide Acetate
Sandostatin LAR.............. 867
Ofatumumab
Arzerra............................106
OFIRMEV............................700
OFLOXACIN 701
OFLOXACIN OTIC 702
Olanzapine
Symbyax...........................928
Zyprexa 1135
Zyprexa Relprevv..............1137
OLEPTRO 703
Olmesartan Medoxomil
Azor.................................139
Benicar............................148
Benicar HCT 149
Tribenzor..........................982
Olopatadine HCl
Patanol............................733
OLUX-E..............................704
Omega-3-Acid Ethyl Esters
Lovaza..............................586
Omeprazole
Prilosec 775
Zegerid...........................1093
Zegerid OTC 1094
OMNARIS............................705
OMNITROPE 706
Ondansetron
Zofran 1114
Zuplenz 1130
ONGLYZA............................707
Oprelvekin
Neumega..........................660
OPSUMIT 708
OPTIVAR.............................709
ORACEA.............................709
ORAVIG 710
ORENCIA 711
Orlistat
Xenical 1075
ORSYTHIA
See Aviane.......................129
ORTHO EVRA 712
ORTHO TRI-CYCLEN 714
ORTHO TRI-CYCLEN LO 716
ORTHO-CYCLEN...................717
Oseltamivir Phosphate
Tamiflu 934
OSENI 718
OSMOPREP........................ 720
OVCON-35...........................721
Oxaliplatin
Eloxatin 348
Oxaprozin
Daypro 278

Oxcarbazepine
  Oxtellar XR 722
  Trileptal 985
OXTELLAR XR 722
Oxybutynin
  Oxytrol 727
OXYBUTYNIN 723
Oxycodone HCl
  OxyContin 725
  Percocet.......................... 745
  Percodan........................ 746
  Roxicet.......................... 859
OXYCODONE TABLETS 724
OXYCONTIN...................... 725
OXYTROL...........................727

P

PACLITAXEL 727
Paclitaxel Protein-bound
  Abraxane............................. 4
Paliperidone
  Invega 506
Paliperidone Palmitate
  Invega Sustenna................ 508
Palonosetron HCl
  Aloxi................................ 54
PAMELOR 729
PANCREAZE 729
Pancrelipase
  Creon 268
  Pancreaze....................... 729
  Zenpep...........................1096
Panitumumab
  Vectibix..........................1022
Pantoprazole Sodium
  Protonix........................... 799
PARCOPA 730
Paricalcitol
  Zemplar Oral...................1095
PARLODEL.......................... 732
Paroxetine HCl
  Paxil 734
  Paxil CR.......................... 735
PATANOL 733
PAXIL 734
PAXIL CR.......................... 735
Pazopanib
  Votrient 1060
PEDIAPRED 736
PEDIARIX........................... 737
PEGASYS........................... 738
Pegfilgrastim
  Neulasta.......................660
Peginterferon alfa-2a
  Pegasys 738
Peginterferon alfa-2b
  PegIntron 740
PEGINTRON...................... 740
Pegloticase
  Krystexxa 539
Pegvisomant
  Somavert........................895

Pemetrexed
  Alimta 52
Penciclovir
  Denavir........................... 281
Penicillin V Potassium
  Penicillin VK..................... 741
PENICILLIN VK.................. 741
PENLAC............................742
PENNSAID 743
PENTASA......................... 744
PEPCID
  See Famotidine................. 396
PERCOCET 745
PERCODAN....................... 746
PERFOROMIST................... 748
Perindopril Erbumine
  Aceon............................ 12
PERJETA.......................... 749
Pertuzumab
  Perjeta........................... 749
Phenadoz
  See Promethazine 790
Phenelzine Sulfate
  Nardil 650
PHENERGAN INJECTION..... 750
Phenobarbital
  Donnatal.......................319
PHENOBARBITAL 751
Phentermine
  Qsymia...........................809
PHENYTEK 752
Phenytoin Sodium
  Dilantin 307
  Phenytek 752
PHOSLYRA 754
Phosphate
  Acetaminophen and Codeine
  Tablets 14
Pimecrolimus
  Elidel.............................. 343
Pioglitazone
  Actoplus Met XR 22
  Actos.............................. 24
  Oseni............................. 718
Pioglitazone HCl
  Duetact 325
Piperacillin
  Zosyn 1128
Pirbuterol Acetate
  Maxair 600
Pitavastatin
  Livalo 569
PLAQUENIL 754
PLAVIX 756
PLETAL............................ 757
Pneumococcal Vaccine
  Polyvalent
  Pneumovax 23 757
PNEUMOVAX 23................. 757
Polyethylene Glycol 3350
  HalfLytely 464
  MiraLax 630

Polymyxin B Sulfate
  Maxitrol..........................604
Posaconazole
  Noxafil........................... 689
POTABA........................... 758
Potassium Chloride
  HalfLytely 464
  Klor-Con M 536
  Micro-K 628
Potassium Sulfate
  Suprep 923
PRADAXA........................ 758
Pramipexole Dihydrochloride
  Mirapex 631
Pramoxine HCl
  Epifoam 365
PRANDIMET...................... 760
PRANDIN.......................... 761
Prasugrel
  Effient 341
PRAVACHOL..................... 762
Pravastatin Sodium
  Pravachol 762
Prazosin HCl
  Minipress........................ 629
PRECEDEX....................... 763
PRECOSE......................... 764
PRED FORTE.................... 765
Prednisolone Acetate
  Pred Forte 765
Prednisolone Sodium Phosphate
  Pediapred 736
PREDNISONE.................... 766
Pregabalin
  Lyrica 594
PREMARIN TABLETS.......... 767
PREMARIN VAGINAL.......... 768
PREMPHASE..................... 770
PREMPRO
  See Premphase................. 770
PREPOPIK........................ 771
PREVACID 772
PREVACID SOLUTAB
  See Prevacid.................... 772
Previfem
  See Ortho-Cyclen.............. 717
PREVPAC......................... 773
PREZISTA.........................774
Prilocaine
  EMLA 351
PRILOSEC........................ 775
PRINIVIL.......................... 777
PRISTIQ 778
PROAIR HFA 779
PROBENECID/COLCHICINE.. 780
PROCARDIA
  See Nifedipine 670
PROCARDIA XL................. 781
PROCENTRA...................... 782
PROCHLORPERAZINE......... 783

PROCRIT............................ 785

PROGRAF........................ 786

Proguanil HCl
  Malarone 597

PROLIA.............................. 788

PROMACTA...................... 789

PROMETH W/ CODEINE
  See Promethazine
  w/Codeine...................... 793

PROMETHAZINE................ 790

Promethazine HCl
  Phenergan Injection 750

PROMETHAZINE VC/
  CODEINE.® 791

PROMETHAZINE W/
  CODEINE........................ 793

Promethegan
  See Promethazine 790

Propafenone HCl
  Rythmol 861
  Rythmol SR...................... 862

PROPECIA 794

PROPRANOLOL................. 795

Propranolol HCl
  Inderal LA....................... 491
  InnoPran XL...................... 497

PROPYLTHIOURACIL 796

PROSCAR 797

PROTAMINE SULFATE........ 798

PROTONIX 799

PROTONIX IV
  See Protonix 799

PROTOPIC 800

PROVENGE....................... 801

PROVERA 802

PROVIGIL.......................... 803

Proxetil
  Cefpodoxime.................... 210

PROZAC........................... 804

Pseudoephedrine Sulfate
  Clarinex-D 233

PULMICORT...................... 806

Pulmicort Flexhaler
  See Pulmicort 806

Pulmicort Respules
  See Pulmicort 806

PYLERA........................... 807

Pyrazinamide
  Rifater............................ 847

Pyridoxine HCl
  Diclegis 298

Q

QSYMIA........................... 809

Quetiapine Fumarate
  Seroquel......................... 877
  Seroquel XR...................... 879

QUILLIVANT XR 810

Quinapril HCl
  Accupril............................10
  Accuretic..........................11

QUINIDINE GLUCONATE
  INJECTION........................811

Quinupristin
  Synercid 930

QUIXIN 812

QUTENZA......................... 813

QVAR.............................. 814

R

Rabeprazole Sodium
  Aciphex...........................15

Radium Ra 223 Dichloride
  Xofigo 1078

Raloxifene HCl
  Evista............................. 386

Raltegravir
  Isentress......................... 511

Ramelteon
  Rozerem.......................... 860

Ramipril
  Altace.............................. 58

RANEXA 815

RANITIDINE...................... 816

Ranolazine
  Ranexa 815

RAPAFLO 817

RAPAMUNE 818

Rasagiline Mesylate
  Azilect............................ 137

RAZADYNE
  See Razadyne ER 819

RAZADYNE ER.................. 819

REBETOL.......................... 820

REBIF 821

RECLAST 822

RECOMBIVAX HB.............. 824

REFLUDAN 824

Reglan Injection
  See Metoclopramide 620

Reglan Tablets
  See Metoclopramide 620

Regorafenib
  Stivarga..........................910

RELENZA.......................... 825

RELISTOR......................... 826

RELPAX 827

REMERON......................... 828

REMERONSOLTAB
  See Remeron 828

REMICADE........................ 829

RENAGEL 831

RENVELA 831

REOPRO........................... 832

Repaglinide
  Prandimet 760
  Prandin........................... 761

REPREXAIN
  See Vicoprofen 1038

REQUIP 833

REQUIP XL
  See Requip 833

RESCRIPTOR 834

RESTASIS........................... 835

RESTORIL.......................... 836

Retapamulin
  Altabax............................ 58

RETAVASE........................ 837

Reteplase
  Retavase......................... 837

RETIN-A........................... 837

RETIN-A MICRO
  See Retin-A 837

RETROVIR 838

REVATIO.......................... 840

REVLIMID 841

REYATAZ 842

RHINOCORT AQUA 844

RIASTAP.......................... 845

Ribavirin
  Copegus 256
  Rebetol........................... 820

RIFAMATE........................ 845

Rifampin
  Rifamate......................... 845
  Rifater............................ 847

RIFATER 847

Rifaximin
  Xifaxan.......................... 1077

Rilpivirine
  Complera......................... 251
  Edurant 339

RILUTEK 848

Riluzole
  Rilutek 848

Riociguat
  Adempas 32

RIOMET 849

Risedronate Sodium
  Actonel 21
  Atelvia........................... 112

RISPERDAL....................... 850

RISPERDAL CONSTA........... 852

RISPERDAL M-TAB
  See Risperdal................... 850

Risperidone
  Risperdal......................... 850
  Risperdal Consta............... 852

RITALIN 853

Ritalin-SR
  See Ritalin 853

Ritonavir
  Kaletra........................... 526
  Norvir............................ 683

RITUXAN 854

Rituximab
  Rituxan........................... 854

Rivaroxaban
  Xarelto 1071

Rivastigmine
  Exelon............................ 389

Rizatriptan Benzoate
  Maxalt 601

ROBAXIN............................. 856
Robaxin Injection
  See Robaxin...................... 856
Robaxin-750
  See Robaxin...................... 856
ROCALTROL 857
ROCEPHIN
  See Ceftriaxone 213
Roflumilast
  Daliresp.......................... 276
Romiplostim
  Nplate............................690
Ropinirole
  Requip............................ 833
Rosiglitazone Maleate
  Avandamet...................... 122
  Avandaryl........................ 124
  Avandia........................... 125
Rosuvastatin Calcium
  Crestor........................... 269
ROTATEQ............................ 858
Rotavirus Vaccine, Live,
  Pentavalent
  RotaTeq.......................... 858
ROWASA
  See SF Rowasa................. 880
ROXICET............................. 859
ROXICODONE
  See Oxycodone Tablets..... 724
ROZEREM 860
Rubella Vaccine Live
  M-M-R II 634
Rufinamide
  Banzel............................144
RYTHMOL........................... 861
RYTHMOL SR...................... 862

S

SABRIL............................... 863
Salmeterol
  Advair Diskus..................... 36
  Advair HFA 37
Salmeterol Xinafoate
  Serevent Diskus 876
SAMSCA............................. 864
SANCTURA
  See Sanctura XR 865
SANCTURA XR.................... 865
SANCUSO.......................... 866
SANDOSTATIN LAR............. 867
SAPHRIS............................ 868
Saquinavir Mesylate
  Invirase........................... 509
SAVELLA 869
Saxagliptin
  Kombiglyze XR 537
  Onglyza........................... 707
Scopolamine
  Transderm Scop................ 974
Scopolamine Hydrobromide
  Donnatal.......................... 319
SEASONIQUE 871

SECTRAL............................ 872
Selegiline
  Emsam 352
SELEGILINE 873
Selegiline HCl
  Zelapar..........................1094
SELZENTRY 874
SENSIPAR.......................... 875
SEREVENT DISKUS 876
SEROQUEL......................... 877
SEROQUEL XR.................... 879
Sertraline HCl
  Zoloft.............................1118
Sevelamer Carbonate
  Renvela 831
Sevelamer HCl
  RenaGel........................... 831
SF ROWASA 880
Sildenafil
  Revatio............................840
Sildenafil Citrate
  Viagra............................1034
SILENOR............................ 881
Silodosin
  Rapaflo............................ 817
SILVADENE 882
Silver Sulfadiazine
  Silvadene......................... 882
SIMBRINZA........................ 883
SIMCOR 884
SIMPONI 885
Simvastatin
  Simcor............................ 884
  Vytorin.......................... 1061
  Zocor.............................1112
SINEMET
  See Sinemet CR 887
SINEMET CR 887
SINGULAIR 888
Sipuleucel-T
  Provenge.........................801
Sirolimus
  Rapamune 818
Sitagliptin
  Janumet 516
  Janumet XR...................... 518
  Januvia............................ 519
SKELAXIN.......................... 889
Sodium Bicarbonate
  HalfLytely........................ 464
  Zegerid..........................1093
  Zegerid OTC 1094
Sodium Chloride
  HalfLytely........................ 464
Sodium Hyaluronate
  Hyalgan 483
Sodium Oxybate
  Xyrem............................1081
Sodium Picosulfate
  Prepopik...........................771
Sodium Sulfate
  Suprep 923

Sofosbuvir
  Sovaldi............................ 898
Solifenacin Succinate
  VESIcare.........................1031
SOLIRIS 890
SOLU-CORTEF.................... 891
SOLU-MEDROL 892
SOMA................................ 894
Somatropin
  Valtropin 1015
Somatropin rDNA origin
  Humatrope 476
  Norditropin...................... 678
  Nutropin.......................... 694
  Omnitrope........................ 706
SOMAVERT 895
SONATA............................ 895
Sorafenib
  Nexavar........................... 664
SORIATANE 896
SORILUX............................ 897
SORINE
  See Betapace.................... 153
Sotalol HCl
  Betapace.......................... 153
  Betapace AF..................... 155
Sotret
  See Amnesteem.................. 71
SOVALDI............................ 898
Spinosad
  Natroba 655
SPIRIVA 899
Spironolactone
  Aldactazide 47
  Aldactone......................... 49
SPORANOX 900
Sprintec
  See Ortho-Cyclen 717
SPRYCEL 901
SSD
  See Silvadene 882
STALEVO............................ 902
STARLIX 904
Stavudine
  Zerit..............................1098
STAVZOR........................... 905
STAXYN 907
STELARA............................ 908
STENDRA 909
STIVARGA.......................... 910
STRATTERA........................ 911
STRIANT............................ 912
STRIBILD 913
SUBOXONE FILM 915
SUBSYS............................. 917
SULAR............................... 918
Sulbactam Sodium
  Unasyn 1004
SULFAMETHOXAZOLE/
  TRIMETHOPRIM................ 918

Sulfasalazine
  Azulfidine 140
  Azulfidine EN-tabs 141
Sulfatrim
  See Sulfamethoxazole/
  Trimethoprim 918
Sumatriptan
  Alsuma 57
  Imitrex 488
  Sumavel Dosepro 920
  Treximet 980
SUMAVEL DOSEPRO 920
Sunitinib Malate
  Sutent 925
SUPRAX 922
SUPREP 923
SUSTIVA 923
SUTENT 925
Syeda
  See Yasmin 1083
SYMBICORT 926
SYMBYAX 928
SYNERA 929
SYNERCID ....,,...... 930
SYNTHROID 931

T

TACHOSIL 933
Tacrolimus
  Hecoria 467
  Prograf 786
  Protopic 800
Tadalafil
  Cialis 222
TAMIFLU 934
TAMOXIFEN 935
Tamsulosin HCl
  Flomax 417
  Jalyn 515
TAPAZOLE 936
Tapentadol
  Nucynta 691
  Nucynta ER 693
TARCEVA 937
TARKA 938
TASIGNA 939
TASMAR 941
TAXOTERE
  See Docetaxel 316
TAZICEF 942
Tazobactam
  Zosyn 1128
TAZTIA XT
  See Tiazac 957
TECFIDERA 943
TEFLARO 944
TEGRETOL 944
Tegretol-XR
  See Tegretol 944
TEKAMLO 946
TEKTURNA 947

TEKTURNA HCT 948
Telaprevir
  Incivek 489
Telavancin
  Vibativ 1035
Telbivudine
  Tyzeka 1000
Telithromycin
  Ketek 532
Telmisartan
  Micardis 626
  Micardis HCT 627
  Twynsta 996
Temazepam
  Restoril 836
TEMODAR 949
Temozolomide
  Temodar 949
Temsirolimus
  Torisel 971
Tenecteplase
  TNKase 965
Tenofovir Disoproxil Fumarate
  Atripla 114
  Complera 251
  Stribild 913
  Truvada 993
  Viread 1051
TENORETIC 951
TENORMIN 952
TERAZOSIN 953
Terbinafine HCl
  Lamisil 543
Teriflunomide
  Aubagio 118
Teriparatide, rDNA origin
  Forteo 429
Tesamorelin
  Egrifta 342
TESSALON 953
Testosterone
  Androderm 81
  Androgel 82
  Axiron 134
  Fortesta 430
  Striant 912
Testosterone Cypionate
  Depo-Testosterone 292
Tetanus Toxoid
  Boostrix 164
  Hiberix 472
  Pediarix 737
Tetracaine
  Synera 929
Tetracycline HCl
  Pylera 807
TEVETEN 954
TEVETEN HCT 955
THEOPHYLLINE ER 956
Thiothixene
  Navane 656
Thyroid
  Armour Thyroid 103

Tiagabine HCl
  Gabitril 442
TIAZAC 957
Ticagrelor
  Brilinta 169
Ticarcillin Disodium
  Timentin 960
TIGAN 958
Tigecycline
  Tygacil 997
TIKOSYN 959
TIMENTIN 960
Timolol
  Betimol 157
TIMOLOL 961
Timolol Maleate
  Combigan 246
  Cosopt 263
  Timoptic 962
TIMOPTIC 962
Timoptic in Ocudose
  See Timoptic 962
Timoptic-XE
  See Timoptic 962
TINDAMAX 963
Tinidazole
  Tindamax 963
Tiotropium Bromide
  Spiriva 899
Tipranavir
  Aptivus 94
Tirofiban HCl
  Aggrastat 43
TIVICAY 964
Tizanidine HCl
  Zanaflex 1088
TNKASE 965
TOBRADEX 966
TOBRADEX ST
  See TobraDex 966
Tobramycin
  Bethkis 156
  TobraDex 966
  Zylet 1133
Tocilizumab
  Actemra 16
Tofacitinib
  Xeljanz 1073
TOFRANIL 967
Tolcapone
  Tasmar 941
Tolterodine Tartrate
  Detrol LA 293
Tolvaptan
  Samsca 864
TOPAMAX 968
TOPAMAX SPRINKLE
  See Topamax 968
Topiramate
  Qsymia 809
  Topamax 968
  Trokendi XR 990

TOPROL-XL......................... 970
TORISEL 971
TORSEMIDE....................... 972
TOVIAZ............................... 973
TRADJENTA....................... 974
Tramadol HCl
  Ultracet 1002
  Ultram.............................1003
Trandolapril
  Mavik............................. 599
  Tarka.............................. 938
TRANSDERM SCOP............ 974
Trastuzumab
  Herceptin....................... 471
TRAVATAN Z...................... 975
Travoprost
  Travatan Z 975
TRAZODONE...................... 976
Trazodone HCl
  Oleptro........................... 703
TREANDA........................... 977
TRECATOR......................... 978
TRELSTAR 979
Tretinoin
  Retin-A........................... 837
  Veltin.............................1023
  Ziana.............................. 1106
TREXIMET.......................... 980
Triamterene
  Dyazide.......................... 333
  Dyrenium........................ 335
  Maxzide......................... 605
Triazolam
  Halcion........................... 463
TRIBENZOR 982
TRICOR.............................. 983
TRIGLIDE........................... 984
TRILEPTAL......................... 985
TRILIPIX............................ 987
Trimethobenzamide HCl
  Tigan.............................. 958
TriNessa
  See Ortho Tri-Cyclen.......... 714
TRIOSTAT 988
Tri-Previfem
  See Ortho Tri-Cyclen.......... 714
Tri-Sprintec
  See Ortho Tri-Cyclen.......... 714
TRIZIVIR 989
TROKENDI XR..................... 990
Trospium Chloride
  Sanctura XR..................... 865
TRUSOPT........................... 992
TRUVADA 993
TUDORZA PRESSAIR 994
TUSSICAPS........................ 995
TWYNSTA........................... 996
TYGACIL............................ 997
TYKERB............................. 998

TYLENOL WITH CODEINE
  See Acetaminophen and
  Codeine Tablets.................. 14
TYSABRI............................ 999
TYZEKA............................. 1000

U

U-CORT
  See Alacort...................... 45
Ulipristal Acetate
  Ella.............................. 346
ULORIC............................. 1001
ULTRACET.........................1002
ULTRAM 1003
ULTRAM ER
  See Ultram......................1003
UNASYN 1004
UNIRETIC...........................1005
UNITHROID........................1007
UNIVASC 1009
UROXATRAL 1010
Ustekinumab
  Stelara...........................908

V

VAGIFEM 1011
Valacyclovir HCl
  Valtrex........................... 1014
VALCYTE...........................1012
Valganciclovir HCl
  Valcyte...........................1012
VALIUM 1013
Valproic Acid
  Depakene 282
  Stavzor...........................905
Valsartan
  Diovan............................311
  Diovan HCT 312
  Exforge 391
  Exforge HCT.................... 392
VALTREX 1014
VALTROPIN.........................1015
VANCOCIN ORAL................1016
Vancomycin HCl
  Vancocin Oral 1016
VANCOMYCIN HCL.............1017
Vandetanib
  Caprelsa 193
VANOS 1018
VANTAS............................1019
Vardenafil HCl
  Levitra........................... 556
  Staxyn...........................907
Varenicline
  Chantix.......................... 221
Varicella Virus Vaccine Live
  Varivax...........................1020
VARIVAX 1020
VASERETIC
  See Enalapril/HCTZ........... 355
VASOTEC...........................1021

VECTIBIX............................1022
VECTICAL...........................1023
VELTIN 1023
Venlafaxine HCl
  Effexor XR....................... 340
VENTOLIN HFA 1024
VERAMYST.........................1025
Verapamil HCl
  Calan..............................184
  Calan SR..........................185
  Covera-HS...................... 266
  Tarka.............................. 938
  Verelan...........................1027
  Verelan PM......................1028
VERDESO 1026
VERELAN 1027
VERELAN PM......................1028
VERSACLOZ........................1030
VESICARE..........................1031
VFEND..............................1032
VIAGRA.............................1034
VIBATIV.............................1035
VIBRAMYCIN 1036
VIBRA-TABS
  See Vibramycin.................1036
VICODIN............................1037
Vicodin ES
  See Vicodin 1037
Vicodin HP
  See Vicodin 1037
VICOPROFEN......................1038
VICTOZA 1040
VICTRELIS 1041
VIDEX
  See Videx EC 1042
VIDEX EC...........................1042
Vigabatrin
  Sabril............................. 863
VIGAMOX 1043
VIIBRYD 1044
Vilanterol
  Breo Ellipta......................166
Vilazodone HCl
  Viibryd 1044
VIMOVO.............................1045
VIMPAT.............................1047
VIRACEPT..........................1048
VIRAMUNE
  See Viramune XR 1049
VIRAMUNE XR....................1049
VIREAD 1051
Vismodegib
  Erivedge......................... 376
VISTIDE 1052
VITRASERT.........................1053
VIVELLE-DOT......................1054
VIVITROL...........................1056
VOLTAREN GEL...................1057
VOLTAREN OPHTHALMIC...1058
VOLTAREN-XR.....................1059

Voriconazole
  Vfend 1032
Vorinostat
  Zolinza 1117
Vortioxetine
  Brintellix 170
VOTRIENT 1060
VYTORIN 1061
VYVANSE 1063

W

Warfarin Sodium
  Coumadin 264
WELCHOL 1064
WELLBUTRIN SR 1065
WELLBUTRIN XL 1067

X

XALATAN 1068
XANAX 1069
XANAX XR 1070
XARELTO 1071
XELJANZ 1073
XELODA 1074
XENICAL 1075
XGEVA 1076
XIFAXAN 1077
XOFIGO 1078
XOLEGEL 1078
XOPENEX HFA 1079
XTANDI 1080
XYREM 1081
XYZAL 1082

Y

YASMIN 1083
YAZ 1084
YERVOY 1086

Z

Zafirlukast
  Accolate 9
Zaleplon
  Sonata 895

ZALTRAP 1087
ZANAFLEX 1088
Zanamivir
  Relenza 825
Zantac Injection
  See Ranitidine 816
Zantac Oral
  See Ranitidine 816
ZARAH 1089
ZARONTIN 1090
ZAROXOLYN 1091
ZEBETA 1092
ZEGERID 1093
ZEGERID OTC 1094
ZELAPAR 1094
ZEMPLAR ORAL 1095
ZENPEP 1096
ZENTRIP 1097
ZERIT 1098
ZESTORETIC 1099
ZESTRIL 1100
ZETIA 1102
ZEVALIN 1103
ZIAC 1104
ZIAGEN 1105
ZIANA 1106
Zidovudine
  Combivir 250
  Retrovir 838
  Trizivir 989
Zileuton
  Zyflo CR 1132
ZINACEF 1107
ZINECARD 1108
Ziprasidone
  Geodon 446
ZIPSOR 1109
ZITHROMAX 1109
Ziv-aflibercept
  Zaltrap 1087
ZMAX 1111
ZOCOR 1112
ZOFRAN 1114

ZOLADEX 1-MONTH 1115
ZOLADEX 3-MONTH 1116
Zoledronic Acid
  Reclast 822
  Zometa 1121
ZOLINZA 1117
Zolmitriptan
  Zomig 1122
ZOLOFT 1118
Zolpidem Tartrate
  Ambien 64
  Ambien CR 65
  Edluar 338
  Intermezzo 501
  Zolpimist 1119
ZOLPIMIST 1119
ZOMETA 1121
ZOMIG 1122
ZOMIG-ZMT
  See Zomig 1122
ZONEGRAN 1123
Zonisamide
  Zonegran 1123
ZORTRESS 1124
ZORVOLEX 1126
ZOSTAVAX 1127
Zoster Vaccine Live
  Zostavax 1127
ZOSYN 1128
ZOVIRAX ORAL 1129
ZUPLENZ 1130
ZYBAN 1131
ZYFLO
  See Zyflo CR 1132
ZYFLO CR 1132
ZYLET 1133
ZYMAR 1134
ZYMAXID 1135
ZYPREXA 1135
ZYPREXA RELPREVV 1137
ZYPREXA ZYDIS
  See Zyprexa 1135
ZYTIGA 1138

Therapeutic Class Index

THERAPEUTIC CLASS INDEX

Organized alphabetically, this index includes the therapeutic class of each drug in the Product Information section. Therapeutic class headings are based on information provided in the drug monographs.

The drug entries listed under each bold therapeutic class are organized alphabetically by brand name or monograph title (shown in capitalized letters), followed by the generic name in parentheses.

A

ACE INHIBITOR
ACCUPRIL
(quinapril HCl) 10
ACEON
(perindopril erbumine) 12
ALTACE
(ramipril) 58
CAPTOPRIL
(captopril) 194
ENALAPRILAT
(enalaprilat) 357
EPANED
(enalapril) 364
FOSINOPRIL
(fosinopril sodium) 433
LOTENSIN
(benazepril HCl) 579
MAVIK
(trandolapril) 599
PRINIVIL
(lisinopril) 777
UNIVASC
(moexipril HCl) 1009
VASOTEC
(enalapril maleate) 1021
ZESTRIL
(lisinopril) 1100

ACE INHIBITOR/CALCIUM CHANNEL BLOCKER (DIHYDROPYRIDINE)
LOTREL
(benazepril HCl-amlodipine besylate) 581

ACE INHIBITOR/CALCIUM CHANNEL BLOCKER (NONDIHYDROPYRIDINE)
TARKA
(verapamil HCl-trandolapril) 938

ACE INHIBITOR/THIAZIDE DIURETIC
ACCURETIC
(quinapril HCl-hydrochlorothiazide) 11
ENALAPRIL/HCTZ
(enalapril maleate-hydrochlorothiazide) 355
FOSINOPRIL/HCTZ
(fosinopril sodium-hydrochlorothiazide) 434
LOTENSIN HCT
(benazepril HCl-hydrochlorothiazide) 580
UNIRETIC
(moexipril HCl-hydrochlorothiazide) 1005
ZESTORETIC
(hydrochlorothiazide-lisinopril) 1099

ACETAMIDE LOCAL ANESTHETIC
EMLA
(lidocaine-prilocaine) 351
LIDODERM PATCH
(lidocaine) 563

ACETYLCHOLINESTERASE INHIBITOR
ARICEPT
(donepezil HCl) 100
EXELON
(rivastigmine) 389
RAZADYNE ER
(galantamine HBr) 819

ALDOSTERONE BLOCKER
ALDACTONE
(spironolactone) 49
INSPRA
(eplerenone) 498

ALDOSTERONE BLOCKER/THIAZIDE DIURETIC
ALDACTAZIDE
(hydrochlorothiazide-spironolactone) 47

ALKYLATING AGENT
TREANDA
(bendamustine HCl) 977

ALKYLATING AGENT (IMIDAZOTETRAZINE DERIVATIVE)
TEMODAR
(temozolomide) 949

ALLYLAMINE ANTIFUNGAL
LAMISIL
(terbinafine HCl) 543

ALPHA-ADRENERGIC AGONIST
CATAPRES
(clonidine HCl) 203

ALPHA-AGONIST/MONOSULFAMYL DIURETIC
CLORPRES
(clonidine HCl-chlorthalidone) 240

ALPHA-GLUCOSIDASE INHIBITOR
GLYSET
(miglitol) 459
PRECOSE
(acarbose) 764

ALPHA$_1$ BLOCKER/NONSELECTIVE BETA-BLOCKER
LABETALOL
(labetalol HCl) 540

ALPHA$_1$/BETA-BLOCKER
COREG CR
(carvedilol phosphate) 260

ALPHA$_1$-ANTAGONIST
FLOMAX
(tamsulosin HCl) 417
RAPAFLO
(silodosin) 817
UROXATRAL
(alfuzosin HCl) 1010

ALPHA₁-BLOCKER (QUINAZOLINE)

CARDURA
(doxazosin mesylate)................................. 200

CARDURA XL
(doxazosin mesylate)................................. 201

MINIPRESS
(prazosin HCl)... 629

TERAZOSIN
(terazosin HCl).. 953

ALPHA₂ₐ-AGONIST

INTUNIV
(guanfacine)... 504

ALPHA₂-AGONIST

KAPVAY
(clonidine HCl).. 528

PRECEDEX
(dexmedetomidine HCl)............................. 763

ZANAFLEX
(tizanidine HCl)....................................... 1088

ALPHA₂-AGONIST/BETA-BLOCKER

COMBIGAN
(timolol maleate-brimonidine tartrate).........246

ALPHA₂-AGONIST/CARBONIC ANHYDRASE INHIBITOR

SIMBRINZA
(brimonidine tartrate-brinzolamide).............883

AMINOGLYCOSIDE

AMIKACIN
(amikacin sulfate)......................................69

BETHKIS
(tobramycin)...156

AMINOGLYCOSIDE/CORTICOSTEROID

TOBRADEX
(dexamethasone-tobramycin)......................966

ZYLET
(loteprednol etabonate-tobramycin)............1133

AMINOKETONE

APLENZIN
(bupropion hydrobromide)...........................89

WELLBUTRIN SR
(bupropion HCl)....................................... 1065

WELLBUTRIN XL
(bupropion HCl)....................................... 1067

ZYBAN
(bupropion HCl)....................................... 1131

AMINOPENICILLIN/BETA LACTAMASE INHIBITOR

AMOXICILLIN/CLAVULANATE 600/42.9
(clavulanate potassium-amoxicillin)............. 73

AUGMENTIN
(clavulanate potassium-amoxicillin)............. 119

AUGMENTIN XR
(clavulanate potassium-amoxicillin)............. 120

AMMONIUM DETOXICANT

ENULOSE
(lactulose)... 363

ANALGESIC

OFIRMEV
(acetaminophen)..................................... 700

QUTENZA
(capsaicin)... 813

ANALGESIC COMBINATION

ROXICET
(oxycodone HCl-acetaminophen)................. 859

ANALGESIC/BARBITURATE

FIORINAL
(caffeine-aspirin-butalbital)........................412

ANDROGEN

ANDRODERM
(testosterone).. 81

ANDROGEL
(testosterone)..82

AXIRON
(testosterone).. 134

DEPO-TESTOSTERONE
(testosterone cypionate).......................... 292

FORTESTA
(testosterone).. 430

STRIANT
(testosterone)..912

ANESTHETIC AGENT

LUSEDRA
(fospropofol disodium)..............................591

ANESTHETIC/CORTICOSTEROID

EPIFOAM
(pramoxine HCl-hydrocortisone acetate)...... 365

ANGIOTENSIN II RECEPTOR ANTAGONIST

ATACAND
(candesartan cilexetil)............................... 110

AVAPRO
(irbesartan)..126

BENICAR
(olmesartan medoxomil)........................... 148

COZAAR
(losartan potassium)................................ 267

DIOVAN
(valsartan)... 311

EDARBI
(azilsartan medoxomil)............................. 336

MICARDIS
(telmisartan)... 626

TEVETEN
(eprosartan mesylate)..............................954

ANGIOTENSIN II RECEPTOR ANTAGONIST/ THIAZIDE DIURETIC

ATACAND HCT
(candesartan cilexetil-hydrochlorothiazide).... 111

AVALIDE
(hydrochlorothiazide-irbesartan).................. 121

BENICAR HCT
(olmesartan medoxomil-hydrochlorothiazide).. 149

DIOVAN HCT
(hydrochlorothiazide-valsartan)...................312

EDARBYCLOR
(azilsartan medoxomil-chlorthalidone).........337

HYZAAR
(losartan potassium-hydrochlorothiazide)....485

MICARDIS HCT
(hydrochlorothiazide-telmisartan)............... 627

TEVETEN HCT
(eprosartan mesylate-hydrochlorothiazide)...955

ANORECTIC SYMPATHOMIMETIC AMINE/ SULFAMATE-SUBSTITUTED MONOSACCHARIDE

QSYMIA
(phentermine-topiramate)......................... 809

ANTHRACYCLINE
DOXIL
(doxorubicin HCl liposome) 323

ANTIBACTERIAL AGENT
VIBATIV
(telavancin) 1035

ANTIBACTERIAL/CORTICOSTEROID COMBINATION
CIPRO HC
(ciprofloxacin HCl-hydrocortisone) 226

CIPRODEX
(dexamethasone-ciprofloxacin) 228

MAXITROL
(neomycin sulfate-polymyxin B sulfate-dexamethasone) 604

ANTIBACTERIAL/KERATOLYTIC
ACANYA
(clindamycin phosphate-benzoyl peroxide) 8

BENZACLIN
(clindamycin phosphate-benzoyl peroxide) ... 151

EPIDUO
(benzoyl peroxide-adapalene) 365

ANTICHOLINERGIC
ATROVENT NASAL
(ipratropium bromide) 117

DICYCLOMINE HCL
(dicyclomine HCl) 300

LEVBID
(hyoscyamine sulfate) 554

OXYBUTYNIN
(oxybutynin chloride) 723

TRANSDERM SCOP
(scopolamine) 974

ANTICHOLINERGIC BRONCHODILATOR
ATROVENT HFA
(ipratropium bromide) 116

SPIRIVA
(tiotropium bromide) 899

TUDORZA PRESSAIR
(aclidinium bromide) 994

ANTICHOLINERGIC/BARBITURATE
DONNATAL
(atropine sulfate-hyoscyamine sulfate-scopolamine hydrobromide-phenobarbital) 319

ANTICHOLINERGIC/BENZODIAZEPINE
LIBRAX
(chlordiazepoxide HCl-clidinium bromide) 561

ANTICHOLINERGIC/BETA₂-AGONIST
COMBIVENT RESPIMAT
(ipratropium bromide-albuterol) 249

DUONEB
(ipratropium bromide-albuterol sulfate) 329

ANTICHOLINERGIC/OPIOID
LOMOTIL
(diphenoxylate HCl-atropine sulfate) 574

ANTIDIARRHEAL
FULYZAQ
(crofelemer) 438

ANTIESTROGEN
TAMOXIFEN
(tamoxifen citrate) 935

ANTIFOLATE
ALIMTA
(pemetrexed) 52

ANTIHISTAMINE
ASTELIN
(azelastine HCl) 109

DIPHENHYDRAMINE INJECTION
(diphenhydramine HCl) 314

ZENTRIP
(meclizine HCl) 1097

ANTIHISTAMINE/OPIOID ANTITUSSIVE
TUSSICAPS
(chlorpheniramine polistirex-hydrocodone polistirex) 995

ANTIHISTAMINE/VITAMIN B6 ANALOG
DICLEGIS
(pyridoxine HCl-doxylamine succinate) 298

ANTI-INFECTIVE/CORTICOSTEROID
ALCORTIN-A
(hydrocortisone-iodoquinol) 47

ANTIMANIC AGENT
LITHIUM ER
(lithium carbonate) 568

ANTIMICROTUBULE AGENT
ABRAXANE
(paclitaxel protein-bound) 4

DOCETAXEL
(docetaxel) 316

HALAVEN
(eribulin mesylate) 462

IXEMPRA
(ixabepilone) 514

JEVTANA
(cabazitaxel) 522

PACLITAXEL
(paclitaxel) 727

ANTIPROTOZOAL AGENT
TINDAMAX
(tinidazole) 963

ANTIPROTOZOAL AGENT/DIHYDROFOLATE REDUCTASE INHIBITOR
MALARONE
(proguanil HCl-atovaquone) 597

ANTITUSSIVE/PHENOTHIAZINE DERIVATIVE
PROMETHAZINE W/ CODEINE
(promethazine HCl-codeine phosphate) 793

ANTITUSSIVE/PHENOTHIAZINE DERIVATIVE/ SYMPATHOMIMETIC
PROMETHAZINE VC/CODEINE
(phenylephrine HCl-promethazine HCl-codeine phosphate) 791

ARB/CALCIUM CHANNEL BLOCKER (DIHYDROPYRIDINE)
AZOR
(olmesartan medoxomil-amlodipine) 139

EXFORGE
(amlodipine-valsartan) 391

TWYNSTA
(amlodipine-telmisartan) 996

ARB/CALCIUM CHANNEL BLOCKER (DIHYDROPYRIDINE)/THIAZIDE DIURETIC
EXFORGE HCT
(hydrochlorothiazide-amlodipine-valsartan). 392
TRIBENZOR
(olmesartan medoxomil-hydrochlorothiazide-amlodipine)..982

ARGININE VASOPRESSIN ANTAGONIST
SAMSCA
(tolvaptan) 864

AROMATASE INACTIVATOR
AROMASIN
(exemestane).. 104

ARTEMISININ-BASED COMBINATION THERAPY
COARTEM
(lumefantrine-artemether)...........................242

ATYPICAL ANXIOLYTIC
BUSPIRONE
(buspirone HCl) 177

AZOLE ANTIFUNGAL
DIFLUCAN ORAL
(fluconazole)..303
EXTINA
(ketoconazole)...394
KETOCONAZOLE TABLETS
(ketoconazole)...533
NOXAFIL
(posaconazole)...689
ORAVIG
(miconazole) 710
SPORANOX
(itraconazole) 900
VFEND
(voriconazole)...1032
XOLEGEL
(ketoconazole)..1078

AZOLE ANTIFUNGAL/CORTICOSTEROID
LOTRISONE
(betamethasone dipropionate-clotrimazole)... 583

B

BACTERIAL PROTEIN SYNTHESIS INHIBITOR
BACTROBAN NASAL
(mupirocin calcium) 142
BACTROBAN TOPICAL
(mupirocin calcium) 143

BARBITURATE
PHENOBARBITAL
(phenobarbital) 751

BENZISOTHIAZOL DERIVATIVE
LATUDA
(lurasidone HCl)..547

BENZISOXAZOLE DERIVATIVE
FANAPT
(iloperidone)...398
GEODON
(ziprasidone) 446
INVEGA
(paliperidone)... 506
INVEGA SUSTENNA
(paliperidone palmitate)...............................508

RISPERDAL
(risperidone)..850
RISPERDAL CONSTA
(risperidone)..852

BENZODIAZEPINE
ATIVAN INJECTION
(lorazepam).. 113
CLONAZEPAM
(clonazepam)..238
HALCION
(triazolam)..463
LIBRIUM
(chlordiazepoxide HCl)..................................562
LORAZEPAM ORAL
(lorazepam)..575
NIRAVAM
(alprazolam)...672
RESTORIL
(temazepam)..836
VALIUM
(diazepam) 1013
XANAX
(alprazolam) 1069
XANAX XR
(alprazolam) 1070

BENZOTHIAZOLE
RILUTEK
(riluzole)..848

BETA-BLOCKER (GROUP II/III ANTIARRHYTHMIC)
BETAPACE
(sotalol HCl)...153
BETAPACE AF
(sotalol HCl)...155

BETA-LACTAMASE INHIBITOR/ BROAD-SPECTRUM PENICILLIN
TIMENTIN
(ticarcillin disodium-clavulanate potassium) .. 960
ZOSYN
(piperacillin-tazobactam) 1128

BETA-LACTAMASE INHIBITOR/ SEMISYNTHETIC PENICILLIN
UNASYN
(ampicillin sodium-sulbactam sodium) 1004

BETA$_2$-AGONIST
ALBUTEROL
(albuterol sulfate)... 46
ARCAPTA
(indacaterol)..98
BROVANA
(arformoterol tartrate)..................................172
FORADIL
(formoterol fumarate) 426
MAXAIR
(pirbuterol acetate) 600
PERFOROMIST
(formoterol fumarate) 748
PROAIR HFA
(albuterol sulfate)..779
SEREVENT DISKUS
(salmeterol xinafoate) 876

VENTOLIN HFA
(albuterol sulfate).....................................1024

XOPENEX HFA
(levalbuterol tartrate)................................1079

BETA$_2$-AGONIST/CORTICOSTEROID

ADVAIR DISKUS
(fluticasone propionate-salmeterol)...............36

ADVAIR HFA
(fluticasone propionate-salmeterol)...............37

BREO ELLIPTA
(fluticasone furoate-vilanterol) 166

DULERA
(formoterol fumarate dihydrate-
mometasone furoate)................................328

SYMBICORT
(formoterol fumarate dihydrate-budesonide)..926

BIGUANIDE

FORTAMET
(metformin HCl)..427

GLUCOPHAGE XR
(metformin HCl)..452

GLUMETZA
(metformin HCl)..457

RIOMET
(metformin HCl)..849

BIGUANIDE/DIPEPTIDYL PEPTIDASE-4 INHIBITOR

JANUMET
(metformin HCl-sitagliptin)..........................516

JANUMET XR
(metformin HCl-sitagliptin)..........................518

JENTADUETO
(metformin HCl-linagliptin)..........................520

KAZANO
(metformin HCl-alogliptin)..........................530

KOMBIGLYZE XR
(metformin HCl-saxagliptin)........................537

BIGUANIDE/MEGLITINIDE

PRANDIMET
(metformin HCl-repaglinide)........................760

BIGUANIDE/SULFONYLUREA

GLUCOVANCE
(metformin HCl-glyburide) 455

BIGUANIDE/THIAZOLIDINEDIONE

ACTOPLUS MET XR
(metformin HCl-pioglitazone) 22

AVANDAMET
(metformin HCl-rosiglitazone maleate).........122

BILE ACID SEQUESTRANT

COLESTID
(colestipol HCl)..246

WELCHOL
(colesevelam HCl) 1064

BIOLOGICAL RESPONSE MODIFIER

EXTAVIA
(interferon beta-1b)...................................393

INFERGEN
(interferon alfacon-1).................................493

INTRON A
(interferon alfa-2b)...................................502

REBIF
(interferon beta-1a)...................................821

BISPHOSPHONATE

ACTONEL
(risedronate sodium)....................................21

ALENDRONATE
(alendronate sodium)...................................51

ATELVIA
(risedronate sodium).................................112

BINOSTO
(alendronate sodium).................................162

BONIVA
(ibandronate sodium).................................163

RECLAST
(zoledronic acid)......................................822

ZOMETA
(zoledronic acid).....................................1121

BISPHOSPHONATE/VITAMIN D ANALOG

FOSAMAX PLUS D
(alendronate sodium-cholecalciferol)...........432

BOWEL CLEANSER

OSMOPREP
(monobasic sodium phosphate monohydrate-
dibasic sodium phosphate) 720

PREPOPIK
(sodium picosulfate-magnesium oxide-
anhydrous citric acid)................................771

SUPREP
(potassium sulfate-magnesium sulfate-
sodium sulfate) 923

BOWEL CLEANSER/STIMULANT LAXATIVE

HALFLYTELY
(polyethylene glycol 3350-sodium
bicarbonate-potassium chloride-
sodium chloride-bisacodyl) 464

BROAD-SPECTRUM ANTIFUNGAL

PENLAC
(ciclopirox) 742

BUTYROPHENONE

HALOPERIDOL
(haloperidol)...465

C

CALCIMIMETIC AGENT

SENSIPAR
(cinacalcet)..875

CALCIUM CHANNEL BLOCKER (DIHYDROPYRIDINE)

ADALAT CC
(nifedipine) 27

CARDENE IV
(nicardipine HCl)......................................197

CARDENE SR
(nicardipine HCl)......................................197

CLEVIPREX
(clevidipine)..235

FELODIPINE ER
(felodipine)...404

NIFEDIPINE
(nifedipine)..670

NORVASC
(amlodipine besylate).................................682

PROCARDIA XL
(nifedipine)...781

SULAR
(nisoldipine)..918

CALCIUM CHANNEL BLOCKER (DIHYDROPYRIDINE)/RENIN INHIBITOR
TEKAMLO
(aliskiren-amlodipine)...................................946

CALCIUM CHANNEL BLOCKER (DIHYDROPYRIDINE)/RENIN INHIBITOR/ THIAZIDE DIURETIC
AMTURNIDE
(aliskiren-hydrochlorothiazide-amlodipine) 78

CALCIUM CHANNEL BLOCKER (NONDIHYDROPYRIDINE)
CALAN
(verapamil HCl)... 184
CALAN SR
(verapamil HCl)...185
CARDIZEM
(diltiazem HCl)... 198
CARDIZEM CD
(diltiazem HCl)... 199
COVERA-HS
(verapamil HCl)..266
DILACOR XR
(diltiazem HCl)..306
DILTIAZEM INJECTION
(diltiazem HCl).. 310
TIAZAC
(diltiazem HCl)...957
VERELAN
(verapamil HCl)...1027
VERELAN PM
(verapamil HCl) 1028

CALCIUM CHANNEL BLOCKER/HMG-COA REDUCTASE INHIBITOR
CADUET
(atorvastatin calcium-amlodipine besylate) ...182

CANNABINOID
CESAMET
(nabilone)...220
MARINOL
(dronabinol)...598

CARBAMOYL PHOSPHATE SYNTHETASE 1
CARBAGLU
(carglumic acid).. 196

CARBAPENEM
DORIBAX
(doripenem)..320
INVANZ
(ertapenem) 505
MERREM
(meropenem).. 611

CARBONIC ANHYDRASE INHIBITOR
AZOPT
(brinzolamide) 138
TRUSOPT
(dorzolamide HCl)...992

CARBONIC ANHYDRASE INHIBITOR/ NONSELECTIVE BETA-BLOCKER
COSOPT
(dorzolamide HCl-timolol maleate).............. 263

CARBOXAMIDE
EQUETRO
(carbamazepine)...373

TEGRETOL
(carbamazepine).. 944

CARBOXYLIC ACID DERIVATIVE
DEPAKENE
(valproic acid).. 282
STAVZOR
(valproic acid)..905

CARDIAC GLYCOSIDE
DIGOXIN ORAL
(digoxin) 304

CCR5 CO-RECEPTOR ANTAGONIST
SELZENTRY
(maraviroc)...874

CD30-DIRECTED ANTIBODY-DRUG CONJUGATE
ADCETRIS
(brentuximab vedotin).....................................28

CENTRAL ACTING ANALGESIC
NUCYNTA
(tapentadol) 691
NUCYNTA ER
(tapentadol) 693
ULTRACET
(tramadol HCl-acetaminophen) 1002
ULTRAM
(tramadol HCl)..1003

CEPHALOSPORIN
TEFLARO
(ceftaroline fosamil)..................................... 944

CEPHALOSPORIN (1ST GENERATION)
CEFADROXIL
(cefadroxil)...207
CEFAZOLIN
(cefazolin)..207
CEPHALEXIN
(cephalexin)...219

CEPHALOSPORIN (2ND GENERATION)
CEFACLOR
(cefaclor)...205
CEFACLOR ER
(cefaclor)...206
CEFOXITIN
(cefoxitin) 209
CEFPROZIL
(cefprozil).. 211
CEFTIN
(cefuroxime axetil) 212
ZINACEF
(cefuroxime sodium) 1107

CEPHALOSPORIN (3RD GENERATION)
CEFDINIR
(cefdinir)...208
CEFPODOXIME
(cefpodoxime proxetil)................................. 210
CEFTRIAXONE
(ceftriaxone sodium) 213
FORTAZ
(ceftazidime) 428
SUPRAX
(cefixime) 922
TAZICEF
(ceftazidime) 942

CEPHALOSPORIN (4TH GENERATION)
MAXIPIME
(cefepime HCl)..602

CFTR POTENTIATOR
KALYDECO
(ivacaftor) 528

CHLORIDE CHANNEL ACTIVATOR
AMITIZA
(lubiprostone)..70

CHOLESTEROL ABSORPTION INHIBITOR
ZETIA
(ezetimibe) 1102

CHOLESTEROL ABSORPTION INHIBITOR/ HMG-COA REDUCTASE INHIBITOR
LIPTRUZET
(ezetimibe-atorvastatin)..............................566
VYTORIN
(ezetimibe-simvastatin)............................1061

CLASS I ANTIARRHYTHMIC
NORPACE
(disopyramide phosphate)..........................681

CLASS IA ANTIARRHYTHMIC/ SCHIZONTICIDE ANTIMALARIAL
QUINIDINE GLUCONATE INJECTION
(quinidine gluconate) 811

CLASS IC ANTIARRHYTHMIC
RYTHMOL
(propafenone HCl) 861
RYTHMOL SR
(propafenone HCl)......................................862

CLASS III ANTIARRHYTHMIC
CORDARONE
(amiodarone HCl).......................................257
CORVERT
(ibutilide fumarate) 262
MULTAQ
(dronedarone)..642
NEXTERONE
(amiodarone HCl).......................................668
TIKOSYN
(dofetilide)..959

CNS DEPRESSANT
XYREM
(sodium oxybate)......................................1081

COMT INHIBITOR
COMTAN
(entacapone)..253
TASMAR
(tolcapone) 941

COMT INHIBITOR/DOPA-DECARBOXYLASE INHIBITOR/DOPAMINE PRECURSOR
STALEVO
(entacapone-levodopa-carbidopa) 902

CORTICOSTEROID
ALACORT
(hydrocortisone)...45
ALREX
(loteprednol etabonate) 56
ASMANEX
(mometasone furoate)................................108

CORDRAN
(flurandrenolide)..259
ELOCON
(mometasone furoate)................................347
ENTOCORT EC
(budesonide) 362
FLONASE
(fluticasone propionate)..............................418
FLOVENT HFA
(fluticasone propionate)..............................419
FLUDROCORTISONE
(fludrocortisone acetate)............................420
FLUTICASONE TOPICAL
(fluticasone propionate)..............................421
LOTEMAX SUSPENSION
(loteprednol etabonate) 578
LUXIQ
(betamethasone valerate)...........................593
NASONEX
(mometasone furoate monohydrate)............651
OLUX-E
(clobetasol propionate)...............................704
PRED FORTE
(prednisolone acetate) 765
PULMICORT
(budesonide) 806
QVAR
(beclomethasone dipropionate)...................814
RHINOCORT AQUA
(budesonide) 844
VANOS
(fluocinonide) 1018
VERAMYST
(fluticasone furoate).................................1025
VERDESO
(desonide) 1026

COX-2 INHIBITOR
CELEBREX
(celecoxib)..215

CYCLIC POLYPEPTIDE IMMUNOSUPPRESSANT
NEORAL
(cyclosporine)...657

CYTOPROTECTIVE AGENT
FUSILEV
(levoleucovorin)..440

D

DEPIGMENTATION AGENT
EPIQUIN MICRO
(hydroquinone)..367

DIBENZAPINE DERIVATIVE
CLOZAPINE
(clozapine)..241
FAZACLO
(clozapine)..401
SAPHRIS
(asenapine)...868
SEROQUEL
(quetiapine fumarate)................................877
SEROQUEL XR
(quetiapine fumarate)................................879
VERSACLOZ
(clozapine)..1030

DIBENZAZEPINE
APTIOM
(eslicarbazepine acetate)............................. 92
OXTELLAR XR
(oxcarbazepine).. 722
TRILEPTAL
(oxcarbazepine).. 985

DICARBAMATE ANTICONVULSANT
FELBATOL
(felbamate)... 403

DIHYDROFOLIC ACID REDUCTASE INHIBITOR
METHOTREXATE INJECTION
(methotrexate)... 617

DIPEPTIDYL PEPTIDASE-4 INHIBITOR
JANUVIA
(sitagliptin).. 519
NESINA
(alogliptin)... 659
ONGLYZA
(saxagliptin)... 707
TRADJENTA
(linagliptin).. 974

**DIPEPTIDYL PEPTIDASE-4 INHIBITOR/
THIAZOLIDINEDIONE**
OSENI
(pioglitazone-alogliptin)............................. 718

DIRECT ACTING SKELETAL MUSCLE RELAXANT
DANTRIUM
(dantrolene sodium)................................... 277

DIRECT THROMBIN INHIBITOR
ANGIOMAX
(bivalirudin)... 85
ARGATROBAN
(argatroban).. 99
PRADAXA
(dabigatran etexilate mesylate)................... 758

DNA METHYLTRANSFERASE INHIBITOR
DACOGEN
(decitabine).. 276

**DOPA-DECARBOXYLASE INHIBITOR/
DOPAMINE PRECURSOR**
PARCOPA
(levodopa-carbidopa)............................... 730
SINEMET CR
(levodopa-carbidopa)............................... 887

DOPAMINE ANTAGONIST/PROKINETIC
METOCLOPRAMIDE
(metoclopramide)..................................... 620

DOPAMINE RECEPTOR AGONIST
AMANTADINE
(amantadine HCl)....................................... 62
PARLODEL
(bromocriptine mesylate)........................... 732

E

ECHINOCANDIN
CANCIDAS
(caspofungin acetate).............................. 192
ERAXIS
(anidulafungin).. 374
MYCAMINE
(micafungin sodium).................................. 643

EDTA DERIVATIVE
ZINECARD
(dexrazoxane).. 1108

EMERGENCY CONTRACEPTIVE KIT
ELLA
(ulipristal acetate)................................... 346

EMETIC RESPONSE MODIFIER
TIGAN
(trimethobenzamide HCl)........................... 958

ENDOGENOUS NUCLEOSIDE
ADENOCARD
(adenosine)... 33

ENDOTHELIN RECEPTOR ANTAGONIST
LETAIRIS
(ambrisentan)... 551
OPSUMIT
(macitentan).. 708

**EPIDERMAL GROWTH FACTOR RECEPTOR
(EGFR) ANTAGONIST**
ERBITUX
(cetuximab) 375

**EPIDERMAL GROWTH FACTOR RECEPTOR
TYROSINE KINASE INHIBITOR**
TARCEVA
(erlotinib) 937

ERYTHROPOIESIS AGENT
FOLIC ACID
(folic acid) 425

ERYTHROPOIESIS STIMULATOR
ARANESP
(darbepoetin alfa).................................... 95
EPOGEN
(epoetin alfa)... 370
PROCRIT
(epoetin alfa)... 785

ESTROGEN
CLIMARA
(estradiol)... 236
DIVIGEL
(estradiol)... 314
ENJUVIA
(conjugated estrogens) 360
ESTRACE
(estradiol)... 378
ESTRADERM
(estradiol)... 380
EVAMIST
(estradiol)... 385
PREMARIN TABLETS
(conjugated estrogens) 767
PREMARIN VAGINAL
(conjugated estrogens) 768
VAGIFEM
(estradiol)... 1011
VIVELLE-DOT
(estradiol)... 1054

ESTROGEN RECEPTOR ANTAGONIST
FASLODEX
(fulvestrant).. 400

ESTROGEN/PROGESTOGEN COMBINATION

ACTIVELLA
(norethindrone acetate-estradiol)................20

ANGELIQ
(drospirenone-estradiol) 84

AVIANE
(ethinyl estradiol-levonorgestrel)................129

BEYAZ
(levomefolate calcium-drospirenone-
ethinyl estradiol)...159

COMBIPATCH
(norethindrone acetate-estradiol)...............248

ESTROSTEP FE
(norethindrone acetate-ferrous fumarate-
ethinyl estradiol)...381

FEMCON FE
(ethinyl estradiol-ferrous fumarate-
norethindrone).. 405

LO/OVRAL
(ethinyl estradiol-norgestrel) 570

LOESTRIN 21
(norethindrone acetate-ethinyl estradiol) 571

LOSEASONIQUE
(ethinyl estradiol-levonorgestrel)................ 577

MIRCETTE
(ethinyl estradiol-desogestrel)....................632

NATAZIA
(estradiol valerate-dienogest)......................653

NORINYL 1/50
(norethindrone-mestranol) 679

NUVARING
(etonogestrel-ethinyl estradiol) 696

ORTHO EVRA
(ethinyl estradiol-norelgestromin)................712

ORTHO TRI-CYCLEN
(ethinyl estradiol-norgestimate)................... 714

ORTHO TRI-CYCLEN LO
(ethinyl estradiol-norgestimate)..................716

ORTHO-CYCLEN
(ethinyl estradiol-norgestimate)..................717

OVCON-35
(ethinyl estradiol-norethindrone) 721

PREMPHASE
(medroxyprogesterone acetate-
conjugated estrogens) 770

SEASONIQUE
(ethinyl estradiol-levonorgestrel)................871

YASMIN
(drospirenone-ethinyl estradiol) 1083

YAZ
(drospirenone-ethinyl estradiol) 1084

ZARAH
(drospirenone-ethinyl estradiol) 1089

F

FIBRIC ACID DERIVATIVE

ANTARA
(fenofibrate) 86

FIBRICOR
(fenofibric acid) 410

LIPOFEN
(fenofibrate) 565

LOFIBRA
(fenofibrate) 573

LOPID
(gemfibrozil)... 575

TRICOR
(fenofibrate)..983

TRIGLIDE
(fenofibrate)..984

TRILIPIX
(fenofibric acid)...987

FIBRINOGEN/TOPICAL THROMBIN

TACHOSIL
(fibrin sealant) 933

5-ALPHA REDUCTASE INHIBITOR/ALPHA ANTAGONIST

JALYN
(tamsulosin HCl-dutasteride).......................515

5-AMINOSALICYLIC ACID DERIVATIVE

APRISO
(mesalamine) 92

ASACOL HD
(mesalamine) 107

CANASA
(mesalamine) 191

COLAZAL
(balsalazide disodium) 244

GIAZO
(balsalazide disodium) 448

LIALDA
(mesalamine)...560

PENTASA
(mesalamine)...744

SF ROWASA
(mesalamine) 880

5-AMINOSALICYLIC ACID DERIVATIVE/ SULFAPYRIDINE

AZULFIDINE
(sulfasalazine)... 140

AZULFIDINE EN-TABS
(sulfasalazine)... 141

5-FLUOROCYTOSINE ANTIFUNGAL

ANCOBON
(flucytosine) 80

5-HT$_1$-AGONIST/NSAID

TREXIMET
(naproxen sodium-sumatriptan)................. 980

5-HT$_{1B/1D}$ AGONIST

ALSUMA
(sumatriptan)..57

AMERGE
(naratriptan HCl)...67

AXERT
(almotriptan malate)....................................133

FROVA
(frovatriptan succinate) 437

IMITREX
(sumatriptan)..488

MAXALT
(rizatriptan benzoate).................................. 601

RELPAX
(eletriptan hydrobromide) 827

SUMAVEL DOSEPRO
(sumatriptan)................................920

ZOMIG
(zolmitriptan)...............................1122

5-HT₃ RECEPTOR ANTAGONIST

ALOXI
(palonosetron HCl).........................54

ANZEMET
(dolasetron mesylate)......................87

GRANISETRON
(granisetron HCl)..........................460

LOTRONEX
(alosetron HCl).............................584

SANCUSO
(granisetron)................................866

ZOFRAN
(ondansetron)..............................1114

ZUPLENZ
(ondansetron)..............................1130

5-LIPOXYGENASE INHIBITOR

ZYFLO CR
(zileuton)...................................1132

FLUOROPYRIMIDINE CARBAMATE

XELODA
(capecitabine).............................1074

FLUOROQUINOLONE

AVELOX
(moxifloxacin HCl).........................128

BESIVANCE
(besifloxacin)..............................152

CILOXAN
(ciprofloxacin HCl).........................224

CIPRO XR
(ciprofloxacin).............................227

CIPROFLOXACIN INJECTION
(ciprofloxacin).............................229

CIPROFLOXACIN ORAL
(ciprofloxacin).............................231

FACTIVE
(gemifloxacin mesylate) 395

LEVAQUIN
(levofloxacin)..............................552

MOXEZA
(moxifloxacin HCl).........................640

NOROXIN
(norfloxacin)...............................680

OFLOXACIN
(ofloxacin).................................701

OFLOXACIN OTIC
(ofloxacin).................................702

QUIXIN
(levofloxacin)..............................812

VIGAMOX
(moxifloxacin HCl)........................1043

ZYMAR
(gatifloxacin) 1134

ZYMAXID
(gatifloxacin) 1135

FUSION INHIBITOR

FUZEON
(enfuvirtide)...............................441

G

GABA ANALOG

GRALISE
(gabapentin) 460

HORIZANT
(gabapentin enacarbil).....................473

LYRICA
(pregabalin)................................594

NEURONTIN
(gabapentin)...............................662

SABRIL
(vigabatrin)................................863

GLUCAGON

GLUCAGON
(glucagon, rdna origin).....................451

GLUCAGON-LIKE PEPTIDE-1 RECEPTOR AGONIST

BYDUREON
(exenatide) 179

BYETTA
(exenatide) 180

VICTOZA
(liraglutide (rdna origin)) 1040

GLUCOCORTICOID

DEPO-MEDROL
(methylprednisolone acetate) 288

DEXAMETHASONE OPHTHALMIC/OTIC
(dexamethasone sodium phosphate)..........294

DEXAMETHASONE ORAL
(dexamethasone) 295

MEDROL
(methylprednisolone) 606

PEDIAPRED
(prednisolone sodium phosphate)...........736

PREDNISONE
(prednisone)...............................766

SOLU-CORTEF
(hydrocortisone sodium succinate) 891

SOLU-MEDROL
(methylprednisolone sodium succinate) 892

GLYCOPROTEIN IIB/IIIA INHIBITOR

AGGRASTAT
(tirofiban HCl)..............................43

INTEGRILIN
(eptifibatide)..............................499

REOPRO
(abciximab)................................832

GLYCOSAMINOGLYCAN

HEPARIN SODIUM
(heparin sodium)...........................469

GLYCYLCYCLINE

TYGACIL
(tigecycline) 997

GRANULOCYTE COLONY-STIMULATING FACTOR

NEULASTA
(pegfilgrastim).............................660

NEUPOGEN
(filgrastim)................................661

GROWTH HORMONE RECEPTOR ANTAGONIST

SOMAVERT
(pegvisomant) 895

GROWTH HORMONE-RELEASING FACTOR
EGRIFTA
(tesamorelin) 342

GUANOSINE NUCLEOSIDE ANALOGUE
BARACLUDE
(entecavir)...145

GUANYLATE CYCLASE-C AGONIST
LINZESS
(linaclotide) 563

H

***H. PYLORI* TREATMENT COMBINATION**
PREVPAC
(clarithromycin-lansoprazole-amoxicillin) 773
PYLERA
(bismuth subcitrate potassium-tetracycline HCl-
metronidazole) 807

HCV NS3/4A PROTEASE INHIBITOR
INCIVEK
(telaprevir) 489
VICTRELIS
(boceprevir) 1041

HEDGEHOG PATHWAY INHIBITOR
ERIVEDGE
(vismodegib) 376

HEPARIN ANTAGONIST
PROTAMINE SULFATE
(protamine sulfate) 798

HISTONE DEACETYLASE INHIBITOR
ZOLINZA
(vorinostat).. 1117

**HIV INTEGRASE STRAND TRANSFER
INHIBITOR/NUCLEOSIDE ANALOGUE
COMBINATION/PHARMACOKINETIC
ENHANCER**
STRIBILD
(tenofovir disoproxil fumarate-emtricitabine-
cobicistat-elvitegravir) 913

HIV-INTEGRASE STRAND TRANSFER INHIBITOR
ISENTRESS
(raltegravir) 511
TIVICAY
(dolutegravir)... 964

HMG-COA REDUCTASE INHIBITOR
ALTOPREV
(lovastatin) 60
CRESTOR
(rosuvastatin calcium)..............................269
LESCOL
(fluvastatin sodium) 549
LIPITOR
(atorvastatin calcium) 564
LIVALO
(pitavastatin)...569
LOVASTATIN
(lovastatin) 584
PRAVACHOL
(pravastatin sodium) 762
ZOCOR
(simvastatin)...1112

**HMG-COA REDUCTASE INHIBITOR/
NICOTINIC ACID**
ADVICOR
(niacin-lovastatin)......................................39
SIMCOR
(niacin-simvastatin)...................................884

H$_1$-ANTAGONIST
ASTEPRO
(azelastine HCl)... 110
BEPREVE
(bepotastine besilate) 152
CLARINEX
(desloratadine) 232
LASTACAFT
(alcaftadine) 545
OPTIVAR
(azelastine HCl)..709
SILENOR
(doxepin) 881
XYZAL
(levocetirizine dihydrochloride) 1082

H$_1$-ANTAGONIST AND MAST CELL STABILIZER
PATANOL
(olopatadine HCl)...................................... 733

H$_1$-ANTAGONIST/SYMPATHOMIMETIC AMINE
CLARINEX-D
(pseudoephedrine sulfate-desloratadine)..... 233

HORMONAL BONE RESORPTION INHIBITOR
FORTICAL
(calcitonin-salmon (rdna origin)).................. 431
MIACALCIN
(calcitonin-salmon) 625

H$_2$-BLOCKER
FAMOTIDINE
(famotidine)..396
NIZATIDINE
(nizatidine) 676
RANITIDINE
(ranitidine HCl) 816

H$_2$-BLOCKER/NSAID
DUEXIS
(famotidine-ibuprofen)..............................326

HUMAN B-TYPE NATRIURETIC PEPTIDE
NATRECOR
(nesiritide) 654

HUMAN GROWTH HORMONE
VALTROPIN
(somatropin)..1015

HYALURONAN AND DERIVATIVES
HYALGAN
(sodium hyaluronate) 483

HYDANTOIN
DILANTIN
(phenytoin sodium)..................................307
PHENYTEK
(phenytoin sodium)...................................752

I

IGG$_2$ MONOCLONAL ANTIBODY
PROLIA
(denosumab) 788
XGEVA
(denosumab) 1076

IMIDAZOLIDINEDIONE ANTIBACTERIAL
MACROBID
(nitrofurantoin monohydrate-nitrofurantoin
macrocrystals)..595
MACRODANTIN
(nitrofurantoin macrocrystals)......................596

IMIDAZOPYRIDINE HYPNOTIC
AMBIEN
(zolpidem tartrate)..64
AMBIEN CR
(zolpidem tartrate)..65
EDLUAR
(zolpidem tartrate)......................................338
INTERMEZZO
(zolpidem tartrate)......................................501
ZOLPIMIST
(zolpidem tartrate)....................................1119

IMMUNE RESPONSE MODIFIER
ALDARA
(imiquimod)..50

IMMUNOMODULATORY AGENT
COPAXONE
(glatiramer acetate)....................................255
PROVENGE
(sipuleucel-T)..801
TECFIDERA
(dimethyl fumarate)....................................943

INOSINE MONOPHOSPHATE DEHYDROGENASE INHIBITOR
CELLCEPT
(mycophenolate mofetil)..............................217
MYFORTIC
(mycophenolic acid)....................................644

INSULIN
APIDRA
(insulin glulisine, rdna origin)........................88
HUMALOG
(insulin lispro, rdna origin)...........................474
HUMALOG MIX 75/25
(insulin lispro protamine, rdna origin-
insulin lispro, rdna origin)............................475
HUMULIN 70/30
(insulin human nph, rdna origin-
insulin human, rdna origin).........................479
HUMULIN N
(insulin human nph, rdna origin).................480
HUMULIN R
(insulin, human regular (rdna origin))..........481
LANTUS
(insulin glargine, rdna origin)......................544
LEVEMIR
(insulin detemir, rdna origin).......................555
NOVOLIN 70/30
(insulin human, rdna origin-insulin,
human
(isophane/regular))....................................685
NOVOLIN R
(insulin, human regular (rdna origin))..........685
NOVOLOG
(insulin aspart, rdna origin).........................686
NOVOLOG MIX 70/30
(insulin aspart, rdna origin-insulin aspart
protamine, rdna origin)...............................688

INTERLEUKIN-6 RECEPTOR ANTAGONIST
ACTEMRA
(tocilizumab)..16

ISONICOTINIC ACID HYDRAZIDE
ISONIAZID
(isoniazid)..512

ISONICOTINIC ACID HYDRAZIDE/ NICOTINAMIDE ANALOGUE/ RIFAMYCIN DERIVATIVE
RIFATER
(pyrazinamide-rifampin-isoniazid)...............847

ISONICOTINIC ACID HYDRAZIDE/ RIFAMYCIN DERIVATIVE
RIFAMATE
(rifampin-isoniazid).....................................845

K

K+ SUPPLEMENT
KLOR-CON M
(potassium chloride)....................................536
MICRO-K
(potassium chloride)....................................628

K+-SPARING DIURETIC
DYRENIUM
(triamterene)...335

K+-SPARING DIURETIC/THIAZIDE DIURETIC
DYAZIDE
(hydrochlorothiazide-triamterene)...............333
MAXZIDE
(hydrochlorothiazide-triamterene)...............605

KETOLIDE ANTIBIOTIC
KETEK
(telithromycin)..532

KINASE INHIBITOR
AFINITOR
(everolimus)...41
INLYTA
(axitinib)..496
SPRYCEL
(dasatinib)..901
TASIGNA
(nilotinib)...939
TYKERB
(lapatinib)..998
XELJANZ
(tofacitinib)..1073

L

LEUKOTRIENE RECEPTOR ANTAGONIST
ACCOLATE
(zafirlukast)...9
SINGULAIR
(montelukast sodium)..................................888

LINCOMYCIN DERIVATIVE
CLEOCIN
(clindamycin)...234
CLINDAGEL
(clindamycin phosphate).............................237
CLINDESSE
(clindamycin phosphate).............................238
EVOCLIN
(clindamycin phosphate).............................387

LINCOSAMIDE DERIVATIVE/RETINOID

VELTIN
(clindamycin phosphate-tretinoin) 1023

ZIANA
(clindamycin phosphate-tretinoin) 1106

LIPASE INHIBITOR

XENICAL
(orlistat) 1075

LIPID-REGULATING AGENT

JUXTAPID
(lomitapide).. 523

LOVAZA
(omega-3-acid ethyl esters)........................... 586

LOCAL ANESTHETIC

SYNERA
(tetracaine-lidocaine)................................... 929

LOOP DIURETIC

BUMETANIDE
(bumetanide).. 173

FUROSEMIDE
(furosemide) 439

TORSEMIDE
(torsemide) 972

LOW MOLECULAR WEIGHT HEPARIN

FRAGMIN
(dalteparin sodium).......................................436

LOVENOX
(enoxaparin sodium) 586

M

**MACROCYCLIC LACTONE
IMMUNOSUPPRESSANT**

RAPAMUNE
(sirolimus)...818

MACROLACTAM ASCOMYCIN DERIVATIVE

ELIDEL
(pimecrolimus).. 343

MACROLIDE

AZASITE
(azithromycin)...136

BIAXIN
(clarithromycin) 160

DIFICID
(fidaxomicin) 302

ERY-TAB
(erythromycin) 377

ZITHROMAX
(azithromycin)...1109

ZMAX
(azithromycin).. 1111

MACROLIDE IMMUNOSUPPRESSANT

HECORIA
(tacrolimus)...467

PROGRAF
(tacrolimus) 786

PROTOPIC
(tacrolimus) 800

ZORTRESS
(everolimus).. 1124

MEGLITINIDE

PRANDIN
(repaglinide)... 761

STARLIX
(nateglinide).. 904

MELATONIN RECEPTOR AGONIST

ROZEREM
(ramelteon)... 860

METHYLXANTHINE

THEOPHYLLINE ER
(theophylline) 956

MISCELLANEOUS ANTIANGINAL

RANEXA
(ranolazine) 815

MISCELLANEOUS ANTIDEPRESSANT

BRINTELLIX
(vortioxetine)..170

MISCELLANEOUS GOUT AGENT

COLCRYS
(colchicine)..244

MONOAMINE OXIDASE INHIBITOR

NARDIL
(phenelzine sulfate)......................................650

MONOAMINE OXIDASE INHIBITOR (TYPE B)

AZILECT
(rasagiline mesylate) 137

EMSAM
(selegiline)... 352

SELEGILINE
(selegiline HCl)... 873

ZELAPAR
(selegiline HCl)..1094

MONOBACTAM

AZACTAM
(aztreonam)...135

CAYSTON
(aztreonam) 204

MONOCLONAL ANTIBODY

STELARA
(ustekinumab)... 908

MONOCLONAL ANTIBODY/BLYS BLOCKER

BENLYSTA
(belimumab)... 150

MONOCLONAL ANTIBODY/CD52-BLOCKER

CAMPATH
(alemtuzumab)...189

MONOCLONAL ANTIBODY/CD20-BLOCKER

ARZERRA
(ofatumumab)... 106

GAZYVA
(obinutuzumab) 444

RITUXAN
(rituximab)..854

ZEVALIN
(ibritumomab tiuxetan) 1103

MONOCLONAL ANTIBODY/CTLA-4 BLOCKER

YERVOY
(ipilimumab) 1086

MONOCLONAL ANTIBODY/EGFR-BLOCKER
VECTIBIX
(panitumumab)..1022

MONOCLONAL ANTIBODY/HER2-BLOCKER
HERCEPTIN
(trastuzumab)..471
PERJETA
(pertuzumab) 749

**MONOCLONAL ANTIBODY/PROTEIN
C5 BLOCKER**
SOLIRIS
(eculizumab)... 890

MONOCLONAL ANTIBODY/TNF-BLOCKER
HUMIRA
(adalimumab) 478
REMICADE
(infliximab) 829
SIMPONI
(golimumab) 885

MONOCLONAL ANTIBODY/VCAM-1 BLOCKER
TYSABRI
(natalizumab)..999

**MONOSULFAMYL DIURETIC/
SELECTIVE BETA₁-BLOCKER**
TENORETIC
(chlorthalidone-atenolol)................................951

MTOR INHIBITOR
TORISEL
(temsirolimus)...971

MULTIKINASE INHIBITOR
CAPRELSA
(vandetanib)..193
NEXAVAR
(sorafenib).. 664
STIVARGA
(regorafenib) 910
SUTENT
(sunitinib malate) 925

MUSCARINIC ANTAGONIST
DETROL LA
(tolterodine tartrate)..................................... 293
ENABLEX
(darifenacin)... 354
OXYTROL
(oxybutynin)... 727
SANCTURA XR
(trospium chloride) 865
TOVIAZ
(fesoterodine fumarate) 973
VESICARE
(solifenacin succinate)...................................1031

MUSCULAR ANALGESIC (CENTRAL-ACTING)
ROBAXIN
(methocarbamol)... 856
SKELAXIN
(metaxalone) 889

N

**NAPHTHOIC ACID DERIVATIVE
(RETINOID-LIKE)**
DIFFERIN
(adapalene) 301

NEURAMINIDASE INHIBITOR
RELENZA
(zanamivir) 825
TAMIFLU
(oseltamivir phosphate).................................. 934

**NICOTINIC ACETYLCHOLINE RECEPTOR
AGONIST**
CHANTIX
(varenicline)..221

NICOTINIC ACID
NIASPAN
(niacin)..669

NIPECOTIC ACID DERIVATIVE
GABITRIL
(tiagabine HCl) 442

NITRATE VASODILATOR
IMDUR
(isosorbide mononitrate)................................ 487
ISOSORBIDE DINITRATE
(isosorbide dinitrate)......................................513
NITRO-DUR
(nitroglycerin)... 673
NITROLINGUAL
(nitroglycerin)... 674
NITROSTAT
(nitroglycerin)... 675

NITROGEN MUSTARD ALKYLATING AGENT
CYCLOPHOSPHAMIDE
(cyclophosphamide)...................................... 272
LEUKERAN
(chlorambucil) 551

NITROIMIDAZOLE
FLAGYL
(metronidazole).. 412
FLAGYL ER
(metronidazole) 414
FLAGYL IV
(metronidazole) 415
METROGEL-VAGINAL
(metronidazole) 624

NMDA RECEPTOR ANTAGONIST
NAMENDA
(memantine HCl)..647

NONBENZODIAZEPINE HYPNOTIC AGENT
LUNESTA
(eszopiclone)..589

NON-ERGOLINE DOPAMINE AGONIST
APOKYN
(apomorphine HCl)... 91
REQUIP
(ropinirole) 833

NON-ERGOT DOPAMINE AGONIST
MIRAPEX
(pramipexole dihydrochloride).....................631

NON-HALOGENATED GLUCOCORTICOID
ALVESCO
(ciclesonide) 61
OMNARIS
(ciclesonide) 705

NON-NARCOTIC ANTITUSSIVE

TESSALON
(benzonatate)...953

NON-NUCLEOSIDE REVERSE TRANSCRIPTASE INHIBITOR

EDURANT
(rilpivirine)..339

INTELENCE
(etravirine)..500

RESCRIPTOR
(delavirdine mesylate)...............................834

SUSTIVA
(efavirenz)..923

VIRAMUNE XR
(nevirapine)...1049

NON-NUCLEOSIDE REVERSE TRANSCRIPTASE INHIBITOR/NUCLEOSIDE ANALOGUE COMBINATION

ATRIPLA
(tenofovir disoproxil fumarate-emtricitabine-efavirenz)...114

COMPLERA
(tenofovir disoproxil fumarate-emtricitabine-rilpivirine)..251

NONSELECTIVE BETA-BLOCKER

BETAGAN
(levobunolol HCl).....................................153

BETIMOL
(timolol)..157

CORGARD
(nadolol)..261

INDERAL LA
(propranolol HCl)......................................491

INNOPRAN XL
(propranolol HCl)......................................497

PROPRANOLOL
(propranolol HCl)......................................795

TIMOLOL
(timolol maleate)......................................961

TIMOPTIC
(timolol maleate)......................................962

NONSTEROIDAL ANTIANDROGEN

CASODEX
(bicalutamide)..201

NILANDRON
(nilutamide)..671

XTANDI
(enzalutamide)...1080

ZYTIGA
(abiraterone acetate).................................1138

NONSTEROIDAL AROMATASE INHIBITOR

ARIMIDEX
(anastrozole)...100

FEMARA
(letrozole)..405

NSAID

ACULAR
(ketorolac tromethamine)............................25

ACULAR LS
(ketorolac tromethamine)............................26

BROMDAY
(bromfenac)..172

CALDOLOR
(ibuprofen)...187

CAMBIA
(diclofenac potassium)................................188

CATAFLAM
(diclofenac potassium)................................202

DAYPRO
(oxaprozin)...278

ETODOLAC
(etodolac)...382

FLECTOR
(diclofenac epolamine)...............................416

INDOMETHACIN
(indomethacin)...492

KETOROLAC
(ketorolac tromethamine)............................534

MOBIC
(meloxicam)..635

NABUMETONE
(nabumetone)..646

NAPRELAN
(naproxen sodium)....................................648

NAPROSYN
(naproxen)..649

NEVANAC
(nepafenac)..663

PENNSAID
(diclofenac sodium)....................................743

VOLTAREN GEL
(diclofenac sodium)....................................1057

VOLTAREN OPHTHALMIC
(diclofenac sodium)....................................1058

VOLTAREN-XR
(diclofenac sodium)....................................1059

ZIPSOR
(diclofenac potassium)................................1109

ZORVOLEX
(diclofenac)...1126

NSAID/PROSTAGLANDIN E$_1$ ANALOGUE

ARTHROTEC
(diclofenac sodium-misoprostol).................104

NSAID/PROTON PUMP INHIBITOR

VIMOVO
(esomeprazole magnesium-naproxen).......1045

NUCLEOSIDE ANALOGUE

COPEGUS
(ribavirin)...256

DENAVIR
(penciclovir)..281

FAMVIR
(famciclovir)..397

REBETOL
(ribavirin)...820

VALTREX
(valacyclovir HCl)......................................1014

ZOVIRAX ORAL
(acyclovir)..1129

NUCLEOSIDE ANALOGUE ANTIMETABOLITE

GEMCITABINE
(gemcitabine)...445

NUCLEOSIDE ANALOGUE COMBINATION
TRUVADA
(tenofovir disoproxil fumarate-
emtricitabine) 993

**NUCLEOSIDE REVERSE TRANSCRIPTASE
INHIBITOR**
COMBIVIR
(zidovudine-lamivudine).............................250
EMTRIVA
(emtricitabine) 353
EPIVIR
(lamivudine) 368
EPIVIR-HBV
(lamivudine) 369
EPZICOM
(abacavir sulfate-lamivudine)........................ 372
RETROVIR
(zidovudine) 838
TRIZIVIR
(abacavir sulfate-zidovudine-lamivudine) 989
TYZEKA
(telbivudine) 1000
VIDEX EC
(didanosine)... 1042
ZERIT
(stavudine) 1098
ZIAGEN
(abacavir sulfate) 1105

NUCLEOTIDE ANALOGUE INHIBITOR
SOVALDI
(sofosbuvir) 898

**NUCLEOTIDE ANALOGUE REVERSE
TRANSCRIPTASE INHIBITOR**
HEPSERA
(adefovir dipivoxil) 470
VIREAD
(tenofovir disoproxil fumarate) 1051

O

OPIOID ANALGESIC
ABSTRAL
(fentanyl) 7
ACETAMINOPHEN AND CODEINE TABLETS
(codeine phosphate-acetaminophen).............. 14
ACTIQ
(fentanyl citrate) 17
AVINZA
(morphine sulfate)....................................... 131
BUPRENEX
(buprenorphine HCl) 174
BUTRANS
(buprenorphine) 177
DEMEROL INJECTION
(meperidine HCl)... 281
DILAUDID ORAL
(hydromorphone HCl) 309
DOLOPHINE
(methadone HCl)... 317
DURAGESIC
(fentanyl) 330
DURAMORPH
(morphine sulfate)....................................... 332

EXALGO
(hydromorphone HCl) 388
FENTANYL INJECTION
(fentanyl citrate) 407
FENTORA
(fentanyl citrate) 408
INFUMORPH
(morphine sulfate)....................................... 495
KADIAN
(morphine sulfate).. 524
LAZANDA
(fentanyl) 548
MEPERIDINE ORAL
(meperidine HCl)... 610
METHADONE ORAL SOLUTION AND
SUSPENSION
(methadone HCl)... 615
MORPHINE
(morphine sulfate)..638
MS CONTIN
(morphine sulfate) 641
NORCO
(hydrocodone bitartrate-acetaminophen) 677
OXYCODONE TABLETS
(oxycodone HCl)... 724
OXYCONTIN
(oxycodone HCl)... 725
PERCOCET
(oxycodone HCl-acetaminophen).................. 745
PERCODAN
(oxycodone HCl-aspirin).............................. 746
SUBSYS
(fentanyl) 917
VICODIN
(hydrocodone bitartrate-acetaminophen) ...1037
VICOPROFEN
(hydrocodone bitartrate-ibuprofen)........... 1038

OPIOID ANTAGONIST
ENTEREG
(alvimopan) 361
RELISTOR
(methylnaltrexone bromide) 826
VIVITROL
(naltrexone) 1056

ORGANOPLATINUM COMPLEX
ELOXATIN
(oxaliplatin) 348

OSMOTIC LAXATIVE
KRISTALOSE
(lactulose) 538
MIRALAX
(polyethylene glycol 3350).......................... 630

P

PANCREATIC ENZYME SUPPLEMENT
CREON
(pancrelipase)..268
PANCREAZE
(pancrelipase)...729
ZENPEP
(pancrelipase).. 1096

PARTIAL D₂/5HT₁ₐ AGONIST/5HT₂ₐ ANTAGONIST

ABILIFY
(aripiprazole)... 1

ABILIFY MAINTENA
(aripiprazole)... 3

PARTIAL OPIOID AGONIST/OPIOID ANTAGONIST

BUPRENORPHINE AND NALOXONE
(naloxone HCl dihydrate-buprenorphine HCl)...175

SUBOXONE FILM
(buprenorphine-naloxone)...........................915

PEDICULOCIDE

NATROBA
(spinosad)..655

PEGYLATED VIRUS PROLIFERATION INHIBITOR

PEGASYS
(peginterferon alfa-2a).............................738

PEGINTRON
(peginterferon alfa-2b).............................740

PENICILLIN

PENICILLIN VK
(penicillin V potassium).............................741

PENICILLIN (PENICILLINASE-RESISTANT)

DICLOXACILLIN
(dicloxacillin sodium)................................299

PENICILLIUM-DERIVED ANTIFUNGAL

GRIS-PEG
(griseofulvin)...461

PEPTIDE SYNTHESIS INHIBITOR

TRECATOR
(ethionamide)...978

PHENOTHIAZINE DERIVATIVE

PHENERGAN INJECTION
(promethazine HCl)....................................750

PROCHLORPERAZINE
(prochlorperazine)......................................783

PROMETHAZINE
(promethazine HCl)....................................790

PHENYLTRIAZINE

LAMICTAL
(lamotrigine)...541

PHOSPHATE BINDER

PHOSLYRA
(calcium acetate).......................................754

RENAGEL
(sevelamer HCl)...831

RENVELA
(sevelamer carbonate)..............................831

PHOSPHODIESTERASE III INHIBITOR

PLETAL
(cilostazol)...757

PHOSPHODIESTERASE TYPE 5 INHIBITOR

CIALIS
(tadalafil)...222

LEVITRA
(vardenafil HCl)...556

REVATIO
(sildenafil)...840

STAXYN
(vardenafil HCl)...907

STENDRA
(avanafil)..909

VIAGRA
(sildenafil citrate)....................................1034

PIPERAZINE ANTIHISTAMINE

HYDROXYZINE HCL
(hydroxyzine HCl)......................................484

PIPERAZINO-AZEPINE

REMERON
(mirtazapine)...828

PLASMA GLYCOPROTEIN

RIASTAP
(fibrinogen concentrate (human))..............845

PLATELET AGGREGATION INHIBITOR

AGGRENOX
(aspirin-dipyridamole)................................44

BRILINTA
(ticagrelor)...169

EFFIENT
(prasugrel)...341

PLAVIX
(clopidogrel bisulfate)................................756

PLATELET-REDUCING AGENT

ANAGRELIDE
(anagrelide HCl)...79

PLEUROMUTILIN ANTIBACTERIAL

ALTABAX
(retapamulin)..58

PODOPHYLLOTOXIN DERIVATIVE

ETOPOPHOS
(etoposide phosphate)...............................384

POLYENE ANTIFUNGAL

ABELCET
(amphotericin B lipid complex).......................1

AMBISOME
(amphotericin B liposome)............................66

AMPHOTEC
(amphotericin B lipid complex).....................74

NYSTATIN ORAL
(nystatin)..699

POTASSIUM CHANNEL BLOCKER

AMPYRA
(dalfampridine)..77

PROGESTERONE

MEGACE ES
(megestrol acetate)...................................608

PROGESTIN CONTRACEPTIVE

DEPO-PROVERA CONTRACEPTIVE INJECTION
(medroxyprogesterone acetate)................290

PROGESTOGEN

DEPO-PROVERA
(medroxyprogesterone acetate)................289

MIRENA
(levonorgestrel)...633

PROVERA
(medroxyprogesterone acetate)................802

PROSTAGLANDIN ANALOG
LATISSE
(bimatoprost) 546
LUMIGAN
(bimatoprost) 588
TRAVATAN Z
(travoprost) 975
XALATAN
(latanoprost) 1068

PROTEASE INHIBITOR
APTIVUS
(tipranavir) 94
CRIXIVAN
(indinavir sulfate) 270
INVIRASE
(saquinavir mesylate) 509
KALETRA
(ritonavir-lopinavir) 526
NORVIR
(ritonavir) 683
PREZISTA
(darunavir)... 774
REYATAZ
(atazanavir sulfate)...................................... 842
VIRACEPT
(nelfinavir mesylate)................................... 1048

PROTEASOME INHIBITOR
KYPROLIS
(carfilzomib) 539

PROTEIN-TYROSINE KINASE INHIBITOR
GLEEVEC
(imatinib mesylate) 449

PROTON PUMP INHIBITOR
ACIPHEX
(rabeprazole sodium) 15
DEXILANT
(dexlansoprazole) 296
NEXIUM IV
(esomeprazole sodium) 665
NEXIUM ORAL
(esomeprazole magnesium)........................ 666
PREVACID
(lansoprazole)... 772
PRILOSEC
(omeprazole) 775
PROTONIX
(pantoprazole sodium) 799

PROTON PUMP INHIBITOR/ANTACID
ZEGERID
(sodium bicarbonate-omeprazole)............. 1093
ZEGERID OTC
(sodium bicarbonate-omeprazole)............. 1094

PYRAZOLOPYRIMIDINE (NON-BENZODIAZEPINE)
SONATA
(zaleplon).. 895

PYRIMIDINE SYNTHESIS INHIBITOR
ARAVA
(leflunomide)... 96
AUBAGIO
(teriflunomide)... 118

PYRROLIDINE DERIVATIVE
KEPPRA XR
(levetiracetam) 531

Q

QUINAZOLINE DIURETIC
ZAROXOLYN
(metolazone) 1091

QUININE DERIVATIVE
PLAQUENIL
(hydroxychloroquine sulfate)...................... 754

QUINOLINEMETHANOL DERIVATIVE
MEFLOQUINE
(mefloquine HCl).. 607

R

RADIOPHARMACEUTICAL AGENT
XOFIGO
(radium ra 223 dichloride) 1078

RECOMBINANT HUMAN GROWTH HORMONE
HUMATROPE
(somatropin rdna origin)............................. 476
NORDITROPIN
(somatropin rdna origin)............................. 678
NUTROPIN
(somatropin rdna origin)............................. 694
OMNITROPE
(somatropin rdna origin)............................. 706

RECOMBINANT HUMAN PARATHYROID HORMONE
FORTEO
(teriparatide, rdna origin) 429

RECOMBINANT URATE-OXIDASE ENZYME
KRYSTEXXA
(pegloticase) 539

RENIN INHIBITOR
TEKTURNA
(aliskiren).. 947

RENIN INHIBITOR/THIAZIDE DIURETIC
TEKTURNA HCT
(aliskiren-hydrochlorothiazide) 948

RETINOID
ABSORICA
(isotretinoin)... 5
AMNESTEEM
(isotretinoin)... 71
RETIN-A
(tretinoin).. 837
SORIATANE
(acitretin).. 896

S

SALICYLATE
BAYER ASPIRIN
(aspirin)... 146

SELECTIVE ALPHA$_2$ AGONIST
ALPHAGAN P
(brimonidine tartrate) 55

SELECTIVE BETA₁-BLOCKER

BETOPTIC S
(betaxolol HCl) 158

BREVIBLOC
(esmolol HCl) 168

BYSTOLIC
(nebivolol) 181

METOPROLOL
(metoprolol tartrate) 621

SECTRAL
(acebutolol HCl) 872

TENORMIN
(atenolol) 952

TOPROL-XL
(metoprolol succinate) 970

ZEBETA
(bisoprolol fumarate) 1092

SELECTIVE BETA₁-BLOCKER/
THIAZIDE DIURETIC

METOPROLOL/HCTZ
(metoprolol tartrate-hydrochlorothiazide).... 623

ZIAC
(bisoprolol fumarate-hydrochlorothiazide).. 1104

SELECTIVE COSTIMULATION MODULATOR

ORENCIA
(abatacept) 711

SELECTIVE ESTROGEN RECEPTOR
MODULATOR

EVISTA
(raloxifene HCl) 386

SELECTIVE FACTOR XA INHIBITOR

ARIXTRA
(fondaparinux sodium) 101

ELIQUIS
(apixaban) 345

XARELTO
(rivaroxaban) 1071

SELECTIVE NOREPINEPHRINE REUPTAKE
INHIBITOR

STRATTERA
(atomoxetine) 911

SELECTIVE PHOSPHODIESTERASE 4 (PDE4)
INHIBITOR

DALIRESP
(roflumilast) 276

SELECTIVE SEROTONIN REUPTAKE INHIBITOR

CELEXA
(citalopram HBr) 216

LEXAPRO
(escitalopram oxalate) 559

LUVOX CR
(fluvoxamine maleate) 592

PAXIL
(paroxetine HCl) 734

PAXIL CR
(paroxetine HCl) 735

PROZAC
(fluoxetine HCl) 804

ZOLOFT
(sertraline HCl) 1118

SELECTIVE SEROTONIN REUPTAKE
INHIBITOR/5-HT₁ₐ-RECEPTOR PARTIAL
AGONIST

VIIBRYD
(vilazodone HCl) 1044

SELECTIVE SEROTONIN REUPTAKE INHIBITOR/
THIENOBENZODIAZEPINE

SYMBYAX
(fluoxetine HCl-olanzapine) 928

SEMISYNTHETIC AMPICILLIN DERIVATIVE

AMOXICILLIN
(amoxicillin) 72

MOXATAG
(amoxicillin) 639

SEMISYNTHETIC PENICILLIN DERIVATIVE

AMPICILLIN INJECTION
(ampicillin sodium) 75

AMPICILLIN ORAL
(ampicillin) 76

SEMISYNTHETIC RIFAMPIN ANALOG

XIFAXAN
(rifaximin) 1077

SEROTONIN AND NOREPINEPHRINE
REUPTAKE INHIBITOR

CYMBALTA
(duloxetine HCl) 273

EFFEXOR XR
(venlafaxine HCl) 340

FETZIMA
(levomilnacipran) 409

PRISTIQ
(desvenlafaxine) 778

SAVELLA
(milnacipran HCl) 869

SEROTONIN 2C RECEPTOR AGONIST

BELVIQ
(lorcaserin HCl) 147

SKELETAL MUSCLE RELAXANT
(CENTRAL-ACTING)

AMRIX
(cyclobenzaprine HCl) 77

CYCLOBENZAPRINE
(cyclobenzaprine HCl) 271

SOMA
(carisoprodol) 894

SODIUM CHANNEL INACTIVATOR

VIMPAT
(lacosamide) 1047

SODIUM-GLUCOSE CO-TRANSPORTER 2
(SGLT2) INHIBITOR

FARXIGA
(dapagliflozin) 400

INVOKANA
(canagliflozin) 510

SOLUBLE GUANYLATE CYCLASE (SGC)
STIMULATOR

ADEMPAS
(riociguat) 32

SOMATOSTATIN ANALOG

SANDOSTATIN LAR
(octreotide acetate) 867

STREPTOGRAMIN
SYNERCID
(quinupristin-dalfopristin)............................930

SUBSTANCE P/NEUROKININ 1 RECEPTOR ANTAGONIST
EMEND CAPSULES
(aprepitant)..349
EMEND FOR INJECTION
(fosaprepitant dimeglumine)........................350

SUCCINIMIDE
ZARONTIN
(ethosuximide)..1090

SULFAMATE-SUBSTITUTED MONOSACCHARIDE ANTIEPILEPTIC
TOPAMAX
(topiramate)..968
TROKENDI XR
(topiramate)..990

SULFONAMIDE
SILVADENE
(silver sulfadiazine)....................................882

SULFONAMIDE ANTICONVULSANT
ZONEGRAN
(zonisamide)..1123

SULFONAMIDE/TETRAHYDROFOLIC ACID INHIBITOR
SULFAMETHOXAZOLE/TRIMETHOPRIM
(sulfamethoxazole-trimethoprim)..................918

SULFONYLUREA (2ND GENERATION)
AMARYL
(glimepiride)...63
DIABETA
(glyburide)..297
GLUCOTROL
(glipizide)...453
GLUCOTROL XL
(glipizide)...454
GLYNASE PRESTAB
(glyburide)..458

SULFONYLUREA/THIAZOLIDINEDIONE
AVANDARYL
(rosiglitazone maleate-glimepiride)...............124
DUETACT
(pioglitazone HCl-glimepiride).....................325

SYMPATHOMIMETIC AMINE
ADDERALL
(amphetamine salt combo).............................29
ADDERALL XR
(amphetamine salt combo).............................30
CONCERTA
(methylphenidate HCl).................................254
DAYTRANA
(methylphenidate)......................................279
FOCALIN
(dexmethylphenidate HCl)...........................422
FOCALIN XR
(dexmethylphenidate HCl)...........................424
METADATE CD
(methylphenidate HCl).................................612
METADATE ER
(methylphenidate HCl).................................613

METHYLIN
(methylphenidate HCl).................................619
PROCENTRA
(dextroamphetamine sulfate).......................782
QUILLIVANT XR
(methylphenidate HCl).................................810
RITALIN
(methylphenidate HCl).................................853
VYVANSE
(lisdexamfetamine dimesylate)...................1063

SYMPATHOMIMETIC CATECHOLAMINE
ADRENACLICK
(epinephrine)...34
ADRENALIN
(epinephrine)...35
EPIPEN
(epinephrine)..366

SYNTHETIC GONADOTROPIN-RELEASING HORMONE ANALOG
ELIGARD
(leuprolide acetate).....................................344
LUPRON DEPOT-PED
(leuprolide acetate).....................................590
TRELSTAR
(triptorelin pamoate)...................................979
VANTAS
(histrelin acetate)......................................1019
ZOLADEX 1-MONTH
(goserelin acetate).....................................1115
ZOLADEX 3-MONTH
(goserelin acetate).....................................1116

SYNTHETIC GUANINE DERIVATIVE NUCLEOSIDE ANALOGUE
VALCYTE
(valganciclovir HCl)....................................1012
VITRASERT
(ganciclovir)...1053

T

TETRACYCLINE DERIVATIVE
DORYX
(doxycycline hyclate)..................................321
DOXYCYCLINE IV
(doxycycline hyclate)..................................324
DYNACIN
(minocycline HCl).......................................334
MONODOX
(doxycycline monohydrate).........................637
ORACEA
(doxycycline)..709
VIBRAMYCIN
(doxycycline)...1036

TETRAENE POLYENE ANTIFUNGAL
NATACYN
(natamycin)...652

THALIDOMIDE ANALOG
REVLIMID
(lenalidomide)..841

THIAZIDE DIURETIC
HYDROCHLOROTHIAZIDE
(hydrochlorothiazide)..................................483
MICROZIDE
(hydrochlorothiazide)..................................629

THIAZOLIDINEDIONE
ACTOS
(pioglitazone)...24
AVANDIA
(rosiglitazone maleate)................................125

THIENOBENZODIAZEPINE
ZYPREXA
(olanzapine)...1135
ZYPREXA RELPREVV
(olanzapine)...1137

THIOUREA-DERIVATIVE ANTITHYROID AGENT
PROPYLTHIOURACIL
(propylthiouracil)...796

THIOXANTHENE
NAVANE
(thiothixene)...656

THROMBIN INHIBITOR
REFLUDAN
(lepirudin)..824

THROMBOLYTIC AGENT
ACTIVASE
(alteplase)..18
RETAVASE
(reteplase)..837
TNKASE
(tenecteplase)..965

THROMBOPOIETIC AGENT
NEUMEGA
(oprelvekin)..660

THROMBOPOIETIN RECEPTOR AGONIST
NPLATE
(romiplostim)...690
PROMACTA
(eltrombopag)...789

THYROID HORMONE SYNTHESIS INHIBITOR
TAPAZOLE
(methimazole)...936

THYROID REPLACEMENT HORMONE
ARMOUR THYROID
(thyroid)...103
CYTOMEL
(liothyronine sodium)...................................275
LEVOXYL
(levothyroxine sodium).................................557
SYNTHROID
(levothyroxine sodium).................................931
TRIOSTAT
(liothyronine sodium)...................................988
UNITHROID
(levothyroxine sodium).................................1007

TNF-BLOCKER
CIMZIA
(certolizumab pegol)....................................225
ENBREL
(etanercept)..358

TOPICAL IMMUNOMODULATOR
RESTASIS
(cyclosporine)...835

TOPOISOMERASE I INHIBITOR
CAMPTOSAR
(irinotecan HCl)..190

TOXOID/VACCINE COMBINATION
BOOSTRIX
(diphtheria toxoid, reduced-acellular pertussis-
tetanus toxoid)..164
PEDIARIX
(acellular pertussis-hepatitis B (recombinant)-
inactivated poliovirus-diphtheria toxoid-
tetanus toxoid)..737

TRIAZOLE DERIVATIVE
BANZEL
(rufinamide)...144

TRIAZOLOPYRIDINE DERIVATIVE
OLEPTRO
(trazodone HCl)..703
TRAZODONE
(trazodone HCl)..976

TRICYCLIC ANTIDEPRESSANT
PAMELOR
(nortriptyline HCl)...729
TOFRANIL
(imipramine HCl)..967

TRICYCLIC GLYCOPEPTIDE ANTIBIOTIC
VANCOCIN ORAL
(vancomycin HCl)..1016
VANCOMYCIN HCL
(vancomycin HCl)..1017

**TYPE I AND II 5 ALPHA-REDUCTASE INHIBITOR
(2ND GENERATION)**
AVODART
(dutasteride)...132

TYPE II 5 ALPHA-REDUCTASE INHIBITOR
PROPECIA
(finasteride)..794
PROSCAR
(finasteride)..797

TYROSINE KINASE INHIBITOR
BOSULIF
(bosutinib)..165
VOTRIENT
(pazopanib)...1060

U

URICOSURIC
PROBENECID/COLCHICINE
(colchicine-probenecid)................................780

V

VACCINE
AFLURIA
(influenza virus vaccine)................................42
CERVARIX
(human papillomavirus recombinant vaccine,
bivalent)...220
ENGERIX-B
(hepatitis B (recombinant))...........................359
GARDASIL
(human papillomavirus recombinant vaccine,
quadrivalent)..443

HAVRIX
(hepatitis A vaccine) 466

HIBERIX
(haemophilus B conjugate-tetanus toxoid) ... 472

MENACTRA
(meningococcal polysaccharide diphtheria
toxoid conjugate vaccine).......................... 609

MENVEO
(meningococcal (groups A, C, Y, and W-135)
oligosaccharide diphtheria crm 197
conjugate) 609

M-M-R II
(rubella vaccine live-measles vaccine live-
mumps vaccine live)....................................634

PNEUMOVAX 23
(pneumococcal vaccine polyvalent)............. 757

RECOMBIVAX HB
(hepatitis B (recombinant))..........................824

ROTATEQ
(rotavirus vaccine, live, pentavalent) 858

VARIVAX
(varicella virus vaccine live) 1020

ZOSTAVAX
(zoster vaccine live) 1127

VALPROATE COMPOUND
DEPAKOTE
(divalproex sodium) 284

DEPAKOTE ER
(divalproex sodium) 286

**VASCULAR ENDOTHELIAL GROWTH FACTOR
(VEGF) INHIBITOR**
AVASTIN
(bevacizumab)... 127

EYLEA
(aflibercept).. 395

ZALTRAP
(ziv-aflibercept) 1087

VIRAL DNA SYNTHESIS INHIBITOR
VISTIDE
(cidofovir)..1052

VITAMIN B COMPLEX
POTABA
(aminobenzoate potassium) 758

VITAMIN D ANALOG
ROCALTROL
(calcitriol).. 857

VECTICAL
(calcitriol)..1023

ZEMPLAR ORAL
(paricalcitol)... 1095

VITAMIN D3 DERIVATIVE
DOVONEX
(calcipotriene) 322

SORILUX
(calcipotriene) 897

**VITAMIN K-DEPENDENT COAGULATION
FACTOR INHIBITOR**
COUMADIN
(warfarin sodium).......................................264

W

WAKEFULNESS-PROMOTING AGENT
NUVIGIL
(armodafinil)...698

PROVIGIL
(modafinil)..803

X

XANTHINE OXIDASE INHIBITOR
ALOPRIM
(allopurinol sodium) 53

ULORIC
(febuxostat)..1001

Visual Identification Guide

VISUAL IDENTIFICATION GUIDE*

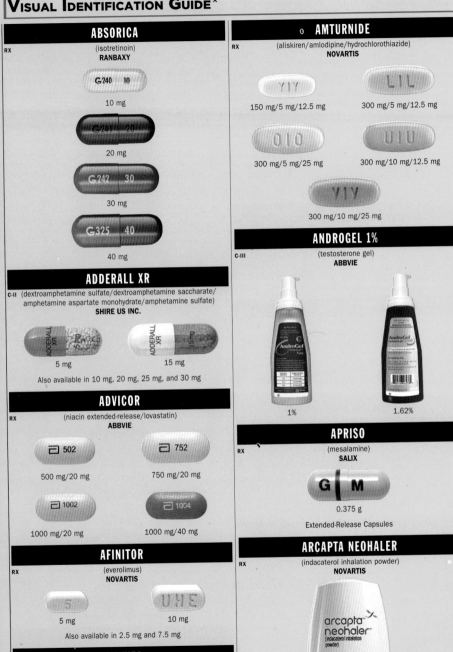

ABSORICA

RX

(isotretinoin)
RANBAXY

G 240   10

10 mg

C-241   20

20 mg

G 242   30

30 mg

G 325   40

40 mg

ADDERALL XR

C-II (dextroamphetamine sulfate/dextroamphetamine saccharate/
amphetamine aspartate monohydrate/amphetamine sulfate)
SHIRE US INC.

ADDERALL XR 5 mg   ADDERALL XR 15 mg

5 mg   15 mg

Also available in 10 mg, 20 mg, 25 mg, and 30 mg

ADVICOR

RX

(niacin extended-release/lovastatin)
ABBVIE

502   752

500 mg/20 mg   750 mg/20 mg

1002   1004

1000 mg/20 mg   1000 mg/40 mg

AFINITOR

RX

(everolimus)
NOVARTIS

5   UHE

5 mg   10 mg

Also available in 2.5 mg and 7.5 mg

AMITIZA

RX

(lubiprostone)
TAKEDA

SPI   SPI

8 mcg   24 mcg

AMTURNIDE

RX

(aliskiren/amlodipine/hydrochlorothiazide)
NOVARTIS

YIY   LIL

150 mg/5 mg/12.5 mg   300 mg/5 mg/12.5 mg

OIO   UIU

300 mg/5 mg/25 mg   300 mg/10 mg/12.5 mg

YIY

300 mg/10 mg/25 mg

ANDROGEL 1%

C-III

(testosterone gel)
ABBVIE

AndroGel   AndroGel

1%   1.62%

APRISO

RX

(mesalamine)
SALIX

G   M

0.375 g

Extended-Release Capsules

ARCAPTA NEOHALER

RX

(indacaterol inhalation powder)
NOVARTIS

arcapta
neohaler
(indacaterol inhalation
powder)

arcapta
neohaler
For use only with Arcapta™ capsules

75 mcg

*Other dosage forms and strengths may be available.

V1

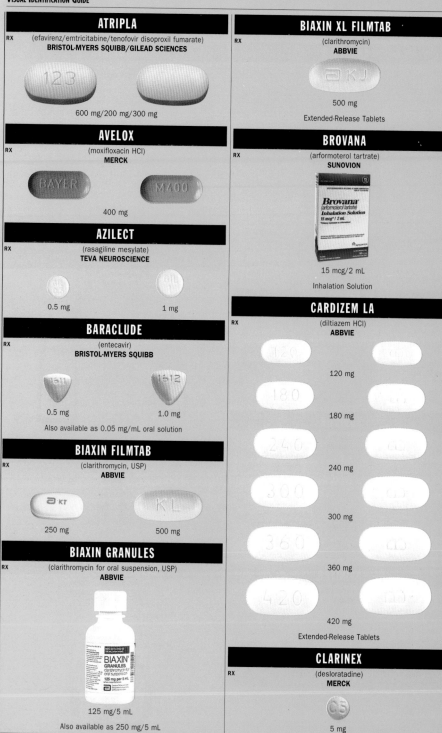

ATRIPLA
RX (efavirenz/emtricitabine/tenofovir disoproxil fumarate)
BRISTOL-MYERS SQUIBB/GILEAD SCIENCES

600 mg/200 mg/300 mg

AVELOX
RX (moxifloxacin HCl)
MERCK

400 mg

AZILECT
RX (rasagiline mesylate)
TEVA NEUROSCIENCE

0.5 mg   1 mg

BARACLUDE
RX (entecavir)
BRISTOL-MYERS SQUIBB

0.5 mg   1.0 mg

Also available as 0.05 mg/mL oral solution

BIAXIN FILMTAB
RX (clarithromycin, USP)
ABBVIE

250 mg   500 mg

BIAXIN GRANULES
RX (clarithromycin for oral suspension, USP)
ABBVIE

125 mg/5 mL

Also available as 250 mg/5 mL

BIAXIN XL FILMTAB
RX (clarithromycin)
ABBVIE

500 mg

Extended-Release Tablets

BROVANA
RX (arformoterol tartrate)
SUNOVION

15 mcg/2 mL

Inhalation Solution

CARDIZEM LA
RX (diltiazem HCl)
ABBVIE

120 mg

180 mg

240 mg

300 mg

360 mg

420 mg

Extended-Release Tablets

CLARINEX
RX (desloratadine)
MERCK

5 mg

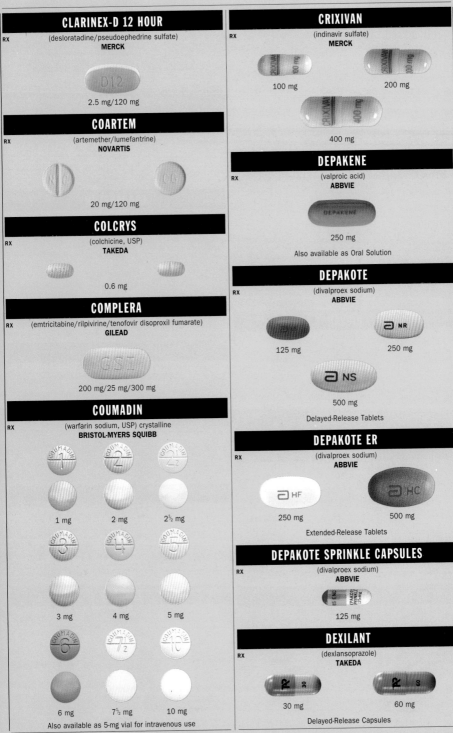

CLARINEX-D 12 HOUR

RX

(desloratadine/pseudoephedrine sulfate)
MERCK

2.5 mg/120 mg

COARTEM

RX

(artemether/lumefantrine)
NOVARTIS

20 mg/120 mg

COLCRYS

RX

(colchicine, USP)
TAKEDA

0.6 mg

COMPLERA

RX

(emtricitabine/rilpivirine/tenofovir disoproxil fumarate)
GILEAD

200 mg/25 mg/300 mg

COUMADIN

RX

(warfarin sodium, USP) crystalline
BRISTOL-MYERS SQUIBB

1 mg   2 mg   2½ mg

3 mg   4 mg   5 mg

6 mg   7½ mg   10 mg

Also available as 5-mg vial for intravenous use

CRIXIVAN

RX

(indinavir sulfate)
MERCK

100 mg   200 mg

400 mg

DEPAKENE

RX

(valproic acid)
ABBVIE

250 mg

Also available as Oral Solution

DEPAKOTE

RX

(divalproex sodium)
ABBVIE

125 mg   250 mg

500 mg

Delayed-Release Tablets

DEPAKOTE ER

RX

(divalproex sodium)
ABBVIE

250 mg   500 mg

Extended-Release Tablets

DEPAKOTE SPRINKLE CAPSULES

RX

(divalproex sodium)
ABBVIE

125 mg

DEXILANT

RX

(dexlansoprazole)
TAKEDA

30 mg   60 mg

Delayed-Release Capsules

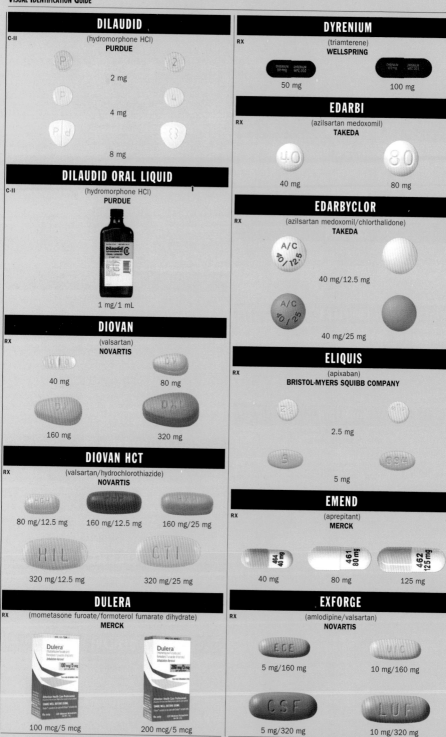

DILAUDID

C-II

(hydromorphone HCl)
PURDUE

2 mg

4 mg

8 mg

DILAUDID ORAL LIQUID

C-II

(hydromorphone HCl)
PURDUE

1 mg/1 mL

DIOVAN

RX

(valsartan)
NOVARTIS

40 mg

80 mg

160 mg

320 mg

DIOVAN HCT

RX

(valsartan/hydrochlorothiazide)
NOVARTIS

80 mg/12.5 mg   160 mg/12.5 mg   160 mg/25 mg

320 mg/12.5 mg   320 mg/25 mg

DULERA

RX

(mometasone furoate/formoterol fumarate dihydrate)
MERCK

100 mcg/5 mcg   200 mcg/5 mcg

DYRENIUM

RX

(triamterene)
WELLSPRING

50 mg   100 mg

EDARBI

RX

(azilsartan medoxomil)
TAKEDA

40 mg   80 mg

EDARBYCLOR

RX

(azilsartan medoxomil/chlorthalidone)
TAKEDA

40 mg/12.5 mg

40 mg/25 mg

ELIQUIS

RX

(apixaban)
BRISTOL-MYERS SQUIBB COMPANY

2.5 mg

5 mg

EMEND

RX

(aprepitant)
MERCK

40 mg   80 mg   125 mg

EXFORGE

RX

(amlodipine/valsartan)
NOVARTIS

5 mg/160 mg   10 mg/160 mg

5 mg/320 mg   10 mg/320 mg

V4

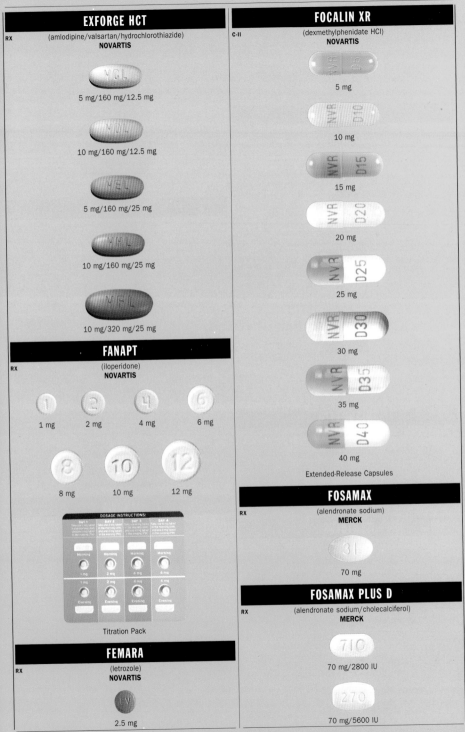

EXFORGE HCT

RX

(amlodipine/valsartan/hydrochlorothiazide)
NOVARTIS

5 mg/160 mg/12.5 mg

10 mg/160 mg/12.5 mg

5 mg/160 mg/25 mg

10 mg/160 mg/25 mg

10 mg/320 mg/25 mg

FANAPT

RX

(iloperidone)
NOVARTIS

1 mg   2 mg   4 mg   6 mg

8 mg   10 mg   12 mg

DOSAGE INSTRUCTIONS

Titration Pack

FEMARA

RX

(letrozole)
NOVARTIS

2.5 mg

FOCALIN XR

C-II

(dexmethylphenidate HCl)
NOVARTIS

5 mg

10 mg

15 mg

20 mg

25 mg

30 mg

35 mg

40 mg

Extended-Release Capsules

FOSAMAX

RX

(alendronate sodium)
MERCK

70 mg

FOSAMAX PLUS D

RX

(alendronate sodium/cholecalciferol)
MERCK

70 mg/2800 IU

70 mg/5600 IU

V5

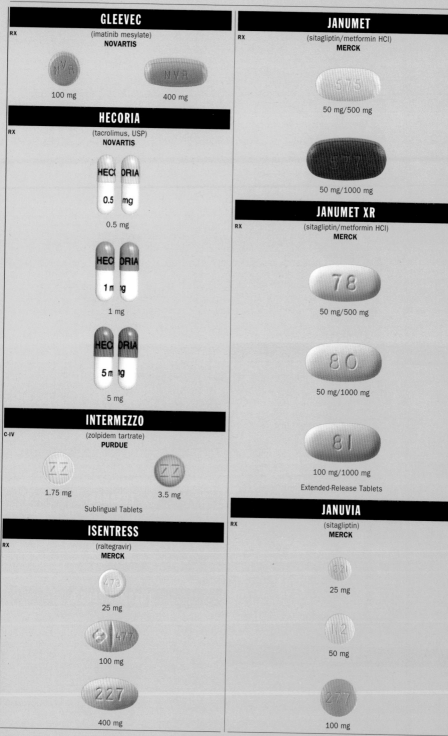

GLEEVEC

RX

(imatinib mesylate)
NOVARTIS

100 mg   400 mg

HECORIA

RX

(tacrolimus, USP)
NOVARTIS

HEC ORIA
0.5 mg
0.5 mg

HEC ORIA
1 m g
1 mg

HEC ORIA
5 m g
5 mg

INTERMEZZO

C-IV

(zolpidem tartrate)
PURDUE

1.75 mg   3.5 mg

Sublingual Tablets

ISENTRESS

RX

(raltegravir)
MERCK

473
25 mg

477
100 mg

227
400 mg

JANUMET

RX

(sitagliptin/metformin HCl)
MERCK

575
50 mg/500 mg

577
50 mg/1000 mg

JANUMET XR

RX

(sitagliptin/metformin HCl)
MERCK

78
50 mg/500 mg

80
50 mg/1000 mg

81
100 mg/1000 mg

Extended-Release Tablets

JANUVIA

RX

(sitagliptin)
MERCK

221
25 mg

112
50 mg

277
100 mg

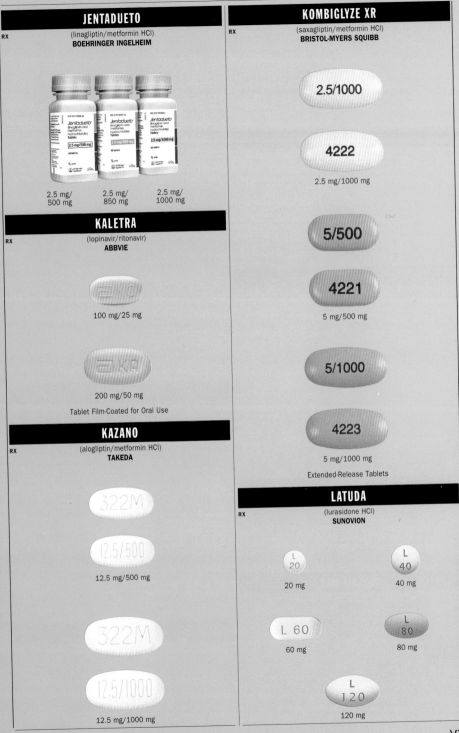

JENTADUETO

RX

(linagliptin/metformin HCl)
BOEHRINGER INGELHEIM

2.5 mg/
500 mg

2.5 mg/
850 mg

2.5 mg/
1000 mg

KALETRA

RX

(lopinavir/ritonavir)
ABBVIE

100 mg/25 mg

200 mg/50 mg

Tablet Film-Coated for Oral Use

KAZANO

RX

(alogliptin/metformin HCl)
TAKEDA

12.5 mg/500 mg

12.5 mg/1000 mg

KOMBIGLYZE XR

RX

(saxagliptin/metformin HCl)
BRISTOL-MYERS SQUIBB

2.5/1000

4222

2.5 mg/1000 mg

5/500

4221

5 mg/500 mg

5/1000

4223

5 mg/1000 mg

Extended-Release Tablets

LATUDA

RX

(lurasidone HCl)
SUNOVION

L 20
20 mg

L 40
40 mg

L 60
60 mg

L 80
80 mg

L 120
120 mg

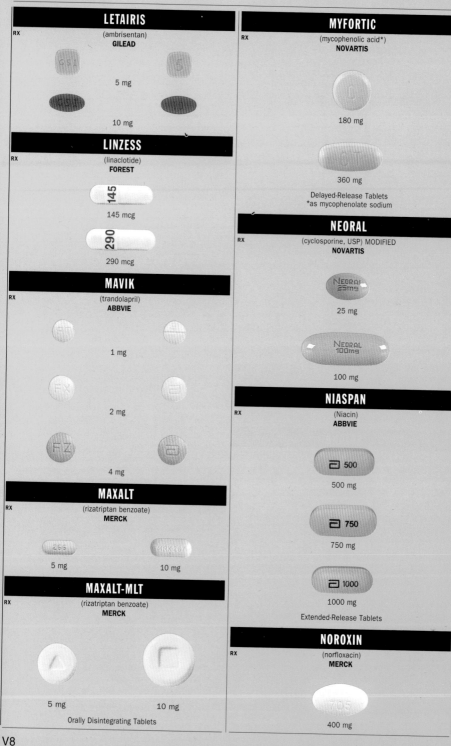

LETAIRIS

RX

(ambrisentan)
GILEAD

5 mg

10 mg

LINZESS

RX

(linaclotide)
FOREST

145 mcg

290 mcg

MAVIK

RX

(trandolapril)
ABBVIE

1 mg

2 mg

4 mg

MAXALT

RX

(rizatriptan benzoate)
MERCK

5 mg   10 mg

MAXALT-MLT

RX

(rizatriptan benzoate)
MERCK

5 mg   10 mg

Orally Disintegrating Tablets

MYFORTIC

RX

(mycophenolic acid*)
NOVARTIS

180 mg

360 mg

Delayed-Release Tablets
*as mycophenolate sodium

NEORAL

RX

(cyclosporine, USP) MODIFIED
NOVARTIS

25 mg

100 mg

NIASPAN

RX

(Niacin)
ABBVIE

500 mg

750 mg

1000 mg

Extended-Release Tablets

NOROXIN

RX

(norfloxacin)
MERCK

400 mg

V8

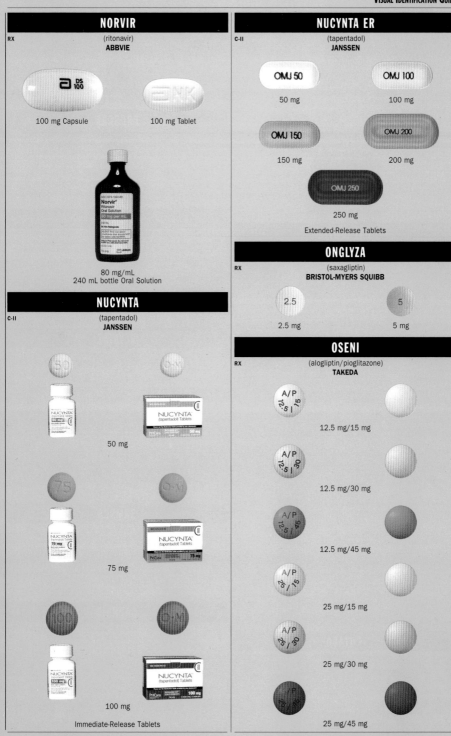

NORVIR
RX

(ritonavir)
ABBVIE

100 mg Capsule   100 mg Tablet

80 mg/mL
240 mL bottle Oral Solution

NUCYNTA
C-II

(tapentadol)
JANSSEN

50 mg

75 mg

100 mg

Immediate-Release Tablets

NUCYNTA ER
C-II

(tapentadol)
JANSSEN

OMJ 50   OMJ 100
50 mg   100 mg

OMJ 150   OMJ 200
150 mg   200 mg

OMJ 250
250 mg

Extended-Release Tablets

ONGLYZA
RX

(saxagliptin)
BRISTOL-MYERS SQUIBB

2.5   5
2.5 mg   5 mg

OSENI
RX

(alogliptin/pioglitazone)
TAKEDA

A/P 12.5 / 15
12.5 mg/15 mg

A/P 12.5 / 30
12.5 mg/30 mg

A/P 12.5 / 45
12.5 mg/45 mg

A/P 25 / 15
25 mg/15 mg

A/P 25 / 30
25 mg/30 mg

25 mg/45 mg

V9

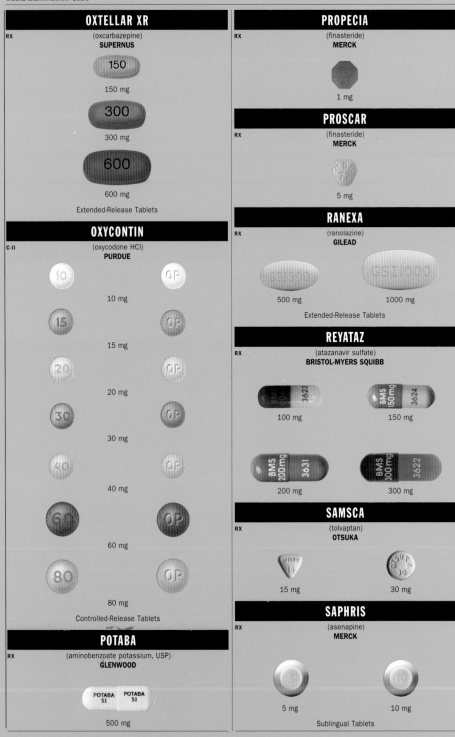

OXTELLAR XR
RX

(oxcarbazepine)
SUPERNUS

150 — 150 mg

300 — 300 mg

600 — 600 mg

Extended-Release Tablets

OXYCONTIN
C-II

(oxycodone HCl)
PURDUE

10 / OP — 10 mg

15 / OP — 15 mg

20 / OP — 20 mg

30 / OP — 30 mg

40 / OP — 40 mg

60 / OP — 60 mg

80 / OP — 80 mg

Controlled-Release Tablets

POTABA
RX

(aminobenzoate potassium, USP)
GLENWOOD

POTABA 51 | POTABA 51 — 500 mg

PROPECIA
RX

(finasteride)
MERCK

1 mg

PROSCAR
RX

(finasteride)
MERCK

MSD 72 — 5 mg

RANEXA
RX

(ranolazine)
GILEAD

GS1 500 — 500 mg

GSI 1000 — 1000 mg

Extended-Release Tablets

REYATAZ
RX

(atazanavir sulfate)
BRISTOL-MYERS SQUIBB

BMS 100mg 3623 — 100 mg

BMS 150 mg 3624 — 150 mg

BMS 200 mg 3631 — 200 mg

BMS 300 mg 3622 — 300 mg

SAMSCA
RX

(tolvaptan)
OTSUKA

OTSUKA 15 — 15 mg

OTSUKA 30 — 30 mg

SAPHRIS
RX

(asenapine)
MERCK

5 — 5 mg

10 — 10 mg

Sublingual Tablets

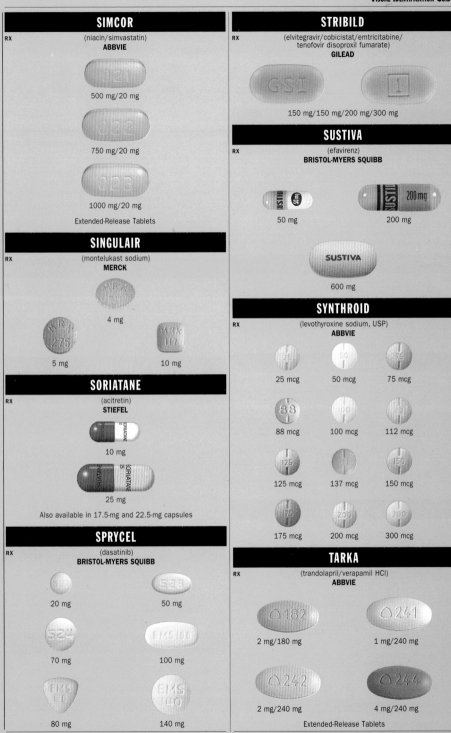

SIMCOR

RX

(niacin/simvastatin)
ABBVIE

500 mg/20 mg

750 mg/20 mg

1000 mg/20 mg

Extended-Release Tablets

SINGULAIR

RX

(montelukast sodium)
MERCK

4 mg

5 mg

10 mg

SORIATANE

RX

(acitretin)
STIEFEL

10 mg

25 mg

Also available in 17.5-mg and 22.5-mg capsules

SPRYCEL

RX

(dasatinib)
BRISTOL-MYERS SQUIBB

20 mg

50 mg

70 mg

100 mg

80 mg

140 mg

STRIBILD

RX

(elvitegravir/cobicistat/emtricitabine/
tenofovir disoproxil fumarate)
GILEAD

150 mg/150 mg/200 mg/300 mg

SUSTIVA

RX

(efavirenz)
BRISTOL-MYERS SQUIBB

50 mg

200 mg

600 mg

SYNTHROID

RX

(levothyroxine sodium, USP)
ABBVIE

25 mcg

50 mcg

75 mcg

88 mcg

100 mcg

112 mcg

125 mcg

137 mcg

150 mcg

175 mcg

200 mcg

300 mcg

TARKA

RX

(trandolapril/verapamil HCl)
ABBVIE

2 mg/180 mg

1 mg/240 mg

2 mg/240 mg

4 mg/240 mg

Extended-Release Tablets

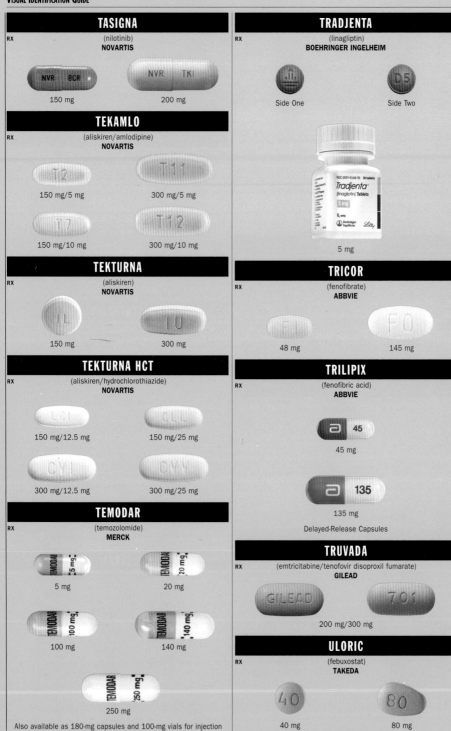

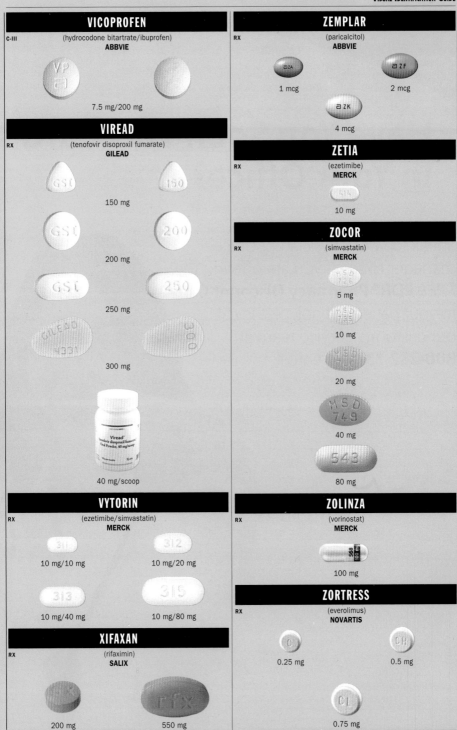

VICOPROFEN
C-III
(hydrocodone bitartrate/ibuprofen)
ABBVIE

7.5 mg/200 mg

VIREAD
RX
(tenofovir disoproxil fumarate)
GILEAD

150 mg

200 mg

250 mg

300 mg

40 mg/scoop

VYTORIN
RX
(ezetimibe/simvastatin)
MERCK

10 mg/10 mg

10 mg/20 mg

10 mg/40 mg

10 mg/80 mg

XIFAXAN
RX
(rifaximin)
SALIX

200 mg

550 mg

ZEMPLAR
RX
(paricalcitol)
ABBVIE

1 mcg

2 mcg

4 mcg

ZETIA
RX
(ezetimibe)
MERCK

10 mg

ZOCOR
RX
(simvastatin)
MERCK

5 mg

10 mg

20 mg

40 mg

80 mg

ZOLINZA
RX
(vorinostat)
MERCK

100 mg

ZORTRESS
RX
(everolimus)
NOVARTIS

0.25 mg

0.5 mg

0.75 mg

Have You Seen This Card In Your Office?

Speak to your physician or office manager to see if you are offering the *FREE* **PDR® Pharmacy Discount Card** to your patients. If not, please call our customer service team at **800-232-7379** to enroll!